Encyclopedia of Data Science and Machine Learning

John Wang
Montclair State University, USA

Volume III

IGI Global
PUBLISHER of TIMELY KNOWLEDGE

Published in the United States of America by
    IGI Global
    Engineering Science Reference (an imprint of IGI Global)
    701 E. Chocolate Avenue
    Hershey PA, USA 17033
    Tel: 717-533-8845
    Fax: 717-533-8661
    E-mail: cust@igi-global.com
    Web site: http://www.igi-global.com

Library of Congress Cataloging-in-Publication Data

Names: Wang, John, 1955- editor.
Title: Encyclopedia of data science and machine learning / John Wang,
   editor.
Description: Hershey, PA : Engineering Science Reference, an imprint of IGI
   Global, [2023] | Includes bibliographical references and index. |
   Summary: "This book examines current, state-of-the-art research in the
   areas of data science, machine learning, data mining, optimization,
   artificial intelligence, statistics, and the interactions, linkages, and
   applications of knowledge-based business with information systems"--
   Provided by publisher.
Identifiers: LCCN 2021027689 (print) | LCCN 2021027690 (ebook) | ISBN
   9781799892205 (h/c) | ISBN 9781799892212 (ebook)
Subjects: LCSH: Big data. | Data mining. | Machine learning.
Classification: LCC QA76.9.B45 E54 2022 (print) | LCC QA76.9.B45 (ebook)
   | DDC 005.7--dc23
LC record available at https://lccn.loc.gov/2021027689
LC ebook record available at https://lccn.loc.gov/2021027690

British Cataloguing in Publication Data
A Cataloguing in Publication record for this book is available from the British Library.

All work contributed to this book is new, previously-unpublished material. The views expressed in this book are those of the authors, but not necessarily of the publisher.

For electronic access to this publication, please contact: eresources@igi-global.com.

Editorial Advisory Board

List of Contributors

Alphabetical Table of Contents

Volume I: 1-618; Volume II: 619-1246; Volume III: 1247-1870; Volume IV: 1871-2498; Volume V: 2499-3143

Table of Contents by Category

Volume I

Section: Accounting Analytics

Wikil Kwak, University of Nebraska at Omaha, USA
Xiaoyan Cheng, University of Nebraska at Omaha, USA
Yong Shi, University of Nebraska at Omaha, USA
Fangyao Liu, Southwest Minzu University, China
Kevin Kwak, University of Nebraska at Omaha, USA

Toshifumi Takada, National Chung Cheng University, Taiwan

Section: Approximation Methods

Jean-Éric Pelet, LARGEPA, Panthéon-Assas University, Paris, France
Santiago Belda, Universidad de Alicante, Spain
Dounia Arezki, Computer Science Faculty, Science and Technology University of Oran, Algeria

Section: Autonomous Learning Systems

Indraneel Dabhade, O Automation, India

Section: Big Data Applications

Section: Big Data as a Service

Section: Big Data Systems and Tools

Section: Business Intelligence

Volume II

Section: Causal Analysis

Section: Chaos Control, Modeling, and Engineering

Section: Cloud Infrastructure

Section: Cognitive Science

Section: Computational Intelligence

Section: Computational Statistics

Section: Computer Vision

Section: Customer Analytics

Section: Data Processing, Data Pipeline, and Data Engineering

Volume III

Section: Data Visualization and Visual Mining

Section: Decision, Support System

Section: Deep Neural Network (DNN) of Deep Learning

Section: E-Learning Technologies and Tools

Section: Emerging Technologies, Applications, and Related Issues

Volume IV

Section: Financial Services Analytics

Section: Fuzzy Logic and Soft Computing

Section: Gradient-Boosting Decision Trees

Section: Graph Learning

Section: High-Throughput Data Analysis

Section: Industry 4.0

Section: Mathematical Optimization

Section: Meta-Analysis and Metamodeling

Section: Multivariate Analysis

Section: Natural Language Processing (NLP)

Section: Nature-Inspired Algorithms

Volume V

Section: Network Modeling and Theory

Section: Object Detection

Section: Performance Metrics

Section: Predictive Analytics

Section: Reinforcement Learning

Section: Simulation and Modeling

Section: Smart City

Section: Social Media Analytics

Section: Supply Chain Analytics and Management

Section: Symbolic Learning

Section: Time Series Analysis

Section: Transfer Learning

Section: Transport Analytics

Section: Unsupervised and Supervised Learning

Foreword

There has been tremendous progress made in Data Science and Machine Learning over the last $10 - 15$ years, leading to the Data Science becoming the major driving force of the Fourth Industrial Revolution and a significant factor in the current cycle of economic expansion. The need for data scientists is growing exponentially and machine learning has become one of the "hottest" professions in the labor market.

The field of Data Science is expanding both in-depth and in-breadth. In particular, we have witnessed widespread adoption of data science methods across a broad class of industries and functional areas, including health sciences and pharmaceuticals, finance, accounting, marketing, human resource management, operations and supply chains. Data-driven approaches have been deployed in such diverse set of applications as drug discovery, analysis of medical data and decision support tools for physicians, financial applications, including robo-advising, predictive maintenance of equipment and defect detection, Internet of Things (IoT), precision agriculture, physics and chemistry, to name a few. All these industries and applications enjoy adoption of a wide range of machine learning methods, the scope of which grew significantly over the last $10 - 15$ years. In addition to the evolutionary growth and expansion of classical machine learning techniques, the last decade has witnessed revolutionary breakthroughs in such areas as Deep Learning, scalable machine learning methods capable of handling Big Data, the size of which grows exponentially over time in many applications, and the analysis of unstructured data, such as text using NLP-based methods, images and videos using Computer Vision techniques, and voice using Speech Recognition methods.

Given all this progress in Machine Learning and Data Science, it is high time to aggregate all this new knowledge "under one roof," and this Encyclopedia of Data Science and Machine Learning serves this purpose. It covers 188 different topics across the whole spectrum of the field written by leading academic scholars and industry practitioners describing the progress made in the respective areas over the last $10 - 15$ years and reflecting the State-of-the-Art for each topic.

Since data science and machine learning are evolving rapidly, the authors also describe the challenges and present promising future research directions in their respective areas, delineating interesting work that lies ahead for the scholars to address these challenges. Therefore, this Encyclopedia remains what it is – a milestone on a long and exciting road that lies ahead of us in Data Science and Machine Learning.

Alexander Tuzhilin
New York University, USA
May 2022

Preface

Big Data and Machine Learning (BDML) are driving and harnessing the power of the Fourth Industrial Revolution, also referred to as Industry 4.0 or 4IR, which revolutionizes the way companies, organizations, and institutions operate and develop. With the age of Big Data upon us, we risk drowning in a flood of digital data. Big Data has now become a critical part of the business world and daily life, as the synthesis and synergy of Machine Learning (ML) and Big Data (BD) have enormous potential.

BDML not only deals with descriptive and predictive analytics but also focuses on prescriptive analytics through digital technology and interconnectivity. It has continuously explored its "depth" and expanded its "breadth". BDML will remain to maximize the citizens' "wealth" while promoting society's "health".

The *Encyclopedia of Data Science and Machine Learning* examines current, state-of-the-art research in the areas of data science, ML, data mining (DM), optimization, artificial intelligence (AI), statistics, and the interactions, linkages, and applications of knowledge-based business with information systems. It provides an international forum for practitioners, educators, and researchers to advance the knowledge and practice of all facets of BDML, emphasizing emerging theories, principles, models, processes, and applications to inspire and circulate cutting-edge findings into research, business, and communities (Wang, 2022).

How can a manager get out of a data-flooded "mire"? How can a confused decision-maker navigate through a "maze"? How can an over-burdened problem solver clean up a "mess"? How can an exhausted scientist bypass a "myth"? The answer to all of the above is to employ BDML.

As Roy et al. (2022) point out, data has become the center point for almost every organization. For quite a long time, we are familiar with Descriptive Analytics (what happened in the past) and Diagnostic Analytics (why something happened in the past), as well as Predictive Analytics (what is most likely to happen in the future). However, BDML could go much above and beyond them with Prescriptive Analytics (what should be done now), which recommends actions companies, and organizations can take to affect those outcomes. The digital transformation, the horizontal and vertical integration of these production systems, as well as the exploitation via optimization models, can make a gigantic jump with this giant digital leverage.

BDML can turn *Data* into *value*; Transform *information* into *intelligence;* Change *patterns* into *profit;* Convert *relationships* into *resources*. Companies and organizations can make *Faster* (real-time or near real-time), *Frequent*, and *Fact-based* decisions. In an ever-evolving market, 4IR with a set of technologies can stimulate innovations and rapid responses. Knowledge workers can proactively take action before an unfriendly event occurs (Wang, 2008).

Having been penetrated and integrated into almost every aspect of our work and life, as well as our society itself, AI and related cutting-edge technologies will enhance human capacities, improve efficiencies, and optimize people's lives. AI would not replace human intelligence, rather than amplify it. As *AI evolves* and *humans* adapt, AI and humans go forward together in the long run because AI and people both bring different capabilities to society.

According to Klaus Schwab, the World Economic Forum Founder and Executive Chairman, 4IR intellectualizes precipitous change to industrial and societal prototypes and processes in the 21st century due to increasing interconnectivity and smart automation and finally blurs the lines among the physical, digital, and biological worlds. Part of the 4IR is the manner in which all types of machines and devices interact, correspond, and cooperate with each other. Even though there will be obvious job losses due to the replacement of tasks that humans have conducted for years by autonomous machines and/or software. On the contrary, there could be new business opportunities and plenty of new jobs for controlling "the new electricity" (Philbeck & Davis, 2018; Moll, 2022).

There are 207 qualified full chapters among 271 accepted proposals. Finally, the encyclopedia contains a collection of 187 high-quality chapters, which were written by an international team of more than 370 experts representing leading scientists and talented young scholars from more than 45 countries and regions, including Algeria, Argentina, Austria, Bangladesh, Brazil, Canada, Chile, China, Colombia, Cuba, Denmark, Egypt, El Salvador, Finland, France, Germany, Ghana, Greece, Hong Kong, Hungary, Indonesia, Iraq, Japan, Lebanon, Macau, Malaysia, Mexico, Netherland, New Zealand, Poland, Portugal, Saudi Arabia, Serbia, Singapore, South Africa, Sweden, Switzerland, Syria, Taiwan, Tunisia, Turkey, UK, USA, Venezuela, Vietnam, etc.

They have contributed great effort to create a source of solid, practical information, informed by the sound underlying theory that should become a resource for all people involved in this dynamic new field. Let's take a peek at a few of them:

Jaydip Sen has published around 300 articles in reputed international journals and referred conference proceedings (IEEE Xplore, ACM Digital Library, Springer LNCS, etc.), and 18 book chapters in books published by internationally renowned publishing houses. He is a Senior Member of ACM, USA a Member of IEEE, USA. He has been listed among the top 2% scientists in the globe as per studies conducted by Stanford University for the last consecutive three years 2019 - 2021. In his contributed chapter Prof. Sen and his co-author, Dutta have evaluated the performance of two risk-based portfolio design algorithms.

Leung - who has authored more than 300 refereed publications on the topics of data science, ML, BDM and analytics, and visual analytics (including those in ACM TODS, IEEE ICDE, and IEEE ICDM) - presents two encyclopedia articles. One of them presents up-to-date definitions in BDM and analytics in the high-performance computing environment and focuses on mining frequent patterns with the MapReduce programming model. Another one provides the latest comprehensive coverage on key concepts and applications for BD visualization; it focuses on visualizing BD, frequent patterns, and association rules.

Lorenzo Magnani is Editor-in-Chief of the Series Sapere, Springer. Thanks to his logico-epistemological and cognitive studies on the problem of abductive cognition (that regards all kinds of reasoning to hypotheses) explained in this chapter both virtues and limitations of some DL applications, taking advantage of the analysis of the famous AlphaGo/AlphaZero program and the concepts of locked and unlocked strategies. Furthermore, he is the author of many important articles and books on epistemology, logic, cognitive science, and the relationships between ethics, technology, and violence.

The chapter 'AI is transforming insurance with five emerging business models' is the culmination of three years of research into how AI is disrupting insurance. Zarifis has recently won a 'best paper award' at a leading conference and Cheng has recently been published in MIS Quarterly for related work. AI is disrupting many distinct parts of our life, but insurance is particularly interesting as some issues like risk and privacy concerns are more important. After several case studies, this chapter identifies that there are five emerging models in insurance that are optimal for AI.

In "Artificial Intelligence, Consumers, and the Experience Economy," Chang and Mukherjee's excellent synthesis of AI and consumers in the modern economy provides a much-needed knowledge base for stakeholders tasked to deploy AI. In "Using Machine Learning Methods to Extract Behavioral Insights from Consumer Data," they present a comprehensive discussion of new data sources and state-of-the-art techniques for researchers and practitioners in computational social science. The chapters are built on their projects supported by the Ministry of Education, Singapore, under its Academic Research Fund (AcRF) Tier 2 Grant No. MOE2019-T2-1-183 and Grant No. MOE2018-T2-1-181, respectively.

Based on many years of application development by CY Pang and S. Pang's cognitive data analysis of many industrial projects, this chapter proposes a programming paradigm specific to BD processing. Pang was the lead architect of a $1.6 billion enterprise software project and was awarded a special architectural design trophy. He has received awards of $20,000 and $5,000 for outstanding innovation from a company he previously worked for. By the way, CY Pang was awarded a Prestige Scholarship from Peter House, Cambridge to complete his Ph.D. at the University of Cambridge, UK.

Vitor provides an excellent overview of multidimensional search methods for optimization and the potential these methods have to solve optimization problems more quickly. With almost ten years of industry experience, Vitor is an expert in optimization methods and the modeling of complex systems using operations research and data analytics techniques. He is also a recipient of the Nebraska EPSCoR FIRST Award, supported by the National Science Foundation to advance the research of early-career tenure-track faculty.

Lee's chapter on evidence-based data-driven pain management bears multi-facet importance. Nearly 40 million anesthetics are administered each year in the United States. And over 10.7% of Americans use prescription pain medication on a regular basis. The findings highlight the optimal safe dose and delivery mechanism to achieve the best outcome. The study showcases the persistence of overprescription of opioid-type drugs, as it finds that the use of fentanyl has little effect on the outcome and should be avoided.

Auditors must evaluate the volatility and uncertainty of the client company at the initial stage of the audit contract because it directly influences the audit risk. Takada contributes to auditing research and accounting education for 40 years. He has been awarded for his research and contributions to his excellent papers and accounting education by the *Chinese Auditing Association* and by the *Japanese Auditing Association*.

Nguyen and Quinn propose an optimal approach to tackle the well-known issue of the imbalance in bankruptcy prediction. Their approach has been evaluated through a rigorous computation including the most popular current methods in the literature. They have also made other main contributions in the area of imbalanced classification by winning the 2020 Literati Awards for Outstanding Author Contribution.

Rodríguez is the Bioethics of Displacement pioneer, a field that merges futurism, belongingness, and life. He has also published analytic papers and fieldwork on crises and big social changes such as pandemics, Anthropocene, AI takeover, cyborgs, digital securitization and terrorist attacks. As a chair, the author leads the research on the first decolonized corruption index. Torres shares his more than 15 years of wealth of experience in Predictive Maintenance management as a speaker at global summits such as Scalable and PMM Tech Dates. The author leads the first non-taxonomic error mode proponent of AI implementation.

Kurpicz-Briki, Glauser, and Schmid are using unique API technologies to measure the impact of online search behavior using several different online channels. Their method allows the identification of the specific channels, where keywords have been searched, and a restriction of regions, using the domains. Such technologies provide a major benefit for different application domains, including public health. In times such as a pandemic crisis, it is highly relevant for different stakeholders to identify the impact of their communications on the user community as well as the well-being of the population. Using the method proposed by the authors, this can be done while fully respecting the privacy of the users.

Sensors sense the environment and process large sets of data. Monitoring the data to detect malicious content is one of the biggest challenges. The previous work used mean variation to ease the surveillance of information. Ambika's proposal minimizes the effort by classifying the streamed data into three subsets. It uses the k-nearest neighbor procedure to accomplish the same. The work conserves 10.77% of energy and tracks 27.58% of more packets. Map-reduce methodology manages large amounts of data to a certain extent. Ambika's other proposal aims to increase processing speed by 29.6% using a hashing methodology.

In today's world, text-based sentiment analysis brings the attention of all. By looking at the people requirement, Tripathy and Sharaff propose a hybridized Genetic Algorithm (GA)-based feature selection method to achieve a better model performance. In the current study, they have customized the GA by using the SVM to evaluate the fitness value of the solutions. The proposed idea is essential as the technique reduces the computational cost by reducing sufficient features without affecting the performance. The proposed model can be implemented in any field to filter out the sentiment from the user's review.

Alberg and Hadad present the novel Interval Gradient Prediction Tree ML Algorithm that can process incoming mean-variance aggregated multivariate temporal data and make stable interval predictions of a target numerical variable. Empirical evaluations of multi-sensor aircraft datasets have demonstrated that this algorithm provides better readability and similar performance compared to other ML regression tree algorithms.

The environmental, societal, and cultural imperatives press for innovative, prompt, and practical solutions for grave humanitarian problems we face in the 21ˢᵗ century. The climate crisis is felt everywhere; natural disasters are rampant. Can technology provide reasonable means to humanitarian supply chains? What potential uses can AI offer in establishing sustainable humanitarian logistics (SHL)? Ülkü, an award-winning professor and the director of CRSSCA-Centre for Research in Sustainable Supply Chain Analytics, and his research associate Oguntola of Dalhousie University - Canada review the latest research on the applications of AI technology on SHL.

Aguiar-Pérez, the leading author of this chapter, provides the audience an insight into what ML is and its relation with AI or DL. He has an extended experience in the field of ML, DL, BD, and IoT in various sectors (automotive, smart roads, agriculture, livestock, heritage, etc.), including collaboration with companies, EU-funded research projects, publications, and postgraduate teaching experience. The rest of the authors work with him in the Data Engineering Research Unit of the University of Valladolid.

Bagui, a highly accomplished author of several books on databases and Oracle, presents a very timely chapter on the improvements made in Oracle 19c's multitenant container architecture and shows how these improvements aid in the management of Big Data from the perspective of application development. The added functionality that comes with the integration of Big Data platforms, alongside the flexibility and improvement that comes with a container and pluggable databases, has allowed Oracle to be in the forefront in the handling of Big Data.

As an internationally renowned interdisciplinary information and data professional, Koltay's chapter on Research Data Management (RDM) is of interest not only for both professionals of DS and ML but is related to any research activity. He is also a widely published author in these fields. In 2021, his contribution to IGI Global books included an entry on information overload. His book, titled Research Data Management and Data Literacy (Chandos, 2021) contains a more detailed explanation of the subjects, contained in this chapter.

Zhao is a DS professional with experience in industry, teaching, and research. He is a leading BD expert in the IR BD & AI Lab in New Jersey, USA. He provides multiple chapters to the book by covering a broad range of BD applications in vast perspectives of urgent demands in DS research objectives, such as DSS, DL, computer vision, BD architecture designs, and applied BD analytics in Covid-19 research. As such, he did excellent work in those chapters and made significant contributions to the book.

Based on their discovery of action rules and meta-actions from client datasets, Duan and Ras propose a strategy for improving the number of promoters and decreasing the number of detractors among customers. Moreover, the improved/enhanced action rules can be utilized in developing actionable strategies for decision makers to reduce customer churn, which will contribute to the overall customer churn study in the business field. The authors target the domain represented by many clients, each one involved with customers in the same type of business. Clients are heavy equipment repair shops, and customers are owners of such equipment.

The A2E Process Model for Data Analytics is simple without being simplistic and comprehensive without being complicated. It balances technology with humanity and theories with practices. This model reflects Jay Wang's decades-long multi-disciplinary training and experience in STEM, Behavioral Science, and Management Science. While existing process models such as CRISP-DM, SEMMA, and KDD were developed for technical professionals with limitations and low adoption rates, the A2E Model is more approachable to subject matter experts, business analysts, and social scientists. The A2E Model will elevate the analytics profession by fostering interdisciplinary collaborations of all stakeholders and increasing the effectiveness and impacts of analytics efforts.

Turuk explores Audio and video-based Emotion Recognition using the Backpropagation Algorithm, which is the backbone of ML and DL architectures. This chapter analyses everyday human emotions such as Happy, Sad, Neutral, and Angry using audio-visual cues. The audio features such as Energy & MFCC and video features using the Gabor filter are extracted. Mutual information is computed using video features. The readers will benefit and motivated to conduct further research in this domain. The application may be extended to a lie detector using Emotions.

Stojanović and Marković-Petrović focus on continuous cyber security risk assessment in Industrial Internet of Things (IIoT) networks, and particularly on possibilities of DL approaches to achieve the goal. The authors successfully complement their previous work regarding the cyber security of industrial control systems. They concisely review the theoretical background and provide an excellent framework for the continuous risk assessment process in the IIoT environment. DL can be integrated into edge-computing-based systems and used for feature extraction and risk classification from massive raw data. The chapter ends with a list of proposals for further studies.

Climate change is a very important issue and each person on our planet must have a culture of keeping it clean. Pollution increased yearly due to the increased consumption of fossil fuels. Alsultanny has many research papers in climate change and renewable energy. He led a UNDP team for writing reports on energy consumption in Bahrain. Alsultanny did an innovative method in his chapter, by utilizing the pollution gases data, these data currently are BD, because they are registered yearly in every minute, and from many monitoring pollutions stations.

Deliyska and Ivanova conducted timely research and practical work representing an important contribution to data modeling in sustainable science. Applying ontological engineering and a coevolutionary approach, a unique metamodel of sustainable development is created containing structured knowledge and mutual links between environmental, social, and economic dimensions in this interdisciplinary area. Specialists in different fields can use the proposed metamodel as a tool for terminology clarification, knowledge extraction, and interchange and for the structuring of ML models of sustainable development processes.

Hedayati and Schniederjans provide a broad spectrum of issues that come into play when using digital technologies to benefit healthcare. This is even more important where the pandemic has forced healthcare models to rapidly adjust towards compliance with local, regional, and national policy. The dissemination and creation of knowledge become paramount when considering the benefits and drawbacks of the rapid changes in technology applications worldwide. The authors consider several insights from the American Hospital Association Compliance to provide some questions researchers and practitioners may consider when addressing knowledge management via digital technology implementation in healthcare settings.

Pratihar and Kundu apply the theory of fuzzy logic to develop a classification and authentication system for beverages. It emphasizes the versatility of fuzzy logic to deal with the higher dimensional and highly non-linear sensor data obtained from e-tongue for different beverage samples. Commonly used mapping techniques (for dimension reduction of a data set) and clustering techniques (for classification) were also briefly discussed. This study provides a perspective on developing a fuzzy logic-based classifier/authenticator system in the future for beverages, foods, and others and their quality control and monitoring.

Drake discusses the use of IoT technology to improve SCM. As firms look to improve their supply chain resilience in response to the COVID-19 pandemic and other disruptions, IoT data increases visibility, traceability, and can help firms to mitigate risks through added agility and responsiveness. The improved decision-making made possible by IoT data creates a competitive advantage in the market.

Today, high-dimensional data (multi-omics data) are widely used. The high dimensionality of the data creates problems (time, cost, diagnosis, and treatment) in studies. Ipekten et al. introduce the existing solutions to these problems and commonly used methods. Also, the authors present the advantages of the methods over each other and enlighten the researchers that using suitable methods in terms of performance can increase the reliability and accuracy of the studies. Finally, the authors advise on what can be done in the future.

Learning analytics (LA), a promising field of study that started more than a decade ago but has blossomed in recent years, addresses the challenges of LA specifically in education, integrating it as a fundamental element of the Smart Classroom. Ifenthaler and Siemens among others discuss the primary features, the benefits, and some experiences. In addition, the team of authors of the chapter has contributed more than twelve publications on this topic in the last 3 years in leading journals and publishers.

Current advances in AI and ML in particular have raised several concerns regarding the trustworthiness and explainability of deployed AI systems. Knowledge-Based approaches based on symbolic representations and reasoning mechanisms can be used to deploy AI systems that are explainable and compliant with corresponding ethical and legal guidelines, thus complementing purely data-driven approaches.

Batsakis and Matsatsinis, both having vast theoretical backgrounds and experience in this research area, offer an overview of knowledge-based AI methods for the interested AI practitioner.

Noteboom and Zeng provide a comprehensive review of applications of AI and ML and data analytics techniques in clinical decision support systems (CDSSs) and make contributions including, 1) the current status of data-driven CDSSs, 2) identification and quantification of the extent to which theories and frameworks have guided the research, 3) understanding the synergy between AI/ML algorithms and modes of data analytics, 4) directions for advancing data-driven CDSSs to realize their potential in healthcare.

Fisogni investigates the emotional environment which is grounded in any human/machine interaction. Through the lenses of metaphysics and system thinking the author sketches a highly valuable insight, for sure an unprecedented challenge for DSs. In fact, only a philosophical foundation of the big issues of this realm can bring about a change in the quality of understanding an increasingly melted environment humans/machines in the Onlife era.

In "Hedonic Hunger and Obesity", Demirok and Uysal touch upon a remarkable topic and explain ways of identification for people with hedonic nutrition and the conditions that are effective in the states that trigger hunger state in humans. In addition, in this text, the authors ensample hormones that suppress and trigger hunger.

Yen and her coauthors contributed a chapter on how ML creates the virtual singer industry. Virtual singers have great market potential and even advantages over their human counterparts. Despite the bright future of virtual singers, the chapter has discussed difficulties virtual singers face, especially their copyright protection by legislation. Literature on the technical aspects of virtual singers is also reviewed, and a list of additional readings is provided for readers interested in the ML algorithms behind virtual singers.

Rastogi is working on Biofeedback therapy and its effect on Diabetes diseases, a currently very active healthcare domain. He brings back the glory of Indian Ancient Vedic Sciences of Jap, Pranayama, Healing techniques, and the effect of Yajna and Mantra science on Diseases and pollution control. Also, He has developed some interesting mathematical models with algorithms on Swarm Intelligence approaches like PSO, ACO BCO, etc. for better human life via Spiritual Index and higher consciousness.

Isikhan presents a comparison of a new proposal for the modeling of Ceiling and Floor Effect dependent variables and classical methods. It has been noticed that there are very few publications evaluating the regression modeling of ceiling and floor effect observations in recent years. The modeling method with regression-based imputation, which clinicians can use as an alternative to classical models for ceiling and floor effective observations, is explained in detail. The performances of the newly proposed imputation-based regression and other classical methods were validated based on both real clinical data, synthetic data, as well as a 500 replicated cross-validation method.

Drignei has extensive experience with time series modeling and analysis. Prior to this work, he addressed statistical modeling aspects of space-time data, such as temperatures recorded over space and time. His research has been published in leading statistics journals. The current work deals with seasonal times series recorded at a large number of time points. Such data sets will become more common in the future, in areas such as business, industry, and science. Therefore, this chapter is timely and important because it sheds new light on modeling aspects of this type of data sets.

Data visualization plays a key role in the decision-making process. Visualization allows for data to be consumable. If data is not consumable, there is a tendency to ignore the facts and rely more on biases. Researchers have found that cognitive biases do exist within data visualizations and can affect decision-making abilities. Anderson and Hardin provide background on cognitive biases related to data visualizations, with a particular interest in visual analytics in BD environments. A review of recent studies related to mitigating cognitive biases is presented. Recommendations for mitigating biases in visualizations are provided to practitioners.

Puzzanghera explores the impact of AI on administrative law. He combines IT systems with administrative activity and researches the processors that prepare content and the implications that arise. He analyzes the European Commission's proposal in regard to the legislation of AI in Europe and the importance of safeguarding human rights in the introduction of AI in administrative activity.

How ML impacts the catering industry? Liu et al. provide a comprehensive vision to readers with real-life examples and academic research. Researchers at business schools may have their attention drawn to the impact of ML on operations, management, and marketing, while scholars with solid ML backgrounds may become aware of industry issues, identify new research questions, and link their expertise to practical problems through reading the chapter.

Di Wang's research interests include 4D printing technology, robot control, remanufactured industry, and energy schedule in the smart city. Combinatorial optimization is a widely applied field at the forefront of combinatorics and theoretical computer science. With BD challenges, deep reinforcement learning opens new doors to solve complex combinatorial optimization problems with overwhelming advantages over traditional methods.

Firmansyah and Harsanto focus on exploring BD and Islamic finance. The utilization of BD in Islamic financial institutions (IFIs) has been perceived as a source of competitive advantage in today's era. Many IFIs have been more dependent on BD technologies than ever before in order to keep up with the changing customers' demands, lifestyles, and preferences.

With his experience of working in both industry and academic research, Indraneel highlights progress made in integrating AI with industry and helps bridge the reality and challenges faced while summarizing the state of Industry 4.0. The author engages audiences from different sectors without overburdening the reader with incoherent technical details. A practitioner in the fields of DS and cybersecurity, the author brings experience interacting with clients and customers from different fields, including manufacturing, legal, and product developers.

Yang, Wu, & Forrest examine the textual aspects of consumer reviews. As a critical source of information for online shoppers, researchers have spent considerable time examining the potential impact of consumer reviews on purchasing behavior. The authors contribute to the existing body of knowledge by proposing a conceptual framework for capturing the internal relationships between major textual features discovered in prior research.

Kara and Gonce Koçken are researchers studying mathematical programming problems in fuzzy environments. In the study, a novel fuzzy solution approach to multi-objective solid transportation problems is developed by using different membership functions, which can help the studies in transportation systems.

Millham demonstrates the various spheres of the emerging 4IR and how they interrelate with the application, opportunities, expectations, and challenges of a smart city. Because many of these smart city applications are very complex and interact with each other using various technologies, several nature-inspired algorithms are introduced as a way to provide intelligent and coordinated management of these entities.

The development of novel measurement and detection techniques is a rapidly growing area, where the generation of vast amounts of information requires novel methods for analysis. Murrieta-Rico explores a new direction of his research by combing the know-how for generating a big dataset from a digital frequency measurement, with the application of the principal component analysis (PCA). As a result, a powerful methodology for data analysis is presented. In addition, these results can be used for extending the capabilities of ML systems based on sensors.

Coimbra, Chimenti, and Nogueira contribute to the debate related to human-machine interaction in social media. The work helped to understand the mechanisms and motivators of this relationship. In addition, the article presented a historical evolution of the debate on the interaction between machines and men in decision-making, distributing the result of the literature review in three historical cycles. The research was carried out through a survey of YouTube users to understand the interaction mechanism along with its motivators.

As a transformational general-purpose technology, AI is impacting marketing as a function, and marketing managers' activities, capabilities, and performance. Oberoi emphasizes how the job of a marketing manager will be evolving into understanding which kind of AI can and should be applied to which kind of marketing actions for better performance. Marketing managers will have to go through a learning curve and acquire new skills.

Singh and Dev have discussed the concepts of data warehouse and OLAP technology to deal with real-life applications efficiently. The topic is useful in the modern digital era as businesses are dealing with data from heterogeneous sources. The chapter presents the case study of the tourism industry as it deals with multidimensional data like tourist, hospitality, and tourist products. This chapter will be helpful in understanding how to generate multi-dimensional reports that will show the information according to the needs of policymakers.

Ramos has made many contributions to the potential of Business Intelligence tools, combined with DM algorithms methods to produce insights about the tourism business, highlighting an aspect of the investment potential of tourism organizations in this type of system, from those related to accommodation, management of tourist destinations, to tourist transport, restaurants, among other businesses complementary to the tourist activity, with a view to innovation and increasing financial performance, which includes examples ranging from the application of OLAP techniques to the application of ML methods.

Balsam depicts the meaning and role of metamodels in defining the abstract syntax of the language by which developers communicate, design, and implement systems including the selection of the design, implementation methods, and techniques for increasingly complex systems to satisfy customers' needs, particularly if the system has to be delivered in a considerably fleeting time. The author highlights different aspects of meta-models standards, categories, the process of creating the metamodel, and challenges in the research of metamodeling.

Dharmapala contributes a novel method to the field of research in 'Classification of employee categories in allocating a reward, with input features from survey responses.' In the past, researchers conducted qualitative and quantitative analyses on this subject as it is an important topic to any organization that strives to boost the morale of its employees. The author opened a new direction in future research on the subject by using ML algorithms, and the results obtained were promising.

Mudrakola identifies the gap and future scope for Breast cancer applications like the impact of chemical therapy, prognosis analysis among various treatment types and stages, etc. From basic to the latest trends, the author's extensive literature survey will direct the root to aspects needed to analyze work on medical applications specific to Breast cancer.

Rani et al. highlight the venues of user-generated content (UGC) in Industry 4.0. This chapter's contribution is highly interesting for any digital content creator and non-paid professionals. The importance of UGC on consumer behavior in the era of Industry 4.0 will be explained, allowing stakeholders to assess their efficacy in Internet communication and enhancing the digital process required for modern marketing. The chapter aims to link existing ideas and provide a holistic picture of UGC by concentrating on future research.

Ibrahim et al. seek to provide an understanding of the relationship between member support exchange behavior and self-disclosure intention in online health support communities using a data-driven literature review. Seeking or providing support in online communities may be useful but having to disclose personal information publicly online is a critical privacy risk – intention counts.

Rusko introduces the main perspectives of industrial revolutions. He found interesting backgrounding details for the chapter about the disruptions of the industrial revolutions. Kosonen updates the paper with the effects of Covid-19 and contemporary digitizing development.

I would like to highlight a number of authors who have received special stunning honors: Eva K Lee has published over 220 research articles, and fifty government and state reports, and has received patents on innovative medical systems and devices. She is frequently tapped by a variety of health and security policymakers in Washington for her expertise in personalized medicine, chronic diseases, healthcare quality, modeling and decision support, vaccine research and national security, pandemic, and medical preparedness. Lee has received multiple prestigious analytics and practice excellence awards including INFORMS Franz Edelman award, Daniel H Wagner prize, and the Caterpillar and Innovative Applications in Analytics Award for novel cancer therapeutics, bioterrorism emergency response, and mass casualty mitigation, personalized disease management, ML for best practice discovery, transforming clinical workflow and patient care, vaccine immunity prediction, and reducing hospital-acquired infections. She is an INFORMS Fellow. She is also inducted into the American Institute for Medical and Biological Engineering (AIMBE) College of Fellows, the first IE/OR engineer to be nominated and elected for this honor. Her work has been funded by CDC, HHS, NIH, NSF, and DTRA. Lee was an NSF CAREER Young Investigator and Whitaker Foundation Young Investigator recipient.

Petry and Yager are both internationally known for their research in computational intelligence, in the area of fuzzy set theory and applications, and are both IEEE Fellows and have received prestigious awards from the IEEE. They have collaborated here as it represents extensions of their previous research on this topic. Hierarchical concept generalization is one important approach to dealing with the complex issues involving BD. This chapter provides insights on how to extend hierarchical generalization to data with interval and intuitionistic forms of uncertainty.

The globalization of the software development industry continues to experience significant growth. The increasing trend of globalization brings new challenges and increases the scope of the core functions of the software development process. Pal introduces a distributed software development knowledge management architecture. Kamalendu has published research articles in the software development community in the ACM SIGMIS Database, Expert Systems with Applications, DSSs, and conferences. Kamalendu was awarded the best research paper on data analytic work at a recent international conference. He is a member of the British Computer Society, the IET, and the IEEE Computer Society.

Badia's research has been funded by the National Science Foundation (including a prestigious CAREER Award) and has resulted in over 50 publications in scientific journals and conferences. His chapter demonstrates how to use SQL in order to prepare data that resides in database tables for analysis. The reader is guided through steps for Exploratory Data Analysis (EDA), data cleaning (including dealing with missing data, outliers, and duplicates), and other tasks that are an integral part of the Data Scientist day-to-day. The references provide a guide for further study.

Srinivasan explains the three components of graph analytics and provides illustrative examples as well as code for implementation. His chapter is one of the few primers of graph DS/analytics that covers a variety of topics in the discipline. The author does active research in graph analytics methods and applications in healthcare, ML explainability, and DL and regularly publishes in top journals and conferences in information systems, healthcare, and computer science. He received best paper awards in INFORMS Workshop on Data Science (2021) and the 6th International Conference on Digital Health (2016), respectively.

Knowledge explosion pushes BDML, a multidisciplinary subject, to ever-expanding regions. Inclusion, omission, emphasis, evolution, and even revolution are part of our professional life. In spite of our efforts to be careful, should you find any ambiguities of perceived inaccuracies, please contact me at prof.johnwang@gmail.com.

John Wang
Montclair State University, USA

REFERENCES

Moll, I. (2022). The Fourth Industrial Revolution: A new ideology. *tripleC: Communication, Capitalism & Critique*, *20*(1), 45–61.

Philbeck, T., & Davis, N. (2018). The Fourth Industrial Revolution: Shaping a new era. *Journal of International Affairs*, *72*(1), 17–22.

Roy, D., Srivastava, R., Jat, M., & Karaca, M. S. (2022). A complete overview of analytics techniques: Descriptive, predictive, and prescriptive. *Decision Intelligence Analytics and the Implementation of Strategic Business Management*, 15-30.

Wang, J. (Ed.). (2008). *Data Warehousing and Mining: Concepts, Methodologies, Tools, and Applications* (Vols. 1–6). IGI Global. doi:10.4018/978-1-59904-951-9

Wang, J. (Ed.). (2022). *Encyclopedia of Data Science and Machine Learning*. IGI Global. https://www.igi-global.com/book/encyclopedia-data-science-machine-learning/276507

Acknowledgment

The editor would like to thank all authors for their insights and excellent contributions to this major volume. I also want to thank the many anonymous reviewers who assisted me in the peer-reviewing process and provided comprehensive and indispensable inputs that improved our book significantly. In particular, the Editorial Advisory Board members, including Xueqi Cheng (Chinese Academy of Science), Verena Kantere (University of Ottawa, Canada), Srikanta Patnaik (SOA University, India), Hongming Wang (Harvard University), and Yanchang Zhao (CSIRO, Australia), have all made immense contributions in terms of advice and assistance, enhancing the quality of this volume. My sincere appreciation also goes to Prof. Alexander Tuzhilin (New York University). Despite his busy schedule, he has written three forewords for my consecutive encyclopaedias, over an 18-year span, in this expanding and exploring area.

In addition, the editor wishes to acknowledge the help of all involved in the development process of this book, without whose support the project could not have been satisfactorily completed. I owe my thanks to the staff at IGI Global, whose support and contributions have been invaluable throughout the entire process, from inception to final publication. Special thanks go to Gianna Walker, Angelina Olivas, Katelyn McLoughlin, and Melissa Wagner, who continuously prodded me via email to keep the project on schedule, and to Jan Travers and Lindsay Wertman, whose enthusiasm motivated me to accept their invitation to take on this project.

I would also like to extend my thanks to my brothers Zhengxian, Shubert (an artist, https://portraitartist. com/detail/6467), and sister Joyce Mu, who stood solidly behind me and contributed in their own unique ways. We are thankful for the scholarships which we have been provided, without which it would not have been possible for all of us to come and study in the U.S.

Finally, I want to thank my family: my parents for supporting me spiritually throughout my life and providing endless encouragement; my wife Hongyu for taking care of two active and rebellious teenagers, conducting all family chores, and not complaining to me too much.

This book was special due to the stresses and difficulties posed by the Covid-19 pandemic. We thank and salute the authors who had to overcome numerous challenges to help make this volume a reality. Our authors had to persevere through unprecedented circumstances to enable this masterful encyclopedia. Now, it is time to celebrate and reap the fruits of our demanding work! Cheese and cheers!

Sustainable Big Data Analytics Process Pipeline Using Apache Ecosystem

S

Jane Cheng
UBS, USA

Peng Zhao
iD https://orcid.org/0000-0003-1458-8266
INTELLIGENTRABBIT LLC, USA

INTRODUCTION

Big data analytics is an automated process which uses a set of techniques or tools to access large-scale data to extract useful information and insight. This process involves a series of customized and proprietary steps. it requires specific knowledge to handle and operate the workflow properly. Due to 4V nature of big data (Volumes, Variety, Velocity and Veracity), it is required to build a robust, reliable and fault-tolerant data processing pipeline . The proposed approach will help application developers to conquer this challenge.

Apache Airflow is a cutting-edge technology for applying big data analytics, which can cooperate the data processing workflows and data warehouses properly. Apache Airflow was developed by Airbnb technical engineers, aiming to manage internal workflows in a productive way. In 2016, Airflow became affiliated by Apache and was made accessible to users as an open source. Airflow is a framework that can conduct the various job of executing, scheduling, distributing, and monitoring. It can handle either interdependent or independent tasks. To operate each job, a directed acyclic graph (DAG) definition file is required. In this definition file, a collection is included for developers to run and sectionalized by relationships and dependencies.

The sustainable automation can consolidate all tasks of ETL, data warehousing, and analytics on one technology platform. The upstream vendor data will be ingested into a data lake, where source data is maintained and gone through the data processing of cleaning, scrubbing, normalization and data insight extraction. In the next step of data mining tasks, data could be processed to perform study analytics for end users. Motivated by the current demand in big data analytics and industrial applications, this chapter is proposed to illustrate and investigate a novel sustainable big data processing pipeline using a variety of big data tools. The proposed data pipeline starts at the standard data processing workflow using Apache Airflow, using GitLab for source code control to facilitate peer code review, and uses CI/CD for continuous integration and deployment. Apache Spark has been used for the data computer process scaling with standardizing data in the data warehousing procedure. With data persistent in HDFS/ADLS, downstream system can choose either data visualization tool or API to access data. The objectives of this chapter are:

- investigating most recent big data tools for constructing the novel data workflow architecture.
- illustrating the major functional components of the proposed system architecture.
- initializing a state-of-the-art data workflow architecture design that can be used in the industrial applications.

DOI: 10.4018/978-1-7998-9220-5.ch073

BACKGROUND

Due to the fast revolutionary of information technologies and systems, avalanche-like growth of data has prompted the emergence of new models and technical methods for distributed data processing, including MapReduce, Dryad, Spark (Khan et al., 2014). For processing large graphs, special purpose systems for distributed computing based on the data-flow approach were introduced (Gonzalez et al., 2014). Some systems focused on batch (offline) data processing, while other systems and services can handle the real-time (online) data processing, such as Storm, Spark Streaming, Kafka Streams, and Apache, which attract more attentions due to the users' demands on its ability of rapid and smart responding to the incoming data (Zaharia et al., 2012). These systems can implement the distributed data processing operations, so that to support large volumes of incoming data and to fulfill high speed of data delivery. For distributed data processing, a crucial feature of existing data-driven software systems is the abstraction of the programmer from the details of the implementation of computations by using ready-made primitives. For example, distributed data-flow-operators use map and reduce. This makes simplification of writing programs possible, which can fit into the proposed model of computations. However, it may be still difficult to implement other classes of applications. MapReduce-based systems may not be an optimal choice for performing iterative algorithms and fully connected applications. Many professional solutions for diverse kinds of applications have been established to figure out the limitations of existing distributed data processing models and technologies (Suleykin & Panfilov, 2019a).

In recent years, the open-source methods have become increasingly popular. Hadoop stack that promoted data processing of MapReduce is one of the most commonly used technologies for big data storage. Hortonworkers Data Platform stack provides 100% open-source global data management and related services, for the customers to manage the full lifecycle of the data. Many large industrial companies widely used this stack for data processing, storage, analysis, and visualization. The technical applications of open-access big data, based on HDP Hadoop ecosystem stack, have discussed and analyzed in current research. HDP Hadoop ecosystem stack can establish data processing workflow with all job dependencies and proceed various jobs from one workflow orchestrator. Based on sample industrial KPIs data, which shows the adaptability of suggested methodology for all the possible real-world data with specific formats, the workflow can be implemented and simulated. A set of interconnected jobs for workflow include Spark jobs, shell jobs and PostgreSQL query commands. Additionally, all the workflow steps can be connected and patterned in one data pipeline.

Most recent studies are concentrated on industrial applications with hybrid approaches using open-source technologies, such as Apache ecosystems and other analytical tools. Suleykin & Panfilov (2019b) introduced a big data processing workflow using Apache Hadoop, Postgre SQL, and Apache Airflow. Such a system architecture can be performed with stages through multiple storage spaces for industrial KPIs of millions of records. A novel big data workflow has been proposed for the scalable execution of data transaction, along with a scalability comparison of the proposed method with that of Argo Workflows (Dessalk et al., 2020). Ramanan et al. (2020) illustrated the features and strengths of a new data workflow framework with real-world deep learning processing using Apache Spark, Beam, Swift/T, and Apache Airflow. Such a system can be applied in terms of ease of authoring, efficiency, scalability, and fault recovery. Similar studies have been represented in the form of discussions of vast applications and system architecture designs using Apache Airflow, ranging from exploration of workflow management (Mitchell et al., 2019), lightweight pipeline decision supporting system (Kotliar et al., 2019), to industrial-level ETL processing with metadata-driven systems (Suleykin & Panfilov, 2020; Panfilov & Suleykin, 2021).

FOCUS OF THE ARTICLE

This chapter provides a comprehensive understanding of the cutting-edge big data workflow technologies that have been widely applied in the industrial applications, covering a broad range of most current big data processing methods and tools, including Hadoop, Hive, MapReduce, Sqoop, Hue, Spark, Cloudera, Airflow, and GitLab. An industrial data workflow pipeline is proposed and investigated in terms of the system architecture, which is designed to meet the needs of data-driven industrial big data analytics applications concentrated on the large-scale data processing. It differs from traditional data pipelines and workflows in its ability of ETL and analytical portals. The proposed data workflow can improve the industrial analytics applications for multiple tasks. This chapter also provides bid data researchers and professionals with an understanding of the challenges facing big data analytics in real-world environments and informs interdisciplinary studies in this field.

SOLUTIONS AND RECOMMENDATIONS

Components of The System Architecture using Apache Hadoop Ecosystem

Apache Spark

Apache Spark is a unified computing engine and a set of libraries for parallel data processing on computer clusters. As of this writing, Spark is the most actively developed open-source engine for this task, making it a standard tool for any developer or data scientist interested in big data (Zaharia et al., 2016). This makes it an easy system to start with and scale-up to big data processing. For MapReduce task, Spark can process 100 times faster than Hadoop. Besides, Multiple programming languages, including Java, Python, Scala, and R, are supported by Spark (Salloum et al., 2016). Spark also supports for integration with HDFS, HBase, Canssandra, Amazon S3, Hive and so on. The user can control the spark cluster by Hadoop YARN or Apache Mesos in command line. Spark Core is the key foundation of the Spark framework for dispatching and scheduling distributed tasks, managing data storage, commanding basic I/O functionalities, and conducting fault tolerance strategy. Resilient Distributed Dataset (RDD) was introduced by Spark for parallel operations, including transformations and actions. Transformation operations work for mapping, filtering, joining, and unionizing on an RDD. The transformation operations in Spark do not calculate the results directly. They only conduct computing after receiving feedback for an action and confirming that the result is ready to the driver. This operation mechanism can promote the computing speed for Spark. Action operations usually can give a certain value using a set of functions, such as reduce, collect, count, first, etc. At the first time the value is computed in an action, it will be stored in memory of the nodes. Before creating an RDD, the user needs to load the input file by Spark-Scala API and then execute word count transformation using map function. Spark SQL is a supportive tool for querying structured and semi-structured data. It enables to use multiple programming languages, including Scala, Python, Java, and NET, to analyze data frames for different data sources. Spark SQL can also combine the SQL queries and transformations together to serve Spark cluster. Based on the reliable scheduling characteristics of Spark Core, Spark Streaming can implement real-time data streaming analytics. Spark Streaming can analyze the web server log status information and diverse messaging queues for social media. After receiving the input streams, Spark Streaming can distribute the data into different batches and then Spark engine can produce the final output stream in batches. Furthermore, in application level, it is easy and feasible for the developers and programmers to work on the streaming data using Spark Streaming API. MLlib is a machine learning library, used in programming languages of Java, Scala, Python, and R, for Spark (Meng et al., 2016). Many algorithms, such as classification, regression, and clustering, can be trained in Spark cluster with streaming data by MLlib. GraphX is a framework for graph processing, which can perform parallel operations on Spark cluster. GraphX supports two different APIs, containing a Pregel abstraction and MapReduce-based API, to carry out parallel algorithms.

Cloudera

Majority of the big data enterprises today use Apache Hadoop in some way or the other. To simplify working with Hadoop, enterprise versions like Cloudera is chosen. Cloudera was founded by three technical engineers from Google, Facebook, and Yahoo! in 2008 (Chawda & Thakur, 2016). Cloudera has an ambition to offer the best Big Data platforms and become a fantastic enterprise data cloud company. Enterprise Data Cloud (EDC) is a strategy to cooperate multiple analytic functions to work on the same data source. EDC help enterprises and governments to achieve productivity through offering multiple clouds, elastic multiple functions, and open-accessible data usage. With the combination of the CDH and HDP services, Cloudera Data Platform (CDP) has been established to manage and access the data lake, data analytics, and machine learning services (Benlachmi & Hasnaoui, 2021). Moreover, CDP public cloud can work as a control center to isolate the used workloads, such as Data Warehouse, Data Streaming, Data Visualization and Operational Database, control workload type, and operate the workload priority. CDP can manage data using a single pane of glass on AWS, Azure and Google Cloud Platform. CDP public cloud services include Data Hub, Data Warehouse, Machine Learning, Data Engineering, Data Visualization, and Operational Database. CDP Data Hub is an analytics service facilitated by Coudera Runtime. Multiple CDP Data Hub clusters can work on the same environment and the connection between each other can make the movement and interaction of the workloads much more flexible. CDP Data Warehouse is an auto-scaling cluster, which was designed for self-service independent DWHs. The main components of CDP Data Warehouse are Database Catalogs and Virtual Warehouses. Besides, it has an obvious advantage on dealing with structured and unstructured data with all sizes and usually can be controlled without using YARN. Machine Learning service provides a self-service machine learning platform, which enables the enterprise users to directly access computing resources and tools. These computing resources and tools include the useful IDEs like Jupiter and Zeppelin, and the commonly used programming languages and modules, like Python, Tensorflow, Scala, and R (Erraissi et al., 2020). The foundation of Cloudera Data Platform architecture is Shared Data Experience, which can help to deliver the data with security and economic costs.

Apache Airflow

Apache Airflow, with the pipelines configured in Python scripts, is an open-source workflow platform that can manage and monitor the workflows (Finnigan & Toner, 2021). In Airflow architecture, DAGs enable the Airflow to operate workflow schedule. DAG can be generated through setting configuration files and file system trees. The user can define the frequency for it to run and trigger rule for each task for DAG. If a DAG fails its task, Airflow will automatically perform retry, even though the number of retries is limited by the DAG ability. The user side can control the work of a DAG, require a retry for the failed task of DAG and check log information through a UI frontend (Mitchell et al., 2019). Moreover, due to alerting system, Airflow can send an email reminder if a failure of DAG happens, and the user can also send an email when a task doesn't follow the defined service level agreement (SLA). Airflow uses SerialExecutor to assign a task to workers, to determine number of tasks to work on simultaneously, and to update the progress status of the tasks. To store the configuration and status information of all DAGs and tasks, Airflow can be set up a database backend to MySQL or PostgresSQL using Hooks to connect (Jurney, 2017). Furthermore, Airflow can track origins of data with lineage support through inlets and outlets of the tasks to check how the workflow goes on over time. In the functional structure of Airflow, operators are building blocks that deal with the real work and conduct tasks in a specific order. The major functions of Airflow can be fulfilled by three categories of operators, including action operators, transfer operators, and sensor operators. Action Operators will execute the work, such as using PythonOperator to compile python script for the application and BashOperator to perform commands in a bash shell. Transfer operators, like S3ToRedshiftOperator, are responsible for moving data from its source to a place that will be processed. Sensor Operators can perceive any external condition that may happen. For example, the ExternalTaskSensor can detect the task status in a DAG and start a new task in its dependent DAG when the current task has been successfully conducted. To meet the customized requirements of the user, Airflow allows the user to generate new operators through defining the parameters for the new operator and adding config values in executing codes.

CI/CD Deployment and GitLab

CI/CD provides an effective method to transform products into market. Continuous integration (CI) helps developers to build and package their software applications (Singh et al., 2019). Continuous delivery (CD) can deliver the code to testing and development environments. CI/CD pipeline performs monitoring to improve the application development process through several stages, including building, packaging, testing, releasing, deploying, and validating. In building stage, a runnable program can be written in multiple programming languages, such as Go, C++, Java. If the program is written in Ruby, Python and JavaScript, the program can work without going through building stage. A test for validation will be conducted in testing stage to check program bugs. Once an implementable program is ready, the deployment environments will be set up by the product team to test application.

GitLab, a web-based Git repository, offers free open and private repositories, which enables users to plan project, manage source code, and monitor the tasks (Choudhury et al., 2021). In 2013, GitLab was divided into GitLab Community Edition and GitLab Enterprise Edition. In 2017, GitLab announced to become completely open-source repository under an MIT License. GitLab has an in-built registry and can be deployed even without configuration settings. Moreover, GitLab has user-friendly UI interface and tools, which is easy for users to use and set up. For the industrial developers or professionals, GitLab allows unlimited accesses of free private repositories. The integration of many API tools and third-party services is convenient for the developer to implement for their application products.

Hadoop, Hive, MapReduce and Impala

With the growth in digital information, traditional database management systems didn't have enough ability to process large data fast. Hadoop Distributed File System (HDFS), developed by Doug Cutting using Java in 2006, solved those challenging tasks, including data creation, data storage, data sharing, data analysis and so on, for Big Data with its advantageous features (Borthakur, 2008). HDFS was a software framework designed for data storage and application implementation on clusters of commodity hardware. Different from the traditional database system, HDFS can handle large amounts of structured and unstructured data fast, since it has more computing nodes working together. Besides, to guarantee the computing quality, fault tolerance mechanism of HDFS will rearrange the tasks to other nodes if any error happens to a node. Adapting to the popularity of multimedia resources, HDFS can directly store unstructured data, such as text, videos, and images, for further use. Its scalability allows the user to update the system easily through adding extra notes to process bigger data. In HDFS, a master-slave architecture works through NameNode and DataNodes. Each cluster has one single NameNode for namespace operations and multiple DataNodes with many blocks to conduct the read and write tasks from the clients. DataNode uses TCP/IP layer to communicate with the clients, while the clients use RPC to give responses. The blocks on DataNotes have the same size, while only last one has the difference size. Based on fault tolerance, the blocks are replicated for the NameNode to make decision (Ghazi & Gangodkar, 2015). To implement the MapReduce tasks, HDFS has JobTracker service that assigns MapReduce tasks for each node and TaskTracker that accepts the tasks, both of which form a complete MapReduce framework to handle large amounts of data. JobTracker is responsible for receiving the job from the client server architecture, scheduling the tasks for each node in a cluster, overseeing them, fixing the error tasks, and giving back the diagnostic feedback to the clients. TaskTracker has a set of slots, which determines how many tasks that it can process. Hive, firstly developed by Facebook and written in Java, is a data warehouse tool that can analyze the huge datasets stored in HDFS. Hive works through SQL-based query language, named HiveQL, to request queries to the MapReduce job and stores the schema in a specific database for data processing. Hive can be configured through manually editing hive-site.xml file, setting the Hive configuration option, or directly using set command.

Sqoop and Hue

Apache Sqoop, with a connector-based architecture, is an important component of the Hadoop ecosystem, which is a tool to import the structured data from relational database systems into Hadoop for MapReduce tasks (Aravinth et al., 2015). In order to transfer data, the data is required to have consistency and be prepared for the following downstream pipeline. Importing data with Apache Sqoop goes through two main steps. The first step is to collect the necessary metadata, and the second step is to submit a map job to the cluster. The imported data is usually stored in text or in Sequence and Avro files as binary data. For the process of exporting data, Sqoop shifts data from HDFS to RDBMS, which is processed through checking for the database and transferring the data. In addition, Sqoop can be utilized by a variety of structured data sources, such as Oracle, Postgres, and can directly load data from Hive and HBase, which make transferring data efficient and cost-effective.

Hadoop Hue is an open-source user interface, through which the users can manage HDFS and MapReduce applications without utilizing the command line (Guttikonda et al., 2019). Developers choose Hue as an optimal choice to operating Hadoop cluster, due to its advantages, including Hadoop API access, presence of HDFS file browser, editor for Hive and Pig query, Hadoop shell access, and so on. One of the most important features of Hue is the capability to access the HDFS Browser. The users can control the works on HDFS through its interface. Besides, the information related to job, including Job ID, Application Type, Name, Job Status, and Job Duration, can be accessed through Job browser. To analyze data, the user can apply SQL Hive queries through the editor and then the browser will present the query result to the user.

Overview of the System Architecture Design

Prior to the advent of big data era, traditional way of extracting raw data into a data analytic has lots of drawback. It relies on processing the data files which satisfy size limit. The job scheduling tool like Autosys or others don't have UI to monitor each step of data processing. Each different type of raw data has its own challenge which makes it hard to standardize processing pipeline. The proposed solution consolidates all ETL, data analytics and data warehousing onto one new big data platform. It empowers developers simplifying the process of building enterprise-grade production data applications. Once the data comes from various source (ftp/sftp/webservice/AWS S3/Amazon data exchange/Sharepoint) is available, it would be loaded into data lake as-is. Then the automated process of cleansing, scrubbing, normalizing and Data quality checking steps would be triggered accordingly.

Apache airflow is used here to achieve the goal. Apache Airflow is one of the most powerful platforms in orchestrating workflows. It is a workflow engine that will easily schedule and run complex data pipelines. It will make sure that each task of data pipeline will get executed in the correct order and each task gets the required resources. Airflow will automatically trigger on defined time, and all the processes get executed in order. With setup of airflow cluster to run across multiple nodes, distributed queue for holding ready-to-execute operators is more efficient. The daemon which accepts HTTP requests and allows user to interact with Airflow UI via a Python Flask Web Application. It provides the ability to pause, un-pause DAGs, manually trigger DAGs, view running DAGs, restart failed DAGs, etc. A running instance of Airflow has several Daemons that work together to provide the full functionality of Airflow. The daemons include the Web Server, Scheduler, Worker, Kerberos, Flower, Celery, and others. The rich user interface of Airflow makes it easy to visualize pipelines running in production, monitor progress and troubleshoot issues when needed.

For data processing, Cloudera Enterprise (CDP) is used. It combines Hadoop with other open-source projects to create a single, massively scalable system in which you can unite storage with an array of powerful processing and analytic frameworks. Cloudera cluster offers a shared infrastructure that provides computing power (CPU cores and memory). It has extra benefits of both private and public cloud with CDP Hybrid Cloud (Chambers & Zaharia, 2018). When we execute spark query, it splits query up into spark tasks and distributed tasks on all the available clusters. The shared computing environment has all the benefits of computing capacity. However, we need to be cognizant of the jobs are shared resource which competing for the resource with other jobs in the system. The time to take for each of the job depends on a few factors such as the speed of cluster resources, computational capacities, the total running tasks, and Data distribution across physical nodes.

The proposed data workflow architecture is illustrated in the data processing chart, as shown in Figure 1, which represents the full cycle of the data flow transaction from external raw data extraction to the data analytics using the hybrid solution with big data tools. Such a novel data workflow architecture can be applied in a variety of real-word applications with the fully automated features of the system. The whole ETL process applies Apache Airflow to ingest various feed and data validation, along with data quality checking, and finally produces data asset using Apache Spark. However, such a system requires the pre-actions to setup Airflow and Cloudera clusters, thereby may cause some unexpected difficulties in initializing the system architecture. Traditional solutions, on the other hand, are easy to implement for smaller datasets, using Autosys, GitHub, Python, Postgres, Greenplum, ftp/stp, webservice, and batch process, however, such a solution relies on manually data checking and intervention, therefore the process is over customized and proprietary in terms of limited file size scales and limitations of Autosys UI. Figure 1 illustrate an Apache Airflow-based pipeline orchestration for Cloudera Data Platform

(CDP) with the flexibility to define scalable transformations with a combination of Spark and Hive. Data engineer can generate curated datasets/analytics for users by any downstream applications efficiently and securely. The pipelines are scheduled and orchestrated by a managed Airflow service without the typical administrative cost of setting up a code is deployed using CI/CD.

Figure 1. Data workflow chart for the proposed system architecture in processing from external data to analytical platforms

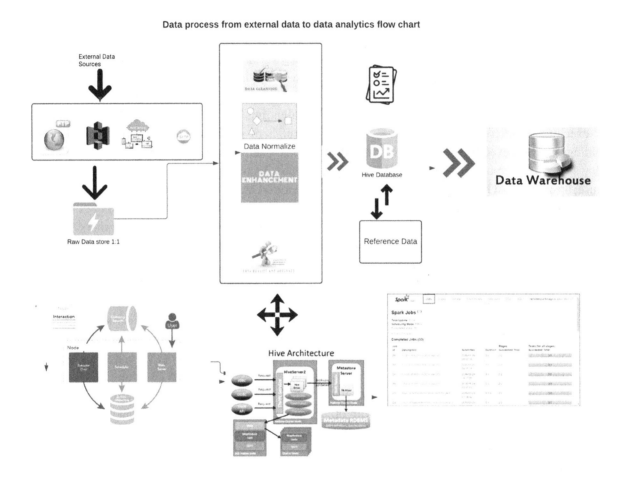

When it comes to working with Big Data in a unified way, at its core is the Spark Engine for both real time and batch. Using Apache Spark in Big Data platforms, another choice is Azure Databricks besides Cloudera CDP. It is fully managed, cloud-based Big Data and Machine Learning platform, Azure Databricks focus on performance and cost-efficiency in the cloud. Several key capabilities to Apache Spark workloads that can increase performance and High-speed connectors to Azure storage services, such as Azure Blob Stor and feature Auto-scaling and auto-termination of Spark clusters to minimize costs, Caching, Indexing, Advanced query optimization

From a high level, the Azure Databricks service launches and manages Apache Spark clusters within Azure subscription. Apache Spark clusters are groups of computers that are treated as a single computer and handle the execution of commands issued from notebooks. We can have the option of using a Serverless Pool. A Serverless Pool is self-managed pool of cloud resources that is auto configured for interactive Spark workloads. You provide the minimum and maximum number of workers and the worker type, and Azure Databricks provisions the compute and local storage based on your usage.

While choosing Databricks as Spark engine, to solve problem the query speed due to data volume increase, Delta Lakecome to help in scalability, reliable and speed. It's a file format that integrates with Spark and has both open-source and managed offerings. helps to combine the capabilities of Data Lake, data warehousing, and a streaming ingestion system. Although Databricks can work with open sources ETL like Airflow, ETL workflow can be operationalized using Azure Data Factory, Azure Data Factory can also be used to ingest data collected from different sources and coordinate processing jobs in Azure Databricks as part of your data pipeline.

FUTURE RESEARCH DIRECTIONS

Current big data tools and systems are powered by a variety of data processing, information gathering, data analytics, data visualization, and machine learning/deep learning. The proposed system architecture enables to extract knowledge and valuable information from internal and external data sources. Nevertheless, such a system needs to be configured by real-world applications, which will be implemented in the future. Various big data tasks can be performed in terms of data integration, distributed storage, centralized management, rapid and interactive analysis, data security, cloud computing capability, and machine learning in the future studies, along with the validation of the system architecture for a multi-task big data analytics. On the other hand, existing big data platforms, as the components of the proposed data workflow architecture, have clearly some limitations and may differ in the offerings and capacities. The future research directions will be ongoing towards optimizing all the aspects of the applied technologies and methods in terms of discussions of multi-streams and other related big data challenges, such as computational capacities, distributions, and environments. Moreover, the prominence of data-driven professionals within industry and research organizations have given rise to teams of data workflow collaborating on extracting useful and insightful information from raw data, as opposed to individual data scientists working alone. However, it is still lack of solid and deeper understanding of how those data professionals work in practice and collaboration, such as data management with data engineering, using Github or Gitlab, data cleaning and model training, etc. Such topics can be the major research direction in the future studies.

CONCLUSION

This chapter illustrates a novel data workflow framework with concentrating on the major components and the system architecture design. Big data characteristics and solutions have been discussed by investigating almost all cutting-edge technologies, such as Hadoop, Hive, MapReduce, Sqoop, Hue, Spark, Cloudera, and Airflow. Besides, different tools and frameworks have been illustrated and compared in terms of their features, advantages, and limitations. The proposed system can be applied in multiple industrial tasks with further examinations in the form of the testing procedure.

REFERENCES

Aravinth, S. S., Begam, A. H., Shanmugapriyaa, S., Sowmya, S., & Arun, E. (2015). An efficient HADOOP frameworks SQOOP and ambari for big data processing. *International Journal for Innovative Research in Science and Technology*, *1*(10), 252–255.

Benlachmi, Y., & Hasnaoui, M. L. (2021). Open source big data platforms and tools: An analysis. *Indonesian Journal of Electrical Engineering and Informatics*, *9*(3), 732–746. doi:10.52549/.v9i3.3170

Borthakur, D. (2008). HDFS architecture guide. *Hadoop Apache Project, 53*(1-13), 2.

Chambers, B., & Zaharia, M. (2018). *Spark: The definitive guide: Big data processing made simple*. O'Reilly Media, Inc.

Chawda, R. K., & Thakur, G. (2016, March). Big data and advanced analytics tools. In 2016 symposium on colossal data analysis and networking (CDAN) (pp. 1-8). IEEE. doi:10.1109/CDAN.2016.7570890

Choudhury, P., Crowston, K., Dahlander, L., Minervini, M. S., & Raghuram, S. (2020). GitLab: Work where you want, when you want. *Journal of Organization Design*, *9*(1), 1–17. doi:10.118641469-020-00087-8

Dessalk, Y. D., Nikolov, N., Matskin, M., Soylu, A., & Roman, D. (2020, November). Scalable execution of big data workflows using software containers. In *Proceedings of the 12th International Conference on Management of Digital EcoSystems* (pp. 76-83). 10.1145/3415958.3433082

Erraissi, A., Banane, M., Belangour, A., & Azzouazi, M. (2020, October). Big data storage using model driven engineering: From big data meta-model to cloudera PSM meta-model. In *2020 International Conference on Data Analytics for Business and Industry: Way Towards a Sustainable Economy (ICDABI)* (pp. 1-5). IEEE. 10.1109/ICDABI51230.2020.9325674

Finnigan, L., & Toner, E. (2021). *Building and maintaining metadata aggregation workflows using Apache Airflow*. Temple University Libraries.

Ghazi, M. R., & Gangodkar, D. (2015). Hadoop, MapReduce and HDFS: A developers perspective. *Procedia Computer Science*, *48*, 45–50. doi:10.1016/j.procs.2015.04.108

Gonzalez, J. E., Xin, R. S., Dave, A., Crankshaw, D., Franklin, M. J., & Stoica, I. (2014). Graphx: Graph processing in a distributed dataflow framework. In *11th USENIX Symposium on Operating Systems Design and Implementation (OSDI 14)* (pp. 599-613). USENIX.

Guttikonda, G., Katamaneni, M., & Pandala, M. (2019, March). Diabetes data prediction using Spark and analysis in Hue over big data. In *2019 3rd International Conference on Computing Methodologies and Communication (ICCMC)* (pp. 1112-1117). IEEE. 10.1109/ICCMC.2019.8819676

Jurney, R. (2017). *Agile data science 2.0: Building full-stack data analytics applications with spark*. O'Reilly Media, Inc.

Khan, N., Yaqoob, I., Hashem, I. A. T., Inayat, Z., Mahmoud Ali, W. K., Alam, M., Shiraz, M., & Gani, A. (2014). Big data: Survey, technologies, opportunities, and challenges. *TheScientificWorldJournal*, *2014*, 2014. doi:10.1155/2014/712826 PMID:25136682

Kotliar, M., Kartashov, A. V., & Barski, A. (2019). CWL-Airflow: A lightweight pipeline manager supporting Common Workflow Language. *GigaScience*, 8(7), giz084. doi:10.1093/gigascience/giz084 PMID:31321430

Meng, X., Bradley, J., Yavuz, B., Sparks, E., Venkataraman, S., Liu, D., ... Talwalkar, A. (2016). Mllib: Machine learning in apache spark. *Journal of Machine Learning Research*, 17(1), 1235–1241.

Mitchell, R., Pottier, L., Jacobs, S., da Silva, R. F., Rynge, M., Vahi, K., & Deelman, E. (2019, December). Exploration of workflow management systems emerging features from users perspectives. In *2019 IEEE International Conference on Big Data (Big Data)* (pp. 4537-4544). IEEE. 10.1109/BigData47090.2019.9005494

Mitchell, R., Pottier, L., Jacobs, S., da Silva, R. F., Rynge, M., Vahi, K., & Deelman, E. (2019, December). Exploration of workflow management systems emerging features from users perspectives. In *2019 IEEE International Conference on Big Data (Big Data)* (pp. 4537-4544). IEEE. 10.1109/BigData47090.2019.9005494

Panfilov, P., & Suleykin, A. (2021). Building resilience into the metadata-based ETL process using open source big data technologies. In *Resilience in the Digital Age* (pp. 139–153). Springer. doi:10.1007/978-3-030-70370-7_8

Ramanan, B., Drabeck, L., Woo, T., Cauble, T., & Rana, A. (2020, December). ~ PB&J~-Easy automation of data science/machine learning workflows. In *2020 IEEE International Conference on Big Data (Big Data)* (pp. 361-371). IEEE. 10.1109/BigData50022.2020.9378128

Salloum, S., Dautov, R., Chen, X., Peng, P. X., & Huang, J. Z. (2016). Big data analytics on Apache Spark. *International Journal of Data Science and Analytics*, 1(3), 145–164. doi:10.100741060-016-0027-9

Singh, C., Gaba, N. S., Kaur, M., & Kaur, B. (2019, January). Comparison of different CI/CD tools integrated with cloud platform. In *2019 9th International Conference on Cloud Computing, Data Science & Engineering (Confluence)* (pp. 7-12). IEEE.

Suleykin, A., & Panfilov, P. (2019a, April). Distributed big data driven framework for cellular network monitoring data. In *2019 24th Conference of Open Innovations Association (FRUCT)* (pp. 430-436). IEEE. 10.23919/FRUCT.2019.8711912

Suleykin, A., & Panfilov, P. (2019b, January). Implementing big data processing workflows using open source Technologies. In *Proceedings of the 30th DAAAM International Symposium* (pp. 394-404). 10.2507/30th.daaam.proceedings.054

Suleykin, A., & Panfilov, P. (2020, December). Metadata-driven industrial-grade ETL system. In *2020 IEEE International Conference on Big Data (Big Data)* (pp. 2433-2442). IEEE. 10.1109/BigData50022.2020.9378367

Zaharia, M., Das, T., Li, H., Shenker, S., & Stoica, I. (2012). Discretized streams: an efficient and fault-tolerant model for stream processing on large clusters. *4th USENIX Workshop on Hot Topics in Cloud Computing (HotCloud 12)*.

Zaharia, M., Xin, R. S., Wendell, P., Das, T., Armbrust, M., Dave, A., Meng, X., Rosen, J., Venkataraman, S., Franklin, M. J., Ghodsi, A., Gonzalez, J., Shenker, S., & Stoica, I. (2016). Apache spark: A unified engine for big data processing. *Communications of the ACM*, 59(11), 56–65. doi:10.1145/2934664

ADDITIONAL READING

Arfat, Y., Usman, S., Mehmood, R., & Katib, I. (2020). Big data tools, technologies, and applications: A survey. In *Smart Infrastructure and Applications* (pp. 453–490). Springer. doi:10.1007/978-3-030-13705-2_19

Baviskar, M. R., Nagargoje, P. N., Deshmukh, P. A., & Baviskar, R. R. (2021). A survey of data science techniques and available tools. *International Research Journal of Engineering and Technology*.

Dasgupta, N. (2018). *Practical big data analytics: Hands-on techniques to implement enterprise analytics and machine learning using Hadoop, Spark, NoSQL and R*. Packt Publishing Ltd.

Du, D. (2018). *Apache Hive Essentials: Essential techniques to help you process, and get unique insights from, big data*. Packt Publishing Ltd.

Grover, M., Malaska, T., Seidman, J., & Shapira, G. (2015). *Hadoop application architectures: Designing real-world big data applications*. O'Reilly Media, Inc.

Jurney, R. (2017). *Agile data science 2.0: Building full-stack data analytics applications with spark*. O'Reilly Media, Inc.

Landset, S., Khoshgoftaar, T. M., Richter, A. N., & Hasanin, T. (2015). A survey of open source tools for machine learning with big data in the Hadoop ecosystem. *Journal of Big Data*, 2(1), 1–36. doi:10.118640537-015-0032-1

Li, K. C., Jiang, H., & Zomaya, A. Y. (Eds.). (2017). *Big data management and processing*. CRC Press. doi:10.1201/9781315154008

Mittal, M., Balas, V. E., Goyal, L. M., & Kumar, R. (Eds.). (2019). *Big data processing using spark in cloud*. Springer. doi:10.1007/978-981-13-0550-4

Rao, T. R., Mitra, P., Bhatt, R., & Goswami, A. (2019). The big data system, components, tools, and technologies: A survey. *Knowledge and Information Systems*, 60(3), 1165–1245. doi:10.100710115-018-1248-0

KEY TERMS AND DEFINITIONS

Apache Airflow: An open-source big data management platform, proposed by Airbnb as one of the most efficient data solutions to manage the industrial-level data workflow challenges.

Apache Spark: An open-source analytical engine for big data processing with an interface for programming entire clusters of implicit data parallelism and fault tolerance.

Big Data Analytics: The usage of analytical tools to deal with large, diverse datasets, including structured, unstructured, and semi-structured data, from multiple data sources, and in efficient and effective transactional processes.

Data Pipeline: A sequence of data processing components connected in series, where the output of one part is the input of the next one, in which the pipeline can be operated in parallel or in time-sliced manner.

Data Workflow: A set of operations that processes information and data from raw to processed.

ETL: Stands for extract, transform, and load, which is the general procedure of delivering data from one data sources to another.

Hadoop Ecosystem: A big data platform which offers a variety of services to solve the big data problems with four main components, such as HDFS, MapReduce, YARN, and Hadoop Common.

HBase: A Hadoop ecosystem part which is a distributed database that is designed to store data in structured formats, which is scalable and distributed.

Section 17
Data Visualization and Visual Mining

An Agent and Pattern-Oriented Approach to Data Visualization

Chung-Yeung Pang

https://orcid.org/0000-0002-7925-4454

Seveco AG, Switzerland

Severin K. Y. Pang

Cognitive Solutions and Innovation AG, Switzerland

INTRODUCTION

The standard style of software development is to analyze the problem, develop a design to solve the underlying problem, and implement the design into an application. As a result, the application is strongly tied to the problem to be solved. With new requirements, the application must be extended to solve the new problem. This way of software development is fine in many cases. However, applications built in this style may not work well when dealing with big data, which contains a wide variety of data types and structures.

In order to be able to handle a large amount of data, the software system must be flexible and agile. This chapter uses an example to show that following traditional standard programming would result in rigid and complex software components. An approach is presented that combines generic programming, pattern-oriented programming, and agent-oriented programming to build flexible and agile software systems. The approach is used to build a data visualization system that can handle a large variety of data. The visualization system is part of a web and mobile geography application. This application has to process thousands of physical and human geography topics with hundreds of data sources from the internet. The focus of this chapter is the general technical approach to building a flexible, scalable, and agile visualization system that can handle this amount of data. Code segments are used for illustration. The programming language used in the presentation is Dart with the Flutter framework. Flutter is a new product from Google and is widely used for web and mobile app development. The Dart language is similar to Javascript. Anyone with programming skills in C, C++, Java or Javascript can easily follow the code segments.

In this chapter, techniques are presented on how software components and patterns can change their behavior depending on the data context through reflection. The main motivation of aspect-oriented programming, the separation of concerns, is also discussed. In order to be able to pursue this approach, a paradigm shift in programming is required. This shift is also presented in this chapter.

The content of this chapter first deals with the background. This is followed by a section on generic programming, a section on patterns and frameworks, and a section on data, context, and agents. At the end, a conclusion is drawn, along with a section on the consequences and applicability of the development approach and a section on future research and direction.

DOI: 10.4018/978-1-7998-9220-5.ch074

Background

This section provides background information about the programming paradigm and the agile development process, the agent, and big data.

Programming, Paradigms, and Agile Development Process

In the early days of software history, programmers tended to develop their programs without documentation in an ad-hoc style. The programs are usually not structured and organized. One result of this programming style was the software crisis of the 1960s, 1970s and 1980s (Software Crisis, 2010).

Structural programming (Jackson, 1975) was introduced in the 1970s to combat spaghetti code resulting from the ad hoc style of programming. Much emphasis has been placed on how a program is well structured. However, it failed to handle the complexities of enterprise applications. At the end of the 1980s, object-oriented (OO) programming began to spread. Software scientists claim that OO languages were designed for programming on a large scale (Wegner, 1989). The OO paradigm with polymorphism and inheritance was a solution to resolve and control the complexity of enterprise applications.

Despite its promises, the OO paradigm was not the ultimate destination of the programming paradigm's journey. Thereafter, various programming paradigms were proposed with great promises. Much research has been carried out on these paradigms. These include aspect-oriented programming, pattern-oriented programming and agent-oriented programming.

Aspect-oriented programming deals with the separation of concerns. For example, technical infrastructure code and business logic code should not be mixed in one software component. AspectJ (AspectJ, 2021) is a practical aspect-oriented extension of the Java programming language. This chapter also takes this concept into account.

We live in a world full of patterns. Our habits are nothing more than repetitively following a series of behavior patterns. The publication of the book by Gamma et al. (1995) made software developers aware of patterns that we use all the time and that should be used in software development. A pattern is defined as the solution to a problem in a specific context. Pattern-oriented programming is a programming approach to identify the problem to be solved and to look for the pattern that provides the solution to the problem in the given context. Patterns in the context of this chapter differ from those of Gamma et al. (1995) and other authors (Weiss, 2003; Hohpe, & Woolfe, 2004). They are not abstractions of a software design. This chapter uses the properties of a pattern proposed by Pang (2020). A pattern can provide a solution through a set of code, composing other patterns together, getting resources, and activating a set of actions to handle a problem in the requests.

Agent-oriented programming (AOP) was introduced by Shoham within his Artificial Intelligence studies in 1990 (Shoham, 1990). His definition of AOP is the following:

AOP can be viewed as a specialization of object-oriented programming. The state of an agent consists of components called beliefs, choices, capabilities, commitments, and possibly others; for this reason, the state of an agent is called its mental state. The mental state of agents is captured formally in an extension of standard epistemic logics: beside temporalizing the knowledge and belief operators, AOP introduces operators for commitment, choice and capability. Agents are controlled by agent programs, which include primitives for communicating with other agents. In the spirit of speech-act theory, each communication primitives is of a certain type: informing, requesting, offering, and so on.

The next subsection contains a detailed description of the agent. AOP is a programming paradigm in which the structure of the software is based on the concept of agents.

The main motivation for research on the programming paradigm is to provide guidelines, standards, disciplines, methods, and software tools that help programmers quickly create software systems that are reliable, sustainable, flexible, extensible, and maintainable. Unfortunately, in practice, standard programming often ends up being too complex, rigid and anything but flexible and agile.

In recent years, the agile software development process (Agile Manifesto Group, 2001) has enjoyed great popularity in the software industry. This process follows the evolutionary and iterative approach to software development (Larman, 2003) and focuses on adapting to change. Software engineers in the agile community claim that they welcome changes in the software systems they develop. In this case, their software systems must be flexible, easy to extend and easy to maintain.

Following a software development process does not really make a software system agile and flexible. Pang (2016) pointed out that a suitable software architecture is essential and that a plug-and-play mechanism must be in place. The architectural design presented in this chapter is based on this concept. The concept is further expanded to cover the programming style required for a flexible and agile software system that is essential for big data processing.

Agents

In his definition of AOP, Shoham did not clearly provide the characteristics of an agent. Russell and Norvig (1995) define an agent is anything that can receive information about its environment or perceive its environment through sensors and then try to choose an appropriate action from available actions and attempt to achieve the expected goals by acting through actuators or effectors. Wooldridge (2009) gave a comprehensive description of an agent in his book. An agent, as described by Wooldridge, is a computer system that can act autonomously in a given environment to achieve a delegated goal. We can think of an agent as being in a close-coupled, continuous interaction with its environment, performing a chain of actions, such as sense-decide-act-sense-decide-act-sense repeatedly. According to Wooldridge, an intelligent agent typically exhibits the following three types of behavior:

- **Reactive** – maintaining an ongoing interaction with its environment
- **Proactive** – generating and attempting to achieve goals; not driven solely by events but taking the initiative
- **Social** – ability to interact cooperate with other agents (and possibly humans) as well as systems and subsystems.

A reactive agent would react to events in its environment and trigger the appropriate actions. A more proactive agent would keep a set of internal states and decide what action to take depending on the combination of the event that occurred and the internal states. An agent that interacts with other agents and people in response to an event is social. A general approach to building an intelligent multi-agent system is to program all possible internal states of the agents and use a mechanism similar to a finite state machine with decision tables for the actions to be taken and state transitions in response to events. Such an approach doesn't work well for data-centric applications. It is not possible to define all possible states and events related to a variety of data.

One approach would be to build agents that can reflect the context of the data and decide what action to take. There are a number of references to reflective agents (Tozicka, Pechoucek, & Rehák, 2007;

Brazier, & Treur, 1995). The issues addressed in these literatures are not actually related to big data analysis. They use Proglog or a similar style to provide reflection capabilities in agents, which doesn't really apply to our use case. However, building agents with reflective behavior is the appropriate approach for big data analysis and visualization, according to us.

Big Data

The world's data volume is growing exponentially over time. Many large companies have already accumulated data of such size and complexity that none of the traditional data management tools can store it or process it efficiently. The greater the amount of data is available worldwide on the Internet. We are dealing with big data.

In a 2001 MetaGroup research publication, Gartner analyst D. Laney presented the 3Vs concept for characterizing big data (Laney, 2012). The 3V stand for "Volume Velocity Variety". Not long after that came the 4th, 5th, 6th, 10th, and so on. The characterization of Big Data is beyond the scope of this chapter.

Many data can be of interest to companies, institutes, governments or individuals. There are many channels to collect this data. In fact, most data can be collected from the Internet. Platforms like Rapidapi facilitate data providers to create data source services using the REST API. Data consumers can access structured data by subscribing to these services. The amount and variety of data is huge. The challenge lies in the analysis of this data. Platforms like Datarobot provide tools for analyzing and visualizing data. However, in many commercial, industrial, and academic use cases like the one presented in this chapter, it is not possible to integrate an external platform into the applications.

The most effective method of data analysis is data visualizations, which consolidate complex datasets into easily digestible graphics. Charts, graphs, and tables are typical data visualization models to choose from (Bekker, 2019; Fedak, 2018; Rishi, 2017). Visualization allows users to look beyond individual datasets and easily see dependencies and correlations hidden in large datasets. Creating a visualization tool for a specific dataset, even if the dataset is huge, is not that difficult. The greater challenge arises when the tool must be able to deal with an unknown variety of data types and structures. The development of a software system for the general analysis and visualization of big data is a great challenge. It has to be extremely flexible. As pointed out by Rishi (Rishi, 2017), scalability is also a major concern. The purpose of this chapter is to present an approach to building a flexible and scalable system that can handle a variety of data.

GENERIC PROGRAMMING

In this section, we look at the traditional and generic programming styles.

Traditional Programming Style

As examples to illustrate the proposed concept for design and implementation, three standard charts, namely the bar chart, the pie chart and the line chart, are used to visualize the data as shown in figure 1. In this example there is a tab bar on top so that the user can switch from one chart to another.

There are many tutorials to create such widgets in Flutter for these diagrams. If we follow the directions of these tutorials (Shah, 2021) we will usually get a standard implementation as shown in the code segment in figure 2. The data entry for these charts can be implemented as shown in figure 3. Basically,

Figure 1. Three different charts for data visualization

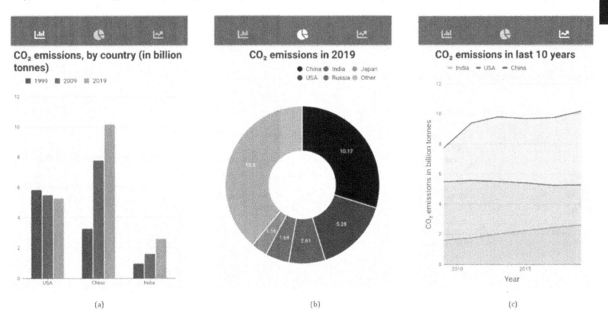

(a) (b) (c)

the Flutter widget structure in figure 2 shows what is required for a 3-tab *TabBar*. The first tab contains a bar chart, the second a pie chart, and the third, not shown in the code segment, contains a time series chart. All diagrams contain legends, which can be seen in figure 1. Flutter enables the nesting of many widgets in a container through the higher-level and subordinate hierarchy. If there are many primitive widgets in it, the structure can easily become very complex.

As shown in Code Segment figure 3, the standard way to set the input for the charts is to create a class like *Pollution*. Objects are instantiated with attributes of the class that are assigned to the input data. The objects serve as input for the series data to be displayed in the diagrams.

In our experience, programs of a similar style are typically provided by external freelance programmers. The next time we need to analyze populations from different countries, we have to program a new class *Population* and reuse the same implementation with a few minor modifications. In fact, the entire process corresponds to the fast iterative programming process with continuous integration into the agile software development approach.

Such an approach can work for small variations in data types. It would still require a full development lifecycle with implementation, testing, deployment, and release on the App Store and Play Store when it comes to mobile apps.

The approach would not work well if we have to process a wide variety of data. Not only would the software development effort be high and the time-to-market would be long, the final software package can also be huge, which can lead to deployment and maintenance issues.

Generic Programming Style

It is pretty easy to make the components generic so that the charts can be applied to different types of data. As shown in figure 3, Dart offers type *dynamics* that can contain any type of object. We can have a list (*List <dynamic>*) and a map (*Map <String, dynamic>*) of different types of objects. The *Map <String, dynamic>* class is very useful for object containers. The structure behind *Map* is similar to

JSON. In fact, a JSON file can be parsed to create a *Map* object. The following code snippet in figure 4 shows how a *Map* Object can be assigned.

Figure 2. Code segment of widget structure of charts

```
class GraphicHomePage extends StatefulWidget {
 final Widget child;
 GraphicHomePage({Key key, this.child}) : super(key: key);
 @override
 _GraphicHomePageState createState() => _GraphicHomePageState();
}

class _GraphicHomePageState extends State<GraphicHomePage> {
 List<charts.Series<Pollution, String>> _seriesData;
 ................
 @override
 Widget build(BuildContext context) {
  return MaterialApp(
     home: DefaultTabController(
        length: 3,
        child: Scaffold(
          appBar: AppBar(backgroundColor: Color(0xff1976d2),
            bottom: TabBar(indicatorColor: Color(0xff9962D0),
              tabs: [Tab(icon: Icon(FontAwesomeIcons.solidChartBar)),
               Tab(icon: Icon(FontAwesomeIcons.chartPie,)),
               Tab(icon: Icon(FontAwesomeIcons.chartLine))]),
            title: Text('Flutter Charts'),
          ),
          body: TabBarView(children: [
          Padding(
            padding: EdgeInsets.all(8.0),
            child: Container(
             child: Center(
              child: Column(
                children: <Widget>[
                Text('CO_2 emissions, by country (in billion tonnes)',
                  style: TextStyle(fontSize: 24.0, fontWeight: FontWeight.bold)),
                Expanded(
                  child: charts.BarChart(
                    _seriesData,
                    barGroupingType: charts.BarGroupingType.grouped,
                    behaviors: [new charts.SeriesLegend()],
                  ),
                ),
               ],
              ),
             ),
            ),
          ),
          Padding(
            padding: EdgeInsets.all(8.0),
            child: Container(
             child: Center(
              child: Column(
                children: <Widget>[
                Text('CO_2 emissions in 2019',
                  style: TextStyle(fontSize: 24.0, fontWeight: FontWeight.bold)),
                SizedBox(height: 10.0),
                Expanded(
                  child: charts.PieChart(_seriesPieData,
          ................
        ),
       }));
   }
 }
}
```

Figure 3. Code segment of data input for visualization

```
class Pollution {
  String country;
  int year;
  double quantity;
  Pollution(this.year, this.country, this.quantity);
}
.................
List<dynamic> list = input["pollution"];
List<List<Pollution>> data = [];
for (Map<String, dynamic> polData in list) {
  List<dynamic> yearList = polData["data"];
  List<Pollution> polList = [];
  for (Map<String, dynamic> countryQuantity in yearList) {
    polList.add(new Pollution(polData["year"], countryQuantity["country"], countryQuantity["quantity"]));
  }
  data.add(polList);
}
int i = 0;
for (List<Pollution> lData in data) {
  Color c = colors[i++];
  _seriesData.add(
    charts.Series(
      domainFn: (Pollution pollution, _) => pollution.country,
      measureFn: (Pollution pollution, _) => pollution.quantity,
      id: lData[0].year.toString(),
      data: lData,
      fillPatternFn: (_, _) => charts.FillPatternType.solid,
      fillColorFn: (_, _) => charts.ColorUtil.fromDartColor(c),
      colorFn: (_, _) => charts.ColorUtil.fromDartColor(c),
    ),
  );
}
```

Figure 4. Code segment illustrating the assignment of a Map object

```
Map<String, dynamic> input = {
  "title": "CO₂ emissions, by country (in billion tonnes)",
  "pollution": [
    {
      "year": 1999,
      "data": [{"country": "USA", "quantity": 5.83}, {"country": "China", "quantity": 3.26}, {"country": "India", "quantity": 0.95}]
    },
    {
      "year": 2009,
      "data": [{"country": "USA", "quantity": 5.49}, {"country": "China", "quantity": 7.76}, {"country": "India", "quantity": 1.61}]
    },
    {
      "year": 2019,
      "data": [{"country": "USA", "quantity": 5.28}, {"country": "China", "quantity": 10.17}, {"country": "India", "quantity": 2.61}]
    }
  ]
};
```

To visualize data in a bar chart, we only need to provide the widget with the data for the horizontal axis and the vertical axis. If the bars are grouped as shown in figure 1 (a), we may need additional information. Instead of input a class such as *Pollution* or *Population*, we can have a generic class *InputData* that contains attributes for the data of the horizontal (*xData*) and vertical (*yData*) axes and a group name (*group*) as shown in figure 5. The modification that changes the original component to a generic one is also shown in the code segment in figure 5.

Figure 5. Code segment of the changes to make the component generic

```
class InputData {                                      int i = 0;
  var xData;                                           for (List<InputData> IData in data) {
  var group;                                             Color c = colors[i++];
  var yData;                                             _seriesData.add(
  InputData(this.xData, this.group, this.yData);           charts.Series(
}                                                            domainFn: (InputData gData, _) => gData.xData,
                                                             measureFn: (InputData gData, _) => gData.yData,
bool grouped = true;                                         id: IData[0].group,
List<charts.Series<InputData, String>> _seriesData;          data: IData,
                                                             fillPatternFn: (_, _) => charts.FillPatternType.solid,
List<dynamic> list;                                          fillColorFn: (_, _) => charts.ColorUtil.fromDartColor(c),
input.values.forEach((value) {                               colorFn: (_, _) => charts.ColorUtil.fromDartColor(c)));
  if (value is List<dynamic>) {                          }
    list = value;
  }                                                    // Change in Bar Chart widget:
});                                                      child: charts.BarChart(
List<List<InputData>> data = [];                           _seriesData,
List<InputData> inputList = [];                            barGroupingType: grouped? charts.BarGroupingType.grouped : null,
List<dynamic> xyList;                                      behaviors: grouped ? [new charts.SeriesLegend()] : null,
for (Map<String, dynamic> groupMap in list) {            ),
  var group;
  groupMap.values.forEach((value) {
    if (value is List<dynamic>) {                      Map<String, dynamic> inputSingle = {
      xyList = value;                                    "title": "CO₂ emissions, by country (in billion tonnes)",
    } else {                                             "pollution": [
      group = value;                                       {"country": "USA", "quantity": 5.83},
    }});                                                   {"country": "China", "quantity": 3.26}, {"country": "India", "quantity": 0.95}]
  if (xyList != null) {                                 };
    List<InputData> groupList = [];
    for (Map<String, dynamic> xyMap in xyList) {
      List<dynamic> mapList = xyMap.values.toList();
      groupList.add(new InputData(mapList[0], group.toString(), mapList[1]));
    }
    data.add(groupList);
  } else {
    List<dynamic> mapList = groupMap.values.toList();
    inputList.add(new InputData(mapList[0], "Bar Chart", mapList[1]));
  }
}
if (xyList == null) {
  grouped = false;
  data.add(inputList);
}
```

To organize the data in a bar chart, we need a title and a list of data. Using the input data shown in figure 4, we have a title and the list of data under the *"Pollution"* key. We can ignore the *"Pollution"* key and just extract the data in the first list of the *Map input* as input to the bar chart. Again, we see that the first attribute of the *Map* in the elements of the list is *"year"* which has a numeric field, but the second is a list under the key *"data"*. The list again contains a map with fields. If we try to fit this data structure into the input data structure for the bar chart, we can see that the *"year"* is the group and the two fields in the elements of *"data"* are the input for the horizontal and vertical axes. In other words, based on the structure, the component can recognize what data in the input should be used for what purpose without checking the actual data itself. The code segment in figure 5 shows how this can be implemented. We have just touched on the design concepts of perception and reflection, which will be further elaborated in the next sections.

The *BarChart* widget can display group data as shown in figure 1 (a). However, it can also display a single set. This would happen when the map *inputSingle* (shown in figure 5) is used as input data and the data structure does not fit into a structure where grouping is required. The component can actually resolve the structure and only display a single record. The legend is also switched off because it is not required for a single data set.

With some modifications, we can implement intelligence into the component so that it recognizes the structure of the input and acts accordingly. In other words, it has different patterns of behavior and changes depending on the context.

PATTERN AND FRAMEWORK

This section contains content for the pattern and framework. A pattern composition topic is described first, followed by pattern configuration and framework topics. The last topic deals with reflective context aware patterns.

Pattern Composition

A pattern is defined as the solution to a problem in a specific context. A pattern-oriented approach would be to identify the problem to be solved and look for the pattern that provides the solution to the problem in the given context. Assuming that our problem is displaying groups of records, our solution may be to use the generic components described in the previous section. Our context is the input data. So we have a pattern for our problem and can give it a name like *TabChart*. However, if we had input data like the one in figure 4, it wouldn't go well with the pie chart which is included in our example in the last section. We can reprogram the component so that we can determine whether to include pie chart based on the input data structure. However, this is not necessarily a good solution. What if we want to include other visualization components like the one shown in figure 6. We cannot extend the *TabChart* component to handle all possible visualization components. We actually need a pattern that can be put together different patterns and components. In order to handle a wide variety of data visualizations and provide rapid integration of new data types, we need a dynamic set of patterns and components to process certain input data.

Regarding our *TabChart* pattern, we need a composition of a pattern that provides the *TabBar* widget and the *TabBarView* widget, and a pattern with containers for the title *Text* widget and the specific *Chart* widget.

To build a composition of patterns, an abstract class *Pattern* is introduced, as shown in figure 7. This class contains a single variable *map* of the type *Map <String, dynamic>*. To instantiate a subclass of *Pattern*, *map* must be provided. The *map* variable is used to transfer parameters that are required by *Pattern*. In other words, *Pattern* must be parameterized before it can be used. This is done by adding the required key-value pairs to the *map* variable that acts as a context container.

The *TabPattern* class shows how a concrete *Pattern* can be implemented. This pattern provides the *TabBar* widget and the *TabBarView* widget that are required for the *TabChart*. It requires that the *tabIconList*, *tabColor* and *tabComponentList* parameters are set in the *map* variable.

Figure 6. Visualization of a complex pattern composition

Figure 7. Code segment showing the implementation of pattern

```
abstract class Pattern {
 final Map<String, dynamic> map;
 Pattern(this.map);
 Widget getWidget(String name);
}

class TabPattern extends Pattern {
 TabPattern(Map<String, dynamic> map) : super(map);
 Widget getWidget(String name) {
  switch (name) {
   case "TabBar":
    List<dynamic> tabIconList = map["tabIconList"];
    List<Tab> tabs = [];
    for (Map<String, dynamic> tabIcon in tabIconList) {
     tabs.add(Tab(icon: tabIcon["icon"]));
    }
    return TabBar(indicatorColor: map["tabColor"], tabs: tabs);
   case "TabBarView":
    return TabBarView(children: map["tabComponentList"]);
   default:
    return null;
  }
 }
}
```

Pattern Configuration and Framework

In order to be able to visualize a wide variety of data types, we may need to implement a number of patterns. It is surprising that the number of basic patterns required for data visualization is not that large. The main types of data visualization can be found on Rockcontent's blogs (Rockcontent, 2020). The next question is how do we configure the composition of patterns and instantiate the object for each pattern for the visualization layout. A good way to do this is to configure the patterns in a JSON file. This JSON file can be downloaded from the web and mobile app server when the apps are running. Therefore, one does not have to release new versions in the App Store and Play Store in order to process new data sets that require a new form of visualization.

Figure 8 shows the JSON configuration of our *TabChart* example. We need a framework that will create the component that contains all the specified widgets in a hierarchical structure. This framework contains a table of preprogrammed patterns. This table can evolve over time. In addition to the patterns, the framework also includes a number of functions such as communicating with external data sources via RESTful APIs, parsing JSON data, as actions that can be performed when needed. Functions and required resources such as icons can be gradually integrated into a framework in the agile manor. An example of the implementation of how the integration of patterns, functions and resources can be integrated into the framework is shown in the Dart code segment in figure 9.

Figure 8. Pattern configuration for the TabChart example

```
{"TabChart": {
    "actions": {
        "getApiString": {"key": "inputString",
            "uri": "https//seveco.com/world/pollution/countries/highestGroup"},
        "parseJSON": {"key": "input", "String": "/inputString"}
    },
    "patternsRequired": [
        {"pattern": "BarChart", "input": "/input"},
        {"pattern": "TimeSeriesChart", "input": "/input"},
        {"key": "TitleComp1", "pattern": "TitleComponent",
            "title": "/input/title", "component": "/BarChart:"},
        {"key": "TitleComp2", "pattern": "TitleComponent",
            "title": "/input/title", "component": "/TimeSeriesChart"}
    ],
    "tabColor": "#/color/#ff9962D0",
    "tabIconList": ["#/icon/solidChartBar", "#/icon/chartLine"],
    "tabComponentList": ["/TitleComp1:", "/TitleComp2:"],
    "pattern": "TabPattern"
    }
}
```

Figure 9. Definition of tables for patterns, actions, and resources

```
Pattern getTabPattern(Map<String, dynamic> map) {        const Map<String, Icon> icons = {
  return TabPattern(map);                                  "solidChartBar": Icon(FontAwesomeIcons.solidChartBar),
}                                                          "chartLine": Icon(FontAwesomeIcons.chartLine),
                                                           "viruses": Icon(FontAwesomeIcons.viruses),
const Map<String, Function> getPattern = {                 "pollution": Icon(FontAwesomeIcons.smog),
  "TabPattern": getTabPattern,                             "population": Icon(FontAwesomeIcons.users),
  "BarChart": getBarChart,                                 ..................
  "PieChart": getPieChart,                                };
  "TimeSeriesChart": getTimeSeriesChart,
  "LineChart": getLineChart,                              const Map<String, Function> getAction = {
  "TitleComponent": getTitleComponent                      "getApiString": getApiString,
  ..................                                        "parseJSON": parseJSON,
};                                                         ..................
                                                          };
```

The main function of the framework is to interpret the JSON configuration like the *TabChart* in figure 8 and create the pattern. A simple prototype is shown in the code segment in figure 10. When the *buildNamePattern ("TabChart", map)* is called, the function fetches the *Map* data from *TabChart* in the JSON configuration file and builds the corresponding pattern object according to the information in the key-value pairs in the *Map* data.

In the *TabChart* example, two actions *getApiString* and *parseJSON* must first be activated. Then the patterns for the *BarChart*, *TimeSeriesChart* and two *TitleComponents* must be created. In addition, the resources required for the *TabChart* must be set. The final step is to create the *TabPattern* pattern that will contain the widgets for the *TabChart*. As shown in figure 10, the framework would perform all of these steps.

A function *getMapData* is used by the *buildNamePattern* method of the framework. The implementation of *getMapData* is not shown in figure 10. The function basically gets the data and objects either from the context container (*map*), the resource table or the input for the main pattern. If necessary, it also pulls the widgets from the pattern. Symbols such as '/' (for parent container), '#' (for resource) and ':' (for widget from a pattern) are used together with the key name so that *getMapData* knows where the data or objects are. All inputs and outputs of actions and patterns are cached in context containers (*map*). Each pattern or action has its own local context container (*childMap* as shown in figure 10). The local context container has a reference to its parent context container, which is the local context container of the parent pattern. In this design, patterns and actions are all autonomous units and functions that would carry out their activities with their inputs and outputs in the containers passed by the framework. The framework would act according to the composition given in the configuration of the main pattern.

To incorporate the pattern into our original program, we only need to make the following code changes in the *_GraphicHomePageState* class shown in figure 2:

```
pattern = buildNamePattern("TabChart", map);
.................
bottom: pattern.getWidget("TabBar"),
.................
body: pattern.getWidget("TabBarView"),
```

Figure 10. Implementation of the pattern builder based on JSON configuration

```
Pattern buildNamePattern(String patternName, Map<String, dynamic> map) {
 Map<String, dynamic> namePattern = PatternConfig[patternName];
 if (namePattern == null) {
  return getPattern[patternName](map);
 }
 String myPatternName;
 Map<String, dynamic> myMap = {"parent": map};
 Pattern myPattern;
 namePattern.forEach((key, value) {
  switch (key) {
   case "actions":
    Map<String, dynamic> actions = value;
    actions.forEach((akey, avalue) {
     Map<String, dynamic> childMap = {"parent": myMap};
     avalue.forEach((vkey, vvalue) {
      childMap[vkey] = getMapData(vvalue, childMap);
     });
     getAction[akey](childMap);
    });
    break;
```
```
   case "patternsRequired":
    List<dynamic> patternRequired = value;
    for (Map<String, dynamic> pat in patternRequired) {
     String pName;
     Map<String, dynamic> childMap = {"parent": myMap};
     pat.forEach((pkey, pvalue) {
      if (pkey == "pattern") {
       pName = pvalue;
      } else {
       childMap[pkey] = getMapData(pvalue, childMap);
      }
     });
     if (pName != null) {
      String k = childMap["key"] ?? pName;
      myMap[k] = buildNamePattern(pName, childMap);
     }
    }
    break;
   case "pattern":
    myPatternName = value;
    break;
   default:
    myMap[key] = getMapData(value, myMap);
    break;
  }
  if (myPatternName != null) {
   myPattern = buildNamePattern(myPatternName, myMap);
  }
 });
 return myPattern;
}
```

Reflective Context Aware Pattern

In the Generic Programming Style subsection of the last section, we show how a component can be implemented so that it changes its behavior depending on its input data. In another phase, the component has the ability to reflect on context. Patterns can also be constructed to have this mechanism. Figure 11 (a) shows a visualization dashboard example of a pattern that provides such a reflective context-aware ability. The pattern composition would change according to the input context. In this example, if the context includes the attribute *description*, the *ColumnPanel* pattern is pieced together to form the *PanelNavi* pattern, resulting in a layout shown in figure 11 (b). If not, the *IconRowPanel* pattern is used instead, resulting in a layout shown in figure 11 (c). In a sense, the reflective context-aware patterns have properties similar to agents, which are discussed in more detail in the next section.

DATA, CONTEXT AND AGENTS

This section first describes the properties and functions of agents. Then the topic of context and messages is discussed.

Figure 11. Illustration of a data visualization dashboard based on reflective context aware pattern

```
{
  "PanelNavi": {
    "context": "#/context/chartContext",
    "patternsRequired": [
    {
      "matchPattern": {
        "ColumnPanel": {"attribute": "description"},
        "IconRowPanel": {}
      },
      "key": "panelComp",
      "element": "/context"
    }
    ],
    "title": "World Statistic Data",
    "component": "panelComp:",
    "pattern": "TitleComponent"
  }
}
```

```
{
  "chartContext": {
    "population": {
      "icon": "population",
      "label": "Population",
      "description": "World population statistic data"
    },
    "pollution": {
      "icon": "pollution",
      "label": "Pollution",
      "description": "CO₂ emissions from top countries"
    },
    "viruses": {
      "icon": "viruses",
      "label": "Covid 19",
      "description": "Covid 19 statistic data"
    }
  }
}
```

(a)

World Statistic Data

World population statistic data

CO_2 emissions from top countries

Covid 19 statistic data

World Statistic Data

Population   Pollution   Covid 19

(b)   (c)

Agent Characteristics and Functions

In the visualization system presented in this chapter, an agent has the properties shown in figure 12. The system provides a set of functions or services to external units or clients of the system as in a service-oriented architecture (SOA). These functions act as sensors for the intelligent agent. The agent perceives the problems triggered by the sensors and analyzes the context of the problems. Based on its reflection mechanism, it develops a solution to the problem and composes patterns of effectors for the solution. It then activates the actions of the effectors.

A typical scenario is that a user makes a request to analyze and visualize a particular data set. The agent would make requests to an external data source and via RESTful APIs. The external data source provides responses to the queries, which in turn triggers the agent's sensor function. The agent analyzes the response message and creates a series of patterns for visualizing the data. The visualization diagram is then displayed to the user. The schematic representation of the process is shown in the activity diagram in figure 13. Because JSON data is used for sample configurations, with the right intelligence, the agent can generate composite sample configurations like the one shown in figure 8 at runtime.

In our context, the definition of an agent is expanded to include the reflective nature of the agent. Reflection in an entity is a function that examines or "introspects" itself and manipulates its internal properties. A brief definition of an agent is as follows:

An agent is anything that can be viewed as perceiving problems occurring in its environment through sensors, reflecting the contexts of the problems, assembling patterns of effectors to form solutions to the problems, and acting upon its environment through the patterns of effectors.

Figure 12. Characteristics of an agent

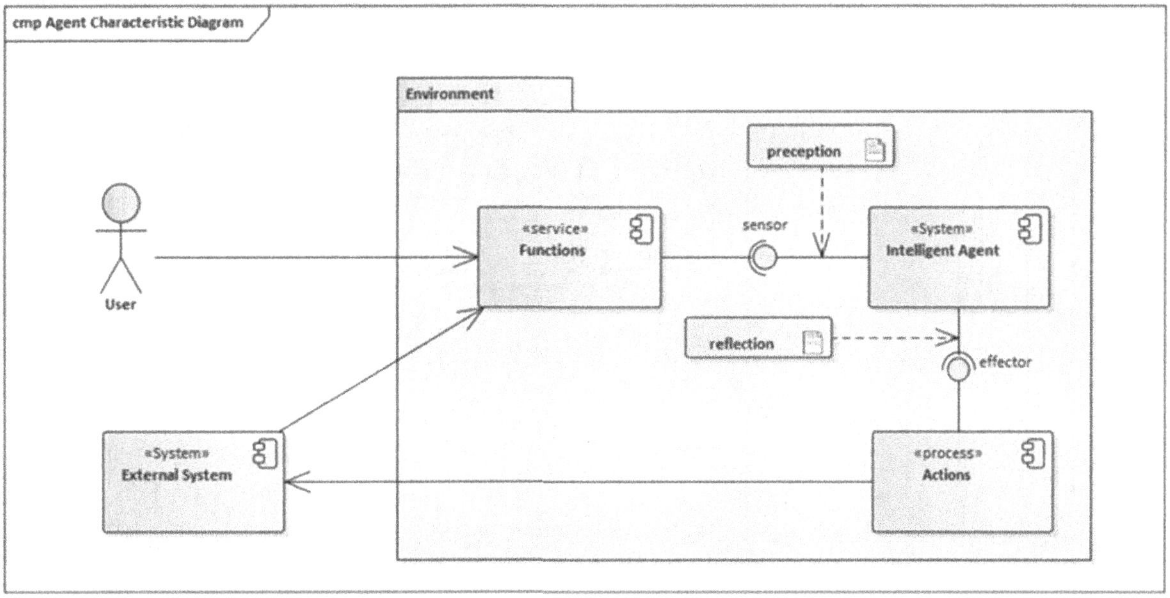

Context and Messages

Figure 11 shows the visualization dashboard of three different types of world data. Dozens or hundreds of different types of data may have to be visualized in a big data system. With a web or mobile app, data is generally obtained from an external data source using RESTful APIs. For each data source, we need to provide a URL as well as the credentials for the connection if necessary. Response messages can vary greatly from one data source to another, even if the same type of information is requested. This is shown in figure 14. This figure lists the URLs, invocation methods, and response messages from three different data sources. The second and third provide similar information for Covid 19. However, their data structures are very different. Even for the same attribute, such as country, the key can be different. The key for the first is *"country_name"*. For the second it is *"country"* and for the third it is *"country_text"*.

Figure 13. Agent function

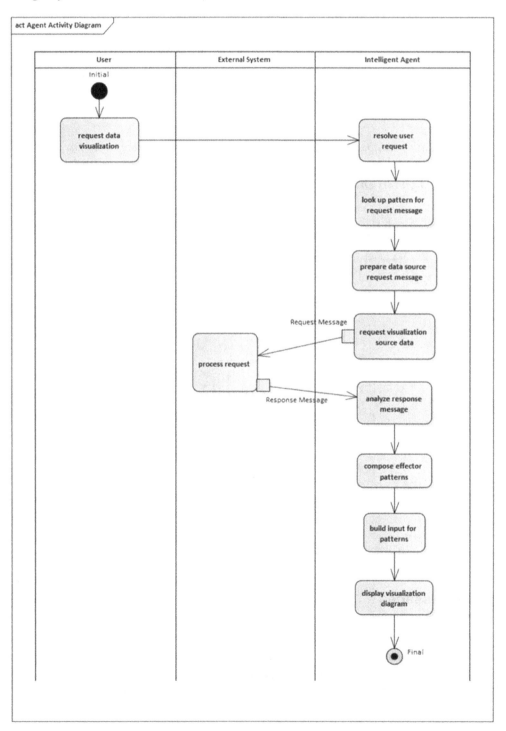

When specifying the URLs that use country as a search parameter, the user can use the following format:

https://covid-19.dataflowkit.com/v1/$country
and
params: {search: '$country'},

To retrieve the data, the user can use a drop-down list to select the country and the agent will replace *$country* with the selected country name in the URL or the *parameter* data.

For the visualization, the user must also specify which data from the response messages should be used. The user can specify the exact keys for the data to be used in each visualization diagram. On the other hand, the user can provide the information of interest such as country, new cases, new deaths, total cases, total deaths, etc. for the Covid-19 data visualization. The user can use the second or third URL. In this case, the agent must have the intelligence to analyze the keys and correlate them with the interests of the user.

In the example in figure 14, three different keys are used for the country. The agent can try to find a *"country"* key in the reply message. If not found, it would try to find the next key with the word country and determine the best match. In this example it is straight forward. There are cases that can make it difficult. For example, we can have both *"country_name"* and *"country_text"* as keys in the message, and *"country_text"* contains a description of the country. In this case, a wider resolution would prefer the one with less text in value. Such rules must be defined in the agent. If there are still doubts, the agent can open a dialog and prompt the user to select the correct key-value pair to use.

In some cases, calculations may need to be performed. The advantages of the architecture proposed in this chapter are that all rules, pattern composition and even calculations can be defined by JSON configurations. They can be uploaded to the server and downloaded from the web or mobile app at runtime. The user can change these definitions while testing the visualization diagrams until the desired result is achieved.

CONSEQUENCES AND APPLICABILITY

In this section we consider the applicability of the flexible agent approach and consequences in software development as well as the resulting paradigm shift in programming.

Flexible Agents to Handle Data and Context

In order to be able to process large varieties of data, we need very flexible applications. Agents with reactive, proactive and social behavior are ideal to create such applications. An agent presented in this chapter reflects the data and context to compose different patterns. The implementation technique for the different patterns would further reflect the data and context to construct different representations of the data using the techniques previously described. Patterns can be built independently on input data structures and integrated into the overall system. They can be integrated via JSON configuration.

As shown in figure 8, a pattern can be configured to trigger actions. Actions can be provided by other agents. Agents can interact with each other. In most applications we use a multi-agent system.

Figure 14. Urls and response messages from different data sources

```
var options = {
  method: 'GET',
  url: 'https://world-population.p.rapidapi.com/population',
  params: {country_name: 'Germany'},
  headers: {
    'x-rapidapi-host': 'world-population.p.rapidapi.com',
    'x-rapidapi-key': '................'
  }
};

var options = {
  method: 'GET',
  url: 'https://covid-193.p.rapidapi.com/countries',
  params: {search: 'Germany'},
  headers: {
    'x-rapidapi-host': 'covid-193.p.rapidapi.com',
    'x-rapidapi-key': '................'
  }
};
```

```
{ "ok": true,
  "body": {
    "country_name": "Germany",
    "population": 83783942,
    "ranking": 19,
    "world_share": 1.0748100278310746}
}

{ "get": "statistics",
  "parameters": {"country": "Germany"},
  "errors": [],
  "results": 1,
  "response": [{
    "continent": "Europe",
    "country": "Germany",
    "population": 84101095,
    "cases": {
      "new": "+6679",
      "active": 150553,
      "critical": 1217,
      "recovered": 3793000,
      "1M_pop": "47996",
      "total": 4036528},
    "deaths": {
      "new": "+26",
      "1M_pop": "1106",
      "total": 92975},
    "tests": {
      "1M_pop": "836841",
      "total": 70379237},
    "day": "2021-09-08",
    "time": "2021-09-08T16:15:02+00:00"}]
}
```

```
https://covid-19.dataflowkit.com/v1/germany
```

```
{ "Active Cases_text": "+8,800",
  "Country_text": "Germany",
  "Last Update": "2021-09-08 16:46",
  "New Cases_text": "6,679",
  "New Deaths_text": "26",
  "Total Cases_text": "4,036,528",
  "Total Deaths_text": "92,975",
  "Total Recovered_text": "3,793,000"
}
```

Agents can interact with users. The interactions can provide some agent learning capabilities. For example, an administrator (non-default user) can request the creation of a new dataset visualization by providing a new data source URL and information like the ones shown in figure 11. The learning agent can generate the JSON configurations for the existing agents to include the new visualization capability.

An agent presented in this chapter is reactive because it would respond to external requests to perform specific functions. It is proactive in that it adapts to the details of its actions that reflect the data and context. It is social in that it can interact with other agents, external data sources, and people. It thus fulfills Wooldridge's requirements for an intelligent agent.

Software Development Approach and Programming Paradigm

In this chapter, the data visualization implementation is provided as an example to demonstrate the underlying architectural concept and implementation techniques to build a flexible, extensible, and maintainable agile software system. In fact, as already mentioned, the implementation of the data visualization is part of a large project for a web and mobile geography application. The application is intended to gradually process many thousands of topics. It has to access many different data sources and process data of all kinds. User interactions are also required for each theme. To give an example of its complexity, it has to analyze the statistics of the last national presidential elections in the US and present the votes of the parties according to different criteria of citizens in different areas.

In the section on generic programming, we see how traditional programming can lead to the construction of inflexible software components that can only deal with a certain data set. As more and more functions are needed, the code base becomes too large and complex, which can ultimately lead to the failure of the software project. Generic programming should help solve some of these problems and it should be applied to the creation of software components. When creating a software component, the question that should always be asked is how the component can be made generic so that it can be used for a variety of data structures and process flows that fall into the component's use category. Generic programming not only provides flexible agile software components, but also increases the reusability of the software components.

In building a complex system, software architects should break down the problems to be solved and try to work out patterns that can provide solutions to the problems. Complex patterns can be compositions of simpler patterns. When designing a pattern, we should consider the variety of similar problems that the pattern can potentially solve. In identifying the diversity of contexts, the pattern should be designed to have reflexive and context-aware capabilities.

For the construction and composition of patterns as well as the activation we need a framework. The framework is generally light and easy to build. One of the authors had built such a framework in a project with a very tight schedule and budget. The result was a great success.

Components should be designed as an autonomous element with a well-defined signature and a contract to be fulfilled (Pang, 2016). Thus, the components would always work and provide the correct output when the correct input is provided. Agents are responsible for ensuring that the output from various components is properly arranged as input to other components. In the design presented in this chapter, data is transferred via context containers. Components should be activated as effectors by agents. Process control should be the task of agents. The process flow should be configurable with the technique presented in this chapter, such as the use of JSON. The architecture supports the agile approach to software development. Components can gradually be developed independently of others and seamlessly integrated into the system.

The demand for flexible agile software systems is increasing, in particular due to the emergence of big data. We need a paradigm shift in programming. Software components should be designed in such a way that they have the properties described above. Software components are plug-and-play elements of the software system. For complex problems, the pattern approach should be used. Patterns must be configurable and composable to handle highly complex problems. A framework should be used that can extract resources, create patterns, and call specific functions. Resources, infrastructure, and technically related functions are separate concerns (aspects) and should be grouped into tables that can be looked up and activated by the framework. Agents should be used for purposes such as process controllers, service dispatchers, executing business and technical rules, parsing and extracting information from messages, assembling patterns, coordinating the propagation of data and objects between components and patterns, and so on. Software components and patterns are effectors for agents that are activated when state data changes due to internal or external events. Following this programming paradigm can result in the creation of a software system that is flexible, agile, easy to extend and maintain, and has high reusability of frameworks, patterns, and components.

FUTURE RESEARCH DIRECTIONS

The authors see the potential of the agent-centered approach in architecture, especially in the design of software architectures, as high. It helps to centralize aspects and concerns in all software components. The software systems are more flexible, maintainable and extensible. The development effort can also be significantly lower. These aspects, along with the ways in which the patterns presented in this chapter are used, should be further explored and the programming paradigm should be spread across the software community.

Big data has become a big topic in the software community. In this chapter only the JSON structure is examined. There is still a need for further research, particularly on unstructured data from different data sources. How natural language processing can be used by an agent to analyze structured and unstructured data is a topic that needs further investigation. Intelligent agent that can source information from around the world is an interesting research topic. In fact, there are many areas in the acquisition, analysis, processing, and visualization of big data that need to be explored.

CONCLUSION

This chapter introduces the design and implementation of a flexible visualization system that can handle a variety of data as in the case of big data. The underlying approach includes generic programming, pattern-oriented programming, and agent-oriented programming. Creating generic component offers great flexibility in handling a wide variety of data required for big data analysis and visualization. With reflection, a component can be programmed to adapt itself to deal with data variation. In the context of this chapter, a component is an autonomous software unit that has a signature and a contract to fulfill. It is an element that can be plugged into the software system and played back.

A pattern is defined as the solution to a problem in a specific context. In the context of this chapter, a pattern is not just an abstraction of a design, but can contain real code that serves a specific purpose. A complex pattern can put together different patterns and the composition can be configured in a JSON file. A framework is required to interpret the pattern composition configuration and create the objects in the pattern at runtime. The framework also gets the resources it needs from resource tables. It also triggers functions that are defined in an action table. Configuring a pattern provides a clear separation of concerns about the use of components, resources, and actions. It also enables reflection with the change in the pattern composition depending on the data context.

A

The definition of an agent is extended compared to the standard definition. An agent would perceive problems that arise in its environment through sensors, reflect on the contexts of the problems in order to put together patterns of effectors to form solutions to the problems, and act on its environment through the patterns of effectors. Agents resolve external inquiries, compile patterns that form the effectors in the environment, control the process flow and compile the output to external systems.

For big data analysis and visualization, building a system with multiple reflecting agents is an appropriate approach. More research needs to be done to study the mechanisms and algorithms of intelligent reflective agents on how to resolve the context of raw data and extract useful information for analysis and visualization.

REFERENCES

Agile Manifesto Group. (2001). *Manifesto for agile software development.* Agile Manifesto. Retrieved March 5, 2022, from http://agilemanifesto.org

Aspect, J. (2021). *AspectJ.* Eclipse Foundation. Retrieved March 5, 2022, from https://www.eclipse.org/aspectj/

Bekker, A. (2019). Big data visualization: value it brings and techniques it requires. *ScienceSoft.* Retrieved March 5, 2022, from https://www.scnsoft.com/blog/big-data-visualization-techniques

Brazier, F. M. T., & Treur, J. (1995). Formal specification of reflective agents. *ResearchGate.* Retrieved March 5, 2022, from https://www.researchgate.net/publication/2426750_Formal_Specification_of_Reflective_Agents

Fedak, V. (2018). Top 4 popular big data visualization Tools. *Towards Data Science.* Retrieved March 5, 2022, from https://towardsdatascience.com/top-4-popular-big-data-visualization-tools-4ee945fe207d

Gamma, E., Helm, R., Johnson, R., & Vlissides, L. (1995). *Design patterns: elements of reusable object-oriented software.* Addison-Wesley.

Hohpe, G., & Woolfe, B. (2004). *Enterprise integration patterns: designing, building, and deploying messaging solutions.* Addison-Wesley.

Jackson, M. A. (1975). *Principles of program design.* Academic Press.

Laney, D. (2012). Gartner's original "Volume-Velocity-Variety" definition of big data. *AIIM Community.* Retrieved March 5, 2022, from https://community.aiim.org/blogs/doug-laney/2012/08/25/deja-vvvu-gartners-original-volume-velocity-variety-definition-of-big-data

Larman, C. (2003). *Agile and iterative development: a manager's guide.* Addison-Wesley.

Pang, C. Y. (2016). An agile architecture for a legacy enterprise IT system. *International Journal of Organizational and Collective Intelligence*, 6(4), 65–97. doi:10.4018/IJOCI.2016100104

Pang, C. Y. (2020). Reuse in agile development process. In C. Y. Pang (Ed.), *Software engineering for agile application development.* IGI Global. doi:10.4018/978-1-7998-2531-9.ch007

Rishi, P. (2017). Big data with visualization and scalable computing. *Analytics Insight.* Retrieved March 5, 2022, from https://www.analyticsinsight.net/big-data-visualization-scalable-computing

Rockcontent. (2020). What are the types of data visualization and when to use them. *Rockcontent*. Retrieved March 5, 2022, from https://rockcontent.com/blog/types-of-data-visualization/

Russell, J., & Norvig, P. (1995). *Artificial intelligence: a modern approach*. Prentice Hall PTR.

Shah, D. (2021). Flutter charts. *Coding with Dhrumil*. Retrieved March 5, 2022, from https://coding-withdhrumil.com/2021/05/flutter-chart-example-tutorial.html

Shoham, Y. (1990). *Agent-oriented programming (technical report STAN-CS-90-1335)*. Stanford University: Computer Science Department.

Software Crisis. (2010). Software crisis. In *Wikipedia*. Retrieved March 5, 2022 from https://en.wikipedia.org/wiki/Software_crisis

Tozicka, J., Pechoucek, M., & Rehák, M. (2007). Multi-agent reflection in autonomic systems. *Proceedings of Holonic and Multi-Agent Systems for Manufacturing, Third International Conference on Industrial Applications of Holonic and Multi-Agent Systems, HoloMAS 2007*.

Wegner, P. (1989). *Concepts and paradigms of object-oriented programming*. Expansion of Oct. 4 OOPSLA-89 Keynote Talk.

Weiss, M. (2003). Pattern-driven design of agent systems: approach and case study. *Proceedings of the 15th International Conference on Advanced Information Systems Engineering*, 711-723. 10.1007/3-540-45017-3_47

Wooldridge, M. (2009). *An introduction to multi-agent systems* (2nd ed.). John Wiley & Son.

ADDITIONAL READING

Agile Manifesto Group. (2001). Manifesto for agile software development. *Agile Manifesto*. http://agilemanifesto.org

Ali Babar, M., Brown, A. W., & Mistrik, I. (2014). *Agile software architecture*. Morgan Kaufmann.

Ambler, S. W. (2010). Agile modeling. *Ambysoft*. Retrieved March 5, 2022, from http://www.agilemodeling.com/

Bass, L., Clements, P., & Kazman, R. (2003). *Software architecture in practice* (2nd ed.). Addison-Wesley.

Bhatia, A. (2018). *Big data analytics*. Retrieved March 5, 2022, from https://github.com/anuradhabhatia/notes

Fowler, M. (2006). *Patterns of enterprise application architecture*. Addison-Wesley.

Gamma, E., Helm, R., Johnson, R., & Vlissides, L. (1995). *Design patterns: elements of reusable object-oriented software*. Addison-Wesley.

Garland, J., & Anthony, R. (2003). *Large-scale software architecture: a practical guide using UML*. John Wiley & Son.

Hohpe, G., & Woolfe, B. (2004). *Enterprise integration patterns: designing, building, and deploying messaging solutions*. Addison-Wesley.

A

Larman, C. (2003). *Agile and iterative development: a manager's guide*. Addison-Wesley.

Russell, J., & Norvig, P. (1995). *Artificial intelligence: a modern approach*. Prentice Hall PTR.

Shoham, Y. (1993). Agent-oriented programming. *Artificial Intelligence, 60*(1), 51–92.

Williamson, J. (2015). *Getting a big data job for dummies*. John Wiley & Son.

Wooldridge, M. (2009). *An introduction to multi-agent systems* (2nd ed.). John Wiley & Son.

KEY TERMS AND DEFINITIONS

Agent-Oriented Programming: Agent-oriented programming (AOP) is a programming paradigm where the construction of the software is centered on the concept of software agents.

Agile Software Development Process: An evolutionary and iterative approach to software development with focuses on adaptation to changes.

Aspect-Oriented Programming: Aspect-oriented programming is a programming paradigm that aims to increase modularity by allowing the separation of cross-cutting concerns.

Big Data: Big data is a field that treats ways to analyze, systematically extract information from, or otherwise deal with data sets that are too large or complex to be dealt with by traditional data-processing application software.

JSON (JavaScript Object Notation): An open-standard file format that uses human-readable text to transmit data objects consisting of attribute–value pairs and array data type.

Pattern: Pattern is defined as the solution to a problem in a specific context.

Pattern-Oriented Programming: Pattern-oriented programming is a programming approach to identify the problem to be solved and to look for the pattern that provides the solution to the problem in the given context.

Software Component: A software unit of functionality that manages a single abstraction.

Software Crisis: A term used in the early days when software projects were notoriously behind schedule and over budget and maintenance costs were exploding.

Big Data Visualization of Association Rules and Frequent Patterns

Carson K. Leung

(iD) https://orcid.org/0000-0002-7541-9127

University of Manitoba, Canada

INTRODUCTION

Big Data and *machine learning* are driving Industry 4.0, which is also known as the Fourth Industrial Revolution. Note that the (First) Industrial Revolution transformed manual production to machine production from the late 18th to mid-19th century. The Technological Revolution, which is also known as the Second Industrial Revolution, further industrialized and modernized the industry from the late 19th century to early 20th century through technological advancements and standardization, installations of extensive railroad and telegraph networks, as well as electrification. The Digital Revolution, which is also known as the Third Industrial Revolution, shifted from mechanical and analogue electronic technology to digital electronics, computing and communication technologies in the late 20th century. Now, Big Data have become one of the greatest sources of power in the 21st century, and they have become a critical part of the business world and daily life. In the current era of Big Data, numerous rich data sources are generating huge volumes of a wide variety of valuable data at a high velocity. These Big Data can be of different levels of veracity: They are precise, whereas some others are imprecise and uncertain. Embedded in these Big Data are implicit, previously unknown and potentially useful information and knowledge. This calls for data science, which makes good use of Big Data mining and analytics, machine learning, mathematics, statistics, visualization, and related techniques to manage, mine, analyze and learn from these Big Data to discover and visualize hidden gems. This, in turn, may maximize the citizens' wealth and/or promote all society's health. As one of the important Big Data mining and analytics tasks, frequent pattern mining aims to discover interesting knowledge in the forms of frequently occurring sets of merchandise items or events. For example, patterns discovered from business transactions may help reveal shopper trends, which in turn enhances inventory, minimizes customers' cost, and maximizes citizens' wealth. As another example, patterns discovered from health records may help reveal important relationships associated with certain diseases, which in turn leads to improve and promote all society's health. To enable users to get better understanding of the discovered patterns in a comprehensive manner, several data visualization and visual analytics tools have been proposed. This encyclopedia article covers *Big Data visualization* with focus on *visualization of association rules and frequent patterns*.

BACKGROUND

Since the introduction of the research problem of *frequent pattern mining* (Agrawal et al., 1993), numerous algorithms have been proposed (Hipp et al., 2000; Ullman, 2000; Ceglar & Roddick, 2006; Aggarwal et al., 2014; Leung et al., 2017b; Alam et al., 2021; Chowdhury et al., 2022). Notable ones include the

DOI: 10.4018/978-1-7998-9220-5.ch075

classical Apriori algorithm (Agrawal & Srikant, 1994) and its variants such as the Partition algorithm (Savasere et al., 1995). The Apriori algorithm uses a level-wise breadth-first bottom-up approach with a candidate generate-and-test paradigm to mine frequent patterns from transactional databases of precise data. The Partition algorithm divides the databases into several partitions and applies the Apriori algorithm to each partition to obtain patterns that are locally frequent in the partition. As being locally frequent is a necessary condition for a pattern to be globally frequent, these locally frequent patterns are tested to see if they are globally frequent in the databases. To avoid the candidate, generate-and-test paradigm, the tree-based FP-growth algorithm (Han et al., 2000) was proposed. It uses a depth-first pattern-growth (i.e., divide-and-conquer) approach to mine frequent patterns using a tree structure that captures the contents of the databases. Specifically, the algorithm recursively extracts appropriate tree paths to form projected databases containing relevant transactions and to discover frequent patterns from these projected databases.

For different real-life business, engineering, healthcare, scientific, and social applications and services in modern organizations and society, the available data are not necessarily *precise* but *imprecise or uncertain* (Leung, 2014; Leung et al., 2014; Rahman et al., 2019; Davashi, 2021; Roy et al., 2022). Examples include sensor data and privacy-preserving data (Leung et al., 2019a; Olawoyin et al., 2021; Pang & Wang, 2021; Jangra & Toshniwal, 2022). Over the past decade, several algorithms have been proposed to mine and analyze these uncertain data. The tree-based UF-growth algorithm (Leung et al., 2008c) is an example.

Moreover, it is not unusual for users to have some phenomenon in mind. For example, a manager in an organization is interested in some promotional items. Hence, it would be more desirable if data mining algorithms return only those patterns containing the promotional items rather than returning all frequent patterns, out of which many may be uninteresting to the manager. It leads to *constrained mining*, in which users can express their interests by specifying constraints and the mining algorithm can reduce the computational effort by focusing on mining those patterns that are interesting to the users.

As we move into the new era of Big Data, these Big Data can be characterized by at least 7Vs—namely, volume, value, velocity, variety, veracity, validity, and visibility. Specifically, volume refers to the huge quantity of Big Data. Value refers to the usefulness of Big Data, as well as information and knowledge discovered from the data. Velocity refers to the rapid rate at which the Big Data are generated or collected. Variety refers to differences in data types (e.g., structured, semi-structured, and/or unstructured data), data contents, data formats (e.g., alphanumeric data, relational data, transactional data, XML, JSON, audio, video), and/or data sources. Veracity refers the quality or trustworthiness of Big Data, especially whether the data are precise vs. imprecise (or uncertain). Validity refers the interpretation of Big Data and of information/knowledge discovered from the data. Visibility refers the visualization of data and of information/knowledge discovered from the data.

Big Data mining and analytics (Leung, 2022) mainly focuses on the first 5V's listed above as it aims to extract valuable information and knowledge from huge volumes of a wide variety of veracious but valuable data that are generated and collected at a high velocity. In contrast, *Big Data visualization* mainly focuses on the last 2V's listed above as it aims to visualize and interpret the valuable data and the information/knowledge that can be discovered from the data. Hence, once Big Data are mined and analyzed to discover valuable information and knowledge (e.g., association rules and frequent patterns), Big Data visualization visualizes these association rules and frequent patterns in a fashion that is comprehendible to users.

Big Data mining and analytics can be executed to discover interesting information and knowledge (e.g., association rules, frequent patterns) from the Big Data. Usually, the discovered knowledge is represented in a textual or tabular form (e.g., a long list of rules or frequent patterns), which may not be comprehendible to many users. As "a picture is worth a thousand words", *Big Data visualization* and *visual analytics* help. Regarding data and result visualization, several tools and systems (Jentner & Keim, 2019) have been developed. On the one hand, some of them were developed to visualize data. Examples include VisDB (Keim & Kriegel, 1996). On the other hand, some others were designed to visualize knowledge—such as clusters (Hassan et al., 2010) and decision trees (Ankerst et al., 1999)—discovered from Big Data.

Association rule mining and frequent pattern mining (which aims to discover interesting knowledge in the forms of rules containing frequently occurring sets of merchandise items or events in the antecedents and consequents of the rules) is one of the important Big Data mining and analytics tasks. Hence, we focus on a few visual analytic systems for Big Data and result visualization (especially, for visualization and visual analytics of association rules and frequent patterns from Big Data). Over the past few years, some tools and techniques have been designed to visualize patterns involving sets of items (i.e., itemsets) and related co-occurring entities.

.

BIG DATA VISUALIZATION FOR ASSOCIATION RULES

To visualize association rules, the R package "arulesViz" (Hahsler, 2017; Hahsler et al., 2021) first loads relevant packages like "arules", which conduct statistical analysis and mine association rules. They provide users with summary information of input transactions such as distributions of transaction length and their statistical measures (e.g., minimum, first quartile, median, third quartile, maximum). They also provide association rules and their interestingness measures (e.g., support, confidence) as output. To visualize these rules, "arulesViz" provides users with the several routines to visualize the rules in different forms. For example, *scatter plot* (Bayardo & Agrawal, 1999) shows the distribution of association rules in terms of their support and confidence. Specially, each association rule is represented by a point in a 2-dimensional space (with *support* of the rule on the *x*-axis and *confidence* on the *y*-axis of the rule). The color intensity of the point represents the *lift* of the rule. As such, the plot shows the distribution of all association rules with respect to the three interestingness measures (i.e., support, confidence, and lift). However, it does not show the details of the rules. For example, it also does not show the cardinality of the rule (i.e., the total numbers of items in both the antecedent and consequent of the rule). To reveal the cardinality, a *two-key plot* (Seno & Karypis, 2005) also represents each association rule by a point in a 2-dimensional space (with *support* of the rule on the *x*-axis and *confidence* on the *y*-axis of the rule). However, it uses color of the point to represent the cardinality of the rule (rather than using the color intensity to represent the lift of the rule).

As an alternative routine, a *2-dimensional matrix* (Ong et al., 2002) lists itemsets in antecedents of all rules on the *x*-axis, and it lists itemsets in consequents of all rules on the *y*-axis. A pixel (or a point) in the intersection of an antecedent and a consequent represents an association rule. The color intensity of the point represents the lift of the rule. As an extension, a *3-dimensional matrix* (Wong et al., 1999; Ong et al., 2002) represents an association rule by a vertical bar (instead of a pixel) rooted from the intersection of an antecedent (on the *x*-axis) and a consequent (on the *y*-axis). It represents the lift of the rule by the height (on the *z*-axis) of the vertical bar (rather than the color intensity of the point in a 2-dimensional space). As another extension of the 2-dimensional matrix, a *grouped matrix* (Hahsler & Chelluboina, 2011; Hahsler & Karpienko 2016) groups similar itemsets on the *x*-axis (and the *y*-axis) based on the Jaccard distance. As such, it reduces the numbers of the itemsets to be listed on the two

B

axes. A pixel (or a point) in the intersection of an antecedent and a consequent represents a group of association rules with similar antecedents (and consequents). The color intensity of the point represents the lift of the group of rules.

Another routine is a *graph* (Csardi & Nepusz, 2006), which represents each itemset (in either the antecedent A or consequent C of a rule A®C) as a vertex in a graph. It represents an association rule as a vertex with incoming directed edges from vertices representing itemsets in the antecedent A and outgoing edges to vertices representing itemsets in the consequent C. The radius of this vertex (representing an association rule) indicates the support of the rule A®C, and the color intensity of this vertex indicates the lift of the rule.

A *parallel coordinate plot* (Yang, 2003, 2005) lists items on the parallel coordinate axes in the y-direction and the sequential index (temporal or others) on the x-axis. As such, it represents an association rule A®C by connecting items on the antecedent A of the rule to items on the consequent C of the rule. n_A items within the antecedent A are connected by polylines over n_A parallel axes, and n_C items within the consequent C are also connected by polylines over n_C parallel axes. To represent an association rule A®C, it uses an arrow to connect the last item in the antecedent A with the first item in the consequent C. As an illustrative example, Figure 1 shows two association rules "$\{a, c, d\} ® e$" and "$\{b, c\} ® d$" in a parallel coordinate plot. Here, a polyline connects items a, c and d in the antecedent $\{a, c, d\}$ and an arrow connects this antecedent to item e in the consequent.

A *double decker plot* (Hofmann et al., 2000) visualizes a single association rule by displaying a contingency table. Specifically, it first builds a contingency table by computing the frequency of all subsets of itemsets in the antecedent A and consequent C of a rule A®C. Then, it vertically splits the items in the antecedent A and horizontally splits the items in the consequent C. Afterwards, the area of any rectangular block shows the support, and the height of the block shows the confidence. Comparison among the heights of different blocks representing different subsets reveals the difference of confidence (Hofmann & Wilhelm, 2001).

Figure 1. An example of parallel coordinate plots

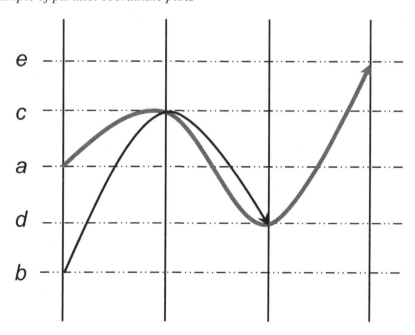

BIG DATA VISUALIZATION FOR FREQUENT PATTERNS

Although the aforementioned parallel coordinate plot (Yang, 2003, 2005) was designed to visualize mainly association rules, it can be adapted for visualizing frequent patterns, in which n items with the same itemset (e.g., in the same shopper basket or shopping cart) are connected by polylines over n parallel vertical axes in a two-dimensional space. All domain items are ranked according to their frequencies and evenly distributed along each axis. Due to the even distribution of the displayed domain items, it may not be easy to comprehend the magnitude of differences in the item frequency. Moreover, a frequent pattern consisting of k items (i.e., a k-itemset) is then represented by a curve that extends from one vertical axis to another connecting k vertical axes. As the frequency of such a pattern is indicated by the thickness of the curve, it is not easy to compare the frequencies of patterns.

Munzner et al. (2005) designed a visualization system called PowerSetViewer (PSV), which provides users with guaranteed visibility of a certain frequent patterns. Out of the entire powerset of domain items (i.e., all combinations of domain items), only those patterns that are frequent are displayed by the PSV. In particular, patterns are first grouped by their cardinality so that they can vertically arranged in non-descending order of cardinality. As such, shorter patterns are displayed on the top of the screen, and longer patterns are displayed on the bottom. Patterns within the same cardinality are sorted lexicographically for easy lookup. As the number of frequent patterns at each cardinality can be different, displayed patterns are wrapped around if they cannot be all fit on the same row. In other words, patterns of the same cardinality may span over multiple rows. Frequency of a pattern is represented by its color. However, PSV does not show the connection between related patterns (e.g., superset-subset relationships).

Line-Based Frequent Pattern Visualizers: FIsViz and WiFIsViz

For easy comparison of pattern frequencies, FIsViz (Leung et al., 2008a) visualizes frequent k-itemsets as polylines connecting k nodes in a two-dimensional space with (x, y)-coordinates, in which domain items are listed on the x-axis and frequency values are indicated by the y-axis. The x-locations of all nodes in the polyline indicate the domain items contained in a frequent pattern Z, and the y-location of the rightmost node of a polyline for Z clearly indicates the frequency of Z. With this representation, prefix-extension relationships can be observed by traversing along the polylines.

Since polylines in FIsViz can be bent and crossed over each other, it may not be easy to distinguish one polyline from another. To solve this problem, WiFIsViz (Leung et al., 2008b) uses two half-screens to visualize frequent patterns. Both half-screens of WiFIsViz are wiring-type diagrams (i.e., orthogonal graphs), which represent frequent patterns as horizontal lines connecting k nodes in a two-dimensional space (where the x-axis lists all the domain items). The left half-screen provides the frequency information by using the y-location of the horizontal line to indicate the frequency of the frequent pattern. The right half-screen lists all frequent patterns in the form of a trie. The same itemsets displayed on both half-screen are linked so that, when user clicks on an itemset on any of two half-screens, the corresponding itemset on another half-screen is highlighted.

Hierarchical Frequent Pattern Visualizers: PyramidViz and FpMapViz

Instead of polylines or wiring-type diagrams (i.e., orthogonal graphs), PyramidViz (Leung et al., 2016b) was designed with an emphasis on showing the prefix-extension relationships among the frequent patterns. In particular, PyramidViz visualizes frequent patterns in a building block layout. The frequent

1-itemsets are located at the bottom of the pyramid, whereas frequent patterns of higher cardinalities are located near the top of the pyramid. Frequent patterns are represented in a hierarchical fashion so that the building blocks representing the extensions of a frequent pattern Z are put on top of the blocks representing the prefixes of Z. The color of the block representing a frequent pattern Z indicates the frequency range of Z.

In contrast, FpMapViz (Leung et al., 2011b) represents frequent patterns as squares in a hierarchical fashion so that extensions of a frequent pattern Z are embedded within squares representing the prefixes of Z. The color of the square representing Z indicates its frequency range, and the size of the square indicates the cardinality of Z.

To recap, both PyramidViz and FpMapViz visualize frequent patterns by using hierarchy. PyramidViz provides a side-view of the hierarchy, whereas FpMapViz provides a top view of the hierarchy.

Circular Frequent Pattern Visualizers: RadialViz, HSVis, and HSLViz

In a collaborative environment, it is not uncommon for collaborators to have face-and-face meetings. Partially due to the emerging of table-top displays as an effective platform for collaboration, information is shared on the table-top surface in the meetings. As such, orientation or view perspective cannot be neglected. Unlike a single-user environment (where orientation may not be an issue), object orientation becomes critical in a multi-user environment because not all users share a common perspective of the displayed information. As information is viewed from different positions, it may be perceived differently. A study (Alallah et al., 2010) showed that user perception (e.g., legibility or readability) of a chart decreases when the chart is not oriented right-side up. For example, a person A has the best view as the chart is oriented right-side up to him. In contrast, both persons B and C who are on either sides have the side view of the chart, but a person D has the worst view as he views the chart upside down. Fortunately, the user perception can be improved by using orientation-free visualizers.

Although RadialViz (Leung & Jiang, 2012; Dubois et al., 2016) also represents frequent patterns in a hierarchical fashion, it uses a radial layout. An advantage of the radial layout is that extensions of a frequent pattern Z are embedded within sectors representing the prefixes of Z. The cardinality of Z is represented by the color of the sector. For ease of visualizing frequent patterns, RadialViz provides users with two visual representations: "radiating out" and "radiating in". For the former, the frequency of Z is represented by the radius (from the center) of the sector representing Z. For the latter (i.e., "radiating in"), the radius is determined by maximum frequency among all frequent patterns, and the frequency of any frequent pattern Z is represented by the direct distance (from circumference toward the center) of the sector representing Z. As an illustrative example, Figure 2 shows how RadialViz visualizes many frequent patterns in a "radiating in" fashion. For example, itemset $\{b, c, d\}$ with frequency 3 lies on top of its prefix itemset $\{b, c\}$ with frequency 5, which lies on top of its prefix itemset $\{b\}$ with frequency 8. The radii of sectors representing these three itemsets are proportional to their frequencies. Their colors indicate their cardinality: Green for 3-itemsets, yellow for 2-itemsets, and red for 1-itemsets.

Observed that a single extremely frequent pattern discovered from a skewed data set (with unevenly frequencies) may lead to undesirable or incomprehensive representation of the frequent patterns (e.g., a spike with a long radius, which makes the radii of the remaining patterns relatively short to be easily visible) in RadialViz. To solve this problem, HSVis (Leung & Zhang, 2019) uses a hue-saturation-value (HSV) color model. Such a model is observed to be more closely aligned with the way human vision perceives color-making attributes than the traditional red-green-blue (RGB) color model (in which red, green and blue light is additively superimposed in various ways to produce a broad range of colors).

Here, hue—with ranges from 0° to 360°, representing colors such as red, (yellowish) green, cyan and violet—shows a color appearance attribute of a visual sensation. Saturation—expressed as a number between 0 and 1 inclusive—shows the purity of a color. It shows colorfulness of a stimulus relative to its own brightness and serves as an indicator of the intensity of a hue. The higher the saturation, the purer is the color. Conversely, the lower the saturation, the more washed out (e.g., the whiter) is the color. Value—also expressed as a number between 0 and 1 inclusive—shows the brightness. The lower the value, the darker (i.e., blacker) is the color.

Note that the HSV color model is a subtractive color model (in which ink or paint can be mixed to form a black color in an extreme case) represented by a single hexacone. To broaden the scope, HSLviz (Leung et al., 2019b) uses the hue-saturation-lightness (HSL) color model—which is an additive color model like the RGB color model in which light sources can be additively superimposed to give a white color in an extreme case—represented by double hexacones. Here, lightness—expressed as a number between 0 and 1 inclusive—shows the perceived brightness. The higher the lightness, the lighter (i.e., whiter) is the color. Moreover, another advantage of HSLviz is that many programs support both the RGB and HSL color models but not the HSV color model. By using the HSL color model, HSLviz avoids extra conversion from one color model to another, and thus saving execution time.

Figure 2. An example of RadialViz

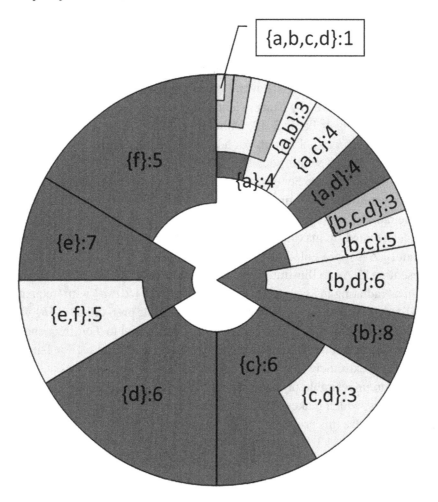

To recap, in both HSVis and HSLviz, characteristics of a frequent pattern Z are represented by different attributes or dimensions of color, hue to represent the cardinality; and a combination of saturation-value (in HSVis), or a combination of saturation-lightness (in HSLviz), to represent the frequency of frequent patterns.

DISCUSSION

Among association rule visualizers in the R package, the scatter plot, two-key plot and grouped matrix plot are capable to analyze large collections of association rules. These routines are interactive to allow users (e.g., Big Data analysts) to zoom and select interesting rules. The matrix can accommodate medium-size collections of association rules. Reordering can be used to improve the presentation. To analyze small collections of association rules, the 3-dimensional matrix, graph and parallel coordinate plots are suitable. Unlike these routines that can visualize multiple association rules, the double decker plot only visualizes a single association rule.

In terms of performance, most—except two (specifically, grouped matrix plot and double decker plot)—of these association rule visualizers take almost the same runtime to display and visualize association rules once these rules are mined and analyzed. In contrast, the grouped matrix plot may run slightly longer due to its extra step in computing the Jaccard distance for grouping itemsets with similar antecedents (or consequents) for visualization, whereas the double decker plot may run slightly shorter as it displays and visualizes only a single association rule (rather than many association rules).

As association rules consist of frequent patterns in the antecedents and consequents of the rules, it is also important to visualize frequent patterns. Among frequent pattern visualizers, key characteristics can be summarized as follows. Both FIsViz and WiFIsViz use lines (e.g., polylines, orthogonal wires) to represent frequent patterns. The number of nodes in the lines show the cardinality of frequent patterns, the y-location of the rightmost node of the lines show their frequency. Extension of a frequent pattern can be found by traversing along the polylines in FIsViz and traversing along the trie on the right half-screen in WiFIsViz. In contrast, PyramidViz and FpMapViz show frequent patterns in a hierarchical manner such that PyramidViz provides a side-view and FpMapViz provides a top view of the hierarchy. The cardinality of a frequent pattern is indicated by its level in PyramidViz or its square area in FpMapViz. The color of the building block (e.g., pyramid block in PyramidViz, square in FpMapViz) indicates its frequency. RadialViz, HSVis and HSLviz all use orientation-free representation to show frequent patterns. RadialViz uses color of the sector to show its cardinality and uses its radius to show its frequency. Although both HSVis and HSLviz uses hue to show its cardinality, the former uses saturation-value whereas the latter uses saturation-lightness to show its frequency.

In terms of performance, these frequent pattern visualizers take almost the same runtime to display and visualize frequent patterns once these patterns are mined and analyzed. However, their functionalities can be different. When comparing with line-based frequent pattern visualizers, hierarchical visualizers clearly show the prefix-extension relationships among the frequent patterns by putting extensions on top of prefixes. Circular visualizers further enhance the comprehensiveness by visualizing frequent patterns in an orientation-free representation.

FUTURE RESEARCH DIRECTIONS

Due to the popularity of Web-based communities and social networking sites, huge volumes of big social media data (including those Facebook, Instagram and Twitter data about an organization) are available. Embedded in these Big Data are rich sets of meaningful knowledge about the social networks (e.g., social networks within an organization, among different organizations). Hence, a future research direction is to visualize results of applying *social media mining and social network analysis* (Leung et al., 2011a, 2013, 2016a; Xu & Li, 2013; Leung, 2018; Al-Shargabi & Selmi, 2021; Hryhoruk & Leung, 2021) to social media data.

With the availability of Big Data in numerous domains besides social media, a second future research direction is to visualize Big Data and the knowledge discovered from the Big Data in various data science and machine learning applications (e.g., business analytics (Ahn et al., 2019), predictive analytics (Morris et al., 2018; Audu et al., 2019; Souza et al., 2020)). Examples include *visualization of other interesting* patterns such as frequent sequences and graphs (Glatz et al., 2014; Abdullah et al., 2020; Alam et al., 2022; Kalamaras et al., 2022; Zhang et al., 2022).

Moreover, a third future research direction is to incorporate interactive mining by applying the concepts of *visual analytics and interactive technologies* (Zhang et al., 2011; Leung et al., 2017a, 2021a, 2021b; Jentner & Keim, 2019; Leung & Zhang, 2019; Bevilacqua et al., 2022; Isichei et al., 2022; Wu et al., 2022).

CONCLUSION

Big Data visualization aims to visualize the Big Data and/or the implicit, previously unknown, and potentially useful information and knowledge that is discovered from the Big Data. Among results of different data science tasks, this encyclopedia article focuses on visualizing frequent pattern mined from Big Data. Knowing the importance of the validity and visibility of Big Data, frequent pattern visualizers support the interpretation and visualization of Big Data and discovered frequent patterns. Among them, line-based visualizers FIsViz and WiFIsViz represent frequent patterns by using polylines and orthogonal wires, respectively. Hierarchical visualizers PyramidViz and FpMapViz represent frequent patterns by building cardinality-based hierarchy of frequent patterns, in which frequent patterns of high cardinality are lied on top of those of low cardinality. Between the two visualizers, PyramidViz provides a side-view of the hierarchy, whereas FpMapViz provides a top view of the hierarchy. Orientation-free visualizers enables user to comprehend the knowledge in any orientations. Among them, RadialViz (with both "radiating out" and "radiating in" versions) also represent frequent patterns in a hierarchical form with frequent patterns of high cardinality lied on top of those of low cardinality. It provides a top view of the hierarchy with patterns either radiating out from the center (for the "radiating out" version) or radiating in toward the center (for the "radiating in" version). In contrast, HSVis and HSLviz represent frequent patterns in rings based on their cardinality. They make good use of the hue-saturation-value (HSV) and hue-saturation-lightness (HSL) color models to represent frequency of the patterns. These frequent pattern visualizers provide users (e.g., executive and management teams of an organization) with a comprehensive representation of data and their discovered frequent patterns. This enhance users' understanding of the Big Data in many real-life data science and machine learning applications.

REFERENCES

B

Abdullah, S.S., Rostamzadeh, N., Sedig, K., Garg, A.X., & McArthur, E. (2020). Multiple regression analysis and frequent itemset mining of electronic medical records: A visual analytics approach using VISA_M3R3. *Data, 5*(2), 33:1-33:24. doi:10.3390/data5020033

Aggarwal, C. C., Bhuiyan, M. A., & Al Hasan, M. (2014). Frequent pattern mining algorithms: a survey. In C. C. Aggarwal & J. Han (Eds.), *Frequent pattern mining* (pp. 19–64). doi:10.1007/978-3-319-07821-2_2

Agrawal, R., Imieliński, T., & Swami, A. (1993). Mining association rules between sets of items in large databases. *Proceedings of ACM SIGMOD 1993*, 207-216. 10.1145/170035.170072

Agrawal, R., & Srikant, R. (1994). Fast algorithms for mining association rules in large databases. *Proceedings of VLDB, 1994*, 487–499.

Ahn, S., Couture, S. V., Cuzzocrea, A., Dam, K., Grasso, G. M., Leung, C. K., McCormick, K. L., & Wodi, B. H. (2019). A fuzzy logic based machine learning tool for supporting big data business analytics in complex artificial intelligence environments. *Proceedings of FUZZ-IEEE, 2019*, 1259–1264. doi:10.1109/FUZZ-IEEE.2019.8858791

Al-Shargabi, A. A., & Selmi, A. (2021). Social network analysis and visualization of Arabic tweets during the COVID-19 pandemic. *IEEE Access: Practical Innovations, Open Solutions, 9*, 90616–90630. doi:10.1109/ACCESS.2021.3091537

Alallah, F., Jin, D., & Irani, P. (2010). OA-graphs: orientation agnostic graphs for improving the legibility of charts on horizontal displays. *Proceedings of ACM ITS 2010*, 211-220. 10.1145/1936652.1936692

Alam, M. T., Ahmed, C. F., Samiullah, M., & Leung, C. K. (2021). Mining frequent patterns from hypergraph databases. *Proceedings of PAKDD, 2021*(Part II), 3–15. doi:10.1007/978-3-030-75765-6_1

Alam, M. T., Roy, A., Ahmed, C. F., Islam, M. A., & Leung, C. K. (2022). UGMINE: Utility-based graph mining. *Applied Intelligence*. Advance online publication. doi:10.100710489-022-03385-8

Ankerst, M., Elsen, C., Ester, M., & Kriegel, H. (1999). Visual classification: an interactive approach to decision tree construction. *Proceedings of ACM KDD 1999*, 392-396. 10.1145/312129.312298

Audu, A. A., Cuzzocrea, A., Leung, C. K., MacLeod, K. A., Ohin, N. I., & Pulgar-Vidal, N. C. (2019). An intelligent predictive analytics system for transportation analytics on open data towards the development of a smart city. *Proceedings of CISIS, 2019*, 224–236. doi:10.1007/978-3-030-22354-0_21

Bayardo, R. J., & Agrawal, R. (1999). Mining the most interesting rules. *Proceedings of ACM KDD 1999*, 145–154. 10.1145/312129.312219

Bevilacqua, M., Paladin, L., Tosatto, S. C. E., & Piovesan, D. (2022). ProSeqViewer: An interactive, responsive and efficient TypeScript library for visualization of sequences and alignments in web applications. *Bioinformatics (Oxford, England), 38*(4), 1129–1130. doi:10.1093/bioinformatics/btab764 PMID:34788797

Ceglar, A., & Roddick, J.F. (2006). Association mining. *ACM Computing Surveys, 38*(2), 5:1-5:42. . doi:10.1145/1132956.1132958

Chen, R., Jankovic, F., Marinsek, N., Foschini, L., Kourtis, L., Signorini, A., Pugh, M., Shen, J., Yaari, R., Maljkovic, V., Sunga, M., Song, H. H., Jung, H. J., Tseng, B., & Trister, A. (2019). Developing measures of cognitive impairment in the real world from consumer-grade multimodal sensor streams. *Proceedings of ACM KDD 2019*, 2145-2155. 10.1145/3292500.3330690

Chowdhury, M.E.S., Ahmed, C.F., & Leung, C.K. (2022). A new approach for mining correlated frequent subgraphs. *ACM Transactions on Management Information Systems, 13*(1), 9:1-9:28. doi:10.1145/3473042

Csardi G., & Nepusz T. (2006). The igraph software package for complex network research. *InterJournal - Complex Systems, 1695*, 1-9.

Davashi, R. (2021). ILUNA: Single-pass incremental method for uncertain frequent pattern mining without false positives. *Information Sciences, 564*, 1–26. doi:10.1016/j.ins.2021.02.067

Dubois, P. M. J., Han, Z., Jiang, F., & Leung, C. K. (2016). An interactive circular visual analytic tool for visualization of web data. *Proceedings of IEEE/WIC/ACM WI 2016*, 709-712. 10.1109/WI.2016.0127

Glatz, E., Mavromatidis, S., Ager, B., & Dimitropoulos, X. A. (2014). Visualizing big network traffic data using frequent pattern mining and hypergraphs. *Computing, 96*(1), 27–38. doi:10.100700607-013-0282-8

Hahsler, M. (2017). arulesViz: Interactive visualization of association rules with R. *The R Journal, 9*(2), 163–175. doi:10.32614/RJ-2017-047

Hahsler, M., Tyler, G., & Chelluboina, S. (2021). *Package 'arulesViz'*. Academic Press.

Han, J., Pei, J., & Yin, Y. (2000). Mining frequent patterns without candidate generation. *Proceedings of ACM SIGMOD 2000*, 1-12. 10.1145/342009.335372

Hassan, M. R., Ramamohanarao, K., Karmakar, C. K., Hossain, M. M., & Bailey, J. (2010). A novel scalable multi-class ROC for effective visualization and computation. *Proceedings of PAKDD, 2010*, 107–120. doi:10.1007/978-3-642-13657-3_14

Hipp, J., Güntzer, U., & Nakhaeizadeh, G. (2000). Algorithms for association rule mining – a general survey and comparison. *SIGKDD Explorations, 2*(1), 58–64. doi:10.1145/360402.360421

Hofmann, H., Siebes, A. P. J. M., & Wilhelm, A. F. X. (2000). Visualizing association rules with interactive mosaic plots. *Proceedings of ACM KDD 2000*, 227–235. 10.1145/347090.347133

Hofmann, H., & Wilhelm, A. (2001). Visual comparison of association rules. *Computational Statistics, 16*(3), 399–415. doi:10.1007001800100075

Hryhoruk, C. C. J., & Leung, C. K. (2021). Compressing and mining social network data. *Proceedings of IEEE/ACM ASONAM 2021*, 545-552. 10.1145/3487351.3489472

Isichei, B. C., Leung, C. K., Nguyen, L. T., Morrow, L. B., Ngo, A. T., Pham, T. D., & Cuzzocrea, A. (2022). Sports data management, mining, and visualization. *Proceedings of AINA, 2022*, 141–153. doi:10.1007/978-3-030-99587-4_13

Jangra, S., & Toshniwal, D. (2022). Efficient algorithms for victim item selection in privacy-preserving utility mining. *Future Generation Computer Systems, 128*, 219–234. doi:10.1016/j.future.2021.10.008

B

Jentner, W., & Keim, D. A. (2019). Visualization and visual analytic techniques for patterns. In P. Fournier-Viger, J. C. Lin, R. Nkambou, B. Vo, & V. S. Tseng (Eds.), *High-utility pattern mining* (pp. 303–337). doi:10.1007/978-3-030-04921-8_12

Kalamaras, I., Glykos, K., Megalooikonomou, V., Votis, K., & Tzovaras, D. (2022). Graph-based visualization of sensitive medical data. *Multimedia Tools and Applications*, *81*(1), 209–236. doi:10.100711042-021-10990-1

Keim, D. A., & Kriegel, H. (1996). Visualization techniques for mining large databases: A comparison. *IEEE Transactions on Knowledge and Data Engineering*, *8*(6), 923–938. doi:10.1109/69.553159

Leung, C. K. (2014). Uncertain frequent pattern mining. In C. C. Aggarwal & J. Han (Eds.), *Frequent pattern mining* (pp. 339–367). doi:10.1007/978-3-319-07821-2_14

Leung, C. K. (2018). Mathematical model for propagation of influence in a social network. In R. Alhajj (Ed.), *Encyclopedia of social network analysis and mining* (2nd ed., pp. 1261–1269). doi:10.1007/978-1-4939-7131-2_110201

Leung, C. K. (2022). Big data analytics and mining for knowledge discovery. Research anthology on big data analytics, architectures, and applications, (pp. 708-721). doi:10.4018/978-1-6684-3662-2.ch033

Leung, C.K., Braun, P., & Cuzzocrea, A. (2019a). AI-based sensor information fusion for supporting deep supervised learning. *Sensors, 19*(6), 1345:1-1345:12. doi:10.3390/s19061345

Leung, C. K., Carmichael, C. L., Johnstone, P., Xing, R. R., & Yuen, D. S. H. (2017a). Interactive visual analytics of big data. In J. Lu (Ed.), *Ontologies and big data considerations for effective intelligence* (pp. 1–26). doi:10.4018/978-1-5225-2058-0.ch001

Leung, C. K., Carmichael, C. L., & Teh, E. W. (2011a). Visual analytics of social networks: mining and visualizing co-authorship networks. *Proceedings of HCII-FAC 2011*, 335-345. 10.1007/978-3-642-21852-1_40

Leung, C. K., Irani, P. P., & Carmichael, C. L. (2008a). FIsViz: A frequent itemset visualizer. *Proceedings of PAKDD, 2008*, 644–652. doi:10.1007/978-3-540-68125-0_60

Leung, C. K., Irani, P. P., & Carmichael, C. L. (2008b). WiFIsViz: Effective visualisation of frequent itemsets. *Proceedings of IEEE ICDM, 2008*, 875–880. doi:10.1109/ICDM.2008.93

Leung, C. K., & Jiang, F. (2012). RadialViz: An orientation-free frequent pattern visualizer. *Proceedings of PAKDD, 2012*(Part II), 322–334. doi:10.1007/978-3-642-30220-6_27

Leung, C. K., Jiang, F., Dela Cruz, E. M., & Elango, V. S. (2017b). Association rule mining in collaborative filtering. In V. Bhatnagar (Ed.), *Collaborative filtering using data mining and analysis* (pp. 159–179). doi:10.4018/978-1-5225-0489-4.ch009

Leung, C. K., Jiang, F., & Irani, P. P. (2011b). FpMapViz: A space-filling visualization for frequent patterns. *Proceedings of IEEE ICDM 2011 Workshops*, 804-811. 10.1109/ICDMW.2011.86

Leung, C. K., Jiang, F., Pazdor, A. G. M., & Peddle, A. M. (2016a). Parallel social network mining for interesting 'following' patterns. *Concurrency and Computation*, *28*(15), 3994–4012. doi:10.1002/cpe.3773

Leung, C. K., Kaufmann, T. N., Wen, Y., Zhao, C., & Zheng, H. (2021a). Revealing COVID-19 data by data mining and visualization. *Proceedings of INCoS, 2021*, 70–83. doi:10.1007/978-3-030-84910-8_8

Leung, C. K., Kononov, V. V., & Pazdor, A. G. M. (2016b). PyramidViz: Visual analytics and big data visualization of frequent patterns. *Proceedings of IEEE DASC-PICom-DataCom-CyberSciTech 2016*, 913-916. 10.1109/DASC-PICom-DataCom-CyberSciTec.2016.158

Leung, C. K., MacKinnon, R. K., & Tanbeer, S. K. (2014). Fast algorithms for frequent itemset mining from uncertain data. *Proceedings of IEEE ICDM, 2014*, 893–898. doi:10.1109/ICDM.2014.146

Leung, C. K., Mateo, M. A. F., & Brajczuk, D. A. (2008c). A tree-based approach for frequent pattern mining from uncertain data. *Proceedings of PAKDD, 2008*, 653–661. doi:10.1007/978-3-540-68125-0_61

Leung, C. K., Medina, I. J. M., & Tanbeer, S. K. (2013). Analyzing social networks to mine important friends. In G. Xu & L. Li (Eds.), *Social media mining and social network analysis: emerging research* (pp. 90–104). doi:10.4018/978-1-4666-2806-9.ch006

Leung, C. K., Wen, Y., Zhao, C., Zheng, H., Jiang, F., & Cuzzocrea, A. (2021b). A visual data science solution for visualization and visual analytics of big sequential data. *Proceedings of IV, 2021*, 224–229. doi:10.1109/IV53921.2021.00044

Leung, C. K., & Zhang, Y. (2019b). An HSV-based visual analytic system for data science on music and beyond. *International Journal of Art, Culture and Design Technologies*, *8*(1), 68–83. doi:10.4018/IJACDT.2019010105

Morris, K. J., Egan, S. D., Linsangan, J. L., Leung, C. K., Cuzzocrea, A., & Hoi, C. S. H. (2018). Token-based adaptive time-series prediction by ensembling linear and non-linear estimators: A machine learning approach for predictive analytics on big stock data. *Proceedings of IEEE ICMLA, 2018*, 1486–1491. doi:10.1109/ICMLA.2018.00242

Munzner, T., Kong, Q., Ng, R. T., Lee, J., Klawe, J., Radulovic, D., & Leung, C. K. (2005). *Visual mining of power sets with large alphabets. Technical report UBC CS TR-2005-25*. University of British Columba.

Olawoyin, A. M., Leung, C. K., & Cuzzocrea, A. (2021). Privacy-preserving publishing and visualization of spatial-temporal information. *Proceedings of IEEE BigData, 2021*, 5420–5429. doi:10.1109/BigData52589.2021.9671564

Ong, H., Ong, K., Ng, K., & Lim, E. P. (2002). CrystalClear: active visualization of association rules. *Proceedings of ICDM 2002 Workshops on Active Mining (AM)*.

Pang, H., & Wang, B. (2021). Privacy-preserving association rule mining using homomorphic encryption in a multikey environment. *IEEE Systems Journal*, *15*(2), 3131–3141. doi:10.1109/JSYST.2020.3001316

Rahman, M. M., Ahmed, C. F., & Leung, C. K. (2019). Mining weighted frequent sequences in uncertain databases. *Information Sciences*, *479*, 76–100. doi:10.1016/j.ins.2018.11.026

Roy, K. K., Moon, M. H. H., Rahman, M. M., Ahmed, C. F., & Leung, C. K. (2022). Mining weighted sequential patterns in incremental uncertain databases. *Information Sciences*, *582*, 865–896. doi:10.1016/j.ins.2021.10.010

Savasere, A., Omiecinski, E., & Navathe, S. (1995). An efficient algorithm for mining association rules in large databases. *Proceedings of VLDB, 1995*, 432–444.

Seno, M., & Karypis, G. (2005). Finding frequent itemsets using length-decreasing support constraints. *Data Mining and Knowledge Discovery*, *10*(3), 197–228. doi:10.100710618-005-0364-0

Souza, J., Leung, C. K., & Cuzzocrea, A. (2020). An innovative big data predictive analytics framework over hybrid big data sources with an application for disease analytics. *Proceedings of AINA*, *2020*, 669–680. doi:10.1007/978-3-030-44041-1_59

Ullman, J. D. (2000). A survey of association-rule mining. *Proceedings of DS*, *2000*, 1–14. doi:10.1007/3-540-44418-1_1

Wong, P. C., Whitney, P., & Thomas, J. (1999). Visualizing association rules for text mining. *Proceedings of IEEE InfoVis 1999*, 120-123. 10.1109/INFVIS.1999.801866

Wu, Y., Chang, R., Hellerstein, J. M., Satyanarayan, A., & Wu, E. (2022). DIEL: Interactive visualization beyond the here and now. *IEEE Transactions on Visualization and Computer Graphics*, *28*(1), 737–746. doi:10.1109/TVCG.2021.3114796 PMID:34587039

Xu, G., & Li, L. (Eds.). (2013). *Social media mining and social network analysis: emerging research.* doi:10.4018/978-1-4666-2806-9

Yang, L. (2003). Visualizing frequent itemsets, association rules, and sequential patterns in parallel coordinates. *Proceedings of ICCSA*, *2003*, 21–30. doi:10.1007/3-540-44839-X_3

Yang, L. (2005). Pruning and visualizing generalized association rules in parallel coordinates. *IEEE Transactions on Knowledge and Data Engineering*, *17*(1), 60–70. doi:10.1109/TKDE.2005.14

Zhang, Q., Segall, R. S., & Cao, M. (Eds.). (2011). *Visual analytics and interactive technologies: data, text and web mining applications.* doi:10.4018/978-1-60960-102-7

Zhang, Y., Liu, H., Dong, X., Li, C., & Zhang, Z. (2022). HyIDSVis: Hybrid intrusion detection visualization analysis based on rare category and association rules. *Journal of Visualization / the Visualization Society of Japan*, *25*(1), 175–190. doi:10.100712650-021-00789-5

ADDITIONAL READING

Aggarwal, C. C., & Han, J. (Eds.). (2014). *Frequent pattern mining.* Springer. doi:10.1007/978-3-319-07821-2

Bilokon, P. A. (2022). *Python, data science and machine learning - from scratch to productivity.* World Scientific.

Hollister, B. E., & Pang, A. (2022). *A concise introduction to scientific visualization - past, present, and future.* Springer. doi:10.1007/978-3-030-86419-4

Kang, M., & Choi, E. (2021). *Machine learning - concepts, tools and data visualization.* World Scientific. doi:10.1142/12037

Kirk, A. (2019). *Data visualisation: a handbook for data driven design* (2nd ed.). SAGE.

Miller, J. D. (2017). *Big data visualization.* Packt Publishing.

Segall, R. S., & Cook, J. S. (Eds.). (2018). *Handbook of research on big data storage and visualization techniques*. IGI Global. doi:10.4018/978-1-5225-3142-5

Ward, M. O., Grinstein, G., & Keim, D. (2015). Interactive data visualization: foundations, techniques, and applications (2nd ed.). A K Peters/CRC Press doi:10.1201/b18379

Wilke, C. O. (2019). *Fundamentals of data visualization*. O'Reilly.

Zaki, M. J., & Meira, W. (2020). *Data mining and machine learning: fundamental concepts and algorithms* (2nd ed.). Cambridge University Press. doi:10.1017/9781108564175

KEY TERMS AND DEFINITIONS

Big Data: High-velocity, valuable, and/or multi-variety data with volumes beyond the ability of commonly used software to capture, manage, and process within a tolerable elapsed time. These Big Data necessitate new forms of processing to deliver high veracity (and low vulnerability) and to enable enhanced decision making, insight, knowledge discovery, and process optimization.

Data Mining: non-trivial extraction of implicit, previously unknown, and potentially useful information from data.

Data Visualization: An interdisciplinary area that deals with the graphic representation of data.

Frequent Pattern (or Frequent Itemset): An itemset or a pattern with its actual support (or expected support) exceeds or equals the user-specified minimum support threshold.

Frequent Pattern Mining: A search and analysis of huge volumes of valuable data for implicit, previously unknown, and potentially useful patterns consisting of frequently co-occurring events or objects. It helps discover frequently co-located trade fairs and frequently purchased bundles of merchandise items.

Itemset: A set of items.

Machine Learning: As a part of artificial intelligence (AI), machine learning aims to improve computer algorithms automatically through experience and by the use of data.

Visual Analytics: An interdisciplinary area that integrates data science, data mining and data visualization. It deals with information visualization and scientific visualization that focuses on analytical reasoning facilitated by interactive visual interfaces.

Cognitive Biases and Data Visualization

Billie Anderson
https://orcid.org/0000-0002-1327-7004
University of Missouri-Kansas City, USA

J. Michael Hardin
Samford University, USA

INTRODUCTION

In 1974, the term *cognitive bias* was coined by Tversky & Kahneman (1974). Since then, there has been an abundance of research in multiple disciplines such as economics, healthcare, social sciences, and psychology that has been impacted by this term (Featherston et al., 2020). Cognitive biases are errors in judgment or decisions that are made by humans when they attempt to process too much information at a time or when they do not have sufficient information to make correct decisions. Cognitive biases can be found in disciplines from accounting to healthcare. Biases such as overconfidence, anchoring, framing, and confirmation can affect an auditor's judgement and decision-making abilities (Chang & Luo, 2021). Gopal et al. (2021) developed a checklist to assist medical providers to guard against bias such as mental shortcuts that can lead to errors in diagnosing and treating patients.

Researchers have identified several cognitive biases and there is no doubt that these cognitive biases have led to poor decisions in a multitude of disciplines. Cognitive biases are pervasive across many disciplines. For example, 75% of clinical errors in internal medicine clinical settings are thought to be rooted in cognitive biases (D O'Sullivan & Schofield, 2018). Another study found that it is impossible for cancer patients to make informed choices owing to the treatment provider's cognitive biases and this is likely to lead to overtreatment (Ozdemir & Finkelstein, 2018). Companies that wish to enter international markets can encounter cognitive biases that, if not overcome, can lead to failure of new product launch (Paul & Mas, 2020).

Data visualization can assist in reducing cognitive biases. Data visualization plays a key role in decision-making process. Visualization allows for data to be consumable, that is, interpretable easily. If data is not consumable, there is a tendency to ignore the facts and rely more on biases. Data visualizations should guard against cognitive biases. However, researchers have found that cognitive biases do exist within data visualizations and can affect decision-making abilities (Padilla et al., 2018). Most recently, there has been interest in designing empirical studies that determine whether cognitive biases can be alleviated (Cho et al., 2017; Dimara et al., 2018; Valdez, Ziefle, & Sedlmair, 2017; Xiong, Van Weelden, & Franconeri, 2019). Some of these studies have provided mitigation strategies to guard against cognitive biases in data visualizations. For example, viewing the data from different positions such as simply reordering the values in a visualization and allowing multiple individuals to critique and provide feedback related to the visualizations (Xiong et al., 2019).

With the advent of big data, practitioners and researchers have become more reliant on data visualizations as a decision-making tool. Telecommunication companies are able to amass large amounts of detailed user data to better understand their customers. Utilities use smart meter data to reduce outages,

DOI: 10.4018/978-1-7998-9220-5.ch076

assign crews, measure energy consumption and meter quality. Governments are able to use data from sensors to monitor road conditions and change the duration of red and green signals of traffic lights according to real-time traffic patterns. With large and complex data, associations, insights, patterns, and errors can be more easily understood with graphical representations than using tables and numbers. The human brain can make sense of pictures more rapidly than tables of numbers. To maximize the impact of big data, it is necessary to incorporate visual analysis at all levels of an organization.

Classical graphing tools do not scale well to big data. However, advances in visual analytics have led to a much broader use of classic visualizations than are normally encountered in small data set environments. Visual analytics goes beyond the traditional dashboard with a few scatterplots and bar charts. They provide more interesting information than classic visualizations. For example, an analytic visualization such as a scatterplot might show an association between women and a certain type of golf club in a particular state. Another analytic visualization could predict the future revenue of golf clubs in a particular geographical area and help determine growth. Sharing reports and dashboards based on analytics conveys more information about future possibilities and promotes collaboration, which leads to more strategic decision making. Visualization technologies that support more complex data and the ability to utilize more cognitive tasks are areas of growth (Borland, Wang, & Gotz, 2018).

When cognitive biases crop up in data visualizations and influence decision-making, the impact can have consequences for the individuals that are affected. College admissions is one such example. The decision to accept or admit a college applicant involves both expertise and heuristics. These heuristics have multiple cognitive biases attached to them (Sukumar & Metoyer, 2018). For example, confirmation bias refers to "the tendency to seek and overweight confirming information in the information gathering and evaluation steps, and to favor conclusions that are consistent with initial beliefs or preferences" (Chang & Luo, 2019, p. 6). The confirmation bias can manifest itself when an admissions reviewer makes up their mind about the accept or rejection status of an applicant before the applicant review process is complete. The reviewer will look for data to support their hypothesis. For example, a reviewer might have decided, based on initial or incomplete data and before the interview process occurs, that an applicant should be rejected. Then, in the interview process, the reviewer will ask questions and look for ways to support the reviewer's early opinion that the applicant should be rejected. The biases can have direct consequences to the applicants themselves but also a larger societal impact. Sukumar & Metoyer (2018) developed visualizations to mitigate biases that occur often in the college admission decision.

Another example of biases influencing decisions that are made using visualizations are climate change implications. Maps are used extensively when displaying data and information related to climate change. Maps are used to display geographical areas of floods, extreme heat, drought, vulnerable animal populations, and sea rise (De Sherbinin et al., 2019). However, maps are an example of how a visual can display and hide information at the same time (McInerny et al., 2014). McInerny et al. (2014) provides an example of how different types of maps can alter the audience's perception of and ability to question data related to jaguar populations in Africa. Luo & Zhao (2021) discuss the importance of visualizations mitigating perceptual biases related to climate change. The authors use the example of greenhouse gases. Many times, people's perception of the effects of greenhouse gases and the reality of these gases are not aligned. To bridge this gap between perception and reality, it is important that visualizations are created with solid design techniques implemented (Luo & Zhao, 2021; Harold et al., 2016).

This chapter provides a background for cognitive biases that are related to data visualizations, with a particular interest toward visual analytics in big data environments. Cognitive biases that crop up in visualizations will be discussed. A review of recent studies related to designing experiments to mitigate cognitive biases in data visualizations will be presented. Recommendations, using applied frameworks that are used to detect and mitigate biases in single visualizations and visual analytic systems, will be provided to practitioners.

BACKGROUND

Human-Computer Interaction (HCI) has a long history of using data visualizations to mitigate cognitive biases. Over 30 years ago, a future application area of HCI was expected to be information visualization (Hartson, 1989). One way that HCI has been able to advance the disciplines of information and data visualization has been through a "pairing analytics" approach (Arias-Hernández et al., 2011). In the "pairing analytics" approach an expert from HCI collaborates with a practitioner that has a real-world data problem to be solved. Arias-Hernández et al. (2011) has worked with expert safety analysts at Boeing to develop a new approach to visualizing and interacting with safety data that was more efficient and cost effective.

Cognitive biases in data visualizations within the HCI discipline has recently received increasing attention. Wall et al. (2019) conducted a study in which metrics were developed that could establish whether an anchoring bias existed using a visual analytical task. An anchoring bias occurs when an individual places too much weight on the first data point provided. These authors (Wall et al., 2019) provide guidelines for applying bias metrics in visual analytical systems and provide the results of a formal study to illustrate how a bias metric can be used to capture whether the bias exists or not. Wesslen et al. (2018) also examined strategies that could be used in data visualizations to mitigate the anchoring bias. The authors (Wesslen et al., 2018) developed and performed a designed experiment to determine the role of an anchoring bias for users of a visual system that assisted in identifying misinformation on Twitter.

Szafir (2018) provides a guide for correcting common mistakes that practitioners make when constructing data visualizations that cause cognitive biases. For example, the author provides the suggestion of using a violin plot in lieu of a bar chart with error bars. The bar chart with error bars creates a within-the-bar-bias, meaning people tend to interpret values inside of a bar as statistically more likely than those outside of the bar (Szafir, 2018).

Branley-Bell, Whitworth, & Coventry (2020) investigated methods for creating explainable output in the form of visualizations available from artificial intelligence systems. This research was an intersection of explainable artificial intelligence (AIX) and HCI. These authors found that even when visualizations are created with algorithms, there are still cognitive biases that exist when humans start using the visualizations for decision-making purposes.

Research on cognitive biases that can be mitigated using data visualizations is a wide open and ongoing area of research, well beyond HCI. Dimara et al. (2018b) provide an overview of cognitive biases that have been studied in the context of data visualization and provide research directions that could facilitate the alleviation of cognitive biases using visualizations. Mitigating cognitive biases means reducing the likelihood that the bias exists. Reduction of bias leads to better decision making. The authors provide 154 types of cognitive biases and indicate whether a study exists to determine if data visualizations can alleviate the biases.

One of the research paths discussed is the experimental determination of whether data visualization can mitigate cognitive bias (Dimara et al. 2018b) using a two-step process as follows:

1. Test whether the bias exists when a standard visualization is used.
2. Test whether the bias can be alleviated using an improved visualization.

There are two studies in literature that provide a detailed process of the aforementioned steps 1 and 2. Dimara et al. (2016) performed a separate study to address Step 1. The authors first identified that there was an attraction effect when making decisions using data visualizations. The attraction effect (decoy effect) is when a person has three choices; two of the choices are incomparable, whereas the third choice is inferior (the decoy) to the other two choices. The inferior choice ends up affecting people's decision when they are in the process of selecting between the non-comparable choices.

Dimara et al. (2016) used two crowdsourcing experiments to test whether the attraction effect was present in visualizations (Step 1). Crowdflower was the crowdsourcing software used (Van Pelt & Sorokin, 2012). Crowdsourcing software is an online platform that recruits subjects for participation in online experiments and surveys. For the first experiment, the authors replicated an experiment in which individuals selected a gym; an attraction effect was found to be present (Malkoc, Hedgcock, & Hoeffler, 2013). The study consisted of subjects selecting between three gyms in which the attributes were the cleanliness and variety of the machines, scaled from −10 to +10, of the gyms. Decoy choices were provided for both the cleanliness and variety attributes. The authors implemented a 3 × 2 between-subjects design using two dependent variables. The first dependent variable used data sets that had no decoy option; the dependent variable was the decision task (choosing the gym). The second dependent variable was the presentation format in which a decoy was present. Either a table or a scatterplot was used to assist subjects in selecting the gym.

The authors admit that performing an experiment with only three choices in a scatterplot does not represent real-world choices that people make using visualizations. The authors refer to a past research that hypothesizes that the number of choices available to subjects could alleviate the attraction effect. Using tables, it is difficult to provide subjects with many choices. However, scatterplots can be designed to offer subjects many choices.

The authors extend their work by conducting another crowdsourcing experiment in which subjects have many choices via a scatterplot using a betting example. Once again, the authors replicate an experiment that was performed in a past research (Wedell, 1991) with a few modifications. Wedell (1991) experimented with subjects choosing between three lottery tickets with two attributes: probability of winning and the prize amount. The two modifications were that the subjects were provided a 10-page tutorial before they began the experiment and there was a monetary gain if the subjects selected the correct lottery ticket.

Once the occurrence of the attraction effect in data visualizations is validated (Dimara et al., 2016), a follow-up was performed to determine whether data visualization can be designed in a manner that reduces or eliminates the attraction effect (Step 2) (Dimara et al., 2018a). Dimara et al. (2018a) revisited the lottery example from their previous paper (Dimara et al., 2016). The same lottery experiment was replicated using the crowdsourcing platform. The difference from the previous study (Dimara et al., 2016) was that in the scatterplots non-comparable options were highlighted. The authors highlighted the non-comparable choices to help the subjects focus on these points. The results from the previous study (Dimara et al., 2016) was used as a baseline. The authors found that highlighting the non-comparable choices weakened the attraction effect. However, it did not eliminate the bias. The authors suggest that a stronger visual cue such as a line be tested to highlight the points.

These two papers (Dimara et al., 2016, 2018a) illustrate how to determine if cognitive biases do exist when individuals use data visualizations and how to conduct a study to determine whether a data visualization can mitigate the bias in a rigorous manner. A researcher could 'pick their favorite bias's and conduct similar types of studies.

BIG DATA AND VISUALIZATION COGNITIVE BIASES

The studies discussed in the previous section are useful for their intended purpose of studying the existence and potential reduction of cognitive biases in data visualizations. However, these studies are not based on big data. Visualizing big data is realistic as organizations deal with big data. Organizations have to visualize complicated spreadsheets, data in non-traditional column and row formats such as social media data, and data that are difficult to access.

An emerging topic in big data visualization is progressive visualization. Progressive visualization is a methodology within the data and information visualization communities that create visualization systems that allow the end-user to interact and build visualizations on extremely large data sets, normally above the gigabyte range. Progressive visualization allows the end-user to visualize partial data from a long-running analysis or computational process (Schulz, Angelini, Santucci, & Schumann, 2015; Stolper, Perer, & Gotz, 2014).

While progressive visualization has many advantages related to being able to visualize big data, it is not without its problems with relation to cognitive biases. Procopio et al. (2021) found that four biases (uncertainty, control, illusion, and anchoring) can occur in progressive visualization. Below is a brief description of these biases.

- **Uncertainty bias** - error made in the presence of not enough information
- **Control bias** - mistake made due to individuals being overconfident because they have control of certain components of creating the visualization
- **Illusion bias** - misconception drawn due to an incorrect pattern or information identified in a visualization
- **Anchoring bias** - inaccurate conclusion from placing too much emphasis on the first piece of information provided

Procopio et al. (2021) provide examples of each of these biases in the context of progressive visualization.

The authors (Procopio et al., 2021) conducted several experiments to assess the impacts of these biases in progressive visualization. The authors found that the magnitude of the biases varied. For example, end-users were able to overcome uncertainty biases by developing strategies to help them make accurate decisions in the presence of not having all the information. The illusion bias affected the end-users the most, particularly when the false information was introduced right at the time the decision was made.

RECOMMENDATIONS FOR A DATA VISUALIZATION FRAMEWORK FOR ORGANIZATIONS: LINK BETWEEN DATA VISUALIZATION AND DATA LITERACY

The link between biases in data visualizations and data visualization literacy (DVL) has been examined with the importance of DVL emphasized (Börner, Bueckle, & Ginda, 2019; Mansoor & Harrison, 2018; Padilla et al., 2018). DVL is how competent individuals are at understanding information presented in graphs. Many individuals are not competent in DVL. For example, Börner et al. (2019) discuss how most individuals have trouble reading most data visualization types. In a recent Accenture study, only 25% of employees felt fully prepared to use data effectively (Stokes, 2021).

DVL is a key factor for making correct decisions with data visualizations within an organization. Given the ever-increasing reliance on data visualizations, it is important for organizations to focus on increasing DVL. However, an organization cannot focus on DVL alone. DVL is part of the larger data culture that needs to be implemented within organizations. Data literacy is the ability to explore, comprehend, and communicate with data. Data literacy is crucial for reducing biases for both the analyst that creates the visualization and the consumer of the visualization.

A framework that allows data literacy to feed into data visualization is provided here. Figure 1 illustrates this framework.

Figure 1.

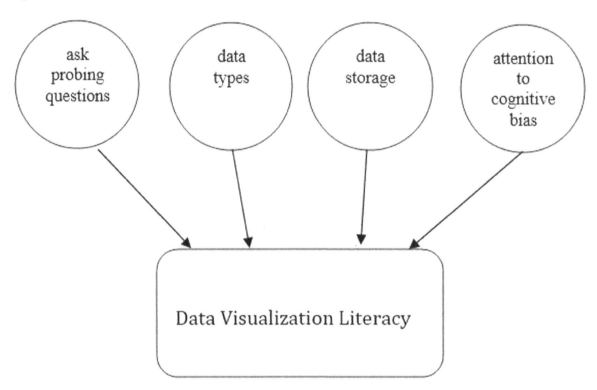

Ask Probing Questions of the Data

Asking critical questions of the data that an organization is collecting is a key part of data literacy. Individuals need to be curious and ask 'how' and 'why' questions of the data. There has been a recent resurgence of adopting a Socratic method of asking questions as it relates to data literacy. Padua (2021) discusses the importance of applying the Socratic questioning method to data analytical problems. Sindhu (2019) provides a list of sample data literacy questions that can be applied to the six types of Socratic questions that stimulate higher-level thinking.

Understand Data Types

The type of data will influence appropriate visualization for the data. Distinguishing between quantitative and qualitative variables is pivotal to understanding which types of graphs are appropriate. Qualitative variables place the values of the variable into categories. Appropriate visualizations for qualitative variables are bar, part-to-whole, or treemap charts. Quantitative variables are variables in which the values are numeric. Examples of appropriate visualizations for quantitative variables are scatterplots, line charts, or box plots. Ryan (2018) provides a comprehensive discussion of which types of visualizations are appropriate for different data types.

Connection Between Data Storage and the Visualization

Each data visualization is connected to a raw data source such as a spreadsheet or database. Identifying the way in which the data is stored can assist with better understanding of the manner in which the visualization is created. A visualization is rarely a display of the raw data The data may have to be aggregated in some manner. Many times, the data has been filtered, new variables created, or original variables may have been transformed to create the visualization. For example, consider a data analyst that works for a University Institute of Research Assessment The analyst may be creating visualizations for a computer science department that illustrates how students performed on a mid-term exam by gender. The exam grades are stored in a spreadsheet in a numerical range from 0 to 100. The analyst might scale these numerical scores using Likert scales to create a butterfly chart shown in Figure 2. It is important that the analyst understand how the original data is stored so that other types of assessment analyses could be performed on this data. For example, since the raw data is stored as numerical values, a two-sample t-test could be performed to determine if there are any significant differences among the gender groups.

Awareness of the Cognitive Biases that Exist in Data Visualizations

It is well-known that biases occur in data visualizations and cause errors to be made all along the decision-making cycle within an organization (Killen, Geraldi, & Kock, 2020; Wesslen et al., 2019; Xiong et al., 2019). Therefore, it is important for organizations to be aware of the errors that cognitive biases can create and design training, processes, and policies to avoid these cognitive biases as much as possible.

The connection between DVL and data literacy should not be ignored by any organization in making decisions using visualizations. It is not an easy task for organizations to build a data literate employee base. It takes time, resources, training, and hiring new individuals with data skills.

FUTURE RESEARCH DIRECTIONS

There is no doubt that data visualization is currently a topic of considerable research interest in a variety of disciplines. Many organizations have amassed large quantities of data, in a variety of formats. That information, once properly visualized, can make a dramatic difference in terms of the accuracy and types of decisions that can be made. However, in years to come, there will be some emerging trends in data visualization that are outlined as follows.

Figure 2.

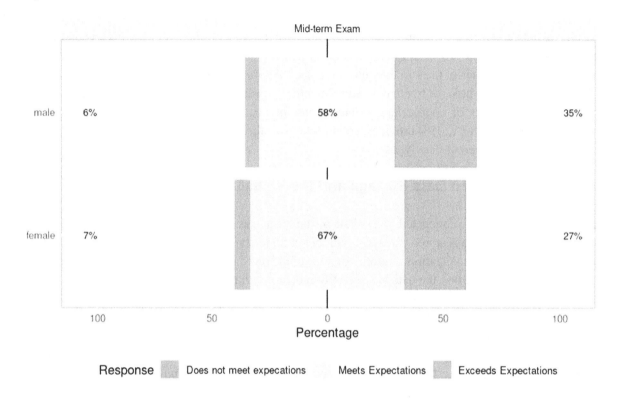

- **Visualizations beyond the basics:** Many organizations still think of data visualization as the basic charts and graphs such as bar charts, histograms, and line charts. Visualizing data must enable organizations to view massive amounts of data and gain substantial insight into their processes. Moritz, Howe, & Heer (2019) developed an interactive visualization system for allowing users to visualize millions to billions of observations with very little latency. Torre-Bastida et al. (2021) discuss how visualizations have not been fully addressed in big data environment due to the cognitive issues as discussed in this chapter. These are going to be the types of studies and advances that will be evolving in the data visualization community in years to come.
- **Additional cognitive bias studies related to data visualizations:** Dimara et al. (2018b) point out that few studies have been conducted on cognitive biases in visualizations and that this is a rich area for future research. The data and information visualization communities are just beginning to scratch the surface in understanding how humans interact, glean information from, and make decisions with visualizations. Further empirical work should be made with observational studies in organizations that wish to design cognitive bias visualization studies. These types of empirical studies could provide insight into the types of visualization tools that are needed to support decisions at all levels of an organization.

CONCLUSION

This chapter has provided an overview and background for cognitive biases in data visualizations. The focus of this chapter was related to cognitive biases that occur in big data and smaller, more traditional sized data sets. The main recommendation to a practitioner or organization is to focus on data literacy. The components of data literacy will assist in thwarting biases that emerge in data visualizations. Implementing data literacy programs within an organization is a first step in cognitive bias mitigation strategies for data visualizations.

Beyond data literacy programs, some other practical bias mitigation strategies could be to provide users a different view of the data to change perspective, peer discussions of hypotheses, and visualize multiple outcomes of the proposed belief or hypotheses (Pohl, 2018).

Data visualizations are a tool that allow individuals with a wide range of backgrounds to interact and work with data. Visualizations can range from static scatterplots and bar charts to interactive visual systems that allow a spacecraft to be monitored in flight in real-time. No matter how simple or complex the visualization, individuals must use their eyes and brains to extract meaning from the visualizations. Therefore, cognitive biases are always likely to occur when interpreting visualizations. The key to mitigating these biases is to deeply understand what people see when they look at a data visualization. More lab and real-world experiments are needed to answer this question. The data visualization community has just started to scratch the surface in performing experiments to understand the cognitive process of humans viewing and interpreting visualizations.

REFERENCES

Arias-Hernández, R., Dill, J., Fisher, B., & Green, T. M. (2011). Visual analytics and human-computer interaction. *Interactions, 18*(1), 51-55.

Borland, D., Wang, W., & Gotz, D. (2018). Contextual visualization. *IEEE Computer Graphics and Applications, 38*(6), 17–23. doi:10.1109/MCG.2018.2874782 PMID:30668452

Börner, K., Bueckle, A., & Ginda, M. (2019). Data visualization literacy: Definitions, conceptual frameworks, exercises, and assessments. *Proceedings of the National Academy of Sciences of the United States of America, 116*(6), 1857–1864. doi:10.1073/pnas.1807180116 PMID:30718386

Branley-Bell, D., Whitworth, R., & Coventry, L. (2020, July). User Trust and Understanding of Explainable AI: Exploring Algorithm Visualisations and User Biases. In *International Conference on Human-Computer Interaction* (pp. 382-399). Springer. 10.1007/978-3-030-49065-2_27

Chang, C. J., & Luo, Y. (2019). Data visualization and cognitive biases in audits. *Managerial Auditing Journal, 36*(1), 1–16. doi:10.1108/MAJ-08-2017-1637

Cho, I., Wesslen, R., Karduni, A., Santhanam, S., Shaikh, S., & Dou, W. (2017). The anchoring effect in decision-making with visual analytics. *2017 IEEE Conference on Visual Analytics Science and Technology (VAST)*, 116–126. 10.1109/VAST.2017.8585665

De Sherbinin, A., Bukvic, A., Rohat, G., Gall, M., McCusker, B., Preston, B., Apotsos, A., Fish, C., Kienberger, S., Muhonda, P., Wilhelmi, O., Macharia, D., Shubert, W., Sliuzas, R., Tomaszewski, B., & Zhang, S. (2019). Climate vulnerability mapping: A systematic review and future prospects. *Wiley Interdisciplinary Reviews: Climate Change, 10*(5), e600. doi:10.1002/wcc.600

Dimara, E., Bailly, G., Bezerianos, A., & Franconeri, S. (2018a). Mitigating the attraction effect with visualizations. *IEEE Transactions on Visualization and Computer Graphics, 25*(1), 850–860. doi:10.1109/TVCG.2018.2865233 PMID:30137000

Dimara, E., Bezerianos, A., & Dragicevic, P. (2016). The attraction effect in information visualization. *IEEE Transactions on Visualization and Computer Graphics*, *23*(1), 471–480. doi:10.1109/TVCG.2016.2598594 PMID:27875163

Dimara, E., Franconeri, S., Plaisant, C., Bezerianos, A., & Dragicevic, P. (2018b). A task-based taxonomy of cognitive biases for information visualization. *IEEE Transactions on Visualization and Computer Graphics*, *26*(2), 1413–1432. doi:10.1109/TVCG.2018.2872577 PMID:30281459

Featherston, R., Downie, L. E., Vogel, A. P., & Galvin, K. L. (2020). Decision making biases in the allied health professions: A systematic scoping review. *PLoS One*, *15*(10), e0240716. doi:10.1371/journal.pone.0240716 PMID:33079949

Gopal, D. P., Chetty, U., O'Donnell, P., Gajria, C., & Blackadder-Weinstein, J. (2021). Implicit bias in healthcare: Clinical practice, research and decision making. *Future Healthcare Journal*, *8*(1), 40–48. doi:10.7861/fhj.2020-0233 PMID:33791459

Harold, J., Lorenzoni, I., Shipley, T. F., & Coventry, K. R. (2016). Cognitive and psychological science insights to improve climate change data visualization. *Nature Climate Change*, *6*(12), 1080–1089. doi:10.1038/nclimate3162

Hartson, H. R. (1998). Human-computer interaction: Interdiscplinary roots and trends. *Journal of Systems and Software*, *43*(2), 103–118. doi:10.1016/S0164-1212(98)10026-2

Killen, C. P., Geraldi, J., & Kock, A. (2020). The role of decision makers' use of visualizations in project portfolio decision making. *International Journal of Project Management*, *38*(5), 267–277. doi:10.1016/j.ijproman.2020.04.002

Malkoc, S. A., Hedgcock, W., & Hoeffler, S. (2013). Between a rock and a hard place: The failure of the attraction effect among unattractive alternatives. *Journal of Consumer Psychology*, *23*(3), 317–329. doi:10.1016/j.jcps.2012.10.008

Mansoor, H., & Harrison, L. (2018). Data visualization literacy and visualization biases: Cases for merging parallel threads. In *Cognitive biases in visualizations* (pp. 87–96). Springer. doi:10.1007/978-3-319-95831-6_7

McInerny, G. J., Chen, M., Freeman, R., Gavaghan, D., Meyer, M., Rowland, F., Spiegelhalter, D. J., Stefaner, M., Tessarolo, G., & Hortal, J. (2014). Information visualisation for science and policy: Engaging users and avoiding bias. *Trends in Ecology & Evolution*, *29*(3), 148–157. doi:10.1016/j.tree.2014.01.003 PMID:24565371

Moritz, D., Howe, B., & Heer, J. (2019). Falcon: Balancing interactive latency and resolution sensitivity for scalable linked visualizations. *Proceedings of the 2019 CHI Conference on Human Factors in Computing Systems*, 1–11. 10.1145/3290605.3300924

O'Sullivan, D., & Schofield, S. J. (2018). Cognitive bias in clinical medicine. *Journal of the Royal College of Physicians of Edinburgh*, *48*(3), 225–231. doi:10.4997/jrcpe.2018.306 PMID:30191910

Ozdemir, S., & Finkelstein, E. A. (2018). Cognitive bias: The downside of shared decision making. *JCO Clinical Cancer Informatics*, *2*(2), 1–10. doi:10.1200/CCI.18.00011 PMID:30652609

Padilla, L. M., Creem-Regehr, S. H., Hegarty, M., & Stefanucci, J. K. (2018). Decision making with visualizations: A cognitive framework across disciplines. *Cognitive Research: Principles and Implications*, *3*(1), 1–25. doi:10.118641235-018-0120-9 PMID:29399620

Padua, L. (2021, November). *Data literacy and the art of asking questions* [Video]. TED. https://www. youtube.com/watch?v=GhqTvWwMOYw

Paul, J., & Mas, E. (2020). Toward a 7-p framework for international marketing. *Journal of Strategic Marketing*, *28*(8), 681–701. doi:10.1080/0965254X.2019.1569111

Pohl, M. (2018). Cognitive biases in visual analytics—a critical reflection. In *Cognitive Biases in Visualizations* (pp. 177–184). Springer. doi:10.1007/978-3-319-95831-6_13

Procopio, M., Mosca, A., Scheidegger, C. E., Wu, E., & Chang, R. (2021). Impact of cognitive biases on progressive visualization. *IEEE Transactions on Visualization and Computer Graphics*. PMID:33434132

Ryan, L. (2018). *Visual data storytelling with tableau: Story points, telling compelling data narratives.* Addison-Wesley Professional.

Schulz, H.-J., Angelini, M., Santucci, G., & Schumann, H. (2015). An enhanced visualization process model for incremental visualization. *IEEE Transactions on Visualization and Computer Graphics*, *22*(7), 1830–1842. doi:10.1109/TVCG.2015.2462356 PMID:27244708

Sindhu, A. (2019). *Data literacy: Using the Socratic method* [Online forum post]. KDnuggets. https:// www.kdnuggets.com/2019/06/data-literacy-socratic-method.html#comments

Stokes, N. (2021). Why your workforce needs data literacy: The key to innovation, growth and problem solving. *Forbes*.

Stolper, C. D., Perer, A., & Gotz, D. (2014). Progressive visual analytics: User-driven visual exploration of in-progress analytics. *IEEE Transactions on Visualization and Computer Graphics*, *20*(12), 1653–1662. doi:10.1109/TVCG.2014.2346574 PMID:26356879

Sukumar, P. T., & Metoyer, R. (2018). A visualization approach to addressing reviewer bias in holistic college admissions. In *Cognitive Biases in Visualizations* (pp. 161–175). Springer. doi:10.1007/978-3-319-95831-6_12

Szafir, D. A. (2018). The good, the bad, and the biased: Five ways visualizations can mislead (and how to fix them). *Interaction*, *25*(4), 26–33. doi:10.1145/3231772

Torre-Bastida, A. I., Díaz-de-Arcaya, J., Osaba, E., Muhammad, K., Camacho, D., & Del Ser, J. (2021). Bio-inspired computation for big data fusion, storage, processing, learning and visualization: State of the art and future directions. *Neural Computing & Applications*, 1–31. doi:10.100700521-021-06332-9 PMID:34366573

Tversky, A., & Kahneman, D. (1974). Judgment under uncertainty: Heuristics and biases. *Science*, *185*(4157), 1124–1131. doi:10.1126cience.185.4157.1124 PMID:17835457

Valdez, A. C., Ziefle, M., & Sedlmair, M. (2017). Priming and anchoring effects in visualization. *IEEE Transactions on Visualization and Computer Graphics*, *24*(1), 584–594. doi:10.1109/TVCG.2017.2744138 PMID:28866525

Van Pelt, C., & Sorokin, A. (2012, May). Designing a scalable crowdsourcing platform. In *Proceedings of the 2012 ACM SIGMOD International Conference on Management of Data* (pp. 765-766). 10.1145/2213836.2213951

Wall, E., Blaha, L., Paul, C., & Endert, A. (2019, September). A formative study of interactive bias metrics in visual analytics using anchoring bias. In *IFIP Conference on Human-Computer Interaction* (pp. 555-575). Springer. 10.1007/978-3-030-29384-0_34

Wedell, D. H. (1991). Distinguishing among models of contextually induced preference reversals. *Journal of Experimental Psychology. Learning, Memory, and Cognition*, *17*(4), 767–778. doi:10.1037/0278-7393.17.4.767

Wesslen, R., Santhanam, S., Karduni, A., Cho, I., Shaikh, S., & Dou, W. (2018). *Anchored in a data storm: How anchoring bias can affect user strategy, confidence, and decisions in visual analytics*. arXiv preprint arXiv:1806.02720.

Wesslen, R., Santhanam, S., Karduni, A., Cho, I., Shaikh, S., & Dou, W. (2019). Investigating effects of visual anchors on decision-making about misinformation. *Computer Graphics Forum*, *38*(3), 161–171. doi:10.1111/cgf.13679

Xiong, C., Van Weelden, L., & Franconeri, S. (2019). The curse of knowledge in visual data communication. *IEEE Transactions on Visualization and Computer Graphics*, *26*(10), 3051–3062. doi:10.1109/TVCG.2019.2917689 PMID:31107654

ADDITIONAL READING

Costa, D. F., de Melo Carvalho, F., de Melo Moreira, B. C., & do Prado, J. W. (2017). Bibliometric analysis on the association between behavioral finance and decision making with cognitive biases such as overconfidence, anchoring effect and confirmation bias. *Scientometrics*, *111*(3), 1775–1799. doi:10.100711192-017-2371-5

Donohoe, D., & Costello, E. (2020). Data visualisation literacy in higher education: An exploratory study of understanding of a learning dashboard tool. *International Journal of Emerging Technologies in Learning*, *15*(17), 115–126. doi:10.3991/ijet.v15i17.15041

Hillemann, E.-C., Nussbaumer, A., & Albert, D. (2015). Visualizations and their effect on cognitive biases in the context of criminal intelligence analysis. *International Conference Computer Graphics, Visualization, Computer Vision & Image Processing*, 313–316.

Kalra, A., Liu, X., & Zhang, W. (2020). The zero bias in target retirement fund choice. *The Journal of Consumer Research*, *47*(4), 500–522. doi:10.1093/jcr/ucaa035

Nussbaumer, A., Verbert, K., Hillemann, E.-C., Bedek, M. A., & Albert, D. (2016). A framework for cognitive bias detection and feedback in a visual analytics environment. *2016 European Intelligence and Security Informatics Conference (EISIC), Intelligence and Security Informatics Conference (EISIC), 2016 European, EISIC*, 148–151. 10.1109/EISIC.2016.038

Wall, E., Blaha, L. M., Franklin, L., & Endert, A. (2017). Warning, bias may occur: A proposed approach to detecting cognitive bias in interactive visual analytics. *2017 IEEE Conference on Visual Analytics Science and Technology (VAST)*, 104–115. 10.1109/VAST.2017.8585669

Wall, E., Stasko, J., & Endert, A. (2019). Toward a design space for mitigating cognitive bias in vis. *2019 IEEE Visualization Conference (VIS)*, 111–115. 10.1109/VISUAL.2019.8933611

Yang, F. (2020). Data visualization for health and risk communication. The handbook of applied communication research, 213-232.

KEY TERMS AND DEFINITIONS

Big Data: Data that is too large to be stored using conventional data storage capabilities. Big data also includes non-traditional types of data such as images, text, weblog searches, and social media data.

Cognitive Bias: An unconscious effect that causes humans to make errors in decision-making tasks.

Data Literacy: The ability to explore, comprehend, and communicate with data.

Data Visualization: A graphical presentation of data and information. The subject is applied in a variety of areas such as business, social science, healthcare, and sports.

Data Visualization Literacy: The ability to understand and interpret data that is presented in a visual format.

Human-Computer Interaction (HCI): The intersection of disciplines such as psychology, information visualization, and artificial intelligence that studies how computers can be more usable to humans.

Information Visualization: A discipline from computer science that deals with efficient methods for displaying data where decision-making is the main objective.

Progressive Visualization: Creating visualizations of big data sets in small pieces. The effect is to create visualizations that display partial results while not sacrificing computing speed.

Data Mining for Visualizing Polluted Gases

Yas A. Alsultanny

🆔 https://orcid.org/0000-0002-6211-7074

Uruk University, Iraq

INTRODUCTION

Big Data Mining (BDM) and Data Visualization (DV) are very important topics in the field of knowledge extraction. Big data required considerable data processing and storage capacity. The big data can be visualized and analyzed to extract knowledge. Big data can be used as a useful tool to enhance decision making (Shumway, 2014). The visual analytical tools have steadily improved during the last years to work with big data. The data age, where data grows exponentially, is a significant struggle to extract knowledge (Zhwan & Zeebaree, 2021). Visual analytics enables the exploration of air quality influence among various traffic scenarios by proper visual means (Bachechi, Po, & Rollo, 2022).

Big data is a term used to describe some of current directions in information technology, as a concept that take into consideration data analysis. The amount of data in the world is huge, in 2020, every person generated 1.7 megabytes per second (Petrov, 2021). It is important to note that most of the big data is unstructured data, where it is not organized and does not fit the usual databases (Smallcombe, 2020).

Data Mining is the technique to get useful knowledge out of databases; data mining requires pre-processing and analytic approach for finding the value. Data mining requires many operations such as data integration, data selection, and so on (Han, Kamber, & Jian, 2012). Selecting a suitable method of data mining is best method for knowledge extraction and forecasting the future (Alsultanny, 2011).

Visual analytic first defined by Thomas and Cook in 2005 as, the science of analytical reasoning facility by interactive visual interface. Murray in 2013 described Data Visualization as; "fortunately, we humans are intensely visual creatures. Few of us can detect patterns among rows of numbers, but even young children can interpret bar charts, extracting meaning from those numbers' visual representations. Visualizing data is the fastest way to communicate it to others." Data Visualization are valuable for the introduction of data in graphical form (Thanuj, Vinitha, & Sumathi, 2021).

Air pollution levels raised risk for diseases such as heart disease, stroke, chronic obstructive pulmonary disease, cancer, and pneumonia, the death every year is 4.2 million due to exposure to ambient (outdoor) air pollution (World Health Organization, 2021a). Air pollution is important in our live; most of the pollutants in the air are a result of emissions from cars, trucks, buses, factories, refineries, and other resources.

The objective of this chapter is to highlight the aspects of Big Data miming to visualize air pollution concentrations and it is relative to meteorological parameters. The data for this chapter collected from stations for monitoring pollution gases. These stations usually have an hourly reading to measure concentrations of gases such as ozone (O_3), nitrogen dioxide (NO_2), sulfur dioxide (SO_2), carbon monoxide (CO), carbon dioxide (CO_2), particulate matter (PM_{10} and $PM_{2.5}$), moreover these stations have an hourly reading for meteorological parameters such as Temperature (Temp), Humidity (Hu), Wind Speed (WS), Wind Direction (WD), and Air Pressure (AP). RapidMiner was used in this chapter to show visually the pollution gases distribution.

DOI: 10.4018/978-1-7998-9220-5.ch077

Background

"Big data" was first known in the 1990s (Hiter, 2021). Big data rises with the huge growth of data. It refers to the storing, processing, and analyzing the vast amounts of data, the speed of information data growth is faster and faster (Guo, Tang, Liu, & Gu, 2021). Big data brings new challenges to visualization because of the speed, size, and diversity of data. One of the most common definitions of big data is data that have volume, variety, and velocity (Dion, AbdelMalik, & Mawudeku, 2015; De Mauro, Greco, & Grimaldi, 2016). The Big data generated may be structured data, Semi Structured, data or unstructured data (Fan & Bifet, 2014).

The term "Big Data" is surrounded by a lot of advertising, where many software vendors claim to have the ability to handle big data with their products (Oracle, 2021). Innovations in hardware technology such as those in network bandwidth, memory, and storage technology have assisted the technology of Big Data. The new innovations coupled with the latent need to analyze the massive unstructured data that stimulated their development (Bhagattjee, 2014). Big data analytics was adopted by many organizations for constructing valuable information from big data to improve operational efficiency (Sivarajah, Kamal, Irani, & Weerakkody, 2017). Large scale data visualization is the best method of utilizing traffic and environmental big data, to improve the efficiency of data analysis, and human-computer interaction (Cao, Wang, & Liu, 2020).

Big data have characteristics 5 Vs (volume, variety, velocity, veracity, and value) (Marr, 2015). These characteristics extended to 10 Vs by adding more 5 Vs (variability, validity, vulnerability, volatility, and visualization) (Firican, 2017). Ability to utilize big data to visualize, analyze, and predict is changing the humanitarian operations and management dramatically (Akter & Wamba, 2019). Big data can be easily, efficiently processed by Map Reduce (Thanekar, Subrahmanyam, & Bagwan, 2016). The global big data market is supported by the growth of big data, which attained USD 208 billion in 2020. The market is expected to grow to attain USD 450 billion by 2026 (Expert Market Research, 2021).

Data analytics helps all types of public and private sector organizations to make better, quicker, and more efficient decisions (Barbero et al., 2016). Data Mining is the field of discovering novel and potentially useful information from large amounts of data (Cheng, Liu, Shi, Jin, & Li, 2016). Data mining defined as the use of analytical tools to discover knowledge in a database. The analytical tools may include machine learning, statistics, artificial intelligence, and information visualization (Redpath, 2000). Data mining categorized into seven categories as Fayyad, Piatetsky-Shapiro, & Smyth, stated in 1996. The important categories of data mining are regression, clustering, summarization, dependency modeling, link analysis, and sequence analysis. Knowledge Discovery in Databases (KDD) is the processing steps used to extract useful information from large collections of data (Frawley, Piatetsky-Shapiro, & Matheus, 1991).

Data mining mainly have two methods: classification is assigns items in a collection to target categories or classes, and clustering is a form of unstructured learning method. Decision trees are types of classifications such as: Reduced Error Pruning (REP) tree, K Nearest Neighbors (KNN), the J48 based on C4.5 algorithm, and M5P algorithm is an improvement of the Quinlan's M5 algorithm (Tan, Steinbach, & Kumar, 2006; Neeb & Kurrus, 2009; Kantardzic, 2011; Witten, Frank, Hall, & Pal, 2017).

Visualization has two meanings, "To form a mental image of something" refers to a cognitive, internal aspect whereas "to make something visible to the eye" refers to an external, perceptual role (Oxford English Dictionary, 2009). Visualization is any kind of technique to present information (Chen, Hardle, & Unwin, 2008; Keim et al., 2008). Data visualization refers to any graphic representation that can examine or communicate the data in any discipline (Few, 2009). Data visualization is the presentation of data in a pictorial or graphical format (SAS.com/offices, 2018). Data visualization used for hundreds of years in research, as it allows researchers to easily get a better insight into complex data they are studying (Djuric, 2014). The 3D visualization is gradually becoming the main trend in many fields including population gases and meteorological parameters (NESSI, 2012).

Climate change as an emerging topic, has been at the forefront of the big climate data analytics (Hassani, Huang, & Silva, 2019). Sophisticated big data analysis methods used to identify the causes of air pollution, and discovering its nexus with environmental parameters (Demertzis, Demertzi, & Demertzis, 2021). WHO's (World Health Organization) recommend air quality measured by the levels of the 6 pollutants (PM, O_3, NO_2, SO_2, CO, CO_2), these pollutants have the most effects on human health (World Health Organization, 2021b).

Data and systems science enables a large amount of socio-environmental heterogeneous data to be processed and interrelated (Sebestyén, Czvetkó, & Abonyi, 2021). Remote sensing is the main source of the massive volumes of real-time data, stored in multiple formats and are provided with high velocity and variety. These data are used in environmental monitoring, to inspect air quality and climate change. (Semlali & El Amrani, 2021). Air pollution is likely to reach levels that create undesirable living conditions. Indoor air data is human future challenges to monitor environment parameters, and create clean indoor environment, which is mainly depends on data mining methods and big data analysis (Iturriza et al., 2020).

The environment pollution is still increasing despite the various efforts of some governments through the world (Gautam et al., 2021). As reported in India the most air pollutants gases are PM_{10}, $PM_{2.5}$, NO_2, O_3 and CO (Deep, Mathur, & Joshi, 2021). The health care expenditure will be increased with the aggravation of air pollution and climate change (Shen, Wang, & Shen, 2021). Air pollution leads to an increase in healthcare expenditure, and reduced life expectancy (Xie, Dai, & Dong, 2018). The diseases combine with air pollution have economic impact and societal impact due to absences the workers from their jobs and reduction in their productivity, the air pollution damages children's health through both chronic and acute effects (Manisalidis et al., 2020; Babaoglu et al., 2022). The particulate matter has a negative effect on trust in the tourism destination and desire for it (Yu et al., 2021).

A study applied on 20 cities across the world, by utilizing both satellite and surface measurements to estimate air pollution, the results of this study proved that the positive effect of COVID 19 lockdown restrictions was the reduction of NO_2, $PM_{2.5}$, and PM_{10} concentration emission, due to decline in traffic volume (Sannigrahi et al., 2021). Sangkham, Thongtip, and Vongruang in (2021) found that the NO and the air quality index decreased during the COVID-19 outbreak, the CO, NO_2, SO_2, O_3, $PM_{2.5}$, and temperature increased, while the relative humidity, absolute humidity, wind speed, and rainfall decreased during the COVID-19 outbreak compared with the previous years.

Data Visualization

Data visualization is the use of computer for visual representations of data. It aims at helping decision maker to detect effectively into big data. Data visualization is an efficient and intuitively accessible approach to identify patterns in large and diverse data sets. Visualization has changed over time and now refers to a graphical representation of data (Alsultanny, 2017). Visually automation of scientific knowledge is important to discover the long-term causes of climate change and reduce its effects (Pauliuk, 2020). Organizations collect data of environmental parameters yearly; non-experts do not have a mental model to extract air quality information visually. In this case the stakeholders unable to interpret these data precisely (Carro et al., 2022).

Urban big data include different types of data, such as air quality data and meteorological parameters, used to measure air pollution status (Zou, Cai, & Cao, 2020). Big data visualization can work well for air quality analysis (Zeng, Chang, & Fang, 2019). The historical air quality must be validated because data quality is crucial when analyzing data for a long period. Visualization of air quality data is important for both the public and decision makers (Mura et al., 2020). MapReduce for visualizing data by one dimensional, two dimensional, and three-dimensional graphs are powerful methods for discovering the relationships between pollutant gases especially for big data (Alsultanny, 2021).

Gases and metrological parameters visualizations can have two goals: Explanatory and Exploratory. Gases and metrological parameters data are usually recorded by automatic stations at regular time intervals. Metrological data is typically multivariate that often consists of many dimensions. Air pollution is a major concern in any city through the world. The visualization technique used to aid visual analysis of the air pollution problem, followed by the challenge of metrological data for knowledge discovery.

There are many steps must be taken to prepare data for visualization, these steps are shown in Figure 1. The steps are stations sensors adjustment, data recording, data filtering, data preprocessing, normalization, aggregation, and visualization.

Figure 1. Big data acquisition and utilization

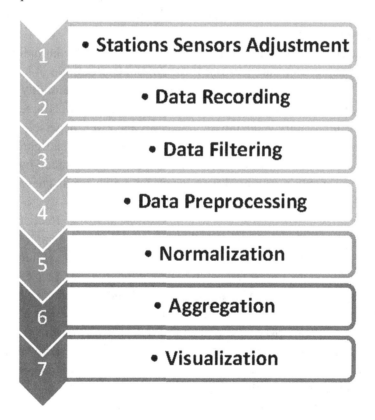

Data Collection and Analysis

The data available for this chapter collected from Arabian Gulf countries stations for air quality monitoring; it was hourly time series data for eleven years, after data filtering and preprocessing, the data for one-year 2019 was analyzed in this chapter. The data represented on an hourly averaged reading, where the yearly readings for each gas or parameter must be 8,760 (24 hr*365 day), but the real readings after filtering and processing are 8,630, with 130 (1.5%) missed reading. The RapidMiner version 9.1 used for processing and visualization the data of this chapter.

Figure 2 in its five sections (Figure 2a, 2b, 2c, 2d, 2e), shows visually in two dimensions and three dimensions the effect of temperature, humidity, and wind speed on the five gases (O_3, NO_2, CO, CO_2, and SO_2) and PM_{10}.

Figure 2a shows the effect of temperature on the concentration of the five gases (O_3, NO_2, CO, CO_2, and SO_2) and PM_{10}. The figure visualizes the data distribution by using two-dimensional diagrams; the temperature has an opposite effect on O_3 and NO_2. The concentration of O_3 increased directly during the hottest hours when the temperature above 40°C. While the temperature has a reverse effect on NO_2, the concentration of this gas became lower during the hottest hours, and its concentration was in its highest levels, when the temperature less than 10°C. The effect of temperature on CO and CO_2 is very limited and this clear in the figure, this indicates the temperature have no effect on these two gases. The hottest hours have a direct effect on SO_2 and PM_{10}, their concentrations usually increased during summer and especially in the hottest hours of a day.

Figure 2b shows the effect of humidity on the five gases and PM_{10}. The humidity has a reverse effect on O_3 and NO_2, their concentrations are increased with lower concentration of humidity, moreover the concentrations of CO, CO_2, and SO_2 increased with lower percentage of humidity. The PM_{10} concentration significantly reduced when the humidity percentage higher than 70%. These results are true, because the highest percentages of humidity, reducing the five gases and PM_{10} disperse.

Figure 2c shows the effect of wind speed on the five gases and PM_{10}, the figure shows the five gases concentrations increased with lower wind speed and these results also stated by Ocak, & Turalioglu, in 2008, while PM_{10} concentration increased with increasing wind speed. These results are very true, because the high wind disperse the five gases, and increase the PM_{10}.

Figure 2d shows the three dimensions scatter diagrams to visualize the effect of both temperature and humidity at the same time on the five gases and PM_{10}. The figure shows again most of the readings of O_3 are concentrated in the region of hottest temperature and low percentage of humidity. The concentrations of NO_2 increased during the lowest temperature and humidity. For CO, CO_2, SO_2, and PM_{10} their readings are concentrated in the region of hottest temperature and low percentage of humidity.

Figure 2e shows the three dimensions scatter diagrams to visualize the effect of both temperature and wind speed on the five gases and PM_{10}. These diagrams indicate that most of the readings of O_3, CO, CO_2, SO_2, and PM_{10} are concentrated in the regions of the hottest temperature with lower wind speed. This indicates that the rising in temperature have a major effect on PM_{10} compared with the wind speed, while NO_2 reading are concentrated in the region of the lower temperature and wind speed.

A decision tree is a predictive model (Rokach & Maimon, 2008; Masethe & Masethe, 2014; Alsultanny, 2020). It was implemented in this chapter to predicate PM_{10}, which is measured in part per million (ppm), by stating the effect of temperature and wind speed. To implement the decision tree the PM_{10}, temperature, and wind speed were classified into different ranges as shown in Table 1. PM_{10} classified into 0=0 to less than 50 ppm, 1=50 to less than 150 ppm, 2=150 to less than 400 ppm, 3=400 to less than 700 ppm, 4=700 to less than 1000 ppm, 5=1000 to less than 1500 ppm, 6=1500 to less than 2500 ppm, 7=2500 ppm and more. The temperature in centigram degree (°C) classified into 0=0 to less than 6 °C, 1=6 to less than 11 °C, 2=11 to less than 16 °C, 3=16 to less than 21 °C, 4=21 to less than 26 °C, 5=26 to less than 35 °C, 6=35 to less than 46 °C, 7=46 °C and more. The wind speed meter per second (m/s) classified into: 0=0 to less than 2 m/s, 1=2 to less than 5 m/s, 2=5 to less than 8 m/s, 3=8 to less than 12 m/s, 4=12 m/s and more.

Figure 2a. Effect of temperature on the five gases and PM$_{10}$

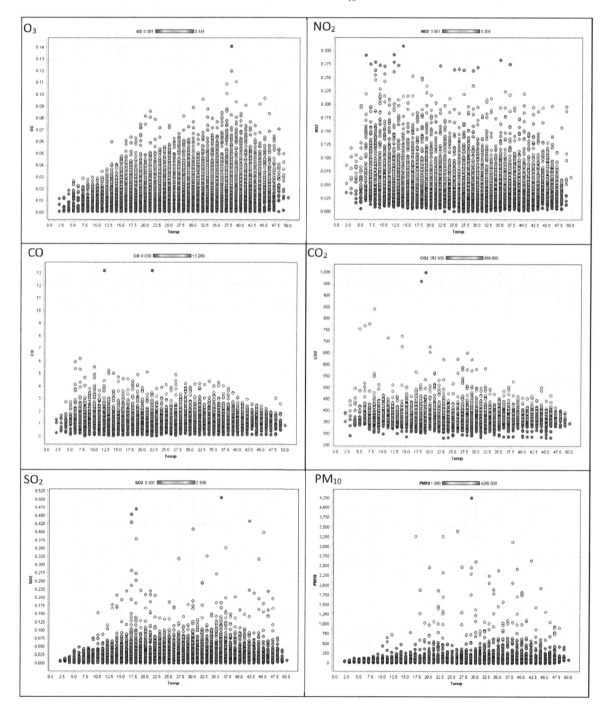

Figure 2b. Effect of humidity on the five gases and PM$_{10}$

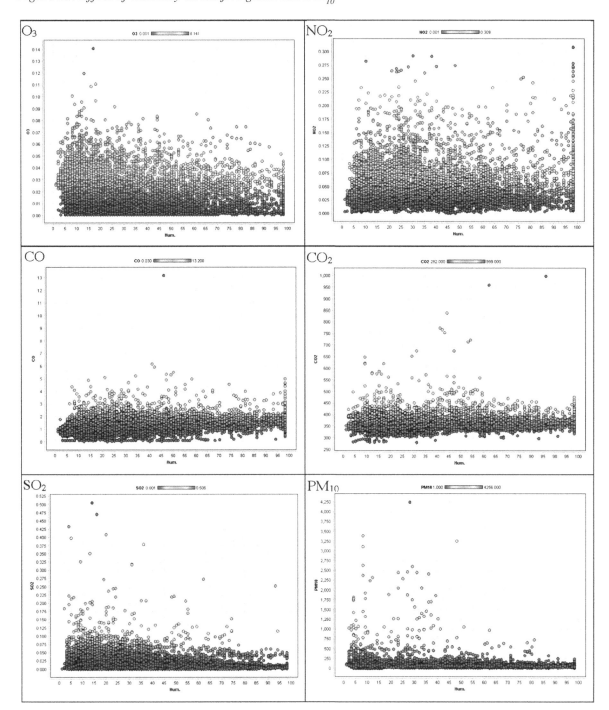

Figure 3 shows the decision tree to predicate PM$_{10}$, as an example by using temperature and wind speed-readings. The decision rules are as follows. It shows when wind speed between 6-12m/s and temperature 22=35 °C, the PM$_{10}$ will be between 151-400 ppm.

Tree

WS > 3.500: 2 {1=0, 0=0, 2=2, 3=2, 7=0, 4=0, 5=1, 6=0}

WS ≤ 3.500

| WS > 2.500

| | Temp > 4.500: 2 {1=15, 0=0, 2=28, 3=8, 7=0, 4=4, 5=4, 6=5}

| | Temp ≤ 4.500: 1 {1=41, 0=11, 2=16, 3=0, 7=2, 4=0, 5=2, 6=3}

| WS ≤ 2.500: 1 {1=4802, 0=1472, 2=634, 3=77, 7=3, 4=23, 5=16, 6=10}

Figure 2c. Effect of wind speed on the five gases and PM$_{10}$

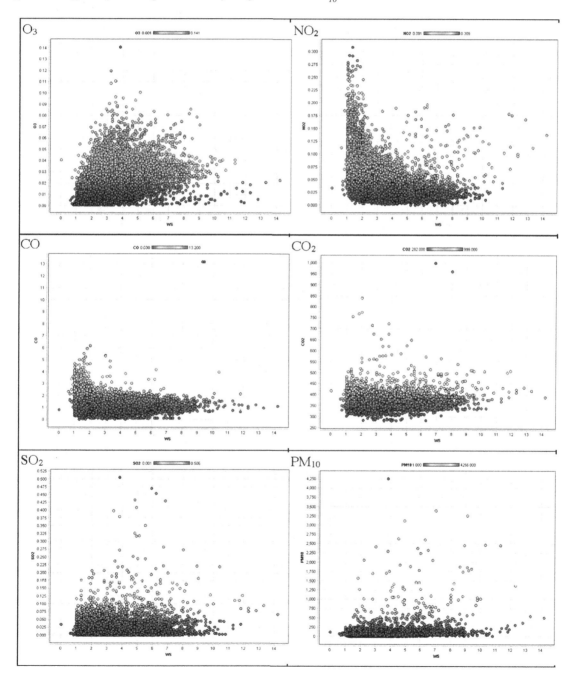

Figure 2d. Effect of temperature and humidity on the five gases and PM$_{10}$

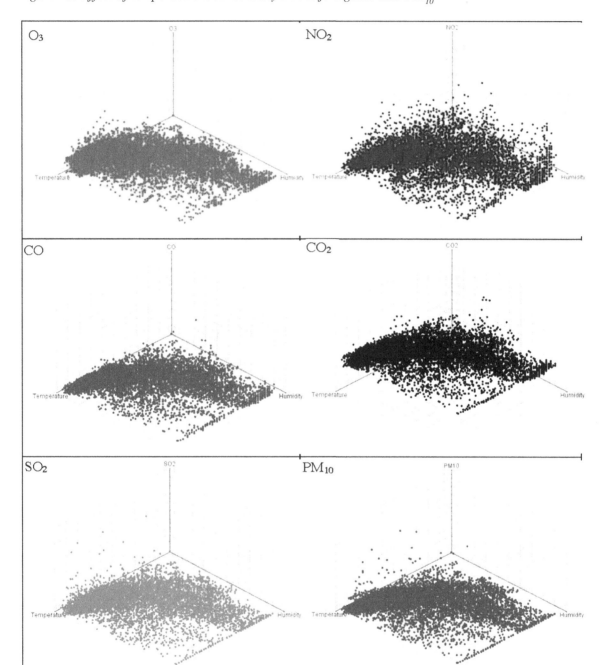

Figure 2e. Effect of temperature and wind speed on the five gases and PM$_{10}$

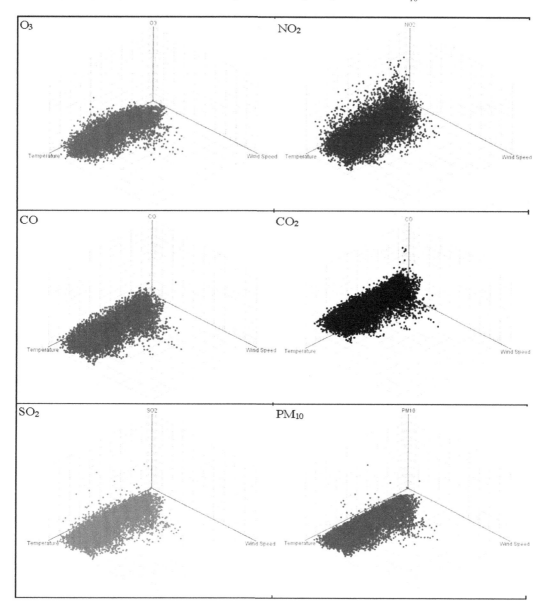

FUTURE RESEARCH DIRECTIONS

The followings are the future research directions:

1. Develop an application that can send a notification for any environmental disasters to any person, who setup this application in anywhere.
2. Using MapReduce to visualize polluted gases online in two and three dimensions.
3. Create culture for climate change disasters in Arab countries, by improving awareness to mitigating the impacts of climate change and natural hazards.

Table 1. Classification for PM$_{10}$, temperature, and wind speed

PM$_{10}$ (ppm)		Temperature (°C)		Wind speed (m/s)	
Class	Range	Class	Range	Class	Range
0	0 to less than 50	0	0 to less than 6	0	0 to less than 2
1	50 to less than 150	1	6 to less than 11	1	2 to less than 5
2	150 to less than 400	2	11 to less than 16	2	5 to less than 8
3	400 to less than 700	3	16 to less than 21	3	8 to less than 12
4	700 to less than 1000	4	21 to less than 26	4	12 and more
5	1000 to less than 1500	5	26 to less than 35		
6	1500 to less than 2500	6	35 to less than 46		
7	2500 and more	7	7=46 more		

Figure 3. Decision tree for prediction PM$_{10}$ by temperature and wind speed

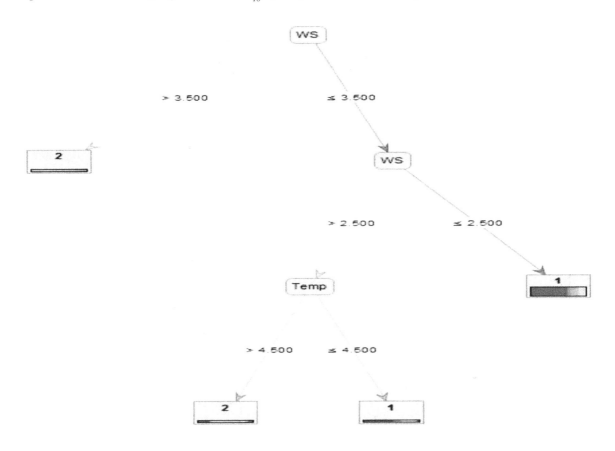

CONCLUSION

Air pollution is a serious global environmental concern, globally the size of data is huge, that are generated and accumulated daily from monitoring stations. Visualization is the best method for monitoring the accumulated data of air pollution daily and yearly. The problem of storing and analysis of big data are facing all the organization through the world, especially the environmental organization interesting on monitoring pollution gases. These organizations have one or more online reading stations installed near industrial cities and oil refinery stations.

Using the 2D and 3D scatter diagram to visualize the data reading is one of the important tools. That can be used by decision makers to explore the concentration of pollutant gases and effect of meteorological parameters, by using these types of visualization the decision makers can take their decision in stopping or reducing the working hours of the factories or refinery stations that cause the major pollution.

There is an urgent necessity of sensors that can monitor pollution gases from any place in the world using IOT and reduces the emissions of harmful substances into the environment, which require a major change in economy and methodology of production and human consumption, staring from electricity power consumption till the method of waste recycling.

We recommend each factory of refinery, using the same methods of visualizing the pollution gases to take their decision to stop their factory of refinery station or reducing the hours of working hours, when the temperature rise to more than 45°C.

REFERENCES

SAS.com/offices (2017). *Data visualization techniques, from basics to big data with SAS-visual analytics, White Paper.* https://www.sas.com/content/dam/SAS/documents/marketing-whitepapers-ebooks/sas-whitepapers/en/data-visualization-techniques-106006.pdf

Akter, S., & Wamba, S. (2019). Big data and disaster management: A systematic review and agenda for future research. *Annals of Operations Research, 283*(1-2), 939–959. doi:10.100710479-017-2584-2

Alsultanny, Y. (2011). Selecting a suitable method of data mining for successful forecasting. *Journal of Targeting, Measurement and Analysis for Marketing, 19*(3/4), 207–225. http://www.palgrave-journals.com/jt/journal/v19/n3/abs/jt201121a.html

Alsultanny, Y. (2017). Data mining and visualization: meteorological parameters and gas concentration use case. In *Proceedings of the 19th International Conference on Data Analytics and Management in Data Intensive Domains (DAMDID)* (pp. 350-353). Moscow State University.

Alsultanny, Y. (2020). Machine learning by data mining REPTree and M5P for predicating novel information for PM_{10}. *Cloud Computing and Data Science, 1*(1), 40-48. https://ojs.wiserpub.com/index.php/CCDS/article/view/418

Alsultanny, Y. (2021). Big data visualization by MapReduce for discovering the relationship between pollutant gases. *Journal Port Science Research, 4*(2), 61–68. doi:10.36371/port.2021.2.3

Babaoglu, U., Ogutcu, H., Erdogdu, M., Taskiran, F., Gullu, G., & Oymak, S. (2022). Assessment of indoor air quality in schools from Anatolia, Turkey. *Pollution, 8*(1), 57–67. doi:10.22059/poll.2021.325240.1112

Bachechi, C., Po, L., & Rollo, F. (2022). Big data analytics and visualization in traffic monitoring, *Big Data Research, 27*. doi:10.1016/j.bdr.2021.100292

Barbero, M., Coutuer, J., Jackers, R., Moueddene, K., Renders, E., Stevens, W., Toninato, Y., Peijl, S., & Versteele, D. (2016). *Big data analytics for policy making.* Report a study prepared for the European Commission DG INFORMATICS (DG DIGIT). *European Union.*

Bhagattjee, B. (2014). *Emergence and taxonomy of big data as a service.* Working Paper CISL# 2014-06. Massachusetts Institute of Technology.

Cao, X., Wang, M., & Liu, X. (2020). Application of Big Data Visualization in Urban Planning. *IOP Conference Series. Earth and Environmental Science, 440*(4), 042066. doi:10.1088/1755-1315/440/4/042066

Carro, G., Schalm, O., Jacobs, W., & Demeyer, S. (2022). Exploring actionable visualizations for environmental data: Air quality assessment of two Belgian locations. *Environmental Modelling & Software, 147.* doi:10.1016/j.envsoft.2021.105230

Chen, C., Hardle, W., & Unwin, A. (2008). *Handbook of Data Visualization.* Springer. doi:10.1007/978-3-540-33037-0

Cheng, S., Liu, B., Shi, Y., Jin, Y., & Li, B. (2016). Evolutionary computation and big data: Key challenges and future directions. *Proceedings of the First International Conference on Data Mining and Big Data*, 3-14. https://link.springer.com/conference/dmbd

De Mauro, A., Greco, M., & Grimaldi, M. (2016). Grimaldi formal definition of big data based on its essential features. *Journal of Library Review, 65*(3), 122–135. doi:10.1108/LR-06-2015-0061

Deep, B., Mathur, I., & Joshi, N. (2021). An approach to forecast pollutants concentration with varied dispersion. *International Journal of Environmental Science and Technology.* Advance online publication. doi:10.100713762-021-03378-z

Demertzis, S., Demertzi, V., & Demertzis, K. (2021). Data analytics for climate and atmospheric science. *International Journal of Big Data Mining for Global Warming, 3*(1), 2150005. doi:10.1142/S2630534821500054

Dion, M., AbdelMalik, P., & Mawudeku, A. (2015). Big data and the global public health intelligence network (GPHIN). *Canada Communicable Disease Report, 41*(9), 209–219. doi:10.14745/ccdr.v41i09a02 PMID:29769954

Djuric, N. (2014). *Big data algorithms for visualization and supervised learning* [Unpublished doctoral dissertation]. Temple University Graduate Board, Philadelphia, PA.

Expert Market Research. (2021). *Global big data market outlook.* https://www.expertmarketresearch.com/reports/big-data-market

Fan, W., & Bifet, A. (2014). Mining big data: Current status, and forecast to the future. *SIGKDD Explorations, 16*(1), 1–5.

Fayyad, G., Piatetsky-Shapiro, G., & Smyth, P. (1996). From data mining to knowledge discovery in databases. *American Association for Artificial Intelligence, 17*(3), 37–54.

Few, S. (2009). *Now you see it: simple visualization techniques for quantitative analysis.* Analytics Press.

Firican, G. (2017). *The 10 Vs of big data. upside where data means business.* https://tdwi.org/articles/2017/02/08/10-vs-of-big-data.aspx

Frawley, J., Piatetsky-Shapiro, G., & Matheus, J. (1991). Knowledge discovery in databases: An overview. *AI Magazine, 13*(3), 57–70.

Gautam, A., Verma, G., Qamar, S., & Shekhar, S. (2021). vehicle pollution monitoring, control and challan system using mq2 sensor based on internet of things. *Wireless Personal Communications*, *116*(2), 1071–1085. doi:10.100711277-019-06936-4

Guo, S., Tang, J., Liu, H., & Gu, X. (2021). Study on landscape architecture model design based on big data intelligence, *Big Data Research, 25*(2). doi:10.1016/j.bdr.2021.100219

Han, J., Kamber, M., & Jian, P. (2012). *Data mining: Concepts and techniques* (3rd ed.). Elsevier Inc.

Hassani, H., Huang, X., & Silva, E. (2019). Big data and climate change. *Big Data Cognitive Computing Journal*, *3*(1), 12. doi:10.3390/bdcc3010012

Hiter, S. (2021). *Big data market review 2021*. https://www.datamation.com/big-data/big-data-market/

Iturriza, M., Labaka, L., Ormazabal, M., & Borges, M. (2020). Awareness-development in the context of climate change resilience. *Urban Climate Journal, 32*. https://www.sciencedirect.com/science/article/pii/S2212095519300392 doi:10.1016/j.uclim.2020.100613

Kantardzic, M. (2011). *Data mining: Concepts, models, methods, and algorithms* (2nd ed.). John Wiley and Sons Inc. doi:10.1002/9781118029145

Keim, A., Mansmann, J., Thomas, S., & Ziegler, H. (2008). Visual *analytics: scope and challenges*. In S. J. Simoff, M. H. Böhlen, & A. Mazeika (Eds.), Lecture Notes in Computer Science: Vol. 4404. *Visual Data Mining*. Springer. doi:10.1007/978-3-540-71080-6_6

Manisalidis, I., Stavropoulou, E., Stavropoulos, A., & Bezirtzoglou, E. (2020). Environmental and health impacts of air pollution: A Review. *Frontiers in Public Health*, *8*, 14. doi:10.3389/fpubh.2020.00014 PMID:32154200

Marr, B. (2015). *Big data: Using SMART big data, analytics and metrics to make better decisions and improve performance*. John Wiley & Sons.

Masethe, M., & Masethe, H. (2014). Prediction of work integrated learning placement using data mining algorithms. In *Proceedings of the World Congress on Engineering and Computer Science* (Vol. 1). WCECS.

Mura, I., Franco, J., Bernal, L., Melo, N., Díaz, J., & Akhavan-Tabatabaei, R. (2020). A Decade of air quality in Bogotá: A descriptive analysis. *Frontiers in Environmental Science*, *8*, 1–12. doi:10.3389/fenvs.2020.00065

Murray, S. (2013). *Interactive data visualization for the web*. O'Reilly Media, Inc.

Neeb, H., & Kurrus, C. (2009). *Distributed K-nearest neighbors*. https://stanford.edu/~rezab/classes/cme323/S16/projects_reports/neeb_kurrus.pdf

NESSI. (2012). *Big data a new world of opportunities*. White Paper. http://www.nessi-europe.com/Files/Private/NESSI_WhitePaper_BigData.pdf

Ocak, S., & Turalioglu, S. (2008). Effect of meteorology on the atmospheric concentrations of traffic-related pollutants in Erzurum, Turkey. *Journal of International Environmental Application and Science*, *3*(5), 325–335.

Oracle. (2021). *What is big data?* https://www.oracle.com/big-data/what-is-big-data/

Oxford English Dictionary. (2009). *Visualization*. Oxford University Press.

Pauliuk, S. (2020). making sustainability science a cumulative effort. *Nature Sustainability, 3*(1), 2–4. doi:10.103841893-019-0443-7

Petrov, C. (2021). *25+ Impressive big data statistics for 2021*. https://techjury.net/author/chris_cleanrank/

Redpath, R. (2000). *A comparative study of visualization techniques for data mining* [Unpublished MSc dissertation]. School of Computer Science and Software Engineering, Monash University, Australia.

Rokach, L., & Maimon, O. (2008). *Data mining with decision trees: Theory and applications*. World Scientific Publishing.

Sangkham, S., Thongtip, S., & Vongruang, P. (2021). Influence of air pollution and meteorological factors on the spread of COVID-19 in the Bangkok Metropolitan Region and air quality during the outbreak. *Environmental Research, 197*. doi:10.1016/j.envres.2021.111104

Sannigrahi, S., Kumar, P., Molter, A., Zhang, Q., Basu, B., Basu, S., & Pilla, F. (2021). Examining the status of improved air quality in world cities due to COVID-19 led temporary reduction in anthropogenic emissions. *Environmental Research, 196*. https://www.sciencedirect.com/science/article/pii/S0013935121002218 doi:10.1016/j.envres.2021.110927

Sebestyén, V., Czvetkó, T., & Abonyi, J. (2021). The applicability of big data in climate change research: The importance of system of systems thinking. *Frontiers in Environmental Science, 9*, 619092. doi:10.3389/fenvs.2021.619092

Semlali, B., & El Amrani, C. (2021). Big data and remote sensing: A new software of ingestion. *Iranian Journal of Electrical and Computer Engineering, 11*(2), 1521–1530. doi:10.11591/ijece.v11i2.pp1521-1530

Shen, J., Wang, Q., & Shen, H. (2021). Does industrial air pollution increase health care expenditure? Evidence from China. *Frontiers in Public Health, 9*, 695664. Advance online publication. doi:10.3389/fpubh.2021.695664 PMID:34222189

Shumway, R. (2014). *One solution for air pollution: big data*. https://www.deseretnews.com/article/865617771/One-solution-for-air-pollution-Big-data.html

Sivarajah, U., Kamal, M., Irani, Z., & Weerakkody, V. (2017). Critical analysis of big data challenges and analytical methods. *Journal of Business Research, 70*, 263-286. doi:10.1016/j.jbusres.2016.08.001

Smallcombe, M. (2020). *Structured vs unstructured data: 5 key differences*. https://www.xplenty.com/blog/structured-vs-unstructured-data-key-differences/

Tan, P., Steinbach, M., & Kumar, V. (2006). *Introduction to data mining*. Pearson Addison Wesley.

Thanekar, S., Subrahmanyam, K., & Bagwan, K. (2016). Big data and MapReduce challenges, opportunities, and trends. *Iranian Journal of Electrical and Computer Engineering, 6*(6), 2911–2919. doi:10.11591/ijece.v6i6.pp2911-2919

Thanuj, S., Vinitha, K., & Sumathi, V. (2021). Data Mining and data visualization for analyzing the rate of bed availability at hospitals due to COVID-19. *Archive of Biomedical Science Engineering, 7*(1), 1-4. doi:10.17352/abse.000023

Thomas, J., & Cook, K. (2005). *Illuminating the path: the research and development agenda for visual analytics.* National Visualization and Analytics Center. https://www.hsdl.org/?view&did=485291

Witten, I., Frank, E., Hall, M., & Pal, C. (2017). *Data mining: Practical machine learning tools and techniques* (4th ed.). Elsevier Inc.

World Health Organization (WHO). (2021a). *New WHO global air quality guidelines aim to save millions of lives from air pollution.* https://www.who.int/news/item/22-09-2021-new-who-global-air-quality-guidelines-aim-to-save-millions-of-lives-from-air-pollution

World Health Organization (WHO). (2021b). https://www.who.int/health-topics/air-pollution

Xie, Y., Dai, H., & Dong, H. (2018). Impacts of SO_2 taxations and renewable energy development on CO_2, NOx and SO^2 emissions. *Journal of Cleaner Production, 171,* 1386–1395. doi:10.1016/j.jclepro.2017.10.057

Yu, J., Lee, K., Ariza-Montes, A., Vega-Muñoz, A., & Han, H. (2021). How do air quality issues caused by particulate matter affect consumers' emotional response to tourism destinations and willingness to visit? *International Journal of Enviroment Research and Public Health, 18*(19), 10364. doi:10.3390/ijerph181910364 PMID:34639667

Zeng, Y., Chang, Y., & Fang, Y. (2019). Data visualization for air quality analysis on big data platform. *2019 International Conference on System Science and Engineering (ICSSE),* 313-317. 10.1109/ICSSE.2019.8823437

Zhwan, Z., & Zeebaree, S. (2021). Big data analysis for data visualization: A review. *International Journal of Science and Business, 5*(2), 64–75.

Zou, Z., Cai, T., & Cao, K. (2020). An urban big data-based air quality index prediction: A case study of routes planning for outdoor activities in Beijing. *Environment and Planning. B, Urban Analytics and City Science, 47*(6), 948–963. doi:10.1177/2399808319862292

ADDITIONAL READING

Deleawe, S., Kusznir, J., Lamb, B., & Cook, D. (2010). Predicting air quality in smart environments. *Journal of Ambient Intelligence and Smart Environments, 2*(2), 145–154. doi:10.3233/AIS-2010-0061 PMID:21617739

Dragomir, E., Oprea, M., Popescu, M., & Mihalache, S. (2016). Particulate matter air pollutants forecasting using inductive learning approach. *Revista de Chimie, 67*(10), 2075–2081.

Fayyad, U., & Uthurusamy, R. (2002). Evolving data into mining solutions for insights. *Communications of the ACM, 45*(8), 28–31. doi:10.1145/545151.545174

Han, J., Chen, M., & Yu, S. (1996). Data mining: An overview from a database perspective. *IEEE Transactions on Knowledge and Data Engineering, 8*(6), 866–883. doi:10.1109/69.553155

Lee, M., Lin, L., Chen, C. Y., Tsao, Y., Yao, T. H., Fei, M. H., & Shih-Hau Fang, S. H. (2020). forecasting air quality in Taiwan by using machine learning. *Scientific Reports, 10*(1), 4153. doi:10.103841598-020-61151-7 PMID:32139787

Vitkar, S. (2017). Comparative analysis of various data mining prediction algorithms demonstrated using air pollution data of Navi Mumbai. *Research Journal of Chemical and Environmental Sciences*, 5(1), 79–85.

Wang, L., Wang, G., & Alexander, A. (2015). Big data and visualization: Methods, challenges and technology progress. *Digital Technologies*, 1(1), 33–38.

KEY TERMS AND DEFINITIONS

Air Pollution: It is the single largest environmental health risk, which is the results of the bad uses of environment resources, which causes harmful effect on humans, animals, plants, and climate change, the major polluted gases are ozone, nitrogen dioxide, carbon monoxide, carbon dioxide, sulfur dioxide, and particulate matter.

Air Quality: Is the degree to which the air is free of harmful substances and must be clean enough for humans, animals, or plants to life healthy.

Big Data: Is a collection of data from polluted gasses monitoring stations in each country that is huge in volume, globally these data growing exponentially with time, the complexity of these data require especial methods for analysis and management.

Climate Change: Is the global phenomenon created by burning fossil fuels, which causes global warming and destroy environment though pollutant gases.

Data Analytics: Are techniques of analyzing raw data to utilizing it in meaningful methods to extract valuable information insights it and draw conclusions.

Data Mining: Is the process of turn raw data into useful information, by finding relationships between variables, especially in big data.

Data Visualization: Is a way to represent data graphically, highlighting patterns, outliers, and trends in data, to help the reader to quickly understand relationships between variables, by using charts, graphs, and maps.

Monitoring Stations: Are stations installed in each country to monitor pollutant gases, working 24/7 to record gases concentration every minute.

Section 18
Decision, Support System

A Systems Analysis for Air Quality in Urban Ecology

Gilbert Ahamer

https://orcid.org/0000-0003-2140-7654

Austrian Academy of Sciences, Austria

Ralf Aschemann

Graz University, Austria

Birgit Pilch

Graz University, Austria

1. INTRODUCTION

The linkage between *data science* and *systems analysis* is a very clear one: on the one hand, fine-tuned data facilitate modelling and thus yield more exact results, on the other hand, detected patterns in time-space can provide a direction in which key interactions between parameters can be detected (Antoniou et al., 2018, Bhardwaj et al., 2015; Gvishiani et al., 2016; Kazieva et al., 2020; Lei et al., 2015; Mondal, 2016; Salazar et al., 2017; Song et al., 2020; Steinwandter & Herwig, 2019; Tripakis, 2018; Weinand et al., 2021).

Moreover, the general architecture of any modelling task in systems analysis and systems dynamics requires understanding, which of the potentially contributing factors can actually exert substantial impact on the results of a model, and hence co-determine meaning of that (quantitatively described) world view (Bentur et al., 2021; Finelli & Narasimhan, 2020; Lee et al., 2020; Medford et al., 2018; Nannapaneni et al., 2015; Tedeschi, 2019; Yang et al., 2015).

A third argument for the relevance of systems dynamics is the need for suitable parametrisation of detected interactions: this needs sound basis drawn from data analysis (Bennett & Clark, 1994; Dominiczak & Khansa, 2018; Idreos & Kraska, 2019; Liebovitch et al., 2019; Parnell et al., 2021; Sheikh et al., 2021; Šoštarić et al., 2021; Wickramage, 2017; Zanin, et al., 2017).

Within systems science, the topic of *urban air quality* is among the most traditional themes because it allows clear systems borders when modelling, namely the city's borders. Within a city, the most dynamic contributing factors can easily be identified, and thus a quick list of remedies can be established – which will suitably lead to rapid decision making on the municipal level. Such a mathematical tool should be short, concise, transparent, easy to understand, quickly manoeuvrable and thus quickly gain sympathy of municipal policy makers such as a mayor and key clerks, who traditionally have a leaning to practical-minded operationalism.

Data scientists are invited to see that (i) a quick conceptual look (ii) based on modelling experience allows to demonstrate the usefulness of gathering data on the local levels.

As topical example after the aggressive war attack by Russia on Ukraine, even states of sustainable peace were modelled (Liebovitch et al., 2019), thus shedding light on the importance of peace and empathy for global conviviality.

DOI: 10.4018/978-1-7998-9220-5.ch078

After this general justification of our theme's presence in this encyclopedia, we turn to the concrete theme: In the field of environmental protection and in any transdisciplinary education, it often becomes apparent that the effect of a certain action is not limited to the directly intended effect (Sterman, 2000; Coyle, 2000; Senge, 1990; Forrester, 1971; Aschemann, 2004; Ahamer and Kumpfmüller, 2013). Side effects can, via detours, spark a much greater dynamic in the overall system than direct effects. Such a characteristic occurs with closed control loops, which can build themselves up (positive feedback) or also stabilize (negative feedback).

For example, the relocation of residential areas into the unpolluted "green" on the outskirts triggers further traffic flows, which in turn cause additional traffic flows that further reduce the quality of life.

To support a clear thought organisation for the system "air pollution control in a city", the main descriptive variables should first be found out and then these should be related to each other.

2. THE DESCRIBING PARAMETERS

A uniform distribution of describing parameters across the entire subject area appears necessary for modelling the system dynamics. Their structure is as follows: the main thematic level consists of the four general themes (1) emitters, (2) the resulting so-called "emission" (i.e., concentration of air pollutants affecting the air quality) or effect on nature, (3) the effect on people and finally (4) the social boundary conditions regarding politics and economy.

Each such main level is divided into three intermediate levels, which can be seen in Table 1. For example, the emitters are divided into transport, energy / industry / trade and finally heat supply. Each of these intermediate levels is usually finally described by three indicators (= variables = parameters). A more detailed description of the individual indicators and units of measurement can be found in an early long version of this work (Pilch et al. 1988, 1992).

3. THE INTERACTIONS

In accordance with the widely differing types of variables from the areas of air chemistry, economics, sociology, etc., a semi-quantitative description of the strengths of interaction is preferred as follows: Effects from "very weak" to "very strong" correspond to the numbers 1 to 5, while positive or negative signs are possible ($-5 \ldots 0 \ldots +5$).

A harmonisation of all occurring strengths in horizontal and vertical direction as well as the restriction to the elementary steps of impacts led to the establishment of the matrix in Table 2. This matrix shows the strength of a parameter listed in a given row onto a parameter listed in a given column.

The most important of these 196 relationships are shown in Figure 1 "emission - transmission – resulting air quality and human health". The totality of all relationships is graphically portrayed in Figure 2.

In accordance with the cybernetic approach of the early Swiss pioneer Frederic Vester (Vester, 1980) and his colleagues, active and passive variables can already be described in this context in view of such a matrix: According to the definition, an active variable has an effect on many others, but itself is only slightly influenced. In the present case, these include the following variables: "Directives, institutions, norms and standards" (4.1.2), "State of technological development" (4.2.1), "Mindsets, models, and social behaviour" (3.3.1), "Land use and spatial planning" (4.3), "Material quality of life" (3.2.1), "Daily and annual concentration of air pollutants" (2.2.1), etc.

Table 1. Air pollution control in urban ecology – list of parameters in its systematic structure

item	Main level	item	Intermediate level	item	Indicator = variable = parameter	Nr.
1	Emitters	1.1	Traffic	1.1.1	Offered means of traffic, as quotient (public/individual)	1
				1.1.2	Demand for means of transport, as quotient (public/indiv.)	2
				1.1.3	Emissions from the means of transport	3
		1.2	Energy, industry, commerce	1.2.1	Diversity of available energy sources	4
				1.2.2	Demand for (ecologically unfavourable) energy sources	5
				1.2.3	Emissions from energy, industry, commerce	6
		1.3	Heat	1.3.1	Diversity of available heating energy carriers	7
				1.3.2	Demand for (ecologically unfavourable) heating sources	8
				1.3.3	Emissions from heating	9
2	nature (air quality)	2.1	Natural environment	2.1.1	Orography	10
				2.1.2	Biomass	11
				2.1.3	Climatic-meteorological framework conditions, geog.basin	12
		2.2	Environmental pressures	2.2.1	Daily and annual concentration of air pollutants	13
				2.2.2	Damage to vegetation, buildings and soil	14
				2.2.3	Systemic delays, synergisms, and secondary damage	15
		2.3	Reduction of loads	2.3.1	Air renewal	16
				2.3.2	Natural sinks for pollutants, filtration	17
3	Effect on humans	3.1	Health	3.1.1	Physical health	18
				3.1.2	Toxicology (= approximately, dangerousness of pollutants)	19
				3.1.3	Intra pollution (pollutants in closed rooms)	20
		3.2	Quality of life	3.2.1	Material quality of life	21
				3.2.2	Social quality of life	22
				3.2.3	Mental health	23
		3.3	Norms and ways of behaviour	3.3.1	Mindsets, models, and social behaviour	24
				3.3.2	Lack of acceptance, citizens' initiatives	25
				3.3.3	Political enforceability of environmental protection measures	26
4	POLICY AND ECONOMY (Border CONDITIONS)	4.1	Community and polity	4.1.1	Household burden, social benefits	27
				4.1.2	Directives, institutions, norms and standards	28
				4.1.3	Public relations, education, participation	29
		4.2	Economy	4.2.1	State of technological development	30
				4.2.2	Competitiveness, Situation of business management	31
				4.2.3	Economic damage, loss of tourism	32
				4.2.4	Quantity and prices of basic and raw materials	33
				4.2.5	Saving and recycling options	34
		4.3	Land use, spatial planning	4.3.1	Share & arrangement of settlements., resident. areas, density	35
				4.3.2	Share & arrangement of commercial and industrial areas	36
				4.3.3	Share & arrangement of traffic areas (flowing and stationary)	37
				4.3.4	Share & arrangement of green spaces	38

Passive variables, on the other hand, are strongly influenced by others but have only few effects themselves: "Daily and annual concentration of air pollutants" (2.2.1), "Demand for means of transport" (1.1.2), etc.

Table 2. The impact matrix. Parameters from one line affect those in one column. For the meaning of the decimally noted parameters, see Table 1.

	1.1.1	1.1.2	1.1.3	1.2.1	1.2.2	1.2.3	1.3.1	1.3.2	1.3.3	2.1.1	2.1.2	2.1.3	2.2.1	2.2.2	2.2.3	2.3.1	2.3.2	3.1.1	3.1.2	3.1.3	3.2.1	3.2.2	3.2.3	3.3.1	3.3.2	3.3.3	4.1.1	4.1.2	4.1.3	4.2.1	4.2.2	4.2.3	4.2.4	4.2.5	4.3.1	4.3.2	4.3.3	4.3.4
1.1.1	0	5	0	0	0	0	0	0	0	0	0	0	0	0	0	0	0	0	0	0	0	0	0	0	0	2	-3	3	0	3	0	0	0	0	3	3	-4	1
1.1.2	4	0	0	0	0	0	0	0	0	0	0	0	0	0	0	0	0	0	0	0	3	0	0	4	0	0	0	0	2	0	0	0	-2	0	4	4	-3	3
1.1.3	0	-5	0	0	0	0	0	0	0	0	0	0	0	0	0	0	0	0	0	0	0	0	0	0	0	0	0	-4	0	-4	0	0	0	0	0	0	0	0
1.2.1	0	0	0	0	4	0	0	0	0	0	0	0	0	0	0	0	0	0	0	0	0	0	0	0	0	2	-2	2	0	2	0	0	0	0	0	3	0	0
1.2.2	0	0	0	-3	0	0	0	0	0	0	0	0	0	0	0	0	0	0	0	0	0	0	0	0	0	0	-2	0	0	-3	0	0	0	0	0	0	0	0
1.2.3	0	0	0	0	5	0	0	0	0	0	0	0	0	0	0	0	0	0	0	0	0	0	0	0	0	0	0	-4	0	-4	0	0	0	-2	0	0	0	0
1.3.1	0	0	0	0	0	0	0	2	0	0	0	0	0	0	0	0	0	0	0	0	0	0	0	0	0	2	-4	4	0	3	0	0	0	0	4	0	0	0
1.3.2	0	0	0	0	0	0	-4	0	0	0	0	4	0	0	0	0	0	0	0	0	1	0	0	-4	0	0	0	0	2	-3	0	0	-1	0	4	0	0	0
1.3.3	0	0	0	0	0	0	0	5	0	0	0	0	0	0	0	0	0	0	0	0	0	0	0	0	0	0	0	-3	0	-4	0	0	0	0	0	0	0	0
2.1.1	0	0	0	0	0	0	0	0	0	0	0	0	0	0	0	0	0	0	0	0	0	0	0	0	0	0	0	0	0	0	0	0	0	0	0	0	0	0
2.1.2	0	0	0	0	0	0	0	0	0	1	0	-1	0	-4	3	0	0	0	0	0	0	0	0	0	0	0	0	0	0	0	0	0	0	0	0	0	0	4
2.1.3	0	0	0	0	0	0	0	0	0	4	-2	0	1	0	2	3	0	0	0	0	0	0	0	0	0	0	0	0	0	0	0	0	0	0	0	0	0	0
2.2.1	0	0	5	0	0	5	0	0	5	0	0	4	0	0	0	-4	-4	0	0	0	0	0	0	0	0	0	0	0	0	0	0	0	0	0	2	2	2	0
2.2.2	0	0	0	0	0	0	0	0	0	0	0	-2	5	0	4	0	0	0	0	0	0	0	0	0	0	0	0	0	0	0	0	0	0	0	0	0	0	3
2.2.3	0	0	0	0	0	0	0	0	0	0	0	3	4	0	0	-1	0	0	0	0	0	0	0	0	0	0	0	0	0	0	0	0	0	0	0	0	0	0
2.3.1	0	0	0	0	0	0	0	0	0	-4	0	-3	0	0	0	0	0	0	0	0	0	0	0	0	0	0	0	0	0	0	0	0	0	0	0	0	0	0
2.3.2	0	0	0	0	0	0	0	0	0	0	4	-3	0	-3	0	0	0	0	0	0	0	0	0	0	0	0	0	0	0	0	0	0	0	0	0	0	0	1
3.1.1	0	0	0	0	0	0	0	0	0	0	0	-2	0	0	0	0	0	0	-5	0	0	0	4	3	0	0	0	0	0	0	0	0	0	0	0	0	0	0
3.1.2	0	0	0	0	0	0	0	0	0	0	0	0	5	0	4	0	0	0	0	5	0	0	0	0	0	0	0	0	0	0	0	0	0	0	0	0	0	0
3.1.3	0	0	0	0	0	0	0	0	0	0	0	0	4	0	0	0	0	-2	0	0	-2	0	0	0	-1	0	0	0	0	0	0	0	0	0	2	2	2	0
3.2.1	0	0	0	0	0	0	0	0	0	0	0	0	0	0	0	0	0	0	0	0	0	0	0	-2	0	0	0	4	0	0	0	0	0	0	0	0	0	0
3.2.2	2	0	0	0	0	0	0	0	0	0	0	0	0	-1	0	0	0	2	0	0	3	0	3	2	0	0	0	0	-1	0	0				2	0	0	0
3.2.3	0	0	0	0	0	0	0	0	0	0	0	2	0	0	0	0	0	3	0	0	4	2	0	3	0	0	0	0	0	0	0	0	0	0	0	0	0	0
3.3.1	0	0	0	0	0	0	0	0	0	0	0	0	3	3	0	0	0	0	0	0	2	3	0	0	0	0	0	0	5	0	0	2	0	0	0	0	0	0
3.3.2	0	0	0	0	0	0	0	0	0	0	0	0	0	0	0	0	0	0	0	0	0	-1	0	5	0	0	0	-2	0	0	0	0	0	0	0	0	0	0
3.3.3	0	0	0	0	0	0	0	0	0	0	0	0	0	0	0	0	0	0	0	0	0	5	0	-4	5	0	0	5	3	0	0	0	0	0	0	0	0	0
4.1.1	0	-2	0	0	0	0	0	-1	0	0	0	0	0	3	0	0	0	4	0	0	-4	0	0	0	0	0	0	2	0	0	-3	3	3	0	0	0	0	0
4.1.2	0	0	0	0	0	0	0	0	0	0	0	0	0	0	0	0	0	0	3	0	0	0	0	0	0	5	3	0	-4	0	0	0	0	0	0	0	0	0
4.1.3	0	0	0	0	0	0	0	0	0	0	0	0	0	0	0	0	0	0	0	0	2	0	0	5	3	0	-4	1	0	0	0	0	0	0	0	0	0	0
4.2.1	0	0	0	0	0	0	0	0	0	0	0	0	0	0	0	0	0	0	0	0	0	0	0	2	0	0	0	4	3	0	3	0	-2	0	0	0	0	0
4.2.2	0	0	0	0	0	0	0	0	0	0	0	0	0	0	0	0	0	-1	0	0	2	0	1	0	0	0	0	-2	0	4	0	-2	-4	4	0	2	0	0
4.2.3	0	0	0	0	0	0	0	0	0	0	0	0	0	4	3	0	0	4	0	0	0	0	0	0	0	0	0	0	0	0	-4	0	0	3	0	0	0	0
4.2.4	0	2	0	0	3	0	0	2	0	0	0	0	0	0	0	0	0	0	0	0	0	0	0	0	0	0	0	-2	0	0	0	0	0	-3	0	0	0	0
4.2.5	0	0	0	0	0	0	0	0	0	0	0	0	0	0	0	0	0	0	0	0	2	0	0	0	0	0	4	0	0	3	0	0	0	0	0	0	0	0
4.3.1	0	0	0	0	0	0	0	0	0	2	0	0	-3	0	0	0	0	0	0	0	5	0	0	0	0	0	0	3	0	0	0	0	0	0	0	1	2	2
4.3.2	0	0	0	2	0	0	0	0	0	-3	0	0	0	0	0	0	0	0	0	0	0	0	0	0	0	0	0	-3	0	0	1	0	0	0	0	0	2	0
4.3.3	-3	0	0	0	0	0	0	0	0	-3	0	0	0	0	0	0	0	0	0	0	0	0	0	0	0	0	0	-3	0	0	0	0	0	0	2	2	0	0
4.3.4	0	0	0	0	0	0	0	0	0	1	0	0	-1	0	0	0	0	0	0	0	2	0	0	0	3	0	0	0	0	0	0	0	0	0	-3	-3	-3	0

Figure 1. Overview of the main and intermediate levels including the most important effects: Emitters -> Nature (air quality) -> Effect on humans.

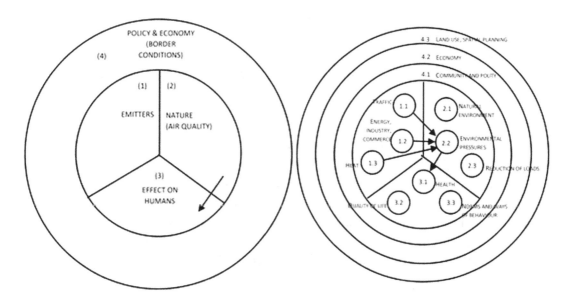

Figure 2. Graphic representation of all effects. The line thickness corresponds to the respective strengths, which are shown as numbers in the matrix from Table 2.

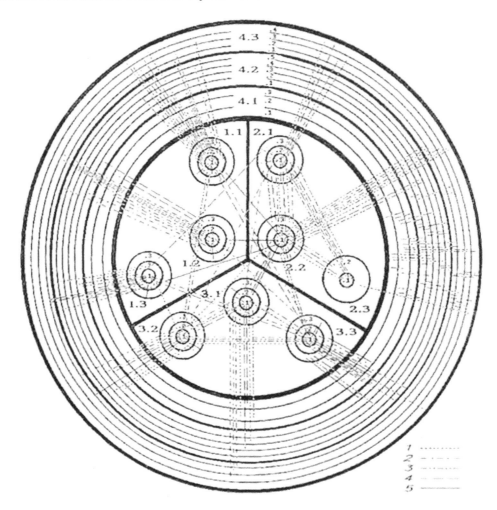

This matrix can also be used to identify indirect effects and chains of effects over several intermediate stages (e.g., 1.1.1 -> 1.1.2 -> 4.3.3 -> 1.1.1 or 4.1.3 -> 3.3.1 -> 1.1. 2 -> 1.1.3) as well as control loops with positive or negative feedback. The former result in a build-up (destabilising) dynamic, which can be advantageous for reinforcing the measures taken in the desired direction. They decisively shape the temporal behaviour of the overall system.

4. SIMULATION OF SIMPLE MEASURES

If the current state of the overall system consisting of 38 parameters is now designated by a vector of 38 numbers with the value zero and a change in the actual state is represented by the percentage change in the relevant variable, then one has a simple means of mathematical description. The vector defined in this way can be multiplied by the matrix in accordance with the usual rules and thus the new state is obtained after a certain time step, in which all effects occur. This new state vector can now in turn be used again for multiplication with the matrix. In this way, the effect of measures can be simulated step by step, which are imprinted on the causal relationship.

Accordingly, we can write:

State vector (t + 1) = state vector (t) + (state vector (t) x
(Evaluation matrix x calibration constant))

The value 0.04 proves to be practical for the calibration constant. Such a step-by-step calculation can be carried out about ten times, at the latest then deficiencies predominate.

A first example is the increase in the availability of public transport in a city (variable 1.1.1) by 5% (Figure 3). The system of means of transport supply - demand for transport, which is fed back positively, has its effect: Both of them increase the most of all parameters; they are indicated by the two upper lines in the diagram. The desired effect is the improvement of air quality, furthermore the mental health is greatly improved due to the increased recreational value of the city.

If one changes a parameter from the social area (variable 4.1.3: Public relations, education, participation), the result is a much more dramatic picture of the desired changes (Figure 4). Because this parameter is embedded in many more feedback loops, it sparks much more dynamic development. The reduction in emissions is almost two times stronger and in air quality three times stronger than in the previous example. It should be pointed out again that the figures given here tend to be of a semi-qualitative character and should have a stimulating effect on one's own thinking but should of course be checked by a knowledgeable reader in the light of own scientifically based experiences.

When reversing the logical direction of the mathematical equation, the optimal measure for a needed result can be computed. Mathematical, this requires the multiplication with the inverse matrix.

Therefore, in Figure 5, several different measures are compared in their effect on parameter 2.2.1 "Daily and annual concentration of air pollutants", meaning "air quality". The extent of the change set is in each case 5% compared to the initial state. Some likely measures could be:

- Increase in the transport offer
- Improvement of the supply for energy sources
- Improvement of the range of space heat carriers
- Stricter guidelines in the ecological sense
- Improving education and public relations
- Promote technical development

It turns out from the model that the air-quality- and health-related situation can best be improved by improving education and adults' education in public, by a tightening of the legal guidelines as well as by increasing the scientific and technical know (parameter 4.1.3. "Public relations, education, participation"). To compute this type of results, it is possible to use the transposed matrix (i.e., mirrored on the main diagonal) to calculate the necessary measures for a set goal. Then, arrows in Figure 2 do not run through the effects from the shaft to the tip, but in the opposite sense.

In this sense, for a desired improvement in quality of life, Figure 6 shows those parameters, the change of which appears most effective: physical health improvement, tightening of guidelines, increasing the level of technological development, followed by improvement in education and a change in the way people think in an ecological sense.

Figure 3. Graphic representation of the twelve most important effects of the measure "increase the offer of public transport (variable 1.1.1) by 5%".

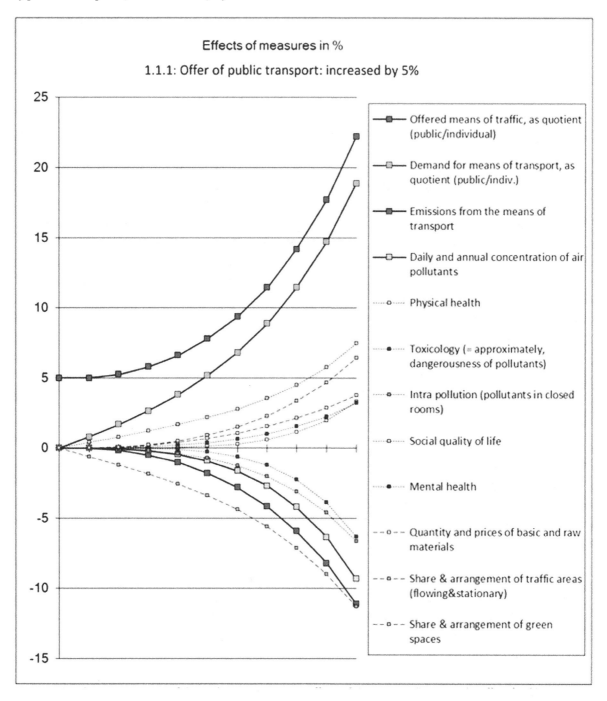

The above-mentioned results show that this interactive tool can be used for students' inspiration and to better perceive transdisciplinary systems dynamics, as needed in present-day projects and policy making (Brudermann et al., 2019; Winkler and Aschemann, 2017; Ahamer and Mayer, 2013; Ahamer and Schrei, 2006; Ahamer, 2013, 2019). Quantitative findings of this tool have always to be interpreted manually and with high levels of personal reflection.

Figure 4. Graphic representation of the twelve most important effects of the measure "increase Public relations, education, participation (variable 4.1.3) by 5%".

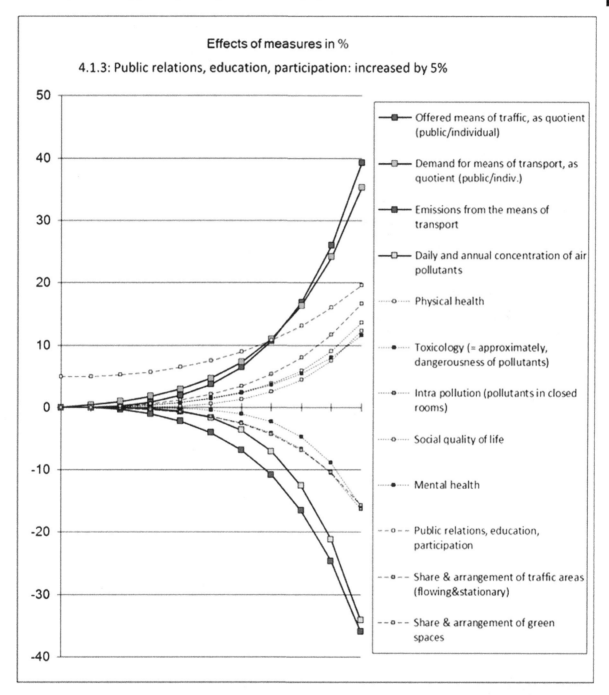

Figure 5. Comparison of the effects of several measures on air quality (parameter 2.2.1)

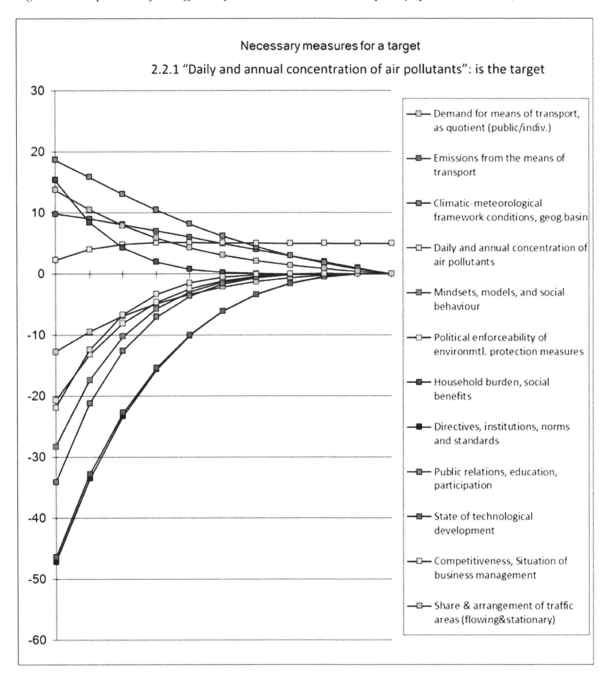

6. CONCLUSION

The graphical and mathematical representation of these interdependencies should serve to be able to keep in mind the way in which a complicated networked system behaves in a concise form. The results of the calculation can keep an expert inspired and a student busy with sufficiently many details in mind and point out any influences that may have been forgotten.

Figure 6. Comparison of the effects of several measures on material quality of life (parameter 3.1.1)

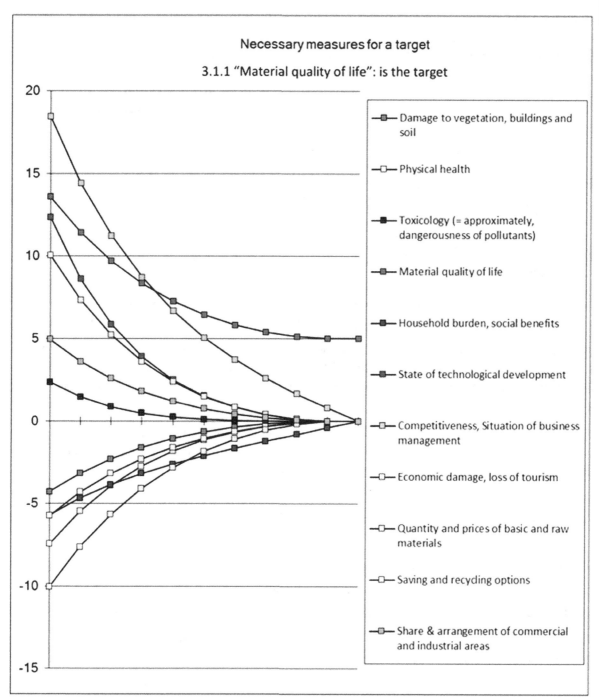

Principally, numbers in this model only give a rough estimate, the quantitative strengths in the matrix could be changed by the reader to the best of their knowledge, in order to experiment, and the entire model can easily be made to run on any PC due to its mathematical simplicity (Santhosh and D'Mello, 2020).

As a result of the matrix (Table 1) and the simulation runs, it can be assessed that only a bundle of measures (as opposed to single measures) promises success if the individual short-, medium- and long-term components are coordinated with one another. The main emitters are in most urban agglomerations (i) motorized individual transport, (ii) industry and (iii) space heating). Therefore, any bundle of measures should comprise (a) short term measures such as technological measures (e.g., applying filtering technologies) and (b) long-term measures such as regional planning in addition to measures on the levels of policy, legislative and public relations.

This model showed that variables such as "the way the population thinks and behaves" (variable 3.3.1 on *mindsets*) turned out to be extraordinarily powerful – in case the time spans for their boosting effect are sufficiently long to unfold.

REFERENCES

Ahamer, G. (2013). Quality assurance in transnational education management – the developmental 'global studies' curriculum. In S. Mukerji & P. Tripathi (Eds.), *Handbook of Research on Transnational Higher Education Management* (Vol. 1, pp. 259–302). IGI Global Publishers. doi:10.4018/978-1-4666-4458-8.ch015

Ahamer, G. (2019). *Mapping global dynamics – Geographic perspectives from local pollution to global evolution*. Springer International Publishing. https://link.springer.com/book/10.1007/978-3-319-51704-9

Ahamer, G., & Kumpfmüller, K. (2013). Education and literature for development in responsibility – partnership hedges globalization. In S. Mukerji & P. Tripathi (Eds.), Handbook of Research on Transnational Higher Education Management (pp.526–584). IGI Global Publishers. doi:10.4018/978-1-4666-4458-8.ch027

Ahamer, G., & Mayer, J. (2013). Forward looking: Structural change and institutions in highest-income countries and globally. *Campus-Wide Information Systems*, *30*(5), 386–403. doi:10.1108/CWIS-08-2013-0034

Ahamer, G., & Schrei, C. (2006). Exercise 'Technology assessment' through a gaming procedure. *Journal of Desert Research*, *5*(2), 224–252. doi:10.1504/JDR.2006.011364

Antoniou, C., Dimitriou, L., & Pereira, F. (2018). Mobility patterns, big data and transport analytics: Tools and applications for modeling. doi:10.1016/C2016-0-03572-6

Aschemann, R. (2004). Lessons learned from Austrian SEAs. *European Environment*, *14*(3), 165–174. doi:10.1002/eet.347

Bennett, M., & Clark, D. (1994). Object oriented modelling of communications systems. *IEE Colloquium (Digest)*, (115) 1/1-1/8.

Bentur, A., Getz, D., & Shacham, O. K. (2021). *System analysis of technology transfer policies and models in higher education.* doi:10.1007/978-3-030-74051-1_8

Bhardwaj, A., Bhattacherjee, S., Chavan, A., Deshpande, A., Elmore, A. J., Madden, S., & Parameswaran, A. (2015). DataHub: Collaborative data science & dataset version management at scale. *CIDR 2015 - 7th Biennial Conference on Innovative Data Systems Research.*

Brudermann, T., Aschemann, R., Füllsack, M., & Posch, A. (2019). Education for sustainable development 4.0: Lessons learned from the University of Graz, Austria. *Sustainability*, *11*(8). doi:10.3390/su11082347

Coyle, G. (2000). Qualitative and quantitative modelling in system dynamics: Some research questions. *System Dynamics Review, 16*(3), 225–244. doi:10.1002/1099-1727(200023)16:3<225::AID-SDR195>3.0.CO;2-D

Dominiczak, J., & Khansa, L. (2018). Principles of automation for patient safety in intensive care: Learning from aviation. *Joint Commission Journal on Quality and Patient Safety, 44*(6), 366–371. doi:10.1016/j.jcjq.2017.11.008 PMID:29793888

Finelli, L. A., & Narasimhan, V. (2020). Leading a digital transformation in the pharmaceutical industry: Reimagining the way we work in global drug development. *Clinical Pharmacology and Therapeutics, 108*(4), 756–761. doi:10.1002/cpt.1850 PMID:32294230

Forrester, J. (1971). Counterintuitive behavior of social systems. *Technology Review, 73*(3), 52–68.

Gvishiani, A., Soloviev, A., Krasnoperov, R., & Lukianova, R. (2016). Automated hardware and software system for monitoring the earth's magnetic environment. *Data Science Journal, 15*, 18. Advance online publication. doi:10.5334/dsj-2016-018

Idreos, S., & Kraska, T. (2019). From auto-tuning one size fits all to self-designed and learned data-intensive systems. *Proceedings of the ACM SIGMOD International Conference on Management of Data*, 2054-2059. 10.1145/3299869.3314034

Kazieva, B., Kaziev, K., Kaziev, V., & Kudaeva, F. (2020). The self-organizational potential of SMART university and its evolution. *CEUR Workshop Proceedings, 2861*, 70-79.

Lee, H., Angelow, D., & Mediavilla, F. A. M. (2020). Data supply chains for data science. *Interconnected Supply Chains in an Era of Innovation - Proceedings of the 8th International Conference on Information Systems, Logistics and Supply Chain, ILS 2020*, 348-355.

Lei, C., Lee, C. H. T., Kwan, T. O., Lee, C. K., Huang, K. B., Kwok, R. Y. K., & Man, K. L. (2015). The design of a smart power conversion system as an undergraduate cross-discipline integrated design project. *ISOCC 2014 - International SoC Design Conference*, 179-180. 10.1109/ISOCC.2014.7087685

Liebovitch, L. S., Coleman, P. T., Bechhofer, A., Colon, C., Donahue, J., Eisenbach, C., Guzmán-Vargas, L., Jacobs, D., Khan, A., Li, C., Maksumov, D., Mucia, J., Persaud, M., Salimi, M., Schweiger, L., & Wang, Q. (2019). Complexity analysis of sustainable peace: Mathematical models and data science measurements. *New Journal of Physics, 21*(7), 073022. Advance online publication. doi:10.1088/1367-2630/ab2a96

Medford, A. J., Kunz, M. R., Ewing, S. M., Borders, T., & Fushimi, R. (2018). Extracting knowledge from data through catalysis informatics. *ACS Catalysis, 8*(8), 7403–7429. doi:10.1021/acscatal.8b01708

Mondal, K. (2016). *Design issues of big data parallelisms.* doi:10.1007/978-81-322-2752-6_20

Nannapaneni, S., Mahadevan, S., Lechevalier, D., Narayanan, A., & Rachuri, S. (2015). Automated uncertainty quantification analysis using a system model and data. *Proceedings - 2015 IEEE International Conference on Big Data, IEEE Big Data, 2015*, 1408–1417. doi:10.1109/BigData.2015.7363901

Parnell, G. S., Kenley, C. R., Whitcomb, C. A., & Palanikumar, K. (2021). System design and engineering trade-off analytics: State of the published practice. *Systems Engineering, 24*(3), 125–143. doi:10.1002ys.21571

Pilch, B., Aschemann, R., & Ahamer, G. (1988). *Air pollution control in urban ecology – connections in the field of air pollution control and derived measures*. Project work as part of the postgraduate curriculum in Technical Environmental Protection, Graz University of Technology. https://www.researchgate.net/publication/318835118_Luftreinhaltung_in_der_Stadtokologie_-_Zusammenhange_im_Bereich_der_Luftreinhaltung_und_abgeleitete_Massnahmen_Air_hygiene_in_a_city_-_contexts_in_air_hygiene_and_deduced_measures

Pilch, B., Aschemann, R., & Ahamer, G. (1992). Eine Systemanalyse zur Luftreinhaltung in der Stadtökologie. *Mitteilungen des Naturwissenschaftlichen Vereines für Steiermark, 122*, 19–28. http://www.landesmuseum.at/pdf_frei_remote/MittNatVerSt_122_0019-0027.pdf

Salazar, B. M., Balczewski, E. A., Ung, C. Y., & Zhu, S. (2017). Neuroblastoma, a paradigm for big data science in pediatric oncology. *International Journal of Molecular Sciences, 18*(1), 37. Advance online publication. doi:10.3390/ijms18010037 PMID:28035989

Santhosh, D. K., & D'Mello, D. A. (2020). Strategies and challenges in big data: A short review. In D. K. Santhosh Kumar (Ed.), *Intelligent Systems Design and Applications* (pp. 34–47)., doi:10.1007/978-3-030-16660-1_4

Senge, P. (1990). *The Fifth Discipline*. Currency.

Sheikh, A., Anderson, M., Albala, S., Casadei, B., Franklin, B. D., Richards, M., Taylor, D., Tibble, H., & Mossialos, E. (2021). Health information technology and digital innovation for national learning health and care systems. *The Lancet. Digital Health, 3*(6), e383–e396. doi:10.1016/S2589-7500(21)00005-4 PMID:33967002

Song, C., Kong, Y., Huang, L., Luo, H., & Zhu, X. (2020). Big data-driven precision medicine: Starting the custom-made era of iatrology. *Biomedicine and Pharmacotherapy, 129*, 110445. Advance online publication. doi:10.1016/j.biopha.2020.110445 PMID:32593132

Šoštarić, M., Vidović, K., Jakovljević, M., & Lale, O. (2021). Data-driven methodology for sustainable urban mobility assessment and improvement. *Sustainability (Switzerland), 13*(13), 7162. Advance online publication. doi:10.3390u13137162

Steinwandter, V., & Herwig, C. (2019). Provable data integrity in the pharmaceutical industry based on version control systems and the blockchain. *PDA Journal of Pharmaceutical Science and Technology, 73*(4), 373–390. doi:10.5731/pdajpst.2018.009407 PMID:30770485

Sterman, J. D. (2000). *Business Dynamics: Systems thinking and modeling for a complex world*. McGraw Hill.

Tedeschi, L. O. (2019). ASN-ASAS symposium: Future of data analytics in nutrition: Mathematical modeling in ruminant nutrition: Approaches and paradigms, extant models, and thoughts for upcoming predictive analytics. *Journal of Animal Science, 97*(5), 1921–1944. doi:10.1093/jaskz092 PMID:30882142

Tripakis, S. (2018). Data-driven and model-based design. *Proceedings - 2018 IEEE Industrial Cyber-Physical Systems, ICPS 2018*, 103-108. 10.1109/ICPHYS.2018.8387644

Vester, F. (1980). *Sensitivitätsmodell* [Sensitivity model]. Regionale Planungsgemeinschaft Untermain.

Weinand, J. M., McKenna, R., Kleinebrahm, M., Scheller, F., & Fichtner, W. (2021). The impact of public acceptance on cost efficiency and environmental sustainability in decentralized energy systems. *Patterns*, 2(7), 100301. Advance online publication. doi:10.1016/j.patter.2021.100301 PMID:34286307

Wickramage, N. (2017). Quality assurance for data science: Making data science more scientific through engaging scientific method. *FTC 2016 - Proceedings of Future Technologies Conference*, 307-309. 10.1109/FTC.2016.7821627

Winkler, T., & Aschemann, R. (2017). Decreasing greenhouse gas emissions of meat products through food waste reduction. A framework for a sustainability assessment approach. In Food waste reduction and valorisation: Sustainability assessment and policy analysis (pp. 43-67). doi:10.1007/978-3-319-50088-1_4

Yang, B., Yamazaki, J., Saito, N., Kokai, Y., & Xie, D. (2015). Big data analytic empowered grid applications - is PMU a big data issue? *International Conference on the European Energy Market, EEM*. 10.1109/EEM.2015.7216718

Zanin, M., Chorbev, I., Stres, B., Stalidzans, E., Vera, J., Tieri, P., Castiglione, F., Groen, D., Zheng, H., Baumbach, J., Schmid, J. A., Basilio, J., Klimek, P., Debeljak, N., Rozman, D., & Schmidt, H. H. H. W. (2017). Community effort endorsing multiscale modelling, multiscale data science and multiscale computing for systems medicine. *Briefings in Bioinformatics*, 20(3), 1057–1062. doi:10.1093/bib/bbx160 PMID:29220509

Automatic Moderation of User–Generated Content

Issa Annamoradnejad
Sharif University of Technology, Iran

Jafar Habibi
Sharif University of Technology, Iran

INTRODUCTION

In recent years, most popular websites, such as Facebook and Wikipedia, emphasize user-generated content, ease of use, participatory culture, and interoperability for end-users (considered as Web 2.0). These websites do not generate systematic content and only depend on user involvement and content generation for their popularity and growth. Due to the vast expanse of these systems in terms of users and posts, manual verification of new content by the administrators or official moderators is not feasible and these systems require scalable solutions. The current strategy is to use crowdsourcing, which usually consists of initial reports by the community on the activities of users and a final decision by the official moderators or experienced users. For example, in community question-answering websites, if a post is against the general rules of the system, other users can flag the post for its violation using a reporting system, which will be entered into a review queue for further processing.

The crowdsourcing strategy has serious problems considering the agility and high impact of new posts (Ipeirotis et al., 2010; Paolacci et al., 2010). The slow handling process of reports is the first problem that exists in all of these systems. In general, the community has to review or simply read a new post, notice its unlawful content, create a flag report for its unlawful content, and wait some time for moderators to review the report that is now in a reporting queue. This process is performed manually by moderators and users, a costly and timely effort that sometimes results in subjective and biased decisions. In addition, some content may never be reported by the community as they are shared privately inside a closed network or not noticed by a large number of readers. This could lead to the usage of platforms as a safe private place for illegal activity, such as terrorism. Finally, users may wrongly report the content of another user because of disagreements and add to the slow handling of reports or cause problems for the target user (because of an automated locking mechanism in case of excessive reports for a user).

Given the need to maintain user rules and the significant problems of crowdsourcing, providing solutions for automatic and fast detection of user violations can resolve the mentioned problems, save time and money, reduce decision subjectivity, increase content quality, and create a safe place for civil debate. In addition, the same automated models can be utilized to develop constructive recommender systems that would help users in new content creation or editing.

In this research, by addressing these problems of manual handling, the authors show the emerging need for automated moderation of user-generated content using the latest machine learning and data science methods. Some recent works that proposed case-by-case solutions will be reviewed and a novel taxonomy of moderation actions will be provided by collecting answers to a new questionnaire. In addition, the authors propose an automated system for recommending the type of required edits to improve

DOI: 10.4018/978-1-7998-9220-5.ch079

the content in a community Q&A website, such as Stack Overflow. Determining the type of required edits for a question would help the asker to fix the problems, reach more readers, and achieve answers to her questions. A more accurate question will help the readers to better understand the context of the problem and provide faster and more accurate answers to the question. Since the proposed approach only uses the question data and does not include previous user achievements or future community feedback on the question (such as upvotes and comments), it can be used as a recommender system for new users and question drafts. The model extracts features by three separate components of feature extraction, which will be fed to feature engineering steps. For the final classification task, the model is trained using a gradient boosting algorithm.

This chapter will present novel ideas to create a real-world recommendation system that can assist system users and moderators in identifying the existing issues of old questions, sharing new high-quality questions, reducing the time needed for performing moderation actions, and improving the overall quality of the system.

BACKGROUND

Previous studies proposed methods to automate a single moderation task in a specific context. Some recent examples include preventing the spread of false content across online social networks (Campan et al, 2017; Shrivastava et al., 2020), spam/ad detection in online encyclopedias (Green & Spezzano, 2017; Yuan et al., 2017), fixing tags (Stanley & Byrne, 2013; Singh et al., 2020; Khezrian et al., 2020), finding low-quality (Tavakoli et al., 2020; Selleras 2020) or duplicate questions (Wang et al., 2020) in community question-answering websites, and predicting punishment for toxic players of competitive games (Blackburn & Kwak, 2014). Majority of these cases use a supervised text classification model to separate unacceptable content or behavior from the rest.

Detecting cyber-bullying and hateful acts is another major concern in online systems, which requires quick and accurate detection and subsequent response. All users, even newly registered ones, can publicly share new posts and comments, which could result in a simple approach for cyber-bullying, racism, and other hateful acts. Several studies focused on the analysis, detection, and prevention strategies (Waseem & Hovy, 2016; Blackwell et al., 2017; Agrawal et al., 2018; Bugueno & Mendoza, 2019).

While the majority of user-generated content is text-based, most platforms allow sharing other types of data, such as voice-chats and gifs. In addition, some systems, like Instagram and YouTube, are completely based on non-textual content. Since user content rules generally apply to all types of data, detecting problematic content would require different machine learning models. Even though, a few studies addressed this challenge for certain types of content in recent years, e.g., moderation of voice-based communities (Jiang et al., 2019), the majority of previous studies on non-textual websites are using lexical and social features for the task (Chancellor et al., 2016; Liu et al., 2018). Non-textual content is more prone to copyright infringement, a study subject since the advent of these systems (Agrawal & Sureka, 2013; Brøvig-Hanssen & Jones, 2021).

In the last few years and with the recent advances in machine learning research, popular online social networks design and use private AI systems to automate a few user and content moderation tasks. These systems use machine learning classifiers trained on large corpora of texts manually annotated. Because of this method of learning, they suffer from bias in training (Binns et al., 2017), a new challenge that needs to be addressed. Recent studies also focus on developing explainable AI for moderation decisions based on AI-led systems to achieve transparency and accountability (Kou & Gui, 2020; Brunk et al.,

2020; Juneja et al., 2020; Annamorad, 2022). This means that people should be given clear explanations on why their user or content has been banned or limited. This feedback would help users to re-evaluate their behavior in the future by learning the norms of the community (Jhaver et al., 2019). From a technical point, in addition to achieving high accuracy, the trained model has to be able to show explanations for making a prediction/decision.

MAIN FOCUS

Understanding the context, aim and frequency of unauthorized actions or content is required for clearly addressing the existing needs and proposing accurate models of detection based on their nature. The authors classify websites with user-generated content to four major types:

- **Online Social Networks (OSNs),** e.g., YouTube and Facebook. While the general definition is very broad, in this chapter, OSNs refer to websites where the content is not forced to be organized and users can share any content publicly or privately. Because of this openness, defining strict rules to separate what is allowed from the rest could be a challenge in some cases for the management.
- **Online Q&A communities**, e.g., Stack Overflow and Quora. These online Q&A sites have attracted many users and have acted as reliable sources for experts from various fields. These systems, in addition to general user rules, have specific rules and guidelines to maintain their content quality and remove out-of-scope or duplicate content.
- **Online Encyclopedias**, e.g., Wikipedia and WikiData. Users have to work together to create high-quality content on topics within the scope and are able to add, edit or remove to the previously existing content.
- **Online Consumer-to-Consumer websites**, e.g., eBay and Airbnb. In these websites, users are able to post their product/service or contact providers. Some rules exist to prevent fraudulent actions or to ensure safety of transactions. In addition, since some of these websites depend on fees from users' business agreements, strict rules may exist to prevent direct contact between users.

To create a proper list of unauthorized content types, the authors created an online questionnaire and asked users of online communities to list the most reoccurring types of content that require moderation. The questionnaire also asked respondents to rate the severity of problems for each of the four types of websites based on their frequency (High/Medium/Low). Severity should be answered only if the action or content is not generally allowed in that website type, e.g., low quality posts are allowed in OSNs. During a week, 95 people completed the questionnaire, based on which the authors created a list of unauthorized content/action and grouped them into seven categories.

Table 1 displays the seven categories of unlawful content/action along with their most general definition. Median severity for each type of websites is included. From the results, false content is the most prevalent illegal posts in all websites; while spams are considered the least sever. Copyright infringement is one of the oldest concerns in social networks, which has been considered as a sub-category of "Duplicate Content".

Unfortunately, there seems to be very little effort to automate moderating actions in popular WEB 2.0 websites. To confirm this, the authors performed clear actions of sock-puppetry and self-promotion in Stack Overflow, Kaggle, and Wikipedia. Using a new user for such actions would result in faster detection by moderators as there seems to be a specific queue for observing the actions of such users. Voting on the same user in the Stack Overflow platform resulted in a warning from the system. Based on unofficial discussions, Kaggle only considers four upvotes from the same user on another user and disregards any further voting. Wikipedia was not able to detect our clear and consecutive self-promotion. From these reports, detecting voting patterns and anomaly detection can be incorporated quicker than detecting textual spams and promotion. Multiple research projects can attack the problem to identify and prevent sock-puppetry and other unlawful actions.

Table 1. Broad categories of illegal content/actions, with their severity of caused problems in each type of websites

#	Title	Description	OSN	Q&A	Encyc	C2C
1	Harassment	Cyber-bullying, racism, sexism, or any hateful act through public/private means toward a specific person or social group	High	Low	Low	Low
2	Sensitive Content	Violent, adult or any prohibited content that would distress the community	High	Low	Low	Low
3	False Content	Any deceptive, outdated or false content published knowingly or by mistake	High	High	High	High
4	Sock Puppetry	Forging multiple user accounts with real or fake identities to attack, promote or any kind of manipulation contrary to accepted practices of the community	Med	High	Low	Med
5	Low Quality Content	Potentially-useful content with problems in citing sources or language usage	-	High	High	Low
6	Duplicate Content	Content that already exist in the website or content under copyright laws	High	High	Low	Med
7	Spam	Unrelated content mostly for self-promotion	-	Low	Low	Med

RECOMMENDING REQUIRED EDITS FOR NEW QUESTIONS

In this section, the authors use a model architecture (from Annamorad et al., 2022) to recommend required edits for new questions. Usually, inexperienced users will fail to properly follow website policies in asking new questions, which results in cold reactions by the community, multiple edits, and sometimes user/content deletion. Thus, determining and recommending the type of edits required for a new question will assist the asker to create a high quality and accurate question, without the need for preliminary community response on the quality of the question. A high-quality question will help the readers to better understand the problem and provide faster and more accurate answers to the question.

Since the goal of the current task is mostly to assist inexperienced users in asking new questions, using user history or achievements is not a proper approach. In addition, community feedback such as comments and up votes cannot be used as inputs for proposing a recommender system for new questions. Thus, the current task is formally defined as a multi-label classification task for suggesting required edit types for new questions only based on the question title and body. The task is considered a multi-label task, as a given subject may require more than one edit type. For the case study, Stack Overflow (SO) is chosen for its large number of questions and availability of up-to-date data.

Step 1. Data

As for data, the authors used *data.stackexchange.com* to perform SQL queries on the majority of the database tables. The new dataset consists of 25,000 Stack Overflow questions from 2016-2020 that consist of (1) 5k well-received questions by the community that require no edits; (2) 20k questions with at least one major edit in one of the four types of edits (Step 3). The data is randomly split into 80% train and 20% test parts, prior to feature engineering.

Step 2. Feature Extraction and Engineering

In machine learning tasks, understanding the context of the problem is an essential step to achieve higher accuracy. This step which can be the result of data visualizations, data analysis or problem comprehension, would lead to better ways to extract features or configure proposed models. The authors argue that a given input (question in a specific Q&A website) has three distinct aspects:

1. The input is a text, meaning that general text-related methods can be applied to comprehend the text or extract features. For example, copy-editing problems related to syntax and semantics can be detected from this aspect of the post, to a great extent.
2. The input is a question, meaning that it has to be formed as a proper fact-seeking question, rather than being informative texts, advertisement, etc. Many question-related qualities, such as the target of the question and the type of the answer, can be utilized as mid-level features.
3. The input is inside a general context, meaning that the website (or sub community) has a topic (such as programming or health) and users cannot ask off-topic questions. It should be noted that even in multi-context Q&A websites, such as Quora or Yahoo Answers, there are smaller communities that have topic-based boundaries to better organize questions.

Based on these aspects, the method extracts several features using advanced state-of-the-art models and predicts the required edit types using Gradient Boosting algorithm. The architecture of the method is shown in Figure 1. First, from the title and body, basic statistical information on letters, words, and sentences are extracted (component A). Main features are *letter count*, *word count, code percentage of the body, sentiment analysis*, and *the type of title as a sentence (Interrogative or not)*. While these values are extracted for the complete question at once, *word count, type of sentence,* and *sentiment analysis* are calculated separately for the first sentence, last sentence, and the mean of all the sentences for their particular importance.

In a recent work, Annamorad et al. (2019) proposed a regression model to predict twenty subjective features of questions (e.g., clearness, intent of the asker, and interestingness). The proposed method has two main components: 1) An input embedding layer (B.1) that extracts contextualized embedding from the BERT-base model for each word in the input sentence. 2) A neural network to predict the targets based on word representations from the previous layer. Component B utilized the trained model to predict the values of these subjective features of questions.

As the last component of feature extraction, Component C uses a Named-Entity-Recognition (NER) model related to the context of the case study and extracts relevant features to the context of the website. Thus, a recent SoftNER model (Tabassum et al., 2020) is used in this component to extract programming and software engineering related features. This is an influential component as the degree of involvement of software-related entities may be crucial in evaluating the quality of a question.

Based on these three components, 74 features (30 text-related features from Component A, 20 question-related features from Component B, and 24 context-related features from Component C) are extracted for a given question, which will be united at Component D. Component D performs two feature-engineering steps. First, it doubles the number of features by applying a numerical function (log) to transform the extracted values. As the second step, since some classifiers, such as kNN-based models, are dependent on their input values, all feature values are normalized to numbers between zero and one.

Step 3. Training

The task is to identify required edit types for a given question. Thus, by assessing edit comments on a sample of Stack Overflow questions, the authors identified four recurring edit types:

- **Lexical/Grammar problems:** The question text should be fixed regarding syntax and grammar usage.
- **Not a question:** The question seems to have no clear question or objective. The question should be concise and clear.
- **Code samples are required:** Some questions cannot be answered without proper code samples to describe the problem. Currently, other system users will note this problem as comments under the question.
- **Hardware/Software specifications are required:** System requirements or context of the problem should be clearly specified. Otherwise, the question would be too broad to answer.

Since the task is defined as a multi-label problem, a model should be able to identify the four issues separately, meaning that the model can label some questions with multiple problems and some others without any identified problem. Thus, 222 normalized numerical values and 4 binary targets will be extracted for a given question. For predicting the final classification, the authors propose to use Gradient Boosting, a strong tree-based method. For implementation, LightGBM python library is utilized which ensures faster training speed while maintaining efficiency. Hyper-parameters are set as follow: *boosting_type='gbdt', max_depth=9, learning_rate=0.02, n_estimators=300.*

Step 4. Evaluation

Table 2 represents the results of comparison between the model and the baseline models evaluated on the test part of the dataset. The model outperforms the state-of-the-art XLNet model in Precision and F1-Score. Even though CNN and Logistic Regression (LR) algorithms performed very well according to the Precision metric, the model achieves a significant lead based on Recall and F1 scores. KNN algorithm was relatively weak according to Precision. As for time performance, all experiments took place on a computer with 16GB RAM and Intel(R) Xeon(R) 2.00GHz CPU.

As for the influence of feature extraction components, removing component B (question-related features) and re-evaluating would decrease F1-score by 4.3%. A similar experiment performed for component C (context-related features) shows 2.7% drop in F1-score.

Figure 1. Architecture of the proposed method

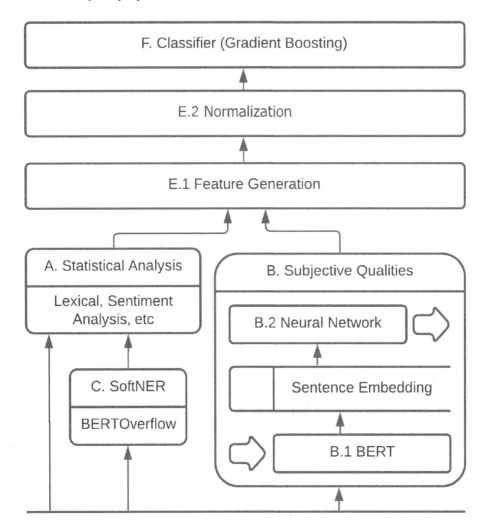

Question Title and Body

Table 2. Performance comparison of the proposed model with the selected baselines.

Model	Precision	Recall	F1-Score	Time (s)
XLNet	65.2	71.2	68.0	2890
CNN	69.2	49.3	57.6	904
KNN	60.1	62.6	61.3	334
LR	67.8	55.9	61.2	26
Proposed	**74.1**	**70.3**	**72.1**	**756**

FUTURE RESEARCH DIRECTIONS

Creating a safe place for online interaction remains a key goal in WEB 2.0 systems. The goal is to achieve systems that are equipped with automated and evolving mechanisms to moderate user content and behavior. Many of the involved tasks, as a result of shortcomings of existing algorithms, remain open and therefore worth investigating:

- **Detecting Sock-puppetry**: As discussed and showcased in the chapter, creating fake users to promote an agenda or another user is quite easy and goes undetected. Considering the vast majority of available data and novel ML approaches, it should be a rewarding task to detect self-promotion, voting discrepancies, and similar actions in popular WEB 2.0 websites.
- **Explainable AI**: Clear explanations on why user or content has been banned or limited would help users to re-evaluate their behavior in the future by learning the norms of the community. While most previous works focused on improving accuracy of the AI systems, i.e. classifiers, another essential pre-requisite for real-world deployment of these systems is to generate trustworthy, dependable and explainable decisions.
- **Transfer learning**: Regarding the paper subject, there are countless small prediction tasks in any popular website that would evolve or multiply with time. Designing, training and deploying proper recommender systems for each of these tasks would be infeasible, time-cost consuming. One solution to overcome this major problem is to use Transfer learning, where a model developed for a task is reused as the starting point for a model on a second task. Current transfer learning approaches for text mining require very little fine-tuning to achieve strong performances, making them a perfect candidate for real use-cases.
- **Unbiased AI**: Proposed ML approaches are considered as supervised learning, where the training is based on the given training data. If the training data is biased itself, the model will act biased and make unfavorable mistakes. This is a less-studied and critical subject and requires deep understanding of the platform, user behavior, subject of bias and ML methods.
- **Multi-media content moderation**: Almost all previous works focused on proposing ML models for user-generated texts. However, many of the current popular websites allow users to share content in multiple data types or in non-textual formats, e.g. Facebook, YouTube, Instagram, Clubhouse, and Spotify.

CONCLUSION

In this chapter, the authors investigated approaches to automatically moderate user-generated content on the Web. High-traffic websites that are built upon user-generated content were classified into four major types, based on their overall goal or behavior. Then, based on the results of a survey, reoccurring unlawful actions/content has been identified and grouped into coarse-grained items along with their frequency in each of the website types. In addition to presenting the taxonomy of moderation actions for user-generated content, the authors used a method for automating moderation actions for predicting required edit types. The method employs state-of-the-art machine learning techniques for supervised classification and considers the usage of context-related and question-related variables in its design. The results showed a promising future for utilizing ML approaches regarding the speed and accuracy of moderation decisions.

This chapter highlights moderation tasks in a structured way to help identify those tasks that have been neglected by machine learning engineers. Furthermore, it helps building recommender systems for real-world scenarios by giving attention to the special intricacies of new content and new users.

REFERENCES

Agrawal, S., & Awekar, A. (2018). Deep learning for detecting cyberbullying across multiple social media platforms. In *European conference on information retrieval*. Springer. 10.1007/978-3-319-76941-7_11

Agrawal, S., & Sureka, A. (2013). Copyright infringement detection of music videos on YouTube by mining video and uploader meta-data. In *International Conference on Big Data Analytics*, 48-67. Springer. 10.1007/978-3-319-03689-2_4

Annamorad, I. (2022). Requirements for Automating Moderation in Community Question-Answering Websites. In *15th Innovations in Software Engineering Conference (ISEC 2022)*. ACM.

Annamorad, I., Fazli, M., & Habibi, J. (2020). Predicting Subjective Features from Questions on QA Websites using BERT. In *2020 6th International Conference on Web Research (ICWR)*. IEEE.

Annamorad, I., Habibi, J., & Fazli, M. (2022). Multi-View Approach to Suggest Moderation Actions in Community Question Answering Sites. *Information Sciences*, *600*(1), 144–154. doi:10.1016/j.ins.2022.03.085

Binns, R., Veale, M., Van Kleek, M., & Shadbolt, N. (2017). Like trainer, like bot? Inheritance of bias in algorithmic content moderation. In *International conference on social informatics*. Springer. 10.1007/978-3-319-67256-4_32

Blackburn, J., & Kwak, H. (2014, April). STFU NOOB! predicting crowdsourced decisions on toxic behavior in online games. *Proceedings of the 23rd international conference on World wide web*, 877-888. 10.1145/2566486.2567987

Blackwell, L., Dimond, J., Schoenebeck, S., & Lampe, C. (2017). Classification and its consequences for online harassment: Design insights from heartmob. *Proceedings of the ACM on Human-Computer Interaction, 1*(CSCW), 1-19. 10.1145/3134659

Brøvig-Hanssen, R., & Jones, E. (2021). Remix's retreat? Content moderation, copyright law and mashup music. *New Media & Society*. Advance online publication. doi:10.1177/14614448211026059

Brunk, J., Mattern, J., & Riehle, D. M. (2019). Effect of transparency and trust on acceptance of automatic online comment moderation systems. In *2019 IEEE 21st Conference on Business Informatics (CBI)*. IEEE. 10.1109/CBI.2019.00056

Bugueño, M. C., & Mendoza, M. (2019). Learning to Detect Online Harassment on Twitter with the Transformer. PKDD/ECML Workshops, 298-306.

Campan, A., Cuzzocrea, A., & Truta, T. M. (2017). Fighting fake news spread in online social networks: Actual trends and future research directions. In *2017 IEEE International Conference on Big Data (Big Data)*. IEEE. 10.1109/BigData.2017.8258484

Chancellor, S., Pater, J. A., Clear, T., Gilbert, E., & De Choudhury, M. (2016). # thyghgapp: Instagram content moderation and lexical variation in pro-eating disorder communities. *Proceedings of the 19th ACM conference on computer-supported cooperative work & social computing*, 1201-1213. 10.1145/2818048.2819963

Green, T., & Spezzano, F. (2017). Spam users identification in wikipedia via editing behavior. *Proceedings of the International AAAI Conference on Web and Social Media*, 11(1).

Ipeirotis, P. G., Provost, F., & Wang, J. (2010). Quality management on amazon mechanical turk. *Proceedings of the ACM SIGKDD workshop on human computation*, 64-67. 10.1145/1837885.1837906

Jhaver, S., Bruckman, A., & Gilbert, E. (2019). Does transparency in moderation really matter? User behavior after content removal explanations on reddit. *Proceedings of the ACM on Human-Computer Interaction, 3*(CSCW), 1-27.

Jiang, J. A., Kiene, C., Middler, S., Brubaker, J. R., & Fiesler, C. (2019). Moderation challenges in voice-based online communities on discord. *Proceedings of the ACM on Human-Computer Interaction, 3*(CSCW), 1-23. 10.1145/3359157

Juneja, P., Rama Subramanian, D., & Mitra, T. (2020). Through the Looking Glass: Study of Transparency in Reddit's Moderation Practices. *Proceedings of the ACM on Human-Computer Interaction, 4*(GROUP), 1-35. 10.1145/3375197

Khezrian, N., Habibi, J., & Annamorad, I. (2020). *Tag Recommendation for Online Q&A Communities based on BERT Pre-Training Technique*. arXiv preprint arXiv:2010.04971.

Kou, Y., & Gui, X. (2020). Mediating Community-AI Interaction through Situated Explanation: The Case of AI-Led Moderation. *Proceedings of the ACM on Human-Computer Interaction, 4*(CSCW2), 1-27. 10.1145/3415173

Liu, P., Guberman, J., Hemphill, L., & Culotta, A. (2018). Forecasting the presence and intensity of hostility on Instagram using linguistic and social features. *Twelfth international aaai conference on web and social media*.

Paolacci, G., Chandler, J., & Ipeirotis, P. G. (2010). Running experiments on amazon mechanical turk. *Judgment and Decision Making, 5*(5), 411–419.

Selleras, R. Q. (2020). *Predictive Model: Using Text Mining for Determining Factors Leading to High-Scoring Answers in Stack Overflow* [Doctoral dissertation]. The George Washington University.

Shrivastava, G., Kumar, P., Ojha, R. P., Srivastava, P. K., Mohan, S., & Srivastava, G. (2020). Defensive modeling of fake news through online social networks. *IEEE Transactions on Computational Social Systems, 7*(5), 1159–1167. doi:10.1109/TCSS.2020.3014135

Singh, P., Chopra, R., Sharma, O., & Singla, R. (2020). Stack Overflow tag prediction using tag associations and code analysis. *Journal of Discrete Mathematical Sciences and Cryptography, 23*(1), 35–43. doi:10.1080/09720529.2020.1721857

Stanley, C., & Byrne, M. D. (2013). Predicting tags for Stack Overflow posts. *Proceedings of ICCM*.

Tavakoli, M., Izadi, M., & Heydarnoori, A. (2020, August). Improving Quality of a Post's Set of Answers in Stack Overflow. In *2020 46th Euromicro Conference on Software Engineering and Advanced Applications* (SEAA). IEEE. 10.1109/SEAA51224.2020.00084

Wang, L., Zhang, L., & Jiang, J. (2020). Duplicate question detection with deep learning in stack overflow. *IEEE Access: Practical Innovations, Open Solutions, 8*, 25964–25975. doi:10.1109/ACCESS.2020.2968391

Waseem, Z., & Hovy, D. (2016). Hateful symbols or hateful people? Predictive features for hate speech detection on twitter. *Proceedings of the NAACL student research workshop*, 88-93. 10.18653/v1/N16-2013

Yuan, S., Zheng, P., Wu, X., & Xiang, Y. (2017). Wikipedia vandal early detection: from user behavior to user embedding. In *Joint European Conference on Machine Learning and Knowledge Discovery in Databases*. Springer. 10.1007/978-3-319-71249-9_50

ADDITIONAL READING

Ashktorab, Z., & Vitak, J. (2016, May). Designing cyberbullying mitigation and prevention solutions through participatory design with teenagers. *Proceedings of the 2016 CHI Conference on Human Factors in Computing Systems*, 3895-3905. 10.1145/2858036.2858548

Chandrasekharan, E., Gandhi, C., Mustelier, M. W., & Gilbert, E. (2019). Crossmod: A cross-community learning-based system to assist reddit moderators. *Proceedings of the ACM on human-computer interaction, 3*(CSCW), 1-30. 10.1145/3359276

Chandrasekharan, E., Samory, M., Srinivasan, A., & Gilbert, E. (2017). The bag of communities: Identifying abusive behavior online with preexisting internet data. *Proceedings of the 2017 CHI Conference on Human Factors in Computing Systems*, 3175-3187. 10.1145/3025453.3026018

Kiene, C., Jiang, J. A., & Hill, B. M. (2019). Technological frames and user innovation: exploring technological change in community moderation teams. *Proceedings of the ACM on Human-Computer Interaction, 3*(CSCW), 1-23. 10.1145/3359146

Kou, Y., & Gui, X. (2021). Flag and Flaggability in Automated Moderation: The Case of Reporting Toxic Behavior in an Online Game Community. In *Proceedings of the 2021 CHI Conference on Human Factors in Computing Systems*, 1-12. 10.1145/3411764.3445279

KEY TERMS AND DEFINITIONS

Community QA Websites: An online question-answering platform where users are able to ask or answer questions, contribute to improving other users' public content or engage in moderation actions.

Cyber-Bullying: Any kind of bullying or harassment using electronic means commonly by posting rumors, threats, sexual remarks, or negative personal information about a victim or disrupting a civil conversation.

Explainable AI: A set of processes and methods that allows human users to comprehend and trust the results and output created by machine learning algorithms.

A

Fake News: False or misleading information presented as news, often to damage the reputation of a person or entity, or making money through advertising revenue.

Sock Puppetry: Forging multiple user accounts with real or fake identities to attack, promote or any kind of manipulation contrary to accepted practices of the community.

Transfer Learning: A machine learning method where a model developed for a task is reused as the starting point for a model on a second task.

Web 2.0: Websites that emphasize user-generated content, ease of use, participatory culture and interoperability for end users.

Bayesian Network–Based Decision Support for Pest Management

Neha Gupta

https://orcid.org/0000-0003-0905-5457

Manav Rachna International Institute of Research and Studies, Faridabad, India

INTRODUCTION

Bayesian Network, a key computer technology dealing with probabilities in Artificial Intelligence is one of the most effective and popular methods of modeling uncertain knowledge expression and reasoning such as environmental management (Bi & Chen, 2011; Uusitalo, 2007). BNs emerged from artificial intelligence research wherein originally, they emerged as formal modes to analyze decision approaches under uncertain conditions (Varis, 1997). New computational methods and techniques keep increasing BN's abilities and range of practical applications (Mead, Paxton & Sojda, 2006).

In contrast to the other approaches or techniques used in environment studies, Bayesian networks use probabilistic expressions rather than deterministic to express the relationships among variables of the system. Bayesian network accounts the lack of knowledge in the network by the usage of Bayesian probability theory which allows the subjective estimation of the probability of occurrence of a particular outcome that is to be combined with more objective data quantifying the frequency of occurrence in finding the conditional probabilistic relationships. Bayesian networks are very appropriate technique to deal with systems where uncertainty is inherently accounted in model as this is an important issue in ecological systems, Pollino & Henderson (2010).

BNs can integrate missing data readily by using Bayes' theorem. They can easily be understood without much mathematical background and knowledge. They have been found to possess good accuracy of prediction with small sample size. BNs can also be applied for predicting the probable values of states of a system for different future scenarios. Bayesian networks are also useful for participatory processes. They can assist in evaluating the alternative decisions to optimize a desired outcome. BNs can also help in processes of social learning. BNs express the system as network of reciprocal actions among system variables from main cause to final outcome; subject to all cause-effect assumptions are clearly made (Pollino & Henderson, 2010). Reasoning approaches are very useful in dealing with uncertain information (Heping & Daniel, 1998).

A Bayesian Network is a combination (G; P) (Jensen & Nielsen, 2007; Kjrulff & Madsen, 2008) where

- G = (V; E) is a DAG where set of nodes V = {X1, X2…Xn} represents the variables of the system and E, a set of arcs represents direct conditional dependencies between the variables(nodes);
- P represents the set of conditional probability distributions comparing conditional probability distribution P (Xi/pa (Xi)) for each variable X given the set of parent's pa (Xi) in the graph.

The joint probability distribution over V can be recovered from the set P of conditional probability distributions by the application of following chain rule:

DOI: 10.4018/978-1-7998-9220-5.ch080

P(X1, X2...Xn) = ∏P (Xi/pa (Xi)) (Singh & Gupta, 2017b)

Conditional probabilities of a BNs can be computed based on the experimental or trial data, results produced by the models and domain expert's knowledge elicitation (Borsuk et al., 2006). Uncertainty is clearly represented by way of presentation of the probabilities (Bromley et al., 2005).

Bayesian Network Theory

BNs are probabilistic graphical model consisting of variables of interest of a system and their conditional relationships (del Águila & del Sagrado, 2012). A BN consists of 'nodes' that represent the set of variables of interest and 'links' represent conditional interdependencies (cause-effect relationship) among nodes via a directed acyclic graph (DAG) (Pearl, 1988). Conditional probability distribution captures the quantum of dependence between system variables and thus explains the relationships between the nodes. For instance, if node A of a system affects another node B, then nodes A and B are linked to each other by an arc having direction from node A to node B. Herein node A is called as parent of node B and node B is referred as child of node A. If node B further affects another node C, then node B be the parent of node C. Figure 1 shows the conditional or causal relationship among nodes A, B and C of a basic Bayesian network.

Figure 1. Conditional or causal relationship among BN nodes
(Source: Landscape logic portal)

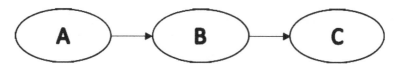

A BN can comprise different kinds of nodes i.e., nature nodes, decision nodes, and utility nodes. Nature nodes are the variables which can be controlled by actions of decision maker and represent the empirical or calculated parameters and the probabilities of occurrence of various states. Input nodes are the nodes without parents and can be expressed in as either constant or categorical states with associated marginal probability distributions. The variables or events which can be directly implemented by the decision makers are represented by a decision node. Decision node represents two or more alternative decision options that a manager can choose from. A decision node does not have probabilities associated with it. Decision nodes should always be accompanied by utility nodes (Singh & Gupta, 2017b). A utility node represents the value of an outcome or a decision. Utility node can be directly linked to the decision node (Kragt, 2009). BNs representing and solving decision problems under uncertainty are also known as Bayesian decision networks (Singh & Gupta, 2017a).

Bayesian network uses Bayes' probability theorem to propagate information/evidence among the nodes. Bayes' theorem defines how observed evidence updates the prior information/knowledge about a hypothesis. In Bayes' theorem, prior probability represents the possibility of an input parameter being in a specific state whereas conditional probability estimates the possibility of a parameter state given the states of input parameters affecting it. Estimate of likelihood of a parameter to be in particular state is the posterior probability, given the input parameters, conditional probabilities and the rules controlling how the probabilities combine. The network is solved using Bayes' Rule:

P (A|B) = P (B|A) P (A)/ P (B)

Where P (A) is the prior probability of parameter A; P (A|B) is the posterior probability, the probability of A given new data B; and P (B|A) the conditional probability of parameter B given existing data A (Pollino & Henderson 2010).

Advantages of Bayesian Networks

Working with BNs has many marked advantages. Learning about causal relationships among the variables of a system is made easier by BNs (Uusitalo, 2007) which can smoothly implemented into decision support systems (Marcot et al., 2001) to provide support in difficult and complex decision-making processes. BNs can also be applied in determining the efficacy of alternate management decisions or policies because of being causal in nature. BNs graphical nature can enable people from a wide variety of domains to discuss the structure of the system and thus can stimulate interdisciplinary discussion among the stakeholders. Moreover, Bayesian network can be easily updated whenever new evidence or knowledge is available. Pest management deals with complex issues and often there is lack of data or information about its processes involved in decision-making. However, BNs allow getting over the limitations of data by incorporation of inputs from various sources. Therefore, they are very helpful means to deal with data uncertainty and integrating simulation models, data observations and expert knowledge (Kragt, 2009). Another advantageous attribute of BNs is that they are capable to learn about system structure and its parameters from data observations. Knowledge about the system structure can provide information of dependent or independent relationship among the system variables as well as the cause-effect direction. BN also assesses the optimal structure on the basis of maximum score of probability of structures of possible candidate based on the given data and possibly penalized because of being complex. Parameter learning involves estimation of CPT at each node based on data structure provided and uses learning algorithms which intend to determine the maximum likelihood for the CPTs in a network. Adequate data observations are required for estimation of conditional probabilities. Availability of data observations is absolutely a constraint in most of the plant protection issues (Kragt, 2009). In case there is lots of data missing, its distribution is to be interpreted which may be depending upon other nodes' states or it may be random distribution.

Bayesian Network Software

Globally, much software is available to develop Bayesian network. Prominent and popular are Analytica, Netica, Hugin and GeNie packages. Each one of this software has its own strengths and limitations, shown in table 1. Norsys Software Corporation developed Netica software; most popular of these packages has been widely used in the development of BNs in the field of natural resource management and environmental modelling world over. This software can be used to build, learn, modify, transform and store networks and can also respond to the queries and can find optimal solutions (Pollino & Henderson, 2010). Netica software updates Bayesian belief that resolves the network by determining the posterior probability of each node (Marcot et al., 2001). One important advantage of Netica software is it having elaborate, flexible and user-friendly graphical interface integrated into the application (Kragt, 2009).

Table 1. Major software available for development of Bayesian Network

Software	Has graphical Interface?	Parameter learning?	Structural learning?	Support for Utility nodes?	Inference algorithm
Analytica	Yes	No	No	Yes	MC sampling
GeNie	Yes	Yes	Yes	Yes	Variousa
Hugin Expert	Yes	Yes	Yes	Yes	Junction tree
Netica	Yes	Yes	No	Yes	Junction tree

BACKGROUND

Major Instances of Bayesian Network in Decision-Making

Bayesian networks (BNs) are widely being used for environmental modeling to integrate multiple issues and components of the system; for utilizing information from various sources; to handle the missing and uncertain data (Singh & Gupta, 2017b). BNs have been adequately used in ecological decision-making (Rivot et al., 2004). They have also been used in agriculture nonetheless; there are very few instances of their usage in pest management (Fabre et al., 2006).

Tari (1996) illustrated about the possible applications of BNs for assessing the yield response of winter wheat to fungicide programs. Therein, experimental data from ADAS trials has been used with some assumptions in order to complete the data.

Gu et al. (1996) applied Bayesian network to handle the uncertainty in climate prediction information for studying risk and benefits to crop production in Scotland. The BN establishes relationship between model of fababean growth and a model of weather generator and thus is able to respond to the queries on fababean production under different climate predictions.

Borsuk, Stow & Reckhow (2002) developed a Bayesian network to know about possible reasons of reduction in the status of health of brown trout population in Switzerland. Further investigation were done by Borsuk, Stow & Reckhow (2004) wherein BN was applied to determine the importance of historical causes of anthropogenic changes and also for predicting the effects of management actions proposed.

Bromley et al. (2005) developed Bayesian network for integrated management of four basins from Europe while focusing on management of water. The project aim was to devise an active and functional method to help the managers in several type of objective decision-makings and simultaneously making sure that various stakeholders actively participate in the process of decision-making.

Ticehurst et al. (2007) built an integrated BN based model framework wherein BNs were applied to determine the sustainability systems of coastal lake-catchment from New South Wales coast. BN based framework developed was implemented in a DSS referred as Coastal Lake Assessment and Management (CLAM)DSS. This provided rapid scenario comparisons and generation of reports to be used for coastal lake planning. Similar to the CLAM DSS, Exploring Climate Impacts on Management (EXCLAIM) DSS was also developed to find out the impact of climate change and its predictions on water flow, quality and ecology of Macquarie River (Pollino and Henderson, 2010).

Koivusalo et al. (2005) built a BN based Decision Support tool that determines the climate change effects on dynamics of the lake. Objective of this was to incorporate simulation models and expert knowledge in the decision support system known as CLIME-DSS. The system details and explains the major results of the project to the interested persons beyond the researchers. The DSS uses a causal Bayesian network that illustrates the relationship between weather variables and lake characteristics.

Smith et al. (2007) also devised a Bayesian network which interacted with expert knowledge and geospatial data about the favored habitats to map the suitability of the Julia Creek dunnart (Sminthopsis douglasi) habitat in north-west Queensland. These were earlier thought to be extinct (Pollino and Henderson, 2010).

Integrated Catchment Assessment and Management (iCAM) Centre of the Australian National University developed and applied Bayesian network in a DSS to find out the climate change impact on natural resource management (NRM) in Central West catchment area. The DSS helps to determine NRM choices under various scenarios of climate change and help in decision-making to reduce the impact on catchment resources.

Chen and Yu (2008) presented application of Bayesian network for development of a disease identification system for Maize crop. Noisy-or model and conversion from certainty to probability were applied in the development of Bayesian network. Thus, a BN based disease identification system for Maize crop was developed. The practice proves Bayesian network as an effective tool for maize disease diagnosis.

Peterson et al. (2008) built a BN based tool to analyze the trade-offs in decision-making. Methodical analysis of when and where purposely use or removal of barriers is most appropriate for decision-making process to manage threats to local fish species from division of habitat and invading by non-native trout species. Unfortunately, management activities to resolve one may produce another.

Pollino & Hart (2008) developed BNs to test risk management action plans of the mining industry. The BNs integrated sand transportation, models of water quality and monitoring data of toxicology and ecology. Model produced various scenario which test the alternate management action plans.

Galan, Matias & Bastante (2009) devised a model of reforestation for woodland in river Liébana basin, NW Spain wherein causal BN was constructed using the relationships between woodland type and other environment variables such as altitude, slope, and rainfall etc.as well as among the environment variables. The resulted predictions were compared with the results produced by classical linear techniques, neural networks and support vector machines. Constructed method is an easy tool of modeling to analyze data and taking appropriate decisions.

Steventon & Daust (2009) developed a BN for modeling the epidemic of mountain pine beetle in north-central British Columbia, Canada. Subsequently, this was applied for examining the response of habitat and population size of pine beetle to management scenarios with built in parameter uncertainty.

Meysam & Mahdi (2010) studied the BN usage for locust pest management. However, it was used to find the effect of various trap plants on population. This was an instance of using Bayesian network for examining the effects of trap plants on locust population.

Douglas & Newton (2014) presented about usage of BNs for supporting protected area management by way of developing habitat suitability models to address the conservation of eight species. The BNs were developed using scientific literature and expert knowledge and were evaluated with the field survey results. Subsequently, they were applied to see the effect of various management practices such as tree cutting, grazing and burning on suitability of habitat of species.

Abbal et al., (2015) developed a DSS tool for vine growers to examine quality of vineyard to be planted. Herein, vineyard quality is determined by the probability of wine sale profitability. Bayesian network being widely used to deal with uncertainty in management of natural resource, was constructed using the relationship between environment and vineyard status parameters. Information for Bayesian network construction was obtained from vine growing experts. BN was validated and thus produced 75%

accurate predictions. The system facilitates the assessment of possible impact of vine grower's decisions on the quality of new vineyards.

INFLUENCE OF BAYESIAN NETWORKS ON DECISION SUPPORT SYSTEMS

In pest management system, the objective of Bayesian network is to select the appropriate pest management option based on the pest relevant agro-ecological information observed from farmers' fields. Once, the objectives are defined, process of construction of BN is initiated which consists of construction of conceptual Bayesian network structure, identification of significant variables of the system and linking them on the basis of relationship among them.

According to the purpose of constructing BN, prior and existing information/knowledge should be synthesized so as to construct conceptual BN of decision-making (also called influence diagram). This broadly helps in visual depiction of how the various factors of decision-making which are considered to be directly or indirectly affecting the final decision or outcome are related to each other. Jakeman, Letcher & Norton (2006) have advised that conceptualization of a system is always good because it helps in finding out the weaknesses in assumptions of the system being modeled. Construction of conceptual BN based on inputs from domain experts and stakeholders greatly helps in establishment of structure of the problem and determination of the causal relationships. Conceptual BN thus structured can be the basis of proposed BN. Once conceptual BN is constructed, it should be reviewed and refined. This helps to find variable missed if any, also in correction of conceptual BN.

CONCEPTUALIZING BAYESIAN NETWORKS FOR PEST MANAGEMENT

Bayesian networks are strictly one-way because they represent a conditional probability distribution that describes the relative likelihood of each value of the "child" node (end of the arrow) conditional on every possible combination of values of the "parent" nodes (start of each arrow). For instance, if a link is directed from node E towards node H as figure 2, then each value of node E conditionally depends upon the possible combination of values of node H since E and F parent nodes are having causal relationship with child node H.

In the network, mutually exclusive states define the values of the nodes (McCann, Marcot & Ellis 2006). BN Structure is usually made of 'box and arrow' diagram. Simplest BN structure having fewer nodes, arc and states should be used to describe a system under consideration. This not only minimizes the computation of probabilities thus restricting to the data availability but also reduces the processing efforts and time. Complex structure of BN consisting of too many nodes, arcs and states can lead to reduction in output accuracy. Similarly, too little details can also decrease representativeness and usefulness of the BN. A BN can be constructed using two approaches:

1.   Using expert knowledge elicitation
2.   Based on data learning

Data learning-based approach is useful to construct BN for complex systems that are difficult to be understood. Pest management decision-making processes are complex in nature wherein quality and comprehensive historical data is rarely available. Hence, it becomes difficult to determine accurate

Figure 2. Basic structure of a Bayesian network
Source: Author

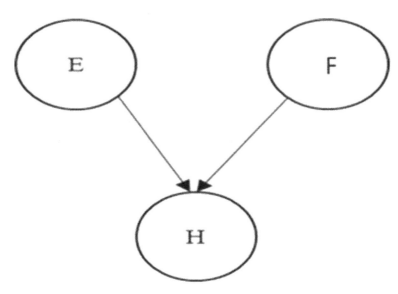

Figure 3. Process of constructing a Bayesian network
Source: Author

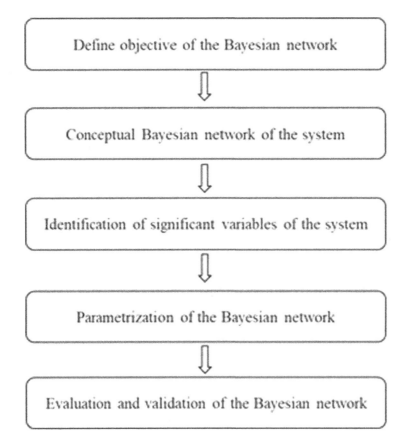

structure on the basis of data learning only. So, the outcome of the data based structural learning can be enhanced by combining it with expert knowledge elicitation together. While developing the conceptual BN structure, all variables (nodes) of the system influencing the outcome of decision-making process are considered.

Process of constructing Bayesian network starts with explanation of the objective. Steps involved in the systematic process of construction of Bayesian network are shown in figure 3.

Structuring Bayesian Networks

Identifying all the variables of the system and establishing links between them results in structure of conceptual Bayesian network representing the system under consideration. Description of pest management framework and knowledge elicited from experts and published literature revealed prominent variables influencing decision-making in pest management system are weather (temperature, rainfall, and humidity), pest activity, presence of pest natural enemies (parasite and predators) and crop condition.

Weather comprising temperature, rainfall, humidity; presence of pest natural enemies comprising predators and parasites; pest activity and crop condition are the broad factors to be considered for determining 'whether and what pest management intervention is required'. Using these variables, structure of conceptual BN for decision-making in pest management was established as shown in figure 4.

Figure 4. Structure of Conceptual BN for decision-making in pest management
Source: Author

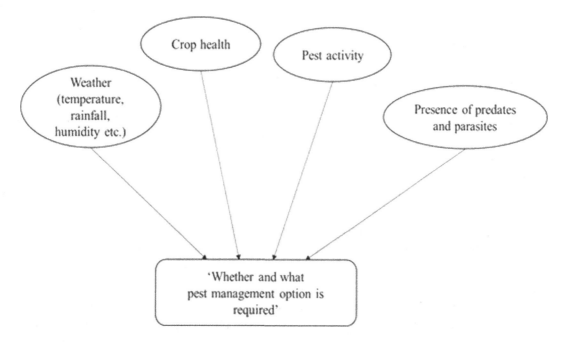

Once structure of the conceptual BN established, we can start with it to have refined version of the network. Identification of significant variables ('nodes') of the system and exclusion of non-significant variables is usually done on the basis of review of literature, data analysis, experts' opinion and discussion with the stakeholders. Nodes must be either measurable or observable or predictable and must have explicit definitions. Once the nodes have been selected, links are revised based on the relationship among them. It is recommended that parent nodes be kept fever i.e. around three so as to limit the dimensions of the CPT (Marcot et al., 2006). If a variable is not at all related to the decision-making in the system, it may be excluded because inclusion of insignificant variables can make the BN structure more complex. Since inclusion of insignificant variables costs extra time and efforts and do not add any value to the BN. Inclusion of higher the number of nodes between the input and output nodes may decrease the sensitivity of output nodes to the input node and may also propagate uncertainty to the final node. Marcot et al. (2006) suggested that a BN should not have more than five layers of nodes if possible. However, inclusion of the number of nodes and its layers depends upon the complexity of the model. Explicit exclusion of the variables may lead to model error. For large complex systems, Bayesian network may be fragmented into sub networks which represent different components of the system (Borsuk, Stow & Reckhow 2004). Usually, it is easier to conceptualize complex systems in terms of smaller, interlinked components. We should strive to make the model structure simpler.

Earlier studies have reported temperature, rainfall and humidity as the most significant weather factors affecting pest activity in the field. Significance of these factors depends upon the location and cropping season. Factors may be significantly affecting pest activity in a particular location and cropping season while other may not be having any significant effect. Similarly, presence of various natural enemies i.e., predators and parasites affecting pest activity too depends upon the crop, cropping season and pesticide load. The same has been endorsed by the published literature as well as the domain experts. Thus, using data records obtained from organizations working in the field of pest management and the knowledge elicited from domain experts and literature, key variables (nodes) of the system relevant to the process of decision-making in pest management and their relationship with each other are identified. The variable which are not significant are excluded and thus the structure of conceptual network is refined. Set of mutually exclusive states of each variable (node) are also determined through the analysis of data records and domain expert inputs.

Parameterization of the Bayesian Network

After identification of nodes, they are assigned the states to be taken by each of them. Each BN node represents either an observable or measurable system variable. Potential values or conditions that can be assumed by a node are represented by its states. Type and quality of available data determines the types of the state and their number. The initial values for each node can be determined using available data records or based on the knowledge elicited from literature or through expert consultation. The states of a node may be categorical e.g., large, medium, small, Boolean e.g., yes or no, discrete such as integers or continuous variables e.g., $<= 10$, >10 and $<=20$ and >20. For instance, in figure 5, the states of node E and node H have been shown as discrete states 'high' or 'low' and 'true' or 'false' respectively. The states of node E and F will determine whether node H is in 'high', 'medium' or 'low' state. However, the decision about the division of range into sub ranges should not be arbitrary rather it should be done on the basis of data analysis such as descriptive, plotting, classification or percentile analysis. Discretization can be useful wherever a variable has specific breakpoint that is significant to management. Domain expert consultation may also be combined with data analysis. Sometimes, defining fewer state of a variable result in information loss and assigning too many states to a variable may complicate the BN. For Bayesian networks of decision-making, states representing the important thresholds can be used as alternatives.

Figure 5. Bayesian network showing nodes with states
Source: Author

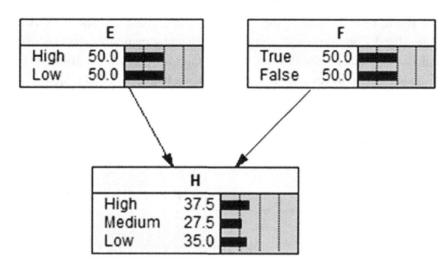

As stated above, weather conditions, presence of pest natural enemies, level of pest activity and crop health are the prominent factors broadly considered for pest management decision-making. Weather conditions are described by a set of variables i.e., maximum temperature, minimum temperature, rainfall, humidity and presence of natural enemies by population of predators and population of parasites as the variables. Whereas pest activity and crop health are not represented as set of variables. Set of possible mutually exclusive states of these variables or nodes in conceptual BN for decision-making in pest management may be categorized as shown in table 2.

Table 2. Possible state values of prominent variables of decision-making in pest management

Variable (s)	Possible state values
Temperature	Extremely hot, hot, warm, cold, frigid
Rainfall	High, moderate or low
Humidity	High, moderate or low
Presence of predators:	Abundant, moderate, low, scarce
Presence of parasites:	Abundant, moderate, low, scarce
Pest activity	High, medium, low
Crop health	Good, average, poor

After defining the state type and its numbers, conditional probabilities for the state values of each child node are estimated based on the state's values of its parent nodes. Probability of priory expecting a node to be into a definite state can be determined from known frequencies or can assume a uniform distribution representing uncertainty, Kragt (2009).

The relationship between parent and child node is defined by the Conditional Probability Table (CPT). The CPT presents the probability value of a node being in a state provided combination of probability values of states of parent nodes. CPT dimension of each node is the multiple of numbers of child node states and its parent nodes states. If a node has no parents, it can be described probabilistically by a marginal probability distribution. Figure 6 shows the CPT of a basic Bayesian network consisting of three nodes. Node H will be in its high, medium and low states, given the states of node E and F in the network. The nodes E and F are root nodes and so are defined by marginal probabilities. H is the child node of E and F nodes and thus probabilities of H node states are conditional given the combination of states of E and F nodes. Parent nodes E and F are the causing factors of child node.

Figure 6. CPT of node in basic structure of a BN
Source: Author

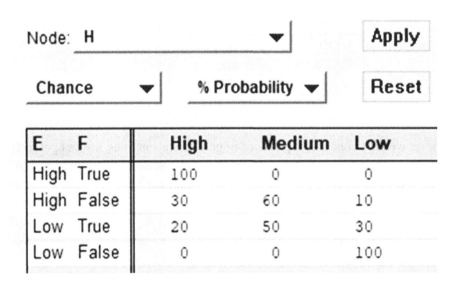

The CPT values associated with each state of a node can be estimated using expert knowledge elicitation, observed data, probabilistic or empirical equations, and results of simulation models or their combination (Pollino, White & Hart, 2007a). Probability distribution quantifies the uncertainties associated with each relationship. It's very important to record probability computation method including any assumptions and limitations. Construction of Bayesian network is complete once the probabilities of all nodes are computed. Once completed, BN used for scenario analysis. Different scenarios be it set of management actions or system observations, can easily be analyzed using the BN. Bayesian networks are simple means of scenario analysis that allows the users to propagate evidence as node input using well defined node distribution. The effect of a scenario is tested through its effect on other nodes of the network by propagating the probabilities. Fast propagation of evidence through the network is one of the main advantages of BNs. Therefore, BNs are used to instantly find the effect of observed conditions or decisions at one node on the whole system. Subsequently the network is evaluated or validated.

Evaluation and Validation of the Bayesian Network

Evaluation and validation of a developed Bayesian network assists in determining whether its results are feasible and satisfactory. The criteria to evaluate or validate BN's performance depends upon its objective. Initially, the interactions of different components of the network can be examined by application of various input scenarios and determine whether the results are logical and reasonable. Expected results can include the network showing realistic performance. Preferably accuracy of the network performance should be examined with empirical data, however many a times data is either not available or is partially available. Data other than that used to develop the Bayesian network should be used for evaluation and validation of the model. Many BN software has the functionalities to allow data to be checked against network predictions. This software revises the probabilities of all the samples within the case, except the unobserved nodes and then produce the beliefs of each unobserved node. These values are compared with actual node value. Another method of BN evaluation is sensitivity analysis, which is done to find sensitive parameters. This analysis ranks the variables according to the importance relative to the variables of the interest. This can be used to confirm whether response of network is correct and matches to the expectations. Sensitivity analysis also assists in identification of the variables having significant influence on the results, and subsequently (Pollino et al., 2007b). There are other forms of evaluation such as critique of assumptions, ability of the model to perform under different scenarios (Jakeman, Letcher & Norton, 2006). Whereas validation of the Bayesian decision network can be done by cross examining the outcome of the BN against the results of existing methods of decision-making.

In case of limited availability or complete unavailability, qualitative forms of evaluation and validation for instance peer review are valuable. By application of different input values, outcome of the network in the form of resulted probabilities can be examined by the reviewers whether it is consistent and logical. Aguilera et al. (2011) did a review of over hundred BN applications in environmental management and found that 38% did not do any validation. This may be because Bayesian network is frequently applied in cases of scarce data availability. Network evaluation should be done even with limited data. In case evaluation or validation results are not logical and reasonable then network structure and its assumptions need to be reassessing that includes readjustment of network structure, refinement of conditional probabilities or variable states (Marcot et al., 2006). Development of BN is an ongoing process. Major advantage of BN is that is can be easily updated. The BNs are very useful in cases of limited data and knowledge availability and thus can be built with scare or incomplete information.

Environmental and crop pest management are the systems complex in nature, where data availability is ether scarce or limited. Therefore, evaluation and validation of BNs developed for these systems can done using combination of data and exert knowledge elicitation.

FUTURE RESEARCH DIRECTIONS

Bayesian Network method developed is the part of an ongoing iterative development process, which could be advanced as more knowledge and primary agro-ecological information relevant to the insect-pest management are available. The work presented would be considered as initial level of development of Bayesian Network based method of support for decision-making in pest management which can be further upgraded. The research work carried out using advanced BN methods and techniques may result in enhanced accuracy in selection of the appropriate pest management options based on uncertain agro-ecological information that farmers provide.

CONCLUSION

Decision Support systems for pest management are static web-based systems comprising of web pages, digital information brochures, technical bulletins, and pest management recommendations. Many of them consist of databases having the records of pest identification, their occurrences and management recommendations or pesticide information and uses them to retrieve the information based on the user's option-based queries. Nevertheless, many dynamic and reliable DSSs are available for pest management providing real-time decision support in the form of crop-pest surveillance/monitoring-based advisories to the farmers. These DSSs use pest ETL as the basis of decision-making in pest management which requires quantitative pest relevant information scientifically observed from farmer fields. In this chapter, process of construction of Bayesian network has been explained in context to the framework of crop pest management system and a conceptual Bayesian network structure for decision-making in pest management system has been established.

REFERENCES

Abbal, P., Sablayrolles, J., Matzner-Lober, E., Boursiquot, J., Baudrit, C., & Carbonneau, A. (2015). A Decision Support System for Vine Growers Based on a Bayesian Network. *Journal of Agricultural Biological & Environmental Statistics*, *21*(1), 131–151. doi:10.100713253-015-0233-2

Aguilera, P. A., Fernández, R., Fernández, A., Rumi, R., & Salmerón, A. (2011). Bayesian networks in environmental modelling. *Environmental Modelling & Software*, *26*(12), 1376–1388. doi:10.1016/j.envsoft.2011.06.004

Bi, C., & Chen, G. (2011). Bayesian Networks Modeling for Crop Diseases. *Computer and Computing Technologies in Agriculture IV, CCTA 2010: 4th IFIP TC 12 Conference proceedings*, 312-320. 10.1007/978-3-642-18333-1_37

Borsuk, M. E., Stow, A. C., & Reckhow, K. H. (2002). *Ecological prediction using causal Bayesian networks: A case study of eutrophication management in the Neuse River estuary*. Duke University.

Borsuk, M. E., Stow, A. C., & Reckhow, K. H. (2004). A Bayesian network of eutrophication models for synthesis, prediction and uncertainty analysis. *Ecological Modelling*, *173*(2-3), 219–239. doi:10.1016/j.ecolmodel.2003.08.020

Bromley, J., Jackson, N. A., Clymer, O. J., Giacomello, A. M., & Jensen, F. V. (2005). The use of Hugin to develop Bayesian networks as an aid to integrated water resource planning. *Environmental Modelling & Software*, *20*(2), 231–242. doi:10.1016/j.envsoft.2003.12.021

Chen, G., & Yu, H. (2008). Bayesian Network and its Application in Maize Diseases Diagnosis. *Computer and Computing Technologies in Agriculture II, CCTA 2007: First IFIP TC 12 International Conference on Computer and Computing Technologies in Agriculture proceedings*, 917-92. 10.1007/978-0-387-77253-0_22

del Águila, I., & del Sagrado, J. (2012). Metamodelling of Bayesian networks for decision-support system development. *8th workshop on knowledge engineering and software engineering (KESE8) proceedings*.

Douglas, S. J., & Newton, A. C. (2014). Evaluation of Bayesian networks for modelling habitat suitability & management of a protected area. *Journal for Nature Conservation*, *22*(3), 235–246. doi:10.1016/j.jnc.2014.01.004

Fabre, F., Pierre, J. S., Dedryver, C. A., & Plantegenest, M. (2006). Barley yellow low dwarf disease risk assessment based on Bayesian modelling of aphid population dynamics. *Ecological Modelling*, *193*(3-4), 457–466. doi:10.1016/j.ecolmodel.2005.08.021

Galan, C. O., Matias, J. M., & Bastante, F. G. (2009). Reforestation planning using Bayesian networks. *Environmental Modelling & Software*, *24*(11), 1285–1292. doi:10.1016/j.envsoft.2009.05.009

Gu, Y., Crawford, J. W., Peiris, D. R., Grashoff, C., McNicol, J. W., & Marshall, B. (1996). Modelling fababean production in an uncertain future climate. *Agricultural and Forest Meteorology*, *79*(4), 289–300. doi:10.1016/0168-1923(95)02285-6

Heping, P., & Daniel, M. (1998). *Fuzzy Causal Probabilistic Networks - A New Ideal & Practical Inference Engine*. http://citeseerx.ist.psu.edu/viewdoc/

Jakeman, A. J., Letcher, R. A., & Norton, J. P. (2006). Ten iterative steps in development & evaluation of environmental models. *Environmental Modelling & Software*, *21*(5), 602–614. doi:10.1016/j.envsoft.2006.01.004

Jensen, F. V., & Nielsen, T. D. (2007). *Bayesian Networks & Decision Graphs* (2nd ed.). Springer-Verlag. doi:10.1007/978-0-387-68282-2

Kjrulff, U. B., & Madsen, A. L. (2008). *Bayesian Networks & Inñuence Diagrams*. Springer-Verlag. doi:10.1007/978-0-387-74101-7

Koivusalo, H., Kokkonen, T., Laine, H., Jolma, A., & Varis, O. (2005). Exploiting simulation model results in parameterizing a Bayesian network – A case study of dissolved organic carbon in catchment runoff. *MODSIM 2005: International Congress on Modelling and Simulation, Proceedings*, 421-427.

Kragt, M. E. (2009). *A beginners guide to Bayesian network modelling for integrated catchment management*. Landscape Logic.

Marcot, B. G., Holthausen, R. S., Raphael, M. G., Rowl, M., & Wisdom, M. (2001). Using Bayesian Belief Networks to Evaluate Fish & Wildlife Population Viability under Land Management Alternatives from an Environmental Impact Statement. *Forest Ecology and Management*, *153*(1-3), 29–42. doi:10.1016/S0378-1127(01)00452-2

Marcot, B. G., Steventon, J., Sutherland, G. D., & McCann, R. K. (2006). Guidelines for developing & updating Bayesian belief networks applied to ecological modeling & conservation. *Canadian Journal of Forest Research*, *36*(12), 3063–3074. doi:10.1139/x06-135

McCann, R. K., Marcot, B. G., & Ellis, R. (2006). Bayesian Belief Networks, Applications in Ecology & Natural Resource Management. *Canadian Journal of Forest Research*, *36*(12), 3053–3062. doi:10.1139/x06-238

Mead, R., Paxton, J., & Sojda, R. (2006, December). Applications of bayesian networks in ecological modeling. *International Conference on Environmental Modelling and Simulation*.

Meysam, M., & Mahdi, S. (2010). Bayesian Network & Pest Management, A case Study of trap plants on locust population. *Advances in Environmental Biology, 4*(2), 147–151.

Pearl, J. (1988). *Probabilistic reasoning in intelligent systems: networks of plausible inference*. Morgan kaufmann.

Peterson, D. P., Rieman, B. E., Dunham, J. B., Fausch, K. D., & Young, M. K. (2008). Analysis of trade-offs between the threat of invasion by non-native brook trout Salvelinus fontinalis& intentional isolation for native westslope cutthroat trout Oncorhynchus clarkii lewisi. *Canadian Journal of Fisheries and Aquatic Sciences, 65*(4), 557–573. doi:10.1139/f07-184

Pollino, C. A., & Hart, B. T. (2008). Developing Bayesian network models within a risk assessment framework. *4th International Congress on Environmental Modelling and Software proceedings*, 372-379.

Pollino, C. A., & Henderson, C. (2010). Bayesian networks: A guide for their application in natural resource management and policy. *Landscape Logic, Technical Report, 14.*

Pollino, C. A., White, K. A., & Hart, B. T. (2007a). Examination of conflicts & improved strategies for the management of an endangered Eucalypt species using Bayesian networks. *Ecological Modelling, 201*(1), 37–59. doi:10.1016/j.ecolmodel.2006.07.032

Pollino, C. A., Woodberry, O., Nicholson, A., Korb, K., & Hart, B. T. (2007b). Parametrization & evaluation of a Bayesian network for use in an ecological risk assessment. *Environmental Modelling & Software, 22*(8), 1140–1152. doi:10.1016/j.envsoft.2006.03.006

Rivot, E., Prevost, E., Parent, E., & Bagliniere, J. L. (2004). A Bayesian state-space modelling framework for fitting a salmon stage-structured population dynamic model to multiple time series of field data. *Ecological Modelling, 179*(4), 463–485. doi:10.1016/j.ecolmodel.2004.05.011

Singh, N., & Gupta, N. (2016). ICT based decision support systems for Integrated Pest Management IPM in India, A review. *Agricultural Reviews (Karnal), 37*(4), 309–316. doi:10.18805/ag.v37i4.6461

Singh, N., & Gupta, N. (2017a). Decision-making in Integrated Pest Management & Bayesian Network. *International Journal of Computer Science and Information Technologies, 9*(2), 31–36. doi:10.5121/ijcsit.2017.9203

Singh, N., & Gupta, N. (2017b). Bayesian network for decision-support on pest management of tomato fruit borer, H. armigera. *IACSIT International Journal of Engineering and Technology, 6*(4), 168–170. doi:10.14419/ijet.v6i4.8583

Singh, N., & Gupta, N. (2017c). Effect of Weather on Fruit Borer, Helicoverpa armigera (Hub.) Activity in Tomato. *Scholars Journal of Agriculture and Veterinary Sciences, 4*(10), 414–417.

Singh, N., & Gupta, N. (2017d). Bayesian Network based Decision support for Leaf Miner Pest Management in Tomato. *American International Journal of Research in Science, Technology, Engineering & Mathematics, 20*(1), 27–30.

Singh, N., & Gupta, N. (2018). Effect of weather on leaf miner, liriomyza trifolii activity in Tomato. *Pestology, 42*(4), 30–33.

Smith, C. S., Howes, A. L., Price, B., & McAlpine, C. A. (2007). Using a Bayesian belief network to predict suitable habitat of an endangered mammal – The Julia Creek dunnart Sminthopsis douglasi. *Biological Conservation, 139*(3-4), 333–347. doi:10.1016/j.biocon.2007.06.025

Steventon, J., & Daust, D. K. (2009). Management strategies for a large-scale mountain pine beetle outbreak, Modelling impacts on American martens. *Forest Ecology and Management, 257*(9), 1976–1985. doi:10.1016/j.foreco.2009.02.013

Tari, F. (1996). A Bayesian network for predicting yield response of winter wheat to fungicide programmes. *Computers and Electronics in Agriculture, 15*(2), 111–121. doi:10.1016/0168-1699(96)00011-7

Ticehurst, J. L., Newham, L. T. H., Rissik, D., Letcher, R. A., & Jakeman, A. J. (2007). A Bayesian network approach for assessing the sustainability of coastal lakes in New South Wales, Australia. *Environmental Modelling & Software, 22*(8), 1129–1139. doi:10.1016/j.envsoft.2006.03.003

Uusitalo, L. (2007). Advantages & challenges of Bayesian networks in environmental modelling. *Ecological Modelling, 2033*(4), 312–318. doi:10.1016/j.ecolmodel.2006.11.033

Varis, O. (1997). Bayesian Decision Analysis for Environmental & Resource Management. *Environmental Modelling & Software, 12*(2-3), 177–185. doi:10.1016/S1364-8152(97)00008-X

ADDITIONAL READING

Bouzembrak, Y., Camenzuli, L., Janssen, E., & Van der Fels-Klerx, H. J. (2018). Application of Bayesian Networks in the development of herbs and spices sampling monitoring system. *Food Control, 83*, 38–44. doi:10.1016/j.foodcont.2017.04.019

Holt, J., Leach, A. W., Johnson, S., Tu, D. M., Nhu, D. T., Anh, N. T., Quinlan, M. M., Whittle, P. J. L., Mengersen, K., & Mumford, J. D. (2018). Bayesian networks to compare pest control interventions on commodities along agricultural production chains. *Risk Analysis, 38*(2), 297–310. doi:10.1111/risa.12852 PMID:28703498

Lawrence, J. M., Hossain, N. U. I., Jaradat, R., & Hamilton, M. (2020). Leveraging a Bayesian network approach to model and analyze supplier vulnerability to severe weather risk: A case study of the US pharmaceutical supply chain following Hurricane Maria. *International Journal of Disaster Risk Reduction, 49*, 101607. doi:10.1016/j.ijdrr.2020.101607 PMID:32346504

Meurisse, N., Marcot, B. G., Woodberry, O., Barratt, B. I., & Todd, J. H. (2021). Risk analysis frameworks used in biological control and introduction of a novel Bayesian network tool. *Risk Analysis*. PMID:34462929

Sciarresi, C. S. (2019). *Optimizing Cover Crop Rotations for Water*. Nitrogen and Weed Management.

Scutari, M., Graafland, C. E., & Gutiérrez, J. M. (2019). Who learns better Bayesian network structures: Accuracy and speed of structure learning algorithms. *International Journal of Approximate Reasoning, 115*, 235–253. doi:10.1016/j.ijar.2019.10.003

Walas, Ł., Ganatsas, P., Iszkuło, G., Thomas, P. A., & Dering, M. (2019). Spatial genetic structure and diversity of natural populations of Aesculus hippocastanum L. in Greece. *PLoS One*, *14*(12), e0226225. doi:10.1371/journal.pone.0226225 PMID:31826015

Zhou, J., Asteris, P. G., Armaghani, D. J., & Pham, B. T. (2020). Prediction of ground vibration induced by blasting operations through the use of the Bayesian Network and random forest models. *Soil Dynamics and Earthquake Engineering*, *139*, 106390. doi:10.1016/j.soildyn.2020.106390

KEY TERMS AND DEFINITIONS

Bayes' Theorem: It defines how observed evidence updates the prior information/knowledge about a hypothesis.

Bayesian Network: A Bayesian network (BN) is a probabilistic graphical model for representing knowledge about an uncertain domain where each node corresponds to a random variable and each edge represents the conditional probability for the corresponding random variables.

Conditional Probability: Conditional probability is a measure of the probability of an event occurring, given that another event (by assumption, presumption, assertion, or evidence) has already occurred.

Decision Support System: Decision support systems (DSSs) are the interactive computer-based information systems that use ICT technologies, information, knowledge, documents, or models to assist the decision makers in identification and solution of a decision-making problem.

Economic Threshold Level: The economic threshold Level (ETL) is the population density at which control measures should be determined to prevent an increasing pest population from reaching the Economic injury level.

Expert System: It is a computer program that uses artificial-intelligence methods to solve problems within a specialized domain that ordinarily requires human expertise.

Pest Management: It is a process to solve pest problems while minimizing risks to people and the environment.

Data–Driven Clinical Decision Support Systems Theory and Research

Cherie Noteboom
Dakota State University, USA

David Zeng
Dakota State University, USA

Kruttika Sutrave
Dakota State University, USA

Andrew Behrens
Dakota State University, USA

Rajesh Godasu
Dakota State University, USA

Akhilesh Chauhan
Dakota State University, USA

INTRODUCTION

Digitization, which has had a significant influence on the healthcare industry, is motivated by the prospect of optimizing performance, reducing costs, and improving the quality of patient care and healthcare (Lee et al., 2017). This digital process has transformed how patients and physicians engage with medical services. Although healthcare has been slow to accept technology, it is now embracing digital transformation. The use of information technology (IT) in the healthcare industry has transformed interactions between physicians and patients, giving way to the implementation and usage of clinical decision support systems (CDSS).

CDSS are examples of the transformative healthcare evolution because they analyze data and assist physicians in making timely patient-related decisions (Agency for Healthcare Research and Quality, 2013)[1]. Healthcare professionals also utilize these systems to enhance treatment by increasing patient safety, eliminating needless testing, and reducing costs. For example, medical errors can decrease through enhanced healthcare, safety, and efficiency. Clinicians use these systems in the preparation of diagnoses and subsequent evaluations and outcomes (Osheroff et al., 2012). Although CDSS have the potential to improve healthcare delivery, it has been a challenge to fully realize their potential (Linder et al., 2006).

Clinical decision making uses descriptive, predictive, and prescriptive analytics. Descriptive analytics analyzes and presents past data regarding patients and treatment (Gensinger, Jr., 2014). This type of analytic utilizes visualization, alerts, and reports to describe patient activities (Gensinger, Jr., 2014). Predictive analytics uses historical data to make predictions by performing an analysis with rule-based or artificial intelligence (AI) techniques like machine learning and deep learning (Bartley, 2017; Gensinger, Jr., 2014). Medical professionals can identify trends and patterns in treatment plans or uncover chronic

DOI: 10.4018/978-1-7998-9220-5.ch081

diseases in patients based on age, location, and ethnicity. Prescriptive analytics recommends actions that can produce the best outcome. This allows healthcare professionals to develop optimal clinical pathways for patient care (Bartley, 2017; Gensinger, Jr., 2014)

A recent Stanford study on the future of AI's impact on society suggests that AI-enabled systems will change the future by replacing tasks rather than eliminating jobs (Grosz & Stone, 2018). In fact, AI technologies and data analytics are transforming the way organizations operate. Tech giants like Google, Microsoft, and Amazon are investing heavily in data collection (Newman, 2020). Organizations are focusing on feeding large datasets into data analytic models to produce predictive and prescriptive information to obtain meaningful projections. This application in the healthcare field facilitates in the reduction of operating costs, improves treatment outcomes, increases access to patients and clinician resources, and optimizes healthcare provider satisfaction (Bartley, 2017). Using predictive and prescriptive analytics in healthcare can improve forecasting, real-time insights, and automated decision making (Bartley, 2017). In turn, physicians and clinicians will experience enhancements in their daily tasks.

Time and external constraints affect clinician and physician decision-making processes (Lynn, 2019; Schwartz & Cato, 2020; Tonekaboni, Joshi, McCradden, & Goldenberg, 2019). Innovative products and accessibility to evidence-based information gives physicians opportunities to identify the most effective options for patients (Moja et al., 2019). The healthcare industry uses diverse methods to collect data about patients (e.g., physical traits, medical history), professional disciplines (e.g., doctors, nurses, administrators, insurers), and treatment options, healthcare delivery processes, and interests of stakeholder groups (Fichman & Kemerer, 1997; Noteboom & Qureshi, 2014). This may prove challenging for the design and implementation of systems. Therefore, contextualizing healthcare systems is key to understanding the integration of information systems (IS) into healthcare organizations (Noteboom & Qureshi, 2014).

A theory is a statement of relations among concepts within a set of boundary assumptions and constraints (Bacharach, 1989; Bhattacherjee, 2012). Theories provide guidance on the analysis, explanation, and prediction of phenomena, as well as design and action guidelines (Bhattacherjee, 2012; Gregor, 2006; Lim, Saldanha, Malladi, & Melville, 2013). IS theories enable users to identify factors that influence intention toward a particular behavior; therefore, they are important to consider in relation to technology adoption and acceptance (Ajzen, 1985; Fishbein & Ajzen, 1975).

Reach, Efficacy, Adoption, Implementation, and Maintenance (RE-AIM) and the Consolidated Framework for Implementation Research (CFIR) are two practitioner-developed frameworks based on theory (Damschroder et al., 2009; Glasgow, Vogt, & Boles, 1999). These systems have the potential to positively impact quality of care and reduce costs. Still, there is a key challenge related to CDSS adoption, implementation, resistance, and acceptance from physicians and clinicians who use the systems to offer high-quality patient care. The users of the system often work with better visualizations, new recommendations, and more accurate predicted information. Although new system features could support the workflow of physicians and clinicians, it can be difficult to incorporate these features into the fabric of healthcare. This challenge opens the door for an investigation into the following research questions:

1. To what extent is data-driven decision making applied in CDSS?
2. What prevalent theories are used in data driven CDSS research?
3. What major system attributes contribute to the theoretical frameworks?

From a theoretical perspective, this study investigates the theories used to inform design and provides a glimpse into the current state of CDSS theory-informed design. The information enables researchers to study CDSS adoption, implementation, acceptance, and resistance more effectively by reframing the discussion around a theory-centered approach. From an analytical perspective, this study shows the current trend of AI-enabled design, including its impact on industry practitioners. It also details the type of analytic used in each design and highlights the current trend of developed systems. The second and third sections discuss the background and methodology. The fourth section demonstrates results. The fifth section explores the findings. Finally, the sixth section concludes with a review, limitations, and recommendations for future research.

BACKGROUND

The terms "descriptive" and "predictive" are often associated with intelligence amplification. Prescriptive analytics are associated with AI (Koerkamp, 2019). Descriptive-level analytics include reporting, such as standard and ad hoc reporting from the data with basic capabilities. The state-of-the-art descriptive level may also contain an advanced query and drilldown capabilities in its reporting systems (Gensinger, Jr., 2014). Pivot tables in Microsoft Excel are examples of advanced queries or drilldown categories. Healthcare providers' multidimensional data can benefit from advanced reporting capabilities like pivot tables because they provide valuable visualization and analysis compared to basic ad hoc reporting (Gensinger, Jr., 2014). Dashboards, scorecards, and alerts are important descriptive analytic tools in CDSS. Dashboards help in the surveillance of the clinical progress. Scorecards facilitate the visualization of clinical metrics. Alerts can be utilized to determine an outbreak of epidemics or pandemics by observing regional laboratory data (Gensinger, Jr., 2014).

Predictive analytics apply statistics and mathematical techniques over huge datasets to gain meaningful insight by deducing patterns and predicting outcomes (Bartley, 2017; Gensinger, Jr., 2014). Simulations, forecasting, and predictive modeling are important tools in predictive analytics (Gensinger, Jr., 2014). Simulations created by mathematical or statistical models predict solutions in multiple scenarios. These simulations can be used to observe behaviors, diseases, healthcare, etc. (Gensinger, Jr., 2014). In forecasting, predictions estimate a changing quantity at some point in the future (Gensinger, Jr., 2014). For instance, a prediction can be used to estimate the total number of people impacted by cancer at some point in future. This type of data mining process employs a mathematical model to generate an accurate prediction (Kuhn & Johnson, 2013). Classification, regression, segmentation, and clustering algorithms are popular approaches to developing predictive models that can then be utilized in various areas of the healthcare field (Bartley, 2017; Gensinger, Jr., 2014; Lopes, Guimarães, & Santos, 2020).

Prescriptive analytics, which are the highest level and most complex of the three analytics, provide a set of actions to determine best paths and optimize clinical decision making to facilitate alternative choices (Gensinger, Jr., 2014; Lopes et al., 2020). The algorithm choices are categorized into a binary search, local search, search based on population, and multiobjective optimization (Lopes et al., 2020). While prescriptive analytics are heavily embedded in the design of well-known applications such as self-driving cars (algorithms analyze real-time data to make optimal driving decisions) and recruitment systems (algorithms help make hiring decisions based on data collected in the interactive hiring process), they are not widely adopted and considered new in the healthcare field. Still, prescriptive analytics provide great potential (Lopes et al., 2020).

There have been a variety of physician attitude surveys on CDSS, with concerns documented back to 1981 (Petkus, Hoogewerf, & Wyatt, 2020; Teach & Shortliffe, 1981). Clinicians and physicians must work with extensive amounts of growing medical data (Chi et al., 2021). According to Liberati et al. (2017), a main barrier is related to the perception of scientific evidence. Often, individual experiences are not enough; therefore, accumulated evidence from different clinical scenarios are applied to drive better patient outcomes (Ostropolets, Chen, Zhang, & Hripcsak, 2020). When designing systems to accumulate evidence, it is also important to consider the three characteristics of clinicians and physicians: (1) complete control over their work; (2) centered on highly specialized knowledge and skills; and (3) a service that is greatly appreciated by society and requires physician-patient confidentiality (Esmaeilzadeh, Sambasivan, Kumar, & Nezakati, 2015; Hoogland & Jochemsen, 2000). These characteristics create groups of medical professionals who collaborate to deliver high levels of care. Consequently, professional groups in the healthcare teams characterize modern healthcare delivery (Mebrahtu et al., 2021). It can, therefore, be a challenge to design systems to effectively meet the needs of the professional groups of physicians and clinicians.

CDSS are designed to improve health and healthcare delivery by enhancing health-related decisions and activities with appropriate, systematic clinical knowledge and patient information (Agency for Healthcare Research and Quality, 2013). The characteristics of an individual patient are paired to a computerized clinical knowledge base. Then, patient-specific evaluations or recommendations are offered to the medical expert for a decision (Osheroff et al., 2012).

Electronic systems have been around since the 1970s; however, they lacked system integration, were time consuming, and restricted academic endeavors. In the early 1990s, hospitals that had established their own IS also developed CDSS systems. Examples include the CPRS/Vista effort at the Veteran's Health Administration (Brown, Lincoln, Groen, & Kolodner, 2003) and the Regenstrief Medical Record System (McDonald et al., 1999). Additionally, some hospitals employed vendor based CDSS systems like HBOC, Meditech, and Lockheed Martin. Furthermore, ethical and legal concerns regarding CDSS were unresolved, including who was to blame if a system with imperfect "explainability" made a recommendation (Sutton et al., 2020).

FOCUS OF THE CHAPTER

Significant advancements continue to evolve. Currently, CDSS systems are embedded in electronic health records (EHRs) or used via desktop, smartphone, and wearable devices. Examples include antibiotic prescribing (Webb et al., 2019), adverse drug event monitoring (Rieckert, Sommerauer, Krumeich, & Sönnichsen, 2018), metabolic diagnosis (Brito et al., 2018), and report formatting (Gil et al., 2016). The health and Medicare acts of the United States government have both acknowledged CDSS.

CDSS can be classified as either AI-enabled or non-AI. Expert knowledge-based systems are represented mainly by if-then rules developed by obtaining data from various sources (i.e., literature, practice, patient-directed) to evaluate the rule and create an action (Tripathi, 2011). Non-knowledge-based systems also use various data sources for data gathering; however, the decision is based on the latest AI branches, including deep learning and machine learning. IT and IS artifacts are often implemented with these new AI branches to better support physicians and clinicians. IS theories have also been utilized to research technology artifacts in the context of acceptance, adoption, avoidance, and resistance.

Theory allows scientists to describe and explain a process or sequence of events (Colquitt & Zapata-Phelan, 2007; DiMaggio, 1995; Mohr, 1982). Therefore, according to Bacharach (1989), theoretical statements aim to organize (parsimoniously) and communicate (clearly). The critical importance of theory in knowledge development would suggest a wellspring of scholarship on theory and its application in IS research (Lim et al., 2013).

The technology acceptance model (TAM) and its subsequent revisions employ the constructs of perceived usefulness and perceived ease of use as antecedents to attitude and behavioral intention and actual system use. TAM, developed by Davis (1989), focuses on system-speciðc attributes. Perceived ease of use is "the degree to which a person believes that using a particular system would be free of effort" (Davis, 1989, p. X). Likewise, perceived usefulness is "the degree to which a person believes that using a particular system would enhance his or her job performance" (Davis, 1989, p. X). However, ease of use is also a potential system feature that would inñuence perceived usefulness. Actual ease of use would also directly inñuence intention to use.

The uniðed theory of acceptance and use of technology (UTAUT), which was built on the theory of reasoned action (TRA), theory of planned behavior (TPB), and TAM models, incorporates several IS and social science models. The constructs of UTAUT are performance expectancy, effort expectancy, social influence, facilitating conditions, and behavioral intention to use (Venkatesh, Morris, Davis, & Davis, 2003). UTAUT2 was created with the additional constructs of hedonic motivation, price value, and habit (Venkatesh, Thong, & Xu, 2012).

The diffusion of innovation (DOI) theory, developed in 1962, is often seen in IS research. Rogers (1995) posited that early adopters start in the beginning and more users eventually join. Finally, late adopters begin to use it after other users have already adopted the system. Agarwal and Prasad (1998), Cooper and Zmud (1990), and Crum, Premkumar, and Ramamurthy (1996) posited that technical compatibility, technical complexity (or ease of use), and relative advantage (perceived need) have a direct effect on IS implementation success (adoption, infusion). DOI posits that innovation must have a clear and unambiguous advantage over usual ways of working to be readily adopted (Brown et al., 2016).

METHODOLOGY

To conduct a comprehensive review, this study followed the guidelines of Kitchenham and Charters (2007) and was in accordance with the Preferred Reporting Items for Systematic Reviews and Meta-Analyses (PRISMA) guidelines (Liberati et al., 2009).

Search Strategy

Identified papers focused on the acceptance or avoidance of CDSS. These publications were retrieved through PubMed, IEEE, and Web of Science from January 1, 2016, to April 20, 2021. The following generic search terms were compiled for each database: ("clinical support system*" OR "clinical information system*" OR "clinical decision support" OR "health information system*") AND (acceptance OR adoption OR avoidance OR resistance). Our search covered title and abstract fields.

Inclusion/Exclusion Criteria

Studies that satisfied the following criteria were considered eligible:

1. Study focused on CDSS
2. CDSS used by medical experts or clinicians
3. Research study

Study Selection

Figure 1 depicts the four-stage process of discovering and selecting relevant material: (1) identification; (2) screening; (3) eligibility; and (4) inclusion. The identification process resulted in the collection of 1,194 articles. The total number of papers was 781 after the removal of duplicates. Next, a coarse-to-fine paper eligibility evaluation was carried out. The articles were screened based on title and abstract; 468 articles were excluded. The remaining 313 articles underwent a full-text review for eligibility based on the inclusion and exclusion criteria. The review excluded 190 articles. The resulting 123 articles were included in the study for synthesis.

Figure 1. PRISMA showing methodological details

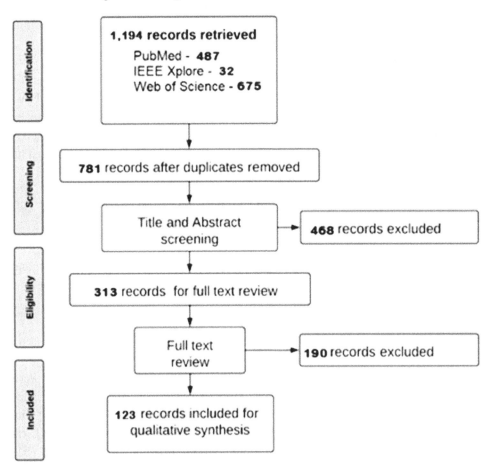

The final set of articles were reviewed by four authors independently. The authors worked in pairs to each review 50% of the articles. Results among the pair were compared and discrepancies were resolved by revisiting the articles. Unresolved articles between a pair were handed to the other pair. If there were additional disagreements, the advisors interfered to make a final decision. This process verified the article assessment process. It resulted in a 94.8% agreement rate and a Cohen's kappa (Cohen, 2016) of 0.89, indicating strong agreement.

SOLUTIONS AND RECOMMENDATIONS

Publication Statistics

There were 16 research studies that were published in 2020, per the distribution of articles by publication year. Excluding 2018, there has been a gradual increase in the number of articles published on CDSS as shown in Table 1. It should be noted that 2021 figures only represent the first few months of the year.

Table 1 shows statistics on the theory in the selected studies. Twelve studies employed UTAUT. In a few papers, UTAUT combined with theories like TAM. Other prevalent theories preferred by researchers were TAM and RE-AIM. Four studies employed more than one theory; some studies used various theories, including the system usability scale (SUS) and structuration theory to analyze the adoption of CDSS. Eighty-two articles neither used a theory nor clarified if a theory was used.

Table 1. Published articles by year and theory

Theory/Year	2016	2017	2018	2019	2020	2021
CFIR				1	3	
DOI	1		1	1		
Human-Computer Trust					1	
PRISM						1
RE-AIM			1	1	4	1
Strong Structuration Theory			1			
TAM		2	1	1	3	2
TTF				1	1	
User- and Context-Dependent Framework		1				
UTAUT		4	2	1	4	1
Total by Year	1	7	6	6	16	5

The analysis of theory use in the literature indicates IS theories and healthcare-adapted theories. Healthcare-adapted theories evolve from IS theories and healthcare-specific frameworks. Most studies utilized one theory or framework. IS-utilized theories were versions of TAM, UTAUT, and DOI. Four instances utilized two theories. Silva et al. (2018) used DOI and TAM. Jung et al. (2020) used TAM and UTAUT to investigate barriers and facilitators. Aljarboah and Miah (2019) investigated the acceptance factors of CDSS using task-technology fit (TTF) and UTAUT. Macheel et al. (2020) used UTAUT and RE-AIM to investigate CDSS interventions.

The emergence of healthcare-adapted frameworks indicates a need to adapt IS theory to the healthcare context. These include CFIR, RE-AIM, PRISM, and user- and context-dependent frameworks.

Figure 2 depicts the distribution of theories across the three types of CDSS. It is evident that prescriptive CDSS are the most prominent analytics included in twelve articles. In addition, it can be observed that six articles do not clearly describe the investigated CDSS. Both descriptive and predictive types of CDSS are used in four articles. Furthermore, UTUAT was used five times and TAM was used three times. These are common in the prescriptive types of CDSS. Apart from UTAUT and TAM, IS and healthcare-adapted theories are combined to understand the acceptance or rejection of prescriptive CDSS. UTAUT is combined with RE-AIM, TTF, and TAM. Regarding descriptive CDSS, most of the articles employ UTAUT. Again, two theories are combinedly used in one of the articles. Regarding predictive CDSS, it is evident that TAM is popular. This is followed by DOI.

Figure 2. Distribution of articles across different analytics

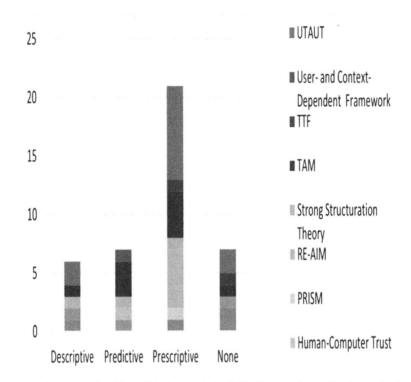

A total of 13 articles employ healthcare-adapted theories and 22 articles utilize IS theories as shown in Table 2. While IS theories and healthcare adapted theories are used, a trend to use both IS and healthcare-adapted theories is identified six times in the literature. This trend is only observed in studies that investigate prescriptive CDSS. Seventeen studies investigated AI-enabled CDSS, and 106 studies investigated rule-based CDSS. Interestingly, AI-enabled CDSS are prominent in predictive CDSS. They are also employed in prescriptive CDSS. However, none of the descriptive CDSS are AI-enabled.

Table 2. AI-enabled CDSS with analytic type

Analytics/AI Enabled	Yes	No
Descriptive		25
Predictive	10	15
Prescriptive	7	56
None		10
Total	17	106

Figure 3 depicts the decision boundary of a classification model trained on the study's dataset. It shows the type of user and variety of CDSS as two variables, which classifies the articles into "those that include a theory" and "those that do not" categories. To improve the visualization of the decision boundary, the study introduced noise to its dataset. Noise is represented by black circles. Blue represents the "no theory" region; orange represents the "theory" region. Histogram gradient boosting is the classification model used to categorize the articles. This method is used in the gradient boosting ensemble to train more efficient decision trees. Categorical variables are supported by this classifier by default. To build this classifier, the study used the scikit-learn machine learning package. Machine learning extensions (Mlxtend) and Matplotlib python libraries were chosen for visualization.

Figure 3. Contour-based decision boundary of histogram gradient boosting

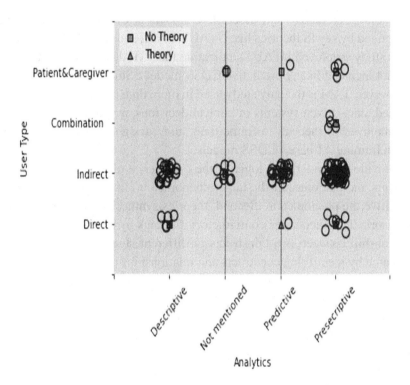

The study extracted four attributes of CDSS as shown in figure 3. This quantifies the strength of the attributes' impact on theoretical frameworks (second part of RQ2). This produced limited results. Limitations included data points or articles, categorical attributes, unbalanced targets, and missing values (for example, the analytics are "not mentioned"). Interestingly, combining the visualized results in the figures identified several connections. Predictive CDSS, some of which are AI- or learning-enabled, are good candidates for carefully chosen theoretic frameworks. Descriptive and prescriptive CDSS, of which most in this study is an expert-system or formula-based, are studied without specific theoretic frameworks. Additionally, the study considers this an important research opportunity to study with additional data.

The IS theories and healthcare-adapted theories are utilized by the three kinds of CDSS. Twenty articles apply IS theories for adoption that are prescriptive. The main theories in this type are UTAUT, TAM, and RE-AIM. There are seven studies that use predictive CDSS that incorporate theory. The main theories include TAM, RE-AIM, and DOI. There are five studies that use descriptive CDSS that and use UTAUT, DOI, RE-AIM, and CFIR. There are 82 studies that do not use a theory or do not clearly state the theory.

This study found that most of the articles study the adoption or resistance of knowledge-based (non-AI) CDSS. Eighteen articles study data-driven or AI-enabled CDSS. Among the 18 AI-enabled articles, three articles utilize theory to inform their design and/or adoption. Further breakdown of this structure provides several outcomes. First, three descriptive CDSS studies use only one theory. One study uses two theories; zero studies use three or more studies. Second, four predictive CDSS studies use one theory. Third, 12 prescriptive CDSS studies use only one theory. Two theories are used in two studies; one study used three or more studies.

Discussion

According to the findings, predictive and descriptive models in CDSS are dominated by prescriptive models. These are guided by key IS theories like UTAUT, TAM, and RE-AIM. Seven of the 20 prescriptive research in this study employed UTAUT, indicating that UTAUT is the most important IS theory. Nevertheless, it is not included in any predictive CDSS models. Studies with predictive models utilize several theories; however, TAM is the only study used in more than one study. While rule-based models are widely researched, data-driven systems in clinical decisions are guided by IS theories. Only three AI-based studies employed IS theories to frame their study design. This indicates a lack of usage of strong IS theories in framing AI-based CDSS models.

First, theories provide the underlying logic of the occurrence of natural or social phenomenon by explaining key drivers and outcomes of the target phenomenon. In addition, it addresses the underlying processes that drive the phenomenon. Second, theories synthesize prior empirical findings within a theoretical framework. This reconciles contradictory findings by discovering contingent factors that influence the relationship between two constructs in different studies. Third, theories provide guidance for future research by identifying constructs and relationships that are worthy of research. Fourth, theories contribute to cumulative knowledge by bridging gaps between theories and causing existing theories to be reevaluated.

Adapted IS theories in healthcare have created frameworks to integrate IS theory with the healthcare domain. CFIR, developed by Damschroder et al. (2009), included constructs associated with successful or effective implementation (https://cfirguide.org/). This adapted theory drew from DOI and a significant compilation of constructs based on the review of 500 published sources across 13 scientific disciplines (CRIF, 2021; Keith et al., 2017). As noted, the CFIR conceptual framework was developed to guide a systematic assessment of multilevel implementation contexts to identify factors that might influence intervention implementation and effectiveness (Damschroder et al., 2009).

The RE-AIM framework was developed in 1999 (https://www.re-aim.org/about/what-is-re-aim/). The framework intended to support the translation of research to practice and policy, as well as improve the impact of health promotion and prevention efforts (Glasgow, 2006, 2013; Glasgow et al., 1999, 2019; Glasgow & Estabrooks, 2018; Harden et al., 2020). Five steps within the framework follow a logical path (Gaglio, Shoup, & Glasgow, 2013):

Reach is the absolute number, proportion, and representativeness of individuals who are willing to participate in a given initiative. Effectiveness is the impact of an intervention on outcomes, including potential negative effects, quality of life, and economic outcomes. Adoption is the absolute number, proportion, and representativeness of settings and intervention agents who are willing to initiate a program.

Implementation refers to the intervention agents' fidelity to the various elements of an intervention's protocol. This includes consistency of delivery as intended and the time and cost of the intervention. Maintenance is the extent to which a program or policy becomes institutionalized or part of the routine organizational practices and policies. Maintenance also has referents at the individual level. At the individual level, it is defined as the long-term effects of a program on outcomes 6 or more months after the most recent intervention contact. (p. 1)

Forty of the 120 reviewed articles included theory. The list of forty articles containing theory categorized by the theory utilized can be found in additional readings section of this chapter. The most prevalent healthcare-adapted theories were CFIR and RE-AIM (four and seven papers, respectively). Prevalent IS theories were UTAUT and TAM (8 and 5 included papers, respectively). The IS specialty sits at an intersection of technology and behavioral sciences; therefore, it is crucial to balance both science (theory) and technology (design artifact) (Baskerville et al., 2018; Eapen, 2020). Walls, Widmeyer, and El Sawy (1992) claimed that CDSS centers around the construction of decision models. In addition, IS theoretical underpinnings are not well known. One decade later, many studies still neglect to infuse theory with design. In 2001, Kaplan's findings claimed that CDSS literature continued to struggle when drawing on theory to understand issues in the development, implementation, and use of CDSS. The current study shows that only 33% of the surveyed articles included theory. Therefore, it is crucial that social and design sciences integrate theory into their research to better inform researchers and practitioners.

FUTURE RESEARCH DIRECTIONS

This study investigated the theories used to inform design and provides a glimpse into the current state of CDSS theory-informed design. Future research should delve into CDSS adoption, implementation, acceptance, and resistance to improve the integration of CDSS technology and benefits into the complex world of healthcare. Additional directions of research include a focus on human-computer interaction, decision design and integration of technology to leverage benefits of automation and human decision-making. In order to achieve better quality of care, the CDSS can provide the transparency needed as physicians utilize the technology to exchange content and patient interaction to improve the of quality of care and the health of populations while reducing costs of health care.

CONCLUSION

Comprehensive and rigorous theory building demands that problems and realms of practice are examined from a comprehensive perspective (Swanson & Chermack, 2013). Often, these problems can be investigated within applied disciplines or realms of study and practice that are fully understood through their use in the functioning world (Swanson & Chermack, 2013). The general method of theory building in applied disciplines (Lynham, 2002; Swanson & Chermack, 2013) fuses information from both perspectives and yields a complete and accurate understanding of the investigated realm.

Prevalent theories utilized in data driven CDSS acceptance, adoption, avoidance, and resistance design are RE-AIM, TAM, UTAUT, and CFIR. TAM and UTAUT are IS behavioral theories; RE-AIM and CFIR are healthcare-adapted theories. These prevalent theories indicate that IS theories are being used to inform the design of healthcare CDSS. Healthcare-adapted theories are informed through IS theories. While these theories are prevalent, they are also scarce compared to the 120 reviewed articles. A call to action is required for authors to integrate theory into behavioral and design sciences. This effort will provide physicians and clinicians with a better understanding of these systems. Theory must be integrated to evolve and build on the current and future literature to recognize and understand the acceptance, adoption, avoidance, and resistance of physicians and clinicians utilizing CDSS.

REFERENCES

Agarwal, R., & Prasad, J. (1998). A conceptual and operational definition of personal innovativeness in the domain of information technology. *Information Systems Research*, *9*(2), 204–215. doi:10.1287/isre.9.2.204

Agency for Healthcare Research and Quality. (2013, February). *Clinical decision support*. Retrieved from https://www.ahrq.gov/cpi/about/otherwebsites/clinical-decision-support/index.html

Ajzen, I. (1985). From intentions to actions: A theory of planned behavior. In J. Kuhl & J. Beckmann (Eds.), *Action control* (pp. 11–39). Springer. doi:10.1007/978-3-642-69746-3_2

Aljarboa, S., & Miah, S. J. (2019). Investigating acceptance factors of clinical decision support systems in a developing country context. *2019 IEEE Asia-Pacific Conference on Computer Science and Data Engineering (CSDE)*, 1-8. 10.1109/CSDE48274.2019.9162388

Bacharach, S. B. (1989). Organizational theories: Some criteria for evaluation. *Academy of Management Review*, *14*(4), 496. doi:10.2307/258555

Bartley, A. (2017). *Predictive analytics in healthcare: A data-driven approach to transforming care delivery* [white paper]. Intel.

Baskerville, R., Baiyere, A., Gregor, S., Hevner, A., & Rossi, M. (2018). Design science research contributions: Finding a balance between artifact and theory. *Journal of the Association for Information Systems*, *19*(5), 358–376. doi:10.17705/1jais.00495

Bhattacherjee, A. (2012). *Social science research: Principles, methods, and practices*. Global Text Project. Retrieved from https://library.biblioboard.com/content/efbf10a8-a0e2-4caf-848c-221afb300b20

Brito, G. C., Fonseca-Pinto, R., Guarino, M. P., Lajes, M., & Lopes, N. V. (2018). CBView: Merging data in metabolic diagnosis. In J. E. Quintela Varajao, M. M. Cruz Cunha, R. Martinho, R. Rijo, D. Domingos, & E. Peres (Eds.), *CENTERIS 2018—International Conference on Enterprise Information Systems / PROJMAN 2018—International Conference on Project Management / HCIST 2018 —International Conference on Health and Social Care Information Systems and Technology, CENTERI* (Vol. 138, pp. 244-249). 10.1016/j.procs.2018.10.035

Brown, B., Cheraghi-Sohi, S., Jaki, T., Su, T.-L., Buchan, I., & Sperrin, M. (2016). Understanding clinical prediction models as "innovations": A mixed methods study in UK family practice. *BMC Medical Informatics and Decision Making*, *16*(1), 106. doi:10.118612911-016-0343-y PMID:27506547

Brown, S. H., Lincoln, M. J., Groen, P. J., & Kolodner, R. M. (2003). VistA—U.S. Department of Veterans Affairs national-scale HIS. *International Journal of Medical Informatics*, *69*(2-3), 135–156. doi:10.1016/S1386-5056(02)00131-4 PMID:12810119

Chi, E. A., Chi, G., Tsui, C. T., Jiang, Y., Jarr, K., Kulkarni, C. V., Zhang, M., Long, J., Ng, A. Y., Rajpurkar, P., & Sinha, S. R. (2021). Development and validation of an artificial intelligence system to optimize clinician review of patient records. *JAMA Network Open*, *4*(7), e2117391. doi:10.1001/jamanetworkopen.2021.17391 PMID:34297075

Cohen, J. (2016). A coefficient of agreement for nominal scales. *Educational and Psychological Measurement*. Advance online publication. doi:10.1177/001316446002000104

Colquitt, J. A., & Zapata-Phelan, C. P. (2007). Trends in theory building and theory testing: A five-decade study of the Academy of Management Journal. *Academy of Management Journal*, *50*(6), 1281–1303. doi:10.5465/amj.2007.28165855

Cooper, R., & Zmud, R. (1990). Information technology implementation research: A technological diffusion approach. *Management Science*, *36*(2), 123–139. doi:10.1287/mnsc.36.2.123

Crum, M. R., Premkumar, G., & Ramamurthy, K. (1996). An assessment of motor carrier adoption, use, and satisfaction with EDI. *Transportation Journal*, *35*(4), 44–57.

Damschroder, L. J., Aron, D. C., Keith, R. E., Kirsh, S. R., Alexander, J. A., & Lowery, J. C. (2009). Fostering implementation of health services research findings into practice: A consolidated framework for advancing implementation science. *Implementation Science; IS*, *4*(1), 50. doi:10.1186/1748-5908-4-50 PMID:19664226

Davis, F. D. (1989). Perceived usefulness, perceived ease of use, and user acceptance of information technology. *Management Information Systems Quarterly*, *13*(3), 319. doi:10.2307/249008

DiMaggio, P. J. (1995). Comments on "What Theory is Not." *Administrative Science Quarterly*, *40*(3), 391. doi:10.2307/2393790

Eapen, B. (2020). *Towards a theory of adoption and design for clinical decision support systems*. McMaster University.

Esmaeilzadeh, P., Sambasivan, M., Kumar, N., & Nezakati, H. (2015). Adoption of clinical decision support systems in a developing country: Antecedents and outcomes of physician's threat to perceived professional autonomy. *International Journal of Medical Informatics*, *84*(8), 548–560. doi:10.1016/j.ijmedinf.2015.03.007 PMID:25920928

Fichman, R. G., & Kemerer, C. F. (1997). The assimilation of software process innovations: An organizational learning perspective. *Management Science*, *43*(10), 1345–1363. doi:10.1287/mnsc.43.10.1345

Fishbein, M. A., & Ajzen, I. (1975). *Belief, attitude, intention and behaviour: An introduction to theory and research*. Addison Wesley. Retrieved from https://www.researchgate.net/publication/233897090_Belief_attitude_intention_and_behaviour_An_introduction_to_theory_and_research

Gaglio, B., Shoup, J. A., & Glasgow, R. E. (2013). The RE-AIM Framework: A systematic review of use over time. *American Journal of Public Health*, *103*(6), e38–e46. doi:10.2105/AJPH.2013.301299 PMID:23597377

Gensinger, R. A. Jr. (2014). *Analytics in healthcare: An introduction*. HIMSS. doi:10.4324/9781498757317

Gil, M., Pinto, P., Simoes, A. S., Povoa, P., Da Silva, M. M., & Lapao, L. V. (2016). Co-design of a computer-assisted medical decision support system to manage antibiotic prescription in an ICU ward. In *Exploring complexity in health: An interdisciplinary systems approach* (Vol. 228, pp. 499–503). doi:10.3233/978-1-61499-678-1-499

Glasgow, R. E. (2006). RE-AIMing research for application: Ways to improve evidence for family medicine. *Journal of the American Board of Family Medicine, 19*(1), 11–19. doi:10.3122/jabfm.19.1.11 PMID:16492000

Glasgow, R. E. (2013). What does it mean to be pragmatic? Pragmatic methods, measures, and models to facilitate research translation. *Health Education & Behavior, 40*(3), 257–265. doi:10.1177/1090198113486805 PMID:23709579

Glasgow, R. E., & Estabrooks, P. E. (2018). Pragmatic applications of RE-AIM for health care initiatives in community and clinical settings. *Preventing Chronic Disease, 15*, 170271. doi:10.5888/pcd15.170271 PMID:29300695

Glasgow, R. E., Harden, S. M., Gaglio, B., Rabin, B., Smith, M. L., Porter, G. C., Ory, M. G., & Estabrooks, P. A. (2019). RE-AIM planning and evaluation framework: Adapting to new science and practice with a 20-year review. *Frontiers in Public Health, 7*, 64. doi:10.3389/fpubh.2019.00064 PMID:30984733

Glasgow, R. E., Vogt, T. M., & Boles, S. M. (1999). Evaluating the public health impact of health promotion interventions: The RE-AIM framework. *American Journal of Public Health, 89*(9), 1322–1327. doi:10.2105/AJPH.89.9.1322 PMID:10474547

Gregor, S. (2006). The nature of theory in information systems. *Management Information Systems Quarterly, 30*(3), 611. doi:10.2307/25148742

Grosz, B., & Stone, P. (2018). A century-long commitment to assessing artificial intelligence and its impact on society. *Communications of the ACM, 61*(12), 68–73. doi:10.1145/3198470

Harden, S. M., Strayer, T. E. III, Smith, M. L., Gaglio, B., Ory, M. G., Rabin, B., Estabrooks, P. A., & Glasgow, R. E. (2020). National working group on the RE-AIM planning and evaluation framework: Goals, resources, and future directions. *Frontiers in Public Health, 7*, 390. doi:10.3389/fpubh.2019.00390 PMID:31998677

Hoogland, J., & Jochemsen, H. (2000). Professional autonomy and the normative structure of medical practice. *Theoretical Medicine and Bioethics, 21*(5), 457–475. doi:10.1023/A:1009925423036 PMID:11142442

Jung, S. Y., Hwang, H., Lee, K., Lee, H.-Y., Kim, E., Kim, M., & Cho, I. Y. (2020). Barriers and facilitators to implementation of medication decision support systems in electronic medical records: Mixed methods approach based on structural equation modeling and qualitative analysis. *JMIR Medical Informatics, 8*(7), e18758. doi:10.2196/18758 PMID:32706717

Kaplan, B. (2001). Evaluating informatics applications—some alternative approaches: Theory, social interactionism, and call for methodological pluralism. *International Journal of Medical Informatics, 64*(1), 39–56. doi:10.1016/S1386-5056(01)00184-8 PMID:11673101

Keith, R. E., Crosson, J. C., O'Malley, A. S., Cromp, D., & Taylor, E. F. (2017). Using the consolidated framework for implementation research (CFIR) to produce actionable findings: A rapid-cycle evaluation approach to improving implementation. *Implementation Science; IS, 12*(1), 15. doi:10.118613012-017-0550-7 PMID:28187747

Kitchenham, B., & Charters, S. (2007). *Guidelines for performing systematic literature reviews in software engineering.* Keele University and Durham University Joint Report. Retrieved from http://www.cs.ecu.edu/gudivada/research/papers/guidelines-for-se-literature-reviews-summary.pdf

Koerkamp, R. M. K. (2019). *The road from analytical CDSS invention to implementation in healthcare.* SAS.

Kuhn, M., & Johnson, K. (2013). *Applied predictive modeling.* Springer. doi:10.1007/978-1-4614-6849-3

Lee, C., Luo, Z., Ngiam, K. Y., Zhang, M., Zheng, K., Chen, G., ... Yip, W. L. J. (2017). Big healthcare data analytics: Challenges and applications. In S. U. Khan, A. Y. Zomaya, & A. Abbas (Eds.), *Handbook of large-scale distributed computing in smart healthcare* (pp. 11–41). Springer International Publishing. doi:10.1007/978-3-319-58280-1_2

Liberati, A., Altman, D. G., Tetzlaff, J., Mulrow, C., Gøtzsche, P. C., Ioannidis, J. P., Clarke, M., Devereaux, P. J., Kleijnen, J., & Moher, D. (2009). The PRISMA statement for reporting systematic reviews and meta-analyses of studies that evaluate health care interventions: Explanation and elaboration. *PLoS Medicine, 6*(7), e1000100. doi:10.1371/journal.pmed.1000100 PMID:19621070

Liberati, E. G., Ruggiero, F., Galuppo, L., Gorli, M., González-Lorenzo, M., Maraldi, M., Ruggieri, P., Polo Friz, H., Scaratti, G., Kwag, K. H., Vespignani, R., & Moja, L. (2017). What hinders the uptake of computerized decision support systems in hospitals? A qualitative study and framework for implementation. *Implementation Science; IS, 12*(1), 113. doi:10.118613012-017-0644-2 PMID:28915822

Lim, S., Saldanha, T. J. V., Malladi, S., & Melville, N. P. (2013). Theories used in information systems research: Insights from complex network analysis. *Journal of Information Technology Theory and Application, 14*(2), 42.

Linder, J. A., Schnipper, J. L., Tsurikova, R., Melnikas, A. J., Volk, L. A., & Middleton, B. (2006). Barriers to electronic health record use during patient visits. *AMIA ... Annual Symposium Proceedings - AMIA Symposium. AMIA Symposium, 2006*, 499–503. PMID:17238391

Lopes, J., Guimarães, T., & Santos, M. F. (2020). Predictive and prescriptive analytics in healthcare: A survey. *Procedia Computer Science, 170*, 1029–1034. doi:10.1016/j.procs.2020.03.078

Lynham, S. A. (2002). The general method of theory-building research in applied disciplines. *Advances in Developing Human Resources, 4*(3), 221–241. doi:10.1177/1523422302043002

Lynn, L. A. (2019). Artificial intelligence systems for complex decision-making in acute care medicine: A review. *Patient Safety in Surgery, 13*(1), 6. doi:10.118613037-019-0188-2 PMID:30733829

Macheel, C., Reicks, P., Sybrant, C., Evans, C., Farhat, J., West, M. A., & Tignanelli, C. J. (2020). Clinical decision support intervention for rib fracture treatment. *Journal of the American College of Surgeons, 231*(2), 249–256.e2. doi:10.1016/j.jamcollsurg.2020.04.023 PMID:32360959

McDonald, C. J., Overhage, J. M., Tierney, W. M., Dexter, P. R., Martin, D. K., Suico, J. G., Zafar, A., Schadow, G., Blevins, L., Glazener, T., Meeks-Johnson, J., Lemmon, L., Warvel, J., Porterfield, B., Warvel, J., Cassidy, P., Lindbergh, D., Belsito, A., Tucker, M., ... Wodniak, C. (1999). The Regenstrief Medical Record System: A quarter century experience. *International Journal of Medical Informatics*, *54*(3), 225–253. doi:10.1016/S1386-5056(99)00009-X PMID:10405881

Mebrahtu, T. F., Bloor, K., Ledward, A., Keenan, A.-M., Andre, D., Randell, R., Skyrme, S., Yang, H., King, H., & Thompson, C. A. (2021). Effects of computerised clinical decision support systems (CDSS) on nursing and allied health professional performance and patient outcomes. *Cochrane Database of Systematic Reviews*. Advance online publication. doi:10.1002/14651858.CD014699 PMID:34911719

Mohr, L. B. (1982). *Explaining organizational behavior*. Jossey-Bass.

Moja, L., Polo Friz, H., Capobussi, M., Kwag, K., Banzi, R., Ruggiero, F., González-Lorenzo, M., Liberati, E. G., Mangia, M., Nyberg, P., Kunnamo, I., Cimminiello, C., Vighi, G., Grimshaw, J. M., Delgrossi, G., & Bonovas, S. (2019). Effectiveness of a hospital-based computerized decision support system on clinician recommendations and patient outcomes: A randomized clinical trial. *JAMA Network Open*, *2*(12), e1917094. doi:10.1001/jamanetworkopen.2019.17094 PMID:31825499

Newman, D. (2020, January 2). *Why the future of data analytics is prescriptive analytics*. Forbes. Retrieved from https://www.forbes.com/sites/danielnewman/2020/01/02/why-the-future-of-data-analytics-is-prescriptive-analytics/

Noteboom, C., & Qureshi, S. (2014). Adaptations of electronic health records to activate physicians' knowledge: How can patient centered care be improved through technology? *Health and Technology*, *4*(1), 59–73. doi:10.100712553-013-0072-5

Osheroff, J., Teich, J., Levick, D., Saldana, L., Velasco, F., Sittig, D., Rogers, K., & Jenders, R. (2012). *Improving outcomes with clinical decision support: An implementer's guide*. Chicago, IL: Healthcare Information and Management Systems Society (HIMSS). Retrieved from https://scholarlyworks.lvhn.org/administration-leadership/54

Ostropolets, A., Chen, R., Zhang, L., & Hripcsak, G. (2020). Characterizing physicians' information needs related to a gap in knowledge unmet by current evidence. *JAMIA Open*, *3*(2), 281–289. doi:10.1093/jamiaopen/ooaa012 PMID:32734169

Petkus, H., Hoogewerf, J., & Wyatt, J. C. (2020). What do senior physicians think about AI and clinical decision support systems: Quantitative and qualitative analysis of data from specialty societies. *Clinical Medicine*, *20*(3), 324–328. doi:10.7861/clinmed.2019-0317 PMID:32414724

Rieckert, A., Sommerauer, C., Krumeich, A., & Sönnichsen, A. (2018). Reduction of inappropriate medication in older populations by electronic decision support (the PRIMA-eDS study): A qualitative study of practical implementation in primary care. *BMC Family Practice*, *19*(1), 110. doi:10.118612875-018-0789-3 PMID:29986668

Rogers, E. M. (1995) Diffusion of Innovations (4th ed.). The Free Press.

Schwartz, J., & Cato, K. (2020). Machine learning based clinical decision support and clinician trust. *2020 IEEE International Conference on Healthcare Informatics (ICHI)*. 10.1109/ICHI48887.2020.9374365

Silva, T. I., Cavalcante, R. B., dos Santos, R. C., Gontijo, T. L., de Azevedo Guimaraes, E. A., & de Oliveira, V. C. (2018). Diffusion of the e-SUS primary care innovation in family health teams. *Revista Brasileira de Enfermagem, 71*(6), 2945–2952. doi:10.1590/0034-7167-2018-0053 PMID:30517397

Sutton, R. T., Pincock, D., Baumgart, D. C., Sadowski, D. C., Fedorak, R. N., & Kroeker, K. I. (2020). An overview of clinical decision support systems: Benefits, risks, and strategies for success. *NPJ Digital Medicine, 3*(1), 17. doi:10.103841746-020-0221-y PMID:32047862

Swanson, R., & Chermack, T. (2013). To hell with gravity. In *Theory building in applied disciplines*. Berrett-Koehler Publishers.

Teach, L., & Shortliffe, H. (1981). An analysis of physician attitudes regarding computer-based clinical consultation systems. *Computers and Biomedical Research, an International Journal, 14*(6), 542–558. doi:10.1016/0010-4809(81)90012-4 PMID:7035062

Tonekaboni, S., Joshi, S., McCradden, M. D., & Goldenberg, A. (2019). What clinicians want: Contextualizing explainable machine learning for clinical end use. *Proceedings of Machine Learning Research*, 21.

Tripathi, K. P. (2011). A review on knowledge-based expert system: Concept and architecture. *IJCA*, (Special Issue), 19–23.

Venkatesh, V., Morris, M. G., Davis, G. B., & Davis, F. D. (2003). User acceptance of information technology: Toward a unified view. *Management Information Systems Quarterly, 27*(3), 425–478. doi:10.2307/30036540

Venkatesh, V., Thong, J., & Xu, X. (2012). Consumer acceptance and use of information technology: Extending the unified theory of acceptance and use of technology. *Management Information Systems Quarterly, 36*(1), 157–178. doi:10.2307/41410412

Walls, J. G., Widmeyer, G. R., & El Sawy, O. A. (1992). Building an information system design theory for vigilant EIS. *Information Systems Research, 3*(1), 36–59. doi:10.1287/isre.3.1.36

Webb, B. J., Sorensen, J., Mecham, I., Buckel, W., Ooi, L., Jephson, A., & Dean, N. C. (2019). Antibiotic use and outcomes after implementation of the drug resistance in pneumonia score in ED patients with community-onset Pneumonia. *Chest, 156*(5), 843–851. doi:10.1016/j.chest.2019.04.093 PMID:31077649

KEY TERMS AND DEFINITIONS

AI-Enabled: Involves feeding datasets into machines to help them achieve near human level intelligence by learning problem-solving, perceiving, and thinking skills.

Clinical Decision Support Systems: Clinical decision support systems (CDSS) are software systems that analyze information from electronic health records (EHRs) and provide recommendations and alerts to help healthcare professionals follow evidence-based clinical standards during treatment.

Data-Driven Decision Making: It is the process of making organizational decisions based on the actual data and analysis instead of just observations.

Descriptive Analytics: Descriptive analytics is used to analyze information in order to answer questions, to organize historical information in order to present it visually.

Healthcare-Adapted Theory: Healthcare-adapted theories evolved from IS theories that utilize healthcare-specific framework.

IS Theory: A theory is a statement of relations among concepts within a set of boundary assumptions and constraints. IS theories enable users to identify factors that influence intention toward a particular behavior.

Predictive Analytics: Data, statistical models, and ML techniques are used in predictive analytics to predict the likelihood of future outcomes based on past data.

Prescriptive Analytics: Prescriptive analytics is a method of analyzing data and making recommendations on how to improve existing processes to meet a variety of predicted outcomes.

ENDNOTE

[1] Comparing to data-driven CDSSs, the limitations of typical expert systems include that expert knowledge is embedded, problem domain is narrow and specialized, data manipulation is symbolic, and decision process is pre-programmed and structured.

Decision–Making Systems

Ghalia Nasserddine
 https://orcid.org/0000-0001-9434-2914
Lebanese International University, Lebanon

Amal A. El Arid
 https://orcid.org/0000-0001-5712-2138
Lebanese International University, Lebanon

INTRODUCTION

Decision-making is one of the steps that humans take in every moment in their lives. When they open their eyes from the early morning, they start making decisions to snooze the alarm or get up. All long the day, decisions make a big part of human life.

After a simultaneous interaction between multiple functional systems differently, decisions are taken; each has its pros and cons. Individuals in organizations use the information collected and processed to make good decisions. These decisions may influence and change the course of the organization and the lives of other employees in this organization. In the business dictionary (Gibson, 2009), decision-making is the thought process of selecting a rational or logical choice from a set of available options. Decision-making theory was first introduced by Simon (Mintrom, 2015). The decision-making process consists of two parts: the actual decision-making process and the implementation process.

In (Scott & Bruce, 1995), the authors proposed four different types of decision-making models: Rational decision-making style, in which thorough research for alternative logical evaluation is done

- Intuitive decision-making style, in which reliance on hunches is the main characteristic
- Dependent decision-making style, which depends directly on advice and direction from others
- Avoidant decision-making style, in which we try to avoid making decisions

The decision-making theory is a multidisciplinary field where philosophers, economists, psychologists, computer scientists, and statisticians are expertise. Generally, two types of decision theory can be distinguished: normative and descriptive decision theory. These theories are studied separately.

- Normative decision theory, which looks for yield instructions about what decision-makers are rationally required or must
- Descriptive decision theories that describe and predict how people make decisions; it is a practical discipline, which was first introduced and experimented with within psychology.

Furthermore, decisions are classified into three categories based on the level at which they happen:

- Strategic decisions adjust the journey of an organization.
- Tactical decisions are the decisions about how things will happen.

DOI: 10.4018/978-1-7998-9220-5.ch082

- Operational decisions refer to the decisions taken daily by employees.

Table 1 shows examples of decisions level within an organization.

Table 1. Examples of decision levels, decision cases, and decision makers

Decision Level	Example	Decision Maker
Strategic Decision	• Merge with another organization to increase profit and globalization. • Create a new product line to ensure business continuity. • Downsize the organization to maintain the continuity of the business.	• Director • CEO
Tactical Decision	• Which employees should be let go during downsizing the organization. • Which employees should be let go during downsizing the organization. • Which employees should be let go during downsizing the organization.	• Manager
Operational Decision	• In addition to face-to-face class, various • Which employees should be let go during downsizing the organization.	• Employee

The main objective of this chapter is to present some existing techniques used in decision-making systems. A background for decision-making technique is represented. Afterward, the decision-making process and existing approaches are introduced. This chapter will conclude with the different models and methods used in decision-making theory.

BACKGROUND

Decision-Making Process

Decision-making is one of the essential activities in different fields: education, health, organization, management, and others. Usually, a decision involves the presence of alternatives and values (Eisenfuhr, 2011). However, the decision-making process requires problem structuring and evaluation of the result. In Scott and Bruce (Scott & Bruce, 1995), four different decision-making models have been proposed: Rational, intuitive dependent, and avoidance decision-making. In this section, the process of rational decision-making is presented. Also, a review of other models is shown.

Decision-making is the process of choosing an action or value from among alternative courses of action, each conduct to different environments or outcomes. Some outcomes are preferable to others, based on the equitable of the decision-maker. This process is presented in Figure 1 (Whitworth, Van de Walle, & Turoff, 2000).

Figure 1. The decision-making structure from analysis to outcome stages

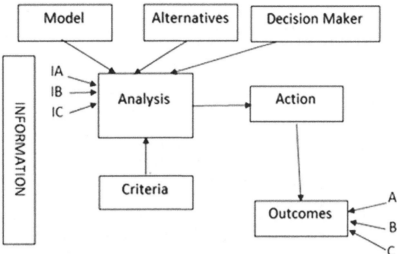

The decision-maker should be able to divine essential properties of the outcomes based on the rational understanding of the environment and the analysis of the problem. The output is the value of the result of the state of the environment that follows the chosen action. The main elements of the rational decision-making structure are (Whitworth, Van de Walle, & Turoff, 2000):

- Alternatives (X): is a set of alternative actions or values that the decision-maker can choose. Each choice can lead to a different outcome environment.
- Criteria (C): is a set of decision criteria that define the properties of the outcomes.
- Model (M): is a model which is predicted logically by processing information about causal factors (A, B, C, etc.) to compute some properties of outcomes like profit and loss.
- Information (I): is the data collected and processed to be used by model M.
- Analysis (A): is the evaluation and analysis of the expected properties of the alternative outcomes in opposition to the decision criteria.
- Decision-maker (D): is the entity that takes the decision.

The process of rational decision-making model can be represented by (Yu, 1979):

$$xf = R(X, C, M, I, A, D)$$

where R represent the rational analysis phase. Table 2 shows the elements of the rational decision making model.

Table 2. The elements of decision-making process

Element	Definition	Recent Advances
Alternatives $(X_0,...,X_n)(t)$	Set of n alternatives outcomes, can change during times. From this set, the decision maker can choose an excepted outcome.	Not necessarily fixed. It can change with time.
Criteria $(C_m,...,C_n)(t)$	Set of m to n criteria that may change during time. These criteria are applied to each choice outcome.	Not necessarily simple linear function. May change with time. Multiple criteria which can be contradict.
Model $(M(t))$	A logical model that allows prediction of the excepted outcome based on the value of the given information and the set of criteria.	Allows subjective estimates. Can be a probabilistic model.
Information $(I_A,...,I_V)(t)$	Information that may change during time. This information should be relevant to the likely outcome of the choice set.	Vary with time
Method $(A(t))$	It is responsible of applying the criteria to the excepted outcome in order to generate the result.	This method may vary according to the situation
Decision maker $(D(t))$	It takes into consideration the current subjective factors in order to make analysis and choose the most likely outcomes.	Accept subjective element.

For a rational decision, alternative options are preferable to be available. If it is not the case, a phase of inspiration and searching for alternative courses of action is required. The making decision process cannot evaluate the unknown action choices. A rational analysis may not generate the best alternative if the better outcomes are associated with the anonymous options). The set of alternatives may not be exhaustive or complete. Some theories like belief function theory cover the case of an uncompleted set of alternatives (Denœux, 2011; Smets & Kennes, 1994).

In the decision-making problem, the decision-maker should know their purpose. This purpose is represented as criteria. Without the requirements, there is no preference for one outcome over the others.

The analysis is based on an available model that predicts the most likely outcomes using the general criteria and the information about certain causal factors.

This model determines the needed set of information in the making decision problem. Usually, the collection of data is unknown, and the model is incomplete. The information gathered should be available and correct. Furthermore, the gathering of data should not affect the situation of the decision-making problem. If it is not the case, the analysis can be invalid (Whitworth, Van de Walle, & Turoff, 2000). In the next section, a presentation of some available techniques of decision-making is shown.

Decision-Making Techniques

Many techniques help decision-maker take the most effective decisions. In this chapter, we will focus on the following three techniques:

- The Five Whys
- The Cause and Effect diagram (Fishbone diagram)
- Decision Trees

THE FIVE WHYS TECHNIQUE

The Five Whys technique is a powerful and straightforward method used to resolve problems by inspecting cause-and-effect relationships (Serrat, 2017). This technique is built on a shell process with the following key elements:

- Contract accurate and complete statements of the given problems
- Answer the question honestly.
- The determination to get to the bottom of the issues and solve them.

The five whys is an elementary and effective method to problem solving that recommend deep thinking through questioning, and can be adapted quickly and applied to all type of problems. It is a systematic problem-solving technique developed by Sakichi Toyoda for the Toyota Industries Corporation (Ohno & Bodek, 2019). Figure 2A shows the general structure of the five whys.

Figure 2. The five whys structure, causes, and effect

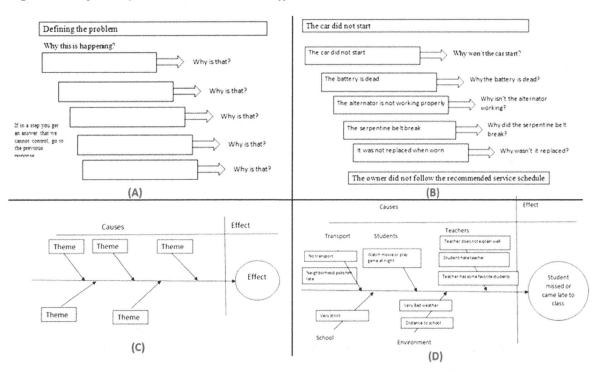

The Five Whys is used for exploring decisions or for reflecting on the root cause of a problem. Whenever something unexpected happens, this technique can serve to make root cause analysis. Even it takes time to master it, but it is easy to apply. Following are the five main steps of this technique (Serrat, 2017).

1. Invite all staff affected or noticed by the issue to a five whys meeting.
2. Select a five Whys master for the meeting who will ask the five questions and assign responsibility for the group's solutions. The rest of the group will answer the five questions and discuss. There are

no special qualifications for the five whys master. He is not necessarily the leader of the project or the manager. The master should note during the meeting unless they would like to assign someone else to do this.

3.   Ask "why?" five times. These steps look very simple, but they can be a bit risky. The master should choose the right "why" to start with. The "first why" is the key. Furthermore, he should Work through each of those five Whys and discover all the practical steps that have been or must be taken.

4.   Answer all the five whys and select the right decision or the root cause of the problem.

5.   Assign the response that will make or survey the solutions and email the result to the whole team

To better understand the five whys technique, let us look at an example from the automotive industry, shown in Figure 2-B, "how to discover the root cause of a car that will not start." To know the root cause, the owner should answer the five whys shown in Figure 2-B. The root cause will be the answer to the last why.

The "five whys" questions are used for simple and moderately complex problems. For highly complex issues, this technique can be used in combination with others. It is highly recommended to use it when problems require human interaction or influence. The "five why" technique has benefits and limitations. In Table 3, some advantages and limitations of this technique are presented.

Table 3. Advantages and limitations of the five whys technique

Advantages	Limitations
• Identify the root cause of a problem • Realize how one action can cause a chain of multiple problems • Find out the relationship between the different root causes • Simple and highly effective without complicated evaluation techniques	• May get different answers from different people for the same question "the cause of the same problem". This issue raises a question about the reliability of this technique. • Related to the knowledge and experience of the staff participated in the five why meeting. • May not wade profound to uncover the correct root cause of the problem.

FISHBONE DIAGRAM

Fishbone diagrams, also called "Ishikawa diagrams" or "cause-and-effect diagrams," were created by Dr. Kaoru Ishikawa (Ishikawa, 1968). A causal diagram shows the potential cause of a specific event (Ishikawa, 1968). To better understand this diagram, it is vital to distinguish between cause and root cause. A cause may continuously affect the system and produce the event. However, a root cause is a direct reason for the event.

A Fishbone diagram is used to show the causes and effects of a particular problem. It helps managers analyze and discuss an affair or situation by looking at the root causes and studying their interconnections. Remarkably, this diagram is very used in diagnosing and examining a particular issue or problem. The construction of the fishbone diagram consists of four main steps:

• Identification of the problem is the consequence or effect of the problem, placed in the head of the fishbone.

• Identification of the factors that contribute to the problem is generally called cause.

- Group the factors into main themes. The different causes of the problem are put together under the main title of the heading. These are the skeleton or prominent bones in the diagram.
- Analysis and discussion: The decision-maker uses the fishbone diagram to discards the causes (factors) that are not considered the root cause of the problem. Therefore, they could select the root cause of the problem.

Figure 2C shows a general form of a fishbone diagram. Fishbone diagram shows the problem (effect) and their root causes (grouped by theme). The problem is shown on the main bone and the causes of the problem are indicated on its branches, respectively.

Decision-making is one of the main problems in an organization. Managers should use a suitable method to make an accurate decision for the organization's success. After identifying the different alternatives and the influential factors regarding the problem, the fishbone (or cause-and-effect) diagram shows the relationship between the problem phenomena. Finally, the analytical hierarchy process analysis is used to determine the priority for the possible solutions; an efficient decision is performed to select the choice with the best outcomes (Yazdani & Tavakkoli-Moghaddam, 2012).

To better understand the fishbone diagram, we will consider the problem of analyzing the main reasons why some students frequently miss school (Amin & Idek, 2019). Students may miss the school day or skip certain classes or come late to classes. It may cause some problems in transportation and with family. Figure 2D shows the fishbone diagram for this problem.

In Table 4, some advantages and limitations of the fishbone diagram are presented.

Table 4. Advantages and limitations of fishbone diagram

Advantages	Limitations
• Identify cause and effect relationships for any given problems, • Facilitate joint brainstorming discussions, • Brainstorming process motivates the team to improve their way of thinking • The process of asking why something happened repeatedly at each stage helps drill down to one or more root causes, • Help prioritize relevant causes, so underlying root causes are addressed first	• Can lead to divergent approach • Need test to prove results. • Based on opinion not evidence • Complex problem can produce sticky diagram

DECISION TREE

A tree consists of root branches and leaves (see Figure 3A). Same structure is used in Decision Tree (See Figure 3B) (Gershman, Meisels, Lüke, Rokach, Schclar, & Sturm, 2010; Jadhav & Channe, 2016).

Generally, the following terminologies are used in the decision tree (Gershman, Meisels, Lüke, Rokach, Schclar, & Sturm, 2010; Jadhav & Channe, 2016):

- **Root node:** this node has no precedent and zeroes incoming edges.
- **Splitting:** the process of dividing a node into two or more sub-nodes. When building the model, the essential input variables are recognized. Then, the variable records are split at the root node and all internal nodes into two or more categories (also called bins) based on the status of these variables. The degree of purity and other characteristics related to the resultant child nodes, like the proportion with the target condition, are used to select one potential input variable. Entropy,

Gini index, classification error, information gain, gain ratio, and towing criteria are examples of these characteristics (Patel & Upadhyay, 2012). The splitting procedure will continue till the determination of the homogeneity or stopping criteria are met. Usually, only some potential input variables are used to construct the decision tree model. However, in some cases, a specific input variable is used multiple times at different levels of the decision tree.

- **Internal node:** each one should have at least one incoming edge and two outcomes edges. All comparisons are made in these nodes.
- **Leaf or terminal node:** this node has one incoming edge and zero outcomes edge. It contains the class label, which represents the result.
- **The branch is a subsection of the tree (also called a sub-tree):** A decision tree model is formed using a hierarchy of branches. Each path from the root node through internal nodes to a leaf node represents a decision rule. These pathways are described as 'if-then" rules. For example, "if condition-1 and condition-2 and condition … and k occur, then outcome j occurs."
- **Parent and Child Node:** A node divided into sub-nodes is called a parent node of sub-nodes, whereas sub-nodes are the child of a parent node.
- **Stopping:** When building a statistical model, the complexity and robustness are considered simultaneously. Generally, the more complex tree will lead to a less reliable result. The goal of building a decision tree is not to represent all records but to fit the existing observation and have a few records on each leaf. Stopping should be applied when building a decision tree to overcome the possibility of getting an overly complex tree. Below are some parameters used in the stopping steps: records in a leaf, number of records in a node before splitting, and number of steps of any leaf from the root node. Stopping parameters depend on the goal of the analysis and the characteristics of the dataset being used. Berry and Linoff (1999) recommend avoiding overfitting and underfitting by fixing the target proportion of records in a leaf node to be between 0.25% and 1.00% of the complete training dataset. This rule is called rule-of-thumb.
- **Pruning:** the process of removing sub-nodes of a decision node (the opposite approach of splitting). Generally, pruning is used in some situations where stopping rules do not work well. In this case, a large tree is built; then, the pruning step is applied to get the optimal size (Friedman, Hastie, & Tibshirani, 2001). One of the most common methods of selecting the best possible subtree from several candidates is to consider the proportion in which the predicted occurrence of the target is incorrect. Another method of choosing the best alternative is to divide the sample data set into two: Training and validation dataset. After creating a model based on the training set, we must test it using the training dataset on the validation dataset. For a small dataset, a cross-validation method is applied. In this method, sample data is divided into ten groups (Called fold), and the model is built using nine folds and tested using the last one. There are two types of pruning: pre-pruning and post-pruning. Pre-pruning uses Chi-square tests or multiple-comparison adjustment methods to prevent the generation of non-significant branches. Post-pruning is used after generating a complete decision tree to remove components to improve the overall classification accuracy when applied to the validation dataset.

Therefore, a decision tree is a tree in which each node manifests an attribute. Each edge, called a branch, shows a rule that helps in making a decision. The outcomes are represented in the leaves. They can be categorical or continuous values (Jadhav & Channe, 2016). Figure 3B shows an example of the decision tree. Node A is a root node, which is split into two sub-nodes: B and C. A is the parent node; B and C are child nodes. B is a terminal node; however, C is a decision node.

Figure 3. The Tree structure and the three examples explained in the context

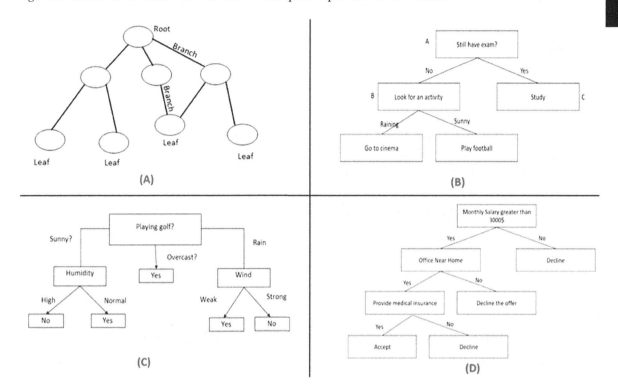

DECISION TREE ALGORITHM

The decision tree algorithm is one of the supervised learning algorithms. However, the decision tree algorithm can resolve the regression and classification problems contrary to other supervised learning algorithms. The primary purpose of the decision tree is to create a training model used to predict an estimation value of the target variable by applying simple learning decision rules deduced from training data (also called prior data). Many algorithms were developed to build a decision tree, including Classification and Regression Trees (CART) (Breiman et al., 2017), C4.5 (Quinlan, 2014), Chi-Squared Automatic Interaction Detection (CHAID) (Kass, 1980), and Quick, Unbiased, Efficient, Statistical Tree (QUEST) (Loh & Shih, 1997).

The CART algorithm is characterized by building binary trees where each internal node has exactly two outgoing edges. The splits are selected using the two criteria, and the obtained tree is pruned by cost–complexity Pruning. When provided, CART can consider misclassification costs in the tree induction. It also enables users to offer prior probability distribution. This algorithm is based on three steps:

1. Find the best feature split. For each feature with K different values, there exist K-1 possible splits. Find the division, which maximizes the splitting criterion. The resulting set of partitions contains the best section (one for each feature).
2. Find the node's best split. Among the best partitions from step *i* find the one, maximizing the splitting criterion.
3. Split the node using the best node split from Step ii and repeat from Step *i* until the stopping criterion is satisfied.

The splitting criterion is built on Gini's impurity index, which is defined for each node t by:

$$i(t) = \sum_{i,j} C(i \mid j) p(i \mid t) p(j \mid t)$$

Where:

1. $C(i|j)$ is the cost of misclassifiying a class i with a class j. Generally, $C(i|j)=1$ if class i different from class j, otherwise $C(i|j)=0$.
2. $p(i|t)$ is the probability that class i drop into node t.

In order to decrease of impurity, Gini impurity criterion must be used. This criterion is defined by:

$$\Delta i(s,t) = i(t) - pLi(tL) - pRi(tR),$$

Where:

1. $\Delta i(s,t)$ is decrease of impurity at node t with split s
2. $pL(pR)$ are probabilities of sending case to the left (right) child node tL (tR)
3. $i(tL)(i(tR))$ is Gini impurity measure for left (right) child node.

The generalization of decision tree is enhanced by using the pruning with combination of cross-validation error rate estimation. The algorithm for pruning is (Breiman, Friedman, Olshen, & Stone, 2017):

1. Divide randomly the training set into folds.
2. Pick the pruning level of tree (level 0 means the full decision tree).
3. Use 9 folds in creation of 9 new pruned trees and estimate error on last 10th fold.
4. Repeat from Step 2 until all pruning levels are used.
5. Find the smallest error and use the pruning level assigned to it.
6. Until pruning level is reached, remove all terminal nodes in the lowest tree level and assign decision class to parent node.

The decision value is equal to class with higher number of cases covered by node.

Table 5 represents a brief comparison about the different algorithms (Bhukya & Ramachandram, 2010) (Lin, Noe, & He, 2006).

A simple example of the accepting job offering is presented. Consider a system that helps in accepting or declining a job. Typically, all positions with monthly salaries smaller than $3000 will be decline. In addition, for timesaving, jobs that need more than 30 minutes of travel to get office are rejected. Additionally, all jobs without medical insurance are declined. The decision tree based on the above rules is presented in Figure 3-D.

Table 5. Comparison between existing decision tree algorithms

Steps	CART	C4.5	CHAID	QUEST
Method used to select input variables	Gini index Twoing criteria	Entropy info-gain	Chi Square	Category variable: Chi Square Continuous variable: J-Way anova
Pruning	Use pre-pruning single pass algorithm	Use pre-pruning single pass algorithm	Use pre-pruning Chi Square test for independence	Post pruning technique
Dependent variable	Categorical or continuous	Categorical or continuous	Categorical	Categorical
Input	Categorical or continuous	Categorical or continuous	Categorical or continuous	Categorical or continuous
Split	BinarySplit with linear combination	Multiple	Multiple	Binary Split with linear combination

CART SIMPLE APPLICATION

This example covers the decision problems of playing golf according to weather status (outlook, temperature, humidity, and winds speed) (Rajesh & Karthikeyan, 2017). Table 6 presents the decision output (Yes or No), based on all the factors.

In this section, the CART algorithm is applied to the playing golf decision problem. First, the Gini index should be computed using:

Gini=1 - $\sum$(*probability$_i$*)^2 for i = 1 to number of classes

Gini index is a metric for classification tasks in CART. It stores sum of squared probabilities of each class.

Table 6. Decision outputs based on weather status, outlook, temperature, humidity, and wind speed

Day	Outlook	Temperature	Humidity	Wind	Decision
1	Sunny	Hot	High	Weak	No
2	Sunny	Hot	High	Strong	No
3	Overcast	Hot	High	Weak	Yes
4	Rain	Mild	High	Weak	Yes
5	Rain	Cool	Normal	Weak	Yes
6	Rain	Cool	Normal	Strong	No
7	Overcast	Cool	Normal	Strong	Yes
8	Sunny	Mild	High	Weak	No
9	Sunny	Cool	Normal	Weak	Yes
10	Rain	Mild	Normal	Weak	Yes
11	Sunny	Mild	Normal	Strong	Yes
12	Overcast	Mild	High	Strong	Yes
13	Overcast	Hot	Normal	Weak	Yes
14	Rain	Mild	High	Strong	No

Outlook

Outlook can take three values: Sunny, Overcast or Rain. Table 7 summarizes the final decisions based on outlook feature.

Table 7. The outlook feature instances

Outlook	Yes	No	Number of instances
Sunny	2	3	5
Overcast	4	0	4
Rain	3	2	5

Using Table 7, Gini index is computed for different values of outlook feature as:

- Sunny: Gini= $1 - (2/5)^2 - (3/5)^2 = 1 - 0.16 - 0.36 = 0.48$
- Overcast: Gini= $1 - (4/4)^2 - (0/4)^2 = 0$
- Rain: Gini = $1 - (3/5)^2 - (2/5)^2 = 1 - 0.36 - 0.16 = 0.48$

The final value of Gini is:

Gini(Outlook) = $(5/14)$ x $0.48 + (4/14)$ x $0 + (5/14)$ x $0.48 = 0.171 + 0 + 0.171 = 0.342$

Where 14 is the total number of instances, 5 is the number of occurrence of each outlook, and 4 is the number of overcast values.

Temperature

The temperature can be Cool, Hot and Mild. Table 8 summarizes the decisions based on the values of the temperature feature.

Table 8. The temperature feature instances

Temperature	Yes	No	Number of instances
Hot	2	2	4
Cold	3	1	4
Mild	4	2	6

The final value of Gini is:

Gini(Outlook) = $(4/14)$ x Gini(Hot) + $(4/14)$ x Gini(Cold) + $(5/14)$ x Gini(Mild) = 0.342

Humidity and Wind

The feature Humidity is a binary feature. It can take only two values high or normal. Table 9 summarizes the decisions based on the value of the humidity feature.

Table 9. The humidity feature instances

Humidity	Yes	No	Number of instances
High	3	4	7
Normal	6	1	7

The final value of Gini according to the humidity is:

Gini(Humidity) = (7/14) x 0.489 + (7/14) x 0.244 = 0.367

Similarly, the Wind feature is a binary feature. It can take only weak and strong (see Table 10).

Table 10. The wind feature instances

Wind	Yes	No	Number of instances
Weak	6	2	8
Strong	3	3	6

The final value of Gini according to the wind is:

Gini(Wind) = (8/14) x 0.375 + (6/14) x 0.5 = 0.428

Decision Summary

Table 11 summarizes the Gini indices for the four studied features.

Table 11. The Gini indices for the features

Feature	Outlook	Temperature	Humidity	Wind
Gini Index	0.342	0.439	0.367	0.428

CART Application Discussion

The Gini index should be calculated based on temperature, humidity and wind features (Temperature, 0.2; Humidity, 0; Wind, 0.466). Thus, the humidity should be taking first in the sunny branch. Decision is always no for high humidity and sunny outlook. On the other hand, decision will always be yes for normal humidity and sunny outlook. This branch is over. Same steps are repeated for Rain branch. For weak wing, all decision is "Yes". In addition, for Strong wind, all decision is "No". Therefore, the final decision tree based on CART algorithm is represented in Figure 3C.

FUTURE RESEARCH DIRECTIONS

Because of data imperfection, it is not easy to choose a suitable method that makes the correct decision from a dataset. Generally, data sets can suffer from ambiguity, incompleteness, inconsistency, imprecision, and uncertainty. Ambiguity information is interpreted in several ways that make statements or outcomes not explicitly defined. Incomplete information means that decision-makers do not know all possible results. Inconsistent information refers to that a part of data may not be compatible or coherent with each other. However, imprecision represents the loss of exactness in the available data, and uncertainty represents the lack of sureness about information or data. Uncertainty may range from short of certainty to an almost complete lack of knowledge about an outcome or result. Thus, it is essential to study more algorithms that handle these types of imperfections in data as a future direction. Additionally, it is necessary to analyze different tools or techniques that manage the deficiency of data like possibility theory, fuzzy logic, and Dempster Shafer theory. Additionally, these techniques are compared to identify the best approach for each type of imperfection.

CONCLUSION

Making-decision process is essential in different domains, including economy, health, education, etc. It is crucial to develop techniques that help analyze stored information to take actions based on specific criteria that suit the situation. Three making-decision models are discussed in this chapter: the five whys, the fishbone diagram, and the decision trees. These techniques are based on defining the problem to solve, asking appropriate questions to reveal some facts about a possible solution, and finally, making a decision. The pros and cons of each making-decision technique are provided. Moreover, the decision tree making-decision system is elaborated in more detail through different decision tree algorithms: CART, C4.5, CHAID, and QUEST. In addition, a numerical example using the CART algorithm is described in detail.

This research received no specific grant from any funding agency in the public, commercial, or not-for-profit sectors.

REFERENCES

Amin, D. A., & Idek, S. (2019). *Analyzing The Main Factors of Students' Chronic Absenteeism Using Fishbone Diagram & Five Whys*. Academic Press.

D

Berry, M., & Linoff, G. (1999). *Mastering data mining: The art and science of customer relationship management*. John Wiley & Sons, Inc.

Bhukya, D. P., & Ramachandram, S. (2010). Decision tree induction-an approach for data classification using AVL–Tree. *International Journal of Computer and Electrical Engineering*, 2(4), 660–665. doi:10.7763/IJCEE.2010.V2.208

Breiman, L., Friedman, J. H., Olshen, R. A., & Stone, C. J. (2017). *Classification and regression trees*. Routledge. doi:10.1201/9781315139470

Denœux, T. (2011). *Introduction to belief functions*. First BFTA Spring School on Belief Functions.

Eisenfuhr, F. (2011). Decision making. *Academy of Management Review*, 19(2), 312–330. PMID:21828162

Friedman, J., Hastie, T., & Tibshirani, R. (2001). *The elements of statistical Learning* (Vol. 1). New York: Springer Series in Statistics.

Gershman, A., Meisels, A., Lüke, K. H., Rokach, L., Schclar, A., & Sturm, A. (2010). A Decision Tree Based Recommender System. *10th International Conferenceon Innovative Internet Community Systems (I2CS)–Jubilee Edition*.

Gibson, K. (2009). BusinessDictionary.com. *Reference Reviews*, 23(2), 25–26. doi:10.1108/09504120910935183

Ishikawa, K. (1968). *Guide to quality control (Japanese): Gemba no QC shuho*. Academic Press.

Jadhav, S. D., & Channe, H. P. (2016). Efficient recommendation system using decision tree classifier and collaborative filtering. *Int. Res. J. Eng. Technol*, 3(8), 2113–2118.

Kass, G. V. (1980). Anexploratory technique for investigating large quantities of categorical data. *ournal of the Royal Statistical Society: Series C. Applied Statistics*, 29(2), 119–127. doi:10.2307/2986296

Lin, N., Noe, D., & He, X. (2006). Tree-based methods and their applications. Springer Handbook of Engineering Statistics, 551-570.

Loh, W. Y., & Shih, Y. S. (1997). Split selection methods for classification trees. *Statistica Sinica*, 815–840.

Mintrom, M. (2015). Herbert A. Simon, administrative behavior: A study of decision-making processes in administrative organization. The Oxford Handbook of Classics in Public Policy and Administration, 12-21.

Ohno, T., & Bodek, N. (2019). *Toyota production system: beyond large-scale production*. Productivity Press. doi:10.4324/9780429273018

Patel, N., & Upadhyay, S. (2012). Study of various decision tree pruning methods with their empirical comparison in WEKA. *International Journal of Computers and Applications*, 60(12).

Quinlan, J. R. (2014). *C4.5: Programs for machine learning*. Elsevier.

Rajesh, P., & Karthikeyan, M. (2017). A comparative study of data mining algorithms for decision tree approaches using weka tool. *Advances in Natural and Applied Sciences*, 11(9), 230–243.

Scott, S., & Bruce, R. (1995). Decision making style: The development and assessment of a new measure. *Educational and Psychological Measurement*, 55(5), 818–831. doi:10.1177/0013164495055005017

Serrat, O. (2017). The Five Whys Technique. *Knowledge Solutions*, 307-310.

Smets, P., & Kennes, R. (1994). The transferable belief model. *Artificial Intelligence*, *66*(2), 191–234. doi:10.1016/0004-3702(94)90026-4

Whitworth, B., Van de Walle, B. A., & Turoff, M. (2000). Beyond rational decision making. *Group Decision and Negotiation*, *2000*, 1–13.

Yazdani, A. A., & Tavakkoli-Moghaddam, R. (2012). Integration of the fish bone diagram, brainstorming, and AHP method for problem solving and decision making—A case study. *International Journal of Advanced Manufacturing Technology*, *63*(5), 651–657. doi:10.100700170-012-3916-7

Yu, P. L. (1979). Second-order game problem: Decision dynamics in gaming phenomena. *Journal of Optimization Theory and Applications*, *27*(1), 147–166. doi:10.1007/BF00933332

ADDITIONAL READING

Brijain, M., Patel, R., Kushik, M. R., & Rana, K. (2014). *A survey on decision tree algorithm for classification*. Academic Press.

Chien-Liang, L., & Ching-Lung, F. (2019). Evaluation of CART, CHAID, and QUEST algorithms: A case study of construction defects in Taiwan. *Journal of Asian Architecture and Building Engineering*, *18*(6), 539–553. doi:10.1080/13467581.2019.1696203

Fülöp, J. (2005). Introduction to decision making methods. BDEI-3 Workshop, 1-15.

Ilie, G., & Ciocoiu, C. N. (2010). Application of fishbone diagram to determine the risk of an event with multiple causes. *Management Research and Practice, 2*(1), 1-20.

Myles, A. J., Feudale, R. N., Liu, Y., Woody, N. A., & Brown, S. D. (2004). An introduction to decision tree modeling. *Journal of Chemometrics: A Journal of the Chemometrics Society, 18*(6), 275-285.

Serrat, O. (2017). The five whys technique. In *Knowledge Solutions* (pp. 307–310). Springer. doi:10.1007/978-981-10-0983-9_32

Song, Y. Y., & Lu, Y. (2015). Decision tree methods: Applications for classification and prediction. *Shanghai Jingshen Yixue*, *27*(2), 130–135. doi:10.11919/10020829215044 PMID:26120265

Yu, P. L. (2013). *Multiple-criteria decision making: concepts, techniques, and extensions* (Vol. 30). Springer Science & Business Media.

KEY TERMS AND DEFINITIONS

Cart: A set of techniques for decision and prediction that build rules for predicting a value of an outcome from known values of predictor.

D

Chaid: A tool that is used to find the relationship between variables. It produces a predictive model in order to determine outcome from a given dependent variables.

Fishbone Diagram: A visual tool that identifies many causes of a particular problem.

Five Whys Technique: An interrogative and repetitive technique, usually used to inspect the cause-and-effect relationships for a particular problem.

Operational Decision: Decisions that are regulated based on the internal and external conditions. Usually this type has influence for no longer than one year.

Quest: A technique able to handle categorical variables and give unbiased feature selection.

Rational Decision: Steps and processes that cover decision-making methods to get the best solution of a problem.

Strategic Decision: A type of decision that has effect over years and even exceed lifetime of the project

Tactical Decision: A: decision type that has a medium-term impact on a company; it covers the details implementation of the director's strategy.

Decision Support Systems and Data Science

Trevor Bihl
Air Force Research Laboratory, USA

William A. Young II
Ohio University, USA

Adam Moyer
Ohio University, USA

INTRODUCTION

Decision support systems (DSSs) are a sub-set of information systems that support human decision-making through computerized systems that provide contextual information. DSSs allow decision-makers to improve their strategic planning and management control. (Yong & Taib, 2009). With the continual expansion of big data (Bihl, Young II, & Weckman, 2016), the expansion of DSSs at the consumer to enterprise level and the increasing demands of senior leaders for an "end-to-end set of information capabilities" (Shelton, 2000), DSS' need and use will continue to expand and grow. This will become an integral part of the data and information environment involving storing the data and information in a database/structure, understanding the information within a given model and presenting it to the user (user interface).

DSSs can be applied in a variety of areas to assist decision-makers as in controlling inventory, assessing consumer behavior, scheduling, forecasting, safety, planning, and risk assessment (Turban, Aronson, & Liang, 2008). From a business standpoint these systems have a wide-range of applications including political analysis (Berg & Rietz, 2003), investigating social implications (Turoff, Hiltz, Cho, Li, & Wang, 2002), medical/clinical decision making (Shaffer & Coustasse, 2012), developing educational programs (Tatnall, 2007), understanding consumer behaviors (Koufaris, Kambil, & Labarbera, 2001), cyber defense (Gutierrez et al., 2018), modeling and simulation result interpretation (Bihl et al., 2009, 2020), evaluating military decisions (Klimack, 2002), assessing environmental policies (Poch et al., 2004), forecast demand (Efendigil, Onut, & Kahraman, 2009), predict stock performance (Kuo, Chen, & Hwang, 2001), and understand power system loads (Santana, et al., 2012). DSSs can further be used as part of a simulation environment, Figure 1, wherein the DSS provides insights into the simulation of a larger system (Bihl et al., 2009). More recently, with the rise of artificial intelligence (AI) and concerns of the black-box nature of AI, DSS interfaces have become of interest to explain AI decisions and inferences (van der Waa et al., 2021; Wanner et al., 2020).

DOI: 10.4018/978-1-7998-9220-5.ch083

Figure 1. Example of a DSS for a satellite power simulation system, the SPECTTRA Viewer from (Bihl et al., 2009)

D

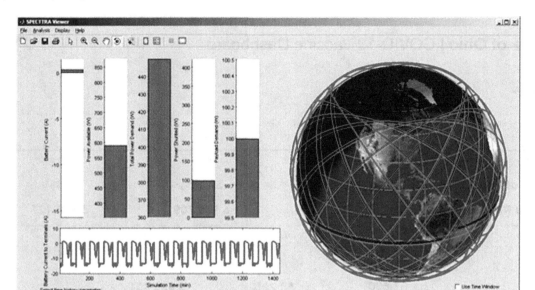

DSS usage, design and development have expanded to near ubiquity with the emergence of business analytics; includes internet listservs, web directories, and Google searches (Lankton, Speier, & Wilson, 2012). This has expanded in the 2010s to include dashboard applications which are embedded in web-pages (O'Brien & Stone, 2020). This expansion and use of DSSs became evident in the public sphere in the COVID-19 pandemic whereby a multitude of DSS systems became available online (Lan et al., 2021), an example of which is presented in Figure 2.

Though there are many types of DSS, considerable value will be gained from DSS that are based on business analytics and optimization strategies (i.e., model driven DSS). The increased application and use of DSS is attributed to the ability to rapidly collected data, perform timely data processing and analysis, continual increases in computing power, and modern software packages which reduce expertise required to developing robust mathematical models. The objective of this chapter is to build upon the work in (Bihl, Young II, & Weckman, 2014) and provide readers with a general background of DSSs, considerations, and their business applications. The intended target audience are those readers who are unfamiliar with DSSs. To provide a starting point for readers, the authors begin this chapter by describing foundational concepts that relate to DSS. The primary focus of this chapter is an overview of the importance and applications of DSSs, model-driven testing practices in the form of verifying and validating DSSs, and evaluation methods. The review of these topics is paramount to avoid the misunderstanding or misuse, of the data and the DSS which result in the reduced utility and benefit of the DSS. Finally, the authors list and describe various applications of DSS to specific data science endeavors for further reading.

Figure 2. The State of Ohio's COVID-19 Vaccine Dashboard
(State of Ohio, 2021)

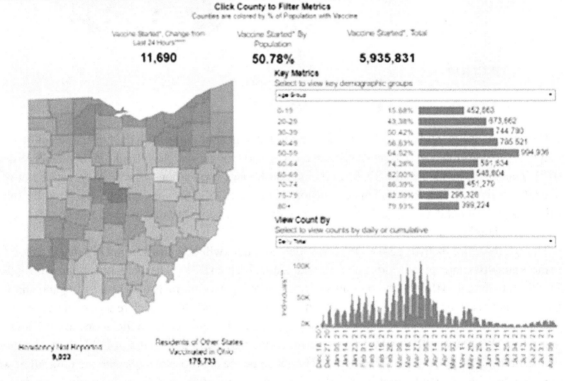

BACKGROUND

D

Development of DSS

The primary goal for DSSs is assisting decision-making through an integration of expert knowledge, data, and mathematical models (Trefil, 2001). The basic framework of a DSS starts with a data or knowledge base, a mathematical model, user interface, and the users themselves (Marakas, 1999). Two of the key components for the DSS are the mathematical models that finds non-obvious trends in data; and the users who through their expert knowledge and interaction with the DSS can understand and apply the results. Modern DSSs often utilize a combination of classical to advanced machine learning methodologies (Kuo, Chen, & Hwang, 2001). DSS development is typically iterative with models used to support decisions continuously or progressively refined until the decision-maker is confident that its components, structure, and values represent a system accurately (McGovern, Samson, & Wirth, 1994). This involves considering the problems being solved, the type of DSS used, and human-factors considerations.

Problem Types

When developing a DSS, it is important to understand the problem being solved. In DSS applications, problems are termed either: unstructured, ill-structured, semi-structured, or structured (Trefil, 2001). These are defined in *Table 1* along a continuum of from structured to unstructured. Generally, DSS find their application at semi-structured problems and below, but with the expanded need for understanding AI systems, structured problems which find a solution through AI could see the need for an eXplainable AI (XAI) DSS to explain decision making.

Table 1. DSS Problem Types (Trefil, 2001)

Type	Description
Structured	· Known system relationships · Lack system ambiguity · Not generally a focus of DSSs
Semi-structured	· Most common area of DSS application · More known and agreed upon than in ill-structured or unstructured · General agreements on either system representative data or system evaluation · Require human knowledge for final decisions
Ill-structured	· Uncertainty exists in the decision-making process
Unstructured	· No consensus on information interpretation · Experts needed to evaluate and implement a solution · Typically involves groups of varying talent and expertise to evaluate candidate solutions · Interactive approaches usually implemented · Solutions are continuously monitored and documented for future use

Taxonomies

Beyond the nature of the problem at hand, understanding the type of DSS needed based on how the user is going to interact with the system and how the system is to provide information to the user must be identified. . This can be illustrated through a few DSS taxonomies as DSSs are very broad in practice and can vary in design. Two primary taxonomies exist for DSSs (Alves, da Silva, & Varela, 2013); first, a simple DSS taxonomy created by (Haettenschwiler, 2001) relating to human interaction and described in *Table 2*; second, a taxonomy developed by (Power, 2002) describing DSSs based on use and described in *Table 3*.

Table 2. DSS Interaction Taxonomy (Haettenschwiler, 2001)

Type	Description
Active	· Provide suggestions or state solutions to complex problems
Cooperative	· Most complicated · Require the most interaction between the DSS and the human decision-makers · Iterative approach: 1. Provide example solution 2. User modifies system parameters 3. DSS refines until arrival at a compromised solution
Passive	· Not designed to determine a solution explicitly for decision-makers

Table 3. DSS Use Taxonomy (Power, 2004)

Type	Description
Communication Driven	· Provide information to groups working on shared tasks
Data Driven	· Emphasize retrieval of real-time (or historic) internal or (extra data)
Document Driven	· Integrates collected stored and processing technologies to assist a decision maker with information retrieval
Knowledge Driven	· Derive specific recommendations for decision makers from computer-driven and expert information
Model Driven	· Provide insight from mathematical models on perceived phenomena

Development of DSS interfaces

Once the problem and general approach is determined for a DSS, it is next critical in developing a useful DSS by paying attention to the user experience. This involves developing appropriate User Interfaces (UI) for Human-Machine Interaction (HMI). While largely a human factors problem, considerations and thought to the UI is critical as HMI involves the complex and cooperative interaction between humans and systems for interpretation, collaboration, and coordination (Booher, 2003) (Lohani, et al., 2017). HMI includes both technical and non-technical accommodations and often employs a user-centric approach (Booher, 2003) (Zacharias, 2019). As discussed in (Bihl & Talbert, 2020), of primary interest in HMI is reducing user workload and displaying information helpfully (Selkowitz, Larios, Lakhmani, & Chen, 2017); thus, in a DSS, this can even involve keeping advanced/mathematical options hidden and focus users to basic visualizations, as seen in (Gutierrez, Bauer, Boehmke, Saie, & Bihl, 2018). Various reviews and considerations of UI for DSS can be found in (Liang, 1987) (Permanasari, Rambli, & Dominic, 2018) (Sgarbossa, Grosse, Neumann, Battini, & Glock, 2020).

Understanding and Evaluating A DSS

D

DSS development is typically an iterative process with models used to support decisions continuously or progressively refined until the decision-maker is confident that its components, structure, UI, and values represent a system accurately (McGovern, Samson, & Wirth, 1994). This involves both vetting objective performance, such as accuracy, and subjective user considerations. Since these systems are often developed with specific metrics in mind, understanding evaluation metrics is critical. However, to address subjective aspects of the UI and the general utility, Likert-surveys are useful for DSSs (Thieme, Song, & Calantone, 2000). In addition, the information, processing models and UI must be reviewed and adjusted to ensure that the DSS continues to accurately display the information and address the continually changing data a, information, and user requirements.

LIMITATIONS AND UNCERTAINTIES

Although DSSs have some application limitations, many DSS practitioners state that DSSs positively influence or augment their decision-making processes (Hillstrom & Hillstrom, 2008). Limitations arise from disconnections between DSS developers and users, care should therefore be taken in composing a DSS (Watson, Boyd-Wilson, & Magal, 1987). Many DSSs use mathematical models known by designers, but not necessarily by end users. Likewise, decision-makers may have specific knowledge needed for decision making but lack capabilities to derive them from or develop an appropriate mathematical model. Thus, collaborative approaches are often desirable for DSS development.

While DSSs can affect decision-making processes and outcomes in a positive manner, human factors considerations should be examined when selecting indicators (Miller, Witlox, & Tribby, 2013). Additionally, many practitioners find an inadequate level of control or, conversely, are overwhelmed with options. For example, providing a wide variety of mathematical options for users inexperienced with math could induce analysis paralysis or result in faulty options. Thus, hiding algorithmic settings behind an "advanced user" setting interface could enable both novice and expert users to use a tool (Gutierrez, Bauer, Boehmke, Saie, & Bihl, 2018).

DSSs can reduce complex, difficult to interpret, information into a single numeric values that represents a system's parameters. While such simplifications are viewed as a requirement by many researchers in the field of decision support theory (Hayes, 2001), a DSS may go out of date or may inaccurately represent the data based on changes that have occurred; this could also include a DSS inadvertently being used to drive certain conclusions based on which information is being presented. An example is seen in the COVID Dashboard of Figure 2 whereby information from prior to the widespread availability of vaccines, as well as using total numbers instead of local or applicable information could drive certain conclusions by the media and political leaders.

In a practical manner, reducing a complicated system to a single level expressed in a DSS is a significant data reduction which can reduce resolution and understanding in a process. Done well, such a data reduction helps explain complex situations and provide for actionable information, for example the river level prediction DSS in Figure 3a. However, done poorly, such a data reduction can be a limitation as it can be extremely difficult for humans to process information represented by a DSS and understand its context. Issues in this area can result from the large number of internal mathematical calculations that are used to formulate a semi-structured problem; interdependencies of a system can cause issues in understanding the results or make it difficult to accurately interpret or represent the information and conclusions. Complex system behavior can become oversimplified with true system relationships and may not adequately address or provide skewed or inaccurate information. In such situations, expert opinions may be needed in order to make assumptions about unknown or dependent behavior. To account for these limitations, DSSs often supply the results of several scenarios, Figure 3b, a modeling practice known as 'what-if' analysis. This practice is exercised because decision-makers often need additional information in order to make an informed decision that involves risk based on unknown system parameters.

Figure 3. a) Example of web-based DSS for river flood stage monitoring with example of the Ohio River with corresponding b) "what-if" analysis
from (National Weather Service, 2022)

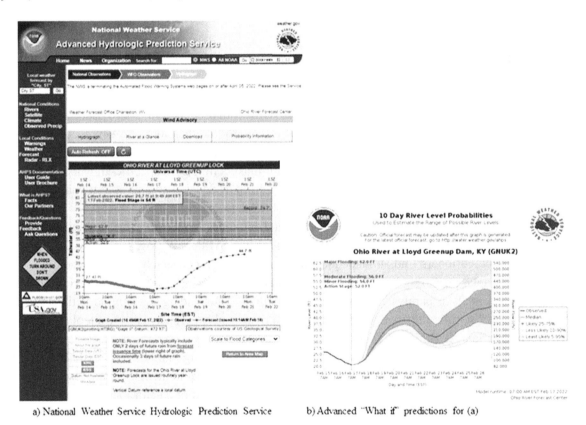

a) National Weather Service Hydrologic Prediction Service   b) Advanced "What if" predictions for (a)

Verification and Validation

In terms of model driven DSSs, verification and validation are critical steps for utility; the various differences between the two steps are described in *Table 4*. Difficulty exists since good decisions can lead to bad outcomes, while bad decisions can result in good outcomes (O'Leary, 1988). Likewise, a poorly built DSS can support decisions accurately in test cases. These situations lead to a 'black-box' relationship between DSSs, decision outcomes, and differences in cognitive biases between decision-makers and DSSs (Kydd, 1989). Additionally, difficulties in validating or verifying DSSs and usefulness can extend from difficulties in finding willing participants; DSS designers are therefore frequently both validators and verifiers, causing potential developmental issues (Papamichail & French, 2005).

Table 4. Validation versus verification

Validation	Verification	Reference
· Model adequacy	· Faithfulness to designer intentions	· (Miser & Quade, 1988)
· Often overlooked	· Common practice	· (Adelman, 1992) · (Borenstein, 1998)
· *"Building the right system"*	· *"Building the system right"*	· (O'Keefe, Balci, & Smith, 1987)

The best practice in validating and verifying DSS includes three phases: technical verification, performance/empirical validation, and subjective assessments (Papamichail & French, 2005); which are described in *Table 5*. To ensure a quality DSS, developing requirements as part of the initial development is ideal with the expectation that requirements are refined overtime along with the final forms and presentation formats being adjusted during development. With the emergence of business analytics, more emphasis is placed on validating the underlying mathematical models in model driven DSSs due to computerized business DSSs being a relatively new practice in decision science theory (Park, et al., 2001).

Table 5. Validation and verification

Type	Description	Evaluation Methods
Technical Verification	· Eliminating coding and dataset errors · Determining subsystem accuracies · Examining knowledge sources	· Compare to a known model
Performance/ Empirical Validation	· Assess system performance · Evaluate decision-maker benefits: better or faster decisions	· Goodness-of-fit
Subjective Assessments	· Establish whether the DSS met decision maker needs	· Questionnaires (Chen & Lee, 2003) (Davis, 1989)

DSS Evaluation Metrics

Various metrics exist to evaluate DSS quality; these are described in *Table 6*. Many of these metrics straight forward interpretation of the information and parameters, and do not need an example of specific application and interpretation, e.g., classification accuracy, other methods are user specific and subjective, such as parsimony. Therefore, goodness-of-fit will be examined to illustrate how models can be evaluated.

Validating DSSs can be difficult depending on the problem nature, but it is a fundamental practice in order to implement and employ DSSs in a practical manner. However, just because a model obtains an attractive numeric measurement does not mean the model is 'correct' or useful (Schunn & Wallach, 2005). Models can perform well on known or historical data but perform poorly on unseen or future data; in its worst case, a model might suffer from overfitting and describe noise rather than data. In terms of validating a DSS with goodness-of-fit metrics, it is clear that a combination of metrics is needed to evaluate the trend and location of a model's accuracy. Applications are critical as well; for example, in stock market analysis, importance is given to how a market is trending across all commodities (stocks, bonds, etc.) or a section of the market, rising or falling in value, rather than the magnitude of change for a single stock (Lakshminarayanan, Snow, & Marvel, 2008).

Table 6. DSS evaluation metrics

Metric	Description
Confidence Intervals (CI)	· Measures trends and relative magnitudes · Has a statistical advantage with large sample sizes to overcome noisy data · Do not indicate how accurately trends are modeled
Classification Accuracy	· How many observations were correctly classified
Goodness-of-fit	· How well a given distribution approaches a reference distribution
Parsimony	· Reducing model dimensionality to lowest possible · Smaller models require less computation time and memory · Accuracy may be improved by removing non-salient information (Bauer, et al., 2000) · Model may not be versatile to new data
Predictive efficiency	· Balance of accuracy and likelihood (van der Heijden, 2012)
r^2 goodness of fit (RSQ)	· noise will negatively affected RSQ · deviation from exact data location

Likert Survey Analysis

Validation can be examined through surveys or questionnaires used to measure agreement in order to quantify participant results. Likert-type questions (Likert, 1932) are common survey instruments, and quantify responses without permitting the users to express or justify their responses (Papamichail & French, 2005).To overcome this particular limitation, a combination of Likert-type and open-ended questions is highly recommended (Adelman, 1992).

Frequently, researchers using a Likert scale assign linear values from ranging from low levels of agreement to the highest level of agreement, respectively; see *Table 7*. Debate exists in the research community about interpreting and handling the Likert scale data. Some advocates suggest that data collected from a Likert survey should be treated as ordinal (Dawis, 1987) and examined using nonparametric over parametric methods (Goldstein & Hersen, 1984); others advocate an interval approach (Sisson & Stocker, 1981), assuming equal distance between the categories (Clason & Dormody, 1994). However, Likert category values are not necessarily considered equal (Mogey, 2010).

Table 7. Likert question responses and values

Response	Value
Strongly Disagree	1
Disagree	2
Neither Agree nor Disagree	3
Agree	4
Strongly Agree	5

Differences also exist in how one should investigate and report findings from Likert data (Clason & Dormody, 1994). Some suggest using only nonparametric tests, e.g., the one sample sign test (Jamieson, 2004; Gibbons, 1993); while others suggest that parametric tests, such as t-tests (Lubke & Muthen, 2004). Additionally, some researchers suggest nonparametric testing can be more straightforward because it does not imply non-observable latent values between Likert categories (Gibbons, 1993). For completeness, when Likert studies are used to validate a DSS, users should apply both parametric and nonparametric testing methods, looking for consistent results (Grace-Martin, 2008).

SOFTWARE AND MEDIUMS/TOOLS FOR DEVELOPING DSS

Tools to support the development and generation of DSS capabilities were originally developed in the 1990s to provide a way to rapidly develop and deploy models for data analysis in GUI platforms (Bhargava, Sridhar, & Herrick, 1999). A variety of methods, such as Analytica, were presented in a review by (Bhargava, Sridhar, & Herrick, 1999) in what might have been the first set of users friendly DSS applications. Since that time, available DSS tools that support data structures, linked to mathematical models and GUI interfaces in a common environment have expanded considerably. The tools now include open-source software, e.g., R, and web-based embedded analytics as well as commercial products and enterprise-level experts that can develop the individual pieces into a user interpretable dashboard for internal or external use depending on the situation. (Gutierrez et al., 2018). Table 8 includes a wide variety of software platforms, which can be divided on dichotomies of software requiring a license and those that are open-sourced, as well as a dichotomy on whether visual development or requiring coding/using functions is needed. The DSS development includes the Software tools that support the end-to-end DSS development. This includes the data access and storage as well as the development environments that enable a user to develop and visualize the results prior to providing a finalized DSS. This allows the developers opportunities to perform rapid iterations and develop the information and workflows for the finalized DSS using developed graphics libraries reducing the development time while providing a robust, polished presentation. Table 9 provides further intersection points on mediums for DSS deployment, which often determines the combination needed (Kim & Eom, 2016)

Table 8. Common software and methods to create DSS

Platform	Availability	Approach	Reference
Analytica	Licensed	Visual	(Bhargava, Sridhar, & Herrick, 1999)
JMP Journals/ Web Reports	Licensed	Visual	(Bihl T., 2017)
KNIME	Open	Visual	(Massaro et la., 2018)
Matlab	Licensed	Function/code	(Mathworks, 2010)
Microsoft Excel/Visual Basic for Applications (VBA)	Licensed	Function/code	(Goldmeier & Duggirala, 2015)
Orange	Open	Visual	(Okagbue et al., 2022)
Qlikview	Licensed	Visual	(Troyansky, Gibson, & Leichtweis, 2015)
Plotly Dash	Licensed	Visual	(Hossain et al., 2019)
R shiny	Open	Function/code	(Wickam, 2021)
Tableau	Licensed	Visual	(Murray, 2013.)

Table 9. Selected new DSS mediums

Medium	Reference
iPads	(Yuan et al., 2013)
Mobile Devices	(Gao, 2013)
Online Games	(Ben-Zvi, 2010)
Smart Phones	(Marling, et al., 2011)

FUTURE RESEARCH DIRECTIONS

Research and developing in DSS is currently expanding in multiple ways. The first is through the democratization of data and methods, e.g., (Garvey, 2018), with the advent of web-based and mobile computing and the corresponding proliferation of DSS facilitating public deliberation over AI and Big Data issues and in having rapid access to information and the ability to draw conclusions and interpret data and information independently from the original DSS. The commonplace example of such a proliferation and democratization of data through DSS is the use of COVID-19 dashboards associated with regional, national, and international pandemic responses and their use in tailorable safety decisions. Further ongoing interests in DSS is also seen in the need to explain AI-based decisions and decision-making processes for human-interpretation and accountability (van der Waa et al., 2021; Wanner et al., 2020). Finally, deploying DSS for personal applications is a further growing area of interest as seen in finance (Deb, 2019) and health (Herrmanny & Torkamaan, 2021) applications.

CONCLUSION

Development of a DSS includes broad considerations of the various types, applications, and user experience developmental considerations a user can begin to consider developing and implementing a DSS. DSSs are found in a variety of domains; it is further expected that more and more model-driven DSSs will be developed due to the expansion and intersection of open-source software and increasing research in business analytics, AI, and data science. However, many applications in these spaces are "dashboards" and not always tied to DSS developmental approaches; thus, appropriate DSS development for decision-making should involve the approaches mentioned in this chapter and include key verification and validation steps developed as part of the development process and evaluated before implementation. In some cases, DSSs are built to aid decision-makers with hard to justify (quantitatively or qualitatively) outcomes.

ACKNOWLEDGMENT

This work was cleared for public release under case AFRL-2022-0897, the views in this work are the view of the authors only and do not represent any position of the US Government, Department of Defense, US Air Force, or Air Force Research Laboratory.

REFERENCES

Adelman, L. (1992). *Evaluating decision support and expert systems*. Wiley.

Alves, C., da Silva, A., & Varela, M. (2013). Web system for supporting project management. *Computational Intelligence and Decision Making*, *61*, 203–214. doi:10.1007/978-94-007-4722-7_19

Ben-Zvi, T. (2010). The efficacy of business simulation games in creating Decision Support Systems. *Decision Support Systems*, *49*(1), 61–69. doi:10.1016/j.dss.2010.01.002

Berg, J., & Rietz, T. (2003). Prediction markets as decision support systems. *Information Systems Frontiers*, *5*(1), 79–93. doi:10.1023/A:1022002107255

Bhargava, H., Sridhar, S., & Herrick, C. (1999). Beyond spreadsheets: Tools for building decision support systems. *Computer*, *32*(3), 31–39. doi:10.1109/2.751326

Bihl, T. (2017). *Biostatistics using JMP: A practical guide*. SAS Institute.

Bihl, T., Gutierrez, R., Bauer, K., Boehmke, B., & Saie, C. (2020). Topological data analysis for enhancing embedded analytics for enterprise cyber log analysis and forensics. *Proceedings of the 53rd Hawaii International Conference on System Sciences*, 1937-1946. 10.24251/HICSS.2020.238

Bihl, T., Heidenreich, J., Allen, D., & Hunt, K. (2009). SPECTTRA: A space power system modeling and simulation tool. *7th International Energy Conversion Engineering Conference*, *4615*. 10.2514/6.2009-4615

Bihl, T., & Talbert, M. (2020). Analytics for autonomous C4ISR within e-Government: A research agenda. *Proceedings of the 53rd Hawaii International Conference on System Sciences*, 2218-2227. 10.24251/HICSS.2020.271

Bihl, T., Young, I. I. W., & Weckman, G. (2014). Decision support systems in business. Encyclopedia of business analytics and optimization, 696-707.

Bihl, T., Young, I. I. W. II, & Weckman, G. (2016). Defining, understanding, and addressing big data. *International Journal of Business Analytics*, *3*(2), 1–32. doi:10.4018/IJBAN.2016040101

Booher, H. (2003). *Handbook of human systems integration*. John Wiley & Sons. doi:10.1002/0471721174

Borenstein, D. (1998). Towards a practical method to validate decision support systems. *Decision Support Systems*, *23*(3), 2270239. doi:10.1016/S0167-9236(98)00046-3

Chen, J., & Lee, S. (2003). An exploratory cognitive DSS for strategic decision making. *Decision Support Systems*, *36*(2), 147–160. doi:10.1016/S0167-9236(02)00139-2

Clason, D., & Dormody, T. (1994). Analyzing data measured by individual Likert-type items. *Journal of Agricultural Education*, *35*(4), 31–35. doi:10.5032/jae.1994.04031

Davis, F. (1989). Perceived usefulness, perceived ease of use, and user acceptance of information technology. *Management Information Systems Quarterly*, *13*(3), 319–340. doi:10.2307/249008

Dawis, R. (1987). Scale construction. *Journal of Counseling Psychology*, *34*(48), 1–489.

Deb, S. (2019). Applying utility theory to improve performance of fuzzy decision support systems for personal financial planning. *IEEE 5th International Conference for Convergence in Technology (I2CT)*, 1-7.

Efendigil, T., Onut, S., & Kahraman, C. (2009). A decision support system for demand forecasting with artificial neural networks and neuro-fuzzy models: A comparative analysis. *Expert Systems with Applications, 36*(3.2), 6697-6707.

Eom, S. (2020). DSS, BI, and data analytics research: Current state and emerging trends (2015–2019). *International Conference on Decision Support System Technology*, 167-179. 10.1007/978-3-030-46224-6_13

Eom, S., & Kim, E. (2006). A survey of decision support system applications (1995–2001). *The Journal of the Operational Research Society, 57*(11), 1264–1278. doi:10.1057/palgrave.jors.2602140

Eom, S., Lee, S., Kim, E., & Somarajan, C. (1998). A survey of decision support system applications (1988–1994). *The Journal of the Operational Research Society, 49*(2), 109–120. doi:10.1057/palgrave.jors.2600507

Eom, S., Lee, S., & Kim, J. (1993). The intellectual structure of decision support systems (1971–1989). *Decision Support Systems, 10*(1), 19–35. doi:10.1016/0167-9236(93)90003-L

Gao, S. (2013). Mobile decision support systems research: A literature analysis. *Journal of Decision Systems, 22*(1), 10–27. doi:10.1080/12460125.2012.760268

Garvey, C. (2018). A framework for evaluating barriers to the democratization of artificial intelligence. *Thirty-Second AAAI Conference on Artificial Intelligence*. 10.1609/aaai.v32i1.12194

Gibbons, J. D. (1993). *Nonparametric statistics: An Introduction*. Sage. doi:10.4135/9781412985314

Goldmeier, J., & Duggirala, P. (2015). *Dashboards for excel*. Apress. doi:10.1007/978-1-4302-4945-0

Goldstein, G., & Hersen, M. (1984). *Handbook of psychological assessment*. Pergamon Press.

Grace-Martin, K. (2008). Can likert scale data ever be continuous? *The Analysis Factor, 3*, 1.

Gutierrez, R., Bauer, K., Boehmke, B., Saie, C., & Bihl, T. (2018). Cyber anomaly detection: Using tabulated vectors and embedded analytics for efficient data mining. *Journal of Algorithms & Computational Technology, 12*(4), 293–310. doi:10.1177/1748301818791503

Haettenschwiler, P. (2001). Neues anwenderfreundliches Konzept der Entscheidungsunterstützung. In Abstrurz im freien Fall - Anlauf zu neuen Hohenflugen (pp. 189–208). vdf Hochschulverlag.

Hayes, H. (2001). Decision support system. *Washington Technology, 16*(13).

Herrmanny, K., & Torkamaan, H. (2021). Towards a user integration framework for personal health decision support and recommender systems. *29th ACM Conference on User Modeling, Adaptation and Personalization*, 65-76. 10.1145/3450613.3456816

Hillstrom, K., & Hillstrom, L. C. (2008). *Small business encyclopedia*. Gale Group, Inc.

Hossain, S., Calloway, C., Lippa, D., Niederhut, D., & Shupe, D. (2019). Visualization of bioinformatics data with dash bio. *Proceedings of the 18th Python in Science Conference*, 126-133. 10.25080/Majora-7ddc1dd1-012

Jamieson, S. (2004). Likert scales: How to (ab)use them. *Medical Education, 38*(12), 1212–1218. doi:10.1111/j.1365-2929.2004.02012.x PMID:15566531

D

Kim, E., & Eom, S. (2016). Decision support systems application development trends (2002–2012). *International Journal of Information Systems in the Service Sector*, *8*(2), 1–13. doi:10.4018/IJISSS.2016040101

Klimack, W. K. (2002). *Robustness of multiple objective decision analysis preference functions* [PhD Dissertation]. Air Force Institute of Technology.

Koufaris, M., Kambil, A., & Labarbera, P. A. (2001). Consumer behavior in web-based commerce: An empirical study. *International Journal of Electronic Commerce*, *6*(2), 115–138. doi:10.1080/1086441 5.2001.11044233

Kuo, R. J., Chen, C. H., & Hwang, Y. C. (2001). An intelligent stock trading decision support system through integration of genetic algorithm based fuzzy neural network and artificial neural network. *Fuzzy Sets and Systems*, *118*(1), 21–45. doi:10.1016/S0165-0114(98)00399-6

Kydd, C. (1989). Cognitive biases in the use of computer-based Decision Support Systems, Omega-International. *Journal of Management Science*, *17*, 335–344.

Lakshminarayanan, S., Snow, A., & Marvel, J. (2008). An integrated stock market forecasting model using neural networks. *International Journal of Business Forecasting and Marketing Intelligence*, *1*(1).

Lan, Y., Desjardins, M., Hohl, A., & Delmelle, E. (2021). Geovisualization of COVID-19: State of the art and opportunities. *Cartographica: The International Journal for Geographic Information and Geovisualization*, *56*(1), 2–13. doi:10.3138/cart-2020-0027

Lankton, N. K., Speier, C., & Wilson, E. V. (2012). Internet-based knowledge acquisition: Task complexity and performance. *Decision Support Systems*, *53*(1), 55–65. doi:10.1016/j.dss.2011.12.004

Liang, T. (1987). User interface design for decision support systems: A self-adaptive approach. *Information & Management*, *12*(4), 181–193. doi:10.1016/0378-7206(87)90041-3

Likert, R. (1932). A technique for the measurement of attitudes. *Archives de Psychologie*, *140*(55).

Lohani, M., Stokes, C., Dashan, N., McCoy, M., Bailey, C., & Rivers, S. (2017). A framework for human-agent social systems: the role of non-technical factors in operation success. *Advances in human factors in robots and unmanned systems*, 137-148.

Lubke, G., & Muthen, B. (2004). Applying multigroup confirmatory factor models for continuous outcomes to Likert scale data complicates meaningful group comparisons. *Structural Equation Modeling*, 514-534.

Marakas, G. M. (1999). Decision support systems in the twenty-first century (P. Hall, Ed.). Academic Press.

Marling, C., Wiley, M., Cooper, T., Bunescu, R., Shubrook, J., & Schwartz, F. (2011). The 4 diabetes support system: A case study in CBR research and development. *Case-Based Reasoning Research and Development*, *6880*, 137–150. doi:10.1007/978-3-642-23291-6_12

Massaro, A., Maritati, V., Galiano, A., Birardi, V., & Pellicani, L. (2018). ESB platform integrating KNIME data mining tool oriented on Industry 4.0 based on artificial neural network predictive maintenance. *International Journal of Artificial Intelligence and Applications*, *9*(3), 1–17. doi:10.5121/ijaia.2018.9301

Mathworks. (2010). *MATLAB version 7.10.0 (R2010a)*. Natick, MA: MathWorks Inc.;.

McGovern, J., Samson, D., & Wirth, A. (1994). Using case-based reasoning for basis development in intelligent decision systems. *European Journal of Operational Research, 77*(1), 40–59. doi:10.1016/0377-2217(94)90027-2

Miller, H., Witlox, F., & Tribby, C. (2013). Developing context-sensitive livability indicators for transportation planning: A measurement framework. *Journal of Transport Geography, 26*, 51–64. doi:10.1016/j.jtrangeo.2012.08.007

Miser, H., & Quade, E. (1988). *Handbook of systems analysis: Craft issues and procedural choices.* Wiley.

Mogey, N. (2010, March 2). *So you want to use a Likert scale?* Retrieved from Learning Technology Dissemination Initiative: http://www.icbl.hw.ac.uk/ltdi/cookbook/info_likert_scale/index.html

Murray, D. (2013). *Tableau your data!: fast and easy visual analysis with tableau software.* John Wiley & Sons.

National Weather Service. (2022, Feb. 17). *National Weather Service Advanced Hydrologic Prediction Service.* Retrieved from National Weather Service: https://water.weather.gov/ahps2/hydrograph.php?gage=gnuk2&wfo=rlx

O'Brien, A., & Stone, D. (2020). Yes, you can import, analyze, and create dashboards and storyboards in Tableau! The GBI case. *Journal of Emerging Technologies in Accounting, 17*(1), 21–31. doi:10.2308/jeta-52760

O'Keefe, R., Balci, O., & Smith, E. (1987). Validating expert system performance. *IEEE Intelligent Systems & their Applications, 2*, 81–90.

O'Leary, D. (1988). Methods of validating expert systems. *Interfaces, 6*, 18.

Okagbue, H., Oguntunde, P., Adamu, P., & Adejumo, A. (2022). Unique clusters of patterns of breast cancer survivorship. *Health and Technology, 12*(2), 1–20. doi:10.100712553-021-00637-4

Papamichail, K., & French, S. (2005). Design and evaluation of an intelligent decision support system of nuclear emergencies. *Decision Support Systems, 41*(1), 84–111. doi:10.1016/j.dss.2004.04.014

Permanasari, A., Rambli, D., & Dominic, P. (2018). User interface design for a zoonosis prediction system. *Journal of Engineering Science and Technology, 13*(2), 347–360.

Poch, M., Cornas, J., Rodriguez-Roda, I., Sanchez-Marre, M., & Cortes, U. (2004). Designing and building real environmental decision support systesm. *Environmental Modelling & Software, 19*(9), 857–873. doi:10.1016/j.envsoft.2003.03.007

Power, D. (2002). *Decision support systems: Concepts and resources for managers.* Quorum Books.

Power, D. (2004). Retrieved 2010, from Free decision support systems glossary: http://dssresources.com/glossary

Santana, A. L., Conde, G. B., Rego, L. P., Rocha, C. A., Cardoso, D. L., Costa, J. C., Bezerra, U. H., & Frances, C. R. (2012). PREDICT – Decision support system for load forecasting and inference: A new undertaking for Brazilian power suppliers. *International Journal of Electrical Power & Energy Systems, 38*(1), 33–45. doi:10.1016/j.ijepes.2011.12.018

D

Schunn, C. D., & Wallach, D. (2005). Evaluating goodness-of-fit in comparison of models to data. In Psychologie der Kognition (pp. 115-154). Reden and Vorträge anlässlich der Emeritierung.

Selkowitz, A., Larios, C., Lakhmani, S., & Chen, J. (2017). Displaying information to support transparency for autonomous platforms. *Advances in Human Factors in Robots and Unmanned Systems*, 161-173.

Sgarbossa, F., Grosse, E., Neumann, W., Battini, D., & Glock, C. (2020). Human factors in production and logistics systems of the future. *Annual Reviews in Control, 49,* 295-305.

Shaffer, J., & Coustasse, A. (2012). Computer physician order entry and clinical decision support systems: Benefits and concerns. *Business and Health Administration Association Annual Conference*, 316-323.

Shelton, H. H. (2000). *Joint vision 2020*. The Pentagon.

Sisson, D., & Stocker, H. (1981). Analyzing and interpreting Likert-type survey data. *Delta Pi Epsilon Journal, 31*(2), 81–85.

State of Ohio. (2021, Aug. 17). *COVID-19 Vaccine Dashboard*. Retrieved from https://coronavirus.ohio.gov/wps/portal/gov/covid-19/dashboards/overview

Tatnall, A. (2007). Experiences in building and using decision support systems in postgraduate university courses. *Interdisciplinary Journal of Information, Knowledge, and Management, 2.*

Thieme, J., Song, M., & Calantone, R. (2000). Artificial neural network decision support systems for new product development project selection. *JMR, Journal of Marketing Research, 37*(4), 499–507. doi:10.1509/jmkr.37.4.499.18790

Trefil, J. (2001). *The encyclopedia of science and technology*. Routledge.

Troyansky, O., Gibson, T., & Leichtweis, C. (2015). *QlikView your business: an expert guide to business discovery with QlikView and Qlik Sense*. John Wiley & Sons. doi:10.1002/9781119182375

Turban, E., Aronson, J., & Liang, T. (2008). *Decision support systems and intelligent systems*. Prentice Hall.

Turoff, M., Hiltz, S., Cho, H., Li, Z., & Wang, Y. (2002). Social decision support systems (SDSS). *Proceedings of the 35th Annual Hawaii International Conference on System Sciences*, 81-90. 10.1109/HICSS.2002.993863

van der Heijden, H. (2012). Decision support for selecting optimal logistic regression models. *Expert Systems with Applications, 39*(10), 8573–8583. doi:10.1016/j.eswa.2012.01.168

van der Waa, J., Nieuwburg, E., Cremers, A., & Neerincx, M. (2021). Evaluating XAI: A comparison of rule-based and example-based explanations. *Artificial Intelligence, 291*, 291. doi:10.1016/j.artint.2020.103404

Wanner, J., Herm, L., Heinrich, K., Janiesch, C., & Zschech, P. (2020). *White, grey, black: Effects of XAI augmentation on the confidence in AI-based decision support systems*. ICIS.

Watson, H. J., Boyd-Wilson, T., & Magal, S. R. (1987). The evaluation of DSS groups. *Information & Management, 12*(2), 79–86. doi:10.1016/0378-7206(87)90063-2

Wickam, H. (2021). *Mastering Shiny*. O'Reilly Media.

Yong, C. C., & Taib, S. M. (2009). Designing a decision support system model for stock investment strategy. *Proceedings of the World Congress on Engineering and Computer Science 2009, 1.*

Yuan, M., Finley, G., Long, J., Mills, C., & Johnson, R. (2013). Evaluation of user interface and workflow design of a bedside nursing clinical decision support system. *Interactive Journal of Medical Research, 2*(1), e4. doi:10.2196/ijmr.2402 PMID:23612350

Zacharias, G. L. (2019). Autonomous horizons the way forward. Air University Press.

KEY TERMS AND DEFINITIONS

Active DSS: One explicitly recommending solutions to a decision maker.

Communication-Driven DSS: One aiding a decision maker with decisions or tasks when there are many individuals working together.

Cooperative DSS: One designed in an iterative manner where recommended solutions are refined by decision makers and sent back for validation. The process is repeated until arriving at a consolidated solution.

Data-Driven DSS: One utilizing data with access being either single or a variety of databases.

Document-Driven DSS: One designed to manage, retrieve, and summarize information from various electronic file formats.

Knowledge-Driven DSS: One designed to leverage expert knowledge on particular decision-making categories; decisions are supported by facts, rules, and procedures based on similar problem structures.

Model-Driven DSS: A DSS utilizing mathematical models built from probability, statistics, and machine learning algorithms and strategies. These DSS manipulate data to assist decision makers.

Passive DSS: One that does not explicitly recommend solutions, but aids a decision maker in the decision making process.

Structured Problems: A problem type with very well-known system relationships. In general, decisions made for structured problems are well defined and documented, requiring no expert knowledge.

Unstructured Problems: A problem type where system relationships are not known; in general, decisions made for unstructured problems are not defined and require expert knowledge.

Decision–Making Approaches for Airport Surrounding Traffic Management

Xiangfen Kong
Civil Aviation University of China, China

Peng Zhao
https://orcid.org/0000-0003-1458-8266
INTELLIGENTRABBIT LLC, USA

INTRODUCTION

The experienced imbalance between demand and supply for airport services forces all air travelers and providers to rethink airport surrounding capacity and its utilization and management of experienced capacity shortages. Although the global airline industry is affected by the Covid-19 pandemic, the issue of airport ground congestion has not been fundamentally solved. The recovery of the air traveling market is expected in the near future, thereby emerging again into the forefront road capacity saturation around major airports. Such a situation triggers considerable costs and negative impacts reflected upon the efficiency of airport managements and the quality of the surrounding road operations. From the public authority's perspective, policy makers and city operators search for optimal airport efficiency and expansion of airport infrastructure to address issues of saturated airport surrounding roads towards implementing environment-friendly solutions and efficiently operational initiatives.

The assessment of the airport landside performance forces the usage of complex modeling and decision support systems in order to extract the manifold measures of the airport operational matrix, including capacity, delays, safety, security, and cost-efficiency, along with their trade-offs. It is important for airport managers and public authorities to consider the airport surrounding traffic congestion involved through the entire airport system. Although existing experiences in models and tools are rich for assessing the operational performance of a variety of airport components, limited elements of the airport operational decision-making process are modeling and formulating. Little is known for modeling traffic congestions and airport landside road system designs. A well-designed decision support system provides an integrated and intelligent view of landside operations and analytics for airport managers and policymakers in terms of the evidence-based decision-making process towards trade-offs among multiple airport operational measures. Existing tools or platforms lack modeling landside capabilities supporting problems and data-driven approaches to airport surrounding traffic management and planning. Advanced landside modeling for decision support of the road traffic prediction should be developed with concentrated on integrating traffic engineering architectures and data-driven approaches.

In response to the demand of the automatic decision-making process for airport surround traffic management, a survey study of the decision support system will be proposed in this chapter, concentrated on the operational management and planning of airport landside traffic congestions. Such a study provides a comprehensive insight to empower decision makers and analysts to discover the road congestion pattern of the landside of the airport in a problem-oriented manner by monitoring the spectrum of the traffic pattern surrounding the airport. The objective of this chapter is to investigate a variety of data-driven

DOI: 10.4018/978-1-7998-9220-5.ch084

approaches that can be applied in constructing the automatic decision-making system by illustrating vast state-of-the-art techniques, such as statistical modeling, data mining, machine learning, and deep learning.

BACKGROUND

Airport operational management and planning assessments are the subject of extensive studies in the field of both airside and landside modeling and optimization, thereby a huge number of existing models and simulations have been made available to both research domains and industrial applications. Existing studies and practices cover a broad range of predictive models for different aspects of decision-making process and multiple categories of airport management operations, both airside and landside, throughout elements and entities involved in the airport flow processes (Zografos et al., 2013; Ravizza et al., 2014; Bruno et al., 2019). However, existing studies about the decision support system are limited in airport surrounding traffic management.

Existing studies in this field mainly focus on investigating the capability of infrastructures in airport surrounding management, e.g., an underground rapid transport system (URTS) has been examined for the international airport hubs (Liu & Liao, 2018). On the other hand, most studies are concentrated on discussing various factors causing traffic congestion. Earlier studies focused on people-centered integrated transport hub (Li & Loo, 2016), whereas most recent studies intensively aim on urban road networks with considering the cascading failure of a complex network system (Wang et al., 2020; Tian et al., 2021; Yin et al., 2021), as the airport surrounding traffic problem is one of the most critical parts in urban traffic system. However, such approaches and investigations are not sufficient for the construction of the automatic decision-making framework in airport surrounding traffic systems as they have not yet incorporated how such a system makes decisions about future or otherwise unknown events.

Predictive analysis, on the other hand, can be applied to simulate future or unknown conditions based on analyzing current and historical facts by encompassing a variety of cutting-edge techniques, such as statistical modeling, data mining, machine learning, and deep learning. With the development of data-driven technologies, big data approaches have also been incorporated in traffic engineering in terms of predicting the traffic congestion in urban road systems (Salazar-Carrillo et al., 2021), whereas similar studies are rare for the airport surrounding traffic management, in particular, traffic congestion predictions. Therefore, a huge gap between the airport surrounding traffic management and big data analytics is significant, along with the discussions in decision-making processes.

FOCUS OF THE ARTICLE

To fill up such a gap, this chapter designed to investigate the automatic decision support system in terms of analyzing airport surrounding road networks. Several decision-making approaches are illustrated and examined based on a board range of data-driven methods, including data mining, machine learning, and deep learning. Each method has been investigated by providing a survey study that involves the most recent and comprehensive understanding in traffic engineering. As a specific problem in urban traffic congestions, airport surrounding traffic management can be referenced from the similar studies in urban traffic congestion. The proposed study can be used in improving the airport services in terms of the operational efficiency and the airport landside management, further supporting the construction of the smart airport.

SOLUTIONS AND RECOMMENDATIONS

D

Data Mining

Data mining is the intersection of statistical modeling, predictive analysis, and database management, in which complex patterns can be extracted and discovered through processing data in large data pools. In traffic engineering research domains, current studies using data mining approaches for decision-making purposes mainly focus on two methods, including statistical modeling and clustering. Statistical modeling is a mathematical method that is commonly applied in predicting traffic congestions by incorporating a variety of probabilistic reasoning approaches, including Markov chains, stochastic processes, and fuzzy logic. Such methods and models relay on the probabilistic reasoning, which has been widely used to deal with uncertainty management and predictive analysis. Other probabilistic models, such as Kalman filter and temporal association rules, have also been applied in predicting traffic congestions, while such methods are discussed by few studies in this field. Common-used models are Hidden Markov Model (HMM), Gaussian probability models, Bayesian methods, and fuzzy logic models. On the other hand, clustering has been widely used in traffic engineering in terms of unsupervised learning tasks. Most studies apply clustering in the data acquisition stage with a fine-tuned model training process.

HMM has been widely used in traffic pattern recognition, of which most of them are focusing on using Pearson Correlation Coefficient for uncovering the relationships between parameters (Zaki et al., 2020). HMM can be used in selecting the best predictors among multiple models with optimal state transition via four major stages, such as initialization, recursion, termination, and backtracking, as illustrated in the adaptive neuron-fuzzy inference system (ANFIS) proposed by Zaki et al. (2019), in which the Viterbi model has been applied to analyze stepwise probabilities through the current state to the previous one. Moreover, the discretized multiple symbol HMM can be applied in traffic prediction for different road segments throughout hidden states of the model, which analyze label results in the next hidden state (Mishra et al., 2016). Besides, HMM is powerful in map-marching, which belongs to the traffic engineering domain using probe vehicle data. Such the ideology can be implemented for mapping the trajectory of observed GPS data points in nearby transportation systems, as introduced by Sun et al. (2019). A set of candidate points has been chosen as the hidden states in HMM, whereas the observation points that are closer to the selected points will obtain the higher transition probability. Despite the advantage of applied HMM in term of the short-term traffic pattern prediction, a significant mismatch for long-term data and similar road systems has been found, thereby the model accuracy may be decreased. Nevertheless, HMM is still applicable for map matching and other transport sectors, such as speed prediction and traffic flow analysis, along with the GPS tracking technology in the era of big data.

One of the most successful stochastic processes for predicting traffic congestions is the Gaussian process, which has been widely used for most regression problems. Existing studies suggest that the Gaussian distribution model can be applied in traffic volume prediction, road safety estimation, and traffic speed analysis using GPS data. The Gaussian distribution model can be implemented for predicting congestion conditions through the decision-making model based on statistical learning. Such the ideology has been employed to calculate the congestion score that is estimated by multiple Gaussian probability models (Yang, 2013). Selecting right mean and variance measurements of Gaussian distribution plays an important role in estimating the probability of the traffic condition distribution, whereas the log-likelihood expectation can be applied to generate the parameters with the maximization (Zhu et al., 2019). Alternatively, Bayesian methods have been widely used as a natural tool for solving congestion problems, such as road uncertainty and traffic complexity, through the directed graphical approach for representing conditional independencies between random variables. The Bayesian model has also been applied to determine congestion factors via initializing and assessing multiple road conditions ranking and prioritizing on different traffic sections (Kim & Wang, 2016), while more complicated models, such as ensemble algorithms and Bayesian networks, have been proposed with the better performance in traffic flow prediction and parameter estimation for signalized intersections (Zhu et al., 2016; Wang et al., 2020).

Fuzzy logic is a common-used method in traffic congestion problems as the traffic data becomes more complicated and nonlinear. A fuzzy logic model usually consists of multiple fuzzy sets based on membership functions, which are determined by different types of the codification shape, including triangular, trapezoidal, and Gaussian function. One of the most popular fuzzy logic methods in traffic engineering is the fuzzy rule-based system, which contains multiple if-then rules generated by input variables associated with outputs. Such rules can make decisions for transforming the real-world traffic system into simple rules combined with the relations among multiple traffic conditions. A broad range of fuzzy models, such as Takagi-Sugeno-Kang model, Mamdani-type model, and Ant Colony Optimization algorithm, have been applied in measuring congestion severity (Cao & Wang, 2019), estimating heterogeneous parameters (Adetiloye & Awasthi, 2019), predicting traffic congestion in real-time (Daissaoui et al., 2015), controlling traffic signals (Collotta et al., 2015), etc., along with the discussions on smart city. Although fuzzy logic models can obtain rule-based outcomes other than binary classifications, few studies have provided logical reasoning on choosing the membership function, thereby may not offer the comprehensive interpretability for traffic congestions.

K-means, fuzzy C-means, and density-based spatial clustering are three popular algorithms in traffic congestion analysis (Chen et al., 2019; He et al., 2019; Wen et al., 2019). In traffic engineering research, datasets are usually large and noisy with missing values and broken data, thereby may not be able to determine the sample distribution. Clustering algorithms can be employed to deal with such limitations by incorporating unsupervised learning, nondeterministic clustering, and data mining. Some clustering algorithms, such as C-means and K-means, require a predefined number of original cluster centers, whereas others (i.e., density-based spatial clustering) can automatically create arbitrary cluster shapes through grouping multiple features of variables. However, several limitations constrain the application of clustering algorithms in traffic congestion predictions. Such models become computationally expensive when the data size is increasing. Besides, the unknown cluster number leads the difficulty in predefining the original centers. On the other hand, clustering algorithms can be used to address outliers without known distributions, therefore, such models are usually applied before the predictive modeling in terms of data preprocessing, feature extraction, and noise filtering, along with additional approaches, such as principal component analysis (PCA), fuzzy logic, and trial/error integration.

Machine Learning

With the development of artificial intelligence, machine learning algorithms have been applied in traffic engineering in the form of computational methods for predicting traffic congestions. A typical study using machine learning is to extract traffic features from multiple input variables, followed by implementing multiple supervised learning models, such as decision tree (DT), support vector machine (SVM), K-nearest neighbor (K-NN), artificial neural network (ANN), etc., whereas the optimal model can be determined by evaluating the model performance matrix per algorithm (Asencio-Cortés et al., 2016). However, such models perform less sensitivity with continuous observations when the dataset has temporal features associated with the time-series data. Regression models, on the other hand, can be applied to solve the problem by incorporating coefficient estimations, auto-regressors, and moving average terms. Therefore, current approaches with machine learning can be split up into two main categories, including the binary classification and the time-series forecasting.

Classical machine learning models can be used to deal with the binary classification problems in terms of traffic congestion prediction, traffic pattern recognition, human-based factor analysis, and ecological environment feature extraction. DT is one of the simplest classification models that can be trained with multiple traffic-related features, such as weather conditions, road conditions, travel times, holiday factors, etc. The idea of using DT is to generate classification rules for interpreting the traffic system by formatting input factors into a tree structure. Common-used DT models, such as CART, C4.5, and random forest, have been applied in predicting traffic congestions (Chen et al., 2019; Asencio-Cortés et al., 2016; Liu & Wu, 2017). The classification results are usually binary in DT, whereas it may not be adoptable when the decision-making aims on the connection level. Moreover, the model performance measures are significantly reduced when the model is trained with nonlinear data and geographical factors (Zhao et al., 2016; Hipps et al., 2017). To deal with such a problem, SVM has been applied in predictive analysis as the model maps the nonlinearity into a higher dimensional linear space where data can be trained linearly. Such a property can be employed in traffic pattern recognition and congestion prediction, e.g., the travel speed prediction with real-time traffic congestion patterns (Tseng et al., 2018), the sustainable system design of transportation urban and ecological environment (Lu & Liu, 2018), and the spatial-temporal analysis for short-term traffic flow prediction (Feng, et al., 2018). Similar studies have been proposed by using alternative machine learning models, such as KNN and ANN, which also make contributions in a range of decision-making processes for a smart traffic system, including traffic congestion prediction (Nadeem & Fowdur, 2018), driver behavior analysis (de Naurois et al., 2019), and vehicle noise control (Nourani et al., 2020).

Regression models, on the other hand, are a set of supervised learning algorithms, which predict real numbers of output values from numerical inputs. Common-used regression model include multiple linear regression (MLR), LASSO regression, exponential regression analysis (ERA), etc. Such models have been applied in traffic engineering, while the model training process usually requires a large volume of data inputs and a higher level of variety of variables, thereby may need to implement efficient tools for computational demands and data flows. Existing studies suggest that big data tools can be one of the most effective solutions for data processing and model training, i.e., predicting traffic congestion with weather information by using MLR with data processing in Hadoop (Lee et al., 2015), estimating origin-destination-based congestion measures using ERA in IBM SPSS (Jain et al., 2017), and predicting peak hour congestion by recognizing electricity usage patterns using LASSO (Zhang & Qian, 2018). Besides, the autoregressive integrated moving average (ARIMA) model is one of the most commonly used regression models in dealing with time-series problems, therefore, such a model can also be applied in predicting traffic congestions with data in time series (Alghamdi et al., 2019).

Deep Learning

From last few years, deep learning has been widely applied in traffic engineering research due to its advantages, such as processing nonlinearity, extracting features without prior information, dealing with complex traffic data with limited inputs etc. Instead of a two-step learning process in machine learning, deep learning integrates feature extraction and model training together, thereby making the congestion prediction easier. Typical deep learning algorithms that have been applied in traffic system analysis include convolutional neural network (CNN), recurrent neural network (RNN), and long short-term memory (LSTM).

A CNN structure consists of five major components, including the input layer, convolutional layers, a max-pooling layer, fully connected layers, and the output layer. CNN has the excellent performance in image recognition, whereas traffic data should be transformed into a 2-dimensional format for model training. Therefore, most studies are analyzing traffic patterns as same as image recognitions with fine-tuning the model structure (Ma et al., 2017), while others apply the partial structure without the pooling layer to deal with the historical traffic data through extracting congestion features of the last time slot in the matrix (Chen et al., 2018). Instead of a 2-dimensional data processing, extra attributes, such as temporal-spatial factors, have been incorporated to produce a 3-dimensional input, which can be trained through convolution-pooling layers (Zhu et al., 2019). Similarly, the raw data has been preprocessed by operating a spatiotemporal feature selection for traffic flow sequence data using convolutional and max-pooling layers (Zhang et al., 2019). Recent studies suggest that CNN performs very well with large scale inputs due to the affective feature extraction and less time on model training, thereby can be applied in most predictive analysis of traffic congestion problems (Ke et al., 2020).

With the evolution of data collection systems and the development of big data analytics, the sequential traffic data is commonly demanded for the decision-making process in traffic engineering. RNN can be applied in dealing with such the data by connecting the nearby neurons. Particularly, as a branch of RNN, LSTM works better since the hidden layer consists of a memory block within multiple fully connected layers, which can store and process the information flow. Earlier studies indicate that RNN can be applied with other models, such as restricted Boltzman machines, for spatiotemporal congestion prediction tasks with vast parameter estimations of the traffic system (Ma et al., 2015), while LSTM and gated recurrent unit (GRU) models have been widely applied by incorporating the memory block characteristics, the unit state, and the hidden state (Sun et al., 2019). The research trend in this field goes different directions, including the fine-tuned LSTM (Lee et al., 2019), the hybrid convolutional LSTM (Di et al., 2019), and LSTM-CNN (Li et al., 2020).

FUTURE RESEARCH DIRECTIONS

Research in airport surrounding traffic system is promising and ongoing, thereby vast potential directions can be discussed in future research. Improving the model performance is obviously one of the most significant directions in any decision-making studies. Numerous predictive analytical approaches have been proposed in forecasting traffic congestions, while such models can be improved by enlarging the sample size for model training. Besides, extracting additional features related to predicting traffic congestions may provide insightful orientations towards the newly proposed decision-making models, in particular, in the age of big data. Such features can be collected from vast information steams and data flows, e.g., using data from social media and smart phones. Nevertheless, related works in airport surrounding traffic management may start from scratch, thereby such discussions can only be referenced for guiding the next stage of the research.

CONCLUSION

Airport surrounding traffic congestion is getting more attention with the development of major cities around would. Automatic decision-making systems allow authorities and airport managers to make plans and take actions in terms of analyzing traffic patterns. Multiple choices are available for research communities and industrial professionals to develop cutting-edge prediction models using artificial intelligence and big data analytics. Despite the effectiveness of using data mining approaches, statistical inference and clustering become more complex while various features that may affect traffic flow may need to consider. Machine learning and deep learning have been widely applied in this domain due to the higher model performance, whereas alternative algorithms are not yet to be investigated. Therefore, opportunities for related works still prevail in terms of the smart airport initiative.

REFERENCES

Adetiloye, T., & Awasthi, A. (2019). Multimodal big data fusion for traffic congestion prediction. In *Multimodal Analytics for Next-Generation Big Data Technologies and Applications* (pp. 319–335). Springer. doi:10.1007/978-3-319-97598-6_13

Alghamdi, T., Elgazzar, K., Bayoumi, M., Sharaf, T., & Shah, S. (2019, June). Forecasting traffic congestion using ARIMA modeling. In 2019 15th International Wireless Communications & Mobile Computing Conference (IWCMC) (pp. 1227-1232). IEEE. doi:10.1109/IWCMC.2019.8766698

Asencio-Cortés, G., Florido, E., Troncoso, A., & Martínez-Álvarez, F. (2016). A novel methodology to predict urban traffic congestion with ensemble learning. *Soft Computing*, *20*(11), 4205–4216. doi:10.100700500-016-2288-6

Bruno, G., Diglio, A., Genovese, A., & Piccolo, C. (2019). A decision support system to improve performances of airport check-in services. *Soft Computing*, *23*(9), 2877–2886. doi:10.100700500-018-3301-z

Cao, W., & Wang, J. (2019, February). Research on traffic flow congestion based on Mamdani fuzzy system. In. AIP Conference Proceedings: Vol. 2073. *No. 1* (p. 020101). AIP Publishing LLC. doi:10.1063/1.5090755

Chen, M., Yu, X., & Liu, Y. (2018). PCNN: Deep convolutional networks for short-term traffic congestion prediction. *IEEE Transactions on Intelligent Transportation Systems*, *19*(11), 3550–3559. doi:10.1109/TITS.2018.2835523

Chen, Z., Jiang, Y., & Sun, D. (2019). Discrimination and prediction of traffic congestion states of urban road network based on spatio-temporal correlation. *IEEE Access: Practical Innovations, Open Solutions*, *8*, 3330–3342. doi:10.1109/ACCESS.2019.2959125

Collotta, M., Bello, L. L., & Pau, G. (2015). A novel approach for dynamic traffic lights management based on Wireless Sensor Networks and multiple fuzzy logic controllers. *Expert Systems with Applications*, *42*(13), 5403–5415. doi:10.1016/j.eswa.2015.02.011

Daissaoui, A., Boulmakoul, A., & Habbas, Z. (2015, December). First specifications of urban traffic-congestion forecasting models. In *2015 27th International Conference on Microelectronics (ICM)* (pp. 249-252). IEEE. 10.1109/ICM.2015.7438035 de Naurois, C. J., Bourdin, C., Stratulat, A., Diaz, E., & Vercher, J. L. (2019). Detection and prediction of driver drowsiness using artificial neural network models. *Accident; Analysis and Prevention*, *126*, 95–104. doi:10.1016/j.aap.2017.11.038 PMID:29203032

Di, X., Xiao, Y., Zhu, C., Deng, Y., Zhao, Q., & Rao, W. (2019, June). Traffic congestion prediction by spatiotemporal propagation patterns. In *2019 20th IEEE International Conference on Mobile Data Management (MDM)* (pp. 298-303). IEEE. 10.1109/MDM.2019.00-45

Feng, X., Ling, X., Zheng, H., Chen, Z., & Xu, Y. (2018). Adaptive multi-kernel SVM with spatial–temporal correlation for short-term traffic flow prediction. *IEEE Transactions on Intelligent Transportation Systems*, *20*(6), 2001–2013. doi:10.1109/TITS.2018.2854913

He, Z., Qi, G., Lu, L., & Chen, Y. (2019). Network-wide identification of turn-level intersection congestion using only low-frequency probe vehicle data. *Transportation Research Part C, Emerging Technologies*, *108*, 320–339. doi:10.1016/j.trc.2019.10.001

Hipps, R., Chopra, T., Zhao, P., Kwartler, E., & Jaume, S. (2017). Geospatial analytics to improve the safety of autonomous vehicles. *International Journal of Knowledge-Based Organizations*, *7*(3), 40–51. doi:10.4018/IJKBO.2017070104

Jain, S., Jain, S. S., & Jain, G. (2017). Traffic congestion modelling based on origin and destination. *Procedia Engineering*, *187*, 442–450. doi:10.1016/j.proeng.2017.04.398

Ke, R., Li, W., Cui, Z., & Wang, Y. (2020). Two-stream multi-channel convolutional neural network for multi-lane traffic speed prediction considering traffic volume impact. *Transportation Research Record: Journal of the Transportation Research Board*, *2674*(4), 459–470. doi:10.1177/0361198120911052

Kim, J., & Wang, G. (2016). Diagnosis and prediction of traffic congestion on urban road networks using Bayesian networks. *Transportation Research Record: Journal of the Transportation Research Board*, *2595*(1), 108–118. doi:10.3141/2595-12

Lee, C., Kim, Y., Jin, S., Kim, D., Maciejewski, R., Ebert, D., & Ko, S. (2019). A visual analytics system for exploring, monitoring, and forecasting road traffic congestion. *IEEE Transactions on Visualization and Computer Graphics*, *26*(11), 3133–3146. doi:10.1109/TVCG.2019.2922597 PMID:31199260

Lee, J., Hong, B., Lee, K., & Jang, Y. J. (2015, December). A prediction model of traffic congestion using weather data. In *2015 IEEE International Conference on Data Science and Data Intensive Systems* (pp. 81-88). IEEE. 10.1109/DSDIS.2015.96

Li, L., & Loo, B. P. (2016). Towards people-centered integrated transport: A case study of Shanghai Hongqiao Comprehensive Transport Hub. *Cities (London, England)*, *58*, 50–58. doi:10.1016/j.cities.2016.05.003

Li, P., Abdel-Aty, M., & Yuan, J. (2020). Real-time crash risk prediction on arterials based on LSTM-CNN. *Accident; Analysis and Prevention*, *135*, 105371. doi:10.1016/j.aap.2019.105371 PMID:31783334

Liu, M. B., & Liao, S. M. (2018). A case study on the underground rapid transport system (URTS) for the international airport hubs: Planning, application and lessons learnt. *Tunnelling and Underground Space Technology*, *80*, 114–122. doi:10.1016/j.tust.2018.06.004

D

Liu, Y., & Wu, H. (2017, December). Prediction of road traffic congestion based on random forest. In *2017 10th International Symposium on Computational Intelligence and Design (ISCID)* (Vol. 2, pp. 361-364). IEEE. 10.1109/ISCID.2017.216

Lu, S., & Liu, Y. (2018). Evaluation system for the sustainable development of urban transportation and ecological environment based on SVM. *Journal of Intelligent & Fuzzy Systems*, *34*(2), 831–838. doi:10.3233/JIFS-169376

Ma, X., Dai, Z., He, Z., Ma, J., Wang, Y., & Wang, Y. (2017). Learning traffic as images: A deep convolutional neural network for large-scale transportation network speed prediction. *Sensors (Basel)*, *17*(4), 818. doi:10.339017040818 PMID:28394270

Ma, X., Yu, H., Wang, Y., & Wang, Y. (2015). Large-scale transportation network congestion evolution prediction using deep learning theory. *PLoS One*, *10*(3), e0119044. doi:10.1371/journal.pone.0119044 PMID:25780910

Mishra, P., Hadfi, R., & Ito, T. (2016, August). Adaptive model for traffic congestion prediction. In *International Conference on Industrial, Engineering and Other Applications of Applied Intelligent Systems* (pp. 782-793). Springer.

Nadeem, K. M., & Fowdur, T. P. (2018). Performance analysis of a real-time adaptive prediction algorithm for traffic congestion. *Journal of Information and Communication Technology*, *17*(3), 493–511. doi:10.32890/jict2018.17.3.5

Nourani, V., Gökçekuş, H., Umar, I. K., & Najafi, H. (2020). An emotional artificial neural network for prediction of vehicular traffic noise. *The Science of the Total Environment*, *707*, 136134. doi:10.1016/j.scitotenv.2019.136134 PMID:31874402

Ravizza, S., Atkin, J. A., & Burke, E. K. (2014). A more realistic approach for airport ground movement optimisation with stand holding. *Journal of Scheduling*, *17*(5), 507–520. doi:10.100710951-013-0323-3

Salazar-Carrillo, J., Torres-Ruiz, M., Davis, C. A. Jr, Quintero, R., Moreno-Ibarra, M., & Guzmán, G. (2021). Traffic congestion analysis based on a web-GIS and data mining of traffic events from Twitter. *Sensors (Basel)*, *21*(9), 2964. doi:10.339021092964 PMID:33922627

Sun, S., Chen, J., & Sun, J. (2019). Traffic congestion prediction based on GPS trajectory data. *International Journal of Distributed Sensor Networks*, *15*(5). doi:10.1177/1550147719847440

Tian, Y., Liu, X., Li, Z., Tang, S., Shang, C., & Wei, L. (2021). Identification of critical links in urban road network considering cascading failures. *Mathematical Problems in Engineering*, *2021*, 2021. doi:10.1155/2021/9994347

Tseng, F. H., Hsueh, J. H., Tseng, C. W., Yang, Y. T., Chao, H. C., & Chou, L. D. (2018). Congestion prediction with big data for real-time highway traffic. *IEEE Access: Practical Innovations, Open Solutions*, *6*, 57311–57323. doi:10.1109/ACCESS.2018.2873569

Wang, P., Lai, J., Huang, Z., Tan, Q., & Lin, T. (2020). Estimating traffic flow in large road networks based on multi-source traffic data. *IEEE Transactions on Intelligent Transportation Systems*.

Wang, S., Huang, W., & Lo, H. K. (2020). Combining shockwave analysis and Bayesian Network for traffic parameter estimation at signalized intersections considering queue spillback. *Transportation Research Part C, Emerging Technologies*, *120*, 102807. doi:10.1016/j.trc.2020.102807

Wen, F., Zhang, G., Sun, L., Wang, X., & Xu, X. (2019). A hybrid temporal association rules mining method for traffic congestion prediction. *Computers & Industrial Engineering*, *130*, 779–787. doi:10.1016/j.cie.2019.03.020

Yang, S. (2013). On feature selection for traffic congestion prediction. *Transportation Research Part C, Emerging Technologies*, *26*, 160–169. doi:10.1016/j.trc.2012.08.005

Yin, R. R., Yuan, H., Wang, J., Zhao, N., & Liu, L. (2021). Modeling and analyzing cascading dynamics of the urban road traffic network. *Physica A*, *566*, 125600. doi:10.1016/j.physa.2020.125600

Zaki, J. F., Ali-Eldin, A., Hussein, S. E., Saraya, S. F., & Areed, F. F. (2020). Traffic congestion prediction based on Hidden Markov Models and contrast measure. *Ain Shams Engineering Journal*, *11*(3), 535–551. doi:10.1016/j.asej.2019.10.006

Zaki, J. F., Ali-Eldin, A. M., Hussein, S. E., Saraya, S. F., & Areed, F. F. (2019). Time aware hybrid hidden Markov models for traffic congestion prediction. *International Journal on Electrical Engineering & Informatics*, *11*(1).

Zhang, P., & Qian, Z. S. (2018). User-centric interdependent urban systems: Using time-of-day electricity usage data to predict morning roadway congestion. *Transportation Research Part C, Emerging Technologies*, *92*, 392–411. doi:10.1016/j.trc.2018.05.008

Zhang, W., Yu, Y., Qi, Y., Shu, F., & Wang, Y. (2019). Short-term traffic flow prediction based on spatio-temporal analysis and CNN deep learning. *Transportmetrica A: Transport Science*, *15*(2), 1688–1711. doi:10.1080/23249935.2019.1637966

Zhao, P., Kapoor, N., Thakur, M., Ty, T., Moskal, E., Michaelson, G., & Jaume, S. (2016). Crime prediction using public transportation data and the random forest algorithm. *International Journal of Decision Science, 7*(1).

Zhu, L., Krishnan, R., Guo, F., Polak, J. W., & Sivakumar, A. (2019, October). Early identification of recurrent congestion in heterogeneous urban traffic. In 2019 IEEE Intelligent Transportation Systems Conference (ITSC) (pp. 4392-4397). IEEE. doi:10.1109/ITSC.2019.8916966

Zhu, Z., Peng, B., Xiong, C., & Zhang, L. (2016). Short-term traffic flow prediction with linear conditional Gaussian Bayesian network. *Journal of Advanced Transportation*, *50*(6), 1111–1123. doi:10.1002/atr.1392

Zografos, K. G., Madas, M. A., & Salouras, Y. (2013). A decision support system for total airport operations management and planning. *Journal of Advanced Transportation*, *47*(2), 170–189. doi:10.1002/atr.154

ADDITIONAL READING

Aggarwal, C. C. (2015). *Data mining: the textbook*. Springer.

Ashford, N. J., Stanton, H. M., Moore, C. A., Pierre Coutu, A. A. E., & Beasley, J. R. (2013). *Airport operations*. McGraw-Hill Education.

Bonczek, R. H., Holsapple, C. W., & Whinston, A. B. (2014). *Foundations of decision support systems.* Academic Press.

Burkov, A. (2019). *The hundred-page machine learning book* (Vol. 1). Andriy Burkov.

Falkowski, L. S. (2019). *Presidents, secretaries of state, and crises in US foreign relations: A model and predictive analysis.* Routledge. doi:10.4324/9780429302985

Goodfellow, I., Bengio, Y., & Courville, A. (2016). *Deep learning.* MIT Press.

Rajapaksha, A., & Jayasuriya, N. (2020). Smart airport: A review on future of the airport operation. *Global Journal of Management and Business Research*, 25–34. doi:10.34257/GJMBRAVOL20IS3PG25

KEY TERMS AND DEFINITIONS

Data Mining: A process of extracting information and recognizing patterns in large datasets by combining statistical learning and database management.

Decision Support System: A computer-based framework that can process and analyze the large scale of data for extracting useful knowledges and information, which can be applied to solve problems in decision-making.

Deep Learning: A subset of machine learning based on artificial neural networks with more layers, which can improve the model performance significantly.

Machine Learning: A subject of artificial intelligence that aims at the task of computational algorithms, which allow machines to learning objects automatically through historical data.

Predictive Analysis: An analytical technique that makes simulations and forecasting in regards to uncertainties and unknown events using a variety of mathematical processes, such as statistical modeling, data mining, machine learning, etc.

Smart Airport: A modern airport ideology that enables to perform planning and operational tasks in digitalized forms using hyper-connected technologies, including IoT, GPS, and sensors.

Traffic Engineering: A subset of transportation engineering that covers a wide range of the traffic planning, road system designs, land uses, and terminal operations.

From DSS to Data Science:
The Effect of Industry 4.0

Natheer Khleaf Gharaibeh

🆔 https://orcid.org/0000-0002-6566-9704

Taibah University, Saudi Arabia

INTRODUCTION

Major evolution of information systems taken place during the second half of the twentieth century during the shift from Industry 3.0 to Industry 4.0, accompanied with transitional period from 20th century to 21st century, jargon and metaphoric words emerged (Laudon and Laudon, 2022). The fields of data science and big data as an example of one of the most important sciences emerging from these transformations are full of jargon and metaphoric words. For example, data lakes represent a single repository of data that includes raw copies of source system data, sensor data through IoT (Internet of Things), social data, and converted data used for reporting, visualization, advanced analytics, and machine learning (Sharda et al., 2021). This is great, but things aren't as beautifully simple as the metaphor of the Lake. If we don't solve the problem of data silos, we may find ourselves facing a data swamp. However, to understand these metaphors we need to know the historical contexts behind these terms. For example, the concept of data silos is information dating back to 1988 (Trkman et al., 2015). The period in which enterprise application emerged, a new era of computing is appearing with more integration and holistic paradigm due to the invention of web in 1990s. This is known as Industry 4.0 technologies, which comes decades after Industry 3.0, in which the big data technologies thrived to integrate more data sources using NoSQL and Hadoop. Data lakes is a good example for of jargon that appeared in this era as an emerging approach to cloud-based big data, in which Enterprises across industries are starting to collect all the different types of data sources through a common ingestion framework like Hadoop-based repository (Stein & Morrison, 2014). This was considered to be 10 to 100 times less expensive to deploy than conventional data warehousing.

The problem of diverse concepts and ambiguous metaphors may be misleading if it is not understood in its proper context. In this chapter, it is proposed that the main reason of this problem is due to isolation between business and technical issues. The good news is that the concepts of DSS still work, and it can bring together all the contradictions. DSS evolved to include what became known as Analytics. The broad and diverse nature of DSS field makes it with high potential to consolidate and provide suitable interpretation for these diverse concepts that evolved through a long period of time.

This methodological suggestion came from the combining and adaptation of commonly used models and procedures in information system research, such as the socio-technical model for information systems. Socio-technical model for information systems views DSS as socio-technical systems with several viewpoints and potential conceptual framework (Hirschheim, Klein, & Lyytinen, 1995). For control or emancipation of effective design (Shim et al., 2002) requires knowledge of both the application domain and the solution domain. The methodology that is used to tackle this dual problem is based on dialectic theory, which was used several times in IS and DSS literature (Elgarah, Haynes, & Courtney, 2002;

DOI: 10.4018/978-1-7998-9220-5.ch085

Haynes, 2001). Further, it was used in similar and related fields, as Boehm did in his Hegelian dialectical (related the German philosopher Hegel) view of the history of the field of software engineering (SE). Boehm (2006) traced evolution of software development methodologies from the classic process models such as waterfall into a spiral model, prototyping and, to agile development methodologies. The latter models seem to have worked well for DSS (Gharaibeh & Soud, 2008; Gharaibeh et al., 2009). In this chapter DSS will be considered as a software system with unique characteristics, from both SE and DSS literature it is found that they have similar beginning, on the one hand power (Shim et al., 2002) in his historical review of DSS field [stated that SAGE (Semi-Automatic Ground Environment- air defense system for North America) is the first computerized DSS, on the other hand, Boehm stated that SAGE was the most ambitious information processing project of the 1950's. By tracing the evolution of concepts, we mitigate the Epistemological rupture (or epistemological break) according to the French philosopher Gaston Bachelard.

There is a general disconnection or gap of concepts between early concepts of DSS and current concepts of data science era. From this viewpoint, there was no research done to investigate the DSS evolution till data science age. This chapter is an extension to the researcher's efforts to push the boundaries of DSS research (Paradice, 2007). DSS evolved to include what became known as Analytics.

In this chapter, section 2 begins with the problem of data silos, and the need for DSS and enterprise applications in solving the problem of data integration and overcoming these silos. Then, section 3 displays the progress in industry which can be portrayed by Kondratieff waves and the four industrial revolutions, showing how to balance between these two concepts and focusing more on the role of IS discipline in industry 4.0. Section 4 and 5 focus on integration shift within the IS discipline and DSS integral position within the IS discipline, they present the solution provided by enterprise applications and how DSS played more comprehensive role within the progress of IS discipline. We finally end with section 6, dialectic of technology and business, which shows the dialectic of technology and business, explaining the thesis of technology-driven and its antithesis of business-driven, then synthesis: a more holistic paradigm in Industry 4.0.

THE PROBLEM AND METHODOLOGY

The Problem of Data Silos

Since the prevalent appearance of data science as a field, its practitioners have asserted that 80% of the work involved is acquiring and preparing data (Wilder-James, 2016). In today's digitized economy and from business perspective, incorporating data as a competitive advantage is necessary for Business, so why is it so hard to get access to the data we need? The biggest obstacle to using analyzing the data is the plain old access to the data in other words the Data Silos, "Organizational silos and a dearth of data specialists are the main obstacles to putting big data to work effectively for decision-making" (Jha, Jha, & O'Brien, 2016). These silos are data islands that make extracting data and putting it to other uses prohibitively expensive. They can occur for a variety of reasons. We need to reduce the impact of data silos on all company activities to shift to higher value uses and preserve a strategic advantage. The capacity to use data effectively is a significant competitive advantage. There's a lot of work to be done in integrating all the data sources to get to a future state of mature analytical proficiency. This is a strategic goal for all businesses, and if correctly addressed, will lead to the development of experience and a data infrastructure that unlocks every subsequent stage.

Data silos research is another area where there is a lot of interest (Gulati, 2007). In which not only big data and analytics are uniquely suited to help, but also the previous legacy of different information systems evolution over the past decades, specifically the DSS and Enterprise Applications, and all the theories and ideas associated with it, which contribute effectively to shedding light on the problem of data integration and overcoming the Silos, all these developments occurred during the transition from third industrial revolution to fourth industrial revolution. Therefore, this chapter will preview the previous progress in Industry represented by Kondratieff waves and the four industrial revolutions, showing how to balance between these two concepts and focusing more on the Role of IS discipline in Industry4.0, It also presents the Integration Shift within the IS discipline representing the solution provided by Enterprise Applications and by showing the more comprehensive role of DSS and its integral position within the IS discipline , therefore there is a need for DSS concepts.

Dialectic Approach

The methodology that is used to tackle this problem is based on dialectic theory, which was used several times in IS and DSS literature (Elgarah et al., 2002; Haynes, 2001). Dialectic refers to the Hegelian idea that organizational entities exist in a pluralistic world of contradicting events, forces or contradictory values that compete with each other over periods of time. Rather than just reaching a compromise, the dialectic process aims to dissolve these oppositions and blend them into a complementing whole. It's an argumentation that aims to clarify the underlying assumptions to produce a deeper synthesis.

The thesis, which is about an issue or problem, is the starting point of a dialectic process. The thesis looks to be inadequate at some point. The antithesis, or the thesis's opposite or negation, develops. The antithesis eventually reveals itself to be inconsistent or insufficient. Both the thesis and the antithesis are one-sided, and in a synthesis, they are brought together in a coherent manner. The synthesis occurs because of discussion and debate about the thesis and antithesis elements, and the process is repeated.

As section 6 will be focused on applying this methodology on dialectic of Technology and Business to be synthesized in the holistic paradigm of DSS in Industry 4.0, before that section 3, 4 and 5 will show consecutive ideas emerged over sequential periods of time, starting from the previous Industrial Revolutions until reaching this end.

BACKGROUND

The first Industrial Revolution began in Britain and spread to Europe and the United States. It is frequently associated with the start of industrialization, the formation of modern societies and escaping the Malthusian trap (Zinkina et al., 2019). New forms of worldwide networks and material that traveled via these networks arose because of the Industrial Revolution. Transportation (railways, steamships) and information transmission (telegraph) innovations provided the foundation for connecting these new networks. The new sorts of content that were traveling through them were diverse, including both material and non-material things. In the face of the modern Technological Revolution, the entire nature of global economic development has undergone significant alterations. Following the Industrial Revolution, modern technical paradigms emerged, as did global economic cycles.

Kondratieff Waves

One of the most distinguishing features of the contemporary Technological Revolution is that it has occurred in waves (Zinkina et al., 2019). The first wave was the Industrial Revolution, which was followed by subsequent waves that can be classified as Kondratieff waves. The many phases of the modern Technological Revolution can be considered as six waves (includes the four previous waves, the current fifth wave, and the impending sixth wave). Each Kondratieff wave is based on a new technological paradigm that is fundamentally different. It first fuels fast expansion, which then declines (as the paradigm's potential is depleted) until the next disruptive technology is released and widely adopted, ushering in a new paradigm. These waves are becoming increasingly global in scope. Long Kondratieff waves (each lasting approximately 50 years) began late in the eighteenth century.

The Six technological paradigms are identified in table in which we combined between the six Kondratieff waves and its equivalent Four Industrial Revolutions, which will be described next.

Table 1. The six Kondratieff waves and its equivalent Four Industrial Revolutions adapted from (Zinkina et al., 2019)

Kondratieff wave	Date	A new mode	Mapping to the four industrial revolutions
The first	1780–1840s	The textile industry	Industry 1.0
The second	1840–1890s	Railway lines, coal, steel	Industry 2.0
The third	1890–1940s	Electricity, chemical industry, and heavy engineering	Industry 2.0 to Industry 3.0
The fourth	1940- the early 1980s	Automobile manufacturing, manmade materials, electronics	Industry 3.0
The fifth	1980s–~2020	Micro-electronics, personal computers	Industry 3.0 to Industry 4.0
The sixth	2020/2030s–2050/2060s	MANBRIC	Industry 4.0

We can note that the fifth wave (early 1980–~2020s) is just finishing, which is representing micro-electronics, personal computers, and biotechnologies; The so-called MANBRIC technological paradigm is thought to be related with the sixth wave (medical, additive, nano, bio, robotics, information, and cognitive technologies).

Four Industrial Revolutions

The modern world's global digital changes are frequently referred to as "the point of non-return" or the "fourth industrial revolution", Klaus Schwab (Schwab & Davis, 2018) a well-known economist and the founder and Executive Director of the World Economic Forum in Davos, made the announcement. According to Klaus Schwab's book "The Fourth Industrial Revolution," the first occurred between 1760 and 1840. It was brought about by the creation of the steam engine. The second industrial revolution occurred between the finish of the nineteenth and the beginning of the twentieth centuries. The spread of electricity, and conveyor manufacture were all factors. The third industrial revolution occurred in the twentieth century, in the 1960s. The spread of semiconductors was the critical point for the evolving computing power.

Figure 1. History of industrial revolutions
(Özen et al., 2020)

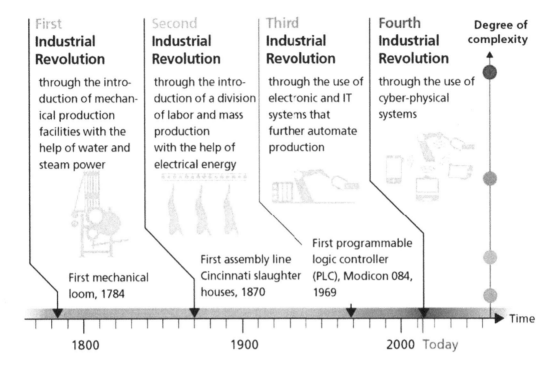

The fourth industrial revolution occurs in our lifetime. Today's industry is undergoing truly dramatic developments across the world.

This fourth industrial revolution is unprecedented in terms of scale, volume, and complexity in human history. The three preceding revolutions were mainly fueled by new technological advancements. The fourth differs significantly from the others due to the rapidity with which technology spreads and the worldwide nature of its dissemination and implementation. The fourth industrial revolution is fundamentally altering human life as we know it, expressing a significant shift in industrial capitalism (Philbeck & Davis, 2018) and blurring the lines between the physical, digital, and biological worlds. The historical sequence of the industrial revolutions is depicted in Figure 1, which lists the essential characteristics while also indicating the degree of complexity.

Weather we are using Kondratieff waves or the four industrial revolutions, the most important is to focus on the role of ICT in this Global evolutionary progress, It should be stated also that some authors do not believe there is a distinction between the third and fourth industrial revolutions, grouping them together as the Third Industrial Revolution (Rifkin, 2013).

One of the most important examples of Indusry4.0 is the movement toward "smart cities" which have been driven by big data analytics (Laudon and Laudon, 2022), Big data analytics is a relatively new technology with a lot of potential for improving smart city infrastructure (Alam et al., 2021). Big data is a massive volume of information gathered from various sensors, smart objects, and smart gadgets connected to IoT. Regional leaders can use smart cities to interact directly with society and local services, as well as track what's going on in the city and how it's progressing, this can be noticed in the Canadian City of Mississauga's e-government program. and in the middle east, these ideas are in the process of being realized in the case of the NEOM smart city in Saudi Arabia (Alam et al., 2021).

The Role of IS Discipline in Industry 4.0

The influence on organizations, industries, and management is inherent in this shift (Sharda et al., 2021), We are seeing Explosive growth and technical advancements in a variety of information and communication technologies (ICTs) fields, including analytics, AI, cognitive computing, robotics, 3D printing, nanotechnology, Cloud Computing, IoT, Deep learning, social media, Big Data, and biotechnology, The Role of IS discipline is critical in the 4th Industrial Revolutions or its synonym: Industry4.0, as it is mentioned in IS literature, will be described more in next sections, in which the most important paradigms is Human Computer Interaction, where People and machines have collaborated automatically. Before the Industry4.0 Manufacturing remained the focus of collaboration until the late of twentieth century. Human–machine collaboration has since expanded to many other areas, including doing mental and cognitive work and cooperating on administrative and executive work, The information and knowledge revolution relies heavily on intelligent systems. Unlike previous slower revolutions.

Integration Shift within the IS discipline

Major evolution of Information Systems taken place during the second half of the twentieth century, the shift from Industry 3.0 to Industry 4.0, during this period the four Major Types of Information Systems emerged (Laudon and Laudon, 2022), Executive Support Systems (ESS), Decision-Support Systems (DSS), Management Information Systems (MIS), Transaction Processing Systems (TPS) and Enterprise systems. TPS was in place until 1960's, MIS had been implemented since 1960's, after that in 1970's there was a shift to DSS and then this led to EIS in 1980's, but it was difficult for business to manage and share all the information in these different systems. it was hard for managers and employees to coordinate their work. further it was costly to maintain them, in the next sections DSS will be discussed as the one that has influenced by many studies and theories that can represent to progress and Evolution of IS discipline.

Cross-functional, dynamic, and global business is the norm nowadays. Most organizations have been attempting to eliminate functional obstacles that have existed for decades since the early 1990s. In today's interconnected world, business process reengineering experts and others have persuaded management that isolation is inefficient and ineffective. Organizations must be customer-focused and cost-effective to compete effectively in today's economy. This necessitates cross-functional collaboration between different systems and Business Units. Enterprise systems (Motiwalla, 2009) like ERP, SCM, CRM and KMS which were used for Linking the Enterprise and eliminating the silo effect. This effect was driven by Process-oriented organizations which break down the barriers of structural departments and try to avoid functional silos (Von Rosing, Von Scheel, and Scheer, 2014). Get rid and keep away from functional or informational Silos can be noted in Converting from the low-levels to up-levels in the Business Process Management (BPM) Maturity Self-Assessment, which is used as a benchmark among the various aspects that are related to the BPM maturity context, as well as a BPM maturity development path.

Figure 2 shows how Enterprise applications transforms the old Management Pyramid of Information Systems that is Categorized by Functional and Hierarchical Models and influenced by side effects of Silos, into new and integrated Management Pyramid, in which there are automated processes that span multiple business functions and organizational levels and may extend outside the organization.

Figure 2. Transformation Hierarchical Models into new and integrated Pyramid

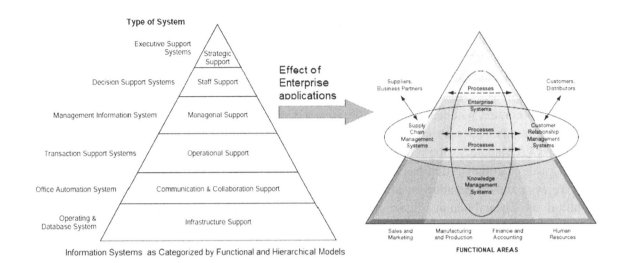

The Need for DSS Concepts

Although enterprise systems like SCM and CRM are very alluring and has a potential value, to obtain this value, business change must be understood to use these systems effectively. Further, enterprise applications technically contain complex pieces of software which almost maybe very expensive in procurement and implementation. So much so, that it may require large companies (e.g., Fortune 500) to spend several years to complete a large-scale implementation of an enterprise system. To bridge the gaps between technical and business views, there is still a need for conceptual views from DSS Theory. In other words, there is still a need for a more holistic paradigm and a "single source of truth."

DSS and its integral position within the IS discipline

DSS alone and more than other kinds of systems is the one that has influenced by many studies and theories. Not only of DSS occupies essential place in the information systems field, but it also stands in an integral position within the IS discipline (Burstein & Holsapple, 2008). The concept DSS grew out as a classical concept in Information Systems in the 1950s and 1960s, as shown in the previous section DSS evolved in 1980s and took several forms, such as EIS, Group Decision Support Systems (GDSS), and Business Intelligence late of 20th century in 1990s.

DSS (Power, 2002) is "an important class of information systems that use data, models and knowledge to help managers solve semi structured and unstructured problems". We would contend that the creation of DSS (Gupta, Forgionne, & Mora, 2007) as a concept was a significant part of this search for a new Hegelian synthesis. The theory of DSS have been evolved (Hayen, Holmes, & Scott, 2004; Arnott & Pervan, 2016) Since the field's foundation, it has evolved into many different directions. Regardless of this variation, it was considered that DSS is a key idea in IS research (Hevner et al., 2008), depending on the special nature of DSS as a boundary object that combine and integrate between technical, people, conceptual and organizational factors. This viewpoint the DSS will help us to tracing the diverse concepts outlined in this chapter.

With the emergence of the Internet and the Web, DSS evolved to include what became known as Analytics, then organizations became more data-driven especially in the era of industry4.0, Bringing together More recent and applied terms like data science, Deep Learning, and Big Data with the prosperity of Networking technologies and advancement of processing power. However, in academic discipline the term of DSS serves as the basic concept of all of today's interest in building applications and technologies that support decisions, therefore, in this chapter, what term we use for a system or software package is a secondary concern. the primary concern will be focused on two perspectives: Thesis of Technology-driven and its antithesis of business-driven as will be shown in section 6. from a technical perspective we want to look at the Information Technology infrastructure that underlines all the technical concepts and products, and from a business perspective by historically tracing all these concepts, in DSS literature, it can be noted simply there was always shifting from silos to more holistic paradigm.

Figure 3. Schematic View of DSS
(Sharda et al., 2021)

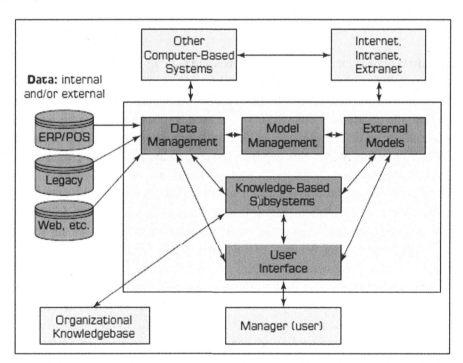

Figure 3 represents Schematic View of DSS components. One the one hand, DSS have been successfully implemented and applied in practice to help in solving complex business problems and being more customer-oriented due to the user interface subsystem component. One the other hand, it is also clear that the DSS field can include many recently technological improvements that have been achieved in AI field, as for example: "knowledge bases, fuzzy logic, multi-agent systems, natural language, genetic algorithms, neural networks and so forth". The presence of AI technologies in DSS is clear from expanding its knowledge-based subsystem component. In addition to spreadsheet, modeling, and database tools, OLAP tools, data warehouses, Web, and many other technologies. What is worth to mention here, is to focus on the interaction between business functions and its underling technological infrastructure, which will be discussed in the next section.

DIALECTIC OF TECHNOLOGY AND BUSINESS

In this section, the discussion will be focused on two perspectives: Thesis of Technology-driven and its antithesis of business-driven, then Synthesis that represents more holistic paradigm in the age of Industry 4.0.

Thesis of Technology-driven and its Antithesis of Business-driven

Before the Dot-com bubble in the 1990s, there was an optimistic look at Information Technology investment, in other words, it was technology driven. In 2003 when Nicholas G. Carr wrote his controversial and shocking paper "IT Doesn't Matter" (Carr, 2003), which accurately was describing the technology world in the post-bubble era, there was a pessimistic look at Information Technology. In other words, the antithesis was shifted to a more "business-driven" approach rather than being technology driven; at that sobering period of consolidation (Laudon and Traver, 2021). Large established corporations learned how to use the internet and web to boost their positions; funding shrank as capital markets rejected new firms; and increasingly complicated services, such as travel and financial services, were launched during this time.

The widespread use of broadband networks in homes and companies, along with the increasing power and cheaper pricing of personal computers, which were the primary way of accessing the Internet, usually from work or home, made this period possible. But even in both sequential periods of Technology-driven and business-driven, the problem of Data Silos still existed, Processing power has increased far faster than the capacity and speed of communication networks throughout the history of utility computing. Due to a lack of sufficient bandwidth, this gap between processing power and communication network speed produces data silos, making data analysis more difficult. to solve this situation, more integration solutions in the context of more holistic paradigm were required, because that gap between processing and networking made it more difficult to analyze the big data, as Eric Schmidt (Carr, 2009) predicted in 1993:" When the network becomes as fast as the processor, the computer hollows out and spreads across the network", so a tipping point was needed but it was delayed until after 2000.

Fiber-optic was not widely used until the 2000s, when utility computing became a reality. Then web applications evolved to the point where they could compete with software programs created for a specific software architecture, such as Hadoop for Big Data. The cloud computing trend of the 2000s was fueled by this maturity, affordable mass storage, and the introduction of service-oriented architecture (SOA) and Microservices. SOA can be viewed as part of a steady progression from the fundamentals of distributed computing and modular programming to modern cloud computing practices (which some see as an extension of SOA).

Synthesis: More Holistic Paradigm in Industry 4.0

The synthesizing of thesis and antithesis waited several years before the explosion of Industry 4.0, which was accompanied by more holistic paradigm, through the emergence of broadband, internet of things, cloud computing, big data, and many other technologies that contributed to balancing the Tradeoff between technical complexity and business model change. What happened after 2005 was the industry 4.0 age, or in Carr's terms "The Big Switch" (Carr, 2009), the situation of the Cloud Computing and everything related to it from big data to the Internet of things in Industry 4.0 is like electrification in the Second Industrial Revolution (1870 and 1914).

Tech boom increased in 2007 with the introduction of the mobile computing represented by smartphones can be reflected as extension of user interface subsystem component of DSS, which was considered together with cloud computing as a disruptive technology and tipping point to the present day. The progress of both DSS and IT has been transformed yet again by the rapid growth of Web 2.0, applications and technologies of online social networks, and the emergence of an on-demand service economy enabled by millions of apps on mobile devices and cloud computing. The advance in mobile computing affected many applications domains, due to the technologies associated with Web 2.0. These include social networking applications, mashups, syndication, tagging, open source, rich Internet applications, web services, virtual worlds and the mobile web. This new kind of more interactive Web-based DSS applications led to creating richer user experiences. Users are doing things and actions on the web and by using mobile that cannot be done in any other way before. For example, mobile augmented reality in the tourism sector (Gharaibeh et al., 2021), Travel Apps (Gharaibeh & Gharaibeh, 2022a), Shopping Applications (Gharaibeh & Gharaibeh, 2021), Mobile Learning (Gharaibeh & Gharaibeh, 2020), Mobile Health Application (Gharaibeh et al., 2020), Mobile Commerce (Gharaibeh et al., 2020), transportation (Gharaibeh & Gharaibeh, 2022b) and Mobile Banking Services (Gharaibeh, Arshad, & Gharaibh, 2018). These diverse applications of mobile applications are driven by mobile, first design principles, and increased the possibilities of solving the last mile problem in logistics in addition to its implications on mobile edge computing and blockchain-based technologies.

All these changes in technologies took place during this age of Industry 4.0, in which not only things and devices are connected, but also ideas and people are more connected and integrated than ever before (Floridi, 2016). The shift from Web 2.0 to Web 3.0, or semantic web (linked data web), is a notable example of these big transformations in which information is given a well-defined meaning, making it easier for machines and people to collaborate.

The semantic web is about two things:

- It is about machines becoming considerably better at processing and 'understanding' the data that they merely show now.
- It's about standard formats for integrating and combining data from many data sources, whereas the original Web was mostly focused on document exchange. This can be considered as expanding of Data, Model and knowledge-based subsystem components of DSS.

As a result, it is thought that the semantic web, in conjunction with other ICTs such as cloud computing, mobile computing, IoT, deep learning, social media, big data, and many others are all contributing to the concept of hyperhistory (Floridi, 2016). These ICTs increasingly record, transfer, and, most importantly, process information autonomously. Human civilizations become increasingly reliant on them and on information as a key resource to thrive. "Innovation, welfare, and added value changed from being ICT-related to being ICT-dependent" around the turn of the third millennium, in this age of Industry 4.0. Next subsections represent the dynamic role still played by DSS despite all these transformations and changes.

FUTURE RESEARCH DIRECTIONS

This chapter is a starting point for further theoretical analysis and more contextual discussion of inter-related concepts in the fields of DSS and data science. In the context of Sprague's DSS development framework (Sprague, 1982), Watson (Watson, 2018) developed a current reference architecture for business intelligence and analytics (BI/A) to be considered as futuristic vision. Although the practices of both decision support and data science are evolving and growing into diverse directions, it can be represented using a maturity model that includes DSS concepts: enterprise data warehousing, real-time data warehousing, big data analytics, and emerging cognition. Even for the coming cognitive generation, the DSS perspective is still viable.

Figure 4 depicts a reference architecture for a modern BI/analytics environment, which can be considered as the modern version of Figure 3 of DSS framework. It displays typical data flows between data sources and data repositories and identifies the data, models/applications, and user's components (i.e., platforms). While Figure 4 is representing more holistic and enterprise-wide view, DSS perspective served as a starting point and a foundation to get to where we are now and even in the future.

Figure 4. An Analytics/DSS Reference Architecture
(Watson, 2018)

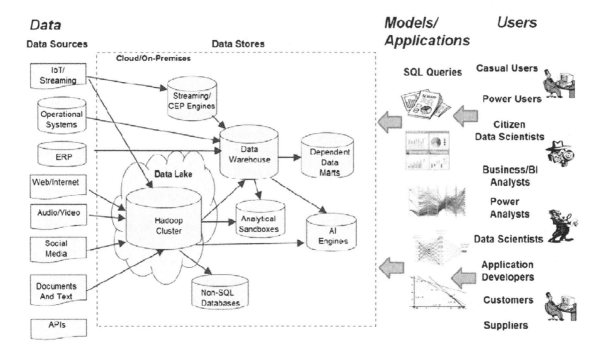

CONCLUSION

Due to the nature of overlapping topics and the gap between technology and business in the context of Industry 4.0, the researcher found it is better to use a dialectic methodology depending on DSS theory to synthesize all the heterogenous concepts and technologies in holistic paradigm.

DSS is continuing to play its important role in current synthesis of technologies and can provide a lot in forming a holistic paradigm. The dialog, data, and models (DDM) paradigm and characteristics of Sprague's DSS development approach (Sprague, 1982). In today's age of business intelligence and big data analytics, the development framework is still relevant. This is clear from viewing the extended reference architecture for business intelligence and analytics developed by Watson (Watson, 2018).

REFERENCES

Alam, T., Khan, M. A., Gharaibeh, N. K., & Gharaibeh, M. K. (2021). Big Data for Smart Cities: A Case Study of NEOM City, Saudi Arabia. In M. A. Khan, F. Algarni, & M. T. Quasim (Eds.), *Smart Cities: A Data Analytics Perspective* (pp. 215–230). Springer International Publishing. doi:10.1007/978-3-030-60922-1_11

Arnott, D., & Pervan, G. (2016). *A critical analysis of decision support systems research revisited: the rise of design science. In Enacting Research Methods in Information Systems*. Springer.

Boehm, B. (2006). A view of 20th and 21st century software engineering. *Proceedings of the 28th international conference on Software engineering*. 10.1145/1134285.1134288

Burstein, F., & Holsapple, C. W. (2008). *Handbook on decision support systems 2: variations*. Springer Science & Business Media.

Carr, N. (2009). *The big switch: Rewiring the world, from Edison to Google*. WW Norton & Company.

Carr, N. G. (2003). IT doesn't matter. *EDUCAUSE Review*, *38*, 24–38. PMID:12747161

Elgarah, W., Haynes, J. D., & Courtney, J. F. (2002, January). A dialectical methodology for decision support systems design. In *Proceedings of the 35th Annual Hawaii International Conference on System Sciences*. IEEE. 10.1109/HICSS.2002.994391

Floridi, L. (2016). *The 4th revolution: How the infosphere is reshaping human reality*. Oxford University Press.

Gharaibeh, M. K., Arshad, M. R. M., & Gharaibh, N. K. (2018). Using the UTAUT2 model to determine factors affecting adoption of mobile banking services: A qualitative approach. *International Journal of Interactive Mobile Technologies*, *12*(4), 123. doi:10.3991/ijim.v12i4.8525

Gharaibeh, M. K., & Gharaibeh, N. K. (2020). An empirical study on factors influencing the intention to use mobile learning. *Advances in Science. Technology and Engineering Systems Journal*, *5*(5), 1261–1265. doi:10.25046/aj0505151

Gharaibeh, M. K., & Gharaibeh, N. K. (2021). Understanding Adoption Intention of Mobile Shopping Applications: Empirical Assessment From IDT–Perceived Risk and Enjoyment. *International Journal of Sociotechnology and Knowledge Development*, *13*(2), 31–47. doi:10.4018/IJSKD.2021040103

Gharaibeh, M. K., & Gharaibeh, N. K. (2022a). A Conceptual Framework for Intention to Use Travel Apps: A Study From Emerging Markets. *International Journal of Service Science, Management, Engineering, and Technology*, *13*(1), 1–16. doi:10.4018/IJSSMET.290333

Gharaibeh, M. K., & Gharaibeh, N. K. (2022b). An Empirical Analysis of User's Continuance Intention (UCI) towards Careem Mobile Application. *International Journal of Interactive Mobile Technologies*, *16*(7), 137–152. doi:10.3991/ijim.v16i07.27055

Gharaibeh, M. K., Gharaibeh, N. K., & De Villiers, M. V. (2020). A qualitative method to explain acceptance of mobile health application: Using innovation diffusion theory. *International Journal of Advanced Science and Technology*, *29*(4), 3426–3432.

Gharaibeh, M. K., Gharaibeh, N. K., Khan, M. A., Abu-ain, W. A. K., & Alqudah, M. K. (2021). Intention to Use Mobile Augmented Reality in the Tourism Sector. *Computer Systems Science and Engineering*, *37*(2), 187–202.

Gharaibeh, N., Abu-Soud, S. M., Bdour, W., & Gharaibeh, I. (2009). *Agile development methodologies: Are they suitable for developing decision support systems.* Paper presented at the 2009 Second International Conference on the Applications of Digital Information and Web Technologies. 10.1109/ICADIWT.2009.5273971

Gharaibeh, N., Gharaibeh, M. K., Gharaibeh, O., & Bdour, W. (2020). Exploring intention to adopt mobile commerce: Integrating UTAUT2 with social media. *International Journal of Scientific and Technology Research*, *9*(3), 3826–3833.

Gharaibeh, N. K., & Soud, S. A. (2008). *Software Development Methodology for Building Intelligent Decision Support Systems.* Paper presented at the DCSOFT.

Gulati, R. (2007). Silo busting: How to execute on the promise of customer focus. *Harvard Business Review*, *85*(5), 98–108, 145. PMID:17494254

Gupta, J. N., Forgionne, G. A., & Mora, M. (2007). *Intelligent decision-making support systems: foundations, applications and challenges.* Springer Science & Business Media.

Hayen, R. L., Holmes, M. C., & Scott, J. P. (2004). Decision support systems in information technology assimilation. *Issues in Information Systems*, *2*, 481–486.

Haynes, J. (2001). Philosophical foundations of a dialectical analysis as a research methodology: transformation of the self in Hegel's dialectic. *AMCIS 2001 Proceedings*, 383.

Hevner, A. R., March, S. T., Park, J., & Ram, S. (2008). Design science in information systems research. *Management Information Systems Quarterly*, *28*(1), 6.

Hirschheim, R., Klein, H. K., & Lyytinen, K. (1995). *Information systems development and data modeling: conceptual and philosophical foundations.* Cambridge University Press. doi:10.1017/CBO9780511895425

Jha, M., Jha, S., & O'Brien, L. (2016). *Combining big data analytics with business process using reengineering.* Paper presented at the 2016 IEEE Tenth International Conference on Research Challenges in Information Science (RCIS). 10.1109/RCIS.2016.7549307

Laudon, K., & Traver, C. G. (2021). *E-commerce: Business, technology, society.* Pearson Education.

Laudon, K. C., & Laudon, J. P. (2022). *Management information systems: Managing the digital firm.* Pearson Educación.

Motiwalla, L. F. (2009). *Enterprise systems for management.* Pearson Education India.

Özen, A., Gürel, F. N., Mhlanga, D., Savić, D., Tosheva, E., Mehmedović, E., . . . Lobejko, S. (2020). *The Impacts of Digital Transformation.* Efe Akademi.

Paradice, D. (2007). *Expanding the boundaries of DSS* (Vol. 43). Elsevier.

Philbeck, T., & Davis, N. (2018). The fourth industrial revolution. *Journal of International Affairs*, *72*(1), 17–22.

Power, D. J. (2002). *Decision support systems: Concepts and resources for managers.* Greenwood Publishing Group.

Rifkin, J. (2013). *The third industrial revolution: How lateral power is transforming energy, the economy, and the world.* Martin's Griffin.

Schwab, K., & Davis, N. (2018). *Shaping the future of the fourth industrial revolution.* Currency.

Sharda, R., Delen, D., & Turban, E. (2021). *Analytics, data science, & artificial intelligence: Systems for decision support.* Pearson Education Limited. doi:10.1201/9781003140351

Shim, J. P., Warkentin, M., Courtney, J. F., Power, D. J., Sharda, R., & Carlsson, C. (2002). Past, present, and future of decision support technology. *Decision Support Systems, 33*(2), 111–126. doi:10.1016/S0167-9236(01)00139-7

Sprague, R. H. C. E. D. (1982). *Building effective decision support systems.* Prentice-Hall.

Stein, B., & Morrison, A. (2014). The enterprise data lake: Better integration and deeper analytics. *PwC Technology Forecast: Rethinking Integration, 1*(1-9), 18.

Trkman, P., Mertens, W., Viaene, S., & Gemmel, P. (2015). From business process management to customer process management. *Business Process Management Journal, 21*(2), 250–266. doi:10.1108/BPMJ-02-2014-0010

Von Rosing, M., Von Scheel, H., & Scheer, A. W. (2014). *The Complete Business Process Handbook: Body of Knowledge from Process Modeling to BPM* (Vol. 1). Morgan Kaufmann.

Watson, H. J. (2018). Revisiting Ralph Spragues Framework for Developing Decision Support Systems. *CAIS Communications of the Association for Information Systems, 42,* 363–385. doi:10.17705/1CAIS.04213

Wilder-James, E. (2016). Breaking down data silos. *Harvard Business Review,* 12.

Zinkina, J., Christian, D., Grinin, L., Ilyin, I., Andreev, A., Aleshkovski, I., & Korotayev, A. (2019). *A big history of globalization: the emergence of a global world system.* Springer. doi:10.1007/978-3-030-05707-7

ADDITIONAL READING

Enders, T. (2018) Exploring the Value of Data–A Research Agenda. In *International Conference on Exploring Service Science* (pp. 274-286). Springer. 10.1007/978-3-030-00713-3_21

Fataliyev, T., & Mehdiyev, S. (2020). Industry 4.0: The oil and gas sector security and personal data protection. *International Journal of Engineering and Manufacturing, 10*(2), 1–14. doi:10.5815/ijem.2020.02.01

Kant, K. (2009). Data center evolution: A tutorial on state of the art, issues, and challenges. *Computer Networks, 53*(17), 2939–2965. doi:10.1016/j.comnct.2009.10.004

Marjanovic, O., & Dinter, B. (2018). Learning from the history of business intelligence and analytics research at HICSS: A semantic text-mining approach. *Communications of the Association for Information Systems, 43*(1), 40. doi:10.17705/1CAIS.04340

Phillips-Wren, G., Daly, M., & Burstein, F. (2021). Reconciling business intelligence, analytics and decision support systems: More data, deeper insight. *Decision Support Systems*, *146*, 113560. doi:10.1016/j.dss.2021.113560

Tansley, S., & Tolle, K. M. (2009). The fourth paradigm: data-intensive scientific discovery (Vol. 1). Microsoft Research.

Watson, H. J. (2019). Update tutorial: Big Data analytics: Concepts, technology, and applications. *Communications of the Association for Information Systems*, *44*(1), 21.

Scrutinizing the Analytic Hierarchy Process (AHP)

S

José G. Hernández R.
Minimax Consultores, Venezuela

María J. García G.
Minimax Consultores, Venezuela

Gilberto J. Hernández G.
Minimax Consultores, Venezuela

INTRODUCTION

Human beings make daily decision making, in which several criteria are involved. The mathematical techniques used to deal with these types of problems are known as multicriteria models. The need to address these problems with multiple criteria has allowed the development of Multiple Criteria Decision Making (MCDM).

MCDMs are found in many fields of human endeavor. Just to mention a few, it has: Industrial maintenance problems (Bigaud, Thibault & Gobert, 2016); Turbine installations (Kolios et al., 2016); Credit evaluation for internet finance companies (Gu et al., 2017); Sustainable renewable energy development (Kunar et al., 217); Evaluation of mutual funds (Mimovic, Jakšić & Leković, 2017); Wind power plant (Ghobadi & Ahmadipari, 2018); Location for a small hydro power project (Patel & Rana, 2018); Location planning of urban distribution center (Sopha, Asih & Nursitasari, 2018); Energy efficiency in automotive engineering (Castro & Parreiras, 2020). And even techniques for group decisions have been developed. (López-Morales & Suárez-Cansino, 2017).

Just as there are multiple applications, MCDMs are made up of a large number of techniques, in particular Wątróbski et al. (2019) list more than forty of them, some, as are the case of ELECTRA and PROMETHEE, contain multiple variants.

Within this wide list, they can be highlighted, following mainly (Kolios et al., 2016): in addition, from ELECTRA and PROMETHEE, to AHP, ANP, DEA, SMART, TOPSIS, VICOR, WPM, WSM and some combinations of some of these methods with fuzzy set.

Additionally, two extremely simple and intuitive methods, but they produce very robust results, should be highlighted. Both are a combination of Weighted Sum Method (WSM), with a slight contribution of Weighted Product Method (WPM). These two methods, presented by Hernández, Hernández & García (2018), are the Matrixes Of Weighing with multiplicative factors (MOWwMf [MDPcFm]) and the Multiattribute Models with multiplicative factors (MMwMf [MMcFm]).

On the other hand, a definition of a MCDM is a procedure that combines the performance of decision alternatives across several, contradicting, qualitative and/or quantitative criteria and results in a compromise solution (Kolios et al., 2016). But Dahdah et al. (2021) point out, relying primarily on Kumar et al. (2017), MCDM is a branch of operations research that aims to find optimal results in complex scenarios that include various indicators, objectives and contradictory criteria. If this last statement is

DOI: 10.4018/978-1-7998-9220-5.ch086

taken into account, any technique that does not allow an optimal result to be obtained, under the conditions indicated, cannot be considered an MCDM.

In this sense, if it pays a little attention to the Analytical Hierarchical Processes (AHP) technique.

The analytic hierarchy process (AHP), also analytical hierarchy process, is a structured technique for organizing and analyzing complex decisions, supported by mathematics and psychology, which is based, mainly, on paired comparisons. On the other hand, the technique derived from it, Analytic Network Process (ANP), can be defined as a more general form of the AHP. The main difference between the two techniques is that AHP structures a decision problem in a hierarchy, while the ANP structures it as a network. Since ANP is an extension of AHP, this second technique inherits all its flaws. Therefore, in this chapter the focus will be mainly and almost exclusively on AHP.

Before continuing, it should be noted that in the literature on mathematical models AHP is presented, as one of the most used techniques for decision making, where multiple criteria intervene. However, in this work, it will be shown that it is necessary, for researchers who make use of this technique and its derivative the ANP, to reflect on the axioms that support it. Since a slight review of them, shows that AHP and therefore ANP, have unsalvable operational failures, which should rule out their use as MCDM techniques.

Despite this last statement there is no denying the great boom, which, over the years, has had this technique of hierarchy, in a part of the scientific community.

If it attends to what was said by Chaudhari, Wasu & Sarode (2020), Saaty developed the AHP at the Pennsylvania University, between 1971-1975. Although the authors of this chapter are not in capacity to certify this. But, if it can cite works by Saaty that evidence the presence of the subject in years very close to these dates (Saaty, 1977; 1979a; 1979b; 1980; 1989; 1991).

Additionally, in his book of 2010 (Saaty, 2010), there are citations to the work of the same author and other authors, where reference is made to the subject, of dates close to those previously mentioned (Belton & Gear, 1983; Dyer, 1990; Dyer & Ravinder, 1983; Harker, 1987; Saaty, 1990; 1996; Saaty & Alexander, 1989; Saaty & Forman, 1993; Wind & Saaty, 1980; Zahir, 1996), some of these quotes come from renowned researchers and published in very prestigious journals.

But the appointments to the AHP, do not remain only in the last century. In more recent years, to name but a few, it can mention the works of: Boutkhoum et al. (2021); Chaudhari, Wasu & Sarode (2020); Ghosh & Kar (2018); Guarini et al. (2017); Hassanpour (2021); Mitjans & Méndez (2020); Panwar et al. (2019); Ristanovic, Primorac & Kozina (2021).

In addition, works by some authors, who have been directly or indirectly critical of AHP and its derivative ANP (Csató, 2017; 2018; Kumar et al., 2017), and others who have been highly critical (Dahdah et al., 2021; Hernández & García, 2018a; 2018b; Hernández, García & Hernández, 2014), as well as some who, at last, have dared to acknowledge and speak publicly about their many faults (Munier & Hontoria, 2021).

In this work there will not be an in depth research on AHP, it will be enough a cursory review of its main axioms, to reach the conclusion that this technique has structural flaws, which should deny its use as a technique of MCDM.

As pointed out by Dahdah et al. (2021) relying on several authors (Hernández, García & Hernández, 2014; Kadoić, Redep & Divjak, 2017; Marković, Kadoić & Kovačić, 2018; Saaty, 2010; Saaty, 2016; Stanković et al., 2017), in general, when talking about axioms of Saaty, reference is made to: Reciprocity, Homogeneity and Synthesis, however, it is impossible to speak, nor to use AHP, without mentioning Consistency, which comes to work, practically, as a fourth axiom.

Except for the first, in this work criticism will be made of the remaining three axioms. These criticisms to axioms of Saaty, allow to enunciate the objective of this work.

Objectives

The general objective of this work is: Analyze the fundamental premises of Analytical Hierarchical Processes and demonstrate that it is not only a technique that has very obvious flaws, but is also used, erroneously, in decision-making for which it is not at all appropriate.

In order to achieve this general objective, the following specific objectives must be completed:

- Analyze, briefly, but critically, three of the four axioms that support the Analytical Hierarchical Processes. And
- Present, because these flaws and a misinterpretation of some of these axioms invalidate that AHP is a multicriteria technique.

Methodology

In order to achieve the overall objective, and its two specific objectives, it follows the Integrated-Adaptable Methodology for the development of Decision Support System (IAMDSS, in Spanish, Metodología Integradora-Adaptable para desarrollar Sistemas de Apoyo a las Decisiones [MIASAD]). As pointed out by Dahdah et al. (2021), García, Hernández & Hernández (2020; 2022) and Hernández, García & Hernández (2022), this methodology, although it was formalized by García, Hernández & Hernández (2014), it is actually the product of an evolutionary process that has as its main characteristic, which it does not handle hypotheses, but a set of steps, which are followed in a very flexible way.

Thanks, mainly, to this great flexibility, it has been shown that MIASAD is extremely useful, in research in different fields of human activity (Barreto et al., 2016; García, Hernández & Hernández, 2018; Schwarz et al., 2016).

As has been done in other works, of similar cut (Dahdah et al., 2021; Garcia et al., 2017; Hernández & García, 2018a, 2018b), of its twenty basic steps only the following will be followed:

1. Define the problem, which as indicated in the overall objective is analyze the fundamental premises of Analytical Hierarchical Processes and demonstrate that it is not only a technique that has very obvious flaws, but is also used, erroneously, in decision-making for which it is not at all appropriate;
2. Develop the first prototype, which, among its first functions, should offer a clear vision of what will be the result of the research. In these works, where the final product is a scientific article, rather than a physical prototype, what is expected is to clearly define who the research is aimed at. What should be translated into being able to identify, before starting the peak of the study, the audience, or, potential readers of the same. In this case, they have identified as possible readers of the article, all those scholars of multicriteria techniques, in particular users and critics of AHP and especially those who see scientific research as a source of knowledge that is based on the critical spirit and the permanent search for knowledge, that is to say those who are not satisfied with following trends. On the other hand, in research such as this one, which does not involve the development of physical structures, part of the time invested in the elaboration of the first prototype is dedicated to establishing some essential parameters. In this case, being a scientific article, the structure of it

was established, which, in addition to this introduction, will consist of a background, which will support the research.

This background will be very brief and reinforce the comments made on AHP in the introduction and will present the four axioms of the AHP. Following this background will show the main chapter of the research, which will discuss the flaws that have three of these four axioms. To close the article will present the conclusions and some possible lines of future research and will culminate with the references relating to the works cited;

3. Get data, which, in this research, the search will be limited to AHP and its four axioms;
4. Establish alternatives, for the achievement of the objectives, that is, it will be presented in the simplest and easiest way, the faults found in the axioms of AHP;
5. Evaluate alternatives, which in this case will focus, on the most concise way to reach clear conclusions about failures of AHP;
6. Select the best alternative, according to the previous evaluation and taking into consideration the secondary objectives, both tacit and explicit. It should be clarified that, in many of these works, the selected alternative may be a set of alternatives or the combination of parts of several of them;
7. Implement the selected alternative; although in these cases, there is no physical implementation as such, if the completion of the article should be guaranteed, having met its general objective and its specific objectives;
8. Establish controls, or mechanisms, that allow to recognize if the solution obtained, is still valid in the course of time. In this case it is a question of measuring the impact that the article has in the scientific and business worlds, especially in the study of multicriteria models.

As part of MIASAD, the scope and limitations of the research are established. In this sense it should be clarified that no field work will be done and that the results will be presented, showing the evidence of the failures of AHP.

Once this introduction has been completed, as clarified in step b, of the methodology, the background of the investigation will then be presented.

BACKGROUND

As indicated in the methodology, in this background the axioms of Analytical Hierarchical Processes (AHP) will be presented very briefly.

These axioms are: Reciprocity, Homogeneity, Synthesis and the Valuation of Consistency.

Following mainly Dahdah et al. (2021), who in turn leaned on Hernandez, Garcia & Hernandez (2014), Saaty (2016) and Stanković et al. (2017), will be said:

To meet the axiom of Reciprocity, the comparative relationship of two elements or criteria to each other, as opposed to their mother criterion, must respect that, if A is k times more important than B, then B must be 1/ k times more important than A.

Of the axioms of AHP, this is the one that makes the most sense, so it is the least questioned in the literature. Therefore, in this work it will not receive any criticism, nor will any other comment be made on it.

With the axiom of Homogeneity, it is expected that the elements or criteria to be compared are very similar to each other, in relation to the property to be measured, so the differences should not be greater than an order of magnitude. As a consequence of this axiom (Saaty, 2016), the Saaty scale arises from 1 to 9.

The elements of the diagonal of the matrix, of paired comparisons, will all be equal to 1.

For the values the Saaty scale is handled, which is:

1 = equal or indifferent with regard to …
3 = slightly more important than …
5 = more important than …
9 = absolutely more important than …

And 2, 4, 6 and 8 represent intermediate values.

Many of the problems of AHP begin with this axiom of Homogeneity and the scale that has just been presented. Saaty, has tried to solve this problem by expanding the scale and making use of clusters (Saaty, 2016), but without achieving a real solution (Dahdah et al., 2021). But the most important thing is in the scale itself, which from the mathematical point of view bears no relation to what it says or thinks it represents. As Dahdah et al. (2021), based mainly on Hernandez & Garcia, (2018b), points out, in mathematics 2 + 2 and 2 x 2 is usually, and should be 4.

The axiom relating to synthesis, on the other hand, means that judgments about the priorities of the elements or criteria in a hierarchy do not depend on the elements of the lower levels.

The axiom Synthesis, says that decisions are not affected neither by previous ones, nor by the following comparisons. In principle it may seem to make sense, since each paired comparison is made independently. However, in AHP, paired comparisons if they are affected by their peers, as will be seen later when making the critical discussion of this axiom. It will be shown that as criteria or alternatives are increased, the normalization values are reduced, even if the new alternatives or criteria do not contribute anything (Hernández, García & Hernández, 2014).

Finally, Consistency refers to the judgments of the "experts" and translates that, if A is better than B and B is better than C, to respect consistency A should be better than C. From the work of Dahdah et al. (2021), having reviewed a large number of studies, most of them, very interesting (Csató, 2018; Guarini et al., 2017; Guillier, 2017; Khatwani & Kar, 2017; Kułakowski & Talaga, 2020; Liang, Brunelli & Rezaei, 2020; Liu et al., 2017; Magalhaes & Silva, 2018; Moslem et al., 2020; Mazurek, 2017; Mu & Pereyra-Rojas, 2017; Zhang, Xu & Liao, 2018) it can see that, in Saaty matrices, Consistency measures nothing but transitivity. But in addition to this limitation, it is important to highlight what is found in an old work (Kwiesielewicz & van Uden, 2004): although a matrix is consistent, it can be contradictory. It should also be noted what Saaty himself pointed out: a madman can be consistent with respect to his fantastic world (Saaty & Ergu, 2015).

In addition, it is very important to note that decisions are not order relations. If on Saturday it is decided that between alternatives A and B A is preferred, and on Sunday it is decided that between alternatives B and C B is preferred, not necessarily, it has to be decided on Monday that between alternatives C and Λ, Λ is preferred. If an order relationship has not been established, there is no reason to expect transitivity to exist.

Presented the four axioms of AHP and made these last comments will move to the main chapter of the work, where there will be a brief, but critical, analysis on three of the four axioms of Saaty.

CRITICAL ANALYSIS OF THREE AXIOMS OF AHP

Observations will be made on Homogeneity, Synthesis and the assessment of Consistency. It starts with Homogeneity.

Failures in the Axiom of Homogeneity

As Dahdah et al. (2021), Hernández & García, (2018a; 2018b) and Hernández, García & Hernández, (2014), have already pointed out, the biggest problems of the Analytical Hierarchical Processes (AHP), are initiated by the misinterpretation of the scale established for the method.

In Table 1 illustrates a paired comparison between Services and Infrastructure made in the work of Hernández & García, (2018b). For more details on these criteria and how the normalization process is carried out, it is recommended to review the work of Dahdah et al. (2021) and the works that preceded it.

Table 1a. Paired comparison and its normalization.

Services and infrastructure	Services	Infrastructure	Services and infrastructure	Services	Infrastructure	Notation (W**)
Services	1	3	Services	0,7500	0,7500	0,7500
Infrastructure	1/ 3	1	Infrastructure	0,2500	0,2500	0,2500

On the left side of Table 1a, paired comparisons were made in three columns and on the right side, in four columns, after normalizing the columns and averaging the new rows, the notation values (W**) were obtained, which is the contribution, in this case of each attribute, to the analyzed criterion. In this simple example the Services attribute is three times better than Infrastructure to meet the criteria being analyzed.

If, as it can see in table 1b, this relationship instead of being three were two, the new values shown there would be obtained.

Table 1b. Paired comparison and its normalization, changing 3 by 2.

Services and infrastructure	Services	Infrastructure	Services and infrastructure	Services	Infrastructure	Notation (W**)
Services	1	2	Services	0,6667	0,6667	0,6667
Infrastructure	1/ 2	1	Infrastructure	0,3333	0,3333	0,3333

If it looks at the Saaty scale, by using three, it is saying that Services is "slightly more important" than Infrastructure. And so, when using two, this relation is less than slightly. In this second case it can be said that it must be practically imperceptible. However, when using three the W** resulted (0.7500; 0.2500) and when two were used the W** resulted (0.6667; 0.3333). That is, in the second case the contribution of Services is twice as much as Infrastructure and in the first is three times. And this has to be so, because in mathematics, when you multiply by 2 you are doubling and when you multiply by 3 you are tripling, at no time are you being slightly better or less than slightly better.

For this simple reason, the whole castle built on this scale, it is to said, everything related to AHP, is a ruined structure, which can never be used for any kind of decision, much less multicriteria decision. But it is unfortunate that, on this false interpretation, a great deal of work has been produced, including doctoral theses, which obviously have no real value. And only because the researchers who used AHP, without making the slightest criticism failed in the first that every researcher should take care of, be critical, above all, of the tools that are being used.

Given the serious error of interpretation that accompanies homogeneity, it will be passed to present the faults of the Synthesis.

Flaws in the Synthesis Axiom

The fault of synthesis is perhaps more obvious than that of homogeneity, but unfortunately a greater number of tables will be needed, so that it can be more easily visualized.

It will be based on the paired comparison of two hypothetical attributes, criteria or alternatives, it is not relevant, the important thing is how AHP makes the comparison. If it were the alternatives A and B, as shown in Table 2, the example will be valid. Similar to the presentation used in Tables 1a and 1b, paired comparison and normalization will be displayed in a joint table. In this case the alternative B, does not represent any contribution, while A meets in a hundred percent with the objective under study, so that A is much higher than B, hence the value of 9 when making the paired comparison.

Table 2. Paired comparison and its normalization, between A and B.

Objective	A	B	Objective	A	B	Notation (W**)
A	1	9	A	0,9000	0,9000	0,9000
B	1/9	1	B	0,1000	0,1000	0,1000

A first observation that can be made is that A, despite being a much superior alternative to B, just because it is next to B, loses part of its contribution, which, instead of being, practically one hundred percent, is reduced to ninety percent. But if this is disturbing, it is more worrying what happens, when a new alternative is added, called C, which, like B has no contribution, as can be seen in table 3a and 3b.

Table 3a. Paired comparison between A, B and C.

Objective	A	B	C
A	1	9	9
B	1/9	1	1
C	1/9	1	1

Table 3b. Normalization, of the paired comparison between A, B and C.

Objective	A	B	C	Notation (W**)
A	0,8182	0,8182	0,8182	0,8182
B	0,0909	0,0909	0,0909	0,0909
C	0,0909	0,0909	0,0909	0,0909

In the case of table 3b, alternative A, due to the presence of the other two alternatives B and C, which are alternatives without any contribution, sees its W** decreased to 0.8182. That is, alternative A, due to the presence of B and C, has lost a little more than eighteen percent of what should be its true contribution. So that the situation can be seen clearer in tables 4a and 4b a similar situation will be presented, but adding a new alternative, the D, which like B and C has no contribution.

Table 4a. Paired comparison between A, B, C and D.

Objective	A	B	C	D
A	1	9	9	9
B	1/9	1	1	1
C	1/9	1	1	1
D	1/9	1	1	1

Table 4b. Normalization, of the paired comparison between A, B, C and D.

Objective	A	B	C	D	W**
A	0,7500	0,7500	0,7500	0,7500	0,7500
B	0.0833	0.0833	0.0833	0.0833	0.0833
C	0.0833	0.0833	0.0833	0.0833	0.0833
D	0.0833	0.0833	0.0833	0.0833	0.0833

In the case of Table 4b, the notation of A is reduced to 0.7500, it is to say a loss of twenty five percent of its contribution, due solely and exclusively to the presence of the other three alternatives B, C and D, which are alternatives with nothing to contribute.

Obviously following this reasoning will be seen, as reflected in Table 5, as next to alternative A are included other alternatives without any value, the contribution of A will be reduced.

Although they were not shown, the authors of this article constructed the other tables that allow to arrive at the values shown in table 5, except the last five that are calculated following the pattern of the previous ones.

Table 5. Contribution of A, according to the number of useless alternatives that accompany it.

A + 0 1,0000	A + 1 0,9000	A + 2 0,8182	A + 3 0,7500	A + 4 0,6923	A + 5 0,6429
A + 6 0,6000	A + 7 0,5625	A + 8 0,5294	A + 9 0,5000	A + 10 *0,4737*	A + 11 *0,4500*
A + 12 *0,4286*	A + 15 *0,3750*	A + 20 *0,3103*	A + 25 *0,2647*	A + 30 *0,2308*	A + 50 *0,1525*

In Table 5, the values of A when accompanied by more than nine alternatives, those indicated in italics, should not make sense, since according to the Saaty scale, it is not advisable to make paired comparisons between more than nine alternatives. However, these values, allow to see that a very good alternative, it could see diluted its impact, by the only fact of being accompanied by other alternatives, although then last do not make any contribution. This obvious conclusion had already been reached in 2010, as can be seen in the references of Hernández, García & Hernández (2014). And it has also been repeated by Hernandez & Garcia, (2018a; 2018b) and by Dahdah et al. (2021). That is, the researchers who have continued to use AHP in recent years, without criticizing the technique, have sinned of negligence, to say the least.

With these critical comments on the axioms of Homogeneity and Synthesis, it is clearly demonstrated that AHP is not a technique to achieve the optimal, so it cannot be considered a multicriteria technique. The sad thing is to see the multitude of works that have been published, making inappropriate use of this technique, when reaching the conclusion shown in Table 5, requires no other effort than to open its eyes, front the tool that is being used.

To conclude these critical comments below will be presented the assessment of consistency.

The Reality of Consistency Calculation

For the analysis of the calculation of Consistency, the reader will refer to the article by Dahdah et al. (2021), which focuses on analyzing this aspect. In this work it can see that the calculation of Consistency, does not present new structural failures, but having to make use of the axioms of Homogeneity and Synthesis, drags the errors introduced with them. But in any case, there are two aspects to point out. The first, Saaty Consistency, as already stated, measures nothing but transitivity, which, as Dahdah et al. (2021) demonstrate, does not have to be necessary. And, second, because the calculation of Consistency requires a series of tedious calculations, as shown in Dahdah et al. (2021), it plays the role of left hand of the magician. It serves as entertainment, so that the public does not see what the right hand does. Consistency only manages to mask, under an apparent sense of objectivity, the obvious errors involved in the use of AHP. The lamentable is that there are many researchers who do not look up, to see what is actually happening.

In addition, Dahdah et al. (2021), make the following observation: it should be remembered that AHP only serves to rank. And they end up making the following approach: although it can be accepted that AHP is a multicriteria model, but it should never be presented as a Multiple Criteria Decision Making (MCDM) model, as is frequently shown in the specialized literature.

Having made the latter comments extracted from Dahdah et al. (2021), it will go on to offer some conclusions and recommendations for future research.

FUTURE RESEARCH DIRECTIONS

Different from what is normally customary, rather than recommending, what kind of research should be done in the future, the first recommendation, in this case, is related to what they should not do, about which they should stop researching. That is, it is recommended not to continue investing time with the Analytical Hierarchical Processes (AHP) and its derivatives.

Therefore, among future research there is no mention of the use of other more proven and better known techniques such as DEA, ELECTRA, PROMETHEE or TOPSIS. However, it is recommended to delve into other techniques than if they are true multicriteria techniques. Just to mention an extremely simple to model and apply those provide very good results, as already mentioned in this paper, it is recommended to deepen the studies on Multiattribute Model with multiplicative Factors (MMwMf) and Matrixes Of Weighing with multiplicative factors (MOWwMf).

CONCLUSION

In this paper, after showing how very popular the Analytical Hierarchical Processes (AHP) technique is, its basic axioms were presented.

Then a critical review was made on three of them, the axioms of Homogeneity, Synthesis and the assessment of Consistency. From a very cursory exploration, given the obviousness of the faults, it was concluded that AHP cannot be considered, under any sense, a Multiple Criteria Decision Making (MCDM) technique.

With this strong conclusion, the objectives of the work were met, both the general objective and the specific objectives. In this work no comment was made on how a multicriteria technique should be chosen, nor was there a critical analysis of cases of AHP applications that have failed, since they were not within the objectives of the same.

REFERENCES

Barreto, O. E. A., Hernández, G. G. J., García, G. M. J., & Hernández, R. J. G. (2016). Security & Safety (S&S) and the Logistics Business. *Proceedings ICIL2016*, 12-23.

Belton, V., & Gear, A. E. (1983). On short-coming of Saaty's method of Analytic hierarchies. *Omega*, *11*(3), 228–230. doi:10.1016/0305-0483(83)90047-6

Bigaud, D., Thibault, F., & Gobert, L. (2016). Decision-making through a fuzzy hybrid AI system for selection of a third-party operations and maintenance provider. *International Journal of Multicriteria Decision Making*, *6*(1), 35–65. doi:10.1504/IJMCDM.2016.075630

Boutkhoum, O., Hanine, M., Nabil, M., El Barakaz, F., Lee, E., Rustam, F., & Ashraf, I. (2021). Analysis and Evaluation of Barriers Influencing Blockchain Implementation in Moroccan Sustainable Supply Chain Management: An Integrated IFAHP-DEMATEL Framework. *Mathematics*, *9*(14), 1601. doi:10.3390/math9141601

Castro, D. M., & Parreiras, F. S. (2020). *A review on multi-criteria decision-making for energy efficiency in automotive engineering*. Applied Computing and Informatics.

Chaudhari, J. S., Wasu, R., & Sarode, A. (2020). Ranking different enablers/drivers of sustainable supply chain management by using AHP in Indian manufacturing industries. *International Journal of the Analytic Hierarchy Process*, *12*(2). Advance online publication. doi:10.13033/ijahp.v12i2.711

Csató, L. (2017). *Characterization of an inconsistency ranking for pairwise comparison matrices.* arXiv:1610.07388v3 [cs.AI].

Csató, L. (2018). *A characterization of the Logarithmic Least Squares Method.* arXiv:1704.05321v5 [math.OC].

Dahdah, A. J. J., Hernández, G. G. J., García, G. M. J., & Hernández, R. J. G. (2021). The Myth of the Importance of Consistency in Analytical Hierarchical Processes. *International Journal of Knowledge-Based Organizations*, *11*(1), 1–13. doi:10.4018/IJKBO.2021010101

Dyer, J. S. (1990). Remarks on the Analytic Hierarchy Process. *Management Science*, *36*(3), 249–258. doi:10.1287/mnsc.36.3.249

Dyer, J. S., & Ravinder, H. V. (1983). *Irrelevant alternatives and the Analytic Hierarchy Process. Working chapter*. The University of Texas at Austin.

García, G. M. J., Hernández, G. G. J., & Hernández, R. J. G. (2014). A Methodology of The Decision Support Systems applied to other projects of Investigation. In M. Khosrow-Pour (Ed.), Encyclopedia of Information Science and Technology, Third Edition. Hershey, PA: IGI Global.

García, G. M. J., Hernández, G. G. J., & Hernández, R. J. G. (2018). Participation of women in logistics through innovation. *International Journal of Sustainable Entrepreneurship and Corporate Social Responsibility*, *3*(2), 32–52. doi:10.4018/IJSECSR.2018070103

García, G. M. J., Hernández, G. G. J., & Hernández, R. J. G. (2020). Marginalization of Women and Mass Markets. In A. Gurtu (Ed.), Recent Advancements in Sustainable Entrepreneurship and Corporate Social Responsibility (pp. 69–87). Academic Press.

García, G. M. J., Hernández, G. G. J., & Hernández, R. J. G. (2022). Looking for an approach to ethics through logistics. *International Journal of Sustainable Entrepreneurship and Corporate Social Responsibility*, *7*(1), 1–17. Advance online publication. doi:10.4018/IJSECSR.287869

García, G. M. J., Schwarz, I. L. M., Schwarz, I. T. M., Hernández, G. G. J., & Hernández, R. J. G. (2017). Inventories control, the Inventory manager and Matrixes Of Weighing with multiplicative factors (MOWwMf). *Journal of Global Business and Technology*, *13*(1), 40–56.

Ghobadi, M., & Ahmadipari, M. (2018). Environmental planning for wind power plant site selection using a Fuzzy PROMETHEE-Based outranking method in geographical information system. *Environmental Energy and Economic Research*, *2*(2), 75–87.

Ghosh, A., & Kar, S. K. (2018). Application of analytical hierarchy process (AHP) for flood risk assessment: A case study in Malda district of West Bengal, India. *Natural Hazards*, *94*(1), 349–368. doi:10.100711069-018-3392-y

Gu, W., Basu, M., Chao, Z., & Wei, L. (2017). A unified framework for credit evaluation for internet finance companies: Multi-criteria analysis through AHP and DEA. *International Journal of Information Technology & Decision Making*, *16*(03), 597–624. doi:10.1142/S0219622017500134

Guarini, M. R., D'Addabbo, N., Morano, P., & Tajani, F. (2017). Multi-Criteria Analysis in Compound Decision Processes: The AHP and the Architectural Competition for the Chamber of Deputies in Rome (Italy). *Buildings*, *7*(38), 1–17. doi:10.3390/buildings8010001

Guillier, F. (2017). French insurance and flood risk: Assessing the impact of prevention through the rating of action programs for flood prevention. *International Journal of Disaster Risk Science*, *8*(3), 284–295. doi:10.100713753-017-0140-y

Harker, P. T., & Vargas, L. G. (1987). The theory of ratio scale estimation: Saaty's Analytical Hierarchy Process. *Management Science*, *33*(14), 1383–1403. doi:10.1287/mnsc.33.11.1383

Hassanpour, M. (2021). An investigation of five generation and regeneration industries DEA. *Operational Research in Engineering Sciences: Theory and Applications*, *4*(1), 19–37. doi:10.31181/oresta2040115h

Hernández, R. J. G., & García, G. M. J. (2018a). *Effect of the use of an ideal alternative in Hierarchical Analytic Processes* [English new version]. Working paper, MXAAAX20-18AA5-AGA0-D19A0I, Minimax Consultores C. A., Caracas, Venezuela.

Hernández, R. J. G., & García, G. M. J. (2018b). *Multicriteria models to evaluate social development projects* [New version]. Working paper, MXAA0020-18AA9-SPAA-D03A0I, Minimax Consultores C. A., Caracas, Venezuela.

Hernández, R. J. G., García, G. M. J., & Hernández, G. G. J. (2014). Shelter Selection with AHP Making Use of the Ideal Alternative. In M. Khosrow-Pour (Ed), Encyclopedia of Information Science and Technology, Third Edition. Hershey, PA: IGI Global.

Hernández, R. J. G., García, G. M. J., & Hernández, G. G. J. (2022). Safety and attention of passengers with disabilities who travel by train. *International Journal of Sustainable Entrepreneurship and Corporate Social Responsibility*, *7*(1), 1–16. Advance online publication. doi:10.4018/IJSECSR.287867

Hernández, R. J. G., Hernández, G. G. J., & García, G. M. J. (2018). The Logistic Model Based on Positions (LoMoBaP [MoLoBaC]) & Industry 4.0. In Handbook of Research on Emerging Developments in Industry 4.0. Hershey, PA: IGI Global.

Kadoić, N., Redep, N. B., & Divjak, B. (2017). Decision making with the Analytic Network Process. SOR 2017, Bled, Ljubljana.

Khatwani, G., & Kar, A. K. (2017). Improving the Cosine Consistency Index for the analytic hierarchy process for solving multi-criteria decision making problems. *Applied Computing and Informatics*, *13*(2), 118–129. doi:10.1016/j.aci.2016.05.001

Kolios, A., Mytilinou, V., Lozano-Minguez, E., & Salonitis, K. (2016). A comparative study of multiple-criteria decision-making methods under stochastic inputs. *Energies*, *9*(7), 566. doi:10.3390/en9070566

Kułakowski, K., & Talaga, D. (2020). Inconsistency indices for incomplete pairwise comparisons matrices. *International Journal of General Systems*, *49*(2), 174–200. Advance online publication. doi:10.1080/03081079.2020.1713116

Kumar, A., Sah, B., Singh, A. R., Deng, Y., He, X., Kumar, P., & Bansal, R. C. (2017). A review of multi criteria decision making (MCDM) towards sustainable renewable energy development. *Renewable & Sustainable Energy Reviews*, *69*, 596–609. doi:10.1016/j.rser.2016.11.191

Kwiesielewicz, M., & van Uden, E. (2004). Inconsistent and Contradictory Judgements in Pairwise Comparison Method in AHP. *Computers & Operations Research*, *31*(5), 713–719. doi:10.1016/S0305-0548(03)00022-4

Liang, F., Brunelli, M., & Rezaei, J. (2020). Consistency issues in the best worst method: Measurements and thresholds. *Omega*, *96*, 102175. Advance online publication. doi:10.1016/j.omega.2019.102175

Liu, F., Peng, Y., Zhang, W., & Pedrycz, W. (2017). On Consistency in AHP and Fuzzy AHP. *Journal of Systems Science and Information*, *5*(2), 128–147. doi:10.21078/JSSI-2017-128-20

López-Morales, V., & Suárez-Cansino, J. (2017). Reliable intervals method in decision-based support models for group decision-making. *International Journal of Information Technology & Decision Making*, *16*(01), 183–204. doi:10.1142/S0219622016500498

Magalhaes, C. D., & Silva, P. F. (2018). *A review on multi-criteria decision-making for energy efficiency in automotive engineering*. Applied Computing and Informatics. doi:10.1016/j.aci.2018.04.004

Marković, M. G., Kadoić, N., & Kovačić, B. (2018). Selection and prioritization of adaptivity criteria in intelligent and adaptive hypermedia e-Learning systems. *TEM Journal.*, *7*(1), 137–146.

Mazurek, J. (2017). *On inconsistency indices and inconsistency axioms in pairwise comparisons*. arXiv preprint arXiv:170305204.

Mimovic, P., Jakšić, M., & Leković, M. (2017). A Multicriteria Decision Making Approach to Performance Evaluation of Mutua Funds: A Case Study in Serbia. *Yugoslav Journal of Operations Research*, *28*(3), 385–414.

Mitjans, F., & Méndez, G. F. (2020). Evaluation of the effects of Climate Change on Air Transmission Lines, using PLS-CADD Software tools and Hierarchical Analytical Processes (AHP). Case: Paraguay. *IOSR Journal of Electrical and Electronics Engineering*, *15*(3-I), 24–33.

Moslem, S., Farooq, D., Omid Ghorbanzadeh, O., & Blaschke, T. (2020). Application of the AHP-BWM Model for Evaluating Driver Behavior Factors Related to Road Safety: A Case Study for Budapest. *Symmetry*, *2020*(12), 243. doi:10.3390ym12020243

Mu, E., & Pereyra-Rojas, M. (2017). Practical Decision Making. An Introduction to the Analytic Hierarchy Process (AHP). In Understanding the Analytic Hierarchy Process. Springer. doi:10.1007/978-3-319-33861-3

Munier, N., & Hontoria, E. (2021). Rationality of the AHP Method. In *Uses and Limitations of the AHP Method. Management for Professionals*. Springer. doi:10.1007/978-3-030-60392-2_4

Panwar, M., Chanda, S., Mohanpurkar, M., Luo, Y., Dias, F., Hovsapian, R., & Srivastava, A. K. (2019). Integration of flow battery for resilience enhancement of advanced distribution grids. *International Journal of Electrical Power & Energy Systems*, *109*, 314–324. doi:10.1016/j.ijepes.2019.01.024

Patel, J. N., & Rana, S. C. (2018). A Selection of the Best Location for a Small Hydro Power Project using the AHP-Weighted Sum and PROMETHEE Method. *Pertanika Journal of Science & Technology*, *26*(4).

Ristanovic, V., Primorac, D., & Kozina, G. (2021). Operational Risk Management Using Multi-Criteria Assessment (AHP Model). *Technical Gazette*, *28*(2), 678–683.

Saaty, R. W. (2016). *Decision Making in complex environments. The Analytic Network Process (ANP) for Dependence and Feedback.* Creative Decisions Foundation.

Saaty, T. L. (1977). A scaling method for priorities in hierarchical structures. *Journal of Mathematical Psychology, 15*(3), 234–281. doi:10.1016/0022-2496(77)90033-5

Saaty, T. L. (1979a). *Optimization by the Analytic Hierarchy Process.* Air Force Office of Scientific Research Bolling AFB DC.

Saaty, T. L. (1979b). *Optimization by the Analytic Hierarchy Process.* doi:10.21236/ADA214804

Saaty, T. L. (1980). *The Analytic Hierarchy Process ± Planning, Priority Setting, Resource Allocation.* McGraw-Hill.

Saaty, T. L. (1989). Group Decision Making and the AHP. *The Analytic Hierarchy Process*, 59-67.

Saaty, T. L. (1990). *Decision Making for Leaders: The Analytical Hierarchy Process for Decision in complex world.* RWS Publications.

Saaty, T. L. (1991). Response to Holder's Comments on the Analytic Hierarchy Process: Response to the Response to the Response. *The Journal of the Operational Research Society, 42*(10), 918–924. doi:10.1057/jors.1991.178

Saaty, T. L. (1996). *Decision Making with dependence and feedback: the Analytical Hierarchy Process for Decision in complex world.* RWS Publications.

Saaty, T. L. (2010). *Principia Mathematica Decernendi. Mathematical Principles of Decision Making.* RWS Publications.

Saaty, T. L., & Alexander, J. (1989). *Conflict resolution: The Analytical Hierarchy Process.* Praeger.

Saaty, T. L., & Ergu, D. (2015). When is a Decision-Making Method trustworthy? Criteria for evaluating Multi-Criteria Decision-Making Methods. *International Journal of Information Technology & Decision Making, 14*(06), 1–17. doi:10.1142/S021962201550025X

Saaty, T. L., & Forman, E. H. (1993). *The Hierarchon – A Dictionary of hierarchies.* RWS Publications.

Schwarz, I. L. M., Schwarz, I. T. M., García, G. M. J., Hernández, G. G. J., & Hernández, R. J. G. (2016). Social Impact of Restrictions on Inventory Management. *Proceedings ICIL2016*, 272-282.

Sopha, B. M., Asih, A. M. S., & Nursitasari, P. D. (2018). Location planning of urban distribution center under uncertainty: A case study of Yogyakarta Special Region Province, Indonesia. *Journal of Industrial Engineering and Management, 11*(3), 542–568. doi:10.3926/jiem.2581

Stanković, J., Džunić, M., Džunić, Ž., & Marinković, S. (2017). A multi-criteria evaluation of the European cities' smart performance: Economic, social and environmental aspects. *Proceedings of Rijeka School of Economics, 35*(2), 519–550. doi:10.18045/zbefri.2017.2.519

Wątróbski, J., Jankowski, J., Ziemba, P., Karczmarczyk, A., & Zioło, M. (2019). Generalised framework for multi-criteria method selection. *Omega, 86*, 107–124. doi:10.1016/j.omega.2018.07.004 PMID:30671511

Wind, Y., & Saaty, T. L. (1980). Marketing applications of the Analytical Hierarchy Process. *Management Science, 26*(7), 641–658. doi:10.1287/mnsc.26.7.641

Zahir, M. S. (1996). Incorporating the uncertainty of decision judgments in the Analytical Hierarchy Process. *European Journal of Operational Research*, *53*(2), 206–216. doi:10.1016/0377-2217(91)90135-I

Zhang, Y., Xu, Z., & Liao, H. (2018). An ordinal consistency-based group decision making process with probabilistic linguistic preference relation. *Information Sciences*, *467*, 179–198. doi:10.1016/j.ins.2018.07.059

Software for Teaching:
Case PROMETHEE

Kenia C. Da Silva F.
Universidad Metropolitana, Venezuela

Coromoto D. M. Raidi Ch.
Universidad Metropolitana, Venezuela

Gilberto J. Hernández G.
Minimax Consultores, Venezuela

María J. García G.
Minimax Consultores, Venezuela

José G. Hernández R.
Minimax Consultores, Venezuela

INTRODUCTION

There is defined a line of research, very open, in the sense of its breadth. With it is pursued to relate different fields of knowledge and human knowledge, to generate new knowledge and disseminate this generated knowledge to the public. Within this line of research, there is a field of work that relates support systems, specifically Teaching support systems (TSS [SAE]) (Abbott et al., 2020; Enslow, Fricke & Vela, 2017; Lin, Xie & Luo, 2021), with different areas of mathematics, among others, multicriteria models (Carnero, 2020; Da Silva et al., 2021; Solodukhin, 2019). This space for research has been translated into tools for teaching. It has been possible to create a series of software to facilitate the teaching of mathematics, particularly in the university environment. Interactive tools, in English and Spanish, have been produced to facilitate the teaching of some fields of linear programming, specifically integer programming (Gamboa et al., 2016) and the transportation problem focused as a flow problem (Castaños, 2015). Software for teaching sequencing was also created (Da Corte, 2015). Additionally, a couple of software were produced to facilitate the teaching of multicriteria problems, specifically, the first of them about Data Envelopment Analysis (DEA) problems (Mata & Sanánez, 2015) and the second to provide some light on the Preference Ranking Organization METHod for Enrichment Evaluations (PROMETHEE) (Da Silva & Raidi, 2016).

In this work it wants to present some comments on the process of creating these software and to illustrate it will use the case of PROMETHEE. Immediately the objectives and the methodology used to achieve them are presented.

DOI: 10.4018/978-1-7998-9220-5.ch087

Objectives

From the aforementioned, the general objective of this work is: to present the process of creating a teaching tool, specifically that of the PROMETHEE case. From this general objective, the following specific objectives are generated:

- Present what it is and some relevant aspects of PROMETHEE.
- Show, through the methodology used, how was the process to create a Teaching support system (SAE) to facilitate the learning of PROMETHEE.

Methodology

The methodology to be used to complete this work will coincide with that used in the development of the tools to be presented. It is the Integrated-Adaptable Methodology for the development of Decision Support System ((IAMDSS, in Spanish, Metodología Integradora-Adaptable para desarrollar Sistemas de Apoyo a las Decisiones [MIASAD]). MIASAD has proven to be very useful, to carry out research in different fields of knowledge (Dahdah et al., 2021; De Burgos et al., 2016; García, Hernández & Hernández, 2018; 2020; 2022; Hernández, García & Hernández, 2018; 2022; Schwarz et al., 2016). This methodology, among other advantages, has the characteristic that it is not dedicated to testing hypotheses, but follows a series of steps, which lead the research and facilitate the achievement of the objectives. However, MIASAD does not oblige the researcher to detail each step of it, but the results are obtained, directly and independently (Dahdah et al., 2021). Thanks, above all, to its flexibility, MIASAD, allows to take from its twenty basic steps only those that are necessary for the respective research that is being conducted. In particular, for this work, following an approach similar to that made in Da Silva & Raidi, 2016; García et al., 2017 and Hernández, Hernández & García, 2018, followed the following steps:

1. Define the problem. Which, as has already been said when stating the objectives is: to present the process of creating a teaching tool, specifically that of the PROMETHEE case;
2. Elaborate a first prototype. Among its first functions is to offer a clear vision of what will be the result of the research. In this case, that the final product, is a scientific article, rather than a physical prototype, what is expected is to clearly define who the work is aimed at. Which it translates in identify, before starting the peak of the investigation, the audience, or, potential readers of it. Of them it can highlight all those concerned with the improvement of teaching-learning processes, in particular those who have concerns about improving the teaching of mathematics, to these would be added those interested in multicriteria models and especially those who have particular interest in PROMETHEE. Additionally, it is expected that the article will be of great benefit to all those who start learning this multicriteria technique.

With the intention of defining clearly the final product, with this first prototype, in these cases of scientific articles, the structure of the same is usually presented. In particular, in addition to this introduction, a background will be presented where some brief comments will be made on the teaching learning processes and on PROMETHEE. Then the central chapter will be presented, which will give some details of the creative process of the tool SAE-PROMETHEE (PROMETHEE Teaching support system). To close the article will present the conclusions and some possible lines of future research and will culminate with the references relating to the works cited;

3. Obtain data. In this case, mainly on the SAE and on PROMETHEE;
4. Define alternatives. It consists of defining the different options for developing an SAE for PROMETHEE;
5. Evaluate alternatives. In accordance with the greatest ease to present the process, in a simple way and that is easy to understand by the public to which the work is directed;
6. Select the best alternative. According to the secondary objectives, tacit or explicit those have been contemplated;
7. Implement the best alternative. Although in these cases, there is no physical implementation as such, if the completion of the article should be guaranteed, having met its general objective and its specific objectives;
8. Establish controls. Mechanisms, it allows to recognize if the solution obtained, remains valid in the course of time.

To close these methodological aspects, it should be noted that field studies will not be done, but will only be narrated, in a very brief way, how the process for the creation and implementation of SAE-PROMETHEE took place.

BACKGROUND

In this work the background is given by the teaching-learning processes, specifically the Teaching support systems (TSS [SAE]) and by the multi-criteria technique that will be used as a case, PROMETHEE. Below, some details on these two aspects will be provided starting with SAE.

Comments on the Teaching-learning Process and Teaching Support Systems

In this work, the interest is focused on the teaching of mathematics, in the university environment, with special emphasis on technological tools and multicriteria models. As mentioned in the introduction, a series of works have been carried out that seek to improve the teaching of mathematical models at university level.

The first of these works, and which, therefore, was responsible for establishing the guidelines to follow, was the work on Data Envelopment Analysis (DEA) problems (Mata & Sanánez, 2015). The study and development of tools for the teaching of mathematics has continued to develop in recent years, as can be seen in a large number of recent works (Ameen, Adeniji, & Abdullahi, 2019; Elugbadebo & Johnson, 2020; Moh, Nurhadi & Darhim, 2021). In addition, the concern to improve teaching-learning processes means that seminars are being organized to discuss these issues. To refer only one, mention will be made of the following works: Drozdek & Rugelj (2018); Leoeste & Heidmets (2018); Mettis & Väljataga (2018); Zhang & Fang (2018), in order to provide a small overview of the discussions taking place in this and other similar seminars. But it should be noted that most of the parameters established by Mata & Sanánez (2015), and that were followed in the remaining tools, which are referred in this work, are still current. Following MIASAD ten fundamental steps were established, which will be discussed in the central chapter, when the process of creating the PROMETHEE Teaching support system (SAE-PROMETHEE) is presented. Among other aspects, from what is followed in these steps, it should be noted that the tool to be created must be: pleasant to the user, this includes, colors, contrasts, text distribution; easy to use; everything that exposes must be verified, to avoid teaching errors; allow the user to go at their own pace; not so simple that it looks uninteresting, nor so complicated, that it calls for discouragement. All these previous aspects, although not discussed in depth, given that none of the authors of this chapter is a specialist in this field, undoubtedly have a psychological component.

In addition, in the case of these works, it was required that it be available in Spanish and English, and that it could be easy to use from very different platforms. Having made these brief comments, then some definitions, about PROMETHEE will be given.

Brief Comments on PROMETHEE

There are, and in this work have been used, different sources on PROMETHEE, both of its theoretical aspects, and of authors who have applied it (Brans & De Smet, 2016; Caldersa & Van Asscheb, 2016; Ghobadi & Ahmadipari, 2018; Govindan, Kadziński & Sivakumar, 2017; Ishizaka & Resce, 2021; Oubahman & Duleb, 2021; Shih, 2021; Steynberg, 2016; Verheyden & De Moor, 2016), however, the information presented below, although, for reasons of space, not all the respective citations are presented, it was taken mainly from Da Silva & Raidi (2016), both from their written work, and from the tool created by them, the which is at the following address: http://ares.unimet.edu.ve/sistemas/fpis05/Profesor/PROMETHEE%20WEB_DEFINITIVO!/index_english.html

The first thing to note, it is that PROMETHEE (Preference Ranking Organisation METHod for Enrichment Evaluations) is one of the many existing multicriteria techniques. Actually, it can be said that PROMETHEE is a set of methods; seven, point Faghihinia & Mollaverdi (2012) and Shih, Chang & Cheng (2016) (PROMETHEE I, II, III, IV, V, VI y GAIA [Geometrical Analysis for Interactive Aid]).

PROMETHEE is a method of "overcoming" (outranking), developed by Brans at the beginning of the eighties of the last century and is based on evaluating the dominance, how much it exceeds, one alternative to another.

To use the PROMETHEE methods, in general, it is important to have: a set of alternatives, the criteria to be considered, a performance matrix, which contains the evaluations or evaluations of the alternatives according to each criterion and a vector of relative importance (RI). In addition, information is required between the different criteria (inter-criteria) and information specific to each criterion (intra-criterion).

In the beginning PROMETHEE I offers a partial classification of the alternatives, while PROMETHEE II presents a complete classification (Mehdiyev et al., 2016), PROMETHEE III classifies the alternatives based on intervals and improves the treatment of the indifference in the classifications, while PROMETHEE IV does it on a continuum. For its part PROMETHEE V, the alternatives are selected considering the set of constraints and PROMETHEE VI offers the decision maker freedom to think of weights as intervals, rather than exact values (Faghihinia & Mollaverdi, 2012). Finally, PROMETHEE GAIA allows a better visualization, at the same time that facilitates the realization of sensitivity analysis (Faghihinia & Mollaverdi, 2012). One must speak of an eighth method PROMETHEE GDSS (Liao, 2014) developed for group decision making.

Simplifying the form concise that Mehdiyev et al., 2016 present the steps to carry out the PROMETHEE application, five steps can be indicated:

1. Determine the amplitude of the deviations.
2. Apply the selected preference function. Faghihinia & Mollaverdi (2012) and Mehdiyev et al. (2016) point out six versions of the preference function.
3. The general index of preference is evaluated.
4. The improvement ranges are defined, both positive and negative and

5. The complete classification of PROMETHEE is determined by calculating the net flow of improvement, as the difference between the flow of positive improvement minus the negative.

Among the advantages of PROMETHEE methods: Integrates benefits of all outranking methods, combined with greater ease of use and less complexity; GAIA offers the decision maker a clear graphic description of the problem, stressing the conflicts between the criteria and the impact of the weights in the final decision and because it is a multicriteria method, it has a large number of application fields.

Two of the main disadvantages, come from its advantages: The GAIA graphical analysis, although it presents a clear description of the problem, the development of the graph can be difficult to perform, so it requires a more advanced mathematical understanding, or the use of specialized GAIA software and although PROMETHEE has the advantage, in front of many of its competitors, that it requires very clear and precise additional information and which can be easily obtained by an analyst in conjunction with the decision maker, however, requiring this additional information can be perceived as a disadvantage when assembling a concise structure of the problem, delaying the solution process.

Regarding the applications of PROMETHEE, they are multiple, to mention just a few Patel & Rana (2018), they use it, along with other techniques to locate Hydro Power. For their part, based on a study from 2010, Shih, Chang & Cheng (2016) point out nine fields of application: (i) environment management, (ii) hydrology and water management, (iii) business and financial management, (iv) chemistry, (v) logistics and transportation, (vi) manufacturing and assembly, (vii) energy management, (viii) social, and (ix) other topics. Other applications include global markets (Lopes & Rodriguez-Lopez, 2021). No more information is available on other applications of PROMETHEE in the university environment, however, it is advisable to read the work of Ishizaka et al. (2020), where the technique is used to rank universities.

In any case, if it wishes to have more details about PROMETHEE methods, it is recommended to review the mentioned works, especially the link included above, where the work of Da Silva & Raidi (2016) is available.

Then, it will offer a brief explanation, of how was the process of creation of the Teaching support system (SAE) to facilitate the teaching of PROMETHEE.

BRIEF OVERVIEW OF THE SAE-PROMETHEE CREATION PROCESS

The process of creating the Teaching support system (SAE) to facilitate the teaching of PROMETHEE (SAE-PROMETHEE) was inspired by previous works, to facilitate the teaching of some topics of operations research, which were mentioned in the introduction. Of these works, the one by Mata & Sanánez (2015) should be highlighted since, like Da Silva & Raidi (2016), they also worked on a multicriteria model.

All these works made use of the Integrated-Adaptable Methodology for the development of Decision Support System (MIASAD). For this reason, to present SAE-PROMETHEE, MIASAD will also be followed, reflecting the steps followed by Da Silva & Raidi (2016):

1. Definition of the problem,
2. Present the first prototype,
3. Collect data,
4. Define the model,
5. Generate the model,
6. Constructed the second prototype,

7. Define the support system,
8. Develop the support system,
9. Test and validate the system and
10. Present an implementation plan.

Here it will present some brief details of each of these steps. Previously, it is necessary to clarify that in the original work of Da Silva & Raidi (2016) the name SAE-PROMETHEE was not used, to identify the tool, as it is done here. It is also important to note that, for reasons of space, although most of the information in this session was obtained from Da Silva & Raidi (2016), appointments will only be made to them, when absolute necessary.

Definition of the Problem

The first thing was to be clear about the objectives that they wanted to achieve with their work. By establishing these objectives, the definition of the problem is achieved: develop a tool that will facilitate the teaching of PROMETHEE, through the Web, that was multi-platform bilingual (English and Spanish), that includes the necessary elements to transmit in a simple way the knowledge related to PROMETHEE methods, including theory, problem solving and some references, which will provide the teacher with additional support to teach PROMETHEE methods, and at the same time, giving students the opportunity to opt for autonomous and online learning, through theory, step-by-step examples, proposed exercises and the use of the tool as support for what is taught in the classes.

Present the First Prototype

Although they had a very clear definition of the problem and it was well known where they wanted to go, the construction of the first prototype was not straightforward.

There were two classes of users, students and teachers. Of the first ones, since they were future students of the subject where they would learn PROMETHEE, they could only be asked for information about how they would like to see the information presented. Therefore, there was a greater exchange of information with the teachers. From all the information collected, the first prototype was reached, which is shown in Figure 1.

Figure 1. First prototype
Source: Da Silva & Raidi (2016).

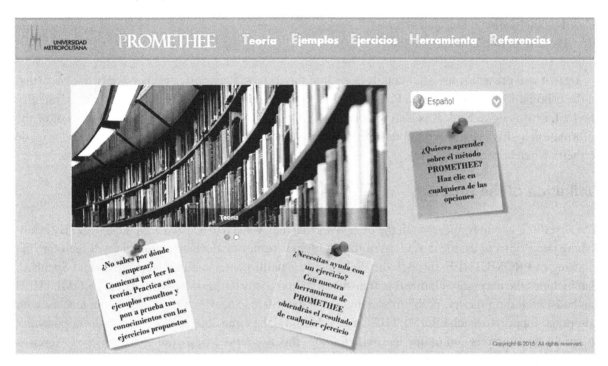

Something was very clear with this first prototype, the visual that should be the tool and that should give the user, especially the student, many facilities to move through it. Additionally, it was known that it should cover aspects of theory, examples, exercises, some tool to facilitate calculations and many references.

Collect Data

This step focused on two fundamental aspects to be able to complete the tool in a satisfactory way, information about PROMETHEE and about techniques to develop an SAE.

An exhaustive research was carried out, through: Google Scholar, bibliographic references on PROMETHEE, and everything that could be found in books, scientific journals, applications of the methods, as well as studies carried out by researchers worldwide, covering some topic of the methods. It was tried, at the same time, to collect examples and exercises where they had applications of PROMETHEE methods.

In addition, those factors that are fundamental in a computer learning system were investigated and other SAEs were reviewed, especially those related to mathematics.

Define the Model

For the definition of the mathematical model, it was necessary to investigate and put into practice, from the beginning, all the information that was obtained in the data collection, to include it in the tool. In fact, a specific mathematical model is not available, but rather, through the revised references, general expressions of the technique of the PROMETHEE methods are followed. To solve the problems related to the PROMETHEE method it is essential that students acquire basic concepts about multicriteria analysis, such as: alternatives, criteria, decision-maker, decision making, weights of the alternatives and additionally they must master the basic mathematical operations.

Generate the Model

As noted in the previous step, there is no proper model, but a set of mathematical expressions that allow the resolution of problems, making use of SEA-PROMETHEE. However, for a better understanding of PROMETHEE methods, the tool should offer a series of examples and practical exercises, of PROMETHEE applications extracted from the bibliographic references consulted. In this case the objective is to provide the student with a detailed guide to the resolution of PROMETHEE problems and then a series of exercises to reinforce knowledge about the technique.

Constructed the Second Prototype

Perhaps this is one of the most relevant steps in the construction of the SEA-PROMETHEE, so that it can be guaranteed that the two primary objectives are met, supporting the teacher, and helping the student to better understand the PROMETHEE methods. After having made the relevant changes referred to the constructive criticisms of the first prototype and above all having understood and incorporated "the mathematical model", a second prototype was made with notable improvements such as a more user-friendly interface. In Figure 2, as a product of this second prototype, the initial screen of the system is shown. It contains: the navigation bar, the logo of the system (PROMETHEE) which when clicked brings to the same home page, the logo of the Metropolitan University which contains a hyperlink to the main page of this institution, a Spanish flag icon indicating that by pressing the flag the page can be viewed in a second language, Spanish (or English if it starts in the Spanish version).

Figure 2. Initial screen of the system, product of the second prototype
Source: Da Silva & Raidi (2016).

In addition, it contains an image presentation or "slideshow" which indicates, in summary, the main content of the page (Theory, Examples, Exercises, Tool and System Language Change), by passing the cursor over each of them. It also has some small boxes with a brief introduction to what is the PROMETHEE model and a small paragraph about the intellectual authors of the system. Finally, in the lower part, not visible in Figure 2, but in Figure 3, are the right of authors of the system and its content.

From the above it can highlight several of the main components of the SAE-PROMETHEE: Theoretical aspects, Examples, Exercises, Tools and References.

- **Theoretical aspects:** It allows the student to delve into the most important points of PROMETHEE methods and thus better understand the practical application of the model. It should be clarified here that, although the tool presents the remaining PROMETHEE models, it is focused on PROMETHEE I and II, mainly the latte.

As can be seen in Figure 3, most of the theoretical lessons have a link at the bottom of the page, which takes the user to a source that offers more information about the topic dealt with in this section. In this way, if the student wishes to have more knowledge and deepen more about the subject, it will be able to access the bibliographic source indicated in the hyperlink.

- **Examples:** There are two examples. These solved examples are shown step-by-step, in different screens. In general, these steps include: The statement, verbally and graphically, The Solution, detailed step-by-step, whenever it is necessary to use some equation, formula or graph, will be provided to the student through a hyperlink in the upper part, which takes it to the theoretical session that covers that aspect, and Answer, where the correct answer to the problem is presented.

Figure 3. Theoretical aspects, product of the second prototype
Source: Da Silva & Raidi (2016).

- **Exercises:** SAE-PROMETHEE has a section of practical exercises, so that the student can practice, clarify all its doubts and reinforce all its knowledge. In the same way these practical exercises will help the user to understand, a little more, the application that PROMETHEE has in matters of daily life.
- **Tools:** Likewise, SAE-PROMETHEE has a tool section, which will help the student solve multicriteria problems through the PROMETHEE method, in an automated way. Starting from the number of alternatives and number of criteria, the tool will demand information from the user, to finally throw a result of the problem raised.
- **References:** In alphabetical order they appear a set of works, some of them used, like material of direct support, by Da Silva & Raidi (2016) and others used in indirect form, but all of them related to the PROMETHEE methods.

Define the Support System

As it is an SAE, the first thing that was verified is that it met the fundamental factors that a computer learning system must contain and in turn, that the necessary tools were integrated to facilitate the learning of the PROMETHEE methods. The system was designed to be interactive with the user, in addition to being a bilingual platform and which, in turn, supports the teacher in terms of teaching a new method of decision making and assessing whether if this knowledge was acquired correctly by the students through theory, step-by-step examples, exercises and the tool implemented. The fundamental aspects of the SAE were already indicated in the previous step: Theoretical aspects, Examples, Exercises, Tools and References.

Develop the Support System

To develop the support system were taken into account, among other aspects: Characteristics of the system, Theoretical component of the system, The examples Step by Step, The Proposed Exercises, The Tool, SAE-PROMETHEE, proper and the References.

- **System features:** SAE-PROMETHEE, being a Web platform, has the great advantage of being able to be accessed from different devices. To achieve this, the system was developed in the HTML5, CSS3 and JavaScript languages. This allowed the tool to be viewed from different devices and browsers. Thanks to the NetBeans tool it was possible to confirm the visualization of this system, so that it was accessed from the following devices: Desktop, Tablet and Smartphone. Ensuring adequate visualization in all of them.
- **Theoretical component of the system:** On the other hand, as has already been pointed out, every SAE must have some characteristics that help it fulfill its main function, which is to facilitate teaching. For this reason, all the SAE-PROMETHEE, but mainly, the theoretical component, had to comply with a couple of characteristics:
  - Colors and Text. The first should be neutral and the second without blank spaces, but without neglecting the aesthetic, avoiding that all the content was agglomerated in one place.
  - Navigability. On each page, both the English and Spanish platforms, the user will be presented with a navigable menu both in the upper part (navigation bar) and in the right side, with which it can go to any section it wants. In addition, if the user clicks on the theory section, in the navigation bar or in the theory image in the slideshow, he will observe in a compressed

way each of the points to be treated in the theoretical section of the system. These points in turn have links that when clicked redirect the user to the corresponding theoretical content page.

- The examples step-by-step. Again, the navigability is very important. If the student clicks the Examples section in the navigation bar or in the theory image in the slideshow, it will observe in a compressed way each of the themes to be discussed in this section. These points in turn have links that, when clicked, redirect the user to corresponding example page. In the example screen, there is a small index just below the title, so that if the user wants to go to a specific part of the example, he can do it without any complications. Likewise, this index presents the link "Examples", in case it wants to go to the initial screen of the examples, and a link "Example 2", in case it wants to see the following example.

In the same way the content has a great importance, and indicate Da Silva & Raidi (2016), that the main reason for which the page of examples step-by-step was designed was to transmit concisely and interactively in a practical way the resolution of problems that make use of PROMETHEE methods. The user will have the opportunity to visualize each of the explicit steps of how to solve the mathematical model in practical problems extracted from the specialized literature. There are two different examples available; one short and one longer.

The short example will be used to introduce the student to the steps of resolving a PROMETHEE problem, identifying the required data and placing the results that are obtained as each step is completed.

The longer example will be used to challenge the student a little more and help him to understand a problem of greater complexity, with more alternatives and more criteria. However, this last example will not be completely resolved by two factors: the space factor, since the page would be very extensive what could cause boredom to the user when observing the resolution of the problem. And there is the learning factor, where the student can practice what they learned both in the theoretical section, as seen in the examples, and thus compare their final results with the system to verify that they have really understood the problem solving process with PROMETHEE.

Da Silva & Raidi (2016) stresses that the resolution process is a bit extensive, so the aim was to make the scroll bar as short as possible, since this plays an important factor in the display of the page by the students. If the scroll bar is very small, it will indicate that the page is very long, so the enthusiasm in reviewing the information will decrease.

- The proposed exercises. A series of proposed exercises are offered so that the user can reinforce what they have learned with the theory and the examples step-by-step. Each one of the proposed problems has its respective answer, which allows the user to solve it with the help of the tool and verify that the answer is correct. With the proposed exercises is not intended to evaluate the student, but simply provide support material and tools for their learning. Because it wanted to reinforce the knowledge acquired in the theoretical section and in the examples, a guide of ten exercises was elaborated, including elementary, intermediate and some more complex exercises. It was made in a pdf format so that the user could easily download it on its computer and in turn could print it if he wished to have it among its notes. It was wanted to avoid that the content of the page was very heavy and very extensive, since they are ten statements of different problems and a considerable number of images are presented.

- The Tool. To support the student, a tool was implemented which made it easier for they to verify the results of the different problems.

All the examples and exercises shown in the system were solved with this tool, to verify that the results were consistent with those presented in the bibliographic references consulted.

This tool works through two simple steps: 1. Enter the number of alternatives and criteria of the problem and 2. Enter the data corresponding to the initial values of the problem. In addition, the necessary parameters must be inserted for the solution of the same, as are the objective function, the type of criterion, the weight and the values of preference (p), indifference (q) or average (s), depending on the case.

To obtain the final solution the user must press accept to be redirected to a new screen that will show as a result: The matrix of preference index, the positive, negative and net flows, and finally the winning alternative. Likewise, the page that shows the final result has a link "Back to Top", which directs the user to the first page of the tool to again introduce the number of alternatives and criteria. This in order to facilitate the user redirection for a new solution, in case if it wants to solve another problem, more quickly.

- SAE-PROMETHEE, properly speaking. It is the product of all the previous steps and is finally the tool for problem solving PROMETHEE, specifically PROMETHEE II. In addition, to provide support to the teacher, offers the student a support to facilitate learning. SAE-PROMETHEE was made using JavaScript and HTML5 together.

- References. With the intention that they serve as additional resources to those interested, this section placed each of the bibliographic references that were used to carry out the development of the tool, as well as those handled in the exhaustive investigation of PROMETHEE methods.

Test and Validate the System

To test and validate the system, a series of tests were performed that demonstrated the correct functionality of the SAE. It was verified in both the English and Spanish platforms that each of the interactive components will perform efficiently when required by the user. Each of the examples step-by-step and proposed exercises were checked, in such a way that they fulfilled the desired operation, and thus, prove that the results that the tool showed were consistent with the questions of the corresponding exercise.

Present an Implementation Plan

This an academic requirement. Although, the students are not required to implement the software, because in some cases it depends on factors outside of them, if they are usually required to present a plan to follow, in order to achieve this implementation. Da Silva & Raidi (2016), fulfilled this requirement, since they not only presented the implementation plan, but SAE-PROMETHEE, is currently operative through the link, previously indicated:

http://ares.unimet.edu.ve/sistemas/fpis05/Profesor/PROMETHEE%20WEB_DEFINITIVO!/index_english.html

With the recommendation to readers, to review this link and have a broader view of the tool, the work is concluded and then some conclusions and recommendations for future research will be presented.

FUTURE RESEARCH DIRECTIONS

The first is to encourage the use of SAE-PROMETHEE, for those who want to start in this important multicriteria technique, as well as those who know the PROMETHEE methods, who want to use the SAE, as support, both to solve problems, and to teach third parties. Additionally, although it is not an objective pursued with the creation of SAE-PROMETHEE, the tool can be used outside the academic field, to solve problems of medium complexity. Unfortunately, the creators of the tool lose control of it and it is left to the hands of the university for which it was created, obtain from it a greater benefit. The latter would be achieved by encouraging students to use it and generating workshops for the teaching of PROMETHEE where SAE-PROMETHEE is used.

In achieving these objectives, it is clear that MIASAD is an excellent methodology to achieve this type of research. Hence arises a second recommendation for future research. Use the MIASAD, to create other tools, similar to the one presented here. These can be for: a) teaching other multicriteria models, b) making other aspects of operations research and decision-making in general and c) teaching other topics that are not directly related to mathematical models.

CONCLUSION

In this paper, following the Integrated-Adaptable Methodology for the development of Decision Support System (MIASAD), the process of creating the Teaching support system (SAE) to facilitate the teaching of PROMETHEE (SAE-PROMETHEE) was presented, thus achieving the proposed general objective.

In addition, some comments were made on what it is and what are some more relevant aspects of the PROMETHEE methods. And having made use of MIASAD, to show the relevant steps in the creation of SAE-PROMETHEE, the specific objectives were achieved.

It is important to note that the tool developed can provide a series of facilities to the students of the university, for which it was developed. Among these facilities, the most important to highlight is the flexibility it offers in the teaching-learning process. Above all, it should be emphasized that SAE-PROMETHEE, can be used anytime, anywhere and under a large number of platforms.

ACKNOWLEDGMENT

This research would not have been possible without the support offered by Minimax Consultores, C. A., especially through its Research Management.

REFERENCES

Abbott, P. A., Brooker, R., Hu, W., Hampton, S., & Reath, J. (2020). I Just Had No Idea What It Was Like to Be in Prison and What Might Be Helpful. *Educator and Learner Views on Clinical Placements in Correctional Health, Teaching and Learning in Medicine*, *32*(3), 259–270. doi:10.1080/10401334.2020.1715804 PMID:32064934

Ameen, S. K., Adeniji, M. S., & Abdullahi, K. (2019). Teachers' and students' level of utilization of ICT tools for teaching and learning mathematics in Ilorin, Nigeria. *African Journal of Educational Studies in Mathematics and Science*, *15*(1), 51–59. doi:10.4314/ajesms.v15i1.5

Brans, J. P., & De Smet, Y. (2016). PROMETHEE Methods. In J. R. Figueira, M. Ehrgott M. & S. Greco (Eds), Multiple criteria decision analysis: State of the art surveys. Springer. doi:10.1007/978-1-4939-3094-4_6

Caldersa, T., & Van Asscheb, D. (2016). *PROMETHEE is Not Quadratic: An O(qn log(n)) Algorithm.* arXiv:1603.00091v1 [cs.DS].

Carnero, M. C. (2020). Fuzzy Multicriteria Models for Decision Making in Gamification. *Mathematics 2020, 8*(5), 1-23. doi:10.3390/math8050682

Castaños, M. (2015). *Sistema de apoyo para facilitar el aprendizaje de los problemas del Agente viajero y de transbordo, como un problema de flujos* [Dissertation]. Universidad Metropolitana, Caracas, Venezuela.

Da Corte, D. (2015). Sistema de apoyo para facilitar la enseñanza de los problemas de secuenciación [Dissertation]. Universidad Metropolitana, Caracas, Venezuela.

Da Silva, F. F., Souza, C. L. M., Silva, F. F., Costa, H. G., Da Hora, H. R. M., & Erthal Junior, M. (2021). Elicitation of criteria weights for multicriteria models: Bibliometrics, typologies, characteristics and applications. *Brazilian Journal of Operations & Production Management, 18*(4), e2021901. doi:10.14488/BJOPM.2021.014

Da Silva, K., & Raidi, C. (2016). *Sistema de apoyo para facilitar la enseñanza del método PROMETHEE*. System Engineering dissertation, Universidad Metropolitana, Caracas, Venezuela.

Dahdah, A. J. J., Hernández, G. G. J., García, G. M. J., & Hernández, R. J. G. (2021). The Myth of the Importance of Consistency in Analytical Hierarchical Processes. *International Journal of Knowledge-Based Organizations, 11*(1), 1–13. doi:10.4018/IJKBO.2021010101

De Burgos, J. J., García, G. M. J., Hernández, G. G. J., & Hernández, R. J. G. (2016). Generation and Management Knowledge. A View from the Manager of Packing. *Proceedings ICIL2016*, 32-44.

Drozdek, S., & Rugelj, J. (2018). Creating multimedia learning materials for improved teacher training. *Proceedings of ICEM 2018 Conference*, 139-156.

Elugbadebo, O., & Johnson, F. (2020). Computer usage proficiency towards pedagogical knowledge and learning improvement. *Ukrainian Journal of Educational Studies and Information Technology, 8*(4), 52–66. doi:10.32919/uesit.2020.04.05

Enslow, E., Fricke, S., & Vela, K. (2017). Providing Health Sciences Services in a Joint-Use Distributed Learning Library System: An Organizational Case Study. *Medical Reference Services Quarterly, 36*(4), 362–376. doi:10.1080/02763869.2017.1369286 PMID:29043936

Faghihinia, E., & Mollaverdi, N. (2012). Building a maintenance policy through a multi-criterion decision-making model. *Journal of Industrial Engineering International, 8*(14), 1–15. doi:10.1186/2251-712X-8-14

Gamboa, B. S. V., Hernández, G. G. J., García G., M. J., & Hernández R., J. G. (2016). Decision Support System to facilitate teaching of Integer Programming. Document presented Eureka 2016, Torreón, México.

García, G. M. J., Hernández, G. G. J., & Hernández, R. J. G. (2018). Participation of women in logistics through innovation. *International Journal of Sustainable Entrepreneurship and Corporate Social Responsibility, 3*(2), 32–52. doi:10.4018/IJSECSR.2018070103

García, G. M. J., Hernández, G. G. J., & Hernández, R. J. G. (2020). Marginalization of Women and Mass Markets. In A. Gurtu (Ed.), Recent Advancements in Sustainable Entrepreneurship and Corporate Social Responsibility (pp. 69–87). Academic Press.

García, G. M. J., Hernández, G. G. J., & Hernández, R. J. G. (2022). Looking for an approach to ethics through logistics. *International Journal of Sustainable Entrepreneurship and Corporate Social Responsibility, 7*(1), 1–17. Advance online publication. doi:10.4018/IJSECSR.287869

García, G. M. J., Schwarz, I. L. M., Schwarz, I. T. M., Hernández, G. G. J., & Hernández, R. J. G. (2017). Inventories control, the Inventory manager and Matrixes Of Weighing with multiplicative factors (MOWwMf). *Journal of Global Business and Technology*, *13*(1), 40–56.

Ghobadi, M., & Ahmadipari, M. (2018). Environmental Planning for Wind Power Plant Site Selection using a Fuzzy PROMETHEE-Based Outranking Method in Geographical Information System. *Environmental Energy and Economic Research*, *2*(2), 75–87.

Govindan, K., Kadziński, M., & Sivakumar, R. (2017). Application of a novel PROMETHEE-based method for construction of a group compromise ranking to prioritization of green suppliers in food supply chain. *Omega*, *71*, 129–145. doi:10.1016/j.omega.2016.10.004

Hernández, R. J. G., García, G. M. J., & Hernández, G. G. J. (2018). Inventories control, state regulations, and The Amplitude Model (TAM). In N. H. Shah & M. Mittal (Eds.), *Handbook of Research on Promoting Business Process Improvement Through Inventory Control Techniques* (pp. 442–467). IGI Global. doi:10.4018/978-1-5225-3232-3.ch023

Hernández, R. J. G., García, G. M. J., & Hernández, G. G. J. (2022). Safety and attention of passengers with disabilities who travel by train. *International Journal of Sustainable Entrepreneurship and Corporate Social Responsibility*, *7*(1), 1–16. Advance online publication. doi:10.4018/IJSECSR.287867

Hernández, R. J. G., Hernández, G. G. J., & García, G. M. J. (2018). The Logistic Model Based on Positions (LoMoBaP [MoLoBaC]) & Industry 4.0. In Handbook of Research on Emerging Developments in Industry 4.0. Hershey, PA: IGI Global.

Ishizaka, A., Pickernell, D., Huang, S., & Senyard, J. M. (2020). Examining knowledge transfer activities in UK universities: Advocating a PROMETHEE-based approach. *International Journal of Entrepreneurial Behaviour & Research*, *26*(6), 1389–1409. Advance online publication. doi:10.1108/IJEBR-01-2020-0028

Ishizaka, A., & Resce, G. (2021). Best-Worst PROMETHEE method for evaluating school performance in the OECD's PISA project. *Socio-Economic Planning Sciences*, *73*, 100799. doi:10.1016/j.seps.2020.100799

Leoeste, J., & Heidmets, M. (2018). The impact of educational robots as learning tools on mathematics learning outcomes in basic education. *Proceedings of ICEM 2018 Conference*, 203-218.

Liao, H., & Xu, Z. (2014). Multi-criteria decision making with intuitionistic fuzzy PROMETHEE. *Journal of Intelligent & Fuzzy Systems*, *27*(4), 1703–1717. doi:10.3233/IFS-141137

Lin, H., Xie, S., & Luo, Y. (2021). Construction of a Teaching Support System Based on 5G Communication Technology. In S. K. Bhatia, S. Tiwari, S. Ruidan, M. C. Trivedi, & K. K. Mishra (Eds.), *Advances in Computer, Communication and Computational Sciences. Advances in Intelligent Systems and Computing, 1158*. Springer. doi:10.1007/978-981-15-4409-5_16

Lopes, A. P., & Rodriguez-Lopez, N. A. (2021). Decision Support Tool for Supplier Evaluation and Selection. *Sustainability*, *13*(22), 12387. doi:10.3390u132212387

Mata, M. A., & Sanánez, F. J. (2015). *Desarrollo de un sistema para facilitar el aprendizaje del análisis envolvente de datos* [Dissertation]. Universidad Metropolitana, Caracas, Venezuela.

Mehdiyev, N., Enke, D., Fettke, P., & Loos, P. (2016). Evaluating forecasting methods by considering Different accuracy measures. *Procedia Computer Science*, *95*, 264–271. doi:10.1016/j.procs.2016.09.332

Mettis, K., & Väljataga, T. (2018). Mapping the challenges of outdoor learning for both students and teachers. *Proceedings of ICEM 2018 Conference*, 51-68.

Moh, N. (2021). Analysis The Ability of Thinking Abstractly of Mathematics And Self-Efficacy Through Tpack. *Journal of Physics: Conference Series*, *1764*(1), 012122. doi:10.1088/1742-6596/1764/1/012122

Oubahman, L., & Duleb, S. (2021). Review of PROMETHEE method in transportation. *Production Engineering Archives*, *27*(1), 69–74. doi:10.30657/pea.2021.27.9

Patel, J. N., & Rana, S. C. (2018). A Selection of the Best Location for a Small Hydro Power Project using the AHP-Weighted Sum and PROMETHEE Method. *Pertanika Journal of Science & Technology*, *26*(4), 1591–1603.

Schwarz, I. L. M., Schwarz, I. L. M., García, G. M. J., Hernández, G. G. J., & Hernández, R. J. G. (2016). Social Impact of Restrictions on Inventory Management. *Proceedings ICIL2016*, 272-282.

Shih, H. (2021). Threshold-Enhanced PROMETHEE Group Decision Support under Uncertainties. *Mathematical Problems in Engineering*, *5594074*, 1–21. Advance online publication. doi:10.1155/2021/5594074

Shih, H., Chang, Y., & Cheng, C. (2016). A Generalized PROMETHEE III with Risk Preferences on Losses and Gains. *International Journal of Information and Management Sciences*, *27*, 117–127.

Solodukhin, K. (2019). Fuzzy Strategic Decision –Making Models Based on Formalized Strategy Maps. Advances in Economics. *Business and Management Research*, *47*, 543–547.

Steynberg, R. (2016). *A framework for identifying the most likely successful underprivileged tertiary bursary applicants* [Master's Dissertation]. Stellenbosch University, South Africa.

Verheyden, T., & De Moor, L. (2016). Process-oriented social responsibility indicator for mutual funds: A multi-criteria decision analysis approach. *International Journal of Multicriteria Decision Making*, *6*(1), 66–99. doi:10.1504/IJMCDM.2016.075610

Zhang, H., & Fang, L. (2018). Project-based learning for statistical literacy: A Gamification approach. *Proceedings of ICEM 2018 Conference*, 3-16.

The Diamond of Innovation

Fernando Ojeda

Universidad Piloto de Colombia, Colombia

INTRODUCTION

This first installment seeks to explain in its basic concepts, the genesis and scientific support of the tool to be used: The Innovation Diamond, with each of the eight points, determines the importance of these as an assessment support against cases related to Innovation, be it for a Country, City, Company or business sector. From the contribution called "Creation of the Diamond", Table No 1 arises, called: GOOD PRACTICES of business models and associated public policy, of the countries of R. P. China, Japan, Vietnam, South Korea, R. China-Taiwan and Singapore. From it, the genesis and beginning of the tool is explained, based on each element that, in terms of Innovation, each of these countries contributes with its unique characteristics, there are nine determining and unique, but determining elements.

To complete the Diamond points, an epistemological study is made around innovation. Contributions from western authors are observed from the eighteenth century, as well as from nations with an innovative vocation, such as from the ancient Chinese nation, ancient Egypt and Sumerian. There the Diamond finally emerges with its eight points. The same is observed, with Table No 2 "Contribution from the Epistemological, to the Diamond of Innovation". Having this construction, the Diamond is shown with its eight points (Figure No. 1), it arrives with its respective indicators that, in addition, allow to be management indicators for each point, and a reference to make a respective traceability for each one.

With the structure of the Diamond, the analytical scope of the tool is explained, which is capable of studying, observing, projecting, etc. This tool and its green versión, remain at the disposal of the global society, which understands that it is essential to generate new and continuous innovations, but its impact on the environment must always be evaluated.

BACKGROUND

The origin of the tool is the product of the work of twelve years, which have been dedicated to studying the business model, associated public policy, culture, education, of the countries of Southeast Asia, and Central Asia. From this investigative work, the tool known as "The Diamond of Innovation" was generated: Of Innovation, of a business structure, its diffusion and investment in machinery and equipment, of a country, city, sector, region.

From the geographic specialization of its industries, accompanied by the construction of spaces in the manner of technology parks, universities and State Institutions of financial, logistical, legal support and continuous specialized Research. From the media and organizations that are part of the State-private sector gear. From the consolidation of companies-brands, inside and outside the country of origin, at an industrial level, consolidating itself as a source of national wealth and creation of patents.

DOI: 10.4018/978-1-7998-9220-5.ch088

From the consolidation of business subsectors, proactive to the continuous added value in their products, supplies, services, processes, source of the "Orange Economy". That every resulting process minimizes the environmental impact, under the strategic principle of Green Innovation.

FOCUS OF THE ARTICLE

The chapter associated with Innovation and the tool called "Diamond of Innovation", has the following main parts: First, the creation of the Diamond, which explains the genesis and origin of the structure of the Diamond. This part has two components, the origin of the Diamond, from the models of Education, State, Company, etc., of South Korea, People's Republic of China, Japan, Vietnam, Singapore and Republic of China-Taiwan, see Table No 1. GOOD PRACTICES of business models and associated public policy, from the countries of R. P. China, Japan, Vietnam, South Korea, R. China-Taiwan and Singapore. The second component, an epistemological support around the concept of innovation, supported by Western authors from the 18th century and ancient nations headed by China.

It ends with the presentation of the Diamond of Innovation and its eight points. The second part explains the origin, structure and scope of the green version of the Diamond or the "Green Diamond".

SOLUTIONS AND RECOMMENDATIONS (chapter-specific Sections)

Having the Diamond as a diagnostic tool and source of strategies associated with the innovation of a City, country, company, business sector, it seeks to answer the following questions:

- What are the paradigms in terms of Innovation to be followed worldwide TODAY?
- What is the State in terms of Innovation, in our country, region, Company, city, business sector?
- What priorities in terms of associated Strategy, SHOULD we implement, in our country, city, region, Company, business sector?
- What are our GREATEST PRIORITIES, in terms of Innovation, that are presented in our country, city, region, Company, business sector?
- What strategic path, should an entrepreneur, academic, state worker, student in the areas of the environment and business have with respect to the innovation of a process, service, input, final good, in a city, country, company, business sector?

DIAMOND CREATION

To get to the construction of the Diamond, it was "fed" in its initial phase of construction, of the business models and the institutions created to support and "raise" the company, through the following books of the FIRMS ASIAN: *The largest city in the world Chongqing* (Ojeda, 2014a); *Takeoff of the great Japanese brands and strategies* (Ojeda, 2014b); *The historical evolution of the Asian Firms model* (Ojeda, 2014c); *The Asian Crisis* (Ojeda, 2014g); *The new Asian miracle, from total destruction and the failed state to the latest model of Asian business success* (Ojeda, 2014d); *Bangalore the Silicon Valley of India* (Ojeda, 2014e); *The business model of 21st century China* (Ojeda, 2014f); *The best kept secret in Asia:*

TAIWAN (Ojeda, 2018); plus, the book on International Business: *International Business Environment* (Ojeda, 2015).

To do this, we must observe Table No 1, called: GOOD PRACTICES of business models and associated public policy, of the countries of R. P. China, Japan, Vietnam, South Korea, R. China-Taiwan and Singapore an see:

Back

It shows a trend, which is observed and it is the end of some dynasties, which, like that of the current P.R. China, is millenary. It implies for Continental China the beginning of the State without Institutions formed under the interest of the royal family or, for the R. China-Taiwan, (SEE Table No 1).

Take Off

It implies new ways of creating and promoting the company (Table 1).

Constitutional Reforms

The highest law (the Constitution) is integrated into the changes where the State is the leader and "captain" of the company and its high value-added sectors. This differential contribution is therefore the support of one of the points and indicators of the Diamond, which promotes the opening of commercial borders within Innovation, under the impulse of private property.

Leading Productive Sectors

Step by step, starting in 1867 in Japan, earlier or later, all these countries gradually choose the sectors that will mark their company concept of the 20th century and the beginning of the 21st century.

Geographic Spaces/ Specialized Contributions in Innovation

The version of specialized and large-scale clusters is the response from these countries around the creation of spaces where value chains are developed from design, to end up as outsourcing, such as MiPymes, and suppliers, which are chained.

Expert Production Zones

Cities, born and structured to specialize and provide products, supplies, services, exclusively for international markets, sometimes satellites, other times of a complementary and continuous port efficiency, (See Table No 1).

Companies, leading Brands

Under the principle that recognizes in the copy, an acknowledgment of what is well done, all these companies, with local markets that serve as tests for years, to adjust and create economies of scale that adjust the cost structure, move to regions to make the leap to global channels and markets, thanks to this experience, national CEOs, low relative prices and continuous innovation, always with high value-added products (See Table No 1).

Human Resource

This resource, aligned in its education, recruitment and then supply with the five-year plans or, if applicable, with its Industrial centers. It is important to highlight the training of a number of engineers, the centers as associations of specialized professionals and a new number of professionals, unbeatable worldwide, especially from science and mathematics, as basic areas of study, (See Table No 1).

State Institutions Focused on Innovation, Integrated to the Company

The State is binding, indivisible, an example to follow, recruiter of the best human resource, leader and credible, in the vast majority of State Institutions associated with the company.

The efficient and respectful use of public resources must also be reflected in economic growth, which is included with the GDP based on PPP valuation. (See Table No 1), associated with this point and the chosen indicator.

EPISTEMOLOGICAL SUPPORT OF THE REST OF THE DIAMOND POINTS

The Diamond of Innovation, in its construction, was complemented with an epistemological study, accompanied by a historical journey of the origin of Innovation in its condition of center and continuous attraction in these countries between company and State. With this mixed contribution, from the Asian models, plus the outstanding and recognized theories of the subject, the Diamond of Innovation (DDI) is built, completing the eight points, with its chosen traceability indicators.

This path, which also seeks not to neglect the contribution that entire nations, companies, authors have historically left behind, in its most important journey, highlights with this contribution the following (Table No 2: "Contribution from the Epistemological, to the Diamond of the innovation".:

The ancient nations from the Sumerians (V BC), the Egyptians (XXXIII to III BC), and ancient China, provide learning and planning methods against the restricted use of all kinds of resources and the construction of skills from the first years, associated with Innovation.

CONSTRUCTION AND SUPPORT OF THE INNOVATION DIAMOND

These points or references of Innovation need an assessment, facilitating their traceability, and subsequent strategic-tactical approach as a reference source, compared to what should be considered as ideal in terms of Innovation, of a business structure, of a country, city, sector or region.

Innovation Indicators

The resulting variables in the face of Innovation, with which the Innovation Diamond has, each one will be evaluated through an Indicator, whose source and credibility is high, both by the study of the respec-

Table 1. Good practices of business models and associated public policy, from the countries of R. P. China, Japan, Vietnam, South Korea, R. China-Taiwan and Singapore

Differential Contributions of each Country	P.R. China	Japan	Vietnam	Suth Korea	Singapore	R. China- Taiwan (ROC)	Relationship to Diamond Points
Back	It originates from the fall of the Qing Dynasty (1644-1912) / 1st October 1949 the PR China is born, after a civil war (1945-1949).	Step to Industrialization, starts from his aristocratic class and within a hereditary monarchical tradition (Meiji Revolution 1867), the oldest in the world- 660 B.C.	End of his last Dynasty that of Nguyen (1802-1945). Armed conflict of 1959-1975, an arm of the Cold War where the United States faces, that supports a pro-capitalist regime, located in the South and the USSR, that supports the establishment of a communist regime.	Termination to one of the oldest Dynasties: the Joseon (1392-1910).	In 1963 it adheres as one of the 14 States of the Malayan Federation. It declares its independence in August 1965.	End of civil war in Continental China (1945-1949) giving rise to the RChina-Taiwan (ROC).	With six Indicators
Take Off	Third Plenary Meeting of the XI Central Committee of the Chinese Communist Party (1978). Take-off sectors are established: agriculture, industry, defence, science and Technology. The new Chinese model takes off: *Market Socialism*.	1945-1952 US occupation The Ministry of International Trade and Industry MITI is born (1949). Zaibatsu is liquidated giving way to the Keiretsu (1950). Take-off sectors are developed (1946-1948): iron and steel, coal.	After a decade of a centrally planned communist model, a new model, from the VI Congress of the Vietnamese Communist Party: Market Economy Oriented to Socialism. It develops through what is called as *Doi Moi* or, (July 13, 2000).	Korea Division. Soviet occupation of North Korea on August 12, 1945. US occupation of South Korea on September 8, 1945. Korean War 1950-1953.	August 9, 1965, with a constitutional amendment, the Parliament of Malaysia recognizes the separation of Singapore, approves the law through which the Independence of the Republic of Singapore is declared.	During the 1950s, under the family business model, its type of company, called "Guanxiqiye", took off. In 1980, the first company dedicated to semiconductors was born as a "spin off" of ITRI, the United Microelectronics Corporation (UMC).	
Constitutional Reforms	The Constitution of the Republic of China is born in 1912. Amendment of December 4, 1982.	Reform towards Constitutional Monarchy (1889); Constitution of Peace (1947).	Reform of 1992, which guarantees the right and respect for private property.	Reform of 1987, since the foundations of a Parliamentary Democracy are established.	Creation on December 22, 1965.	Creation on December 22, 1965. Between 1868 and 1947, adopts the Japanese Constitutio.	Index of Economic Freedom.

continued on following page

Table 1. Continued

Differential Contributions of each Country	P.R. China	Japan	Vietnam	South Korea	Singapore	R. China- Taiwan (ROC)	Relationship to Diamond Points
Leading productive sectors	Aeronautics, telecommunications, nanotechnology, agribusiness, mining, logistics structure, household appliances, automotive, military, clean energy, aerospace, financial.	Insurance, Banking, Telecommunications, Electronics, automotive, high-speed mass transportation, nuclear energy, robotics, semiconductor, clean energy, biochemistry.	Agribusiness, forestry, livestock, fertilizers, fishing, fish farming, sporting goods, oil-refinery, tourism and banking.	Electronics, nanotechnology, Agribusiness, Shipyards, cosmetology, light chemicals, fertilizers, clean energy, Aerospace.	Financial Services (Financial and Business- F&B services), Information Technolog, agrotechnology, biotechnology.	SMEs, Biomedical Technology, Disaster, Development, Military, Clean Energy, Ocean Exploratio, and precision machinery.	
Geographic Spaces/ Specialized Contributions in Innovation	Shanghai's Silicon Valley (Pudong-1990); Zhongguancung (Beijing High-Technology Industry Development Experimental Zone-1988). Zhongguancung The "Silicon Valley" of PRChina.	Artificial Islands with multimodal transportation: Omura City and its international airport. Osaka City and its Kansai airport, Kobe City and its airport, Tokoname City.	Tan Thuan Export Processing Zone (TTZ), Ho Chi Minh (EPZ), Linh Trung (EPZ). Ho Chi Minh City University of Agriculture and Foresty. Vietnam Foresty University, Hanoi.	Science Cities from Daeduck Science park (Taejon, DSP-1973); Digital Media City, Kaesong* with North Korea, Changwon National Industrial Complex.	Singapore Science park (SSP-1980); One-North Science Habitat (1N-2005); Biopolis (Buona Vista in shared space with the National University of Singapore.	Tainan Science Park (1996), Hsinchu Science and Industrial Park (1980), Kaohsiung Science Park (2000), Central Research Academy.	Index of Economic Freedom; The Global Competitiveness Index 2014-2015; Higher Education & Training 2014- 2015; GDP based on PPP. Per capita.
Expert Production Zones	Today Shanghai has the largest tonnage and container port in the world. Guangzhou area is the pole of attraction for labor that joins the leading factories of Toys, electronics, plastic products, clothing. The area is Shenzhen, is in the catchment area of Guangzhou and Hong Kong. Research.	Honshu Island-SMEs, Nagoya-Automotive, Toyota Shi-Automotive, Technopolitan Areas (1986). Artificial Islands with multimodal transportation: Omura City and its international airport, Osaka City and its Kansai airport, Kobe City and its airport. Chofu and Tokyo, aerospace research.	The manufacture of electronic elements, nanotechnology, software in Hanoi the capital, Danang and Ho Chi Minh. Gold, Bauxite, in the Pleiku area; Bauxite in the Gio Nghia area; Coal in Bang Son area.	In the city of Daegu, companies are developed from the textile and machinery sectors, origin of Chaebol Samsung. Research and Development, plus disciplinary education on the subject of Agro in North Jeolla Province with the National University de Chonbuk.	In the Singapore Science Park, located on the southwestern side of the country, is the Institute of Microelectronics, petrochemicals, biomedical sciences, food technology.	Biotechnology, Information Technology with; Optoelectronics and electronic circuits in the Tainan and Kaohsiung Industrial Parks; chemicals, metals, agrobusiness in Linhai Park; in Tainan City Xinhua District. Clean Energy.	
Companies-Leading Brands	Galanz (1978), TCL Corporation (1981), Haier (1984), ZTE (1985), Huawei (1987), Lenovo (1990), Aigo (1993), Alibabá (1999), Xiaomi (2011), TCL Corporation (1981), China Mobile (1997).	From holding company such as Matsushita (Panasonic, Akai), Mitsubishi (Honda). Mitsui (Toshiba, Toyota, Hino), Sanwa (Daihatsu, NEC); Global brands like Nissan, SONY, Casio, Yamaha, Kawasaki, Suzuki, Seven Eleven.	Vietin Bank, Agribank, Vietcombank, Petrovietnam, VINAPI, Huu Nghi, Minh Long I, Viet Tiep, Duc Thanh, VNP, VINATEX, Vinamilk, Bao Viet Holding, Thanh Cong Textile (TCG).	Hyundai, LG, Kia, Samsung, Missha, Millimeter Milligram, Daewoo.	Singapore Airlines, Sing Tel, Media Corp., Klok, Temasek Holding, SAP Singapore, Tiger Airways, Keppel Corporation.	Asus, HTC, Acer, Foxconn, Taiwan Semiconductor Manufacturing Company, United Microelectronics Corporation.	

continued on following page

T

Table 1. Continued

Diferential Contributions of each Country	P.R. China	Japan	Vietnam	Suth Korea	Singapore	R. China- Taiwan (ROC)	Relationship to Diamond Points
Human Resource	By the year 2000, about 300,000 engineers were graduating, ten times more than in Germany.	Establishes JUSE, the Japanese Union of Scientists and Engineers, for the transfer and adaptation of knowledge and technology, as at the time it began with William E. Deming (1900-1993). As of 2015, it graduates about 168,000 engineers per year. (1)	Close to 90% of its inhabitants who work are in the private sector, showing a move away from the communist model of more than two decades ago. In 2014, the average salary of a Vietnamese engineer was about 40% cheaper than one in China PR and about 60% cheaper than one in Japan. As of 2015, it graduates nearly 100,000 engineers per year. (1)	According to the OECD, it is the second developed country in which more hours are worked per year. Students from South Korea, together with those from Singapore, obtained the best results in 2014 in the PISA tests focused on creative problem solving. As of 2015, there are about 148,000 engineers, graduates per year. (1)	Since the 1990s, the Singapore workforce has had a high percentage of foreigners, at the end of this era around 16% of the total. Of almost 5,000,000 inhabitants around 2,000,000 are foreigners, the first decade of the millennium reached about 34%, that is, it doubled in two decades (Singapore Department of Statistics.	Second decade of the millennium, the workforce is characterized by developing skills associated with interpersonal relationships, the ability to adapt to changing work situations. Your indicator for Science, Technology, Engineering and Mathematics will be used, which are part of the so-called "STEM", by the first letters corresponding to the words in English that treat each of these areas. (4)	Engineers - year
Instituciones del Estado, Integradas a la Empresa e Innovación	Bank of China, Industrial and Commercial Bank of China, Agricultural Bank of China, China Construction Bank, China Railway Group, Chinese Academy of Sciences. As of 2017, it has 21 "cybersecurity" Institutes. (2)	Ministry of International Trade and Industry (MITI), Japan Union of Scientists and Engineers (JUSE), Japan Industrial Robot Association (JIRA), Agency of Japan International Cooperation (JICA). Japan Aerospace Exploration Agency (JAXA).	Ministry of Planning and Investment (MPI), Union of Industry and Trade Associations (HCMC), Center for Science and Information Technology (CESTI). National Institute for Science and Technology Policy and Strategic Studies (NISTPASS).	Korea Trade Promotion Corporation (KOTRA), Korea; Korea Aerospace Research Institute (KARI), Gastech Young Engineers Foundation (GYEF). In terms of Cybersecurity, according to the GlobalCibersecurity Index of 2017, it ranked No. 13, among 165 countries. (3)	Ministry of Home Affairs, Research, Innovation and Enterprise Council (PMO), Ministry of Trade and Industry, Microelectronics Institute of Singapore, Enterprise Social Business Centre of Excellence, Singapore Innovation & Productivity Institute (SiPi).	SINICA Academy, National Applied Research Laboratories NARLabs, Taiwan External Trade Development Council (TAITRA), Industrial Technology Research Institute (ITRI), National Synchrontron Radiation Research Centre.	Corruption Perception Index (CPI); GDP based on PPP valuation.

SOURCE: (Ojeda, 2015, 2018)
1. (McCarthy, 2015)
2. (Demchak et al., 2015)
3. (International Telecommunication Union, [ITU], 2017)
4. (Midrack, 2022)

tive subject, and by the systematic monitoring supported by Institutions supranational, national, regional, public and private capital. The chosen Indicators with their respective variables that they represent are:

The Global Competitiveness Index (GCI)

Established by the World Economic Forum, it focuses on the analysis of Global Competitiveness, clearly marking its relationship with Innovation. Its last report was that of 2018, its sub-indicators or pillars are: macroeconomic environment, Institutions, Infrastructure, health and Education, efficiency in the goods market, efficiency in the labor market, market size, business sophistication, financial market development, technological preparation, education and training of High Quality and the same Innovation, (Schwab, 2018).

GDP

This indicator of Wealth of the countries is created annually by the World Bank, recognized worldwide as GDP or Gross Domestic Product. It makes use of the indicator of purchasing power parity (PPP), this technical element, manages to compare this value between countries of the world, avoiding having as a barrier, the price levels of each country, according to the internal inflation of each one (World Bank, n.d.).

Open Economy (ILC)

Its indicator is the Index of Economic Freedom (ILC), which observes the degree of closure or opening of an economy, calculated annually, is created by the Heritage Foundation and the Wall Street Journal (WSJ). Its four sub-indices or pillars are: Rule of Law, Government Size, Regulatory Efficiency and Market Opening (Consejo Nacional de Competitividad, 2019).

Also known as the "OPEN ECONOMY" indicator. Determinant as observed, the degree of openness and its tendency that facilitates the exchange of goods, services, inputs, of a country with the rest of the world. Likewise, due to the tendency towards open innovation, it is important to be flexible with the commercial opening of the territory under study, (OECD, 2010).

Corruption Perception Index (IPC)

Known as the Corruption Perceptions Index (CPC), this indicator seeks to absorb the perception of Corruption in a country. In countries like the R.P. China, this type of crime is punishable by the death penalty, or under the modality of life imprisonment and forced labor (Ebdrup, 2014). This indicator is associated with the use of public resources and respect for their due use, which, in our case, is to observe their use and their application in Plans, programs associated with Innovation. Its latest version, that of the year 2018. Its generator is the NGO known as Transparency International (International).

Year Engineers (IA)

For the document and the Diamond, Science, Technology, Engineering and Mathematics will be used as indicators, which are part of the so-called "STEM", by the first letters corresponding to the words in English that treat each of these areas (Midrack, 2022).

Global Cibersecurity Index (GCI)

In the information society and corporate Big data, respect for the use and implementation of data collection systems is decisive, generating an environment of trust towards the company and the technological environment that surrounds it. Its Indicator the Global Cybersecurity for this point of the Diamond, is emanated from the United Nations and its organism in charge of Telecommunications, International Telecommunications Union or ITU (ITU, International Telecomunications Union).

Global Index of Cognitive Skills and Educational Achievement

Therefore, a new indicator is used that takes the aforementioned elements, called the Global Skills Index 2020 (GSI). Its analytical base is sourced from sixty countries, which collected information from about eighty million students, using the COURSERA platform, created in 2012 by Stanford University professors, Andrew Ng and Daphne Koller, which became a platform for courses from the Universities of Pennsylvania, Michigan, Princenton and of course Stanford. Today, there are about 220 world-class universities that offer their courses in this way, to fifty-five countries, an increasingly general trend from COVID-19 in the World.

World Intellectual Property Indicators (PI)

Created in an Academic-supranational association, by Cornell University, INSEAD and the World Intellectual Property Organization (WIPO), it takes up the different forms associated with Intellectual Property (IP), such as patents, copyrights, trademarks, industrial designs.

The Innovation Diamond Figure

Each of these points represents, groups, the variables on which Innovation depends, according to the information that was collected, from the STATE OF THE ART (Ojeda, 2019) and the Asian Innovation model, the basis for the formation of the Innovation Diamond, (Figure 1).

From this scientific structure, which has been explained up to here, the Origin of Innovation (DDI) is built in its final version, which has as supports, pillars or points, Intellectual Property, Growth, Education, Resource Human- Engineering, the Open Economy, Competitiveness, Transparency and Cybersecurity.

With these eight points, tools emerge that dynamize and turn Innovation into a continuous source of information and successful production.

THE GREEN DIAMOND: INNOVATION, WITH MINIMUM IMPACT ON THE ENVIRONMENT

Continuing with the research on the use and strategic impact of the Innovation Diamond, the second year of the Work, part of the Innovation Diamond and its eight points, so that they achieve one by one determine the impact of innovation on the environment, within a country, city, business group or company (as is the case study).

Figure 1. The Innovation Diamond
SOURCE: the author based on data that gave rise to the Innovation Diamond.

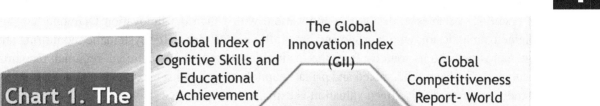

Chart 1. The Innovation Diamond

- Global Index of Cognitive Skills and Educational Achievement
- The Global Innovation Index (GII)
- Global Competitiveness Report- World Economic Forum (GCI)
- Global Cibersecurity Index (GCI)
- PIB (PPA)- (World Bank)
- Science Technology, Engineering & Mathematics
- Corruption Perceptions Index (CPI)
- Index of Economic Freedom

Figure 2. The Green Diamond of Innovation
SOURCE: Author, The Environmental Impact, as a point of reference for the Innovation Diamond. Research Project: THE SUSTAINABLE REFERENCE OF THE COMPANY IN COLOMBIA: support of the Innovation of the XXI Century. Business Administration Program. Research Office. Pilot University of Colombia.

		Does the use of it imply payment of "bribes" to be able to use it? YES / NO. Explain and specify the process.		
		CORRUPTION		
Its start-up, does it include import-export processes, donation? YES / NO. If the answer is YES, explain if you are careful against possible environmental impacts	**OPEN ECONOMY**		**ENGINEERS**	How many of the staff are engaged in green technology processes? Which of these are engineers? Which ones belong to another professional profile?
Who participates in this, in their position as operators, directors, creators, how many are? Technician? Technologists? Basic education? higher?	**EDUCATION**		**ECONOMIC GROWTH**	Do you contribute to green, clean public policies, or associated with Clean Industry? YES / NO. If your answer is YES, briefly explain which of the modalities.
Is insider information associated with their green innovation tracked-cyber-controlled? YES / NO. If the answer is YES, briefly explain the process	**CIBERSECURITY**		**INTELLECTUAL PROPERTY**	In recent years, have you developed an innovation associated with a product, service, input, that minimizes environmental impact? Five years? two years? last year?
		COMPETITIVENESS		
		In terms of MOBILITY, final products, inputs, in processes with suppliers, clients, workers, it seeks to minimize DIRECT emissions that come from fuels used in transportation, gas leaks from the production plant, from any other area of the company? YES / NO If your answer is YES or NO, please specify.		

Innovation Diamond Green Indicators

The resulting variables in the face of Innovation, with which the Innovation Diamond has, have, as explained, an indicator, whose origin and credibility is high, due to the systematic monitoring and coverage that is made to its sources, from the Institutions supranational, national, regional, recognized by the subject, whether public, mixed and private capital organizations. Next, its basic origins are retaken, and then, its passage to its green valuation is explained, see Figure 2.

To reach this "green conversion", each of the sub-indicators that are part of the central indicator, which are part of each of the eight points, is taken, subjecting them to an evaluation of the environmental impact before the implementation of the Innovation, see Figure 2.

Valuation-Construction of the Green Diamond

An update of the Innovation Diamond was developed, in terms of its eight points, thereby making it possible to show the importance of each of them, compared to Innovation and its ability to evaluate it in a city, region, country, sector, company, allowing to formulate the questions that allow knowing the degree of environmental impact of an Innovation, resulting in its final version, Figure 2.

Environmental Impact Levels

Once the evaluation face is finished, the questions are applied by each point of the Diamond, after the respective evaluation, it will be possible to know the environmental impact that an Innovation in progress, to be put into operation, can create in a country, city, business sector, company. According to the results, suggestions may be made, prioritizing them, according to the results that can be considered in three levels: green innovation, innovation to be reformed, innovation rejected.

Evaluation: Testing, of the Green Impact from the Diamond Points

Experimenting with the Innovation Diamond to bring it to its "green" structure is done through the evaluation of the process - products, services to be placed in the country, city, business sector, company, point to point, with the respective questions, Figure 1: from the Point of Corruption, Human Resource- Engineers, Education, Open Economy, Economic Growth, Cybersecurity associated with green innovation, Intellectual Property with innovations associated with the control of waste throughout the operation / process, Competitiveness with the mobility of products / supplies / clients / workers and ecologically productive areas.

Organizational Achievements of the Green Approach

At a macro level, the Diamond showed its ability to detect the existence of "good practices at the global level", observing in this regard, what has been achieved by example countries at the eight-point level and its impact on innovation, at the level of: Cybersecurity, Open Economy, Education, Transparency, Economic Growth, Competitiveness, Intellectual Property and contribution of Human Resources. After detecting the difference between good practices worldwide and what has been done in the country, or in a city, chosen, chosen, where the companies or the company to be analyzed are located (called this space, as "The Gap of Innovation" see Key Terms), within the resulting graph (Cobweb of Innovation, see Figure 3), we look for those priorities that are in the red space of part of the country, city analyzed, and propose strategies to follow.

FUTURE RESEARCH DIRECTIONS

Currently, research called *Implementation of the Methodology for Innovation in "Micavdi" Value Chains with Internationalization Processes of Agroindustrial Products: Case Studies* is being developed.

It seeks to explore and analyze the structure of issues associated with innovation of a population group of women entrepreneurs in Colombia.

CONCLUSION

The "Innovation Diamond" tool, in its original version, as well as in its "green" version, or "Green Diamond", is a diagnostic support, and allows detecting the strategies to follow and knowing which one or which of them, they must work for a country, city, company, business sector, as priorities.

Therefore, the scope of the Tool manages to remake, adapt the strategic plan of the country, city, company, focused on integral processes that include making, structuring green value chains behind sub-brands and proposing strategies for displaying products and associated processes. to "Clean Industry".

Likewise, the Diamond of Innovation manages to establish the weaknesses or strengths to work on, in terms of State institutions, at the national, regional, and local levels, which, after observing them, allow proposing actions to improve them.

It allows proposing strategies that manage to propose improvements and / or, determine the option of assuming them from the business sector (of public and private capital), in innovation and complementary structures associated with cybersecurity, intellectual property, the transparent use of public resources aimed at programs associated with innovation.

At a macro level, the Diamond showed its ability to detect the existence of "good practices at a global level", observing in this regard, what has been achieved by example countries at the level of eight points and its impact on innovation, at the level of: Cybersecurity, Open Economy, Education, Transparency, Economic Growth, Competitiveness, Intellectual Property and contribution of Human Resources.

After detecting the difference between good practices worldwide and what has been done in the country, or in a chosen city, where the companies or the company to be analyzed are located (called this space, as the INNOVATION GAP or "The Innovation Gap), proposes, through the Strategic Mother Matrix, concrete and priority actions to close these gaps in a concrete and forceful way.

It has a logical and structured methodology, so that regardless of the state of wealth or resources, a country, city, business sector, company from anywhere in the world, manages to build a strategy that involves specific objectives and goals on the subject. of innovation.

REFERENCES

Consejo Nacional de Competitividad. (2019). *Index of economic freedom* [Índice de libertad económica]. Retrieved from http://www.competitividad.org.do/wp-content/uploads/2019/03/%C3%8Dndice-de-Libertad-Econ%C3%B3mica-2019-1.pdf

Demchak, C., Kerben, J., McArdle, J., & Spidalieri, F. (2015). *Cyber readiness index 2.0*. Retrieved from https://www.belfercenter.org/sites/default/files/legacy/files/cyber-readiness-index-2.0-web-2016.pdf

Ebdrup, N. (2014). *Minimal corruption in Denmark began with the absolute monarchy*. Science Nordic. Available at https://sciencenordic.com/minimal-corruption-denmark-began-absolute-monarchy

ITU, International Telecomunications Union. (n.d.). *Global Cybersecurity Index*. Retrieved from https://www.itu.int/en/ITU-D/Cybersecurity/Pages/global-cybersecurity-index.aspx

McCarthy, N. (2015). The Countries With The Most Engineering Graduates. *Forbes. Business (Atlanta, Ga.)*, *8*(1), 33–38.

Midrack, R. L. (2022, June 26). *What is STEM (science technology engineering math)?* Lifewire. Retrieved from https://www.lifewire.com/what-is-stem-4150175

OECD. (2010). *SMEs. Entrepreneurship and Innovation*. Retrieved from https://www.oecd.org/berlin/45493007.pdf

Ojeda, F. A. (2014a). *The largest city in the world Chogqing* [La ciudad más grande del mundo Chogqing]. Bogotá: Universidad Piloto de Colombia. Obtenido de https://www.unipiloto.edu.co/chonquin-la-ciudad-mas-grande-del-mundo/

Ojeda, F. A. (2014b). *Take-off of the big Japanese brands and strategies: Contributions to a way of doing business and building companies for life* [Despegue de las grandes marcas y estrategias Japonesas: Aportes a una manera de hacer los negocios y construir empresas para toda la vida]. Bogotá, Colombia: Universidad Piloto de Colombia. Obtenido de https://www.unipiloto.edu.co/wp-content/uploads/2013/11/FA-No.1-Japon.pdf

Ojeda, F. A. (2014c). *The historical evolution of the Asian Firms model* [La evolución histórica del modelo de las Firmas Asiáticas]. Universidad Piloto de Colombia. Obtenido de., https://www.unipiloto.edu.co/la-evolucion-historica-del-modelo-de-las-firmas-asiaticas/

Ojeda, F. A. (2014e). *Bangalore the Silicon Valley of India: In a city that manages to enhance its competitive and historical comparative possibilities at the level of the great ones in the world* [Bangalore el Silicon Valley de la India: In a ciudad que logra potenciar sus posibilidades competitivas y comparativas históricas al nivel de las grandes del mundo]. Bogotá, Colombia: Universidad Piloto de Colombia. Obtenido de https://www.unipiloto.edu.co/wp-content/uploads/2013/11/FA-No.3-bangalore.pdf

Ojeda, F. A. (2014f). *The business model of twenty-first century China* [El modelo empresarial de la China del siglo XXI]. Universidad Piloto de Colombia. Obtenido de. https://www.unipiloto.edu.co/el-modelo-empresarial-de-la-china-del-siglo-xxi-2/

Ojeda, F. A. (2014g). *The Asian crisis* [La crisis Asiática]. Bogotá: Universidad Piloto de Colombia. Obtenido de http://repository.unipiloto.edu.co/handle/20.500.12277/4459?show=full

Ojeda, F. A. (2015). *Business environment* [Entorno de los negocios]. Bogotá: Universidad Piloto de Colombia. Obtenido de https://www.unipiloto.edu.co/descargas/Entorno-de-los-negocios.pdf

Ojeda, F. A. (2018). *The best gaurdado secret in Asia: Taiwan* [El secreto mejor gaurdado de Asia: Taiwan]. Bogotá: Universidad Piloto de Colombia. Obtenido de https://www.amazon.com/gp/product/B07JZQHCFK/ref=as_li_tl?ie=UTF8&creativeASIN=B07JZQHCFK&linkCode=as2

Ojeda, F. A. (2019). *State of the art and theoretical framework, companies as a benchmark in terms of innovation and international commercial management: a vision in the face of exchanges from Bogotá, Colombia* [Estado del Arte y Marco Teórico, las empresas como referente en materia de innovación y de gestion comercial internacional: Una visión frente a los intercambios desde Bogotá, Colombia.]. Presentado al Programa de Administración de Empresas y la Oficina de Investigación, Universidad Piloto de Colombia, Universidad Piloto de Colombia.

Ojeda, F. A. (2020). Analysis and Strategic Projection of the Dairy Sector- Cundinamarca, to aprtir of an approach, of the Diamond of Innovation [Análisis y Proyección Estratégica del Sector Lácteo- Cundinamarca, a aprtir de un enfoque, del Diamante de la Innovación]. Universidad Piloto de Colombia, Proyección Social. Bogotá: Universidad Piloto de Colombia.

Ojeda, F. A. (2014d). *El nuevo milagro asiático, del destrozo total y el estado fallido al último modelo del éxito empresarial asiático.* Bogotá: Universidad Piloto de Colombia. Obtenido de https://www.unipiloto.edu.co/el-nuevo-milagro-asiatico-del-destrozo-total-y-el-estado-fallido-al-ultimo-modelo-de-exito-empresarial-asiatico/

Schwab, K. (2018). *The Global Competitiveness Report 2018.* World Economic Forum. Retrieved from https://www3.weforum.org/docs/GCR2018/05FullReport/TheGlobalCompetitivenessReport2018.pdf

World Bank. (n.d.). *GDP (current US$).* Retrieved from https://data.worldbank.org/indicator/ny.gdp.mktp.cd

ADDITIONAL READING

Córdoba, S., García, J., Aley, H. Y. M., Mora, M., Santamaría, L., Fuentes, K., ... & Ojeda, F. (2019). La innovación en Colombia 4.0: un reto de ocho estrategias para los empresarios del siglo XXI. *Ensayos: Revista de Estudiantes de Administración de Empresas, 11*(1).

Herrera, M. M., Carvajal-Prieto, L. A., Uriona-Maldonado, M., & Ojeda, F. (2019). Modeling the Customer Value Generation in the Industry's Supply Chain. *International Journal of System Dynamics Applications, 8*(4), 1–13. doi:10.4018/IJSDA.2019100101

Lingard, B. (2015 December 9). *The Learning Curve of Pearson.* Retrieved from https://worldsofeducation.org/en/woe_homepage/woe_detail/4829/the-learning-curve-of-pearson

Ojeda, F. A. (2018). *The best gaurdado secret in Asia: Taiwan* [El secreto mejor gaurdado de Asia: Taiwan]. Universidad Piloto de Colombia. Obtenido de https://www.amazon.com/gp/product/B07JZQHCFK/ref=as_li_tl?ie=UTF8&creativeASIN=B07JZQHCFK&linkCode=as2

Ojeda, F. A. (2019). *The Asian entrepreneurship of the XXL century and the keys to its current positioning. Value chains, specialized education, massive participation of women, strategic accompaniment and mysticism* [El emprendimiento asiático del siglo XXL y las claves para su posicionamiento actual. Cadenas de valor, educación especializada, participación masiva de la mujer, acompañamiento estratégico y misticismo]. Retrieved from http://repository.unipiloto.edu.co/handle/20.500.12277/8086

Ojeda, F. A. (2021). Cybersecurity, An Axis On Which Management Innovation Must Turn. In *The 21st Century.* Reference Of Good Practices For Latin America In Clean Industry.

KEY TERMS AND DEFINITIONS

Cobweb of Innovation: The so-called Cobweb of Innovation has as its main objective to rank countries, cities, under three levels, according to the score given by each of the eight points of the Diamond. Its possibilities are three levels: high, medium, and low. To locate the countries, cities, at each level, the scores given by each indicator are taken into account. Thus, if the score is 100 points at most, being in the 100-80 point range, it will correspond to a high level, it will correspond to the Green Strip or space.

Contribution to the Diamond of Innovation (CDI): These are the contributions that authors, nations, studios, and companies make to the Diamond of Innovation and its eight points from the epistemological point of view.

Environmental PPP Alliances: They are strategic alliances, which include organizations, of public and private capital, whose purpose is the search to generate processes, value chaines, products, services, supplies, with low environmental impact.

Green Innovation: It is one that meets at least 80% of the requirements, evaluated by the Green Diamond. It can and should be put into action. It must have instruments for continuous monitoring and, if necessary, adjustments.

Green Version of the Diamond: It is the version of the Diamond of Innovation, which evaluates the environmental impact of the use of an innovation in a product, service, process, raw material, in a project or start-up phase, or in search of an improvement, for a company, group of companies, city and country or group of countries.

Innovation Gap: Within the Web of Innovation, it is the space that exists, between the country, city, etc., observed and the world references. It reveals the distance in achievements and strategies that the country, city studied, has with respect to the leading countries for each point of the Diamond. Knowing the determining aspects of this "GAP of Innovation" will serve to have a reference of the Company that we are analyzing according to its geographical location according to the country, city, where it is located. These results will be able to show us, in the end, how this Firm, Company, Farm, Business at a global, national level, etc., are facing Innovation, and therefore what strategic priorities it must face in the matter. Therefore, their data help the resulting Mother Matrix.

Innovation Rejected: It is one that does not meet at least 40% of the requirements, evaluated by the Green Diamond. It cannot and must not be set in motion. Their actions could create serious environmental damage. Its structure should be reviewed and a new version should be considered from scratch, emphasizing the unfulfilled items.

Innovation to Reform: It is one that meets at least 40% of the requirements, evaluated by the Green Diamond. It cannot and must not be set in motion. You need to make the suggested changes to reach at least 80% of the assessed requirements. Likewise, it must have continuous monitoring instruments and determine a schedule of actions and personnel in charge, associated with the required modifications.

Levels of the Web of Innovation: The levels mark the strategic priority. If it is at a high level (Green Strip), it will have a score of 1 in the so-called Strategic Mother Matrix, which will be explained later, in the "Strategic Priority Rating" Column, that is, this item is at a higher level. for the analyzed variable, close to the reference countries, or with the highest score in the analyzed indicator, which has in the second column (from left to right) called "International", the maximum scores and in the box a black dot, which highlights the highest score. Figure No 3.

T

Poll on the Points of the Innovation Diamond: This survey collects data on the analyzed population, be it company, city, etc., and on the behavior or state of affairs, of each of the eight Diamond points for the case and population under analysis. If the status is critical, it will correspond to a red dot in the "Strategic Mother Matrix". If it has a black dot in this matrix, it is because that item of any of the eight Diamond points is a reference to follow as a "Best Practice" worldwide.

Strategic Mother Matrix: This matrix, based on the results analyzed in the Web of Innovation for each of the eight points, locates for each point (of the eight) of the Diamond, which allows knowing if these are a priority (Red Stripe, score 3), average level of to observe (Yellow Strip), at the level of reference of good practices in the world (Green Strip). The first column from left to right has the main indicator and its sub-indicators. The second, called "International" are the scores of good practices recognized as "Good Practices" or reference to follow. Then follows the country that is being studied, it can be a City. Next comes the company or business group and lastly, the strategic priority, where "3" is the maximum" and with a double asterisk, it means immediate application, See Table 3.

APPENDIX

Figure 3. The cobweb of innovation
Source: The author based on data that gave rise to the Innovation Diamond.

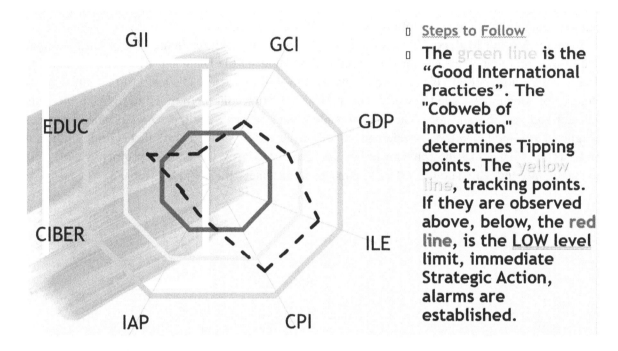

Table 3. Example of a strategic mother matrix, with the sub-indicator "The Global Competitivines"

STRATEGIC MOTHER MATRIX				
Indicator (Pillar/ Source)				
The Global Competitiviness	**INTERNATIONAL**	**COLOMBIA**	**GROUP SASA***	**STRATEGIC PRIORITY**
Finance System	●			1
Innovation Ecosystem	●		●	3
Macroeconomic Stability	●		●	3
Infraestructure	●	●	●	3**
Products Market	●		●	3
Institutions	●	●		2
Information Technology and Communication	●	●	●	3
Education	●			2
Health	●			2
Entertainment	●			2

Source: (Ojeda, 2019). Analysis and Strategic Projection of GRUPO SASA S.A.S, based on an approach, contributed by the Innovation Diamond. Research Project: COMPANIES AS A REFERENCE IN THE MATTER OF INNOVATION AND INTERNATIONAL COMMERCIAL MANAGEMENT: a vision in front of the exchanges from Bogotá, Colombia. Business Administration Program. Research Office. Pilot University of Colombia.

Section 19
Deep Neural Network (DNN) of Deep Learning

Machine Learning Approach to Art Authentication

Bryan Todd Dobbs

https://orcid.org/0000-0001-6711-6962

University of North Carolina at Charlotte, USA

Zbigniew W. Ras

https://orcid.org/0000-0002-8619-914X

University of North Carolina at Charlotte, USA

INTRODUCTION

When buying or selling a piece of art, it is common to require proof of the artwork's authenticity. Proof of authenticity is normally accomplished through artifact provenance which consist of documentation such as certificate of authenticity, past ownership, artist signature, and other physical attributes such as dimension, medium, and title. The value of artwork is directly proportional to proper authentication. Therefore, proper art authentication impacts all parties involved with a piece of art such as artist, buyer, seller, curator, appraiser, and insurance adjuster.

Conversely, there are issues with artwork authentication when artifact provenance is fraudulent or missing. For 15 years, Ann Freedman, the president of Knoedler & Company, unknowingly owned $80 million of fraudulent art. Glafira Rosales commissioned fraudulent reproductions of Rothko, Mother-well, and Pollock masterpieces from a local artist and sold them to Freedman. Rosales walked away with $20 million before FBI forensics on the masterpieces revealed historically inconsistent chemicals (Panero, 2013). The German army stole numerous amounts of art between 1938 and 1945 during their invasion of Europe (Henson, 2001). Paris and Vienna were areas of interest for the German army due to the lavish collections held by private collectors and galleries in the area (Feliciano & Felliciano, 1997). Wissbroecker (2004) discuss the litigation attempts of recovering art during this time period. Some of this art that was not destroyed still exists by holders aware and unaware of the art asset. When one of these missing pieces of art surfaces, provenance may be missing.

Blockchain and digital rights management (DRM) are new ways to address art authentication. Wang et al. (2019) developed a system that leverages the provenance capability of blockchain to protect a unique identifier assigned to a digital art asset. Zhaofeng, Weihua, and Hongmin (2018) developed a digital watermarking algorithm to protect digital assets. This algorithm is based on discrete cosine transfer (DCT), the Arnold transform, the human vision system (HVS) model, and Watson model. Both methods address art authentication of digital assets and are easily applied to contemporary art or art with existing authentication and digital representation. However, these methods cannot be used for physical art that is fraudulent, has missing provenance, or is produced by an artist unwilling to use a supervised technical method for art authentication. The need for a supervised method to authenticate digital art assets derived from physical art still exists. The objective of this chapter is to discuss the state-of-the-art approach to meet this need.

DOI: 10.4018/978-1-7998-9220-5.ch089

BACKGROUND

With the popularity of digital image processing and supervised machine learning, Johnson et al. (2008) provides objective measures for determining Van Gogh's artistic style. This work branched off into numerous research efforts analyzing artistic style thus providing a basis to mitigate the issues of missing provenance with a digital signature of an artist's work. The success of Russakovsky et al. (2015) winning the ImageNet challenge pushed image classification to new performance standards. From an artist classification perspective, Viswanathan and Stanford (2017) and Dobbs, Benedict, and Ras (2021) build on the success of ImageNet winners by applying residual neural networks to increase the performance of artist classification using the WikiArt data set. Likewise, Mensink and van Gemert (2014) and van Noord, Hendriks, and Postma (2015) apply machine learning algorithms to increase the performance of artist classification using the Rijksmuseum data set. The Rijksmuseum is the national museum of the Netherlands. They tell the story of 800 years of Dutch history, from 1200 to now. In addition, they organize several exhibitions per year from their own collection and with (inter) national loans (Rijksmuseum, 2021). The focus of this chapter relates to the Rijksmuseum dataset and ResNet 101 algorithm. (Dobbs et al., 2021) discuss additional background related to the OmniArt and WikiArt datasets and lower performing algorithms.

MACHINE LEARNING ART AUTHENTICATOIN METHODOLOGY

Applying machine learning to the art authentication problem requires five things. First, a source of data with sufficient samples for experiments is required. Second, a residual neural network method that can be customized is needed. Third, a custom method of annealing results between data subsets is required. Fourth, a high-performance cluster is needed to run experiments. Last, a method for measuring the performance of experiments is needed. These five requirements should be constructed in a manner that is easy to repeat if any step needs to be redone.

Data Source

The data source for experiments should be publicly available for research. For example, data available from the Rijksmuseum consists of 112,039 artworks from 6,629 artists. Each artwork has a corresponding image and xml metadata file. The high-quality images are stored as 300 dpi compressed jpeg and were taken in a controlled environment (Mensink & van Gemert, 2014). Special organization and translation scripts developed in Matlab can prepare the data for experimentation. For experiments, images from all types of artworks can be used for artists with more than ten artworks. Artwork types can include images of paintings, prints, photographs, ceramics, furniture, silverware, doll's houses, and miniatures. Artworks from anonymous and unknown artists can be included in experiments even though these two categories are not relevant to art authentication. Since both anonymous and unknown classes contain multiple artists, they provide a group for which an artist should not identify.

Residual Neural Network

Like Kim (2017), Matlab's implementation of Residual Neural Networks (He, Zhang, Ren, & Sun, 2016) can be used to train, validate, and test output models. Matlab provides an extensible scripting method which facilitates the implementation. Images can be resized to 224x224x3 to match network input size. Typically, 70% of artwork images are used for training, 10% are used for validation, and 20% are used for test. Models are produced from training and validation data. Test data is used for accuracy metrics on the model thus proving that the models are not overfitting. Images can undergo random rotation, scaling, and reflection to prevent overfitting. Training makes a pass through all images in batches of 128 for up to 30 times or epochs and validation occurs after 50 iterations within each epoch. After each epoch, training data typically shuffles paintings to handle the situation where the mini batch size does not equally partition the data. Once a training model is generated, predictions are made using the model and generate a confusion matrix from the ground truth and output predictions.

Additional parameters from Matlab can be used. Transfer learning is used by utilizing Matlab's pre-trained networks which are based on models from ImageNet (Deng et al., 2009). These models provide an optimal starting point for experimentation. Matlab recommended hyper parameters are a good place to start experiments. The solver used is stochastic gradient descent with momentum (SGDM) with a learning rate of 0.01 and a momentum of 0.9. To reduce overfitting, a weight decay regularization term with a value of .0001 to the loss function is used.

The theoretical foundations of experiments are derived from transfer learning and deep residual neural networks. Traditionally, these theories are applied to practical applications which classify images or objects within an image (Deng et al., 2009). These experiments leverage these theories to classify artists given images of their paintings. Two practical developments come from these theoretical foundations. First, higher classification performance amongst many classes will extend support for art authentication in situations of good and bad art provenance (Dobbs et al., 2021). Second, improving performance extends the labeling and querying organizational applications of the Rijksmuseum challenge (Mensink & van Gemert, 2014).

Transfer Learning

Torrey and Shavlik (2010) describe transfer learning as a technique used to transfer knowledge from a source task to improve the learning rate in a target task by allowing the training process to start with higher start, slope, and asymptotic characteristics. Transfer learning from ImageNet models should be used when running experiments. The ImageNet model is generated from classifying whole images and objects within images based on a large lexical database of English called WordNet (Miller, 1995).

Table 1. Annealing parameters example from van Noord et al. (2015)

Artist Count	Artist Loss
958	0
197	761
97	100
34	63

Table 2. Annealing parameters example from Mensink and van Gemert (2014)

Artist Count	Artist Loss
374	0
300	74
200	100
100	100

Deep Residual Neural Network

He et al. (2016) solves the exploding and vanishing gradient problem of deep neural networks with a deep residual learning framework which allows for much deeper networks using the concept of skip connections. Philipp, Song, and Carbonell (2018) provide mathematical proof demonstrating how skip connections can largely circumvent the exploding and vanishing gradient problem. With admissible, deeper neural networks, performance is improved from previous work that did not take advantage of these theories. Specifically, experiments should at least use the ResNet 101 algorithm.

Annealing

Matlab can be used to apply a custom annealing process to harden results based on performance. Annealing takes place after a ResNet model is generated. Class counts from baseline experiments determine how many times annealing takes place. If the annealing step is removed, artists with high performing collections can be lost, and the overall multi-classification performance will not be optimal. Table 1 and Table 2 show example annealing parameters.

High Performance Cluster

The time to train models from over 112,039 images for 1,199 artist classes is prohibitive for a personal computer. If a personal computer is used, it could take weeks or months to get results and prohibit the use of the personal computer on a day-to-day basis. Moreover, any type of interruption such as coding bugs and power outage would interrupt the process, and the process would need to start over. Therefore, a high-performance cluster from an academic institution or cloud compute provider is needed for experiments. Targeting a node with 128 gigabytes (GB) of memory and four graphics processing units (GPUs) for experiments should provide results in adequate time.

Performance Measurement

Once experiments are complete, Matlab can be used to calculate the performance of models based on the output confusion matrix of each experiment. A mean class average (MCA) metric is calculated, and this is the same performance metric used for these types of experiments (Mensink & van Gemert, 2014; van Noord et al., 2015). Balanced MCA is used in (Dobbs et al., 2021) and (Dobbs & Ras, 2021) and is shown to reduce metric values to account for balanced data issues so manipulation of input data via over and under sampling is not needed.

SOLUTIONS AND RECOMMENDATIONS

The methodology described in this chapter has most recently been implemented using the ResNet 101 algorithm with WikiArt and Rijksmuseum by (Dobbs et al., 2021) and (Dobbs & Ras, 2021) respectively. The focus of this chapter is on (Dobbs & Ras, 2021) as it is state of the art and aligns with the background and examples used in this chapter. It is important to note that performance results are consistent using the same ResNet 101 algorithm with WikiArt and Rijksmuseum datasets which have no artists and therefore artworks in common. Five artifacts are produced after running a machine learning, art authentication experiment. These artifacts consist of overall performance metrics, confusion matrices, training metrics, classification labels, and classification models.

Performance Metrics

The ten experiments in (Dobbs & Ras, 2021) are performed in two HPC and take a combined time of 2.65 days to produce ten models for artists with ten or more artwork images. The first job run produces seven results for class count 34 to 368 and the second job run picks up three results with larger class counts of 1199, 958, and 374.

Confusion Matrices

The ten experiments in (Dobbs & Ras, 2021) produce ten confusion matrices. From these matrices, core result measures are calculated. The list of primary MCA performance measure results for the experiments are listed in table 3 and table 4. Results are split into two tables to align to the baseline experiment results from Mensink and van Gemert (2014) and van Noord et al. (2015) respectively. The results table displays class or artists count, baseline performance, experiment performance, and the increase in performance.

Regarding the MCA result calculations, Dobbs et al. (2021) determine the optimal method for calculating ResNet art authentication MCA as using a balanced micro method. Micro calculations (subscript of μ) aggregate measures before the final class measure calculation. Macro calculations (subscript of M) aggregate after each individual class calculation (Sokolova & Lapalme, 2009). The micro version is used for increased performance and its propensity to handle undefined calculations. Undefined calculations occur when a class has a true positive and false negative value of zero which causes a division by zero situation. These are real situations which cause issues in the macro calculation. Balanced accuracy (subscript of β) addresses class imbalance as described in Grandini, Bagli, and Visani (2008). Data classes are imbalanced, so the same technique is utilized. Both techniques are combined and represented with equation 1 where l is class count, fp is false positive, fn is false negative, tp is true positive, and tn is true negative.

$$MCA_{\beta\mu} = \frac{\dfrac{\sum_{i=1}^{l} tp_i}{\sum_{i=1}^{l} tp_i + fn_i} + \dfrac{\sum_{i=1}^{l} tn_i}{\sum_{i=1}^{l} tn_i + fp_i}}{2} \tag{1}$$

Table 3. Performance of ResNet 101 with annealing compared to van Noord et al. (2015) baseline

Artist Count	Baseline Performance	Performance	Increase
958	52.50%	67.06%	21.71%
197	68.20%	81.66%	16.48%
97	74.50%	87.32%	14.68%
34	78.30%	91.58%	14.50%

Table 4. Performance of ResNet 101 with annealing compared to Mensink and van Gemert (2014) baseline

Artist Count	Baseline Performance	Performance	Increase
374	66.50%	74.26%	10.45%
300	68.70%	75.97%	9.57%
200	72.10%	80.94%	10.92%
100	76.30%	87.72%	13.02%

Results of error rate and the macro and micro versions of precision, recall, and F1 score are omitted. The performance of these calculations is not applicable to this research because they are not significant, and the baseline research does not report these measures.

Neither baseline addresses art authentication for all artists with ten or more artworks. An additional experiment is run to initialize the van Noord et al. (2015) baseline and obtain an MCA of 61.49% for 1,199 artists.

Training Metrics

The training artifacts from the ten experiments in (Dobbs & Ras, 2021) consists of training/validation accuracy and loss along with information for base learn rate and aggregate validation accuracy and loss. Validation accuracy is not useful to visualize due to undefined data, and aggregate measures are not useful for reporting performance since the aggregated data does not consider previous learning. The base learn rate is not useful because it stays constant. There is a focus on training accuracy because it provides a good visualization for the time and rate for which each experiment completes. It is important to point out that the training measures do not take data balance into account and over fitting often occurs when generating the model. These issues are addressed by using test data to produce final performance on the training models. The results of the test measures consider data imbalance and over fitting.

Table 5 displays the iterations taken for each experiment. Note, the iteration gap between 368 and 374. The gap is a direct result from breaking up experiments into two jobs. The reason for doing this is discussed in the conclusion section. Note that the counts are in proportion with the learning rate of the respective jobs.

Table 5. Iteration count for each experiment

Artist Count	Iteration Count
34	1,020
97	3,090
100	3,120
197	6,450
200	6,480
300	12,150
368	13,440
374	3,060
958	15,120
1199	16,380

In table 6 and table 7 the top performers are shown with corresponding artwork count for each classification experiment. Due to the required space, the top performers with less than 20 artworks are not shown in table 7. Note, there are not as many top performers in table 6 because the artwork cutoff is 50. Whereas the artwork cutoff in table 7 is 10.

Table 6. Top performers for each experiment in first HPC job

Artist Count	Top Performing Artist(s)	Artwork Count
34	Hausdorff	66
	Voet-430	61
97	Hausdorff	66
	No´e Michel	54
	Voet-430	61
100	Hausdorff	66
	No´e Michel	54
197	Breen Adam-van	84
	Hausdorff	66
	Voet-430	61
200	Hausdorff	66
	Voet-430	61
300	Den-Haag Porseleinfabriek	66
	Hausdorff	66
368	Hausdorff	66

Training performance results are compiled for each of the ten models. As expected, the slope and asymptote of the training curve reduces as the number of classes increase. The time also increases with the number of classes. This is seen best when comparing the 200-class experiment with the 1199 class experiment. For the most part, each step of the experiments is in proportion. The only exception being class count 374. This is a special situation that benefits from the learning of class 1,199 and 958 models which puts it in line with class 100 learning rate. This is likely the cause for the small increase between 374 and 300 in table 4.

Classification Labels

For the ten experiments in (Dobbs & Ras, 2021), classification labels are collected for each experiment to assist with reproducing and extending results in future research. As expected, the number of classification labels reduce with each experiment by an expected amount due to the annealing process. The only exception to this rule occurs between the 374 and 368 class experiments where only 84 classes are in common. The reason for this is explained in more detail in the conclusion section.

Table 7. Top performers for each experiment in second HPC job

Artist Count	Top Performing Artist(s)	Artwork Count
374	Corvinus Johann-August	34
	Fuchs Adam	25
	Hausdorff	66
	Meester-van-Antwerpen-(I)	29
	Montano Giovanni-Battista	37
	Ravesteyn Jan-Antonisz-van	28
958	Adam Richard	20
	Crespi Giuseppe-Maria	23
	Fuchs Adam	25
	Groenning Gerard-P	31
	Hausdorff	66
	Ikku Jippensha	26
	Kunimasa Utagawa	23
	Le-Gouaz Yves-Marie	20
	Matteini Teodoro	25
	Montano Giovanni-Battista	37
	Naiwincx Herman	21
	Rabel Daniel	25
1199	Adam Richard	20
	Den-Haag Porseleinfabriek	66
	Fuchs Adam	25
	Ikku Jippensha	26
	Kunimasa Utagawa	23
	Naiwincx Herman	21
	No´e Michel	54

Classification Models

For the ten experiments in (Dobbs & Ras, 2021), a classification model is collected for each experiment. Each experiment leverages its model to produce a confusion matrix based on the ground truths and applying the classification model to each test case. These models are not shared because they are too large for a code repository and sharing the models in this manner defeats the purpose of required result duplication of this research.

FUTURE RESEARCH DIRECTIONS

Future work with art authentication and machine learning will likely occur in six areas. First, similar experiments need to be conducted with contemporary art to determine if performance and multi-class counts align within a reasonable margin of error. Disparate datasets producing similar performance further verifies the ability of an algorithm to learn artist style. Second, the investigation of adversarial attacks on art authentication will be useful to understand. As algorithmic methods for understanding artistic style are better understood, adversarial algorithms will be produced to leverage this understanding. Third, a thorough investigation of the saliency maps that support art authentication need to be understood in depth. Experiments producing optimal visualization techniques for these saliency maps will aid understanding. Fourth, an investigation on how increased performance estimates with multi-class classification using pairwise coupling techniques could yield better performance results for individual artist binary classification. Fifth, an investigation of the use of recommender systems and action rules with art authentication could produce promising applications with art recommendation requirements. Sixth, it is very likely that performance opportunities exist by tweaking the algorithm, hyper parameters, and transfer learning models of current experiments. For example, the ResNet 152 algorithm can be leveraged, and different transfer learning models could be used including the models produced during the annealing process.

CONCLUSION

This chapter discussed art authentication using the Rijksmuseum data set by applying a performance annealing residual neural network to baseline experiments. The experiments in (Dobbs & Ras, 2021) demonstrate an improvement of the artist classification aspect of the Rijksmuseum challenge. The best increase is 21% for 958 artists. The conclusion discusses the experiments and results in more detail. First, the significance of this work and contribution is reviewed. Second, the results of an experiment that can be easy visualized is reviewed. While result measures are extensible up to the larger 1,199 class experiment, the resultant confusion matrix is difficult to visualize. Third, potential data congruence concerns with experiments are noted.

Contribution

The significance of the experiments is self-evident from a performance perspective. All experiments listed in table 3 and table 4 produce performance gains over the baseline ranging from 9.57% to 21.71%. While there are no specific baseline comparisons for 1,199 artists, it is noted that related work does not indicate any artist classification baselines for an artwork data set that performs better than 61.49% MCA for 1,199 artist classes. These results have a strong correlation to similar ResNet 101 experiments on different art collections. For example, (Dobbs et al., 2021) report 87.31% MCA on 90 artist classes from WikiArt which is in line with the 87.32% and 87.72% MCA reported in this chapter for 97 and 100 artist classes, respectively. The actual experiments discussed in this chapter extend the solution to the art authentication problem by increasing performance. An increase in performance has a direct correlation to the value of art which benefits all interested parties.

It is noteworthy to point out how the ResNet model outperforms the baseline. Both baseline approaches use traditional algorithms to extract features and perform classification. The ResNet approach uses a deep convolutional neural network which efficiently uses a general feature extraction approach over multiple convolutions of an image to build a model for classification. Efficiency gains are realized by reducing the number of fully connected layers and identity or skip blocks.

Artist Confusion

As expected, performance is inversely related to the number of artists. This relationship is apparent since the probability of an artist's style will be confused with another artist's style naturally increases as the number of artists classified increases. The research of Dobbs et al. (2021) shows that similar Resnet 101 performance experiments show no correlation to similarity (SSIM), estimator quality (MSE), or artwork count which gives us further confidence of the validity of artist confusion through learning.

Artist confusion is demonstrated via a confusion matrix for 34 artist classes. Visualization for artists classes greater than 34 is prohibitive due to presentation space. Table 8 lists the most confused artists for each experiment. The most confused artist is defined by extracting the two artists that correspond to the item with the maximum value in a confusion matrix excluding diagonal values. Duplicate values are included. Diagonal values are excluded because these represent true positives or an artist that is not being confused with another.

The two artists confused for each artist count experiment are noted, and the corresponding HPC job is shown to support the fact that intermingling the HPC job runs with baseline experiments does not have an impact on results in a meaningful way. For example, it is shown that both jobs have experiments with similar confusion between anoniem/Scherm Laurens and GordonRobertJacob/Meissener-Porzellan-Manufaktur. The 200-class experiment confuses Picart Bernard with Houbraken Jacob and Tanj´e Pieter to the same degree. It is also noted that the initial runs of both HPC jobs have an artist being confused with anoniem or anonymous. After each annealing step completes, the two artists most confused tighten up to two unique artists. Given a confusion matrix and a cross referenced to table 8 it is seen that 34 instances where Jacob Houbraken, is predicted, but Rober Nanteuil is the correct class. Likewise, Rober Nanteuil is predicted, but the true class is Jacob Houbraken, albeit to the lesser degree of one. The fact that these two artists are confused with one another is no surprise as they are both portrait artists.

Table 8. Artist most confused with each experiment

Artist Count	Artist 1	Artist 2	HPC Job
34	Houbraken-Jacob	Nanteuil Robert	1
97	Galle Philips	Lepautre Jean	1
100	Gordon Robert-Jacob	Meissener-Porzellan-Manufaktur	1
197	Coornhert Dirck-Volckertsz	Cort Cornelis	1
200	Houbraken-Jacob	Picart Bernard	1
	Tanj´e Pieter	Picart Bernard	1
300	anoniem	Harrewijn Jacobus	1
368	anoniem	Scherm Laurens	1
374	Gordon Robert-Jacob	Meissener-Porzellan-Manufaktur	2
958	anoniem	Scherm Laurens	2
1199	anoniem	Scherm Laurens	2

Further inspection reveals that Arnoud van Halen has the falsest negatives, and Robert Nanteuil has the falsest positives. Both artists are portrait artists. Meissen porcelain manufacturer has most true positives. This art consists of images of porcelain pieces. The features from these pieces are visually distinctive which contributes to the art providing the best performance. These results support the van Noord et al. (2015) experiments. Specifically, Meissen porcelain manufacturer accuracy in the baseline is 97.5% and this accuracy is increased by (Dobbs & Ras, 2021) to 99.8%. The top performing true positives for each experiment are displayed in table 9.

Table 9. Artist with most true positives for each experiment

Artists	Artist	True Positive Count
34	Meissener-Porzellan-Manufaktur	201
97	Rembrandt-Harmensz-van-Rijn	249
100	Rembrandt-Harmensz-van-Rijn	231
197	Rembrandt-Harmensz-van-Rijn	201
200	Rembrandt-Harmensz-van-Rijn	215
300	anoniem	1718
368	anoniem	1494
374	Rembrandt-Harmensz-van-Rijn	213
958	anoniem	1087
1199	anoniem	819

Data Congruence

In (Dobbs & Ras, 2021), it is important to make several observations on potential artwork gaps in the data that feeds MCA results and baseline MCA results. The complete domain of artwork used to produce experiments is the same as the baseline. Experiments initialize with artists having the same number of artworks. This equates to 50 artworks for the Mensink and van Gemert (2014) experiment which ensures at least ten artworks per artist for testing which implies a 35/5/10 split for the first experiment. This equates to 10 artworks for the van Noord et al. (2015) experiment which is the same starting point. However, there may be a margin of error with the artwork domain selection due to the interpretation of which artists make initial and subsequent performance cuts. For example, the same criteria are used to select 374 artists as Mensink and van Gemert (2014), but the selection produces 368 artists. To get the 374 artists performance number, a special annealing step is included after the 958 experiments when running experiments with respect to van Noord et al. (2015). This is a necessary step to produce the measure. The exception step results in an intersection of 84 classes between class experiment 374 and 368 which would normally result in a six-class difference. A similar discrepancy occurs with van Noord et al. (2015) where initial selection of artists with ten or more artworks starts experiments with 1,199 artists instead of 958 artists. Artist domain shear may also be present with each annealing step. Without the exact artist and art selection for each point of analysis and the code to reproduce these relative states, it's impossible to know if the exact same images are used between baseline and current experiments. Moreover, the annealing process only takes performance into account when generating the artists classes for each experiment. Whereas the baseline takes both performance and artwork count into consideration.

This is clearly seen in class 34 and 97 measures of table 6 where the artwork shows counts in the 60s where the baseline has counts between 128 and 256. Despite these data discrepancies, the performance increase supports an advancement due its significance over the baseline and curve. To assist with research that would extend results in the future, artist selection from annealing, training progress, and confusion matrices are shared via open repository.

REFERENCES

Deng, J., Dong, W., Socher, R., Li, L.-J., Li, K., & Li, F.-F. (2009). ImageNet: A large-scale hierarchical image database. In *2009 IEEE conference on computer vision and pattern recognition* (pp. 248–255). IEEE. https://ieeexplore.ieee.org/document/ 5206848/

Dobbs, T., Benedict, A., & Ras, Z. (2022). Jumping into the artistic deep end: Building the catalogue raisonné. *AI & Society, 37*(3), 1–16. doi:10.100700146-021-01370-2

Dobbs, & Ras. (in review). On art authentication and the rijksmuseum challenge. *Expert Systems With Applications.*

Feliciano, H., & Felliciano, H. (1997). *The lost museum: the nazi conspiracy to steal the world's greatest works of art.* Basic Books.

Grandini, M., Bagli, E., & Visani, G. (2008). *Metrics for multi-class classification: an overview.* https:// arxiv.org/abs/2008.05756

He, K., Zhang, X., Ren, S., & Sun, J. (2016). Deep residual learning for image recognition. In *Proceedings of the IEEE conference on computer vision and pattern recognition* (pp. 770–778). Retrieved 2020-10-08, from !--INSERTPICT-->HeDeepResidualLearningCVPR2016paper.html">https://openaccess. thecvf.com/content cvpr 2016/html/ He Deep Residual Learning CVPR 2016 paper.html

Henson, E. J. (2001). The last prisoners of war: Returning world war ii art to its rightful owners-can moral obligations be translated into legal duties. *De Paul Law Review, 51,* 1103.

Johnson, C., Hendriks, E., Berezhnoy, I., Brevdo, E., Hughes, S., Daubechies, I., Li, J., Postma, E., & Wang, J. (2008). Image processing for artist identification. *IEEE Signal Processing Magazine, 25*(4), 37–48. doi:10.1109/MSP.2008.923513

Kim, P. (2017). *MATLAB deep learning: with machine learning, neural networks and artificial intelligence.* Apress.

Mensink, T., & van Gemert, J. (2014). The Rijksmuseum challenge: Museumcentered visual recognition. In *Proceedings of international conference on multimedia retrieval.* Association for Computing Machinery. 10.1145/2578726.2578791

Miller, G. A. (1995). Wordnet: A lexical database for english. *Communications of the ACM, 38*(11), 39–41. doi:10.1145/219717.219748

Panero, J. (2013). "i am the central victim": Art dealer ann freedman on selling $63 million in fake paintings. *New York Magazine, 27.*

Philipp, G., Song, D., & Carbonell, J. G. (2018). Gradients explode-deep networks are shallow-resnet explained. *arXiv*.

Rijksmuseum. (2021, April). *Rijksmuseum.* https://www.rijksmuseum.nl

Russakovsky, O., Deng, J., Su, H., Krause, J., Satheesh, S., Ma, S., . . . Fei-Fei, L. (2015). *ImageNet large scale visual recognition challenge.* http://arxiv.org/ abs/1409.0575

Sokolova, M., & Lapalme, G. (2009). A systematic analysis of performance measures for classification tasks. *Information Processing & Management*, *45*(4), 427–437. doi:10.1016/j.ipm.2009.03.002

Torrey, L., & Shavlik, J. (2010). Transfer learning. In *Handbook of research on machine learning applications and trends: algorithms, methods, and techniques* (pp. 242–264). IGI global. doi:10.4018/978-1-60566-766-9.ch011

van Noord, N., Hendriks, E., & Postma, E. (2015). Toward discovery of the artist's style: Learning to recognize artists by their artworks. *IEEE Signal Processing Magazine*, *32*(4), 46–54. doi:10.1109/MSP.2015.2406955

Viswanathan, N., & Stanford. (2017). *Artist identification with convolutional neural networks.* https://www.semanticscholar.org/paper/Artist-Identification-with-Convolutional-Neural-Viswanathan-Stanford/dafe87bf57c4413d769de46af78f7e4305087838

Wang, Z., Yang, L., Wang, Q., Liu, D., Xu, Z., & Liu, S. (2019). Artchain: blockchain-enabled platform for art marketplace. In 2019 IEEE international conference on blockchain (blockchain) (pp. 447–454). IEEE. doi:10.1109/Blockchain.2019.00068

Wissbroecker, D. (2004). Six klimts, a picasso, & (and) a schiele: Recent litigation attempts to recover nazi stolen art. *DePaul-LCA J. Art & Ent. L.*, *14*, 39.

Zhaofeng, M., Weihua, H., & Hongmin, G. (2018). A new blockchain-based trusted drm scheme for built-in content protection. *EURASIP Journal on Image and Video Processing*, *2018*(1), 1–12. doi:10.118613640-018-0327-1

ADDITIONAL READING

Blessing, A., & Wen, K. (2010). *Using Machine Learning for Identiðcation of Art Paintings*. Academic Press.

Cetinic, E., Lipic, T., & Grgic, S. (2018). Fine-tuning Convolutional Neural Networks for fine art classification. *Expert Systems with Applications*, *114*, 107–118. doi:10.1016/j.eswa.2018.07.026

Chen, J. (2018). *Comparison of Machine Learning Techniques for Artist Identification.* https://www.semanticscholar.org/paper/Comparison-of-Machine-Learning-Techniques-for-Chen/8cf70f05a9582fb3383c6c465bd4e7a608631dc2

Jou, J., & Agrawal, S. (2011). *Artist Identification for Renaissance Paintings.* https://www.semanticscholar.org/paper/Artist-Identification-for-Renaissance-Paintings-Jou-Agrawal/399c6be15a90e94cc3610121566147e29520c9ea

Kondo, K., & Hasegawa, T. (2020). CNN-based Criteria for Classifying Artists by Illustration Style. *Proceedings of the 2020 2nd International Conference on Image, Video and Signal Processing*, 93–98. 10.1145/3388818.3389163

Leonarduzzi, R., Liu, H., & Wang, Y. (2018). Scattering transform and sparse linear classifiers for art authentication. *Signal Processing*, *150*, 11–19. doi:10.1016/j.sigpro.2018.03.012

Liu, H., Chan, R. H., & Yao, Y. (2016). Geometric tight frame based stylometry for art authentication of van Gogh paintings. *Applied and Computational Harmonic Analysis*, *41*(2), 590–602. doi:10.1016/j.acha.2015.11.005

Łydżba-Kopczyńska, B. I., & Szwabiński, J. (2021). Attribution Markers and Data Mining in Art Authentication. *Molecules (Basel, Switzerland)*, *27*(1), 70. doi:10.3390/molecules27010070

Pirrone, R., Cannella, V., Gambino, O., Pipitone, A., & Russo, G. (2009). WikiArt: An Ontology-Based Information Retrieval System for Arts. *2009 Ninth International Conference on Intelligent Systems Design and Applications*, 913–918.

Strezoski, G., & Worring, M. (2017). *OmniArt: Multi-task Deep Learning for Artistic Data Analysis.* https://arxiv.org/abs/1708.00684

Strezoski, G., & Worring, M. (2018). *OmniArt: A Large-scale Artistic Benchmark.* Association for Computing Machinery., doi:10.1145/3273022

KEY TERMS AND DEFINITIONS

Art Authentication: The process of proving a piece of art to be created by an artist.

Confusion Matrix: A table of actual and predicted classes such that the intersection of said classes statistically define the corresponding level of confusion.

Deep Learning: A type of machine learning which leverages a layered pipeline of neural networks which progressively extract features from input data.

Digital Image Processing: The process of applying computer algorithms to digital images to satisfy a visual related computing task.

Machine Learning: The application of statistical computer algorithms such that inference is used rather than explicit instruction to accomplish a task.

Supervised Machine Learning: A type of machine learning for which labeled input data is used to train a model to determine an output classification.

Transfer Learning: The process of leveraging existing learning models to facilitate the initial learning of related new problems.

Machine Learning for Decision Support in the ICU

Yu-Wei Lin

Gies College of Business, University of Illinois at Urbana-Champaign, USA

Hsin-Lu Chang

National Chengchi University, Taiwan

Prasanna Karhade

University of Hawai'i at Mānoa, USA

Michael J. Shaw

Gies College of Business, University of Illinois at Urbana-Champaign, USA

INTRODUCTION

Overview of Healthcare Decision Support Ecosystems

Machine learning (ML) technologies have altered the way consumers and businesses interact (Karhade & Kathuria, 2020; Karhade et al., 2015; Kathuria et al., 2020). Using ML models to understand healthcare data is an emerging research area in many disciplines, including information systems. Both researchers and the industry are excited about the potential influence that ever-evolving health care technologies can have on the delivery and operation of healthcare. The future of healthcare is becoming dependent on our ability to integrate ML into healthcare organizations. However, given the constrained resources available, the adoption of ML models into the process of healthcare decision support is not a trivial task for healthcare providers, as the adoption of new technologies require significant changes in their operations, and its benefits remains unclear. Therefore, we need to have a clear picture of the ecosystem of healthcare decision support to determine the best use of these applications in healthcare. We show an overview of the healthcare decision support ecosystem in Figure 1, introducing the ecosystem's three major components: beneficiaries, data, and models.

DOI: 10.4018/978-1-7998-9220-5.ch090

Figure 1. Healthcare decision support ecosystem

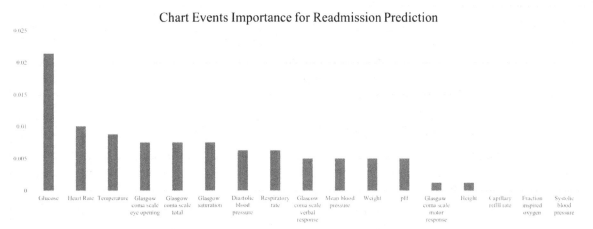

Beneficiaries: Doctors, Patients, Platforms

The goal of the healthcare decision support systems (HDSS) is to improve healthcare delivery by integrating different healthcare data, including patient information, patient activities, healthcare knowledge, and other clinical information (Sutton et al., 2020). According to the Office of the National Coordinator for Health IT (ONC), HDSS "provides clinicians, staff, patients or other individuals with knowledge and person-specific information, intelligently filtered or presented at appropriate times, to enhance health and health care."[1] It is necessary to understand whose decision-making can be enhanced and therefore improve healthcare delivery.

Healthcare systems are comprised of providers (e.g., doctors, nurses, hospital managers), consumers (e.g., patients), and platforms (e.g., wearables and mobile device applications, online appointment platforms). These are the three main parties that can benefit from the improvement of HDSS. In the past, doctors used to treat their patients based on their individual experiences—resulting in doctors with less experience being more likely to make poor decisions. Computer-based HDSS can improve clinical decisions by making faster, safer, and better treatment choices with fewer human errors and improve practitioners' overall performance (van Baalen et al., 2021). Given the urgency to make weighted decisions of healthcare, with the help of HDSS, medical providers can consider all available healthcare data, and healthcare knowledge management and transmission is made easier (Wood et al., 2019). HDSS benefits physicians by supporting them during diagnosis, treatment, and follow-up of patients. This support comes in the form of alerts, reminders, diagnostic suggestions, treatment options, and prescribing recommendations, to name a few. For example, HDSS provides alerts and reminders by analyzing changes in vital signs to capture increasing risks to hospitalized patients.

We now turn our attention to the healthcare consumer, patients. In the traditional healthcare model, information flows one way: from physicians to patients. It was acceptable for physicians to recommend a single treatment plan without mentioning alternatives. Under this treatment model, there is little or no input from the patients. Including patients in the decision process has proven to improve healthcare quality. "Empowering patients" is the concept described as giving patients greater control over their healthcare decisions and actions and has been shown to have positive consequences by healthcare research. Patients who actively participate in medical decisions tend to be more satisfied with their care

(Moyer & Salovey, 1998), enjoy a better life (Haynes et al., 1996), and are more likely to adhere to doctors' suggestions (Street Jr & Voigt, 1997).

The doctor-patient relationship has evolved and is closer now, due to hospitals' adoption of patient-centered HDSS, which changes how patients and doctors interact during treatment processes. According to an industry report[2], 70% of patients say they have become more engaged in the past few years. Patient-centered HDSS allows patients to participate in their own health-related decisions. Patient-centered decision support tools (e.g., brochures, websites, and mobile apps) can not only improve the communication between patients and their care providers, but also empower patients with the knowledge and ability to participate in their own healthcare decision-making process to make the best healthcare choices. Such support tools to provide (1) the condition and disease information, (2) the decisions that the patient needs to make, (3) clear information on the treatment options, potential outcomes, risks, and benefits (Ngo et al., 2020).

Healthcare platforms are the third party that can benefit from HDSS in terms of better healthcare delivery. ML-based HDSS also empower healthcare platforms to provide better services. For instance, ML-enabled wearable platforms not only can track the users' health status, but also can analyze the data collected by the devices to detect hidden variations within the users' health status. Moreover, advanced sensors can even provide suggestions to improve users' health, such as how much they need to eat, how much they should exercise, and how they should train to improve their fitness. In addition to wearables devices, online appointment platforms can also benefit from the AI-enabled HDSS. Those platforms now utilize ML-based natural language analysis to make patients' doctor searches easier. The ML techniques serve as a bridge to connect the healthcare industry and humans by translating patients' search texts into professional medical language and helping patients find the specialists they need.

Data: Primary Dataset and Secondary Dataset

Data access is the foundation for ML-based development (Karhade & Shaw, 2007; Karhade et al., 2018; Karhade et al., 2009a, 2009b). The "Big Data" revolution makes it possible for people to acquire large amounts of healthcare data for medical use. The first kind of data source is patients' *primary data*, which is comprised of patients' medical records. These data include observed symptoms, diagnostic reports, doctors' notes, etc. For *primary data*, the source of large-scale data comes from patients' electronic health records (EHRs). The implementation of EHR systems dramatically increases the availability of healthcare primary data. According to ONC, more than 90% of US hospitals and physician offices implement some form of EHR, and even higher adoption rates are seen globally.

In addition to primary data sets, *secondary data* are further used to enhance healthcare services. *Secondary data* comprises data external to the healthcare system. Common sources of *secondary data* for healthcare include censuses, information collected by government departments, or social media activities (De Silva et al., 2018). The content of *secondary data* includes the patient's emotions, activity habits, food and drinking habits, sensitivity to certain allergens, etc. (Kumar & Jayadev, 2020).

Both *primary data* and *secondary data* sources contain great amounts of healthcare information, which removes the main barrier of AI-based decision system adoptions. Greater access to these large-scale healthcare data generates new opportunities, but also new challenges to overcome. For healthcare organizations, their problems now are how to equip themselves with the right suite of HDSS to turn raw data into informed action at the point of care.

Models: ML Models

With the rapid developments in ML algorithms and improvements in hardware performances (Karhade et al., 2021; Malik, Jaiswal, et al.; Malik, Karhade, et al.), ML technologies are expected to be able to effectively analyze and utilize extensive amounts of health and medical data. The goal is to convert those healthcare data into actionable recommendations that can then be used to provide better care, keep better track of patients' vital signs, involve patients more in their own health, and empower them with the tools to do so.

Deep learning (DL), a type of complex ML that mimics how the human brain functions, can learn from data without any supervision. Here, we introduce two types of DL models that are especially useful in analyzing healthcare data: Long Short-Term Memory (LSTM) and convolution neural networks (CNNs).

LSTM is well-suited to make predictions based on time series data (Choi et al., 2016a). LSTM is a recurrent neural network equipped with memory cells to store information at each time step, at which point the LSTM model reads an input, updates the memory cell, and moderates the memory that needs to be passed to the output.

CNNs are another type of powerful DL in healthcare data analysis. CNNs are made of multiple convolutional filters, which are responsible to learn and extract necessary features. CNN-based models are not only effective in medical image understanding, but also in analyzing longitudinal EHR data. In our ICU readmission paper (Lin et al., 2019b), we use the multi-filter CNN structure introduced by (Zhang & Wallace, 2015) to analyze patients' EHR data for readmission prediction.

CONCEPTUAL BACKGROUND

Major Breakthroughs of ML in Healthcare Applications

ML-based HDSS is based on algorithms with self-learning neural networks that are able to increase the quality of treatment by analyzing data of patients. Various applications are emerging for ML-based HDSS.

First, ML is providing excellent solutions in analyzing medical images for image segmentation tasks. For example, using DL techniques, researchers in the Google Brain developed an AI-powered diabetic eye disease detection method that can examine large numbers of fundus photographs and automatically detect Diabetic Retinopathy and diabetic macular edema with a high degree of accuracy (Gulshan et al., 2016). Also, researchers at Stanford University created an algorithm to diagnose skin cancer. When the algorithm was cross-referenced with 21 board-certified dermatologists, the convolutional neural network was able to classify cancer at a similar level as that of the trained dermatologists (Esteva et al., 2017).

Second, ML is able to successfully capture the hidden features in patients' medical vital sign trajectories and the impacts of those hidden features on patients' healthcare outcomes. For example, we use the combination of LSTM and CNN to analyze ICU patients' vital sign trajectories and successfully predict ICU patients' readmission (Lin et al., 2019b). Hannun et al. (2019) used deep neural networks to detect and classify cardiologist-level arrhythmias in ambulatory electrocardiograms (Hannun et al., 2019).

Third, ML and natural language processing (NLP) technology have the potential to reveal insights that before were buried in medical jargon. For example, we use sentiment analysis technique to analyze patients' reviews in cancer online support groups (OSGs) to help OSG platforms identify those who are more likely to share their knowledge and experience with other patients (Lin et al., 2019a). Recently, Tsui et al. (2021) propose using NLP and ML for unstructured clinical notes and EHR data to predict patients' first-time suicide attempts (Tsui et al., 2021). Practically, online appointment platforms can also benefit from the ML and NLP techniques. Those platforms (e.g., Zocdoc) now utilize ML-based natural language analysis to make patients' doctor searches easier and helping patients find the specialists they need.

Challenges of Healthcare Decision Support

Although there are several successful ML applications in healthcare, ML-based HDSS also faces many challenges. We describe three of those challenges below.

Data Complexity

Healthcare data are composed of different structured and unstructured data types, each with complementary information. The issue is how to adjust HDSS to leverage these heterogeneous data types to generate useful information for decision support. Verma et al. (2016) propose that the integration of heterogeneous data in structured, semi-structured, and unstructured data types is needed for sophisticated knowledge mining tasks. Gheisari et al. (2017) also highlight the data heterogeneity problem in DL, noting that massive data are produced in unknown and untuneful patterns (e.g., text, audio, images, video, and social media).

The issue of data heterogeneity in electronic health records (EHRs) also has been discussed by researchers (Shickel et al., 2017). EHR data is available in different forms, varying from structured physiologic states (e.g., temperature, pulse, respiratory rate, and blood pressure, etc.) to unstructured handwritten text. Moreover, clinical texts contain abbreviations and shorthand notations, and vary from one clinician to another. This variation must be parsed and processed before being plugged into ML algorithms.

Decision Criticality

Healthcare is often a matter of life and death. Unlike e-commerce, there is no room for mistakes. Clearly, diagnostic accuracy should be a major priority in healthcare. Research has shown that rapid and accurate diagnosis is the key to improving treatment efficiency and decreasing the length of the hospital stay. On the other hand, diagnostic errors can result in patient safety hazards such as care gaps, unnecessary procedures, and medical resource waste. Therefore, the diagnostic of ML-based HDSS needs to be accurate to support doctors' decisions.

Moreover, diagnostic accuracy can also be a driving force to enhance patient acceptability of ML-based HDSS. Literature has shown that by informing patients of the potential of the HDSS to improve diagnostic accuracy, patient's acceptance of HDSS will be enhanced (Porat et al., 2017).

Model Explainability

Explainability might be one of the most important dilemmas when it comes to the application of ML in healthcare. When an ML model is being used as part of a healthcare service, among the concerns the experts raised are bias, transparency, accountability, fairness, privacy, and security (Topol, 2019). Since medical decisions greatly influence human health, it is necessary to understand how such decisions are made before putting the algorithms into practice (Arrieta et al., 2020).

Explainable AI (XAI), frameworks to help human experts understand and interpret predictions made by AI technology, is proposed to solve the problem (Samek et al., 2017). XAI is even more important now that DL technologies have made recent major breakthroughs. Samek et al. (2016) summarized that verification of the system, improvement of the system, learning from the system, and compliance to legislation are key factors to understanding AI's learning process.

SOLUTIONS AND RECOMMENDATIONS

In this section, we propose applying decision support in ICU to show how the three main challenges of ML-based HDSS can be overcome. Unplanned hospital readmission is an indicator of patients' exposure to risk and avoidable waste of medical resources. In addition to hospital readmission, ICU readmission brings further financial risk, along with morbidity and mortality risks (Chen et al., 1998). Premature ICU discharge may potentially expose patients to the risks of unsuitable treatment, which further leads to avoidable mortality (Rubins & Moskowitz, 1988; Xue et al., 2019). Surprisingly, even in developed countries, hospitals suffer from high ICU readmission rates; about 10% of patients will be readmitted to ICU within a hospital stay (Chen et al., 1998). To reduce avoidable ICU readmission, hospitals need to identify patients with a higher risk of ICU readmission (Jamei et al., 2017). In this study, we focus on the analysis and prediction of unplanned ICU readmission, using recent DL techniques and utilizing the time series feature of data.

The Data Complexity Issue

The readmission dataset is constructed from the MIMIC-III Critical Care Database (Johnson et al., 2016). Following the data-screening process stated in (Kim et al., 2010), we first screen out the patients under age 18 and remove the patients who died in the ICU. This results in a total of 35,334 patients with 48,393 ICU stays. We then split the processed patients into training (80%), validation (10%), and testing (10%) partitions to train our model and conduct fivefold cross-validation.

Our readmission prediction model combines three categories of features: chart events, ICD-9, and demographic information of the patients. We extract time series features from chart events within a 48-hour window. The last 48 hours before the patient is discharged or transferred are found to be the most informative data for the prediction of readmission (Brown et al., 2013). To cope with the problem of data missingness, we use the Last-Observation-Carried-Forward (LOCF) imputation method. In cases where the last hour is missing, we include an indicator for missingness. We also create a binary indicator feature, appended to each chart event feature. This feature indicates whether the record for each type of chart event exists at that given hour.

We extract 17 types of time series features from chart events within a 48-hour window. The raw features include both numerical (e.g., diastolic blood pressure) and categorical items (e.g., capillary refill rate). Details of these 17 features and their dimensions are shown in Table 1, along with their normal median value. We use the normal values later in the discussion section for ML model interpretation. In total, we construct 59 dimensions from the chart events; the increased number is due to the one-hot encoding of the categorical features. To identify and overcome the missing records in the chart events, we create a 17-dim binary indicator feature, appended to the chart events feature. This feature indicates whether the record for each type of chart event exists.

Table 1. 17 types of features in the chart events

Chart Events	Dim	Normal
1. Glasgow coma scale eye opening	8	4 Spontaneously
2. Glasgow coma scale verbal response	12	5 Oriented
3. Glasgow coma scale motor response	12	6 Obeys Commands
4. Glasgow coma scale total	13	15
5. Capillary refill rate	2	Normal < 3 secs
6. Diastolic blood pressure	1	70.0
7. Systolic blood pressure	1	105.0
8. Mean blood pressure	1	87.5
9. Heart Rate	1	80.0
10. Glucose	1	85.0
11. Fraction inspired oxygen	1	0.21
12. Oxygen saturation	1	97.5
13. Respiratory rate	1	15.0
14. Body Temperature	1	37.0
15. pH	1	7.4
16. Weight	1	80.7
17. Height	1	168.8

Note DT: Data Type, Dim: Dimension, Normal: Normal Value.

To address the data sparsity of disease information in disease information, we adopt a disease-embedding method proposed by (Choi et al., 2016b). The disease-embedding method is an embedding algorithm that creates low-dimensional vectors to represent medical concepts from ICD-9 in EHRs. Utilizing a lower-dimensional embedding of ICD-9 benefits the model training process by avoiding a sparse representation and applying the relationship information among different diseases. For a patient with multiple diseases, we simply add embeddings of all the diseases to construct the feature.

The demographic features consist of the patient's' gender, age, race, and insurance type. Details of this category and its corresponding dimensions are summarized in Table 2. We include the insurance type, as it could potentially influence the discharge/transfer rate. For example, although unlikely, the insurance type "uninsured" could lead to insufficient payment and might result in an unexpected discharge. In total, there are 14 dimensions for the demographic category.

Table 2. Demographic features

Chart Events	Dim	Option
1. Gender	2	Male/Female
2. Age	1	18-120
3. Insurance Type	5	Government, Self, Medicare, Private, Medicaid
4. Race	6	Asian, Black, Hispanic, White, Other, No Information

Note. Dim: Dimension.

The Decision Criticality Issue

To enhance the predictive model by incorporating the time series data, we use a bidirectional LSTM combined with an additional LSTM layer, followed by a dense decision layer with one output neuron activated by a sigmoid function. We also implement a CNN-based model for comparison to the LSTM model. Moreover, we combine the LSTM and the CNN models. There are two combinations: (1) CNN+LSTM model and (2) LSTM+CNN model. In the CNN+LSTM model, the CNN follows a multi-filter convolution computation with zero paddings to maintain the timestamp consistency for different groups of feature maps. The following LSTM only outputs the hidden units of the last timestamp. As for the LSTM+CNN model, CNN computes the feature maps without zero paddings after receiving the output hidden unit sequence from LSTM.

To evaluate the prediction power of DL-based CNN and temporal LSTM models, we compare them with conventional models (logistic regression [LR], random forest [RF], Naive Bayes [NB], and Support Vector Machine [SVM]). For the baseline models, we use the slopes and intercepts of the regression line (a and b in y = ax + b) as features to characterize the linear trend for continuous data, including the numerical chart events.

The results are shown in Table 3. Our experimental results reveal that LSTM followed by a CNN, utilizing all the feature sets, obtains a higher positive recall rate and overall prediction performance. The proposed LSTM+CNN model outperforms the conventional ML approaches and baseline models. For our baselines, SVM outperforms other traditional methods in terms of positive recall and AUC under the ROC curve.

Table 3. Performance comparison of various ML models on different sets of features

Model	Features	Re-1 (95% C.I.)	A.R (95% C.I.)
(a) Baseline Models			
LR-L2	L48-h STAT + ICD9	0.670 (0.647 - 0.694)	0.770 (0.758 - 0.782)
LR-L1	L48-h STAT + ICD9	0.669 (0.647 - 0.691)	0.775 (0.764 - 0.786)
NB	L48-h STAT + ICD9 + D	0.453 (0.434 - 0.472)	0.709 (0.702 - 0.716)
RF	L48-h STAT + ICD9 + D	0.563 (0.548 - 0.578)	0.714 (0.703 - 0.725)
SVM	L48-h STAT + ICD9 + D	0.701 (0.686 - 0.715)	0.775 (0.765 - 0.785)
(b) DL Models			
LSTM	L48-h CE + ICD9 + D	0.733 (0.698 - 0.768)	0.787 (0.771 - 0.802)
CNN	L48-h CE + ICD9 + D	0.735 (0.676 - 0.794)	0.784 (0.773 - 0.794)
CNN+LSTM	L48-h CE + ICD9 + D	0.710 (0.648 - 0.771)	0.787 (0.775 - 0.799)
LSTM+CNN	L48-h CE + ICD9 + D	**0.742 (0.718 - 0.766)**	**0.791 (0.782 - 0.800)**

Note. Acc: Accuracy. Pre: Precision. Re: Recall. A.R: AUC under ROC. A.P: AUC under PRC. L48: Last 48 hours. CE: Chart Events. D: Demographic features. C.I.: 95% confidence interval. STAT (statistical features): slope and intercept.

The Model Explainability Issue

We conduct the feature ablation test on the chart events to better understand the underlying logic of our proposed LSTM+CNN model. For each case, we iterate over all the chart events each time, changing only one event to its normal value in the humans, and record the number of cases that are falsely predicted due to the change. Figure 2 shows the results of the feature ablation test based on the changing ratio of the prediction results after we replace the original feature with its normal value. We see that glucose is the most important factor learned by the DL model for the readmission prediction task, while capillary refill rate, fraction-inspired oxygen, and systolic blood pressure do not have a significant influence on the prediction results. The underlying logic of our DL model, as well as the most important features identified by the model, are in line with the existing clinical literature.

Figure 2. The results of the feature ablation test. The importance of chart events for predicting ICU readmission

Note: The y-axis shows the changing ratio of the prediction results after we replace the original feature with its normal value.

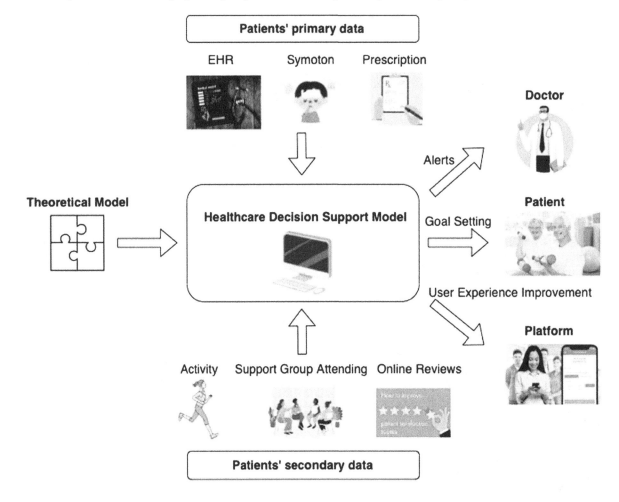

FUTURE RESEARCH DIRECTIONS

IT is facilitating digital transformation in a wide variety of industries (Dong et al., 2021; Karhade & Dong, 2020, 2021) We believe that ML-based HDSS has an important role to play in healthcare service delivery in the future. From the perspective of financing, according to the McKinsey report, it is estimated that big data analytics can account for more than $300 billion in savings per year in U.S. healthcare spending[3].

The gradual maturation of artificial intelligence applications in healthcare paves the way to faster and more accurate clinical decision-making. As this happens, the questions will shift from the technology itself to the iteration between the technology and adopters (Lin et al., 2021). First, understanding how to operate artificial intelligence algorithms may take up a lot of doctors' time and add more responsibilities, thereby exacerbating doctors' burnout. Second, the healthcare providers then need to consider how to integrate AI-based HDSS into daily clinical practices. For instance, how can they incorporate and utilize AI platforms with their existing HER system may? Finally, HDSS needs to enable agile communications between healthcare providers, systems, and data. For example, artificial intelligence systems may be too sensitive in their alarm systems, causing doctors to experience alarm fatigue. The system needs to be able to adjust flexibly. Therefore, the next goal for AI developers is not only making AI-based HDSS user-friendly, but also supporting healthcare providers in integrating this new system into their decision-making process.

As noted earlier, AI/ML highly relies on large-scale and high-quality datasets. Data privacy will become a more and more important concern. By nature, privacy within healthcare is extremely sensitive and, thus, confidential. The perspective of healthcare data privacy should be considered from both cyber security and regulation perspectives. Protection and security must be included in HDSS to ensure data privacy and protection from hackers. Unfortunately, according to the *HIPAA Journal*[4], more than 3,705 healthcare data breaches happened between 2009 and 2020, resulting in over 268 million personal records becoming vulnerable to fraud and identity theft. With legislators gradually putting more emphasis on the use of digitalized healthcare data, the use of artificial intelligence inevitably will involve the Health Insurance Portability and Accountability Act (HIPAA) as well as privacy and security regulations related to such data, and these data may need to be de-identified. Moreover, laws that give personal data ownership back to individuals, such as the General Data Protection Regulation (GDPR), have recently been passed in Europe. Under GDPR law, individuals own the rights to their data, including data collection and use of the data.

Trust is a key factor when designing interactive intelligent agents, because it significantly affects interactions between people. In the field of healthcare, the trust issue between AI and humans is even more crucial, because healthcare is about life and death. A significant challenge is that many doctors adopt some AI practices they don't fully understand, partly because of the risk of medical malpractice suits. To gain physicians' trust, AI software developers will have to clearly demonstrate that when the solutions are integrated into the clinical decision-making process, they help the clinical team do a better job. Theoretically, researchers may want to develop a quantitative measure for the optimal level of trust between clinicians and AI systems to make the most accurate and reliable clinical decisions and link this optimal level of trust to specific design attributes of the systems.

CONCLUSION

This chapter focuses on the role of ML-based HDSS in shaping the relationship between healthcare providers, patients, and healthcare-related platforms. The rapid developments in ML algorithms are expected to be able to effectively utilize extensive health and medical data for clinical decision supports. We review the major breakthroughs and important trends of ML in healthcare: (1) medical image analysis, (2) medical vital sign trajectories analysis, and (3) medical text analysis. Knowing the potential at stake and the opportunities AI offers to improve the clinical decision-making process, we overview the whole ecosystem of health decision support and identify the challenges, which are (1) data complexity, (2) decision criticality, and (3) model explainability.

We then use unplanned ICU readmission predictions to explore how to overcome the three main challenges of ML-based HDSS. We tackle the data sparsity issue through ICD-9 embeddings. To address the decision criticality issue, we propose the combination of the LSTM and CNN models to boost prediction accuracy of ICU readmissions. Finally, we unpack the model explainability issue by performing an in-depth DL performance analysis.

We highlight the ability of machine learning models to improve healthcare delivery in hospitals. These data-driven solutions hold the potential for substantial clinical impact by augmenting clinical decision-making for physicians and ICU specialists. We anticipate that ML-based HDSS will improve patient counseling, hospital administration, allocation of healthcare resources, and ultimately individualized clinical care. Further research is necessary to evaluate performance in a real-world, clinical setting, in order to validate this technique across varying critical care practices.

Finally, we would like to discuss the limitations of this chapter, and future works that it can spawn. In reality, vital signs are complicated, and most are dependent on each other. However, while we uncover the myth of a black box model, we assume all the features are independent from each other. Our model does not capture the characteristics of a multivariate time series, because the complicated interaction among vital signs needs the knowledge and input from healthcare professionals. Future studies should consider the possibility of covariance of multiple vital signs in matched or misclassified groups to further explore the knowledge from the prediction results.

REFERENCES

Arrieta, A. B., Díaz-Rodríguez, N., Del Ser, J., Bennetot, A., Tabik, S., Barbado, A., ... Benjamins, R. (2020). Explainable Artificial Intelligence (XAI): Concepts, taxonomies, opportunities and challenges toward responsible AI. *Information Fusion*, *58*, 82–115. doi:10.1016/j.inffus.2019.12.012

Brown, S. E., Ratcliffe, S. J., & Halpern, S. D. (2013). An empirical derivation of the optimal time interval for defining ICU readmissions. *Medical Care*, *51*(8), 706–714. doi:10.1097/MLR.0b013e318293c2fa PMID:23698182

Chen, L. M., Martin, C. M., Keenan, S. P., & Sibbald, W. J. (1998). Patients readmitted to the intensive care unit during the same hospitalization: Clinical features and outcomes. *Critical Care Medicine*, *26*(11), 1834–1841. doi:10.1097/00003246-199811000-00025 PMID:9824076

Choi, E., Bahadori, M. T., Schuetz, A., Stewart, W. F., & Sun, J. (2016a). Doctor AI: Predicting clinical events via recurrent neural networks. *Proceedings of Machine Learning Research*, *2016*, 301–318. PMID:28286600

Choi, Y., Chiu, C. Y.-I., & Sontag, D. (2016b). Learning low-dimensional representations of medical concepts. *AMIA Joint Summits on Translational Science Proceedings AMIA Summit on Translational Science, 2016*, 41. PMID:27570647

De Silva, D., Ranasinghe, W., Bandaragoda, T., Adikari, A., Mills, N., Iddamalgoda, L., Alahakoon, D., Lawrentschuk, N., Persad, R., Osipov, E., Gray, R., & Bolton, D. (2018). Machine learning to support social media empowered patients in cancer care and cancer treatment decisions. *PLoS One, 13*(10), e0205855. doi:10.1371/journal.pone.0205855 PMID:30335805

Dong, J. Q., Karhade, P. P., Rai, A., & Xu, S. X. (2021). How firms make information technology investment decisions: Toward a behavioral agency theory. *Journal of Management Information Systems, 38*(1), 29–58. doi:10.1080/07421222.2021.1870382

Esteva, A., Kuprel, B., Novoa, R. A., Ko, J., Swetter, S. M., Blau, H. M., & Thrun, S. (2017). Dermatologist-level classification of skin cancer with deep neural networks. *Nature, 542*(7639), 115–118. doi:10.1038/nature21056 PMID:28117445

Gheisari, M., Wang, G., & Bhuiyan, M. Z. A. (2017). *A survey on deep learning in big data. In 2017 IEEE international conference on computational science and engineering (CSE) and IEEE international conference on embedded and ubiquitous computing.* EUC.

Gulshan, V., Peng, L., Coram, M., Stumpe, M. C., Wu, D., Narayanaswamy, A., ... Cuadros, J. (2016). Development and validation of a deep learning algorithm for detection of diabetic retinopathy in retinal fundus photographs. *Journal of the American Medical Association, 316*(22), 2402–2410. doi:10.1001/jama.2016.17216 PMID:27898976

Hannun, A. Y., Rajpurkar, P., Haghpanahi, M., Tison, G. H., Bourn, C., Turakhia, M. P., & Ng, A. Y. (2019). Cardiologist-level arrhythmia detection and classification in ambulatory electrocardiograms using a deep neural network. *Nature Medicine, 25*(1), 65–69. doi:10.103841591-018-0268-3 PMID:30617320

Haynes, R. B., McKibbon, K. A., & Kanani, R. (1996). Systematic review of randomised trials of interventions to assist patients to follow prescriptions for medications. *Lancet, 348*(9024), 383–386. doi:10.1016/S0140-6736(96)01073-2 PMID:8709739

Jamei, M., Nisnevich, A., Wetchler, E., Sudat, S., & Liu, E. (2017). Predicting all-cause risk of 30-day hospital readmission using artificial neural networks. *PLoS One, 12*(7), e0181173. doi:10.1371/journal.pone.0181173 PMID:28708848

Johnson, A. E., Pollard, T. J., Shen, L., Li-Wei, H. L., Feng, M., Ghassemi, M., ... Mark, R. G. (2016). MIMIC-III, a freely accessible critical care database. *Scientific Data, 3*(1), 1–9. doi:10.1038data.2016.35 PMID:27219127

Karhade, P., & Dong, J. Q. (2020). Information technology investment and commercialized innovation performance: Dynamic adjustment costs and curvilinear impacts. *Management Information Systems Quarterly, 45*(3), 1007–1024. doi:10.25300/MISQ/2021/14368

Karhade, P., & Dong, J. Q. (2021). Innovation outcomes of digitally enabled collaborative problemistic search capability. *Management Information Systems Quarterly, 45*(2), 693–718. doi:10.25300/MISQ/2021/12202

Karhade, P., & Kathuria, A. (2020). Missing impact of ratings on platform participation in India: A Call for Research in GREAT Domains. *Communications of the Association for Information Systems*, *47*(1), 19. doi:10.17705/1CAIS.04717

Karhade, P., Kathuria, A., & Konsynski, B. (2021). When Choice Matters: Assortment and Participation for Performance on Digital Platforms. *Proceedings of the 54th Hawaii International Conference on System Sciences*. 10.24251/HICSS.2021.218

Karhade, P., & Shaw, M. (2007). Rejection and selection decisions in the IT portfolio composition process: An enterprise risk management based perspective. AMCIS 2007 Proceedings, 221.

Karhade, P., Shaw, M. J., & Subramanyam, R. (2015). Patterns in information systems portfolio prioritization. *Management Information Systems Quarterly*, *39*(2), 413–434. doi:10.25300/MISQ/2015/39.2.07

Karhade, P., Subramanyam, R., & Shaw, M. J. (2018). Adaptation of Decision Rules: Responding to Complexity of Information Systems Portfolio Planning. In Academy of Management Proceedings (Vol. 2018, No. 1, p. 15499). Academy of Management.

Karhade, P. P., Shaw, M. J., & Subramanyam, R. (2009a). Evolution of decision rules used for IT portfolio management: An inductive approach. In *SIGeBIZ track of the Americas Conference on Information Systems* (pp. 307-320). Springer.

Karhade, P. P., Shaw, M. J., & Subramanyam, R. (2009b). Patterns in strategic IS planning decisions: An inductive approach. *AMCIS 2009 Proceedings*, 397.

Kathuria, A., Karhade, P. P., & Konsynski, B. R. (2020). In the realm of hungry ghosts: Multi-level theory for supplier participation on digital platforms. *Journal of Management Information Systems*, *37*(2), 396–430. doi:10.1080/07421222.2020.1759349

Kim, H., Ross, J. S., Melkus, G. D., Zhao, Z., & Boockvar, K. (2010). Scheduled and unscheduled hospital readmissions among diabetes patients. *The American Journal of Managed Care*, *16*(10), 760. PMID:20964472

Kumar, E. S., & Jayadev, P. S. (2020). Deep learning for clinical decision support systems: A review from the panorama of smart healthcare. *Deep Learning Techniques for Biomedical and Health Informatics*, 79-99.

Lin, Y.W., Ahsen, M. E., Shaw, M., & Seshadri, S. (2019a). The impacts of patients' sentiment trajectory features on their willingness to share in online support groups. *ICIS 2019 Proceedings,* 15.

Lin, Y.W., Ivanov, A., Chang, H.-L., & Shaw, M. J. (2021). Role of Telehealth Adoption in Shaping Perceived Quality of Care: Empirical Analysis. *ICIS 2021 Proceedings*, 22.

Lin, Y. W., Zhou, Y., Faghri, F., Shaw, M. J., & Campbell, R. H. (2019b). Analysis and prediction of unplanned intensive care unit readmission using recurrent neural networks with long short-term memory. *PLoS One*, *14*(7), e0218942. doi:10.1371/journal.pone.0218942 PMID:31283759

Malik, O., Jaiswal, A., Kathuria, A., & Karhade, P. Leveraging BI Systems to Overcome Infobesity: A Comparative Analysis of Incumbent and New Entrant firms. *Proceedings of the 55th Annual Hawaii International Conference on System Sciences*. 10.24251/HICSS.2022.034

Malik, O., Karhade, P., Kathuria, A., Jaiswal, A., & Yen, B. Unravelling the Origins of Infobesity: The Impact of Frequency on Intensity. *Proceedings of the 55th Annual Hawaii International Conference on System Sciences.* 10.24251/HICSS.2022.016

Moyer, A., & Salovey, P. (1998). Patient participation in treatment decision making and the psychological consequences of breast cancer surgery. *Women's Health (Hillsdale, N.J.), 4*(2), 103–116. PMID:9659000

Ngo, E., Truong, M. B.-T., & Nordeng, H. (2020). Use of decision support tools to empower pregnant women: Systematic review. *Journal of Medical Internet Research, 22*(9), e19436. doi:10.2196/19436 PMID:32924961

Porat, T., Delaney, B., & Kostopoulou, O. (2017). The impact of a diagnostic decision support system on the consultation: Perceptions of GPs and patients. *BMC Medical Informatics and Decision Making, 17*(1), 1–9. doi:10.118612911-017-0477-6 PMID:28576145

Rubins, H. B., & Moskowitz, M. A. (1988). Discharge decision-making in a medical intensive care unit: Identifying patients at high risk of unexpected death or unit readmission. *The American Journal of Medicine, 84*(5), 863–869. doi:10.1016/0002-9343(88)90064-2 PMID:3364445

Samek, W., Wiegand, T., & Müller, K.-R. (2017). *Explainable artificial intelligence: Understanding, visualizing and interpreting deep learning models.* arXiv preprint arXiv:1708.08296.

Shickel, B., Tighe, P. J., Bihorac, A., & Rashidi, P. (2017). Deep I: A survey of recent advances in deep learning techniques for electronic health record (I) analysis. *IEEE Journal of Biomedical and Health Informatics, 22*(5), 1589–1604. doi:10.1109/JBHI.2017.2767063 PMID:29989977

Street, R. L. Jr, & Voigt, B. (1997). Patient participation in deciding breast cancer treatment and subsequent quality of life. *Medical Decision Making, 17*(3), 298–306. doi:10.1177/0272989X9701700306 PMID:9219190

Sutton, R. T., Pincock, D., Baumgart, D. C., Sadowski, D. C., Fedorak, R. N., & Kroeker, K. I. (2020). An overview of clinical decision support systems: Benefits, risks, and strategies for success. *NPJ Digital Medicine, 3*(1), 1–10. doi:10.103841746-020-0221-y PMID:32047862

Topol, E. J. (2019). High-performance medicine: The convergence of human and artificial intelligence. *Nature Medicine, 25*(1), 44–56. doi:10.103841591-018-0300-7 PMID:30617339

Tsui, F. R., Shi, L., Ruiz, V., Ryan, N. D., Biernesser, C., Iyengar, S., . . . Brent, D. A. (2021). Natural language processing and machine learning of electronic health records for prediction of first-time suicide attempts. *JAMIA Open, 4*(1). doi:10.1093/jamiaopen/ooab011

van Baalen, S., Boon, M., & Verhoef, P. (2021). From clinical decision support to clinical reasoning support systems. *Journal of Evaluation in Clinical Practice, 27*(3), 520–528. doi:10.1111/jep.13541 PMID:33554432

Verma, J. P., Agrawal, S., Patel, B., & Patel, A. (2016). Big data analytics: Challenges and applications for text, audio, video, and social media data. *International Journal on Soft Computing. Artificial Intelligence and Applications (Commerce, Calif.), 5*(1), 41–51.

Wood, C. S., Thomas, M. R., Budd, J., Mashamba-Thompson, T. P., Herbst, K., Pillay, D., Peeling, R. W., Johnson, A. M., McKendry, R. A., & Stevens, M. M. (2019). Taking connected mobile-health diagnostics of infectious diseases to the field. *Nature*, *566*(7745), 467–474. doi:10.103841586-019-0956-2 PMID:30814711

Zhang, Y., & Wallace, B. (2015). *A sensitivity analysis of (and practitioners' guide to) convolutional neural networks for sentence classification*. https://arxiv.org/abs/1510.03820

ADDITIONAL READING

Chen, D., Liu, S., Kingsbury, P., Sohn, S., Storlie, C. B., Habermann, E. B., Naessens, J. M., Larson, D. W., & Liu, H. (2019). Deep learning and alternative learning strategies for retrospective real-world clinical data. *NPJ Digital Medicine*, *2*(1), 1–5. doi:10.103841746-019-0122-0 PMID:31304389

Esteva, A., Robicquet, A., Ramsundar, B., Kuleshov, V., DePristo, M., Chou, K., Cui, C., Corrado, G., Thrun, S., & Dean, J. (2019). A guide to deep learning in healthcare. *Nature Medicine*, *25*(1), 24–29. doi:10.103841591-018-0316-z PMID:30617335

Faust, O., Hagiwara, Y., Hong, T. J., Lih, O. S., & Acharya, U. R. (2018). Deep learning for healthcare applications based on physiological signals: A review. *Computer Methods and Programs in Biomedicine*, *161*, 1–13. doi:10.1016/j.cmpb.2018.04.005 PMID:29852952

Miotto, R., Wang, F., Wang, S., Jiang, X., & Dudley, J. T. (2018). Deep learning for healthcare: Review, opportunities and challenges. *Briefings in Bioinformatics*, *19*(6), 1236–1246. doi:10.1093/bib/bbx044 PMID:28481991

Norgeot, B., Glicksberg, B. S., & Butte, A. J. (2019). A call for deep-learning healthcare. *Nature Medicine*, *25*(1), 14–15. doi:10.103841591-018-0320-3 PMID:30617337

Pham, T., Tran, T., Phung, D., & Venkatesh, S. (2017). Predicting healthcare trajectories from medical records: A deep learning approach. *Journal of Biomedical Informatics*, *69*, 218–229. doi:10.1016/j.jbi.2017.04.001 PMID:28410981

Prosperi, M., Guo, Y., Sperrin, M., Koopman, J. S., Min, J. S., He, X., Rich, S., Wang, M., Buchan, I. E., & Bian, J. (2020). Causal inference and counterfactual prediction in machine learning for actionable healthcare. *Nature Machine Intelligence*, *2*(7), 369–375. doi:10.103842256-020-0197-y

Rajkomar, A., Oren, E., Chen, K., Dai, A. M., Hajaj, N., Hardt, M., ... Sun, M. (2018). Scalable and accurate deep learning with electronic health records. *NPJ Digital Medicine*, *1*(1), 1–10. doi:10.103841746-018-0029-1 PMID:31304302

KEY TERMS AND DEFINITIONS

Decision Support Systems: A decision support system is an information system used to support the courses of decisions in an organization or a business.

Deep Learning: Deep learning is a subset of machine learning, which is a neural network imitating the structure of a human brain.

Healthcare Data Analytics: A process of applying various analytical tools on historical healthcare data to identify patterns and get actionable insights to treat diseases.

Healthcare Decision Support: A kind of decision support system to improve healthcare delivery by integrating different healthcare data, including patient information, patient activities, healthcare knowledge, and other clinical information.

Healthcare Decision Support Ecosystem: Healthcare decision support ecosystem include three major components: beneficiaries, data, and models.

Machine Learning: Machine learning is a kind of algorithm that provides systems the ability to automatically learn and improve from data without human intervention.

Unplanned ICU Readmission: Unplanned ICU readmissions are defined as ICU patients who were rehospitalized within 30 days of hospital discharge.

ENDNOTES

[1]   https://www.healthit.gov/topic/safety/clinical-decision-support

[2]   https://www.cdw.com/content/cdw/en/newsroom/archive/patient-engagement-on-the-rise.html

[3]   https://www.mckinsey.com/industries/healthcare-systems-and-services/our-insights/the-big-data-revolution-in-us-health-care

[4]   https://www.hipaajournal.com/healthcare-data-breach-statistics/

Section 20
E–Learning Technologies and Tools

Artificial Intelligence in E-Learning Systems

Roberto Marmo

University of Pavia, Italy

INTRODUCTION

Education is one the most essential sectors of society. It is linked with all of the other sectors and its impact on them is substantial. E-learning - or electronic learning - has been referred to as technology-enhanced learning, it describes a set of technology-mediated methods that can be applied to support student learning and can include elements of assessment, tutoring, and instruction.

With the traditional training approach, there is a single learning path, and the instructor/course creator defines the same order of content for all students equally, content is generic, and content is not adapted in relation to the interests of each person. With the traditional training approach, students can get bored, teachers have difficulty in analyzing the individual learning path, teachers have fewer resources to create teaching material.

As more and more students gain learning experience with computers, it is possible to record data on their progress and it is necessary to engage the student with learning materials.

The adaptive educational systems within e-learning platforms are built in response to the fact that the learning process is different for every learner. In order to provide adaptive e-learning services and study materials, that are tailor-made for adaptive learning, this type of educational approach seeks to combine the ability to comprehend and detect a person's specific needs in the context of learning with the expertise required to use appropriate learning pedagogy and enhance the learning process. Thus, it is critical to create accurate student profiles and models based upon analysis of their affective states, knowledge level, and their individual personality traits and skills. In this sense, it is necessary to give the system dynamic self-learning capabilities from the behaviors exhibited by the teachers and students to create the appropriate pedagogy and automatically adjust the e-learning environments to suit the pedagogies.

Artificial Intelligence changes the nature of industries, transport, health, finance etc. included education, so the prospect of personalized e-learning is quickly becoming a reality, allowing to determine how individual students understand the material and to develop more personalized curricula, while helping teachers identify problem areas of students, helping to provide the right content to the right student at the right time, to customize content based on each student's existing knowledge, to create eLearning courses in less time. Therefore, Artificial Intelligence has the power to optimize both learning and teaching, helping the education sector evolve to better benefit students and teachers alike. It is important to admit the current limits of technology and admit that AI is not (yet) ready to replace teachers but is presenting the real possibility to augment them.

The aim of this contribution is to describe some technologies and methodologies to execute personalized e-learning using Artificial Intelligence as specific approach, it also discusses background, knowledge, challenges, and critical factors necessary for successful implementation. The impact of the development of Artificial Intelligence on the role of educators is detailed.

DOI: 10.4018/978-1-7998-9220-5.ch091

Background

Humans are lifelong learners. From our first breaths to our last, we are constantly learning: we learn about the world around us, we learn about each other, we gather new knowledge. To help us in this never-ending task, e-learning can be viewed as a system of electronic learning whereby instructions are devised or formatted to support learning and then delivered to the intended beneficiaries through digital devices that normally come in the form of computers or mobile devices.

The traditional model presents some common difficulties, including:

- too much content and way too long, this overwhelms people very easily;
- lack of personalized experiences, courses are often too generic and do not adapt to the specific needs of each student;
- don't really track the program's effectiveness, result estimation involves time-consuming data collection and entry processes;
- the student prefer to self-manage the learning experiences.

Artificial Intelligence is useful to improve the student experience of learning, and allows educators to analyze the performance and to create enhanced multimedia content in less time. Artificial Intelligence-based eLearning platform is a machine/system that possesses the ability to perform different tasks requiring human intelligence. It has the ability to offer solutions to human-related problems, like speech recognition, translations, decision making, and much more.

E-Learning Approach

E-learning may be designed in two forms where one form of e-learning is designed as an instructor-led type of learning known as synchronous e-learning, while the other is designed in a format that is a self-paced individual study, known as asynchronous e-learning. In asynchronous e-learning, when the learners take up a course study that utilizes spoken or printed texts that come in the form of illustrations, photos, animation, or video as learning materials, and with which evaluations are made, the learners are then given the opportunity to control the time and place as well as the pace at which they want to undertake their own learning. The other e-learning format, known as synchronous e-learning, is real-time instructor-led training that is designed for instructions on the learning to be delivered or facilitated by an instructor to take place in a real time. In adaptive educational systems, the learner characteristics are monitored, and the instructional milieu is appropriately adjusted to offer support and to make improvements to the learning process.

People can now access educational materials with just a click on their phones and laptop. Today, students do not need to leave the warmth of their beds on winter mornings to be physically present in class. All they need is a computer and a smooth internet connection, and they are good to go.

There are abundant e-learning systems and methods (knows as Learning Management Systems) that can be utilized to deliver online courses.

Educational Data Mining

Educational Data Mining is an emerging interdisciplinary research area that deals with the development of methods to explore data originating in an educational context. It uses computational approaches to analyze educational data, to study educational questions. Peña-Ayala (2014) and Muttathil (2015) survey the most relevant studies. Educational data mining and learning analytics, although experiencing an upsurge in exploration and use, continue to elude precise definition; the two terms are often interchangeably used. This could be because the two fields exhibit common thematic elements. One avenue to provide clarity, uniformity, and consistency around the two fields, is to identify similarities and differences in topics between the two evolving fields. Lemay et al. (2021) describe a topic modeling analysis of articles related to educational data mining and learning analytics to reveal thematic features of the two fields.

Artificial Intelligence

Artificial Intelligence (AI) allows machines to learn from previous experiences. The Oxford dictionary defines artificial intelligence as "The theory and development of computer systems able to perform tasks normally requiring human intelligence, such as visual perception, speech recognition, decision-making, and translation between languages." AI is a machine which possesses the ability to solve problems that can be solved only by the human brain. In this way, AI can increase Educational Data Mining, can support on content creation and other learning problems.

There are various AI techniques that have been used in adaptive educational systems, such as Fuzzy Logic, Decision tree, Bayesian networks, Neural Networks, Genetic algorithms, and Hidden Markov Models. These techniques can manage the inherent uncertainty that human decision making has, and they are innovative approaches that can deal with impression, uncertainty, and partial truth. In this respect, these AI techniques are useful for several reasons, including that they are capable of developing and imitating the human decision-making process and building automatic and accurate teaching-learning models.

Journals and Conferences

The conference "AIED: Artificial Intelligence in Education" detailed at http://www.wikicfp.com/cfp/program?id=102 and related proceedings are useful sources of research paper in many educational contexts, known for high quality and innovative research on intelligent systems and cognitive science approaches for educational computing applications.

"The journal Computers & Education: Artificial Intelligence" is an open access and peer reviewed journal available online at https://www.journals.elsevier.com/computers-and-education-artificial-intelligence aims at affording a world-wide platform for researchers, developers, and educators to present their research studies, exchange new ideas, and demonstrate novel systems and pedagogical innovations on the research topics in relation to applications of artificial intelligence (AI) in education and AI education.

"Education and Information Technologies" is the official journal of the IFIP Technical Committee on Education publishes papers from all sectors of education on all aspects of information technology and information systems, available at https://www.springer.com/journal/10639. It has been proposed in order to meet the demand for an international publication which addresses all aspects of education and information systems. As users are aware the new technologies can liberate the learner and teacher and allow their time to be used more efficiently.

The journal IEEE Transactions on Learning Technologies (TLT) on https://ieeexplore.ieee.org/xpl/RecentIssue.jsp?punumber=4620076 covers research on such topics as Innovative online learning systems, Intelligent tutors, Educational software applications and games, and Simulation systems for education and training.

WAYS OF SUPPORTING EDUCATION

AI is improving the student experience of learning, at the same time, is extending better support for educators to analyze the performance and to create enhanced multimedia content in less time.

AI in education has been undergoing several paradigmatic shifts, which are characterized into three paradigms detailed in Ouyang et al. (2021): AI-directed, learner-as-recipient, AI-supported, learner-as-collaborator, and AI-empowered, learner-as-leader. In three paradigms, AI techniques are used to address educational and learning issues in varied ways. AI is used to represent knowledge models and direct cognitive learning while learners are recipients of AI service in Paradigm One; AI is used to support learning while learners work as collaborators with AI in Paradigm Two; AI is used to empower learning while learners take agency to learn in Paradigm Three. Overall, the development trend of AI has been developing to empower learner agency and personalization, enable learners to reflect on learning and inform AI systems to adapt accordingly, and lead to an iterative development of the learner-centered, data-driven, personalized learning.

Here are some of the ways AI and machine learning is supporting education and taking it to new heights. The following technologies can be grouped according to student, teacher, administrative roles, in this way:

Administrative role:
- Guidance Service;
- Recruiting and hiring;
- School management;

Student:
- Exploration;
- Guidance Service;
- Learner profiles;
- Personalize learning;
- Practical mentoring;
- Real-time questioning;
- Recruiting and hiring;
- Video Contents;

Teacher:
- Accessibility:
- Assessment and grading;
- Assignment writing;
- Content creation;
- Learner profiles;
- MOOC;
- Natural Language Processing;
- Personalize learning;
- Professional learning;
- Real-time questioning;
- Video Contents;
- Voice Analysis.

Accessibility

Accessibility is the practice of making your websites usable by as many people as possible. We traditionally think of this as being about people with disabilities, but the practice of making sites accessible also benefits other groups such as those using mobile devices, or those with slow network connections.

AI has also been used to improve the lives of people with disabilities, such as: to narrate the world to the blind, to read text, to recognize products, to act as a virtual assistant who responds to voice commands to individuals who deal with mobility issues, to convert spoken language into captions and transcripts helping the hearing-impaired comprehend the subject easily, to describe scenes, currencies and describe the person standing in front of student.

Assessment and Grading

After consuming the informational course assets, students are generally invited to apply the new knowledge through hands-on exercises. Since every student is dynamic, it is only unfair that everyone comes under the same grading system. But the impossible has been made possible with the inclusion of AI bringing in welcoming changes in the way a student is assessed. With adaptive testing, educators and trainers can now monitor a student's progress and measure skills beyond the grades they have scored in their academic papers.

Current ways in which assessment is carried out in most learning platforms regards: 1) auto-graded content with predefined answers (e.g., multiple-choice questions, numerical questions, short-answers with limited solutions, etc.); 2) auto-graded content with open-ended answers (e.g. essays, derivations, programming); and 3) peer-graded content with open-ended or non-trivial answers. Current AI research is focuses on solutions for the last two points, as well as providing tools to instructors to help with assessment.

Programming is the domain that has received the most attention. Drummond et al. (2014) consider a program to be constituted of multiple code fragments and measuring the distance between fragments of different students through appropriate distance metrics. By relying on previously graded programs, a quality score is assigned (i.e., programs that have a small neighboring distance should be of similar quality).

However, most works related to programming focus on how to automatically provide feedback to learners. Piech et al. (2015) predict how an instructor would encourage a learner to progress towards the correct solution to automatically generate hints. They use Desirable Path algorithms to model the best paths that can lead to the correct solution and steer learners in that direction. Singh et al. (2013) developed a technique that uses an error model describing the potential corrections and constraint-based synthesis to compute minimal corrections to student's incorrect solutions, enabling them to automatically provide feedback to learners. Their results show that relatively simple error models can correct a good number of incorrect solutions. Gulwani et al. (2014) use a dynamic analysis-based approach to test whether a student's program matches a teacher's specification. After manually identifying specifications and their associated feedback, the algorithm matches a program with a specification and automatically generates the relevant feedback.

Sadigh et al. (2012) investigates how to automate exercise creation, solution generation and grading. They do so by generalizing existing exercises from textbooks into templates that capture the common structure. They then adapt previously developed techniques for verification and synthesis to generate new problems and their solutions.

Lan et al. (2015) investigates how to automatically grade open response mathematical questions. They leverage the high number of solutions created by learners to evaluate the correctness of their solutions, assign partial-credit scores, and provide feedback to each learner.

Clustering can be a powerful tool to quickly see what learners understood, to identify patterns in solutions, and to provide feedback at scale. Glassman (2014) and Glassman et al. (2014) develop a clustering-based visualization tool that enables one to view functionally similar programming solutions. Their algorithm is unsupervised, meaning it does not require any human input to operate.

Assignment Writing

An assignment is a task, or a piece of work allocated to someone as part of job or course of study. Feedback systems like Grammarly, Turnitin, and Write to Learn are being powered by AI to offer better and more accurate guidance to students. There are several online perfect essay writing service brands too that are using machine learning to provide customized solutions that reflect the literary voice of the students. Students can also use test prep tools like Quizlet and Magoosh for personalized question papers designed to target the areas that a student is weak in.

Content Creation

AI is being experimented to create or generate new content. For example, the Sci-Fi short film 'Sunspring' was entirely scripted by an AI, including the title and song. Students can now look up for study course material on the internet, often free of cost or at minimal charges. AI can help to organize and even generate supporting materials. To enable more flexible navigation and easier retrieval, AI can be used to label and index materials. Collaborative semantic filtering technologies are used to enrich learning materials with semantics, thus enabling collaborative labelling and indexing.

AI can be used to find and reuse existing contents. There already exist many open learning resources on the Internet, which represents a great opportunity to reduce time in creating new contents. However, finding such resources and their integration is often difficult. The use of taxonomies, ontologies, and semantic technologies can help. Piedra et al. (2014) discuss the main aspects needed to support the discovery, accessibility, visibility, and reuse of open resources in MOOCs. Their framework, based on semantic web technologies, apply the principles of Linked Data for these tasks.

Exploration

Education is now changing in many ways. Some students succeed in reading the given materials, while others are hindered by a wall of text that is easier to understand when they are speaking in a lecture form.

By identifying these trends in student data, students can obtain more accessible material that can improve learning outcomes.

Thanks to AI becoming a norm in schools and universities, more kids are getting the opportunity to learn in an environment supported by augmented and virtual reality. Since the tech era is all about machines, the close association with gadgets and Virtual Reality will only help them survive in this fast-changing world. Moreover, Virtual Reality is including gesture and voice recognition and image rendering experiences for differently abled students with special needs.

Guidance Service

The only way to reap the benefits of your years of perseverance and effort is to get the dream job. Two important networks provide guidance services, in order to find job: the network of educational services, the network of employment services. Talent and recruiting platforms like LinkedIn and Ziprecruiter are suing AI to match a potential candidate with the fitting employers. AI, therefore, is playing an important role in paving rapid pathways to eradicating unemployment.

Learner Profiles

A student's learning profile is the complete picture of his/her learning preferences, strengths, and challenges and is shaped by the categories of learning style, intelligence preference, culture, and gender. With AI into the picture, interoperability to support competency management is being aided by extended comparisons of comprehensive profiles formed via grade books and portfolios. Although human reviewers and distributed ledgers will continue to form the chunk, machine learning tools are being used alongside to review larger profiles–both submitted and scraped.

MOOC

Massive Open Online Courses (MOOCs) have gained tremendous popularity in the last few years. Thanks to MOOCs, millions of learners from all over the world have taken thousands of high-quality courses for free. Putting together an excellent MOOC ecosystem is a multidisciplinary endeavor that requires contributions from many different fields. AI can greatly improve student experience and learning outcomes. There already exists a large body of AI research for this purpose, which we break down into three aspects:

1. modelling engagement and learning behaviors, to better understand how learners engage with MOOC resources and tools;
2. modelling, predicting and influencing learners' achievement to better understand what leads to learner achievement;
3. modelling learners knowledge to deliver new skills and knowledge to learners.

Fauvel et al. (2016) review the state-of-the-art AI and data mining research applied to MOOCs, emphasizing how AI and data mining tools and techniques can improve student engagement, learning outcomes, and our understanding of the MOOC ecosystem. The paper shows how AI and data mining are seamlessly embedded in virtually every aspect of the MOOC ecosystem as we know it today, then it provides an overview of key trends and important future research in AI and data mining for MOOCs so that they can reach their full potential.

Natural Language Processing

Natural Language Processing, or NLP, is the sub-field of AI that is focused on enabling computers to understand and process human languages. It is an effective approach for teachers, students, authors, and educators for providing assistance for writing, analysis, and assessment procedures. Application of NLP in education is also effective for mining, information retrieval, and quality assessment. By integrating

NLP, student can ask queries and clarify doubts in the preferred human language in the similar way as talking to human teacher.

Personalize Learning

Delivering the same form of content to every single learner is a very common approach in corporate training. But this one-size-fits-all approach is not appropriate as everybody has their own style and pace of learning. AI can be used to track the previous performance of an individual and use that data to alter the current learning material, thus providing a personalized learning experience. Within an eLearning course, AI can track learners' progress, which will help identify the areas where each learner lacks proficiency thus altering the material accordingly.

Singh et al. (2014) proposes a reinforcement learning based algorithm to analyze every learner's profile. Using both implicit and explicit feedback, they infer learners' needs and capabilities and then recommend an appropriate learning sequence. They validated their results by asking learners to rate the usefulness of recommended learning objects, showing that ratings were higher after recommendation compared to before.

Brinton et al. (2015) build their learner model by using machine learning techniques on behavioral data. They then provide personalized content based on this model. Preliminary results indicate that learners subjectively prefer the adaptive platform over a traditional one, and that they statistically view more content.

Instead of trying to model each learner individually, Sonwalkar (2013) classify them in one of five distinct learning strategies through an assessment tool. They then provide an adaptive sequence for each strategy. The sequences must be provided by an instructor. No results are reported about the effectiveness of this system.

Venkataraman et al. (2014) relies on open repositories of learning objects to build adaptive sequences. Collaborative filtering is used to model learner preferences. Based on these preferences, repositories are queried by exploiting the metadata attached to each learning object.

Practical Mentoring

Mentoring is a highly personal and individual process, in which mentees take advantage of expertise and experience to expand their knowledge and to achieve individual goals. Connecting the stalwarts and mentors of the industry to the students at the right time is what project-based mentoring is all about. While e-learning brands like Nepris Learning and Educurious have already taken to this kind of online mentoring, several colleges are welcoming members from the college alumni associations aboard to work in tandem with the bench of educators.

Professional Learning

We will never be able to make the most of AI if the educators are not familiar with the applications of AI. The onus here lies with institutional boards and IT companies to prepare teachers as AI instructors by providing them with the required curriculums. Several schools are striking deals with tech moguls for teachers' training programs.

Real-time Questioning

One of the major issues an individual comes across when learning is the inability to clear their doubts as soon as they pop up in their minds. AI can act as a virtual tutor and answer questions on the fly. By integrating AI, the necessity to walk up to the trainer or look up the Internet every time a slight confusion/doubt arises during learning can be avoided. All one would have to do is ask the AI engine and receive the appropriate answer.

Recruiting and Hiring

Although the world moves towards a new dawn of technology, the basic scepter of imparting education rests in the hands of teachers and trainers. To hire the best minds, who can lead the adults of tomorrow onto the right path, institutions are using machine learning for corporate recruiting. For example, Frontline Education is a smart platform that uses analytics to improve the efficiency of recruiting and matching.

School Management

As the number of micro-schools grows in the west along with low-cost private schools in developing countries, the need for a robust school management platform becomes more pressing. With AI and Cloud Technology paired up, administrative tasks like recruitment, collecting and maintaining student information, tacking attendance, and journaling payment have become less tedious and time-consuming.

Video Contents

Videos are undoubtedly the most prominent learning content available to MOOC learners. AI can analyze video production features and correlate them with measures of engagement: how long learners watch a given video, and whether they attempt a post-video exercise. In this way, several useful observations can help instructors create more impactful MOOC videos. These observations mention that shorter videos lead to more engagement and specify production styles that can lead to more engagement. AI can support authors to takes all the hard work out of turning content into a storytelling video, takes care of the tedious work and inspires creativity. AI can create an avatar, no actors or camera needed, simply to type text in many languages, no voiceover needed, AI video will be created in minutes.

Voice Analysis

AI can perform analysis of voice and pronunciation of certain words that students pronounce when learning them. Most word learning applications analyze which words or phrases the student makes mistakes on and revise them at the next study session. There are automatic spell-checking, grammar, and punctuation apps such as Grammarly https://www.grammarly.com/. This approach saves teachers time when checking students' writing and helps students prepare for the written part of the exam without the help of a teacher. Of course, it does not fix all mistakes, and sometimes it is wrong.

Cyber and Physical Security

Schools are major target for ransomware attacks. Just as it's important to implement the correct technology for cyber security in education organizations, so too is it important for them to carry out policies on campus which encourage safe cyber security practices. According to a Cisco report, available at https://www.itgovernance.co.uk/blog/artificial-intelligence-in-cyber-security/, school security professionals are spending more on AI-powered tools to learn to automatically detect unusual patterns within IoT environments with encrypted web traffic. AI is also being used to identify patterns in student behavior that could foreshadow violence.

PRIVACY ISSUES

Using tracking approaches on the majority of e-learning platforms to monitor learners' activities raises many privacy questions. As for learners, knowing that their personal data are being used, even for educational purposes, they could radically change their perception on e-learning technologies.

Whenever implementing new technology that involves the collection of sensitive data, the GDPR requires identifying and mitigating any risks that could lead to misuse of personal data. These assessments are particularly necessary when handling children's data, which is especially sensitive.

Failing to protect sensitive data can lead to serious financial and legal troubles, and it can also damage your reputation and put your ethics into question.

Education providers usually already have a privacy policy in place to cover the usual data processing. It is necessary to consider a section defining precisely what personal data is captured through online learning platforms and explain what you're using it for, where it's stored, and for how long you'll retain it.

In order to legally collect personal data, you must obtain consent, but don't forget that consent should also be updated as your privacy policy changes. Being transparent and keeping everyone from your staff to parents informed about your privacy policy is not only a legal requirement and a good ethical practice, but it can also help you avoid cyber security threats.

May and Iksal et al. (2016) discuss a study on privacy issues in e-learning, based on both existing research findings and an experiment conducted with the participation of students from three universities in France and one university in Germany. The study covers two main aspects. First, it outlines various tracking approaches in e-learning. Second, it analyzes how the participants perceive the use of their tracking data and the related privacy issues. The major contribution of this paper is the awareness-raising of privacy concerns, which are often overlooked by researchers and e-learning content providers.

Ivanova (2015) discuss a data privacy model created after explorations related to the measures for security of private information in different online transactional fields including in the area of eLearning and after results summarization of students' opinion. The findings show that privacy in eLearning could be achieved through a combination of actions from student's side, third parties' side and appropriate design of educational software.

THE CHANGING ROLE OF THE TEACHER

Naturally, there is some hesitation when it comes to the use of AI in the classroom. It may be tempting to assume that AI can replace classroom teachers. Even though most experts believe the critical presence of teachers is irreplaceable, there will be many changes to a teacher's job and to educational best practices.

Machines are horrible when it comes to tasks that require emotional intelligence, which are the skills needed to educate a diverse student body.

AI in front of an audience could be a recipe for disaster, as students who don't want to learn can play with artificial intelligence, thereby destroying all the educational benefits it provides.

Instead, AI is designed to free the educator from the most time-consuming and monotonous tasks, such as certification exams and plagiarism tests.

Any teacher will confirm that this work takes up most of his time, time that could be better spent on more important things.

If AI helps teachers, not replace them, then AI education can free up educators so that they can make full use of their training in ways that were simply not possible before. In fact, AI can drive efficiency, personalization and streamline admin tasks to allow teachers the time and freedom to provide understanding and adaptability.

Appropriate familiarity and training of teachers on how to use these new tools in the classroom can significantly reduce the anxiety that such technology can cause.

AI Providers cannot and should not replace teachers. Still, thanks to personalized curricula and the fact that AI helps the teacher by eliminating lengthy paperwork, they can be transformative and liberating innovations in education.

The more commonplace AI becomes, the more people will find innovative ways to put it to use. Educators should keep their eyes out for industry-disrupting use-cases—or maybe even consider becoming the disruptor themselves.

It is important to focus further research on the new roles of educators on new learning pathways for students, with a new set of graduate attributes, with a focus on imagination, creativity, and innovation, that is, the set of abilities and skills that can hardly be ever replicated by machines.

FUTURE RESEARCH DIRECTIONS

As AI educational solutions continue to mature, the hope is that AI can help fill needs gaps in learning and teaching and allow schools and teachers to do more than ever before. It is expected that AI in U.S. Education will grow by 47.5% from 2017-2021 according to the Artificial Intelligence Market in the US Education Sector report available online at https://www.researchandmarkets.com/research/5lshzz/artificial

AI can be used to generate the entire content of an eLearning course, taking away a huge load from the instructional designers.

E-learning research looking at better understanding learners is concerned with engagement, achievement, and how students navigate through platforms. A lot of work remains to be done before e-learning can achieve their true potential, and AI still has an important role to play.

There already exists a large body of work on education for online paradigms, and an even larger body of research on education in general. So far, AI has not exploited this well. Few tools that have proven effective in online learning systems (such as intelligent agents) have been tested or integrated. Research from learning analytics has not been leveraged.

AI has improved significantly recently but there are still a number of challenges that it is unable to solve. For such challenges, combining the power of AI with humans (a concept known as crowdsourcing) could prove game changing. One important problem is the fact that most data is unlabeled. This makes it much harder to draw causation links in the data. Supervised algorithms must thus rely on the small amount of labelled data, either provided by student surveys or researchers themselves, both approaches are expensive. Examples of data labelling through crowdsourcing include allowing students to rate different portions of a video to assist curriculum redesign, gathering insights about navigation behavior through short pop-up questions, collaborative materials annotation to label contents, and more.

Personalization is important so that every learner has a fruitful experience, current research is somewhat limited and generally requires significant human input to achieve adaptability, more automated approaches that are generalizable would provide high value. Other forms of personalization could be valuable. Intelligent agent has the potential to help in all aspects of e-learning, because such agents can mitigate the lack of instructor resources by taking some of their responsibilities. For example, affective agents could help students stay engaged and motivated throughout the course by offering personalized support, teachable agents could enable students to gather knowledge through the framework framework learning-by-teaching,

The study needs to be tested statistically for better understanding and to make the findings more generalized in the future.

CONCLUSION

With the development of computing and information processing techniques, Artificial Intelligence (AI) has been extensively applied in education. Advances in Artificial Intelligence open to new opportunities, potentials, and challenges for teaching and learning in education, with the potential to fundamentally change governance and the internal architecture of institutions of education.

This chapter reviewed the state-of-the-art AI research applied to e-learning system, emphasizing how AI tools and techniques can improve student engagement, learning outcomes, teaching abilities, assessment of the quality of learning materials, as well as in adaptive learning mechanisms. The impact will be felt right from the lowest levels of education to the higher grades of learning institutions. While adding personalization features has some clear benefits, their potential negative impacts and privacy problems should also be evaluated. It is important to admit the current limits of technology and admit that AI is not (yet) ready to replace teachers but is presenting the real possibility to augment them.

REFERENCES

Brinton, C. G., Rill, R., Ha, S., Chiang, M., Smith, R., & Ju, W. (2015). Individualization for education at scale: MIIC design and preliminary evaluation. *IEEE Transactions on Learning Technologies*, 8(1), 136–148. doi:10.1109/TLT.2014.2370635

Drummond, A., Lu, Y., Chaudhuri, S., Jermaine, C., Warren, J., & Rixner, S. (2014). Learning to grade student programs in a Massive Open Online Course. *Proceedings of the IEEE International Conference on Data Mining*, 785-790. 10.1109/ICDM.2014.142

Fauvel, S., & Yu, H. (2016). *A Survey on Artificial Intelligence and Data Mining for MOOCs*. Retrieved October 13, 2021 from https://arxiv.org/abs/1601.06862

Glassman, E. L. (2014). Interacting with Massive numbers of student solutions. *Proceedings of the 27th annual ACM symposium on User interface software and technology*, 17-20. 10.1145/2658779.2661167

Glassman, E. L., Scott, J., Miller, R. C., & Guo, P. (2014). OverCode: Visualizing variation in student solutions to programming problems at scale. *ACM Transactions on Computer-Human Interaction*, 22(2), 129–130.

Gulwani, S., Radiček, I., & Zuleger, F. (2014). *Feedback generation for performance problems in introductory programming assignments*. doi:10.1145/2635868.2635912

Ivanova, M., Grosseck, G., & Holotescu, C. (2015). Researching data privacy models in eLearning. *Proceedings of the International Conference on Information Technology Based Higher Education and Training (ITHET)*, 1-6.

Lan, A. S., Vats, D., Waters, A. E., & Baraniuk, R. G. (2015). Mathematical language processing: Automatic grading and feedback for open response mathematical questions. *Proceedings of the ACM Conference on Learning at Scale*, 167-176. 10.1145/2724660.2724664

Lemay, D. J., Baek, C., & Doleck, T. (2021). Comparison of learning analytics and educational data mining: A topic modeling approach. *Computers and Education: Artificial Intelligence*, 2, 100016. doi:10.1016/j.caeai.2021.100016

May, M., Iksal, S., & Usener, C. (2016). Learning tracking data analysis - how privacy issues affect student perception on e-learning? *Proceedings of the 8th International Conference on Computer Supported Education (CSEDU)*, 1, 154-161. 10.5220/0005810801540161

Muttathil, A., & Zubair Rahman, A. M. J. (2015). A Comprehensive survey on Educational Data Mining and use of Data Mining Techniques for Improving teaching and predicting student performance. *Proceedings of the International Conference on Innovative Engineering and Technologies*, 59-88.

Ouyang, F., & Jiao, P. (2021). Artificial intelligence in education: The three paradigms. *Computers and Education: Artificial Intelligence*, 2, 100020. Retrieved October 13, 2021 from https://www.sciencedirect.com/science/article/pii/S2666920X2100014X

Peña-Ayala, A. (2014). Educational Data Mining: A survey and a Data Mining-based analysis of recent works. *Expert Systems with Applications*, 41(4), 1432–1462. doi:10.1016/j.eswa.2013.08.042

Piech, C., & Guibas, L. (2015). Autonomously generating hints by inferring problem solving policies. *Proceedings of the Second ACM Conference on Learning*, 195-204. 10.1145/2724660.2724668

Piedra, N., Chicaiza, J. A., López, J., & Tovar, E. (2014). An architecture based on linked data technologies for the integration and reuse of OER in MOOCs Context. *Open Prax*, 6(2), 171–187. doi:10.5944/openpraxis.6.2.122

Sadigh, D., Seshia, S., & Gupta, M. (2012). Automating exercise generation: A step towards meeting the MOOC challenge for embedded systems. *Proceedings of the Workshop on Embedded and Cyber-Physical Systems Education*, 2-9.

Singh, R., Gulwani, S., & Solar-Lezama, A. (2013). Automated feedback generation for introductory programming assignments. *Proceedings of the 34th ACM SIGPLAN Conference on Programming Language Design and Implementation*, 15-26. 10.1145/2491956.2462195

Sonwalkar, N. (2013). The First Adaptive MOOC: A case study on Pedagogy Framework and Scalable Cloud Architecture—Part I. *MOOCs Forum*, 22-29. Retrieved October 13, 2021 from https://online. liebertpub.com/doi/abs/10.1089/mooc.2013.0007

Venkataraman, G., & Elias, S. (2014). Context-aware authoring and presentation from Open E-Learning Repository. *Proceedings of the IEEE International Conference on MOOC, Innovation and Technology in Education (MITE)*, 301-307. 10.1109/MITE.2014.7020292

ADDITIONAL READING

Anouar Tadlaoui, M., & Khaldi, M. (2019). *Personalization and collaboration in Adaptive E-Learning*. IGI Global. Retrieved October 13, 2021 from https://www.igi-global.com/book/personalization-collaboration-adaptive-learning/233148

Rienties, B., Køhler Simonsen, H., & Herodotou, C. (2020). *Defining the boundaries between Artificial Intelligence in Education, Computer-Supported Collaborative Learning, Educational Data Mining, and Learning Analytics: A need for coherence*. Retrieved October 13, 2021 from https://www.frontiersin. org/articles/10.3389/feduc.2020.00128/full

Seel, N. M. (2012). *Encyclopedia of the sciences of learning*. Springer. Retrieved October 13, 2021 from https://link.springer.com/referencework/10.1007/978-1-4419-1428-6

Singh, T., & Khanna, S. (2014). Reinforcement learning approach towards effective content recommendation in MOOC environments. *Proceedings of the IEEE International Conference on MOOC, Innovation and Technology in Education (MITE)*, 285-289.

Tatnall, A. (2020). *Encyclopedia of education and information technologies*. Springer. Retrieved October 13, 2021 from https://link.springer.com/referencework/10.1007/978-3-030-10576

KEY TERMS AND DEFINITIONS

Adaptive Educational System: Emphasize the importance of individual differences in modelling the ideal online learning environment.

Artificial Intelligence (AI): Intelligence demonstrated by machines, as opposed to the natural intelligence displayed by animals including humans, allows machines to learn from previous experiences.

E-Learning: any form of learning conducted via electronic media, typically the Internet, it focuses on utilizing the knowledge of professors in such a way that educational systems and courses can be delivered anytime and anywhere.

E-Learning Theory: Describes the cognitive science principles of effective multimedia learning using electronic educational technology.

A

Educational Data Mining: Methods for exploring the unique and increasingly large-scale data that come from educational settings and using those methods to better understand students, and the settings which they learn in.

Educational Technology: Combined use of computer hardware, software, and educational theory and practice to facilitate learning.

Learning Analytics: Compilation, quantification, analysis, and notification of information related to students in relation to their individual characteristics.

MOOC: Massive Open Online Courses, open and free learning system available on internet.

Converging International Cooperation Supported by Data Structures

Gilbert Ahamer

ⓘD https://orcid.org/0000-0003-2140-7654

Graz University, Austria

INTRODUCTION

The organizations involved in the following cases include universities, university clusters, transnational university partnerships, international environmental NGOs, and the European Union's external policy. These organizations range from public to private and from idealistic to pragmatic. All of them plan to "change the world" and for that target they undertake to *exchange views and perspectives* among the stakeholders concerned. This paper approaches to find answers to the specific set of questions through cases of international collaborative educational projects.

SETTING THE STAGE

Learning is Dialogue

As a starting point, we look at the core element of any social progress, namely at "dialogue". Dialogue leads to reflection and reflection, in turn, leads to awareness.

The final target of evolution (encompassing amongst others the evolution of mankind) is to *build consciousness* (Ahamer & Strobl, 2009, Toutain et al., 2020, Heuer & Toro, 2019, Janus, 2020, Koumpis et al., 2018, Love, 2018, Padilla & Lagercrantz, 2020). Consciousness governs procedures in the material world (Strigin 2019, Cherdymova et al., 2019, Cominelli et al., 2018, della Volpe et al., 2018).

Dialogue is a suitable means to approximate divergent views – which is one of the main issues of learning – and to ultimately facilitate changes in consciousness (Akhmetova et al., 2021, Aviv & Spires, 2021, Geraci et al., 2021, Krishnendu et al., 2021, Lodge, 2021, Sergin, 2021, Smith & Schillaci, 2021, West, 2021, Woiwode et al., 2021).

Regarding learning, we may distinguish between *individual* learning and *societal* learning. Regarding the multiplicity of learning objects and learners (Baqui et al., 2021, Bojjireddy et al., 2021, Chaku et al., 2021, Duram 2021, Francesconi et al., 2021, Groves et al., 2021, Hansen et al., 2021, Hasni & Faiz, 2021, Huntington et al., 2021, Kannan et al., 2021, Kunkel & Settersten, 2021, Leach et al., 2021, Rinnooy Kan et al., 2021, Sumell et al., 2021), we distinguish the following types of learning:

- Individual learning
  - traditional learning (1:1)
  - interdisciplinary learning (1:n)
  - intercultural learning (n:m)

DOI: 10.4018/978-1-7998-9220-5.ch092

- Societal learning, e.g.
  - responding to climate change
  - political integration (globally, Europe-wide).

We are traditionally used to approach learning objects from one perspective (1:1) and consider it a progress to view objects from several, interdisciplinary perspectives (1:n). A still more advanced learning procedure would take into account the *multitude of learning subjects* (m) in addition to the *multiplicity of learning objects* (n), we will refer to it as *intercultural learning* (m:n) in this text because subjects are considered to be rooted and coached in their respective cultures inducing the subject to see and view reality as they decide to.

Useful training situations are spatial planning exercises and other space-related procedures that are open to GIS applications, or political, technological, civil engineering, cultural or peace negotiations in the classroom (Ahamer, 2004, 2008, 2012a).

Learning Means Converging Divergent World Views

For very complex, interdisciplinary and intercultural learning issues a purely cognitive approach (an individual learner cognises a well-defined object of learning) appears too simple and the approach of "converging individual perspectives" (Ahamer, 2019, ch. 9, Beames et al., 2021, Claverie, 2021, Greenlees & Cornelius, 2021, Haaker et al., 2021) seems more appropriate. Here, the object of learning is not regarded as something unchangeable (such as facts in natural sciences), but rather as the result of a constructivist procedure.

Learning Means Evolution of Spaces of Understanding

Also, practical-minded disciplines take a similar stance: Taylor (2007, p. 198) stems from spatial planning. He says that *spaces are constructed*: "The most influential recent writer on the social construction of space is Manuel Castells who argues that, in an emerging network society, 'a new spatial logic', 'spaces of flows', is superseding the former logic, 'spaces of places' (Castells, 1996, p. 378). Both of these spatial forms are created through material practices. In his social theory, 'space is the material support of time-sharing practices'. That is to say, social spaces are created to bring together practices requiring simultaneous attention."

Castells is reported to condense this view to the statement "Our societies are increasingly structured around the bipolar opposition of the *Net* and the *Self*". The Net means the new, networked forms of organization which are replacing vertically integrated hierarchies as the dominant form of social organization. The Self, on the other hand, relates to the multiple practices through which people try to reaffirm identity and meaning in a landscape of rapid change. Castells also coined the term 4th World for the poorest nations. Castells is defining space as the physical support of the way we live in time. The space and time we are used to, "real world time", is referred to by him as a space of places.

Manuel Castells (2001) himself says:

So, what we have, for instance, in the case of Europe, is a complex system of institutional relations, which I call the network state, because, in fact, it's a network of interactions of shared sovereignty. In a world of global flows of wealth, power, and images, the search for identity - collective or individual, ascribed or constructed - becomes the fundamental source of social meaning.

Such views come close to Matthias Horx's emerging "*society of meaning*", Renard's "mental structures" and the evolution towards a societal structure autopoietically optimizing towards values such as sense and human well-being (Ahamer & Strobl, 2009: Fig. 4). On this basis we can say: *the ultimate civilisatoric aim is to create meaning*, be it called "sense of life", "quality of life" or other immaterial values.

Castells writes in his famous trilogy (1996-1998) what is comparable to the above-mentioned evolutionist views:

- "Social movements in the Information Age are essentially mobilized around *cultural values*. The struggle to change the *codes of meaning* in the institutions and practice of the society is the essential struggle in the process of social change in the new historical context, movements to seize the power of the minds, not state power."
- "The networks are not programmed by technology; technological tools are programmed by minds. So the *human consciousness is the source*, because everything now depends on our ability to generate knowledge and process information in every domain and activity. Knowledge and information are cognitive qualities from the human mind."
- "Now, therefore, in a world in which signals, processed by our minds, are constantly shaping and reshaping what we do, the ability to influence, to change the categories through which we think our world (here, what I call the code of our culture) -- this becomes the essential battle. If you win the battle of minds, you win the battle of politics, the battle of the economy, because people will decide what they want to buy or what they don't want to buy, for instance."
- "So, it's a *battle*, but ideas and talents are, ultimately, the source of productivity and competitiveness. The same thing is true in terms of the overall social organization, how people *change their minds* determines how they change their behavior. And the change of behavior would, ultimately, translate into changes in the overall social organization."

Castells says according to Stalder (2000):

New social formations emerge around primary identities. These identities are often seen as biologically or socially unchangeable. In the interplay of the Net and the Self the conditions of human life and experience around the world are deeply reconfigured.

The first assumption structures Castells' account of the rise of the Net: the dialectical interaction of social relations and technological innovation, or, in Castells' terminology, modes of production and modes of development. The second assumption underlines the importance of the Self: the way social groups define their identity shapes the institutions of society. As Castells (1997, pp. 6-8) notes "each type of identity-building process leads to a different outcome in constituting society". - "Identity-building itself is a dynamic motor in forming society. *Identity* is defined as the *process of construction of meaning* on the basis of a cultural attribute, or a related set of cultural attributes that are given priority over other sources of meaning". – Remember here that the final result of the GCDB analyses (Ahamer & Strobl, 2009) was "to accelerate (social as compared to physical) time" in order to allow for more sustainability in society building.

Before the start of the following *practical chapter* containing the "case descriptions" we link both chapters by stating that all cases implement the above main guiding ideas of dialogue and discourse for societal learning. The network society is implemented by mapping controversial perspective into one interdisciplinary and intercultural synthetic view. New common spaces of understanding are stretched out and new and common identities are synthesised as structural capital.

Case UNINET

The *Eurasia-Pacific Uninet* established between Austrian and Asian universities is the largest of its kind in the world and reunites a total of 113 member institutions. This university network promotes multilateral scientific cooperation, joint research projects, conferences as well as faculty and student exchange. Contacts stemming from the Salzburg-based GIS cluster (Strobl et al., 2008) led to international institution building among others in India, Central Asia (ACA*GIS in Bishkek/Kyrgyz Republic), Southeast Asia, China, and other countries.

A small office of five has developed out of the China Center of Salzburg University and has managed to establish the largest existing Europe-Asia-university network. Funded by the Austrian ministry of science, annually almost hundred study visits, conferences, workshops, scholarships, preparatory missions, are attended by members of Austrian and Asian universities, who have gradually succeeded in building a network structure and even distinctly institutionalised branches of research and teaching.

Dialogue is occurring during the typically week-long visits and study tours. The foundation of collaboration is created by such structured discourse, whereas the content only acts as intermediary means for building such structures. The target of Uninet is not to hold conferences as a target in itself, but to create structures that might be institutionalised using personal contacts in such conferences. Hence Uninet might be the most constructivist of all case studies mentioned here. Difficulties encountered might be political instability or a subcritical mass of too few involved persons on either side of the network.

Case Kyrgyzstan

The Austrian-Central Asian Centre for Geographic Information Science (ACA*GIS) was founded in 2008 in Bishkek (Kyrgyzstan) as an offspring of both Unigis and Uninet activities. Starting from this Kyrgyz cooperation, the workshop openSolar'09 (www.aca-giscience.org/opensolar) is organized in August 2009 together with the annual Central Asian GIS conference GISCA'09. Again, its target is to create sufficient personal links between stakeholders in order to promote institutionalising of solar-oriented collaboration: construction and deployment of thermal and photovoltaic solar cells, cooperation in research and in legal matters. For this target, high-ranking officials from administration are expected to enhance solar implementation in Kyrgyzstan.

Regarding solar energy applications, the necessity to bridge standpoints occurs (1) between Central Asian and European views to consider for example to what extent the Kyrgyz economy should master the modernisation of the energy system (Ahamer, 2001) by its own force and (2) among Central Asian standpoints themselves, for example regarding the question of the water management of the Syr-Darya river, if water from the Toktogul reservoir should be released during summer for the needs of the Uzbek cotton plantations or during winter for the needs of the Kyrgyz electricity generation. As another example, the tariff for electricity in Kyrgyztan is presently still so low, that it does not at all cover the cost of electricity generation, which holds back the engagement of foreign investors to exploit the huge hydroelectricity potential of Kyrgyztan. Additionally, an escape from the deadlock of the Kyrgyz electricity market cannot be imagined without external help: the Kyrgyz viewpoint might be too restricted, so that raising electricity tariffs is only seen as socially negative, whereas the World Bank report identifying weak financial sustainability and corruption as prime obstacle might be seen as capitalistically inspired.

Foreign experts are useful in such a situation not only for delivering know-how but also because they are not part of the pattern of interest of the respective country. Therefore, they can play the role of a social catalyst. The very essence of such consultancy work is to bring the social procedures beyond the point of a deadlock when opposing national interests bring national planning efforts to a standstill. The mere fulfilment of World Bank advice does not always seem a possible strategy for everyday politics, especially because the so-called "Tulip-Revolution" in 2003 was initiated among others by a rise in electricity tariffs.

Dialogue and discourse in this case may construct a real-world escape from an unsatisfying situation after the collapse of the Soviet Empire.

The technological substrate of this type of collaboration is a web site containing the lectures of Austrian authors and also a web space containing the contributions of the workshop attendants who have computed the solar energy potential of their respective Central Asian home country, such as Kyrgyztan, Uzbekistan, Kazakhstan, Tajikistan, and Turkmenistan. Continued interlacing of social webs in Austria and Central Asia will be performed during a discussion session on the last day of the workshop, where professors from both sides take part and also industrial actors and development helpers in order to prepare concrete implementation of solar energy in Kyrgyztan.

Case Nepal

Both Austria and the Himalayan countries have special experience with problems in high mountain ranges: natural disasters, earth slides, climate change. Therefore, a long cooperation between Austrians and members of a centre of mountain research has been developed and led to the joint organization of an annual conference. Additionally, Himalayan countries might encounter political difficulties when cooperating among themselves; they reach from Afghanistan to Myanmar. Therefore, it is important to have a joint platform for discussing scientific and environmental issues without disturbances due to different political systems. Such a platform allows to adopt different viewpoints and to go beyond limited national views. Additionally, the presence of Austrian experts has enlarged the scope of existing perspectives. This annual conference is also organized through Uninet, in this case the scientific output and the technological support were comparable to a conventional conference.

Case Tajikistan

Geographic Information Systems are a suitable IT tool for solving practical energy related questions for the Central Asian country of Tajikistan. Deprived of fossil resources, its important hydro energy potentials are worth being analysed in a geo-referenced manner as planned in a GIS workshop (enerGIS, 2010).

Not only generation of electricity is a highly georeferenced issue but also transport of electricity (i) across the "oasis" of Ferghana Valley with the shared borders of Uzbekistan, Kyrgyzstan and Tajikistan and (ii) across the Pamir-Alai mountain ridges to the emerging markets of Pakistan – quite unlikely economic ties when considering Russia in line with the former Soviet structure of interdependency.

Case Twinning in Slovakia

An example for an early Twinning project during the early phase of accession is one of the first hundred Twinnings: "Strengthening of Institutions in the Air Quality Sector" in Slovakia in 2000-2001 led by the Austrian Federal Environment Agency.

Initially planned as a technical investment project to provide 40 PCs for the Slovak air monitoring system, this project became a full-fledged Twinning and was later unofficially named "the best Twinning in Slovakia". It produced over twelve concise reports on air quality measurement methodologies that were very positively received by the European Court of Auditors. However, some of the possible shortcomings of Twinnings played a considerable role here: during the planning process, all three involved actors (Slovakia, Austria, and European Commission) contributed to delays during the preparative phase of preparing the Twinning contract (Twinning Covenant). During these early years the Twinning tool was not yet fully developed, the rules were subject to change, and all involved actors lacked experience. The resulting delay of more than one year prompted the beneficiary country to assume that it would no longer need a Twinning at all.

However, the ongoing legal analysis of the "Act on Air" text of the Slovak Republic revealed that there were still considerable shortcomings of the transposition of the EU legal texts (the EU Framework Directive on Air Quality and their related daughter directives). As a consequence, during long periods of this Twinning, the Slovak partners showed considerable reluctance to sufficiently collaborate with the Austrian partners because the beneficiary thought it had sufficiently accomplished transposition (Ahamer, 2013a, b, c). Nonetheless, more gaps emerged in the field of implementation, and even more in enforcement – these three steps are the main phases of any Twinning procedure.

Ultimately, this single Twinning reflected very well the subjective perceptions of the civil society on both sides of the former "Iron Curtain", namely that each one thought the processes on their own side to be much more mature than perceived by the other side. Slovaks considered themselves over-matured to approach the EU, whereas Austrians felt alleged backwardness of any Central or Eastern European country. This fundamental bias of perception of the role of one's own country with respect to the role of the partner country led to a decrease in factual collaboration during the Twinning process. In contradiction to the mutually agreed plans, the Twinning reports were authored by Austrian experts to 95%, whereas Slovak experts restricted themselves to delivering data in cases they have been asked for expressly. As a result, the Twinning targets, that actually are understood as "guaranteed results" were watered down and fulfilled either too late or only formally or not at all. Such severe assessment comes from a long-term expert who is one of the authors. The Slovak administration repeatedly declared that it was willing to achieve only the minimum performance in transposition of the acquis into Slovak legislation.

During the same time period, another Twinning on water quality in Slovakia was very successful due to the high level of dedication of the Slovak project leader and his team. A third Twinning on waste suffered from distributed responsibilities among several Slovak ministries. In general, Slovak administration was severely understaffed (that was partly triggered by EU advice to cut down costly administrative staff in ministries) and severely underpaid which resulted in a brain drain towards private economy. Ten years after the Velvet Revolution, a change of working atmosphere, the degree of taking responsibilities and self-guidedness of civil servants had not yet reached a sufficient level. This is only one of the conclusions after having spent a year in another working culture. Another conclusion was that after returning home many aspects of administrative life in the home country resembled considerably the unsatisfactory impressions in the beneficiary country. Consequently, the returning long-term expert perceived his own country as a "developing country" - only at a different stage of development. Any country that is reluctant to develop further its social structures and institutions is in danger of creating bottlenecks for fruitful societal evolution.

What were the lasting benefits of such a project? Firstly, training on the technical level of how to fulfil the reporting duties for air quality matters, secondly, personal knowledge of the environmental administration in the partner country and thirdly, and foremostly, the ability to step out of the perspective of one's own country and to adopt the perspective of a member of the other country. This latter *ability of "switching roles and switching perspectives"* is the *core of social learning* in such *intercultural* interdisciplinary projects.

Case Twinning in Slovenia

A different country with a different history and a different phase in the overall accession process has led to very different experiences, self-conceptions and resulting interpersonal relationships. One year after the accession of Slovakia to the EU had already taken place, the Twinning on "Pricing of Water According to the EU Water Framework Directive" has been performed by a mixed German-Austrian team from 2005 to 2006. For half a year of the Twinning period, Slovenia itself adopted the role of EU presidency and fulfilled its duties in a highly respected manner.

A rather complex issue was selected, namely the question of how market mechanisms could control the amount of water consumption as a function of the water price. The aim of the project was to use different levels of water pricing to determine the levels of water consumption in different geographic areas of Slovakia with its only two million inhabitants. The task of the Twinning experts was to develop an algorithm of computing water prices that would sufficiently take into account the ecological ("external") costs linked to the supply of fresh water and subsequent management of wastewater.

The selection procedures by the Slovenian administration revealed later on that existing personal contacts had led to the decisions which partner to select.

During the entire Twinning a friendly interpersonal atmosphere prevailed among the experts. However, the collaboration among the RTAs and project leaders was not always without problems. Lack of knowledge of the subject itself might have led to a visibly formalistic attitude on one side of the Twinning partnership.

The fulfilment of the "guaranteed results" in this Twinning was endangered by the interdisciplinary complicatedness of the field and the audacious underlying assumption of controlling water demand by the price level. A very positive aspect was that Slovenia's very young staff in administration saw an active collaboration in this international project as a chance to advance their own careers and showed ongoing consistent activity that was only hampered by the generally very high workload imposed on the exhausted staff of this small EU member country. Different working attitudes were no problem at all, given the folkloristic designation of Slovenes as "the Prussians of the Balkan" based on the century-long common history with its northern neighbours. There were no frictions between the EU member state senior partner (Germany) and junior partner (Austria) due to the friendly overall attitude of the resident Twinning advisor (RTA). His fair and empathic attitude might have added to a low level of clarity and resistance against the formalistic behaviour exhibited by the other partner. As in all such cases of international projects, final reports reflect mainly the harmonious side of completed projects. The role as EU presidency has prohibited Slovenia to succumb to a role of the recipient of "good advice". Patterns of interaction within the senior member state partner were overshadowed by relationships to the original workplace in the home country, which brought about an inclination to solve strategic issues around a small table "behind closed doors". Also here, social interactions during this exercise of social learning were not ideal, but they did not hamper the overall project success at all.

Case Twinning for Armenia

When the tool of Twinning had been transferred to the countries of the "European Neighbourhood Policy" (ENP), an additional item was introduced: authoring of the so-called "Twinning Fiche" (the tendering document clearly defining the targets and contents of the Twinning project) was also transferred to a team of two or three consultants from the European Union member states, because administrations in the ENP did not usually dispose of sufficient knowledge of EU procedures and institutions to draft this text on their own.

One of the first three Twinning fiches drafted for the Ex-Soviet Republic of Armenia was on aviation safety. For this target, two missions of two weeks and one week respectively took place and comprised mainly visits to Armenian officials in the responsible ministries in descending order of hierarchy. This process ensured the active involvement of the local government and enhanced the spirit of ownership of the institution demanding assistance before the target of meeting the criteria of the international aviation association. The main phase of this preparatory project consisted in long-hour conversations with the national experts on aviation that revealed and precisely defined the real needs of the beneficiary country for EU assistance (Ahamer, 2012c). The findings of these conversations were moulded into a clear work plan containing clearly defined tasks for the future Twinning project.

During the month between the first and second mission the Armenian experts had the chance to review in detail the draft fiche that has also been translated into Armenian language by the translator who was part of the consultant's team. Additionally, the relative amount of manpower flowing into each expert's area of responsibility has also been clarified during a hearing convening all Armenian experts. In such a way the philosophy of partnership and peer activity was guaranteed.

In a subsequent procedure, the line DGs in Brussels expressed their review comments on the draft fiche. After these last comments had been taken into account by the team of experts, the fiche was published, and the bidding procedure was able to start.

Given the highly difficult traffic situation of Armenia it is understandable that one of the first Twinnings related to aviation in order to secure the country's accessibility.

Generally, the level of intercultural understanding between European and Armenian experts was very high and no severe mismatches in working attitudes occurred.

Case Twinning for Georgia

Half a year later, a Twinning fiche preparation project on the same subject matter of aviation safety was held in Georgia. The same geopolitical circumstances were prevailing, namely the wish of a country to have access to European Union traffic schemes. Additionally, in Georgia the wish to adhere to the European Union's system of values, democratic principles and political organizations was very developed, as could be seen during numerous encounters with the local population. In a similar procedure of two missions a first draft fiche was prepared, and then reviewed by the Georgian partners and finally completed by adding a very concrete work plan that defined targets and volume of numerous short-term missions (Ahamer & Mayer, 2013).

In both these Caucasian aviation Twinnings, the task of creating a precise and adequate list of "guaranteed results" was relatively simple, because the targets of the European aviation requirements are precise, independent of the country's characteristics and well-documented. Neither the existence of the working targets nor their concrete definition is questioned – and could not have been questioned, because they lie out of the reach of both actors (Ahamer, 2014, 2015). Rather, working targets are defined by an international institution that is responsible for civil aviation safety. Consequently, the task of defining the workload boiled down to attributing numbers of weekly missions to each one of the subdivisions of aviation safety requirements.

Also, in this case there occurred no cultural inconsistencies between the partners as a function of different working attitudes, despite the large geographic distance. It was visible both from the numbers of European flags on public buildings and from the behaviour of "people on the street" that Georgian self-understanding was truly European. However, considerable weakening of Georgian integrity was perceived to have occurred by recent military and political issues in two northern territories of Georgia.

Not even the presence of three different international bodies of observers seemed to have been able to help out of this impasse.

Case Twinning for Azerbaijan

A third project preparing a Twinning fiche took place recently in the third and largest Caucasian republic of Azerbaijan. The theme of Twinning in this case was "Vocational Education in the Field of Agriculture". At a first glance, almost all the parameters guaranteeing project success seemed to have been lower in this case: possibly a lower level of involvement on part of the beneficiary, possibly a less clear division of responsibilities among the ministries, possibly lower clarity in communication with the Twinning team and in general, and possibly a lower degree of experience with clear, objective, personality-independent ways of working.

Such first impressions have been corroborated by personal experiences with the police on the street, who took money out of our wallets during the course of a passport inspection and during other incidents with street police, who halted taxis on the highway without visible reason but only in order to bluntly ask for money from the taxi driver. An elevated level of informal economic behaviour and corruption is reported by outside perspectives, but not always by spectators from inside the country (Ahamer & Kumpfmüller, 2013). Azerbaijan is highly ranked in the international corruption index. In almost any office of mid-level civil servants, a dozen of devotional objects such as photos, portraits, books and videos of political leaders were present in a very self-understood manner.

In parallel to this internal situation, a frozen military and political conflict with the neighbour country was perceived by citizens in an astonishing manner, taking into account only one's own national lines of argumentation and not seeing or perceiving arguments brought forth by the conflict partner.

During the first week of the mission, the impression arose among the European experts that Azerbaijani counterparts were not particularly interested in the project at all. However, with time and as a result of a repeated attempt to communicate by telephone rather than by email (typically officials have no administrative email addresses but only public domain addresses like Gmail and Yahoo) the success of communication increased substantially. Therefore, the assumption became more convincing that not a substantial lack of interest, but maybe just general self-constraint and caution were the reason for unsuccessful communication in the first place.

In total, the communicative procedures in Azerbaijan were far more difficult than in the case of the other two Caucasian republics. However, final results will be achieved also there, and the prospects are promising that during the three weeks of the project dedication of the actors can be generated and enhanced, even if it might not be present right from the outset.

CONCLUSION

This article provided an overview of "transdisciplinary, dialogue-based learning". For complex interdisciplinary and intercultural issues, "learning" is seen as converging different and divergent world views into a common synthetic perspective on reality. Manuel Castells' concept of the "network society" combines easily with such concept.

Another target of this contribution is transcultural learning. Cultures may be delimited spatially, politically, or also mentally such as different scientific disciplines. But dialogue enhances their options to develop further.

Consequently, the described cases in this contribution

- extending on both individual and societal learning
- comprising aspects of interdisciplinary and intercultural learning settings

all attempt to illustrate that a suitable way to make a change in our world is to exchange and adapt our world views.

REFERENCES

Ahamer, G. (2001). A structured basket of models for global change. In C. Rautenstrauch & S. Patig (Eds.), *Environmental Information Systems in Industry and Public Administration* (pp. 101–136). Idea Group Publishing. doi:10.4018/978-1-930708-02-0.ch006

Ahamer, G. (2004). Negotiate your future: Web based role play. *Campus-Wide Information Systems*, *21*(1), 35–58. doi:10.1108/10650740410512329

Ahamer, G. (2008). Virtual Structures for mutual review promote understanding of opposed standpoints. *The Turkish Online Journal of Distance Education*, *9*(1), 17-43. https://tojde.anadolu.edu.tr/

Ahamer, G. (2012a). Training to Bridge Multicultural Geographies of Perspectives. *Campus-Wide Information Systems*, *29*(1), 21–44. doi:10.1108/10650741211192037

Ahamer, G. (2012c). Geo-referenceable model for the transfer of radioactive fallout from sediments to plants. *Water, Air, and Soil Pollution*, *223*(5), 2511–2524. doi:10.100711270-011-1044-x

Ahamer, G. (2014). Kon-Tiki: Spatio-temporal maps for socio-economic sustainability. *Journal for Multicultural Education*, *8*(3), 206–223. doi:10.1108/JME-05-2014-0022

Ahamer, G. (2015). Applying student-generated theories about global change and energy demand. *International Journal of Information and Learning Technology*, *32*(5), 258–271. doi:10.1108/IJILT-01-2015-0002

Ahamer, G. (2019). *Mapping global dynamics – Geographic perspectives from local pollution to global evolution*. Springer International Publishing. https://link.springer.com/book/10.1007/978-3-319-51704-9

Ahamer, G. (2022). Interparadigmatic social spaces are supported by data structures. In Encyclopedia of Data Science and Machine Learning. IGI Global.

Ahamer, G., & Kumpfmüller, K. (2013). Education and literature for development in responsibility – Partnership hedges globalization. In Handbook of Research on Transnational Higher Education Management. IGI Global.

Ahamer, G., & Mayer, J. (2013). Forward looking: Structural change and institutions in highest-income countries and globally. *Campus-Wide Information Systems*, *30*(5), 386–403. doi:10.1108/CWIS-08-2013-0034

Ahamer, G., & Strobl, J. (2009). Learning across social spaces. In S. Mukerji & P. Tripathi (Eds.), *Cases on Transnational Learning and Technologically Enabled Environments* (pp. 1–26). IGI Global.

Akhmetova, D. Z., Morozova, I. G., & Suchkov, M. A. (2021). Ethno-cultural aspects of inclusive education development in the context of globalization and digitalization. *Education and Self Development*, *16*(2), 165–181. doi:10.26907/esd.16.2.11

Aviv, E., & Spires, K. (2021). Buddhism and cognitive sciences in dialogue: Pedagogical reflections on teaching across disciplines. *Religions*, *12*(5), 303. Advance online publication. doi:10.3390/rel12050303

Baqui, P., Marra, V., Alaa, A. M., Bica, I., Ercole, A., & van der Schaar, M. (2021). Comparing COVID-19 risk factors in Brazil using machine learning: The importance of socioeconomic, demographic and structural factors. *Scientific Reports*, *11*(1), 15591. Advance online publication. doi:10.103841598-021-95004-8 PMID:34341397

Beames, J. R., Kikas, K., & Werner-Seidler, A. (2021). Prevention and early intervention of depression in young people: An integrated narrative review of affective awareness and ecological momentary assessment. *BMC Psychology*, *9*(1), 113. Advance online publication. doi:10.118640359-021-00614-6 PMID:34392830

Bojjireddy, S., Chun, S. A., & Geller, J. (2021). Machine learning approach to detect fake news, misinformation in COVID-19 pandemic. *ACM International Conference Proceeding Series*, 575-578. 10.1145/3463677.3463762

Castells, M. (1996-8). *The information age: Economy, society and culture*. Cambridge, MA: Blackwell.

Chaku, N., Kelly, D. P., & Beltz, A. M. (2021). Individualized learning potential in stressful times: How to leverage intensive longitudinal data to inform online learning. *Computers in Human Behavior*, *121*, 106772. Advance online publication. doi:10.1016/j.chb.2021.106772 PMID:33927470

Cherdymova, E. I., Faleeva, L. V., Ilkevich, T. G., Sharonov, I. A., Sayfutdinova, G. B., Leusenko, I. V., & Popova, O. V. (2019). Socio-psychological factors that contribute to and impede the process of student eco-vocational consciousness formation. *Ekoloji*, *28*(107), 133–140.

Claverie, B. (2021). Ethical postures in relation to new technologies: Classification, miscommunication, and perspectives [Postures éthiques face aux néotechnologies: Plan de classification, incommunication et perspectives]. *L'Information Psychiatrique*, *97*(2), 147–155. doi:10.1684/ipe.2021.2220

Cominelli, L., Mazzei, D., & De Rossi, D. E. (2018). SEAI: Social emotional artificial intelligence based on damasio's theory of mind. *Frontiers in Robotics and AI*, *5*(FEB), 6. Advance online publication. doi:10.3389/frobt.2018.00006 PMID:33500893

della Volpe, M., Elia, A., & Esposito, F. (2018). *Semantic predicates in the business language* doi:10.1007/978-3-319-73420-0_9

Duram, L. A. (2021). Teaching a social science course on climate change: Suggestions for active learning. *Bulletin of the American Meteorological Society*, *102*(8), E1494–E1498. doi:10.1175/BAMS-D-21-0035.1

enerGIS. (2010). *Staff development workshop on geographic information systems (GIS) for energy issues in Central Asia*. Tajik Agrarian University, Dushanbe. Program and lectures at https://www.researchgate.net/publication/232834905_Workbook_enerGIS'10_-_Staff_Development_Workshop_Geographic_Information_Systems_GIS_for_Energy_Issues_in_Central_Asia

Francesconi, D., Symeonidis, V., & Agostini, E. (2021). FridaysForFuture as an enactive network: Collective agency for the transition towards sustainable development. *Frontiers in Education, 6.* Advance online publication. doi:10.3389/feduc.2021.636067

Geraci, A., D'Amico, A., Pipitone, A., Seidita, V., & Chella, A. (2021). Automation inner speech as an anthropomorphic feature affecting human trust: Current issues and future directions. *Frontiers in Robotics and AI, 8.* Advance online publication. doi:10.3389/frobt.2021.620026

Greenlees, K., & Cornelius, R. (2021). The promise of panarchy in managed retreat: Converging psychological perspectives and complex adaptive systems theory. *Journal of Environmental Studies and Sciences, 11*(3), 503–510. doi:10.100713412-021-00686-1

Groves, C., Henwood, K., Pidgeon, N., Cherry, C., Roberts, E., Shirani, F., & Thomas, G. (2021). The future is flexible? exploring expert visions of energy system decarbonisation. *Futures, 130.* Advance online publication. doi:10.1016/j.futures.2021.102753

Haaker, J., Diaz-Mataix, L., Guillazo-Blanch, G., Stark, S. A., Kern, L., LeDoux, J. E., & Olsson, A. (2021). Observation of others' threat reactions recovers memories previously shaped by firsthand experiences. *Proceedings of the National Academy of Sciences of the United States of America, 118*(30). Advance online publication. doi:10.1073/pnas.2101290118

Haberman, J., & Suresh, S. (2021). Ensemble size judgments account for size constancy. *Attention, Perception & Psychophysics, 83*(3), 925–933. doi:10.375813414-020-02144-6

Hansen, P., Fourie, I., & Meyer, A. (2021). *Third space, information sharing, and participatory design.* doi:10.2200/S01096ED1V01Y202105ICR074

Hasni, S., & Faiz, S. (2021). Word embeddings and deep learning for location prediction: Tracking coronavirus from British and American tweets. *Social Network Analysis and Mining, 11*(1). Advance online publication. doi:10.100713278-021-00777-5

Heuer, K., & Toro, R. (2019). Role of mechanical morphogenesis in the development and evolution of the neocortex. *Physics of Life Reviews, 31,* 233–239. doi:10.1016/j.plrev.2019.01.012

Huntington, H. P., Raymond-Yakoubian, J., Noongwook, G., Naylor, N., Harris, C., Harcharek, Q., & Adams, B. (2021). "We never get stuck:" A collaborative analysis of change and coastal community subsistence practices in the northern Bering and Chukchi seas, Alaska. *Arctic, 74*(2), 113–126. doi:10.14430/arctic72446

Kannan, R., Swaminathan, S., Anutariya, C., & Saravanan, V. (2021). Exploiting multilingual neural linguistic representation for sentiment classification of political tweets in code-mix language. *ACM International Conference Proceeding Series.* doi:10.1145/3468784.3470787

Koumpis, A., Christoforaki, M., & Handschuh, S. (2018). *The robot who loved me: Building consciousness models for use in human robot interaction following a collaborative systems approach.* doi:10.1007/978-3-319-99127-6_35

Krishnendu, G., Wadekar, S., Majumdar, S., & Patnaik, A. K. (2021). Common sense, habitus, and social imaginary: Case studies from India. *Economic and Political Weekly, 56*(26), 84–91.

Kunkel, S. R., & Settersten, R. A. (2021). Aging, society, and the life course: Sixth edition. doi:80353 doi:10.1891/97808261

Leach, S., Xue, Y., Sridhar, R., Paal, S., Wang, Z., & Murphy, R. (2021). Data augmentation for improving deep learning models in building inspections or postdisaster evaluation. *Journal of Performance of Constructed Facilities*, *35*(4). Advance online publication. doi:10.1061/(ASCE)CF.1943-5509.0001594

Lodge, W. (2021). Confronting repressive ideologies with critical pedagogy in science classrooms. *Cultural Studies of Science Education*, *16*(2), 609–620. doi:10.100711422-021-10047-7

Love, K. S. (2018). Too shame to look: Learning to trust mirrors and healing the lived experience of shame in alice walker's the color purple. *Hypatia*, *33*(3), 521–536. doi:10.1111/hypa.12430

Padilla, N., & Lagercrantz, H. (2020). Making of the mind. *Acta Paediatrica. International Journal of Pediatrics*, *109*(5), 883–892. doi:10.1111/apa.15167

Rinnooy Kan, W. F., März, V., Volman, M., & Dijkstra, A. B. (2021). Learning from, through and about differences: A multiple case study on schools as practice grounds for citizenship. *Social Sciences*, *10*(6). Advance online publication. doi:10.3390ocsci10060200

Sergin, V. Y. (2021). Autoidentification and sensorimotor rehearsal as physiological mechanisms of consciousness. *Neuroscience and Behavioral Physiology*, *51*(5), 648–665. doi:10.100711055-021-01118-x

Smith, D. H., & Schillaci, G. (2021). Why build a robot with artificial consciousness? how to begin? A cross-disciplinary dialogue on the design and implementation of a synthetic model of consciousness. *Frontiers in Psychology*, *12*. Advance online publication. doi:10.3389/fpsyg.2021.530560

Stalder, F. (2000). The Network Paradigm: Social Formations in the Age of Information. *The Information Society*, *14*(1). http://www.indiana.edu:80/~tisj/readers/full-text/14-4%20Stalder.html

Strigin, M. B. (2019). World conscience. model of a social crystal. *Journal of Environmental Treatment Techniques*, *7*(4), 647–653.

Sumell, A. J., Chiang, E. P., Koch, S., Mangeloja, E., Sun, J., & Pédussel Wu, J. (2021). A cultural comparison of mindfulness and student performance: Evidence from university students in five countries. *International Review of Economics Education*, *37*. Advance online publication. doi:10.1016/j.iree.2021.100213

Taylor, P. J., Derudder, B., García, C. G., & Witlox, F. (2007). From North-South to 'Global' South An investigation of a changing 'South' using airline flows between cities, 1970-2005. *Geography Compass*, *3*(2), 836–855.

Toutain, T. G., Baptista, A. F., Japyassú, H. F., Rosário, R. S., Porto, J. A., Campbell, F. Q., & Miranda, J. G. V. (2020). Does meditation lead to a stable mind? synchronous stability and time-varying graphs in meditators. *Journal of Complex Networks*, *8*(6), 1–14. doi:10.1093/comnet/cnaa049

West, D. E. (2021). The dialogic nature of double consciousness and double stimulation: Implications from Peirce and Vygotsky. *Sign Systems Studies*, *49*(1), 235–261. doi:10.12697/SSS.2021.49.1-2.10

Woiwode, C., Schäpke, N., Bina, O., Veciana, S., Kunze, I., Parodi, O., ... Wamsler, C. (2021). Inner transformation to sustainability as a deep leverage point: Fostering new avenues for change through dialogue and reflection. *Sustainability Science*, *16*(3), 841–858. doi:10.100711625-020-00882-y

Online Educational Video Recommendation System Analysis

Parvathi R.
Vellore Institute of Technology, Chennai, India

Aarushi Siri Agarwal
Vellore Institute of Technology, Chennai, India

Urmila Singh
Vellore Institute of Technology, Chennai, India

INTRODUCTION

Recommendation systems usually filter large amounts of available data and select items that are most likely to be interesting and attractive to users. Recommendation methods are classified into three categories: content-based, collaborative filtering and hybrid methods. The most preferred and popular among the three methods is content-based methods, it looks at the user's history and suggests other items in the same or a similar category to increase user retention and increase in customer base. For example, news recommendations find similarities by considering words or terms in articles.

Content-based filtering is the use of certain features on the basis of likes, comments, reactions and explicit feedback to escalate recommendation for other items. Collaborative filtering uses user ratings and gives more personalized recommendations (Ni et al., 2022). Hybrid method is a combination of content based and collaborative filtering methods.

For generations, humans have looked outwards at others for inspiration, individuals of great intellect and accomplishment have been regarded as heroes and model citizens. However, this kind of admiration has not always been shared equally amongst the diverse set of people in the world. As such, with growing awareness, it is often pondered whether the data we are recommended to solve the issue of finding what we need in the ever growing products and services options online, also known as information overload (Beede et al., 2011) is subjected to any form of bias. A particular focus is on popularity bias caused by recommendation systems (Boring, 2017) leading to extreme disparity. Popularity bias results in the popular videos that have more views and likes to become even more popular while the long-tailed videos remain long-tailed. By investigating user ratings of speakers in TED talks, a popular lecture series that are widely shared for approachable discussions from various experts. The aim is to explore whether a platform primarily served to distribute educational content is subject to potential unconscious biases (Veletsianos et al., 2022) and if certain types of content are systematically more recommended than others. In order to achieve this aim we try finding the different correlations between parameters of uploaded talk videos and visually represent these correlations for better understanding (Pedersen and Duin, 2022).

DOI: 10.4018/978-1-7998-9220-5.ch093

BACKGROUND

Systems designed based on content-based recommendation explicitly analyze parameters, considering feedback, descriptions of previously rated items, and work on further building a model based on the candidate specification and similarity metrics. Several channels can be used up for generating relevant feedback and specifications required. New interesting items are then recommended on the basis of the structure model developed. Highly positive and accurate recommendations require good hand-engineered features. Semantic analysis (lexicons and ontologies) are used by other members of Content-based RSs for enhanced and accurate item representation. Furthermore (Kempe et al., 2003) discussed one of the most popular algorithms for extracting clusters in a graph is proposed by New-man and Girvan (Newman and Girvan, 2004), which is based on modularity. (Zhou et al., 2016), developed a modularity based graph clustering approach, which can help users discover common interests of other users quite effectively. It obtains an undirected weighted tag-graph for each user. One of other methods is the Content-based video retrieval (CBVR) technique, which has been widely used in content-based video lecture recommendation systems (Zhou et al., 2016). OCR, ASR techniques, and folksonomy are very widely used in annotation tasks for information retrieval for user preference. In most of the related works, the solidity and consistency problems are caused by varying accuracy of different analysis engines (Yang and Meinel, 2014), which has not been thoroughly discussed. (Wingrove 2022; Holland et al., 2022).

Artificial intelligence like Iris AI is known for indexing academic resources. The system further recommends scientific papers and speeches using a model trained with TED Talks videos which is related to the field of interest of this research paper. In a paper by Yang and Meinel, 2014), the authors applied automatic video segmentation and key-frame detection for the video lecture content navigation.

Latent Dirichlet Allocation (LDA) (Shiokawa et al., 2013) has also been used to ðnd the topics in a particular website and those in a particular video. Wang and Blei combined probabilistic topic modeling with collaborative ðltering to recommend scientiðc papers. Chen, Cooper, Joshi, and Girod have proposed a Multi-modal Language Model (MLM) that uses latent variable techniques to explore the co-occurrence relation between multi-modal data (Chen et al., 2014).

Clauset et al. (2004) proposed a greedy modularity-based algorithm, called CNM which is one of the most widely used methods recently. Blondel et al. (2008) proposed an efficient greedy algorithm BGLL. To the best of our knowledge, BGLL is representative of the state-of-the-art algorithm; it achieves fast clustering with higher modularity than the other algorithms. In contrast to CNM, it computes the modularity gain only for the adjoined vertex pairs as a local maximization (Newman and Girvan, 2004).

In the literature survey, a variety of content-based recommendation algorithms have been proposed. A traditional example is the "k-nearest neighbours" approach (KNN) that computes the preference of a user for an unknown item by comparing it against all the items known by the user in the catalogue (Tang and Yu, 2022). Similarity of the known to the unknown items, helps in predicting the preference score. Dot Product or similarity metrics is a common parameter to mark the similarity. Relevant works include models for user's interest and recommendation based on Bayesian approach, IR (Information Retrieval), or a product of IR, i.e., Relevance Feedback method.

FEASIBILITY STUDY

The analysis parameters for an online video recommendation system could be of any form: title, main speaker, film date, opening words related to the videos. Here, we specifically study and build our model over our own dataset. Some of the areas of motivation are general application of speaker recommendation to a particular user, to find the most used words by speaker which draw in the viewers which leads to high video recommendation, if there is the possible bias in the content online and its recommendation system and is the recommendation based on the speaker's popularity or is it based on herd psychology which can be seen through the number of views and comments. A few popular videos possess the most view counts, but most videos have lower view counts. This is an example of the Pareto Principle, or 80/20 rule. In other words, the top 20 most popular (Yang and Meinel, 2014) videos are watched by the most people, a phenomenon of interest in numerous studies focused on the popularity of videos, which further strengthens the herd psychology.

Recommendation systems play a critically important role in helping users to discover interesting contents. For example, it has been shown in our previous work (Farrell and McHugh, 2017) that approximately thirty percent of the views on YouTube are contributed by the YouTube recommendation system. The most feasible solution to go through the proper analysis is to check for herd psychology in the recommendation system or if the system is a random jumble of latest uploaded videos first and then gets adjusted based on the user viewing habits. To find out which of the two it is we can look at the various parameters that can point towards herd psychology and if the recommendation system is not based on our assumptions, we can say that it is recommending based on individual tests. This is of course assuming we collect the data for various users and both experienced and new to the platform.

ABOUT THE DATASET

The dataset is created by using a web scraper program to collect valuable information stored as the metadata for each video, which is most recommended on the ted talks website. the metadata information is referred to as features in this paper. The dataset contains metadata for more than 4800 videos uploaded before April 2021. The initial dataset contained 51 features which also included various other information such as talk url, speaker id, speaker description, reason to listen to this speaker, if talk has been featured, language in which the talk is, if it has subtitles and much more. out of these 51 features only the handful is used for the analysis described in this paper. these selected features include Main speaker name, speaker occupation, title of TED Talk, number of views, number of comments, tags that are associated with the video, list of related Talk videos to the current talk, filming and publishing dates of the talks, description of the talk, duration of the talk, event of which the talk was a part of user ratings and transcript. The list of "related talks" to watch for each TED talk is according to the recommended talk links on the actual website for current talk that is shown in the main page.

Further detailed explanation on the present initial features, based on what criteria the features are selected and how each is used for analysis. A basic idea of why only certain features are chosen is given in the following feature components for analysis section followed by steps taken in implementation analysis for this paper in section 5.1 and section 5.2 under the design and flow of modules section.

Feature Components for Analysis

While creating recommender systems for an online platform there is often the problem of lack of data. This is not due to enough features not being collected in the metadata, but it occurs due to null values being stored in those features instead of actual usable data (Lee et al., 2022). Therefore in order to recommend videos and subsequently also to analyze how videos are recommended the best approach would be to look at the implicit data that is generated by the platform and stored in the metadata and at the explicit metadata, which is provided by the users, that is most likely to be present.

If a dummy example is considered and first analyzed for what could be the possible online educational video related parameters that are stored and on the basis of which we can analyze the data.

Every online video database based on educational videos often contains features such as video publishing date, views, comments, duration, title, category, owner or speaker in the video and most times also the profession of the speaker (Khalid et al., 2022).

Based on this we can say that the video collection and correspondingly its recommendation may be strongly related to and also possibly biased based on the views, comments and likes of the video, which could result in popularity bias (Boring, 2017) or it can be biased based on profession of speaker, which can result in a particular profession related videos being recommended a lot just because people prefer listening to a particular good speaker. It can be biased based on topics or categories of video, resulting in an inverse effect compared to the previous point where many good speakers' videos are not watched because they are not of the recommended topic or category.

To check if recommendation is biased in these aspects, we sort the videos based on recommendation frequency and correspondingly check the distribution of the videos based on the three categories. the distribution and pattern based on the number of views and comments which can play a big part in recommendation systems as it is possible that the video liked by most people will also be liked by new users of the platform and hence increase the number of platform users (Katsamakas et al., 2022).

Design and Flow of Models

For the collection of data and analysis of recommendation systems, certain methods, analysis parameters and procedures are used. the procedure for collection of data, cleaning and analyzing the collected recommended videos data is as described in the following modules:

Figure 1. Design and Flow of Model

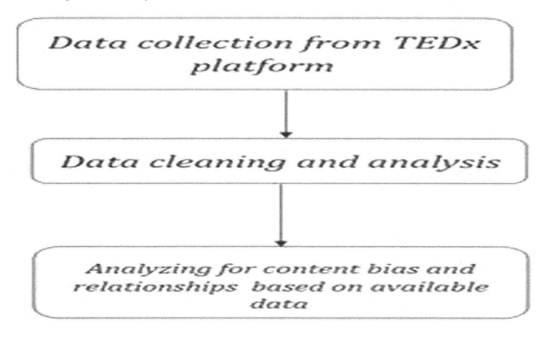

Module 1: Data Collection

In this module the URL links text file has been made for all the videos on the home page which gives the recommended Ted talks list and then downloaded the meta data in the URLs to extract video information from them using a web scraper program. The URL link text file is created such that the talks are in order of recommendation on the platform and then the program takes the related talk that gets recommended on watching the current talk and adds the related talks URL to the list if not already present. After getting the metadata the information for each video is extracted and stored in csv file format. The meta data includes the data about the video title, views, comments, tags, related videos (videos usually recommended alongside the given video), duration, publishing date, transcript and also the speaker details like speaker name and speaker profession.

One strong point to note about the collection process is that the videos which are most recommended are put first in the database. Hence the database is sorted in order of most recommended talks. .

Module 2: Data Cleaning and Dataset Analysis

Once the data is available, it needs to be cleaned and analyzed. After this it can be easily planned which parameters to analyze to find out the recommendation system used on the platform. As discussed in the previous section on feature components for analysis, it needs to be made sure that features are taken that have usable values and not features which mostly contain null values. Availability of valid values has been the main method to select the parameters for further analysis in this paper. on feature analysis of individual records in the dataset, it was found that the features Main speaker name, speaker occupation, title of TED Talk, number of views, number of comments, tags that are associated with the video, list of related Talk videos to the current talk, filming and publishing dates of the talks, description of the talk and duration of the talk contained least number of null values. Hence these features were selected for further analysis.

In order to analyze and understand which domain most of the recommended videos belong to, video transcripts are used to directly extract keywords in the talk and then identify possible domains rather than rely on the category metadata alone. As the objective is to find the general domain of multiple recommended videos and not any single video, accuracy of identified domain is not necessary and finding keywords helps reduce dealing with the number of categories the videos are related to. It also removes dependency on having correct categorization of the videos and helps identify if there is a theme based bias in the recommendation system of the platform.

Module 3: Analysis and Visualization from Dataset

The features from the obtained dataset are compared with each other to find correlations and dependencies and then these are visualized using different types of graphs. The graphs obtained are then studied in detail to obtain further observations to see to what factor each attribute influences the recommendation system and which attributes are dependent and independent. Also find if the features are contributing towards a possible biased recommendation. Most common type of bias that recommendation systems are prone to is popularity bias. A common way to declare a video popular is if it has a large number of views and correspondingly a large number of comments, which is shown in section 3.1. the next most common bias to check is bias based on profession, which results in talks of one particular profession being recommended because certain speakers in that profession are popular. This also indirectly points towards popularity bias. It can also be considered a cause of herd psychology, where more users watch only a certain kind of videos because it is recommended to them when they first enter the platform. section 3.2 checks for this bias. The third bias check is based on if videos of a certain category are more recommended, causing some good talks from less popular categories to not be recommended. This is checked in section 3.3.

Module 3.1: Checking Bias Based on Views and Comments

The relation between the views and the comments and their effect on the recommended videos is checked in this subsection. Also, the effect of more views and less comments usually signifies the possibility of hate comments or dissatisfaction with the talk. if such videos are recommended it could have a negative impact on the platforms' reputation. Hence by finding the correlation between comments and views the recommendation systems are checked for popularity bias and for a false positive classification of a talk as a popular video. Also features like time duration can also be taken into account. The more the duration of the talk, the less likely it is to be watched

Module 3.2: Checking Bias Based on Profession

The distribution of videos based on the speaker profession is first checked, to check if there is bias based on availability of talks by different professions on the platform. since bias based on profession is indirectly related to popularity bias, which is measured by the views. Then it's seen how the videos are recommended based on whether views play a central role in the recommendation system.

Module 3.3: Bias Based on Content or Talk Category

Since the transcripts were found, they can be used in TF-IDF to first get the unique and important words used in the entire collected video data and to convert this unique word dataset into numerical form. This removes the dependency on category features and helps identify hidden general topics that the talks are related to. TF-IDF is a short term of term frequency - inverse document frequency. TFIDF is mostly used for information retrieval. It can be defined as a method to find how relevant a word is in a text document by counting its frequency of occurrence after removing common words like "is", "the", "a" and so on. term frequency tells the frequency of the word by the number of unique words. Inverse document frequency is given by taking a log value of the number of documents containing current word by frequency of current word across documents. Following keyword extraction algorithms like PCA (principal component algorithm) can be used to reduce its dimensionality which can be used in clustering algorithms to find out the various clusters the uploaded videos belong to based on the content of the talks. The number of general categories of videos uploaded can be checked by checking the silhouette scoring for different numbers of clusters formed using appropriate clustering algorithms. Silhouette scoring is one of the most convenient, accurate and well-defined methods to be used.

3.3.1 PCA Algorithm

The Principal Component Analysis (PCA) is one of the methods often used to reduce the dimensions of a large dataset. It does so by transforming a large set of variables into a smaller set of variables that are the most relevant and hence retains most of the information from the large set. In order to free our analysis from being biased it is critical to perform standardization of data prior to PCA, as variables with large ranges tend to dominate over variables with slammer ranges. So, transforming the data to comparable scales can prevent this problem.

Principal components are new variables that are constructed as linear combinations or mixtures of the initial variables. The variables are combined as such that they contain most of the information from the large dataset which is compressed into the components and at the same time they are uncorrelated. In order to determine the principal components of the data we need to compute the Eigenvectors and eigenvalues from the covariance matrix.

The principal components are used to show the directions of the data that captures the maximum amount of information from the data. Here information and variance show a relationship that can be explained as the larger the variance in the line the higher the dispersion along the line hence resulting in more information provided by it.

3.3.2. K-means

Once the keywords have been converted to numeric dataset and the dimensionality is reduced using PCA method, the keywords need to be grouped into clusters. the aim here is to find the least number of distinct categories of talks we can find on the platform and then using the keywords identify what these categories are. to ensure that distinct categories are being made and all words are taken into account this paper uses kmeans. kmeans is a simple yet efficient clustering algorithm that uses a hard membership function and equally considers all data points. Hard membership functions ensure that the data points belong to one cluster alone and not to multiple clusters, in order to find the optimal number of categories there are 2 commonly used methods.

The elbow method, which repeatedly applies k means and averages the distances of all the data points from their centroids. then plots all the k values and chooses the value where there is a sharp drop in average distance. The second method is silhouette analysis, which is done over the calculated kmean clusters. it checks how similar each datapoint is to its own cluster when compared to other clusters. hence providing a way to assess parameters like number of clusters visually, which the elbow method cannot provide. Also it can find outliers in a cluster, if any present.Silhouette analysis is easy to implement as well since it's readily available as part of scikit in python.

K-means algorithm is a simple and efficient centroid based algorithm which uses hard membership function and divides all the data points into K groups without any overlapping subgroups. It has an equal weight function which helps with including outliers as well. It tries to achieve two goals which is to keep the k clusters as different as possible while keeping the data points within a cluster as similar as possible. The way K-means algorithm works is as follows:

1. set the required cluster numbers K.
2. Initialize centroids by shuffling and randomly selecting K unique datapoints as centroids.
3. Compute the sum of the squared distance between data points and all centroids.
4. Assign each data point to the cluster for centroid it is closest to.
5. Recalculate the centroids and repeat the process till the centroids do not change.

Compute the centroids for the clusters by taking the average of the all-data points that belong to each cluster.

The objective function is given in Equation (1)

$$J = \sum_{i=1}^{m}\sum_{k=1}^{K} w_{ik} x^i - \mu k^2 \tag{1}$$

There are many better performing variations to kmeans that are present such as those mentioned in (1), where most of these try using soft membership functions. Also there are some other clustering algorithms such as BIRCH, K-Medoids which can be used in cases where there is a larger dataset as they are faster and more accurate even with huge numbers of clusters unlike k means which loses accuracy after a certain number of clusters are formed. In this paper since the keywords extracted does not form a huge dataset and is within a range of 2500-3000 data points, traditional k means clustering algorithm is used. OPTICS and DBSCAN are some other well-known alternatives to k means that can be used with larger dataset and do not require separately finding optimal number of clusters, but these algorithms tend to discard the outliers. An alternative to k means clustering of text can be using hierarchical clustering such as Divisive Hierarchical clustering algorithm, which starts with one large root cluster and breaks into the individual clusters after that or using Agglomerative Hierarchy clustering algorithm where each does the opposite of what divisive clustering does. Both these clustering algorithms increase complexity and are not required in this analysis.

RISK ANALYSIS

Due to the vast amount of data in online video content platforms like TEDx gathering accurate data on videos on all fields might be tough. Hence, we have taken the data on a considerable size but not containing all the videos on the platform as this can affect our analysis for bias based on time of publishing hence we have not analyzed based on time of upload or publishing of video. Also, we might not get other datasets besides TEDx platform for comparing our analysis with recommendation systems used on educational online video platforms.

EXPERIMENTATION

First import the libraries to better analyze the data set, applying dimensionality reduction to find the important feature for further analysis. Figure 2 show the initial features in the dataset before applying dimensionality reduction and Figure 3 shows the important features extracted using dimensionality reduction.

Correlation Analysis

Then analyze the correlation of each column or parameter in our dataset with the other parameters using heat map as shown in the Figure 4. Figure 5 shows the correlation between view and comment count, it is assumed that there is always a high possibility of views and comments being used in recommendation of a video. Those parameters and correlations are checked first.

Figure 2. Data set before reducing dimensionality

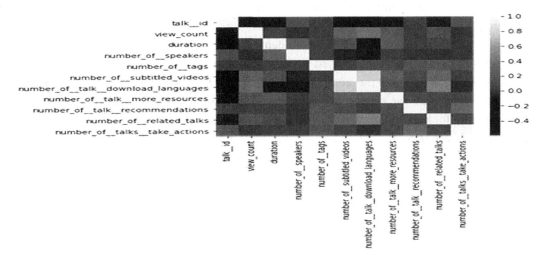

```
TedTalks.dtypes
talk_id                                                       int64
talk_name                                                     object
talk_description                                              object
view_count                                                    int64
comment_count                                                 float64
duration                                                      int64
transcript                                                    object
video_type_name                                               object
event                                                         object
number_of_speakers                                            int64
speaker_id                                                    float64
speaker_name                                                  object
speaker_description                                           object
speaker_who_he_is                                             object
speaker_why_listen                                            object
speaker_what_others_say                                       object
speaker_is_published                                          float64
all_speakers_details                                          object
is_talk_featured                                              bool
has_talk_citation                                             float64
recording_date                                                object
published_timestamp                                           object
talk_tags                                                     object
number_of_tags                                                int64
language                                                      object
native_language                                               object
language_swap                                                 bool
is_subtitle_required                                          bool
url_webpage                                                   object
url_audio                                                     object
url_video                                                     object
url_photo_talk                                                object
url_photo_speaker                                             object
number_of_subtitled_videos                                    int64
talk_download_languages                                       object
number_of_talk_download_languages                             int64
talk_more_resources                                           object
number_of_talk_more_resources                                 int64
talk_recommendations_blurb                                    object
talk_recommendations                                          object
number_of_talk_recommendations                                int64
related_talks                                                 object
number_of_related_talks                                       int64
intro_duration                                                float64
post_ad_duration                                              float64
ad_duration                                                   float64
external_duration                                             float64
external_start_time                                           float64
talks_player_talks_resources_h264_00_bitrate                 float64
talks_take_action                                             object
number_of_talks_take_actions                                  int64
dtype: object
```

Figure 3. Features selected after reducing dimensionality

```
1 #15 most viewed
2 df = pd.read_csv('ted_main.csv')
3 print(df.columns)
4 df["film_date"]=df["film_date"].apply(lambda x: datetime.datetime.fromtimestamp(int(x)).strftime('%d-%m-%Y'))
5 df["published_date"]=df["published_date"].apply(lambda x: datetime.datetime.fromtimestamp(int(x)).strftime('%d-%m-%Y'))
6
7 pop_talks=df[["name","title","main_speaker","views","film_date"]].sort_values("views",ascending=False)[:15]
8 pop_talks
```

```
Index(['comments', 'description', 'duration', 'event', 'film_date',
       'languages', 'main_speaker', 'name', 'num_speaker', 'published_date',
       'ratings', 'related_talks', 'speaker_occupation', 'tags', 'title',
       'url', 'views'],
      dtype='object')
```

| | name | title | main speaker | vi |

Figure 4. Correlation between View and Comment

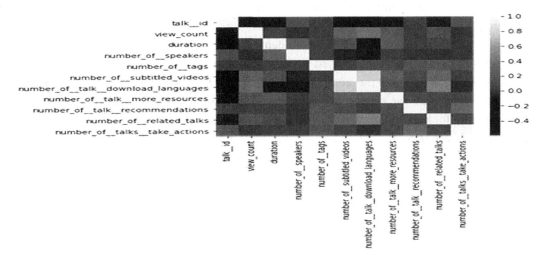

It is seen that there is a strong correlation between the views and the comments as expected. As discussed in previous sections that there is always a high possibility of views and comments being used in recommendation of a video. Those parameters and correlations are checked first. It is seen that there is a strong correlation between the views and the comments as expected. There are very few talks where the number of comments is too high compared to the views and vice versa.

Another common recommendation factor can be the correlation with the time duration as more the time duration less likely that the user be patient and listen to the whole talk without getting bored. hence, we also analyze based on the talk duration as shown in Figure 5 and Figure 6

*Figure 5. Correlation between View and Comment Count and Popularity Bias_*

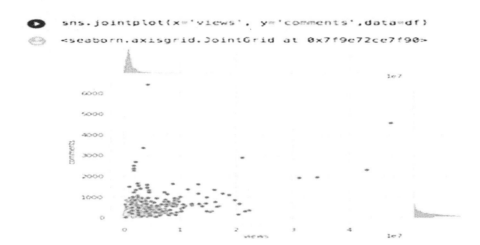

Views and Comments Distribution

On analysis it was found that the assumption was wrong as the time duration parameter does not strongly correlate with the views and comments. After finding how strongly correlated the views and comments are, there relation to the recommendation system also needs to be checked. to check this their distribution is seen based on the sorted talks dataset. For this we use a violent plot. The violin plots a method of plotting numeric data. It is similar to a box plot, with the addition of a rotated kernel density plot on each side. Violin plots are similar to box plots, except that they also show the probability density of the data at different values, usually smoothed by a kernel density estimator.

The distribution shows that the number of comments and views are more for the highly recommended videos. the dataset is a list of the videos based on their recommendation likelihood and a wider violin plot says that the mean of the data is in the area closer to the start of the dataset where the more recommended videos are. this shows that the number of views does play a big role in the recommendation system, since the violin plot for views is shows extreme density towards entries at the start of the list compared to the comments. hence there is a possibility of popularity bias which in turn can cause herd behavior.

Figure 6. Comparison of Views, Comments, Duration

```
1 df["duration"]=df["duration"]/60 #minutes
2 sns.pairplot(data=df, vars=["views", "comments", "duration"])
3 display(df[["views", "comments", "duration"]].corr())
```

	views	comments	duration
views	1.000000	0.530939	0.048740
comments	0.530939	1.000000	0.140694
duration	0.048740	0.140694	1.000000

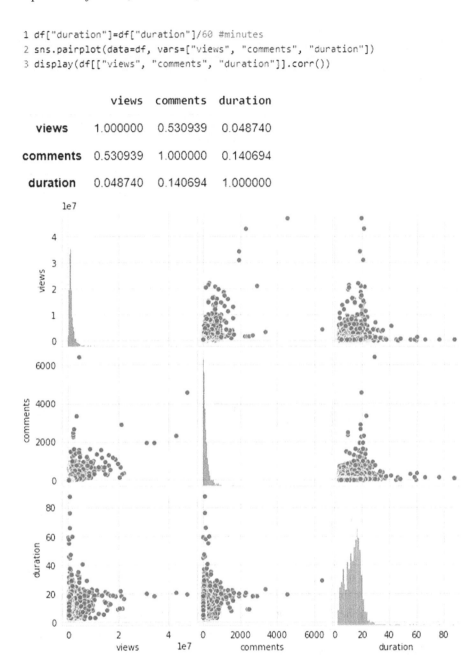

Based on the Speaker Profession

Often, we can see that the online platforms don't have equal content in different categories or if they do, they might be biased based on the type of content that is recommended. one parameter where such bias can be seen is in the speaker profession.

Figure 7. Violent plot for Views Distribution

```
2 fig, ax = plt.subplots(figsize =(9, 7))
3
4
5 sns.violinplot( ax = ax, y = df["views"] )
```

‹matplotlib.axes._subplots.AxesSubplot at 0x7f9e672dab90›

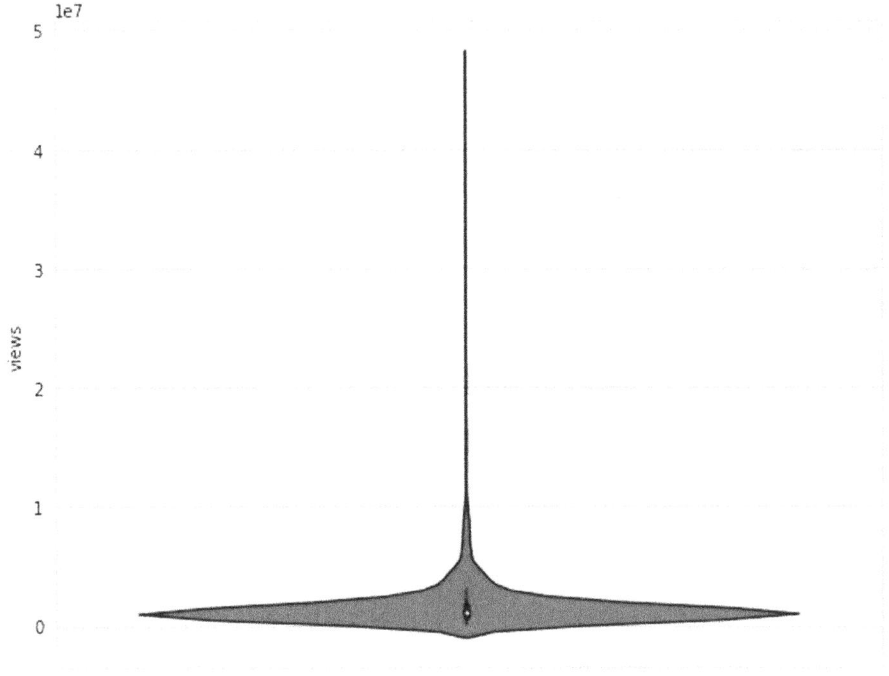

Just analyzing based on appearance gives us the count of videos in each profession but we also need to know its distribution based on the number of views since we had confirmed that views play a central role in recommendation of a video. The table shows that the professions with more videos like writers have the highest number of views but also that the profession like artists despite having a high number of videos does not have a high number of counts and is not recommended as much as videos on talks by psychologists. This might be due to people tending to watch talk by psychologists more than artists. This signals the possibility of a herd behavior followed by recommendation as well. Since people tend to watch more talks given by psychologists than artists over time, talks on the former receive more views and comments and hence get recommended more.

We can see in the above data that has been analyzed that in almost all the scenarios, there has been a bias created on the videos with maximum recommendation and the type of content curated by the performer for its audience. For example, a psychologist who has shown up the second least number of times has got the views and likes(recommendation) equal to a writer's, who has shown up the maximum number of times. Hence, it can be concluded there are a lot of factors affecting the analysis as well and in order to analyze better a look at the direct content of the talk is also necessary.

Figure 8. Violent plot for Comments Distribution

```
2 fig, ax = plt.subplots(figsize =(9, 7))
3
4 ax.set_ylim([0,1000])
5 sns.violinplot( ax = ax, y = df["comments"] )
```

```
<matplotlib.axes._subplots.AxesSubplot at 0x7f9e638c6950>
```

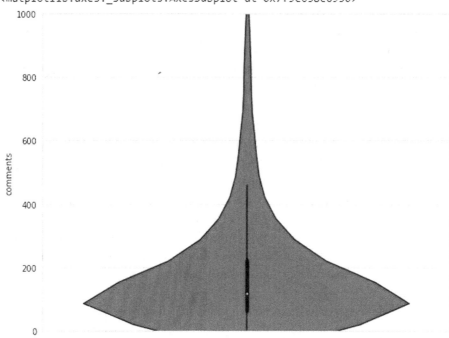

Figure 9. Views for Videos of Different Profession

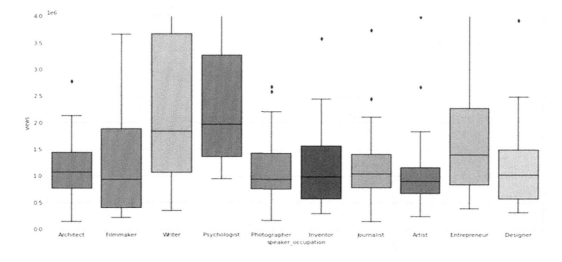

Based on Content Category

Since the videos are not divided into the type of content, they talk about the transcript of video collected earlier is used to extract the unique and important words used in the talks. This is done by getting the TF-IDF score for individual videos and then taking a select number of the words. In the most recent times, Word2Vec has been a more useful approach, which is a neural network processing the data. It also consists of algorithms such as CBOW and skip-gram and should be used frivolously. Then use variance and similarity between these words to get the different content category clusters for their classification. Once classified it is possible to determine any bias based on content category for the videos online. Also, later on we make a tag cloud of these words to see the most used words in a particular category. To analyze if the videos are recommended equally for all categories and if there are enough videos in all categories a common tag cloud can be made and the word size which corresponds to its occurrence in the dataset can be seen as representation of equal contribution or talks in all categories. Transformed keyword matrix has 2550 observations, matching our original data frame, and 440 features, each of which correspond to a unique word. There are a total of 440 unique words across all the talk keyword sets.

A common first step in unsupervised learning is to reduce the dimensions of your data. Unsupervised learning are machine learning techniques where the model does not require a training dataset or a dataset where the data is labelled into different categories. The model finds insights and hidden patterns from the given data on its own by grouping and finding clusters in the given data or finding associations in the given dataset. While in supervised learning a labeled training and testing dataset is used. In supervised learning we already know what the correct data looks like and just want to classify some new data based on previous knowledge.

Once dimensionality is reduced the data can be plotted in 2 dimensions to visualize it and get a sense of what is going on. Principal component analysis (PCA) is a method which finds the axes of highest variance in the data and rotates the data so that the first dimension corresponds to the greatest variance, the second dimension corresponds to the second greatest variance, and so on. Running PCA on the data it's possible to visualize the distribution of talks in this dimensionally reduced PC space.

Figure 10. Visualization of PCA

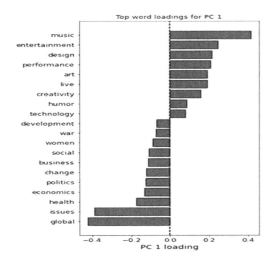
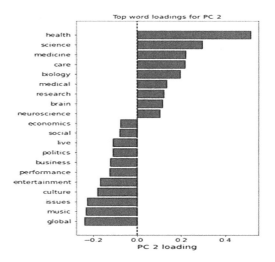

The bar plot shows that there are three possible clusters that can be formed. One pertaining to politics, second pertaining to art and third pertaining to the medical field. Also, in both PC1 and PC2 around the middle where x axis value is 0, we see topics related to technology and science.

To categorize the videos an unsupervised clustering algorithm is required. This paper uses k means clustering for this purpose. K-means clustering is an unsupervised learning algorithm that finds k clusters in a data set by minimizing the distance(which creates the final operations set with numbers) of each point to its assigned cluster center.

But there is a problem of how to set the number of clusters, k, in the K-means algorithm. One way is to find the average silhouette score across all observations and choose k such that the silhouette score is maximized. The silhouette score essentially weighs the inter vs. intra-cluster distances. A high score indicates more unambiguous cluster assignments, and low scores indicate ambiguous or incorrect cluster assignments. The silhouette score is defined on [-1, 1]. To get the number of clusters to form, different values of the number of clusters are used and silhouette scores are analyzed. in the images for clusters 3,4,5,6 the red dotted line represents the average silhouette score for all the clusters a cluster going above the line represents strong clustering and vice versa. Also the cluster size can be determined visually using by the thickness of each silhouette plot. For example, in the plot for k=3 clusters cluster 3 (yellow cluster) is unusually thick indicating it's probably having 2 or 3 sub clusters grouped together and hence is not a good clustering.A good cluster would be represented by a plot where most of the individual cluster silhouette plots have similar thickness and all are above the average silhouette line, as in cluster 4. in k=5 and k=6 the cluster 4 and 2 silhouette plots become too thin compared to the other clusters.

Figure 11. Silhouette Score Analysis

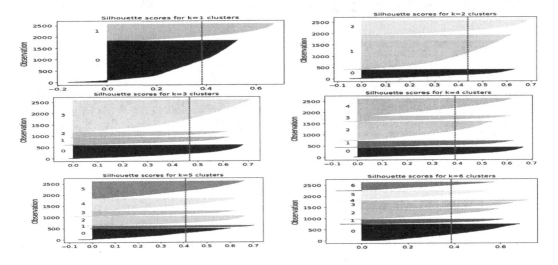

When plotting the different values of k that were tested and the corresponding mean silhouette scores, the silhouette score peaks at 4 clusters. Choosing k is not an exact science and could also be informed by our prior knowledge of the expected number of clusters based on PC1 and PC2 top words analysis.

K-means has essentially divided the observations based on physical location in PC space. Now word clouds for each cluster can be used to see what topics each cluster roughly show

Figure 12. Kmeans Clustering for k = 4 on PCA output

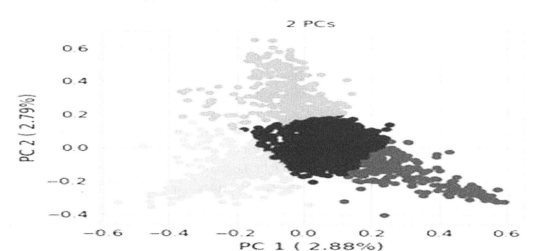

Figure 13. Word Cloud for 4 clusters

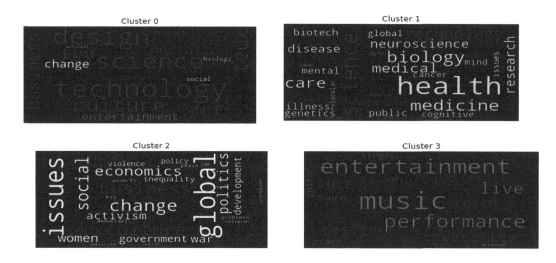

In the word clouds above each word is colored by the cluster in which it is most frequently found. the cluster 0 (colored maroon), which resides in the bottom left region of our PC space plot, contains words like global, issues, and politics, which matches with our understanding of PC 1 from earlier. Cluster 1 (colored peach) resides in the center of PC space and contains words like technology, design, and culture. And clusters 2 (colored green) and 3 (colored purple) reside in the top and bottom right of PC space, respectively. As expected from our understanding of PC space, cluster 2 contains science, and specifically biomedical, related words, and cluster 3 contains words pertaining to art, music and entertainment.

The above analysis can be suitably extended to many other situations where user preference predictions might make a great impact and enhance a firm's competitive advantage. Spreading vast information through online streaming services has become a very popular concept. From the educational models of Byju's, Vedantu, Twitter, Youtube; Entertainment models like Tik Tok, Instagram reels, Facebook, Netflix, Amazon Prime etc. to brands own personal websites with videos, understanding user preference is the key to increased customer engagement and satisfaction. Hence, the above methods do not only help analyse data on a deep level but also understand the market demands and strategies accordingly for the growth of the company.

FURTHER RESEARCH

The above analysis can be suitably extended to many other situations where user preference predictions might make a great impact and enhance a firm's competitive advantage. Spreading vast information through online streaming services has become a very popular concept. From the educational models of Byju's, Vedantu, Twitter, Youtube; Entertainment models like Tik Tok, Instagram reels, Facebook, Netflix, Amazon Prime etc. to brands own personal websites with videos, understanding user preference is the key to increased customer engagement and satisfaction. Hence, the above methods do not only help analyze data on a deep level but also understand the market demands and strategies accordingly for the growth of the company.

CONCLUSION

No matter how different the subjects of the talks are, the common theme of spreading ideas and inspiring people seems to be an adhesive force between them.

TED speeches seem to place a lot of emphasis on knowledge, insight, the present and of course, the people. After analyzing all the important parameters it can be concluded that the TEDX platform in recommending Videos has one major flaw and that's popularity bias which causes herd behavior. This means that rather than recommending videos according to individual tastes and history, the TEDX platform looks at videos which have the most views, comments etc. and on the basis of this recommends videos to each user who have just logged in, as they have no history of talks watched yet that could be used to personalize recommendations.

This method thus leads to many users being recommended videos which are not of their interest and thus these videos lose viewership and popularity. here using collaborative filtering is also not the solution as that might lead to users only being recommended what they have seen before and cause dissatisfaction when the user would like to watch something

The easiest way of rectifying this situation is to look at individual preferences and accordingly suggest the videos resulting in increasing popularity of those currently long-tail videos as well on the platform. They could also try getting categories of talk videos that interest them and the using group recommender systems as talked extensively in order to remove the popularity bias when recommending to new users, hence preventing herd psychology in recommendation systems.

REFERENCES

Beede, D. N., Julian, T. A., Langdon, D., McKittrick, G., Khan, B., & Doms, M. E. (2011). Women in STEM: A gender gap to innovation. *Economics and Statistics Administration Issue Brief*, (04-11).

Blondel, V. D., Guillaume, J. L., Lambiotte, R., & Lefebvre, E. (2008). Fast unfolding of communities in large networks. *Journal of Statistical Mechanics*, *2008*(10), P10008.

Boring, A. (2017). Gender biases in student evaluations of teaching. *Journal of Public Economics*, *145*, 27–41. doi:10.1016/j.jpubeco.2016.11.006

Chen, H., Cooper, M., Joshi, D., & Girod, B. (2014, November). Multi-modal language models for lecture video retrieval. In *Proceedings of the 22nd ACM international conference on Multimedia* (pp. 1081-1084). 10.1145/2647868.2654964

Clauset, A., Newman, M. E., & Moore, C. (2004). Finding community structure in very large networks. *Physical Review. E*, *70*(6), 066111. doi:10.1103/PhysRevE.70.066111 PMID:15697438

Farrell, L., & McHugh, L. (2017). Examining gender-STEM bias among STEM and non-STEM students using the Implicit Relational Assessment Procedure (IRAP). *Journal of Contextual Behavioral Science*, *6*(1), 80–90. doi:10.1016/j.jcbs.2017.02.001

Holland, M. L., Brock, S. E., Oren, T., & van Eckhardt, M. (2022). Assessment, Resources, and Conclusion. In *Burnout and Trauma Related Employment Stress* (pp. 99–107). Springer.

Katsamakas, E., Miliaresis, K., & Pavlov, O. V. (2022). Digital platforms for the common good: Social innovation for active citizenship and ESG. *Sustainability*, *14*(2), 639.

Kempe, D., Kleinberg, J., & Tardos, É. (2003, August). Maximizing the spread of influence through a social network. In *Proceedings of the ninth ACM SIGKDD international conference on Knowledge discovery and data mining* (pp. 137-146). 10.1145/956750.956769

Khalid, A., Lundqvist, K., & Yates, A. (2022). A literature review of implemented recommendation techniques used in Massive Open online Courses. *Expert Systems with Applications*, *187*, 115926.

Lee, K., Fanguy, M., Bligh, B., & Lu, X. S. (2022). Adoption of online teaching during the COVID-19 Pandemic: A systematic analysis of changes in university teaching activity. *Educational Review*, 1–24.

Newman, M. E., & Girvan, M. (2004). Finding and evaluating community structure in networks. *Physical Review. E*, *69*(2), 026113. doi:10.1103/PhysRevE.69.026113 PMID:14995526

Ni, J., Huang, Z., Hu, Y., & Lin, C. (2022). A two-stage embedding model for recommendation with multimodal auxiliary information. *Information Sciences*, *582*, 22–37.

Pedersen, I., & Duin, A. (2022, January). AI Agents, Humans and Untangling the Marketing of Artificial Intelligence in Learning Environments. *Proceedings of the 55th Hawaii International Conference on System Sciences*.

Shiokawa, H., Fujiwara, Y., & Onizuka, M. (2013, June). Fast algorithm for modularity-based graph clustering. *Proceedings of the AAAI Conference on Artificial Intelligence*, *27*(1), 1170–1176. doi:10.1609/aaai.v27i1.8455

Tang, Y., & Yu, Y. (2022). A personalized recommendation system for English teaching resources based on multi-K nearest neighbor regression algorithm. *Security and Communication Networks*.

Veletsianos, G., Kimmons, R., Larsen, R., Dousay, T. A., & Lowenthal, P. R. (2022). Public comment sentiment on educational videos. *Education Research*.

Wingrove, P. (2022). Academic lexical coverage in TED talks and academic lectures. *English for Specific Purposes*, *65*, 79–94.

Yang, H., & Meinel, C. (2014). Content based lecture video retrieval using speech and video text information. *IEEE Transactions on Learning Technologies*, 7(2), 142–154. doi:10.1109/TLT.2014.2307305

Zhou, R., Khemmarat, S., Gao, L., Wan, J., Zhang, J., Yin, Y., & Yu, J. (2016). Boosting video popularity through keyword suggestion and recommendation systems. *Neurocomputing*, *205*, 529–541. doi:10.1016/j.neucom.2016.05.002

ADDITIONAL READING

Abdollahpouri, H., Mansoury, M., Burke, R., & Mobasher, B. (2019). *The unfairness of popularity bias in recommendation*. arXiv preprint arXiv:1907.13286.

Baltrunas, L., Makcinskas, T., & Ricci, F. (2010, September). Group recommendations with rank aggregation and collaborative filtering. In *Proceedings of the fourth ACM conference on Recommender systems* (pp. 119-126). 10.1145/1864708.1864733

Bawden, D., & Robinson, L. (2020). Information overload: An introduction. Oxford Research Encyclopedia of Politics.

Elahi, M., Kholgh, D. K., Kiarostami, M. S., Saghari, S., Rad, S. P., & Tkalčič, M. (2021). Investigating the impact of recommender systems on user-based and item-based popularity bias. *Information Processing & Management*, *58*(5), 102655. doi:10.1016/j.ipm.2021.102655

Yalcin, E., & Bilge, A. (2021). Investigating and counteracting popularity bias in group recommendations. *Information Processing & Management*, *58*(5), 102608. doi:10.1016/j.ipm.2021.102608

KEY TERMS AND DEFINITIONS

Clustering Algorithm: A machine learning algorithm used to segregate data into groups.

Collaborative Filtering: Uses user ratings and gives more personalized recommendations.

Content-Based Filtering: The use of certain features on the basis of likes, comments, reactions and explicit feedback to escalate recommendation for other items.

K-Means Clustering: Used to partition n observations into k groups, where each observation belongs to cluster with nearest mean.

Principal Component Analysis: A method often used to reduce the dimensions of a large dataset.

Term Frequency: Inverse document frequency used to get important words in a set of documents by calculating frequency of occurrence for unique words in the document Silhouette score method to validate consistency within a cluster of data.

Word Cloud: A visual representation of text data and keywords in a particular corpus.

Tools and Techniques of Digital Education

Gautam Srivastava

(iD) https://orcid.org/0000-0002-8614-6718

G. L. Bajaj Institute of Technology and Management, India

Surajit Bag

(iD) https://orcid.org/0000-0002-2344-9551

Institute of Management Technology, Ghaziabad, India

INTRODUCTION

Education is one of the basic needs of the people and the digitalization in education is a necessity and also a current trend which is shaping the learning of the students and making them more focused on learning. Digitalization in education can be understood as the utilization of various modes like desktop, mobile, software applications and various other digital education tools for delivering education. Digitalization has transformed the education system in the present scenario (Starkey, 2011). Over the past few years digitalization has penetrated the education sector. A significant change has been observed in the teaching and learning process throughout the globe. Digitalization is revolutionizing education (Williamson, 2016). It is important to transform the education system as it is the backbone of any country. Modern education boosts the economy of the country which in turn helps the people of the country to grow, develop and have a high standard of living. This whole process requires the up gradation of the education system through digitalized tools (Edwards, 2015). The traditional education system has limited resources which has put limitations. In the pre- digitalized era classroom, libraries etc. were the only tools to teach the students but now apart from these tools, there are multiple digitalized tools which impart education even in remote areas. Digitalization in education helps the students to gain knowledge easily and also in a different way than it was before. Digitalization also saves a lot of time for the learners and hence they can focus on other things at the same time. Digitalization has changed the traditional way of learning (Loveless, 2011). People were dependent on textbooks and lecture notes before digitalization stepped into the education system (Dillenbourg, 2016). But the whole learning system has been upgraded as now the students can easily find all the textbooks and the study material on the internet and also it is readily available which was limited to classroom education before. The entire world is moving towards a knowledge society (Kyaw et al., 2019). In today's modern world, education is given the highest priority in society. Digitalization has opened multiple avenues in the teaching and learning process (Pozzi et al., 2020).

Due to digitalized tools and techniques education reached every part of the world and ICT become an integral part of education. Information and communication technology has a significant impact on the modernization of education. Adopting technologies is in the favour of learners. Digital education is creating new opportunities for teachers and students (Oakley, 2020). The teachers are also benefitted as they can share the recorded lectures with the student which can be used by the students for future references. The students are also able to learn at their own pace and they can have self-directed learning. Digitalization adds fluidity to the education system which is very important in the current scenario

DOI: 10.4018/978-1-7998-9220-5.ch094

(Emejulu & McGregor, 2019). Digital education is a need of time, especially in a country like India where population density is very high. Digital education provides assistance to give education to the students of remote areas. It is also cost-effective (Ozga, 2016). Digital education provides a platform for the weaker section of students to get a world-class education anywhere, anytime. Digital education transforms the teaching and learning process. Educators construct a positive approach for the students toward digital education.

Digitalization in Education

The 21st century has witnessed rapid development which only resulted due to digitalization. Technology has taken place in every corner and niche which is also seen in the education sector (Buchanan, 2011). Digitalization is penetrating the education system. It is widely seen that a digital strategy is also needed to reframe the education system. Due to increasing population and competition, the education sector needs a cost-effective mode to impart education to everyone (Robin, 2016). To overcome this problem most countries are focusing on the digitalization of higher education. Digitalization in higher education has become indispensable as it allows innovation in the education system which is needed for transforming the future (Irvine and Barlow, 1998).

Digitalization makes the way of teaching more convenient and easier. The education sector is also not untouched by digitalization. Digitalization especially the internet is transforming the traditional way of teaching. In the present digitalized world, students and teachers interact with each other on the digital platform (Malott, 2020). These digital platforms are replacing the physical classroom with the digital classroom. Education is undergoing a rapid expansion and thus digitalization has emerged as a boon for the higher education system (Selwyn, 2013). The appropriate theoretical model helps the teachers and students understand and learn the tools and techniques of digital education. Measuring the effectiveness of digital education is also very essential, so we can do the necessary amendments required in digital education. Digital education has a wide variety of methodologies (Lane, 2012). Those methodologies need to be evaluated and analysed for their effectiveness.

Covid-19 hit the world at the beginning of 2019. Due to this all the colleges and schools had shut down. But the pandemic widened the scope of digital learning in education. During the pandemic, online education increases broadly. The physical classroom has shifted to the virtual classroom. Tools and techniques of digital education play a crucial role to minimize the impact of a pandemic on the teaching and learning process. Pandemic has accelerated the use of digital technology in modern education. Now, online education become an integral part of our education system.

Digital education platform has changed the way of teaching and learning process. In pandemics, online education has grown exponentially and become indispensable. The concept of online teaching has greater relevance during a pandemic. Apart from digital teaching and learning, students are also getting their degrees through online mode. Even online orientation program has also been organized which is a new experience for both students and teachers.

Research Questions

- RQ1: How digital education changing the traditional way of teaching and learning process?
- RQ2: What are the different tools and techniques of digital educations?

The rest of the sections talks about various facets in digital education.

BACKGROUND

Digitalization in education focuses on the imaginative use of digital tools in the education system (Duke et al., 2013). This use of technology in education is termed digital learning or Technology Enhanced Learning. Digital learning can be understood as the learning which is backed up by various digital tools which have made learning easy, and the students have also overcome various barriers related to the time, place, learning pace and the path (Khitskov, 2017). Traditional education is highly replaced by digital education with each passing day. There are numerous advantages of digitalization in education.

Digitalization in Education has Helped the Students to get Smarter than Before

The students can grow and develop through self-directed learning (Noble, 1998). The students have become smarter as they utilize the technology to learn at their own pace and also, they utilize the tools to enhance their learning as they want which was not possible in the traditional learning system. They are also able to gain more knowledge through self-learning (Gibson et al., 2015). The students are more interested in learning as digital education has removed all the barriers that they were facing in the traditional system of education (Gros, 2007). They are also able to retain knowledge as they learn through their interest. Digitalization also helps them to develop various skills including critical thinking which is very important for the students for having a vibrant future.

Information Sharing has Become more Convenient and Easier

Digitalization in education has helped the students to get customized information which could help in solving the problems which are aroused in the path of learning (Papastergiou, 2009). The students are also able to learn at their own pace which creates a sense of understanding and thus helps them to remain competitive (Brown, 2000). Real-time data sharing is also possible through digitalization in education which has helped the students to learn more (Hiltz & Turoff, 2005). The barrier of distance is also removed as students can access the content from anywhere and in any part of the world. The students can share information and can access data which are helpful for them to gain knowledge.

Collaborative Learning Approach is Created through Digitalization in Education

The students get wider areas of learning (Green, 2007). It is found in a report that through the traditional method of learning the students merely retain 5% of the education while imparting education through digital aids helps in increasing the retaining power to 80%.

Digital Education Helps in Imparting Vocational Education to the Students

The students can learn a lot of new techniques like writing etiquettes, making presentations etc. which is not possible in the traditional learning system (Selwyn & Facer, 2014).

Disadvantages of Digitalization in Education

Imparting Education through Digital Technology may Distract the Students

The use of technology can be considered as addictive as alcohol or other drugs (Blikstein, 2013). If the students get addicted to the use of the internet it will hamper their education and learning will also be hampered.

It will Restrict the Social Interaction of the Students

Educating through digital aids will increase the online connectivity and the students may lack face-to-face interaction with their peers (Zuckerman et al., 2005). It will socially disconnect them. This is one of the major concerns which have emerged due to the changing trend of education and more focus on digitalization in the education system.

The Students may Develop the Habit of Cheating

The communication barrier is removed with the advent of technology and therefore the students may use it to cheat. The students will likely tend to cheat in the exams which is a natural-born urge in them (Kirriemuir, 2002). The best way to rule this out is to focus more on the assignments which are related to presenting personal ideas and individual perspectives.

The Students can Also Rely on Unreliable Sources of Education

The various assignment helps which are available online can be used by the students which will hamper their learning (Buckingham, 2007a). These assignments are already done and the students just copy them which is of no use. It will affect their speed of learning and their ability to critical thinking (Allen, 2017).

FOCUS OF THE ARTICLE

This chapter is focusing on the importance of digital tools and technologies for the teaching and learning process. Digital education is easily accessible by the students. This chapter elaborates on the importance of digital education for modern society. It covers the various theoretical framework of digital education. The discussed theoretical models are Bloom's taxonomy, Behavior Learning Theory, Cognitive Learning Theory, and Online Collaborative Theory. The chapter also describes the applications of different digital tools used in digital education. The challenges of digital education are also elaborated on in this chapter.

THEORETICAL FRAMEWORK

The theoretical framework of digital education is a combination of several theoretical frameworks and models of digital education. Theoretical framework enhances the capability of trainers to understand the tools, techniques, and methodology of digital education.

Digital Pedagogy

Digital pedagogy is a contemporary of digital tools and techniques. It enables teachers to use and learn digital tools for content creation (Blackwell et al., 2014). In the digital era, teachers create online content, and pdf content and use digital tools to teach mass students. This digital pedagogy is much more effective in comparison to the traditional way. Digital pedagogy also enables both teachers and students to work together (McLellan, 2007). Effective digital pedagogy must be well structured and informative for the learners. It offers potential learning elements to the students.

Context of use and Evaluation Digital Education

The context of use and evaluation is also a key element of digital education. Making appropriate context and evaluation plays an important role in digital education (Buckingham, 2007b). Appropriate content can be made in the form of audio and videos for the students. Digital evaluation speed up the evaluation process and is able to give the result in the least possible time in comparison to the traditional method. Digital materials are more suitable and can be accessible to the students in less time (Hanna, 1998). These contents may be available for the students for long last. Recorded content is one of the most important benefits of online learning. It means that if the students miss any lecture, they can understand the topic with the help of it.

Bloom's Taxonomy

Blooms Taxonomy is the combination of the hierarchical model. This model is used to classify learning objectives into different complex levels (Forehand, 2010). The three-level of Bloom's Taxonomy are cognitive, affective, and sensory.

Figure 1. Bloom's Taxonomy

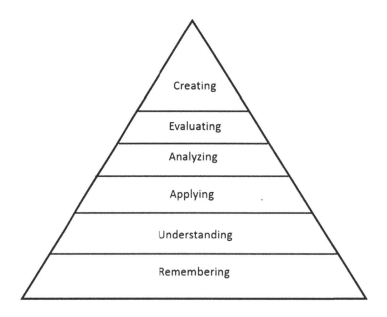

Remembering

Recalling the learning knowledge for a long period. Digitally recorded videos help the student to remember the content for a long time (Huitt, 2004). They can also revise the content wherever they want with the help of digital tools.

Understanding

Developing constructive and understanding digital materials for the students. Interpretation of the content through graphical representations. Explaining the concept more appropriately so students can easily grab the concept (Churches, 2008). Innovative software allows the students to learn the topics in their way. Information technologies help the students of remote areas to learn their content in an easier and best possible way.

Applying

Suitable strategies adopted to implement digital education. Effective and efficient digital tools and techniques are required to implement the procedure of digital education. The digital education system is an advanced practice that helps the bulk of students to get an education despite going to school physically. It utilizes wide technology-based education strategies. Digital education strategies are the combination of personal learning, flipped learning, blended learning etc.

Analyzing

Creating the study material for the digital education system is the biggest challenge. Formulation of the proper structure of digital education is very much essential. There should be proper mechanisms and support for its tools for digital education. Then only it will be able to achieve its objectives. At first, the online materials are broken into different parts and then make a proper linkage of one part with another. Then it will become easier for the students to understand the concepts.

Evaluating

Evaluation is the most crucial part of the teaching and learning process. The development of an efficient framework for evaluation is requisite. It is a mandatory part of the formal evaluation process (Overbaugh, 2008). In the case of digital education, this process becomes a little bit complicated. So, in digital education, the evaluation process is tested before going for full-fledged implementation. The major components which should be taken into consideration for digital evaluation are engagement, digital literacy, communication, efficacy, diversity and cultural understanding. The elements should be common for all students. An appropriate evaluation framework helps the teachers to know the effectiveness of the online lecture.

Creating

All the information is compiled together in a new pattern. Digital tools and techniques support the modern education system to enhance the creativity of the teaching and learning process. Digital education also enhances the capability of the students to propose new innovative solutions to the questions (Hanna, 2007). Digital learning is based on a practical approach to different topics. Students get in-depth knowledge and practical exposure to how to implement the learned theories in a real-time situation. This creativity-based learning system enables the students and enhance their capabilities as per the requirements of the corporate world.

Behavior Learning Theory

Behavior theory also supports digital education. This theory emphasizes on behavior aspects of the teaching and learning process. This theory believes in operant conditioning. This theory is based on practice and rewards which motivate the students and engage them and make their Behavior positive towards the learning process (Eysenck, 1959). Digital technologies and the education system drastically change the behavior of students towards their education. Digital education provides an innovative way of learning and gives the freedom the students to learn in their ways (Ballantyne and Packer, 2005). Behavior philosophy is based on changing behavior throw learning. It is incorporated with digital education to make the education system more attractive. This theory helps the teachers to shape the behavior of the students more deliberately (Limberg and Sundin, 2006). Behavior can be linked-to stresses scientific information rather than subjective. This theory is based on stimuli which change the cognitive Behavior of the students. Behavior theory is used in digital education to change the Behavior of the students towards desirable action.

Cognitive Learning Theory

Cognitive theory is based on the way people think. Mental thinking is the main element of this theory. In this theory, we try to understand how people think. It proposes that behavior is influenced by internal and external forces (Efland, 1995). This theory can be adopted in digital education to understand and change the Behavior of the students towards education. Most of the students in remote areas are not able to go to school. Due to this their behavior towards education becomes obsolete. It's become very difficult to change the negative behavior of the students (Nabavi, 2012). Digital education helps to overcome this problem. It assists the students to reshape their Behavior of students in an innovative way. Digital platforms provide the option to the students to get an education in their way. Digital tools and techniques help the trainers to make the teaching and learning process more attractive and effective.

Online Collaborative Theory

The unanimity of the learning approach and the development of the internet has led to the development of a new theory called collaborative learning theory. This theory is based on computer-mediated communication, constructive teaching, and digital education has given birth to online collaborative theory (Smith, 2005). It provides a framework to encourage and support the students to learn in their way. This theory provides a constructive and structured teaching methodology that replaces the old version of the teaching process. Students collectively solve the problem and learn in their way. Digital education is an innovative form of teaching and learning. Online collaboration is the process of communicating digitally. Developing higher learning thinking is one of the major importance of online collaborative theory (Xu et al., 2015). The different tools which are used in this theory are video conferencing, learning management systems, enterprise resource planning, online classes, learning materials in soft format etc. Online education doesn't have any limitations on distance. Digital education helps to provide quality education to those students who are not able to attend the class physically (Zhu et al., 2010). This theory provides an appropriate model for the student to encourage them and creates their interest in the teaching and learning process.

Connectivism

Connectivism is an innovative learning theory. This theory is still in its developing phase. The Connectivism theory of learning is based on the connectivity approach to the teaching and learning process. It helps to develop the appropriate content through a mutual understanding between teachers and students (Siemens & Conole, 2011). The main aim of this theory is to provide the initial learning environment to the students. In digital education, the scope of connectivism theory increases. Digital tools and techniques can be used to connect the teachers and students irrespective of their geographical locations. MOOC and other online courses are examples of the theory of connectivism. These types of learning are more appropriate for students living in remote areas (Kop & Hill, 2008). More practice in digital teaching and learning process improve its viability and scope.

Constructivism

Constructivism theory is based on the elements of cognitive. Learning and Behavior are important components of this theory. This theory believes in the practical approach of the education system, where students can actively participate to create their motifs by connecting new concepts of learning motives (Steffe & Gale, 1995). In digital education theory of constructivism play a significant role. It encourages the students toward collaborative learning. Constructivism theory is classified into two parts: cognitive constructivism and social constructivism. It develops advanced skills among the students (Jones & Brader, 2002). In digital education, the trainer can serve their students in three important ways: making proper procedures for online education, the objective should be well defined and there should be a proper timetable for the students, so the students know well in advance that when they have their online classes.

Objectives of Digitalized Education

Increase Productivity of Teachers and Students

Digitalized education system reduced the paperwork. Even the entire process of school and colleges become paperless through digitalization. It saves a lot of time and teachers can utilize their maximum time in the teaching and learning process. It also enhances the coordination among the different stakeholders of the education system and increases productivity.

Reduces the Cost

Digital education is paperless, so it reduces the cost of operations. In traditional education, there is various cost like records on the register, equipment of the management and other physical maintenance costs. All this physical equipment's replaced by the electronic database management system.

Easily Accessible

Documents stored in an electronic database is easily accessible from anywhere through cloud computing or the internet. Time management is extremely essential in the education sector. Technology has smoothened the process of education.

Figure 2. Challenges of Digital Education

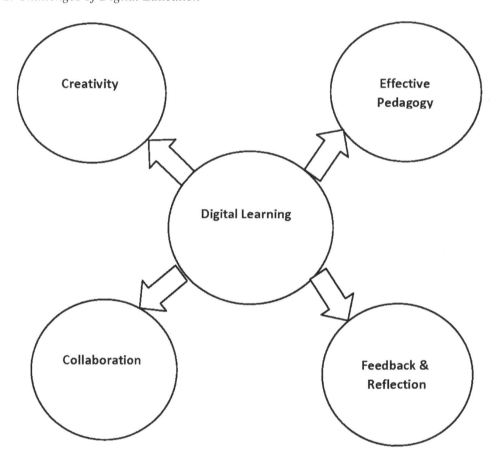

Challenges of Digital Education

Creativity

The combination of creativity and digitalization is accelerating the development and success of society. It has been observed in many countries that the education system failed to generate creativity among the students. This is due to the lack of digital equipment. Digital education has unique pedagogy which boosts creativity among the students. Creativity is essential for applied knowledge of subjects.

Effective Pedagogy

In the modern education system, traditional pedagogy is moving towards digital pedagogy. Digital pedagogy is more effective in comparison to traditional ones. It used digital tools and techniques for the teaching and learning process. Advanced digital pedagogy is more effective to shape the students. A more positive significant role can be played by the teachers to motivate, promote, and trained the students.

Collaboration

Members of the teaching and learning system collaborate to provide education to the students. Digital technologies are used for collaboration in digital education. It is different from traditional collaboration and provides a better network among the participants and instructors. Digital collaboration provides an opportunity for the students to learn and grow with each other. This helps the teachers to develop higher thinking among the students and accelerate the pace of the teaching and learning process.

Feedback and Reflection

Feedback and reflection are an important part of students learning. Digital tools provide an edge to the students to get the feedback instant and do the self-evaluation. It is an important part of students learning and should be very specific to develop the skills in the students.

Need of Digital Education

Digitalization is penetrating the education system which helps to face the challenges of the future education system. It helps to impart education to all. In the digitalized education system, there is no limitation on the number of enrollments, and it is also cost-effective. Even the students of developing and poor countries can interlink their universities to the world's top-ranking universities and improve the quality of education. Digitalized tools and techniques are transforming the education system. Even the working people could also update their skills through digital education, it provides the flexibility of timing. Participants can watch the video lecture according to their convenience. Digital technologies provide a digital space where instructors and learners interact.

TOOLS OF DIGITAL EDUCATION

Information and Communication Tools (ICT)

The information and communication technologies such as computers and the internet are powerful digital tools to do the reforms in education. ICT has made a lot of changes in our daily life and education is one of them. Digitalized resources are being used by teachers to impart education to their students (Webb & Cox, 2004). The use of ICT in education has become the policy of many countries. Digitalization has a very strong presence in developed countries and developing countries adopting these policies at an accelerated pace (Jones and Shao, 2011). Now it's become essential for the teachers to become digitally equipped.

Massive Open Online Courses (MOOC)

In recent years, the enrolment of students has accelerated in massive open online courses (MOOC). In MOOC, technology is used to deliver online lectures. It is flexible and designed for mass participation of the students. Students can access the online class through the internet from any part of the world. IT enables the education system to be the most advanced recent development in education (Heikkilä et al., 2017). Students can also access online material through a digital platform. MOOC becomes the most important platform to provide online education. MOOC has huge potential. In recent years, tremendous enrolment has been observed in MOOC courses worldwide (Castaño et al., 2018). This platform can engage a large number of students at a time. Students can also re-watch the online videos which help them to revise their subjects easily.

Figure 3. Functionality of MOOC

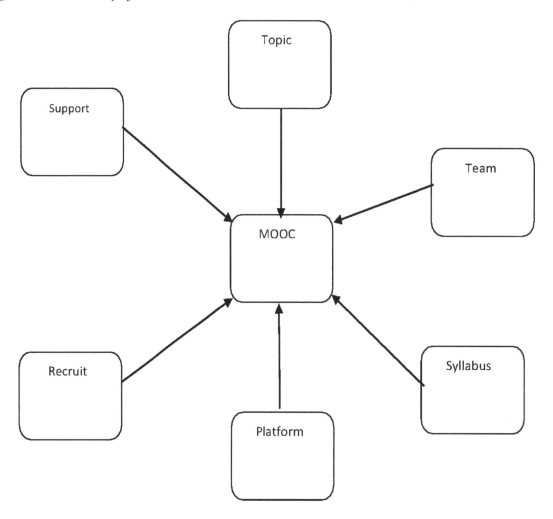

Advantages of MOOC

Learning Management System (LMS)

A learning Management System is a digital platform used to deliver resources, materials etc. It allows instructors to post additional study materials, assignments, etc. for the enrolled participants (Hoffman, 2018). It provides support to multiple learning modes. Participants can also access the materials in the form of video, audio, research articles etc. Moodle is the most widely used LMS in the world (Turnbull et al., 2021).

Advantages of Learning Management System (LMS)

Flexibility

LMS can be accessed anywhere in the world via the internet. It is flexible for both, the learners as well as for instructors. Participants in remote areas get tremendous benefits from LMS.

Supporting Content in Multiple Format

An instructor could upload the study materials in many formats on LMS. It may be in the form of audio, video, or text. Quiz, etc. The uploaded material could be easily updated, and students can instantly access it. All the study materials and activities can store in the database for re-use, so it saves the time for the instructors.

Individualized Learning

In this system, it is easy for the instructor to offer choices to the participants, so students could develop their learning framework.

Reduces Time

It reduces learning and development time. In place of sitting long hours in the classroom, students can simply click on online classes and absorb the knowledge by staying at their homes.

Integrated Learning Experience

It provides an integrated e-learning strategy. Instructors can link it to the social networking platform and could promote their e-learning courses. It helps the instructor attract new learners.

Figure 4. Functionality of Learning Management System

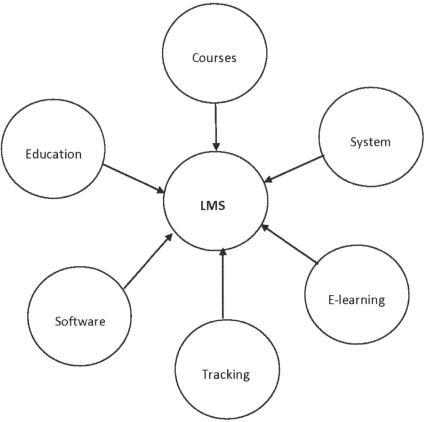

Transformation of Education System through Digitalization

Smart Classes

Teaching with chalk and dusters become past now. The teaching pedagogy is shifted toward e-learning systems, DVD, VCD and video lectures. Now smart classes are equipped with smart TV and projector. This electronic equipment motivates the students toward the lecture. It also enhanced the efficiency of the teachers to deliver the lecture. Online teaching enhanced the capability of the teacher. They can take the live video lecture of the bulk of students which is not possible through traditional classroom teaching. Students and teachers interact on the digital platform.

E- Learning Resources

Books are converted into soft-copy forms like pdf etc. which can be easily accessed through laptops, desktops, tabs or smartphones. These are the digital way to encourage the students to e-learning study.

Online Test

From time-to-time online tests can create a positive environment for the students. Taking tests through online mode can also create enthusiasm for the students.

Promoting Online Research

Online research is promoting research in different areas, especially in the marketing area. It is also creating huge job opportunities in marketing research. Now, a large number of study materials are available on the digital platform related to different areas. Asking students to find the data online encourages the students towards online research. Rewarding students for their online findings motivate them.

Creating Online Communities

The relationship between students and teachers does not end in the classroom. Both can continue with their online communities for a new project or research work. Teachers can establish an online community to discuss their ideas, project or research work. These activities encourage students to focus more on outside of the school.

Types of Digital Learning

Digital learning is the process of learning based on technology applied to the learning process. Digital technology allows participants to learn anytime from anywhere. Digital technology has multiple advantages. Some important digital education resources and techniques are as follows:

Gamification

Gamification is the process of applying game design in non-gaming activities. It is also used in digital education to make the learning process more attractive. Gamification boosts motivation in digital education and creates fun in the learning process. It engages and entertains the students in the learning process.

Adaptive Learning or Adaptive Teaching

Adaptive learning or Adaptive teaching is an educational method based on the customization process. It is a personalized learning or teaching technique which uses a computer algorithm to provide customized learning to the participants.

Flipped Learning

Flipped learning is the pedagogy through which students can watch the recorded videos as many times as they want. In this, the instruction directly moves from an online group to an individual learner. It creates an interactive learning and teaching environment among the students.

Social Media

Social media also helps the students to create their group for an assignment or project and share their views and answers. It provides a digital platform for the students to sharpen their skills. It is the direct communication tool through which teachers and learners interact with each other and is used as a digital classroom.

Google Classroom

Google Classroom is an online virtual platform by which teachers can create a classroom, communicate with a group of students, and give them an assignment. It helps the students to get real feedback from the teachers. Teachers can share videos and text materials in their virtual classrooms.

SOLUTIONS AND RECOMMENDATIONS

It has been found that the scope of digital education is much wider than traditional education. Digital education provides an opportunity for all the students and a better pace of learning in a new digital environment. We are living in the digital era where life is rapidly changed by the digital revolution. The education industry is also in its transformation process. Digital education is transforming the education system from classroom learning to virtual learning classes. Classroom teaching is not as effective as virtual teaching. Virtual classroom uses an innovative way of learning. Students can learn their lessons in their ways. The digital format can customize the teaching and learning process and it is advantageous for those students also who physically cannot come to the classroom.

The digital education system is more holistic and productive leading to a better quality of students. The Internet is the backbone of digital education. Without the internet, it is not possible to spread digital education in a wide area. Digital tools and techniques give a wider range to the students to learn from them. The content in the form of audio, video, gamification etc. helps the students to learn their lesson more appropriately. Digital education does not only benefit the students but also provides an opportunity for the trainers to enhance their teaching capabilities as per the requirements of the 21st century of the education system. Digital technologies enhance performance and optimize the outcome of digital education. In the nearby future, artificial intelligence enhances the digital ecosystem for learning systems which provides an innovative solution to the problems faced by teachers and students. The transition in digital education motivates the students toward the teaching and learning process. Digital platforms made the learning process more competent and enhance the standard of education. A Digital learning system helps to produce more quality students. It focuses on the practical approach to the teaching and learning process.

FUTURE RESEARCH DIRECTIONS

Digital technologies are rapidly changing the framework of the education system. In urban areas, digital education is deeply penetrated. In rural areas, it is still in the growth face. The impact of digital education in rural areas could be the future scope of the study. Digital education is more beneficial for the students of rural areas. So, it will be very interesting to know how digital education is changing teaching and learning practices in rural areas.

FINDINGS

Digital education is the need of the hour in the present global scenario. Now, due to the digital revolution in digital education, the distance would not be a barrier to getting an education. Students of rural and remote areas can easily educate through digital tools and techniques. It is replacing the old classroom traditional methods of teaching. The smartphone revolution also accelerates the pace of digital education. A student who does not afford computers or laptops can easily access their digital class through smartphones. Social sites can be used to connect the students and make the classroom more interesting. Gamification is also used in digital education to create interest among the students. Students of the lower class could be attracted by using gamification in online education. Digital tools and technologies enable students to develop self-learning skills among students. The different elements of digital education increase the efficiency of online education. Apart from teaching, developing interest among the students in education is the most important aspect of digital tools and techniques. Different educational software tries to develop in such a way that they would create interest among the students. This software should be unique and different from other software. Students who are involved in digital education are more engaged in their learning process.

Digital education plays a significant role in the teaching and learning process. Learning digital tools makes the teachers easier to manage their virtual classes. In higher education, digital learning should be based on a problem-solving learning approach, then only it will be more effective and able to prepare the students as per the corporate requirements. Digital learning tools and techniques fill the gap which was not possible through traditional education. Online learning is also flexible in comparison to traditional tools. The productivity of digital education is much higher than in traditional education. Student learning through digital mode is more engaged in their learning process. Digital tools and techniques have revolutionized the whole education system.

CONCLUSION

Digital education is the future of the teaching and learning process. The education system is adopting digital tools and technologies to impart education to everyone. Digital education is cost-effective in comparison to traditional classroom teaching. Digital education can impart education to those students who are living in remote areas. Digital education helps to bridge the gap between instructors and learners. It also motivates the students to learn through fun. Digital education is redefining the teaching and learning process. Digital education can increase the efficiency and effectiveness of the education system. Digital education is continuously replacing traditional education and creating a new digital environment for the teaching and learning process.

Digital education becomes very much popular among the youth because it is more convenient than the traditional education system. Even students need not travel a long distance, they can just log in to their virtual classroom from anywhere. Online education is cost-effective, and students who are serious about their learning and improving skills are getting attracted to this online education. Digital tools and techniques make online education more effective in comparison to traditional education. In digital education, the retention rates of students are higher than in traditional education. Soft copies of study materials and online tests regularly can engage the students and make digital education more attractive. Apart from engaging the students, digital education also sharpens critical thinking of the students. Online education is more effective for those students who are not able to attend a physical classroom. Digital technologies made online education accessible to the students who are living in remote areas, they can easily access quality lectures with the laptop and internet. Due to digital education, students are becoming self-motivated and more accountable. Digital tools and techniques enable the students to develop self-directed learning skills. Students can identify the online courses as per their requirements. They can evaluate the online platform and chooses the best one as per their needs. It enhances the productivity and efficiency of the students.

REFERENCES

Allen, I. E., & Seaman, J. (2017). *Digital Compass Learning: Distance Education Enrollment Report 2017*. Babson Survey Research Group.

Ballantyne, R., & Packer, J. (2005). Promoting environmentally sustainable attitudes and Behavior through free-choice learning experiences: What is the state of the game? *Environmental Education Research*, *11*(3), 281–295. doi:10.1080/13504620500081145

Blackwell, C. K., Lauricella, A. R., & Wartella, E. (2014). Factors influencing digital technology use in early childhood education. *Computers & Education*, *77*, 82–90. doi:10.1016/j.compedu.2014.04.013

Blikstein, P. (2013). Digital fabrication and 'making 'in education: The democratization of invention. *FabLabs: Of Machines. Makers and Inventors*, *4*(1), 1–21.

Brown, J. S. (2000). Growing up: Digital: How the web changes work, education, and the ways people learn. *Change: The Magazine of Higher Learning*, *32*(2), 11–20. doi:10.1080/00091380009601719

Buchanan, R. (2011). Paradox, Promise and Public Pedagogy: Implications of the Federal Government's Digital Education Revolution. *The Australian Journal of Teacher Education*, *36*(2), 67–78. doi:10.14221/ajte.2011v36n2.6

Buckingham, D. (2007a). Digital Media Literacies: Rethinking media education in the age of the Internet. *Research in Comparative and International Education*, *2*(1), 43–55. doi:10.2304/rcie.2007.2.1.43

Buckingham, D. (2007b). Media education goes digital: An introduction. *Learning, Media and Technology*, *32*(2), 111–119. doi:10.1080/17439880701343006

Castaño-Muñoz, J., Kalz, M., Kreijns, K., & Punie, Y. (2018). Who is taking MOOCs for teachers' professional development on the use of ICT? A cross-sectional study from Spain. *Technology, Pedagogy and Education*, *27*(5), 607–624. doi:10.1080/1475939X.2018.1528997

Churches, A. (2008). Bloom's taxonomy blooms digitally. *Tech & Learning*, *1*, 1–6.

Dillenbourg, P. (2016). The evolution of research on digital education. *International Journal of Artificial Intelligence in Education*, *26*(2), 544–560. doi:10.100740593-016-0106-z

Duke, B., Harper, G., & Johnston, M. (2013). Connectivism as a digital age learning theory. *The International HETL Review*, 4-13.

Edwards, R. (2015). Software and the hidden curriculum in digital education. *Pedagogy, Culture & Society, 23*(2), 265–279. doi:10.1080/14681366.2014.977809

Efland, A. D. (1995). The spiral and the lattice: Changes in cognitive learning theory with implications for art education. *Studies in Art Education, 36*(3), 134–153. doi:10.2307/1320905

Emejulu, A., & McGregor, C. (2019). Towards a radical digital citizenship in digital education. *Critical Studies in Education, 60*(1), 131–147. doi:10.1080/17508487.2016.1234494

Eysenck, H. J. (1959). Learning theory and Behavior therapy. *The Journal of Mental Science, 105*(438), 61–75. doi:10.1192/bjp.105.438.61 PMID:13641957

Forehand, M. (2010). Bloom's taxonomy. *Emerging Perspectives on Learning, Teaching, and Technology, 41*(4), 47–56.

Gibson, D., Ostashewski, N., Flintoff, K., Grant, S., & Knight, E. (2015). Digital badges in education. *Education and Information Technologies, 20*(2), 403–410. doi:10.100710639-013-9291-7

Green, H., & Hannon, C. (2007). *Their space: Education for a digital generation.* Academic Press.

Gros, B. (2007). Digital games in education: The design of games-based learning environments. *Journal of Research on Technology in Education, 40*(1), 23–38. doi:10.1080/15391523.2007.10782494

Hanna, D. E. (1998). Higher education in an era of digital competition: Emerging organizational models. *Journal of Asynchronous Learning Networks, 2*(1), 66–95.

Hanna, W. (2007). The new Bloom's taxonomy: Implications for music education. *Arts Education Policy Review, 108*(4), 7–16. doi:10.3200/AEPR.108.4.7-16

Heikkilä, A. S., Vuopala, E., & Leinonen, T. (2017). Design-driven education in primary and secondary school contexts. A qualitative study on teachers' conceptions on designing. *Technology, Pedagogy and Education, 26*(4), 471–483. doi:10.1080/1475939X.2017.1322529

Hiltz, S. R., & Turoff, M. (2005). Education goes digital: The evolution of online learning and the revolution in higher education. *Communications of the ACM, 48*(10), 59–64. doi:10.1145/1089107.1089139

Hoffman, E. B. (2018). Untangling the talk: A new multimodal discourse analysis method to investigate synchronous online learning. *Journal of Digital Learning in Teacher Education, 34*(3), 179–195. doi:10.1080/21532974.2018.1453895

Huitt, W. (2004). Bloom et al.'s taxonomy of the cognitive domain. *Educational Psychology Interactive, 22*.

Irvine, S. E., & Barlow, J. (1998). The digital portfolio in education: An innovative learning and assessment tool. *Journal of Information Technology for Teacher Education, 7*(3), 321–330. doi:10.1080/14759399800200045

Jones, C., & Shao, B. (2011). *The net generation and digital natives: Implications for higher education.* Academic Press.

Jones, M. G., & Brader-Araje, L. (2002). The impact of constructivism on education: Language, discourse, and meaning. *American Communication Journal, 5*(3), 1–10.

Khitskov, E. A., Veretekhina, S. V., Medvedeva, A. V., Mnatsakanyan, O. L., Shmakova, E. G., & Kotenev, A. (2017). Digital transformation of society: Problems entering in the digital economy. *Eurasian Journal of Analytical Chemistry, 12*(5), 855–873. doi:10.12973/ejac.2017.00216a

Kirriemuir, J. (2002). Video gaming, education and digital learning technologies. *D-Lib Magazine: the Magazine of the Digital Library Forum, 8*(2), 7. doi:10.1045/february2002-kirriemuir

Kop, R., & Hill, A. (2008). Connectivism: Learning theory of the future or vestige of the past? *The International Review of Research in Open and Distributed Learning, 9*(3). Advance online publication. doi:10.19173/irrodl.v9i3.523

Kyaw, B. M., Saxena, N., Posadzki, P., Vseteckova, J., Nikolaou, C. K., George, P. P., & Car, L. T. (2019). Virtual reality for health professions education: Systematic review and meta-analysis by the digital health education collaboration. *Journal of Medical Internet Research, 21*(1), e12959. doi:10.2196/12959 PMID:30668519

Lane, J. M. (2012). Developing the vision: Preparing teachers to deliver a digital world-class education system. *The Australian Journal of Teacher Education, 37*(4), 59–74. doi:10.14221/ajte.2012v37n4.7

Limberg, L., & Sundin, O. (2006). Teaching information seeking: Relating information literacy education to theories of information Behavior. *Information Research, 12*(1).

Loveless, A. (2011). Technology, pedagogy and education: Reflections on the accomplishment of what teachers know, do and believe in a digital age. *Technology, Pedagogy and Education, 20*(3), 301–316. doi:10.1080/1475939X.2011.610931

Malott, C. (2020). The sublation of digital education. *Post Digital Science and Education, 2*(2), 365–379. doi:10.100742438-019-00083-6

McLellan, H. (2007). Digital storytelling in higher education. *Journal of Computing in Higher Education, 19*(1), 65–79. doi:10.1007/BF03033420

Nabavi, R. T. (2012). Bandura's social learning theory & social cognitive learning theory. *Theory of Developmental Psychology*, 1-24.

Noble, D. F. (1998). Digital diploma mills: The automation of higher education. *Science as Culture, 7*(3), 355–368. doi:10.1080/09505439809526510

Oakley, G. (2020). Developing pre-service teachers' technological, pedagogical and content knowledge through the creation of digital storybooks for use in early years classrooms. *Technology, Pedagogy and Education, 29*(2), 163–175. doi:10.1080/1475939X.2020.1729234

Overbaugh, R. C., & Schultz, L. (2008). *Bloom's Taxonomy.* Academic Press.

Ozga, J. (2016). Trust in numbers? Digital education governance and the inspection process. *European Educational Research Journal, 15*(1), 69–81. doi:10.1177/1474904115616629

Papastergiou, M. (2009). Digital game-based learning in high school computer science education: Impact on educational effectiveness and student motivation. *Computers & Education, 52*(1), 1–12. doi:10.1016/j.compedu.2008.06.004

Pozzi, F., Asensio-Perez, J. I., Ceregini, A., Dagnino, F. M., Dimitriadis, Y., & Earp, J. (2020). Supporting and representing Learning Design with digital tools: In between guidance and flexibility. *Technology, Pedagogy and Education*, *29*(1), 109–128. doi:10.1080/1475939X.2020.1714708

Robin, B. R. (2016). The power of digital storytelling to support teaching and learning. *Digital Education Review*, *30*, 17–29.

Selwyn, N. (2013). Discourses of digital 'disruption' in education: a critical analysis. *Fifth International Roundtable on Discourse Analysis,* 23-25.

Selwyn, N., & Facer, K. (2014). The sociology of education and digital technology: Past, present and future. *Oxford Review of Education*, *40*(4), 482–496. doi:10.1080/03054985.2014.933005

Siemens, G., & Conole, G. (2011). Connectivism: Design and delivery of social networked learning. *International Review of Research in Open and Distance Learning*, *12*(3).

Smith, R. O. (2005). Working with difference in online collaborative groups. *Adult Education Quarterly*, *55*(3), 182–199. doi:10.1177/0741713605274627

Starkey, L. (2011). Evaluating learning in the 21st century: A digital age learning matrix. *Technology, Pedagogy and Education*, *20*(1), 19–39. doi:10.1080/1475939X.2011.554021

Steffe, L. P., & Gale, J. E. (1995). *Constructivism in Education*. Psychology Press.

Turnbull, D., Chugh, R., & Luck, J. (2021). Learning management systems: A review of the research methodology literature in Australia and China. *International Journal of Research & Method in Education*, *44*(2), 164–178. doi:10.1080/1743727X.2020.1737002

Webb, M., & Cox, M. (2004). A review of pedagogy related to information and communications technology. *Technology, Pedagogy and Education*, *13*(3), 235–286. doi:10.1080/14759390400200183

Williamson, B. (2016). Digital education governance: Data visualization, predictive analytics, and 'real-time' policy instruments. *Journal of Education Policy*, *31*(2), 123–141. doi:10.1080/02680939.2015.1035758

Xu, J., Du, J., & Fan, X. (2015). Students' groupwork management in online collaborative learning environments. *Journal of Educational Technology & Society*, *18*(2), 195–205.

Zhu, C., Valcke, M., & Schellens, T. (2010). A cross-cultural study of teacher perspectives on teacher roles and adoption of online collaborative learning in higher education. *European Journal of Teacher Education*, *33*(2), 147–165. doi:10.1080/02619761003631849

Zuckerman, O., Arida, S., & Resnick, M. (2005). Extending tangible interfaces for education: digital montessori-inspired manipulatives. *Proceedings of the SIGCHI conference on Human factors in computing systems*. 859-868. 10.1145/1054972.1055093

ADDITIONAL READING

Goldin, T., Rauch, E., Pacher, C., & Woschank, M. (2022). Reference Architecture for an Integrated and Synergetic Use of Digital Tools in Education 4.0. *Procedia Computer Science*, *200*, 407–417. doi:10.1016/j.procs.2022.01.239

Greener, S., & Wakefield, C. (2015). Developing confidence in the use of digital tools in teaching. *Electronic Journal of E-Learning*, *13*(4), 260–267.

Meirbekov, A., Maslova, I., & Gallyamova, Z. (2022). Digital education tools for critical thinking development. *Thinking Skills and Creativity*, *44*, 101023. doi:10.1016/j.tsc.2022.101023

Mohammed, Q. A., Naidu, V. R., Hasan, R., Mustafa, M., & Jesrani, K. A. (2019). Digital Education using Free and Open-Source Tools to Enhance Collaborative Learning. *IJAEDU-International E-Journal of Advances in Education*, *5*(13), 50–57. doi:10.18768/ijaedu.531636

Ross, J. (2017). Speculative method in digital education research. *Learning, Media and Technology*, *42*(2), 214–229. doi:10.1080/17439884.2016.1160927

Soomro, S. A., Casakin, H., & Georgiev, G. V. (2021). Sustainable Design and Prototyping Using Digital Fabrication Tools for Education. *Sustainability*, *13*(3), 1196. doi:10.3390u13031196

Williamson, B. (2016). Digital education governance: An introduction. *European Educational Research Journal*, *15*(1), 3–13. doi:10.1177/1474904115616630

Williamson, B. (2016). Digital education governance: Data visualization, predictive analytics, and 'real-time' policy instruments. *Journal of Education Policy*, *31*(2), 123–141. doi:10.1080/02680939.2015.1035758

KEY TERMS AND DEFINITIONS

Bloom's Taxonomy: Bloom's taxonomy is the classification of the education model based on the levels of specificity and complexity.

Digital Education: Digital education is the process of using digital technologies to assist the modern education system.

Digital Learning: Digital learning is a method of learning that incorporates the use of digital technologies.

Digital Pedagogy: The process of using digital technologies in the teaching and learning process is known as digital pedagogy.

Digital Technologies: Digital technologies are the devices, systems, resources and electronic tools used for data processing and data transferring.

Digitalization: The procedure of transforming the information into a digital format is known as digitalization.

Gamification: The process of incorporating game mechanics into non-game activities is known as gamification.

Section 21
Emerging Technologies, Applications, and Related Issues

Artificial Intelligence Into Democratic Decision Making

Takis Vidalis

Hellenic National Commission for Bioethics and Technoethics, Greece

INTRODUCTION

The expanded use of artificial intelligence in decision-making nowadays involves the most critical sectors of social activity, from economic life, communications, and crime prevention, to education, health, and scientific research. With the term "artificial intelligence" (AI), we mean, here, "machine-based systems that can, for a given set of human-defined objectives, make predictions, recommendations, or decisions influencing real or virtual environments" (OECD, 2019).

In a complex world requiring rapid, accurate, transparent, and unbiased decisions, the benefits are obvious; the systems of artificial intelligence make it possible to avoid obstacles inherent to human decision-making, due to various reasons, like limited access to relevant data, bureaucratic restraints, waste of time, and even unethical motivation. On the other hand, the involvement of algorithms in decision-making presents a major risk which may be described as a fundamental lack of adaptability to specific conditions, unforeseen at the time of the algorithm development. That problem affects directly the responsibility of those entrusting decisions to AI systems and, in legal terms, their liability. So far, no alternatives to the traditional responsibility of humans exist to capture decisions escaping from the direct human control as those of AI systems; humans remain responsible for these decisions too, and this may discourage the use of AI systems.

The above remarks make inevitable a permanent work of risk/benefit balancing regarding the use of AI in specific sectors of social activity. However, the sector of political decision-making illustrates, here, a striking exemption. Indeed, the world of politicians, persons undertaking critical decisions with massive influence at the scale of populations, looks unattainable considering the presence of AI applications in policy- and- law-making at any level. This happens although the relevance of AI is extensively investigated, over the last thirty years (Duffy & Tucker, 1995; der Voort et al., 2019, p. 27; Hochtl et al., 2016, pp.154-156 et seq.; Rubinstein et al., 2016; Poel et al., 2018; Castelluccia & Le Métayer, 2019, p. 19 et seq.), to the extent that examples of "digital politicians" and "virtual embassies" (a Swedish initiative) (Efthymiou et al., 2020, pp. 49-50) are also discussed.

On the one hand, this seems reasonable if we take into account the specific nature of political decisions requiring direct relation to the will of political representatives for ensuring their accountability before the people, at least in modern democracies. On the other, it is evident that numerous (and often crucial) political decisions either fail to regulate or even, they provoke damage in terms of public interest they are supposed to serve due to problems of misjudging, delaying, corruption, or just personal incapacity, all related to the human nature of decision-makers.

In general, we can explain such problems as a) lack of information crucial for a certain decision, b) biased evaluation of the relevant data (even if sufficient), c) incapacity of distinguishing and calculating important data in complex cases. Assuming that prevention of problems belonging to any of the three categories could be feasible if we entrusted applications of AI, it looks reasonable to explore a possibility

DOI: 10.4018/978-1-7998-9220-5.ch095

of removing a portion of political decision-making from the direct will of our political representatives or officers, following the example of other sectors of social life.

We must note, however, that numerous contributions argue that a positive stance concerning the involvement of AI in political decisions is not evident (Unver, 2018; der Voort et al., 2019; p. 28 et seq.; Savaget et al., 2019, p. 370 et seq., Starke & Lunich, 2020, p. e165, Cavaliere & Romeo, 2022, pp.18-19, Valladao, 2018, p. 16 et seq, Adamova et al., 2021, pp. 412-413). In a wider sense, the use of AI in politics has been heavily criticized, after the Cambridge Analytica case and the confirmed influence on voters' political attitudes in the U.S. presidential elections (Unver, 2018, pp. 2, 8), which is one among other similar examples (Savaget et al., 2019, p. 370), although positive opinions regarding that use are also expressed (Kane, 2019). Yet, this example highlights a different dimension, that of shaping political expressions, not decision-making as such. Regarding the latter, there are specific critiques stressing undesired potential effects, from the uncontrolled designing of algorithms that may drive to biased decisions (Olteanu et al., 2019), favoring for instance social discriminations (Corbett-Davies et al., 2017), including also the influence of diverging interests between data analysts and decision-makers (der Voort et al., 2019, pp. 28, 30, 36-37, Unver, 2018, pp. 4, 14), to the emergence of a dystopic new totalitarianism centrally organized on the basis of massive data control by the governmental power (Unver, 2018, p. 4 et seq., Adamova et al., 2021, p. 412, Valladao, 2018, p. 16 et seq.). Examples, like the UK's "Karma Police" surveillance system, highly controversial in terms of citizens' privacy respect, or the AI use from the Chinese administration for evaluating the citizens' activity in the social media to promote discriminatory decisions on the basis of restrictions on the freedom of expression (Unver, 2018, pp. 7, 9), or even various systems of citizens' scoring, based on the development of biased algorithms reflecting social prejudices (Dencik et al., 2019, p. 3 et seq.), are characteristic here.

Still, opposite examples seem to justify a positive attitude, suggesting that if the introduction of AI in political decision-making follows rationale terms, the benefits compared to conventional procedures are uncontestable. This has been confirmed in several occasions, like for example in the case of crime prevention; a local administration in the Netherlands developed a data-driven system of criminal investigation and accurate police intervention based on transparent procedures of controls in the algorithms designing and use (der Voort et al., 2019, pp. 31-33). Another example is the use of AI systems in the U.S. and Canada for monitoring immigration and making predictions as to the social incorporation of migrants, including risk evaluation for potential threats related to national security. In that example, particular attention is paid to the development of algorithms for avoiding implicit biases that may generate human rights violations, forms of direct or indirect discriminations, etc. (Cavaliere & Romeo, 2022, pp. 13-14. A similar case of AI use is that supporting the social distribution of refugees, as shown by a pilot study performed in the U.S. and Switzerland resulted in significantly improved rates of refugees' employment (Bansak et al., 2018). Also, the determination of priorities in the political agenda (Poel et al., 2018) seems to represent a topic where the use of AI does not meet any serious criticism.

In any case, this contradictory image makes it necessary to reflect on the issue of the AI legitimacy when it comes to political decision-making, or in other words to frame the discussion in a context of ethical and constitutional conditions. We can define as "ethical conditions" those referring to the general principles for the organization of any modern democratic society, no matter if these are explicitly stated in legal instruments (respect of human dignity, protection of human rights, equal treatment of citizens, political transparency, political accountability, etc.). With "constitutional conditions", we mean explicitly recognized rules existing in constitutional texts that detail the ethical conditions (due process of law, representational mandate of elected politicians, parliamentary responsibility, etc.).

Indeed, the use of AI in political decision-making should be in line with the essential elements of representative democracies, which means that legal representatives always remain responsible for any political decision, thus they need to control the AI involvement directly. Is that direct control possible without the problems that we intend to solve with the introduction of AI in the first place?

This paper explores that normative framework for a "democracy-friendly" AI in political decision-making, focusing on three questions in relevance:

1. The **constitutional question** raises issues concerning the legal margin that modern democratic constitutions (and international instruments on political rights) recognize for introducing algorithms in political decision-making, particularly in law-making and critical decisions of the administration.

In that topic, we need to identify a) the common constitutional elements that characterize the process of political decision-making in modern representative democracies and b) fields of regulation fitting the application of AI without compromising constitutional requirements. An interesting issue is, also, that of the introduction of AI as a necessary condition in political decision-making, possibly on the basis of an explicit constitutional stipulation.

2. The **data collection question** is related to the legitimate process of gathering personal data for public interest purposes, such as regulation (European Commission, 2017, pp. 16-34). To develop algorithms suitable for reaching decisions really influential at the scale of populations presupposes the extensive processing of massive information of various origins. Collections with the four characteristic elements of Big Data (volume, variety, velocity, veracity) (Hochtl et al., 2016, pp. 151-152) are necessary for making feasible any meaningful effort in that prospect, on condition that the quality of this data (particularly its transformation into a structured form) (Hochtl et al., 2016, pp. 152-153, 160) is ensured. Usually, such collections contain scientific data, statistical data, and empirical data deriving from similar experiences of other countries, in most cases freely accessible as "open data" (European Commission, 2017, p. 48; Savaget et al., 2019, pp. 369, 371, 374 et seq.).

Still, apart from these categories of non-identifiable data, access to existing collections of personal data is often a valuable condition for designing new legislation in fields such as taxation, health, insurance, banking, housing, etc. This raises the problem of data protection, even if the purpose of data processing is regulation for the public interest. The laws on data protection refer to that problem, but with no particular attention to regulation as a public interest topic. We need then to investigate conditions that could be suitable for ensuring a fair balance between personal data protection and the necessity of such data processing in the specific field of political decision-making.

3. The third **question on accountability** concerns the control of political decisions by the citizens when these decisions involve the use of algorithms. Here, we address the issue of responsibility regarding, first, the formation of algorithms, and second, the necessity of their implementation to specific objects of regulation; or, in other words, the freedom of politicians to regulate with no such use, based on their personal considerations.

Concerning both issues, a very interesting problem is that of advanced AI systems' potential use, particularly of unsupervised self-learning AI systems, that in principle escape from direct control of the human decision-maker. We cannot exclude the involvement of unsupervised systems in future scenarios of political decision-making, if continuous monitoring of regulatory effects in a certain field feed with new data the relevant algorithms, enabling the system to provide updated proposals of regulatory amendments with no human intervention. In such cases, decision-makers (representatives or political officers) who decide to follow the system's proposals, may have no direct control over the algorithms' self-updating process, although they remain politically accountable for the final decisions.

Constitutional Considerations: Is AI Compatible with Representative Democracy?

Modern representative democracies are structured on the basis of decision-making delegation from the citizens to periodically elected political representatives. The mandate of representatives is open ("representational mandate"), that is, they are not bound by any specific wishes of citizens regarding the decisions' content (Van der Hulst, 2000: 8-9). Any representative is, in principle, considered free to evaluate a certain social, economic, or political situation and decide accordingly on potential regulation. This is so, even if most representatives participate in political parties acting in compliance with the framework of their programs and under a fixed political hierarchy. On the other hand, representatives are politically responsible for their decisions before the citizens, who dispose of the ultimate power to renew or cease the representational mandate in periodical general elections. Therefore, the idea of political representation concerns a mandate to a certain person only, not to specific acts or decisions as it happens with the type of "imperative mandate" (Van der Hulst, 2000, pp. 9-10).

That general idea of representation characterizes, in particular, the democratic systems of governance and administration. Regardless of the sort of governmental system in modern democracies (presidential, mostly in the world, parliamentary in almost all European countries) (Sargentich, 1993, pp. 579-582), the political party that wins the general elections holds the power of governmental decision-making at both levels of legislation and administrative norms. The Government supported by the representatives in the parliamentary bodies enacts decisions binding for the community in the form of legal rules backed by sanctions in case of a breach.

In principle, the governmental power is limited only by the constitutional framework, in the sense that all political decisions need to comply with the constitutional principles and the fundamental rights that are explicitly mentioned in the national Constitution's text; they need also to respect the procedural stipulations of the Constitution, that is, the rules of democratic procedures, regarding, in particular, the election or assignment of persons and organs competent for political decision-making. Further limitations of the governmental power do not exist, given that any government has the option to change any law by introducing a relevant proposal before the parliamentary bodies. What balances that broad governmental power is the system of political accountability in the context of which decision-makers should justify their choices and respond to criticism before the parliamentary bodies and ultimately before the citizens in general elections (Palumbo & Bellamy, 2010).

The introduction of AI in political decision-making challenges this broad governmental power to the extent that, besides a legal limitation (that of the Constitution), there is also a technical limitation of data processing. Data relevant to a certain topic of regulation are not submitted anymore to subjective assessments of the responsible politicians, but they become subject of processing guided by algorithms leading to unbiased recommendations for decision-making. On the one hand, this restricts the constitutionally guaranteed discretion of decision-makers, on the other, it may enhance the reliability of decisions in terms of scientific consistency, and therefore reduce the possibility of rational criticism. Two issues emerge here:

1. The broad governmental power in decision-making is justified not only as of the "award" that the citizens' majority attributes to the winners of elections in the democratic process; it is also justified in terms of efficiency, as it may ensure flexibility of decisions when these are dependent on multiple unpredictable social conditions. Therefore, the Government must provide quick responses in urgent circumstances, even if the data remain insufficient or unstable for mobilizing AI methods. From the citizens' point of view, that necessity could be seen as a critical dimension of the mandate they entrust to the politicians. In fact, there are only a few areas of everyday governmental activity that allow the collection and processing of significant data before reaching the final regulatory choices; usually, these involve major reforms with the expectation of a long-run influence.

2. The elaboration of algorithms for the processing of data and their involvement in decision-making is not necessarily a "neutral" task, based on scientific parameters only. The political program of the Government plays a crucial role here; elements of the relevant political ideology may affect substantially the algorithms' content. This is reasonable since the majority of citizens entrust the Government on the basis of a specific political program characterized by certain ideological principles. In other words, there are no "neutral" algorithms that may serve equally right-wing and left-wing political programs and relevant decision-making regarding, for instance, the national health system, the educational policy, the tax policy, or the public investments. In that sense, the involvement of specific elements of political ideology in the creation of algorithms may be seen as a prerequisite corresponding to the concrete mandate that the citizens entrusted to the political decision-makers. However, this does not mean that, under this condition, the mobilization of algorithms produces biased decisions; under the light of a certain political ideology, there is always room for rational decision-making that might be criticized only from the general point of view of a different political ideology, but not from a scientific point of view. Furthermore, the involvement of politically "neutral" algorithms in decision-making is always possible when it comes to routine decisions of administration where ideological variations are rather irrelevant. It is worth noting that, there are also examples suggesting even ideologically "neutral" political programs (like that of Emmanuel Macron's LREM, in France) (Valladao, 2018, p. 19). Decisions of such a nature, often characterized by poor data processing, subjective preferences, unjust assessments, and even corrupting practices, may be rationalized with the application of AI systems driven by neutral algorithms; this may be described as "evidence-based policy" (Hochtl, et al., 2016, p. 157).

We may conclude, then, that the basic constitutional requirement in any modern representative democracy that characterizes political decision-making is the representational mandate entrusted by the citizens to the elected politicians. On the one hand, that mandate acknowledges the freedom of choices, on the other, it always refers to a specific political program and relevant ideological principles. The governmental power, in particular, should be compliant to the nature of the representational mandate. Decisions on regulation, that is, legislative or administrative acts, and the introduction of AI in decision-making need to be addressed under this normative framework. The most that we can expect from the algorithms, thus, is to rationalize that process, not to delete ideological differences and political programs. Ideological and political criticism will continue to play a crucial role in decision-making, but mostly at the level of each specific policy's principles, assuming that the AI will be in place to ensure a rational development and implementation of that policy.

Under this view, potential topics of AI involvement in political decision-making could be certainly those requiring assessment of multi-factorial information at the scale of Big Data. Public policies in the fields of taxation, employment, insurance, education, health, agriculture, competition, land uses, and environmental protection, in which the flow of relevant data from multiple sources is rapid and needs continuous monitoring (European Commission, 2017: 87, 93-94), are prominent examples here. Usually, these policies require decisions vulnerable to misleading or poor information, or influence from multiple pressure groups and lobbies, and even personal corruption. Even if such decisions may be reasonable, their implementation often becomes difficult or even impossible, due to the significant role that personal attitudes play in conventional decision-making. On the other hand, there are still few areas of governmental action with intense political nature, like foreign affairs, parliamentary affairs, and the electoral regulation, in which the application of AI seems less useful; decision-making in these areas is not based on quantitative assessments or evidence and has little technocratic significance.

Can we suppose that political decision-makers at any level have an institutional obligation to introduce AI systems for better support and evidence of their decisions? The answer to that question is difficult, because, if affirmative, it looks challenging the freedom of the politicians' action which is based on their representational mandate. Nevertheless, the AI systems in political decision-making should serve the interests of the political community "by design". This means that the algorithms involved need to be structured around common interests specifically determined and well justified before the citizens, following the political program that they have approved in the elections. If, for instance, that common interest is the mitigation of carbon-related energy consumption and the corresponding increase of renewable sources of energy at a certain rate, the relevant algorithm needs to focus on the processing of comparative data regarding the benefits and environmental, economic, social, etc., implications of both sources of energy in order to indicate a range of potential choices serving that particular and well-determined goal. Similarly, in the area of public financing, such a common interest could be the determination of the best rate of taxation for increasing investments at a certain rate in the fields of IT technology, or car industry, or winter tourism, etc.

Assuming that common interests like the above have been presented to the citizens and approved by them as part of a party's political program, we can argue that there is a sort of "presumed requirement" from the part of the citizens for the introduction of AI to the relevant decision-making process if the algorithms involved are identified as proof-of-concept tools for reaching the best possible choices. Indeed, if other means of decision-making in these areas cannot demonstrate the same level of feasibility (because they involve subjective elements or poor data documentation), there is no room for decision-makers to insist on their original freedom based on the representational mandate: If a tool promising strong evidence for the best outcomes regarding a goal of common interest is available, that original freedom becomes meaningless, and the politician is in fact engaged to use the relevant AI application.

This, of course, does not mean that this politician is also obliged to comply with one of the choices recommended by the system. There may be other considerations that influence the final decision, particularly considerations regarding the personal political carrier of any politician or prioritizations regarding the implementation of a political party's program. Still, the voters will know the reasons for which their political representative declined a certain decision, although its rationality is confirmed by the engagement of AI systems. Certainly, this improves transparency in decision-making, prevents populistic behavior, and facilitates political accountability. In that sense, an autonomous role of AI systems in political decision-making is not ethically acceptable (Cavaliere & Romeo, 2022, pp. 8-9, Starke & Lunich, 2020, p. 11 et seq), and the "accountability of algorithmic decision systems" (Castelluccia & Le Métayer, 2019, p. 72 et seq) could not mean something more than requirements of transparent functioning.

Taking into account these points, it would be not absurd to defend a position according to which the engagement of AI systems in political decision-making should be understood as an expression of the representational mandate that the citizens entrust to political decision-makers, that is, a new dimension of the citizens' political rights in representative democracies (Bach-Golecka, 2018, pp. 89-93). A provisional conclusion is, then, that the democratic process as expressed in political decision-making needs to take advantage of technological applications suitable for reaching choices serving the common good; this does not reflect a mere wishful thought but rather a real institutional duty.

On that basis, it would not be absurd to defend even the explicit recognition in the constitutional text of a relevant guarantee regarding the involvement of AI in political decision-making, particularly in law-making procedures. Although such a guarantee would inevitably be dependent on specific conditions of feasibility (regarding the objective of regulation or the availability of adequate systems), a constitutional guidance could encourage the use of means that may ensure transparency and unbiased decisions.

Table 1.

Ideology /Political program	Ideologically determined policies	AI suitable for ideologically compliant, evidence-based decisions
No ideology	Neutral policies	AI suitable for evidence-based decisions
-	Quick actions (no time for data collection)	AI unsuitable
Ideology /Political program	Policies requiring sophisticated data processing	AI as an institutional prerequisite

Data Collection

Assuming that personal data constitute a significant part of the whole data pool that supports the development of AI systems in political decision-making, we need to address problems regarding their protection.

Sources of such data may be either already existing public or private collections originally created for serving other purposes (in health, insurance, urbanization, taxation, commerce, etc.) or even new collections specifically created for supporting concrete policies and relevant legislation.

According to the data protection laws, in principle, the "secondary use" of existing personal data collections for purposes other than the original ones must be based upon a fresh specific consent of the data subjects, if their identities remain accessible in the context of the new data use. Nevertheless, accepts the secondary use of existing data without fresh consent, on condition that measures ensuring confidential processing are in place, such as the data anonymization (that is, with no possibility of access to the subjects' identity) or pseudonymization (i.e., permitting access only to certified persons). This is the current trend in regulation characterizing the laws in the EU (General Data Protection Regulation/GDPR 2016, Art. 6 para 4, 9 para 2 j), U.S. (Privacy Act 1974/2020, 552a (b), U.S. Department of Justice, 2020: 64 et seq), Canada (PIPEDA 2015, Div. 1, 7), and Australia (Privacy Act 1988/2020, Sched. 1, part. 2, 3.3). On the other hand, new data can be collected on the basis of their subjects' informed consent that, in principle, should be specific, that is, pertinent to the purposes of their collection. However, in the EU, the GDPR (as the only legislation detailing more that issue), accepts a sort of generic consent also, particularly regarding data use for research purposes, that is, consent pertinent to a broader area of research purposes but still with relevance to the specific original research purpose (GDPR, recital 33). That generic sort of the subjects' consent facilitates any further secondary use of the data collected (within the context of a research objective, though) with no need to obtain fresh consent fitting a specific research protocol.

Therefore, we can consider two possibilities in relevance that ensure data protection, as a common regulatory trend nowadays in western legal systems

Table 2.

Existing data	Measures of confidential processing are required	No necessary consent for secondary use
New data		Consent is required

This is the general regulatory framework for the use of data which would be applicable also to the context of AI development with the purpose to support political decision-making. Hence, for the creation of a pool of personal data that may be considered as necessary for feeding algorithms in order to yield political or regulatory proposals, it looks that all the above means of a collection might be mobilized following the existing legal prerequisites. This is also true for the generic consent exemption, applicable only to the use of data for research purposes, at least for certain political decisions that require previous scientific research seeking to measure or evaluate the efficiency of regulation in certain areas (urbanization, taxation, insurance, etc.).

The above laws do not mention political decision-making as a specific topic that justifies data processing. There are, of course, multiple explicit references to issues of public interest, like health, national security, defense, public security, etc. that involve political decisions; therefore, they justify not only collections and further processing of personal data but also derogations regarding the exercise of the data subjects' relevant rights. This is the normative gate through which politicians may have access to personal data. The laws do not make any distinction between governmental and other political decisions in that context. Not only governments (expressing the majority of citizens) in their regulatory authority but also the other political parties have, in principle, legitimate interest to have access to citizens' personal data, to the extent that they also elaborate proposals of public policy.

This ample possibility that data protection laws recognize to political decision-makers creates a general question: Is it necessary to suggest any limits for the sake of the citizens' data protection? The problem becomes critical if we suppose that data collections would be available for extensive processing applications in the context of AI systems. Knowing that questions on confidential handling of data arise even under the direct control of human processors, the degree of uncertainty when involving AI systems becomes much higher here due to the evident complexity of these.

All the above legal systems accept two sorts of conventional limitations regarding the legitimate processing of data. First, there is an institutional limitation requiring the implementation of the proportionality principle, a principle which is applicable to any regulation of fundamental rights, meaning that processing is legitimate only if the data is necessary for the original purpose of collection. Second, a technical requirement is also recognized, according to which measures ensuring confidentiality must be in place, to secure the data collections (pseudonymization, anonymization, encryption, etc.). Also, all the above laws designate persons involved in data management determining in detail their responsibility under the control of state authorities.

However, the fact that multiple political organizations (or even individual politicians) may have a special interest in personal data processing for political decision-making, besides the Government or the administrative authorities, raises risks in terms of data protection. This is because references to public policies in the text of legal instruments do not contain substantial reservations regarding the possibility of data processing. In other words, if the Government or a political party, or a politician consider it necessary to collect and process personal data to an undetermined extent for elaborating decisions of public policy (in national security, defense, economy, education, health, etc.), there are no legal limits for securing the citizens' privacy, others than the above-mentioned conventional ones. This could be a problem, particularly if AI systems are involved in political decision-making, as the processing and possible uses (and misuses) of the data collected are practically uncontrolled by the data subjects. By nature, the potential purposes of any public policy are not always strictly determined, and they usually refer to general political aspirations (like economic growth, equal opportunities in education, the quality of healthcare, etc.). As a consequence, this makes it almost impossible to determine the volume of data that may serve these purposes and the legitimate extent of data processing. Therefore, substantial safeguards for data protection (as mentioned in current laws) become practically inactive, and relevant risks are obvious.

Considering the possibility of AI involvement in political decision-making, as a factor that multiplies the options and accelerates the process of data processing, raising the risk of misuse, we need to reflect on specific safeguards for anew balancing the data subjects' interests with the interests of decision-makers when designing public policies. Such a safeguard could be the relocation of the subject's specific informed consent as a necessary prerequisite for allowing access to personal data when the purpose of collection and processing is the elaboration of political decisions. Under this view, the possibility of access with generic consent or without consent (on the basis of data pseudo- or anonymization for secondary uses) would be banned. Alternatively, enhanced security measures for preventing potentially unauthorized data flow in the context of AI applications need to be developed, possibly in combination with a stricter approach of the data managers' liability.

Political Accountability

As mentioned already, the freedom to make political decisions that politicians enjoy under the view of the representational mandate is associated with their political accountability (Ferejohn, 1999). Politicians are accountable to the citizens and subjects to political blame because they have full discretion in evaluating a certain situation of public interest and make political proposals, which in the case of governance include also regulatory decisions, binding for all. Political accountability is distinct from the legal responsibility of politicians, which involves legal sanctions if political acts violate a certain law (European Commission for Democracy Through Law, 2013, pp. 4-7, Chang et al., 2010). Sanctions of political nature, that is, expressions of citizens' disapproval are pertinent to acts that propose or introduce new laws or even pertinent to unaccepted political behavior in a broader sense. In that meaning, the ultimate political sanction is the denial of election or re-election by the citizens. Therefore, to blame politicians in decision-making presupposes that they could act "differently" either in evaluating a certain situation or in pursuing a certain goal with appropriate decisions.

However, the above scheme fits the conventional process of political decision-making where human control is present and influences any step of that process directly. In the conventional process, politicians are accountable for their decisions because, at any time, they may stop, modify, speed up or simply enact them. They remain responsible for acts of their executive collaborators intending to determine the details for making or implementing a certain decision, and for acts of the administrative personnel and civil servants if politicians are members of the Government. Therefore, the accountability always corresponds to the extent of the decisions' control that the politician holds.

Supposing that the implementation of AI systems contributes substantially to the process of political decision-making, being a reliable (or the most reliable) means for evaluating massive data and reaching rational outcomes (as appropriate recommendations for political decisions), the question is whether we can recognize the same degree of accountability for politicians using such systems in their political activity. This is because, to some extent, they are unable to control the process of data processing and the development of respective recommendations. We can examine, here, three relevant conditions.

The first is when a decision-maker has no institutional obligation to involve AI in the process. In that case, the control over the process remains direct, in the sense that the politician opted for decision-making support by a certain AI system, although there was always the option to act differently. Here, the extent of accountability cannot be limited, even if the politician is not in place to control (or even understand) the algorithms' structure, the data processing course, or the final outcomes' development. It is sufficient that the one responsible for decision-making entrusted the system and proceeded thus partially to a kind of self-restricting freedom of choices regarding decision-making. Moreover, when the system provides more alternative recommendations for decision-making and the politician evaluates them, picking the best according to subjective criteria, the accountability remains unaffected, as the option to "act differently" is present not only at the beginning but at the end of the process as well.

The second condition refers to the decision-makers' accountability when there is an institutional (legal) obligation to involve AI in the process. In such a case, it would be reasonable to assume that the system of AI should be known to the citizens and the political opponents (the minority in Parliament, if decision-makers are members of the Government), for transparency reasons. A mandatory mobilization of AI, here, would lead to a certain reduction of political responsibility regarding the use of the system, as the politician is obliged to take into account the system's outcomes. Still, the extent of accountability is not influenced, if decision-makers have to opt between more recommendations that the algorithms provide after the data processing since they always remain able to decide "differently".

The third condition is that of unsupervised AI systems' involvement, that is, self-learning systems capable to automatically adapt their algorithms according to the input of data they receive, without the need for human control or intervention. In such cases, we address problems of "black box" in decision-making, where the human user faces a certain opacity regarding the system's function (Rudin, 2019, Castelluccia & Le Métayer, 2019, p. 47 et seq, Starke & Lunich, 2020, p. e166, Cavaliere & Romeo, 2022, p. 20 et seq., Unver, 2018, pp. 12-13). By definition, that condition reduces human responsibility, but only at the level of the system's functioning. On the contrary, decision-makers remain fully responsible, first, if they have the freedom to choose support from unsupervised AI, and, second, if they need to select between more recommendations that the system provides. However, in political decision-making, more serious issues of legal implications (liability) do not emerge (as they do, for instance, in medical decision-making, when involving unsupervised AI applications) (Vidalis, 2021).

To summarize the above considerations:

Table 3.

Optional use of AI	Option to "act differently"	Full political responsibility	Full accountability
Required use of AI	Not always option to "act differently"	Limited political responsibility	Full accountability (if more recommendations from the system exist)
Optional use of unsupervised systems	Option to "act differently"	Full political responsibility	Full accountability

CONCLUSION

Although the importance of political decisions is indisputable in any society, a substantial degree of irrational elements occurring in the process of these decisions' development obstructs their feasibility. This is due to various reasons but mostly to insufficient data regarding their objective or the poor or even biased evaluation of this data by responsible politicians. The idea of supporting political decision-making with AI applications focuses exactly on the necessity to reduce the degree of irrationality and boost the practical value of decisions.

There is no question, here, to seek the "best" decisions for coping with problems of public interest. The AI cannot promise this, since the "best" decisions for a certain society clearly differ according to political ideologies or philosophical systems. What the application of AI may truly promise, is to reach "better" decisions than those expected by ordinary politicians, under the framework of a given political attitude or philosophical approach.

The formation of algorithms and the amount and quality of data that feed the system will continue to rely on human interventions; thus, they will remain exposed to irrational considerations, although in advanced democracies there are procedures that may prevent such practices including parliamentary procedures, or party procedures guaranteeing free political debates, and collective decision-making (Cavaliere & Romeo, 2022, pp. 17-18). Still, an AI system can ensure the best data evaluation and accuracy of the recommendations issued, which is a huge benefit in political decision-making anyway. Transparency is an additional benefit, here, particularly when AI systems with certified characteristics established by specific legal regulation (European Commission, 2021; Sherer, 2016) are used by the government in law-making procedures. To decline evidence-based recommendations issued by reliable AI applications certainly gives room to political opponents for exercising criticism and may deeply affect the political accountability of decision-makers.

With no doubt, there are difficult problems that need special attention before involving machines in political decisions, such as, for example, the use of unsupervised AI systems, the institutional (or even constitutional) status of AI in the procedures of representative democracy, structured around the free mandate of our political representatives, and so on. This study shows why solutions to these problems are not impossible. If we agree on the merits of AI in political decision-making, we need to promote the creation of interdisciplinary fora to explore realistic prospects in relevance, where AI experts, lawyers, ethicists, politicians, and also laypersons would have to provide valuable input.

REFERENCES

Adamova, M. A., Kardanova, M. L., Yakusheva, A. V., Dyakonova, M. A., & Mankieva, A. V. (2021). Artificial Intelligence in Politics. *Meta-Scientific Study of Artificial Intelligence*, 409 – 417.

Bach-Golecka, D. (2018). The Emerging Right to Good Governance. *The Emerging Right to Good Governance, American J. Of International Law Unbound, 112*, 89–93. doi:10.1017/aju.2018.37

Bansak, K., Ferwerda, J., Hainmueller, J., Dillon, A., Hangartner, D., Lawrence, D., & Weinstein, J. (2018). Improving refugee integration through data-driven algorithmic assignment. *Science, 359*(6373), 325–329. doi:10.1126cience.aao4408 PMID:29348237

Castelluccia, C., & Le Métayer, D. (2019). *Understanding algorithmic decision-making: Opportunities and challenges.* European Parliament.

Cavaliere, P., & Romeo, G. (2022). From Poisons to Antidotes: Algorithms as Democracy Boosters. *European Journal of Risk Regulation*, 1–25.

Chang, E. C., Golden, M. A., & Hill, S. J. (2010). Legislative malfeasance and political accountability. *World Politics, 62*(2), 177–220. doi:10.1017/S0043887110000031

Corbett-Davies, S., Pierson, E., Feller, A., Goel, S., & Huq, A. (2017). Algorithmic decision making and the cost of fairness. *Proceedings of the 23rd acm sigkdd international conference on knowledge discovery and data mining*, 797-806. 10.1145/3097983.3098095

Dencik, L., Redden, J., Hintz, A., & Warne, H. (2019). The 'golden view': Data-driven governance in the scoring society. *Internet Policy Review, 8*(2), 1–24. doi:10.14763/2019.2.1413

Duffy, G., & Tucker, S. A. (1995). Political science: Artificial intelligence applications. *Social Science Computer Review, 13*(1), 1–20. doi:10.1177/089443939501300101

Efthymiou-Egleton, I. P., Egleton, T. W. E., & Sidiropoulos, S. (2020). Artificial Intelligence (AI) in Politics: Should Political AI be Controlled? *International Journal of Innovative Science and Research Technology, 5*(2), 49–51.

European Commission. (2017). *Quality of Public Administration. A Toolbox for Practitioners. Theme I: Policy-making, Implementation and Innovation.* Office of the EU.

European Commission for Democracy Through Law (Venice Commission). (2013). *Report on the Relationship between Political and Criminal Ministerial Responsibility.* Council of Europe. https://www.venice.coe.int/webforms/documents/default.aspx?pdffile=CDL-AD(2013)001-e

Ferejohn, J. (1999). Accountability and Authority: Toward a Theory of Political Accountability. In Democracy, accountability, and representation (Vol. 2). Cambridge University Press.

Höchtl, J., Parycek, P., & Schöllhammer, R. (2016). Big data in the policy cycle: Policy decision making in the digital era. *Journal of Organizational Computing and Electronic Commerce, 26*(1-2), 147–169. doi:10.1080/10919392.2015.1125187

Kane, T. B. (2019). Artificial Intelligence in Politics: Establishing Ethics. *IEEE Technology and Society Magazine, 38*(1), 72–80. doi:10.1109/MTS.2019.2894474

OECD, Recommendation of the Council on Artificial Intelligence, C/MIN(2019)3/FINAL (5/ 22, 2019)

Olteanu, A., Castillo, C., Diaz, F., & Kıcıman, E. (2019). Social data: Biases, methodological pitfalls, and ethical boundaries. *Frontiers in Big Data, 2*, 13. doi:10.3389/fdata.2019.00013 PMID:33693336

Palumbo, A., & Bellamy, R. (Eds.). (2010). *Political Accountability.* Routledge.

Poel, M., Meyer, E. T., & Schroeder, R. (2018). Big data for policymaking: Great expectations, but with limited progress? *Policy and Internet*, *10*(3), 347–367. doi:10.1002/poi3.176

Proposal for a Regulation of the European Parliament and of the Council, Laying Down Harmonized Rules on Artificial Intelligence (Artificial Intelligence Act) and Amending Certain Union Legislative Acts (2021). https://eur-lex.europa.eu/legal-content/EN/TXT/HTML/?uri=CELEX:52021PC0206&from=EN

Rubinstein, M., Meyer, E., Schroeder, R., Poel, M., Treperman, J., van Barneveld, J., Biesma-Pickles, A., Mahieu, B., Potau, X., & Svetachova, M. (2016). *Ten Use Cases of Innovative Data-Driven Approaches for Policymaking at EU Level*. Tecnopolis Group.

Rudin, C. (2019). Stop explaining black box machine learning models for high stakes decisions and use interpretable models instead. *Nature Machine Intelligence*, *1*(5), 206–215. doi:10.103842256-019-0048-x PMID:35603010

Sargentich, T. O. (1993). The Presidential and Parliamentary Models of National Government, American University International. *Law Review*, *8*(2/3), 579–592.

Savaget, P., Chiarini, T., & Evans, S. (2019). Empowering political participation through artificial intelligence. *Science & Public Policy*, *46*(3), 369–380. doi:10.1093cipolcy064 PMID:33583994

Sherer, M. U. (2016). Regulating Artificial Intelligence Systems: Risks, Challenges, Competencies, and Strategies. *Harvard Journal of Law & Technology*, *29*, 353–400.

Starke, C., & Lünich, M. (2020). Artificial intelligence for political decision-making in the European Union: Effects on citizens' perceptions of input, throughput, and output legitimacy. *Data & Policy*, *2*, e16. Advance online publication. doi:10.1017/dap.2020.19

United States Department of Justice. (2020). *Overview of the Privacy Act of 1974*. https://www.justice.gov/opcl/overview-privacy-act-1974-2020-edition

Unver, A. (2018). *Artificial intelligence, authoritarianism and the future of political systems*. EDAM Research Reports.

Valladao, A. G. (2018). *Artificial Intelligence and Political Science*. OCP Policy Paper.

Van der Hulst, M. (2000). *The Parliamentary Mandate. A Global Comparative Study*. Inter-Parliamentary Union.

Van der Voort, H. G., Klievink, A. J., Arnaboldi, M., & Meijer, A. J. (2019). Rationality and politics of algorithms. Will the promise of big data survive the dynamics of public decision making? *Government Information Quarterly*, *36*(1), 27–38. doi:10.1016/j.giq.2018.10.011

Vidalis, T. (2021). Artificial Intelligence in Biomedicine: A Legal Insight. *BioTech*, *10*(3), 15. doi:10.3390/biotech10030015 PMID:35822769

ADDITIONAL READING

Braun, R. (2019). *Artificial intelligence: socio-political challenges of delegating human decision-making to machines* (No. 6). IHS Working Paper

Daly, A., Hagendorff, T., Li, H., Mann, M., Marda, V., Wagner, B., ... Witteborn, S. (2019). *Artificial intelligence, governance and ethics: Global perspectives*. The Chinese university of Hong Kong faculty of law research paper, (2019-15)

De Fine Licht, K., & De Fine Licht, J. (2020). Artificial intelligence, transparency, and public decision-making. *AI & Society, 35*(4), 917–926.

Duan, Y., Edwards, J. S., & Dwivedi, Y. K. (2019). Artificial intelligence for decision making in the era of Big Data–evolution, challenges and research agenda. *International Journal of Information Management, 48*, 63–71.

Elliot, V. H., Paananen, M., & Staron, M. (2020). Artificial intelligence for decision-makers. *Journal of Emerging Technologies in Accounting, 17*(1), 51–55.

Greene, D., Hoffmann, A. L., & Stark, L. (2019, January). Better, nicer, clearer, fairer: A critical assessment of the movement for ethical artificial intelligence and machine learning. *Proceedings of the 52nd Hawaii international conference on system sciences*.

Hudson, V. M. (2019). *Artificial intelligence and international politics*. Routledge.

Reis, J., Santo, P., & Melão, N. (2020). Artificial intelligence research and its contributions to the European Union's political governance: Comparative study between member states. *Social Sciences, 9*(11), 207.

Renda, A. (2019). *Artificial Intelligence. Ethics, governance and policy challenges*. CEPS Centre for European Policy Studies.

Sætra, H. S. (2020). A shallow defence of a technocracy of artificial intelligence: Examining the political harms of algorithmic governance in the domain of government. *Technology in Society, 62*, 101283.

KEY TERMS AND DEFINITIONS

Constitutional Conditions: Explicitly recognized rules existing in constitutional texts that detail ethical requirements.

Ethical Conditions: General principles for the organization of any modern democratic society, no matter if these are explicitly stated in legal instruments.

Evidence-Based Policy: Policy-making procedures based on AI systems driven by neutral algorithms.

Identifiable Data: Personal data revealing directly or indirectly its subject's identity.

Political Accountability: The responsibility of politicians to justify their decisions that involves the possibility of political sanctions by the citizens.

Representational Mandate: The mandate entrusting decisions for the common good to the free discretion of elected representatives.

Unsupervised AI Systems: Self-learning systems capable to automatically adapt their algorithms, without the need for human intervention.

Change Management Science Innovation Methodologies

Nuno Geada

(iD) https://orcid.org/0000-0003-3755-0711

ISCTE - University Institute of Lisboa, Portugal

INTRODUCTION

Digital Transformation permits new businesses implement, digital business models, and processes. Innovation is used as a key to companies for competitiveness, it is the way forward for firms that want to grow in today's complex and turbulent environment (Andrew, et al, 2009; Barsh, et al, 2007). Whether organizations are long established or new, those that manage to grasp leading positions are the ones that innovate faster and possess the relevant knowledge to uphold their innovativeness (Desouza et al., 2009).

Organizations faces two simultaneous challenges:

1. They constantly perform and innovate to sustain their position on the marketplace and secondly, they must transform themselves so that they can navigate fundamental shifts in their environment in terms of market and technology (Garud et al., 2006). In other words, they have to re-design themselves with agility to anticipate and adapt to changes, searching constantly for innovation while sustaining performance daily.
2. In other way of analysis, recent literature echoes the emerging role of social media – a new practice for harnessing the power of mass collaboration, shaping new modes of behavior and facilitating knowledge flows in networks across organizational boundaries; all of these features are essential for company innovativeness (Noteboom, 2000; Weinberg et al., 2013).

The use of social media applies methodologies constantly prints the essence, throw continuous improvement, of the Knowledge Management and Change Management. Through its capacity is to build up a model of intelligence from human interactions and processes, turning lead to collaboration if trust and reciprocity are at work (Boughzala et al., 2010). The relationships between the design requirements for an innovative enterprise and the implementation of the emerging practice of social media takes the form of a layered cycle and draws a distinction between sectors, processes and components that delivers digital infrastructure, and create digital services, and consume digital services/infrastructure. Digital infrastructure consists of data as the raw material, the network sector, the data center sector, and the cloud and hosting sector. Digital services are created and delivered by software and digital companies. Digital data, infrastructure and services are purchased by businesses, consumers, and the government (digital consumption), facilitated by linking on-premises IT infrastructure and devices such as smartphones, tablets. (Alaerds et al., 2017) social media (SM) has become very popular, etymologically speaking, social media dates from the ascent of humankind, since humans have always looked for different ways to communicate, and to change. Today, social media can be understood as "a group of Internet-based applications that build on the ideological and technological foundations of Web 2.0, and that allow the creation and exchange of user generated content" (Kaplan & Haenlein, 2010).

DOI: 10.4018/978-1-7998-9220-5.ch096

Consequently, organizations are required to adapt their operations, infrastructures, and strategies in coordination with challenges imposed by the intensive changes prevailing in the global environment and business. This can be achieved by adopting a continuous improvement methodologies approach, through which organizations can monitor and integrate all advancements in technology and business tools into their operations targeting efficient and effective business results (Hashem 2020; Albrecht et al., 2020). According to the author the challenges of automating component integration, which can be summarized as the need for particular protocols and lower costs of hardware, software, and middleware tools to ease the knowledge exchange of integrators (Manesh et al., 2021).

BACKGROUND

The Change Challenge

According to Turner et al. (2009), It should be noted that these elements are most often not pertinent to manage an organizational change, however they are an integral and fundamental part of its success. This management model recognizes the need to reject old behaviors, structures, processes, and cultures before successfully adopting new approaches. Employees of organizations must bear in mind the concepts related to the hard and soft aspects regarding organizational changes as they are fundamental for the success of its implementation. The importance of the human side of change, according to Galpin (2000), presents a change management model, which, as a differentiating element, reconciles the soft aspects and the hard aspects. Turner et al. (2009) also reinforces the importance of applying a holistic approach to change management models, which focuses on both hard and soft systems.

Figure 1. Adapted from
(Turner et al., 2009)

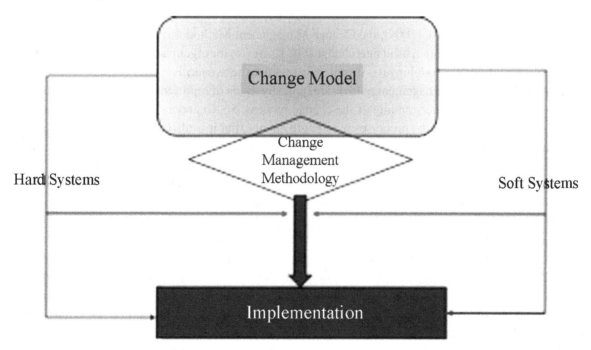

The value that is generated by this approach is the permanence and flexibility it provides organizations and their managers to adapt and be able to respond to changes. In practical terms, leveraging a change management methodology requires that organizations' leaders understand and synergistically apply the organization's hard and soft systems. The table below describes the synergy of activities related to the hard and soft system in order to manage change:

Figure 2. Application of the Hard and Soft System in Change Management
adapted from Turner et al. (2009)

Hard Systems Implementation		Soft Systems Implementation
Define a desired outcome (vision)		Create dialogue around desired outcome
Prescribe the Steops		Manage in between the steps
Manage the event		Facilitate the change process
Measure quantitative results		Measure qualitative results
Create structure		Experience participative management
Name the change		Experience the transition

According to Turner et al. (2009), the Change Management Methodology and the Change Management Model are two terms often used interchangeably. However, for organizations trying to use a change management model or methodology it is useful to distinguish the two terms as they correlate and complement each other. Change management models are typically a way of representing and describing a series of steps in a theoretical understanding of the change process. So, to understand the planned change, it is not enough to understand the processes inherent to change, but it is also necessary to understand the states through which the organization has to go, in order to move from an unsatisfactory present state to a desired future state (Gawke, Gorgievski, and Bakker, 2019; Nasiri et al., 2020; Albrecht et al., 2020). The authors also pointed out challenges in the areas of employee recruitment and qualification, and they highlighted the importance of companies' ability to develop the know-how required to seize digitalization opportunities.

A methodology differs from a model in that it typically does not attempt to explain phenomena, but rather represents a set of activities or procedures that define the completion of an event or task. Another way to define the methodology is effectively comparing it to a repository of methods and problem solving that are governed by a common set of principles, rules, or philosophy for solving targeted problems (Kettinger et al., 1997). Kettinger et al. (1997) verified and consolidated the additional differentiation between methodology, techniques, and tools. Methodology is represented as the highest level of abstraction followed by techniques that are defined as a set of specific steps or procedures and, finally, at the lowest level are tools, which refer to specific items that allow a task to be performed as software or an evaluation.

METHODOLOGY OF CHANGE

In addition to change management models, there are also methodologies that, when correlated with the models, become an extremely powerful support and support tool. The ITIL methodology is widely used by top management, and worldwide today, and is associated with increased competitiveness between organizations. In order to apply good practices and control the existing change processes within the IS, ITIL is a tool to support methodologies. ITIL (Cartlidge et al., 2007) is a methodology created in the late 1980s (initially it was called CCTA (Central Computer and Telecommunications Agency), which is based on the management of IT services, applying best practices to help companies to achieve their business goals, with the support of IS Services. Therefore, these managers thus face additional challenges, compared to most organizations, which derive from various factors:

1. Existence of multiple functions, such as providing health care to the population, maintaining fiscal solvency and constituting a primary employer in the community (Golden, 2006);
2. Convergence of professions, namely doctors, nurses, physiotherapists, pharmacists and administrators, and other diverse stakeholders (for example, users and the government itself), with incompatible interests and perspectives (Golden, 2006; Iles & Sutherland, 2001);
3. The interdependence of individuals and teams, whose goals depend on collaboration with other individuals or teams (Iles & Sutherland, 2001);
4. The power and autonomy of health professionals, whose decisions and performance largely influence both the quality-of-service provision and, influencing user satisfaction, such as health expenses (Golden, 2006);
5. The constant changes in the environment, especially in terms of the market, the global economy, social values and politics (Rego & Nunes, 2010; Applebaum & Wohl, 2000; Church et al., 1996);
6. Need to keep up with major technological changes in the health area, in terms of processes, diagnosis, treatment and IS (Iles & Sutherland, 2001; Applebaum & Wohl, 2000);
7. Growing demands of customer groups, with different needs, expectations and increasingly informed (Iles & Sutherland, 2001; Applebaum & Wohl, 2000);
8. Government and regulatory requirements regarding the performance and quality of health services provided (DGS, 2004-2010);
9. Investors' demands regarding performance and results (Applebaum & Wohl, 2000);
10. Lack of information needed to manage change processes in healthcare organizations (Golden, 2006);
11. Past change experiences of employees that had unintended and unintended consequences, giving rise to resistance to new change initiatives (Iles & Sutherland, 2001).

CHANGE MANAGEMENT AND HEALTH SERVICES

In fact, IS progressively support automation processes in most activities and in modernization. However, this modernization is related to the levels of innovation of the various economic sectors, in each of the organizations impacting the operational dynamics and their interactions with the market. Therefore, the introduction of technological innovations in the functioning of hospital units still requires structural, organizational, functional, informational, and decision-making adaptations.

The systemic perspective under which hospital operation and dynamics are due should make it possible to question, in each innovation and consequent need for adaptation, the existing status quo. This logic of approach must allow management to open up competitive opportunities for change. Competitive opportunities can be driven internally by the fact that innovations provide reductions in the cost structure or efficiency gains in organizational dynamics. However, when addressing the issue of change management, it should be emphasized that these benefits cannot be achieved if economic organizations cannot match the innovation potential achieved by their competitors. Change management includes, among other variables, the identification and management of the gap between a given organizational context and the desired one. The latter, the desired context, should be seen in the possibility of introducing innovation in processes, in systems integration, in the development of new products and services, in cultural change, in the introduction of new models and instruments.

As we are in an essentially digital age, the rate of applicability of changes is increasing. Therefore, whatever the change, it needs to be managed in all areas, namely the technological one. Therefore, this is a challenge both for IT departments, who need to manage projects of constant adaptation and innovation, as well as for top management, who need to deal with business requirements and people management in order to balance changes with new expectations and needs.

As a tool, methodologies are used, which make it possible to gather a set of world best practices for the operation of IS services. The methodologies provide Change Management guidelines that make it easier for IT professionals to implement and prioritize changes efficiently, without negative impacts to customers (users).In the field of management, innovation within the scope of change must be assimilated at the strategic level and, at that level, the frequent need to rethink organizational logic and dynamics to improve economic performance, the adequacy of communication with the market, the differentiation of the commercial offer, among others. The successful implementation of a change within the IS largely depends on the commitment and commitment of its users, as the reactions of end users to the introduction of changes in their daily work routines are critical success factors for any project, since the IS do not increase organizational performance per se, but with the help of users and managers.

In this way, the introduction or alteration of an information system implies a change process that, if not properly managed, can cause the project to fail, so when analyzing the influence of the IS in the change processes, it is concluded that the introduction of the information system is effectively relegated to the background. Thus, giving greater weight to the restructuring of processes and to people's awareness as core factors affecting change. In the first instance, when we talk about changes brought about by the information system, we are talking about cultural change in terms of user habits. For example, the simple automation of tasks causes profound changes in the internal organizational functioning, requiring extra care regarding internal communications (horizontal and vertical), as only in this way is it possible to help users to identify and understand the benefits that the change will provoke when the IS expansion to other functional areas. Change is inevitable and necessary, as the individual, organizations and society are destined to live with the transformations unequivocally. The process of change is made up of various technological innovations associated with knowledge and global competitiveness. IS provide organizations with a way to build and plan a greater connection with organizational processes, providing more agility in development, thus contributing to improved performance and decision support. When you want to make changes in an organization, managing this change is as relevant and precious as the project in its essence and object, so the expectations created by a process of change can go down substantially for the simple fact that users do not understand them their object, or effectively resist the project. The operationalization of the change must be preceded by the identification and evaluation of the factors associated with it. In addition to the set of steps presented in the different models for change management, it is necessary to ensure the presence of these projects or processes that have a very strong cultural dimension.

Understanding the existing culture, regarding formal and informal rules, policies, norms, and habits, represents a critical success factor in change management, therefore, and to corroborate this premise advocates the following phases (Albrecht et al. 2020; Lin et al. 2019; Giannoccaro 2018):

- Establish the need for change.
- Define the purpose of the planned change.
- Diagnose and analyze the current situation.
- Create recommendations.
- Detail the recommendations.
- Create a pilot based on these recommendations.
- Prepare roll-out recommendations.
- Distribute the recommendations.
- Measure, reinforce and redefine change.

Even so, it is necessary to mention that the IS are dynamic, so it is necessary that their implementation process is duly accompanied by a process of continuous and coordinated change using tools and methodologies that enable apply good practices, such as ITIL, constantly involving people, information, and technology.

Challenge to use Telehealth

According to Smith et al. (2020), the number of cases of coronavirus disease 2019 (COVID-19) Is increasing rapidly and, as of 11 March 2020, the World Health Organization has declared that this can be characterized as a pandemic. Outside of emergency situations, the overall uptake of telehealth has been slow and fragmented. Substantial efforts have gone into scaling-up the routine use of telehealth, often with limited success. In Australia, despite the introduction of generous financial incentives for specialist video consultations, telehealth represented less than 1% of all specialist consultations provided. The experience in the USA has been similar, where less than 1% of people living in rural areas have ever experienced telehealth. Reasons for the low uptake of telehealth are multifaceted and diverse, but factors such as clinician willingness, financial reimbursement and (re)organization of the health system may be to blame (Smith and Beretta 2021; Smith et al., 2020).

SOLUTIONS AND RECOMMENDATIONS

Once you know exactly what you want to achieve and why, you will need to determine the impacts of the change at various organizational levels. It is very useful to analyze the effect on each business unit. It is equally important to understand how changes cascade through the organizational structure to the employee. The information obtained in this analysis will help to plan the training and support needed to mitigate the impacts. All employees must be involved in the change management process. But the first step will be to define the key employees to whom you must communicate the changes. It is necessary to determine the most effective means of communication for the group or individually. The communication strategy should include a timeline of how the change will be incrementally communicated, key messages, as well as the communication channels you intend to use. With the message of change out in the open, it's important that your employees know they're going to be trained. It will allow them to gain the knowledge they need to operate efficiently as the change is implemented. The training may include a set of online microlearning modules or a face-to-face approach. For effective change management, it is also necessary to ensure that your company has a support team. It should help employees adapt to change and develop the behaviors and technical skills needed to achieve desired business results. Regardless of whether the changes result in redundancies or restructuring, you must view support as fundamental to the company's success. Throughout the process, a framework must be in place to measure the impact of changes on the business. It will ensure that there are opportunities for continuous reinforcement to create knowledge. It should also evaluate the change management plan to determine its effectiveness and document the experiences gained. Effective change management reduces the risk of the new system or other change being rejected by the company. In addition, it increases the teamwork required for the organization to accept change and operate more efficiently. Change management exists to help businesses plan for their transformations, rather than just reacting to them. Change management is the discipline that guides the agency to prepare, equip, and assist individuals to successfully adopt changes toward results for the organization. While all changes are unique and no two people are the same, it is evident that there are steps we can take to influence people in their metamorphoses. Change management provides a structured approach to helping your employees move from their current state to the future. There are basically three levels of change management. Even though it is a natural human psychological and physiological reaction to resist change, we are very resilient creatures. When we have support in times of change, we can be wonderfully adaptable. Individual change management requires understanding how people experience change and what needs to change. It also requires knowing what will make people transition successfully: what messages they need to hear and from whom, when is the best time to teach someone a new skill, how to instruct them to show new behaviors, and how to make those changes "stick to their own" in someone's work. While change happens at the individual level, it is virtually impossible for a project leader to manage change on a person-to-person basis. Organizational change management provides us with a guide with actions to take to impact the entire agency. This involves first identifying groups and people who will need to change because of your project, and how they will need to embrace these transitions.

This management encompasses the creation of a customized plan to ensure that impacted employees receive attention, leadership, and training to proceed with their processes. Driving successful individual transitions should be the primary focus of your organizational change management activities. This level corresponds to an organization's core competence, which provides competitive differentiation and the ability to effectively adapt to a constantly changing world. The enterprise's change management capability means that change is built into your agency's job competencies, structure, processes, projects, and leadership. In this way, process management is constantly applied to initiatives, leaders have the skills to guide teams in times of change, and employees know what to ask for to succeed. The result of a communication agency capable of managing change is individuals who embrace change faster and organizations better able to respond to market changes, launch strategic initiatives and adopt new management technologies with less impact on production. In this world where change is imperative, not adapting to the new times is being forgotten and left behind. But it's not enough just to adhere to all the trends that appear, but to have full control over the transitions your agency will go through. In this way, change management generates several benefits for the optimization of the company. Every transformation involves personal issues, as new leaders will be summoned to participate in the process, the roles of some teams and collaborators are changed and new skills will have to be developed. This can cause employees to look to the future of the business with uncertainty and become resistant to proposed changes. Keep in mind that ignoring the human side carries a huge risk for the company. When the idea is to implement management software, for example, and the focus is only on meeting the technical requirements, leaving aside the issues related to the adoption and use of the solution, there are chances that the team cannot handle the tool well which results in losses for the agency. Therefore, dealing with these issues reactively, that is, thinking about them only when they become a problem, is too dangerous. In this sense, it is essential to carry out a formal approach to change management, starting with the leadership teams and, later, working on actions with leaders and key stakeholders. Everything must be done in advance and with strategic planning. It is necessary to collect a lot of data, carefully analyze and plan the execution of the redesign of the company's strategies, processes, or systems. Ideally, the change management approach should be integrated into internal program development and decision-making strategies.

Expands Possibilities for Innovation

Organizations that apply well-established change management have a greater entrepreneurial orientation — which means that they are always researching and integrating new things, which increases the chances of innovation and business growth. Those companies that are not afraid to change cannot be compared with the "discouraged" companies, who have been pushing the same processes with their stomachs for several years due to the fear of innovating and failing. Having the courage to change is an act that is rewarded by new opportunities and above-average growth.

Improves the Team's Quality of Life

A change management that considers human issues aims to establish processes that help improve the activities provided by the team, eliminating bureaucracy, and improving time management, for example. All this increases the quality of life of employees, as it excludes stressful factors, in addition to facilitating the process of adapting to changes. By proactively supporting employees in times of change, you show with actions that you value them, which stimulates engagement and motivation daily.

Benefits Internal Communication

Communication failures cause rework and cause losses for companies. In some cases, change leaders err in believing that people are inside their heads and feel as they do that it's time to change. Even the best change programs offer no guarantee of success. Therefore, they reinforce not only the main messages, but also regular advice on simple points. One aspect that every company has to understand is that communication flows from the top down. With this, management makes business decisions, communicates to those who occupy management positions, and the information is directed to employees at the right time. For this, it is necessary to set up a large communication scheme, which uses different channels and often transmits redundant data. Such actions avoid the occurrence of failures and delays in deliveries.

Increases Profitability

The vision theory, which is based on resources, sees the company as a set of resources, including human, material, and financial ones. In view of this, the agency learns to strategically organize all these items, being able to establish the necessary changes. This theory also points to another benefit of change management: the ability to evaluate and reorganize all the company's resources, joining them in a strategic way, according to the interests of the enterprise. This allows for the elimination of unnecessary expenses and better investments, increasing the company's profits.

Raises Productivity

By defining new processes and improving the company's strategies, value can be added to the business. This is because change is only chosen if it provides a competitive advantage for the company. However, none of this works if there is no employee engagement. In change management, teams are prepared and trained to interact with new processes and structures, so there is little impact on productivity and a quick recovery of the desired results by the agency is also guaranteed.

Generates Competitive Advantage

Undoubtedly, one of the great advantages of understanding what change management really is and applying it correctly in the company is the increase in competitiveness. The great speed with which people can access information and new technologies today, plus the characteristics of the new global economy, are forcing organizations to quickly change the way they carry out their activities locally and remotely. The company that cannot adapt and keep up with the dynamism of the market ends up being left behind — after all, there will always be a competitor that successfully promotes change. In this scenario, agencies must react quickly and efficiently to follow market changes, without impacting productivity. Employees need to be empowered to learn to deal with new processes in order to reduce resistance to innovation. Discuss solutions and recommendations in dealing with the issues, controversies, or problems presented in the preceding section.

FUTURE RESEARCH DIRECTIONS

This chapter is about the failure of general programs of change and, due to the scarcity of empirical research on the management of change within organizations, it is recommended that more research on the management of organizational change is conducted. In this sense, research of nature exploration should be prioritized to increase knowledge of the management of the organizational change. These studies should allow a critical analysis of the factor's success of change management. It is also suggested a work that elaborates indicators to assess and measure the success rate of change initiatives in organizations. "As Change Managers today, we have access to more information than ever before, and the amount of available information is growing exponentially. As a profession, our collective competency is higher than ever. However, many organizations say that change is not done well and/or the leadership of change is lacking and/or that change isn't happening fast enough." Change is an element present in organizations and affects, the business structure. There is a consensus among the authors studied that that the pace of change in today's business environments is constantly evolving. Therefore, successful change management is a necessary and desired skill for all the organizations. Perhaps investigate a construct named performance to achieve some more efficient assumptions.

CONCLUSION

Health organizations manage a diversity and heterogeneity of essential information for the performance of their sensitive public activity, in the provision of health care. The paradigm shift in healthcare has profoundly changed behavior and the way healthcare organizations relate to and understand their surroundings, thus triggering needs and new forms of internal organization. The management of hospitals, as top management bodies, reveal strategic characteristics of concern with the impacts of change and the application of best practice methodologies. it is possible to discern that there is a strong concern on the part of Management to ensure a strategic change management policy within the IS that is based on a methodology, in this case ITIL, which makes it possible to apply good practices. While we may not be able to accurately predict the timing of natural disasters and infectious pandemics, we can be sure that they will present again in the future. The COVID-19 experience is not a first, and nor will it be the last. Telehealth does have a critical role in emergency responses (Krishnamurthy, 2020).

REFERENCES

Alaerds, R., Grove, S., Besteman, S., & Bilderbeek, P. (2017). *The Foundations of our Digital Economy.* Wouter Pegtel & Splend.

Albrecht, S. L., Connaughton, S., Foster, K., Furlong, S., & Yeow, C. J. L. (2020). Change Engagement, Change Resources, and Change Demands: A Model for Positive Employee Orientations to Organizational Change. *Frontiers in Psychology, 11*, 531944. doi:10.3389/fpsyg.2020.531944 PMID:33240144

Andrew, J., Haanæs, K., Michael, D. C., Sirkin, H. L., & Taylor, A. (2009). *Making Hard Decisions in the Downturn.* Consulting Group.

Applebaum, S., & Wohl, L. (2000). Transformation or change: Some prescriptions for health care organizations. *Managing Service Quality, 10*(5), 279–298. doi:10.1108/09604520010345768

Barsh, J., Capozzi, M. M., & Davidson, J. (2008). Leadership and innovation. *The McKinsey Quarterly, 1*, 36.

Cartlidge, A., Hanna, A., Rudd, C., Macfarlane, I., Windebank, J., & Rance, S. (2007). An introductory overview of ITIL V3. *The UK Chapter of the itSMF, 64.*

Church, A. H., Siegal, W., Javitch, M., Waclawski, J., & Burke, W. W. (1996). Managing organizational change: What you don't know might hurt you. *Career Development International, 1*(2), 25–30. doi:10.1108/13620439610114315

Gawke, J. C., Gorgievski, M. J., & Bakker, A. B. (2019). Measuring intrapreneurship at the individual level: Development and validation of the Employee Intrapreneurship Scale (EIS). *European Management Journal, 37*(6), 806–817. doi:10.1016/j.emj.2019.03.001

Giannoccaro, I. (2018). Centralized vs. decentralized supply chains: The importance of decision maker's cognitive ability and resistance to change. *Industrial Marketing Management*, *73*, 59–69. Advance online publication. doi:10.1016/j.indmarman.2018.01.034

Golden, B. (2006). Change: Transforming health organizations. *Healthcare Quarterly*, *10*(sp), 10–19. doi:10.12927/hcq..18490 PMID:17163111

Hashem, G. (2020). Organizational enablers of business process reengineering implementation An empirical study on the service sector. *International Journal of Productivity and Performance Management*. . doi:10.1108/IJPPM-11-2018-0383

Iles, V., & Sutherland, K. (2001). *Organizational Change: A Review for Health Care Managers, Professionals and Researchers*. London: NHS Service Delivery and Organization R&D, NCCSDO.

Kaplan, B., & Duchon, D. (1994). Combining Qualitative and Quantitative Methods in Information Systems Research: A Case Study. In J. Anderson, C. Aydin, & S. Jay (Eds.), *Evaluating Health Care Information Systems: Methods and Applications*. Sage.

Krishnamurthy, S. (2020). The Future of Business Education: A Commentary in the Shadow of the Covid-19 Pandemic. *Journal of Business Research*, *117*, 1–5. doi:10.1016/j.jbusres.2020.05.034 PMID:32501309

Lin, H., Qu, T., Li, L., & Tian, Y. (2019). The paradox of stability and change: A case study. *Chinese Management Studies*, *14*(1), 185–213. doi:10.1108/CMS-10-2018-0725

Manesh, M. F., Pellegrini, M. M., Marzi, G., & Dabic, M. (2020). Knowledge management in the fourth industrial revolution: Mapping the literature and scoping future avenues. *IEEE Transactions on Engineering Management*, *68*(1), 289–300. doi:10.1109/TEM.2019.2963489

Nasiri, M., Saunila, M., Ukko, J., Rantala, T., & Rantanen, H. (2020). Shaping digital innovation via digital-related capabilities. *Information Systems Frontiers*, 1–18.

Rego, G., & Nunes, R. (2010). *Health Management* [Gestão da Saúde]. Prata & Rodrigues.

Smith, A. C., Thomas, E., Snoswell, C. L., Haydon, H., Mehrotra, A., Clemensen, J., & Caffery, L. J. (2020). Telehealth for global emergencies: Implications for coronavirus disease 2019 (COVID-19). *Journal of Telemedicine and Telecare*, *26*(5), 309–313. doi:10.1177/1357633X20916567 PMID:32196391

Smith, P., & Beretta, M. (2021). The gordian knot of practicing digital transformation: Coping with emergent paradoxes in ambidextrous organizing structures. *Journal of Product Innovation Management*, *38*(1), 166–191. doi:10.1111/jpim.12548

ADDITIONAL READING

Dwivedi, Y. K., Hughes, D. L., Coombs, C., Constantiou, I., Duan, Y., Edwards, J. S., Gupta, B., Lal, B., Misra, S., Prashant, P., Raman, R., Rana, N. P., Sharma, S. K., & Upadhyay, N. (2020). Impact of COVID-19 pandemic on information management research and practice: Transforming education, work and life. *International Journal of Information Management*, *55*, 102211. doi:10.1016/j.ijinfomgt.2020.102211

Fahrenbach, F., & Kragulj, F. (2019). *The Ever-Changing Personality: Revisiting the Concept of Triple-Loop Learning*. doi:10.1108/TLO-01-2019-0016

Geada, N. (2021). Management of Change: Pandemic Impacts in IT. *International Journal of Enterprise Information Systems*, *17*(2), 92–104. doi:10.4018/IJEIS.2021040105

Geada, N., & Anunciação, P. (2020). *Change Management Projects in Information Systems: The Impact of the Methodology Information Technology Infrastructure Library (ITIL) (change-management-projects-in-information-systems)*. Https://Services.Igi-Global.Com/Resolvedoi/Resolve.Aspx?Doi=10.4018/978-1-5225-9993-7.Ch011

Hu, Z., Tariq, S., & Zayed, T. (2021). A comprehensive review of acoustic based leak localization method in pressurized pipelines. *Mechanical Systems and Signal Processing*, *161*, 107994. doi:10.1016/j.ymssp.2021.107994

Kay, M. C., Burroughs, J., Askew, S., Bennett, G. G., Armstrong, S., & Steinberg, D. M. (2018). Digital weight loss intervention for parents of children being treated for obesity: A prospective cohort feasibility trial. *Journal of Medical Internet Research*, *20*(12), e11093. doi:10.2196/11093 PMID:30573449

Kling, R., & Lamb, R. (1999). IT and Organizational Change in Digital Economies. A Socio-Technical Approach, 17-25.

Kondakci, Y., Kurtay, M. Z., & Caliskan, O. (2019). Antecedents of continuous change in educational organizations. *International Journal of Educational Management*. Advance online publication. doi:10.1108/IJEM-11-2018-0349

Koschate-Fischer, N., Hoyer, W. D., Stokburger-Sauer, N. E., & Engling, J. (2018). Do life events always lead to change in purchase? The mediating role of change in consumer innovativeness, the variety seeking tendency, and price consciousness. *Journal of the Academy of Marketing Science*, *46*(3), 516–536. doi:10.100711747-017-0548-3

Kucirkova, N., Littleton, K., & Kyparissiadis, A. (2018). The influence of children's gender and age on children's use of digital media at home. *British Journal of Educational Technology*, *49*(3), 545–559. doi:10.1111/bjet.12543

Movahed, S. M. A., & Sarmah, A. K. (2021). Global trends and characteristics of nano-and micro-bubbles research in environmental engineering over the past two decades: A scientometric analysis. *The Science of the Total Environment*, *785*, 147362. doi:10.1016/j.scitotenv.2021.147362 PMID:33957600

Plugge, A., Nikou, S., & Bouwman, H. (2020). The revitalization of service orientation: A business services model. *Business Process Management Journal*.

Schiavo, G., Leonardi, C., & Zancanaro, M. (2020). *Values and Practices behind Collaborative Childcare in Knowledge-based Organizations*. Academic Press.

Silk, D., Mazzali, B., Gargalo, C. L., Pinelo, M., Udugama, I. A., & Mansouri, S. S. (2020). A decision-support framework for techno-economic-sustainability assessment of resource recovery alternatives. *Journal of Cleaner Production*, *266*, 121854. doi:10.1016/j.jclepro.2020.121854

Thomson, L., Kamalaldin, A., Sjödin, D., & Parida, V. (2022). A maturity framework for autonomous solutions in manufacturing firms: The interplay of technology, ecosystem, and business model. *The International Entrepreneurship and Management Journal*, *18*(1), 125–152. doi:10.100711365-020-00717-3

Varriale, V., Cammarano, A., Michelino, F., & Caputo, M. (2021). New organizational changes with blockchain: A focus on the supply chain. *Journal of Organizational Change Management*, *34*(2), 420–438. doi:10.1108/JOCM-08-2020-0249

Wimelius, H., Mathiassen, L., Holmström, J., & Keil, M. (2021). A paradoxical perspective on technology renewal in digital transformation. *Information Systems Journal*, *31*(1), 198–225. doi:10.1111/isj.12307

KEY TERMS AND DEFINITIONS

Change Management: It is a process of allocating resources, to transform the organization, with the objective of improving its effectiveness.

Digital Sustainability: In concrete terms, this means that digital information must be financially, organizationally, and technically modifiable and available to all.

Digital Transformation: It is a change of mentality that companies go through to become more modern and keep up with the technological advances that are constantly emerging.

Digitalization: Is the process of turning analog processes and physical objects into digital.

Information Systems: The collection of technical and human resources that provide the storage, computing, distribution, and communication for the information required by all or some part of an enterprise.

Information Technology Infrastructure Library (ITIL): ITIL, an acronym for Information Technology Infrastructure Library, is a best practice guide, developed by the British government's Central Computer and Telecommunications Agency (CCTA), on managing of information technology services that focuses on aligning services with business needs. Developed in the 1980s with last update in 2019 (ITIL 4) The guide underpins the foundations of ISO/IEC 20000, the international standard for managing IT services (International Service Management Standard), becoming the most widely adopted IT service management in companies. ITIL describes processes, procedures, tasks, and checklists that are neither organization-specific nor technology-specific but can be applied by an organization to establish integration with the organization's strategy, delivering value and maintaining a minimum level of competence. It allows the organization to establish a baseline from which to plan, implement and measure. It is used to demonstrate compliance and measure improvement. There is no independent third-party compliance assessment available for ITIL compliance in an organization. ITIL certification is available to individuals only.

Processes: Integration of components for collection, storage, and processing of data of which the data is used to provide information, contribute to knowledge as well as digital products that facilitate decision making.

Developing Machine Learning Skills With No-Code Machine Learning Tools

Emmanuel Djaba

Ghana Institute of Management and Public Administration, Ghana

Joseph Budu

 https://orcid.org/0000-0002-0003-5807

Ghana Institute of Management and Public Administration, Ghana

INTRODUCTION

Building a machine learning (ML) model involves multiple complex skill sets. In the most minimal form, the standard protocol for building and using ML models involves at least three steps. Firstly, data must be collected and preprocessed. Secondly, a model must be trained using the preprocessed data, and thirdly, the trained model must be deployed in some form of application (Ramos et al., 2020). Generally, each step in this process requires advanced technical skills such as data collection, data preprocessing, model training, and model performance evaluation. In addition to their complexity, these required skills are cognitively demanding to acquire and use and are thus often restricted to experts. If we take into account the fact that, most models have to be updated regularly to accommodate for evolutions in the data (concept drift), the entire ML process then becomes expensive and unattainable for organizations and individuals without extensive resources and skills.

Against this backdrop, No-code ML (NML) tools have emerged as avenues for individuals to build ML models without possessing the requisite technical knowledge and skills (García-Ortiz and Sánchez-Viteri, 2021). This is because NML tools commonly exist as visual programming tools for ML (von Wangenheim et al., 2021). Hence NML tools considerably reduce the cognitive effort needed to create ML models. The reduction in effort is achieved because users focus on the logic of the system being developed instead of the textual elements (programming language syntax and semantics). More specifically, NML tools allow users to train ML models either by using a drag-and-drop interface to place visual elements on a canvas; or by specifying input, output parameters, and values in a few clicks. Furthermore, where visual elements are employed, they are largely used in the form of blocks or flows. This approach improves users' ability to learn by helping them prevent errors and improving their understanding of the concepts at hand. Consequently, NML tools allow one to build models relatively quickly. Additionally, NML tools reduce the financial barriers to using ML. This is mainly due to their features, mode of packaging, and distribution. Quite a substantial number of NML tools are free to download and free to use. Also, some are available over the web as cloud-based tools, and as such, they substantially reduce the necessity of using specialized hardware for training.

Naturally, the emergence of NML tools has generated discourse in academic research. Extant literature highlights the potential of no-code ML tools in developing relevant ML skills, knowledge, and attitudes. For instance, Lao (2020) provides empirical evidence of the use of NML tools in teaching high-school students how to create ML models and troubleshoot their performance. Similarly, García et al. (2020) and Rodríguez-García et al. (2021) identify ML knowledge and computational skills as possible learn-

DOI: 10.4018/978-1-7998-9220-5.ch097

ing outcomes of introducing NML tools to high school students. The foregoing indicates that ML skills can be learned using NML tools. Despite this invaluable knowledge, what remains unclear is how NML tools contribute to the acquisition of ML skills. From a technology affordances perspective, the authors conceive that there is a gap in the explanation of how the affordances generated when learners interact with NML tools, lead to the development of ML skills. An explanation that fills this gap exposes the positive mechanisms embedded in NML tools that lead to the generation of ML skills. Subsequently, developers of NML tools will be able to identify and grow these mechanisms to maximize learning outcomes. Thus, in this chapter, we draw on the technology affordance theory to explain how NML tools afford the development of ML skills.

This chapter has six sections. The first section provides the rationale and motivation for this chapter, while the second provides an overview of NML and reviews relevant literature on the subject. The third section expounds on the theory of technology affordances and constraints while the fourth section outlines our methodology for this work. The fifth, and sixth sections present the core findings of the chapter by covering the results, analysis, and discussions respectively. To conclude, we identify avenues for future research and summarize our arguments and findings.

BACKGROUND

In the introductory section, we have seen that NML tools allow users without computer programming skills and knowledge to develop ML algorithms and projects to solve problems. However, not all NML tools are made the same. While some enable data preprocessing, others focus exclusively on model training and deployment. During model training, an interface is provided for users to load data. The generally accepted forms of data include text, audio, video, and images (Carney et al., 2020). After loading data, the type of ML task to be performed is selected. Here, the user may choose to perform clustering, image classification, sound classification, and so forth. It should be noted that while some NML tools provide access to a wide variety of ML tasks, others focus on enabling very specific tasks. After the task to be performed has been selected, the user can train the model for the selected task using the data provided. Finally, the user can evaluate the model to determine how well it performs. Support for model evaluation is provided in different ways. Some tools enable evaluation by providing detailed graphs on a host of preselected evaluation metrics. Alternatively, other tools allow users to evaluate models by trying them out on sample input data to determine how often the model performs the task correctly (Ozan, 2021).

In supporting model deployment NML tools enable users to export the trained models in easily reusable formats. Usually, this is done by saving models in formats supported by popular ML frameworks and libraries. Thus, it is common to see NML tools export trained models to formats supported by popular ML libraries such as Tensorflow. Consequently, NML tools can support a so-called "low-code" mode of ML deployment where no computer programming is done for training models, but some code is written to incorporate trained models into other computer programs (Carvalho & Harris, 2020).

At the core, NML tools have the potential to enable the wider ML community to overcome three major problems. Firstly, they can address the dire, and yet unsatisfied need for ML experts in various industries. Since its inception, the initial adoption of ML has been by technology-focused organizations such as Google and Microsoft. However, over time, a wide array of organizations have begun to adopt ML. From exemplars in governance, banking, health, and the retail industry (Lamberti et al., 2019; Mikalef et al., 2021), the potential of ML to improve operations and create value in new and interesting ways has been highlighted. However, this rise in adoption has not been accompanied by a similar rise in the number of qualified ML experts who would aid ML adopters and innovators in their quest for value generation. Subsequently, the rise of NML could lead to a reduction in the level of expertise needed to be productive with ML. This then means that with minimal training, organizations can start exploring ML and developing appropriate use cases that could lead to the generation of value. Furthermore, the ability of NML tools to facilitate such experimentation at a relatively low cost would facilitate organizational adoption as evidence exists that experimentation facilitates adoption (Kolbjørnsrud et al., 2017).

Secondly, NML tools have the potential to democratize ML. Democratizing ML has been extensively discussed in the existing literature. While these discussions focus on diverse perspectives and conceptualizations, they usually revolve around the central idea of empowerment. For Ahmed et al. (2020) democratizing ML involves dispersing the high concentration of ML technology, power, and expertise that exists in a few powerful organizations to reduce their propensity for creating marginalization and inequalities. In effect, Ahmed et al. (2020) advocate for the empowerment of nations and organizations that have not been historically dominant in ML to aid them to excel in the forthcoming fourth industrial revolution where advanced technologies like ML would be pivotal in value creation. Similar to Ahmed et al. (2020), Bagrow (2020) argues for empowering non-ML-experts who are often instrumental in generating and sometimes labeling the data used for training models but are not able to use the same data they generate to meet their own needs. By their nature, NML tools respond to the views expressed by both authors.

Finally, NML tools have the potential to facilitate the teaching and learning of ML. Across the world, several nations have realized the potential of ML to radically change the future. As such, they have developed programs and policies to ensure that they are better positioned to maximize the benefits of ML. One of such common policies involves public education on the development and use of ML. In this regard, training programs have been developed to enable students at various levels of education learn ML (Touretzky et al., 2019). As a component of such programs, NML tools have proven to be effective in teaching and learning ML knowledge and skills, especially when used in an active learning approach. In such scenarios, students learn by developing, using, analyzing, and remixing (García-Ortiz and Sánchez-Viteri, 2021). Furthermore, students with non-technical backgrounds can also use these tools to build simple models various tasks without necessarily understanding the details of ML. Thus, NML enables ML education on a wide scale that will enable a wide array of users to become conscientious creators and users of intelligent systems. In the next section, we introduce the technology affordance and constraints theory as a lens to explain how NML tools lead to the generation of ML skills.

TECHNOLOGY AFFORDANCES AND CONSTRAINTS

Generally, different users may perceive and use an information system differently. The different perceptions and use may consequently lead to the generation of different outcomes. For instance, crashworthiness managers at Autoworks perceived CrashLab – a mesh model pre-processing tool – differently from engineers and management (Leonardi, 2011). Hence, differing users' perceptions result from differing users' goals. These differing goals affect how users interact with a system, and subsequently, the related outcomes. Understanding the outcomes associated with the introduction and use of information systems in general, and NML tools specifically, can be achieved by uncovering their associated generative mechanisms. Generative mechanisms are "the causal powers and liabilities of objects or relations" (Sayer, 2010). These mechanisms can be uncovered by working backward from observable empirical events to the underlying mechanism that could have logically produced those events (Danermark et al., 2019).

By digging behind the observable empirical events to identify generative mechanisms, we gain causal explanations for how and why things happen (Volkoff & Strong, 2013). Consequently, in searching for the mechanisms that generate the attainment of ML skills when learners interact with NML tools, we need a theoretical lens that would be most useful.

In information systems research, the concept of affordances has been proposed as "a helpful way to conceive of the generative mechanisms associated with technical artifacts used in organizations. This is because affordances are particularly appropriate for middle-range theories that involve actors (with their intentions and skills) and technical objects (with their specific features)" (Volkoff & Strong, 2013). Consequently, prominent scholars have accepted and drawn on the concept of affordances as an analytical construct to identify and analyze mechanisms. For instance, the concept of affordances formed the foundation of a theoretical framework to identify four functional affordances that originate in the pursuit of environmental sustainability transformations using information systems (Seidel et al., 2013). Seidel and colleagues conceptualized two categories of affordances, namely, organizational sensemaking affordances, and sustainable practicing affordances. Each broad category has two functional affordances; organizational sensemaking affordances have reflective disclosure and information democratization, while sustainable practicing affordances include output management and delocalization. Delocalisation affordances enable work practices to become location-independent, thereby reducing the negative sustainability impact arising from moving resources to the location of work. Other scholars also used affordances to conceptualize connective affordances as a way of explaining how user interdependence affects what users can do with technology, specifically social media (Vaast et al., 2017). By looking at technologies as sets of affordances and constraints for particular actors, IS researchers can explain how and why a technology creates different outcomes in different contexts, thus creating deeper and richer general and substantive IS theories (Majchrzak et al., 2016). We define and discuss the components of affordances in the following sections.

Understanding Technology Affordances and Constraints

The affordance lens is particularly useful for understanding the mechanisms that arise when users relate with technology because both the technology and the users are explicitly accounted for concurrently, but distinctively (Bygstad et al., 2016). Affordance theory is based on the ideas of Gestalt theory and originated from ecological psychology (Gibson, 1969, 1986). The theory's central concept of affordance defines the possibilities and limits for action that material objects offer to actors. Gibson coined and included the term affordance as a core concept in his theory of ecologically based visual perception, which explains how organisms perceive and interact with their environments. He believed that an explanation of visual perception had to include both the affordances of the external environment and the psychological process within an individual. He states that:

The affordances of the environment are what it offers the animal, what it provides or furnishes, either for good or ill. ...I mean by it something that refers to both the environment and the animal in a way that no existing term does. It implies the complementarity of the animal and the environment (Gibson, 1986)

Hence, the concept underpins functional explanations of how material objects are implicated in human activity. Functional explanations identify the group of an object's features that meet an actor's goals, because its presence in the past, generated some positive consequences (Hovorka et al., 2008). Other scholars have also suggested the "affordance" concept as a theoretical approach for specifying the

D

possibilities and limitations for action that different features of an IT artifact as a material object offer to an individual user (Leonardi, 2012, 2013; Vaast et al., 2017). From the foregoing, we can imply that IT objects exist because a particular functional need was identified for which the artifact was designed and implemented. However, the intentions of an IT artifact's designer are not always understood by its users, nor realized in use nor are understood or shared by the artifact's users. Instead, users can use some of the IT's features and ignore others or work around others based on their own goals. We propose that the intended and unintended consequences of technology uses or workarounds are realized in a three-stage process. The first stage is *familiarisation* i.e. users' recognition of the IT artifact's potential to meet their goals. The second stage is *utilization*, during which the user experiments with those features to achieve a goal. Further during the third stage, *administration*, the user settles on and can manage the features and use of a specific NML tool to manage ML projects. These three processes culminate in the user's attainment of ML skills. According to Lao (2020), the necessary achievable ML skills include (i) the ability to decipher when using ML would be appropriate in solving problems; (ii) the ability to plan a solution to identified ML problems; (iii) the ability to create ML artifacts; (iv) the ability to analyze the intentions and results of ML; (v) the ability to critically engage with the ML community; and finally (vi) the ability to engage in independent ML learning. While this set of skills may not be exhaustive, we argue that they provide appropriate benchmarks for evaluating and planning ML training.

METHODOLOGY

As stated in the foregoing, this work draws on the theory of technology affordances and constraints to identify the generative mechanisms that NML tools possess. Subsequently, we explain how these mechanisms can lead to the generation of ML skills. To achieve our goals, this work proceeds in three steps. Firstly, we identify publicly available NML tools. Secondly, a sample of these tools is selected and subjected to qualitative analysis. Finally, we present the findings from our report below.

In selecting NML tools for this work, we first performed a Google search using the keywords "no-code ML" and "no-code AI". Our initial search returned 17 tools. Next, we filtered the results to exclude tools that were developed for specific use cases such as RunwayML (a tool for editing videos) and Nanonets (a tool for automating data entry). Also, we removed tools that could neither be used with the Windows operating system nor over the web through a browser. Finally, we randomly selected two applications from the remaining ones. The final tools used for this study are thus Lobe and Teachable Machine. The sample applications were extensively used for one month each to gather enough evidence for their evaluation. Subsequently, evaluation was performed using artifact analysis since it provides an appropriate method of investigating man-made artifacts. Thus, we draw on Saldana & Omasta (2017) to perform our analysis using two frames. Firstly, for each of the graphical user interfaces (GUI) of a selected artifact, we analyze each element on the interface – an individual element – then subsequently, then together with the other elements. This enables us to determine the tasks that can be performed with the interface and how the relationships between elements can generate or restrict affordances. Secondly, we analyzed the major processes that each tool supports to enable us to connect tasks performed on the interface with more conceptual actions required during ML. The following section outlines our results for each of the tools studied.

RESULTS

Overview of Selected Tools

Lobe

Lobe is a free desktop application developed by Microsoft to make it easy to train ML models. It was first launched in October 2020 (Microsoft, 2021). At the time of writing, it only supports image classification. Lobe enables users to quickly create and label datasets by dragging and dropping images into the application. After the images have been labeled, the application trains a model privately on the user's computer without uploading the data to the cloud. The models are trained automatically after images are labeled and as such do not require user input in any way. The trained model can be evaluated by uploading previously unused images for prediction. For each test image, the model predicts its class based on the available labels. The user then has a chance to provide feedback on whether the predicted label is right or wrong. If the predicted label is wrong, the model is instantly retrained with the corrected label as provided by the user. Finally, Lobe enables users to export the trained model in formats supported by popular machine learning frameworks and programming libraries.

Teachable Machine

Teachable Machine is a web-based application that was initially developed by Google in 2017 to provide people with an avenue to explore machine learning without writing computer programs. The initial version released in 2017 focused exclusively on image classification with 3 prelabelled classes. Currently, the application has been expanded to support image, sound, and pose classification with an unlimited number of classes. To use the tool, a user has to navigate to the Teachable machine website and create a project. For each project, the user would first have to indicate the type of data that would be used for training. Subsequently, the user is sent to an interface where they can upload and label training data. The uploaded data is used to train a model which the user can then test with sample input. Similar to Lobe, for each sample provided, Teachable Machine predicts the class of the input and provides a level of confidence for that prediction. However, unlike Lobe, Teachable Machine provides the option for advanced evaluation and tuning of the model during training. Users can specify training parameters such as the number of epochs, batch size, and learning rate. Also, they can evaluate trained models using a confusion matrix and a loss per epoch graph.

ANALYSIS AND FINDINGS

A close evaluation of the selected artefacts reveals that, while the interface of each artifact is organized differently, there is a significant amount of overlap in the processes that they enable users to perform. Subsequently, we identify 11 processes that can be performed with both artifacts. Of these processes, 10 are common to both Lobe and Teachable Machine while 1 is restricted to Lobe. We outline and discuss the processes below.

In this study, we find that features of NML tools enable users to learn about the fundamentals of ML. For Lobe, this is made possible by viewing the video tutorial which can be accessed by clicking on the "Tour" button. Also, through the frequently asked questions (FAQ) feature, users can learn how to properly use the tool. Furthermore, users are also able to view sample projects. These sample projects are either provided by the developers of the tool as inspiration to new users or, provided by the community as successful use cases. Beyond the learning-related processes outlined in the foregoing, NML tools also enable users to train, evaluate and export ML models. While Lobe automatically starts training a model when images are added to the dataset of a project, Teachable Machine allows users to fine-tune model training by providing the ability to set the learning rate, epoch, and batch size. Also, both tools make it possible to export trained models and well-labeled datasets for use in external applications. Finally, NML tools possess features that enable users to manage individual ML projects as well as to manage the tool itself. For instance, through the menu feature, NML tools selected for this study enable users to send feedback to the developers and set their preferences for using the tool. Also, the menu feature enables users to create, save and update individual ML projects. In addition to the processes outlined above, Lobe enables users to perform one more process that is unique to it. By linking to a Reddit group dedicated to the tool, Lobe enables users to engage with each other in a virtual community. To summarize, we present tables 1 and 2 below. Table 1 lists some processes and the features that enable them whereas table 2 depicts the actions users take with each tool and the processes related to these actions.

Table 1. Tool features and processes

Tool	Feature	Description
Teachable Machine	Menu	Helps the user to manage the tool
	FAQ	Teaches the user about ML
	Landing Page	Teaches the user about ML
	Made with Teachable Machine	Users can view sample ML projects
Microsoft Lobe	Tour	Teaches the user about the ML tool
	Documentation	Teaches the user about ML
	Examples	Users can view sample ML projects
	Community	Enables users to engage with the ML Community

Table 2. Tool features and processes

Process	Related feature in Lobe	Related feature in Teachable Machine
A. Learning ML	Click on a button and get directed to the web page to watch the Lobe Tour video	Click on a video player to watch a video titled "What is Teachable Machine"
B. Learning about the Tool		
C. View Potential Projects	Click on a button and get redirected to the examples page on the website	View example projects onsite
D. Package model for external use	Click on a button to open a window. Select format for export of model	Click on a button to export the model to TensorFlowjs or TensorFlow for python
E. Create and label training data	Click on a to open a dialog box. Then upload image(s) and apply labels.	Click a button to capture from image web camera or import images from the computer
F. Assess model performance	View information about model accuracy in the project window	Click a button to view graphs of model performance
G. Train model	Training happens automatically after images are loaded	Click a button to perform training
H. Engage with ML Community	Click a button to be redirected to a virtual community	-
I. Use the model to make predictions	Click on a button to open a dialog box. Then, upload an image or take a picture.	Click on a button to capture images from a web camera or import images from a file
J. Manage the tool	Click on a button to check for software updates	Click on a button to open a dialog box. Type in feedback and hit send
K. Manage ML project.	Click on a button to start a new ML project	Click on a button to open a project from Google Drive

DISCUSSIONS

In this section, we analyze our findings and identify the affordances NML tools provide for the development of ML skills. Furthermore, we also explain how the affordances identified can lead to the generation of ML skills.

Categorizing Processes into Affordances

Our findings suggest that the processes outlined in the preceding section lead to the formation of three categories of affordances. We identify these affordances as familiarization affordances, utilization affordances, and, administrative affordances. Familiarization affordances are offered when the user is either learning the fundamentals of ML, learning about the NML tool being used or when the user views sample ML projects. These three processes clarify the concept of ML to the user and among other things, enable the user to identify the role that the tool plays in developing ML models. Also, by viewing sample projects, a user may develop an understanding of what types of problems are ripe for exploitation with ML. Utilization affordances refer to the opportunities the NML tool presents for creating and sharing ML artifacts. Thus, utilization affordances are supported by the following processes: creating labeled datasets, training a model, assessing model performance, exporting models for external use, using the model to make predictions, and engaging with the ML community. We add community engagement to this group because through it, a user can share completed projects, participate in the discussion of the relevant issue to the ML community and even acquire or share software, models, and other ML artifacts. Finally, administration affordances refer to the processes that allow the user to effectively use the NML tool. They include processes for managing the tool and those for creating, updating, and deleting ML projects. Table 3 outlines the affordances and associated processes.

Table 3. Affordances and processes

Familiarization	Utilization	Administration
Learning about ML	Package model for external use	Manage the tool
Learning about the tool	Create and label training data.	Manage a project.
View potential projects	Assess model performance	
	Train model	
	Engage with ML Community	
	Use model	

From Affordances to Skills

In earlier sections, we have outlined six relevant skills that ML practitioners should have. In this section, we would argue that the affordances identified in this work can lead to the generation of these skills.

As a skill, ML advocacy refers to the ability of ML practitioners to engage with organizations, communities, and governments on issues that are pertinent to ML. These issues include policies, the creation and use of ML products as well as ML education. To possess this skill, an individual must understand the ML process and be able to identify the direct or indirect implications of using ML. Thus, the process of learning about ML afforded by NML tools can be instrumental in the development of this skill. For instance, on the homepage of Teachable Machine, there are links to resources that discuss the concept of machine learning and its societal impact. Similarly, the documentation feature in Lobe contains links to similar resources. Thus, we envision that learning about ML can lead to the formation of ML advocacy skills.

Secondly, aside from ML advocacy, another important skill for practitioners to possess is the ability to determine which problems can be addressed with ML. Given the hype often associated with ML, an ML practitioner needs to be able to look beyond the hype and properly ascertain where ML can deliver value to individuals and organisations. We argue here that, by viewing the sample projects provided by no-code ML tools, a user can develop this skill. The "Examples" feature of Lobe and the "Made with Teachable Machine" feature of Teachable Machine both contain a diversity of sample projects from various industries. Thus, a user can for instance determine that image classification is good for detecting different human activities.

Thirdly, given a specific problem, an ML practitioner should be able to plan an ML project that trains and deploys a model to solve the problem. This skill is referred to as ML project planning. It enables the practitioner to understand the requirements of a given project and the necessary resources (data, algorithms) that are needed to implement the project. Our findings suggest that the learning processes identified as part of familiarization affordances can lead to the generation of this skill. This is because, given that NML tools are designed to support model development, several features are specifically dedicated to this. Subsequently, learning how to use these features invariable translates to learning how to plan and implement an ML project. In Lobe, for instance, the documentation feature contains a section on gathering data, training a model, and using a model. These steps are fundamental to the ML process.

Subsequently, learning about them in the order in which they are presented would lead to an understanding of how to plan an ML project.

Fourthly, as part of any ML project, certain artifacts are developed. These artefacts include labeled datasets, ML models, and the applications that use the models. The skill of creating these artefacts can be developed with NML tools. Firstly, features that enable users to learn about the tool inform the user on how to generate these artefacts. Thus, this skill can be gained through familiarization affordances. Secondly, this skill is directly enabled by the utilization affordances that enable users to gather data, label it, and also to train and evaluate models. As an example, the utilization affordances present in Teachable Machine and Lobe enable users to export the trained models as a TensorFlow saved model. This would enable the model to be used outside the tool in external applications. Furthermore, both tools also contain sample code that users can experiment with while building their ML artifacts.

After any ML model is developed, it would be used in one form or the other. ML practitioners should be able to evaluate the use of these artefacts taking into consideration their implicit and explicit design objectives. ML practitioners should be able to answer questions like: What is this model intended to do? How well is this model performing in line with its design intentions? The skills needed to answer these questions can be developed when users learn about ML or when they learn how to use the tool to evaluate ML models. For instance, in the Tour feature of Lobe, some guidance is provided on evaluating models and improving their performance. Beyond the familiarization affordances presented in the latter, utilization affordances also lead to the development of these skills. For instance, Teachable Machine has a feature that provides users with information on model performance in form of a confusion matrix and loss graphs. Furthermore, for each input provided visual feedback is provided which indicates the output of the model and the confidence of the model in the returned output.

Finally, using NML tools can foster the development of independent learning skills. This skill is especially enabled by Lobe through its community feature which enables the user to view and comment on posts on the dedicated Reddit group. Such interactions expose users to issues and challenges associated with using the tool. Furthermore, they also provide the user with the opportunity to explore how these challenges may be addressed beyond the immediate affordances of the tool.

In summary, familiarisation affordances lead to the formation of ML advocacy, ML problem scoping, and ML project planning skills. They also enable users to create ML artifacts and evaluate their performance. On the other hand, utilization affordances enable users to develop ML artifacts, evaluate their performance and engage with the ML community. Figure 2 below summarises our discussion in this section.

Figure 1. Conceptual framework of NML tool affordances and ML skill development

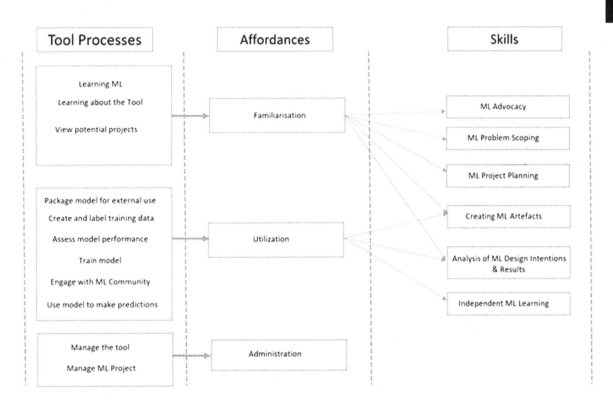

FUTURE RESEARCH DIRECTIONS

This chapter supports the general literature on NML tools and ML skill development. More specifically, it explains how the use of NML tools could lead to the acquisition of relevant ML skills. To enhance the outcomes of this study, future work may focus on developing appropriate assessment tools that can measure the extent to which a given NML tool supports the acquisition of the skills outlined herein. While these assessment tools would be important in evaluating the effectiveness of existing NML tools, they can also guide the design of future NML tools and provide preliminary feedback to tool designers. Secondly, given that previous research García-Ortiz and Sánchez-Viteri (2021) uses NML tools in imparting ML skills, assessment tools may also provide an avenue for evaluating the outcomes of such interventions.

CONCLUSION

In summary, we proffer that learning ML skills using NML tools happens in three stages. Before this work, it was unclear how NML tools contribute to the acquisition of ML skills. Extant literature (Lao, 2020; Rodríguez-García et al., 2020, 2021) only indicated that NML tools lead to the creation of some ML skills, however, no explanation was provided as to how these skills are acquired. To fill this gap, this work outlines how NML tools generate affordances that lead to the generation of ML skills. Subsequently, we organize these affordances into a process for learning ML skills displayed below.

Figure 2. A Process Model of how NML tools lead to the generation of skills

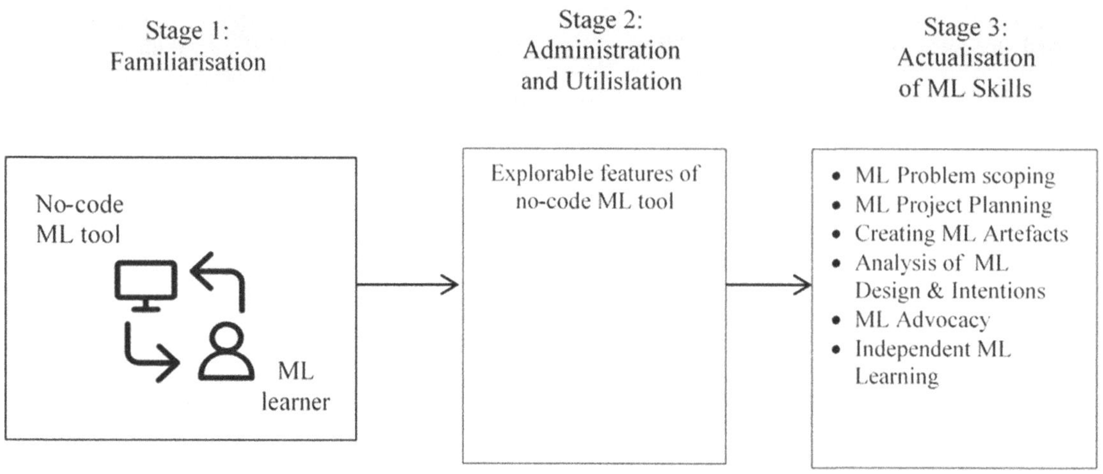

In the first stage, which we call familiarization, users explore the tool's features in three ways. First, they learn about the fundamental concepts of ML. Secondly, they learn how the specific NML tool being used facilitates the development of ML models. Then, they explore some exemplar projects that have been developed using the tool. In the second stage, users explore the administration and utilization affordances of the tool and create ML projects where they gather data, label them, and, subsequently use the data for training and evaluating models. In this stage, users have the option of exporting their models for further use outside the tool. They can also engage with the wider ML community and undertake independent learning. In the second stage i.e. administration and utilization, the user manages to apply the features to a specific ML project, leading to the third stage in which the user's ML skills manifest.

REFERENCES

Ahmed, S., Mula, R. S., & Dhavala, S. S. (2020). A Framework for Democratizing AI. *ArXiv Preprint*. https://arxiv.org/abs/2001.00818

Bagrow, J. P. (2020). Democratizing AI: Non-expert design of prediction tasks. *PeerJ. Computer Science*, *6*, e296. doi:10.7717/peerj-cs.296 PMID:33816947

Bygstad, B., Munkvold, B. E., & Volkoff, O. (2016). Identifying generative mechanisms through affordances: A framework for critical realist data analysis. *Journal of Information Technology*, *31*(1), 83–96. doi:10.1057/jit.2015.13

Carney, M., Webster, B., Alvarado, I., Phillips, K., Howell, N., Griffith, J., Jongejan, J., Pitaru, A., & Chen, A. (2020). Teachable machine: Approachable web-based tool for exploring machine learning classification. *Conference on Human Factors in Computing Systems - Proceedings*. 10.1145/3334480.3382839

Carvalho, A., & Harris, L. (2020). Off-the-Shelf technologies for sentiment analysis of social media data: Two empirical studies. *26th Americas Conference on Information Systems, AMCIS 2020*. https://www.ibm.com/cloud/watson-natural-language-understanding

D

Danermark, B., Ekström, M., & Karlsson, J. C. (2019). *Explaining society: Critical realism in the social sciences*. Routledge.

García, J. D. R., Moreno-León, J., Román-González, M., & Robles, G. (2020). Learningml: A tool to foster computational thinking skills through practical artificial intelligence projects. *Revista de Educación a Distancia (RED), 20*(63).

García-Ortiz, J., & Sánchez-Viteri, S. (2021). Identification of the Factors That Influence University Learning with Low-Code/No-Code Artificial Intelligence Techniques. *Electronics (Basel), 10*(10), 1192. doi:10.3390/electronics10101192

Gibson, J. J. (1969). *The Senses Considered as Perceptual Systems* (Vol. 3, Issue 1). Praeger. doi:10.2307/3331482

Gibson, J. J. (1986). The Ecological Approach to Visual Perception. In The Ecological Approach to Visual Perception. doi:10.4324/9781315740218

Gresse von Wangenheim, C., Hauck, J. C. R., Pacheco, F. S., & Bertonceli Bueno, M. F. (2021). Visual tools for teaching machine learning in K-12: A ten-year systematic mapping. *Education and Information Technologies, 26*(5), 5733–5778. Advance online publication. doi:10.100710639-021-10570-8 PMID:33967587

Hovorka, D. S., Germonprez, M., & Larsen, K. R. (2008). Explanation in information systems. *Information Systems Journal, 18*(1), 23–43. doi:10.1111/j.1365-2575.2007.00271.x

Kolbjørnsrud, V., Amico, R., & Thomas, R. J. (2017). Partnering with AI: How organizations can win over skeptical managers. *Strategy and Leadership, 45*(1), 37–43. doi:10.1108/SL-12-2016-0085

Lamberti, M. J., Wilkinson, M., Donzanti, B. A., Wohlhieter, G. E., Parikh, S., Wilkins, R. G., & Getz, K. (2019). A Study on the Application and Use of Artificial Intelligence to Support Drug Development. *Clinical Therapeutics, 41*(8), 1414–1426. doi:10.1016/j.clinthera.2019.05.018 PMID:31248680

Lao, N. (2020). *Reorienting Machine Learning Education Towards Tinkerers and ML-Engaged Citizens*. http://appinventor.mit.edu/assets/files/NatalieLao_PhD_Dissertation.pdf

Leonardi, P. M. (2011). When flexible routines meet flexible technologies: Affordance, constraint, and the imbrication of human and material agencies. *MIS Quarterly: Management Information Systems, 35*(1), 147–167. doi:10.2307/23043493

Leonardi, P. M. (2012). Materiality, sociomateriality, and socio-technical systems: What do these terms mean? How are they different? Do we need them. *Materiality and Organizing: Social Interaction in a Technological World, 25*, 10–1093. doi:10.1093/acprof:oso/9780199664054.003.0002

Leonardi, P. M. (2013). Theoretical foundations for the study of sociomateriality. *Information and Organization, 23*(2), 59–76. doi:10.1016/j.infoandorg.2013.02.002

Majchrzak, A., Markus, M. L., & Wareham, J. (2016). Designing for Digital Transformation: Lessons for Information Systems Research from the Study of ICT and Societal Challenges. *Management Information Systems Quarterly, 40*(2), 267–277. doi:10.25300/MISQ/2016/40:2.03

Microsoft. (2021). *Lobe | Machine Learning Made Easy*. https://www.lobe.ai/blog

Mikalef, P., Lemmer, K., Schaefer, C., Ylinen, M., Fjørtoft, S. O., Torvatn, H. Y., Gupta, M., & Nie-haves, B. (2021). Enabling AI capabilities in government agencies: A study of determinants for European municipalities. *Government Information Quarterly*, *101596*, 101596. Advance online publication. doi:10.1016/j.giq.2021.101596

Ozan, E. (2021). A Novel Browser-based No-code Machine Learning Application Development Tool. *2021 IEEE World AI IoT Congress*, 282–284. 10.1109/AIIoT52608.2021.9454239

Ramos, G., Meek, C., Simard, P., Suh, J., & Ghorashi, S. (2020). Interactive machine teaching: A human-centered approach to building machine-learned models. *Human-Computer Interaction*, *35*(5–6), 413–451. doi:10.1080/07370024.2020.1734931

Rodríguez-García, J. D., Moreno-León, J., Román-González, M., & Robles, G. (2020). Introducing Artificial Intelligence Fundamentals with LearningML: Artificial Intelligence made easy. *ACM International Conference Proceeding Series*, 18–20. 10.1145/3434780.3436705

Rodríguez-García, J. D., Moreno-León, J., Román-González, M., & Robles, G. (2021). Evaluation of an Online Intervention to Teach Artificial Intelligence with LearningML to 10-16-Year-Old Students. *Proceedings of the 52nd ACM Technical Symposium on Computer Science Education*, 177–183. 10.1145/3408877.3432393

Saldana, J., & Omasta, M. (2017). Analyzing documents, artifacts, and visual materials. In *Qualitative Research* (Vol. 63). Analyzing Life.

Sayer, A. (2010). Method in Social Science: A Realist Approach: Revised Second Edition. doi:10.4324/9780203850374

Seidel, S., Recker, J., & Vom Brocke, J. (2013). Sensemaking and sustainable practicing: Functional affordances of information systems in green transformations. *MIS Quarterly: Management Information Systems*, *37*(4), 1275–1299. doi:10.25300/MISQ/2013/37.4.13

Touretzky, D., Gardner-McCune, C., Martin, F., & Seehorn, D. (2019). Envisioning AI for K-12: What Should Every Child Know about AI? *Proceedings of the AAAI Conference on Artificial Intelligence*, *33*(01), 9795–9799. doi:10.1609/aaai.v33i01.33019795

Vaast, E., Safadi, H., Lapointe, L., & Negoita, B. (2017). Social media affordances for connective action: An examination of microblogging use during the Gulf of Mexico oil spill. *MIS Quarterly: Management Information Systems*, *41*(4), 1179–1206. doi:10.25300/MISQ/2017/41.4.08

Volkoff, O., & Strong, D. M. (2013). Critical realism and affordances: Theorizing IT-associated organizational change processes. *MIS Quarterly: Management Information Systems*, *37*(3), 819–834. doi:10.25300/MISQ/2013/37.3.07

ADDITIONAL READING

Di Ruscio, D., Kolovos, D., de Lara, J., Pierantonio, A., Tisi, M., & Wimmer, M. (2022). Low-code development and model-driven engineering: Two sides of the same coin? *Software & Systems Modeling*, ●●●, 1–10.

Hurlburt, G. F. (2021). Low-Code, No-Code, What's Under the Hood? *IT Professional, 23*(6), 4–7.

Li, Y., Zhang, H., Jiang, S., Yang, F., Wen, Y., & Luo, Y. (2021). *ModelPS: An Interactive and Collaborative Platform for Editing Pre-trained Models at Scale.* arXiv preprint arXiv:2105.08275.

Redchuk, A., & Walas Mateo, F. (2022). New Business Models on Artificial Intelligence—The Case of the Optimization of a Blast Furnace in the Steel Industry by a Machine Learning Solution. *Applied System Innovation, 5*(1), 6.

Ullrich, C., Lata, T., & Geyer-Klingeberg, J. (2021). *Celonis Studio–A Low-Code Development Platform for Citizen Developers.* BPM.

Xin, D., Wu, E. Y., Lee, D. J. L., Salehi, N., & Parameswaran, A. (2021, May). Whither automl? understanding the role of automation in machine learning workflows. In *Proceedings of the 2021 CHI Conference on Human Factors in Computing Systems* (pp. 1-16). ACM.

Zhuang, W., Gan, X., Wen, Y., & Zhang, S. (2022). *Easyfl: A low-code federated learning platform for dummies.* IEEE Internet of Things Journal.

Zöller, M. A., & Huber, M. F. (2021). Benchmark and survey of automated machine learning frameworks. *Journal of Artificial Intelligence Research, 70*, 409–472. doi:10.1613/jair.1.11854

KEY TERMS AND DEFINITIONS

Batch Size: A hyperparameter that determines the number of samples used for training before the internal parameters of a model is updated during the training of neural networks.

Clustering: A computational approach for grouping data points in a dataset such that, data points in the same group are more similar to each other and differ from those in other groups.

Concept Drift: A significant change in the statistical attributes of the data that a machine learning model has been trained to predict which may lead to a reduction in the performance of the model.

Data Preprocessing: The manipulation of raw gathered data to remove redundant, unreliable, or incorrect data points to make a dataset more suitable for machine learning tasks.

Epoch: A hyperparameter that determines the number of complete passes that a training algorithm makes over the training dataset during the training of neural networks.

Learning Rate: A hyperparameter that is used to determine the magnitude by which model weights are updated during the training of neural networks.

Tensorflow: An open-source software library developed and distributed by Google that enables developers to train and use machine learning models.

Educational Data Mining and Learning Analytics in the 21st Century

Georgios Lampropoulos

https://orcid.org/0000-0002-5719-2125

International Hellenic University, Greece

INTRODUCTION

The digitalization of everyday life and the rapid technological advancements have helped the new generation of students be familiar with and accustomed to digital technologies from a young age. As a result, their educational needs and requirements as well as their viewpoints regarding what effective learning is have drastically changed. Moreover, while the need for basic education is becoming urgent, the current educational system struggles to satisfy the new educational requirements (Prensky, 2001) and students' need for more personalized learning experiences.

Simultaneously, an exponentially increasing amount of heterogeneous data which is characterized by its volume, variety, veracity, velocity and value is being generated (McAfee et al., 2012). This vast volume of data is called Big Data and it paves the way for technological advances. Data mining is a scientific field which has experienced drastic advancements due to the rise of Big Data and its being more broadly applied in a wide variety of domains.

Data mining, also known as Knowledge Discovery in Databases (KDD), utilizes a variety of algorithms, techniques and methods in order to generate knowledge by discovering novel and useful information, patterns, relationships or structures from large data collections (Fayyad et al., 1996; Witten & Frank, 2002). Therefore, it can be used as an invaluable tool that supports and enhances decision-making (Peña-Ayala, 2014). As a result, data mining along with the necessary analysis tools are utilized in various sectors. The educational domain is no exception to that as data mining can offer several benefits.

The main aim of this chapter is to offer an overview of educational data mining and learning analytics and their essential role in improving 21st century education while capitalizing on the emergence of data science. For that reason, it presents and analyzes the concepts of learning analytics and educational data mining, their evolution as well as their role in modern education and highlights the impact of machine learning on them. Moreover, the chapter goes over the recent literature and extracts invaluable information according to the results and outcomes of related studies. Furthermore, it discusses their use as useful tools in educational settings and as a means to offer intelligent personalized learning in order to meet the new and upcoming educational needs and requirements. In addition, it goes over the merits that they can yield, and it suggests ways to address some of the current open challenges and limitations. Finally, it presents the summary of the main findings, drawn conclusions and provides directions for future research.

DOI: 10.4018/978-1-7998-9220-5.ch098

BACKGROUND

E

A lot of emphasis is put on the collection, processing and analysis of data so as to better comprehend and optimize the learning and teaching process and outcomes. Educational data mining and learning analytics are two fields which are becoming more popular due to this fact.

Educational data mining is a specialized form of data mining which focuses on educational environments. It aims at addressing educational issues by analyzing data and developing models that enhance the overall learning experience and outcomes and increase the institutional effectiveness (Baker and Yacef, 2009; Dutt et al., 2017). It is worth noting that due to its nature, it can be applied at all educational levels (Saa, 2016). According to the Educational Data Mining community, educational data mining can be defined as "an emerging discipline, concerned with developing methods for exploring the unique and increasingly large-scale data that come from educational settings and using those methods to better understand students, and the settings which they learn in" (Educational Data Mining Community, 2021). Based on this particular definition, it is apparent that educational data mining constitutes an interdisciplinary field. Therefore, it exploits machine learning, statistics, information retrieval, recommender systems and other innovative technologies and techniques (Romero & Ventura, 2010).

As a part of Technology-Enhanced Learning (TEL) research, learning analytics is another interdisciplinary scientific field which is gaining ground as it can enhance the existing education models (Ferguson, 2012; Siemens & Baker, 2012). It can be regarded as a powerful tool which explores how the large volume of data can be used to enhance the overall learning quality and to address a variety of educational challenges and issues (Bakharia et al., 2016; Pardo et al., 2019). Particularly, learning analytics involves the collection, analysis and visualization of data with a view to better comprehending and improving both learning experience and environment (Ferguson, 2012; Lang et al., 2017; Liñán & Pérez, 2015; Romero & Ventura, 2020; Siemens, 2013). The analysis and visualization of data can provide invaluable feedback for both students and teachers (Clow, 2013) and assist in fulfilling the new educational needs as well as positively affecting students' learning and progression (Slade & Prinsloo, 2013). Therefore, it can be regarded as an essential educational tool which can be further improved as the amount of data increases and machine learning algorithms and models become more advanced.

Even though these two fields seem similar at first sight, there are some distinct differences between them. Particularly, educational data mining follows a bottom-up approach as it aims at finding new patterns in data and developing new models while learning analytics follows a top-down approach to assess the learning theories and the educational process by utilizing existing models (Baker and Yacef, 2009; Bienkowski et al., 2012). Moreover, there are various distinctions between educational data mining and learning analytics regarding their origins, reduction and holism approaches, knowledge discovery aims and methods, adaptation and personalization strategies as well as the overall techniques and methods used (Liñán & Pérez, 2015; Siemens, 2012). It can be said that educational data mining focuses more on the technical challenges while learning analytics on the educational ones (Ferguson, 2012). Despite their main focus points, their successful implementation in educational settings can bring about numerous innovative and positive changes and yield several merits to satisfy the new educational needs and students' requirements.

FOCUS OF THE ARTICLE

With the multitude of sensory data that contains various semantics, formats and structures, the general field of data science is rapidly evolving. Due to its nature, it affects several domains, such as healthcare (Raghupathi & Raghupathi, 2014), industry (Lampropoulos et al., 2018), transportation (Zhu et al., 2018) etc. Particular interest is noticed in the field of education. As the educational sector employs a data-driven approach, both learning analytics and educational data mining are being widely accepted and adopted since they constitute powerful analytical and statistical tools that offer invaluable predictive models and decision-making systems and rules and enable educational institutions to stay ahead of the global competition by reducing their costs, increasing their income and productivity and providing education of higher quality (Liñán & Pérez, 2015).

SOLUTIONS AND RECOMMENDATIONS

As educational data mining aims at detecting patterns within large collections of data originating from educational environments (Hann & Kamber, 2000), it is closely connected with the fields of machine learning and deep learning (Hernández-Blanco et al., 2019). Particularly, machine learning constitutes a sub-field of artificial intelligence which aims at creating models that imitate the way that humans perceive things and learn by using data and algorithms while deep learning is a specialized form of machine learning with a multitude of layers through which the data is transformed (Lampropoulos et al., 2020). Moreover, it is worth noting that as traditional data mining algorithms satisfy only specific objectives and functions in order for them to be applied in educational problems, customized preprocessing algorithms need to be enforced first (Dutt et al., 2017).

Educational data mining can assist in assessing, predicting and analyzing students' academic performance and outcomes (Asif et al., 2017; Baradwaj & Pal, 2012; Fernandes et al., 2019) and it can provide ways to profile and group students, assess and grade students in an unbiased manner, detect undesirable behaviors, create concept maps and student models as well as to generate recommendations and evaluations (Bakhshinategh et al., 2018; Hernández-Blanco et al., 2019; Romero & Ventura, 2010; Salloum et al., 2020). In addition, educational data mining can be applied to improve student-centered and specific domain models, to assist in exploring pedagogical approaches as well as in supporting the implementation and justification of scientific research into learning and teaching activities (Baker, 2010; Baker and Yacef, 2009). Moreover, it creates methods to better assess and evaluate students' performance and the educational material used, provides learning recommendations based on specific and personalized students' needs and behaviors and constitutes a means that provides advanced feedback for both students and teachers (Castro et al., 2007).

With the aim of improving the educational process, learning analytics is used to generate actionable intelligence and reveal hidden information and patterns from raw data that derive from educational environments (Campbell et al., 2007; Siemens, 2012). Moreover, they can increase our comprehension regarding the learning and teaching processes as well as the educational environment itself by providing invaluable insight into learners' performance, behavior, interaction and learning paths (Vahdat et al., 2015). Particularly, with a view to optimizing learning, learning analytics enables the collection, process, measurement, analysis, reporting and visualization of educational data (Romero et al., 2010).

Learning analytics puts emphasis on performance management, metrics and quantification and utilizes statistical and computational methods and tools to manage and analyze large data sets that derive

E

from the increasing number of learning activities that take place within learning management systems and virtual learning environments (Clow, 2013). Techniques and applications are the main overlapping components of learning analytics with techniques referring to specific models and algorithms while applications to how the specific techniques are implemented to improve the educational process (Siemens, 2013). When used in a student-centered way, learning analytics can constitute a useful educational tool that assesses and evaluates teachers' and instructors' pedagogical intent within learning and teaching activities and provides invaluable insights regarding their impact on students (Lockyer et al., 2013). Moreover, learning analytics supports adaptive learning, quality assurance and quality improvement, boosts retention rates, improves the quality of teaching, enables students to take control of their own learning and is positively perceived by students (Sclater et al., 2016).

Both educational data mining and learning analytics can enhance the educational process by providing computer-supported learning, behavioral, predictive and visualization analytics and by improving collaborative learning and social networking analysis (Aldowah et al., 2019). Additionally, they need to take the educational context into consideration, to be integrated into current e-learning systems and to be designed in a flexible and simple way so that it would be easier for the educators to learn and use them (Romero & Ventura, 2010). Understanding better how people learn and utilizing these methods efficiently can lead to designing more effective and smarter learning environments that will boost both learning and teaching activities (Baker, 2014). Moreover, in both cases, the primary areas of analysis can be categorized into: (i) prediction, (ii) clustering, (iii) relationship mining, (iv) discovery with models and (v) data distillation for human judgment (Baker et al., 2009). Furthermore, their areas of application can be grouped into: (i) trend analysis, (ii) personalization and adaptation, (iii) user profiling, (iv) knowledge domain modeling and (v) users' knowledge, behavior and experience modeling (Bienkowski et al., 2012).

FUTURE RESEARCH DIRECTIONS

Since both educational data mining and learning analytics are new research fields there still remain several issues and open research questions that need to be explored and addressed. As the fields evolve, there is a need for both analytic approaches and outputs to be aligned with conceptual frames of reference as well as the necessary for each case educational contexts (Bakharia et al., 2016; Gašević et al., 2015).

Moreover, as they both have strong roots and are interrelated with several fields of data mining, statistics and analytics, it is difficult to detect and retrieve the crucial for the comprehension of the learning process information regarding pedagogy, cognition and metacognition (Ferguson, 2012; Vahdat et al., 2015). Consequently, it is vital to enforce effective pedagogical methods, approaches and strategies. As a result, there is a great need to build strong connections with the learning sciences, concentrate on learners' perspectives and needs and create methods that can be applied in a wide variety of data sets (Ferguson, 2012).

It is evident that teachers and instructors lack the theoretical and practical knowledge regarding the use of the necessary tools (Liñán & Pérez, 2015). Therefore, in order for learning analytics and educational data mining to further advance, it is crucial to develop more freely available tools as well as general purpose ones and to enhance the promotion, adoption and development of a data-driven culture within educational environments and institutions (Romero & Ventura, 2013, 2020).

Moreover, both educational data mining and learning analytics can be particularly useful in cases where traditional informal monitoring is not possible such as online learning, as they can provide crucial monitoring, knowledge and decision-making support (Romero & Ventura, 2007). As online learning and virtual learning environments are becoming more widely utilized, developing and using advanced analytical and monitoring tools that can assist the overall educational process is vital. This is particularly helpful when augmented reality (AR), virtual reality (VR) and immersive 360-degree videos are utilized in the educational process so as to achieve a better understanding of the impact and benefits they can yield as they constitute innovative solutions that can enhance the educational process in an interactive, engaging and student-centered manner (Lampropoulos et al., 2021). Additionally, the majority of recent studies concentrated on predicting, grouping, modeling and monitoring learning activities solely based on classification, clustering, association rules, statistics and visualization techniques (Aldowah et al., 2019). Hence, there is a profound need for more customized and powerful educational data classification and clustering algorithms and methods to be developed (Dutt et al., 2017).

The majority of systems being used and studied are developed to address specific use cases or courses and for that reason, they cannot be generalized (Mohamad & Tasir, 2013). Therefore, it is apparent that in order to provide generalized results, future research should emphasize the collaboration of different fields so as to create broader use cases that will be able to be applied in various contexts, courses and educational environments. Additionally, more effort should be put into the increased collaboration among researchers and practitioners so as to develop more student-centered and advanced tools and techniques, to assess data related issues and enhance analytics performance and interpretation (Siemens, 2012).

According to Leitner et al. (2019), in order for learning analytics and educational data mining to be fully realized in higher education institutions, the challenges that need to be successfully met can be categorized into: (i) purpose and gain, (ii) representation and actions, (iii) data, (iv) IT infrastructure, (v) development and operation, (vi) privacy and (vii) ethics. Moreover, based on the study conducted by Baker (2019), some of the main general challenges that need to be addressed refer to: (i) transferability, (ii) effectiveness, (iii) interpretability, (iv) applicability and (v) generalizability.

It is worthwhile to mention that the majority of issues and challenges faced by analytics within the educational domain are mainly focused on data related issues such as openness, accuracy, quality and sufficiency (Siemens, 2013). Furthermore, due to data ethical and privacy concerns as well as a lack of a standardized representation, it is difficult to make the data available for research purposes despite the fact that more and more data is being collected from learning environments (Siemens, 2013; Verbert et al., 2012). Consequently, a specific emphasis should be put on addressing the open research questions regarding ethical and privacy principles, issues, dilemmas and practices for both educational data mining (Ihantola et al., 2015; Siemens, 2012) and learning analytics (Pardo & Siemens, 2014; Slade & Prinsloo, 2013). Ethics and privacy should be greatly taken into consideration in all stages, that is from the data retrieval and collection to the analysis, interpretation and decision making (Greller & Drachsler, 2012).

CONCLUSION

Nowadays, with a view to improving the educational process and addressing students' needs and requirements, more emphasis is put on the collection, process, analysis and visualization of data. Furthermore, the exponentially increasing volume of data has brought about not only new challenges but also new opportunities for innovative applications and solutions. Educational data mining and learning analytics are two of the most rapidly growing scientific fields which aim at providing insights into educational matters based on the analysis of data.

As learning analytics and educational data mining mature and provide enhanced insights into learning and teaching processes, they will be more widely used by the educational community. Additionally, as more educational institutions develop and adopt a data-driven culture that utilizes tools which provide predictive, diagnostic and descriptive analytics, more personalized, advanced and smarter learning environments that are able to offer customized experiences and meet students' specific needs can be developed.

All in all, both educational data mining and learning analytics have the potential to significantly influence the current educational system and provide opportunities for new learner-centered tools, methodologies and techniques to be developed. Nonetheless, there still remain open research issues and challenges that need to be met in order for them to be fully implemented in educational settings. Future studies should focus on these issues while also showcasing the potentials and benefits that learning analytics and educational data mining can render to further enhance their adoption, implementation and advancement.

FUNDING

The research work was supported by the Hellenic Foundation for Research and Innovation (HFRI) under the 3rd Call for HFRI PhD Fellowships (Fellowship Number: 6454).

REFERENCES

Aldowah, H., Al-Samarraie, H., & Fauzy, W. M. (2019). Educational data mining and learning analytics for 21st century higher education: A review and synthesis. *Telematics and Informatics*, *37*, 13–49. doi:10.1016/j.tele.2019.01.007

Asif, R., Merceron, A., Ali, S. A., & Haider, N. G. (2017). Analyzing undergraduate students' performance using educational data mining. *Computers & Education*, *113*, 177–194. doi:10.1016/j.compedu.2017.05.007

Baker, R. S. (2014). Educational data mining: An advance for intelligent systems in education. *IEEE Intelligent Systems*, *29*(3), 78–82. doi:10.1109/MIS.2014.42

Baker, R. S. (2019). Challenges for the future of educational data mining: The Baker learning analytics prizes. *Journal of Educational Data Mining*, *11*(1), 1–17.

Baker, R. S., & Yacef, K. (2009). The state of educational data mining in 2009: A review and future visions. *Journal of Educational Data Mining, 1*(1), 3-17.

Baker, R. S. J. D. (2010). Data mining for education. *International Encyclopedia of Education, 7*(3), 112-118.

Bakharia, A., Corrin, L., De Barba, P., Kennedy, G., Gašević, D., Mulder, R., Williams, D., Dawson, S., & Lockyer, L. (2016). A conceptual framework linking learning design with learning analytics. *Proceedings of the Sixth International Conference on Learning Analytics & Knowledge*, 329–338. 10.1145/2883851.2883944

Bakhshinategh, B., Zaiane, O. R., ElAtia, S., & Ipperciel, D. (2018). Educational data mining applications and tasks: A survey of the last 10 years. *Education and Information Technologies*, *23*(1), 537–553. doi:10.100710639-017-9616-z

Baradwaj, B. K., & Pal, S. (2012). *Mining educational data to analyze students' performance.* arXiv Preprint arXiv:1201.3417.

Bienkowski, M., Feng, M., & Means, B. (2012). *Enhancing teaching and learning through educational data mining and learning analytics: An issue brief.* Office of Educational Technology, US Department of Education.

Campbell, J. P., DeBlois, P. B., & Oblinger, D. G. (2007). Academic analytics: A new tool for a new era. *EDUCAUSE Review, 42*(4), 40.

Castro, F., Vellido, A., Nebot, A., & Mugica, F. (2007). Applying data mining techniques to e-learning problems. In *Evolution of teaching and learning paradigms in intelligent environment* (pp. 183–221). Springer. doi:10.1007/978-3-540-71974-8_8

Clow, D. (2013). An overview of learning analytics. *Teaching in Higher Education, 18*(6), 683–695. doi:10.1080/13562517.2013.827653

Dutt, A., Ismail, M. A., & Herawan, T. (2017). A systematic review on educational data mining. *IEEE Access: Practical Innovations, Open Solutions, 5,* 15991–16005. doi:10.1109/ACCESS.2017.2654247

Educational data mining community. (2021). https://educationaldatamining.org/

Fayyad, U., Piatetsky-Shapiro, G., & Smyth, P. (1996). From data mining to knowledge discovery in databases. *AI Magazine, 17*(3), 37–37.

Ferguson, R. (2012). Learning analytics: Drivers, developments and challenges. *International Journal of Technology Enhanced Learning, 4*(5-6), 304–317. doi:10.1504/IJTEL.2012.051816

Fernandes, E., Holanda, M., Victorino, M., Borges, V., Carvalho, R., & Van Erven, G. (2019). Educational data mining: Predictive analysis of academic performance of public school students in the capital of brazil. *Journal of Business Research, 94,* 335–343. doi:10.1016/j.jbusres.2018.02.012

Gašević, D., Dawson, S., & Siemens, G. (2015). Let's not forget: Learning analytics are about learning. *TechTrends, 59*(1), 64–71. doi:10.100711528-014-0822-x

Greller, W., & Drachsler, H. (2012). Translating learning into numbers: A generic framework for learning analytics. *Journal of Educational Technology & Society, 15*(3), 42–57.

Hann, J., & Kamber, M. (2000). *Data mining: Concepts and techniques.* Morgan Kaufman Publish.

Hernández-Blanco, A., Herrera-Flores, B., Tomás, D., & Navarro-Colorado, B. (2019). A systematic review of deep learning approaches to educational data mining. *Complexity, 2019,* 1–22. Advance online publication. doi:10.1155/2019/1306039

Ihantola, P., Vihavainen, A., Ahadi, A., Butler, M., Börstler, J., Edwards, S. H., Isohanni, E., Korhonen, A., Petersen, A., Rivers, K., & ... (2015). Educational data mining and learning analytics in programming: Literature review and case studies. *Proceedings of the 2015 ITiCSE on Working Group Reports,* 41–63. 10.1145/2858796.2858798

Lampropoulos, G., Barkoukis, V., Burden, K., & Anastasiadis, T. (2021). 360-degree video in education: An overview and a comparative social media data analysis of the last decade. *Smart Learning Environments, 8*(20), 1–24. doi:10.118640561-021-00165-8

Lampropoulos, G., Keramopoulos, E., & Diamantaras, K. (2020). Enhancing the functionality of augmented reality using deep learning, semantic web and knowledge graphs: A review. *Visual Informatics*, *4*(1), 32–42. doi:10.1016/j.visinf.2020.01.001

Lampropoulos, G., Siakas, K., & Anastasiadis, T. (2018). Internet of things (IoT) in industry: Contemporary application domains, innovative technologies and intelligent manufacturing. *International Journal of Advances in Scientific Research and Engineering*, *4*(10), 109–118. doi:10.31695/IJASRE.2018.32910

Lang, C., Siemens, G., Wise, A., & Gasevic, D. (2017). Handbook of learning analytics. SOLAR, Society for Learning Analytics. doi:10.18608/hla17

Leitner, P., Ebner, M., & Ebner, M. (2019). Learning analytics challenges to overcome in higher education institutions. In *Utilizing learning analytics to support study success* (pp. 91–104). Springer. doi:10.1007/978-3-319-64792-0_6

Liñán, L. C., & Pérez, Á. A. J. (2015). Educational data mining and learning analytics: Differences, similarities, and time evolution. *International Journal of Educational Technology in Higher Education*, *12*(3), 98–112. doi:10.7238/rusc.v12i3.2515

Lockyer, L., Heathcote, E., & Dawson, S. (2013). Informing pedagogical action: Aligning learning analytics with learning design. *The American Behavioral Scientist*, *57*(10), 1439–1459. doi:10.1177/0002764213479367

McAfee, A., Brynjolfsson, E., Davenport, T. H., Patil, D., & Barton, D. (2012). Big data: The management revolution. *Harvard Business Review*, *90*(10), 60–68. PMID:23074865

Mohamad, S. K., & Tasir, Z. (2013). Educational data mining: A review. *Procedia: Social and Behavioral Sciences*, *97*, 320–324. doi:10.1016/j.sbspro.2013.10.240

Pardo, A., Jovanovic, J., Dawson, S., Gašević, D., & Mirriahi, N. (2019). Using learning analytics to scale the provision of personalised feedback. *British Journal of Educational Technology*, *50*(1), 128–138. doi:10.1111/bjet.12592

Pardo, A., & Siemens, G. (2014). Ethical and privacy principles for learning analytics. *British Journal of Educational Technology*, *45*(3), 438–450. doi:10.1111/bjet.12152

Peña-Ayala, A. (2014). Educational data mining: A survey and a data mining-based analysis of recent works. *Expert Systems with Applications*, *41*(4), 1432–1462. doi:10.1016/j.eswa.2013.08.042

Prensky, M. (2001). Digital natives, digital immigrants. *On the Horizon*, *9*(5), 1–6. doi:10.1108/10748120110424816

Raghupathi, W., & Raghupathi, V. (2014). Big data analytics in healthcare: Promise and potential. *Health Information Science and Systems*, *2*(1), 1–10. doi:10.1186/2047-2501-2-3 PMID:25825667

Romero, C., & Ventura, S. (2007). Educational data mining: A survey from 1995 to 2005. *Expert Systems with Applications*, *33*(1), 135–146. doi:10.1016/j.eswa.2006.04.005

Romero, C., & Ventura, S. (2010). Educational data mining: A review of the state of the art. *IEEE Transactions on Systems, Man and Cybernetics. Part C, Applications and Reviews*, *40*(6), 601–618. doi:10.1109/TSMCC.2010.2053532

Romero, C., & Ventura, S. (2013). Data mining in education. *Wiley Interdisciplinary Reviews. Data Mining and Knowledge Discovery*, *3*(1), 12–27. doi:10.1002/widm.1075

Romero, C., & Ventura, S. (2020). Educational data mining and learning analytics: An updated survey. *Wiley Interdisciplinary Reviews. Data Mining and Knowledge Discovery*, *10*(3), e1355. doi:10.1002/widm.1355

Romero, C., Ventura, S., Pechenizkiy, M., & Baker, R. S. (2010). Handbook of educational data mining. CRC Press.

Saa, A. A. (2016). Educational data mining & students' performance prediction. *International Journal of Advanced Computer Science and Applications*, *7*(5), 212–220. doi:10.14569/IJACSA.2016.070531

Salloum, S. A., Alshurideh, M., Elnagar, A., & Shaalan, K. (2020). Mining in educational data: Review and future directions. *AICV*, 92–102.

Sclater, N., Peasgood, A., & Mullan, J. (2016). Learning analytics in higher education: A review of UK and international practice. *JISC, 8*(2017), 176.

Siemens, G. (2012). Learning analytics: Envisioning a research discipline and a domain of practice. *Proceedings of the 2nd International Conference on Learning Analytics and Knowledge*, 4–8. 10.1145/2330601.2330605

Siemens, G. (2013). Learning analytics: The emergence of a discipline. *The American Behavioral Scientist*, *57*(10), 1380–1400. doi:10.1177/0002764213498851

Siemens, G., & Baker, R. S. d. (2012). Learning analytics and educational data mining: Towards communication and collaboration. *Proceedings of the 2nd International Conference on Learning Analytics and Knowledge*, 252–254. 10.1145/2330601.2330661

Slade, S., & Prinsloo, P. (2013). Learning analytics: Ethical issues and dilemmas. *The American Behavioral Scientist*, *57*(10), 1510–1529. doi:10.1177/0002764213479366

Vahdat, M., Ghio, A., Oneto, L., Anguita, D., Funk, M., & Rauterberg, M. (2015). Advances in learning analytics and educational data mining. *Proc. Of Esann*, *2015*, 297–306.

Verbert, K., Manouselis, N., Ochoa, X., Wolpers, M., Drachsler, H., Bosnic, I., & Duval, E. (2012). Context-aware recommender systems for learning: A survey and future challenges. *IEEE Transactions on Learning Technologies*, *5*(4), 318–335. doi:10.1109/TLT.2012.11

Witten, I. H., & Frank, E. (2002). Data mining: Practical machine learning tools and techniques with java implementations. *SIGMOD Record*, *31*(1), 76–77. doi:10.1145/507338.507355

Zhu, L., Yu, F. R., Wang, Y., Ning, B., & Tang, T. (2018). Big data analytics in intelligent transportation systems: A survey. *IEEE Transactions on Intelligent Transportation Systems*, *20*(1), 383–398. doi:10.1109/TITS.2018.2815678

ADDITIONAL READING

Ahuja, R., Jha, A., Maurya, R., & Srivastava, R. (2019). Analysis of educational data mining. In *Harmony Search and Nature Inspired Optimization Algorithms* (pp. 897–907). Springer. doi:10.1007/978-981-13-0761-4_85

Freire, M., Serrano-Laguna, Á., Manero, B., Martínez-Ortiz, I., Moreno-Ger, P., & Fernández-Manjón, B. (2016). Game learning analytics: learning analytics for serious games. In *Learning, design, and technology* (pp. 1–29). Springer Nature Switzerland AG. doi:10.1007/978-3-319-17727-4_21-1

Knight, S., & Shum, S. B. (2017). Theory and learning analytics. Handbook of learning analytics, 17-22. doi:10.18608/hla17.001

Leitner, P., Khalil, M., & Ebner, M. (2017). Learning analytics in higher education—a literature review. *Learning analytics: Fundaments, applications, and trends*, 1-23. doi:10.1007/978-3-319-52977-6_1

Slater, S., Joksimović, S., Kovanovic, V., Baker, R. S., & Gasevic, D. (2017). Tools for educational data mining: A review. *Journal of Educational and Behavioral Statistics*, *42*(1), 85–106. doi:10.3102/1076998616666808

KEY TERMS AND DEFINITIONS

Big Data: An exponentially increasing volume of heterogeneous data which is differentiated from traditional data based on its volume, variety, veracity, velocity, and value.

Data Mining: It is also known as Knowledge Discovery in Databases (KDD) and refers to the use of algorithms, techniques, and methods in order to generate knowledge by discovering novel and useful information, patterns, relationships or structures from large data collections.

Educational Data Mining: It is a specialized form of data mining which focuses on utilizing data that derives from educational environments and aims at addressing educational issues and enhancing the overall learning experience, performance, and outcomes.

Learning Analytics: It is an interdisciplinary scientific field which examines the way in which data can be used to improve the overall learning quality and to address a variety of educational challenges and issues.

Emerging Tools and Technologies in Data Science

Mahmud Ullah

(iD) https://orcid.org/0000-0001-7472-2477

Department of Marketing, University of Dhaka, Bangladesh

Nayem Rahman

Anderson College of Business and Computing, Regis University, USA

INTRODUCTION

Necessary and reasonable use of data to produce authentic and effective information to run different government, nongovernment, nonprofit organizations, and mainly large size businesses had always been there up to certain extent. Every phase of industrial revolution had added new dimensions to increase the size and frequencies of data usage, making it unmanageable at times to deal with the required data by the existing knowledge of the time.

Consequently, every phase of industrial revolution gave birth of many new fields of knowledge related to dealing with data or data management, which may be collectively termed as 'Data Science'. After the invention of information technology, now in the rapidly growing current phase of industrial revolution, which is technically termed by the professionals, and popularly known to people as Fourth Industrial Revolution, referred as Industry 4.0 in brief as well, every single entity in the world is immersed in the large oceans of data, data, and data only, irrespective of any entity's consent to be so.

Hence it is becoming even more & more difficult every day to manage the huge volume of data we have to deal with as an individual, or as a small or large scale business, or as government, nongovernment, and nonprofit organizations. The term 'Big Data' has evolved to refer to the sheer size of data, and the scope, importance, usefulness etc. of these data we have deal with in our everyday lives nowadays.

Luckily, new knowledge on tools and technologies to handle these big data, an obvious reality of this industry 4.0 era, is also evolving simultaneously. The big question is, how useful this continuous addition & learning of new knowledge in the field of data science are, in terms of wide spread availability, easy accessibility, smooth understanding, price structure, cost saving / cutting, effectiveness, efficiency, user friendliness etc., and how to make the optimum use of the ever increasingly emerging knowledge on tools and technologies in the field of data science, the most important field for every single country, organization, and individual around the world.

This is the most desirable field of knowledge as well, mainly to the younger generation everywhere around the world. Everybody would love to have some expertise at least in dealing with data scientifically using the most up to date tools and technologies of data management, which is virtually pushing the field of data science to flourish more rapidly than ever before.

In this context, the authors prepared this paper covering the nature of ever increasing evolution of overwhelming knowledge in the field of data science, focusing mainly on the discovery or emergence of tools and technologies to deal with data, on the basis of their experience and expertise of doing or being involved in similar kind of multiple research projects or activities in small scale in the field of data

DOI: 10.4018/978-1-7998-9220-5.ch099

science. They believe that this paper would be worth reading for the professionals and academicians to have an in-depth idea of the continuing development in the field of data science, and choose the best possible tools or technologies for their respective organizations corresponding to their specific purposes.

BACKGROUND

The advent of computing technologies, software engineering, data warehousing technologies, cloud computing, etc., and very rapid emergence and adoption of smart-phone around the globe, have made modern day business environment much more competitive than ever before. To survive and sustain facing the immense competition due to all these fast emerging technologies, businesses have to make informed decision by analyzing business data using the most effective, efficient, and up to date data dealing tool, which will ultimately ensure the use of the least expensive data handling procedure. This paper will try to identify the most economic ways of using data handling tools and technologies.

Data analyses are mainly done using data stored in the enterprise data warehouses, which (data) are mainly created in, and collected from operational data stores. Everybody wants to have faster access to information but not quite eager to pay as much. Business enterprises struggle continuously to make a balance between these two conflicting expectations. This paper aims to identify the best possible ways to make this balance, e.g. switching to cloud computing from maintaining enterprises' own data warehouse.

Handling huge data volume, which is referred as big data, and coming from different sources like social media, videos, mobile phone etc., is a real challenge. Fortunately, new tools and parallel processing database engines are now available to assist with overcoming that challenge. This paper attempts to identify the existing and emerging technologies of data storage, retrieval, parallel processing etc. with as much details as possible to help people choose the most suitable one for any person, or organization to handle these large data.

Thus, this chapter aims to make an exhaustive list of all the existing and emerging technologies to deal with data of any volume - big, large, or huge, by displaying the required details in a systematic manner classifying and categorizing those, making those easy to comprehend and compare. Exhaustive literature review has been done to start with. Information has been collected from all the stakeholders involved in producing, marketing, and using data handling / managing / interpreting tools and technologies to generate authentic information by systematically storing, instantly retrieving, and objectively analyzing different types of data of different volume, mostly large or huge referred as big data.

Global nature of modern business, triggered and facilitated mainly by the drastic development in the ever changing digital devices and software engineering has made the business environment much more competitive, and consequently kind of volatile in many senses, especially in this era of industry 4.0, evolving with an extraordinary pace unlike the other phases of industrial revolution. Making informed decisions on the basis of authentic data and information has hence become obvious for the organizations to survive, sustain, and succeed.

Companies typically create and collect data in operational data stores. This data is then moved to the enterprise data warehouse for various analytical needs. There is a push to access information faster, often as soon as it is created. To achieve that, database engines need to have a faster processing capability (Rahman, 2007). While organizations want a state of the art data warehousing and Business Intelligence (BI) environment, they also continuously strive to bring down their IT infrastructure budget. Data warehouse and BI tools involve huge capital expenditure. Small and medium-sized companies cannot afford that. With the advent of cloud computing data warehouse infrastructure costs could be avoided as cloud services allow companies to pay-for-use avoiding the need to own a data warehouse, which can be both costly and time consuming (Armstrong, 1997) to build. Organizations have started to move from traditional server-based data warehousing to a private cloud.

Businesses are facing challenges in today's environment while data volume grows every year. Consequently, data storage and retrieval response time increases. So, data warehousing tools and database needs to be more powerful with parallel processing capability to expedite refreshing data warehouses. Fortunately, new tools and parallel processing database engines (Sen & Sinha, 2005) are now available to assist with overcoming that challenge. Business organizations find business value in unstructured data which are in a huge volume – mostly a few terabytes to hundreds of terabytes. This data comes from many sources including mobile, social media, videos, sensors and surveillance (TechAmerican Foundation, 2012) and has a new name called 'big data' as opposed to normal data.

Conventional databases are used to store, process, and manage structured data. For big data, which is mostly unstructured and in huge volume, a completely new set of computing technologies have emerged (Chandramouly and Stinson, 2013). Business organizations are showing special interest in big data to generate new business out of it. To view, analyze, and visualize both structured and unstructured data BI and visualization tools have emerged. The smart phone and tablets have brought Mobile BI into picture (Power, 2013; Haghighi, 2013).

Business organizations need to deploy emerging technologies in data warehousing (one with a parallel processing capability) and state of the art BI tools (e.g., in-memory analytics capability) to achieve faster data processing of, business intelligence to help making strategic decisions (Cooper et al., 2000) at the right time. To facilitate businesses to make right decisions at the right time, a series of new technologies have emerged. In this article, the authors will cover the latest database and business intelligence technologies.

FOCUS OF THE PAPER

Literature Review

In today's data-driven business decision making environment data science and business intelligence play a significant role and are dependent on each other (C. Eden and V. Padmanabhan, 2006). Data warehousing is deemed one of the six physical capability clusters of IT-infrastructure (Weill, Subramani, Broadbent, 2012). Data science / warehousing has been a research topic for the last two decades (Brobst, McIntire, and Rado, 2008; Lam and Lee, 2006; Payton and Handfield, 2004; Storey and Goldstein, 1993; Widom, 1993). Business intelligence is also gaining growing significance (Lonnqvist and Pirttimaki, 2006; Watson, 2009) over the last one decade. Data warehouse maintenance (Rundensteiner, Koeller, and Zhang, 2000), implementation (Rahman, 2008) and best practices have been explored (Wixom and Watson, 2001; Rahman, 2007). Researchers and practitioners have written papers on business intelligence design (Jourdan, Rainer, and Marshall, 2008; Sandu, 2008; Yermish et al., 2010; Rutz, NelaKanti, and Rahman, 2012; Chaudhuri, Dayal, and Narasayya, 2011). BI tools (Hagerty, Sallam, and Richardson, 2012; Spy, 2007; Vesset, 2011) have flourished significantly.

In business organizations the data volume has been increasing significantly every year. Data warehouse users express concern about slowness of access to time-critical data (Tank et al., 2010). This has been putting continuous pressure on IT departments to improve performance (Mithas, Ramasubbu, and Sambamurthy, 2011) and efficiency of IT infrastructures. There is a strong correlation between information technology capability and organizational agility (Lu and Ramamurthy, 2011). To speed up ETL processing in data warehousing Tank et al. (2010) suggests techniques to join operations and data aggregation. Allen & Parsons (2010) propose adjusting and reusing existing queries to help improve performance of data warehouse data retrieval process.

Chen et al. (2012) states that business intelligence and analytics has emerged as an important area of study to solve data viewing related problems with both 'normal' and big data in business organizations. Watson et al. (2006) emphasizes that "to be successful with real-time BI, organizations must overcome both organizational and technical challenges." Business organizations need to adopt emerging technologies to overcome technical and performance issues with traditional tools. The real-time BI helps in making right time business decisions which in turn allows for potential increase of revenues (Watson et al., 2006). Ramakrishnan et al. (2012) examines how external pressures influence the relationship between an organization's business intelligence (BI) data collection strategy and the purpose for which BI is implemented. Steiger (2010) asserts that "BI techniques can be applied to knowledge creation as an enabling technology."

In this paper, the authors show the latest technologies that emerged in data warehousing, BI, big data analytics and in cloud computing, and how they help support faster decision making. These technologies help in decreasing latency in data warehouse refreshes and without impacting performance and resources consumption. These technologies allow for achieving maximum benefits in terms of efficiency, revenue generation and cost avoidance.

Parallel Processing DBMS as Emerging Technology

Teradata® (a data warehousing DBMS) is the pioneer of a parallel processing data warehousing architecture (Teradata Corporation, 2006). Lately, other DBMS companies, including Oracle®, have been trying to implement similar kinds of technology. As we see tremendous data growth in medium to large companies, current commercial databases encounter huge amounts of data that need to be processed in loading and business intelligence purposes. Most of the commercial databases are not capable of processing millions of rows within a few seconds to support business intelligence decision making. Parallel processing architecture of DBMS is the right technology towards that endeavor.

In this article, the authors provide an overview of Teradata® parallel processing architecture. Figure 1 shows the parser engine (PE) at the top of hierarchy. The parser of the PE parses and optimizes SQL requests and then dispatches the optimized plan to AMPs over BYNET. After SQL request is processed the query results are returned back to the requesting user via the BYNET. The Teradata BYNET loosely couples Symmetric Multiprocessing (SMP) nodes in a multi-node system. There are two network links for each node. The AMPs and PEs send and receive messages using BYNET. It provides communication path among nodes. It merges SQL answer sets back to PE. The BYNET enables Teradata parallelism.

Figure 1. A Parallel Processing DBMS

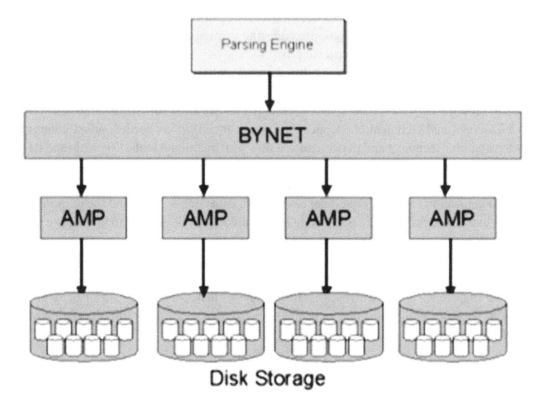

In a parallel processing DBMS architecture, a large number of individual access module processors (AMP) are used. The AMPs in Teradata DBMS work in parallel. This is also called shared nothing architecture. The data of a table does not get stored into a single AMP and instead is distributed across all AMPs. A hash algorithm decides which record to go to which AMP based on primary index (PI) of the table and during data retrieval all required AMPs participate in the data retrieval process based on a SQL query.

That is how a parallel processing DBMS maintains parallelism during both data store and retrieval processes. The data access module processor (AMP) stores and retrieves the distributed data in parallel. In data retrieval process each AMP is only responsible for the rows it stores. A particular AMP cannot pull rows that belong to a different AMP. As far as the AMPs are concerned, it owns all of the rows. The AMPs cannot access each other's data due to shared nothing architecture. The AMPs are designed to work in parallel and return the request results in the shortest possible time.

In SQL writing the ETL programmers must make sure that their SQL takes the parallel processing architecture of DBMS into consideration. Parallel processing database system is a key technology to adopt in handling large volumes of data when loading data warehouses as well as retrieving data from data warehouses for business intelligence purposes using reporting and data mining tools.

FINDINGS AND ANALYSES

Emerging Technologies in Big Data

Big data refers to dataset, which conventional DBMS cannot store, manage, or analyze. So big data is not limited to analytics (Ricknäs, 2012) and it is about taking care of everything such as collection, storing, organizing, analyzing and sharing. All these aspects pose a great challenge in big data system. Big data comes from so many sources including sensors embedded in the processes or systems consisting of operational data, images, videos, documents, mobile devices, and the Internet. Big data is not something that emerged all of a sudden. Organizations have been encountering large volumes of data for years. With the maturity of computing technology, processing power, and other data processing and BI tools, nowadays organizations leverage big data to provide greater insights with assessing new business opportunities and for better decision making. Studies show that organizations that adopt data-driven decision making have been successful in increasing productivity 5-6% higher than competition (Oracle Corporation, 2011). Big data is used to empower organizations to improve their predictive capabilities (Ricknäs, 2012).

Table 1. Big data with emphasis on 5 V's

Characteristic	Description	Influencer
Volume	A few terabytes to hundreds of terabytes of data need to be captured, processed, stored, and analyzed	Data volume keeps growing in source
Velocity	Given the volumn the data need to captured, processed, and displayed faster for right time business intelligence and decsion making	Increase in data sources. Improved computing, processing, BI & Visualization technologies
Variety	Includes a variety of data sources with unstructured, semistructured, and structured data. More than 90% unstructured	Sensors, social media sites, digital pictures, video, transaction records, and communication surveillance
Veracity	The quality and provenance of received data. As data most cases data is no structured data consistency is an issue	Data-based decisions require traceability and justification
Value	Provides greater insights generating new business value	Corporate business value

Big Data is identified by five factors - volume, velocity, variety, veracity and value. As the name says big data references an enormous amount of data which cannot be handled by conventional database systems and associated tools. Given the volume of data, it has become important to have the capability of receiving, processing and storing data faster (velocity). Big data also refers to data that comes from many sources and in different formats (variety). The data is unstructured (more than 90%), semi structured and structured.

This unstructured nature of data invalidates conventional database systems, which are meant for managing structured data. As data is mostly unstructured data consistency issue comes into picture (veracity). Again, that is due to the nature of source data (mostly unstructured). Business finds value as long as there is traceability and data processing is done by following some standard processes. With regards to the characteristic, business organizations find business opportunity in big data. One good example is predictive analytics using big data. Big data system provides capabilities for analyzing a greater breadth and depth of data (TechAmerican Foundation, 2012).

The big data challenge compels computer scientists, programmers, and information technology professionals to come up with a new paradigm. It is about a complete set of new technology, tools and techniques to receive large volume of data, process them, organize, store and display. There are several technological advancements that have recently occurred which effectively deal with 5 V's of big data. HBase database has emerged as a column oriented database scaling to billions of rows. To handle large volume of data open source framework, Hadoop provides a distributed file system (HDFS). To process large volume of data MapReduce is used for parallel computation on server clusters.

Thus big data is distributed and a small portion of data resides on each node. This is shared nothing architecture. Each node possesses its own autonomic unit of CPU, RAM and storage. Not much data movement is needed as the processing occurs where data resides. MapReduce allows lower cost processing of massive data. Hive provides capability of data warehouse with SQL-like access. On the data mining front Mahout provides a library of machine learning and data mining algorithms.

Sqoop is used to import data from relational databases. Zookeeper tool is used as a configuration management and coordination. From big data capable database systems there are a couple of new database systems including Hbase and in-memory database. Teradata is also used among current commercial database systems to store structured data. Teradata is best suited for big data because it has parallel processing architecture.

Business organizations have been conducting a variety of test cases using big data to prove usefulness and fulfill business needs. In one of our test cases we faced computing and scalability issue with existing technologies (database and other applications) in comparing all pairs of a few million proteins. This search and comparison activities overburdened the conventional database tables. Later we needed to do this comparison between 20 million proteins. We realized that this cannot be accomplished with existing technology.

Here, Big Data technologies come into picture – Hadoop, Map Reduce, Hbase, Hive, etc. Our experiments show that big data technologies have to do the said comparison and analysis by reducing the processing time from days to hours. Another use case was about dealing with medical monitoring data to improve patient outcomes. "The patients routinely are connected to equipment that continuously monitors vital signs, such as blood pressure, heart rate and temperature. The equipment issues an alert when any vital sign goes out of the normal range, prompting hospital staff to take action immediately.

The use case result is an early warning that gives caregivers the ability to proactively deal with potential complications, such as detecting infections in premature infants up to 24 hours before they exhibit symptoms" (TechAmerican Foundation, 2012). We conducted another use case to come up with a smart traffic intelligence system, a predictive analytics using Hadoop technologies. The challenge was to analyze city traffic data to derive statistics for crime prevention, information sharing, and predictive traffic analysis. By using real time traffic data predictive analytics was performed. The big data technologies helped with generating automated queries for traffic violation, data mining of fake licenses in a minute based on data captured for a week. This has improved the predictive traffic forecasting capability of city authority.

Chandramouly & Stinson (2013) provide an architectural overview of big data solution that allows for effective use of BI tools to run business with operational efficiency and competitive advantage. While big data holds hidden information, business analysts need to read or view that business information using some analytical and visualization tools. Heer and Kandel (2012) suggest some interactive analysis tools for big data to empower data analysts to formulate and assess hypothesis in a rapid manner.

To make meaningful information from big data, visualization matters. Visualization of data helps us to understand data, see patterns, spot trends and detect outliers (Heer, Bostock, and Ogievetsky, 2010). Heer and Shneiderman (2012) emphasize several visualization techniques of big data. They propose a taxonomy of interactive dynamics for visual analysis consisting of data view specification, view manipulation and processes.

In-Memory Analytics in Business Analytics and DBMS

In-memory data processing is a very new technology that has recently emerged. It's been used in both database and business intelligence space. Exasol® (Beyer et al., 2012) has first in-memory column-store DBMS available and primarily used as a data mart for analytic applications. In-memory has several key performance benefits (Gartner, Inc., 2009): dramatic performance improvements; cost-effective alternative to data warehouses; discover new insights; and connect insight with action.

Table 2. Capabilities of in-memory analytics

Read and Write Capabilities
Centrally Managed Data, Business Hierarchies, Rules and Calculations
Empower Business Users to Analyze any Combination of Data
High Impact Visualizations
Extend and Transform Excel
Designed for Modern 64 bit Architectures
Easy to Insall and Easy to Use

The IBM Cognos (Gartner, Inc., 2009) provides several capabilities with in-memory analytics. These include read and write capabilities; centrally managed data, business hierarchies, rules and calculations; empower business users to analyze any combination of data; high impact visualizations; extend and transform excel; designed for modern 64 bit architectures; and easy to install and easy to use. SAP Hana has come up with in-memory database technology which provides better performance of analytics and transactional applications. SAP Hana is even positioned to handle big data in terms of several terabytes of data in memory for analytical purposes.

Oracle, a leading commercial database company, has launched its in-memory database and business analytics technology. Oracle's In-Memory machine features an optimized BI foundation suite and its 'TimesTen' In-Memory database. The Oracle BI Foundation takes "advantage of large memory, processors, concurrency, storage, networking, kernel, and system configuration of the Oracle exalytics hardware. This optimization results in better query responsiveness, higher user scalability (Oracle Corporation, 2011)".

Data Science and Business Intelligence with Cloud Computing

Data warehousing projects are very expensive. Normally medium to large companies maintain their own data warehouse. On the other hand, companies of all sizes have data growing over the years. Data warehouse and BI on the cloud have opened the door for all sizes of companies to use these technologies. The Cloud is transforming the economics of BI and opening up many new possibilities for organizations of all sizes (Vertica Systems Inc., 2008). With cloud, business organizations will find it relatively easy to fund data warehousing projects given the low cost and no maintenance involved. For cloud-based data warehousing long term capital expenditures is not needed. Businesses can pay for cloud service on a weekly, monthly or pay per service basis.

Cloud data warehousing and BI will allow business organizations to conduct more short-term ad-hoc analysis. Building an organization's own data warehouse takes a long time to set up infrastructure and line up resources. With cloud individual business organizations do not have to worry about infrastructure and logistics. With cloud technology it takes a few hours or days to get an initial data warehouse created.

Cloud-based data warehouse is economically suitable for sandbox kind of development and testing as well as short-lived projects. Cloud-based analytic databases will enable small companies to warehouse and analyze a large volume of data even though their BI budgets and staff are much smaller than larger enterprises. On the other hand, analytic SaaS market will develop faster (Jaspersoft, 2011). Amazon is the leading provider of cloud services. All leading commercial database companies have teamed up with Amazon to run their databases on the cloud platform (Amazon EC2).

Cloud service providers provide both public and private cloud services. Given that most of the business organizations have financial and other mission critical data, using public cloud is not a good choice as public cloud is shared by anyone sharing the same network, server, software and hardware. Data security is the biggest concern. While cloud provides financial advantage, data security on the cloud is a big concern. Industry experts suggest using private cloud from the standpoint of data security. They also suggest using multiple layers of data protection (e.g., password encryption) and the higher levels of security (Bair, 2013) to ensure compliance requirements of individual business organizations.

As emerging technology, the Amazon Web Services (AWS) recently announced a new cloud-based data warehousing and BI tool called Amazon Redshift (Butler, 2012). This service provides service in big data analytics as well. The customers can pay per service basis to make it affordable to small and medium-sized businesses (Narcisi, 2012). Besides Amazon's entry into cloud-based data warehousing, the data warehouse vendors such as Teradata® and HP Vertica ® are already on the market (Bair, 2013) with cloud-based data warehouse appliance offering. So with the offering of cloud-based data warehousing and BI technology by these leading companies, the adoption of data warehousing and BI should expand much faster (Jaspersoft, 2011).

FUTURE RESEARCH DIRECTIONS

Recent development in smart phone has opened the possibilities of getting up to the minutes business information. This has a positive impact in the business intelligence field. Industry survey shows that mobile BI is getting more popularity. According to a recent survey, "24% of enterprises already use or are piloting mobile BI applications, while 37% are considering mobile BI for near-term implementations" (Tabbitt, 2013). In another survey it was observed that "87% of the respondents reported that they planned to use a mobile device to help make purchasing decisions during holiday shopping" (Power, 2013).

E

The trend of computer-based reports is changing with the emergence of Business Intelligence system applications that run on mobile devices, such as smart-phones and tablet computers (Business Intelligence Strategy, 2013). The Gartner research findings indicate that one third of BI functionality will be consumed through hand-held devices. There are many positive developments occurring in smart phone and other mobile devices. With the growing popularity of the tablet, the adoption rate of mobile BI is expected to soar (Robb, 2011). The proliferation of iPad apps has allowed access to BI information at anywhere and anytime. These smart-phones have downloading capabilities faster than expected. Finally, touch-screens have improved the user experience (Jaspersoft, 2011). All these speak for business intelligence in the Mobile era as opposed to desktop-based business intelligence.

Robb (2012) reports top ten mobile intelligence apps including MicroStrategy Mobile, SAP Business Objects, Roambi, BIRT Mobile, IBM Cognos 8 Go! Mobile, and SAS Mobile (Robb, 2011). All these apps operate on iPhone, iPad, Blackberry, and Windows Mobile. Each of these apps has several great features. SAS Mobile applications have the ability to navigate through displays with interactive graphs, tables and charts. BIRT Mobile by Actuate extends BIRT-based data visualization to mobile devices. Roambi Enterprise Server 3 (ES3) by MeLLmo bundles server software, the Roambi Publisher utility and the Roambi mobile app. It integrates with most BI platforms and data warehouses. MicroStrategy Mobile extends graphs, grids, enterprise reports and information dashboards and its features also include out-of-the-box integration with Google maps (Robb, 2011).

With the advent of smart phone and tablets the Mobile Decision Support System (MDSS) has emerged as a new decision support system in this early 21st century. Haghighi suggests that MDSS can be beneficial to application domains where critical decisions need to be made under time pressure and the decision-makers are on the move (Haghighi, 2013). There are some potential industries that might use the emerging mobile BI technologies. These include mobile healthcare, emergency management, mobile commerce, mobile banking (Haghighi, 2013), purchase and selection decisions, and negotiations (Power, 2013).

CONCLUSION

The authors made sincere effort to present the latest information about the most advanced tools & technologies along with the traditional weapons among the both existing and emerging ones on big data, cloud computing, parallel processing data base management system (DBMS), in-memory analytics, data warehousing etc.

They have also tried to explore the emerging technologies in data storing and business intelligence. The benefits of using these new technologies have also been discussed. These emerging technologies and methods are very likely to be adopted by the business organizations steadily in the near future. Use of these new technologies in data warehousing and business intelligence will help organizations increase their revenues by providing data based or informative assistance in making strategic and tactical decisions in the right manner at the right time.

Thus, this paper / chapter is expected to help people as individual, or representing any organization, government or private, profit or nonprofit, to learn about the alternative tools and technologies to manage the structured or unstructured data they have to manage, their sources, cost, usage, etc., which will help them find the ways to choose the best possible technology for their purposes of managing their data most effectively, and efficiently in terms of time, cost, and comfort.

REFERENCES

Allen, G., & Parsons, J. (2010). Is query reuse potentially harmful? Anchoring and adjustment in adapting existing database queries. *Information Systems Research, 21*(1), 56–77. doi:10.1287/isre.1080.0189

Armstrong, R. (1997). Data warehousing: Dealing with the growing pains. *IEEE Proceedings, 97*, 199-205.

Bair, J. (2013). *Emerging cloud appliances for business intelligence and data warehousing: 6 challenges and opportunities.* http://www.b-eye-network.com/view/16915.2013/04/24

Beyer, M. A., Feinberg, D., Adrian, M., & Edjlali, R. (2012). Magic quadrant for data warehouse database management systems. Gartner Inc.

Brobst, S., McIntire, M., & Rado, E. (2008). Agile data warehousing with integrated sandboxing. *Business Intelligence Journal, 13*(1).

Business Intelligence Strategy. (2013). *Smarter mobile devices drive demand for mobile business intelligence applications.* http://www.businessintelligencestrategy.com.au/news-views/mobile-business-intelligence/

Butler, B. (2012). *Is the cloud the right place for your data warehouse?* https://www.networkworld.com/news/2012/121012-aws-data-warehouse-264957

Chandramouly, A., & Stinson, K. (2013). *Enabling big data solutions with centralized data management.* Intel Information Technology White Paper. www.intel.com/it

Chaudhuri, S., Dayal, U., & Narasayya, V. (2011). An Overview of Business Intelligence Technology. *Communications of the ACM, 54*(8), 88–98. doi:10.1145/1978542.1978562

Chen, H., Chiang, R. H. L., & Storey, V. C. (2012). Business intelligence and analytics: From big data to big impact. *Management Information Systems Quarterly, 36*(4), 1165–1188. doi:10.2307/41703503

Cooper, B. L., Watson, H. J., Wixom, B. H., & Goodhue, D. L. (2000). Data warehousing supports corporate strategy at first American corporation. *Management Information Systems Quarterly, 24*(4), 547–567. doi:10.2307/3250947

Eden, C., & Padmanabhan, V. (2006). *Building an enterprise data warehouse and business intelligence solution.* Intel Information Technology White Paper, (2006), 1-11. www.intel.com/it

Gartner, Inc. (2009). *In-Memory Analytics: Leveraging Emerging Technologies for Business Intelligence.* http://download.boulder.ibm.com/ibmdl/pub/software/data/sw-library/cognos/pdfs/ar_inmemory_analytics_leveraging_emerging_technologies_for_business_intelligence.pdf

Hagerty, J., Sallam, R. L., & Richardson, J. (2012). Magic quadrant for business intelligence platforms. Gartner Inc.

Haghighi, P. D. (2013). The new era of mobile decision support systems. *Journal of Decision Systems, 22*(1), 1–3. doi:10.1080/12460125.2013.764063

Heer, J., Bostock, M., & Ogievetsky, V. (2010). A tour through the visualization zoo. *Communications of the ACM, 53*(6), 59–67. doi:10.1145/1743546.1743567

Heer, J., & Kandel, S. (2012). Interactive analysis of big data. *ACM Crossroads, 19*(1), 50–54. doi:10.1145/2331042.2331058

Heer, J., & Shneiderman, B. (2012). Interactive dynamics for visual analysis. *Communications of the ACM*, 55(4), 45–54. doi:10.1145/2133806.2133821

Jaspersoft. (2011). *Seven trends that will change business intelligence as we know it.* http://resources.idgenterprise.com/original/AST-0043754_Jaspersoft_eBook.pdf

Jourdan, Z., Rainer, R. K., & Marshall, T. E. (2008). Business intelligence: An analysis of the literature. *Information Systems Management*, 25(2), 121–131. doi:10.1080/10580530801941512

Kandel, S., Paepcke, A., Hellerstein, J. M., & Heer, J. (2012). Enterprise data analysis and visualization: An interview study. *IEEE Transactions on Visualization and Computer Graphics*, 18(12), 2917–2926. doi:10.1109/TVCG.2012.219 PMID:26357201

Lam, K., & Lee, V. C. S. (2006). On consistent reading of entire databases. *IEEE Transactions on Knowledge and Data Engineering*, 18(4), 569–572. doi:10.1109/TKDE.2006.1599393

Lonnqvist, A., & Pirttimaki, V. (2006). The measurement of business intelligence. *Information Systems Management*, 23(1), 32–35. doi:10.1201/1078.10580530/45769.23.1.20061201/91770.4

Lu, Y., & Ramamurthy, K. (2011). Understanding the link between information technology capability and organizational agility: An empirical examination. *Management Information Systems Quarterly*, 35(4), 931–954. doi:10.2307/41409967

Mithas, S., Ramasubbu, N., & Sambamurthy, V. (2011). How information management capability influences firm performance. *Management Information Systems Quarterly*, 35(1), 237–256. doi:10.2307/23043496

Narcisi, G. (2012). *AWS introduces Redshift big data and business intelligence service.* https://search-cloudprovider.techtarget.com/news/2240173984/AWS-introduces-Redshift-big-data-and-business-intelligence-service

Oracle Corporation. (2013). *Oracle exalytics in-memory machine: A brief introduction.* An Oracle White Paper, (2013/07), 1-18.

Payton, F., & Handfield, R. (2004). Strategies for data warehousing. *MIT Sloan Management Review*.

Power, D. J. (2013). Mobile decision support and business intelligence: An overview. *Journal of Decision Systems*, 22(1), 4–9. doi:10.1080/12460125.2012.760267

Rahman, N. (2007). Refreshing data warehouses with near real-time updates. *Journal of Computer Information Systems*, 47(3), 71–80.

Rahman, N. (2008). Updating data warehouses with temporal data. *American Conference on Information Systems (AMCIS) Proceedings*, 323. https://aisel.aisnet.org/amcis2008/323

Ramakrishnan, T., Jones, M. C., & Sidorova, A. (2012). Factors influencing business intelligence (BI) data collection strategies: An empirical investigation. *Decision Support Systems*, 52(2), 486–496. doi:10.1016/j.dss.2011.10.009

Ricknäs, M. (2012). *Big data not just about the analytics.* https://www.computerworld.com/s/article/9224986/Big_data_not_just_about_the_analytics_says_Amazon_CTO. 2013/04/16.

Robb, D. (2011). *Ten great mobile business intelligence Apps.* http://www.enterpriseappstoday.com/business-intelligence/ten-great-mobile-business intelligence-apps-1.html, 2011.

Rundensteiner, E. A., Koeller, A., & Zhang, X. (2000). Maintaining data warehouses over changing information sources. *Communications of the ACM, 43*(6), 57–62. doi:10.1145/336460.336475

Rutz, D., NelaKanti, T., & Rahman, N. (2012). Practical implications of real time business intelligence. *Journal of Computing and Information Technology – CIT, 20*(4), 257-264. doi:10.2498/cit.1002081

Sandu, D. I. (2008). Operational and real-time Business Intelligence. *Revista Informatica Economică, 3*(47), 33–36.

Sen, A., & Sinha, A. P. (2005). A comparison of data warehousing methodologies. *Communications of the ACM, 48*(3), 79–84. doi:10.1145/1047671.1047673

Spy, D. (2007). *5 top business intelligence tool vendors according to IDC.* http://www.enterprise-dashboard.com/top-5-business-intelligence-tool-vendors-2007/

Steiger, D. M. (2010). Decision support as knowledge creation: A business intelligence design theory. *International Journal of Business Intelligence Research, 1*(1), 29–47. doi:10.4018/jbir.2010071703

Storey, V. C., & Goldstein, R. C. (1993). Knowledge-based approaches to database design. *Management Information Systems Quarterly, 17*(1), 25–46. doi:10.2307/249508

Tabbitt, S. (2013). *Mobile business intelligence: Here at last?* http://www.informationweek.com/software/business-intelligence/mobile-business-intelligence-here-at-las/240146333

Tank, D. M., Ganatra, A., Kosta, Y. P., & Bhensdadia, C. K. (2010). Speeding ETL processing in data warehouses using high-performance joins for changed data capture (CDC). *2010 International Conference on Advances in Recent Technologies in Communication and Computing,* 2010(63), 365-368. DOI: 10.1109/ARTCom.2010.63

Tech American Foundation. (2012). *Demystifying big data: A practical guide to transforming the business of government.* https://www.techamerica.org/Docs/fileManager.cfm?f=techamerica-bigdatareport-final.pdf

Teradata Corporation. (2006). *Teradata solution technical overview.* www.teradata.com/WorkArea/DownloadAsset.aspx?id=4650

Vertica Systems Inc. (2013). *Cloud transforms economics of data warehousing -vertica.pdf, 2008.* https://www.vertica.com/wpcontent/uploads

Vertica Systems Inc. (2013). *Transforming the economics of data warehousing with cloud computing.* https://www.vertica.com/wpcontent/uploads/2011/01

Vesset, D. (2011). Competitive analysis: Worldwide business intelligence tools 2010 vendor shares. *IDC Analyze the Future, 1,* 1-16. http://www.sas.com/news/analysts/103115_0611.pdf

Watson, H. J. (2009). Tutorial: Business intelligence – past, present, and future. *Communications of the Association for Information Systems, 25*(39), 487–510. doi:10.17705/1CAIS.02539

Watson, H. J., Wixom, B. H., Hoffer, J. A., Anderson-Lehman, R., & Reynolds, A. M. (2006). Real-time business intelligence: Best practices at continental airlines. *Information Systems Management, 23*(1), 7–18. doi:10.1201/1078.10580530/45769.23.1.20061201/91768.2

Weill, W., Subramani, M., & Broadbent, M. (2012). Building IT Infrastructure for Strategic Agility. *MIT Sloan Management Review.*

Widom, J. (1995). Research problems in data warehousing. *Proceedings of the 4th Int'l Conference on Information and Knowledge Management (CIKM)*.

Wixom, B. H., & Watson, H. J. (2001). An empirical investigation of the factors affecting data warehousing success. *Management Information Systems Quarterly*, *25*(1), 17–44. doi:10.2307/3250957

Yermish, I., Miori, V., Yi, J., Malhotra, R., & Klimberg, R. (2010). Business plus intelligence plus technology equals business intelligence. *International Journal of Business Intelligence Research*, *1*(1), 48–63. doi:10.4018/jbir.2010071704

ADDITIONAL READING

Agarwal, R., & Dhar, V. (2014). Editorial - Big data, data science, and analytics: The opportunity and challenge for IS research. *Information Systems Research*, *25*(3), 443–448. doi:10.1287/isre.2014.0546

Alugubelli, R. (2018). Visualization for data analytics and data science. *Journal of Emerging Technologies and Innovative Research*, *5*(3), 586–594.

Bharath, K. (2021). *10 Best tools and technologies for data science.* https://towardsdatascience.com/10-best-tools-and-technologies-for-data-science-e335fb99c2f2

Dilmegani, C. (2022). *The ultimate guide to top 10 data science tools in 2022.* https://research.aimultiple.com/data-science-tools/

Fairfield, J., & Shtein, H. (2014). Big data, big problems: Emerging issues in the ethics of data science and journalism. *Journal of Mass Media Ethics*, *29*(1), 38–51. doi:10.1080/08900523.2014.863126

Goyal, D., Goyal, R., Malik, S., Rekha, G., & Tyagi, A. K. (2020). Emerging trends and challenges in data science and big data analytics. In *Proceedings of 2020 International Conference on Emerging Trends in Information Technology and Engineering (ic-ETITE)* (pp 1-8). IEEE. 10.1109/ic-ETITE47903.2020.316

Jose, C. G. J., Brewer, S., Wiktorski, T., & Demchenko, Y. (2019). EDISON data science framework (EDSF) extension to address transversal skills required by emerging industry 4.0 transformation. In *Proceeding of 2019 15th International Conference on eScience (eScience)* (pp. 553-559). IEEE.

Nadikattu, R. R. (2020). Research on data science, data analytics and big data. *International Journal of Engineering, Science, and Mathematics*, *9*(5), 99–105. doi:10.2139srn.3622844

Pole, G., & Gera, P. (2016). A recent study of emerging tools and technologies boosting big data analytics. In H. Saini, R. Sayal, & S. Rawat (Eds.), *Innovations in Computer Science and Engineering. Advances in Intelligent Systems and Computing* (Vol. 413). Springer. doi:10.1007/978-981-10-0419-3_4

Prasad, P. (2020). Role of big data science in the emerging world. *International Journal of Trend in Scientific Research and Development*, *4*(5), 215–217.

Pratt, M. K. (2022). *18 data science tools to consider using in 2022.* https://www.techtarget.com/searchbusinessanalytics/feature/15-data-science-tools-to-consider-using

Provost, F., & Fawcett, T. (2013). Data Science and its relationship to big data and data-driven decision making. *Big Data,* *1*(1), 51-59. doi:10.1089/big.2013.1508

Shivam, N. (2021). *Emerging trends and technologies in data science for 2022.* https://www.naukri.com/learning/articles/emerging-trends-technologies-in-data-science/

KEY TERMS AND DEFINITIONS

Big Data: Big data – a simple word turned into a technical jargon now-a-days to many common people because of its extensive use in the computing world with both its implicit and explicit meanings. The connotation of the term does not mean only the size of the raw facts the concerned people have to deal with, it also gives an impression about the scope and importance of those facts, budget, tools, technologies, and expertise to process those unstructured facts, and an apprehension of the utility of the information to be derived from those raw facts.

Business Intelligence: The whole process or system of providing the refined and smart information to the business people or organizations based on properly processed pure data, to help them make accurate and timely decisions on the major and critical issues to sustain and succeed.

Cloud Computing: These kinds of terminologies / nomenclatures in the field of computer science, or data science are very interesting because of their association with some easily understandable regularly used very common and familiar words. Natural cloud being free to all irrespective of nationality, color, ethnicity etc., and making the computing or data science resources available to many users at the same time at no cost, or at a minimum cost as the total cost being distributed among all the users seems to be pretty similar to natural cloud, and hence the whole process of collective or shared usage of common computing resources has been named cloud computing very logically and befittingly.

Data Science: The field of knowledge dealing with the total processing viz. collection, classification, comprehension, interpretation, etc., of raw facts in any discipline to convert those into the required information to be used by different government, non-government, non-profit, profit or business organizations working in or involved with the corresponding discipline, to make informative decision on the basis of authentic data. Using this sorts of data supports to make data based decisions is known as Decision Support System (DSS)

Emerging: Any living or non-living entity, product, service etc., that becomes evident to exist from a non-existing, unseen, or unimagined entity, or as a revised and improved version of any existing entity, product, or service; and which is usually welcomed and widely excepted by the concerned community with a positive thought of seeing high potential of performance in the upcoming or would be entity, product, or service.

Parallel Processing: Parallel processing basically means multi-tasking in a word, with the purpose of increasing efficiency of doing a task up to the highest possible level of its standard set in an industry or working field, in terms of both time and cost, by approaching to do that task from all possible cost & time effective avenues simultaneously, within the limits of the existing performance facilities, and the environmental factors.

Tools and Technologies: A device along with the art and techniques of using that device to facilitate task performances by replacing or supplementing the manual method of doing a particular task. Tools and technologies help people to do huge amount of work which could not be even imagined to be performed manually, although those very tools and technologies might have been built absolutely manually at the early stages of the evolution of those.

Explainable Artificial Intelligence

Vanessa Keppeler
PwC, Germany

Matthias Lederer
Technical University of Applied Sciences Amberg-Weiden, Germany

Ulli Alexander Leucht
PwC, Germany

INTRODUCTION

Artificial intelligence (AI) can be used in almost all areas of a modern digital enterprise. While the very first AI systems were easy to interpret, increasingly opaque decision-making systems have emerged in recent years (Arrieta et al., 2019). This is largely due to the fact that their tremendous progress in performance has made them increasingly complex, making it difficult to understand how they come to a decision or outcome (Biran et al., 2017). AI systems are therefore often referred to as a 'black box' (Bauer et al., 2021). These complex and non-transparent models present a significant challenge to many companies when it comes to assuming responsibility and ensuring the traceability of decisions.

The explainability of AI thus represents one of the central barriers for the comprehensive use of the new technology. While there is widespread agreement on the basic requirement of explainability, the design of an appropriate explanation is rarely well defined and the definition of what 'explainable' means is less clear. There are different ways to formulate explanations, but it is not defined which formulation is considered appropriate to make AI explainable (Gilpin et al., 2019).

The comprehensibility and explainability of AI systems and their results is a basic prerequisite for the use and acceptance of the technology in many companies (Manikonda et al., 2020). In the research field of 'Explainable AI', the generation of explanations and the establishment of comprehensibility for AI systems is being researched intensively (Bauer et al. 2021). This includes all decisions being prepared or performed by highly complex AI models (Arya et al., 2019).

This contribution shows that there are numerous approaches for explanations, with varying relevance for different interest groups. Furthermore, the quality of explanations for artificial intelligence is described in more detail and evaluated with respect to completeness of an explanation as well as its interpretability.

BACKGROUND

Explanations

Explanations serve to make facts interpretable for human beings (Keil, 2006; Bechtel et al., 2005; Chater et al., 2006). Accordingly, an explanation is a mean or an instrument that helps people comprehend and understand decisions (Arrieta et al., 2019).

DOI: 10.4018/978-1-7998-9220-5.ch100

According to Karl Popper (Popper, 1935), an explanation serves to describe the cause of a decision by formulating its logical and causal relations. This is done by deductively deriving its laws and boundary conditions.

Popper attributes two essential components to an explanation. On the one hand that is a general hypothesis, e.g., 'everytime something happens, it has this same consequence', somewhat of a law for the case in question. The second component comprises particular statements, valid only for one specific occurrence, e.g., 'this happened' and 'this was the consequence in that case'. These case-specific statements represent the boundary conditions (Popper, 1935).

A causal explanation as such includes all components or factors related to a particular issue in a fully comprehensive way (Herman, 2019). However, for the explanation of a specific issue, people usually prefer short, selective explanations. They do not expect all causes to be fully included in an explanation, but rather that the most important ones are summarized (Molnar, 2020).

Furthermore, explanations are social interactions between the explainer and the receiver of the explanation (Confalonieri et al., 2020). Therefore, the social context has a great influence on the actual content of the explanation. Depending on the recipient, explanations are shaped differently (Van den Berg et al., 2020).

The quality of an explanation can be evaluated in two ways (Gilpin et al., 2019):

- **Interpretability**: The goal of interpretability is to provide an explanation for a decision that is as comprehensible as possible for humans (Doshi-Velez et al., 2017). The success of this goal depends on the perception, knowledge, and personal bias of the recipient (Miller, 2018). Therefore, for something to be interpretable, it must be described in a way that is simple enough for a person to understand, using vocabulary that makes sense to the counterpart (Gilpin et al., 2019).
- **Completeness**: The completeness of an explanation aims at describing an issue as precisely and accurately as possible. An explanation is more complete the better it makes an issue (e.g., a decision, a system, or an outcome) predictable in multiple situations (Gilpin et al., 2019).

There is a general trade-off between interpretability and completeness (Hoffmann et al., 2019). The most accurate explanations are not easy for people to interpret and, adversely, explanations that are particularly easy to interpret often do not offer extensive predictive power (Doshi-Velez et al., 2017).

Herman (2019) points out that the quality of an explanation for establishing interpretability therefore should not be assessed solely on the basis of human judgments and perceptions, because human judgments imply a strong and specific bias against simpler descriptions. In practice, this can lead to the presentation of simplified descriptions of complex systems to increase the confidence of recipients without them knowing the limits of the simplification (Doran, 2017).

To avoid this ethical dilemma, explanations should allow a trade-off between interpretability and completeness (Doshi-Velez et al., 2017). Depending on the recipient, an explanation should be able to be simplified. Vice versa, it should be able to be completed and expanded to include details, even though it then loses interpretability for humans. The evaluation of an explanation should be based on how it performs on the curve between maximum interpretability and maximum completeness (Doshi-Velez et al., 2017).

Artificial intelligence

There is widespread disagreement in the literature regarding the definition of the term 'artificial intelligence' (Arrieta et al., 2019). AI can be defined as the ability of a machine to perform cognitive functions that we associate with the human mind, such as perception, reasoning, learning, interaction with the environment, problem solving, and even the exercise of creativity (European Banking Federation, 2019).

In this context, an AI system is 'stronger' the more it approaches the capabilities of a human, with all the intelligence, emotions, and broad applicability of a human's knowledge (Jordan, 2019).

However, the majority of what is referred to as artificial intelligence today is still far from what is understood by 'strong' AI.

The commonly used definition of AI already in use today ('weak AI') often refers to machine learning (BaFin, 2018a).

- **Machine learning**: can be defined as a method of designing a sequence of actions to solve a problem, known as algorithms, that automatically optimize themselves through experience with limited or no human intervention (Financial Stability Board, 2017).
- **Supervised Learning**: In supervised learning, the algorithm is given labeled training data, i.e. pairs $(x1, y1)$, ..., (xn, yn), $x1, ...,xn \hat{I} X$, $y1, ...,yn \hat{I} Y$, which contain correlations. With these pairs, the algorithm is trained and learns to recognize the correlations. The algorithm learns to predict the variable y (Dixon et al., 2020). Its accuracy is then checked with a test data set (Guidotti, 2018). A label can be both a nominal feature (e.g., customer receives a loan or not) or a numerical feature (e.g., default amount). In the first case, the algorithm deals with a classification problem (Mohri et al., 2018). Supervised learning methods that deal with classification problems are, for example, K-Nearest-Neighbors, rule-based algorithms or Bayesian models (Thamm et al., 2020). If numerical features are involved, the algorithm deals with a regression problem (BaFin, 2018a). Examples are algorithms of linear or logistic regression (Thamm et al., 2020). In both cases, the goal is for the algorithm to learn the relationship between x and y and then apply it to previously unknown cases (Dixon et al., 2020).
- **Unsupervised Learning**: In unsupervised learning, the algorithm is given data without labels $(x1, x2, ..., xn)$. The goal is to obtain exploratory information about the data, group similar observations, or detect hidden patterns, so-called 'clustering' (Dixon et al., 2020). Unsupervised learning methods include, for example, K-Means clustering or anomaly detection methods (Thamm et al., 2020).
- **Reinforcement Learning**: In contrast to supervised learning, which considers only a single action at any point in time, reinforcement learning is concerned with the optimal sequence of actions. It is therefore a form of dynamic programming that leads to optimal execution of actions over a given horizon (Dixon et al., 2020). In reinforcement learning, an algorithm learns by interacting with its environment (Mohri et al., 2018). It typically selects an action and its environment responds by presenting rewards and moving it to the next situation. In reinforcement learning, an algorithm determines how to change its action selection strategy as a result of its experience. Its goal in doing so is to maximize future rewards (Feher da Silva et al., 2018). For example, Monte Carlo methods and temporal difference learning are used in reinforcement learning (Thamm et al., 2020).
- **Deep Learning**: Deep learning is a form of machine learning that uses algorithms that operate in layers, inspired by the structure and function of the brain. Deep learning algorithms, whose

structure is called deep artificial neural networks, can be used for supervised, unsupervised, or reinforcement learning. Deep neural networks are designed according to the number and width of layers as well as the connections between them (BaFin, 2018a).

APPROACHES OF EXPLAINABLE AI

Machine learning methods, especially Deep Learning, are in many ways incomprehensible to the user compared to simpler tools and solutions in practice (Lipton, 2017). They are often referred to as 'black boxes' because the user usually has no direct way of knowing why or how the algorithm made a particular decision or produced a result (Molnar, 2020). Deep learning algorithms are considered a particular challenge due to their high complexity (BaFin, 2018a).

Explainability of AI is particularly relevant in areas or for decisions that have financial, security, or personal output/implications for a person (Doran, 2017). For example, if the decision to grant a loan depends on an AI system, the consequences of a rejection may have financial or personal implications for the applicant (Manikonda, 2020).

Models without significant effects rarely require an explanation for their results. For example, if an AI decides on the type of advertising that is sent to an end customer, this usually has little impact and is rarely questioned (Molnar, 2020).

The explainability of artificial intelligence in general is important due to a variety of reasons (Arrieta et al., 2019):

- **Compliance with laws and regulations**: To enable the use of AI models in highly regulated sectors, even with very complex models to at least provide insights into how the model works and why decisions are made.
- **Improving the algorithms**: To improve an AI system, it must be possible to understand its weaknesses. Bias, discrimination, or unfair judgments in the model are easier to identify if it is understable what the model does and why. The better the understanding of a system, the easier it is to improve the system (Samek et al., 2017).
- **Increasing the trustworthiness of AI**: Trustworthiness can be considered as the confidence that a model will act as intended in a given problem. It is easier for users to have confidence in the correctness of the results the better they can understand them (Doshi-Velez et al., 2017).
- **Transferability of findings**: Explainability facilitates the transferability of recognized approaches to problem solving to other models and further development through new algorithms (Arrieta et al., 2019).
- **Provision of decision-relevant information**: AI models are, among other things, used with the intention of supporting decision-making. In doing so, humans remain ultimately responsible and therefore demand an explanation for the solution or decision recommended by the AI (Arrieta et al., 2019).

The explainability of artificial intelligence is often determined by the philosophical and social scientific definition of an "explanation" and "interpretability" (Miller, 2018).

According to Miller (2018), the term 'explainable AI' refers to an explanatory agent revealing underlying causes to its or another agent's decision making. The explanatory agent in this case is the explanation itself, as the instrument by which a decision made by AI is made interpretable to humans. The agent making the decisions is the AI (Miller, 2018).

Artificial intelligence is considered 'explainable' or 'interpretable' to the degree that an observer or user can understand the cause of a decision (by formulating an explanation) (Biran et al., 2017) or also to the degree that a user can correctly and efficiently predict the results of the method by providing an explanation (Kim et al., 2016).

Arrieta et al. (2019) argue that the nature and scope of the explanation depend on the audience to which it is presented. Similarly, the evaluation of the explanation in terms of its comprehensibility is also dependent on the audience to whom it is presented. They therefore add the factor of the recipient of an explanation to the definition of explainability in the context of AI: Given a certain audience, explainability refers to the details and reasons a model gives to make its functioning clear or easy to understand (Arrieta et al., 2019).

Explainability by conception refers to specific models, such as linear regression or decision trees, as summarized in Figure 1. Post-hoc explainability can be considered both for specific models and 'model-agnostic', that is, independent of the model (Brochado, 2019). The two approaches are presented below.

Figure 1. Overview of categories and methods of explainable AI
Arrieta et al. (2019)

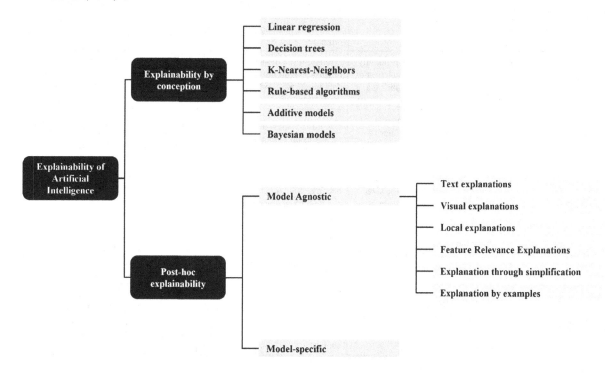

Explainability by Conception

The simplest way to achieve explainability is to use only the subset of algorithms that create 'explainable models'. A model is explainable by conception if it is directly understandable for an observer without further intervention (Arrieta et al., 2019). Because of the ease with which models can be understood, they are often referred to as 'transparent models'. According to Lipton (2017), transparency can be given on three different levels:

- **Entire model**: This means that a model is completely and directly comprehensible by a human being and can therefore be simulated.
- **Individual components**: This means a model is decomposable into its individual components (input, parameters and output) and these individual components can be explained.
- **Algorithm**: This means that the process followed by the model to produce any output from its input data is readily understandable to the user.

Linear regression, decision trees, K-nearest neighbors, rule-based algorithms, additive models, and Bayesian models are commonly used interpretable models (Molnar 2020).

Table 1. AI models explainable by conception (Arrieta et al., 2019)

Model	Transparency of the entire model	Transparency of individual components	Transparency of the Algorithm
Linear regression	Given if the variables are human readable and the interactions between them are kept to a minimum.	If the variables are still readable, but the number of interactions and predictors involved in them is too high, decomposition is required.	Variables and interactions can be too complex to analyze without mathematical tools.
Decision trees	Given if a human can independently simulate and obtain the prediction of a decision tree without requiring a mathematical background.	Possible if the model consists of rules that do not change the data in any way and preserve its readability.	Human-readable rules that explain what is learned from the data and provide a direct understanding of the prediction process.
K-Nearest-Neighbors	Given if the set of variables is not too large and/or the similarity measure is not too complex to fully simulate the model.	Possible by analyzing similarity measures and input variables separately.	If the similarity measure cannot be decomposed and/or the number of variables is too high, the user must resort to mathematical tools.
Rule based algorithms	Given if the variables contained in the rules are readable and the size of the rule set is manageable by a human user without external help.	If the size of the rule set becomes too large to analyze, it can be broken down into small rule chunks to make sense of it.	If the rules become so complicated and/or the size of the rule set is too large, mathematical tools are needed to study the model behavior.
Additive models	Given if the variables and the interaction between them are constrained or minimized.	When the interactions become too complex to simulate, decomposition techniques are required to analyze the model.	Due to their complexity, variables and interactions cannot be analyzed without the application of mathematical and statistical tools.
Bayesian models	Given if statistical relationships that are modeled between variables and the variables themselves are directly understandable to humans.	When statistical relationships involve too many variables, they must be decomposed into marginals to facilitate their analysis.	Statistical relationships cannot be interpreted even if they are already decomposed, and the predictors are so complex that the model can only be analyzed with mathematical tools.

Table 1 illustrates the models that can be explained by conception and describes their transparency at the different levels (Arrieta et al., 2019). The first column 'Transparency of the entire model' describes under which conditions this level of transparency is given. The second column explains whether the model is decomposable, and under which conditions the individual components can be made explainable. The third column on 'Transparency of the Algorithm' shows for which models the algorithm can be transparent. This is often not possible without additional statistical or mathematical tools (Arrieta et al., 2019).

E

Models that are explainable by conception merely require communication of their mode of operation in a way that is appropriate for the addressee. They no longer need to be explained separately (Lipton, 2017). Therefore, they will not be the focus of the present work in the following. It will also not be further considered at this point how these models function. It should only be made clear to which degree or on which level they are considered transparent.

There is generally a trade-off between accuracy and explainability (see Figure 2).

Figure 2. Trade-off between accuracy and explainability of AI models
Arrieta et al. (2019)

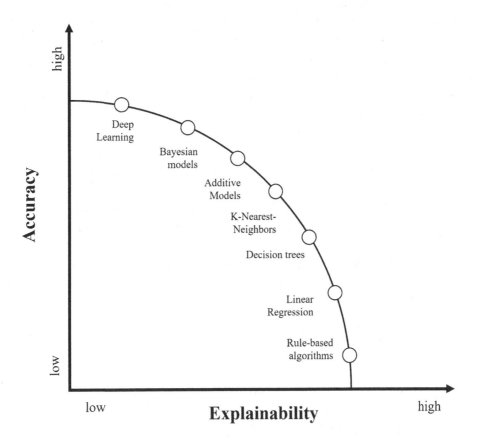

The quality of an explanation can be evaluated on the basis of its interpretability and its completeness. Explanations should allow a compromise between interpretability and completeness. The transfer of this principle to AI models also leads to a trade-off, as shown in Figure 2. This relates to the accuracy of the models, in the sense of complete and accurate results, and the explainability of the models (Arrieta et al., 2019). Rule-based algorithms represent a possible extreme on the curve between maximum accuracy and maximum explainability in terms of explainability, since they are explainable by design and easily interpretable by humans (Manikonda et al., 2020). However, they therefore belong to the less performant or accurate algorithms (Ribeiro et al., 2016). Deep learning algorithms, on the other hand, can be very good in terms of performance. However, they are difficult to explain (Manikonda et al. 2020). In practice, high-performing AI models are used to either make work easier or create significant added value. However, in order for even highly complex and efficient systems to be used and made explainable, methods are needed to establish or at least improve this explainability without having to make significant sacrifices in accuracy (Lundberg and Lee, 2017).

Post Hoc Explainability

Post-hoc explainability targets all those models that are not explainable by conception. These include, for example, support vector machines, multi-layer neural networks, convolutional neural networks, and recurrent neural networks (Van den Berg et al., 2020). For this purpose, various means are resorted to such as textual explanations, visual explanations, local explanations, explanations by examples, explanations by simplification, and feature explanation techniques (Adadi et al., 2018).

Although post-hoc explanations often do not elucidate exactly how a model works, they can still provide useful information for end users and contribute to comprehensibility (Lipton, 2017). For models that are not per se comprehensible to a human, post-hoc explanations create the necessary tools to help the recipient understand why a particular result was achieved (Arrieta et al., 2019). It is less relevant how accurate or complete the explanation is in the sense of Karl Popper (Popper 1935). What is more important is that it presents an accurate description of how things work or a rationale for the result that is understandable to humans, without the AI model itself having to sacrifice accuracy in favor of explainability (Doshi-Velez et al., 2017).

A distinction is made between model-specific and model-agnostic methods (Brochado, 2019):

- **Model-specific methods** are those methods that have only been designed for specific machine learning models and therefore have the disadvantage that they cannot be transferred to other models (Molnar, 2020).
- **Model-agnostic methods**, on the other hand, were designed to be applied to any type of model. In practice, they can be combined and designed in such a way that they are understandable for the recipient (Arrieta et al., 2019).

Due to their flexibility, the focus in the following will be on model-agnostic xAI methods. The models used in practice are diverse and subject to constant change (Bauer et al., 2021). Formulating requirements for explainability along model-agnostic methods has the advantage that they can be implemented independently of the model used and thus provide more stable guidelines in the long term (Molnar, 2020).

Model-agnostic methods for explaining artificial intelligence separate the explanation from the model used, that is, they are independent of the model. The major advantage of these methods is therefore their flexibility (Ribeiro et al., 2016). Mittelstadt et al. (2018) point out that post-hoc methods often generate only approximations or simpler models and then call them 'explanations'. In doing so, they suggest to the user reliable and exact knowledge about how a complex model works.

The goal of model-agnostic methods is to provide a representation to help the recipient understand how the 'black box model' works and/or why the model produces certain results (Guidotti et al., 2018).

In the following, the 'black box model', as shown in Figure 3, is defined in terms of three components to illustrate the different methods:

- 'x' as input factors, i.e., all data that serve as the basis for calculations in the model,
- 'M' as the trained black box model itself, regardless of which algorithm is applied; and
- 'y' as output factors, that is, all results based on the input factors 'x' calculated by the model 'M'.

Figure 3. Illustrative representation of a black box
Arrieta et al. (2019)

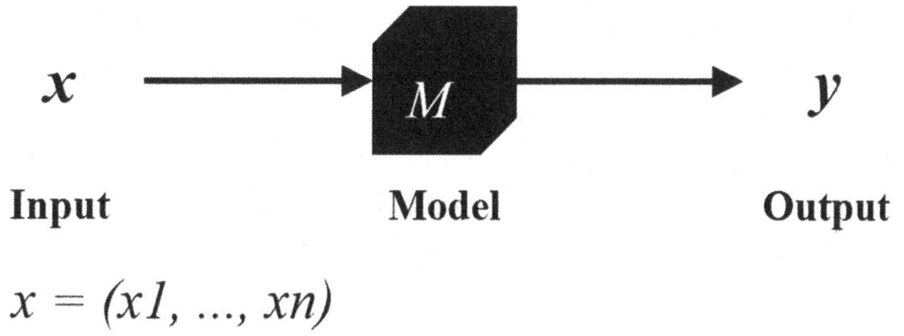

E

$$x \longrightarrow \boxed{M} \longrightarrow y$$

Input   **Model**   **Output**

$$x = (x1, ..., xn)$$

Text Explanations

Verbal reasoning is one of the most natural ways for humans to explain results or decisions (Lipton, 2017). Text explanations as an explanation method for AI models deal with creating model explainability by generating text segments from the trained model, or with an additional model, in such a way that they make the results verbally understandable to a user (Krening et al., 2017). The basic idea is that a textual explanation (shown in Figure 4) is generated that, for a given outcome or decision, verbally states the causality of the outcome (Bennetot et al., 2019).

Figure 4. Illustrative representation of a text explanation
Arrieta et al. (2019)

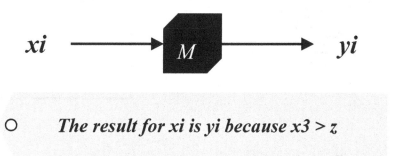

Alternatively, the extraction of decision rules used by the model can be used as text explanation, as illustrated in Figure 5. This type of text explanation is much easier to implement in practice by extracting rules (Hailesilassie, 2016).

Figure 5. Illustrative representation of a rule-based text explanation
Hailesilassie (2016)

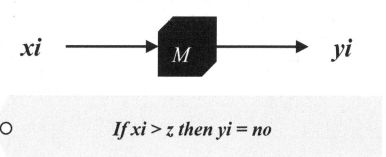

Visual Explanations

Visual explanation techniques for post hoc explanations aim to illustrate the behavior of a model (Adadi et al., 2018). In doing so, they are often accompanied by dimensionality reduction techniques that provide a simple visualization that can be interpreted by humans (Arrieta et al., 2019). Visualizations are considered the most appropriate way to show complex interactions within the variables involved in the model to users who are not familiar with AI modeling (Hendricks et al., 2016). Figure 6 shows an example of visualization of 'clusters'. Technical tools for visualization include sensitivity analysis (Cortez et al., 2013) and 'Individual Conditional Expectation (ICE)' (Goldstein et al., 2015).

Visual explanations are less common in the field of model-agnostic techniques for post hoc explainability (Adadi et al., 2018). They are often used to visually represent other methods, such as feature relevance (Arrieta et al., 2019). Without linking them to another method for explanation, as a purely visual representation of the black box, they are difficult to implement (Bennetot et al., 2019). To visualize the black box as such, based on the input and output of a black box model alone, a graph would have to be created to make the result understandable. This is a sufficiently complex task and is rarely pursued in practice (Arrieta et al., 2019).

Figure 6. Illustrative representation of a visual explanation
Arrieta et al. (2019)

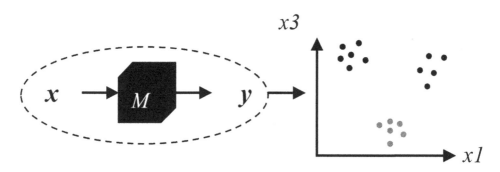

Feature Relevance Explanations

The goal of feature relevance explanation methods is to make the functioning of a model understandable by calculating a relative relevance score for the input variables (called features). Each feature is given a quantitative value that describes how important the feature was to the outcome of the model. By comparing the score values, it is then possible to evaluate which input variable had a particularly large influence on the result and which was less influential (Arrieta et al., 2019).

Figure 7 illustrates the comparison of the feature relevancies for the black box model 'M' with the input factors 'x'. It also shows why visualization techniques and feature relevance often coincide. The visual comparison of the score values is a popular way to present them to the recipient (Lipton, 2017).

Within feature relevance explanations, various algorithmic approaches can be found. One of the most popular and widely used approaches is 'SHapley Additive exPlanations' (SHAP) (Lundberg and Lee, 2017). The authors present a method to compute an additive feature importance for each outcome (output) with a set of desirable properties (local accuracy, irrelevance of missing inputs, and consistency)

Figure 7. Illustrative representation of a feature relevance explanation
Arrieta et al. (2019)

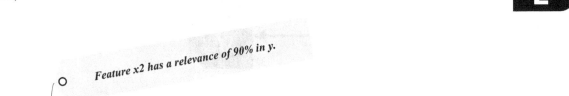

that they found lacking in their predecessors (Molnar, 2020). SHAP values assign the change in expected outcome to each characteristic, provided that the characteristic in question is accounted for by the model. They explain how to get from the baseline value $E[f(z)]$, to the output $f(x)$ (Lundberg and Lee, 2017).

Figure 8 shows how SHAP values are regularly visualized. The coloring of the arrows is typical: blue represents the positive variables and red those that are negative (Lundberg and Lee 2017).

Figure 8. Feature relevance representation with SHAP values
Lundberg and Lee (2017)

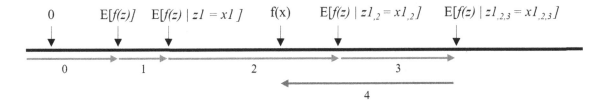

Local Declarations

Local explanations address explainability by segmenting the solution space and generating explanations of less complex solution subspaces that are relevant to the entire model. They consider the influence of input variables on the outcome for individual decisions, as illustrated in Figure 9 (Molnar, 2020).

These types of explanations can be generated using techniques that are characterized by explaining only part of how the entire system works. A commonly used example for the generation of local explanations is the 'local interpretable model-agnostic explanations (LIME algorithm) (Bracke et al., 2019).

LIME explains the results of any model by approximating the actual model locally (i.e., for one outcome or single case) with an interpretable model (Ribeiro et al., 2016). In doing so, LIME tests what happens to the results when the model receives variations in the input data. LIME then generates a new data set consisting of the variations in the input data and the corresponding results of the model. On this basis, LIME generates an interpretable surrogate model (a model that is explainable by conception) to

Figure 9. Illustrative representation of a local declaration (Arrieta et al., 2019)

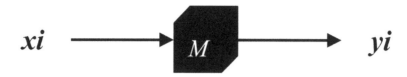

What happens to the forecast for yi when we change xi?

analyze the weighting of the input variables according to their importance for the individual outcome (Molnar, 2020).

It is particularly advantageous that the output of LIME can be in the form of a bar chart (see Figure 10). It identifies which variables, with which weight and how (positive or negative) affect the model result. This brings together local explanations, feature relevance explanations, and visualization techniques (Molnar, 2020).

Figure 10. Example of LIME feature relevance visualization
Dancho (2018)

Case: 1
Prediction: y1
Explanation fit: 0.12

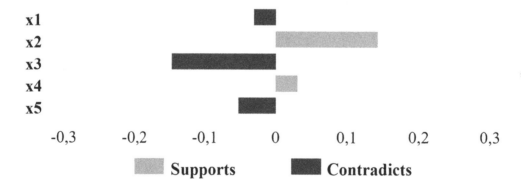

Explanation by Simplification

Almost all techniques of textual, visual, feature relevance, or local explanations also fall into the category of explanations by simplification. Complex models are usually simplified (as illustrated in Figure 11) to make them easier to interpret, and then presented in textual or visual form (Arrieta et al., 2019).

Simplification of complex models involves building a new model based on the trained model to be explained. In doing so, the new, simplified model attempts to optimize its similarity to the function of the predecessor model while reducing its complexity and aiming for a similar result (Bracke, 2019).

Figure 11. Illustrative representation of an explanation by simplification
Arrieta et al. (2019)

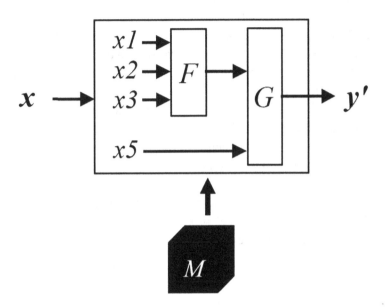

Explanation by Examples

Explanations by example consider the extraction of data examples that relate to the outcome of a model to gain a better understanding of the model itself, as illustrated in Figure 12 (Molnar, 2020). These types of explanations, in addition to the actual explanation for the trained model or the case, additionally draw on analogous or similar decisions as precedent to justify the decision (Lipton, 2017).

Figure 12. Illustrative representation of an explanation by examples
Arrieta et al. (2019)

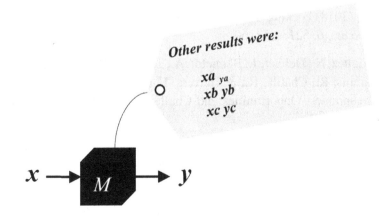

FUTURE RESEARCH DIRECTIONS

Traceability, in the context of decision-making processes supported by some form of AI, should no longer be an obstacle to the use of new technologies in an organization. This requires a common understanding of what constitutes an appropriate explanation. In the future, it will be an important task of many companies to establish explanation procedures and propose them in practical application. Finally, industries or domains need a normative expectation for the scope and design for the explainability of AI.

The explanatory schemes presented can be further refined in the future. In addition to further elaboration of the explanatory schemes, the derived designs can also be explored for their technical feasibility in practice. Various technical tools have already been investigated and designed in research for the various explanatory methods. These include sensitivity analyses (Cortez and Embrechts, 2013), Individual Conditional Expectation (Goldstein et al., 2015), SHAP values (Lundberg and Lee, 2017), and the LIME algorithm (Ribeiro et al., 2016). In addition to the techniques listed, various other approaches exist (Adadi and Berrada, 2018; Arrieta et al., 2019; Guidotti et al., 2018), which can be analyzed and tested for their suitability for a technical implementation. In particular, it is necessary to investigate whether the requirements established in this paper are technically feasible. Increasing regulation of AI will make further research of the field essential. Laws and standards could lead to a situation where, in addition to post hoc explainability, explainability by conception becomes the subject of future research. The goal here would have to be to create models that can be explained by conception and thus advance explainability without sacrificing model accuracy.

CONCLUSION

For the proper organization of a modern company, decisions, both within the organization and increasingly for external parties, must be comprehensible, especially when they involve risky decisions. For an increasing number of industries, traceability depends on the different requirements for the scope and design of declarations imposed by the various stakeholders. This contribution presents an overview of current approaches to providing good and comprehensible explanations for the complex field of AI. This provides a basis for establishing explanation procedures in companies and for developing them in practical applications.

REFERENCES

Adadi, A.; Berrada, M. (2018) Peeking inside the black-box: A survey on Explainable Artificial Intelligence (XAI). *IEEE Access, 6*, 52138-52160.

Arrieta, A., Díaz-Rodríguez, N., Del Ser, J., Bennetot, A., Tabik, S., Barbado, A., García, S., Gil-López, S., Molina, D., Benjamins, R., Chatila, R., & Herrera, F. (2019). Explainable Artificial Intelligence (XAI) - Concepts, Taxonomies, Opportunities and Challenges towards Responsible AI. *Information Fusion, 58*(20), 82–115.

BaFin. (2018a): *Big Data meets artificial intelligence - Challenges and implications for supervision and regulation of financial services.* https://www.bafin.de/SharedDocs/Downloads/ DE/dl_bdai_studie.pdf?__blob=publicationFileandv=9

Bauer, K., Hinz, O., & Weber, P. (2021): KI in der Finanzbranche: Im Spannungsfeld zwischen technologischer Innovation und regulatorischer Anforderung. *SAFE White Paper 80.* http://nbn-resolving. de/urn:nbn:de:hebis:30:3-568799

Bechtel, W., & Abrahamsen, A. (2005). Explanation: A mechanist alternative. *Studies in History and Philosophy of Science Part C Studies in History and Philosophy of Biological and Biomedical Sciences*, *36*(2), 421–441. doi:10.1016/j.shpsc.2005.03.010 PMID:19260199

Bennetot, A., Laurent, J.-L., Chatila, R., & Díaz-Rodríguez, N. (2019). *Towards Explainable Neural-Symbolic Visual Reasoning.* https://arxiv.org/pdf/1909.09065.pdf

Biran, O., & Cotton, C. V. (2017). Explanation and Justification in Machine Learning: A Survey. *Workshop on Explainable Artificial Intelligence.*

Bracke, P., Datta, A., Jung, C., & Sen, S. (2019). *Machine learning explainability in finance: an application to default risk analysis.* https://www.bankofengland.co.uk/working-paper/2019/machine-learning-explainability-in-finance-an-application-to-default-risk-analysis

Brochado, N. (2019). *Explainable AI is indispensable in areas where liability is an issue.* https://philar-chive.org/archive/BROEAI-3v3

Chater, N., & Oaksford, M. (2005). Mental mechanisms: Speculations on Human Causal Learning and Reasoning. *Information sampling and adaptive cognition*, 210-236.

Confalonieri, R., Coba, L., Wagner, B., & Besold, T. (2020). A historical perspective of explainable Artificial Intelligence - WIREs. *Data Mining and Knowledge Discovery.* Advance online publication. doi:10.1002/widm.1391

Cortez, P., & Embrechts, M. J. (2013). Using sensitivity analysis and visualization techniques to open black box data mining models. *Information Sciences*, *225*(10), 1–17. doi:10.1016/j.ins.2012.10.039

Dancho, M. (2018): *Deep Learning With Keras To Predict Customer Churn.* https://blogs.rstudio.com/ai/posts/2018-01-11-keras-customer-churn/

Dixon, M., Halperin, I., & Bilokon, P. (2020). *Machine Learning in Finance - From Theory to Practice.* Springer. doi:10.1007/978-3-030-41068-1

Doran, D., Schulz, S., & Besold, T. (2017). What Does Explainable AI Really Mean? A New Conceptualization of Perspectives. *CEUR Workshop Proceedings.*

Doshi-Velez, F., & Kim, B. (2017). *Towards a rigorous science of interpretable machine learning.* https://arxiv.org/pdf/1702.08608.pdf

Feher da Silva, C., Yuan-Wei, Y., & Hare, T. A. (2018). *Can model-free reinforcement learning operate over information stored in working-memory?* doi:10.1101/107698

Financial Stability Board. (2017). *Artificial intelligence and machine learning in financial ser-vices - Market developments and financial stability implications.* https://www.fsb.org/wp-content/uploads/P011117.pdf

Gilpin, L., Bau, D., Yuan, B., Bajwa, A., Specter, M., & Kagal, L. (2019): Explaining Explana-tions: An Overview of Interpretability of Machine Learning. *Proceedings of the IEEE International Conference on Data Science and Advanced Analytics.*

Goldstein, A., Kapelner, A., Bleich, J., & Pitkin, E. (2015). Peeking inside the black box: Visu-alizing statistical learning with plots of individual conditional expectation. *Journal of Computational and Graphical Statistics, 24*(1), 44–65. doi:10.1080/10618600.2014.907095

Guidotti, R., Monreale, A., Ruggieri, S., Turini, F., Pedreschi, D., & Giannotti, F. (2018). A Survey Of Methods For Explaining Black Box Models. *ACM Computing Surveys, 51*, 1-42.

Hailesilassie, T. (2016). Rule Extraction Algorithm for Deep Neural Networks: A Review. *International Journal of Computer Science and Information Security, 14*(7), 371–381.

Hendricks, L. A., Akata, Z., Rohrbach, M., Donahue, J., Schiele, B., & Darrell, T. (2016): Gene-rating Visual Explanations. In Computervision-ECCV 2016 (pp. 3-19). Cham: Springer International Publishing.

Herman, B. (2019): The Promise and Peril of Human Evaluation for Model Interpretability. *Proceedings of the NIPS 2017 Symposium on Interpretable Machine Learning.*

Hoffman, R., Mueller, S., Klein, G., & Litman, J. (2019): *Metrics for Explainable AI: Challenges and Prospects.* https://arxiv.org/abs/1812.04608

Jordan, M.I. (2019). Artificial intelligence - the revolution hasn't happened yet. *Harvard Data Science Review, 1*(1).

Keil, F. (2006). Explanation and understanding. *Annual Review of Psychology, 2006*(1), 227–254. doi:10.1146/annurev.psych.57.102904.190100 PMID:16318595

Kim, B., Khanna, R., & Koyejo, O. (2016). Examples are not enough, learn to criticize! Criticism for interpretability. *Advances in Neural Information Processing Systems, 9*, 2288–2296.

Krening, S., Harrison, B., Feigh, K., Isbell, C., Riedl, M., & Thomaz, A. (2017). *Learning from expla-nations using sentiment and advice in RL. IIEE Transactions on Cognitive and Developmental Systems.* doi:10.1109/TCDS.2016.2628365

Lipton, Z. (2017): The Myth of Model Interpretability. *Proceedings of the ICML Workshop on Human Interpretability in Machine Learning.*

Lundberg, S., & Lee, S.-I. (2017). A Unified Approach to Interpreting Model Predictions. *Proceedings of the NIPS 2017 Symposium on Interpretable Machine Learning.*

Manikonda, P., Poon, K., & Nguyen, C. (2020). *Explainable Machine Learning for Credit Lending.* https://www.cse.scu.edu/~mwang2/projects/ML_explainableCreditLend ing_20s.pdf

Miller, T. (2018). Explanation in artificial intelligence: Insights from the social sciences. *Artificial Intel-ligence, 267*, 1–66. doi:10.1016/j.artint.2018.07.007

Mittelstadt, B., Russel, C., & Wachter, S. (2018): Explaining Explanations in AI. *Proceedings of the conference on fairness, accountability, and transparency*, 279-288.

Mohri, M., Rostamizadeh, A., & Talwalkar, A. (2018). *Foundations of Machine Learning* (2nd ed.). The MIT Press.

Molnar, C. (2020). *Interpretable Machine Learning - A Guide for Making Black Box Models Explainable*. Leanpub.

Patton, M. (2007). *Sampling, qualitative (purposive)*. Blackwell. doi:10.1002/9781405165518.wbeoss012

Popper, K. (1935). *Logik der Forschung - Zur Erkenntnistheorie der Modernen Naturwis-senschaft*. Springer.

Ribeiro, M., Singh, S., & Guestrin, C. (2016). Why Should I Trust You? Explaining the Predictions of Any Classifier. *Proceedings of the 22nd International Conference on Knowledge Discovery and Data Mining*. 10.18653/v1/N16-3020

Samek, W., Wiegand, T., & Müller, K. (2017). Explainable Artificial Intelligence: Understanding, Visualizing and Interpreting Deep Learning Models. *ITU Journal*, *1*(13), 39–48.

Thamm, A., Gramlich, M., & Borek, A. (2020). *The Ultimate Data and AI Guide*. Data AI Press.

Van den Berg, M., & Kuiper, O. (2020). *XAI in the Financial Sector. A Conceptual Framework for Explainable AI (XAI)*. Hogeschool.

ADDITIONAL READING

Confalonieri, R., Coba, L., Wagner, B., & Besold, T. (2020). A historical perspective of explainable Artificial Intelligence - WIREs. *Data Mining and Knowledge Discovery*. Advance online publication. doi:10.1002/widm.1391

Doran, D., Schulz, S., & Besold, T. (2017). What Does Explainable AI Really Mean? A New Conceptualization of Perspectives. *CEUR Workshop Proceedings*.

Gilpin, L., Bau, D., Yuan, B., Bajwa, A., Specter, M., & Kagal, L. (2019): Explaining Explana-tions: An Overview of Interpretability of Machine Learning. *Proceedings of the IEEE International Conference on Data Science and Advanced Analytics*.

Miller, T. (2018). Explanation in artificial intelligence: Insights from the social sciences. *Artificial Intelligence*, *267*, 1–66. doi:10.1016/j.artint.2018.07.007

Mittelstadt, B., Russel, C., & Wachter, S. (2018): Explaining Explanations in AI. *Proceedings of the conference on fairness, accountability, and transparency*, 279-288.

Samek, W., Wiegand, T., & Müller, K. (2017). Explainable Artificial Intelligence: Understanding, Visualizing and Interpreting Deep Learning Models. *ITU Journal*, *1*(13), 39–48.

KEY TERMS AND DEFINITIONS

Artificial Intelligence: Ability of a machine to perform cognitive functions that we associate with the human mind.

Back Box: Component of a system, of which only the external behavior is known, but not the content.

Completeness: Characteristic of a good explanation that aims to describe a fact as precisely and accurately as possible (Gilpin et al., 2019).

Explainability: Degree to which an observer or user can understand the cause of a decision by formulating an explanation.

Explainable AI: Explanatory agent revealing underlying causes to its or another agent's decision making.

Explanation: Information to describe the cause of a state of affairs by formulating its logical and causal relations.

Interpretability: Characteristic of a good explanation to provide a fact as comprehensible as possible for humans (Doshi-Velez et al., 2017).

F

Fairness Challenges in Artificial Intelligence

Shuvro Chakrobartty
Dakota State University, USA

Omar El-Gayar
 https://orcid.org/0000-0001-8657-8732
Dakota State University, USA

INTRODUCTION

Massive amounts of data and its cheap storage combined with vast computing power, efficient and improved machine learning algorithms to process the data, powered the development of the various Artificial Intelligence (AI) and Machine Learning (ML) applications. However, concern has been raised about the decisions made by these AI systems, especially where the AI system's decisions impact human life. One such example is the recidivism risk prediction tool COMPAS used by the United States Department of Justice, where it has been observed that recidivism risk prediction was biased against black Americans. It should be noted that the COMPAS system used a proxy of prior arrests and friend/family arrests that measured risk for crime (Suresh & Guttag, 2020). Because of cases like this, there has been a focus in the AI research discipline on algorithmic fairness.

Fairness is a highly desirable human value in day-to-day decisions that affect human life. In recent years many successful applications of AI systems have been developed, and increasingly, AI methods are becoming part of many new applications for decision-making tasks that were previously carried out by human beings. Questions have been raised 1) can the decision be trusted? 2) is it fair? Overall, are AI-based systems making fair decisions, or are they increasing the unfairness in society?

Accordingly, this chapter presents a systematic literature review (SLR) of existing works on AI fairness challenges. Towards this end, a conceptual bias mitigation framework for organizing and discussing AI fairness-related research is developed and presented. The systematic review provides a mapping of the AI fairness challenges to components of a proposed framework based on the suggested solutions within the literature. Future research opportunities are also identified. The rest of the chapter is organized as follows: first, AI fairness is elaborated, then a conceptual framework for an AI fairness challenge category and bias mitigation framework is presented. Later, the review protocol applied in the study is described. Following that, the results are discussed. Finally, a set of future research directions and a summary of key findings are described.

BACKGROUND

In recent years discrimination through bias in AI systems has made headlines multiple times across multiple industries. For example, in 2018, Amazon's recruiting algorithm was flagged for penalizing applications that contained the word "women's" (Dastin, 2018). The AI models were trained to vet ap-

DOI: 10.4018/978-1-7998-9220-5.ch101

plicants by observing patterns in resumes submitted to the company over ten years. Amazon's AI system had taught itself that male candidates were preferable because most applications came from men, reflecting the tech industry's male dominance. Bartlett et al. (2021) investigated and found that the mode of lending discrimination has shifted from human bias to algorithmic bias in the USA, where even the online lending backed by algorithmic decision making caused the minority lenders to be charged higher interest rates for African Americans and Latino borrowers.

There is no apparent consensus within the literature as to what the definition of fairness is, and the fairness metrics for any given ML model should be given in each situation (Mehrabi et al., 2021; Verma & Rubin, 2018). This is because defining fairness is not easy, as stakeholders are unlikely to agree on "fair" in different spheres of life. Moreover, something may be deemed fair in one context but may seem unfair in another context. For example, ethnic affinity (one's affinity for a specific ethnic group without identifying their ethnicity) based ads targeting for selling products may not be wrong. However, the same would be deemed unfair when targeting the same ethnic affinity to advertising for credit, housing, jobs, or other opportunities that impacts human life. This would even be illegal if the algorithm could identify a person's actual ethnicity. However, it is understood that fairness is the absence of any prejudice or favoritism towards an individual or a group based on their intrinsic or acquired traits in the context of decision-making (Makhlouf et al., 2021). Even though fairness is an incredibly desirable quality in society, it can be surprisingly difficult to achieve in practice (Mehrabi et al., 2021). Multiple definitions of fairness and mathematical formulas have been proposed, such as equal odds, positive predictive parity, counterfactual fairness, etc. Verma and Rubin (2018) collected the most prominent definitions of fairness for the algorithmic classification problem explaining the rationale behind these definitions and demonstrated them on a single unifying case study. In real-life scenarios, fairness measurement may not be as simple since no algorithm can pass all of these notions of fairness tests because the critical notions of fairness are incompatible with each other (Kleinberg et al., 2016).

Fairness is closely related to bias, and bias can come from data used to train AI algorithms. An early review article on computer bias by Friedman & Nissenbaum (1996) identified three kinds of biases:

1. Preexisting biases based on social practices and attitudes.
2. Technical bias based on design constraints in hardware and software.
3. The emergent bias that arises from changing the use of context.

These biases remain as a guideline for building fair AI systems. More recently, Mehrabi et al. (2021) categorized biases in data, algorithm, and user interaction identifying the feedback loop that goes from data to algorithm, the algorithm to user interaction, and user interaction producing more biased data that gets fed into the algorithm again. In AI systems, data biases arise from sensitive or protected attributes. Protected attributes define the aspects of data that are socio-culturally sensitive for the application of ML. Some examples of such variables are age, ethnicity, gender, marital status, religion etc. Additionally, these sensitive variables' synonyms (i.e., proxy variables) should also be treated as protected. However, the notion of a protected variable can encompass any feature of the data that involves or concerns human beings. Most approaches to mitigate unfairness, bias, or discrimination are based on the notion of protected or sensitive variables and unprivileged groups (Caton & Haas, 2020). The dimension of fairness ensures that algorithmic decisions do not display unjust or biased behavior concerning sensitive or protected attributes. It accounts for the ethical and legal risk of discrimination against specific collectives or minority groups (Unceta et al., 2020). Further, ML algorithms operate by learning models from historical data and generalizing them to unseen new data (Suresh & Guttag, 2020). The increased

F

reliance on algorithmic decision-making in socially impactful processes has intensified the calls for unbiased and procedurally fair algorithms (Berkel et al., 2019). Zhou et al. (2020) investigated fundamental ethical principles of AI and their implementations, suggesting that ethical principles need to be combined with every stage of the AI lifecycle to ensure that the AI system is designed, implemented, and deployed ethically.

Fairness has implications for ethics, and all major tech companies and research institutes have published their stance on responsible AI. Table 1 lists a few notable published responsible/ethical AI principles. The list depicts how different organizations have identified fairness as foundational in their responsible and trustworthy AI principles. Each recognizes that data used for training automated decision-making systems can contain biases, creating systems that might discriminate against certain groups of people and adhere to the idea that AI systems should treat all people fairly. Google recognizes that AI algorithms and datasets can reflect, reinforce, or reduce unfair biases. While distinguishing fair from unfair biases is not always straightforward and differs across cultures and societies, Google is committed to avoiding unjust impacts on people, particularly those related to sensitive characteristics such as race, ethnicity, gender, nationality, income, sexual orientation, ability, and political or religious belief (Google, 2018). Moreover, fairness and bias can be defined in more than one way, and it may not be either desirable or feasible to arrive at a single definition that would be applied in all circumstances (Chatila & Havens, 2019). IEEE's trust principles such as effectiveness, competence, accountability, and transparency are defined such that they will provide information that will allow the testing of an application of A/IS against any fairness criteria. It is also recognized that sometimes complex and unsettled issues of fairness arise when social norms of fairness change regionally and over time. Microsoft, Google, and IBM all have published their fairness assessment toolkit for assessing the fairness of ML models.

Table 1. Organizations and their AI principles

Organization	Stance on AI research and development
Microsoft	Responsible AI (Microsoft, 2021)
Google	AI at Google: our principles (Google, 2018)
IBM	IBM's Principles for Trust and Transparency (IBM, 2018)
IEEE	Ethically Aligned Design (Chatila & Havens, 2019)

Prior survey studies have been conducted on AI fairness and ethics (Caton & Haas, 2020; Mehrabi et al., 2019; Qandi & Rakhmawati, 2020; Zhou et al., 2020) on general AI bias and fairness topic defining a taxonomy for fairness definitions. Caton & Haas (2020) organized these approaches into a framework of pre-processing, in-processing, and post-processing methods, subcategorizing them into eleven method areas. Mehrabi et al. (2021) investigated different real-world applications that have shown biases in various ways and how data biases can affect AI applications while providing a feedback loop model of data, algorithm, and user interaction. Moreover, Tommasi et al. (2017) looked at the dataset bias from an image processing perspective, and they analyzed Convolutional Neural Networks (CNN) as it has emerged as a reliable and robust image processing ML model. However, there remains a gap in the literature of integrating the sociotechnical challenges with governance and regulation for implementing fair AI. In this review, the AI fairness challenges are discussed from a holistic perspective.

CONCEPTUAL FRAMEWORK

Fairness is a concern for many of the ML classification problems. This section presents a conceptual framework for organizing and discussing AI fairness-related research and providing directions for future research. The framework relies on a conceptualization of AI fairness challenges and sources of bias as described below.

AI Fairness Challenge Categories

From the social point of view throughout literature, fairness has been categized into three categories 1) individual 2) group 3) subgroup fairness. Individual fairness emphasizes that similar predictions be given to similar individuals (Dwork et al., 2012). Thus, it is a fairness characteristic that examines whether similar people are categorized in the same way. For example, an academic institution might want to ensure that two students with comparable grades and standardized test results have an equal chance of being accepted. As a result, individual fairness is solely determined by how similarity is defined. It takes important precautions while determining the similarity measures; otherwise, fairness cannot be guaranteed. For example, if a student's grades and test scores were solely assessed while ignoring the student's curriculum, it may not ensure fairness because there may be significant differences in the rigor of the student's curriculum.

Group fairness is about the parity of treating different groups equally within a dataset; i.e., the proportion of members in a protected group receiving positive (or negative) classification is identical to the proportion in the population as a whole (Zemel et al., 2013). Thus, group fairness attempts to define fairness in terms of statistical parity criteria that are imposed on the predictions produced by the ML model. For example, to ensure group fairness, the academic institutions' admission decision cannot discriminate against a certain ethnic group (e.g., African American) by giving acceptance decisions for the ethnic students' group that is less percentage than the non-ethnic student group.

Subgroup fairness is a special case of group fairness. It comes into the picture when a classifier appears to be fair on each group; however, it violates the fairness constraint on one or more structured subgroups defined over the protected attributes considering certain combinations of protected attribute values (Kearns et al., 2017). Thus, subgroup fairness is intended to bridge the gap between statistical and individual notions of fairness (Kearns et al., 2019). Subgroup fairness is relatively a new topic within the literature. Kearns et al. (2017) proposed subgroup fairness which tries to establish statistical notions of fairness across infinitely many subgroups, defined by a structured class of functions over the protected attributes. It picks a group fairness constraint like equalizing false positive and asks whether this constraint holds over a large collection of subgroups (Mehrabi et al., 2021).

Data, Algorithm, and User Interaction as Source of Bias

From a technical point of view, unfairness causing bias can emerge from three different categories: data, algorithm and user interaction (Mehrabi et al., 2021). Data could contribute to unfairness for decision outcomes of ML models because of the inherent biases present in the dataset. Measurement, representation, omitted variable, aggregation, sampling are various types of dataset biases, to name a few.

While many different dataset biases have been reported throughout the literature (Hinnefeld et al., 2018; Olteanu et al., 2019; Torralba & Efros, 2011). Mehrabi et al. (2021) describe various dataset biases commonly encountered in the feedback loop between data, algorithm and user interaction. Few dataset biases mentioned in the list of articles categorized in Table 3 for AI fairness challenges are:

- Historical bias arises when there is a misalignment between the world as it is and the values or objectives to be encoded and propagated in a model. Even with perfect sampling and feature selection, this bias can happen (Suresh & Guttag, 2020). Historical bias often involves evaluating the representational harm (such as reinforcing a stereotype) to a particular identity group.
- Representation bias arises while defining and sampling from a population. It occurs when a sample population under-represents and subsequently fails to generalize well (Suresh & Guttag, 2020). This can happen when the sampling methods only reach a portion of the population, or the population of interest has changed or is distinct from the population used during model training.
- Cross-dataset bias can arise when an AI algorithm has been only tested on a small and biased dataset, however, would be used as a generalized model across many datasets (Thambawita et al., 2020). It is a type of representation bias that happens when a model was trained and intended to be used with a specific dataset but subsequently used in a more generalized setup.

Algorithmic bias occurs when the bias is introduced only by the algorithm and is not present in the raw data. The use of certain optimization functions, regularizations, and whether to apply regression models to the data as a whole or subgroups, as well as the general use of statistically biased estimators in algorithms, can all contribute to biased algorithmic decisions that can bias the algorithms' outcomes (Mehrabi et al., 2021).

User interaction bias occurs because many of the data sources used to train machine learning models are created by users. Users' innate prejudices may be reflected in the data they produce. Furthermore, any biases in the algorithm that affect or modulate user behavior may induce bias in the data generation process (Mehrabi et al., 2021).

A Bias Mitigation and Fair AI Framework

Figure 1 depicts the fairness challenge mitigation framework by combining the technical approaches to AI with the elements of a typical machine learning model building lifecycle while incorporating the concerns of the biases arising from the feedback loop identified by Mehrabi et al. (2021).

Figure 1. AI Fairness challenge mitigation framework

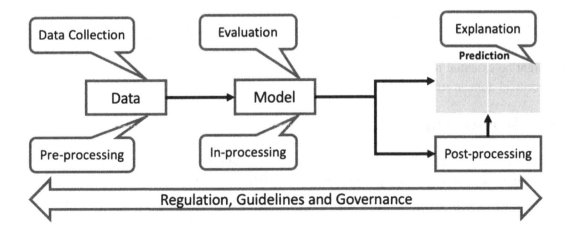

Technical aspects of fairness in AI has been classified along the following three approaches (Caton & Haas, 2020; Mujtaba & Mahapatra, 2019):

- Pre-processing recognizes and deals with data itself in terms of distributions of specific sensitive or protected variables that could be biased, discriminatory, and/or imbalanced (Caton & Haas, 2020). Therefore, pre-processing steps transform data to alter the sample distributions of protected variables. With this approach preprocessed data can be used for any downstream task without modifying the classifier. Also, it doesn't require to access sensitive attributes at test time like the post-processing approach.
- In-processing recognizes that modeling techniques can become biased by dominant features. So, in-processing approaches introduce one or more fairness metrics into the model optimization functions resulting in a model parameterization that satisfies performance and fairness maximization (Caton & Haas, 2020). This approach can provide flexibility to choose the trade-off between accuracy and fairness measures for specific model. Like post-processing, it doesn't require to access sensitive attributes at test time.
- Post-processing recognizes that the original ML model's output could be unfair to one or more protected variables and/or subgroup(s), therefore, it applies transformations to model output to improve prediction fairness (Caton & Haas, 2020). This approach can be applied for any classifiers without modification. However, it requires test-time access to the protected attribute is not being flexible for picking a desired trade-off between accuracy vs. fairness.

In this framework, the historical bias happens during the data generation and collection time. Representation bias occurs in the preprocessing step while defining and sampling a development population that under-represents and subsequently fails to generalize well for some part of the user population (Suresh & Guttag, 2020). During the model development, the in-processing approach allows the flexibility to choose any fairness measures, injecting model-specific fairness metrics. Moreover, in-processing is the phase where algorithmic biases are mitigated by selecting the correct optimization functions, regularizations, unbiased statistical estimators etc. In the model evaluation step model's performance is evaluated with unseen data, and other available benchmark datasets for robustness. Cross-dataset validation test would also be performed at this step to measure models' generalization ability across many datasets. Post-processing can be used when the original ML model's output is unfair to one or more protected variables and/or subgroup(s), and further transformations to model output is done to improve prediction fairness. Explanation or interpretation of the prediction allows for better understandings of the reasons that affect fairness. The regulation and governance cuts across all various steps in the machine learning model development and deployment lifecycle. Within the literature (Bærøe et al., 2020; C. W. L. Ho et al., 2020; Jacobson et al., 2020; Vayena et al., 2018), regulation and governance have been identified as an important element for implementing fair AI systems as regulatory protections against algorithmic bias might be essential to maintain the safety and efficacy of ML-based algorithms especially within safety-critical domain such as medical domain.

Review Methodology

This research's methodological framework can be divided into three essential phases: research definition, research methodology, and research analysis, as depicted in Figure 2. In the research definition phase, the expected research goal and the research scope are determined. The research area is academic research on AI fairness challenges, proposed solution methods and techniques, and recent development. Through a systematic literature review, the research goal is to provide a bias mitigation framework, map the identified articles to the framework's components for fair AI prediction, and suggest directions for future research. The research scope is the literature on the AI fairness challenges, proposed solution methods and techniques, summarized to aid the further creation and accumulation of knowledge in this area. As the research on this topic is relatively recent, the scope of this investigation is limited to the time frame of 2008 to 2021.

The research methodology phase defined the criteria for searching and selecting articles and creating a framework for classifying the selected articles. Three online academic databases (ACM Digital Library, IEEE Explorer, and Academic Search Premier) were searched to provide a comprehensive listing of research articles, as the nature of fair AI methods and techniques research makes it difficult to confine the search to specific disciplines. These databases cover most academic journals in English available in full-text versions. This literature search was based on the descriptors "fair", "fairness", "fairness and bias", "bias and fairness", "fairness and accuracy", "accuracy and fairness", "fairness-aware", "fairness-", "justice", "ethical", "accountable", "accountability", "trustworthy", "trustworthiness", "dataset bias" AND "artificial intelligence", "machine learning", "deep learning", "AI", "ML", "DL". Boolean expressions were used to apply these terms and publication dates to a search of online databases. Only articles related to AI fairness challenges, proposed solution methods, and techniques were included. Further, each article was carefully examined to ensure that it met the following two selection criteria. First, the articles must have been published in academic journals for which the full-text versions are available. Duplicate articles, non-research articles, master or doctoral dissertations, textbooks, survey articles, and unpublished working papers were excluded. Second, the articles had to present or discuss AI fairness challenges solution methods, techniques, recent development, and challenges in general or specific use cases. Overall, eleven articles were selected for further analysis.

Figure 2. Methodological framework for research - adapted from (Ngai et al., 2011)

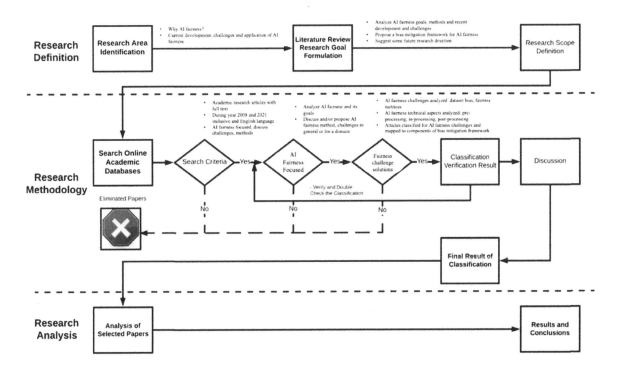

RESULT

Figure 3 describes the flow diagram of article selection and filtration for the study according to the methodology. The search initially produced approximately 380 articles. Table 2 summarizes the search result article counts for the three databases and the distribution of total, research, other, and initially selected article counts before applying the elimination criteria. As shown in figure 3, upon applying the exclusion and inclusion criteria, 11 articles are selected for analysis. Categorizing the articles in terms of the domain results in four articles related to ethical AI, three articles related to medicine or health care, and four articles related to other areas.

Table 2. Search result for various databases

Database name	Total article count	Research articles	Other articles (magazine, book, newspaper, reviews etc.)	Initial selected (count) excluding unavailability of full text before further elimination
ACM	170	96	74	94
IEEE explorer	82	65	17	65
Academic search premier	128	97	31	16

Table 3 shows the classification of the eleven journal articles based on the challenges identified and the solution proposed for those challenges while mapping them to the components of the proposed framework for bias mitigation. In these articles, the authors focus on the ethics and robustness of artificial intelligence, including fairness for developing such technologies and potential governance policies, rather than how to deal with the legal issues that may arise from the deficiencies of these systems.

Figure 3. Flow diagram of study selection

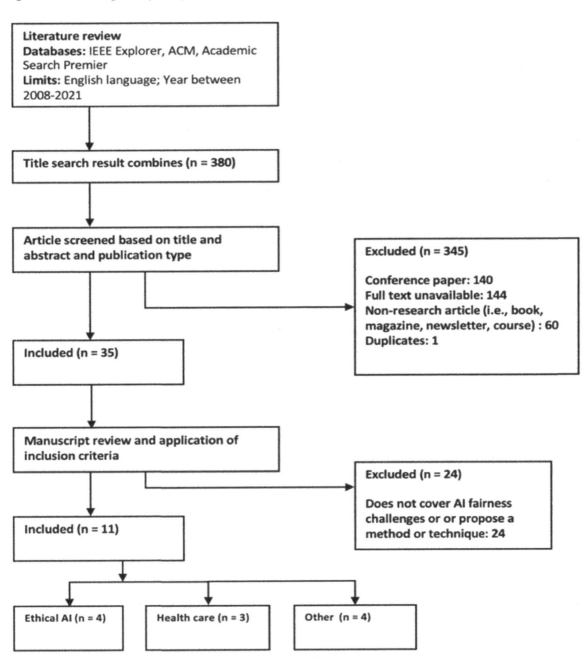

Table 3. List of journal papers discussing AI fairness challenges

Article	AI fairness challenges	Challenge category	Challenge mitigation framework component
Deep Ethical Learning: Taking the Interplay of Human and Artificial Intelligence Seriously (A. Ho, 2019)	Systems optimized for task performance without considering fairness can inadvertently induce or perpetuate biases.	Group fairness / Data representation bias	Pre-processing; overall technical design
Ensuring trustworthy use of artificial intelligence and big data analytics in health insurance (C. W. L. Ho et al., 2020)	Bias arising from the limited number of data sets could penalize already vulnerable individuals.	Individual and group fairness / Data representation bias.	Regulation, guidelines, and governance
Ethical dilemmas posed by mobile health and machine learning in psychiatry research (Jacobson et al., 2020)	Data being sampled reflects societal inequalities (i.e., historical bias) or if the sampling methods result in the underrepresentation of certain groups (i.e., representation bias).	Group fairness / Historical data and representation bias.	Pre-processing; Regulation, guidelines, and governance
How to achieve trustworthy artificial intelligence for health (Bærøe et al., 2020)	The potential for bias in the data used to train artificial intelligence algorithms.	Algorithm and Dataset bias	Regulation, guidelines, and governance
Machine learning in medicine: Addressing ethical challenges (Vayena et al., 2018)	Poorly representative training data sets can introduce biases because data sources themselves do not reflect true epidemiology within a given demographic. Also, data set that does not contain enough members of a given demographic.	Group fairness / Data representation bias.	Dataset bias; Regulation, guidelines, and governance
An Extensive Study on Cross-Dataset Bias and Evaluation Metrics Interpretation for Machine Learning Applied to Gastrointestinal Tract Abnormality Classification (Thambawita et al., 2020)	Algorithms are often only tested on small and biased datasets, and cross-dataset evaluations are rarely performed. ML Model generalization capacity is questionable.	Group fairness / Cross-dataset bias.	In-processing; post-processing
Bridging the Gap Between Ethics and Practice: Guidelines for Reliable, Safe, and Trustworthy Human-centered AI Systems. (Shneiderman, 2020)	Biased decision making, unfair treatment of minority groups raising human rights challenges.	Group fairness / Dataset bias.	Pre-processing; Post-processing
Crowdsourcing Perceptions of Fair Predictors for Machine Learning: A Recidivism Case Study (Berkel et al., 2019)	Obtaining insight on the perceived fairness of predictors for Machine Learning (ML) models.	Individual fairness / Data and algorithmic bias	In-processing; Evaluation with fairness metrics
Improving Machine Learning Fairness with Sampling and Adversarial Learning (Amend & Spurlock, 2021)	How to increase the fairness of machine learning based classification with respect to a sensitive attribute?	Individual fairness / Data and algorithmic bias	In-processing; Evaluation with fairness metrics
Contrastive Fairness in Machine Learning (Chakraborti et al., 2020)	How to answer the contrastive question "why this and not that?" of a decision.	Individual and sub-group fairness / Data bias	In-processing; Evaluation with fairness metrics
Fairness in Deep Learning: A Computational Perspective (Du et al., 2020)	How to design bias detection and mitigation approaches for Deep Neural Network (DNN)?	Group fairness / Data representation bias.	Pre-processing; In-processing; post-processing

FUTURE RESEARCH DIRECTIONS

Overall, dataset bias cuts across all various fairness challenges and is identified as the major cause of fairness issues in AI. Vayena et al. (2018) identified that dataset bias in the medical domain could happen either with the data sources themselves not reflecting true epidemiology within a given demographic or dataset that does not contain enough members of a given demographic. Moreover, based on certain operational conditions, ML system results can vary. For example, a chest x-rays based pneumonia detection AI system was found to provide varied results across hospitals depending on the x-ray machine, unrelated patient characteristics, and even the angle of the machine (Shneiderman, 2020). This finding informs that care needs to be taken in selecting a dataset to build an AI system based on that dataset. The organization or people responsible for building the system should pay particular attention and analyze how data is being collected and what pre-processing is needed for the specific application using that dataset.

Representation bias has been identified frequently as a cause of fairness issues. Optimizing learning systems for performance and without adequate care for ensuring fairness can unintentionally induce or perpetuate existing biases in data that do not properly represent all groups. Criminal-sentencing and hiring-decision algorithms have been shown to discriminate against people of certain ethnic or gender backgrounds because of representation bias (Du et al., 2020; Ho, 2019). In that regard, Jacobson et al. (2020) investigated historical and representation bias where concerns were mentioned for a machine learning model trained using the electronic health records of medical visits but used to predict psychiatric conditions in immigrant populations that avoid interacting with the healthcare system. In this case, according to the authors, the model might not be able to give accurate predictions because of representation bias. This finding informs that historical and representation bias can emerge when a model built with a training dataset from a specific group of people was then used to make predictions for other groups. The organization or people responsible for building the system should pay particular attention and ensure the system is only used with the intended audience and not extended to a population that has not been part of the training dataset.

Group fairness is a common concern within the AI research community, multiple articles (Du et al., 2020; Ho, 2019; Ho et al., 2020; Jacobson et al., 2020; Shneiderman, 2020; Vayena et al., 2018) focused on group fairness. Du et al. (2020) show that interpretability could significantly contribute to better understandings of the reasons that affect the fairness, and they suggest fairness mitigation strategies categorized into three stages of the deep learning life-cycle. Further, Chakraborti et al. (2020) proposed the concept of contrastive fairness, where fairness is assessed by asking the contrastive question "why this and not that?" for a decision. Contrastive fairness is important to show and defend the fairness of algorithmic decisions in tasks where a person or sub-group of people is chosen over another, such as job recruitment, university admission, etc. (Chakraborti et al., 2020).

The need for regulation, governance, and guidelines was highlighted as a potential solution for many of the concerns raised for the AI fairness issue. Jacobson et al. (2020) identified that there need to be regulations for monitoring changes in adaptive algorithms as they continuously learn from real-world data. Moreover, there need to be protocols in place for addressing risks that might result from changes to an algorithm's operations. For example, in the health insurance domain, a clear and effective data governance framework is needed while the insurers and governance bodies, including regulators and policymakers, work together to ensure that the big data analytics-based AI systems are developed transparently and accurately (Ho et al., 2020). Scientific societies and regulatory agencies must develop standards and best practices based on ethical principles such as the European Union expert group framework for recognizing and minimizing the AI fairness issues (Bærøe et al., 2020; Vayena et al., 2018). To reduce the effects of biased training datasets, institutional review boards, ethics review committees, and health technology assessment organizations should check for compliance with such standards (Vayena et al., 2018). This finding informs that regulation and governance should be integral for building and operationalizing fair AI. From that aspect, the organization, and people responsible for building AI systems should consult regulations and guidelines at the constituency level where it would be operational such as a country, state, etc. Additionally, they should build the system adhering to respective industry-level policy and rules and seek certification approval where necessary.

Significance to Management and Practice

AI fairness challenges and the need for identifying and mitigating bias for more fair predictive results from AI systems are well documented in the literature. A holistic perspective is needed integrating the technical and societal issues into governance and regulation. The proposed conceptual bias mitigation framework integrates all these aspects. Overall, implications to management and practice of AI systems development and deployment include:

- Helping the implementer of an AI system identify their specific use case, the relevant fairness challenge, and provide a reference solution for mitigating it. This is accomplished via the systematic mapping of AI fairness challenges to suggested solution in extant literature.
- Highlighting the need for careful attention and analysis to select a dataset to build an AI system as dataset challenges significantly impact fairness. This is discussed earlier regarding the correctness, historical, and representation bias that impede fair AI development.
- Identifying the need for regulation, governance, and guidelines as a potential solution for many of the concerns raised from the cited literature. This helps explicitly highlight the importance of governance and regulatory requirements.

Directions for Future Research

Despite the increase in AI ethics and fairness research, there remain opportunities for further research. In the following paragraphs, a list of future research opportunities are summarized.

Handling Dataset Bias with Pre-processing

Dataset bias remains the most critical issue in AI fairness. Du et al. (2020) identified several open problems around bias detection and mitigation, such as designing benchmark datasets for each deep neural network (DNN) application, the investigation of intersectional fairness, i.e., a combination of multiple sensitive attributes, the balance between fairness and utility trade-off, fairness measurements which could meet the specific requirements of each application domain.

Data pre-processing is an essential step to prepare training data. If there are multiple plausible ways in which a dataset can be processed to generate training data for an algorithm, it makes sense to provide performance metrics for more than one of the possible choices. Accordingly, when ML algorithms are being compared to each other, care needs to be taken to ensure they are being compared based on the same pre-processing. Overall, there are opportunities to formalize the pre-processing and the performance comparison methods for all types of dataset biases.

Further, when ML models use a dataset that gets updated regularly or continuously, it can present a substantial challenge (Shneiderman, 2020). Data curation that ensures that the data is still representative is very important. More research is needed to investigate possible ways to ensure optimal model performance and bias metrics in the face of changing datasets.

Fairness Evaluation Metrics for In-processing

There are many different metrics to measure fairness in an ML model. New metrics are being proposed regularly in the literature for various use cases. Unfortunately, there is no consensus on the approach to quantifying fairness. Additionally, there is generally a trade-off between model accuracy and different fairness metrics (Amend & Spurlock, 2021). For the gastrointestinal (GI) tract image dataset to predict cancers, Thambawita et al. (2020) proposed an evaluation method using six measures to minimize cross-dataset bias. The six measures are recall (sensitivity), accuracy, Matthew's correlation coefficient, F1-score, R_k correlation coefficient, and frames per second. Only cross-dataset evaluations can help determine the real capabilities of ML models before using them in clinical settings (Thambawita et al., 2020). More research needs to be done for other use cases on finding and incorporating evaluation metrics that are relevant for the specific scenario. Moreover, emphasizing the dependence of the ML models on training datasets, Shneiderman (2020) suggested that different datasets need to be collected for each context to increase accuracy and reduce biases – more research is needed as to how to optimize both metrics for a specific algorithm and what does the dataset look like for the specific context.

Scope for Guidelines, Regulations, and Governance

AI is now being used for various use cases across many industries and addresses a complex and diverse problem space with varying degrees of impact concerning ethical and fairness issues. First, there needs to be industry and use case-related ethical regulation and governance guidelines defined. These ethical principles and bias awareness need to be converted into action, which begins with in-depth testing of training datasets to verify that the data is current and has a fair distribution of records (Shneiderman, 2020). At a broad oversight level, the government, civil society organization, professional organizations, and research institutes need to work in sync to lead on industry-wide efforts that include government interventions and regulation, accounting firms conducting external audits, insurance companies compensating for failures, nongovernmental and civil society organizations advancing design principles, and professional organizations and research institutes developing standards, policies, and novel ideas - the larger goal of effective governance should be to limit the dangers and increase the benefits of Human-centered AI (HCAI) to individuals, organizations, and society (Shneiderman, 2020). Up until now, there has been much work done on defining the responsible AI principles (Chatila & Havens, 2019; Google, 2018; IBM, 2018; Microsoft, 2021). However, there remain opportunities to establish a coherent structure for governing AI to maximize its benefit for society at large. Opportunities also remain at the technical implementation level to define guidelines and governance processes on how to build responsible and fair AI.

CONCLUSION

This systematic literature review focused on the AI fairness challenges for modern AI systems. Further, and to better organize and discuss extant literature, a conceptual bias mitigation framework is presented and is used to map the identified challenges to components of the framework. Opportunities for AI fairness research were also identified, most notably in the areas of handling dataset biases, fairness evaluation metrics, and scope for guidelines, regulations, and governance.

Some limitations of this study are as follows: 1) a shortlist of query terms has been used within the article title, and 2) the literature search has been limited to only three databases. While such limitations are commensurate with the scope of the review, namely providing a synopsis of AI fairness challenges, a comprehensive review will entail extending the review to other databases, expanding the search query and scope, and including snowballing (tracking forward and backward citations). Opportunities exist to potentially enhance the conceptual framework and classify articles at a finer level of abstraction for challenges and solutions.

In conclusion, fairness in AI systems is a critical and timely field of research within AI. The proposed conceptual framework and the findings from the SLR provide a perspective on the current state of the art and insights for future research of AI fairness.

REFERENCES

Amend, J. J., & Spurlock, S. (2021). Improving Machine Learning Fairness with Sampling and Adversarial Learning. *Journal of Computing Sciences in Colleges*, *36*(5), 14–23.

Bærøe, K., Miyata-Sturm, A., & Henden, E. (2020). How to achieve trustworthy artificial intelligence for health. *Bulletin of the World Health Organization*, *98*(4), 257–262. doi:10.2471/BLT.19.237289 PMID:32284649

Bartlett, R., Morse, A., Stanton, R., & Wallace, N. (2021). Consumer-lending discrimination in the FinTech Era. *Journal of Financial Economics*. Advance online publication. doi:10.1016/j.jfineco.2021.05.047

Berkel, N., Goncalves, J., Hettiachchi, D., Wijenayake, S., Kelly, R. M., & Kostakos, V. (2019). Crowdsourcing Perceptions of Fair Predictors for Machine Learning: A Recidivism Case Study. *Proceedings of the ACM on Human-Computer Interaction, 3*(CSCW), 1–21. 10.1145/3359130

Caton, S., & Haas, C. (2020). *Fairness in Machine Learning: A Survey*. https://arxiv.org/abs/2010.04053

Chakraborti, T., Patra, A., & Noble, J. A. (2020). Contrastive Fairness in Machine Learning. *IEEE Letters of the Computer Society*, *3*(2), 38–41. doi:10.1109/LOCS.2020.3007845

Chatila, R., & Havens, J. C. (2019). The IEEE Global Initiative on Ethics of Autonomous and Intelligent Systems. In M. I. Aldinhas Ferreira, J. Silva Sequeira, G. Singh Virk, M. O. Tokhi, & E. E. Kadar (Eds.), *Robotics and Well-Being* (Vol. 95, pp. 11–16). Springer International Publishing. doi:10.1007/978-3-030-12524-0_2

Chen, J., Kallus, N., Mao, X., Svacha, G., & Udell, M. (2019). Fairness Under Unawareness: Assessing Disparity When Protected Class Is Unobserved. *Proceedings of the Conference on Fairness, Accountability, and Transparency*, 339–348. 10.1145/3287560.3287594

Corbett-Davies, S., Pierson, E., Feller, A., Goel, S., & Huq, A. (2017). *Algorithmic decision making and the cost of fairness*. doi:10.1145/3097983.3098095

Dastin, J. (2018, October 10). *Amazon scraps secret AI recruiting tool that showed bias against women*. https://www.reuters.com/article/us-amazon-com-jobs-automation-insight/amazon-scraps-secret-ai-recruiting-tool-that-showed-bias-against-women-idUSKCN1MK08G

Du, M., Yang, F., Zou, N., & Hu, X. (2020). Fairness in Deep Learning: A Computational Perspective. *IEEE Intelligent Systems*, 1–1. doi:10.1109/MIS.2020.3000681

Dwork, C., Hardt, M., Pitassi, T., Reingold, O., & Zemel, R. (2012). Fairness through awareness. *Proceedings of the 3rd Innovations in Theoretical Computer Science Conference on - ITCS '12*, 214–226. 10.1145/2090236.2090255

Friedman, B., & Nissenbaum, H. (1996). Bias in Computer Systems. *ACM Transactions on Information Systems*, 14(3), 330–347. doi:10.1145/230538.230561

Google. (2018, June). *AI at Google: Our principles*. https://www.blog.google/technology/ai/ai-principles/

Hemment, D., Belle, V., Aylett, R., Murray-Rust, D., Pschetz, L., & Broz, F. (2019). Toward Fairness, Morality and Transparency in Artificial Intelligence through Experiential AI. *Leonardo*, 52(5), 426–426. doi:10.1162/leon_a_01795

Hinnefeld, J. H., Cooman, P., Mammo, N., & Deese, R. (2018). *Evaluating Fairness Metrics in the Presence of Dataset Bias*. https://arxiv.org/abs/1809.09245

Ho, A. (2019). Deep Ethical Learning: Taking the Interplay of Human and Artificial Intelligence Seriously. *The Hastings Center Report*, 49(1), 36–39. doi:10.1002/hast.977 PMID:30790317

Ho, C. W. L., Ali, J., & Caals, K. (2020). Ensuring trustworthy use of artificial intelligence and big data analytics in health insurance. *Bulletin of the World Health Organization*, 98(4), 263–269. doi:10.2471/BLT.19.234732 PMID:32284650

IBM. (2018). *IBM'S Principles for Data Trust and Transparency*. https://www.ibm.com/blogs/policy/trust-principles/

Jacobson, N. C., Bentley, K. H., Walton, A., Wang, S. B., Fortgang, R. G., Millner, A. J., Coombs, G. III, Rodman, A. M., & Coppersmith, D. D. L. (2020). Ethical dilemmas posed by mobile health and machine learning in psychiatry research. *Bulletin of the World Health Organization*, 98(4), 270–276. doi:10.2471/BLT.19.237107 PMID:32284651

Kearns, M., Neel, S., Roth, A., & Wu, Z. (2017). *Preventing Fairness Gerrymandering: Auditing and Learning for Subgroup Fairness*. Academic Press.

Kearns, M., Neel, S., Roth, A., & Wu, Z. S. (2019). An Empirical Study of Rich Subgroup Fairness for Machine Learning. *Proceedings of the Conference on Fairness, Accountability, and Transparency*, 100–109. 10.1145/3287560.3287592

Kleinberg, J., Mullainathan, S., & Raghavan, M. (2016). *Inherent Trade-Offs in the Fair Determination of Risk Scores*. https://arxiv.org/abs/1609.05807

Kusner, M. J., Loftus, J. R., Russell, C., & Silva, R. (2018). *Counterfactual Fairness*. https://arxiv.org/abs/1703.06856

Liu, Y., Radanovic, G., Dimitrakakis, C., Mandal, D., & Parkes, D. (2017). *Calibrated Fairness in Bandits*. ArXiv, abs/1707.01875.

Makhlouf, K., Zhioua, S., & Palamidessi, C. (2021). On the Applicability of Machine Learning Fairness Notions. *SIGKDD Explorations*, 23(1), 14–23. doi:10.1145/3468507.3468511

Mehrabi, N., Morstatter, F., Saxena, N., Lerman, K., & Galstyan, A. (2019). *A Survey on Bias and Fairness in Machine Learning*. https://arxiv.org/abs/1908.09635

Mehrabi, N., Morstatter, F., Saxena, N., Lerman, K., & Galstyan, A. (2021). A Survey on Bias and Fairness in Machine Learning. *ACM Computing Surveys*, *54*(6), 1–35. doi:10.1145/3457607

Microsoft. (2021). *Responsible AI principles from Microsoft*. https://www.microsoft.com/en-us/ai/responsible-ai?activetab=pivot1%3aprimaryr6

Mujtaba, D. F., & Mahapatra, N. R. (2019). Ethical Considerations in AI-Based Recruitment. *2019 IEEE International Symposium on Technology and Society (ISTAS)*, 1–7. 10.1109/ISTAS48451.2019.8937920

Ngai, E. W. T., Hu, Y., Wong, Y. H., Chen, Y., & Sun, X. (2011). The application of data mining techniques in financial fraud detection: A classification framework and an academic review of literature. *Decision Support Systems*, *50*(3), 559–569. doi:10.1016/j.dss.2010.08.006

Olteanu, A., Castillo, C., Diaz, F., & Kıcıman, E. (2019). Social Data: Biases, Methodological Pitfalls, and Ethical Boundaries. *Frontiers in Big Data*, *2*, 13. doi:10.3389/fdata.2019.00013 PMID:33693336

Qandi, G. A., & Rakhmawati, N. A. (2020). Survey of Fairness in Machine Learning for Indonesian General Election Research. *2020 3rd International Conference on Computer and Informatics Engineering (IC2IE)*, 19–24. 10.1109/IC2IE50715.2020.9274583

Shneiderman, B. (2020). Bridging the Gap Between Ethics and Practice: Guidelines for Reliable, Safe, and Trustworthy Human-centered AI Systems. *ACM Transactions on Interactive Intelligent Systems*, *10*(4), 1–31. doi:10.1145/3419764

Suresh, H., & Guttag, J. V. (2020). *A Framework for Understanding Unintended Consequences of Machine Learning*. https://arxiv.org/abs/1901.10002

Thambawita, V., Jha, D., Hammer, H. L., Johansen, H. D., Johansen, D., Halvorsen, P., & Riegler, M. A. (2020). An Extensive Study on Cross-Dataset Bias and Evaluation Metrics Interpretation for Machine Learning Applied to Gastrointestinal Tract Abnormality Classification. *ACM Transactions on Computing for Healthcare*, *1*(3), 1–29. doi:10.1145/3386295

Tommasi, T., Patricia, N., Caputo, B., & Tuytelaars, T. (2017). A Deeper Look at Dataset Bias. In G. Csurka (Ed.), *Domain Adaptation in Computer Vision Applications* (pp. 37–55). Springer International Publishing. doi:10.1007/978-3-319-58347-1_2

Torralba, A., & Efros, A. A. (2011). Unbiased look at dataset bias. *CVPR*, *2011*, 1521–1528. doi:10.1109/CVPR.2011.5995347

Unceta, I., Nin, J., & Pujol, O. (2020). Risk mitigation in algorithmic accountability: The role of machine learning copies. *PLoS One*, *15*(11), e0241286. doi:10.1371/journal.pone.0241286 PMID:33141844

Vayena, E., Blasimme, A., & Cohen, I. G. (2018). Machine learning in medicine: Addressing ethical challenges. *PLoS Medicine*, *15*(11), e1002689. doi:10.1371/journal.pmed.1002689 PMID:30399149

Verma, S., & Rubin, J. (2018). Fairness definitions explained. *Proceedings of the International Workshop on Software Fairness*, 1–7. 10.1145/3194770.3194776

Zemel, R., Wu, L. Y., Swersky, K., Pitassi, T., & Dwork, C. (2013). *Learning Fair Representations*. ICML.

Zhou, J., Chen, F., Berry, A., Reed, M., Zhang, S., & Savage, S. (2020). A Survey on Ethical Principles of AI and Implementations. *2020 IEEE Symposium Series on Computational Intelligence (SSCI)*, 3010–3017. 10.1109/SSCI47803.2020.9308437

ADDITIONAL READING

Kusner, M. J., Loftus, J. R., Russell, C., & Silva, R. (2018). *Counterfactual Fairness.* https://arxiv.org/abs/1703.06856

Corbett-Davies, S., Pierson, E., Feller, A., Goel, S., & Huq, A. (2017). *Algorithmic decision making and the cost of fairness.* doi:10.1145/3097983.3098095

Liu, Y., Radanovic, G., Dimitrakakis, C., Mandal, D., & Parkes, D. (2017). *Calibrated Fairness in Bandits.* ArXiv, abs/1707.01875.

Verma, S., & Rubin, J. (2018). Fairness definitions explained. *Proceedings of the International Workshop on Software Fairness*, 1–7. 10.1145/3194770.3194776

Dwork, C., Hardt, M., Pitassi, T., Reingold, O., & Zemel, R. (2012). Fairness through awareness. *Proceedings of the 3rd Innovations in Theoretical Computer Science Conference on - ITCS '12*, 214–226. 10.1145/2090236.2090255

Torralba, A., & Efros, A. A. (2011). Unbiased look at dataset bias. *CVPR, 2011*, 1521–1528. doi:10.1109/CVPR.2011.5995347

Hinnefeld, J. H., Cooman, P., Mammo, N., & Deese, R. (2018). *Evaluating Fairness Metrics in the Presence of Dataset Bias.* https://arxiv.org/abs/1809.09245

Chen, J., Kallus, N., Mao, X., Svacha, G., & Udell, M. (2019). Fairness Under Unawareness: Assessing Disparity When Protected Class Is Unobserved. *Proceedings of the Conference on Fairness, Accountability, and Transparency*, 339–348. 10.1145/3287560.3287594

Friedman, B., & Nissenbaum, H. (1996). Bias in Computer Systems. *ACM Transactions on Information Systems*, *14*(3), 330–347. doi:10.1145/230538.230561

Hemment, D., Belle, V., Aylett, R., Murray-Rust, D., Pschetz, L., & Broz, F. (2019). Toward Fairness, Morality and Transparency in Artificial Intelligence through Experiential AI. *Leonardo*, *52*(5), 426–426. doi:10.1162/leon_a_01795

KEY TERMS AND DEFINITIONS

Artificial Neural Network (ANN): ANNs are a class of machine learning algorithms and are at the heart of deep learning. ANNs are comprised of node layers, containing an input layer, one or more hidden layers, and an output layer.

Counterfactual Fairness: A fairness metric that checks whether a classifier produces the same result for one individual as it does for another individual who is identical to the first, except with respect to one or more sensitive attributes.

Deep Learning (DL): DL is also ML relying on DNN.

Deep Neural Network (DNN): DNNs are ANN of multiple hidden layers.

Demographic Parity: A fairness metric that is satisfied if the results of a model's classification are not dependent on a given sensitive attribute.

Equalized Odds: A fairness metric that checks if, for any label and attribute, a classifier predicts that label equally well for all values of that attribute.

Fairness Constraint: Applying constraints to an algorithm to ensure one or more definitions of fairness are satisfied.

Fairness Metric: Fairness metrices are measurable notion of "fairness" with a mathematical definition. Some commonly used fairness metrics include equalized odds, predictive parity, counterfactual fairness, demographic parity, etc.

Machine Learning (ML): ML commonly used alongside AI and is a subset of AI. ML refers to systems that can learn from data, i.e., systems that get smarter by learning over time without direct human intervention.

Predictive Parity: A fairness metric that checks whether, for a given classifier, the precision rates are equivalent for subgroups under consideration.

Integration of Knowledge Management in Digital Healthcare Industries

Mehrnaz Khalaj Hedayati
Georgia College and State University, USA

Dara G. Schniederjans
University of Rhode Island, USA

INTRODUCTION

In service industries, organizational assets are in the staff experience and knowledge, rather than in their factories or equipment (Tsui et al., 2009). According to Tsui et al. (2009), offered services may vary in nature to accommodate different customer needs. These days, service firms manage and use knowledge, rather than raw materials, in order to provide customized services (Agrifoglio et al., 2017). The collaboration and sharing of knowledge and information between various actors throughout the network of service firms provide customer value and improve processes. Using emergent digital capabilities can provide higher levels of customization to consumers and higher levels of customer satisfaction as a result (Agrifoglio et al., 2017). Managing the pandemic and the increase in COVID-19 cases has presented major challenges to the healthcare system, which has prompted a more aggressive effort to develop and deploy digital healthcare services with the aim of ensuring value-based outcomes (Sermontyte-Baniule et al., 2022). In addition, learning from the past, knowledge management can be applied in the context of COVID-19 crisis which is marked by great uncertainty. Since the advent of the Fourth Industrial Revolution and emerging new digital technologies, we are experiencing unprecedented changes in our external environment, including speed and scale (Tomé & Hatch, 2022). In response to the pandemic, healthcare systems have been reimagined according to the prevention principle, which is characterized by the use of advanced technology, which has the potential to reshape markets and public policy regarding healthcare globally (Lauri, 2022). As a result, Countries with developed healthcare systems have adopted digital health technology to improve the practice of healthcare professionals, and to provide a positive experience to consumers and the community. On the other hand, accepting, embracing, and uptaking digital technologies is going to be challenging for healthcare professionals due to concerns about managing a large amount of data while maintaining the privacy and security of personal information. The main purpose of embracing digital technologies in healthcare is to transform and create value for the healthcare system and hospital facilities, empower patients to access their health records, communicate and control their personal health records and make better health and well-being decisions (Medhekar & Nguyen, 2022; McCarthy, 2022).

Emerging digital technologies by their distinctive characteristics are profoundly changing how the service industry and in particular healthcare processes are managed. It provides value by promoting and enhancing cooperation among several healthcare actors. For example, although record-keeping and updating through centralized programs (e.g., electronic medical records) has provided many advantages for the healthcare industry such as convenient and continuous documentation of care records, improved decision making and coordination, and reduced redundant services, the system still needs

DOI: 10.4018/978-1-7998-9220-5.ch102

advancements to overcome the current challenges for patients such as privacy issues and ethical and legal consequences as a result. Privacy concerns in healthcare services and palliative and hospice care may result in reducing patients' trust regarding properly protecting their care and health records and maintaining confidentiality. This may also undermine public trust in the healthcare system (Azogu et al., 2019). Considering the increased need to store private data in the healthcare industry in an increasingly digitalized environment, the need for high-level trust is more vital than ever. Fortunately, blockchain technology as a new emergent digital technology is considered to be one mechanism for enhancing trust throughout the healthcare network.

In the literature about the digitization eco-system, what distinguishes the new digital era is the trend toward decentralized information sharing and automation. A blockchain is a decentralized and transparent database for recording transactional data. It cannot be changed, and for any correction or change, a new block must be added to the network. The history of changes is therefore preserved in the system, so it is referred to as an incorruptible ledger for a secure and transparent form of sharing transactional data (Tapscott and Tapscott, 2016; Underwood, 2016). One specific application of blockchain in healthcare is allowing patients to have agency over who can access their healthcare data (Angraal et al., 2017, P. 2). Blockchain provides benefits for value creation through trust in decision-making for businesses.

According to Khalajhedayati et al. (2020), hospice professionals suggest that digitization may impede the creation of knowledge by standardizing electronic documents without allowing personalized, qualitative, and/or visual evidence (i.e., body language). They believe for hospice as a service industry, face-to-face communications are very important, and describing narratives can come through face-to-face communications. Particularly in urgent and vital situations, the relationship between patients and team members is essential. They described how digital initiatives may impede this relationship without having visual communication. However, there are potentials for visual collaboration through technologies such as Cisco WebEx telepresence services, video robots, and telehealth. Digitization, as defined in this proposal, is facilitated by digital technologies such as Internet of Things (IoT), Augmented Reality (AR), Artificial Intelligence (AI), 3D printing, blockchain technology, etc., which are used to provide a well-connected network and to improve digital communications. An Internet of Things (IoT) society involves people, devices, and systems interconnected via the internet and integrated communication. In the definition of IoT, "things" encompass people, devices, computers, and digitalized systems that link the digital and physical worlds (Bolton et al., 2016). People play a pivotal role in the ecosystem of "things" within an IoT-connected network. Incorporating human intelligence into the IoT eco-system, combined with AI capabilities, can provide the opportunity for computerized decision-makers to make decisions on behalf of human players (Bolton et al., 2016). The Internet of Things provides an integrated, well-connected system for connecting people and things anywhere at any time (Wang et al., 2015). An IoT concept can be generalized to include ideas and information exchanged from a service provider to a service receiver within a digital environment. People are a key component of communications systems that foster and drive the dissemination of knowledge (Bolton et al., 2016). Having IoT connectivity can benefit hospice services in several ways, including monitoring patient health and providing access to emergency alarm devices to family and patients.

Furthermore, healthcare services and processes highly rely on information and knowledge as well (Lenz et al., 2012; Laurenza et al., 2018). Knowledge management and digital technology management are crucial factors in the healthcare industry. (Laurenza et al., 2018). Additionally, healthcare and caregiver organizations face challenges more than any other, including resource restrictions and an expanding regulatory framework. Caregiver companies such as hospices strive to provide higher quality service and reduce costs to maximize value. Hospice care involves treating medical conditions requiring interdisciplinary expertise and multiple interventions (Porter et al., 2010). Value is created by an interdisciplinary team working together throughout the entire care cycle (Laurenza et al., 2018). Healthcare industries are constantly challenging themselves to simplify processes, deliver high quality and reduce response times. Therefore, the enormous changes in healthcare require creating a new business model to create value (Laurenza et al., 2018). Applying the field of knowledge management to digital healthcare industries through a knowledge management theoretical framework, this chapter provides an integrative conceptual approach to highlight the enhancement of digital healthcare performance using knowledge management.

Although digital technologies provide many advantages and opportunities for storing, processing, and sharing information in real-time, disseminating and managing knowledge are critical for value creation. A deeper understanding of the tools and processes as drivers of knowledge creation can also have a significant impact on service quality in the healthcare industry. Knowledge management theories presuppose an essential aspect of knowledge relates to human processing, challenging the technology basis of digital healthcare. Without the ability to leverage digital technologies through knowledge management, the creation of value is minimal. Following this, this study provides future research avenues by integrating knowledge management and digital healthcare. To achieve this goal, this study provides a conceptual Knowledge Management Digital Capability Model (KMDCM) in order to enhance digital healthcare performance.

BACKGROUND

Digitization converts the physical or analog signal to a digital form to provide electronic accessibility, processing capability, and data storage (Kayikci, 2018). "Digitization makes information and communication available anywhere, anytime, within any context, and for any user using any device and type of access" (Kayikci, 2018, p.2) and therefore, this means a higher level of digitization provides more access to information and business processes. This study defines digitization as the use of emerging digital technologies to provide value for the stakeholders. Based on this definition, digital technologies include anything from cloud computing, advanced robotics, internet of things (IoT), artificial intelligence (AI), augmented reality (AR), machine learning, drones, blockchain, sensors, etc. The goal is to provide a well-interconnected network through decentralized technology processes with high ability of collecting, storing, sharing, and using information to facilitate business decision making processes and be more productive.

According to Tsui et al. (2009), the knowledge and experience of an organization is its most valuable asset, rather than the factory or equipment that makes it work (Tsui et al., 2009). Provided services by service industries often vary in nature to address numerous customers' needs and demands (Tsui et al., 2009). In recent years, firms more deal with managing information rather than raw materials for the purpose of providing customized services for their customers (Agrifoglio et al., 2017). Collaborating and sharing information between numerous actors in a firm network provides value for the consumers and enhances processes. Utilizing emergent technologies and their capabilities can provide higher levels of information sharing across the entire network and customization to consumers (Agrifoglio et al., 2017).

As digital technologies emerge, they are profoundly changing the process of managing service industries, and specifically healthcare. The use of digital technologies, which provide general frameworks for developing solutions in which quality data is the core, facilitates the management of knowledge in healthcare delivery (Gyaase et al., 2021). Advanced knowledge management systems are based on integrating digital technologies into corporate strategies to improve decision making and quality service

(Di Vaio et al., 2021). Knowing that knowledge is a critical resource for any company, it is of interest to learn how knowledge management systems, by leveraging digital innovation, can lead the corporate strategy toward new, innovative business models, improving value creation in the long run. (Di Vaio etal., 2021). Digital healthcare systems are characterized by decentralized interconnected digital technologies to provide new healthcare models to get better service performance and to create value for the healthcare services and their stakeholders (Tortorella et al., 2021). Information and knowledge are essential to the processes and services of healthcare (Lenz et al., 2012; Laurenza et al., 2018). Thus, healthcare industry management and support of new digital technologies as well as information and knowledge management of these crucial services are vital (Laurenza et al., 2018).

Furthermore, the healthcare industry is being challenged more than others by resource constraints and growing regulations. Healthcare organizations and caregiver companies such as hospices and palliative care strive to maximize value and provide a high level of service while simultaneously reducing costs. Treatment of medical conditions requiring numerous interdisciplinary experts and various interventions is a part of healthcare services (Porter et al., 2010). Healthcare interdisciplinary team members work together to create value for patients over the entire cycle of care (Laurenza et al., 2018). They place a high value on process management, delivering high-quality care, and decreasing response times. Therefore, this industry needs to create a new value-producing business model that can provide high-quality services and enable it to perform better (Laurenza et al., 2018).

While digital technologies provide many advantages and opportunities for collecting, processing, storing, and real-time sharing information, distributing and managing knowledge is vital to create value. Based on the current literature, there is limited human knowledge of how to implement, apply, and utilize a huge amount of data to attain strategic value through knowledge and information sharing in an organizational network (Feng and Shanthikumar, 2018).

In the new computing era, persistent managing and sharing of data are essential. However, there is a lack of knowledge transfer and experience in these new systems and environments. People involved in healthcare networks need to extract knowledge and information from the data to optimize the utilization of digital technologies to improve healthcare services (Schniederjans et al., 2019).

MAIN FOCUS OF THE CHAPTER

Knowledge Management in Healthcare Industries

Knowledge Management (KM) connects information demand and supply to support learning processes as a means of improving organizational performance (Curado and Bontis, 2011). According to Polanyi (1962), there are two types of knowledge: tacit and explicit. As tacit knowledge is deeply rooted in action, involvement, and commitment, it is difficult to formalize and communicate. The explicit knowledge is codified and transmitted through formal, systematic language; so, it is captured in libraries, archives, and databases (Nonaka, 1994). It is believed that tacit and explicit knowledge are constantly in dialogue with each other, moving from individuals to groups and organizations; and then back again to individuals (Nonaka and Toyama, 2003). According to the theory of knowledge creation (Nonaka, 1994), by continuous learning, organizations increase their knowledge and understanding through socialization, externalization, combination, and internalization. Face-to-face communication and exchanging tacit knowledge among organization members is essential for socialization to occur. Externalization requires individuals to transform tacit knowledge into explicit knowledge, which enables other members of the organization to capture it. Combination is the process of transforming explicit knowledge into more complex forms, while internalization converts explicit knowledge back into tacit form, enabling individuals to incorporate it into their daily routine (Curado and Bontis, 2011). As a result of such a theory, a major step in the creation of knowledge is human interaction, which challenges healthcare digitization technology.

Knowledge management is a process of managing the tension between exploration and exploitation, according to March (1991). While exploration involves developing new organizational routines and solutions, exploitation involves leveraging existing routines to refine solutions and pre-existing knowledge. It is essential to apply both knowledge management strategies to sustain competitive advantage. Achieving the correct balance can be challenging because companies learn from experience how to allocate resources between exploration and exploitation (Curado and Bontis, 2011). The acquisition, management, and transfer of knowledge require technology, processes, and people, according to Carrión et al. (2004). These three aspects are considered as three pillars of knowledge management. Both exploration and exploitation are conducted through knowledge management processes. According to Alavi and Leidner (2001), knowledge management processes include knowledge creation, knowledge storage/ retrieval, knowledge transfer, and knowledge application, to create value by leveraging the knowledge assets of the firm processes.

Knowledge management involves the technical capabilities of managers and workers and social networks to design, modify, and execute flows thus enabling the circulation of knowledge in internal processes and to reach search engines for capture and application of external knowledge (Rojas et al., 2017). The use of information and communication technologies (ICT) helps routines that support knowledge management practices within healthcare applications (Shahmoradi et al., 2017). While there are some advantages by implementing digital technologies, there are some managerial challenges of digitization including change and leadership, strategy and analysis, business models, planning and implementation, human resources, and cooperation and networks (Schneider Electric, 2017). In order to cope with these challenges, firms should combine the three pillars of knowledge management i.e., people, processes, and technology.

In general, knowledge management relates to healthcare by providing the tools necessary to manage large amounts of data generated by healthcare providers and their customers. Every single day, healthcare providers, face an overwhelming amount of knowledge and information processing, and thus, integrating knowledge management into healthcare organizations by providing appropriate tools and methods to collect, manage, share, and store the huge amount of data is vital (Schniederjans et al., 2019 Shahmoradi et al., 2017).

Healthcare services need managers to understand, monitor, and control operations in the entire healthcare network, and all these tasks involve managing knowledge not only from the technology side through information and communication technologies (Tortorella et al., 2021; Aceto et al., 2018) but also the quality of knowledge provided in the healthcare services through knowledge management and data analytics, considering either tacit or explicit knowledge. As a result, knowledge management contributes to healthcare services allowing healthcare providers to improve the quality of care as well as responding to internal and external stakeholder needs (Shahmoradi et al., 2017). While the role of knowledge management in healthcare services is established in existing literature, the role of knowledge management as it relates to digital healthcare has yet to be fully explored. A general understanding is needed on the digital healthcare ecosystem. This chapter, integrating digital healthcare and knowledge management proposes a general conceptual model and provides future research avenues for further exploration of enhancing digital healthcare performance to create value.

Capability Approach in Digital Healthcare

Capability approach is used to understand and theorize the effect of digital technologies on development (Nikou et al. 2020; Sahay et al., 2017). In this sense, digital technologies are the resources that enable people can accomplish valuable goals, and capabilities are defined as what people can do by using digital technology features (Nikou et al., 2020).

A capability approach allows researchers to evaluate how digital technologies influence development, allowing them to consider the impact of digital technologies on the wellbeing and agency of individuals rather than merely maximizing access to technology. Capability approach is popular in ICT4D as a powerful perspective to evaluate the effect of ICT on people's wellbeing (Nikou et al., 2020; Zheng, 2009). This viewpoint supports our claim to understand how digital healthcare provides value to its stakeholders.

Considering the digital capability model, the knowledge management approach by Alavi and Leidner (2001) is applied to digital healthcare to propose an integrative approach to improve the digitization of healthcare industries. This integrative model is presented in Figure 1 to highlight the digital healthcare optimization and benefits through the use of knowledge management (Schniederjans et al., 2019).

Figure 1. Proposed integrated model for digital healthcare and knowledge management (Borrowed from Schniederjans et al., 2019)

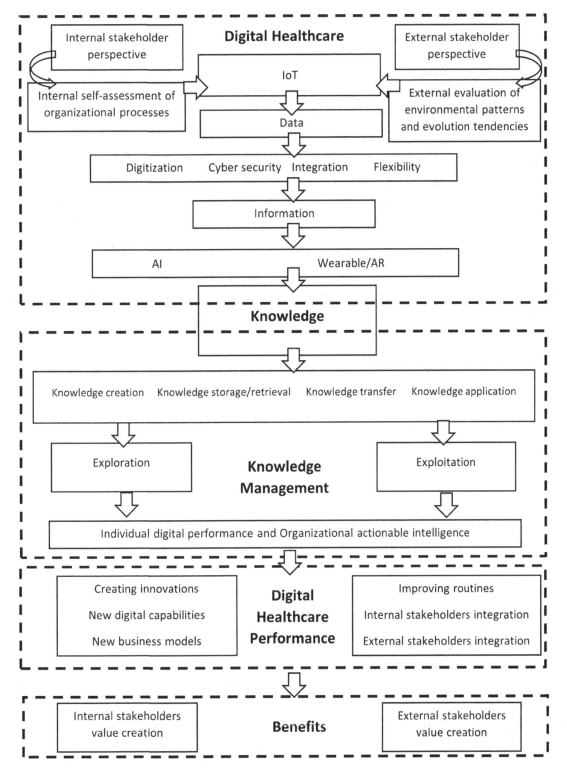

SOLUTIONS AND RECOMMENDATIONS

Digital technologies such as artificial intelligence, mobile health applications, and wearable electronic devices are used to deliver remote care to patients due to the increasing burden on healthcare (Vuong et al., 2022). What distinguishes the new era of digitization, according to the literature on the digitization eco-system, is the development of a decentralized information sharing and automation system. For recording transactional data, blockchain technology acts as a decentralized distributed ledger. As the ledger cannot be changed and for any changes or corrections, a new block needs to be added to the system; its history of changes is therefore preserved, making it an incorruptible digital ledger for secure and transparent sharing of transactional data (Tapscott and Tapscott, 2016; Underwood, 2016).

Due to the decentralized nature of blockchain technology, all individuals involved in the care network have direct access to each other. In other words, the information stored in a blockchain is not controlled by any central authority and, as a consequence, it can be reviewed by network participants who have access to the system, ensuring proper redundancy (Azogu et al., 2019; Atzori, 2015). A specific example of blockchain application in healthcare services can be the capability of "giving patients the ability to have agency over and knowledge of who access their healthcare data (Angraal et al., 2017, P. 2). Businesses can also create value through blockchain's trust-based decision-making benefits. By creating transparency between parties in an ecosystem, blockchain reduces the need for third-party intermediaries. Blockchain technology can be an appropriate solution if service providers seek to establish an immutable system (Hughes et al., 2019). Utilizing blockchain technology allows for automatic authentication and verification of each block. A specific application in healthcare industries is the process of sending messages to the members in the healthcare network who are involved in the care processes for the patients. Blockchain technology with its unique characteristics can allow people to keep track of activities and update in a secure and trustworthy manner.

Additionally, digital technology can provide visual collaboration through integrated services such as Cisco WebEx telepresence, robotics, telemedicine, etc. Based on the definition of digitization in this study, emerging Internet of Things (IoT) technologies are used to provide a well-connected network and to improve digital communications. IoT is a system of internet connectivity and integrated communication that enables everyday interactions between individuals, devices, and systems. According to the definition of IoT, 'things' include people, machines, computers, and digitized systems which connect a digital world to an analog one (Bolton et al., 2016). Within the ecosystem of 'things' created by the Internet of Things, people play an essential role. Incorporating humans into the digital IoT eco-system by incorporating artificial intelligence (AI) capabilities could produce benefits for computerized decision makers working in place of humans (Bolton et al., 2016). The Internet of Things provides a well-connected integrated system that provides connectivity among people and things at anytime, anywhere (Wang et al., 2015). In a digital environment, the concept of IoT can also be applied to the exchange of information and ideas between service providers. Communication systems are driven by people who disseminate knowledge (Bolton et al., 2016). Connectivity from IoT devices can offer many advantages for healthcare services and patient care such as the ability to monitor patient's health and provide emergency alarms to the responsible members. The emergence of IoT and AI applications in many industries has been the subject of a great deal of research since Shah & Chircu (2018) published their systematic literature review. In their study, the authors examine a wide range of publications in order to gauge the impact of IoT and AI in the healthcare industry. Another important technological change in the healthcare sector is the use of wearable devices through IoT connectivity. Innovative uses of emerging technologies include tracking and monitoring of patients via wearable devices, and remote diagnosis, which facilitate emergency detection, treatment management, and expert medical advice (Vongsingthong and Smanchat, 2014).

Another application in the systematic literature review by Shah & Chircu (2018) reveals a high emphasis on wearable sensors in elderly care. Konstantinidis et al. (2015) provided in the overview of their study, that low-cost, easily accessible, and easy-to-use controllers are suitable for the care of elderly interventions like Wii remotes and pressure sensors. Integrating smart TVs into the care system will allow for real-time monitoring of patients and alerting the involved members to patients' condition in healthcare services and palliative or hospice cares. Moreover, they can implement a system of games that can promote exercise and enable daily life management and independence. Furthermore, these devices facilitate continuous monitoring, remote diagnosis, and data exchange through mobile health applications, which are essential in healthcare services (Sun et al., 2016; Shah and Chircu, 2018; Konstantinidis et al., 2015).

Although cutting-edge digital technologies like blockchain, artificial intelligence, and IoT wearables can offer many benefits, technological risks and threats persist and must also be investigated. In addition, further research is needed to investigate the impact of applying digital technologies on ethical issues, legislations, privacy and security, data collection and storage, and their reliability and accuracy. Future research can explore further customization of digital technologies in healthcare to provide patients with more convenient and quality services. These issues need to be addressed to successfully enhance value added changes in digital healthcare.

CONCLUSION AND FUTURE RESEARCH DIRECTIONS

It is important to ascertain that even though digital technologies offer various benefits to healthcare, there is a broad spectrum of issues that come into play. This is especially considering the current state, where a pandemic has forced healthcare models to rapidly adjust towards compliance with local, regional, and national policy.

The dissemination and creation of knowledge, practice, and understanding become paramount when considering the benefits but also the drawbacks of the rapid changes in policy and practicality of technology application worldwide. Below we consider several insights from the American Hospital Association Compliance Topics[1]. The following is a summary of questions researchers and practitioners may consider when addressing knowledge management via digital technology implementation in healthcare settings:

- The Health Insurance Portability and Accountability Act (HIPAA) established standards of confidentiality, security, and transmissibility of health care information. How can we leverage theoretical insights from the theory of knowledge creation while maintaining patient privacy via digital technology tools (i.e., blockchain, cybersecurity, cloud computing)?
- Clinical integration is necessary to facilitate the coordination of patient care across a variety of providers. Yet, legal barriers often impeded reform efforts. How might digital technology be leveraged to enhance clinical integration?
- Policy in the use of digital technology in healthcare settings has yet to be matured. How might a model be created to develop policy for the broad use of digital technology across national borders?
- Healthcare access is currently being reduced by physicians moving in and out of states with increasing insurance costs, how might digital technologies be leveraged to enhance access to healthcare?

- Approximately $50 to $100 billion is spent on defensive medicine annually. These are services provided to mitigate the risk of physician liability and are not based on the primary purpose of the well being of the patient. How might knowledge management be leveraged for liability reform?
- While applications and benefits of digital technology are seemingly transparent in literature, what is less transparent are the negative implications of technology, specifically in "technostress" for patients, providers, insurance companies, nurses, physicians, etc. What are the aspects of digital technology that can lead to technostress? And how might theory in knowledge management be used to mitigate these issues?

REFERENCES

Aceto, G., Persico, V., & Pescapé, A. (2018). The role of information and communication technologies in healthcare: Taxonomies, perspectives, and challenges. *Journal of Network and Computer Applications*, *107*, 125–154. doi:10.1016/j.jnca.2018.02.008

Agrifoglio, R., Cannavale, C., Laurenza, E., & Metallo, C. (2017). How emerging digital technologies affect operations management through co-creation. empirical evidence from the maritime industry. *Production Planning and Control*, *28*(16), 1298–1306. doi:10.1080/09537287.2017.1375150

Alavi, M., & Leidner, D. E. (2001). Knowledge management and knowledge management systems: Conceptual foundations and research issues. *Management Information Systems Quarterly*, *25*(1), 107–136. doi:10.2307/3250961

Angraal, S., Krumholz, H. M., & Schulz, W. L. (2017). Blockchain technology: Applications in health care. *Circulation: Cardiovascular Quality and Outcomes*, *10*(9), e003800. doi:10.1161/CIRCOUTCOMES.117.003800 PMID:28912202

AtzoriM. (2015). Blockchain technology and decentralized governance: Is the state still necessary? *Available at* SSRN 2709713. doi:10.2139/ssrn.2709713

Azogu, I., Norta, A., Papper, I., Longo, J., & Draheim, D. (2019). A framework for the adoption of blockchain technology in healthcare information management systems: A case study of Nigeria. *Proceedings of the 12th International Conference on Theory and Practice of Electronic Governance*, 310–316. 10.1145/3326365.3326405

Bolton, A., Goosen, L., & Kritzinger, E. (2016). Enterprise digitization enablement through unified communication & collaboration. *Proceedings of the Annual Conference of the South African Institute of Computer Scientists and Information Technologists*, 1–10. 10.1145/2987491.2987516

Carrion, G. C., Gonzalez, J. L. G., & Leal, A. (2004). Identifying key knowledge area in the professional services industry: A case study. *Journal of Knowledge Management*.

Curado, C., & Bontis, N. (2011). Parallels in knowledge cycles. *Computers in Human Behavior*, *27*(4), 1438–1444. doi:10.1016/j.chb.2010.09.011

Di Vaio, A., Palladino, R., Pezzi, A., & Kalisz, D. E. (2021). The role of digital innovation in knowledge management systems: A systematic literature review. *Journal of Business Research*, *123*, 220–231. doi:10.1016/j.jbusres.2020.09.042

Feng, Q., & Shanthikumar, J. G. (2018). How research in production and operations management may evolve in the era of big data. *Production and Operations Management*, 27(9), 1670–1684. doi:10.1111/poms.12836

Gyaase, P. O., Boye-Doe, J. T., & Okantey, C. (2021). An Assessment of the Quality of Data From the EPI for Knowledge Management in Healthcare in Ghana. Digital Technology Advancements in Knowledge Management, 195-216.

Hughes, A., Park, A., Kietzmann, J., & Archer-Brown, C. (2019). Beyond bit- coin: What blockchain and distributed ledger technologies mean for firms. *Business Horizons*, 62(3), 273–281. doi:10.1016/j.bushor.2019.01.002

Kayikci, Y. (2018). Sustainability impact of digitization in logistics. *Procedia Manufacturing*, 21, 782–789. doi:10.1016/j.promfg.2018.02.184

Konstantinidis, E. I., Antoniou, P. E., Bamparopoulos, G., & Bamidis, P. D. (2015). A lightweight framework for transparent cross platform communication of controller data in ambient assisted living environments. *Information Sciences*, 300, 124–139. doi:10.1016/j.ins.2014.10.070

Laurenza, E., Quintano, M., Schiavone, F., & Vrontis, D. (2018). The effect of digital technologies adoption in healthcare industry: A case based analysis. *Business Process Management Journal*, 24(5), 1124–1144. doi:10.1108/BPMJ-04-2017-0084

Lauri, C. (2022). Smart health from the hospital to the city: regulatory challenges for upcoming digital healthcare systems. Smart Cities and Machine Learning in Urban Health, 1-19.

Lenz, R., Peleg, M., & Reichert, M. (2012). Healthcare process support: Achievements, challenges, current research. *International Journal of Knowledge-Based Organizations*, 2(4).

March, J. G. (1991). Exploration and exploitation in organizational learning. *Organization Science*, 2(1), 71–87. doi:10.1287/orsc.2.1.71

McCarthy, S. E. (2022). The Digitisation of Healthcare in a Global Pandemic: Implications for Healthcare Quality From Patient, Clinician, and Provider Perspectives. In Handbook of Research on Cyberchondria, Health Literacy, and the Role of Media in Society's Perception of Medical Information (pp. 55-71). Academic Press.

McCormick, J., & Shah, A. (2020). Hospitals monitor some coronavirus patients at home. *World Street J*. https://www.wsj.com/articles/hospitals-monitor-somecoronavirus-patients-at-home-11586856604

Medhekar, A., & Nguyen, J. (2022). My digital healthcare record: innovation, challenge, and patient empowerment. Research Anthology on Improving Health Literacy Through Patient Communication and Mass Media, 538-557. doi:10.4018/978-1-6684-2414-8.ch030

Nikou, S., Agahari, W., Keijzer-Broers, W., & de Reuver, M. (2020). Digital healthcare technology adoption by elderly people: A capability approach model. *Telematics and Informatics*, 53, 101315. doi:10.1016/j.tele.2019.101315

Nonaka, I. (1994). A dynamic theory of organizational knowledge creation. *Organization Science*, 5(1), 14–37. doi:10.1287/orsc.5.1.14

Nonaka, I., Toyama, R., & Byosi'ere, P. (2003). Handbook of organizational learning and knowledge, a theory of organizational knowledge creation: Understanding the dynamic process of creating knowledge. Academic Press.

Park, Y., Lee, C., & Jung, J. Y. (2022). Digital healthcare for airway diseases from personal environmental exposure. *Yonsei Medical Journal*, *63*(Suppl), S1–S0. doi:10.3349/ymj.2022.63.S1 PMID:35040601

Polanyi, M. (1962). Tacit knowing: Its bearing on some problems of philosophy. *Reviews of Modern Physics*, *34*(4), 601–616. doi:10.1103/RevModPhys.34.601

Porter, M. E. (2010). What is value in health care. *The New England Journal of Medicine*, *363*(26), 2477–2481. doi:10.1056/NEJMp1011024 PMID:21142528

Rojas, R., Morales, V. J., Sánchez, E., & Jiménez, A. E. (2017). El aprendizaje colaborativo enla docencia sobre empresa. *Dialnet*, 235–235. Retrieved from. https://dialnet.unirioja.es/servlet/articulo?codigo=6274710

Sahay, S., Sein, M. K., & Urquhart, C. (2017). Flipping the context: ICT4D, the next grand challenge for is research and practice. *Journal of the Association for Information Systems*, *18*(12), 837–847. doi:10.17705/1jais.00479

Schneider Electric. (2017). *IoT EcoStruxureTM Ensures Efficiency for CNBM - YouTube*. Retrieved from https://www.youtube.com/watch?v=zV7l-wavtCA

Schniederjans, D. G., Curado, C., & Khalajhedayati, M. (2019). Supply chain digitisation trends: An integration of knowledge management. *International Journal of Production Economics*, *220*, 107439. doi:10.1016/j.ijpe.2019.07.012

Sermontyte-Baniule, R., Pundziene, A., Giménez, V., & Narbón-Perpiñá, I. (2022). Role of cultural dimensions and dynamic capabilities in the value-based performance of digital healthcare services. *Technological Forecasting and Social Change*, *176*, 121490. doi:10.1016/j.techfore.2022.121490

Shah, R., & Chircu, A. (2018). IoT and AI in healthcare: A systematic literature review. *Information Systems*, *19*(3).

Shahmoradi, L., Safadari, R., & Jimma, W. (2017). Knowledge management implementation and the tools utilized in healthcare for evidence-based decision making: A systematic review. *Ethiopian Journal of Health Sciences*, *27*(5), 541–558. doi:10.4314/ejhs.v27i5.13 PMID:29217960

Sun, J., Guo, Y., Wang, X., & Zeng, Q. (2016). Mhealth for aging china: Opportunities and challenges. *Aging and Disease*, *7*(1), 53. doi:10.14336/AD.2015.1011 PMID:26816664

Tapscott, D., & Tapscott, A. (2016). *Blockchain revolution: how the technology behind bitcoin is changing money*. Business, and the World.

Tomé, E., Gromova, E., & Hatch, A. (2022). Knowledge management and COVID-19: Technology, people and processes. *Knowledge and Process Management*.

Tortorella, G. L., Fogliatto, F. S., Saurin, T. A., Tonetto, L. M., & McFarlane, D. (2021). Contributions of healthcare 4.0 digital applications to the resilience of healthcare organizations during the COVID-19 outbreak. *Technovation*, 102379.

Tsui, E., Fong, P. S., & Choi, S. K. (2009). The processes of knowledge management in professional services firms in the construction industry: A critical assessment of both theory and practice. *Journal of Knowledge Management, 13*(2), 110–126. doi:10.1108/13673270910942736

Underwood, S. (2016). Blockchain beyond bitcoin. *Communications of the ACM, 59*(11), 15–17. doi:10.1145/2994581

Vongsingthong, S., & Smanchat, S. (2014). Internet of things: A review of applications & technologies. *Warasan Technology Suranaree, 21*(4), 359–374.

Vuong, Q. H., Le, T. T., La, V. P., Nguyen, H. T. T., Ho, M. T., Van Khuc, Q., & Nguyen, M. H. (2022). Covid-19 vaccines production and societal immunization under the serendipity-mindsponge-3D knowledge management theory and conceptual framework. *Humanities and Social Sciences Communications, 9*(1), 1–12. doi:10.105741599-022-01034-6

Wang, D., Lo, D., Bhimani, J., & Sugiura, K. (2015). AnyControl--IoT based home appliances monitoring and controlling. *2015 IEEE 39th Annual Computer Software and Applications Conference, 3*, 487–492.

Zheng, Y. (2009). Different spaces for e-development: What can we learn from the capability approach? *Information Technology for Development, 15*(2), 66–82. doi:10.1002/itdj.20115

ADDITIONAL READING

de Bem Machado, A., Secinaro, S., Calandra, D., & Lanzalonga, F. (2022). Knowledge management and digital transformation for Industry 4.0: A structured literature review. *Knowledge Management Research and Practice, 20*(2), 1–19. doi:10.1080/14778238.2021.2015261

El Morr, C., & Subercaze, J. (2010). Knowledge management in healthcare. In *Handbook of research on developments in e-health and telemedicine: technological and social perspectives* (pp. 490–510). IGI Global. doi:10.4018/978-1-61520-670-4.ch023

Ferraris, A., Mazzoleni, A., Devalle, A., & Couturier, J. (2018). Big data analytics capabilities and knowledge management: Impact on firm performance. *Management Decision*.

Fu, L., Zhang, W., & Li, L. (2022). Big Data Analytics for Healthcare Information System: Field Study in an US Hospital. In Frontiers of Data and Knowledge Management for Convergence of ICT, Healthcare, and Telecommunication Services (pp. 25-44). Springer.

Jayaraman, P. P., Forkan, A. R. M., Morshed, A., Haghighi, P. D., & Kang, Y. B. (2020). Healthcare 4.0: A review of frontiers in digital health. *Wiley Interdisciplinary Reviews. Data Mining and Knowledge Discovery, 10*(2), e1350. doi:10.1002/widm.1350

Kraus, S., Schiavone, F., Pluzhnikova, A., & Invernizzi, A. C. (2021). Digital transformation in healthcare: Analyzing the current state-of-research. *Journal of Business Research, 123*, 557–567. doi:10.1016/j.jbusres.2020.10.030

Mohanta, B., Das, P., & Patnaik, S. (2019, May). Healthcare 5.0: A paradigm shift in digital healthcare system using Artificial Intelligence, IOT and 5G Communication. In *2019 International Conference on Applied Machine Learning (ICAML)* (pp. 191-196). IEEE. 10.1109/ICAML48257.2019.00044

Wang, Q., Su, M., Zhang, M., & Li, R. (2021). Integrating digital technologies and public health to fight Covid-19 pandemic: Key technologies, applications, challenges and outlook of digital health-care. *International Journal of Environmental Research and Public Health*, *18*(11), 6053. doi:10.3390/ijerph18116053 PMID:34199831

KEY TERMS AND DEFINITIONS

Digital Capability Approach: Capabilities as defined in this study are what people can do by using digital technology features, and capability approach is used to evaluate how digital technologies impact on the wellbeing of individuals to support understanding of how digital healthcare provides value to its stakeholders.

Digital Healthcare: Digital healthcare in this study is defined as using decentralized interconnected digital technologies (mentioned above) to develop new digital healthcare models in order to improve healthcare service performance and to create value for the healthcare services and their stakeholders.

Digitization: This study defines digitization as the use of emerging digital technologies to provide value for the stakeholders.

Emerging Digital Technologies: Emerging digital technologies are defined as anything from cloud computing, advanced robotics, internet of things (IoT), artificial intelligence (AI), augmented reality (AR), machine learning, drones, blockchain, sensors, etc.

Healthcare Knowledge Management: Knowledge management relates to healthcare by providing the tools necessary to manage large amounts of data generated by healthcare providers and their customers.

Integrative Approach: This chapter applies the field of knowledge management to digital healthcare industries through a knowledge management theoretical framework to develop an integrative conceptual approach to highlight the enhancement of digital healthcare performance using knowledge management.

Knowledge Management Digital Capability Model (KMDCM): This study by integrating knowledge management approach to digital healthcare, proposes an integrative Knowledge Management Digital Capability Model (KMDCM) to highlight the digital healthcare optimization and benefits through the use of knowledge management.

ENDNOTE

[1]   Compliance | AHA.

Learning Analytics for Smart Classrooms

Cèlia Llurba
 https://orcid.org/0000-0003-1192-8579
University Rovira i Virgili, Spain

Ramon Palau
 https://orcid.org/0000-0002-9843-3116
University Rovira i Virgili, Spain

Jordi Mogas
 https://orcid.org/0000-0003-3385-5534
University Rovira i Virgili, Spain

INTRODUCTION

Big data and LA are poised to transform personalized learning once again (Shemshack, & Spector, 2020) which can help students to increase motivation and engagement.

The modern digital era, which includes LA, has not changed this fundamental aspect of a teacher day in a class because teachers' target has always been to enhance learning by getting answers to tailored questions, scoring attendance on a sheet of paper and comparing this with test scores supported by triage (Dollinger et al., 2019); although teachers have always used different types of data about students, data analysis tools are useful for having more information and presumably much faster (Naujokaitiene et al., 2020).

In recent years, when researching and conducting studies on this topic, it has been found that the tools provided the teacher with improbable data such as: predictive analytics to help determine which students are at-risk (Joksimovic, Kovanovic, & Dawson, 2019; Larrabee et al., 2019); to use the student's past data and current data to determine what is likely to happen next, such as identifying underperforming students; and prescriptive analytics to provide teachers with data which can then use to make actionable decisions, as providing alternative suggestions to make teaching more effective (Admiraal, Vermeulen, & Bulterman-Bos, 2020). These examples have been taken to improve the work of the teacher in the classroom. Saving time and data that teacher can also easily store. Even though Naidu et al. (2017) affirm the model will be effective in making traditional classrooms to SC equipped with LA. Taking into account the definition of SC, which is according to Cebrián, Palau, & Mogas (2020), an educational space endowed with digital devices and learning software, sensor networks, gathering data and offering insights to help decision making for better and faster learning, to provide more convenient teaching and learning conditions for educators and students. Therefore, LA are intimately linked to SC, which integrates in an unobtrusive manner the sensor and communication technology, and artificial intelligence (AI), among others, into the classroom (Aguilar et al., 2018) collecting data to improve the learning process and the student's academic performance.

The overarching aim of this review is to know the benefits of data analysis, main features, claiming if the practice has been carried out, and which contributions or experiences about LA and SC are already made. Even though systematic review focuses on LA for supporting study success, there have been a

DOI: 10.4018/978-1-7998-9220-5.ch103

number of research focused on LA (Atif et al., 2013), on practices (Sclater, Peasgood, & Mullan, 2016) and policies (Gasevi et al., 2019). But, according to Ifenthaler, & Yau (2020), the success of LA in improving student learning has not yet been systematically and empirically demonstrated. Yet not much is known about the practice. It is important to note that many of the implementations described in these papers studied the importance of using LA in SC at different educational levels in higher education, such as high schools or at Universities. Nevertheless, there remains a significant gap in the research concerning LA adoption in high schools (Joksimovic et al., 2019), and almost no practice found in elementary schools.

BACKGROUND

Material and Method

Following the steps used by Vangrieken et al. (2015) were determined to meet the criteria for inclusion of the work in the final set to be reviewed. The first step was the initial search, in the results of the present review the authors searched for several keywords, specifically five combinations of keywords, which were: "LA and SC", "LA and teaching", "LA and learning", "LA and learning processes" and finally "LA and smart school". The keywords were linked obtaining more precise results that improve the search. Also in this phase of the systematic review only included papers published in the last five years, filtered years to 2016 – 2020 to review papers which have been related to the topic for their search. English and Spanish were the selected languages.

The filtering criteria used during the second step of searching was to remove by title; the keywords and titles of each initial search result were reviewed and those that appeared related to the term were included. The third search step was an attentive read of the abstract of each article to determine the main underlying focus.

The fourth step consisted of downloading all these articles to Mendeley. The downloaded literature was indexed based on full text pdf files; thereafter the review search string was applied on the indexed literature. Each article that met the inclusion criteria was read in its entirety a second time to validate the article's decision in the final data set.

Table 1. Number of reviewed articles selected from two scientific databases

Database	LA	LA & SC	LA & TEACHING	LA & LEARNING	LA & LEARNING PROCESSES	LA & SC	Total
Scopus	459	24	10	19	3	1	57
Web of Science	546	5	13	7	3	1	31
Total	1005	29	23	26	8	2	88

The results grouped by studies according to the term used, as shown in Table 1, which started among two of the main scientific databases in educational science, with only one keyword, which was LA, therefore came out with 1005 articles. Papers met in the research field and were examined in detail; the results grouped by studies according to the term used, a combination of keywords were made: 29 of them use classroom, 23 teaching, 26 learning, 8 learning processes, and 2 smart schools as the main term in the paper. A total of 88 articles were selected from the scientific data-bases.

Data Collection

This study reporting LA intervention was first collected via two different reputable citation databases: Scopus and the Web of Science using the key terms (——LA-AND——......) for filtered years to the period 2016–2020. Most of the articles were published in 2020 (12), and 12 more articles in 2019, followed by four in 2018, 2017 (3) and 4 in 2016. An initial search on these databases shows that the number of published papers on LA in SC has progressively increased year by year; especially there is a jump in 2019 as seen in Figure 1.

Figure 1. The growth trend of LA in SC by year

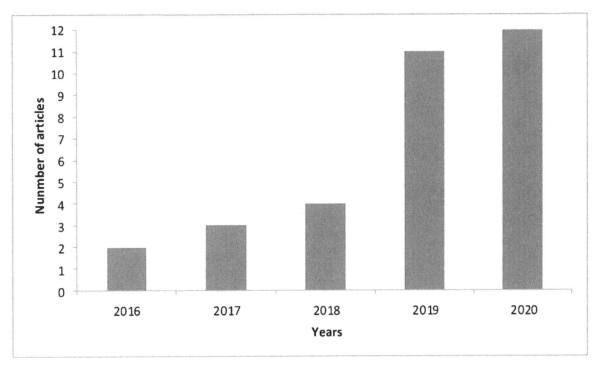

A number of papers have begun to be examined; exactly 1005 papers were reviewed in total. These papers were directly related to one keyword, LA; which 459 were published on Scopus, 546 on the Web of Science, and those that were related to the chosen topic and followed these criteria of this keyword but now associated with another word making a combination of two keywords ended up being 88.

Of these 88, 10 were repeated and removed, 10 more were discarded for the title as it did not fit, for the summary another 28 were subtracted, and finally 6 did not refer to the criteria and were deleted upon reading the conclusion. All these selected papers were identified and saved in Mendeley, a bibliographic reference multi-platform tool for the study review. Finally, after reading references of the mentioned articles, 9 extra papers were added for meeting the selection criteria. In total 35 studies were chosen out of 88 relevant studies identified through database searching for this systematic literature review. In Figure 2, the diagram shows the results of each step using a PRISMA 2009 flow diagram.

Figure 2. PRISMA 2009 flow diagram

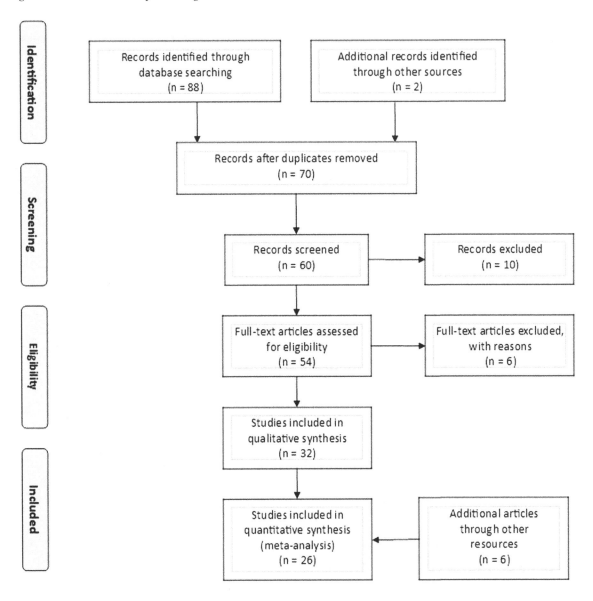

As, having analyzed research on LA in SC published in the period from 2016 to 2020; the date range of 2016 to the present day was chosen as this is when the term LA in SC started to gain more research attention due to the increased use of technology in education.

RESULTS

Elias (2011) described LA as an emerging field, which had sophisticated tools for improving learning and education; (Siemens and Long, 2011) added LA are used to collecting, analyzing and reporting data of learners, thus optimizing the learning and learning environment. As well as Siemens (2013) suggested that LA used intelligent data, learning product data and analytical models for getting information and could predict and advise on learning. According to the JISC report (Sclater et al., 2016) LA have the capability to transform the way to measure impact and results in learning environments facilitating to develop new ways of accomplishing supremacy in teaching and learning, and bringing students with new information to make the best decisions about their education. Moreover, Suchithra, Vadihehi, and Iyer (2015) listed as LA help educators/teachers to understand the students, at the same time learning capabilities can be improved for the learners. Even so, in the literature of Ramos De Melo et al., (2014), the term tends to be growing to ensure the process of personalizing the content which allows mechanisms to identify student characteristics and associate them with a learning pattern.

Particularly, there is a list of intervention methods of LA reported in different institutions. There are alternative models described in various papers, however there is no one that stands out more than the others, but the most part of the intervention is concentrated on universities, followed by high schools, and few on primary schools, as seen on Table 2.

Table 2. Distribution of articles according to the educational level across the experiences discussed

Educational level	Number of data sources	References
Primary school	2	Admiraal et al. (2020); Salas-Pilco & Yang (2020)
High school	5	Klašnja-Milićević, & Ivanović (2018); Larrabee et al. (2019); Salas-Pilco & Yang (2020); Sclater et al. (2018); Wong & Li (2020)
University	18	Aguilar et al. (2018); Erdemci & Karal (2020); Gasevic et al. (2019); Hernández-Lara et al. (2019); Hoyos & Velasquez (2020); Ifenthaler & Yau (2020); Nguyen et al. (2020); Klašnja-Milićević & Ivanović (2018); Mangaroska et al. (2019), Nganji et al. (2020); Salas-Pilco & Yang (2020); Samuelsen et al. (2019); Sclater et al. (2016); Aguilar & Valdiviezo (2017); Uskov et al. (2019); Ochoa et al. (2016); Wong & Li (2020); Zhang et al. (2018)

Another way of grouping the observed sources are words related to the definition of LA, which involves the application of different data analysis strategies, and the interrelation between them. At the same time, the benefits of LA for teachers, students and institutions have been outlined, and an opportunity for LA to support success in studies has been provided. It should be noted that not all educational data are equivalent.

Table 3. Research approaches. Words related to the definition of LA

Words related to the definition of LA	improving	learning	environment student	teaching	learning capabilities	style or learning pattern
References	Elias (2011)					
		Siemens (2013)				
	Siemens, & Long (2011)	Siemens, & Long (2011)	Siemens, & Long (2011)			
	Sclater et al., (2018)	Sclater et al., (2018)	Sclater et al., (2018)	Sclater et al., (2018)		
	Suchithra, Vadihehi, and Iyer (2015)				Suchithra, Vadihehi, and Iyer (2015)	
						Ramos de Melo et al., (2014)

That is, as seen on different sources written on Table 3, the majority of authors affirm that LA are useful for improving in education, either learning or learning environment. In contrast, the most modern source also includes that LA improve the way of teaching, a term which was not included in any definition mentioned in these articles until that moment.

At the same time, this paper was aimed to address responses based on the following question criteria:

1. What assumptions are made about the benefits (in teaching and learning) of using LA?
2. What are the main characteristics/elements of LA in the studies provided?
3. Are there research or experiences about LA and SC or smart schools and which models or contributions do they make?

Benefits in Teaching and Learning Using LA

Different authors show the benefits of LA in teaching and learning processes. Some of them from the teaching perspective as Erdemci, & Karal (2020), allowing instructors to make a self-evaluation about themselves and their teaching processes, through the modification of content to be aligned with students' desire (Ifenthaler, 2016). Some other from the student perspective as Salas-Pilco, & Yang (2020) that showed that LA helped to improve students' achievement, such as academic performance, developing oral and behavioral skills, and reversing students' dropout risk. Accordingly, it allows students to pay attention and to act quickly to achieve better academic performance, having the opportunity to identify their learning process, or Aguilar et al. (2018) when highlighted that LA can examine learning processes, and examine students' behavior. Ifenthaler (2016) indicated that LA could help understand learning habits of students, obtain real-time feedback and real-time insight, promoting their success. Moreover, the same author, a few years later added that the automated adaptive LA support systems reduce a learner's self-regulation and perceived autonomy and can give opportunities for personalization (Ifenthaler, 2020). All combined for reaching the global goal: improve the learning experiences.

Finally other authors see both perspectives as a whole topic. Eckerson (2011) manifests that the use of LA assist to enhance the teaching and learning of the students so as to understand well. Therefore, it also brings profit to other elements of the education process (Siemens and Long, 2011), such as providing to help teachers in terms of the effectiveness of the process of learning and determining students at risk. At the same time, the achievement targets of learning become more rapidly through providing the accessible tools to let the learners and teachers to assess their performances progress and get the best result. Hadhrami (2017) indicates that LA not only will help to improve the students' performance, but teachers' time and effort, whereas by providing the information on which students need to uptick good knowledge and enhance skills. Furthermore, Siemens (2013) claimed that one of the main reasons why LA were gaining popularity in education was due to deeper understanding of teaching, learning, intelligent content, personalized learning and adaptive learning.

All of these findings demonstrate the potential uses of LA for improving the quality of education in a smart school. Thus, it is interesting to include LA in the classroom, so the learning-teaching process can have a positive impact on, which contributes to determining this teaching process (Halibas, Sathyaseelan, & Shahzad, 2019), post-educational employment opportunities, and improved research in the field of education (Avella et al., 2016).

The Main Characteristics of LA in the Studies Provided

Based on Aguilar et al. statement (2018), learning analytic goal in a SC is to extract knowledge for a better understanding of the students and the manner of how they learn, then it should be clear and concise, teacher must understand why student success or failure, otherwise supposition and default positions may not be controlled (Archer & Prinsloo, 2020). Meanwhile, it must take into consideration the long-term effects of our judgments and assessments. The authors need to seriously commit to the understanding that our assessment (whether formative or summative, observational, behavioral, or learning analytic) is a representation of the real learning experience of learners in a given context and at a given time (Archer & Prinsloo, 2020). Moreover, as shown by data analysis, there is a contrast between traditional and blended or online learning styles. In another study relatively similar to that of Samuelsen, Chen, & Wasson, (2019), where LA provide teachers with data to help them improve learning design, the most commonly used data source is the learning management system (LMS), the most commonly used data type is the activity log, and the most important challenge is real-time multimodal recording and analysis for immediate teacher action (Hoyos & Velasquez, 2020).

Table 4. The main characteristics of LA according to the authors

References	Main characteristics of LA
Aguilar et al., (2018)	The goal is to extract knowledge for a better understanding of the students and the manner of how they learn.
Archer & Prinsloo (2020)	Data may be controlled if teacher must understand why student success or failure.
Hoyos & Velasquez (2020)	The most important challenge is real-time multimodal recording and analysis for immediate teacher action.
Samuelsen et al., (2019)	Provides teachers with data to help them improve learning design.

Experiences About LA and SC

According to Naidu et al. (2017) the learning environment of SC is enhanced by various technological interventions, these as the Learning Management System (LMS), which is implemented to provide a common platform for information sharing; academic engagement according to the results from the data provided by the system logs, tutoring systems and educational platforms through combination of traditional and blended learning style (Klašnja-Milićević, & Ivanović, 2018). Furthermore, possible LA objectives such as monitoring, analysis, prediction, intervention, assessment, evaluation, feedback, adaptation, personalization, recommendation, and reflection can be acquired (Lukarov et al., 2014).

However, there are still few works dealing with SC, and most of them approach this topic from a theoretical perspective (Martín, Alario-Hoyos, & Kloos, 2019). Even after the research, some models are still described for (Joksimovic et al., 2019) such as a predictive model on which is based on LMS engagement activity, demographics, and past academic performance; it is called Course Signals and consists to detect students' risk of school failure and a dashboard that uses the traffic light analogy to visualize each student's risk of failure (green: no risk, yellow: moderate risk, red: high risk). Another approach is a discourse analysis which has also been widely used to examine synchronous student communication, such as the use of online chat platforms. Another one focuses on using sensors to capture various aspects of student engagement and learning processes, works by gesture recognition method, based on gyroscope and accelerometer sensors using deep convolution and recurrent neural networks; it is a survey data to incorporate various sensor data streams that capture gestures, gaze, or speech (Azevedo, 2015; Ochoa et al., 2016). Another uses multimodal analytics, in a real-time learning analysis of gesture recognition, voice recognition, image recognition, body movements, facial expressions and eye movements; or as Junokas et al. (2018) who created a system based on multimodal educational environments that integrate gesture recognition systems and found it to be effective in enhancing the learning experience. Furthermore, there is a model that develops new methodologies for personalized training for higher education, based on AI (Xiao & Yi, 2020). Also a method relying on IoT devices such as cameras generating a huge amount of images for face recognition systems based on deep neural networks which are processed in a cloud environment to recognize the person for personalized education reform, working through local binary patterns. To say more, use of wearable devices to estimate levels of stress and sleep quality or other biometrical signals captured with sensors. Academic success prediction based on emotion modeling, sentiment analysis.

FUTURE RESEARCH DIRECTIONS

After analyzing all selected articles and searching for the meaning of LA, LA can be defined as Sclater et al. (2016), a suitable technology which helps teachers for improving and managing the learning processes of the students, whilst giving and proposing methods to support them; in particular, as stated by Larrabee Sønderlund et al. (2019) the effectiveness of LA targeting student underperformance, experience and discontinuation, enclosed in making use of information that brings the learning activities in order to enhance the learning processes of students. Since the definition of LA conform among researchers, as shown in table 3, LA provide teachers with data in real-time for immediate action to help them improve learning design, a better understanding of the students, and how students learn and why success or failure. But Mckenna, Pouska, Moraes, & Folkestad, (2019) added that teachers, educators, institutions must be behind the technology, taking control if LA are to succeed in our educational environment. As Ulrich Hoppe, & Suthers (2014) said, a soft technology since it involves the orchestration of human processes.

There are certain authors as (Nguyen et al., 2020; Samuelsen et al., 2019; Mckenna et al., 2019; Wise & Jung, 2019), that provide us how to collect data from students for a better understanding of how LA can be achieved and how the technology can be used to enhance students' learning; such as Gasevic et al., (2019) which indicated that the analysis of digital traces of learning and teaching may reveal benefits for learners, teachers, learning environments, or the organization. Besides, students appreciate information about the status and prognostic of skills in a course (Uskov et al., 2019). Further and related to the learning process and due to learners' experience and knowledge, Yildirim, & Gülbahar (2022) showed that prior knowledge has a significant positive impact on final performance, on interactions and technical skills; aside from that, having a strategic planning is more likely to achieve personal course goals; however, final performance does not seem to be related to students' motivation, attitude and self-regulation skills.

Although the majority of the studies only mention the strengths of using LA in a SC adapting to the changing needs of students, having positive consequences identifying and helping students who are at risk, it's not all about profit. It must be pointed out that there were detected studies with evidence of disadvantages on the use of LA. More educational data does not always make better educational decisions (Ifenthaler, & Yau, 2020); but instead, more information will help us achieve a better analysis if we ask the right questions and maintain a growth mindset (Rodriguez, 2022); emphasizing that it is important to take care to release the information and no matter how much information you have, you must know how to use it. Another weakness is that students expressed their concerns about data privacy issues and ethical aspects of LA in cases when unnamed data of a particular student, difficult to implement in some countries like many in Latin America (Salas-Pilco, & Yang, 2020), especially when considering data privacy protection law; in addition, O'Donoghue (2022) points out that large amounts of data are collected, which creates a tension between the principles of autonomy and the principle of beneficence. These are about student privacy, informed consent and data justice, meaning that many of the current practices around LA in higher education can be violating the standards. Nganji, Hosseini, & Okoye, (2020) also explained there may be a controversy between the different data, which can be misunderstood, can be a lack of information, insufficient qualitative results and even too much information. Additionally, as higher education institutions increasingly make use of algorithmic decision-making systems, Archer, & Prinsloo (2020) submit, students can be wrongly identified as high-performing or not at-risk, followed by an unchecked assessment that may have an adverse effect on students.

Regarding another aim of the review which relates to the main characteristics, LA technologies and their applications in the educational environment are rapidly gaining popularity among academic institutions in the world (Uskov et al., 2019). Additionally, Hadhrami (2017) mentioned there is an increasing interest in the use of LA as an indicator of student performance. But probably here lies the fundamental importance of LA; understanding the students, their strengths and their weaknesses, only in this path can we move forward in a positive way with the help and use of these LA.

Another trend is a contrast between traditional and blended learning style or even the comparison with online learning. The result demonstrates that eLearning and conventional learning are not equal in information gathering. Considering classroom learning with teaching presence is much more effective than doing it online to ensure learners' engagement (Naujokaitiene et al., 2020). Above all, as documented by Seufert, Guggemos, & Sonderegger, (2019) guidelines need to be designed for pedagogically effective learning analysis interventions. Whilst LA are mainly implemented as a data-driven method for detecting at-risk students as International Association for Development of the Information Society (IADIS), Spector, Ifenthaler, & Isaias, (n.d.) reported. From its authors can also affirm that from online learning is easily to obtain data, such as how many times the student logs into the platform, what they visualize, the time they spend on the platform, among others; with a quick glance at the results in the diagrams, statistics,... a lot of data is recorded. On the other hand, data obtained from students during a conventional class, requires to be a SC, having a variety of devices in the classroom connected to an interface to obtain information of each student, individually, and to know if the student is bored, confused, distracted, and any other emotional feeling, and warn the teacher somehow with the dashboard regardless of whether teacher has noticed or not it before with their own eyes.

For that reason and regarding the models described above in the present research, the authors can describe several techniques with special attention in the LA literature in the last few years in high schools. Classified by Brown (2012) as predictors and indicators, visualizations and interventions; such as text analysis, process mining and social network analysis to identify broad outcomes. Viberg et al. (2018) added, the most common method is interpretive, then data collection methods, product description and surveys. Adding another point of view, (Wong & Li, 2020) say that providing personalized recommendations was the most frequent method, followed by visualization of learning data and personalized reports. Therefore, authors can emphasize the most common methods are statistics (time online, total number of visits, number of visits per page, distribution of visits over time), information visualization (charts, scatterplot, 3D representations), data mining (data-bases, text, images), social network analysis (support networked learning, tools that enable to manage), classification, regression and correlation (Samuelsen et al., 2019). It is worth to say all of these initiatives demonstrated the potential uses of LA for improving the quality of education in a smart school. In addition, integrating data from multiple sources is a challenge (Samuelsen et al., 2019).

While there is much interest in LA, the paper summarizes with several remarks that reinforce the critical points for future work related to the adoption of LA; as Gasevic et al. (2019) said, the vast majority of institutions have not yet fully exploited the use of the learner and have not addressed the educational challenges.

CONCLUSION

Higher education institutions are collecting lots of data using different educational platforms through a combination of traditional and blended learning styles (Klašnja-Milićević, & Ivanović, 2018). But, in connection with the types of LA applied in a smart school, it must be said that there are few studies explaining how they have managed to collect with the system design, analyze, do the development and the implementation (Dollinger et al., 2019).

As a whole, the results of the review show that is enough information to explain LA and its characteristics, but although the findings showed that there were a certain type of significant benefits on the use of LA, most of the articles brings to teaching-learning a large amount of positive outcomes, such as tackle to identify struggling students earlier and helping to improve students' performance in real-time, developing oral and behavioral skills, giving support or advice and motivation and reversing students' dropout risk; there are also a number of authors who commented on the weaknesses of data analytics in a smart school. Students expressed their concerns about data privacy issues and ethical aspects; the collected data can be misunderstood, can be a lack of information, insufficient qualitative results and even too much information. One aspect that is also emphasized is the participatory design of the LA tools which must be approved at the same time by the teachers and students themselves, who will be the ones to use them after all; thus, to achieve optimal results, LA should not be designed only by researchers and designers.

This article also aimed at models that talk about how to get data from AI, others about IoT devices, motion capture, gestures, voice, feelings, how many times they have logged into the platform, what they have looked at; endless data that provide us with information to be able to improve performance in a SC. Nevertheless, LA and its related technologies are still at a relatively early stage of development and application especially with regard to innovation in educational processes (Nganji et al., 2020) but are rapidly developing the processes for its use. Meanwhile the data collected in papers with experiences in a SC can be distinguished in two discernible objectives, to analyze the learning process, such as the analytics extracted from online systems and platforms (LMS, CLS, VLE,...) and the results of to analyze students' behavior in the classroom, as gestures, gaze, voice, movements,.. requiring a camera or sensors connected to a computer for this purpose. Aguilar et al., (2018) said both must be combined for reaching the global goal: improve the learning experiences.

There is still research on how to collect data from students in class, how to collect if students are focused, listening to the teacher, motivated, and eager to learn. More research is needed about LA and SC. Future research could be done and know what option is the best to improve the performance of students who do not follow the class with interest. As well as aim to get a better understanding of how schools, upper and lower levels, can make sense of the information of LA, to get feedback on their learning skills, either to encourage their strengths or to work on their weaknesses.

REFERENCES

Admiraal, W., Vermeulen, J., & Bulterman-Bos, J. (2020). Teaching with learning analytics: How to connect computer-based assessment data with classroom instruction? *Technology, Pedagogy and Education*, *29*(5), 577–591. Advance online publication. doi:10.1080/1475939X.2020.1825992

Aguilar, J., Sánchez, M., Cordero, J., Valdiviezo-Díaz, P., Barba-Guamán, L., & Chamba-Eras, L. (2018). Learning analytics tasks as services in smart classrooms. *Universal Access in the Information Society*, *17*(4), 693–709. doi:10.100710209-017-0525-0

Al Hadhrami, G. A. (2017). Learning Analytics Dashboard to Improve Students' Performance and Success. *IOSR Journal of Research & Method in Education*, *07*(01), 39–45. doi:10.9790/7388-0701053945

Archer, E., & Prinsloo, P. (2020). Speaking the unspoken in learning analytics: Troubling the defaults. *Assessment & Evaluation in Higher Education*, *45*(6), 888–900. doi:10.1080/02602938.2019.1694863

Atif, A., Richards, D., Bilgin, A., & Marrone, M. (2013). *Learning Analytics in Higher Education: A Summary of Tools and Approaches Human-Agent Teamwork in Collaborative Virtual Environments View project PACE Workloads Project View Project*. https://www.researchgate.net/publication/280860450

Avella, J. T., Kebritchi, M., Nunn, S. G., & Kanai, T. (2016). Learning Analytics Methods, Benefits, and Challenges in Higher Education: A Systematic Literature Review. *Online Learn*, *20*(2), 13–29.

Azevedo, R. (2015). Defining and Measuring Engagement and Learning in Science: Conceptual, Theoretical, Methodological, and Analytical Issues. *Educational Psychologist*, *50*(1), 84–94. doi:10.1080/00461520.2015.1004069

Brown, M. (2012). *Learning Analytics: Moving from Concept to Practice*. Academic Press.

Cebrián, G., Palau, R., & Mogas, J. (2020). The smart classroom as a means to the development of ESD methodologies. *Sustainability*, *12*(7), 3010. Advance online publication. doi:10.3390u12073010

Dollinger, M., Liu, D., Arthars, N., & Lodge, J. M. (2019). Working together in learning analytics towards the co-creation of value. *Journal of Learning Analytics*, *6*(2), 10–26. doi:10.18608/jla.2019.62.2

Eckerson, W. W. (2011). *Performance dashboards: Measuring, monitoring, and managing your business*. Wiley.

Elias, T. (2011). *Learning Analytics: Definitions*. Processes and Potential.

Erdemci, H., & Karal, H. (2020). Examination of instructors' experiences for the use of learning analytics. *International Journal of Information and Learning Technology*. doi:10.1108/IJILT-05-2020-0076

Gasevic, D., Tsai, Y. S., Dawson, S., & Pardo, A. (2019). How do we start? An approach to learning analytics adoption in higher education. In *International Journal of Information and Learning Technology 36(4), 342–353*. Emerald Group Publishing Ltd., doi:10.1108/IJILT-02-2019-0024

Halibas, A. S., Sathyaseelan, B., & Shahzad, M. (2019). Learning Analytics: Developing a Data-Centric Teaching-Research Skill. Advances in Science, Technology and Innovation, 213–219. doi:10.1007/978-3-030-01659-3_24

Hoyos, A. A. C., & Velásquez, J. D. (2020). Teaching Analytics: Current Challenges and Future Development. *Revista Iberoamericana de Tecnologías del Aprendizaje, 15*(1), 1–9. doi:10.1109/RITA.2020.2979245

Ifenthaler, D. (2016). Are Higher Education Institutions Prepared for Learning Analytics? *TechTrends, 61*(4), 366–371. doi:10.100711528-016-0154-0

Ifenthaler, D., & Yau, J. Y. K. (2020). Utilising learning analytics to support study success in higher education: A systematic review. *Educational Technology Research and Development, 68*(4), 1961–1990. Advance online publication. doi:10.100711423-020-09788-z

Joksimovic, S., Kovanovic, V., & Dawson, S. (2019). Learning analytics assessment of cognitive presence MOOCs literature analysis View project The Journey of Learning Analytics. In HERDSA. *Review of Higher Education, 6*. www.herdsa.org.au/herdsa-review-higher-education-vol-6/37-63

Junokas, M. J., Lindgren, R., Kang, J., & Morphew, J. W. (2018). Enhancing multimodal learning through personalized gesture recognition. *Journal of Computer Assisted Learning, 34*(4), 350–357. doi:10.1111/jcal.12262

Klašnja-Milićević, A., & Ivanović, M. (2018). Learning analytics - New flavor and benefits for educational environments. *Informatics in Education, 17*(2), 285–300. doi:10.15388/infedu.2018.15

Larrabee Sønderlund, A., Hughes, E., & Smith, J. (2019). The efficacy of learning analytics interventions in higher education: A systematic review. *British Journal of Educational Technology, 50(5), 2594–2618.* doi:10.1111/bjet.12720

Lukarov, V., Muslim, A., Mohamed, A., Yousef, F., Wahid, U., Chatti, M. A., Thüs, H., Greven, C., Chakrabarti, A., & Schroeder, U. (2014). *Learning Analytics: Challenges and Future Research Directions.* https://www.researchgate.net/publication/278712499

Mangaroska, K., Vesin, B., & Giannakos, M. (2019). Cross-platform analytics: A step towards personalization and adaptation in education. *ACM International Conference Proceeding Series*, 71-75. 10.1145/3303772.3303825

Martín, A., Alario-Hoyos, C., & Kloos, C. (2019). Smart Education: A Review and Future Research Directions. *Proceedings, 31*(1), 57. doi:10.3390/proceedings2019031057

Mckenna, K., Pouska, B., Moraes, M. C., & Folkestad, J. E. (2019). Visual-Form Learning Analytics: A Tool for Critical Reflection and Feedback. *Contemporary Educational Technology, 10*(3), 214–228. doi:10.30935/cet.589989

Naidu, V. R., Singh, B., Hasan, R., & Al Hadrami, G. (2017). *Learning Analytics for Smart Classrooms in Higher Education. IJAEDU- International E-Journal of Advances in Education.* doi:10.18768/ijaedu.338514

Naujokaitiene, J., Tamoliune, G., Volungeviciene, A., & Duart, J. M. (2020). Using learning analytics to engage students: Improving teaching practices through informed interactions. *Journal of New Approaches in Educational Research, 9*(2), 231. Advance online publication. doi:10.7821/naer.2020.7.561

Nganji, J. T., Hosseini, S., & Okoye, K. (2020). Learning Analytics for Educational Innovation: A Systematic Mapping Study of Early Indicators and Success Factors. *International Journal of Computer Information Systems and Industrial Management Applications.* https://www.researchgate.net/publication/341323827

Nguyen, A., Tuunanen, T., Gardner, L., & Sheridan, D. (2020). Design principles for learning analytics information systems in higher education. *European Journal of Information Systems.* Advance online publication. doi:10.1080/0960085X.2020.1816144

O'Donoghue, K. (2022). Learning Analytics within Higher Education: Autonomy, Beneficence and Non-maleficence. *Journal of Academic Ethics.* Advance online publication. doi:10.100710805-021-09444-y

Ochoa, X., Weibel, N., Worsley, M., & Oviatt, S. (2016). Multimodal learning analytics data challenges. *ACM International Conference Proceeding Series*, 498–499. 10.1145/2883851.2883913

Ramos De Melo, F., Flôres, E. L., Diniz De Carvalho, S., Gonçalves De Teixeira, R. A., Batista Loja, L., & Rodriguez Jugo, M. (2022). Learning Analytics: A Science in Rapid Expansion That Is Shaping the Future of Education. In S. Iñiguez & P. Lorange (Eds.), *Executive Education after the Pandemic.* Palgrave Macmillan. doi:10.1007/978-3-030-82343-6_27

Ramos de Melo, F., Flôres, E. L., Diniz de Carvalho, S., Gonçalves de Teixeira, R. A., Batista Loja, L. F., & de Sousa Gomide, R. (2014). Computational organization of didactic contents for personalized virtual learning environments. *Computers & Education, 79*(1), 126-137. https://www.learntechlib.org/p/200892/

Salas-Pilco, S. Z., & Yang, Y. (2020). Learning analytics initiatives in Latin America: Implications for educational researchers, practitioners and decision makers. *British Journal of Educational Technology, 51*(4), 875–891. doi:10.1111/bjet.12952

Samuelsen, J., Chen, W., & Wasson, B. (2019). Integrating multiple data sources for learning analytics—Review of literature. *Research and Practice in Technology Enhanced Learning, 14*(1), 11. Advance online publication. doi:10.118641039-019-0105-4

Sclater, N., Peasgood, A., & Mullan, J. (2016). *Learning Analytics in Higher Education: A review of UK and international practice Full report.* Academic Press.

Seufert, S., Guggemos, J., & Sonderegger, S. (2019). Learning analytics in higher education using peer-feedback and self-assessment: Use case of an academic writing course. *CSEDU 2019 - Proceedings of the 11th International Conference on Computer Supported Education, 2*, 315–322. 10.5220/0007714603150322

Shemshack, A., & Spector, J. M. (2020). A systematic literature review of personalized learning terms. In Smart Learning Environments, 7(1). doi:10.118640561-020-00140-9

Siemens, G. (2013). Learning Analytics: The Emergence of a Discipline. *The American Behavioral Scientist, 57*(10), 1380–1400. doi:10.1177/0002764213498851

Siemens, G., & Long, P. (2011). Penetrating the fog: Analytics in learning and education. *EDUCAUSE Review, 46*(5), 30.

Spector, J. M., Ifenthaler, D., & Isaias, P., & International Association for Development of the Information Society (IADIS). (n.d.). *International Conference on Cognition and Exploratory Learning in the Digital Age (CELDA) (12th, Maynooth, Greater Dublin, Ireland, October 24-26, 2015).* Academic Press.

Suchithra, R., Vaidhehi, V., & Iyer, N. E. (2015). Survey of learning analytics based on purpose and techniques for improving student performance. *International Journal of Computers and Applications*, *111*(1).

Ulrich Hoppe, H., & Suthers, D. D. (2014). Computational approaches to connecting levels of analysis in networked learning communities. *ACM International Conference Proceeding Series*, 285–286. 10.1145/2567574.2567588

Uskov, V. L., Bakken, J. P., Aluri, L., Rayala, N., Uskova, M., Sharma, K., & Rachakonda, R. (2019). Learning analytics based smart pedagogy: Student feedback. *Smart Innovation. Systems and Technologies*, *99*, 117–131. doi:10.1007/978-3-319-92363-5_11

Vangrieken, K., Dochy, F., Raes, E., & Kyndt, E. (2015). Teacher collaboration: A systematic review. In *Educational Research Review, 15, 17–40*. Elsevier Ltd. doi:10.1016/j.edurev.2015.04.002

Viberg, O., Hatakka, M., Bälter, O., & Mavroudi, A. (2018). The current landscape of learning analytics in higher education. *Computers in Human Behavior*, *89*, 98–110. Advance online publication. doi:10.1016/j.chb.2018.07.027

Wise, A. F., & Jung, Y. (2019). Teaching with analytics: Towards a situated model of instructional decision-making. *Journal of Learning Analytics*, *6*(2), 53–69. doi:10.18608/jla.2019.62.4

Wong, B. T., Ming, & Li, K. C. (2020). A review of learning analytics intervention in higher education (2011–2018). Journal of Computers in Education, 7(1), 7–28. doi:10.100740692-019-00143-7

Xiao, M., & Yi, H. (2020). Building an efficient artificial intelligence model for personalized training in colleges and universities. *Computer Applications in Engineering Education*. Advance online publication. doi:10.1002/cae.22235

Yildirim, D., & Gülbahar, Y. (2022). *Implementation of learning analytics indicators for increasing learners' final performance*. Tech Know Learn. doi:10.100710758-021-09583-6

ADDITIONAL READING

Aguilar, J., Buendia, O., Pinto, A., & Gutiérrez, J. (2019). Social learning analytics for determining learning styles in a smart classroom. *Interactive Learning Environments*. Advance online publication. doi:10.1080/10494820.2019.1651745

Bao, H., Li, Y., Su, Y., Xing, S., Chen, N. S., & Rosé, C. (2021). The effects of a learning analytics dashboard on teachers' diagnosis and intervention in computer-supported collaborative learning. *Technology, Pedagogy and Education*, *30*(2), 1–17. doi:10.1080/1475939X.2021.1902383

Biernacka, K., & Pinkwart, N. (2021). *Opportunities for Adopting Open Research Data in Learning Analytics*. doi:10.4018/978-1-7998-7103-3.ch002

Duart, J.M., Misiulien, R., Naujokaitienė, J., Tamoliūnė, G., & Volungevičienė, A. (2019). Learning Analitycs: Learning to think and and make desciions. *Journal of Educators Online*.

Georgiadis, K., & Van Lankveld, G., & Bahreini, K., & Westera, W. (2019). *Learning Analytics Should Analyse the Learning: Proposing a Generic Stealth Assessment Tool*. doi:10.1109/CIG.2019.8847960

Li, K., & Wong, B. (2021). Research landscape of smart education: A bibliometric analysis. *Interactive Technology and Smart Education*. ahead-of-print. doi:10.1108/ITSE-05-2021-0083

Prestes, P. A. N., Silva, T., & Barroso, G. C. (2021). Correlation Analysis using Teaching and Learning Analytics. *Heliyon*, *7*(11), e08435. Advance online publication. doi:10.1016/j.heliyon.2021.e08435 PMID:34877427

Zheng, L., Niu, J., & Zhong, L. (2021). Effects of a learning analytics-based real-time feedback approach on knowledge elaboration, knowledge convergence, interactive relationships and group performance in CSCL. *British Journal of Educational Technology*. Advance online publication. doi:10.1111/bjet.13156

KEY TERMS AND DEFINITIONS

Algorithmic Decision-Making Systems: Analysis of large amounts of personal data to obtain information and considered useful for decision making.

Big Data: Large amount of data, procedures, and computer applications, processed at high speed and stored for analysis.

Data Analysis: Statistical analysis methods for analyzing large amounts of information.

Educational Environment: The way, in which students are educated, depending on the physical, emotional, and intellectual environment.

Learning Analytics: Measurement, collection, and analysis of data on learners and their context, to optimize learning and improve educational practice.

Process Mining: Assist in the analysis of processes and converts data into ideas and actions.

Smart Classroom: Learning space designed with the aim of improving the experience of the students and their knowledge achievement.

Machine Learning in the Real World

Stylianos Kampakis
Centre for Blockchain Technologies, University College London, UK

INTRODUCTION

Data science cannot be disentangled from organizational demands. A famous graph (Figure 1) produced by Brendan Tierney (2012) demonstrates how data science is integrated within an organization.

Figure 1. A concise summary of what data science is (Tierney, 2012)

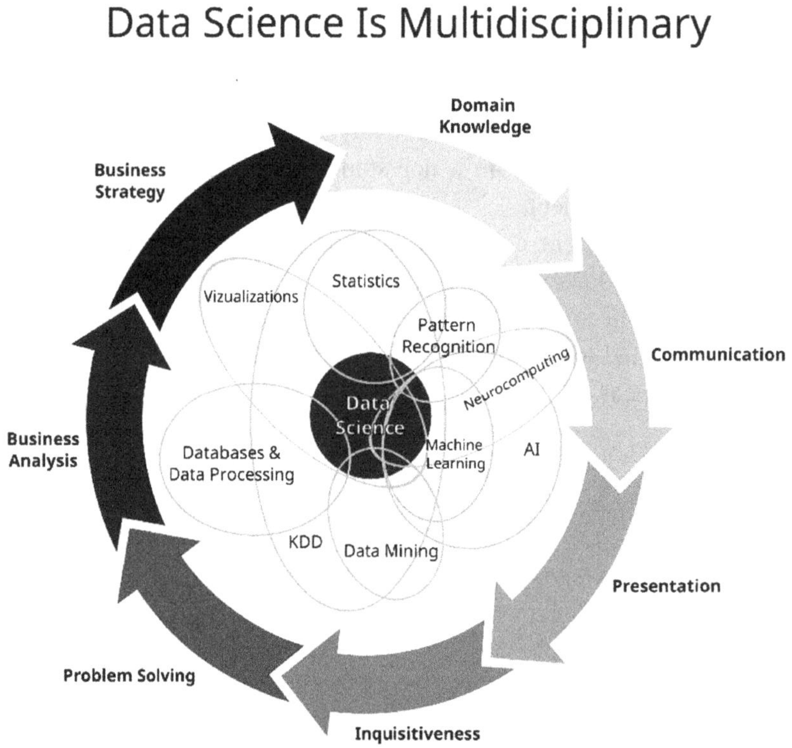

This well-known diagram shows that data science is surrounded by a cycle of "soft skills" and business-related terms like "business strategy." What this diagram demonstrates is that data science is an applied discipline. Data science aims to bring impact within an organization.

When machine learning is seen in isolation, it can be treated as an academic exercise, and it is acceptable for the researcher to deal with questions such as convergence bounds and metrics like categorical cross-entropy. On the other hand, when machine learning is used in practice, it is called data science, and

DOI: 10.4018/978-1-7998-9220-5.ch104

research questions are essential only when converted into revenue. Metrics like the RMSE are replaced with KPIs, and the end-to-end process needs to translate into tangible impact for an enterprise.

The successful application of data science requires a set of steps within the organization.

Data science and machine learning are often taught in isolation as if the successful practice of those disciplines simply is about implementing algorithms. However, experience has demonstrated that the successful implementation of data science requires covering other aspects, like data strategy.

This chapter aims to assist data scientists and machine learning practitioners in engaging with the larger picture.

BACKGROUND

The first step is the successful design and execution of a data strategy. Data strategy refers to the long-term plan and goals of a business with regard to its data. Data strategy encapsulates business strategy, data governance, and data science and requires the participation of business leaders and technical experts.

The second step is the successful choice and implementation of a data science process. A data science process represents a structured approach to data science and machine learning projects. For example, methodologies like AGILE (Dingsøyr et al., 2012) and SCRUM (Hossain et al., 2011) have helped structure and define the work of software developers. Similar methodologies have appeared in the last few years in data science, whose requirements are different from the requirements of traditional software development.

The third step is to consider recent developments in machine learning and AI, like MLOps, which streamline machine learning training, deployment, and execution. MLOps stands for machine learning operations and is an acronym borrowed from Devops. Devops is defined on the official website of Amazon AWS (one of the pioneers of this field) as:

DevOps is the combination of cultural philosophies, practices, and tools that increases an organization's ability to deliver applications and services at high velocity: evolving and improving products at a faster pace than organizations using traditional software development and infrastructure management processes. This speed enables organizations to better serve their customers and compete more effectively in the market. (Amazon Web Services, n.d.)

In a similar spirit, MLOps combined a set of philosophies and practices to streamline the development, testing, and deployment of machine learning algorithms.

DATA STRATEGY: AN OVERVIEW

Companies must be able to manage vast quantities of data to succeed in the current business environment. Unfortunately, despite many companies instituting data-management and chief data officer roles, they are still playing catch-up.

Studies show that most businesses use less than half of their structured data in the decision-making process and use less than 1% of their unstructured data. Furthermore, over 70% of employees can access data they should not, and analysts spend 80% of their time discovering and preparing data (DalleMule & Davenport, 2017). Unfortunately, as the figures show, most companies do not have a coherent plan to tackle their data effectively (DalleMule & Davenport, 2017). Instead, they have a vague idea of what they need, hire people to fill the roles, and then waste their resources because they do not have a clear data strategy in place.

What Is a Data Strategy?

Data strategy has varying definitions online, but the most comprehensive one is the following:

A data strategy is a living document that defines how the business is setting itself up, both from a technical and organizational perspective, to proactively manage and leverage data towards the long-term business strategy.

This definition explains precisely what a data strategy should be. First, it should not be a static document that is created and then abandoned. Instead, it should be fluid and constantly updated as the business changes and grows. Furthermore, an effective data strategy must address how one approaches the infrastructure and engineering aspects. It must also cover how one will structure the teams and the organization to fully capitalize on the data. By creating a data strategy as early as possible, a business becomes proactive in shoring up resilience and gaining a competitive advantage. Finally, this definition reveals that a data strategy is not an island. In other words, it should not be a separate entity from the business. Instead, it should be focused on the overall business strategy, as should all plans.

The Importance of an Effective Data Strategy

Data has become an essential asset for any business if it is used effectively. It can add value by helping identify ways to streamline operations, provide customer insights, and even generate alternative revenue streams. In terms of operational improvements, data can be used to streamline or even completely automate various business processes. Netflix, for example, has invested heavily in optimizing its production process to create original content at scale, thereby providing a competitive edge (Kumar et al., 2018). Data can also provide vital customer insights. Most of the popular services we use rely on data to create better experiences for their customers. Amazon uses a customer's past purchases and browsing history to recommend products they might be interested in. Spotify's Discover Weekly does something similar for music recommendations, using data and machine learning to do so (Tawanghar, 2020). Businesses can also use data to create a new revenue stream once they have scaled to thousands of users and generated massive data. For example, a global retailer converted its customer data into a revenue stream by creating a digital advertising business that allows advertisers to create personalized and targeted ads based on their data (Keely, 2021). Understanding the power of data is critical to building an effective data strategy. Without one, fully capitalizing on gathered data will be challenging. Furthermore, data collection could lead to a waste of resources if not done right (Kampakis, 2019). Collecting data can be costly, especially for a young business. By creating a data strategy, an organization can collect the data that will provide the most critical insights. However, a business leader will also be able to keep an eye on the future and what data they might need as the business grows.

How to Develop a Data Strategy

M

A data strategy is vital to a business. However, how does one create such a strategy? Many data strategy frameworks are available, including the data strategy canvas (Competence Center Corporate Data Quality, n.d.) and the Single Source of Truth (SSOT) – Multiple Versions of the Truth (MVOT) model (DalleMule & Davenport, 2017). The approach we will be delving into, though, is one that we have found effective for small and medium-sized businesses.

Starting with Business Strategy

As our definition of data strategy shows, having a clear business strategy is essential. The goals the business must achieve in the short- to medium-term will dictate what data must be collected, how it will be analyzed, and what insights are required. Consider a start-up that will soon be launching its first product. Naturally, one priority will be customer acquisition but also keeping retention and engagement rates high.

To do so, rapid iteration is essential to ensure the product aligns with customer expectations and demands. That means collecting and analyzing the right data, thereby making it an essential part of the data strategy. Of course, business strategies are never static. Goals and objectives might change, and the data strategy must also change accordingly.

How to Determine Strategic Priorities

The first step is to figure out why the company exists, also known as a *vision*. The company's vision must answer the question: "What will the world look like in 10 years with our company?"

It must be grand and bold. It must be a big dream because that is what inspires people. Of course, it might never come to pass. However, when one has a grand vision, simply getting close will mean far more progress than one could achieve with a small vision. J.F. Kennedy told Congress in 1961(NASA History Office, n.d.) that they would put a man on the moon by the end of the decade. Of course, everyone warned him that it could not be done, especially in such a short timeframe.

What happened? On July 20, 1969, two American astronauts landed on the moon. That is because everyone had a sense of direction and purpose, and they were led by a big dream.

Next comes the mission statement, which should answer the following questions:

- Why does the business do what it does?
- What does the business do?
- Who does the business do it for?
- How does the business do it?

A mission statement is more focused on the immediate future and should be something that the organization is currently working towards. In other words, it is a stepping-stone on the path towards the vision. Defining a vision and mission statement is essential because it helps determine the destination and the path one must take to get there. That path represents the strategy. The final step is to convert the strategy into clear priorities. When we work with business owners, we like to break the business down into its essential parts to analyze what can be improved. Our usual breakdown consists of:

- Product

- Growth Marketing / Sales
- Internal Operations
- Business Model / Finance

Of course, a different breakdown might apply, depending on the type of business. Once the individual elements have been defined, it is time to brainstorm. At this point, one must develop ideas where improvements can be made. It would help to involve people from other areas of the business to provide more perspectives. However, if too many people are involved, the brainstorming workshop will become longer, and it will be more challenging to do a deep dive into each person's opinion. As a result of this workshop, the business leader will better understand what to focus on to improve and grow the business. Subsequently, all these thoughts should be clustered into logical groups defined by their themes. Then, the business leader must decide which area to focus on first, and the chosen cluster will become the foundation of the business strategy.

Creating Data-Use Cases

Once the business' strategic priorities have been set, data-use cases must be developed to achieve those goals. A data-use case represents a contained, well-defined project connected to achieving one strategic objective. Some examples of data-use cases include:

- Reducing delivery costs for a product
- Improving the personalization of the customer experience
- Increasing customer retention rates.

The data-use cases an organization develops should become priorities for the following year. These data-use cases will also make planning data activities more effective. The practitioner should not go overboard with the number of data-use cases. However, underestimating what can be achieved is also a mistake. Ideally, one should consider between three and five cases for a year, of which one or two should be quick wins. A quick win is essential because it provides motivation and shows the rest of the business how valuable data is. A small project is also practical because it can reveal issues before starting on a larger project. Now, it is time to look at each data-use case to determine what will be needed to achieve the objectives of each. Some of the areas to consider include:

- Data Requirements – what data is necessary to deliver the project? The help of a data scientist will be invaluable here.
- Key Project Resources – who needs to be involved in the project? Consider all the roles necessary, including data scientists and analysts, data engineers, business owners, product managers, and other stakeholders.
- Technology – do any technical issues need to be addressed before implementing the project? Also, any modifications necessary to the data architecture/infrastructure to ensure the right data is obtained must be considered.

Once the requirements for each data-use case have been considered, they must be compared to identify any overlap across projects for better resource coordination.

Data Architecture

As the business grows, so will the amount of data in the organization. This data growth will often be non-linear because every new user might be creating more data than previous ones as the product expands and improves. Switching architectures or databases when the company is still in its infancy is far more cost-efficient – and requires acceptable levels of downtime – than if one were to wait until the business has grown. For example, it took Slack three years to migrate their data architecture from active-active clusters to Vitess. A start-up with fewer than 1,000 users will have a far easier time migrating to a new system. We can learn from Slack's experience that it pays to carefully consider the architecture of the data and systems from the beginning (Ganguli et al., 2020). Otherwise, a business might end up like one of the many organizations that have wasted millions trying to fix problems and missed out on a slew of opportunities due to their slow reaction times. While effective data architecture design is vital, speed is also of the essence. Without a clear idea of what the product will look like in the future, obsessing over the perfect architecture is a wasted endeavor. Instead, it is far more critical to move fast, test assumptions, and continue to iterate to create an effective product.

Data Governance

A data governance program is also an essential part of the data strategy as it helps to ensure data traceability. It also allows for data that is clearly defined, as well as making sure the right people can access the information. However, as before, obsessing over creating the perfect data governance program is a mistake. Instead, it should be kept proportional to the amount of data a business has. Otherwise, too many processes will slow down reaction times, nullifying the competitive benefits of being data-driven. A data dictionary is an excellent place to start in the beginning. It is a living document where all the raw and derived data in the business is clearly defined. Derived data should include notes on the source and any modifications. The goal of the dictionary is to clear up any potential confusion or misunderstandings about the data. It should also ensure that everyone knows where to look for data to work out metrics or create reports.

It is also wise to put someone in charge of each data source to provide further guidance or fix problems if they arise. Legal regulations, such as the General Data Protection Regulation (GDPR) (2016) or the California Consumer Privacy Act (CCPA) (2018), are also essential. A dictionary will help because it will allow one to determine the type of personal data the organization holds and provide essential answers like why the data is needed, how long the data will be archived, and what other independent software the data is shared with.

DATA SCIENCE PROCESSES

Data science processes help formalize some of the necessary steps involved in implementing data science projects. While there are many approaches, some actions are critical, leading to the birth of these processes.

We will be looking at some data science processes in this section. While they differ slightly, they are all guided by the same principles. In the end, it is the principles that matter, as the project's style and requirements will dictate the process.

In other words, adapt the process to the project rather than the project to the process. Instead of being set in stone, these processes consist of guidelines and best practices, so they must be adapted to the project's needs.

Cross-Industry Standard Process for Data Mining (CRISP-DM)

The goal with Cross-Industry Standard Process for Data Mining (CRISP-DM) is to clearly define a project's stages and understand how those stages interact with each other (IBM, n.d.).

This approach represents a high-level framework rather than focusing on the nitty-gritty, such as team roles and responsibilities or work management. In other words, CRISP-DM provides insight into the type of work necessary for each phase, along with what deliverables can be expected.

Most importantly, though, CRISP-DM is flexible enough to allow the process to quickly be adapted to new findings as it considers that data projects are iterative.

CRISP-DM consists of six main phases:

1. Business Understanding
2. Data Understanding
3. Data Preparation
4. Modeling
5. Evaluation
6. Deployment

A summary of this process can be seen in Figure 2.

Figure 2. Summary of CRISP-DM (Jensen, 2012)

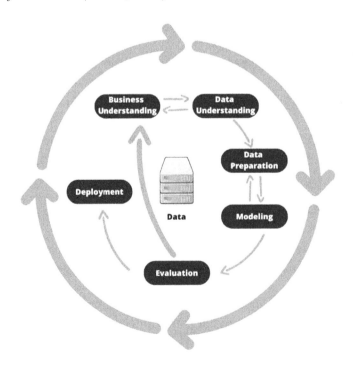

Business Understanding

M

CRIPS-DM starts with the Business Understanding phase, in which the project's context is determined. Thus, in this phase, business objectives will be defined, project requirements will be determined, and a plan will be created. Establishing business objectives is essential because they will drive the entire process. Business objectives are, in essence, the destination the organization must reach. It is similar to an airplane. Pilots constantly make adjustments to ensure they stay on course. They can only do that if they know where they are going. The same applies to a business.

Once the main goal has been established, business leaders can make the right decisions to ensure they are moving closer to achieving their objectives. Related questions that might require answers should also be considered at this point. The next step is to determine the most effective metrics to track progress accurately. Defining goals that cannot be measured is a mistake. Without clear metrics, the team will be uncertain whether they are making any progress, which can be demoralizing and lead to a lack of results. Furthermore, if they do not have a clearly defined destination, the team might go off on a tangent, making it difficult to achieve the primary objective.

Once the objectives are clear, the project's essential requirements and dependencies must be determined. These can be categorized in various ways, including project resources, data, and computing resources. At this point, a data scientist can help as they can determine whether the project is feasible based on the available data and resources. In some cases, it might also help to develop an overview plan with key milestones. It is essential to be realistic as delays can occur and could derail the project's timeline.

Data Understanding

The goal of the Data Understanding phase is to determine whether sufficient data of good enough quality exists to build an accurate model.

For example, some issues one might encounter with the data include missing values for variables, noise in the data due to errors in the data-gathering phase, and not collecting the correct data for the project. All issues must be identified in this phase, and the assumptions regarding what the data describes must be validated. Then, the resulting report should detail any actions needed to fix these problems with the data.

Data Preparation

At this point, a data scientist will choose the correct data from the different sources, clean it, and wrangle it into shape so it can be inputted into a data science model. This phase will likely be repeated a few times to improve the model's results through experimentation with various data points and processing methods. Generally, there will be more significant levels of improvement from a more judicious choice of the input data and its processing methodology than from tweaking the model.

Modeling

The modeling phase is the best model for the project is developed. Therefore, it should start with defining the metrics to evaluate and choose the best model for the application. While a simple model is a good idea, to begin with, the model the practitioner chooses will depend on the project and how much any errors might cost. It is important to note that data might have to be processed differently for each model since every model uses somewhat different assumptions.

Evaluation

In the Evaluation phase, the practitioner analyses how well the project aligns with the objectives laid out in the first phase. Of course, by now, there is a better understanding of the data and the intricacies of the project. So, the business leader might decide to re-evaluate the goals to a certain degree based on the new insights. It is also an excellent time to test the model as it might perform well in a development environment, but issues might arise in a production environment.

Deployment

The Deployment phase is when the practitioner decides how to run the model in production. Some of the factors that will be considered at this point include:

- The frequency with which the model will be run in real-time
- The communication method between input and output systems
- The methodology for monitoring the model's performance
- The frequency with which the model must be retrained.

Microsoft Team Data Science Process

According to Microsoft, the Team Data Science Process (TDSP):

…is an agile, iterative data science methodology to deliver predictive analytics solutions and intelligent applications efficiently. TDSP helps improve team collaboration and learning by suggesting how team roles work best together. TDSP includes best practices and structures from Microsoft and other industry leaders to help toward successful implementation of data science initiatives. The goal is to help companies fully realize the benefits of their analytics program. (Microsoft, 2020)

TDSP consists of four key components, namely:

1. A data science lifecycle definition
2. A standardized project structure
3. Infrastructure and resources for data science projects
4. Tools and utilities for project execution.

The focus of this section is solely on the lifecycle. The remaining three components are helpful, but they are focused on the implementation phase.
According to TDSP, the lifecycle consists of four main phases, namely:

- Business Understanding
- Data Acquisition and Understanding
- Modeling
- Deployment

These are seen in Figure 3.

Figure 3. The data science lifecycle (Microsoft, 2020)

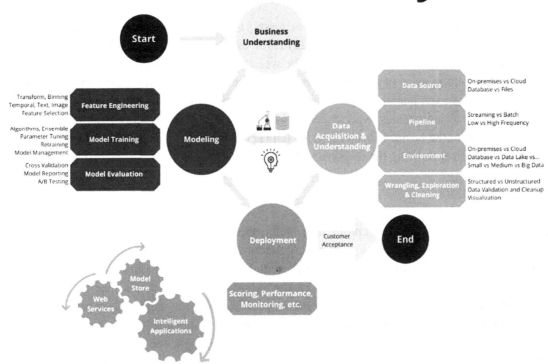

While similar to CRISP-DM's phases, TDSP emphasizes the iterative nature of the process, with a focus on iterating between each step and not just the complete cycle. Agility in data science development makes delivering quality results on schedule easier. Rarely will organizations go through the process just once because that assumes they can define the problem perfectly from the get-go, they know precisely what data is necessary, and they have managed to develop and deploy the perfect model. It does not happen. Unexpected situations will occur, and practitioners will gain more insight, so they can better perfect every aspect of the process.

Thus, in the Business Understanding phase, a plan will be developed to solve the problem, which will include the data necessary to train the model. It must then be verified whether sufficient data of high-enough quality is available. After this phase, the organization will gain vital insights, such as if data is missing or if the training examples are skewed. This makes it essential to update the assumptions and suggested approaches defined in the plan created in the Business Understanding phase. The most frequent iterations will occur between the second and third phases. Typically, the process starts with the simplest model. Simple, however, means that the model might not be as accurate as it should be. Other data points that could improve the model's accuracy might be discovered by exploring these errors. As different data points are tested, the findings should be noted. A record of what was attempted, what worked, and what did not is vital to maximizing efficiency. Finally, there will be some iteration between the Modeling, Data Acquisition and Understanding, and Deployment phases to determine the best deployment methodology for the model. To learn more about the process and start implementing it, check out the Github repository released by Microsoft (2016).

Tesseract Academy's 2-Actor Process

The previous two processes focused on the steps necessary to complete a data science project. Conversely, the Tesseract Academy's 2-Actor Process (2021) revolves around the people involved, along with the challenges and misinterpretations that can arise between the data scientist and the business stakeholder. This 2-Actor Process is more of a complement to the other two and is an excellent way to determine potential issues. However, it assumes that the business does not have a data science role, so it might not be the best option for companies experienced in working with data. The process includes two actors: the domain expert or the business leader and the data scientist or the data science team lead. There are also four steps, with each being the responsibility of one or both actors.

Problem Definition

The first step is to define the critical problem, which is the responsibility of the domain expert. The domain expert understands the business, so they are better positioned to define the problems and challenges that need to be address. However, a data scientist with experience in the same field can provide great ideas too. It is still imperative for the domain expert to have a clear idea of the specific business issues to be tackled. While one does not need to be 100% specific, being too vague might make it difficult to precisely explain what must be solved to the data scientist. After all, if the data scientist does not know the destination at the end of the journey, they will not be able to make the proper course corrections to ensure it is reached.

Choosing the Right Data (Data Management)

The domain expert and the data scientist need to work together. A business that has followed an effective data strategy from the beginning will have fewer issues. However, this is rarely the case, and most companies' data will have missing values, lack essential variables, and have data collected at the wrong granularity level. The most effective approach is for the domain expert and the data scientist to communicate constantly and avoid making assumptions. For example, one must not assume that the data is accurate or there is no noise, or that the data is correct. Furthermore, early results that are highly successful results must be treated with much skepticism.

Great results right off the bat are more likely to result from data leakage than outstanding data. Data leakage can be something like having an input variable that correlates highly with the output variable but is not generally available at test time.

Solving the Problem

This phase is the data scientist's responsibility. If everything has gone well so far, the practitioner will have a clear definition of the problem and the business, as well as a good, clean data set.

The data scientist must now determine the key success metrics and solve the problem using the most relevant and effective data science methods.

Creating Value Through Actionable Insights

The final phase also requires the domain expert and data scientist to work together. The data scientist's job is to show the business leader how the solution they have developed solves the defined problem. The solution must be able to generate measurable results. The domain expert can incorporate the solution into the overall business strategy, and the data scientist will have benchmark metrics against which future improvements can be measured.

MLOPS

MLOps defines a set of practices and tools that replicate the philosophy of DevOps in the domains of machine learning and data science. Google Cloud's official webpage on the topic splits down MLOps in 3 key areas:

1. Continuous integration
2. Continuous delivery
3. Continuous training

Continuous integration is a DevOps term that refers to the integration of code from multiple team members many times a day (Fowler, 2006).

Continuous delivery refers to the production of software in short cycles, which enables a software development team to constantly release new updates (Shahin et al., 2017). While there are many tools to train and test models effectively, the cycle of retaining and deployment can be a time-consuming and error-prone task. The practices of MLOps try to automate this process as much as possible and speed up the deployment of machine learning systems. The following image demonstrates that the ML code is only one part of a system composed of many different interconnected entities within the enterprise's production code.

Machine learning systems have some key differences compared to standard software.

One of the key differences is that machine learning pipelines are born out of experimentation. As the name implies, data science is a "science," which means that it is impossible to predefine the results of a certain experiment in most cases. The practitioner will have to work on many ill-defined variables, which are quite often educated guesses:

- How much data is required to train a successful model?
- Which model is the best?
- What type of maximum performance are we looking at?

Another challenge behind data science and machine learning systems is that, whereas bugs in software will manifest as obvious malfunctions, bugs in a machine learning system are more inconspicuous. For example, if a model is trained on the wrong dataset, then the performance in the real world might be worse than it should be, but it might take weeks or months until someone notices. This is because the machine learning model will not issue a compile error. Instead, it will simply produce suboptimal results. Another consideration is the continuous monitoring of systems to detect drift (Gama et al., 2004), the monitoring of data quality, and the retraining of the model.

Figure 4. Representation of the enterprise production code (Google Cloud, n.d.)

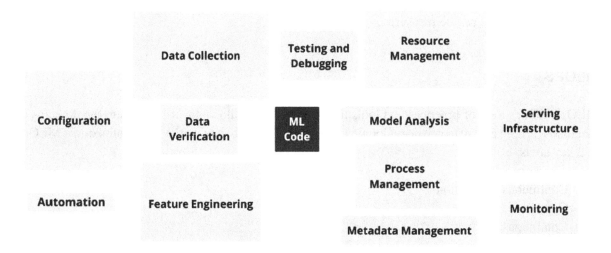

FUTURE RESEARCH DIRECTIONS

The future of data strategy, data processes, and MLOps is not just about the tools. It is also about the people who use them. Data scientists and MLOps engineers are in high demand, but there are not enough to meet the demand. This is why it is crucial to invest in training programs for these professionals.

Many research directions can be taken to improve data strategy and MLOps. One of them would be to study how different types of data sources affect the performance of ML models. Another one would be to investigate how different algorithms perform on different types of datasets and their limitations and strengths.

Another direction seems to be given by the recent surge of the NoCode trend. The NoCode trend is a new way of doing data science. It is a way to do data science without code. The idea behind this trend is that many people want to do data science but do not know how to code.

NoCode is an approach that allows non-technical people to do data science without coding skills. It is a new way of doing data science, which means it is not just about the tools one uses, but also about how one thinks and works. This trend has been popularized by the launch of MIT's App Inventor and MIT App Inventor 2 (MIT, n.d.), both NoCode tools. These tools allow people to build apps without any knowledge of coding languages like Java or Python.

The NoCode trend will likely accelerate the adoption of data science processes and assist in disseminating the concept of data strategy.

CONCLUSION

The practice of machine learning and data science in the real world brings to the front challenges which can be very different from the ones that data scientists are trained one during the years of their academic degree. The correct application of data science and machine learning within an organization requires the careful balancing of many different requirements, ranging from product to business KPIs. In this chapter, we covered some of the topics that will play a key role in the application of data science in the next few years, like data strategy and MLOps. There are other topics like product management/development and data engineering that we didn't mention but might also play a key role in the near future. A holistic data scientist should aim to be aware of all these areas and aspire to have at least some basic skills in some of them, in addition to excellent algorithmic and coding skills.

REFERENCES

Amazon Web Services. (n.d.). *What is DevOps?* Amazon Web Services, Inc. https://aws.amazon.com/devops/what-is-devops/

Competence Center Corporate Data Quality. (2020, September 11). *Data Strategy to Manage Data Successfully*. Competence Center Corporate Data Quality. https://www.cc-cdq.ch/data-strategy

DalleMule, L., & Davenport, T. H. (2017, May 1). What's Your Data Strategy? *Harvard Business Review*. https://hbr.org/2017/05/whats-your-data-strategy

Dingsøyr, T., Nerur, S., Balijepally, V., & Moe, N. B. (2012). A decade of agile methodologies: Towards explaining agile software development. *Journal of Systems and Software*, *85*(6), 1213–1221. doi:10.1016/j.jss.2012.02.033

Fowler, M. (2006, May 1). *Continuous Integration*. https://martinfowler.com/articles/continuousIntegration.html

Gama, J., Medas, P., Castillo, G., & Rodrigues, P. (2004). Learning with Drift Detection. In A. L. C. Bazzan & S. Labidi (Eds.), *Advances in Artificial Intelligence – SBIA 2004* (pp. 286–295). Springer. doi:10.1007/978-3-540-28645-5_29

Ganguli, A., Iaquinti, G., Zhou, M., & Chacon, R. (2020, December 1). *Scaling Datastores at Slack with Vitess*. Slack Engineering. https://slack.engineering/scaling-datastores-at-slack-with-vitess/

General Data Protection Regulation. (2016). https://data.europa.eu/eli/reg/2016/679/2016-05-04/eng

Google Cloud. (n.d.). *MLOps: Continuous delivery and automation pipelines in machine learning*. Google Cloud. https://cloud.google.com/architecture/mlops-continuous-delivery-and-automation-pipelines-in-machine-learning

Hossain, E., Bannerman, P. L., & Jeffery, D. R. (2011). Scrum Practices in Global Software Development: A Research Framework. In D. Caivano, M. Oivo, M. T. Baldassarre, & G. Visaggio (Eds.), *Product-Focused Software Process Improvement* (pp. 88–102). Springer. doi:10.1007/978-3-642-21843-9_9

IBM. (2021, August 17). *CRISP-DM Help Overview*. IBM. https://prod.ibmdocs-production-dal-6099123ce774e592a519d7c33db8265e-0000.us-south.containers.appdomain.cloud/docs/en/spss-modeler/SaaS?topic=dm-crisp-help-overview

Jensen, K. (2012). *A diagram showing the relationship between the different phases of CRISP-DM and illustrates the recursive nature of a data mining project.* https://commons.wikimedia.org/wiki/File:CRISP-DM_Process_Diagram.png

Kampakis, S. (2019). *The Decision Maker's Handbook to Data Science: A Guide for Non-Technical Executives, Managers, and Founders*. https://search.ebscohost.com/login.aspx?direct=true&scope=site&db=nlebk&db=nlabk&AN=2319566

Keely, L. C. (2021, March 1). *How retailers can leverage data as an alternative profit source*. EY Parthenon. https://www.ey.com/en_us/consumer-products-retail/retailers-can-use-data-as-an-alternative-profit-source

Kumar, R., Misra, V., Walraven, J., Sharan, L., Azarnoush, B., Chen, B., & Govind, N. (2018, March 27). *Data Science and the Art of Producing Entertainment at Netflix*. Netflix Technology Blog. https://netflixtechblog.com/studio-production-data-science-646ee2cc21a1

Massachusetts Institute of Technology. (n.d.). *MIT App Inventor | Explore MIT App Inventor*. MIT App Inventor. https://appinventor.mit.edu/

Microsoft. (2021, November 12). *What is the Team Data Science Process?* Microsoft. https://docs.microsoft.com/en-us/azure/architecture/data-science-process/overview

Microsoft. (2022). *TDSP Project Structure, and Documents and Artifact Templates*. Microsoft Azure. https://github.com/Azure/Azure-TDSP-ProjectTemplate

National Aeronautics and Space Administration History Office. (n.d.). *The Decision to Go to the Moon: President John F. Kennedy's May 25, 1961 Speech before Congress*. National Aeronautics and Space Administration. https://history.nasa.gov/moondec.html

Shahin, M., Ali Babar, M., & Zhu, L. (2017). Continuous Integration, Delivery and Deployment: A Systematic Review on Approaches, Tools, Challenges and Practices. *IEEE Access: Practical Innovations, Open Solutions, 5*, 3909–3943. doi:10.1109/ACCESS.2017.2685629

Tawanghar, A. (2020, June 16). *Spotify's Discover Weekly: How machine learning finds your new music*. LinkedIn. https://www.linkedin.com/pulse/spotifys-discover-weekly-how-machine-learning-finds-your-tawanghar/

Tesseract Academy. (2021). *Data analytics consulting services*. Tesseract Academy. https://tesseract.academy

The California Consumer Privacy Act, 375, California State Assembly, Civil Code (2018). https://leginfo.legislature.ca.gov/faces/billTextClient.xhtml?bill_id=201720180AB375

Tierney, B. (2012, June 13). Data Science Is Multidisciplinary. *Oralytics*. https://oralytics.com/2012/06/13/data-science-is-multidisciplinary/

ADDITIONAL READING

Alla, S., & Adari, S. K. (2021). What is mlops? In *Beginning MLOps with MLFlow* (pp. 79–124). Apress. doi:10.1007/978-1-4842-6549-9_3

Elshawi, R., Sakr, S., Talia, D., & Trunfio, P. (2018). Big data systems meet machine learning challenges: towards big data science as a service. *Big Data Research, 14*, 1-11.

Fleckenstein, M., Fellows, L., & Ferrante, K. (2018). *Modern data strategy*. Springer International Publishing. doi:10.1007/978-3-319-68993-7

Kotu, V., & Deshpande, B. (2018). *Data science: concepts and practice*. Morgan Kaufmann.

Mahanti, R. (2019). *Data Quality: Dimensions, Measurement, Strategy, Management, and Governance.* Quality Press.

Mäkinen, S., Skogström, H., Laaksonen, E., & Mikkonen, T. (2021, May). Who Needs MLOps: Opresnik, D., & Taisch, M. (2015). The value of big data in servitization. *International Journal of Production Economics*, *165*, 174–184.

KEY TERMS AND DEFINITIONS

Business Strategy: Business strategy is a term used to describe the process of defining the direction and scope of a business. It is also the process of developing and implementing the plans for achieving these goals.

Data Science Lifecycle: The data science lifecycle is a process that starts with the collection of raw data, followed by cleaning and processing, then modeling and prediction, and finally deployment.

Data Science Process: A general guideline which advises data science teams and stakeholders on how to design and execute data science projects.

Data Strategy: The design of processes for data collection and manipulation with the objective to add value to a business objective.

MLOps: MLOps (shortcut for machine learning operations) refers to the automation and streamlining of machine learning pipelines within a deployment setting.

The Artificial Intelligence in the Sphere of the Administrative Law

Alessandro Puzzanghera

University for Foreigners "Dante Alighieri" of Reggio Calabria, Italy

INTRODUCTION

The extraordinary development of Artificial Intelligence (from now simply AI) in the context of administrative law, both in policy and in the main sectors of its organisational, administrative and jurisdictional activity, begins a new era. The term AI contains a series of notions: machine-learning, robotics, game theory, the development of complex algorithms, artificial neutral networks, etc. Administrative sector organizations has addressed the influence of AI on decision-making process, looking mainly at efficiency and rationalization. However, recent adoptions of AI have been challenged because of their discriminatory nature. As a result, questions emerged on the accountability of AI supported decision-making processes in the public sector. This process generates a lot of issues, with particular regard to the intermediation of the administrative provision. The so-called administrative relationship that is established between citizen and administration, rendered functional by the issue of a legislative measure, is affected by this process even before a provision is issued, not to mention the effects on the interaction between an administrative decision and its consequent effects on judicial review.

The automated administrative measure generates a series of advantages but also hides pitfalls not only for the public administration but also for the citizen himself. A computerised decision must not damage citizens but must be open to control. We are, therefore, faced with a double challenge, both technological and legal. A wise use of AI systems and programs should increase efficiency and performance in public service, while at the same time complying with constitutional and legal requirements and those norms in general that characterise administrative law. A legal challenge must restrict the use of new forms of technology and determine its application without placing unjustified and unnecessary obstacles in the way of technological development. AI will not only help the administrative assistant in the preliminary phases of the administrative process, concerning the admissibility, eligibility, validity and compatibility of applications, but also play a much more important role in the decision-making phases. However, this highly idealized and simplified vision risks undermining the fundamentals of administrative action inherent in the identification of the public interest in practice and the weighting in decision-making as well as the possible distortions of the administrative function.

The aim of this research is, therefore, to investigate, with a critical approach, the impact and the resulting effect that artificial intelligence has had in the sphere of Italian administrative law, also in relation to specific national circumstances within the EU area. On the 21 April 2021 European Commision proposed a new Union legislation to regulate AI. The Commission's proposal marks a defining moment in the history of AI, since it will ultimately lead to the first comprehensive legislative measure globally containing binding rules on AI.

DOI: 10.4018/978-1-7998-9220-5.ch105

BACKGROUND

Artificial Intelligence: "The Science of Making Machines do Things"

The research in the IT field on "artificial intelligence" is aimed at deepening the theoretical foundations, the methodologies and techniques that allow the design of hardware and software systems capable of providing the electronic processor with performance that, for a common observer, would be of exclusive competence of human intelligence (Amigoni, Schiaffonati, & Somalvico, 2008). AI was programmatically established as a discipline in 1956 during a seminar held at Dartmouth College in Hanover in New Hampshire. Marvin Minsky, a famous American mathematician and scientist, gave the following definition to the AI: *"artificial intelligence is the science of making machines do things that would require intelligence if done by men"* (Stonier, 1992).

Through "artificial neural networks", which transmit the connections of the human brain to the computer, the machine should be able to understand the natural language, to learn and interpolate incomplete information and self-perfecting (Buscema, 1993). The automation of activities is becoming more and more widespread. There is no human involvement in the automated decision making so data is taken by a computer program equipped with an appropriate algorithm. AI is responsible for a given final result of the data analysis based on certain rules. These rules can be economic indicators, medical quantifiers, or the law and therefore an algorithm. It is crucial, that a computer program prepares the final solution on the basis of the output data, without human intervention.

The technical possibilities of using automated decision making have expanded considerably and thus seem to be created for use by public authorities in repetitive activities. The progress in machine learning and the possibility of using large and diverse sets of variable data (Big Data) allows for a wide use of AI in decision-making processes. Most often, within the automated decision making framework a distinction is made between processes that are relatively simple in nature, processes that are more complex in nature, and processes that require abstract thinking. It should be remembered, however, that administrative law is not a binary code that can be easily and simply algorithmized (Bateman, 2020), but a law that serves the collective and individual needs of citizens resulting from the coexistence of people in communities, with all the cultural and social heritage that will or will not be possible to convert into a binary code, and thus to automate administrative processes. It is interesting to observe the relationship between the automated decision and the discipline of the processing of personal data. The General Data Protection Regulation (new EU regulation 2016/679 on personal data), recalls the right of the interested party not to be subjected to a decision that may include a measure, which assesses personal aspects that concern him, which is based solely on automated processing and that produces legal effects that affect him. In particular, pursuant to art. 22, paragraph 1 of the GDPR, the interested party has the right not to be subjected to a decision based solely on automated processing, which produces legal effects that affect him or that affect his person.

Therefore, the right of the interested party not to be subjected to decisions based solely on automated processing can, however, be limited by any legislative measures, necessary and proportionate, aimed at safeguarding public interests such as national security, defense, prevention, the investigation, detection and prosecution of crimes.

But any state can give the administrations, through suitable legal provisions and in limited circumstances, a power of adopting decisions based solely on automated data processing (Pizzetti, 2016). As part of the administrative activity, numerous applications of the AI in the exercise of public functions and in the provision of services. In Australia, for example, there is the use of automated information systems in the provision and management of public services (Sartor, 2008). As it has been repeatedly stressed, the processing capacity of computers is progressing exponentially, therefore it is hoped that discretionary public decision-making processes will not encounter, in principle, technological obstacles due to the constant tension of computer studies towards the reproduction of human dialectical reasoning. Given the computing capacity of computers and the possibility for these machines to large quantities of information in real time, in order to reach the best solution for the concrete case, we could witness a transformation of the public decision model: "*from intuitive policy making, into model-based policy design*" (Civitarese Matteucci & Torchia, 2015). Many academics adapt the theory of balancing constitutional rights (Alexy, 2003) to the activity of comparing interests proper to the exercise of discretion, formulate an algorithm whose application should ensure maximum satisfaction (Lucatuorto & Bianchini, 2009). Other academics, on the other hand, consider the possibility of an automated administrative decision when, through the software, valid criteria are introduced to guide the exercise of power on a case-by-case basis (Masucci, 2011). In these cases, the administration's discretion would be exercised through the predetermination of the criteria as well as the principles and therefore the computer should examine the information material in making the decision (Saitta, 2003).

We are getting closer to the so-called "Automated decision", given the numerous applications of AI that, using "reasoning" techniques and knowledge to solve complex problems, explain and justify the reasons for the chosen solution (Lucatuorto, 2009). We are faced with an "automated legal consultant" who has overturned the classic scheme of human-machine interrogation, capable of asking questions to the user (as, for example, a public official does), to acquire factual data and necessary information aimed at identifying the applicable abstract discipline and arriving at a decision (Morollo, 2015) which must be fully motivated and suggested to the owner of the body to use the relevant provision. The administrative network is the one that, at least in theory, best lends itself to computerization and automation (Marongiu, 2005). And it is precisely its "procedural" character typical of the activity, together with its character of "globally relevant function", which combines with the rules of the algorithms and with which it presents singular analogies. Despite AI is growing more and more exponentially, there is still a stumbling block between administrative activity and computerization, which concerns its character or not "discretionary", that much cited "administrative discretion" (Gorgerino, 2018).

Administrative Decision

Administrative activity has undergone important transformations in recent decades due to the increasing use of new technologies and information technology. The Public Administration has deployed AI tools in order to reach better informed and more rapid decision-making in multiple service domains: from policing to home office, from criminal justice to healthcare. The application of the tools of AI is examined from the aspect of the basic activities carried out by public administration institutions. AI solutions may be used in the area of defining institutional policies and strategies, making administrative decisions and providing information, as well as for other institutional activities and internal daily routine tasks. Administrative decisions, which may be initiated by both citizens and authorities, form an area of high priority in our article. Administrative decisions always involve the making of some kind of decisions. We can talk about cases without deliberation (normative regulations), and cases with deliberation. The use of new technologies on administrative activity has given rise to two different worlds that have joined together, on the one hand the use of the computer as a database (a reductive and minimal use given its power), on the other hand, the use of the computer to process administrative documents electronically and digitally.

We are facing a transformation of a progressive nature for the administrative activity that leads the jurist to a double reflection projected with a look at the present, as regards the study and interpretation of current uses combined with the power of IT tools, which have been implemented by positive law, based on administrative decisions; and with another towards the future (Otranto, 2018).

It is legitimate to ask whether, information and communication technologies will be used to codify the decision-making process in order to arrive at an automated decision. It should contain all information required for the identification of the competent authority, the clients and the case, ascertained facts of the case, the evidence available, explanation for the specialist authority's assessment, the reasons for deliberation and the decision and the specific statutory provisions on the basis of which the decision was adopted. To elaborate a decision that defines the structure of relationships and interests according to the provisions of the law, it is necessary to provide the machine with the appropriate instructions, that is, the logical-mathematical rules derived from a path of rationalization of human activity based on a certain factual situation and certain legal conditions. Machine learning is considered a tool of AI. Its algorithms build mathematical models based on sample data, and make predictions or form opinions without being explicitly programmed to do so. The most important machine learning methods are: supervised learning, unsupervised learning, reinforced learning, deep learning (Burns, 2020). Machine learning algorithms map input data to output data, but do not show the method of mapping, they operate as black boxes.

Consequently, they are not suitable for making direct and independent administrative decisions but may do the preparations and offer support. In Italy the hypothesis of an electronically processed administrative act, less problematic and more easily accessible, is the so-called act bound. This experiment is already present in a 1978 paper by an italian Professor, who addressed the close link between the tied act and the possibility of entrusting the processing of the provision to a computer (Duni, 1978). The fact of limiting oneself to the so-called acts constrained, given what can be seen from the practical writings relating to the underlying problem, it can be deduced from the strong theoretical awareness and concrete experience that had in the administrative practice of the time and which therefore had determined the extension of automation to get to the issuing of tied documents (Ravalli, 1989). The doctrinal evolution has elaborated a more complete reconstructive framework, while nevertheless limiting itself only to the application of the category of electronic processing documents so-called bound. By way of example, the machine that has been set up according to technical parameters concerning the content of the rules on speed limits in road traffic, once it has been verified that the limit has been exceeded through technologies, imposes the administrative sanction conceived for this hypothesis and elaborates the related provision. Once the data has been entered, the machine transforms the quantifiable data (input) into output data (output) without carrying out any autonomous "reasoning", but using an algorithm (man's intelligible computational procedure), which subsequently transforms it in a program (intelligible computational procedure of the machine).

We are faced with the classic norm-fact-effect scheme (Capaccioli, 1983), as the decision will be automatable only if the regulatory provision can be effectively and univocally codified, so that there is the appropriate instruction to determine the content of the act (Saitta, 2003); if it is possible to identify and enclose a series of logical steps connected by a link of consequentiality, so that a univocal result can be achieved given the problem, according to a syllogistic scheme. Therefore, only what is attributable to a conditional judgment by which conditionality "A" occurs, then the effect "B" must be produced (Morollo, 2015). In order for the automated system to be able to carry out the activities that a public official would carry out with uniformity, versatility, efficiency, it must be free of administrative discretion and with an abstract case built around analytical legal concepts useful for quantifying reality (Follieri, 2017). There can be a double level of administrative decision: a first level is that which takes place in the absence of legal provisions which provide for the mandatory administrative act. In this case, the administration decides to exercise its function by adopting a software that, through pre-established rules and compliant with the law, transforms inputs into outputs. For most of the doctrine, the legal basis of the administration's power to use software for the automation of the tied activity is the result of an independent choice made by each entity (Masucci, 2011). Such an organizational choice would still comply with the principle of reasonableness and logic (Saitta, 2003), as the automated decision undoubtedly brings about advantages in terms of reducing the risks of unequal treatment, compliance with the law, protection from corruption, completeness at the preliminary level and, finally, what better tool to achieve the impartiality and good performance of the administration (Costantino, 2013). The second level of decision concerns, however, the content of the commands structured in the algorithm that are translated into software.

Non-analytical legal concepts are used to construct the normative case, so that an acceptable hermeneutic option is identified, the result will be a decision that, translated into the software, will produce its effects in a uniform manner in the arrangement of relationships and interests affected by the automated act (Follieri, 2017). The passage to the automation of decisions also depends on the need to have an accurate language that makes the related statements more reducible to an algorithm, so much so that automation as well as the tightening of legal language (Frosini, 1988) risks eliminating the benefits that "adaptive behaviors" bring about the functioning of complex organizations (Civitarese Matteucci & Torchia, 2015).

The automated act, despite having some advantages in terms of efficiency, cost-effectiveness and effectiveness of the action, as well as being a guarantee of uniform treatment and non-contradiction, at the same time does not in itself entail legitimacy. It will be illegitimate, for example, if the instructions provided to the computer through the software are incorrect, or when the software has programming defects (Orofino, 2002) or in the case of hardware malfunction. In the event of an error by the administration or the private entity, which prepared the program, all acts of that type would be affected, avoiding different solutions, since the illegitimacy would not depend on the execution of the commands given on a case-by-case basis (and therefore on the machine), but from the choices that were made in the construction of the algorithm and its translation into software. In order to be able to syndicate compliance with the fact-effect scheme envisaged by the standard and, therefore, establish any defects in the algorithm (or software), it is necessary to have full knowledge of the instructions that the administration has provided to the electronic processor.

The Tar Lazio in a recent judgment (22 March 2017, n. 3769) recognized the applicants' right to access the algorithm of the program used to carry out the entire procedure and also affirmed the full legitimacy of the administration's choice to manage the procedure through a "Electronic processing act". However, despite the choice of the administration, the right of access of the interested parties must remain unchanged. It is not sufficient that the administration, in response to the request for access, describes the algorithm used, since, in order for there to be full effectiveness, it is necessary that it be made available to the interested parties, the structure and the so-called "source code", that is, the text of an algorithm of a program written in a language and in the programming phase is included in a source file. The Tar's choice to adopt an electronic administrative procedure cannot negate the protections and guarantees, since the use of technology must be balanced by constant reference to the principles and institutions that make up the right procedure. The observance and reference to the rules of the fair procedure guarantee the citizen's relationship with the public administration in cases where a discretionary decision (Giannini, 1939) is considered that is subject to electronic processing. Although part of the doctrine tends to exclude any discretionary provision for electronic processing, it is undeniable, however, that technology is making giant strides and is advancing at an incessant rhythm that distorts consolidated relationships and interests.

It should be noted that the effects that could derive from the automation of administrative choices on constitutional balances and on the administrative function itself in the structure of the State are not yet clearly configurable.

Accountability

The increased concerns with regards to the discriminating effects of PA decisions mediated by AI systems raises the call to question AI accountability i.e. to explain and justify how AI impacts PA decisions (de Sousa et al., 2019). The lack of accountability of AI decision-making systems have raised concerns on the use of AI to support public sector service delivery (de Fine & de Fine, 2020). These concerns mainly deal with ethical and legal aspects (Helbing et al., 2019). The search for AI accountability in this context has been framed as a human/technology control dilemma: humans are not accountable since they are not in full control of AI (Matthias, 2004); or humans are accountable for the technology despite their control over AI (De George, 2003). It is important to shed light on the complex effects of AI systems on the decision-making logics followed by public sector organisations.

The starting point of the liability for compensation from an administrative act prepared electronically, finds application in a logical procedure that ends up directly attributing the accountability to the administrative authority which, in the issuing of the administrative acts, has decided to make use of the IT aid. The technology is not a neutral tool of transformation: rather, technology reflects but also transcend decision-making drivers of the context where it is deployed. Accordingly, AI systems adopted to support decision-making processes in the PA generate organizational, legal, and institutional, transformations that deeply impact on the logics driving public decision-making (Cordella & Iannacci, 2010). To prove the traceability of the will of the computerized act to the authority, it must be kept in mind that, the will of the computer is at the same time the will of the authority. Through the program, the authority previously prepares the "decision" for an indeterminate number of cases and even if this decision occurs later, it always remains attributable to the authority.

However, attributing responsibility to the authority is not the resolution of the problem, as for other cases, in fact, it is necessary to treat the subjective element of the compensation case and this is where the problems begin to arise. As noted by authoritative doctrine: "it is certainly problematic to envisage a responsibility of the public administration for the adoption and / or execution of an illegitimate IT administrative act. If the art. 2043 of the Italian civil code requires that the willful misconduct or fault of whoever acted for the authority arises, this finding is particularly difficult in the case of an administrative act carried out with IT equipment" (Masucci, 1993). To apply the provisions of art. 2043 of the Italian civil code is somewhat difficult, if not impossible. Given that the context that led to the computerization of the act is characterized by the presence of multiple public and private agents, as well as the great difficulty of accurately identifying the causes and those responsible for the damage.

According to what has been said by authoritative doctrine, administrative power is not exercised by the single official, but by an automated administrative system. The will of the IT administrative act, is not attributable to a single person but to a multitude of people. Databases which are autonomous from an organizational point of view with respect to the deciding authorities, supply the same large parts of their data and information needs. In this regard, the preparation of the programs is entrusted by the authority to concessionary companies, which make use of the mere collaboration of officials of the competent offices for the activity in question.

For this reason, it is therefore difficult to find the official's willfulness or guilt, and still to make the detection of the fault still more difficult, it must be added that we are often faced with mere machine errors that are in no way attributable to the official (D'Angelosante, 2015). A further complication can be found in the fact that the doctrine has proposed framing the case of the administrative act with electronic processing in the categories of the Digital Administration Code (Legislative Decree of the 7 March 2005, n. 82; so-called C.A.D.). The application of the C.A.D. the electronic processing administrative act is also justified by attachment 1 to the Presidential Decree November 13, 2014 which defines the "automatic generation" of IT documents as the formation of IT documents carried out directly by the IT system upon the occurrence of certain conditions and by the administrative jurisprudence relating to the right of access to the IT program (D'Angelosante, 2015). It should be added to the above that there could be a computer language used by the official in charge of the procedure and, therefore, could reduce the possibility of controlling the final result for the manager.

This problem which will tend to increase as the systems become more complex. In this perspective, it is unreal to believe that the user knows exactly what his computer system will do. This knowledge is prevented by a series of factors, for example the ignorance of the circumstances of the different contexts in which the computer system will operate as well as the impossibility of reproducing, at least for sufficiently complex agents, all the processing operations that the software will perform under each of these circumstances.

Furthermore, the user does not have all the information that is or will be available to his computer system. It will be impossible for the user to foresee (at least for his computer system who can learn, and therefore modify themselves) which data and which instructions will be part of the computer system when it operates (Sartor, 2003). In practice, the problem remains the same, namely the protection restrictions that derive from the application to the p.a. of the provisions of art. 2043 of the Italian Civil Code, rather than applying strict liability, as provided for in other legal systems.

The only desirable solution in order to avoid a reduction of guarantees for the recipients of the administrative action and at the same time a new "immunity for authority" seems to be specific legislation, which provides for a hypothesis of objective liability of the public administration for damages caused by carrying out the administrative tasks through electronic computers (Masucci, 1993). Morollo also commented on this point, pointing out how one could think of a liability for damages caused in the conduct of an electronic procedure which is released from the fault requirement and based solely on objective elements: for example, a reference criterion could be the risk, so-called "IT risk" (Morollo, 2015). The attempts of strict responsibility have already been reported by authoritative doctrine, which proposed the case of the model referred to in art. 2050 of the Italian Civil Code according to which the responsibility must be placed on the one who can avoid damages (or at least insure against them). An unpredictable liability, even for events that go beyond the control, and that could be placed on the developer, owner or user (Sartor, 2003). It is important to underline that, the passage to an objective responsibility does not necessarily presuppose the approval of a law and that the same can be reached by interpretation; the doctrine stated that what is provided for by art. 2050 of the Italian Civil Code it can also be applied with reference to the so-called dangerous activities cd. "Atypical" and whose danger is ascertained in concrete case by case by the judge (Salvi, 1998). And finally, given the complexity of the matter and the difficulties that could be faced by the injured and the "dangerous" nature of the use of information technology for electronically processed administrative documents, what has been said by the jurisprudence that has been expressed to solve the problem waiting for an unlikely intervention by the legislator.

SOLUTIONS AND RECOMMENDATIONS

A EU Legislation to Regulate Artificial Intelligence

The use of the A.I., as a complex algorithmic evolution, represents, with all the doubts of the case, a fascinating legal challenge as well as being a challenge for our society. The Commission's proposal of new Union legislation to regulate AI distinguishes three categories of AI, namely certain uses of AI that it bans, high-risk AI which it regulates in detail, and low-risk AI which it addresses to a limited extent. Since the first two categories are relatively narrowly circumscribed, the vast majority of existing intelligent algorithms falls into the third category where the proposed regulation essentially requires AI to be flagged. The proposed regulation prohibits certain uses of AI. It bans the use of AI: a) to materially distort a person's behaviour; b) to exploit the vulnerabilities of a specific group of persons; c) public social scoring and d) for real time remote biometric identification in public places. The ban is limited to the use of AI. It does not preclude the development of AI which could potentially be used in cases covered by the ban. The material distortion of behaviour (a) and the exploitation of vulnerabilities (b) are only banned, if they causally affect a human person's physical or psychological harm, or if they are likely to do so. This condition qualifies the ban and makes it narrower but the ban is still rather vague and broad with regard to these two categories. Importantly, the ban of biometric recognition is not absolute. Derogations from it are possible broadly speaking in case of public security concerns. In particular Article 5 specifically lists the search for individual potential victims of crimes; the concrete looming threat to life or physical safety of human persons or a terrorism threat; and the finding or prosecution of suspects or criminals in case of certain crimes as grounds for legitimate derogation. Restrictions of fundamental and human rights, for instance, can regularly be justified on grounds other than the protection of public security. The ban of biometric recognition is furthermore subject to an assessment of the circumstances of the situation, the potential harm as well as necessity, proportionality and an authorization to be granted by an independent national authority. In Italy for example the Council of State recently re-expressed (Judgment n. 2270 of 2019) itself on the use of algorithms in the administrative procedure with a new sentence (Judgment n. 8472 of 2019). On this occasion, the Council of State returned to dealing with the issue, reiterating the importance of the use by the public administration of computer algorithms that can bring benefits in terms of greater efficiency and greater neutrality of the administrative action.

The public administration has already been overwhelmed by this powerful innovation which, in the future, will lead to a progressive automation of administrative procedures. There will be greater dynamism regarding the private sector, greater speed of procedure, all to the advantage of an improvement not only in terms of quality, but also in terms of quantity, of administrative action.

It will be essential to adapt the public administration to private standards both technologically and professionally, so as not to create damage to the community in general.

The choice to use computerized procedures must be encouraged, as it allows a reduction in procedural timing for merely repetitive operations and without discretion, also avoiding any interference or errors eventually committed by the official. The use of AI in the administrative procedure is traced back to the concrete and current application of art. 97 of the Constitution as it is likely to implement the good performance techniques by which the P.A. manages to operate according to the known criteria of efficiency, efficacy and economy. At present, A.I. systems are not able to replace a jurist completely.

However, these systems are able to prepare - with the minimum collaboration of a human being - simple or repetitive legal acts, extract rules, judicial precedents, maxims, arguments, or to analyze documents regarding states of reality and understand them as a human operator for the limited purposes for which their knowledge is useful. Despite the doubts that may arise regarding the judicial protection "against" those measures adopted by an administration "technically set" to comply with the law, it must, however, be taken into account that an electronic act will make almost nothing residual, or better yet, almost nothing. the hypothesis of defects of violation of the law and incompetence, since it will decide according to rules of logic, non-contradiction and equal treatment (D'Angelosante, 2015). Although there are benefits for the state will have (and for people) once the transition to an automated administration is complete, it is important to analyze what has been said by authoritative doctrine regarding the risks of such a process. The doctrine has highlighted those risks deriving from a block of functionality of the IT systems (*crash down*), as well as the inclusion of private powers (such as owners and managers of IT technologies, very often subtracted from any form of control by the State) in the exercise of public functions, in addition to the possible prejudices that could result from data storage in case of *cloud computing* (Cardarelli, 2015). A further issue concerns, any damage that could result from attacks (including terrorist attacks) on computer systems. At the moment, the Italian administration is equipping itself with IT consultants capable of investigating the evolution of AI, on the exercise of public functions. Furthermore, at the legislative level, the debate on the impact of robotics and artificial intelligence within society remains open and in the initial phase.

Therefore, the jurist is called to a double reflection: on the one hand, towards the present, and therefore to the study and interpretation of current and potential uses of IT techniques and tools, as they are accepted by positive law also in terms of administrative decisions increasingly effectively participated and shared by citizens; on the other hand, however, it will be important to look towards the future of the administration which, as has been highlighted in the previous discussion, cannot take the contemporary legal systems unprepared. The proposed regulation does not preclude AI that is learning live and on the go while being in use (adaptive AI), but imposes some additional obligations beyond those already applicable to high-risk AI in which the learning is frozen when it is put into circulation. AI that was trained exclusively with data stemming from the Union benefits from a presumption of compliance with the regional specificity requirement applicable to training data.

Indeed, some further aspects of the proposed regulation should be highlighted. A careful analysis is necessary to determine whether the Europeean Union has the power to adopt the regulation with the content proposed. It is not clear whether articles 16 of the Treaty on the Functioning of the European Union on data protection and article 114 TFEU, which requires a link to the establishment and the functioning of the internal market, together can serve as foundation for the whole regulation. While the power to impose penalties remains with the Member States, article 72 of the proposed regulation determines that certain behaviour, including contravention of the ban of certain uses of AI within the sense of article 5. In conclusion, in order to increase efficiency and to establish an official point of contact with the public and other counterparties, each Member State will have to designate one or more National Supervisory Authorities.

The Commission's goal of managing the AI market well in Europe and avoiding any side effects of a globalized market without rules seems to be perfectly in line with the provisions of the proposal.

AI In Administrative Procedure Around The World

With the development of technology and the continuous growth of robotics, the automation of public administration has become one of the issues in politics and science. Advances in the field of AI are leading to a new level of computing in which systems will have the capability to act as autonomous agents and learn to learn independently. In the administrative sphere, the term 'automated decision-making' has come into use. In the legislation of some countries there are examples of regulations which show that legislators have standardised automatic issuance of administrative decisions, and therefore the automatic decision-making process. The Article 28 of the Swedish Administrative Procedure Act 2017 stipulates that an administrative decision may be made by an official, a group of officials, or automatically. The latter is taken without the participation of a human being. This is how, for example, the individual risk calculation for taking out a loan is assessed. AI is also used to assess the validity of compensation claims against airline companies for changes due to delayed or cancelled flights. In turn, the Swedes use an AI system called *Exoplore* which analyses the way children read and their eye movements when reading text from a screen in order to detect dyslexia. Although some disadvantages of this way of issuing decisions are recognised, such as the lack of clear and transparent documentation illustrating the process, it is emphasized that it is efficient and effective. The application of artificial intelligence is designed to automate procedure activities in routine and repetitive cases. Undoubtedly, therefore, it can apply to inherently uncomplicated cases with a simple factual and legal background. Thus, in those cases where it is not beyond the capabilities of an automated system to make certain determinations. So far, Polish lawmakers have not introduced general regulations corresponding to the Hungarian or Swedish norms on automatic issuance of decisions in certain types of cases. However, the use of the automated decision making system in cases related to imposing traffic penalties may be noticed. In Poland, the nationwide radar system CANARD (Centre for Automatic Traffic Supervision) has been operating since 2015. It is linked to an IT system that uses image analysis algorithms to read license plates before automatically imposing fines on speeding drivers.

FUTURE RESEARCH DIRECTIONS

The importance of AI is to automate various processes and make decisions based on an algorithm that processes large volumes of data. These activities have so far mostly been carried out by a human being/ public servant/officer. This is not without an impact on human rights, if only because it creates a strong need to share as well as to protect data. The positive aspects of the application of AI include the reduction of operating costs and the elimination of errors or abuses committed by humans, if only due to subjectivity. The decisions issued by AI are seen as more balanced and fairer. By applying AI in the decision-making process, timeliness is improved. The AI literature and implications for public administration raise issues concerning a number of classic dilemmas relevant to administrative discretion, including responsiveness, judgement, and accountability. The literature provides few answers to the question of how government and public administration should respond to the great challenges associated with AI and use regulation to prevent harm. What has been noted so far clearly shows how the use of AI in public administration requires a re-examination (if not an amendment) of legal institutions and of the organisational principles and regulations of administrative activity.

Against this background and by way of example, attention should be focused on giving structure to procedural dynamics and the relationship between administrative procedure and legality. For this reason, and in light of what has been observed in the preceding paragraphs, a doubt remains. Can a system of principles and legal institutions, conceived and built around an individual, a 'human being', be so easily transferable and adaptable to a world of algorithms and intelligent machines?

AI functionally simplifies and closes administrative processes. As a consequence, AI has impacts that transform the logic underlining the decision-making processes. Hence, AI can produce outcomes which do not reflect relevant factual circumstances. When these outcomes are used as inputs to support public sector decision-making, issues of accountability arise. Public administration will certainly become more efficient, but it may be completely deprived of that element of humanity that makes administrative activity acceptable to its beneficiaries, despite its elements of one-sidedness.

However, in order to answer this question fully, it is necessary to establish if there is a room for AI in a context where administrative action is characterised by a right to good governance, as detailed in Article 41 of the EU Charter of Fundamental Rights, in a summary of the procedural rights of a citizen that is, guided by an obligation to provide clarifications that leaves no room for defined algorithmic systems.

CONCLUSION

The greater challenge is to make administrative decisions that are based on valuation rules, general clauses and administrative recognition. Theoretically, machine learning can break this barrier, but introducing automatic solutions in this area requires some testing and checking if the algorithms are able to work not only objectively and legally, but also in accordance with the values presented by the public administration, such as transparency, equality, justice and others. Past experience shows that algorithms are as subjective as the designers who create them. Therefore it is important that everyone should be able to say why a public administration body made this decision and not another. In other words, an AI making automatic decisions on behalf of the State cannot be a black box that generates a decision, but must be a tool that supports the execution of public tasks for the citizens. The author, in view of what has been analysed in this work, is optimistic. It is certain that AI is on the verge of such sophisticated evolution that it will easily interact with human intelligence. It appears necessary, instead, to establish the appropriate means of integrating AI and man, so that even where professional systems are in use, man may continue to provide those cognitive skills lacking in a machine, while maintaining control over the information that is transmitted and the process of its application.

REFERENCES

Alexy, R. (2003). On balancing and subsumption. A structural comparison. *Ratio Juris*, *16*(4), 433–449. doi:10.1046/j.0952-1917.2003.00244.x

Amigoni, F., Schiaffonati, V., & Somalvico, M. (2008). *Artificial intelligence* [Intelligenza artificiale]. Rome: Enciclopedia della scienza e della tecnica.

Barone, G. (1989). *Discretion (administrative law)* [Discrezionalità (diritto amministrativo)]. Enciclopedia Giuridica.

Bateman, W. (2020). Algorithmic decision-making and legality: Public law dimensions. *The Australian Law Journal*.

Burns, E. (2020). *In-depth guide to Machine Learning in the enterprise*. TechTarget.

Buscema, V. (1993). *Administrative discretion and artificial neural networks* [Discrezionalità amministrativa e reti neurali artificiali]. Foro Amministrativo.

Capaccioli, E. (1983). Manual of Administrative Law [Manuale di diritto amministrativo]. Academic Press.

Cardarelli, F. (2015). Digital administration, transparency and the principle of legality [Amministrazione digitale, trasparenza e principio di legalità]. *Il Diritto Dellinformazione e Dellinformatica, 31*(2), 227–273.

Civitarese Matteucci, S., & Torchia, L. (2017). *The technicalization of administration* [La tecnificazione dell'amministrazione]. Firenze University Press.

Cordella, A., & Iannacci, F. (2010). Information systems in the public sector: The e-Government enactment framework. *The Journal of Strategic Information Systems, 19*(1), 52–66. doi:10.1016/j.jsis.2010.01.001

Costantino, F. (2012). *Autonomy of administration and digital innovation* [Autonomia dell'amministrazione e innovazione digitale]. Jovene.

D'Angelosante, M. (2017). The consistency of the 'invisible' administration model in the age of technology: from decision-making to responsibility for decisions [La consistenza del modello dell'amministrazione 'invisibile' nell'età della tecnificazione: dalla formazione delle decisioni alla responsabilità per le decisioni]. *La tecnificazione*, 155.

De Fine Licht, K., & De Fine Licht, J. (2020). Artificial intelligence, transparency, and public decision-making. *AI & Society, 35*(4), 917–926. doi:10.100700146-020-00960-w

De George, R. T. (2003). *The ethics of information technology and business.* Blackwell. doi:10.1002/9780470774144

De Sousa, W. G., de Melo, E., Bermejo, P., Farias, R., & Gomes, A. (2019). How and where is artificial intelligence in the public sector going? A literature review and research agenda. *Government Information Quarterly, 36*(4), 101392. doi:10.1016/j.giq.2019.07.004

Duni, G. (1978). L'utilizzabilità delle tecniche elettroniche nell'emanazione degli atti e nei procedimenti amministrativi. *Spunto per una teoria dell'atto emanato nella forma elettronica.*

Fantigrossi, U. (1993). Automation and public administration [Automazione e pubblica amministrazione]. Profili giuridici. Bologna: Il Mulino.

Follieri, F. (2017). *Administrative decision and binding act* [Decisione amministrativa ed atto vincolato]. Federalismi.

Frosini, V. (1988). *Informatics law and society* [Informatica diritto e società]. A. Giuffrè.

Galetta, D. U. (2005). *The right to a good European administration as a source of essential procedural guarantees against the Public Administration* [Il diritto ad una buona amministrazione europea come fonte di essenziali garanzie procedimentali nei confronti della Pubblica Amministrazione]. Academic Press.

Giannini, M. S. (1939). The discretionary power of the public administration [Il potere discrezionale della pubblica amministrazione]. *Concetto e problemi.*

Gorgerino, F. (2018). *Administrative discretion and legal hermeneutics* [Discrezionalità amministrativa ed ermeneutica giuridica]. Academic Press.

Helbing, D. (2019). Will Democracy Survive Big Data and Artificial Intelligence? In Towards Digital Enlightenment. Springer.

Lucatuorto, P.L.M. (2006). Artificial intelligence and law: the legal applications of expert systems [Intelligenza artificiale e diritto: le applicazioni giuridiche dei sistemi esperti]. *Cyberspazio e diritto.*

Lucatuorto, P.L.M., & Bianchini, S. (2009). Discretion and balancing of interests in the decision-making processes of the Digital Administration [Discrezionalità e contemperamento degli interessi nei processi decisionali dell'Amministrazione digitale]. *Cyberspazio e diritto*.

Maddalena, M. L. (2016). The digitalization of the life of the administration and the process [La digitalizzazione della vita dell'amministrazione e del processo]. *Foro amm*, (10), 2535.

Marongiu, V. D. (2005). The automated administrative activity [L'attività amministrativa automatizzata]. Academic Press.

Masucci, A. (1993). *The computer administrative act. First features of a reconstruction* [L'atto amministrativo informatico. Prima lineamenti di una ricostruzione]. Jovene.

Masucci, A. (2011). Administrative procedure and new technologies [Procedimento amministrativo e nuove tecnologie]. Academic Press.

Matthias, A. (2004). The responsibility gap: Ascribing responsibility for the actions of learning automata. *Ethics and Information Technology*, 6(3), 175–183. doi:10.100710676-004-3422-1

Morollo, F. (2015). *Electronic document between e-government and artificial intelligence* [Documento elettronico fra e-government e artificial intelligence]. Federalismi.

Mortati, C. (1960). *Discretion* [Discrezionalità]. Novissimo Digesto Italiano.

Orofino, A. G. (2002). *The pathology of the electronic administrative act: judicial review and protection tools* [La patologia dell'atto amministrativo elettronico: sindacato giurisdizionale e strumenti di tutela]. Academic Press.

Otranto, P. (2018). Administrative decision and digitalization of the PA [Decisione amministrativa e digitalizzazione della pa]. *federalismi. it, 2*.

Pizzetti, F. (2016). Privacy and the European right to the protection of personal data [Privacy e il diritto europeo alla protezione dei dati personali]. Il Regolamento europeo 2016/679.

Pruyt, E. (2015). From building a model to adaptive robust decision making using systems modeling. In *Policy practice and digital science* (pp. 75–93). Springer. doi:10.1007/978-3-319-12784-2_5

Ravalli, A. (1989). *Administrative acts issued through computer systems: issues related to judicial protection* [Atti amministrativi emanati mediante sistemi informatici: problematiche relative alla tutela giurisdizionale]. Academic Press.

Saitta, F. (2003). The pathologies of the electronic administrative act and the review of the administrative judge [Le patologie dell'atto amministrativo elettronico e il sindacato del giudice amministrativo]. *Rivista di Diritto amministrativo elettronico*.

Salvi, C. (1998). *Civil liability* [La responsabilità civile]. Giuffrè.

Sartor, G. (2003). The intentionality of computer systems and the law [L'intenzionalità dei sistemi informatici e il diritto]. *Rivista trimestrale di diritto e procedura civile*.

Stonier, T. (1992). *The evolution of machine intelligence*. Springer. doi:10.1007/978-1-4471-1835-0_6

ADDITIONAL READING

Avanzini, G. (2019). *Algorithmic decisions and computer algorithms: predetermination, predictive analysis and new forms of intelligibility* [Decisioni algoritmiche e algoritmi informatici: predeterminazione, analisi predittiva e nuove forme di intellegibilità]. Editoriale Scientifica.

Carullo, G. (2017). *Management, use and dissemination of digital administration data and administrative function* [Gestione, fruizione e diffusione dei dati dell'amministrazione digitale e funzione amministrativa]. Giappichelli.

Dean, T., Allen, J., & Aloimonos, Y. (1995). *Artificial intelligence: Theory and practice*. Benjamin Cummings.

Galetta, D. U. (2020). *Algorithms, administrative procedure and guarantees: brief reflections, also in the light of the latest jurisprudential arrests on the subject* [Algoritmi, procedimento amministrativo e garanzie: brevi riflessioni, anche alla luce degli ultimi arresti giurisprudenziali in materia]. Rivista Italiana di Diritto Pubblico Comunitario.

Haugeland, J. (1985). *Artificial intelligence: The very idea*. MIT Press.

Luger, G., & Stubblefield, W. (1993). *Artificial intelligence: Structures and strategies for complex problem solving*. Benjamin/Cummings.

Masucci, A. (2011). *Administrative procedure and new technologies. The electronic administrative procedure at the request of a party* [Procedimento amministrativo e nuove tecnologie. Il procedimento ammi-nistrativo elettronico ad istanza di parte]. Giappichelli.

KEY TERMS AND DEFINITIONS

Administrative Decision: It can be described as the application of general rules to individual cases, often in the context of performing public tasks.

Algorithm: It is an extended subset of machine learning that tells the computer how to learn to operate on its own.

Artificial Intelligence: It is an increasingly popular concept, although it is often used only as a marketing tool to label activities that are very far from AI.

Automatic Decision Making: Should be one of the stages in the development and improvement of public administration.

Machine Learning: It is an application of artificial intelligence that provides systems the ability to automatically learn and improve from experience without being explicitly programmed.

Neural Network: It is a method in artificial intelligence that teaches computers to process data in a way that is inspired by the human brain.

Public Administration: We should not speak of public administration but of public administrations, as the concept should diversify according to the purposes for which it should be used.

Trust Management Mechanism in Blockchain Data Science

Ge Gao

https://orcid.org/0000-0002-5881-319X

Zhuhai College of Science and Technology, Jilin University, China

Ran Liu

https://orcid.org/0000-0003-4663-4861

Central Connecticut State University, USA

INTRODUCTION

With the development of new technologies, e.g., the Internet of Things (IoT), Big Data, and blockchain data technology, economic development relies on refined specialization (Slamet et al., 2017; Tian et al., 2018; Xie et al., 2019). Meanwhile, the interaction between supply chain enterprises is becoming increasingly more comprehensive. More and more companies are seeking supply chain partners globally to achieve complementary advantages, cooperation potentials, and to integrate the enterprises with the upstream and downstream players of the supply chain to form a supply chain alliance (Nyaga et al., 2010; Wallenburg & Schäffler, 2014). However, with the extension and increasing complexity of supply chains, trust becomes a big issue between supply chain partners. For instance, due to the immature credit system and inconsistent punishment mechanism under the traditional supply chain model, each member holds limited information that is difficult to share. Additionally, the lack of trust between members leads to a failure rate of 50% to 70% of actual supply chain transactions (Kale et al., 2002; Taylor, 2005; Mingang et al., 2017). Part of the reason is supply chain partners have interests that are not aligned with one another, which may lead to potential opportunistic behaviors, resulting in failures in collaborations (Das & Rahman, 2010; Gerwin, 2004). Therefore, new technologies and management models are urgently needed to solve this issue.

The cutting-edge development in information and data technology plays an increasingly essential role in any market decision and firms' performance (liu et al, 2021). The emerging blockchain data technology provides new opportunities and ways to solve the trust issue in supply chain system. First, the decentralized nature of blockchain data is very suitable for supply chain systems. With blockchain data, supply chain partners can trade without knowing one another's basic information, achieving a high level of trust without establishing a trust relationship. Trust can be achieved through the technical architecture of blockchain data, including smart contracts, making transactions between members determined by intelligent machines and related algorithms automatically. Furthermore, each participant of the supply chain system can establish a mutually beneficial and coordinated mechanism of trust using the blockchain data consensus mechanism. This can guide enterprises' operating a dynamic block supply chain alliance while realizing the value creation of the supply chain, eliminating the various risks caused by lack of trust.

This combination's rationality and feasibility are discussed from the three dimensions of trust, including cultural, social, and economic attributes. This paper further explores the smart contracts' operation

DOI: 10.4018/978-1-7998-9220-5.ch106

mechanism, mutual trust mechanism, and related technologies in supply chain trust management with the proposed framework. Layer by layer then enumerates the specific smart contract application types and introduces a blockchain data consensus mechanism suitable for supply chain trust management.

Supply Chain Trust Issues

Supply chain trust issues have been around for a long time, from a personal level to an organizational level, and intertwined throughout the entire supply chain system. Scholars have carried out relevant research on the trust problem in the supply chain from different angles. Initially, most academic research was focused on the cognitive aspects of trust in the cooperation of members in supply chain systems. Leng et al. (2019) interpreted trust in supply chains as a kind of emotional judgment and evaluation of interpersonal communication. In social communications, it is the interpersonal attitude formed by the interaction of rational thinking and irrational emotions. Scholars have proposed different solutions on how to improve and solve the trust problem in supply chain systems. Kwon and Suh (2004) started with the relationship between trust and commitment and proposed establishing a trust mechanism with information sharing to improve the efficiency of cooperation among members of the supply chain. Das and Rahman (2010) found that opportunism among partners in a supply chain is mainly determined by economic factors such as payoff inequity, relational factors such as cultural diversity, and other factors such as time. Meanwhile, the establishment of trust needs to consider multi-stakeholders, such as buyer, seller, technology, and customers, and its construction needs a process orientation to form a multi-dimensional model. On the basis of this, Özer et al. (2014) further analyzed the impact of trust and supply chain system credibility level on global supply chain partnership management from two main factors: geography and culture. Zhang and Zhang (2017) explored the rigid management mechanism of mutual trust in a supply chain system and revealed the influence of institutional trust deviation on the willingness of secondary cooperation among supply chain nodes. Li et al (2018) empirically tested the positive effect of supply chain inter-firm calculate-trust and kindness trust on supply chain companies' improvisation ability and studied the mediation role of supply chain flexibility.

The status of trust in a supply chain system is not just a singular form (Marsh & Dibben, 2005). Li & Sun (2011) studied the trust crisis in supply chain cooperation in China and proposed a multi-agent grey diagnosis method for diagnosing organizational trust crisis possibilities in supply chains. For different trust issues, this method can effectively diagnose the source of the trust problem. Based on analyzing massive speculator behaviors caused by changes in market supply and demand, Li et al. (2014) introduced the speculative crisis of trust as an objective in an optimization model and obtained the supplier's optimal pricing strategy and the equilibrium number of speculators. Mora-Monge et al. (2019) found that in the context of web-enabled supply chains, trust, and integration, rather than trading partner power, significantly impact business performance, and establishing successful trust relationships with suppliers has proven to be a critical competitive advantage.

From the review of the research presented, it can be seen that although the trust problem in the supply chain system and consumer behaviors has been in existence for a long time, relevant research is still in its infancy (Irshad et al., 2020). Under complicated market conditions, the supply chain trust problem may cause a series of chain reactions, affecting the supply chain enterprises' normal operation. Therefore, an effective way or technology to manage supply chain trust is needed.

Application of Blockchain data in Supply Chains

The application of blockchain data technology in the supply chain is also a "hundred schools of thought contend." Toyoda et al. (2017) proposed a product ownership management system based on blockchain data technology, which significantly reduces the management cost of product ownership while ensuring the authenticity of supply chain products. Nakasumi (2017) proposed a supply chain information sharing management system based on blockchain data technology for the current supply chain management system's problems. The system guarantees the authenticity of information and solves insufficient supply under the double marginalization effects. Yang et al. (2018) discussed the application of the blockchain data smart contract in the supply chain, designed a new consensus mechanism named Stochastic Delegate Proof of Stake (SDPoS) based on blockchain data technology, and analyzed the advantages of blockchain data technology applied in a real business scenario and its supply chain information system.

Blockchain data is seen as a trust machine that can be used as a basis for drug data flow to create transparent drug transaction data in terms of supply chain governance, thereby changing the drug supply chain's governance model and enabling every node in the drug supply chain to participate in the chain's governance. From the perspective of a social contract, Wallenburg and Schäffler (2014) analyzed the interaction between relational governance and formal control in horizontal alliances, which helps to curb opportunism and achieve higher supply chain performance. Li and Liu (2017) proposed a supply chain intelligent governance mechanism based on blockchain data technology, which provides a new perspective for solving the opportunistic risks and trust issues in supply chain governance. Weber et al. (2016) built a decentralized supply chain mutual trust and cooperation model by means of the smart contract mechanism in the blockchain data, which enhances the flexibility of supply chain governance while promoting information interaction and sharing among entities in the supply chain system.

In supply chain finance, O'Leary (2017) purported the use of blockchain data technology can further improve the traditional inventory transaction detection mechanism, enabling the supply chain to obtain more favorable financing terms at lower signal costs. In addition, Zhu et al. (2018) noted blockchain data technology can simplify the paper application process in traditional supply chain finance and solve core enterprises' credit endorsement by combining the intelligent contract mechanism. New technologies, such as Big Data, the Io T, and blockchain data are readily adopted in supply chain finance. While transforming supply chain finance, blockchain data technology can unearth more transparent and shareable social credit information, which has promoted the construction of the credit value system (Wu & Deng, 2018).

From the literature review, it can be inferred there are only a handful of blockchain data applications in the supply chain. Most of them are focused on supply chain governance and management mode optimization or on supply chain finance. Yet, few scholars do integration research, making it difficult for blockchain data technology to play its role in the layer of integrated use value and exchange value. Further, there are few studies on the trust problem of the supply chain system; however, to date, no scholar has built a supply chain trust framework based on blockchain data technology. This study aimed to build a framework of a trust management mechanism in the supply chain by using blockchain data technology and solving supply chain trust at the technical level.

BLOCKCHAIN DATA AND THE LINK WITH TRUST

Blockchain data is a decentralized, distributed, shared network ledger technology based on a computer encryption algorithm, which involves vital technologies such as Merkle tree, Hash function, P2P network, propagation mechanism, and various proof mechanisms. The process is based on decentralized, trustless, open, transparent, and tamper-proof features (Feng et al., 2019; Swan, 2015). As the core supporting technology of bitcoin transactions, the complete blockchain data consists of two parts: the block header and the block body, as shown in Figure 1. The block header includes hash values, proof of work (POW) difficulty targets, and timestamp technology. Hash values are used to implement the docking between the block and the previous block. The POW difficulty targets are the difficulty coefficient set by the "miner" to mine the next block. The timestamp is used to record the block's time and add a time mark for the data information. The block body contains the block trading mechanism and its transaction data ledger.

Figure 1. Blockchain data random hash transaction structure

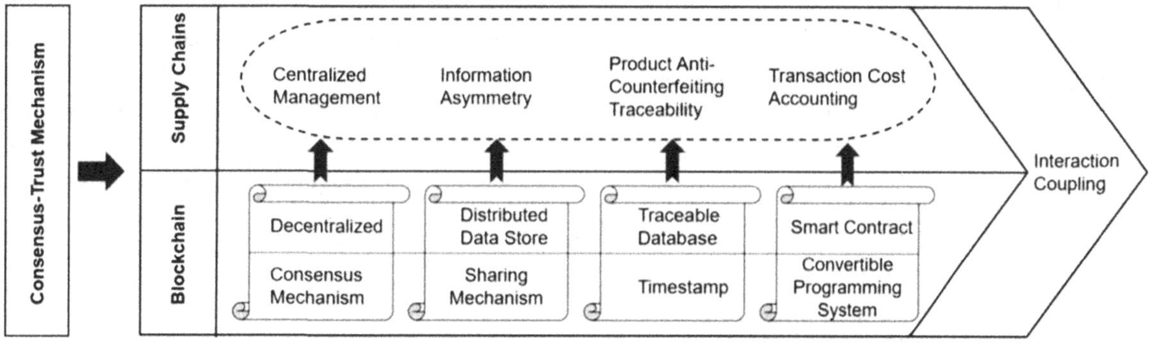

For owner 2 in Figure 1, the transaction information sent to him/her is first verified by owner 1's public key (the transaction information with the private key signature of owner 1), and owner 1 is authenticated. Next, owner 2 re-decomposes the verified transaction information, uses the private key to sign and seal the decomposed information, and then sends it to owner 3 through the public key of owner 3. By that analogy, digital signatures of transaction information with random hashes are transmitted along each block. Thus, the transaction information contained in the blockchain data is generated. Finally, the block containing the transaction information (the current block's random hash), contains the previous block's timestamp information. The random hash values are broadcasted on the whole network. Each transaction is then subject to joint supervision and verification, which strengthens each block's credibility and enhances the timestamp information of each block.

From the description given, blockchain data can force the trading parties to eliminate the traditional model of relying on personality and third-party institutions to establish trust. Owners of each block can trade without knowing the other party's relevant information, and only need to rely on the blockchain data random hash trading principle to achieve "trust transaction without trust." This trading mechanism changes the trust management model centered on core enterprises or third-party intermediaries in the traditional supply chain. All blockchain data participants do not need to deliberately pursue mutual trust and determine the identity and trading mode of both parties by protocols, rules, and public keys encryption, etc., establishing an algorithmic trust relationship (Shin, 2019). Thus, blockchain data technology, by nature, has genes for building a world of trust. Freedom, equality, openness, and sharing are the spiritual concepts behind it. These concepts have surpassed the value embodied in the technology itself, which is the inexhaustible motive force for blockchain data's rapid development. Core features, such as decentralization, autonomy, and unchangeability, provide the technical foundation for the trust mechanism. The side chain also leaves enough room for the flexible management of trust, makes the specific trust mechanism not stick to the blockchain data's technical framework, and opens up the connection between the blockchain data and the external world. Therefore, what blockchain data brings is a change of thinking mode and a great mission to reconstruct the world of trust.

COUPLING ANALYSIS OF BLOCKCHAIN DATA AND SUPPLY CHAIN TRUST MANAGEMENT

The trust of supply chain members refers to risk sharing, cooperation, mutual benefit of each member, and no opportunistic behavior that harms other members' interests. The core enterprise's expectations and confidence are used to maintain the supply chain network (Wang, 2010). However, trust is not formed spontaneously through the expectations of the supply chain system. In other words, trust still needs a specific technology or method to manage. Some scholars define supply chain trust management as the management of the whole process of the formation of trust in the supply chain system based on trust attributes from the perspective of the supply chain system (Lei & Yu, 2009). Trust attributes include cultural attributes, social attributes, and economic attributes. The relationship between the three attributes is shown in Figure 2. The three attributes will be used to analyze the coupling relationship between blockchain data and supply chain trust management.

Figure 2. Relationship of trust attributes

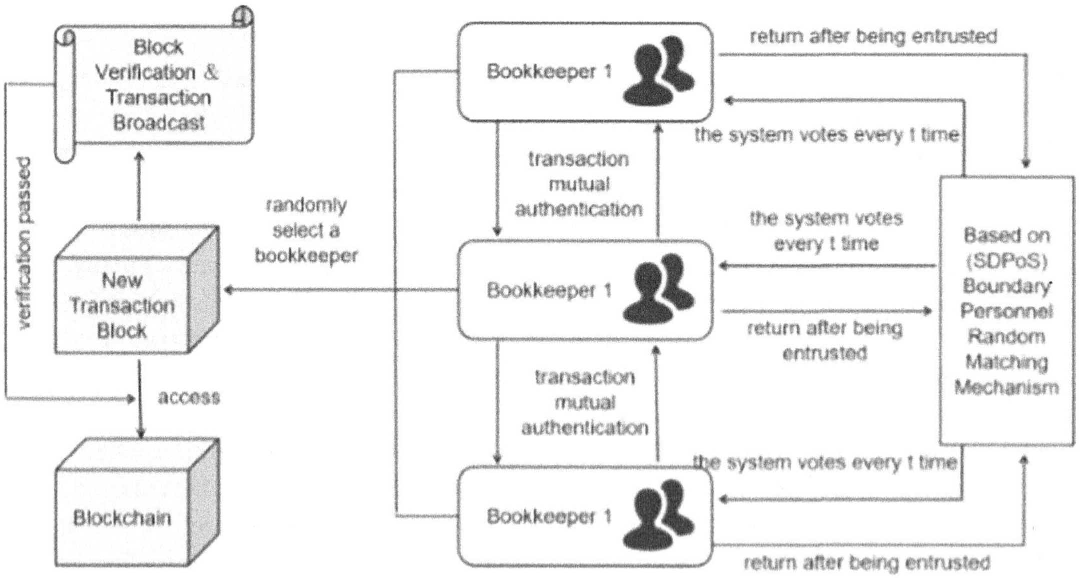

Value Coupling Based on Cultural Attributes

Since its inception, blockchain data technology has produced countless brilliant achievements (Grover et al., 2019; Kshetri, 2017, 2018). It is called a revolutionary technology comparable to the Internet. However, it is not the blockchain data technology itself that brings change, but the values and concepts behind it, such as openness, transparency, sharing, and mutual benefits. This standpoint is consistent with scholars' interpretation of group trusts among society members, including supply chains. They believe that supply chain members are based on shared values, and trust is one of them (Dyer & Singh, 1998; Joshi & Campbell, 2003). In practical terms, a supply chain system is a hierarchical and diversified chain organization, which realizes resource sharing through information exchange among various subjects (Bharadwaj, 2000; Fiala, 2005; Prajogo & Olhager, 2012). It can be seen that from the cultural attributes of trust, there is a coupling relationship between the blockchain data and the supply chain, as shown in Figure 3. Based on the common openness, transparency, sharing, and reciprocity attributes, the coupling between the blockchain data system and the supply chain system have a cultural basis. In applying the blockchain data to the supply chain, the two constantly interact and feedback to optimize the overall system.

Figure 3. Value coupling under the interaction between blockchain data and supply chains

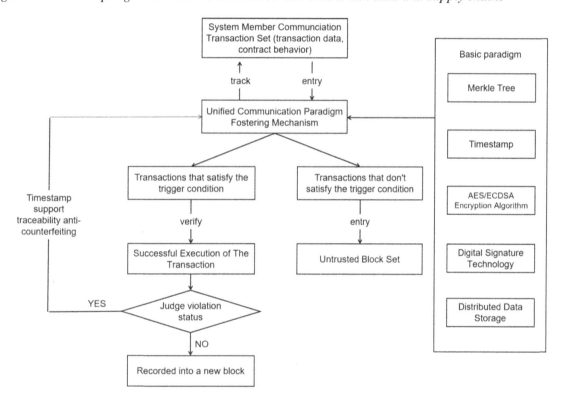

Coupling of Consensus-Trust Mechanism Based on Social Attributes

Blockchain data platforms possess a specific mechanism that ensures data immutability along the ledger called consensus. The consensus's particular scope is to maintain a general agreement between the nodes of the network about all submitted transaction information (Litke et al., 2019). The transactions between members of the supply chain are complex and changeable. They are subject to a centralized management model, with limited information sharing between members and product anti-counterfeiting traceability. The asymmetrical information and the members' limitation on knowledge and rationality may result in a chain system full of uncertainty and risk. From the social attributes of trust, we know that trust is a processing mechanism for when people face uncertainty and risk. Trust is undoubtedly a rational choice to mitigate the risks if there is no other way to reduce or avoid them. From the perspective of the social attributes of trust, blockchain data's technical characteristics, such as decentralization and distributed storage, effectively solve the problem of trust caused by centralized management and information asymmetry in supply chain management. Thus, there is a coupling relationship between the blockchain data and the supply chain in the consensus-trust mechanism, as shown in Figure 4.

Figure 4. Coupling of consensus-trust mechanism between blockchain data and supply chains

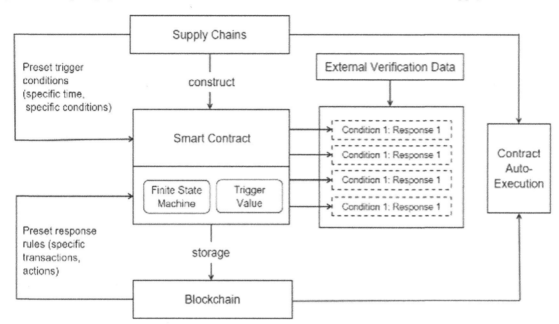

Incentive Coupling Based on Economic Attributes

Trust between members of the supply chain is dependent upon whether or not the economic benefits increase. The ultimate goal of supply chain trust management is to ensure that all members' interests are not damaged. Based on rational choice theory, we know that all system members are rational and calculate the credibility of one another through the available information, and then try to maximize the utility of the system by obtaining mutual trust (Simon, 1955).

From the economic attributes, trust is a choice driven by the interest incentive of the supply chain members. Blockchain data can construct, and process various smart contracts based on its related mechanisms (storage mechanism, transaction processing mechanism, and complete state machine). The supply chain members accessing the smart contract do not have to rely on hard-to-obtain information to calculate each other's trustworthiness, which ensures the automatic execution of transactions within the supply chain system by triggering the complete state machine of the smart contract. Therefore, irrational human intervention is avoided, and overall benefits increase under rational action. Besides, the blockchain data has a coupling relationship in realizing the benefit incentive of supply chain trust management (see Figure 5). Supply chain member transactions mainly rely on establishing contracts and punishment mechanisms to promote the establishment and maintenance of trust. Contracts are an indispensable element in the formation of trust in the supply chain and the carrier of the economic attributes of trust in the process of trust formation. The blockchain data establishes satisfactory contracts for the supply chain members through smart contracts, urges each "fractal element" in the supply chain system to fulfill the responsibilities stipulated in the contract, and reduces the cost of negotiations among enterprises.

Figure 5. Coupling of interest motives under the interaction of blockchain data and supply chains

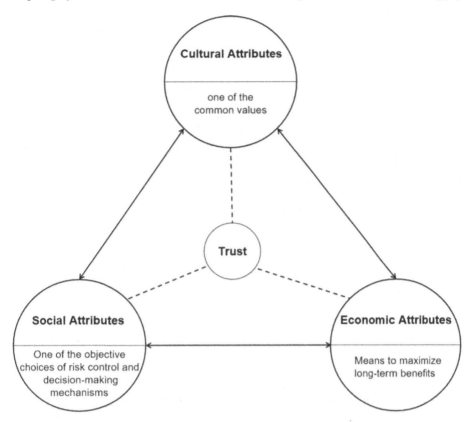

SOLUTIONS AND RECOMMENDATIONS

Based on the analysis of the coupling of blockchain data and supply chain trust management presented, the blockchain data's technical characteristics and the problems to be solved are coupling with one another. As a complex open system integrating economic and social attributes, the supply chain aims to increase the enterprises' value on the entire chain. Trust management aims to promote a high degree of trust between members in the supply chain system, and then promote the supply chain system's evolution to a higher level. Therefore, supply chain trust management must strictly meet the requirements of the supply chain system. To address this, the study develops a credit management mechanism in the supply chain in a blockchain data model based on systems theory principles. It promotes the realization of trust in the supply chain system (see Figure 6).

Figure 6. Supply chain trust management mechanism based on blockchain data technology

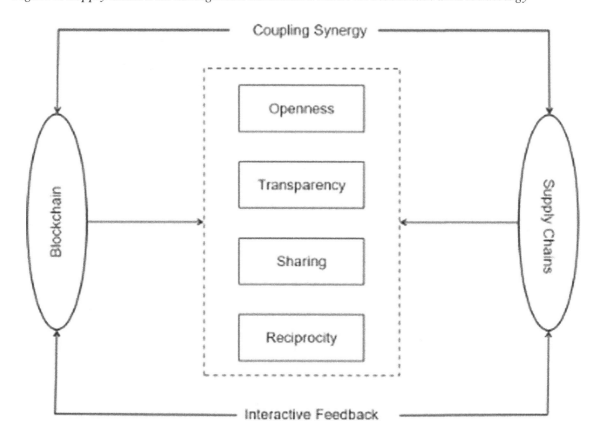

Figure 6 illustrates how the trust management mechanism in the supply chain consists of two parts: the rigid management mechanism of supply chain trust, and the flexible management mechanism of supply chain trust. These two parts jointly contribute to the formation of high trust in the supply chain. Starting from the supply chain system's operation mechanism and combining the related theories of supply chain trust management, the two parts were divided into five components that can directly link to the blockchain data technology. Combined with blockchain data technology, the whole framework is divided into three layers, namely the contract layer, the consensus layer, and the data layer.

Contract Layer

In the blockchain data architecture, the contract layer encapsulates classification scripts, algorithms, and smart contracts, which are the basis of the blockchain data programmable features. The smart contract is the core part of the entire contract layer. The relevant parties jointly formulate contract content, construct the contract trigger mechanism through programming to achieve the contract's coding, and finally embed it in the blockchain data to complete the intelligent implementation of the contract. As shown in Figure 7, the contract layer contains two sub-items of system members': satisfaction contract and the system punishment and incentive mechanism, which are the most direct embodiments of the supply chain system's economic attributes. A satisfaction contract means that the supply chain system members formulate collaboration agreements to meet one another's interests under the principle of "satisfaction" to eliminate significant opinion differences over the objectives, reducing collaboration failure. Since trust between system members arises from transactions between organizations that are necessarily accompanied by the agreement and execution of contracts, the contract is both the basis for the standardization of transactions and the best measure of credibility among members of the system. Therefore, in the supply chain trust management, the system "satisfaction" contract should be implemented in smart contracts, making the contract execution more scientific while saving the workforce and improving efficiency. Moreover, any contract's actual execution process is bound to be accompanied by the risk of breaching the contract. For the members of the system to implement the contract well, the punishment and incentive measures must also be packaged into the smart contract as the contract content. In the event of default or dishonesty, the penalty mechanism will be triggered, and the smart contracts will impose penalties on this behavior in accordance with the content of the agreement.

Figure 7. The operational mechanism of the contract layer

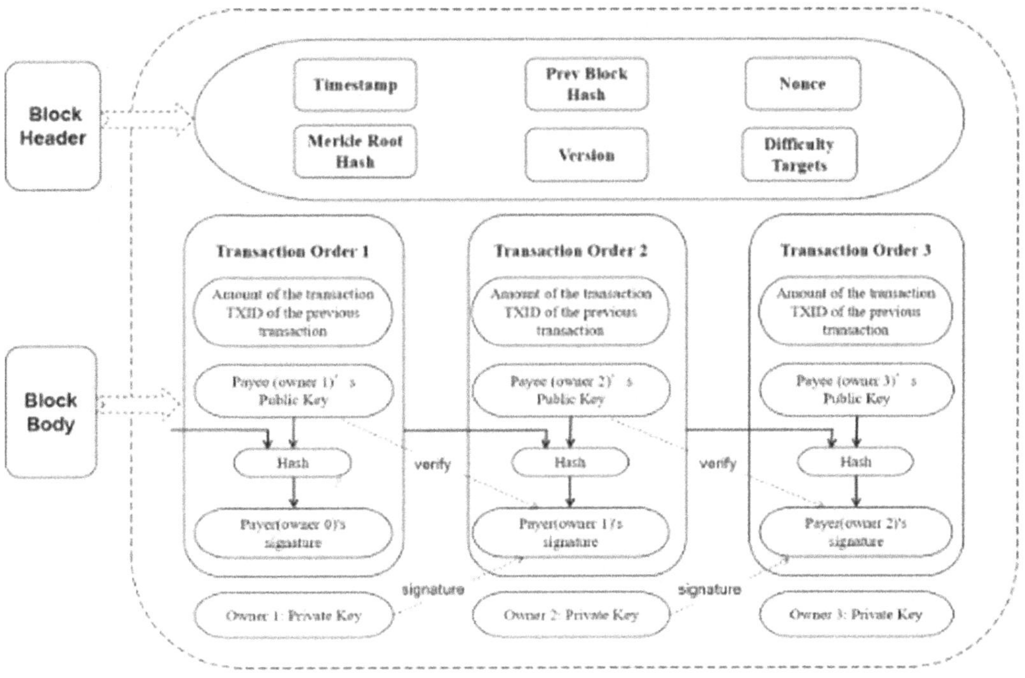

Consensus Layer

The consensus layer in the blockchain data architecture primarily includes the consensus algorithm and its mechanism. The hierarchy's main function is to allow the distributed nodes to communicate with one another in the decentralized blockchain data network and reach a consensus on the validity of the block data. It is the core technology of the blockchain data and the governance mechanism of the blockchain data community. Researchers have proposed various consensus mechanisms, and the characteristics and application scenarios of different consensus mechanisms are also different. Therefore, considering the multi-center characteristics of supply chain alliances, Yang et al. (2018) proposed a Stochastic Delegate Proof of Stake (SDPoS), which will hold a vote at a specific time to select the fiduciary bookkeepers of the supply chain system (i.e., the boundary personnel of the supply chain system). After the transaction occurs between the supply chain nodes, the system will entrust the selected two to three bookkeepers to perform two-way verification of the transaction and randomly assign one person to record the system transaction and generate a new block. Due to the random dynamic nature of the mechanism, voting will be re-scheduled at specific times, significantly improving transaction information reliability while effectively preventing the bookkeepers from cheating. The ideas behind the mechanism and its operating mechanism are conducive to establishing the boundary personnel's interpersonal trust in the supply chain nodes and can cultivate the shared values of the supply chain system. It is technically feasible to encapsulate the establishment of interpersonal trust of border personnel and the cultivation of common values into the consensus layer (Figure 8).

Figure 8. Operational mechanism of the consensus layer

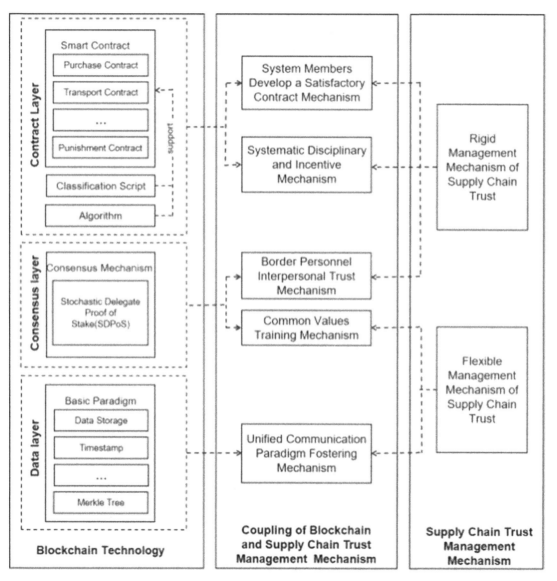

First, it is essentially the result of "rigid" management relying on the various types of smart contracts included in the contract layer and the system trust formed by the reward and punishment mechanism. Nevertheless, this trust based on the unmanned intelligent code mechanism often lacks "flexibility" and "human interest." Because the blockchain data technology itself is relatively easy to meet the rigid management of the supply chain, ignoring the cultural and social attributes of trust and neglecting the requirements of the supply chain system's social role. Therefore, this study constructs the interpersonal trust mechanism of the boundary personnel with "flexibility" and "human interest" and realizes the mechanism's establishment and operational process through the SDPoS consensus mechanism so that the trust management of the supply chain system can be both flexible and rigid.

Second, from the perspective of trust's cultural attributes, trust also arises from the cultivation of shared values among organizations. As a multi-node complex system, the supply chain is no exception. Establishing common values will help the formation and consolidation of supply chain trust. However, the primary condition for the formation of common values resides in consensus and shared knowledge. Combined with the spirit of openness, transparency, sharing, and reciprocity embodied in the blockchain data technology itself, the SDPoS consensus mechanism creates such conditions for forming common values and is technically feasible.

Data Layer

In the blockchain data architecture, the data layer is the lowest-level technology, but it is the foundation of the entire blockchain data system. It includes the data storage paradigm Merkle tree, AES and ECDSA encryption algorithms, and digital signature technology such as a timestamp (Yang et al., 2019). It laid the foundation for cultivating a unified communication paradigm for the supply chain system. The consensus mechanism can gradually form the shared values of the supply chain system. As time goes on, it will eventually become the consensus of all nodes, but the interaction between systems is happening all the time. The theory of public relations shows that the unified communication paradigm of system members, such as how and the method of dealing with business or solving problems, will directly affect the establishment of trust between systems (Grunig, 1989). The blockchain data data layer's storage technologies are equivalent to providing a unified credit paradigm for members of the supply chain system. As shown in Figure 9, the technologies are embedded in the unified communication paradigm cultivating mechanism; the unified data storage rules that the Merkle tree can establish, and the digital signature technology jointly held by the system members can print standard timestamps for the data. After the mechanism uniformly filters the system transaction set, the new block's compliance date will be written. The data generated by the violation transaction can be returned to the state before the entry under the timestamp technology's support. The responsible party for the loss of trust is found according to the traceability of the data. The untrustworthy behavior is recorded in the untrusted block set, thus preventing untrustworthy behavior at the root.

Therefore, the data layer establishes the basic principles and methods of "doing things" for the supply chain system. The system unified communication paradigm and system common values established on this basis complement one another, jointly promote the formation of a trust culture in the supply chain system, and play an essential supporting role in forming a trust management mechanism in the supply chain.

Figure 9. Operational mechanism of the data layer

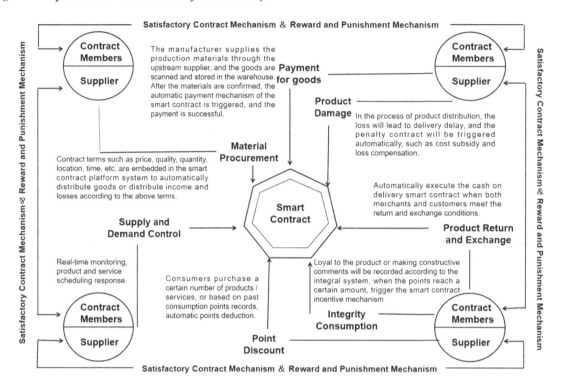

FUTURE RESEARCH DIRECTIONS

To tackle the increasing issue of opportunistic behavior in supply chain management, it is essential to identify the underlying processes and theoretical possibilities of how building a high level of trust improves the stability and efficiency using blockchain technology. While this work examines the data encryption technology of blockchain, it does not provide sufficient proof in traditional statistical modelling. Future research may examine the robustness of the finding by collecting data from the business field across different cultural contexts. Statistical significance is anticipated for the connection between blockchain technology and the supply chain's trust management. In addition, the significant association between varied management mechanism types in forming supply chain trust is plausible and should be verified by future experimental studies.\

CONCLUSION

From the perspective of system coupling, the study innovatively applied blockchain data technology to the supply chain's trust management mechanism, which solved the supply chain trust crisis brought on by new opportunism. The main research conclusions are as follows:

First, blockchain data technology's application to the supply chain's trust management mechanism is technically reasonable and feasible. According to the cultural, social, and economic attributes of trust, it is concluded that blockchain data and supply chain trust management are highly coupled in terms of value concept, consensus-trust mechanism, and interest motivation.

Second, system members formulate satisfactory contracts, systematic punishment and incentives, and interpersonal trust of border personnel, which constitute a rigid management mechanism for supply chain trust. The cultivation of shared values and the cultivation of a unified communication paradigm constitutes a flexible management mechanism for supply chain trust. Both management mechanisms jointly promote a high level of trust in the supply chain system under blockchain data technology.

Third, the contract layer's three technical architecture levels, the consensus layer, and the data layer of the blockchain data constitute the trust management's internal operation mechanism in the supply chain. The data layer is the foundation of the blockchain data system, which provides essential technical support for supply chain trust management. The unified data storage rules and data encryption technology lays the foundation for cultivating system members' unified communication paradigm. The consensus layer is the core of the blockchain data architecture, promoting the close connection between the core value concept of the blockchain data, the shared value fostering mechanism, and the border personnel's interpersonal trust mechanism. The contract layer is the intelligent extension layer of the blockchain data architecture. The encapsulated smart contract provides technical support for the operation of the supply chain's trust rigid management mechanism.

The analysis provides theoretical justifications for the role of trust management mechanisms in blockchain data science and uncovers the underlying technical process of how trust could be built using blockchain data technologies. The coupling relationship between blockchain data and trust management provides novel implications for building trust among opportunistic behaviors through supply chain management techniques.

REFERENCES

Bharadwaj, A. S. (2000). A resource-based perspective on information technology capability and firm performance: An empirical investigation. *Management Information Systems Quarterly*, *24*(1), 169–196. doi:10.2307/3250983

Das, T. K., & Rahman, N. (2010). Determinants of partner opportunism in strategic alliances: A conceptual framework. *Journal of Business and Psychology*, *25*(1), 55–74. doi:10.100710869-009-9132-2

Dyer, J. H., & Singh, H. (1998). The relational view: Cooperative strategy and sources of interorganizational competitive advantage. *Academy of Management Review*, *23*(4), 660–679. doi:10.5465/amr.1998.1255632

Feng, Q., He, D., Zeadally, S., Khan, M. K., & Kumar, N. (2019). A survey on privacy protection in blockchain data system. *Journal of Network and Computer Applications*, *126*(1), 45–58. doi:10.1016/j.jnca.2018.10.020

Fiala, P. (2005). Information sharing in supply chains. *Omega: The International Journal of Management Science*, *33*(5), 419–423. doi:10.1016/j.omega.2004.07.006

Gerwin, D. (2004). Coordinating new product development in strategic alliances. *Academy of Management Review*, *29*(2), 241–257. doi:10.2307/20159031

Grover, P., Kar, A. K., Janssen, M., & Ilavarasan, P. V. (2019). Perceived usefulness, ease of use and user acceptance of blockchain data technology for digital transactions–insights from user-generated content on Twitter. *Enterprise Information Systems*, *13*(6), 771–800. doi:10.1080/17517575.2019.1599446

Irshad, M., Ahmad, M. S., & Malik, O. F. (2020). Understanding consumers' trust in social media marketing environment. *International Journal of Retail & Distribution Management, 48*(11), 1195–1212. doi:10.1108/IJRDM-07-2019-0225

Joshi, A. W., & Campbell, A. J. (2003). Effect of environmental dynamism on relational governance in manufacturer-supplier relationships: A contingency framework and an empirical test. *Journal of the Academy of Marketing Science, 31*(2), 176–188. doi:10.1177/0092070302250901

Kale, P., Dyer, J. H., & Singh, H. (2002). Alliance capability, stock market response, and long-term alliance success: The role of the alliance function. *Strategic Management Journal, 23*(8), 747–767. doi:10.1002mj.248

Kshetri, N. (2017). Blockchain data's roles in strengthening cybersecurity and protecting privacy. *Telecommunications Policy, 41*(10), 1027–1038. doi:10.1016/j.telpol.2017.09.003

Kshetri, N. (2018). 1 Blockchain data's roles in meeting key supply chain management objectives. *International Journal of Information Management, 39*(1), 80–89. doi:10.1016/j.ijinfomgt.2017.12.005

Kwon, I. W. G., & Suh, T. (2004). Factors affecting the level of trust and commitment in supply chain relationships. *The Journal of Supply Chain Management, 40*(1), 4–14. doi:10.1111/j.1745-493X.2004.tb00165.x

Lei, X., & Yu, L. (2009). Research on the construction of supply chain trust management system. *Contemporary Finance and Economics*, 78-81.

Leng, Y., Dai, A., & Li, J. (2019). Research on the trust cultivation mechanism of China's agricultural product supply chain. *Shandong Social Science*, 137-142.

Li, H., & Sun, J. (2011). Grey group diagnosis method for supply chain organization trust crisis. *Journal of Industrial Engineering and Engineering Management, 25*(1), 155–160.

Li, J., Luo, X., & Xu, M. (2014). Supply chain optimization strategy introducing speculative trust crisis. *Journal of Industrial Engineering and Engineering Management, 28*(1), 137–144.

Li, T., Qiao, L., & Yang, P. (2018). Research on the influence mechanism of inter-firm trust on supply chain enterprise organization impromptu—The mediating role of supply chain flexibility and the adjustment function of interactive memory system. *Nankai Management Review, 21*(1), 74–84.

Litke, A., Anagnostopoulos, D., & Varvarigou, T. (2019). Blockchain datas for supply chain management: Architectural elements and challenges towards a global scale deployment. *Logistics, 3*(1), 5. doi:10.3390/logistics3010005

Liu, R., An, E., & Zhou, W. (2021). The effect of online search volume on financial performance: Marketing insight from Google trends data of the top five US technology firms. *Journal of Marketing Theory and Practice, 4*(29), 1–12. doi:10.1080/10696679.2020.1867478

Liu, Y., Liu, J., & Zhang, Z. (2019). Review of research on blockchain data consensus mechanism. *Chinese Journal of Cryptography*, 395-432.

Marsh, S., & Dibben, M. R. (2005). Trust, untrust, distrust and mistrust–An exploration of the dark(er) side. In *International conference on trust management* (pp. 17-33). Springer. 10.1007/11429760_2

Mingang, Z., Qian, L., Huanwen, P., & Jia, Z. (2017). The relationship among information technology capability, trust and supply chain integration. *Management Review*, *29*(12), 217. http://journal05.magtech. org.cn/jweb_glpl/ EN/abstract/abstract949.shtml

Mora-Monge, C., Quesada, G., Gonzalez, M. E., & Davis, J. M. (2019). Trust, power and supply chain integration in web-enabled supply chains. *Supply Chain Management*, *24*(4), 524–539. Advance online publication. doi:10.1108/SCM-02-2018-0078

Nakasumi, M. N. M. (2017, July). Information sharing for supply chain management based on block chain technology. In *2017 IEEE 19th conference on business informatics (CBI)* (Vol. 1, pp. 140-149). IEEE. 10.1109/CBI.2017.56

Nyaga, G. N., Whipple, J. M., & Lynch, D. F. (2010). Examining supply chain relationships: Do buyer and supplier perspectives on collaborative relationships differ? *Journal of Operations Management*, *28*(2), 101–114. doi:10.1016/j.jom.2009.07.005

O'Leary, D. E. (2017). Configuring blockchain data architectures for transaction information in blockchain data consortiums: The case of accounting and supply chain systems. *Intelligent Systems in Accounting, Finance & Management*, *24*(4), 138–147. doi:10.1002/isaf.1417

Özer, Ö., Zheng, Y., & Ren, Y. (2014). Trust, trustworthiness, and information sharing in supply chains bridging China and the United States. *Management Science*, *60*(10), 2435–2460. doi:10.1287/ mnsc.2014.1905

Prajogo, D., & Olhager, J. (2012). Supply chain integration and performance: The effects of long-term relationships, information technology and sharing, and logistics integration. *International Journal of Production Economics*, *135*(1), 514–522. doi:10.1016/j.ijpe.2011.09.001

Qrunig, J. E., & Qrunig, L. S. (1989). Toward a theory of the public relations behavior of organizations: Review of a program of research. *Public Relations Research Annual*, *1*(1), 27–63. Advance online publication. doi:10.12071532754xjprr0101-4_2

Shin, D. D. (2019). Blockchain data: The emerging technology of digital trust. *Telematics and Informatics*, *45*, 101278. doi:10.1016/j.tele.2019.101278

Simon, H. A. (1955). A behavioral model of rational choice. *The Quarterly Journal of Economics*, *69*(1), 99–118. doi:10.2307/1884852

Slamet, W. S. W., Made, K. M. K., Tubagus, P., Agus, S., & Wiwoho, M. S. (2017). Internet of things (IoT) as green city economic development smart transportation system. In *MATEC Web of Conferences* (Vol. 138, p. 07015). EDP Sciences. 10.1051/matecconf/201713807015

Swan, M. (2015). *Blockchain data: Blueprint for a new economy*. O'Reilly Media, Inc.

Taylor, A. (2005). An operations perspective on strategic alliance success factors: An exploratory study of alliance managers in the software industry. *International Journal of Operations & Production Management*, *25*(5), 469–490. Advance online publication. doi:10.1108/01443570510593157

Tian, Z., Hassan, A. F. S., & Razak, N. H. A. (2018. May). Big data and SME financing in China. In Journal of Physics: Conference Series (Vol. 1018, No. 1, p. 012002). IOP Publishing. doi:10.1088/1742-6596/1018/1/012002

Toyoda, K., Mathiopoulos, P. T., Sasase, I., & Ohtsuki, T. (2017). A novel blockchain data-based product ownership management system (POMS) for anti-counterfeits in the post supply chain. *IEEE Access: Practical Innovations, Open Solutions*, *5*(1), 17465–17477. doi:10.1109/ACCESS.2017.2720760

Wallenburg, C. M., & Schäffler, T. (2014). The interplay of relational governance and formal control in horizontal alliances: A social contract perspective. *The Journal of Supply Chain Management*, *50*(2), 41–58. doi:10.1111/jscm.12041

Wang, L. (2010). Analysis of the formation and governance mechanism of the trust relationship in supply chain based on game theory. *Soft Science*, *24*(2), 56–59.

Weber, I., Xu, X., Riveret, R., Governatori, G., Ponomarev, A., & Mendling, J. (2016). Untrusted business process monitoring and execution using blockchain data. In *International Conference on Business Process Management* (pp. 329-347). Springer. 10.1007/978-3-319-45348-4_19

Wu, R., & Deng, J. (2018). Internet + supply chain finance: New ideas for SME financing. *Enterprise Economy*, *37*(1), 108–114.

Xie, J., Tang, H., Huang, T., Yu, F. R., Xie, R., Liu, J., & Liu, Y. (2019). A survey of blockchain data technology applied to smart cities: Research issues and challenges. *IEEE Communications Surveys and Tutorials*, *21*(3), 2794–2830. doi:10.1109/COMST.2019.2899617

Yang, H., Sun, L., & Zhao, X. (2018) Building a trust and supply chain information platform based on blockchain data technology. *Science & Technology Progress and Policy*, 21-31.

Yang, X., Liu, J., & Li, X. (2019). Research and analysis of blockchain data data. In Journal of Physics: Conference Series (Vol.1237, No. 2, p. 22084). IOP Publishing. doi:10.1088/1742-6596/1237/2/022084

Zhang, H., & Zhang, Z. (2017). Empirical study on the influence of institutional trust deviation on re-cooperation willingness. *Soft Science*, *31*(1), 38–41.

Zhu, X., He, Q., & Guo, S. (2018). Application of blockchain data technology in supply chain finance. *China Circulation Economy*, *32*(1), 111–119.

Using Machine Learning to Extract Insights From Consumer Data

Hannah H. Chang
Singapore Management University, Singapore

Anirban Mukherjee
Cornell University, USA

INTRODUCTION

Advances in digital technology have led to the digitization of everyday activities of billions of people around the world, generating vast amounts of data on human behavior. From what people buy, to what information they search for, to how they navigate the social, digital, and physical world, human behavior can now be measured at a scale and level of precision that human history has not witnessed before. These developments have created unprecedented opportunities for those interested in understanding observable human behavior–social scientists, businesses, and policymakers—to (re)examine theoretical and substantive questions regarding people's behavior. Moreover, technology has led to the emergence of new forms of consumer marketplace—crowdfunding (whereby entrepreneurs obtaining funds from an anonymous online crowd; Mukherjee, Chang, & Chattopadhyay 2019) and crowdsourcing (whereby organizations gather new ideas and business solutions from an anonymous online crowd; Mukherjee, Xiao, Wang, & Contractor, 2018)—which not only details people's behavior in exchange of products and services but also led to new behavior.

Making sense of the vast amount of fine-grained data about consumer behavior, however, poses nontrivial challenges for marketing researchers and practitioners. In the past, behavioral data about consumers originated from sources such as point-of-purchase scanner data, customer attitude or satisfaction surveys, consumer purchase panels, and laboratory-based experiments. These traditional sources of consumer data are much smaller in scale, much more structured (e.g., in numbers-based data formats which can be directly analyzed), and measured to purpose, than new consumer data sources. Consequently, many of the methods used to analyze traditional customer data—such as conventional econometric and statistical methods—are not designed to deal with the breadth, precision, and scale of the new consumer data sources publicly available, which tend to be unstructured—written texts, images, audios, and videos—and require parsing and processing before data can be analyzed.

Fortunately, a parallel trend to the emergence of "big data" on consumer behavior has been the emergence of computational methods and analysis techniques needed to deal with these new sources of behavioral data—which tend to be more unstructured, of much larger scale, and noisier. Specifically, data on consumers come in four basic forms: (1) structured data, (e.g., number of likes on Facebook), (2) textual data (e.g., tweets on Twitter), (3) audial data (e.g., Spotify radio advertisements), and (4) visual data (e.g., photos on TripAdvisor). Consumer data can involve only one form, such as textual messages (e.g., tweets on Twitter) and visual images (e.g., Instagram photos). Consumer data can also involve more than one form. Video data, which are increasingly prevalent, combine a series of visual images (typically, 24 visual frames per second) and an audio track. Many publicly available sources of consumer relevant

DOI: 10.4018/978-1-7998-9220-5.ch107

data detailing people's consumption behavior involve multiple data elements. For example, consumer data from YouTube combines all four of these basic forms—audial and visual data in the video, textual data in the comments, and structured data in the number of views and likes. For each of these four data elements, new machine learning and big data methods enable us to simply and easily parse the data to uncover consumer insights if analysts are equipped with the right toolkit.

BACKGROUND

As both the availability of large-scale behavioral data and computational analysis methods are recent and emerging developments, many behavioral scientists and practitioners may be unaware or unfamiliar with (1) new sources of secondary data and types of data that are available to extracts insights about consumer behavior, and (2) new analysis techniques to study consumer behavior at scale. Therefore, motivated by these recent developments and opportunities, the main objective of this book chapter is to discuss computational methods (specifically, machine learning methods) for researchers and practitioners interested in addressing customer-relevant questions using new secondary data sources that are publicly available. This chapter offers a primer on the application of computational social science for understanding consumer data for both researchers and practitioners.

The rest of this chapter is organized as follows. First, types of unstructured data pertaining to consumer behavior—including the information that consumers are exposed to and their digital footprints in the modern marketplace—will be decomposed to their underlying data elements. Next, machine learning and computational techniques to parse and process unstructured customer data are described. Finally, potential directions for future research using consumer data are discussed.

TYPES OF CUSTOMER-RELEVANT DATA

Consumers today have unprecedented access to numerous types of information and media. New forms of information environments, often fueled by technology, have also emerged since the 2010s. For example, reward-based crowdfunding platforms like Kickstarter and Indiegogo post videos and text descriptions about new product innovations (Dhanani & Mukherjee, 2017; Allon & Babich, 2020). Debt-based crowdfunding platforms such as Lending Club and Funding Societies post text descriptions about business loans (Lee, Chang, & Mukherjee, 2020). As self-contained marketplaces, crowdfunding data include comprehensive descriptions of the factors that influence consumers and investors as well as detailed accounts of purchase and exchange behavior (Mukherjee et al., 2019). App-based ecosystems enable marketers to promote "green" initiatives as a part of their corporate social responsibility strategy (Merrill, Chang, Liang, Lan and Wong 2019). These platforms offer a wealth of detailed data to study emerging consumer behavior in new marketplaces. New voice assistants such as Amazon's Alexa and Apple's Siri allows consumers to search for product information through voice based commands, simplifying consumers' purchase journey, which led to changing customer behavior. This development also led to emerging forms of voice-assisted retail shopping that is often dubbed "voice commerce" (i.e., v-commerce), all of which offer a wealth of data to study emerging customer behavior in new marketplaces. Moreover, new digital channels help facilitate communication among businesses, consumers, investors, and other stakeholders.

Much of customer-relevant data today are publicly available, giving researchers' and 2 unprecedented access to study modern consumer behavior and generate behavioral insights. For example, Yelp released an academic dataset which contains description of patrons' ratings, reviews, and images of restaurants and businesses on its platform, while Twitter offered an API that facilitates data collection of tweets posted on Twitter. Spotify also released its web API to allow easier data access for researchers to collect people's music listening behavior on the platform. Many other customer-facing firms similarly provided opportunities for researchers and analysts to access their data.

Consumers information environment—including information and media that consumers are exposed to in learning about brands and products as well as data generated by consumers' behavior—can be decomposed to four basic data elements: structured (numbers), textual, audio, and visual data. Table 1 outlines examples of customer-relevant data along the four basic data elements. They are discussed next.

Table 1. Overview of customer-relevant data in the modern marketplace

Data elements	Sample sources of such data from information shown to consumers in the marketplace	Sample sources of such data captured from consumer behavior	Common computational techniques for data processing
Structured data	● Price ● Consumer reports product ratings ● Product quantity ● Classification systems used to describe products (e.g., product categories)	● Customer review ratings ● Attitude surveys ● Satisfaction surveys	● Standard statistical models ● Standard econometrics models
Textual data	● Product descriptions ● Consumer reports product reviews ● Packaging labels	● Product reviews ● Email inquiries to customer services ● Social media posts (e.g., tweets on Twitter)	● Linguistic inquiry and word count (LIWC) ● Natural language processing ● Sentiment analysis ● Topic modeling
Audial data	● Audiobooks ● Earnings conference call ● Music ● Social audio app (e.g., Clubhouse) ● Sonic branding ● Radio ● Podcasts ● Voice assistants (e.g., Apple's Siri, Amazon's Alexa)	● Customer service calls ● Conversation log with voice assistants ● Voice search	● Automatic speech recognition ● Waveform analysis
Visual data	● Brand logos ● Digital ads ● Print ads ● Product images ● Visual frames sampled from videos	● Social media photos (e.g., Instagram photos) ● Influencer videos	● Computer vision ● Image analysis and processing

Structured Data

Structured data are represented by numbers across the measurement scales (nominal, ordinal, internal, and ratio scales) and are typically denoted as quantitative data. Structured data is typical and common in settings where it is feasible to directly measure the intensity and extent of communications and interactions. For example, on Tripadvisor, it is possible to measure the number of reviews that were posted for a hotel property and the rating (e.g., a 5-point scale in which five points represent highest rating) that was given by users to the hotel property, in order to understand customer engagement with the brand and property and customer satisfaction with the property. In another example, on a common crowdsourcing website (Threadless.com), users upload new designs, rate each other's designs, and purchase selected designs. On this website, it is possible to measure the ratings given by users to different designs and to relate these to sales (Mukherjee et al., 2018). Furthermore, a key source of structured data (from both online and offline sources) is data on consumers' transactions, including descriptors of what the consumer purchased, how and when the purchase was consumed, and the consumer's satisfaction with the purchase. These data frequently are the dependent variable in financial models of the firms' decision calculus such as deciding on pricing and promotions, which are used to accurately and holistically measure firms' performance (Lee et al., 2020).

Textual Data

Communication is an integral part of the marketplace. It fundamentally shapes the relationships, and the transmission of information, between businesses, consumers, investors, public agencies, and the society at large. Among the various types of unstructured data, extant research on communication—spanning marketing, psychology, computer science, economics, and information systems—has primarily focused on written (text-based) communication such as product reviews (e.g., Tirunillai & Tellis, 2014; Van Laer et al., 2019), product descriptions (e.g., Chang & Pham, 2018; Mukherjee & Chang, 2022), movie storylines (e.g., Toubia, Iyengar, Bunnell, & Lemaire, 2019; Mukherjee et al. 2018), consumer application forms (e.g., Netzer, Lemaire, & Herzenstein, 2019), advertising slogans, social media posts (e.g., Hamilton, Schlosser, & Chen, 2017; Chang & Hung, 2018), marketing communication from businesses to consumers (e.g., Culotta & Cutler, 2016; Villarroel Ordenes et al., 2019), and newspapers or reference articles (e.g., Mikolov et al., 2013; Chen et al., 2017). While these written communications are readily available on the Internet for data collection, digitization of information has further increased the availability of textual data.

Audial Data

Audial data represent another fruitful opportunity for understanding consumer behavior, as this type of data is becoming more common and readily available in the marketplace. On one end of the marketplace, audial data originates from businesses' audio communication with other stakeholders include audiobooks for consumers, earnings conference call to investors, music (in ads and as products), social audio app in which consumers can listen in to conversation between other experts and consumers on a specific topic (e.g., Clubhouse), radios, podcasts, voice assistants (such as Apple's Siri and Amazon's Alexa), and sonic branding (sounds that are used as brands' audio signature, such as the distinctive synthesized glissandos of THX's sound trademark "Deep Note" that is often played in the cinema). In recent years, the popularity of audio communication has grown, positively contributing to the availability of audial data. Brands like GE, Microsoft, Johnson & Johnson, and Sephora communicate their brand messages directly with customers through each brand's online podcasting ("The Message," "future," "Innovation," and "#LIPSTORIES," respectively). Meanwhile, consumers also seem to increasingly embrace the consumption of audio information. For example, in 2008, 9% of Americans aged 12 and older reported listening to a podcast while 21% reported listening to online radio (Pew Research, 2021). In 2018, a decade later, 26% of Americans aged 12 and older reported listening to a podcast while 64%

reported listening to online radio (Pew Research, 2021). Radio reaches more Americans each week (92%) than other channels—such as TV (87%), smartphone (81%), computers (54%), TV-connected devices (52%), and tablets (46%)—across all age groups (Nielsen, 2019). On the other end of the marketplace, consumers are also generating audial data such as customer service calls, voice search, and conversation log with voice assistants such as Siri and Alexa. Thus, audial data represents a promising but currently underutilized data source for extracting consumer insights (cf. Chang et al., 2021; Chang et al., 2022; Dahl, 2010; Meyers-Levy et al., 2010).

Visual (Image) Data

Mobile and other digital technology, as well as social media platforms, have contributed to a tremendous surge in the presence and use of digital images and digital videos. Typical examples of visual data generated by consumers include photos and videos posted by consumers on social media as well as influencer videos. Video sharing sites such as YouTube and TikTok generate exabytes of visual data each hour, most of which is archived but not systematically utilized for any form of meaningful analysis to extract behavioral insights. Consumers, particularly younger consumers, like to create, watch, and share content on these video and image sharing platforms (e.g., Instagram, TikTok) both to enrich their own lives and to create their social image. Consequently, it is now typical and common for brands to engage these consumers using videos on these websites by contracting influencers to create advertisements and product placements, and in creating and promoting content that is viewed as on point for the brand. In addition, image data produced by businesses for consumers include brand logos, digital and print ads, product visuals, and visual frames sampled from videos.

OVERVIEW OF MACHINE LEARNING METHODS FOR VARIOUS TYPES OF CUSTOMER DATA

The various types of information that customers are exposed to and in turn post digitally are typically unstructured elements such as videos, text descriptions, audio clips, and images. These various data elements are ubiquitous in the modern information environment. However, because such data are unstructured (e.g., audio, video), they are challenging to analyze. One estimate indicates that about 80% to 95% of the data that businesses have access to are unstructured (Gandomi & Haider, 2015).

Recent advancements in computational methods and analysis techniques help facilitate data processing and analysis to study customer-relevant questions. In particular, several classes of methods—natural language processing, computational linguistics, automatic speech recognition, waveform analysis, computer vision, and image analysis—are useful to parse and process unstructured elements (videos, texts, audios, visuals) that customers are exposed to and also post online (Athey and Imbens, 2019; Chang et al., 2022). Consequently, behavioral researchers and practitioners have just begun to leverage unstructured data that customers are exposed to in the marketplace (e.g., product videos posted on brands' social media accounts).

These machine learning, natural language processing, and data processing tools allow researchers and practitioners to examine consequential customer behavior at scale, leveraging new secondary data sources (as described in earlier section) and types of data (e.g., product videos in a leading online crowdfunding platform). They also allow large-scale structured data and computationally demanding unstructured data be analyzed in a fairly straightforward and cost-effective manner. These various techniques are described next.

Big (Structured) Data

While unstructured data (such as written texts, music, and visual images) poses the challenge that they cannot be directly statistically modelled and understood mathematically, and therefore are not a good fit for conventional econometric, statistical, and psychometric methods (e.g., Lancaster, 1966; Mukherjee & Kadiyali, 2011, 2018), modern large-scale structured data is primarily difficult to deal with due to the overwhelming volume, variety, and velocity of such data. For example, consider the modern social media eco-system. In this eco-system, it is typical for consumers to generate tera-bytes of data describing a wealth of activities from the likes on comments, to shared posts, to geographical traces of where the consumer logged into the website or used the app. Each of these individual use-cases is simple to analyze for both descriptive purposes (e.g., to compute the count of likes) and for statistical modeling (e.g., to regress the count of likes on time of day to work out when a post is most likely to be liked). To facilitate the training of a statistical learning model using large-scale structured data, researchers can leverage established machine learning methods—supervised (e.g., random forest, LASSO regressions), unsupervised (e.g., clustering, autoencoders), and semi-supervised learning (e.g., transductive support vector machine)—to help make predictions for data-driven decisions (see Athey & Imbens, 2019 for a discussion on recent machine learning methods for empirical research and econometrics). With sufficient data for model training, these methods are straightforward to implement as there are many readily available packages in Python and R to simplify the implementation of these popular machine learning algorithms.

Often, the key analytical challenge with large-scale structured data is to determine how to organize the data analysis such that the data can be collected, stored, and analyzed in a principled workflow (see Lazer et al., 2009). Fortunately, the rise of cloud services provides both managers and researchers with the requisite toolkit. Specifically, services like Google Cloud Storage offer space in the cloud that allows for the storage and retrieval of large-scale data while other cloud services such as Google BigQuery enable such activities to be paired with software such as Tableau and AutoML to enable analysis without requiring the researcher or practitioner to know how to write code. Furthermore, modern analysis models such as neural networks, as implemented in software frameworks such as PyTorch and TensorFlow, enable the analyst to "let the data speak" – they enable relaxing functional form restrictions and the discovery of higher-level structure in high dimensional data.

Textual Data: Text Mining and Natural Language Processing

Unlike structured data, textual data is unstructured and needs to be converted into structured, numbers-based formats for further analysis. Typically, text mining is used initially to collect and convert unstructured textual data (e.g., text descriptions of a product innovation on a crowdfunding webpage; Younkin & Kuppuswamy, 2018) into structured formats for subsequent processing and analysis. Numerous models and approaches have been developed to analyze textual data, typically with the following aims: (1) to extract meaning of a word (or n-gram) based on count, co-location, or co-occurrence (e.g., "entity extraction" via using human-validated dictionaries and classification tools via pre-determined rules or machine learning; e.g., Pennebaker et al., 2007); (2) to extract higher-level, general themes shared across the texts (e.g., latent semantic analysis, topic modelling, and poisson factorization; e.g., see Toubia et al., 2019; Toubia, 2021); (3) to identify higher-order relations among extracted words or entities (e.g., "relation extraction" through deep learning and embedding; e.g., Toubia & Netzer, 2017).

Today, the term "text analysis" is often used synonymously with natural language processing (NLP), a class of techniques aimed to understand human languages. The original natural language processing toolkit for text analysis was relatively simple and rudimentary and primarily based on word counts, which simply counts words of different types to construct measures such as the extent of positivity and negativity in the text (e.g., sentiment analysis). These models often rely on dictionaries that are generated and validated by human participants, whose inputs are then used to infer the psychological constructs. Research in computational linguistics has led to development of statistical models that link the use of words and phrases in a communication to higher-order psychological constructs such as agreeableness in the message sender and recipient (Fast & Funder 2008; Pennebaker et al., 2003). A classic linguistic-analysis model builds on a seminal method by Pennebaker et al. (2001) that is commercially available as the Linguistic Inquiry and Word Count (LIWC; Pennebaker et al., 2015). LIWC has been widely used across disciplines, such as psychology, communications, and marketing, to study the relationship between linguistic characteristics of texts and individuals' behavior, such as in consumption (e.g., Cavanaugh et al., 2015) or lending (e.g., Netzer et al., 2019). In addition to LIWC, many other dictionary-based tools are readily available for application.

These methods have now been supplanted by the use of machine learning and deep learning (neural networks based) models that use more advanced techniques such as Transformers (Vaswani et al., 2017) to provide a much more fine-grained analysis of the text. Deep-learning (neural networks) based language models take into account the context—that is, the surrounding words to the focal word (e.g., through co-occurrence) and the remaining texts in the documents—to derive meaning of the focal word (Mikolov et al., 2013; Mukherjee & Chang, 2022). Moreover, in the last few years research has shown that pairing context-sensitive word embeddings with neural network (deep learning) models for sequential data (e.g. recurrent neural networks) leads to significant improvements in downstream performance on tasks as diverse as language inference and paraphrasing (see Peters et al., 2018; Devlin et al., 2018). Researchers can select among a wide range of NLP methods to train their context-specific language models using the textual data they have on hand, if they have sufficient data. Existing tools are available as suites of libraries and programs on Python and R, such as the popular Natural Language Toolkit (NLTK) for Python. Alternatively, many cloud service providers (e.g., IBM Watson, Google cloud, Amazon cloud, among others) and commercially available services (e.g., Hedonometer, Diction 5.0) offer pre-trained language models that are developed using existing text corpora (e.g., Wikipedia, Google news) and already validated by human participants. For example, IBM Watson offers two versions of its linguistic-analysis model, a version trained using general text documents and another trained using extant customer service dialogs. The linguistic-analysis model takes as input several lexical features commonly used in computational linguistics, including lexical features from LIWC (among other dictionaries developed and validated by human participants). IBM's linguistic-analysis model comprises of Support-Vector Machine models (a machine learning model) that were trained independently to classify each tone using a One-Versus-Rest strategy on large corpora of documents. During prediction, the linguistic-analysis model identifies the tones that are predicted with at least 0.5 probability as the final output. As a result, the model measures tones corresponding to language ("Analytical," "Confident," and "Tentative"), social propensity ("Agreeableness," "Conscientiousness," "Emotional Range," "Extraversion," and "Openness"), and emotion ("Anger," "Disgust," "Fear," "Joy," and "Sadness"; see Kaminski 2017). The wide range of readily available toolkits make analyzing large amounts of textual data much more accessible to researchers and analysts.

Audial Data: Automatic Speech Recognition and Waveform Analysis

Audial data in the marketplace can be decomposed to spoken narration (verbal content), voice conveying the narration (nonverbal content), music, and background sound. This type of unstructured data is typically captured in acoustic waveform in its raw form. To parse and process audial data, researchers and practitioners need to first identify the research focus, specifying the audial features to characterize (for feature extraction). For example, podcast advertising typically includes a voiceover narration—narrators' voices conveying spoken content—music and other sounds (Chang et al. 2022). These different audial components require different data processing techniques prior to data analyses. Researchers dealing with spoken narration can apply automatic speech recognition (ASR), a process by which a computer system maps acoustic speech signals to texts. ASR generates text transcription of the spoken verbal content and deduces speaker identity as model outputs.

Intuitively, speech recognition models involve pattern recognition through speech detection, segmentation, and clustering of spoken utterances. ASRs operate through multiple phases. First, the model detects which audial patterns in the waveform is speech. Next, the model detects when speakers in the audial utterances change by examining variations in the acoustic spectrum (through vocal features such as pitch and timbre). Finally, the model identifies what was said by each speaker in the entire acoustic waveform, through audial features characterizing each speaker. Thus, through a procedure known as speaker diarization via sequence transduction, ASRs operate on the acoustic waveform from which they extract the data features attributed to the identity of different speakers and to identify the words spoken by each speaker in the audio track.

The current state-of-the-art speech recognition model leverages deep learning (in particular, recurrent neural network (RNN)) methods to accomplish these tasks, automating transcription of audial speech data to text-based data (Graves, Mohamed, & Hinton, 2013). Whereas non-machine-learning-based ASRs use gaussian mixture models, hidden markov models, or their combination to map speech fragments with audial bits, modern ASRs use a much larger latent state-spaces to capture long-term dependencies in sequential data such as speech, given that the focal spoken word depends on what was said before and what was said after. Because deep neural networks such as RNNs are able to infer the word that is spoken from both the sequence of spoken syllables and the sequence of spoken words, deep-learning-based speech recognition models can achieve greater computational efficiency and accuracy than conventional speech recognition models (Chelba et al., 2013). ASRs are relatively mature in their development among the recent techniques for unstructured data, with many commercially available toolkits. Some of the most popular ones include speech-to-text APIs and commercially available services from Speechmatics, Otter.ai, and Google's cloud services. Given that a main output from ASRs is the text transcription of spoken content in the acoustic waveform, researchers can then use text analysis and natural language processing methods (discussed in the earlier section on textual data) to treat the resulting textual data for analysis of spoken content.

Besides spoken content, researchers and analysts may be interested in deriving acoustic characteristics of speech, music, and background sounds in the raw audio waveform. Typically, audial characteristics are described by (1) physical features (e.g., spectral features, volume), (2) perceptual features (e.g., pitch), and (3) signal features (e.g., zero-crossing rate; Fant, 1960). Numerous toolkits are readily are available to help measure audial characteristics, based on researchers' and analysts' focus of audial elements. For example, many tools are accessible derive acoustic features of songs and music, such as sonic API, Discogs API, Spotify API, and Last.fm API. To measure more general acoustic features of audio waveforms, toolkits such as the Librosa library in Python and NVIDIA's Data Loading Library (DALI)

API (for Python and PyTorch) can help derive physical features characterizing the audio spectrogram (i.e., a representation of an audio signal of the frequency spectrum over time) such as short-time fast fourier transform (the process of dividing the audio signal in short term sequences of certain sizes and computing these) and spectral centroid (location of the center of mass of the spectrum). These toolkits can also help derive signal features such as zero-crossing rate (a measure of the rate at which the signal is crossing the zero line between negative and positive signal; Chang et al. 2021).

Visual Data: Computer Vision and Image Analysis

Visual images are unstructured and require processing to represent them in numbers for statistical analyses. An image is essentially a 2D or 3D function of spatial coordinates, with its amplitude at a particular value of spatial coordinates determining the intensity of an image at that point. An image is represented by an array of pixels arranged in vectors, where pixels are elements that contain information about intensity and color. Basic image analysis methods can help measure pixel-by-pixel variation to account for data features of visual characteristics, such as variation in visual imagery (without knowing the visual content and objects in the image) and resolution (number of pixels in the image, which is linked to image detail). These methods can also help transform an image by varying these data elements of a visual image.

Recent developments in new algorithms, digital images, and computing power have jointly contributed to new machine learning methods which allow computer systems to detect, identify, and understand visual images. A popular class of machine learning methods typically used to process digital images is computer vision. Broadly speaking, computer vision concepts constitute three levels of techniques, with varying focus on data outputs (and increasing sophistication) for each level. Low level computer vision techniques derive basic data features of the image content, extracting fundamental image primitives such as edge detection (by detecting discontinuities in brightness), corner detection, shapes, morphology, and filtering. It is typically used to preprocess images. Middle level computer vision aims to infer visual geometry and motion, which require computer systems to compare more than one images. Finally, high level computer vision techniques attempt to understand the "semantics"—the content of visual images—such as object recognition and scene understanding. In other words, higher level computer vision techniques attempt to mimic human visual systems and higher-order cognitive processes and are computationally more intensive.

In higher level computer vision, deep-learning-based visual recognition models typically use convolutional neural networks (CNNs) that are trained on large corpora of labelled images (such as ImageNet) to derive the data features (e.g., colors, lines, and curves) corresponding to images of common objects (e.g., tables, humans, cats; Krizhevsky, Sutskever, & Hinton, 2012), which allow computers to make probabilistic inferences on the visual contents of the images.

There are many readily available open-source libraries for Python and R, as well as commercially available services, with built-in algorithms and pre-trained models for common computer vision tasks. Among open-source libraries (for Python or R), OpenCV and Scipy are useful for a wide range of lower and higher level computer vision tasks such as object recognition and face detection, whereas Python image library (PIL), FFmpeg, and Numpy are useful for lower level image processing tasks such as filtering, measuring of pixels, and manipulating images. Other open source APIs, such as NVIDIA's DALI API, can also help carry out common image processing tasks. Higher level computer vision tasks such as object identification and face recognition can be completed using commercially available services, Clarifai, Google cloud services, and Lionbridge AI. For example, researchers and analysts can leverage a visual-recognition model developed by Clarifai (a state-of-the-art CNN architecture trained over billions of training samples) to identify the visual elements (common objects) present in each image frame. The model operates automatically on the images and outputs a vector of words describing each frame (e.g., tables, people, cats, etc.). These automated image analysis techniques can help parse and process image data for subsequent data analysis using standard statistical and econometrics models (see Chang et al., 2022).

FUTURE RESEARCH DIRECTIONS

Information display and media can combine more than one data element. For example, a print ad can include an image of the product and a text-based message about the product. Video is another form of audio-visual data. For decades, companies have relied on television commercials to communicate their brands and products to consumers. Advances in internet and digital technology have added to the popularity of newer forms of marketing communications carrying audio-visual content, such as product videos (e.g., new product introduction or product review videos) and branded vlogs. Consumers also add to the availability of video data by posting short videos on social media.

A video is composed of an audio track and a sequence of images (frames). Broadly speaking, video analysis is a combination of analyzing audio track and visual images. To analyze videos, researchers and analysts need to first decouple the audio track from the visual frames. This can be easily done using any of the image analysis libraries, APIs, and commercial services (for lower level computer vision techniques) discussed earlier. Depending on the length of the video, it may be necessary to sample the visual frames as a video typically has 24 frames per seconds and analyzing each visual frame is computationally more costly than standard data analysis of numbers. A series of deep-learning models (in automatic speech recognition, computational linguistics, and computer vision) can then be applied to the audio tracks and visual frames, which allows researchers to parse the unstructured multimedia data and measure the focal and control variables for empirical analyses (e.g., Chang et al., 2022). As video analysis is one of the exciting areas receiving much research attention in computer science and artificial intelligence, it is likely that the current empirical challenge with detailed analysis of large-scale video datasets would be solved in the foreseeable future.

CONCLUSION

This chapter presents an overview of new sources of customer-relevant data that are publicly available—such as purchase behavior in popular crowdfunding platforms and social media posts (texts, images, videos). These data sources present fruitful opportunities for researchers and practitioners to better understand modern consumer behavior in the evolving information environments. Not only would resulting insights be theoretically interesting, they can also offer practical benefits for extracting insights about customer behavior and for designing the information environment that the modern consumers face. Finally, the availability of new types of secondary data and the use of machine learning methods create new fruitful avenues to study emerging consumer behavior. These tools allow us to examine consequential consumer behavior in the marketplace at scale, leveraging new secondary data sources and types of data. Machine learning methods facilitate data processing and analyses of data sources that were challenging to analyze just a few years ago, leading to new possibilities for researchers and analysts to extract novel behavioral insights about individuals and groups at scale. These developments create exciting opportunities for behavioral researchers, social scientists, practitioners, and businesses going forward.

ACKNOWLEDGMENT

This research was supported by the Ministry of Education, Singapore, under its Academic Research Fund (AcRF) Tier 2 Grant No. MOE2018-T2-1-181. Any opinions, findings, and conclusions or recommendations expressed in this material are those of the authors and do not necessarily reflect the views of the Singapore Ministry of Education.

REFERENCES

Allon, G., & Babich, V. (2020). Crowdsourcing and crowdfunding in the manufacturing and services sectors. *Manufacturing & Service Operations Management*, 22(1), 102–112. doi:10.1287/msom.2019.0825

Athey, S., & Imbens, G. W. (2019). Machine learning methods that economists should know about. *Annual Review of Economics*, 11(1), 685–725. doi:10.1146/annurev-economics-080217-053433

Cavanaugh, L. A., Bettman, J. R., & Luce, M. F. (2015). Feeling love and doing more for distant others: Specific positive emotions differentially affect prosocial consumption. *JMR, Journal of Marketing Research*, 52(5), 657–673. doi:10.1509/jmr.10.0219

Chang, H. H., & Hung, I. W. (2018). Mirror, mirror on the retail wall: Self-focused attention promotes reliance on feelings in consumer decisions. *JMR, Journal of Marketing Research*, 55(4), 403–428. doi:10.1509/jmr.15.0080

Chang, H. H., & Pham, M. T. (2018). Affective boundaries of scope insensitivity. *The Journal of Consumer Research*, 45(2), 403–428. doi:10.1093/jcr/ucy007

Chang, H. H., Mukherjee, A., & Chattopadhyay, A. (2021). The impact of single versus multiple narrating voices in persuasive videos. In T. Bradford, A. Keinan, & M. Thomson (Eds.), Advances in consumer research (pp. 388-389). Association for Consumer Research.

Chang, H. H., Mukherjee, A., & Chattopadhyay, A. (2022). Designing persuasive voiceover narration in crowdfunding videos. In A. Humphreys, G. Packard, & K. Gielens (Eds.), *AMA winter academic conference proceedings* (pp. 217-218). American Marketing Association.

Chen, D., Fisch, A., Weston, J., & Bordes, A. (2017). *Reading Wikipedia to answer open-domain questions*. doi:10.18653/v1/P17-1171

Chelba, C., Mikolov, T., Schuster, M., Ge, Q., Brants, T., Koehn, P., & Robinson, T. (2013). *One billion word benchmark for measuring progress in statistical language modeling*. arXiv preprint arXiv:1312.3005.

Culotta, A., & Cutler, J. (2016). Mining brand perceptions from twitter social networks. *Marketing Science*, 35(3), 343–362. doi:10.1287/mksc.2015.0968

Dahl, D. W. (2010). Understanding the role of spokesperson voice in broadcast advertising. In A. Krishna (Ed.), *Sensory marketing: Research on the sensuality of products* (pp. 169–182). Routledge.

Devlin, J., Chang, M. W., Lee, K., & Toutanova, K. (2018). *BERT: Pre-training of deep bidirectional transformers for language understanding.* arXiv preprint arXiv:1810.04805.

Dhanani, Q., & Mukherjee, A. (2019). *Is crowdfunding the silver bullet to expanding innovation in the developing world?* https://blogs.worldbank.org/psd/crowdfunding-silver-bullet-expanding-innovation-developing-world

Fast, L. A., & Funder, D. C. (2008). Personality as manifest in word use: Correlations with self-report, acquaintance report, and behavior. *Journal of Personality and Social Psychology*, *94*(2), 334–346. doi:10.1037/0022-3514.94.2.334 PMID:18211181

Gandomi, A., & Haider, M. (2015). Beyond the hype: Big data concepts, methods, and analytics. *International Journal of Information Management*, *35*(2), 137–144. doi:10.1016/j.ijinfomgt.2014.10.007

Graves, A., Mohamed, A., & Hinton, G. (2013). Speech recognition with deep recurrent neural networks. In *Proceedings of international conference on acoustic, speech, and signal processing* (pp. 6645-6649). 10.1109/ICASSP.2013.6638947

Hamilton, R. W., Schlosser, A., & Chen, Y. J. (2017). Who's driving this conversation? Systematic biases in the content of online consumer discussions. *JMR, Journal of Marketing Research*, *54*(4), 540–555. doi:10.1509/jmr.14.0012

Kaminski, J. (2017). *The Science behind the service.* https://github.com/IBM-Bluemix-Docs/tone-analyzer/

Krizhevsky, A., Sutskever, I., & Hinton, G. E. (2012). Imagenet classification with deep convolutional neural networks. In Advances in neural information processing system (pp. 1097-1105). Academic Press.

Lancaster, K. J. (1966). A new approach to consumer theory. *Journal of Political Economy*, *74*(2), 132–157. doi:10.1086/259131

Lazer, D., Pentland, A., Adamic, L., Aral, S., Barabasi, A. L., Brewer, D., Christakis, N., Contractor, N., Fowler, J., Gutmann, M., Jebara, T., King, G., Macy, M., Roy, D., & Van Alstyne, M. (2009). Social science. Computational social science. *Science*, *323*(5915), 721–723. doi:10.1126cience.1167742 PMID:19197046

Lee, M. P., Chang, H. H., & Mukherjee, A. (2020). *Funding societies: Using fintech to support small businesses in Singapore.* SMU813-PDF-ENG. https://hbsp.harvard.edu/product/SMU813-PDF-ENG

Merrill, R., Chang, H. H., Liang, H. H., Lan, Y., & Wong, A. (2020). *Growing a global forest: Ant financial, Alipay, and the Ant Forest.* SMU515-PDF-ENG. https://hbsp.harvard.edu/product/SMU515-PDF-ENG

Meyers-Levy, J., Bublitz, M. G., & Peracchio, L. A. (2010). The sounds of the marketplace: The role of audition in marketing. In A. Krishna (Ed.), *Sensory marketing: Research on the sensuality of products* (pp. 167–186). Routledge.

Mikolov, T., Sutskever, I., Chen, K., Corrado, G. S., & Dean, J. (2013). Distributed representations of words and phrases and their compositionality. In Advances in neural information processing systems (pp. 3111-3119). Academic Press.

Mukherjee, A., Chang, H. H., & Chattopadhyay, A. (2019). Crowdfunding: sharing the entrepreneurial journey. In R. W. Belk, G. M. Eckhardt, & F. Bardhi (Eds.), *Handbook of the sharing economy* (pp. 152–162). Edward Elgar Publishing. doi:10.4337/9781788110549.00019

Mukherjee, A., & Chang, H. H. (2022). Describing rosé: An embedding-based method for measuring preferences. In A. Humphreys, G. Packard, & K. Gielens (Eds.), *AMA winter academic conference proceedings* (pp. 150-151). American Marketing Association.

Mukherjee, A., & Kadiyali, V. (2018). The competitive dynamics of new DVD releases. *Management Science, 64*(8), 3536–3553. doi:10.1287/mnsc.2017.2795

Mukherjee, A., & Kadiyali, V. (2011). Modeling multichannel home video demand in the U.S. motion picture industry. *JMR, Journal of Marketing Research, 48*(6), 985–995. doi:10.1509/jmr.07.0359

Mukherjee, A., Xiao, P., Wang, L., & Contractor, N. (2018). Does the opinion of the crowd predict commercial success? Evidence from Threadless. In Academy of management proceedings (pp. 12728). Academy of Management. doi:10.5465/AMBPP.2018.12728abstract

Netzer, O., Lemaire, A., & Herzenstein, M. (2019). When words sweat: Identifying signals for loan default in the text of loan applications. *JMR, Journal of Marketing Research, 56*(6), 960–980. doi:10.1177/0022243719852959

Nielsen. (2019). *Audio today 2019: How America listens.* The Nielsen Company (US). https://www.nielsen.com/us/en/insights/report/2019/audio-today-2019/#

Pennebaker, J. W., Francis, M. E., & Booth, R. J. (2001). *Linguistic inquiry and word count: LIWC 2001.* Lawrence Erlbaum Associates.

Pennebaker, J. W., Boyd, R. L., Jordan, K., & Blackburn, K. (2015). *The development and psychometric properties of LIWC2015.* Academic Press.

Peters, M., Neumann, M., Zettlemoyer, L., & Yih, W. (2018). *Dissecting contextual word embeddings: Architecture and representation.* doi:10.18653/v1/D18-1179

Pew Research Centre. (2021). *Audio and Podcasting Fact Sheet.* Pew Research Centre. https://www.pewresearch.org/journalism/fact-sheet/audio-and-podcasting/

Tirunillai, S., & Tellis, G. J. (2014). Mining marketing meaning from online chatter: Strategic brand analysis of big data using latent dirichlet allocation. *JMR, Journal of Marketing Research, 51*(4), 463–479. doi:10.1509/jmr.12.0106

Toubia, O. (2021). A Poisson factorization topic model for the study of creative documents (and their summaries). *JMR, Journal of Marketing Research, 58*(6), 1142–1158. doi:10.1177/0022243720943209

Toubia, O., Iyengar, G., Bunnell, R., & Lemaire, A. (2019). Extracting features of entertainment products: A guided latent dirichlet allocation approach informed by the psychology of media consumption. *JMR, Journal of Marketing Research, 56*(1), 18–36. doi:10.1177/0022243718820559

Toubia, O., & Netzer, O. (2017). Idea generation, creativity, and prototypicality. *Marketing Science, 36*(1), 1–20. doi:10.1287/mksc.2016.0994

Van Laer, T., Edson Escalas, J., Ludwig, S., & Van Den Hende, E. A. (2019). What happens in Vegas stays on TripAdvisor? A theory and technique to understand narrativity in consumer reviews. *The Journal of Consumer Research, 46*(2), 267–285.

Vaswani, A., Shazeer, N., Parmar, N., Uszkoreit, J., Jones, L., Gomez, A. N., Kaiser, L., & Polosukhin, I. (2017). Attention is all you need. In Advances in neural information processing systems (pp. 5998-6008). Academic Press.

Villarroel Ordenes, F., Grewal, D., Ludwig, S., Ruyter, K. D., Mahr, D., & Wetzels, M. (2019). Cutting through content clutter: How speech and image acts drive consumer sharing of social media brand messages. *The Journal of Consumer Research*, *45*(5), 988–1012. doi:10.1093/jcr/ucy032

Younkin, P., & Kuppuswamy, V. (2018). The colorblind crowd? Founder race and performance in crowd-funding. *Management Science*, *64*(7), 3269–3287. doi:10.1287/mnsc.2017.2774

ADDITIONAL READING

Chang, H. H., & Tuan Pham, M. (2013). Affect as a decision-making system of the present. *The Journal of Consumer Research*, *40*(1), 42–63. doi:10.1086/668644

Liu, X., Singh, P. V., & Srinivasan, K. (2016). A structured analysis of unstructured big data by leveraging cloud computing. *Marketing Science*, *35*(3), 363–388. doi:10.1287/mksc.2015.0972

MukherjeeA.XiaoP.ChangH. H.WangL.ContractorN. (2017). Plebeian Bias: Selecting Crowdsourced Creative Designs for Commercialization. doi:10.2139/ssrn.3038775

Netzer, O., Feldman, R., Goldenberg, J., & Fresko, M. (2012). Mine your own business: Market-structure surveillance through text mining. *Marketing Science*, *31*(3), 521–543. doi:10.1287/mksc.1120.0713

KEY TERMS AND DEFINITIONS

Automatic Speech Recognition: A field of computer science and class of methods which enables the recognition and translation of spoken language into written text that is processed by computer systems.

Computational Linguistics: A field of study and class of methods which allow computer systems to process and make sense of natural (human) language.

Computational Social Science: An emerging field of study which leverages computational techniques to study social and behavioral phenomena of individuals, groups, and societies.

Computer Vision: A field of computer science and class of methods which allow computer systems to process and make sense of visual images, akin to human vision system.

Customer-Relevant Data: Data in relation to information that customers are exposed to in the marketplace as well as data generated by customer's behavior.

Machine Learning: An approach to derive computer algorithms and statistical models that can learn to improve their performance based on use of data, without explicit instructions (data-generative models).

Natural Language Processing: A field of study to derive computational approaches to process and analyze large amounts of textual data on human (natural) language.

Structured Data: Data that is predefined through number-based formats and typically considered quantitative data, such as total revenues, counts of likes on a social media post, number of products sold, customer satisfaction ratings, and so on. Their measurement scales could be nominal, ordinal, interval, and ratio.

Text Mining: The process of identifying, retrieving, and preparing unstructured textual data into a structured format for data analysis.

Unstructured Data: Data that is not predefined through structured, number-based systems, such as texts, sounds, visual images, or videos.

Waveform Analysis: Analysis of the acoustic features of the raw waveform file containing audio (sound and speech).

Section 22
Ensemble Learning

Effective Bankruptcy Prediction Models for North American Companies

Rachel Cardarelli
Bryant University, USA

Son Nguyen
Bryant University, USA

Rick Gorvett
Bryant University, USA

John Quinn
Bryant University, USA

INTRODUCTION

The study of bankruptcy prediction aims to provide risk assessment in order to reduce the likelihood of financial distress for individual companies and the macroeconomy. It provides creditors and investors with insight when making financial decisions, and the timely recognition of the potential for bankruptcy is important for mitigating its potential costs to many parties.

For decades, this subject has been flooded with new research, benefiting from the continuously evolving field of data science, and because of this has seen numerous advancements including the implementation of highly accurate modeling, feature selection, and ensemble techniques. However, one facet of bankruptcy prediction that has not been researched as thoroughly is the imbalance problem. If there are 100 observations in a dataset, with 99 of them being positive and 1 being negative, a model could predict that the entire dataset is positive with 99% accuracy.

However, this disregards the minority, negative observation altogether. And as the ratio of majority to minority samples increases, this problem worsens. So, this paper proposes a new technique to address the imbalance problem.

The proposed method undersamples the training data at various levels of imbalance (defined as the ratio of the number of majority points to the number of minority points). It performs this on 200 bagged samples, and each resulting training set is used to train a random forest. Then, a majority voting procedure determines the final prediction.

The Background section contains a literature review and concludes with the motivation for this study. The Methodology section contains descriptions of and the rationale for this study's experimental settings as well as the details of the proposed Bagging Undersampling method. The Results section provides an evaluation of each model's performance and the support for the proposed sampling method. Finally, the Conclusions section discusses the results and suggests ideas for future study.

DOI: 10.4018/978-1-7998-9220-5.ch108

BACKGROUND

In this review of bankruptcy prediction literature, there is a discussion of commonly used predictive models, feature selection techniques, model tuning, ensemble learning, and other distinctive topics studied in the literature. The review concludes with an overview of methods used to handle the imbalance problem.

Predictive Models

Bankruptcy prediction models can be divided into two main classes. The first consists of statistical methods which began with Beaver in 1966 followed by Altman in 1968 who applied univariate discriminant analysis and multivariate linear regression respectively. It continued with stochastic models such as logit regression (Ohlson, 1980) and probit-regression (Zmijewski, 1984). The second class consists of artificial intelligence (AI) methods. This class has been used in a large number of studies and in application to bankruptcy prediction since the 1990's. AI methods include decision tree, genetic algorithm (GA), support vector machine (SVM), and several kinds of neural networks such as BPNN (back propagation trained neural network), PNN (probabilistic neural networks), and ANN (artificial neural networks) (Min and Jeong, 2009).

According to a 2014 review written by Sun, Li, Huang, and He, AI models have dominated more recent studies because of their superior accuracy and mapping abilities (Sun et al., 2014) (Kumar et al., 2007). In a review of studies from 1968-2005, the authors found that SVM and neural network (NN) (especially BPNN) are objectively more powerful than other methods, especially statistical methods. They also suggest that decision trees, while less powerful, are underused but recommended due to their "if-then" rule-based interpretation (Kumar et al., 2007). Another review of corporate failure and financial failure from 2014 agrees with these assertions and adds that decision trees (DT) are easy to interpret and powerful, especially in combination with an ensemble method, but they only work best for short term use and are easy to overfit (Sun et al., 2014). Evolutionary algorithms (EA) such as genetic algorithms (GA) are rule-based and more easily interpreted, but usually do not perform as well as NN and SVM. (Sun et al., 2014). The review also argues that statistical single classifier methods such as Altman's and Beaver's, which require normality, as well as the logit regression model which requires independent variables (i.e., no multicollinearity, which is hard to achieve with accounting data) are not preferred due to the assumptions that they require (Sun et al., 2014).

Finally, on the note of linear models and linear mapping in general, one study by Barboza, et. al compares statistical methods versus AI and ensemble methods confirmed what the review stated (i.e., that statistical methods cannot perform as well as machine learning models) and drew other conclusions, including that linear models perform worse as the number of variables increases and SVM with linear kernels perform just as badly as linear models, thus confirming that models with more complex mapping abilities are preferred (Barboza et al., 2017).

Feature Selection

Feature selection is another facet of bankruptcy prediction that has been widely studied. Features can be selected empirically with the methods for doing so falling under two categories: wrapper and filter feature selection. Wrapper feature selection methods assess the subsets of features according to their usefulness to a given predictor, by following a searching process for a good feature subset. They are best suited for smaller datasets because the searching process becomes more challenging as the size increases and becomes prone to overfitting. The other type of feature selection is filter feature selection which attempts to select the most "relevant" features from a larger feature set. Unlike wrapper methods, this selection process is independent from the classifier used to build the prediction model and can be implemented when the feature set is large. However, these methods do not always help yield the most accurate prediction because "the filter approach ignores the interaction with the classification algorithm used to build the predictor," and "do[es] not model the feature dependency" (Lin et al., 2014).

There are widely used methods such as LASSO, which one study by Tian et. al uses to select variables for two previous studies' hazard models to address the multicollinearity problem when using accounting variables. The authors also say that LASSO is good for stabilization in the face of "perturbations in the data" and its results give insight into the relative importance of the variables that it selects (Tian et al., 2015). However, other studies often chose the variables that the models found to be most important and by majority voting. The following are examples of this.

Using an AdaBoost ensemble of ANN, one study by Fedorova, Gilenko, and Dovzhenko selected variables that were the two most significant variables received from multivariate discriminant analysis (MDA), classification and regression tree, and logit regression (LR) (Fedorova et al., 2013). A similar study employed "several statistical methods including independent sample t-test, discriminant analysis, logistic regression (stepwise), decision tree, and factor analysis" to select their features (Min and Jeong, 2009). Brezigar-Masten et al. (2012) studied CART-based selection of bankruptcy predictors for the logit model. They first generated the principal component of each type of variable. Taking the principal components with highest loadings and with statistical significance, they used CART decision trees with dummy variables to select predictors (Brezigar-Masten et al., 2012). And yet another study by Wang, Ma, and Yang selected features using a boosted decision tree ensemble (Wang et al., 2014). Some other current works on using boosting algorithm for bankruptcy prediction include the works of Jabeur and Stef (Ben Jabeur et al., 2022), Shetty, Musa and Bredart (Shetty et al., 2022).

Another approach is to combine expert opinion and empirical methods. One study by Lin, Liang, Yeh, and Huang implements a feature selection method that combines expert knowledge and wrapper feature selection. It categorizes financial features into seven classes according to their "financial semantics" based on experts' domain knowledge from the literature. It then applies the wrapper method to search for "good" feature subsets that contain the top candidates from each feature class. The search space of the wrapper method effectively shrinks because features have been pre-classified before the wrapper method was applied (Lin et al., 2014).

Model Tuning

Empirical methods for model tuning are also a common theme in the study of bankruptcy prediction. The previously mentioned 2014 review also details studies that employed hybrid classifiers, which use other methods or algorithms to optimize the classifier being studied, to optimize parameters for the other classification algorithm. One study that performed well created a genetic algorithm support vector machine (GA-SVM) hybrid model that used GA to optimize both feature selection and SVM parameters (Sun et al., 2014). Another study by Jeong, Minb, and Kim uses a hybrid of grid search to find local optimum and GA to find global optimum to select the number of hidden nodes and the weight decay parameter of a NN (Jeong et al., 2012).

Ensemble Methods

Ensemble is a machine learning concept where multiple learners are trained to solve the same problem (Wang et al., 2014). Three of the most common ensemble methods are boosting, bagging and random subspace. Boosting constructs a composite classifier by training base classifiers while increasing weight on their misclassified observations. The observations that are incorrectly classified are chosen more often than examples that were correctly classified to produce new classifiers that are better able to predict observations that previously led to poor performance. Boosting combines predictions with weighted majority voting by giving more weights to more accurate predictions (Kim et al., 2010). Bagging, which stands for Bootstrap Aggregating is an intuitive and simple ensemble method. Diverse bags are obtained by bootstrapping different training data sets (i.e., randomly drawn with replacement). Subsequently, a classifier is built for each training data set and their predictions are combined by a majority vote (Abellán et al., 2014). The random subspace ensemble consists of several classifiers that use randomly chosen sets of the original dataset and combines the classifiers into a final decision rule by majority vote. However, each single classifier uses only a subset of the available features in the data set for training and testing, and these features are chosen uniformly at random from the full set of features (Abellán et al., 2014)

In terms of ensemble techniques, the 2014 review on corporate failure and financial distress discusses parallel and serial ensemble methods. Beginning with parallel methods, which use majority voting on the results of multiple classifiers, there are ensembles with different algorithms, ensembles with one algorithm under different samples or features, and ensembles with one algorithm under different parameters. Serial methods arrange several base classifiers in sequence and selects the result of one base classifier as the final output according to certain principles They include well-studied techniques like bagging, boosting and AdaBoost (although, the study stresses that AdaBoost performs best with weak learners) (Sun et al., 2014).

Employing bagging and boosting decision tree ensembles, Kim et al. (2010) compare ensemble methods to a NN tuned by back propagation learning algorithm. The ensemble methods removed generalization error and reduced overfitting. Overall, the bagging ensemble performed the best followed by the boosting ensemble (Kim et al., 2010).

One study by Abellán and Mantas uses credal decision trees (CDT) that are, "based on imprecise probabilities (more specifically, on the Imprecise Dirichlet Model (IDM)," in random subspace and bagging ensembles to improve their accuracy. They found that, because the split criterion used to build a credal decision tree has a different treatment of the imprecision than the one used for the classic split criteria, it improved the ensemble's ability to learn (Abellán et al., 2014).

Other Topics in Bankruptcy Studies

Bankruptcy prediction literature knows no bounds and the facets that researchers have studied are varied. The 2014 review suggests that future studies look at the problem of bankruptcy on a spectrum from mild financial distress or a temporary cash flow difficulty to business failure or bankruptcy, and that future studies broaden their definition of bankruptcy from a dichotomous outcome to a metric that encompasses the timeframe and intensity of financial distress before bankruptcy (Sun et al., 2014). The following studies explore these topics and other miscellaneous topics.

One study by Režňáková and Karas attempted to construct dynamic indicators of bankruptcy, assuming that the development of financial ratios is not very dynamic over the years (Režňáková et al., 2014). To avoid assuming that their data is normal and does not have meaningful outliers, they used non-parametric boosted decision trees ("non-parametric" meaning it does not need assumptions about parameters) to select predictors for an LDA. It used boosted decision trees because they are nonparametric (i.e., they do not need to be normally distributed, allow for outliers, and can capture non-linear relationships between inputs). They found that, despite not seeing improved accuracy, the models were able to identify, "bankruptcy symptoms," before actual bankruptcy (Režňáková et al., 2014).

Another study by Tinoco and Wilson endeavored to detect financial distress as opposed to bankruptcy. The timeframe for a company to be considered bankrupt can be a lengthy process where the "legal" date of failure can differ from the "economic"/ "real" date of failure by up to two years. This model looks for financial distress because it can still cost a firm a lot of money and it includes the time that a company cannot meet its financial needs even before bankruptcy, potentially as a warning that bankruptcy is eminent. However, financial distress does not always end in bankruptcy as, "there are several stages that a firm can go through before it is defined as dead: financial distress, insolvency, filing of bankruptcy, and administrative receivership (in order to avoid filing for bankruptcy), for instance." Using accounting, macroeconomic and market variables, the study compares five models: one using only accounting variables, one using accounting and macroeconomic variables, one using only market variables, one using market and macroeconomic and one using all variables. It found that macroeconomic variables improved the model marginally yet positively and that market variables considerably increased model accuracy (Tinoco and Wilson, 2013).

Along the same lines, one study conducted by Zhou, Tam, and Fujita uses multi-class classification to predict the listing status of Chinese listed companies using ensembles of binary classifiers, random undersampling, and VIF feature selection process. Their feature selection process aided in correctly classifying delisted status rather than correctly classifying healthy status, and their selected variables performed well with several different ensemble methods (retaining low standard deviation across the board) (Zhou et al., 2016).

The Imbalance Problem

The imbalance problem is of great significance to bankruptcy prediction studies because, while there are generally more instances of healthy companies rather than bankrupt companies in a given dataset, "any degree of imbalance somewhat damages a method's prediction capacity (Veganzones et al., 2018)." Below are examples of how past studies have dealt with this issue.

In a study that compares the performance of 5 models, Wu, Gaunt, and Gra balance the data by "matched-pair" methods. A pair of points (one from the minority class and the other from the majority class) are matched by the size of the firm (Wu et al., 2010).

One study by Zhou compares several sampling techniques when considering the imbalance problem. For oversampling techniques, it looked at random oversampling with replication (ROWR) and Synthetic Minority Over-sampling Technique (SMOTE). SMOTE oversamples the minority class by taking each minority class sample and introducing synthetic examples along the line segments joining any of the k minority class nearest neighbors. For undersampling techniques, it looked at random undersampling (RU), Undersampling Based on Clustering from Nearest Neighbor (UBOCFNN) and Undersampling Based on Clustering from Gaussian Mixture Distribution (UBOCFGMD). UBOCFNN partitions the points in a sample space into k clusters and selects the point which is the nearest to the central point of each cluster to represent the whole cluster. (UBOCFGMD) is clustering based on Gaussian Mixture distribution using the Expectation Maximization (EM) algorithm to estimate the parameters. In a Gaussian mixture model with k components for data in the majority class, the EM algorithm will estimate its parameters and then that data will be partitioned into k clusters in terms of the k components of Gaussian mixture distribution (Zhou, 2013). In this study, k in UBOCFGMD and UBOCFNN was equal to the size of the minority population. UBOCFNN selected the point nearest to the central point of each cluster and resulted in a training set that was double the size of the minority population. For UBOCFGMD, in the case that no points are partitioned into one cluster, for each cluster with points, one point is randomly selected to represent that cluster and for the clusters without points, one point was randomly selected from the nearest cluster with points. In general, the study found that undersampling techniques (RU and UBOCFGMD with NN and SVM) are generally better for datasets with larger minority populations and oversampling techniques (logistic regression with SVM) are generally better for datasets with smaller minority populations (Zhou, 2013).

When considering the imbalance problem, one study by Kim, Kang, and Kim examined the difference between arithmetic and geometric means in boosting algorithms to minimize the decision boundary of the majority class invading the decision boundary of the minority class. Their method starts by sampling five portions of the data with different imbalance ratios. It then performs classification experiments using AdaBoost, cost-sensitive boosting and GMBoost of SVM classifiers and compares the performances after using SMOTE to balance the imbalanced sets. Cost-sensitive boosting uses a cost to punish for positive and negative misclassifications, and normally these costs are the same, but in this algorithm, they are different and calculated using geometric accuracy rather than arithmetic accuracy. The results showed that in the

AdaBoost ensemble, higher imbalance ratios led to higher arithmetic accuracy for the majority population but lower arithmetic accuracy for the minority population. The inverse effect was seen for geometric accuracy. In the CostBoost ensemble, the geometric accuracy was higher than that of AdaBoost, but it had a lower arithmetic accuracy. Its average accuracies for the two most imbalanced sets were lower than a random guess. However, the GMBoost ensemble had better, more stable arithmetic accuracies than the previous methods as well as a better geometric accuracy. The geometric accuracy was significantly better when comparing the results of the most imbalanced samples (Kim et al., 2014).

Cluster-based undersampling was used by Lin, Tsai, Hu, and Jhang to deal with data imbalance in a general sense (i.e., not just with bankruptcy data). The study's algorithm set the number of clusters in the majority class equal to the number of data points in the minority class. Then, one version of the algorithm (referred to as "centers") used the cluster centers as the representative of the majority class, but another version (referred to as "centers_nn") used the nearest neighbors of the cluster centers to represent the cluster. Using clustering as a replacement for another undersampling strategy has two main benefits. The first is that the elements of the clusters are relatively homogeneous. The second is that it preserves some of the information that may have been lost if another undersampling technique was used to remove some of the data points. When applying these two algorithms to multilayer perceptron classifier and decision tree classifier AdaBoost ensembles, the centers_nn algorithm used in combination with the decision tree ensemble produced the highest rate of classification accuracy. Furthermore, the results showed statistically significant improvements in both small-scale and large-scale datasets (Lin et al., 2017).

With the goal of reducing noise and overcoming imbalance between and within classes, Douzas, Bacao, and Last implemented a hybrid k-means and SMOTE clustering algorithm to deal with the imbalance issue. This study's algorithm uses k-means to generate clusters and then, "a filter step chooses clusters to be oversampled and determines how many samples are to be generated in each cluster (Douzas et al., 2018)." It then applies SMOTE to oversample the minority class.

Motivation

The literature surrounding bankruptcy prediction encompasses a variety of topics. Some studies focus on variable selection, others the performance of different models, etc. However, although the imbalance issue is prevalent in any real-world dataset, where the count of non-bankrupt companies is almost always greater than the count of bankrupt companies, the literature regarding how to deal with the imbalance issue is noticeably sparse. Many studies barely mention the issue or rely on empirical methods to hand-pick the points in the training sets (e.g., the "matched-pair" method used by Wu et al., 2010). So, this study aims to further the research on how to handle the imbalance issue in a way that can be applied globally to any study, regardless of its purpose.

METHODOLOGY

The Data

The data comes from COMPUSTAT which is a database of financial, statistical and market information on active and inactive global companies. The data provides quarterly SEC filing information for companies in the USA and Canada from 2009-2019. Half of the dataset contains information for the companies within the same year and the other half contains information for one year in advance. The variables include the target variable, which is whether a company is bankrupt or not, and the most popular variables used in bankruptcy prediction models: Return on Assets, Net Income, Retained Earnings, Total Assets, Working Capital, Earnings Before Interest and Taxes, Net Sales, Cash, Current Assets, Total Stockholder's Equity, Total Debt, and Total Current Liabilities. The target variable is severely imbalanced as each dataset has 78,321 nonbankrupt entries, but the dataset for one year in advance has 426 bankrupt points while the dataset within the same year has 353 bankrupt points.

Pre-Existing Sampling Techniques Used in This Study

There are two main categories of sampling methods: undersampling and oversampling. Undersampling reduces the size of the majority class to match the size of the minority class. The most basic form of undersampling, random undersampling, picks a subset of the majority class points randomly in order to have the same number of points as the minority class. The other type of sampling, oversampling, increases the size of the minority class to meet the size of the majority class. Random oversampling duplicates points from the minority population randomly until there are just as many minority points as there are majority points. While this study compares the results of the proposed method to both random undersampling and random oversampling, it compares SMOTE-based oversampling techniques as well.

One of the most popular oversampling methods is Synthetic Minority Over-sampling Technique, or SMOTE, which creates new samples of the minority class based on the other minority samples around it. The algorithm starts by selecting a minority point and drawing lines between it and the closest minority points around it. It then imagines new points along those connecting lines.

SMOTE is widely used, even outside the field of bankruptcy prediction, for the following reasons. First, as with oversampling in general, none of the information in any of the majority points is discarded, like in undersampling. Next, SMOTE has been shown to be less prone to overfitting than random oversampling. With random oversampling, points that already exist in the dataset are duplicated, and in the case of bankruptcy data, a model would only understand the type of companies that are represented by these points. But, because SMOTE generates points that are different than the points in the original minority class with features that other similar companies may have, a model would have a better chance of recognizing not only the companies in the original minority population of the dataset but also bankrupt companies that are similar.

The downsides to SMOTE are as follows. First, it tends to generate noise. If the points that SMOTE generates are not useful nor representative of the minority population, they may lead inaccurate predictions. Second, while SMOTE is not as prone as random oversampling to overfitting, it is still possible for it to lead to overfitting, especially with extremely imbalanced data.

This study also compares the Bagging Undersampling results with several other algorithms that are variations of SMOTE. Each of the following algorithms follows the aforementioned SMOTE procedures apart from the changes that follow. Adaptive Neighbor SMOTE (ANS) changes the number of lines drawn from each minority point depending on number of minority points around it. So, if a point is an outlier and does not have any minority points close to it, ANS will only draw one line between it and its closest point. The goal of this is to reduce noise while still including the information captured in outliers (Siriseriwan et al., 2017). Borderline

SMOTE (BLSMOTE) generates more points from minority points that are near majority points. The algorithm takes each "pocket" of minority points and selects the points on the border of these pockets to generate more points from them. Because these borderline points are closer to non-bankrupt points, they are often more easily misclassified as majority class by a model. The goal is to produce more of these points so that the model can learn that they are minority points. Finally, Density Based SMOTE (DBSMOTE), starts by clustering the minority points and then generates samples on the line between each point and the closest cluster's centroid. The goal is to segment the bankrupt points into clusters to capture points with similar features within these clusters. Then by only drawing one line between each point and the cluster center, noise is reduced because the points generated along this line should be within the cluster that, ideally, represents a type of company that the algorithm will see again (Bunkhumpornpat et al., 2012).

Metrics for Model Performance

Each of the metrics uses information from the following confusion matrix. Sensitivity, otherwise known as the true positive rate, shows how well the model predicted on the minority population by taking the number of points that were predicted to be positive and are in fact positive and dividing it by the number of points that are actually positive regardless of what the model predicted.

Specificity, or the true negative rate, shows how well the model predicted on the majority population by taking the number of points that were predicted to be negative and are in fact negative and dividing it by the number of points that are actually negative regardless of what the model predicted. Balanced accuracy is a metric that evaluates both sensitivity and specificity by averaging them. It is used to account for how well the model predicts for both the majority and minority populations.

Model Selection

There are three types of models that are used in bankruptcy prediction studies: statistical models, AI models, and ensemble methods. However, because statistical methods and linear models do not perform as well as machine learning models, this study will focus on machine learning models (Barboza et. al.

2017) (Sun et al., 2014) (Kumar et al., 2007). While numerous models have been tested in bankruptcy studies, one that the review in 2014 praised highly for its power and interpretability is the decision tree, and the study suggested using them in ensemble methods (Sun et al., 2014). This is one of the reasons why this study chooses to implement a random forest, which is an ensemble of decision trees after bagging. Bagging, or bootstrap aggregating entails sampling from the data with replacement (bootstrapping) and then training and testing decision trees on these samples, taking a majority vote to make a prediction for each testing point (aggregating). Random forest uses a combination of the results of many decision trees as its final prediction with the hope of increasing predictive ability. The more bags, or samples, that are taken, and the more models that are trained, the less likely the random forest is to miss out on information from the data. The only thing this model forfeits is the interpretability that is characteristic of decision trees. However, its predictive ability is much higher than that of a decision tree.

To solidify the decision to use a random forest in this study, a random forest is compared to several other machine learning algorithms including a fast implementation of AdaBoost, logistic regression, naïve Bayes, decision tree, and support vector machine.

Proposed Sampling Method

After splitting the data with a 70/30 training/testing split, the study compares the five oversampling techniques (random oversampling, SMOTE, and the three SMOTE variations) and random undersampling. It also tests these with different imbalance ratios, meaning the sampling algorithms are used to generate different ratios of majority to minority points, and compares the results of the random forest across different levels of imbalance. The range of the imbalanced ratios used was 1 to 183, with 183 being the original imbalance ratio of the full dataset. The proposed Bagging Undersampling technique undersamples the majority population to yield a certain imbalance ratio and then repeats this on 200 bagged samples from the training set. The resulting 200 training set samples are used to train and test 200 random forests, and the resulting predictions are yielded by a majority voting procedure.

Algorithm

For imbalance ratio ($\dfrac{\sum majority\, observations}{\sum minority\, observations}$) = 1, 2,…mm where mm equals the original imbalance ratio of the dataset:

1. Apply random undersampling to yield an imbalance ratio of k 200 times yielding 200 trainings sets.
2. Train 200 random forests on the 200 training subsets, and then receive a prediction on the testing set from each of the random forests.
3. Perform majority vote, where the most common prediction among the 200 models is used as the final prediction for each observation in the testing set.
4. Next k.

RESULTS

Oversampling Techniques

The oversampling methods were prone to overfitting. Figure 1 shows the balanced accuracy (i.e., the y-axis) for each imbalance ratio (i.e., x-axis) after applying each oversampling technique on the portion of the data that is trying to predict bankruptcy within the same year. The balanced accuracy on the training set is in blue and on the testing set is in orange. The trend of the training balanced accuracy to slope upward while the testing balanced accuracy slopes downward is indicative of overfitting. ANS is the best of these methods, but it is still overfit.

Bagging Undersampling

Figure 2 shows the balanced accuracy after applying Bagging Undersampling for predictions within the same year on the left and for one year in advance on the right. For an imbalance ratio of 1.2, the model yields the best balanced accuracy and is not yet overfit because the curve of the testing points (orange) starts as an upwards slope, increasing simultaneously with the training balanced accuracy (blue). It peaks at an imbalance ratio of 1.2 and afterwards starts to slope downwards while the training curve continues to increase. In other words, it starts to overfit.

Figure 3 compares the performance of the aforementioned oversampling techniques with random undersampling and Bagging Undersampling. It shows the balanced accuracy on the testing set for each of these methods. For both the models that predicted bankruptcy within the same year (orange bars) and the models that predicted one year in advance (blue bars), Bagging Undersampling yields the best balanced accuracies.

FUTURE RESEARCH DIRECTIONS

For future study, our results suggest the use and exploration of undersampling techniques as there are many other options that this study did not investigate. The use of undersampling might be combined with different strategies to rank or weight the importance of regions in the dataset to set the degree of elimination in each region. We also suggest using ensemble techniques to tune the balanced ratios in the desired undersampled dataset.

CONCLUSION

In this study, we implement a variety of resampling techniques to handle the imbalance issues in bankruptcy prediction. We have found that the oversampling techniques tends to lead to overfitting. Our study shows that out of all the implemented oversampling methods, the ANS method yields the least overfit models. We also proposed a method that combine the idea of undersampling and oversampling and illustrated that our method was able to avoid overfitting and yield a notable balanced accuracy.

Figure 1. Balanced accuracy for models predicting bankruptcy within the same year after applying oversampling techniques. Note that the axes for each of the diagrams is the same

SMOTE

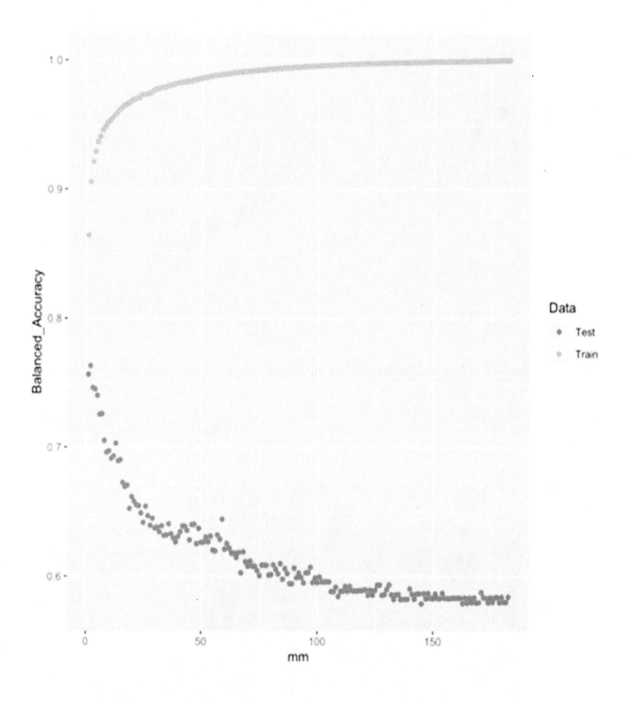

Figure 2. Training and testing balanced accuracy for models predicting within the same year and for one year in advance after applying Bagging Undersampling to the training data

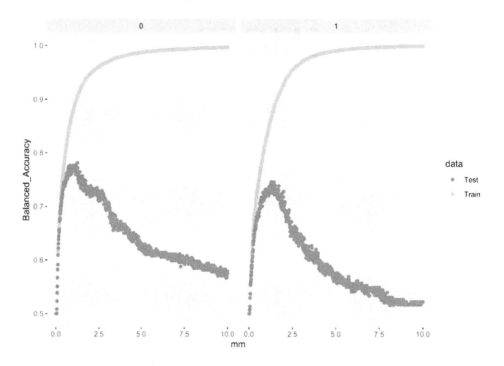

Figure 3. Comparison of balanced accuracies on the testing sets after applying each of the sampling techniques

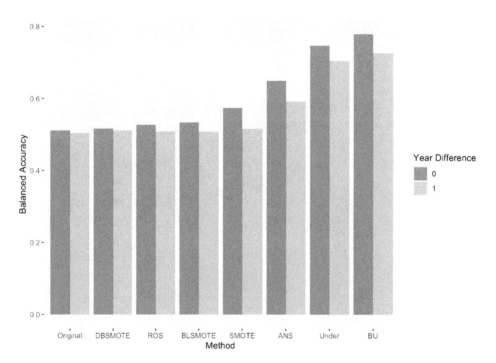

REFERENCES

Abellán, J., & Mantas, C. J. (2014). Improving experimental studies about ensembles of classifiers for bankruptcy prediction and credit scoring. *Expert Systems with Applications*, *41*(8), 3825–3830. doi:10.1016/j.eswa.2013.12.003

Altman, E. I. (1968). Financial ratios, discriminant analysis and the prediction of corporate bankruptcy. *The Journal of Finance*, *23*(4), 589–609. doi:10.1111/j.1540-6261.1968.tb00843.x

Barboza, F., Kimura, H., & Altman, E. (2017). Machine learning models and bankruptcy prediction. *Expert Systems with Applications*, *83*, 405–417. doi:10.1016/j.eswa.2017.04.006

Beaver, W. H. (1966). Financial ratios as predictors of failure. *Journal of Accounting Research*, *4*, 71–111. doi:10.2307/2490171

Ben Jabeur, S., Stef, N., & Carmona, P. (2022). Bankruptcy Prediction using the XGBoost Algorithm and Variable Importance Feature Engineering. *Computational Economics*, 1–27. doi:10.100710614-021-10227-1

Brezigar-Masten, A., & Masten, I. (2012). CART-based selection of bankruptcy predictors for the logit model. *Expert Systems with Applications*, *39*(11), 10153–10159. doi:10.1016/j.eswa.2012.02.125

Bunkhumpornpat, C., Sinapiromsaran, K., & Lursinsap, C. (2012). DBSMOTE: Density-based synthetic minority over-sampling technique. *Applied Intelligence*, *36*(3), 664–684. doi:10.100710489-011-0287-y

Douzas, G., Bacao, F., & Last, F. (2018). Improving imbalanced learning through a heuristic oversampling method based on k-means and SMOTE. *Information Sciences*, *465*, 1–20. doi:10.1016/j.ins.2018.06.056

Fedorova, E., Gilenko, E., & Dovzhenko, S. (2013). Bankruptcy prediction for Russian companies: Application of combined classifiers. *Expert Systems with Applications*, *40*(18), 7285–7293. doi:10.1016/j.eswa.2013.07.032

Jeong, C., Min, J. H., & Kim, M. S. (2012). A tuning method for the architecture of neural network models incorporating GAM and GA as applied to bankruptcy prediction. *Expert Systems with Applications*, *39*(3), 3650–3658. doi:10.1016/j.eswa.2011.09.056

Kim, M. J., & Kang, D. K. (2010). Ensemble with neural networks for bankruptcy prediction. *Expert Systems with Applications*, *37*(4), 3373–3379. doi:10.1016/j.eswa.2009.10.012

Kim, M. J., Kang, D. K., & Kim, H. B. (2015). Geometric mean based boosting algorithm with over-sampling to resolve data imbalance problem for bankruptcy prediction. *Expert Systems with Applications*, *42*(3), 1074–1082. doi:10.1016/j.eswa.2014.08.025

Kumar, P. R., & Ravi, V. (2007). Bankruptcy prediction in banks and firms via statistical and intelligent techniques–A review. *European Journal of Operational Research*, *180*(1), 1–28. doi:10.1016/j.ejor.2006.08.043

Lin, F., Liang, D., Yeh, C. C., & Huang, J. C. (2014). Novel feature selection methods to financial distress prediction. *Expert Systems with Applications*, *41*(5), 2472–2483. doi:10.1016/j.eswa.2013.09.047

Lin, W. C., Tsai, C. F., Hu, Y. H., & Jhang, J. S. (2017). Clustering-based undersampling in class-imbalanced data. *Information Sciences*, *409*, 17–26. doi:10.1016/j.ins.2017.05.008

Min, J. H., & Jeong, C. (2009). A binary classification method for bankruptcy prediction. *Expert Systems with Applications*, *36*(3), 5256–5263. doi:10.1016/j.eswa.2008.06.073

Ohlson, J. A. (1980). Financial ratios and the probabilistic prediction of bankruptcy. *Journal of Accounting Research*, *18*(1), 109–131. doi:10.2307/2490395

Režňáková, M., & Karas, M. (2014). Bankruptcy prediction models: Can the prediction power of the models be improved by using dynamic indicators? *Procedia Economics and Finance*, *12*, 565–574. doi:10.1016/S2212-5671(14)00380-3

Shetty, S., Musa, M., & Brédart, X. (2022). Bankruptcy Prediction Using Machine Learning Techniques. *Journal of Risk and Financial Management*, *15*(1), 35. doi:10.3390/jrfm15010035

Siriseriwan, W., & Sinapiromsaran, K. (2017). Adaptive neighbor synthetic minority oversampling technique under 1NN outcast handling. *Songklanakarin Journal of Science and Technology*, *39*(5), 565–576.

Sun, J., Li, H., Huang, Q. H., & He, K. Y. (2014). Predicting financial distress and corporate failure: A review from the state-of-the-art definitions, modeling, sampling, and featuring approaches. *Knowledge-Based Systems*, *57*, 41–56. doi:10.1016/j.knosys.2013.12.006

Tian, S., Yu, Y., & Guo, H. (2015). Variable selection and corporate bankruptcy forecasts. *Journal of Banking & Finance*, *52*, 89–100. doi:10.1016/j.jbankfin.2014.12.003

Tinoco, M. H., & Wilson, N. (2013). Financial distress and bankruptcy prediction among listed companies using accounting, market and macroeconomic variables. *International Review of Financial Analysis*, *30*, 394–419. doi:10.1016/j.irfa.2013.02.013

Veganzones, D., & Séverin, E. (2018). An investigation of bankruptcy prediction in imbalanced datasets. *Decision Support Systems*, *112*, 111–124. doi:10.1016/j.dss.2018.06.011

Wang, G., Ma, J., & Yang, S. (2014). An improved boosting based on feature selection for corporate bankruptcy prediction. *Expert Systems with Applications*, *41*(5), 2353–2361. doi:10.1016/j.eswa.2013.09.033

Wu, Y., Gaunt, C., & Gray, S. (2010). A comparison of alternative bankruptcy prediction models. *Journal of Contemporary Accounting & Economics*, *6*(1), 34–45. doi:10.1016/j.jcae.2010.04.002

Zhou, L. (2013). Performance of corporate bankruptcy prediction models on imbalanced dataset: The effect of sampling methods. *Knowledge-Based Systems*, *41*, 16–25. doi:10.1016/j.knosys.2012.12.007

Zhou, L., Tam, K. P., & Fujita, H. (2016). Predicting the listing status of Chinese listed companies with multi-class classification models. *Information Sciences*, *328*, 222–236. doi:10.1016/j.ins.2015.08.036

Zmijewski, M. E. (1984). Methodological issues related to the estimation of financial distress prediction models. *Journal of Accounting Research*, *22*, 59–82. doi:10.2307/2490859

ADDITIONAL READING

Bellovary, J. L., Giacomino, D. E., & Akers, M. D. (2007). A review of bankruptcy prediction studies: 1930 to present. *Journal of Financial Education*, 1-42.

E

Chava, S., & Jarrow, R. A. (2004). Bankruptcy prediction with industry effects. *Review of Finance*, 8(4), 537–569. doi:10.1093/rof/8.4.537

Odom, M. D., & Sharda, R. (1990, June). A neural network model for bankruptcy prediction. In *1990 IJCNN International Joint Conference on neural networks* (pp. 163-168). IEEE. 10.1109/IJCNN.1990.137710

Shin, K. S., Lee, T. S., & Kim, H. J. (2005). An application of support vector machines in bankruptcy prediction model. *Expert Systems with Applications*, 28(1), 127–135. doi:10.1016/j.eswa.2004.08.009

Shin, K. S., & Lee, Y. J. (2002). A genetic algorithm application in bankruptcy prediction modeling. *Expert Systems with Applications*, 23(3), 321–328. doi:10.1016/S0957-4174(02)00051-9

Wilson, R. L., & Sharda, R. (1994). Bankruptcy prediction using neural networks. *Decision Support Systems*, 11(5), 545–557. doi:10.1016/0167-9236(94)90024-8

Wu, Y., Gaunt, C., & Gray, S. (2010). A comparison of alternative bankruptcy prediction models. *Journal of Contemporary Accounting & Economics*, 6(1), 34–45. doi:10.1016/j.jcae.2010.04.002

Zhang, G., Hu, M. Y., Patuwo, B. E., & Indro, D. C. (1999). Artificial neural networks in bankruptcy prediction: General framework and cross-validation analysis. *European Journal of Operational Research*, 116(1), 16–32. doi:10.1016/S0377-2217(98)00051-4

KEY TERMS AND DEFINITIONS

Balanced Accuracy: The average of the true positive rate and the true negative rate of a predictive model. Balanced accuracy is often used as a measure of a predictive model trained on an imbalanced dataset.

Classification Random Forest: A classification models using the majority votes of multiple classification trees to predict. A split of a tree in a random forest is determined using only by considering a pre-selected number of variables in the dataset.

Classification Tree: A classification model that breaks the data into regions using hyperplanes (in two-dimension hyperplanes are lines) then assigns labels to the regions by majority voting.

Imbalanced Classification: The problem of classifying a dataset into different categories where the distribution of sizes of the categories is not uniform, i.e., one category may have too many observations while other categories may have too few observations.

Oversampling: The process of randomly adding duplicate observations in the minority class until the minority class has the same observations as the majority class.

Resampling: The process of balancing the majority class and the minority class so that the ratio of the sizes of these two classes reaches a desired number.

Undersampling: The process of randomly eliminating observations in the majority class until the majority class has the same observations as the minority class.

Ensemble Methods and Their Applications

M. Govindarajan

Annamalai University, India

INTRODUCTION

Considering the variety of ensemble techniques and the large number of combination schemes proposed in literature, it is not surprising that a very large number of ensemble methods and algorithms are now available to the research community. To help the researchers and practitioners to get their bearings and to develop new methods and techniques, several taxonomies of ensemble methods have been proposed. Indeed, ensemble methods are characterized by two basic features: 1) the algorithms by which different base learners are combined; 2) the techniques by which different and diverse base learners are generated. This chapter basically distinguishes between non-generative ensemble methods that mainly rely on the former feature of ensemble methods, and generative ensembles that mainly focus on the latter. It is worth noting that the "combination" and the "generation" of base learners are somehow both present in all ensemble methods: the distinction between these two large classes depends on the predominance of the combination or of the generation component of the ensemble algorithm. More precisely, non-generative ensemble methods confine themselves to combine a set of possibly well-designed base classifiers: they do not actively generate new base learners but try to combine in a suitable way a set of existing base classifiers. On the contrary, generative ensemble methods generate sets of base learners acting on the base learning algorithm or on the structure of the data set to try to actively improve diversity and accuracy of the base learners. In this case the emphasis is placed on the way diverse base learners are constructed, while the combination technique does not represent the main issue of the ensemble algorithm. The main aim of this chapter is to explain the detailed characteristics of each ensemble methods and to provide an overview of the main application areas of ensemble methods. The rest of the chapter is organized as follows: the background section describes the related work. A brief description of ensemble methods reported in the literature, distinguishing between generative and non-generative methods, main application areas of ensemble methods is presented in section of main focus of the chapter. Finally, the chapter concludes with future research directions.

BACKGROUND

Patil et al., (2016) attempts to build robust data mining models to predict the defaulters using data obtained from one of finance company and various ensemble algorithms like bagging, boosting and stacking are implemented. Araque et al., (2017) seek to improve the performance of deep learning techniques integrating them with traditional surface approaches based on manually extracted features. Chubato Wondaferaw Yohannese et al. (2018) are to conduct large scale comprehensive experiments to study the effect of resolving those challenges in Software Fault Prediction in three stages in order to improve the practice and performance of Software Fault Prediction. Silas Nzuva et al., (2019) review the superiority exhibited by ensemble learning algorithms based on the past that has been carried out over

DOI: 10.4018/978-1-7998-9220-5.ch109

the years. Gupta et al., (2019) proposed an approach for Facial Expression Recognition using Ensemble Learning Technique. In the proposed method, initially the features are extracted from static images using color histograms. This process is done for all images gathered in the training dataset. The ensemble technique is then applied on the featured dataset in order to categorize a given image into one of the six emotions, happy, sad, fear, angry, disgust, and surprise. Peterson et al., (2019) introduce the application of canonical correlation analysis fusion as a method for water-based spectral analysis to overcome the low signal-to-noise ratio of the data. Water-quality variables and spectral reflectance were used to create predictive models via machine learning regression models, including multiple linear regression, partial least-squares regression, Gaussian process regression, support vector machine regression, and extreme learning machine regression. The models were then combined using decision-level fusion. Thanh and Lang (2019) analyzes and evaluates the performance of using known ensemble techniques such as Bagging, AdaBoost, Stacking, Decorate, Random Forest and Voting to detect DoS attacks on UNSW-NB15 dataset, created by the Australian Cyber Security Center 2015. Singh et al., (2020) have developed a model to combine the results of each individual base learner using Bagging and Boosting ensemble methods. The results obtained using bagging and boosting ensemble techniques were compared to select the best model. Yu et al., (2020) propose an end-to-end deep ensemble learning based on the weight optimization (DELWO) model. It contributes to fusing the deep information derived from multiple models automatically from the data. Huang et al., (2020) proposes an ensemble-learning-approach-based solution of integrating a rich body of features derived from high resolution satellite images, street-view images, building footprints, points-of-interest (POIs) and social media check-ins for the urban land use mapping task. The proposed approach can statistically differentiate the importance of input feature variables and provides a good explanation for the relationships between land cover, socioeconomic activities and land use categories. Rajagopal et al., (2020) present an ensemble model using meta classification approach enabled by stacked generalization. Akhter et al., (2021) use five ensemble learning methods to ensemble the base-predictors' predictions to improve the fake news detection system's overall performance. Gaikwad (2021) proposed a novel ensemble classifier using rule combination method for intrusion detection system. Ensemble classifier is designed using three rule learners as base classifiers. The benefits and feasibility of the proposed ensemble classifier have demonstrated by means of KDD'98 datasets. The main novelty of the proposed approach is based on three rule learner combination using rule of combination method of ensemble and feature selector. These three base classifiers are separately trained and combined using average probabilities rule combination. Mehmet Akif Yamana et al., (2021) presented different algorithms employing skin color for face detection, histogram tor the feature extraction and ensemble methods for recognition part. Hence, the developed Bagging and Boosting has thoroughly presented their superiority over FERET database. Advanced classification capabilities of the ensemble classifiers are having better accuracy than the existing methods in the face recognition. Jafarzadeh et al., (2021) investigates the capability of different EL algorithms, generally known as bagging and boosting algorithms, including Adaptive Boosting (AdaBoost), Gradient Boosting Machine (GBM), XGBoost, LightGBM, and Random Forest (RF), for the classification of Remote Sensing (RS) data.

FOCUS OF THE ARTICLE

Ensemble Learning

Ensemble learning is a machine learning technique where multiple learners are trained to solve the same problem and their predictions are combined with a single output that probably has better performance on average than any individual ensemble member. The fundamental idea behind ensemble learning is to combine weak learners into one, a strong learner, who has a better generalization error and is less sensitive to overfitting in the presence of noise or small sample size. This is because different classifiers can sometimes misclassify different patterns and accuracy can be improved by combining the decisions of complementary classifiers.

The Concept Behind Ensemble Learning Models

The training of ensemble learning models is based on the psychological model of training humans for teamwork. For example, in a competition, an individual might not know the answer for all the questions asked to him/her. The individual will rely on guessing the answer, which will make the individual prone to failure. However, in a team, while one team member doesn't know the answer of any particular topic, the rest of his/her team members might be aware of the answers for the said question. Let's say if three members of the team are confident to conclude a similar answer for the question and three are making varied assumptions regarding the answer, the probability of giving the wrong answer gets distributed. The team will pick the confident answer ensuring reliability. Furthermore, the wrong guesses are distributed to the individuals having all the wrong answers, thus cancelling each other out. And the correct guess will be clustered around the correct answer. Similarly, as multiple machine learning models are trained in ensemble learning technique, the incidents of making errors get distributed. For example, if a machine learning model has insufficient data to be trained on, this issue will be negated by the models that have sufficient or large amount of data. This implies less room for making mistakes with improved accuracy. Since all models are prone to make different errors to a different extent, the errors get distributed across the thread of models, instead of getting clustered to a particular one. Instead of data clustering over the single model, the data also gets distributed across the thread of machine learning models, thus reducing the incidents of errors and improving accuracy.

Elements of an Ensemble Classifier

A typical ensemble framework for classification tasks contains four fundamental components described as follows:

- **Training set:** a training set is a special set of labeled examples providing known information that are used for training.
- **Base inducer(s) or base classifier(s):** an inducer is a learning algorithm that is used to learn from a training set. A base inducer obtains a training set and constructs a classifier that generalizes relationship between the input features and the target outcome.
- **Diversity generator:** it is clear that nothing is gained from an ensemble model if all ensemble members are identical. The diversity generator is responsible for generating the diverse classifiers and decides the type of every base classifier that differs from each other. Diversity can be realized

in different ways depending on the accuracy of individual classifiers for the improved classification performance. Common diversity creation approaches are using different training sets, (ii) combining different inducers, and (iii) using different parameters for a single inducer.

- **Combiner:** the task of the combiner is to produce the final decision by combining all classification results of the various base inducers. There are two main methods of combining: weighting methods and meta-learning methods. *Weighting methods* give each classifier a weight proportional to its strength and combine their votes based on these weights. The weights can be fixed or dynamically determined when classifying an instance. Common weighting methods are majority voting, performance weighting, Bayesian combination, and vogging. *Meta-learning methods* learn from new training data created from the predictions of a set of base classifiers. The most well-known meta-learning methods are stacking and grading. While weighting methods are useful when combining classifiers built from a single learning algorithm and they have comparable success, meta-learning is a good choice for cases in which base classifiers consistently classify correctly or consistently misclassify.

Ensemble Strategies

In order to construct an ensemble model, any of the following strategies can be performed:

- **Strategy 1: different training sets using random sampling with replacement:** One ensemble strategy is to train different base learners by different subsets of the training set. This can be done by random resampling of a dataset (i.e., *bagging*). When multiple base learners are trained with different training sets, it is possible to reduce variance and therefore error.
- **Strategy 2: different training sets obtained by random instance and feature subset selection:** The combination of bagged decision trees is constructed similar to Strategy 1 using one significant adjustment that random feature subsets are used (i.e., *random forest*). When there are enough trees in the forest, random forest classifier is less likely overfit the model. It is also useful to reduce the variance of low-bias models, besides handling missing values easily.
- **Strategy 3: different training sets using random sampling with replacement over weighted data:** This ensemble strategy can be implemented by weighted resampling of the dataset serially by focusing on difficult examples which are not correctly classified in the previous steps (i.e., *boosting*). Boosting helps to decrease the bias of otherwise stable learners such as linear classifiers or univariate decision trees also known as decision stumps.
- **Strategy 4: different algorithms:**The other ensemble strategy (i.e., *voting*) is to use different learning algorithms to train different base learners on the same dataset. So, the ensemble includes diverse algorithms that each takes a completely different approach. The main idea behind this kind of ensemble learning is taking advantage of classification algorithms' diversity to face complex data.

Taxonomies of Ensemble Methods

A large number of combination schemes and ensemble methods have been proposed in literature. Combination techniques can be grouped and analysed in different ways, depending on the main classification criterion adopted. If the representation of the input patterns is considered as the main criterion, two distinct large groups, one that uses the same and one that uses different representations of the inputs can be identified. (JKittler, 1998; Kittler et al., 1998). Table 1 provides a high-level scheme of the taxonomy of ensemble methods discussed in this chapter.

Assuming the architecture of the ensemble as the main criterion, serial, parallel and hierarchical schemes can be distinguished (Lam, 2000), and if the base learners are selected or not by the ensemble algorithm, selection oriented and combiner-oriented ensemble methods can be separated (Jain et al., 2000; Kuncheva et al., 2001). In this brief overview an approach similar to the one cited above is adopted in order to distinguish between non-generative and generative ensemble methods. Non-generative ensemble methods confine their selves to combine a set of given possibly well-designed base learners: they do not actively generate new base learners but try to combine in a suitable way a set of existing base classifiers. Generative ensemble methods generate sets of base learners acting on the base learning algorithm or on the structure of the data set and try to actively improve diversity and accuracy of the base learners.

Table 1. A taxonomy for ensemble methods

Non generative ensembles	Ensemble fusion methods	- Majority voting - Naive Bayes rule - Behavior-Knowledge-Space - Algebraic operators fusion - Fuzzy fusion - Decision Template - Meta Learning - Multi-label hierarchical methods
	Ensemble selection methods	- Test and select - Cascading classifiers - Dynamic classifier selection - Clustering based selection - Pruning by statistical tests - Pruning by semidef. programming - Forward/Backward selection
Generative ensembles	Resampling methods	- Bagging - Boosting - Arcing - Cross-validated committees
	Feature selection and extraction methods	- Random Subspace - Similarity based selection - Input decimation - Feature subset search - Rotation forests
	Mixture of experts	- Gating network selection - Hierarchical mixture of experts - Hybrid experts
	Output Coding methods	- One Per Class - Pairwise and Correcting Classifiers - ECOC - Data driven ECOC
	Randomized methods	- Randomized decision trees - Random forests - Pasting small votes

Non-generative Ensemble Methods

The subdivisions of non-generative strategies are ensemble fusion and ensemble selection methods. Both these approaches share the very general common property of using a predetermined set of learning machines previously trained with suitable algorithms. The base learners are then put together by a combiner module that may vary depending on the requirement of the output of the individual learning machines: for instance, the combiner may need the labels of the classes, or a ranking of the classes, or a support (e.g., the a posteriori probability estimation) for each class (Xu et al., 1992). Moreover, combiners that are trainable and not trainable may be distinguished (Duin, 2002). Very schematically ensemble fusion methods combine all the outputs of the base classifiers, while ensemble selection methods try to choose the "best classifiers" among the set of the available base learners.

Ensemble Fusion Methods

The most popular ensemble fusion method is represented by the *majority voting* ensemble, by which each base classifier "votes" for a specific class, and the class that collects the majority of votes is predicted by the ensemble. Other simple operators such as Minimum, Maximum, Average, Product and Ordered Weight Averaging have been applied to combine multiple classifiers. Ensemble fusion can be performed also by second-level trainable combiners, through meta-learning techniques. For instance, in stacking methods the outputs of the base learners are interpreted as features in an intermediate space: the outputs are fed into a second-level machine to perform a trained combination of the base learners

Ensemble Selection Methods

This general approach tries to identify the "best" base classifier among the set of base learners for a specified input, and the output of the ensemble is the output of the selected best classifier. From a more general standpoint also a subset of base classifiers can be chosen. In this case their needs to pick one of the selected outputs as the ensemble output, or to combine the output of the base learners, according, e.g., to one of the ensemble fusion methods described in the previous section. To design an ensemble selection method, how to build the individual classifiers, how to evaluate the competence of each classifier on a specific input, what selection strategy to use should be decided. The test and select methodology relies on a greedy approach, by which a new learner is added to the ensemble only if the resulting squared error is reduced, but in principle any optimization technique can be used to select the "best" component of the ensemble, including genetic algorithms. Another possible approach is represented by cascading classifiers. The base learners are applied sequentially, and if the confidence of the first classifier is high, its prediction is taken, otherwise the prediction is recursively demanded to the next classifier and so on. This "cascade" model is useful especially with real-time systems, since most of the inputs need to be processed by a few classifiers. Other greedy search methods are based on a ranking that gives preference to classifiers that are able to correct the incorrect predictions of the ensemble, as in *Orientation Ordering* ensembles, thus assuring the selection of base learners able to improve the prediction of the overall ensemble. Ensembles of heterogeneous classifiers can also be pruned by statistical procedures that select only those classifiers with significantly better performances, combined in a second step through majority voting.

Generative Ensemble Methods

In this section, ensemble methods are introduced that can generate base learners by acting on the base learning algorithm or on the structure of the data set to try to actively boost diversity and accuracy of the base learners. These methods can perturb the structure and the characteristics of the available input data, as in *resampling* methods or in *feature selection/subsampling* methods or can manipulate the aggregation and the coding of the classes (*Output Coding* methods), or can select base learners specialized for a specific input region (*mixture of experts* methods). They can also randomly modify the base learning algorithm or apply randomized procedures to the learning processes to improve the diversity or to avoid local minima of the error (*randomized* methods).

Resampling Methods

Bagging

Bagging is a "bootstrap" ensemble method that creates individuals for its ensemble by training each classifier on a random redistribution of the training set. Each classifier's training set is generated by randomly drawing, with replacement, t, N examples – where N is the size of the original training set; many of the original examples may be repeated in the resulting training set while others may be left out. Each individual classifier in the ensemble is generated with a different random sampling of the training set.

Boosting

Boosting is a general method for improving the accuracy of any given learning algorithm. Boosting's roots are in a theoretical framework for studying machine learning called the PAC learning model. In 1999, a boosting algorithm called AdaBoost, which stands for adaptive boost. AdaBoost also uses perturbation and combination. But it adopts the way of adaptively resample and combining so that the weights in the resampling are increased for those cases most often misclassified. Combining is done by weighted voting. For AdaBoost, a set of weights is maintained over the training set. One way to implement AdaBoost in practice is to resample the dataset based on the weights of the instances. This weight for each instance is adjusted in each round according to whether the instance is correctly classified or not. After a family of classifiers is built based on the adaptively resampled replicates, they are combined using weighted voting.

Arcing

Breiman introduced Arcing ('Adaptive Resampling and Combining') as a generalization of Bagging and Boosting. In Arcing, as Breiman puts it, "modified training sets are formed by resampling from the original training set, classifiers constructed using these training sets and then combined by voting. In this research, the variants of voting methods are analyzed in Arcing. Arcing is a more complex procedure. Again, multiple classifiers are constructed and vote for classes. But the construction is sequential, with the construction of the $(k+1)^{st}$ classifier depending on the performance of the k previously constructed classifiers. At the start of each construction, there is a probability distribution $\{p(n)\}$ on the cases in the training set. A training set T' is constructed by sampling N times from this distribution. Then the probabilities are updated depending on how the cases in T are classified by C(x,T'). A factor $\beta > 1$ is defined which depends on the misclassification rate. If the nth case in T is misclassified by C(x,T'), then put weight βp(n) on that case. Otherwise define the weight to be p(n). Now divide each weight by the sum of the weights to get the updated probabilities for the next round of sampling. After a fixed number of classifiers have been constructed, voting is done for the class.

Feature Selection/Extraction Methods

Reducing the number of input features of the base learners can contrast the effects of the classical curse of dimensionality problem that characterize high-dimensional and sparse data. For instance, by applying feature selection algorithms or subsampling methods to draw subsets of features from the available data, sets of diverse base classifiers can be constructed that can be combined through appropriate ensemble fusion techniques. A random strategy can be applied to select sets of features. In Random Subspace methods, a subset of features is randomly selected and assigned to an arbitrary learning algorithm: a random subspace of the original feature space is obtained, and classifiers are constructed inside this reduced subspace. The aggregation is usually performed using weighted voting on the basis of the base classifier's accuracy, but other techniques could be in principle applied. Another effective method that relies on feature extraction techniques is represented by the rotation forests. Features are randomly split into n subsets, and n axis rotations are performed to encourage simultaneously individual accuracy and diversity within the ensemble.

Mixtures of Expert's Methods

The recombination of the base learners can be governed by a supervisor learning machine that selects the most appropriate element of the ensemble on the basis of the available input data. This idea led to the mixture of expert's methods (Jacobs, et al., 1991; Jacobs, 1995), where a gating network performs the division of the input space and small neural networks perform the effective calculation at each assigned region separately. An extension of this approach is the hierarchical mixture of expert's method, where the outputs of the different experts are non-linearly combined by different supervisor gating networks hierarchically organized (Jordan et al., 1992, 1994; Jacobs, 1995).

Output Coding Methods

By manipulating the coding of classes in multi-class classification problems, ensembles can be constructed that are able to partially correct errors committed by the base learners, exploiting the redundancy in the bit-string representation of the classes. More precisely, Output Coding (OC) methods decompose a multiclass-classification problem in a set of two-class sub problems, and then recompose the original problem combining them to achieve the class label. An equivalent way of thinking about these methods consists in encoding each class as a bit string (named codeword), and in training a different two-class base learner (dichotomizer) in order to separately learn each codeword bit. When the dichotomizers are applied to classify new points, a suitable measure of dissimilarity between the codeword computed by the ensemble and the codeword classes is used to predict the class (e.g. Hamming distance). Error Correcting Output Coding (ECOC) is the most studied OC method, and has been successfully applied to several classification problems. This decomposition method tries to improve the error correcting capabilities of the codes generated by the decomposition through the maximization of the minimum distance between each pair of codewords. This goal is achieved by means of the redundancy of the coding scheme.

Randomized Ensemble Methods

Injecting randomness into the learning algorithm is another general method to generate ensembles of learning machines. Several experimental results showed that randomized learning algorithms used to generate base elements of ensembles improve the performances of single non-randomized classifiers. For instance, in (Dietterich, 2000b) randomized decision tree ensembles outperform single C4.5 decision trees (Quinlan, 1993), and adding gaussian noise to the data inputs, together with bootstrap and weight regularization can achieve large improvements in classification accuracy (Raviv et al., 1996).

Evaluation of Ensemble Methods

A successful ensemble could be described as having accurate predictors and commits errors in the different parts of the input space. An important factor in measuring the performance of an ensemble lies in the generalization error. Generalization error measures how a learning module performs on out of sample data. It is measured as the difference between the prediction of the module and the actual results. Analyzing the generalization errors allows us to understand the source of the error and the correct technique to minimize it. Understanding the generation error also allows probing the base predictors underlying characteristics causing this error. To improve the forecasting accuracy of an ensemble, the generalization error should be minimized by increasing the ambiguity yet without increasing the bias. In practice, such an approach could be challenging to achieve. Ambiguity is improved by increasing the diversity of the base learners where a more diverse set of parameters is used to induce the learning process. As the diversity increases, the space for prediction function also increases. A larger space for prediction improves the accuracy of the prediction function given the more diverse set of parameters used to induce learning. The larger space of input given for the prediction models improves the accuracy on the cost of a larger generalization error. Brown provides a good discussion on the relation between ambiguity and co-variance (Brown 2004). An important result obtained from the study of this relation is the confirmation that it is not possible to maximize the ensemble ambiguity without affecting the ensemble bias component as well, i.e., it is not possible to maximize the ambiguity component and minimize the bias component simultaneously (Moreira,et al. 2012). Dietterich (2000a) states an important criterion for successful ensemble methods is to construct individual learning algorithms with prediction accuracy above 50% whose errors are at least somewhat uncorrelated.

Applications of Ensemble Methods

Numerous academic studies analyzed the success of ensemble methods in diverse application fields such as medicine (Polikar et al., 2008), climate forecasting (Scott and Forest, 2007), image retrieval (Tsoumakas etal., 2005) and astrophysics (Bazell and Aha, 2001).

Remote Sensing

As satellite/sensor technology has improved, the amount of remote sensing data collected has expanded both in sheer volume (e.g., terabytes) and detail (e.g., hundreds of spectral bands). As a consequence, this domain poses distinct challenges to classification algorithms. The hyper-spectral data classification is particularly well suited to the divide and conquers approach of classifier ensembles, where different classifiers with different properties can extract the necessary information from the raw data before an ensemble puts it all together. This allows for the inputs and/or features to be sampled to reduce the difficulty each classifier faces; the data labels to be estimated; and the multi class problems to be reduced to multiple two-class problems.

Person Recognition

Person recognition is the problem of verifying the identity of a person using characteristics of that person, typically for security applications. Examples include iris recognition, fingerprint recognition, face recognition, and behaviour recognition (such as speech and handwriting) recognizing characteristics of a person, as opposed to depending upon specific knowledge that the person may have (such as usernames and passwords for computer account access). Person recognition has historically been one of the most frequent applications of ensemble learning methods.

There are many facets to the person recognition problem, some of which make it especially well-suited to be addressed by ensemble methods. Person recognition can involve multiple types of features. In case of iris, fingerprint, and face recognition, the features are those that are often used in computer vision. Of- ten, such as in face recognition, Principal Components Analysis (PCA) is used to identify a set of features that is smaller than the entire image but is nevertheless more informative. In speech recognition, characteristics of the speech signal such as frequencies and amplitudes must be captured and appropriate new features extracted or selected. Speech and other behavioral characteristics, unlike more static features such as fingerprints and faces, also can be represented as time series. Combining such diverse feature types into one recognizer is difficult because they have different scales. Ensembles consisting of individual recognizers for each modality would work better because they combine at the decision level where the scales would be the same.

Another facet to the person recognition problem is the difficulty in collecting good data. The environment and data collection instruments introduce noise, which is common to many applications. However, some environments are particularly difficult. For example, Erdogan et al., (2005) perform person recognition in a vehicle. If person recognition is to be performed during vehicle operation, then obviously the data collection method must not interfere with vehicle operation, must be non-intrusive, and must be robust to the noise typical of roads and highways.

In person recognition, just as in medical applications and certain anomaly detection applications, there are different misclassification costs. For example, in person recognition, denying system access to a legitimate user who should be given such access may be less costly than allowing access to an illegitimate user. In some systems, it may be possible for the recognition system to defer to a human in cases where the recognition system cannot firmly decide whether the person seeking access is a legitimate or illegitimate user.

Intrusion Detection

The intrusion detection problem can be cast as either a target detection or anomaly detection problem. When intrusion detection problems are cast as target detection problems, they are sometimes referred to as misuse detection. In these problems, models of known attacks are devised, and if current computer system activity matches that described by any attack model, then it is assumed that the corresponding type of attack is taking place. The disadvantage of this method is that it requires knowledge of and data representing all the types of attacks that one expects. If one does not have this, then one can expect a large false negative rate because the system will miss attacks of the types that it does not know about.

Anomaly detection methods work by modeling normal system behavior and flagging significant deviations from normal behavior as examples of attacks. This avoids the problem of having to model every type of attack; however, anomaly detection systems are prone to high false alarm rates, since any legitimate activity that is not modeled may be needlessly flagged as an attack.

Medical Applications

There are many examples of medical applications of machine learning. These examples include many different types of problems, such as analyzing x-ray images, human genome analysis, and examining sets of medical test data to look for anomalies. However, the root of all these problems is in assessing the health of human beings. This root brings about several characteristics of medical applications that make them particularly difficult problems.

Other Applications

There are other areas in which ensemble systems have been used and/or proposed, and the list is continuously growing at what appears to be a healthy rate. Some of the more promising ones include using ensemble systems in non-stationary environments (Kuncheva, 2004), in clustering applications (Ayad et al., 2005; Monti et al., 2003; Strehl and Ghosh, 2002), and countless work on theoretical analyses of such systems, such as on incremental learning, improving diversity, bias-variance analysis, etc. Specific practical applications of ensemble systems—whether used for biomedical, financial, remote sensing, genomic, oceanographic, chemical or other types of data analysis problems are also rapidly growing.

SOLUTIONS AND RECOMMENDATIONS

Machine learning models, a subset of artificial Intelligence require voluminous data to train the datasets. Though the data that gets collected every day by organizations is huge, data becomes a persistent problem for machine learning models to train the datasets. The data collected is either too less or too huge for training the datasets, which ultimately influences the decision-making capability of the models. An inaccurate amount of data results in undesired outcomes. Moreover, the entire process becomes disrupted. Organizations are rendered to face such challenges often. To eradicate such problems ensemble learning comes to the rescue. Ensemble Learning is the technique of machine learning, where diverse multiple machine learning models or classifiers are trained at the same time with their combining outputs. The different models are used as a base to create one predictive model. Moreover owing to the diverse machine learning models involved, it ensures enhanced reliability, improved stability and accurate predictions. They are strategically generated and combined to solve the computational process, which is otherwise not possible using a single model. Since different machine learning models are trained on a varied data population, using different modeling techniques, the result ensures accuracy. Moreover, the ensemble learning focuses on improving the classification prediction, functions of a model and reduces the instances of making a bad decision. These ensemble learning models are trained by using simple and advanced techniques.

FUTURE RESEARCH DIRECTIONS

Ensemble learning is a procedure that is employed to train numerous learning machines and combining their outputs to obtain a better composite global model with more accurate and reliable decisions than can be accomplished through a single model. The theory, algorithms, and applications of ensemble learning continue to be active areas of research. Based on the work surveyed in this chapter and the current state of ensemble learning, three major research areas will receive more attention in the future.

First, the sheer amount of available data is exploding as both data collection and processing algorithms handle amounts of data that would have been inconceivable a decade ago. Yet, most of the classification and ensemble algorithms do not address this issue directly. Though several of the applications have dealt with this problem indirectly (e.g. remote sensing, intrusion detection), new ensemble methods that use this richness of the data rather than aim to avoid it are needed. Indeed, were there methods available that could handle hundreds of classifiers trained on diverse data sets at different times and at different physical locations, many new application domains would open up to ensemble methods.

Second, there are many domains that are well-suited to unsupervised learning algorithms, such as clustering algorithms that have not benefitted from the bulk of the classifier ensemble results. The central concept of clustering is that data points are partitioned into separate clusters so that data points within a cluster are "close" to each other, while data points from different clusters are "far" from each other. This concept is of great practical interest in terms of summarizing data, reaching quick decisions and flagging certain patterns for further study.

Third, all the ensemble algorithms discussed in this chapter are based on "passive" combining, in that the classification decisions are made based on static classifier outputs, assuming all the data is available at a centralized location at the same time. Distributed classifier ensembles using "active" or agent-based methods can overcome this difficulty by allowing agents to decide on a final ensemble classification based on multiple factors (e.g., classification, confidence). This approach can be viewed as "active" stacking in that a second layer of decision making is introduced. In addition to providing more flexibility and incorporating spatially and temporally separated data, such an approach will allow the infusion of prior information (as a "base" classifier with set decisions) and be applicable to both supervised and unsupervised learning.

All three extensions of classifier ensembles highlighted above address the different aspects of the problem arising from the complexity and richness of the data generated by new applications. In many ways, such applications will not only provide new domains for ensembles, but also provide the impetus for developing new ensemble methods. Research into such classifier ensembles for such domains offers the promise of new solutions to a multitude of problems including remote sensing, person recognition, intrusion detection and biological applications.

CONCLUSION

Ensemble methods have shown to be effective in many applicative domains and can be considered as one of the main current directions in machine learning research. This chapter presents an overview of the ensemble methods, showing the main areas of research in this discipline, and the fundamental reasons why ensemble methods are able to outperform any single classifier within the ensemble. A general taxonomy, distinguishing between generative and non–generative ensemble methods, has been discussed, considering the different ways base learners can be generated or combined together. This chapter also discussed about the broad application domains that have received particular attention from the classifier ensemble community: remote sensing, person recognition, intrusion detection, and medical/biological applications. In each of these applications, harnessing a set of reasonable performing but diverse set of base models yields a combined classifier that performs better than any individual classifier.

REFERENCES

Akhter, M. P., Zheng, J., Afzal, F., Lin, H., Riaz, S., & Mehmood, A. (2021). Supervised ensemble learning methods towards automatically filtering Urdu fake news within social media. *PeerJ. Computer Science*, 7(e425), 1–24. doi:10.7717/peerj-cs.425 PMID:33817059

Patil, Aghav, & Sareen. (2016). An Overview of Classification Algorithms and Ensemble Methods in Personal Credit Scoring. *International Journal of Computer Science And Technology*, 7(2), 183–188.

Araque, O., Corcuera-Platas, I., Sánchez-Rada, F., & Iglesias, C. A. (2017). Enhancing deep learning sentiment analysis with ensemble techniques in social applications. *Expert Systems with Applications*, 77, 236–246. doi:10.1016/j.eswa.2017.02.002

Ayad, H. G., & Kamel, M. S. (2005). Cluster-Based Cumulative Ensembles. *6th Int. Workshop on Multiple Classifier Sys., Lecture Notes in Computer Science*, 3541, 236–245. 10.1007/11494683_24

Bazell, D., & Aha, D. W. W. (2001). Ensembles of Classifiers for Morphological Galaxy Classification. *The Astrophysical Journal*, 548(1), 219–223. doi:10.1086/318696

Brown, G. (2004). *Diversity in Neural Network Ensembles* [PhD thesis]. University of Birmingham.

Dietterich, T. G. (2000a). Ensemble Methods in Machine Learning. In J. Kittler & F. Roli (Eds.), *Multiple Classifier Systems* (pp. 1–15). Springer-Verlag. doi:10.1007/3-540-45014-9_1

Dietterich, T. G. (2000b). An experimental comparison of three methods for constructing ensembles of decision tress: Bagging, boosting and randomization. *Machine Learning*, 40(2), 139–158. doi:10.1023/A:1007607513941

Duin, R. (2002). The combining classifier: to train or not to train? *Proc. of the 16th Int. Conf. on Pattern Recognition, ICPR'02*, 765-770. 10.1109/ICPR.2002.1048415

Erdogan, H., Eril, A., Ekenel, H. K., Bilgin, S. Y., Eden, I., Kirisi, M., & Abut, H. (2005). Multi-modal person recognition for vehicular applications. *Proceedings of the Sixth International Workshop on Multiple Classifier Systems*, 366-375. 10.1007/11494683_37

Gaikwad, D. P. (2021). Intrusion Detection System Using Ensemble of Rule Learners and First Search Algorithm as Feature Selectors. *I. J. Computer Network and Information Security*, 4(4), 26–34. doi:10.5815/ijcnis.2021.04.03

Gupta, A., & Purohit, A. (2019). Facial Expression Recognition using Ensemble Learning Technique. *International Journal of Recent Technology and Engineering*, 8(4), 10274–10278. doi:10.35940/ijrte.D4508.118419

Huang, Z., Qi, H., Kang, C., Su, Y., & Liu, Y. (2020). An Ensemble Learning Approach for Urban Land Use Mapping Based on Remote Sensing Imagery and Social Sensing Data. *Remote Sensing*, *12*(3254), 1–18. doi:10.3390/rs12193254

Jacobs, R. A. (1995). Methods for combining experts probability assessment. *Neural Computation*, *7*(5), 867–888. doi:10.1162/neco.1995.7.5.867 PMID:7584890

Jacobs, R. A., Jordan, M. I., Nowlan, S. J., & Hinton, G. E. (1991). Adaptive mixtures of local experts. *Neural Computation*, *3*(1), 125–130. doi:10.1162/neco.1991.3.1.79 PMID:31141872

Jafarzadeh, H., Mahdianpari, M., Gill, E., Mohammadimanesh, F., & Homayouni, S. (2021). Bagging and Boosting Ensemble Classifiers for Classification of Multispectral, Hyperspectral and PolSAR Data: A Comparative Evaluation. *Remote Sensing*, *13*(4405), 1–22. doi:10.3390/rs13214405

Jain, A., Duin, R., & Mao, J. (2000). Statistical pattern recognition: A review. *IEEE Transactions on Pattern Analysis and Machine Intelligence*, *22*(1), 4–37. doi:10.1109/34.824819

Jordan, M., & Jacobs, R. (1992). Hierarchies of adaptive experts. In Advances in Neural Information Processing Systems (Vol. 4, pp. 985–992). Morgan Kauffman.

Jordan, M. I., & Jacobs, R. A. (1994). Hierarchical mixture of experts and the em algorithm. *Neural Computation*, *6*(2), 181–214. doi:10.1162/neco.1994.6.2.181

Kittler, J. (1998). Combining classifiers: A theoretical framework. *Pattern Analysis & Applications*, *1*(1), 18–27. doi:10.1007/BF01238023

Kittler, J., Hatef, M., Duin, R. P. W., & Matas, J. (1998). On combining classifiers. *IEEE Transactions on Pattern Analysis and Machine Intelligence*, *20*(3), 226–239. doi:10.1109/34.667881

Kuncheva, L. I. (2004). Classifier ensembles for changing environments. *5th Int. Workshop on Multiple Classifier Systems, Lecture Notes in Computer Science*, *3077*, 1–15.

Kuncheva, L. I., Bezdek, J. C., & Duin, R. P. W. (2001). Decision templates for multiple classifier fusion: An experimental comparison. *Pattern Recognition*, *34*(2), 299–314. doi:10.1016/S0031-3203(99)00223-X

Kyle, T. (2019). Machine Learning-Based Ensemble Prediction of Water-Quality Variables Using Feature-Level and Decision-Level Fusion with Proximal Remote Sensing. *Photogrammetric Engineering and Remote Sensing*, *85*(4), 269–280. doi:10.14358/PERS.85.4.269

Lam, L. (2000). Classifier combinations: Implementations and theoretical issues. *Lecture Notes in Computer Science*, *1857*, 77–86.

Monti, S., Tamayo, P., Mesirov, J., & Golub, T. (2003). Consensus Clustering: A Resampling-Based Method for Class Discovery and Visualization of Gene Expression Microarray Data. *Machine Learning*, *52*(1–2), 91–118. doi:10.1023/A:1023949509487

Moreira, J., Soares, C., Jorge, A., & De Sousa, J. (2012). Ensemble Approaches for Regression: A Survey. Faculty of Economics, University of Porto. *ACM Computing Surveys*, *45*(1), 1–40. doi:10.1145/2379776.2379786

Nzuva, S., & Nderu, L. (2019). The Superiority of the Ensemble Classification Methods: A Comprehensive Review. *Journal of Information Engineering and Applications*, *9*(5), 43–53.

Polikar, R. A., Topalis, D., Parikh, D., Green, D., Frymiare, J., Kounios, J., & Clark, C. (2008). An Ensemble Based Data Fusion Approach for Early Diagnosis of Alzheimer's Disease. *Information Fusion*, *9*(1), 83–95. doi:10.1016/j.inffus.2006.09.003

Quinlan, J. R. (1993). *C4.5 Programs for Machine Learning*. Morgan Kauffman.

Rajagopal, S., Kundapur, P. P., & Hareesha, K. S. (2020). A Stacking Ensemble for Network Intrusion Detection Using Heterogeneous Datasets. *Security and Communication Networks*, *2020*, 1–9. doi:10.1155/2020/4586875

Raviv, Y., & Intrator, N. (1996). Bootstrapping with noise: An effective regularization technique. *Connection Science*, *8*(3/4), 355–372. doi:10.1080/095400996116811

Scott, P. A., & Forest, C. E. (2007). Ensemble Climate Predictions Using Climate Models and Observational Constraints. *Mathematical, Physical, and Engineering Sciences, 365*(1857), 52.

Singh, R., & Pal, S. (2020). Machine Learning Algorithms and Ensemble Technique to Improve Prediction of Students Performance. *International Journal of Advanced Trends in Computer Science and Engineering*, *9*(3), 3970–3976. doi:10.30534/ijatcse/2020/221932020

Strehl, A., & Ghosh, J. (2002). Cluster Ensembles-A Knowledge Reuse Framework for Combining Multiple Partitions. *Journal of Machine Learning Research*, *3*, 583–617.

Thanh, H. N., & Van Lang, T. (2019). Use the ensemble methods when detecting DoS attacks in Network Intrusion Detection Systems. *EAI Endorsed Transactions on Context-aware Systems and Applications*, *6*(19), 1–7. doi:10.4108/eai.29-11-2019.163484

Tsoumakas, G., Angelis, L., & Vlahavas, I. (2005). Selective Fusion of Heterogeneous Classifiers. *Intelligent Data Analysis*, *9*(6), 511–525. doi:10.3233/IDA-2005-9602

Xu, L., Krzyzak, C., & Suen, C. (1992). Methods of combining multiple classifiers and their applications to handwritting recognition. *IEEE Transactions on Systems, Man, and Cybernetics*, *22*(3), 418–435. doi:10.1109/21.155943

Yamana, M. A., Rattayb, F., & Subasic, A. (2021). Comparison of Bagging and Boosting Ensemble Machine Learning Methods for Face Recognition. *Procedia Computer Science*, *194*, 202–209. doi:10.1016/j.procs.2021.10.074

Yohannese, C. W., Li, T., & Bashir, K. (2018). A Three-Stage Based Ensemble Learning for Improved Software Fault Prediction: An Empirical Comparative Study. *International Journal of Computational Intelligence Systems*, *11*(1), 1229–1247. doi:10.2991/ijcis.11.1.92

Yu, X., Zhang, Z., Wu, L., Pang, W., Chen, H., Yu, Z., & Li, B. (2020). Deep Ensemble Learning for Human Action Recognition in Still Images. *Complexity*, *2020*, 1–23. doi:10.1155/2020/9428612

KEY TERMS AND DEFINITIONS

Base Inducer(s) or Base Classifier(s): An inducer is a learning algorithm that is used to learn from a training set. A base inducer obtains a training set and constructs a classifier that generalizes relationship between the input features and the target outcome.

E

Combiner: The task of the combiner is to produce the final decision by combining all classification results of the various base inducers.

Ensemble Learning: Ensemble learning is a machine learning technique where multiple learners are trained to solve the same problem and their predictions are combined with a single output that probably has better performance on average than any individual ensemble member.

Generalization Error: Generalization error measures how a learning module performs on out of sample data. It is measured as the difference between the prediction of the module and the actual results.

Generative Ensemble Methods: Generative ensemble methods generate sets of base learners acting on the base learning algorithm or on the structure of the data set to try to actively improve diversity and accuracy of the base learners.

Non-Generative Ensemble Methods: Non-generative ensemble methods confine themselves to combine a set of possibly well-designed base classifiers: they do not actively generate new base learners but try to combine in a suitable way a set of existing base classifiers.

Person Recognition: Person recognition is the problem of verifying the identity of a person using characteristics of that person, typically for security applications.

How to Structure Data for Humanitarian Learning

Gilbert Ahamer

🆔 https://orcid.org/0000-0003-2140-7654

Graz University, Austria

INTRODUCTION

What is Learning?

Several basic approaches can be taken towards learning. The direction in which one understands learning predetermines the learning setting considered as optimal. Consequently, it is a prerequisite to reach clarity about how one might understand "learning". This chapter proposes:

- learning as mental structural change (psychological approach)
- learning as leapfrogging biological and evolutionary cycles (evolutionist approach)
- learning as creating new (mental, existential) spaces by reflection (ontological approach).

In any case, it will be useful to keep in mind both *learning of individuals* and *learning of society*.

Learning is Mental Structural Change

According to a psychological approach, learning is understood as *mental structural change* that leads to change in real-world behaviour. In this view, learning would be only successful if it results in changes of the person's real actions. Let us undertake a "tour d'horizon", in which contexts we may find a similar viewpoint and how fixed or loose border conditions for such learning should be:

Here we examine any type of learning, especially life-long learning for adults (Chen & Gao, 2021, Eynon et al., 2021, Sieglova & Stejskalova, 2021, Cheng et al., 2012, King, 2002, Shapiro et al., 2017) and we draw conclusions from decades of our own teaching, learning and training experience in both roles, active and passive. Often, learning is most productive when taking the role of a trainer. We adopt a constructivist stance, under the philosophical auspices of John Dewey's *Pragmatism* (Maboloc, 2021, Pyysiäinen, 2021, Racine et al., 2021, Waight, 2021, Ahamer, 2008, Berding, 2000, Haack, 2004, Grippe, 2002). In the resulting picture, in order to reach the mentioned structural mental change, the *core action is dialogue* and *exchange of views in a discourse*, constituting Dewey's "education for responsible democracy".

As does democracy, education deeply involves ethics: it is based on the "principle of responsibility" (Insanguine Mingarro, 2020, Mourelo, 2021, Jonas, 1984, Stähli, 1998, 2005, Werner, 2003). Here, preference is given to *teleologic* (target oriented) ethics as opposed to *deontologic* (duty oriented) ethics – stressing the result of any human action as preferred to theoretical and subjective conviction.

For facilitating such dialogue, a very helpful approach is: "learning through gaming" (Prensky, 2001, Ahamer, 2013d, 2019: ch. 9, 25, Croxton & Kortemeyer, 2018, Padmanabhan et al., 2019, Ryu, 2013,

DOI: 10.4018/978-1-7998-9220-5.ch110

Shirsekar, 2019, Soneji, 2019, Venter & Coetzee, 2014, Viola et al., 2021, Volejnikova-Wenger et al., 2021). Symbolically, a gaming setting means to leave a "play" in the rigid mechanisms of traditional reproduction of content by allowing for trial and error in a modelled ("game") scenario. Coherent with the affiliation of the authors, such endeavour of responsibility-oriented teaching encompasses both the area of e-learning and (human) geography (Popke, 2003: 298, Cloke, 2002: 589). An *"ethics of encounter"* (Popke, 2003: 300) is both facilitated by *e-learning tools* and *geo-referenced* in a multicultural sense. Supported by web-based tools and e-learning didactics (and especially by planet-wide data structures: Ahamer, 2013a), we are led to say: "out of sight, but *in* mind".

Let us consider another perspective on learning: according to design literature, iterative oscillation occurs between the *problem* space and the *solution* space (Maher, 2003; Dorst & Cross, 2001: 434). Such loose type of oscillating interaction between the two "spaces", namely to act and to reflect, is also well characterized by the pedagogic concept of *"reflection-in-action"*, a pedagogical and managerial principle combining sequences of contemplative and actionist aspects (Cattaneo & Motta, 2021, Jung et al., 2021, Schön, 1983, 1986: 62, Lawless & Roth, 2001) that has been applied to learning individuals but also to learning organisations.

In an influential article that has prompted a series of responses and comments, Roth et al. (2001) instead propose the notion of *"Spielraum"* – a word that the Canadian authors import into English language from German. It has the meaning "room to play" both in the sense of game-based learning (Ahamer, 2012a, Ahamer & Kumpfmüller, 2013) and in the sense of machinery as the desired clearance a joint has in order to allow for motion. So, there should be a playful element or "game" in learning in both senses. The symbolic usage of the word "play" suggests allowing students to enjoy a near-to-real-life situation without fearing the merciless real-world sanctions of suboptimal behaviour (Fresner et al., 2007: 21).

Concluding from the above, "leeway for wits and senses" (Tröhler, 2007) should be allowed in any learning setting. *Spielraum* is "elbow room" (an effective existence radius of the self) according to Jaros (2007) who stems from spatial planning and argues that "the self depends for its ability to recognise itself primarily on collisions that suspend the flow of spatialised complexity".

After decades of classroom experience narrated in vivid examples, Roth et al. (2001: 183) "propose 'Spielraum' as room to manoeuvre, as a concept that describes the reality of teaching much better than reflection-in-action, especially when there is no time out for reflection." They "therefore see [themselves as teachers] always at some point in time and space which means for them to take into account the specific individual situation of students in the given classroom. Readiness for appropriate action, whatever the unfolding events, means that the agent has Spielraum, the room to manoeuvre appropriately in the current situation. According to Heidegger (1977), *Dasein* (being here) "combines self and world into a single irreducible entity, being-in-the-world, in the face of all the contingencies real-time interactions pose to the participants involved" (Adani, 2021, Brito et al., 2021, Grollo, 2021, Periñán, 2021, Pirc & Weber, 2021, Ross, 2021, Rouse, 2021, Roth et al. 2001: 186) and "constitutes the location from which a person negotiates the world" (Popke, 2003, 302). Not the teacher's but "the students' own questions guide or scaffold students because they always test the outer edge of their students' current reality. The questions therefore can neither be completely in the teacher's reality nor completely internal to students' reality, but always along the interface of the two. Students are the builders of their own reality" (Roth et al., 2001: 186-201).

Summing up this above subchapter, readers may believe that the following views are helpful:

1. learners construct their own reality
2. learners benefit from less pressure of real-life consequences

3. in the optimal case, trainers and teachers have a set of reactions at their disposal ready to implement them even without lengthy reflections
4. learning individuals proceed on a largely unpredictable path; and trying to understand learners' unforeseen explanatory constructions dissolves and replaces immature concepts in teachers' mind-sets. No theory whatsoever sufficiently describes real learning paths of individuals.

To continue, we propose one step of reasoning: what applied to individual learning (i.e. of students), may apply also to societal learning, namely to the long-term evolution of countries.

The findings for individual learning deduced from this section in the above four bullets will be adapted to societal learning in the four bullets of the following subchapter.

Learning is Leapfrogging Biological and Evolutionary Cycles

Recently several universities have launched initiatives in "intercultural learning" (Arvanitis et al., 2021, Heggernes, 2021, Huang, 2021, Kongot & Matz, 2021, Markey et al., 2021, Permatasari & Andriyanti, 2021, Tham et al., 2021, Tonner-Saunders & Shimi, 2021, Global Studies, 2009) which means that students are trained to better understand divergent cultural and ethical concepts. Thinking of states, countries, economies and cultures (instead of students), we may conclude:

1. countries construct their own realities and their own national rationalities and sense – which might harmonise or not with concepts of sense in other countries or other populations (Castells & Arsenault, 2006: 285)
2. the understanding of other cultures and their civilisational trajectories is likely to benefit from loosening the tightness of pre-fabricated explanatory patterns – for example macro-economic theories of one kind or another that state "how economies develop and grow" (Coats, 1985: 1718) and believe to be correct even in a historical sense (Heilbronner, 1990: 1097)
3. the ones considering themselves as leaders are not likely to act based on thorough, reflected or even scientific understanding of ongoing complex procedures but rather based on "preconceptive understandings", visions, or "preanalytic cognitive acts" (Schumpeter, 1949, Heilbronner, 1990: 1109), similar to an elbow room in the strict sense
4. economies proceed on a largely unpredictable path when developing; trying to understand such real techno-socio-economic development quickly unveils the tremendous limitations of economic theories, be they (neo-)classical or Keynesian. No theory whatsoever sufficiently describes real learning paths of societies.

As a consequence, it is proposed to follow the real-world paths of evolutionary development instead of following the results of theoretical concepts boiled down to a set of formulas. Purely formula-centred understanding of economics tumbles down the abyss of non-perceived complexity, it remains painfully simple. *Priority to phenomena!* Freedom from formulas! To promote "reflective science", the sociologist Bourdieu has created a method of letting the phenomena speak for themselves (Robbins, 2007: 87).

Complexity is the major challenge in multi-actor networks where one actor forms the framework condition and context for the other. Complexity might be seen as a major challenge of slowly maturing rational science (Ahamer 2013b). Robust knowledge is always situated and situating (Roth et al., 2001: 203). Foresight has to be trained especially for entrepreneurs as an art involving intuition and creativity (Fontela et al., 2006: 11).

Current Theorising on Global Structural Evolution

Learning on the societal level means also the creation, development and strengthening of new emerging societal institutions (Papenhausen, 2009: 5). These might be likely to appear cyclically (Freeman & Louca, 2001), according to Kondratieff's famous analysis of economic long waves that he performed in the 1920s. Which other shape could a developing trend show? Linear, curvilinear, a sequence of saturation states (Menzel, 1996: 35ff, Wagner-Döbler, 1998: 67) or just a complex pattern of syndromes? No single "theory" (reducing itself to a simple cause-and-effect style) is capable of explaining consistently the complexity of global historical dynamics – even if several explanatory patterns were applied, such as the unsatisfying "climatic explanation" for differences in economic and cultural development (Landes, 2000, Mokyr, 1990).

HOW TO LEARN

Based on the theoretical deliberations in the first section, in this part of the article, their practical implications are analysed in a structured manner, following the four basic characteristics of learning put forth by (Mukerji & Tripathi, 2009) – these are equivalent to the STEP factors described in the following four sub-sections.

Social Factor S: The Procedural Factors for Learning

The social factors (S) largely correspond to the procedural factors for learning and answer the question: how to design learning?

They coincide with Castell's *space of flows* and they regulate the *interaction* between students and trainers and among students. We propose to:

- facilitate an interactive *dialogue* between trainers & learners and among learners
- make use of the chances of open distance learning (ODL) to render the exchange of "flows" more massive
- allow for *self-guidedness* of learners (key word of self-adaptive e-learning material)
- suitably *rhythmise* procedures in order to facilitate optimal learning as suggested by "Surfing Global Change" SGC (Ahamer & Schrei, 2004)
- establish clear and well-defined procedural rules and criteria for success for students in order to safeguard quality control
- use the concept of *"spatial citizens"* to denote the approach of personal responsibility of learners
- to make use of evolutionary long-term trends for the target of learning
- to promote *leap-frogging* matter-centred *evolution* by faster evolving mental and social reorganization of a country (inner re-crystallisation of a country's society).

Technological Factor T: The Tools for Learning

- Web platforms (such WebCT, Moodle or others) have been the object of suitability studies already a decade ago and have entered their annual routine at most universities. From being a critical bottleneck for communication-centred e-learning (because of alleged self-restriction to a mere

behaviourist learning model) most platforms have made a consistent step forward to enabling communication-centred learning
- For the UniGIS curriculum the decision was made to use two technologies (Blackboard & MS live) in order to enhance e-literacy of learners.
- Promote formation of teachers and trainers to incorporate peer communication among learners
- To enhance autopoiesis, i.e. self-creation of (knowledge) structures such as wikis
- Include digital globes for learning.

Economic Factor E: The Material Basis for Learning

- Which resources are necessary for learning? In Europe, many universities provide each resource in the necessary amount.
- In the view of the GCDB analysis (section titled "The example of the global economic structure"): Education is part of the sector "social services" encompassing personal care-taking, (mental) health and communication services and can be expected to grow further as a long-term global tendency. Analysis of the evolution of forerunning economic sectors calls for suitable maturity of both learning infrastructures and learning motivation, namely to "create meaning by education".
- In the view of the section on social space life meant the generation of meaning and sense. "Sense" equals forward-linking of values into the future (in Latin: re-ligio). Investments in e-learning therefore are based on a minimum accountability and foreseeability of individual careers. Vice versa, e-learning should foster skills that are independent of short-term business cycles.
- Evolutionarily, we slide into an "era of a society of sense": acting in order to produce meaning becomes gradually more important than acting for a material target – to the extent that material targets are already fulfilled. A "natural succession" of life's targets for any learner may be hypothesized.

Political Factor T: The Structural Basis for Learning

- Connectedness to other organisational entities on the labour market, among firms, within administration is the materialization of the "network society" (section "Learning means to create new spaces by reflection)
- Human, social, institutional structures and tissues complement traditional "hard skills"
- The reliability and openness of political structures must guarantee that learners can implement their democratic social skills in real-life careers in real-life institutions.

THE CASES

List of Cases

The following cases are explained in the coming sections. More insight is available from the literature and the links provided as well as in (Ahamer & Jekel, 2010):

- UniGIS ("Learn, but learn together") – a collaborative web-based study framework

- Twinning Projects ("Learn while living together") are the main programming tools for EU accession and applied also to European Neighbourhood Nations: examples with the authors' collaboration range from Slovakia and Slovenia to Armenia, Georgia and Azerbaijan.
- "Global Studies" are curriculum initiatives in Graz, Vienna and Salzburg ("Learn, how to live together") training professionally for intercultural understanding and in-depth cooperation.
- UniNET ("Live together, but while learning") is the largest bilateral university network between a European country and Asia; the authors have organized several conferences in Kyrgyzstan and Nepal
- ESD (= European Forum for the Promotion of Sustainable Development) creates radically new visions prompted by the economic-environmental crisis by dialogic authoring of a book
- Environmental Systems Analysis (USW) is a unique curriculum in Graz focusing on interdisciplinary dialogue.

Details on characteristics and on results of these cases can be found in Table 1.

UniGIS

What started as several local initiatives for open and distance learning (ODL) of Geographic Information Science and Systems (GIS) has become the largest global network of highly professional GIS curricula (Unigis, 2009) that are internationally not only recognised but defining standards.

The characteristic is a very clear definition of rules, criteria and procedures which allows to reach standardisation across a wide range of countries, universities and related working styles and cultures.

This networked and networking social system keeps proliferating: last year, the Central Asian node was formally founded as the "Austria-Central Asia Centre for GIScience" ACA*GIS (2009) in Bishkek, Kyrgyzstan after a series of preparatory workshops, conferences, projects and common projects that have constituted an evolution of networking flows.

Twinning Projects

We move from the world of education to the world of administration and national strategies. The European Union has developed a successful "tool" called "Twinning" for enhancing institution building in neighbouring countries that has been initially applied to preparing candidate countries for their accession to the Union. The core issue is "institution building" (EU, 2009) – again very similar to the intention of the present volume.

Twinning principles are: "Twinning must aim at developing structural reforms. At the end of a project, any new or adapted system must be self-sufficient and function under the auspices of the beneficiary country" (EU, 2009).

A very clearly defined set of procedural rules has been moulded into a "Twinning handbook" a decade ago. Annually, over 100 Twinning projects with a typical budget of 1M€ take place on almost any aspect of administrative life (Ahamer & Mayer, 2013; Ahamer, 2015). In the meantime, this instrument for strengthening institutions by sourcing from the own strength and conviction of the beneficiary country is also applied to interested non-candidate countries in the so-called European Neighbourhood Policy.

The main strategy is to create understanding by (i) daily collaboration for complex issues by peer-oriented collaboration with equal rights and mutual respect, (ii) keeping the driving force the main interest of the beneficiary administration, (iii) generous funding by the European Commission, (iv) personal contacts emerging after week-long repeated on-site collaboration of experts and (v) clear focus on voluntary adoption of parts of the European legal system for easier bilateral exchange.

One author has worked during the last decades in such Twinnings on the subjects of air quality (Slovakia, 2000-01), water quality (Slovenia, 2007-08); and prepared Twinnings on the subjects of aviation security (Armenia, Georgia, 2008) and vocational formation (Azerbaijan, 2009) and is convinced of high suitability and appropriateness of such programmes of international co-operation.

Relevance of the STEP Structure for these Cases

This section views the described institutional case studies along the four criteria proposed by the editors of this book: S, T, E, P (= Social, Technological, Economic and Political): *Table 1*.

Table 1. How the STEP factors apply to the cases of this article; these are explained in the earlier section

Cases	S = Social factors	T=Technological factors	E = Economical factors	P = Political factors
UniGIS	Easy access for individuals, international network embeds	normalised catalogue of criteria for achievements	Costs paid by learners and supporting institutions	UniGIS is embedded in intl. and EU networks
UniNet	Lecturers and students are networking agents	Thematic orientation is secondary, real persons travel	One-way financial transfer from Austria to Asian universities	Developmental aid on academic level in mutual partnership
- Kyrgyzstan	Promote GIS and solar energy	Strengthen local institutions	~ODA + own effort to organise	Young democratic republic
- Nepal	Apply GIS for mountain areas	Divert natural hazards' menaces	Cooperation with Himalaya states	Strengthen local self-governance
- Tajikistan	Teach GIS for energy	Raise IT formation & awareness	ACA*GIScience: regional GIS hub	Enhance university network
Global Studies	Response to increasing students' awareness and NGO work	Partly e-learning, but focus on face2face, students travelling	Efforts made by students who also participate in practicals	The guiding idea of global collaboration is implemented
ESD	An NGO creates itself and provides orientation to others	Only "social software" directs interplay of self-responsible actors	No economic weight. "Just" development of societal strategies	Includes senior political figures with high profile & individualism
USW (= Environmental Systems Analysis)	Institutionalising a pioneering university curriculum	Strong e-learning component but only as blended learning	Synergism with classical curricula boosts attractivity for students	Slow diffusion through the traditional university system
Twinning tool	Main tool of EU enlargement & reduce barriers	Self-motivated implementation of EU legislation	Better mutual exchange increases development	Smooth transition from EU to neighb. countries
- Slovakia	Candidate country wants to join	Improve air quality legislation	Reduced pollution improves life	Ex-communist country's rebirth
- Slovenia	New EU member state joined	Implement water quality legislation	Water price covers external costs	New market economy stabilises
- Armenia	Discontinue Soviet safety syst.	Aviation security must be compatible	Switch from old to EU system	European neighbourhood policy
- Georgia	Leave behind Soviet security	Aviation will be compatible to EU	Integration in larger aviation area	Equilibration of strategic contacts
- Azerbaijan	Re-build agr. vocational training	Agriculture employs 40% of pop.	Agricult. value added is minimal	Wish to modernise non-oil sect.

Practical experiences from these case studies are described from the perspective of "learners" (Table 2) and the perspective of "trainers" (Table 3) while approximately using the STEP factors.

*Table 2. Experiences with the cases of this article ordered approximately along the STEP factors, while taking the perspective as seen from the "**learners**"*

Cases	S ~ collaboration	T ~ dialogue tech.	E ~interculturality	P ~ results
UniGIS	Occasional questions among individual learners	An internal discussion forum + annual meetings	Only among German speaking students	Technical & background GIS knowledge
UniNet	Among occasional Austro-Asian working groups	Co-author future project proposals with Asia	On the university level only; scientific exchange	Transfer of knowledge and skills
- Kyrgyzstan	Bridge heads in civil engineering university	Along annual conferences and staff exchanges	Review of papers in a scientific journal	Common publiccation and mutual insight
- Nepal	Bridge to an Asian multilateral research centre	Only personal exchange on the conference	Very broad range of cultures along the Himalayas	Scientific assessment harmonised on a conference
- Tajikistan	Cross-link Central Asian agents of modernisation	Pre-conference online exams as academic selection	Interest in GIS bridges local cultural tensions	Understand criteria-based review culture
Global Studies	Students with strong multicultural inclination	Integrative core lectures + isolated specialised lectures	Interculturality extends to different scient. culture	Integration of explicitly opposing views
ESD	Panel of self-motivated idealists & authors	Discussing chapters of the own visionary book	Representatives from academia & industry discuss	Consensus view on very radical societal changes
USW (= Environmental Systems Analysis)	Five disciplines: economics, business administrat., chemistry, physics, geography	30% integrative core lectures done jointly plus 70% specialised lectures done in isolation	Offering a systemic approach to overcome barriers between social & natural sci.	Environmental scientists mastering divergent scientific approaches
Twinning tool	Administrative representatives from EU & candidate countries	Clear definition of deliberable results worked out in 2 years project	Experts from diverse political cultures collaborate personally	Harmonisation of legal systems and their factual implementation
- Slovakia (SK)	8 SK + 8 AT authors:12 reports	Monthly 1-day visits during 1 year	Ex-communist working habits	Air quality laws are on EU level
- Slovenia (SI)	10 SI + 10 DE + 6 AT authors: 3 r.	Permanent 3-days visits during 1 yr.	Similar approach, democratic state	Water quality & pricing law is ok
- Armenia	Define workplan for EU aviation	Daily interviews with AM experts	Clear technical targets are easy	Defined results for future Twinn.
- Georgia	Define workplan for EU aviation	Daily interviews with GE experts	Clear technical targets are easy	Defined results for future Twinn.
- Azerbaijan	Define workplan for vocational education in agriculture	Trying to identify partners for daily interviews with AZ experts	Difficulties due to unclarity of own targets, low familiarity w. EU	Defined results for future Twinning including pilot voc. school

*Table 3. Experiences with the cases of this article ordered approximately along the STEP factors, while taking the perspective as seen from the "**trainers**"*

Cases	S ~ How the (social, economic, technological) space is bridged	T ~what kind of difficulties are encountered in practice	E ~ how/whether technology helped in overcoming barriers	P ~ how to learn from such international interventions
UniGIS	By a tight compulsory schedule & clear exercises	Lack of previous experience with GIS can be fatal	Online chats, webspace, tutors, annual meetings	Create strong personal initial committment
UniNet	By own developmental interest	Shortage of time during pers. visits	Joint proceedings define achievemt.	A clear, narrow discipline helps
Global Studies	By being in the same curriculum	Initially romantic attitudes prevail	Only personal experience ripens	Own long-year studies equilibrate
ESD	Weekly structured discussion rounds	Divergent value systems preferred	Book publication focused all ideas	Intensive personal dedication
USW (= Environmental Systems Analysis)	By drawing own identity from the first pioneering student generation	Lack of enthusiasm and working motivation of some students	Web platforms allow detailed communication between courses	To create a strong identity as pioneering entity within university
Twinning tool	By jointly defining the targets of the Twinning future project	Fundamentally different political views in different countries	Dialogic review during joint authoring of legislation and reports	Online cooperation helps only if intact personal ties exist

CONCLUSION

This text has provided an extensive overview of diverse concepts, philosophies and views.

Based on multiple experiences of "learning" of individuals and societies, a general view of the sense and the procedure of learning is proposed in this contribution: The target of learning is to maximise the change of real-world behaviour. Consequently, an optimal learning methodology is to put learners in a situation of dialogue with stakeholders having another view of the complex interdisciplinary issue at stake.

Such conclusion of seeing "facilitated dialogue" in the centre of any learning endeavour results from all three understandings proposed here (psychological, evolutionist and ontological approaches). Dialogue is the unit activity of approximating world views between persons.

The role of technology receives a clear place, namely to facilitate dialogue and discourse. Such has been corroborated by a series of cases of individual, societal and international learning.

Attempts to implement technology-centred learning environments without foregoing generation of the strong wish and persistent will of learners to reflect, exchange, discuss and reformulate own convictions would not yield optimal learning results.

This sequence seems promising: first create human attitudes for a dialogue and second support such dialogue by technological means.

Dialogue is the key element and the will to arrive at a consensus is the key motor for learning.

When designed in this order, technological support may become valuable for learning which is a deeply human act of questioning oneself and redirecting one's behaviour.

A symbolic description of such learning effect is "to create new spaces of understanding".

REFERENCES

ACA*GIS. (2009). *Austria-Central Asia Centre for GIScience*. Retrieved from https://www.aca-giscience.org/

Adani, A. C. O. (2021). *Adapting Heidegger's notion of authentic existence to analyze and inspire everyday experiences of individuals for societal transformation in Nigeria*. doi:10.3726/b17217

Ahamer, G. (1994). Influence of an Enhanced Use of Biomass for Energy on the CO_2 Concentration in the Atmosphere. *International Journal of Global Energy Issues*, 6(1/2), 112–131.

Ahamer, G. (2008). Virtual Structures for mutual review promote understanding of opposed standpoints. *The Turkish Online Journal of Distance Education*, 9(1), 17-43. https://tojde.anadolu.edu.tr/

Ahamer, G. (2012a). A four-dimensional Maxwell equation for social processes in web-based learning and teaching – windrose dynamics as GIS: Games' intrinsic spaces. *International Journal of Web-Based Learning and Teaching Technologies*, 7(3), 1–19. doi:10.4018/jwltt.2012070101

Ahamer, G. (2013a). A Planet-Wide Information System. *Campus-Wide Information Systems*, 30(5), 369-378. DOI . doi:10.1108/CWIS-08-2013-0032

Ahamer, G. (2013b). GISS and GISP facilitate higher education and cooperative learning design. In Handbook of Research on Transnational Higher Education Management. IGI Global. DOI doi:10.4018/978-1-4666-4458-8.ch001

Ahamer, G. (2013c). Quality assurance in transnational education management – the developmental "Global Studies" curriculum. In Handbook of Research on Transnational Higher Education Management. IGI Global. Doi:10.4018/978-1-4666-4458-8.ch015

Ahamer, G. (2013d). Game, not fight: Change climate change! *Simulation and Gaming –. International Journal (Toronto, Ont.)*, 44(2-3), 272–301. doi:10.1177/1046878112470541

Ahamer, G. (2015). Applying student-generated theories about global change and energy demand. *International Journal of Information and Learning Technology*, 32(5), 258–271. doi:10.1108/IJILT-01-2015-0002

Ahamer, G. (2019). *Mapping Global Dynamics – Geographic Perspectives from Local Pollution to Global Evolution*. Springer International Publishing. https://link.springer.com/book/10.1007/978-3-319-51704-9

Ahamer, G., & Jekel, T. (2010). Make a Change by Exchanging Views. In S. Mukerji & P. Tripathi (Eds.), Cases on Transnational Learning and Technologically Enabled Environments (pp. 1–20). Academic Press.

Ahamer, G., & Kumpfmüller, K. (2013). Education and literature for development in responsibility – Partnership hedges globalization. In Handbook of Research on Transnational Higher Education Management. IGI Global.

Ahamer, G., & Mayer, J. (2013). Forward looking: Structural change and institutions in highest-income countries and globally. *Campus-Wide Information Systems*, 30(5), 386–403. doi:10.1108/CWIS-08-2013-0034

Ahamer, G., & Schrei, C. (2004). Exercise 'Technology Assessment' through a gaming procedure. *Journal of Desert Research*, 5(2), 224–252.

Arvanitis, E. (2021). Educating 'others': Drawing on the collective wisdom of intercultural experts. *British Educational Research Journal, 47*(4), 922–941. doi:10.1002/berj.3731

Berding, J. W. A. (2000). John Dewey's participatory philosophy of education – Education, experience and curriculum. In *The history of education and childhood*. Nijmegen University. http://www.socsci. kun.nl/ped/whp/histeduc/misc/dewey01.html

Brito, R., Joseph, S., & Sellman, E. (2021). Exploring mindfulness in/as education from a heideggerian perspective. *Journal of Philosophy of Education, 55*(2), 302–313. doi:10.1111/1467-9752.12553

Castells, M., & Arsenault, A. (2006). Conquering the Minds, Conquering Iraq. *Information Communication and Society, 9*(3), 284–307. https://annenberg.usc.edu/Home/Faculty/Communication/~/media/ Faculty/Facpdfs/Castells%20Iraq%20misinformation%20pdf.ashx

Cattaneo, A. A. P., & Motta, E. (2021). "I reflect, therefore I am... a good professional". on the relationship between reflection-on-action, reflection-in-action and professional performance in vocational education. *Vocations and Learning, 14*(2), 185–204. doi:10.100712186-020-09259-9

Chen, Y., & Gao, Q. (2021). *How do older adults learn informally via social media? A pilot study of Chinese urban older adults*. doi:10.1007/978-3-030-78108-8_28

Cheng, B., Wang, M., Moormann, J., Olaniran, B. A., & Chen, N. (2012). The effects of organizational learning environment factors on e-learning acceptance. *Computers & Education, 58*(3), 885–899. doi:10.1016/j.compedu.2011.10.014

Cloke, P. (2002). Deliver us from evil? Prospects for living ethically and acting politically in human geography. *Progress in Human Geography, 26*(5), 587–604.

Coats, A. W. (1985). The American Economic Association and the Economics Profession. *Journal of Economic Literature, 23*(4), 1697–1727.

Croxton, D., & Kortemeyer, G. (2018). Informal physics learning from video games: A case study using gameplay videos. *Physics Education, 53*(1). Advance online publication. doi:10.1088/1361-6552/aa8eb0

Dorst, K., & Cross, N. (2001). Creativity in the design process: Co-evolution of problem-solution. *Design Studies, 22*(5), 425–437.

EU. (2009). *Boosting Co-operation through Twinning*. European Commission, EuropeAid. Retrieved from https://ec.europa.eu/europeaid/where/neighbourhood/overview/twinning_en.htm

Eynon, R., & Malmberg, L. (2021). Lifelong learning and the internet: Who benefits most from learning online? *British Journal of Educational Technology, 52*(2), 569–583. doi:10.1111/bjet.13041

Fontela, E., Guzmán, J., Pérez, M., & Santos, F. J. (2006). The art of entrepreneurial foresight. *Foresight, 8*(6), 3–13. http://www.emeraldinsight.com/

Fresner, J., Angerbauer, C., Möller, M., Wolf, P., Dielacher, T., & Schnitzer, H. (2007). *ZERMEG III – Decision guidance for the visualisation of the achievements of sustainable corporate strategies*. Final report by STENUM, Austrian Federal Ministry of Traffic, Infrastructure and Technology. Retrieved from http://www.fabrikderzukunft.at/results.html/id4132

Global Studies. (2009). *Bundle of Electives on "Global Studies" at Graz University*. Retrieved from https://www.uni-graz.at/en/vre1www/vre1www-wfs.htm

Grippe, E. J. (2002). Pragmatism, Perspectivism and Education: A Critique of Habitual Social Constructivism. *Insights, 34*(3), 2–14.

Grollo, S. G. (2021). Thinking the event in Heidegger's "black notebooks". *Philosophy Today, 65*(1), 89–104. doi:10.5840/philtoday202129385

Haack, S. (2004). Pragmatism, Old and New. *Contemporary Pragmatism, 1*(1), 3–41.

Heggernes, S. L. (2021). A critical review of the role of texts in fostering intercultural communicative competence in the English language classroom. *Educational Research Review, 33*. Advance online publication. doi:10.1016/j.edurev.2021.100390

Heidegger, M. (1977). Sein und Zeit. Academic Press.

Huang, L.-D. (2021). Developing intercultural communicative competence in foreign language classrooms – A study of EFL learners in Taiwan. *International Journal of Intercultural Relations, 83*, 55–66. doi:10.1016/j.ijintrel.2021.04.015

Insanguine Mingarro, F. A. (2020). Towards a reconstruction of the concept of bioethics [Per una ricostruzione del concetto di bioetica]. *Ragion Pratica*, (2), 557-586. doi:10.1415/98607

Jonas, H. (1984). The Imperative of Responsibility. In *Search of Ethics for the Technological Age*. University of Chicago Press. https://www.hans-jonas-zentrum.de/

Jung, I., Omori, S., Dawson, W. P., Yamaguchi, T., & Lee, S. J. (2021). Faculty as reflective practitioners in emergency online teaching: An autoethnography. *International Journal of Educational Technology in Higher Education, 18*(1). Advance online publication. doi:10.118641239-021-00261-2

King, K. P. (2002). Educational technology professional development as transformative learning opportunities. *Computers & Education, 39*(3), 283–297. doi:10.1016/S0360-1315(02)00073-8

Kongot, A., & Matz, A. (2021). Perfectly imperfect: A speculation about wabi-sabi inspired user experience design: Wabi-sabi inspired UX design. *Conference on Human Factors in Computing Systems – Proceedings*. doi:10.1145/3411763.3450370

Landes, D. S. (2000). *The Wealth and Poverty of Nations: Why Some Are So Rich and Some So Poor*. W.W. Norton.

Lawless, D. V., & Roth, W.-M. (2001). The Spiel on "Spielraum and Teaching". *Curriculum Inquiry, 31*(2), 229–235.

Maboloc, C. R. (2021). Deep thinking or resistance? on finding a middle ground between paolo Freire's critical pedagogy and john Dewey's pragmatism. *Philosophia (United States), 49*(3), 1097–1108. doi:10.100711406-020-00292-5

Maher, M. L., & Tang, H.-H. (2003). Co-evolution as a computational and cognitive model of design. *Research in Engineering Design, 14*(1), 47–63.

Markey, D. K., O' Brien, D. B., Kouta, D. C., Okantey, C., & O' Donnell, D. C. (2021). Embracing classroom cultural diversity: Innovations for nurturing inclusive intercultural learning and culturally responsive teaching. *Teaching and Learning in Nursing, 16*(3), 258–262. doi:10.1016/j.teln.2021.01.008

Menzel, U. (1996). *Lange Wellen und Hegemonie.* Inst. for Social Science. TU Brunswick. http://www-public.tu-bs.de:8080/~umenzel/inhalt/forschungsberichte/BlaueReihe13.PDF

Mokyr, J. (1990). *The lever of riches. Technological creativity and economic progress.* Oxford University Press.

Mourelo, S. G. (2021). The «principle of responsibility» in adolphe Gesché's theology [El «principio de responsabilidad» en la teología de Adolphe Gesché]. *Estudios Eclesiasticos, 96*(376), 87–131. doi:10.14422/EE.V96.I376.Y2021.003

Mukerji, S., & Tripathi, P. (2009). *Editorial: Cases on Technological Adaptability and Transnational Learning: Issues & Challenges.* Retrieved from https://www.igi-global.com/requests/details.asp?ID=588

Padmanabhan, J., Geetha Bala, P., & Rajkumar, S. (2019). Learning based approximation algorithm: A case study in learning through gaming. *Proceedings of the 11th International Conference on Advanced Computing, ICoAC 2019*, 404-408. doi:10.1109/ICoAC48765.2019.24687

Papenhausen, C. (2009). A cyclical model of institutional change. *Foresight, 11*(3), 4–13.

Periñán, J. J. G. (2021). Conscience and selfhood: A phenomenological analysis of being and time, 54-60. *Tópicos (México)*, (61), 145–170. doi:10.21555/TOP.V0I61.1171

Permatasari, I., & Andriyanti, E. (2021). Developing students' intercultural communicative competence through cultural text-based teaching. *Indonesian Journal of Applied Linguistics, 11*(1), 72–82. doi:10.17509/ijal.v11i1.34611

Pirc, T., & Weber, M. B. (2021). The ontological status of animals: A deconstruction of anthropocentric metaphysics [Ontološki status živali: Dekonstrukcija antropocentrične metafizike]. *Ars Et Humanitas, 15*(1), 183–195. doi:10.4312/ARS.15.1.183-195

Popke, E. J. (2003). Poststructuralist ethics: Subjectivity, responsibility and the space of community. *Progress in Human Geography, 27*(3), 298–316.

Prensky, M. (2001). *Digital Game-Based Learning.* McGraw-Hill.

Pyysiäinen, J. (2021). Sociocultural affordances and enactment of agency: A transactional view. *Theory & Psychology, 31*(4), 491–512. doi:10.1177/0959354321989431

Racine, E., Kusch, S., Cascio, M. A., & Bogossian, A. (2021). Making autonomy an instrument: A pragmatist account of contextualized autonomy. *Humanities and Social Sciences Communications, 8*(1). Advance online publication. doi:10.105741599-021-00811-z

Robbins, D. (2007). Sociology as reflective science - On Bourdieu's Project. *Theory, Culture & Society, 24*(5), 77–98.

Ross, D. (2021). Care and carelessness in the Anthropocene: Bernard Stiegler's three conversions and their accompanying Heideggers. *Cultural Politics, 17*(2), 145. doi:10.1215/17432197-8947851

Roth, W.-M., Lawless, D. V., & Masciotra, D. (2001). Spielraum and Teaching. *Curriculum Inquiry,* *31*(2), 183–207.

Rouse, J. (2021). Stance and being. *Journal of the American Philosophical Association, 7*(1), 20–39. doi:10.1017/apa.2020.5

Ryu, D. (2013). Play to learn, learn to play: Language learning through gaming culture. *ReCALL, 25*(2), 286–301. doi:10.1017/S0958344013000050

Schön, D. (1983). *The reflective practitioner.* Basic Books.

Schön, D. A. (1986). Leadership as Reflection-in-Action. In T. J. Sergiovanni & J. E. Corbally (Eds.), *Leadership and Organizational Culture: New Perspectives on Administrative Theory and Practice* (p. 59). University of Illinois Press.

Schumpeter, J. A. (1949). *The theory of economic development.* Harvard Univ. Press.

Shapiro, H. B., Lee, C. H., Wyman Roth, N. E., Li, K., Çetinkaya-Rundel, M., & Canelas, D. A. (2017). Understanding the massive open online course (MOOC) student experience: An examination of attitudes, motivations, and barriers. *Computers & Education, 110,* 35–50. doi:10.1016/j.compedu.2017.03.003

Shirsekar, S. S. (2019). *Learning through gaming? Comparative innovative educational games of children (an on-going research project).* doi:10.1007/978-981-13-5977-4_75

Sieglova, D., & Stejskalova, L. (2021). Designing language courses for twenty-first century competences: A model of teaching toward learner autonomy implemented in a university context in the czech republic. *Language Learning in Higher Education, 11*(1), 33–49. doi:10.1515/cercles-2021-2004

Soneji, C. (2019). Learning through gaming. *British Dental Journal, 227*(12), 1011–1012. doi:10.103841415-019-1106-9

Stähli, F. (1998). *Ingenieurethik an Fachhochschulen* [Ethics for Engineers at Universities of Applied Science]. Fortis FH, Verlag Sauerländer AG.

Stähli, F. (2005). *Warum muss Technik ein Gegenstand der Ethik sein?* [Why must technology be an object of ethics?]. Aarau. Retrieved from http://web.fhnw.ch/personenseiten/fridolin.staehli/_html/publ.html

Tham, J., Duin, A. H., Veeramoothoo, S. C., & Fuglsby, B. J. (2021). Connectivism for writing pedagogy: Strategic networked approaches to promote international collaborations and intercultural learning. *Computers and Composition, 60.* Advance online publication. doi:10.1016/j.compcom.2021.102643

Tonner-Saunders, S., & Shimi, J. (2021). Hands of the world intercultural project: Developing student teachers' digital competences through contextualised learning [El proyecto intercultural "Hands of the World": Desarrollando las competencias digitales de estudiantes de magisterio a través del aprendizaje contextualizado]. *Pixel-Bit, Revista De Medios y Educacion,* (61), 7-35. doi:10.12795/PIXELBIT.88177

Tripathi, P., & Mukerji, S. (2008). Access and Equity to Education in India through Synergy of Conventional and ODL Systems: A Step towards Democratization of Education. *IGNOU.* Retrieved from http://www.distanceetdroitaleducation.org/contents/OP2008-IGNOU.pdf

Tröhler, M. (2007). Leeway for wits and sense [Spielraum für Sinne und Sinn]. *Du: Zeitschrift der Kultur, 778,* 45-61. Retrieved from http://www.du-magazin.com/

UniGIS. (2009). UNIGIS International Association. *Curricula*. Retrieved from https://www.unigis.net/

Venter, C. J., & Coetzee, J. (2014). Interactive learning through gaming simulation in an integrated land use-transportation planning course. *Journal of Professional Issues in Engineering Education and Practice, 140*(1). Advance online publication. doi:10.1061/(ASCE)EI.1943-5541.0000171

Viola, I., Aiello, P., Di Tore, S., & Sibilio, M. (2021). Learning through gaming in times of COVID-19: The pedagogical value of edugames. *ACM International Conference Proceeding Series*, 140-144. doi:10.1145/3450148.3450170

Volejnikova-Wenger, S., Andersen, P., & Clarke, K. (2021). Student nurses' experience using a serious game to learn environmental hazard and safety assessment. *Nurse Education Today, 98*. Advance online publication. doi:10.1016/j.nedt.2020.104739

Wagner-Döbler, R. (1998). Innovationsebben und Innovationsfluten: xxx. In S. Greif, H. Laitko, & H. Parthey (Eds.), *Wissenschaftsforschung: Yearbook 96/97*. BdWi-Verlag.

Waight, H. (2021). Recovering John Dewey's lost vision for social science in contemporary American sociology. *The American Sociologist, 52*(2), 420–448. doi:10.100712108-021-09482-4

Werner, M. H. (2003). Hans Jonas' Prinzip Verantwortung [H. Jonas' principle of responsibility]. In M. Düwell & K. Steigleder (Eds.), *Bioethik: Eine Einführung* (pp. 41–56). Suhrkamp. Retrieved from https://www.micha-h-werner.de/jonas.pdf

Stock Price Prediction:
Fuzzy Clustering–Based Approach

S

Ahmet Tezcan Tekin
Istanbul Technical University, Turkey

Ferhan Çebi
Istanbul Technical University, Turkey

Tolga Kaya
Istanbul Technical University, Turkey

INTRODUCTION

Forecasting the stock market index and index movements is one of the most challenging time series analysis obstacles. Investors use two types of analysis, fundamental and technical analysis, before investing in stocks. With fundamental analysis, investors decide whether to invest, taking into account indicators such as the stock's actual value, the political climate, the industry's performance, and the economy. In technical analysis, the evaluation of stocks is provided by using statistics created by market movements such as historical values and transaction volumes (Pabuççu, 2019).

Investors are beginning to rely on forecasting systems to make critical business decisions. There is a lot of research done in this field, but no complete solution has yet been found. Difficulty in predicting the stock market depends not only on the influence of social, political and economic reasons but also on a vast amount of historical data about the stocks and currency (Iqbal et al., 2013). This study consists of many states of the art machine learning techniques to find optimum solutions for predicting stock values.

In the literature, there are two types of approaches to forecasting a stock price. These are qualitative and quantitative approaches. The quantitative approach uses past stock prices, such as the closing and opening price, the amount exchanged, neighbouring closing rates of the stock etc., to forecast the stock's future price. In the qualitative approach, the analysis is based on external factors: economic and political factors, company's identity, company's and general market situation etc. In this approach, textual information published in the magazine or web and social media blogs are used, written by economic experts (Hur et al., 2006).

This study aims to predict bank stocks: AKBNK, GARAN, HALKB, YKBNK and VAKBN in BIST 30 index. For that reason, the authors use the last three years' BIST 30 index values for predicting those stocks values. Also, the fuzzy clustering technique is applied to the dataset to find stocks in BIST 30 index and have similar characteristics with predicted bank stocks. The main reason for this approach is to test whether enlarging the data set to be used in the prediction phase positively affects the performance of the algorithms.

The authors applied classical machine learning algorithms such as Random Forest, Support Vector Machine etc. But, ensembling types of machine learning algorithms such as XGBoost, Catboost, LightGBM and GBDT produced more promising results with different hyperparameters for the prediction. Besides, the most successful models with their hyperparameters were ensembled according to their er-

DOI: 10.4018/978-1-7998-9220-5.ch111

ror rate's reciprocal for better prediction performance. These results were compared with the traditional methods, and it is discussed in the methodology section.

In this paper, the details of the methodology are provided in Section 2. Section 3 discusses the result of the findings, and Section 4 concludes the article.

BACKGROUND

In the era of big data and machine learning, with historical data usage, there are many studies conducted on the literature for predicting stock prices in several stock markets such as NASDAQ, Chinese Market etc. Recent works show us machine learning and deep learning technics can be used for predicting future stock prices. Li et al. (2017) and Oyeyemi et al. (2007) used neural networks such as Convolutional Neural Network (CNN), Artificial Neural Network (ANN), Long Short-Term Memory (LSTM) and Recurrent Neural Network (RNN) for predicting stock prices. Due to high-level noise in stock markets, Shen and Shafiq combined a customized deep learning-based system for predicting stock market price trends (Shen et al., 2020). Thus Artificial Neural Networks proves to be successful in predicting stock price; Wang et al. applied artificial neural networks for stock market price prediction with the dataset related to the S&P 500 (Xiaohua et al., 2003). Kim and Han also used ANN with genetic algorithms for predicting stock price index (Kim et al., 2000). Besides, RNN and LSTM prove to be successful in stock market price prediction. Selvin et al. built a comparative model approach for stock price prediction using LSTM, RNN and CNN-sliding window models (Selvin et al., 2017). Zhuge et al. (2017) used LSTM with Emotional Analysis to predict stock price. Jaiswal et al. (2022) applied a comparative analysis on stock price prediction model using deep learning technology. In addition to deep learning technics, machine learning technics are applied to solve stock price prediction problems. Shen et al. (2012) Hongming (2020), and Rajeswar et al. (2022) applied traditional machine learning algorithms such as SVM and Logistic Regression, Linear Regression to predict stock prices. Also, Khan et al. (2020) used the Random Forest classifier to improve forecasting accuracy using social media and news with natural language processing techniques. Known from the literature, ensembling machine learning algorithms have promising results in machine learning problems. Hongming (2020) applied ensembling type boosting algorithms such as Extreme Gradient Boosting etc., to stock data for predicting stock price prediction. Akşehir and Kılıç (2019) use some bank stocks in BIST market data for predicting their stock prices with machine learning technics. Demirel (2019) applies machine learning and deep learning techniques to predict stock prices in the BIST 100 index. Pabuçcu (2019) aims to predict stock market movement using ANN and machine learning algorithms such as Naive Bayes and SVM in BIST 100 index. Deep learning technics and ensemble learning technics are also used together for predicting stock prices in the literature. Kumar and Lokesh (2022) use ensemble learning technics and Deep learning technics together for predicting stock prices.

Fuzzy logic is an area of great importance in the literature on its own. Although its use in machine learning approaches has increased recently, the number of fuzzy machine learning studies in the literature is insufficient. Not all of the features used in machine learning problems contain certainties such as 1 or 0. Combining the power of the fuzzy logic approach with machine learning can increase the success rate in prediction. Besides, Fuzzy logic is commonly utilized in the literature to expand machine learning and data mining research. Fuzzy logic methods are used for this purpose, particularly in clustering and association rule mining research.

PROPOSED METHODOLOGY

Description of Data

The authors used the last four years' bank stock values which are in BIST 30. The dataset consists of hourly opening, closing, highest, lowest, last day value metrics of stocks. Also, technical indicators, which are Relative Strength Index (RSI), Moving Average, Moving Average Convergence/Divergence (MACD) etc., are used for better accuracy. Besides, because of the investors' investment preferences, the authors also added one gram gold value in TRY, USD-TRY parity and the bank index value in the BIST 30. The details of the base features which are used in this study are shown in Table 1.

Table 1. Base features in prediction

Feature	Description
Open	It is the price at which financial security first trades on the market.
High	It is the highest price of a stock in the last trading interval.
Low	It is the lowest price of a stock in the last trading interval.
Close	It is the price at which financial security last trades on the market.
MAV	It is the average price of a stock over a set period.
MACD	It's a trend-following momentum indicator that shows how two stocks' price moving averages are linked.
Trigger	It is generally a market situation, such as an increase or decrease in an index or asset price.
RSI	It's a momentum oscillator that monitors price movement speed and change
TS	It is the overall direction of a market or an asset's price.
VLT	It is a statistical measure of a security's or market index's return dispersion.
BIST30	It is the value of the BIST 30 index.
BIST100	It is the value of the BIST 100 index.
XBANK	It is the bank index value in the BIST 30.
GOLDGR	It is the one gram gold value in TRY.
USDTRY	It is USD TRY parity.

Ensembling Type Algorithms

Ensembling type machine learning algorithms are very commonly used in predictions nowadays. For that reason boosting type ensembling machine learning algorithms such as Catboost, Extreme Gradient Boosting (XGBoost), Light Gradient Boosting (LGBM), Gradient Boosting Decision Trees (GBDT) are used in this study. These algorithms are briefly explained below.

Light Gradient Boosting Machine

Light Gradient Boosting algorithm is a new version of GBDT. It is very commonly used in many different kinds of modelling problems, such as classification and regression. Two new strategies are used in LightGBM: Gradient-based One-Side Sampling and Exclusive Function Bundling to accommodate a large number of data instances and a large number of functions (Ke et al., 2017). Comparing to the base gradient boosting strategies or Extreme Gradient Boosting, LightGBM extends the decision tree vertically, while others extend the decision tree horizontally. This feature makes LightGBM effective in processing large scale data.

Catboost

Catboost is a new version of the gradient boosting type algorithm proposed by Prokhorenkova (2018). Catboost efficiently operates for categorical functionality with the lowest knowledge loss. CatBoost differs from other gradient boosting algorithms such as Extreme Gradient Boosting and LightGBM because it uses ordered boosting, an effective modification of gradient boosting algorithms, to solve the issue of target leakage (Dorogoush et al., 2018). Besides, Dorogush states that Catboost tries to prevent overfitting problems caused by gradient boosting algorithms by performing random permutations to adjust leaf values when choosing the tree structure. The estimated output of Catboost is described in Equation 1.

$$Z = H(x_i) = \sum J_j = 1c_j1\left\{x \in R_j\right\} \tag{1}$$

where $H(X_i)$ is a decision tree function of the explanatory variables x_i, and R_j is the disjoint region corresponding to the tree's leaves (Prokhorenkova, 2018).

Extreme Gradient Boosting

Extreme Gradient Boosting (XGBoost) is a prevalent version of gradient boosting type algorithms proposed by Chen and Guestrin (Chen et al., 2016). XGBoost is an improved GBDT (Gradient Boosting Decision Trees) algorithm that involves multiple decision trees and is used frequently in the classification and regression field. XGBoost adds a regularization concept to maximize the size of the classification function of the tree to be more reproducible. Furthermore, regularization helps to predict the function value, which plays a crucial role in big data problems. The estimated output of XGBoost is described in Equation 2.

$$Z=F(x_i)=\sum T_t=1f_t(x_i) \tag{2}$$

where x_i denotes the explanatory variables, and $f_t(x_i)$ is the output function of each tree.

Gradient Boosting Machine

Gradient Boosting Machine (GBM), the base version of Catboost, XGBoost and LightGBM, is proposed by Friedman (Friedman, 2001). It is a tree type learning algorithm that efficiently and scalable implementation of a gradient boosting framework. GBM is one of the most popular machine learning algorithms, and it has been stated that it performs very accurate in both regression and classification problems in the literature. GBM aims to reduce bias-variance using base learner as a weighted sum and reweight the misclassified data. Also, it uses decision trees as base learners for reducing the loss function. The estimated output of GBM is described in Equation 3.

$$Z=F(x_i)=\sum M_j=1\beta_jh \tag{3}$$

where the function $h(x; bj)$ is the base learner, x is the explanatory variables, βj is the expansion coefficients, and bj is the model's parameters.

FUZZY CLUSTERING TECHNIQUES

Fuzzy logic, which is essential in the literature, is frequently utilized in machine learning issues. One of the primary reasons for this is that the solutions to real-world problems do not consist solely of 0 and 1 single values, as is the case with machine learning methods to real-world problems.

Lofti Zadeh discovered fuzzy logic (Zadeh 1965; Zadeh 1968; Zadeh 1973) in 1965. Zadeh thought that analytical and computer-based approaches could be used to tackle all real-world issues (Kumar et al., 2015). Fuzzy logic is essentially a way for defining intermediate values between standard assessments such as true/false or yes/no.

The concept of fuzzy logic is often encountered in clustering problems in machine learning problems. In this context, there are many studies in the literature. Clustering algorithms are divided into two as hard clustering and soft clustering (Nasibov et al., 2019). Fuzzy clustering is in the soft clustering category. In the hard clustering method, each observation set can belong to only one cluster, while in the soft clustering methods, it can belong to more than one cluster simultaneously (Sujamol et al., 2017). The soft clustering approach is also known as fuzzy clustering in the literature. The membership level for each observation value is determined using the fuzzy clustering approach. This level ranges from 0 to 1.

There are several fuzzy clustering algorithms in the literature but, Fuzzy C-Means (FCM) is one of the most widely used fuzzy clustering algorithms. Because the implementation of FCM is easy, the authors preferred to use FCM in this study. FCM clustering was developed by Dunn in 1973 (Dunn, 1973) and improved by Bezdek in 1981 (Bezdek, 1981). This method improves on prior clustering techniques. FCM assigns data points to a predetermined number of distinct clusters as they populate multidimensional space. The primary feature of FCM is that it enables data points for cluster memberships with degrees ranging from 0 to 1. The FCM algorithm is based on a minimization objective function. This function can be written as

$$J_m = \sum_{i=1}^{N}\sum_{j=1}^{C} u_{ij}^m x_i - c_j^2, 1 \leq m < \infty \tag{4}$$

where u_{ij} is the degree of membership of x_i in the cluster, x_i denotes that i th of d-dimensional measured data, c_j is the dimension centre of the cluster (Bora et al., 2014). FCM distinguishes from K-means clustering, which is one of the most popular hard clustering techniques in the literature by the addition of the membership values w_{ij} and the fuzzifier, $m \in R$, with $m \geq 1$. m determines the level of cluster fuzziness.

HYPERPARAMETER OPTIMIZATION

The algorithms' performances in solving machine learning problems are generally dependent on the hyperparameters selected while these algorithms are run (Klein et al., 2019). Because default hyperparameters cannot ensure machine learning model performance, adjusting hyperparameters becomes the primary procedure for machine learning techniques (Thiede et al., 2019).

To achieve the optimum configuration of hyperparameters, several tuning techniques such as empirical approaches and manual search have been developed. However, the following challenges remain.

- Tuning hyperparameters is primarily dependent on professional expertise and time-consuming empirical study. These are making it time-consuming and labour-intensive.
- The adjustment procedure must be repeated when applied to a new dataset; determining the hyperparameter setting range is difficult.
- There are countless hyperparameter combinations in the high dimension, and finding the optimal combination is difficult. As a result, the tuning process is time-consuming and labour-intensive, and the outcomes of the tuning process quickly converge to inferior hyperparameter configurations.

The most prominent hyperparameter optimization approaches used in the literature are grid search, random search and Bayesian optimization, and hyperparameter optimization has been applied in many areas in the literature. Shi et al. applied a grid search for several hyperparameter settings to improve the accuracy of tilt angle tracking (Shi et al., 2019). Hao et al. used the Random Search method to optimize the serval control hyperparameters for efficiency (Hao et al., 2018). McParland et al.; tried to improve the success rates of algorithms used to estimate wear rates with Bayesian optimization (McParland et al., 2019). Compared to empirical research and manual search, hyperparameter optimization methods are easy to use and can also achieve state-of-the-art results on some tasks.

Hyperparameter optimization methods are practical and efficient, but they need to be further improved when hyperparameter spaces are complex, as in high dimension with hyperparameters gap, continuous, combinatorial and conditional hyperparameter types for workpiece quality prediction model (Wen et al., 2020).

Grid search, random search, evolutionary algorithms and Bayesian optimization, which are among the hyperparameter optimization methods, have been used in many areas in the literature. If we look at these methods in more detail;

- **Grid search:** The grid search method tries every possibility among all candidate parameter combinations and selects the most successful candidate combination as the final result. The grid search method is reliable in low-dimensional space. However, the increase in the size of the super parameter to be optimized increases the computational complexity exponentially (Xie et al., 2019).
- **Random search:** The random search method is similar to the grid search method, except that it randomly selects the points to be optimized from within the given range. According to the studies conducted by Schaer et al. and Bhat et al., they state that it is much more efficient than the grid search method in high-dimensional spaces (Schaer et al., 2016; Bhat et al., 2018). Due to the lack of routing, the random search method cannot easily approach the optimum configuration.
- **Evolutionary algorithms:** Evolutionary algorithms such as genetic algorithms and particle swarm optimization achieve the best configurations based on population information sharing and evolution. They are easy to implement in parallel (Falkner et al., 2018) but require much more time (Assad and Deep, 2018; Gobeyn et al., 2019). Other methods, such as annealing, require less computation time but tend to fall into the local optimum.
- **Bayesian Optimization:** Bayesian optimization uses Bayes' theorem to find optimal hyperparameter configurations (Li et al., 2020). A surrogate model is constructed based on the final prob-

ability distribution, and the next most potential point is chosen by maximizing the acquisition function. Its calculation is simple and has been applied in some areas in the literature (Letham et al., 2019; Chen et al., 2018).

SOLUTIONS AND RECOMMENDATIONS

To evaluate the effectiveness of the models, the authors use regression models' main performance metrics such as Mean Absolute Error (MAE), Root Mean Squared Error (RMSE), R Squared Value (R2) and Mean Absolute Percentage Error (MAPE). The details of these metrics and their calculation equations are briefly described below.

MAE: The MAE is defined by Equation 4. MAE averages the absolute differences between predicted and actual values. The smaller amount of MAE means that prediction is more accurate.

$$MAE = \frac{1}{n} \sum_{i=1}^{n} \left| y_i - \widehat{y_i} \right| \tag{5}$$

In this equation, n represents the number of samples, and the value is determined by adding the absolute values of the discrepancies between the actual and predicted values.

RMSE: This measure closely resembles MAE. It may also be used to calculate the difference between expected and actual values. The distinction between MAE and RMSE is that RMSE takes the square of the error and penalizes larger discrepancies between expected and actual values. RMSE is defined by Equation 6.

$$RMSE = \sqrt{\frac{\sum_{i=1}^{n} \left(y_i - \hat{y}_i \right)^2}{n}} \tag{6}$$

R2: This statistic measures how closely expected and actual values match each other. R2 is a numeric value between 0 and 1. When this number approaches one, it indicates that prediction accuracy is improving. It is computed by subtracting from one the fraction of explained variation to total variation. R2 is defined by Equation 7.

$$R^2 = 1 - \frac{\sum_{i=1}^{n} \left(y_i - \hat{y}_i \right)^2}{\sum_{i=1}^{n} \left(y_i - \overline{y}_i \right)^2} \tag{7}$$

MAPE: In statistics, it measures a forecasting system's prediction accuracy, such as in trend estimation, and is frequently used as a loss function for machine learning regression issues. The actual value is At, while the predicted value is Ft. The MAPE is typically expressed as a percentage, which is the next calculation multiplied by 100. T The real value of At breaks the gap between At and Ft once again. The absolute value in this equation is summed and divided by the number of fitted points n at each predicted point in time. MAPE is defined by Equation 8.

$$M = \frac{1}{n} \sum_{t=1}^{n} \left| \frac{A_t - F_t}{A_t} \right| \tag{8}$$

The authors added the last thirty-hour values of base features added to the dataset to predict the correspondent stock's next hour's closing value. This feature extension procedure supplies meaningful data about the trends of stocks values. After this step, the authors apply commonly used machine learning algorithms in the literature and achieve a comparison matrix of machine learning algorithms' performance results. These results are shown in Table 2. The results show that Light Gradient Boosting Machine has the best performance, with the lowest error rate in applied algorithms with a 0.3663 RMSE value. The results also demonstrate that boosting type ensemble learning methods outperform other algorithms.

Table 2. Algorithms' results for the prediction

Model	MAE	RMSE	R2	MAPE
Light Gradient Boosting Machine	0.2387	0.3663	0.9499	0.0419
CatBoost Regressor	0.2650	0.3902	0.9441	0.0472
Gradient Boosting Regressor	0.3769	0.5438	0.9124	0.0648
Extreme Gradient Boosting	0.3780	0.5450	0.9114	0.0652
Random Forest	0.4613	0.6917	0.8692	0.0854
Support Vector Machine	0.5465	0.7726	0.8432	0.0943

Then, the FCM algorithm was applied to the dataset for increasing the observation count. This process aims to improve the learning curve of machine learning algorithms. With this method, some of the BIST 30 stocks which are not in the banking industry and have similar characteristics with the banking industry stocks are added to the dataset. But, before applying FCM to the dataset, firstly, the authors aim to find optimum fuzzifier parameters, which is crucial for fuzzy clustering and cluster count. Default fuzzifier parameter "m" was set to 2 in FCM, so different "m" values and different cluster seeds are tested, and their Fuzzy Partition Coefficient (FPC) values are compared. FPC is a metric that uses the fuzzy partition matrix to quantify the fuzzy degree of final split clusters; the higher the value, the better the partition outcome (Bezdek, 1974). The comparison results are shown in Table 3.

Table 3. FPC scores with different cluster counts and different fuzzifier parameters

	c=2	c=3	c=5	c=7	c=9
m=1.2	0.8657	0.8421	0.8290	0.7523	0.7433
m=1.5	0.9402	0.9265	0.9064	0.8577	0.8431
m=2	0.9532	0.9386	0.9124	0.8637	0.8548
m=2.5	0.9186	0.8954	0.8702	0.8258	0.7865

The comparison results show that m=2 and c=2 have the most optimum fuzzifier value and cluster count. With these results, different seven stocks values which are not in the banking industry have similar characteristics with banking industry stocks. So, these stocks' values are added to the dataset and algorithms were reapplied to the dataset. The results are shown in Table 4.

Table 4. Algorithms' results with the extended dataset for the prediction

Model	MAE	RMSE	R2	MAPE
Light Gradient Boosting Machine	0.2340	0.3591	0.9689	0.0411
CatBoost Regressor	0.2593	0.3818	0.9649	0.0462
Gradient Boosting Regressor	0.3691	0.5326	0.9316	0.0635
Extreme Gradient Boosting	0.3699	0.5333	0.9315	0.0638
Random Forest	0.4505	0.6755	0.8901	0.0834
Support Vector Machine	0.5343	0.7552	0.8626	0.0922

The results indicate that algorithms have better performance with the extended dataset. The R Squared Values for the best-performed algorithm, Light Gradient Boosting Machine, improved nearly 2 per cent.

In the last step of the modelling phase, the authors intend to tune LGBM hyperparameters to increase modelling performance. In general, the algorithms' efficiency in solving machine learning problems depends on the hyperparameters chosen when the algorithms are run (Klein, et al., 2019). The hyperparameters setting is the primary mechanism for machine learning techniques, as the default hyperparameters do not guarantee the efficiency of machine learning models (Thiede et al., 2019). Various modification approaches such as trial and error and manual search have been developed to obtain hyperparameters' best configuration. So, the authors applied hyperparameter optimization for the top three algorithms with the best prediction results. The authors have used k-fold cross-validation to assess the models' stability. The optimization method of hyperparameters has a positive prediction effect. The results of different hyperparameters of the top three best-performed algorithms' performance outcomes are shown in Table 5.

The results show that hyperparameter optimization has a positive effect on decreasing the error rate in the prediction. Also, with the hyperparameter optimization, a variation of the Catboost Regressor has better performance than many of the other algorithm variations.

Besides, the weighted average method is applied to the best performed three algorithms variations which are LGBM learning_rate:0.3 - n_estimator:200, LGBM learning_rate:0.3 - n_estimator:100, Catboost Regressor depth:4 - learning_rate:0.01 for ensembling these algorithms. With this method, authors try to optimize model performance. The weight calculation is defined by Equation 9.

$$\text{Weight}_{r_i} = \frac{1}{\text{RMSE}_{r_i}} \tag{9}$$

After that, the ensemble prediction was produced, and the results were compared to the results of the other model and parameter groups. The performance of our ensembled model is 0.3433 RMSE. As a result, the authors claim that the ensembled model performs somewhat better than the other methods.

After the modelling and hyperparameter tuning phase, the authors tested our ensembled model with the following sixty-hour stock prices for YKBNK, AKBNK, GARAN, HALKB and VAKBN stocks which are in BIST 30 index. The actual and predicted values for correspondent stocks are given in Figure 1, Figure 2, Figure 3. While the blue line in the figures states the actual result, the red line states the prediction results. When the figures examined, it is seen that blue and red lines are fit into one another. This situation shows us the prediction that bank stocks are successful.

Table 5. Different hyperparameters' results of the top three best-performed algorithms

Algorithm	Parameters	RMSE
Light Gradient Boosting Machine	learning_rate:0.1, n_estimator:200	0.3561
Light Gradient Boosting Machine	learning_rate:0.1, n_estimator:100	0.3503
Light Gradient Boosting Machine	learning_rate:0.3, n_estimator:200	**0.3442**
Light Gradient Boosting Machine	learning_rate:0.3, n_estimator:100	**0.3470**
Catboost Regressor	depth:4, learning_rate:0.01	**0.3466**
Catboost Regressor	depth:8, learning_rate:0.01	0.3571
Catboost Regressor	depth:4, learning_rate:0.1	0.3703
Catboost Regressor	depth:8 learning_rate:0.1	0.3766
Gradient Boosting Regressor	learning_rate:0.1, n_estimator:500	0.4723
Gradient Boosting Regressor	learning_rate:0.1, n_estimator:1000	0.4711
Gradient Boosting Regressor	learning_rate:0.01, n_estimator:500	0.4987
Gradient Boosting Regressor	learning_rate:0.01, n_estimator:1000	0.5054

Figure 1. YKBNK and AKBNK Stock's Actual and Predicted Values

Figure 2. VAKBN and GARAN Stock's Actual and Predicted Values

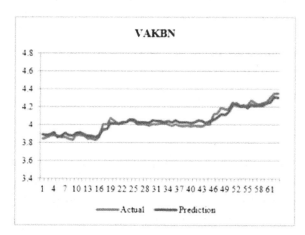

Figure 3. HALKB Stock's Actual and Predicted Values

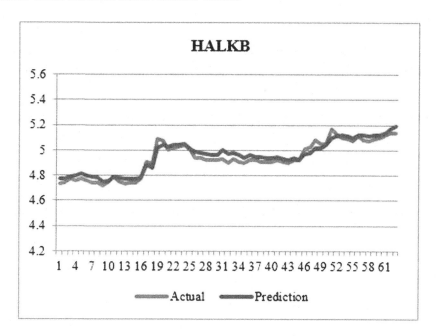

CONCLUSION

This study intends to predict the stock prices of GARAN, HALKB, YKBNK, AKBNK, and VAKBN bank in BIST 30. To this end, firstly, the last four years of stock indexes values were collected. After that, the authors extended our dataset with one gram gold value in TRY, USD-TRY parity and the bank index value in the BIST 30. Then, the last thirty-hour values of base features were added to the dataset to predict the correspondent stock's next hour's closing value.

In the modelling section, extended features as input for machine learning algorithms were used. After applying more than ten regression algorithms, the results show that the ensembled model has the best performance for minimizing the error in the prediction with a 0.3433 RMSE value. Also, the results show us boosting type ensemble learning algorithms have better performance than other algorithms. Then the authors apply hyperparameter optimization LGBM, which has the lowest error rate in prediction for improving prediction performance.

Then the authors tested our tuned model for each bank stock index. As we show in figures, actual and predicted value lines are fit into one another. So, it is possible to deduce our prediction is successful.

FEATURE RESEARCH DIRECTIONS

The authors will try to extend the dataset with different stock values in the BIST 100 index for future works. Then, other fuzzy clustering techniques, which are Possibilistic C-Means Clustering, Fuzzy Possibilistic C-Means Clustering, Possibilistic Fuzzy C-Means Clustering, will also be applied to the dataset to find similar stocks as characteristics. This will supply more training data for getting better performance in the prediction.

REFERENCES

Akşehir, Z. D., & Kılıç, E. (2019, September). Prediction of bank stocks price with reduced technical indicators. In *2019 4th International Conference on Computer Science and Engineering (UBMK)* (pp. 206-210). IEEE. 10.1109/UBMK.2019.8906999

Assad, A., & Deep, K. (2018). A hybrid harmony search and simulated annealing algorithm for continuous optimization. *Information Sciences*, *450*, 246–266. doi:10.1016/j.ins.2018.03.042

Bezdek, J. C. (1974). Numerical taxonomy with fuzzy sets. *Journal of Mathematical Biology*, *1*(1), 57–71. doi:10.1007/BF02339490

Bezdek, J. C. (1981). *Pattern recognition with fuzzy objective function algorithms*. doi:10.1007/978-1-4757-0450-1

Bhat, P. C., Prosper, H. B., Sekmen, S., & Stewart, C. (2018). Optimizing event selection with the random grid search. *Computer Physics Communications*, *228*, 245–257. doi:10.1016/j.cpc.2018.02.018

Bora, D. J., Gupta, D., & Kumar, A. (2014). *A comparative study between fuzzy clustering algorithm and hard clustering algorithm.* arXiv preprint arXiv:1404.6059.

Chen, T., He, T., & Benesty, M. (2015). *Xgboost: extreme gradient boosting*. R package version 0.4-2.

Chen, T., & Guestrin, C. (2016, August). Xgboost: A scalable tree boosting system. In *Proceedings of the 22nd acm sigkdd international conference on knowledge discovery and data mining* (pp. 785-794). 10.1145/2939672.2939785

Demirel, U. (2019). *Hisse senedi fiyatlarının makine öğrenmesi yöntemleri ve derin öğrenme algoritmaları ile tahmini* (Master's thesis). Sosyal Bilimler Enstitüsü.

Dorogush, A. V., Ershov, V., & Gulin, A. (2018). *CatBoost: gradient boosting with categorical features.* https://arxiv. org/pdf/1810.11363. pdf

Dunn, J. C. (1973). *A fuzzy relative of the ISODATA process and its use in detecting compact well-separated clusters*. Academic Press.

Falkner, S., Klein, A., & Hutter, F. (2018). BOHB: Robust and efficient hyperparameter optimization at scale. In *International Conference on Machine Learning* (pp. 1437-1446). PMLR.

Friedman, J. H. (2001). Greedy function approximation: A gradient boosting machine. *Annals of Statistics*, *29*(5), 1189–1232. doi:10.1214/aos/1013203451

Gobeyn, S., Mouton, A. M., Cord, A. F., Kaim, A., Volk, M., & Goethals, P. L. (2019). Evolutionary algorithms for species distribution modelling: A review in the context of machine learning. *Ecological Modelling*, *392*, 179–195. doi:10.1016/j.ecolmodel.2018.11.013

Hao, M. R., Ahmad, M. A., Raja Ismail, R. M. T., & Nasir, A. N. K. (2018). Performance evaluation of random search based methods on model-free wind farm control. In *Intelligent Manufacturing & Mechatronics* (pp. 657–670). Springer. doi:10.1007/978-981-10-8788-2_60

Hur, J., Raj, M., & Riyanto, Y. E. (2006). Finance and trade: A cross-country empirical analysis on the impact of financial development and asset tangibility on international trade. *World Development*, *34*(10), 1728–1741. doi:10.1016/j.worlddev.2006.02.003

Iqbal, Z., Ilyas, R., Shahzad, W., Mahmood, Z., & Anjum, J. (2013). Efficient machine learning techniques for stock market prediction. *International Journal of Engineering Research and Applications*, *3*(6), 855–867.

Jaiswal, R., Mahato, K., Kapoor, P., & Pal, S. B. (2022). A Comparative Analysis on Stock Price Prediction Model using Deep Learning Technology. *American Journal of Electronics & Communication*, *2*(3), 12–19. doi:10.15864/ajec.2303

Ke, G., Meng, Q., Finley, T., Wang, T., Chen, W., Ma, W., ... Liu, T. Y. (2017). Lightgbm: A highly efficient gradient boosting decision tree. *Advances in Neural Information Processing Systems*, 30.

Khan, W., Ghazanfar, M. A., Azam, M. A., Karami, A., Alyoubi, K. H., & Alfakeeh, A. S. (2020). Stock market prediction using machine learning classifiers and social media. *Journal of Ambient Intelligence and Humanized Computing*, 1–24.

Kim, K. J., & Han, I. (2000). Genetic algorithms approach to feature discretization in artificial neural networks for the prediction of stock price index. *Expert Systems with Applications*, *19*(2), 125–132. doi:10.1016/S0957-4174(00)00027-0

Klein, A., Dai, Z., Hutter, F., Lawrence, N., & Gonzalez, J. (2019). Meta-surrogate benchmarking for hyperparameter optimization. *Advances in Neural Information Processing Systems*, 32.

Kumar, M., Misra, L., & Shekhar, G. (2015). Survey in fuzzy logic: An introduction. *Int. J. Sci. Res. Dev*, *3*(6), 822–824.

Kumar, R., & Shrivastav, L. K. (2022). An Ensemble of Random Forest Gradient Boosting Machine and Deep Learning Methods for Stock Price Prediction. *Journal of Information Technology Research*, *15*(1), 1–19. doi:10.4018/JITR.299947

Letham, B., Karrer, B., Ottoni, G., & Bakshy, E. (2019). Constrained Bayesian optimization with noisy experiments. *Bayesian Analysis*, *14*(2), 495–519. doi:10.1214/18-BA1110

Li, L., Wu, Y., Ou, Y., Li, Q., Zhou, Y., & Chen, D. (2017, October). Research on machine learning algorithms and feature extraction for time series. In *2017 IEEE 28th annual international symposium on personal, indoor, and mobile radio communications (PIMRC)* (pp. 1-5). IEEE. 10.1109/PIMRC.2017.8292668

Li, Y., Liu, G., Lu, G., Jiao, L., Marturi, N., & Shang, R. (2019). Hyper-parameter optimization using MARS surrogate for machine-learning algorithms. *IEEE Transactions on Emerging Topics in Computational Intelligence, 4*(3), 287–297. doi:10.1109/TETCI.2019.2918509

McParland, D., Baron, S., O'Rourke, S., Dowling, D., Ahearne, E., & Parnell, A. (2019). Prediction of tool-wear in turning of medical grade cobalt chromium molybdenum alloy (ASTM F75) using non-parametric Bayesian models. *Journal of Intelligent Manufacturing, 30*(3), 1259–1270. doi:10.100710845-017-1317-3

Nasibov, E., & Ordin, B. (2019). An incremental fuzzy algorithm for data clustering problems. *Balıkesir Üniversitesi Fen Bilimleri Enstitüsü Dergisi, 21*(1), 169–183.

Oyeyemi, E. O., McKinnell, L. A., & Poole, A. W. (2007). Neural network-based prediction techniques for global modeling of M (3000) F2 ionospheric parameter. *Advances in Space Research, 39*(5), 643–650. doi:10.1016/j.asr.2006.09.038

Pabuççu, H. (2019). Borsa Endeksi Hareketlerinin Makine Öğrenme Algoritmaları ile Tahmini. *Uluslararası İktisadi ve İdari İncelemeler Dergisi*, (23), 179–190.

Prokhorenkova, L., Gusev, G., Vorobev, A., Dorogush, A. V., & Gulin, A. (2018). CatBoost: Unbiased boosting with categorical features. *Advances in Neural Information Processing Systems*, 31.

Rajeswar, S., Ramalingam, P., & SudalaiMuthu, T. (2022, January). Comparative analysis of stock market price behaviors using machine learning techniques. In *AIP Conference Proceedings* (Vol. 2385, No. 1, p. 050007). AIP Publishing LLC.

Schaer, R., Müller, H., & Depeursinge, A. (2016). Optimized distributed hyperparameter search and simulation for lung texture classification in ct using hadoop. *Journal of Imaging, 2*(2), 19. doi:10.3390/jimaging2020019

Selvin, S., Vinayakumar, R., Gopalakrishnan, E. A., Menon, V. K., & Soman, K. P. (2017, September). *Stock price prediction using LSTM, RNN and CNN-sliding window model. In 2017 international conference on advances in computing, communications and informatics (icacci)*. IEEE.

Shen, J., & Shafiq, M. O. (2020). Short-term stock market price trend prediction using a comprehensive deep learning system. *Journal of Big Data, 7*(1), 1–33. doi:10.118640537-020-00333-6 PMID:32923309

Shen, S., Jiang, H., & Zhang, T. (2012). *Stock market forecasting using machine learning algorithms*. Department of Electrical Engineering, Stanford University.

Shi, L., He, Y., Li, B., Cheng, T., Huang, Y., & Sui, Y. (2019). Tilt angle monitoring by using sparse residual LSTM network and grid search. *IEEE Sensors Journal, 19*(19), 8803–8812. doi:10.1109/JSEN.2019.2921356

Sujamol, S., Ashok, S., & Kumar, U. K. (2017). Fuzzy based machine learning: A promising approach. *CSI Commun. Knowl. Digest for IT Community, 41*(8), 21–25.

Thiede, L. A., & Parlitz, U. (2019). Gradient based hyperparameter optimization in echo state networks. *Neural Networks, 115*, 23–29. doi:10.1016/j.neunet.2019.02.001 PMID:30921562

S

Wang, H. (2020, July). Stock price prediction based on machine learning approaches. In *Proceedings of the 3rd International Conference on Data Science and Information Technology* (pp. 1-5). 10.1145/3414274.3414275

Wang, X., Phua, P. K. H., & Lin, W. (2003, July). Stock market prediction using neural networks: Does trading volume help in short-term prediction? In *Proceedings of the International Joint Conference on Neural Networks*, 2003 (Vol. 4, pp. 2438-2442). IEEE.

Wen, L., Ye, X., & Gao, L. (2020). A new automatic machine learning based hyperparameter optimization for workpiece quality prediction. *Measurement and Control, 53*(7-8), 1088–1098. doi:10.1177/0020294020932347

Xie, G., Zhao, Y., Xie, S., Huang, M., & Zhang, Y. (2019). Multi-classification method for determining coastal water quality based on SVM with grid search and KNN. *International Journal of Performability Engineering, 15*(10), 2618. doi:10.23940/ijpe.19.10.p7.26182627

Zadeh, L. A. (1965). Information and control. *Fuzzy Sets, 8*(3), 338-353.

Zadeh, L. A. (1968). Fuzzy algorithms. *Info & Ctl., 12*, 94–102.

Zadeh, L. A. (1973). Outline of a new approach to the analysis of complex systems and decision processes. *IEEE Transactions on Systems, Man, and Cybernetics, SMC-3*(1), 28–44. doi:10.1109/TSMC.1973.5408575

Zhuge, Q., Xu, L., & Zhang, G. (2017). LSTM Neural Network with Emotional Analysis for prediction of stock price. *Engineering Letters, 25*(2).

ADDITIONAL READING

Freund, Y., & Schapire, R. E. (1997). A decision-theoretic generalization of on-line learning and an application to boosting. *Journal of Computer and System Sciences, 55*(1), 119–139. doi:10.1006/jcss.1997.1504

Krishnapuram, R., & Keller, J. M. (1996). The possibilistic c-means algorithm: Insights and recommendations. *IEEE Transactions on Fuzzy Systems, 4*(3), 385–393. doi:10.1109/91.531779

Kuncheva, L. (2000). *Fuzzy classifier design* (Vol. 49). Springer Science & Business Media. doi:10.1007/978-3-7908-1850-5

Mendes-Moreira, J., Soares, C., Jorge, A. M., & Sousa, J. F. D. (2012). Ensemble approaches for regression: A survey. *ACM Computing Surveys, 45*(1), 1–40. doi:10.1145/2379776.2379786

Pal, N. R., Pal, K., & Bezdek, J. C. (1997, July). A mixed c-means clustering model. In *Proceedings of 6th international fuzzy systems conference* (Vol. 1, pp. 11-21). IEEE. 10.1109/FUZZY.1997.616338

Pal, N. R., Pal, K., Keller, J. M., & Bezdek, J. C. (2005). A possibilistic fuzzy c-means clustering algorithm. *IEEE Transactions on Fuzzy Systems, 13*(4), 517–530. doi:10.1109/TFUZZ.2004.840099

Ridgeway, G., Madigan, D., & Richardson, T. S. (1999, January). Boosting methodology for regression problems. In *Seventh International Workshop on Artificial Intelligence and Statistics*. PMLR.

Tekin, A. T., & Cebi, F. (2020). Click and sales prediction for OTAs' digital advertisements: Fuzzy clustering based approach. *Journal of Intelligent & Fuzzy Systems*, *39*(5), 6619–6627. doi:10.3233/JIFS-189123

Tekin, A. T., Kaya, T., & Çebi, F. (2020). Click prediction in digital advertisements: a fuzzy approach to model selection. In *International Conference on Intelligent and Fuzzy Systems* (pp. 213-220). Springe.

KEY TERMS AND DEFINITIONS

FCM: Fuzzy C-means clustering.
FPC: Fuzzy partition coefficient.
FPCM: Fuzzy possibilistic c-means clustering.
LGBM: Light gradient boosting machine.
MAE: Mean absolute error.
MAPE: Mean absolute percentage error.
PCM: Possibilistic c-means clustering.
PFCM: Possibilistic fuzzy c-means clustering.
R^2: R-squared value.
RMSE: Root mean squared error.

Section 23
Feature Engineering

A Hybridized GA–Based Feature Selection for Text Sentiment Analysis

Gyananjaya Tripathy
National Institute of Technology, Raipur, India

Aakanksha Sharaff
National Institute of Technology, Raipur, India

INTRODUCTION

The advancement of today's internet technology has changed the lifestyle of society. Due to this advancement, the current generation has upgraded their lifestyle up to a certain extent. Different social forums are commonly used to share helpful information and new ideas for advertisement and service improvement. The social platform is often watched with various perspectives. These include compiling business marketing strategies for product and promotional services, observing harmful actions to detect and reduce cyber-attacks, and sentiment analysis to analyze human responses and feedback (Saberi & Saad, 2017). Sentiment analysis is often referred to as archaeology, uprooting and classifying sentiments from text using Natural Language Processing (NLP), mathematics, or Machine Learning (ML) methods. ML methods use various approaches and a database that can be trained to distinguish and find sentiments (Fiok et al., 2021). Authors have widely studied the field of sentiment analysis over the past few years. In this state of affairs, different methods have been tested after development. The most usual process is ML which requires a robust database to train and learn the relationship between various aspects and sentiments.

Sentiment analysis is a form of written assessment or language spoken to determine whether speaking is negative, positive, or neutral and to what extent. Current analysis Market tools can handle a lot of price customer criticism honestly and accurately. Collectively, sentiment analysis finds customers' ideas on various topics, including procurement, the provision of services, or the presentation of promotions (Alsaeedi & Khan, 2019). Sentiment analysis is often used in the case of a review. Reviews can be taken from various resources for various reasons, such as product reviews, political reviews, and community reviews. When feedback from customers using any product, further questions will be included: Is the product usable? Is this product satisfactory? Is this product worth the money? Some helpful information always comes out of updates in positive or negative feedback (Birjali et al., 2021). Sentiments need to be learned using these practical answers. The semantic position estimates submission and ideas in the text data. The rules-based analysis searches for different words in a text and categorizes them based on positivity and negativity.

The proposed paper is based on Amazon's review dataset's hybrid sentiment analysis process. The dataset contains several responses and equally separates the positive and negative labels. Authors have developed an integrated novel algorithm based on the Genetic Algorithm (GA) to minimize the feature (Iqbal et al., 2019). Iqbal et al. (2019) have explained the feature selection method using GA by evaluating the fitness value with sentiment score whereas in the proposed model the fitness of each solution is evaluated using the accuracy score of each feature subsets. Support Vector Machine (SVM) (Preeti et al.,

DOI: 10.4018/978-1-7998-9220-5.ch112

2020) is used to check the validity of the words concerning the label to find an effective solution. This evolutionary process of selecting the right element improves accuracy with increasing scalability. This customized method offers a 45% reduced feature set with better accuracy. In addition to demonstrating the feasibility of this proposed method, the authors conducted a detailed study with other mitigation strategies such as Principal Component Analysis (PCA) and Singular Value Decomposition (SVD). Using these two algorithms as a comparison, the authors obtained the proposed model results, which provides up to 14.5% increased accuracy over PCA and 16.2% increased accuracy over SVD through the Naïve Bayes learning process and this reduction feature strategies. As a comparison of the number of features of all three feature reduction strategies, the proposed method gives 13% better results compared to PCA and a 10% better result compared to SVD. With a small amount of variable set, the proposed system exceeds the other two algorithms.

The main contributions to the proposed work are as follows:

- Text reviews are undergone pre-processing before being applied to the proposed framework. This pre-processing includes 'stop words removal', 'lemmatization,' and 'tokenization.'
- The authors have designed, developed, and evaluated a hybridized sentiment analysis model by integrating dictionary-based methods and ML methods to perform better than each individual.
- The authors have proposed a hybrid feature minimization method using a GA-based technique with a customized fitness calculation. Fitness calculation uses SVM to explore feasible solutions that improve system performance.
- The authors have analyzed the proposed method that demonstrates improved accuracy compared to the existing feature reduction algorithms.
- The authors have examined the novel algorithm to decrease the number of features to an excellent yield with an increment in accuracy esteem.

In evaluating the results of the suggested model, execution is performed with the Amazon cell review dataset (discussed in section 5) using Python language. The evaluation process is dependent on several measuring parameters like precision, recall, F1_Score, and accuracy. By applying all these performance measuring parameters, the proposed hybrid model outperforms the other two techniques. The further portion is divided in different sections where section 2 represents the work done in the related field. Section 3 represent the architecture behind the proposed model. Section 4 explains the proposed algorithm. Section 5 gives the insight of result analysis. Section 6 shows the future research direction and the final Section concludes the proposed work.

BACKGROUND

This section focused on outstanding correlated research performed in sentimental and textual analysis mines. The proposed comparison method is based on two factors discussed earlier. The important thing is to check how the user's feedback and social practices can help analyze the current circumstances.

Medhat et al. (2014) have proposed a novel technique in sentiment analysis. Fields related to transfer reading, sentimental acquisition, and construction resources were also their discussion point. The authors have attempted to provide a complete picture of the sentiment analysis approach. Khan et al. (2011) have proposed a method that detached different sentiments like objective or subjective directly from the review and blog feedback. SentiWordNet helped to evaluate points and determine the polarity. The proposed model outperforms the ML-based approach with an increasing accuracy value of 76.9% at the feedback level and 86.7% at the whole sentence level. Zhao et al. (2021) have proposed a model by taking feature reduction into account. The authors took different data processing techniques for the data pre-processing and feature selection stages. Finally, the authors classified customer reviews' sentiment into positive, negative, and neutral. Halim et al. (2021) has designed a method that stores a lot of unique data related to a small number of features. The study provided a preferred way to improve the GA to improve the accuracy of classifiers by taking the help of the feature selection approach in intrusion detection and network security. Zhao et al. (2021) describe overfitting as a critical issue that negatively impacts the accuracy of an ML model where there are a vast number of attributes in the data. In addition, having an enormous number of attributes means the necessity for additional memory and calculation costs. The most suitable way to handle a significant issue is to minimize the size of a particular database, referred to as feature reduction. The feature reduction process can be made by feature selection. The feature selection process converts many prominent data features into a unique feature subset with a smaller size. Feature selection refers to selecting a subset of the most appropriate feature from a given input feature vector that properly helps the ML model train. In real-world situations, datasets come with unwanted data that creates insignificant features. Canning such unwanted data from the data can positively affect the learning rate and accuracy of the classifier while reducing FP and FN.

Njolstad et al. (2014) have explained and examined different ML techniques to train their dataset to achieve phase accuracy up to 71.1%. Compared to other approaches, J48 produced very high results nearer to Random Forest. Shafipour et al. (2021) proposed a feature reduction method that raised the particle level depending on the particle range from controlled and uncontrolled particles and used it for component level calculation. The shape and frequency of the particles are updated with the new revision rule, which depends on the feature variables included in the vector. The features of the suggested method are statistically proven and are based on testing. The proposed feature reduction method was tested on a different dataset with five other models for feature reduction. The experiments have shown the dominating performance of suggested methods over regularly used methods. Sharaff and Srinivasarao (2020) have proposed their model, which removes inactive and unwanted attributes that do not relate to model accuracy using feature selection methods. The model complexity was reduced in that model as only a few attributes were required. Njølstad et al. (2014) have discussed three selection options categories: filter, wrapper, and embedded strategies based on various selection strategies. The first two phases work differently and later apply both the techniques. In the wrapper approach, the method depends on the predicted result of the learning method defined in the explanation of a particular problem. The selected attributes are checked using the performance measure. The wrapping strategy has two stages. First, it explores a subset of features and, in the second stage, examines the selected attributes using a learning approach. These stages are repeated until the conditions of the stopping criteria are met. The problem with wrapping is that the search space is 2n for any n features, which is a big challenge for too large datasets. To address this, various strategies, such as the 'hill-climbing,' 'best-first search,' 'branch-and-bound search,' and GA, can help improve the effectiveness of local learning. In the proposed model, the authors have used GA to address the issue of search space.

Halim et al. (2021) represent the task of compiling the most suitable attribute selection method for a particular situation to obtain an optimal feature subset. The authors combine multiple feature selections to find a standard solution. The experimentation was done using UCI repository data and a few real-life datasets. Garate-Escamila et al. (2020) describe the PCA, selecting features that keep the essential details by apprehending high variance. Many analyses have utilized PCA to analyze textual sentiment as a feature reduction technique. The authors describe two features that can be sparse and informative for prediction so that no one can be deleted. Using SVD, features can be reduced from n-elements to k-elements, each of which will be the original n combination. The method used in SVD is a feature reduction task, just like feature selection. In the proposed work, the GA-based hybrid technique provides the well-fitted features for achieving a better accuracy level.

PROPOSED ARCHITECTURE

In this proposed work, all the essential components required for the experiment execution are discussed. This approach offers a variety of sentiment analysis options with the optimization technique. The proposed framework has different elements which control the functioning of the model. A step-wise approach is used for data cleaning, pre-processing, hybrid approach-based feature processing, and sentiment evaluation to make the whole structure automated. Mainly three stages are essential in this framework. Firstly, data cleaning part, then pre-processing, and finally the data analysis stage. Figure 1 shows the architecture of the proposed model.

- **Data Cleaning:** Data cleaning is the first stage to be executed. The required data is extracted from the Amazon review dataset (discussed in section 5) and stored for cleaning in this stage. Data cleaning stage follows some sub-stages.
  - **Stopword Elimination:** In the stop word elimination stage, ubiquitous words like "a," "an," "the," "about," etc., are removed. These words have less impact on sentiment. So, it is better to remove these words to reduce the complexity of the execution. Better accuracy can be achieved by eliminating these common unrelated words. NLTK (Natural Language Toolkit) in python lists stopwords stored in 16 various languages. The stopword list can be found in the nltk_data directory. In the execution of the proposed model NLTK library from python is used for removing the stopwords.
  - **Garbage Elimination:** Typically, real-world data is noisy and may contain elements that do not correlate well with dependent variables. The idea behind the feature selection is to study this relationship and then select only the variables that show a strong correlation. With the help of regular expression, URLs, links, and web addresses are removed from the data.
- **Data Pre-processing:** Before using the data as input, it needs to be pre-processed. This stage works on different NLP tasks. It includes word tokenization, word stemming, and vectorization.
  - **Tokenization:** Tokenization plays a vital role in dealing with text data. Tokenization is the process of dividing a piece of text into smaller units called tokens. Tokenization is the process of converting text into tokens before transforming it into vectors. It is also easy to filter out unwanted tokens. For example, a document into paragraphs or sentences into words. The word 'token' can be words, letters, or subwords. Since tokens are elements of standard language construction, the most usual method of processing raw data occurs at the level of token. In the present study the reviews are tokenised into words. In the proposed model the 'Treebank tokenizer' is used which uses regular expressions to tokenize text.
  - **Stemming:** In stemming, the word is reduced to its original form. In the present work, the 'stemmer' can be used, but to get the better accuracy of the model, the researcher needs to focus on the correct form of the word. To get proper meaning, 'lemmatizer' is used instead of 'stemmer.' 'lemmatizer' uses the dictionary to collect the correct form of a word. It will take more time than 'stemmer,' but it will provide better accuracy for this classification.

Lemmatization usually seems more instructive than simple stemming. In contrast to stemming, lemmatization looks beyond word reduction and looks for complete grammar in terms of morphological analysis of words.

- ○ **Vectorization:** In this process, all tokens are converted into vector form. So further stages can be applied to the output. For this purpose, the authors have used the 'TF-IDF vectorizer' (Term Frequency–Inverse Document Frequency). Different vectorizers are available to convert data into vector form, but in other cases, the same priority is given to all the words present in the data. In 'TF-IDF,' the words are given a different priority based upon their frequency level.

- **Data Analysis:** Data Analysis is the most crucial part of the proposed work. The complete data is analyzed in this stage, and the final sentiment is evaluated from provided data. In the proposed work, the hybrid approach-based analysis is used to assess the sentiment of the availed data.

  - ○ **Hybridized Feature Reduction:** The usual methods such as ML classifiers get worse as the size of the database grows more prominent. Specially while working with review dataset the reviews are broke in to tokens and the tokens are considered as features after data pre-processing. This process will create a large volume of features. If the number of features is high, then it will be more complex, and in the other hand, if the number of elements is low, it will produce very low accuracy. An effective process is proposed to reduce the size of the attribute setup to get a solution for the downgrading problem. In this proposed work, the authors work on the hybridized GA to perform the available data task. Without selecting all tokens, select a set of tokens such as discarded tokens that do not affect the calculated overall sentiment of the desired data. In particular, authors aim to reduce attribute set size by extracting those tokens related to the sentiment level of the whole document and leaving the keywords that do not affect the sentiment. Once the feature selection process is done, this feature is used to perform the analysis using a machine learning classifier. Firstly, some candidate solutions are created randomly to start the research. Those candidate solutions are called the chromosomes. The chromosomes are nothing but a collection of 0's and 1's which is created randomly using NumPy library from Python. The length of each chromosome is the same with the number of features generated from the vectorization stage. To start the execution of the proposed model total 8 such randomly generated chromosomes are taken into consideration as the initial population (discussed in section 4). With the help of these chromosomes, GA-based analysis will begin. These selected groups of chromosomes are now called the new population. In this population, crossover and mutation are applied. Crossover is a genetic operator used to vary the programming of a chromosome or chromosomes from one generation to the next. Two strings are picked from the mating pool at random to crossover in order to produce superior offspring. From different crossover methods 'one point crossover' is used in the proposed model and the middle point of the chromosomes is used as crossover point. The key idea behind mutation is to insert random genes in offspring to maintain the diversity in the population to avoid premature convergence. In the proposed work, 'bit flip mutation' is used as the current study uses binary encoded GA. In the bit flip mutation, one or more random bits are selected and flipped. In each iteration, the fitness value of each chromosome is calculated by considering only those features for which the bit value is 1, and based on those fitness values; the fittest parents are selected for mating. Finally, after all the iterations the chromosome with highest fitness value is considered as the best solution and the features correspond to the 1's present in the chromosome is collected as the final feature subset.

- **Feature Optimization Technique:** Extract features using the results of the 'TF-IDF' data architecture at the size of the most significant feature because all the keywords having related sentiments are included in the attribute vector. However, this process has a scalability problem when using an extensive database. A feature vector needs to be added by bringing down its size while preserving accuracy to resolve this issue. In this segment, a solution is proposed using the hybrid method of Genetic Algorithm.

  - **Problem Articulation:** Let P be a group of all keywords in the document. Authors wish to create a subset Q, added to the feature setup, of P should give the same polarity value with the sentiments labeled without compromising accuracy. The process is crucial for the scalability of the method. If all possible attributes are included, then the vector attribute of more significant data will be large enough that memory will be insufficient. Therefore, authors need to add an attribute selection process to resolve this issue. As already discussed earlier, GA, because of its evolutionary nature, is such a perfect fit for the non-polynomial complications.

  - **Fitness Evaluation:** The binary string is selected as a genotype to use GA in the process. Fitness calculation is a crucial part of the feature reduction based on GA. The process regulates the best options to produce offspring and get through to the upcoming generation. It is designed to strengthen it so that you have to make a solution that comes together from the early generation. Strength work to check the suitability of a group of selected attributes depending on the value of accuracy determined with the help of SVM. The higher the accuracy, the more likely it is the current solution. Therefore, it is possible to survive in the next generation.

  - **Algorithm and Analysis:** GA-based attribute selection algorithm, as indicated in section 4, the authors execute the simulation up to number m iterations so that the whole population could be transformed into one right solution. In each iteration, different GA function processes are performed, including crossover, mutation, successor creation, and fitness calculation. The duration of GA depends on the strength of the fitness function. In two ways, this issue can be processed; either iteration will continue to achieve a solution or adjust the number of iterations to a large enough value to get the solution before the limit is reached. For convenience, the limit is set to a value n, as per the later one concept. In this case, n is set to 4000, and the starting population is set to 8. This is the starting population, and the group will be redesigned to accept a new population. As per Algorithm 1, the loop operates up to m iteration, and each execution builds the next generation.

Figure 1. Architecture of the proposed model

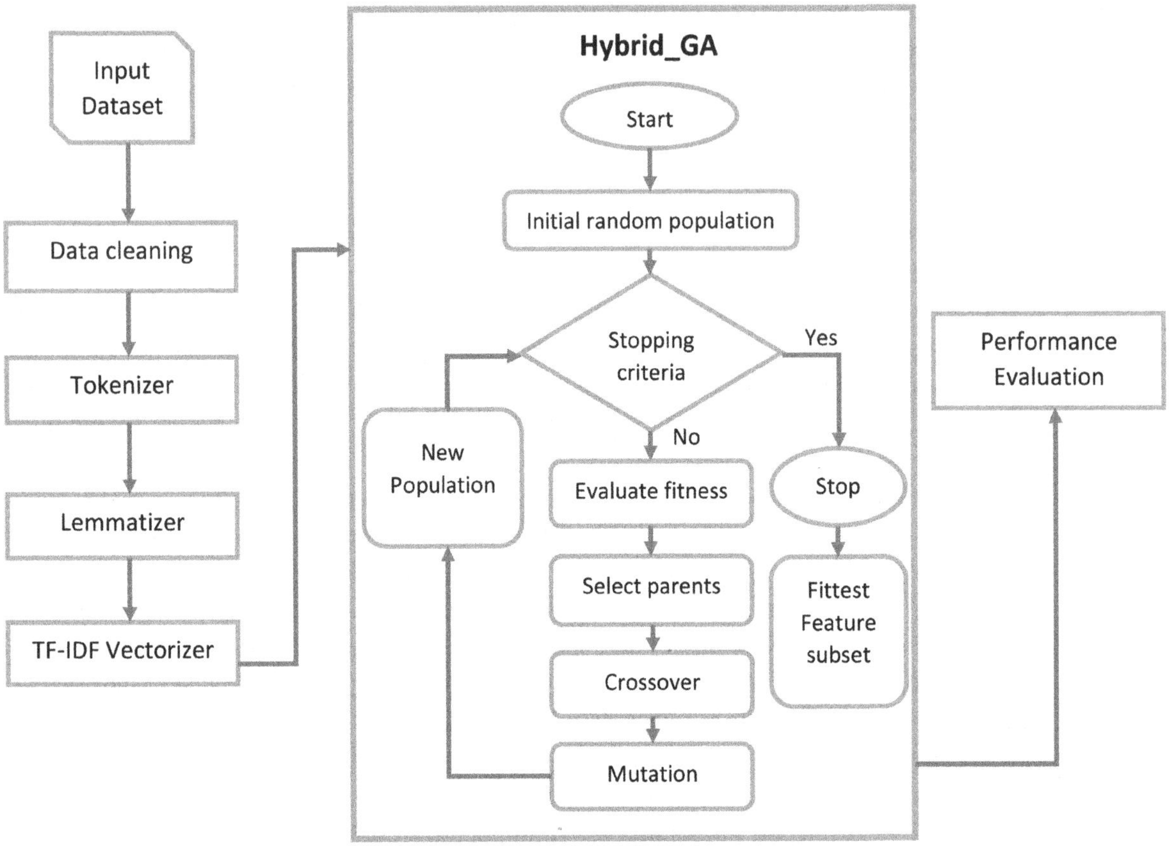

Algorithm 1: Hybrid_GA

Input: Initial population P and target T

 Initialize *population_size, matingpool_size, mutate_number* and *num_generation*

 Let P_n be the new population randomly generated based on *population_size*.

$outputs \leftarrow \varnothing$

foreach $generation \in num\_generation$ **do**

$fitness \leftarrow P_n \ cal\_pop\_fitness \ ()$

$outputs.add(maximum(fitness))$

 Selection of the best individuals in the current generation as parents to develop the successor of the upcoming generation based on *matingpool_size*.

$parent1 \leftarrow fittest_1$

$parent2 \leftarrow fittest_2$

A

Perform *uniform crossover* on *parent1* and *parent2* with *0.5* probability to generate two new offspring.

$num\_mutations \leftarrow 2$

Mutation changes a gene in each offspring randomly and generate *offspring1* and *offspring2*. Creating the new population based on the parents and offspring.

$P_{n1} \leftarrow parent1$

$P_{n2} \leftarrow parent2$

$P_{n3} \leftarrow offspring1$

$P_{n4} \leftarrow offspring2$

This new population P_n is now go for next iteration.
end
$fitness \leftarrow P_n\ cal\_pop\_fitness\ ()$
$best\_match \leftarrow maximum(fitness)$
$P \leftarrow best\_match$
return

SOLUTIONS AND RECOMMENDATIONS

The findings are presented in this stage. It includes the hardware and software testing setup discussion. Later, the effectiveness of the proposed technique is discussed on some parameters. Some evaluation metrics, namely, precision, recall, F1_Score, and accuracy, are used for the comparison of performance with different techniques.

- **Experimental Setup:** The experiment is performed on a computer with a Core i7 frequency of 2.6 GHz, Ram of 12GB, and 1TB disk drive space. The framework is developed using Python with Jupyter Notebook as a workbench.
- **Dataset Gathering:** In this section, the experiments were performed on the Amazon review dataset, which has been collected from the Kaggle repository https://www.kaggle.com/marklvl/ sentiment-labelled-sentences-data-set/amazon_cells_labelled.txt. This database contains 1000 instances labeled with 1 or 0 for positive and negative sentiments, respectively. Performance evaluation has been done on the basis of accuracy, precision, recall, and F1_Score metrics.
- **ML Classifier with GA Optimization:** In the proposed model, the authors have taken the Naïve Bayes classifier to classify the review data, and based on this classifier; the performance is measured. Naive Bayes classifiers are simple 'probabilistic' based on the Bayes' theorem with powerful ideas of freedom between the elements. The Bayesian network can achieve a high value of

accuracy while dealing with the population density of the kernel. The network is highly scalable and requires linear number dependent variables for learning. It takes a limited amount of time, rather than costly scaling as used in many other types of classifiers.

- **Defining Parameters:** The proposed algorithm needs some parameters to execute. Before executing the algorithm, all these parameters need to be initialized. The definition of all the parameters is provided in table 1.

Table 1. Parameter definition for the proposed algorithm

Parameter	Explanation	Value
P	Total Population	Vector matrix of 1000 instances
T	Target Value	Target variable
population_size	Size of randomly generated population	8
matingpool_size	Size of mating pool for parents	4
mutate_number	Mutation value	0.015
num_generation	Number of iterations for the algorithm	4000
P_n	Randomly generated initial population	Vector matrix of 8 instances

- **Effectiveness of GA with SVD and PCA:** In the last part of the experiment, authors show that GA-based attribute reduction strategies work better than Feature reduction based on PCA and SVD. Figure 2 shows the graph of all three methods used in reducing the feature in the Amazon dataset. In the present research the GA-based technique has, on average, 14.5% increased accuracy over PCA and 16.2% increased accuracy over SVD. Based on these observations, it can be concluded that the GA-based approach outperforms other two known methods available for the feature reduction. Table 2 represents the proficiency of the proposed model over other two feature reduction techniques.

Table 2. Performance measurement on Amazon review dataset

	Accuracy	Precision	Recall	F1_Score
Proposed_GA	**77.67**	**80.69**	**75.00**	**77.74**
PCA	62.50	74.63	48.08	58.48
SVD	61.00	69.12	45.19	54.65

This proposed work measures the recall, precision, and F1_Score along with accuracy as this is not sufficient to measure accuracy alone because for an unlabeled dataset a bad model can also give a better accuracy. Figure 2 indicates the margin of proficiency of the proposed work compared to the other two feature reduction techniques. For simplicity, all three measuring parameters are highlighted on the same bar graph representing their performance using the Naïve Bayes classifier. In the measurement of recall and F1_Score, the margin is very high compared to the other two techniques. While calculating the F1_Score percentage, the proposed method shows a value nearer to 78%, whereas PCA stands near 58% and SVD shows nearer to 54%. It shows the efficiency of the proposed work.

Figure 2. Performance comparison of different feature reduction techniques

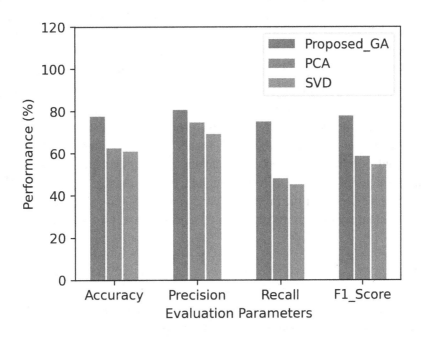

FUTURE RESEARCH DIRECTIONS

The present research uses the Naïve Bayes classifier as a classification model, but this work can be extended by using a more significant number of classifiers. On the other hand, the proposed GA-based hybrid approach can be modified using different crossover methods. To calculate the fitness function, other techniques can be used to reduce the features effectively. Other advantages of GA-based optimization include reducing feature size improving efficiency over time, maintaining inequality. In the future, the aim should be to improve this model for cyber intelligence to aid recommendations of law enforcement agencies supported user comments. So, instead of manually investigating the suspicious comments, law enforcement agencies can get a recommendation automatically from the user opinion.

CONCLUSION

The proposed work comprehensively represents the integrated sentimental evaluation model's construction, development, and exploration. Many current research works have illustrated the significance of various sentiment-diversification methods, from simple dictionary-based techniques to complex machine learning techniques. While dictionary-based methods suffer from a deficiency of dictionary and label knowledge, machine learning methods lack accuracy. The authors have developed an integrated framework that bridges the breach between dictionary-based and ML methods to attain high accuracy and greater flexibility in this study. This proposed hybrid algorithm design is presented to resolve the problem of failure that occurs as the attribute set grows. In the proposed model, a Genetic Algorithm is used in an integrated qualitative test. In the current study, the authors have approached a different method to evaluate the fitness value of the feature subset. Instead of considering only the sentiment score of the features, the authors have calculated the accuracy of each feature subset as their fitness value. With the help of this novel method, authors can reduce the size of a specified element by achieving outstanding accuracy. The current study represents that the authors have compared the proposed feature reduction technique, PCA and SVD value. In addition, the proposed sentiment analysis model is tested on other parameters, including recall, precision, F1_Score, and attribute size.

To exhibit the benefits of using the proposed attribute selection algorithm over other attribute reduction strategies, provided a differentiation of GA-based hybridized method with SVD and PCA. Results revealed that the proposed GA-based selection factor offered a 14.5% accuracy value using PCA and up to a 16.2% increase in accuracy value using SVD. The result reinforces the claim the proposed technique is scalable and accurate even if the database grows bigger. In the measurement of recall and F1_Score, the margin is very high compared to the other two techniques. While ascertaining the F1_Score rate, the proposed technique shows worth closer to 78%, though PCA remains close to 58% and SVD shows closer to 54%. It shows the proficiency of the proposed work. In conclusion, the proposed sentiment analysis framework is an excellent addition to the direction of sentiment analysis, which provides flexibility.

REFERENCES

Alsaeedi, A., & Khan, M. Z. (2019). A study on sentiment analysis techniques of Twitter data. *International Journal of Advanced Computer Science and Applications*, *10*(2), 361–374. doi:10.14569/IJACSA.2019.0100248

Birjali, M., Kasri, M., & Beni-Hssane, A. (2021). A comprehensive survey on sentiment analysis: Approaches, challenges and trends. *Knowledge-Based Systems*, *226*, 107134. doi:10.1016/j.knosys.2021.107134

Fiok, K., Karwowski, W., Gutierrez, E., & Wilamowski, M. (2021). Analysis of sentiment in tweets addressed to a single domain-specific Twitter account: Comparison of model performance and explainability of predictions. *Expert Systems with Applications*, *186*, 115771. doi:10.1016/j.eswa.2021.115771

Garate-Escamila, A. K., Hassani, A. H. E., & Andres, E. (2020). Classification models for heart disease prediction using feature selection and PCA. *Informatics in Medicine Unlocked*, *19*, 100330. doi:10.1016/j.imu.2020.100330

Halim, Z., Yousaf, M. N., Waqas, M., Sulaiman, M., Abbas, G., Hussain, M., Ahmad, I., & Hanif, M. (2021). An effective genetic algorithm-based feature selection method for intrusion detection systems. *Computers & Security*, *110*, 102448. doi:10.1016/j.cose.2021.102448

Iqbal, F., Hashmi, J. M., Fung, B. C. M., Batool, R., Khattak, A. M., Aleem, S., Patrick, C. K., & Hung, P. C. K. (2019). A hybrid framework for sentiment analysis using genetic algorithm-based feature reduction. *IEEE Access: Practical Innovations, Open Solutions*, *7*, 14637–14652. doi:10.1109/ACCESS.2019.2892852

Kaghazgarian, M. (2018). *Sentiment labelled sentences data set* [Data set]. https://www.kaggle.com/marklvl/sentiment-labelled-sentences-data-set/amazon_cells_labelled.txt

Khan, A., Baharudin, B., & Khairullah, K. (2011). Sentiment classification using sentence-level lexical based semantic orientation of online reviews. *Trends in Applied Sciences Research*, *6*(10), 1141–1157. doi:10.3923/tasr.2011.1141.1157

Medhat, W., Hassan, A., & Korashy, H. (2014). Sentiment analysis algorithms and applications: A survey. *Ain Shams Engineering Journal*, *5*(4), 1093–1113. doi:10.1016/j.asej.2014.04.011

Njølstad, P. C. S., Høysæter, L. S., Wei, W., & Gulla, J. A. (2014). Evaluating feature sets and classifiers for sentiment analysis of financial news. *Proc. IEEE/WIC/ACM International Joint Conference on Web Intelligence (WI) and Intelligent Agent Technology (IAT)*, *2*, 71-78. 10.1109/WI-IAT.2014.82

Preeti, B., & Kaur, R. (2020). Sentiment analysis using different techniques. *International Journal of Advance Science and Technology*, *29*, 2439–2443.

Saberi, B., & Saad, S. (2017). Sentiment analysis or opinion mining: A review. *International Journal on Advanced Science, Engineering and Information Technology*, *7*(5), 1660–1666. doi:10.18517/ijaseit.7.5.2137

Shafipour, M., Rashno, A., & Fadaei, S. (2021). Particle distance rank feature selection by particle swarm optimization. *Expert Systems with Applications*, *185*, 115620. doi:10.1016/j.eswa.2021.115620

Sharaff, A., & Srinivasarao, U. (2020). Spam detection in SMS based on feature selection techniques. *Emerging Technologies in Data Mining and Information Security*, *813*, 555–563. doi:10.1007/978-981-13-1498-8_49

Zhao, H., Liu, Z., Yao, X., & Yang, Q. (2021). A machine learning-based sentiment analysis of online product reviews with a novel term weighting and feature selection approach. *Information Processing & Management*, *58*(5), 102656. doi:10.1016/j.ipm.2021.102656

ADDITIONAL READING

Bifet, A., & Frank, E. (2010). Sentiment knowledge discovery in twitter streaming data. *Proc. International Conference on Discovery Science*, 1-15. 10.1007/978-3-642-16184-1_1

Esuli, A., & Sebastiani, F. (2006). SentiWordNet: A publicly available lexical resource for opinion mining. *Proc. International Conference on Language Resources and Evaluation*, *6*, 417-422.

Fang, X., & Zhan, J. (2015). Sentiment analysis using product review data. *Journal of Big Data*, *2*(1), 5. doi:10.118640537-015-0015-2

Hu, X., Tang, J., Gao, H., & Liu, H. (2013). Unsupervised sentiment analysis with emotional signals. *Proc. 22nd International Conference on the World-Wide Web*, 607-618. 10.1145/2488388.2488442

Jain, P. K., Pamula, R., & Srivastava, G. (2021). A systematic literature review on machine learning applications for consumer sentiment analysis using online reviews. *Computer Science Review*, *41*, 100413. doi:10.1016/j.cosrev.2021.100413

Nanli, Z., Ping, Z., Weiguo, L., & Meng, C. (2012). Sentiment analysis: A literature review. *Proc. International Symposium on Management of Technology. (ISMOT)*, 572-576.

Prabowo, R., & Thelwall, M. (2009). Sentiment analysis: A combined approach. *Journal of Informetrics*, *3*(2), 143–157. doi:10.1016/j.joi.2009.01.003

Ridhwan, K. M., & Hargreaves, C. A. (2021). Leveraging Twitter data to understand public sentiment for the COVID-19 outbreak in Singapore. *International Journal of Information Management Data Insights*, *1*(2), 100021. doi:10.1016/j.jjimei.2021.100021

Schmitt, L. M. (2001). Theory of genetic algorithms. *Theoretical Computer Science*, *259*(1-2), 1–61. doi:10.1016/S0304-3975(00)00406-0

Zhang, Y. Z., & Law, R. (2009). Sentiment classification of online reviews to travel destinations by supervised machine learning approaches. *Expert Systems with Applications*, *36*(3), 6527–6535. doi:10.1016/j.eswa.2008.07.035

KEY TERMS AND DEFINITIONS

Chromosome: Set of parameters which is a suggested solution to the complication that Genetic Algorithm is trying to resolve.

Classification: This is the technique used to separate the categorical values on the basis of their positivity and negativity.

Crossover: One kind of genetic operator used to convert the chromosome from one generation to another. By doing so, high quality offspring can be collected.

Feature Optimization: The technique used towards the dimensionality reduction. As an optimized feature reduction, this will only select the features which have more impact on the target variable.

Fitness Calculation: This is the core part of the algorithm. It is an objective function which is used to find the optimal one. This will calculate the fitness to select new parents for mating.

Mutation: Mutations convert one or more genes from a chromosome from its original state. In the resolution of the solution, the solution may change completely from the previous solution.

Population: A bunch of attributes that converges towards the best solution with the certain iteration to take care of the issue.

About the Contributors

John Wang is a professor in the Department of Information Management and Business Analytics at Montclair State University, USA. Having received a scholarship award, he came to the USA and completed his Ph.D. in operations research at Temple University. Due to his extraordinary contributions beyond a tenured full professor, Dr. Wang has been honored with two special range adjustments in 2006 and 2009, respectively. He has published over 100 refereed papers and seventeen books. He has also developed several computer software programs based on his research findings.

* * *

Nassir Abba-Aji, PhD, is a Senior Lecturer at the Department of Mass Communication, University of Maiduguri, Borno State, Nigeria, and the Sub-Dean, Faculty of Social Sciences of the university. He is a one-time Chairman, Jere Local Government Area, Borno State, as well as Commissioner for Religious Affairs during the Senator Ali Modu Sheriff Administration in Borno State. Dr Nassir has published several articles and book chapters, and has presented papers at several conferences.

Peter Abraldes completed his BA in political science at the University of Pittsburgh. He completed graduate work in statistics and earned his masters in data analytics at the Pennsylvania State University. Peter also spent time studying development economics in Argentina and Brazil, especially how international trade impacts developing countries. His studies include labor economics, trade export policies, and national industrial development policies. He is a maritime trade analyst for the Philadelphia Regional Port Authority, focused on optimizing the organization's cargo development strategy. The strategy includes understanding how the port can differentiate itself and make it more resilient to supply chain disruptions and international policy changes. He has been the scholarship chair for the World Trade Association of Philadelphia since 2018.

Anal Acharya is currently Assistant Professor in Computer Science department in St. Xavier's College, Kolkata. His current research interest is Educational Data Mining.

Prageet Aeron is presently an Assistant Professor at the department of Information Management at MDI Gurgaon. He is a Fellow (FPM) of Computers and Information Systems Group from the Indian Institute of Management Ahmedabad, and a B.Tech from the Indian Institute of Technology-BHU, Varanasi. He has over 10 years of teaching experience across various B-schools in NCR and is actively engaged in teaching and research in the areas of Entrepreneurship, Strategic Information Systems, e-Commerce and Big Data Applications in Management. His research work has been regularly accepted in reputed International Journals and Conferences.

Javier M. Aguiar Pérez is Associate Professor at University of Valladolid, and Head of the Data Engineering Research Unit. His research is focused on Big Data, Artificial Intelligence, and Internet of Things. He has managed international research projects and he has contributed in the standardisation field as expert at the European Telecommunications Standards Institute. He serves as editor, guest editor and reviewer, and author in several international journals, books and conferences. Furthermore, he has been involved as reviewer and rapporteur in several international research initiatives.

Gilbert Ahamer is inclined to analyse fundamentals of philosophy for the target of designing new paradigms driven by foresight when it comes to develop policies for mastering globalisation. As a physicist, environmentalist, economist, technologist, and geographer, he suggests that radically new concepts might beneficially contribute to solving the pressing problems of global change. He co-founded the 'Global Studies' curriculum at Graz University, Austria, studied and established global long-term scenarios when affiliated to the International Institute for Applied Systems Analysis IIASA, and is active in institutionalised dialogue-building for the Environment Agency Austria in Central Asia, Ukraine, and Georgia since his earlier affiliation to the Austrian Academy of Sciences.

Md. Omar Al-Zadid is currently working as a Senior Officer in Bank Asia Limited, Dhaka, Bangladesh. He began his career as a corporate professional in The Daily 'Prothom Alo', one of the top ranking newspapers in Bangladesh. His primary responsibilities in Prothom Alo included key account management and customer relationship management in advertisement department. He achieved 2nd Category Ptak Prize Award in recognition of global supply chain understanding and leadership in the young supply chain community organized by International Supply Chain Education Alliance (ISCEA) in 2013. He obtained Certificate of Achievement for completion of ITES Foundation Skills Training on Digital Marketing under NASSCOM IT-ITES sector Skill Council Certification in 2015. He holds an MBA in Marketing from the University of Dhaka, Bangladesh. His principal research interests include marketing analytics, innovation adoption, digital marketing, online banking, consumer behavior and psychology, Blue Ocean marketing strategy etc.

İnci Albayrak is an Professor in the Department of Mathematical Engineering at Yildiz Technical University (YTU),Turkey, where she has been a faculty member since 1992. She received her BS in 1990, MS in 1993 and PhD in 1997 in Mathematical Engineering from Yildiz Technical University. She had studied spectral theory and operator theory. She has lots of papers in these areas. In recent years, she has collaborated actively with researchers and focused on fuzzy mathematics. She has ongoing research projects about fuzzy linear equation systems and fuzzy linear programming problem.

Dima Alberg is a Researcher in SCE – Shamoon College of Engineering. His areas of specialty are financial data mining, scientific programming, and simulation methods. His current and future research plans focus on developing new models and tools that allow researchers and practitioners to analyze and solve practical problems in data science research areas.

Miguel Alonso Felipe received his M.S. degrees in telecommunication engineering from the University of Valladolid, Spain. In addition, he is PhD Candidate at University of Valladolid and Researcher of the Data Engineering Research Unit. His research is mainly focused on Big Data, Artificial Intelligence, and Internet of Things. Besides, he is co-author of some publications in journals, dealing with topics related to his lines of research.

Yas Alsultanny is the scientist of machine learning, data mining, and quantitative analysis, he is a computer engineering and data analysis PhD holder. He was spent his past 30 years of his life dedicated to the advancement of technological convergence and knowledge transfer to students. He was developed a high standard of research methods for graduate students and MBA through his supervising 100 MSc and PhD theses, and consulting 140 MBA projects, moreover he supervised 40 higher diploma projects and 100 BSc projects. Professor Alsultanny served for a reputed university in Bahrain: Arabian Gulf University (AGU), French Arabian Business School, and University of Bahrain. In Jordan: Applied Science University (ASU), Amman Arab University, Al-Balqa Applied University, and the Arab Academy for Banking and Financial Sciences. In Iraq: University of Baghdad, University of Technology, Al-Mustansiriya University, and Institute of Technology. In Germany: Arab German Academy for Science and Technology (online). Besides these, he was held position director of the AGU University Consultations, Community Services, Training, and Continuous Teaching Centre in Bahrain. And the position of head of the Computer Information Systems department and vice dean College of Information Technology in ASU University in Jordan. Alsultanny was worked a chair of statistical and KPIs committees in AGU University, chair of quality assurance and accreditation committee in Amman Arab University, member of quality assurance and accreditation committee in ASU and AGU Universities, member of establishing PhD Innovation Management programme in AGU University, member of establishing the college of Information Technology, ASU University, member of establishing Graduate College of Computing Studies, Amman Arab University, member of developing MSc Technology Management programme, member council of College of Graduate Studies, AGU University, and member council of College of Information Technology, ASU University. He is a trainer and a consultant for several public and private organizations, he led more than 100 workshops, and main speaker in many symposiums and conferences. He is a main writer of the UN Environment report, as well as member of writing AGU university strategic plans. In addition, he is reviewer and editor for various international journals.

Gerardo Amador Soto is a PhD student in Energy Systems from the National University of Colombia, Researcher in Energy Efficiency for Complex Systems.

Billie Anderson is an Assistant Professor of Applied Statistics at UMKC's Henry W. Bloch School of Management. Billie earned her Ph.D. in Applied Statistics from the University of Alabama, Masters of Mathematics and Statistics from the University of South Alabama, and her Bachelor of Mathematics from Spring Hill College. Before entering academia, Billie was a Research Statistician for SAS. SAS is a statistical software company headquartered in North Carolina. Billie wrote data mining algorithms for the banking and insurance industries. Billie maintained a consultancy relationship with SAS as an analytical trainer from 2012-2020. In this role, she taught analytical-based classes to professionals in organizations to help promote best statistical practices. And, she has consulted with different companies like Ann Taylor, Dunn & Bradstreet, Blue Cross Blue Shield of Michigan, Lowes Home Improvement Store, and Starbucks. She assisted these organizations in applying analytics to solve their business problems. Billie's research focus is in the statistical modeling of credit scoring with a particular interest in reject inference.

Issa Annamoradnejad is a Ph.D. candidate at the Sharif University of Technology, Tehran, Iran.

Rahimberdi Annamoradnejad wrote a chapter on the current and potential application of machine learning for predicting housing prices. He is an Iranian urban planner and an associate professor of geography and urban planning at the University of Mazandaran.

Joel Antúnez-García was born in Ensenada B. C., México, in 1975. He received the B. Sc. degree in Physics from Universidad Autónoma de Baja California (UABC), México, in 1999. The M. Sc. from Centro de Investigación Científica y de Educación Superior de Ensenada (CICESE), México, in 2004. The Ph. D. in Physical-Industrial Engineering from Universidad Autónoma de Nuevo Léon (UANL), Méxio, in 2010. From 2012 to 2013, he did a postdoctoral stay at Centro de Nanociencias y Nanotecnología at UNAM, working on DFT calculations to obtain different zeolites' electronic properties. From 2013-2015 he worked as a professor at Centro de Enseñanza Técnica y Superior (CETYS university). From 2016 to date, he has been involved in the theoretical study of bi-and tri-metallic catalysts based on MoS2 compounds and zeolites.

Dounia Arezki (), after obtaining an MSc in Artificial Intelligence, pursued her Ph.D. program in information technology at the Computer Science faculty of Science and Technology university of Oran (USTO) from 2017 to 2021. January 2022, she started an MSc program in international business. Presently her research interests are focused on spatial data processing, clustering algorithms, data analysis, risk, and project management.

Heba Atteya is the Senior Director of Business Intelligence and Data Analytics unit at The American University in Cairo (AUC). She led the founding team who built AUC's enterprise data-warehouse and business intelligence (BI) platform. In her current role, she manages the full-spectrum of the BI process including: setting AUC's BI roadmap, leading the data architecture and modeling functions, as well as the automated data extraction from the different source systems. Heba completed her MSc in Computer Science at AUC in Spring 2017 in the topic of visualizing large datasets. She earned her bachelor of science in Information Systems with honors in 2010 and joined AUC as a full-time staff member since 2011. She had a successful track record of achievements which qualified her for the position of BI and Data Analytics Director in 2017. Ever since then, she has successfully expanded the BI platform to extract data from the main ERP of the University, the main student information system, and the university CRM, as well as several other source systems providing a 360-degree view of student, faculty, staff and alumni of the University. Recently, she has led the efforts of the AUC's first big data project, analyzing Wi-Fi big data streams to support COVID-19 contact tracing process, as well as AUC's first AI-powered Chat-bot supporting the IT Help Desk function. She has always found inspiration in working with data and finding its underlying hidden patterns. She believes that informed decision-making is what every institution needs to compete in this highly competitive market.

Antonio Badia is an Associate Professor in the Computer Science and Engineering department at the Speed School of Engineering, University of Louisville. His research focuses on database systems and data science; his previous projects have been funded by the National Science Foundation and US Navy. He's the author of over 50 publications and 2 books.

Youakim Badr is an Associate Professor of Data Analytics in the Great Valley campus of the Pennsylvania State University, USA. He earned his Ph.D. in computer science from the National Institute of Applied Sciences (INSA-Lyon), where he worked as an associate professor in the computer science and engineering department. Over the course of his research, Dr. Badr has worked extensively in the area of service computing (distributed systems) and information security. His current research strategy aims at developing a new software engineering approach for designing and deploying "smart connected devices" and building "smart service systems" for the Internet of Things.

Surajit Bag is an Associate Professor at the Institute of Management and Technology, Ghaziabad, India (AACSB accredited). He is also working as a Visiting Associate Professor in the Department of Transport and Supply Chain Management, University of Johannesburg, South Africa. He has 11 years of industry experience. He has teaching experince from India, Morocco, South Africa and U.K. Educationally, Dr. Surajit earned his second Ph.D. in Information Management from the Postgraduate School of Engineering Management, University of Johannesburg, South Africa, and holds his first Ph.D. in Supply Chain Management from the School of Business, University of Petroleum and Energy Studies, India. Prior to getting a Ph.D., he obtained an MBA in Marketing Management (major) from MAKAUT (formerly the West Bengal University of Technology), India. His substantive areas of interest include Industry 4.0, big data, artificial intelligence applications in marketing and supply chain, sustainability. His expertise lies in the areas of Multivariate Data Analysis Techniques, Mediation Analysis, Moderation Analysis, and Structural Equation Modeling. He is familiar with data analysis software such as WarpPLS, PLS-SEM, SPSS, and Python. Surajit has published some of the most cited papers in the Industrial Marketing Management, International Journal of Production Economics, International Journal of Production Research, Technological Forecasting & Social Change, Production, Planning & Control, IEEE Transactions on Engineering Management, Journal of Cleaner Production, Annals of Operations Research, Information Systems Frontiers, Journal of Business Research, and Supply Chain Management: An International Journal. He is the proud recipient of the "AIMS-IRMA Young Management Researcher Award 2016" for his significant contribution to management research. He is the proud recipient of best "Doctoral Research Award 2020" from the Postgraduate School of Engineering Management, University of Johannesburg in recognition of the outstanding academic excellence. Dr. Surajit was listed in World's Top 2% Scientists which was released by Stanford University. He is a professional member of the Association of International Business, (AIB), Chartered Institute of Procurement and Supply (CIPS); Association for Supply Chain Management (ASCM); Institute of Electrical and Electronics Engineers (IEEE); Indian Rubber Institute; Association of Indian Management Scholars (AIMS International); and Operational Research Society of India (ORSI).

Sikha Bagui is Professor and Askew Fellow in the Department of Computer Science, at The University West Florida, Pensacola, Florida. Dr. Bagui is active in publishing peer reviewed journal articles in the areas of database design, data mining, Big Data analytics, machine learning and AI. Dr. Bagui has worked on funded as well unfunded research projects and has 85+ peer reviewed publications, some in highly selected journals and conferences. She has also co-authored several books on database and SQL. Bagui also serves as Associate Editor and is on the editorial board of several journals.

Samir Bandyopadhyay is presently a distinguished professor of The Bhawanipur Education Society College.

Soumya Banerjee is the Chief Technical Advisor & Board member of Must with specialised on ML & Security.

Sarang Bang is currently Studying at Vellore Institute of Technology, Vellore (India) pursuing Btech in Computer Science with Specialization in Data Science. He completed his schooling from Bhavan's Bhagwandas Purohit Vidya Mandir, Nagpur wherein he secured 10 cgpa in 10th grade and few other merit awards . He has been District Level Volleyball player during his schooling year. After choosing PCM and completing his 12th grade with 86.7 percentage he developed a lot of interest in coding and hence chose Computer Science as his career. In VIT, he is core committee member at VIT Mathematical Association Student chapter and also member at Lions Club International Leo Club Victory, Nagpur. He is passionate about Web Development and has worked on many projects as well as contributed to Hackathons as a front end developer. He also has interest in flutter development, machine learning. He wants to focus on a career in research and is currently exploring Machine learning and Artificial Intelligence.

Bazila Banu is a Professor and Head in the Department of Artificial Intelligence and Machine Learning at Bannari Amman Institute of Technology, India. She received her PhD degree in Information and Communication Engineering at Anna University, India in 2015 and guiding PhD Scholars. She holds 16 years of professional experience including academic and software Industry. She published 15 articles in National and International journals . She is an active reviewer and Guest Editor for International journals and technical committee member for International conferences. Her research interest includes Big Data and Data Analytics. She has filed three National level Patents and received grants from AICTE for Margdarshan scheme (19 Lakhs) and National Commission for women.

Isak Barbopoulos, PhD, has worked as a research psychologist studying the situational activation of consumer motives. He is currently working as a data scientist at Insert Coin, where he is developing and implementing a system for adaptive gamification.

Mikel Barrio Conde is a PhD candidate at University of Valladolid, who received his M.S. degrees in telecommunication engineering from the University of Valladolid, Spain. He is researcher of the Data Engineering Research Unit and his research is focused on Artificial Intelligence, and Internet of Things. Also, he is co-author of some publications in journals, dealing with topics related to his lines of his research.

Sotiris Batsakis is a Laboratory Teaching member of the Technical University of Crete, Greece and he has worked as Affiliated Senior Researcher and Senior Lecturer at the University of Huddersfield, UK. He received a diploma in Computer Engineering and Informatics from the University of Patras, Greece with highest distinction, and a Master's degree and a Ph.D. in Electronic and Computer Engineering from the Technical University of Crete Greece. He is an experienced researcher having participated on various research projects and with over 50 research publications in the areas of Knowledge Representation, Artificial Intelligence and Information Retrieval.

Andrew Behrens is an Instructor of business analytics courses at Dakota State University and is pursuing a Ph.D. in Information Systems at Dakota State University. He has worked with Cherie Noteboom for three years and has published in IS Conferences (MWAIS, IACIS, and AMCIS).

Santiago Belda https://orcid.org/0000-0003-3739-6056 (ORCID ID) From 2011 to 2015, he engaged in a PhD in Mathematical Methods and Modeling in Science and Engineering at Universidad de Alicante. He worked in various projects and is currently affiliated to Universidad de Alicante as a Distinguished postdoc researcher Presently his research interests are Astronomy, VLBI, Earth Orientation Parameters, Terrestrial and Celestial Reference Frames. Santiago Belda was partially supported by Generalitat Valenciana SEJIGENT program (SEJIGENT/2021/001), European Union – NextGenerationEU (ZAMBRANO 21-04) and European Research Council (ERC) under the ERC-2017-STG SENTIFLEX project grant number 755617.

Zakaria Bendaoud is an associate professor at the University of Saida. His research focuses on information retrieval, supply chain and transportation.

Mustapha Benramdane is a Ph.D. student in Computer Science at CNAM. His main research domains are matchmaking and Intent-based Contextual Orchestration inside Digital Business Ecosystems and Platforms.

Níssia Bergiante is a Doctor in Transportation Engineering (COPPE UFRJ– Federal University of Rio de Janeiro - Brazil). Production Engineer with a Master in Production Engineering (UFF-Brazil). Background in Production Engineering, focusing on Operational Management and Operational Research, acting on the following subjects: Decision Analysis and Soft Operation Research (Problem Structuring Methods); Operation Management and Process improvement.

Aditi A. Bhoir is a final year undergraduate student, currently pursuing Bachelor of Technology (B. Tech.) in Mechanical Engineering, at Sardar Patel College of Engineering, Mumbai, India. She will be doing Master of Science (MS) in abroad from fall 2022. Her focus research interest is design and robotics.

Trevor J. Bihl is a Senior Research Engineer with the Air Force Research Laboratory, Sensors Directorate where he leads a diverse portfolio in artificial intelligence (AI) and autonomy. Dr. Bihl earned his doctorate in Electrical Engineering from the Air Force Institute of Technology, Wright Patterson AFB, OH, and he also received a bachelor's and master's degree in Electrical Engineering at Ohio University, Athens, OH. Dr. Bihl is a Senior Member of IEEE and he has served as a board member as Vice President of Chapters/Fora for INFORMS (The Institute of Operations Research and the Management Sciences). His research interests include artificial intelligence, autonomous systems, machine learning, and operations research.

Sanjay Krishno Biswas is a faculty of Anthropology at Shahjalal University of Science and Technology, Bangladesh. He is currently pursuing his Ph.D. His academic interest includes Anthropological Theory, Mobility, and Migration, Diaspora and Transnationality, Ethnicity and Marginality, and Ecology and Climate Change. Mr. Biswas has a number of articles in reputed journals and book chapters from reputed publishers including Routledge.

Karim Bouamrane received the PhD Degree in computer science from the Oran University in 2006. He is full Professor of computer Science at the same university. He is member of computer science laboratory (LIO). He is the head of the team decision and piloting system. His current research interests deal with decision support system, transportation system, risk management, Health system, bio-inspired approach. He participates in several scientific committees' international/national conferences in Algeria and others countries in the same domain and collaborate in Algerian-French scientific projects. He is co-author of more than 60 scientific publications and communications.

Samia Bouzefrane is Professor at the Conservatoire National des Arts et Métiers (Cnam) of Paris. She received her PhD in Computer Science from the University of Poitiers (France) in 1998. After four years at the University of Le Havre (France), she joined in 2002 the CEDRIC Lab of Cnam. She is the co-author of many books (Operating Systems, Smart Cards, and Identity Management Systems). She is a lead expert in the French ministry. She is involved in many scientific workshops and conferences. Her current research areas cover Security and AI Internet of Thing.

Paul Bracewell is Co-Founder of New Zealand-based data science firm, DOT loves data and Adjunct Research Fellow at Victoria University of Wellington. He received his PhD in Statistics from Massey University and has contributed to more than 50 peer reviewed publications.

James Braman is an Associate Professor in the Computer Science/Information Technology Department at the Community College of Baltimore County for the School of Business, Technology and Law. He earned a B.S. and M.S. in Computer Science and D.Sc. in Information Technology from Towson University. He is currently pursuing a M.S. in Thanatology from Marian University. From 2009 to 2017 he was a joint editor-in-chief for the European Alliance for Innovation (EAI) endorsed Transactions on E-Learning with Dr. Giovanni Vincenti. Dr. Braman's research interests include thanatechnology, virtual and augmented reality, e-Learning, affective computing, agent-based technologies, and information retrieval.

Alexis D. Brown is an Assistant Professor in the Computer Science & Information Technology Department at the Community College of Baltimore County. They hold a master's degree in Management Information Systems from the University of Maryland Baltimore County. Their main research interests focus on education and instructional technology but includes varied technology-related topics.

Joseph Budu is an award-winning research scholar within the information systems discipline. He received the University of Ghana Vice Chancellor award for the outstanding doctoral dissertation for the humanities for the 2019/2020 academic year. Prior to this feat, he has undertaken several academic research and consultancies. Dr. Budu has written one mini-book, and one research workbook to guide students in conducting academic research. See https://bit.ly/BuduContentfolio for various contents Joseph has produced (e.g. manuals, blog posts, lead magnets, and presentations).

Rachel Cardarelli graduated from Bryant University with a degree in Actuarial Mathematics and concentration in Applied Statistics. Since graduating, she has been working as an Actuarial Analyst.

Ferhan Çebi is a Professor in Istanbul Technical University Faculty of Management, Management Engineering Department. She holds a B.S. in Chemical Engineering from ITU, a M.S. and a Ph.D. in Management Engineering from ITU. She gives the lectures on Operations Research and Operations Management at the undergraduate level and graduate level. Her main research areas are application of Operations Research techniques to the manufacturing and service problems, production planning and control, fuzziness and mathematical modelling, decision analysis, decision support systems, information technology for competitiveness. She is acting scientific committee member and organization committee member for a number of national & international conferences. Ferhan Cebi is member of editorial boards of International Journal of Information Systems in the Service Sector, International Journal of Information & Decision Sciences, and International Journal of Data Sciences. Her works have been published in several international and national conference proceedings and journals such as Computers and Industrial Engineering, Information Sciences, Information Systems Frontiers, Journal of Enterprise Information Management, Logistics Information Management, International Journal of Information and Decision Sciences.

Shuvro Chakrobartty has made significant contributions to identifying, conceptualizing, and formulating the research objective and methodology, the proposed framework, and the analysis of the findings. With a prior educational background in Computer Science and Business, currently, he is a Ph.D. student of Information Systems at Dakota State University. His research interests lie in responsible AI and data analytics. He has work experience in multiple industries within the software, cloud, and data engineering domain. He is a member of the Association for Information Systems (AIS) professional organizations and serves as a peer-reviewer for multiple conferences, books, and journal publications.

Hannah H. Chang is Associate Professor of Marketing at Lee Kong Chian School of Business, Singapore Management University. She received a PhD in Marketing from Graduate School of Business, Columbia University.

Hsin-Lu Chang is a professor in the Department of Management Information Systems, National Chengchi University. She received a Ph.D. in information systems at the School of Commerce, the University of Illinois at Urbana-Champaign. Her research areas are in E-Commerce, IT value, and technology adoption. She has published in Decision Support Systems, Information Systems Journal, International Journal of Electronic Commerce, Journal of Organizational Computing and Electronic Commerce, and Information Systems and e-Business Management.

D. K. Chaturvedi is Professor in Electrical Engineering at DEI, Agra, India.

Akhilesh Chauhan is a fourth-year Ph.D. (IS) student in the College of Business and Information Systems at the Dakota State University (Madison, S.D., USA). He is received a master's degree in Analytics from Dakota State University. He is currently working as a graduate research assistant at DSU. His current research interest includes association rule mining, machine learning, healthcare informatics, transfer learning, text mining, and data mining.

Tanvi Chawla completed her B.Tech in Information Technology (IT) from MDU, Rohtak in 2012 and received her M.Tech in Software Engineering (SE) from ITM University, Gurgaon in 2014. She has completed her Ph.D. in Computer Science and Engineering (CSE) from Malaviya National Institute of Technology (MNIT), Jaipur in 2022. During her Ph.D. she published articles in premier journals and conferences. Her research interests are Semantic Web, Big Data, Distributed Data Storage, and Processing.

Xi Chen is a lecturer in the College of Humanities at Beijing University of Civil Engineering and Architecture. She is also a research assistant in the Beijing Research Base for Architectural Culture. Her current research interests include English academic writing, settlement evolution, and urbanization in China and the U.S., etc.

Xiaoyan Cheng is a professor at University of Nebraska at Omaha. Dr. Cheng's research has been published in Auditing: A Journal of Practice & Theory, Advances in Accounting, Review of Quantitative Finance and Accounting, Research in Accounting Regulation, Global Finance Journal, Asian Review of Accounting, and Review of Pacific Basin Financial Markets and Policies.

Xusen Cheng is a Professor of Information Systems in the School of Information at Renmin University of China in Beijing. He obtained his PhD degree from the University of Manchester, UK. His research is in the areas of information systems and management particularly focusing on online collaboration, global teams, the sharing economy, e-commerce, and e-learning.

Paula Chimenti is an Associate Professor of Strategy and Innovation at COPPEAD graduate school of business, Federal University of Rio de Janeiro, Brazil. She holds a PhD in Administration from Coppead. She is the coordinator of the Center of Studies in Strategy and Innovation, where she develops research about the impact of disruptive innovations on business ecosystems. She has several works published in journals in Brazil and abroad, such as JGIM and JCR. Her article on Business Ecosystems received the first prize in one of the most important academic conferences in Brazil. She teaches Management Networked Businesses, Digital Marketing and Research Methodology in the Executive MBA, Master's and Doctorate programs at COPPEAD / UFRJ. She coordinated the Master program and Executive MBA programs at COPPEAD. Paula is the cases for teaching Editor for RAC - Revista de Administração Contemporânea, one of the top journals in Brasil.

Jahid Siraz Chowdhuy is a Fellow Ph.D. the program, Department of Social Administration and Justice, Faculty of Arts and Social Sciences, University of Malaya, 50603, Kuala Lumpur, Malaysia and Ex-faculty of Anthropology, Shahjalal University of Science and Technology, Bangladesh.

Parvathi Chundi is a professor of computer science at University of Nebraska at Omaha. Her primary research interests are in the fields of data mining, big data, and computer vision. She is currently focused on developing algorithms for automatic labeling of data for semantic and instance segmentation of biofilm images.

William Chung is an associate professor of Management Sciences at the City University of Hong Kong. He earned his Ph.D. in Management Sciences at the University of Waterloo, Canada. His personal research interests mainly focus on developing mathematical methodologies for energy-environmental policy problems, like large-scale equilibrium models, benchmarking methods for the energy consumption performance of buildings, and decomposition analysis of energy intensity. His papers can be found in the following journals: Operations Research, European Journal of Operational Research (EJOR), Computational Economics, Energy Economics, Energy Policy, Energy, Applied Energy, and Energy and Buildings. In addition, he is the director and founder of the Energy and Environmental Policy Research

Unit at the City University of Hong Kong. He was a visiting professor of the Center for International Energy and Environment Strategy Studies, Renmin University of China.

Mateus Coimbra holds a PhD in Administration from COPPEAD school of business in Federal University of Rio de Janeiro, Brazil.

Mirko Čubrilo is BSc in Mathematics, MSc in Mathematics, PhD in Computer Science (all from Zagreb University, Croatia). Full professor with tenure (Zagreb University, Croatia). Currently engaged at the University of the North (Varaždin, Croatia). Scientific interest includes mathematical logic, theory of algorithms, logic programming, artificial intelligence in a broad context, including neural nets and deep learning. Author of two books on the topics of mathematical logic and programming and more than fifty papers, published in journals and conference proceedings around the world (Germany, Japan, UK, USA, Egypt, Slovakia, Greece, Italy).

Marcin Czajkowski received his Master's degree (2007) and his PhD with honours (2015) in Computer Science from the Bialystok University of Technology, Poland. His research activity mainly concerns bioinformatics, machine learning and data mining, in particular, decision trees, evolutionary algorithms and relative expression analysis.

Jeya Mala D. has a Ph.D. in Software Engineering with Specialization on Software Testing and is currently working as 'Associate Professor Senior' in Vellore Institute of Technology, Chennai, India. She had been in the industry for about 4 years. She has a profound teaching and research experience of more than 24 years. She has published a book on "Object Oriented Analysis and Design using UML" for Tata McGraw Hill Publishers, also she has published 2 edited books for IGI Global, USA. She has published more than 70 papers about her research works at leading international journals and conferences such as IET, ACM, Springer, World Scientific, Computing and Informatics etc. As a researcher, Dr. Jeya Mala had investigated practical aspects of software engineering and object oriented paradigms for effective software development. Her work on Software Testing has fetched grants from UGC under Major Research Project scheme. Her dissertation has been listed as one of the best Ph.D. thesis in the CSIR – Indian Science Abstracts. She has successfully guided numerous Software Development based projects for the IBM- The Great Mind Challenge (TGMC) contest. The project she has mentored during 2007, has received national level Best Top 10 Project Award – 2007, from IBM. Currently she is guiding Ph.D. and M.Phil research scholars under the areas of Software Engineering and optimization techniques. She is a life member of Computer Society of India and an invited member of ACEEE. She forms the reviewer board in Journals like IEEE Transactions on Software Engineering, Elsevier – Information Sciences, Springer, World Scientific, International Journal of Metaheuristics etc. She has organized several sponsored national level conferences and workshops, notably she is one of the organizers of "Research Ideas in Software Engineering and Security (RISES'13) – A run-up event of ICSE 2014 sponsored by Computer Society of India". She has been listed in Marquis Who's Who list in 2011. She has completed certification on Software Testing Fundamentals, Brain bench certification on Java 1.1 programming, IBM certification as Associate Developer Websphere Application Studio. She is a proud recipient of several laurels from industries like Honeywell, IBM and Microsoft for her remarkable contributions in the field of Software Development and Object Orientation.

Karim Dabbabi is currently working as an assistant professor at the Faculty of Sciences of Tunis (FST). He held the postdoctoral position for a year and a half at the same faculty. He obtained his doctorate degree in electronics in July 2019 from the FST in addition to that of a research master's degree in automatic and signal processing from the National School of Engineers of Tunis in 2014. He has worked on various research projects in Automatic Speech Recognition (ASR), speaker diarization, automatic indexing of audio documents, audio segmentation and natural language processing (NLP) in general. In addition, he has worked on the identification of different neurological diseases, including Parkinson's and Alzheimer's using different voice features.

Indraneel Dabhade completed his M.S. in Engineering at Clemson University. He is a CISSP and has studied Cybersecurity from the Massachusetts Institute of Technology Center for Professional Education. He is currently pursuing an advanced certification in information security at the Stanford Center for Professional Development. Indraneel is a published author in Data Science, Human Factors, and Intellectual Property Rights. He has over 7 years of industry experience. Currently, Indraneel heads an automation firm (O Automation) in India.

Debabrata Datta is currently an Assistant Professor In Computer Science at St. Xavier's College (Autonomous), Kolkata. His research interest is Data Analytics and Natural Language Processing.

Magdalene Delighta Angeline D. is currently in the Department of Computer Science and Engineering as Assistant Professor, Joginpally B.R Engineering College, Hyderabad, India. Her research area includes data mining, computer networks. She has a good number of research publications.

Boryana Deliyska is professor retired in Department of Computer Systems and Informatics of University of Forestry, Sofia, Bulgaria. She obtained a PHD Degree in Computer Science from Technical University of Sofia, BG. She has long-standing research and practical experience in Semantic Web technologies, e-learning, computer lexicography, ontology engineering, web design and programming, geographical information systems (GIS), databases and information systems. She teaches information technologies, programming, CAD, computer graphics and computer networks. She is an author of 4 monographies, 7 Elsevier's dictionaries, 18 textbooks, more of 130 journal articles and conference papers.

Javier Del-Pozo-Velázquez received his M.S. degrees in telecommunication engineering from the University of Valladolid, Spain. In addition, he is PhD Candidate at University of Valladolid and Researcher of the Data Engineering Research Unit. His research is mainly focused on Big Data, Artificial Intelligence and Internet of Things. Besides, he is co-author of some publications in journals, dealing with topics related to his lines of research.

Chitra A. Dhawale (Ph.D in Computer Science) is currently working as a Professor Department of Computer Engineering P.R. Pote College of Engineering and Management, Amravati (MS), India. Earlier She worked as a Professor at Symbiosis International University, Pune (MS). To her credit, 06 research scholars have been awarded PhD. so far under her guidance, by S.G.B. Amravati and R.T.M. Nagpur University. Her research interests include Image and Video Processing, Machine Learning, Deep Learning, Multi-Biometric, Big Data Analytics. She has developed many projects for Machine Learning, Deep Learning, Natural Language Processing Algorithms using python. She also has hands on experience in

R-Programming, Hadoop-MapReduce, Apache Spark, Tableau. She has published 02 books, 08 Book Chapters, 26 Research papers in Journals (02- SCI-Indexed,15-Scopus Indexed, 06-UGC Journals and 03 in other research journals) and presented 35 papers in International Conferences (Abroad Conference-08, IEEE-18, ACM-02, Elsevier-01,Springer-04, Others-02) and 19 papers in National Conferences. She has reviewed 09 books for various publishers.

Kritika Dhawale is working as Deep Learning Engineer at SkyLark Drones, Bangalore. She has published 2 book chapters on Deep Learning. Her Research interest is Deep Learning and Cloud Computing.

Harini Dissanayake is a research student at Victoria University of Wellington, New Zealand working on her project 'Data informed decision bias.' The project focuses on identifying discriminatory bias in operational algorithms and remedying sample selection bias in datasets used for informing both commercial and government decisions.

Emmanuel Djaba is an early-stage academic with an avid interest in data science and machine learning. With extensive experience in industry, he is interested in doing innovative research that can be readily applied to interesting problems. He is currently a PhD student at the University of Ghana where he is pursuing a PhD in information systems.

Matt Drake has been a researcher in supply chain management for twenty years, focusing mainly on the areas of supply chain education and ethics. He has published over 30 articles and book chapters during this time. His chapter discusses the use of IoT technology to improve supply chain management. As firms look to improve their supply chain resilience in response to the COVID-19 pandemic and other disruptions, IoT data increases visibility, traceability, and can help firms to mitigate risks through added agility and responsiveness. The improved decision making made possible from IoT data creates a competitive advantage in the market.

Dorin Drignei received his PhD in Statistics from Iowa State University in 2004. Following his graduation, he was a postdoctoral researcher at the National Center for Atmospheric Research for two years. In 2006 he joined Oakland University where he is currently a Professor of Statistics. His current research interests include statistical modeling of big time series data.

Yuehua Duan is a PhD student in Computer Science Department at the University of North Carolina, Charlotte. Her research interests include recommender systems, business analytics, data mining, natural language processing, and machine learning.

Dishit Duggar is currently Studying at Vellore Institute of Technology, Vellore (India) pursuing Btech in Computer Science with Specialization in Information Security. He completed his schooling from Delhi Public School, Jaipur wherein he secured 10 cgpa in 10th grade and was a gold medal recipient for being a scholar for 6 consecutive years. After choosing PCM and completing his 12th grade with 93.8 percentage, He developed a lot of interest in coding and hence chose Computer Science as his career. In VIT, he is the App Lead of VinnovateIT which is a lab setup by Cognizant and also a member at Student Technical Community which is backed by Microsoft. He is passionate about Apps, Blockchain and Machine Learning and has worked on many projects as well as contributed and lead teams in multiple Hackathons. He wants to focus on a career in research and is currently exploring Cyber Security and Artificial Intelligence.

Ankur Dumka is working as Associate Professor and head of department in Women Institute of Technology, Dehradun. He is having more than 10 years of academic and industrial experience. He is having more than 60 research papers in reputed journals and conferences of repute. He contributed 4 books and 12 book chapters with reputed publisher. He is also associated with many reputed journals in the capacity of editorial board members and editor.

Abhishek Dutta has completed BS in Computer Science from Calcutta University and MS in Data Science and Analytics from Maulana Abul Kalam Azad University of Technology, Kolkata, India in 2020. He has authored seven conference papers which are published in IEEE Xplore and Springer Link. His research areas include Machine Learning, Deep Learning and AI applications in Finance.

Santosha Kumar Dwivedy received the Ph.D. in Mechanical Engineering from Indian Institute of Technology Kharagpur (IIT Kharagpur), India in 2000. He is currently Professor in Department of Mechanical Engineering at Indian Institute of Technology Guwahati (IIT Guwahati). He was also a Visiting Professor at Institute of Engineering and Computational Mechanics, University of Stuttgart, Germany under DAAD-IIT faculty exchange scheme. He has over 180 journal and conference publications with a focus on integrating robotics and dynamics in various fields. His research interests include both industrial and medical robotics, biomechanics, nonlinear vibration, and control along with the applications.

Brent M. Egan, MD, is Vice-President, Cardiovascular Disease Prevention in the Improving Health Outcomes group of the American Medical Association. He also serves as Professor of Medicine at the University of South Carolina School of Medicine, Greenville and as Past-President of the South Carolina Upstate affiliate of the American Heart Association. He received his medical degree and training in medicine and hypertension at the University of Michigan. He also served on the Board of Directors and President of the International Society of Hypertension in Blacks for many years. His professional interests center on hypertension, metabolic syndrome and vascular disease, which led to some 350 original papers and reviews. Dr. Egan remains committed to working with colleagues to translate the evidence-base into better cardiovascular health, especially for medically underserved populations.

Amal El Arid has earned a Masters' degree in Electrical and Computer Engineering from the American University of Beirut. She has been an instructor in the Department of Computer Science and Information Technology at the Lebanese International University since 2012. In addition, she specializes in programming and networking fields, earning a trainer certificate from the CISCO organization as a CCNA instructor since 2016. She is now working in the artificial intelligence and machine learning research field.

Houda El Bouhissi graduated with an engineering degree in computer science from Sidi-Bel-Abbes University - Algeria, in 1995. She received her M. Sc. and Ph. D. in computer science from the University of Sidi-Bel-Abbes, Algeria, in 2008 and 2015, respectively. Also, she received an M. Sc. in eLearning from the University of sciences and technologies, Lille1, France. Currently, she is an Assistant Professor at the University of Bejaia, Algeria. Her research interests include recommender systems, sentiments analysis, information systems interoperability, ontology engineering, and machine learning.

Mohamed El Touhamy is a Senior Data Engineer at The American University in Cairo (AUC). He completed his undergraduate studies at the Faculty of Computers and Information, Cairo University, earning a bachelor's degree in Computer Science. Mohamed started his journey in data science in 2017, participating in and leading many mega projects. He has excellent experience in big data engineering, data extraction using different technologies, data quality checks automation, and data warehouse enterprise solution management. He is also a graduate student at The American University in Cairo, seeking his master's degree in Computer Science.

Caner Erden, currently working as Assistant Professor in the Faculty of Applied Sciences, Sakarya University of Applied Sciences, Sakarya, Turkey. He worked as resarch assistant of Industrial Engineering at Sakarya University and researcher at Sakarya University Artificial Intelligence Systems Application and Research between 2012-2020. He holds a PhD degree in Industrial Engineering from Natural Science Institue Industrial Engineering Department, Sakarya University, Turkey with thesis titled "Dynamic Integrated Process Planning, Scheduling and Due Date Assignment". His research interests include scheduling, discrete event simulation, meta-heuristic algorithms, modelling and optimization, decision-making under uncertainty, machine learning and deep learning.

Omar El-Gayar has made a significant contribution to the conceptualization and formulation of the research objective and methodology, the proposed framework, and the interpretation of the findings. He is a Professor of Information Systems at Dakota State University. His research interests include analytics, business intelligence, and decision support. His numerous publications appear in various information technology-related venues. Dr. El-Gayar serves as a peer and program evaluator for accrediting agencies such as the Higher Learning Commission and ABET and as a peer reviewer for numerous journals and conferences. He is a member of the association for Information Systems (AIS).

Gozde Erturk Zararsiz is a faculty member in Biostatistics Department of Erciyes University. Her research mostly focuses on statistical modeling, method comparison, survival analysis and machine learning. Zararsiz completed her M.Sc. from Cukurova University, Institute of Health Sciences, Department of Biostatistics with the thesis entitled as "Evolution of Competing Risks Based on Both Dependent-Independent Real and Simulated Data by Using Self-Developed R Program". In 2015, Zararsiz has started her Ph.D. in Department of Biostatistics of Eskisehir Osmangazi University. During her Ph.D. in 2016, Zararsiz worked as a visiting researcher under the supervision of Prof. Dr. Christoph Klein at the laboratory of the Dr von Hauner Children's Hospital, LMU in Munich. During her research period, Zararsiz has published international papers and received awards. Zararsiz completed her PhD with the thesis entitled as "Bootstrap-Based Regression Approaches in Comparing Laboratory Methods".

Tasnia Fatin is a PhD Candidate in Management at Putra Business School, UPM, Malaysia. She has been a Lecturer of Marketing at Northern University Bangladesh (BBA, MBA) where she has taught Brand Management, Strategic Marketing, Principles of Marketing and Marketing Management. She had also been a Lecturer at Independent University Bangladesh. She takes keen interest in Entrepreneurship and has been running her own Business Solutions Agency and a Skill Training Institute. She holds an

MBA in Marketing from the University of Dhaka. She has also worked as a Strategic Marketing Manager for Prasaad Group of Companies to develop real estate projects home and abroad. She has also separately worked on projects in Urban Waste Management and Sustainable Agriculture that has been presented at George Washington University (USA), MIT (USA), Queens University (Canada) and at KLCC (Malaysia). Her research interests include digital marketing, disruptive innovations and the way they shape the world, IoT (Internet of Things), and sustainable business practices. She participated in several national level, Government level, and International level Youth Conferences and Forums home and abroad mentored by Industry leaders, experts, and professors from Harvard, Oxford, and many other prestigious institutions.

Arafat Febriandirza is a junior researcher at the Research Center for Informatics, The Indonesia Institute of Sciences (LIPI), Indonesia since 2020. He obtained his bachelor degree in Electrical Engineering from University of General Achmad Yani, Indonesia in 2008. He earned a Master's degree in Information Technology from the University of Indonesia in 2011 and a Doctorate in Communication and Transportation Engineering from Wuhan university of Technology in 2018. Arafat Febriandirza's research interests include issues in the field of Machine Learning, Modeling, Simulation, and Social Informatics.

Egi Arvian Firmansyah is a permanent lecturer at the Faculty of Economics and Business Universitas Padjadjaran, Indonesia. He has been published numerous journal articles and conferences proceedings. He is also a finance and managing editor at Jurnal Bisnis dan Manajemen, which is an accredited and reputable journal in Indonesia. Currently, he is a Ph.D student in finance at Universiti Brunei Darussalam.

Robert Leslie Fisher was educated in New York City. He attended Stuyvesant High School, a special science high school, has a bachelors degree (cum laude) in sociology from City College of New York, and a graduate degree in sociology from Columbia University. He is the author of several books including "Invisible Student Scientists (2013)" and the forthcoming Educating Public Interest Professionals and the Student Loan Debt Crisis." He has previously contributed chapters to encyclopedias and handbooks published by IGI Global including John Wang International Handbook of Business Analytics and Optimization as well as the International Encyclopedia of Information Sciences and Technology, and the International Encyclopedia of Modern Educational Technologies, Applications, and Management (both edited by Mehdi Khosrow-Pour). Mr. Fisher resides in the USA. He is an independent contractor.

Wendy Flores-Fuentes received the bachelor's degree in electronic engineering from the Autonomous University of Baja California in 2001, the master's degree in engineering from Technological Institute of Mexicali in 2006, and the Ph.D. degree in science, applied physics, with emphasis on Optoelectronic Scanning Systems for SHM, from Autonomous University of Baja California in June 2014. By now she is the author of 36 journal articles in Elsevier, IEEE, Emerald and Springer, 18 book chapters and 8 books in Springer, Intech, IGI global Lambert Academic and Springer, 46 proceedings articles in IEEE ISIE 2014-2021, IECON 2014, 2018, 2019, the World Congress on Engineering and Computer Science (IAENG 2013), IEEE Section Mexico IEEE ROCC2011, and the VII International Conference on Industrial Engineering ARGOS 2014. Recently, she has organized and participated as Chair of Special Session on ''Machine Vision, Control and Navigation'' at IEEE ISIE 2015-2021 and IECON 2018, 2019. She has participated has Guest Editor at Journal of Sensors with Hindawi, The International Journal of Advanced

Robotic Systems with SAGE, IEEE Sensors, and Elsevier Measurement. She holds 1 patent of Mexico and 1 patent of Ukraine. She has been a reviewer of several articles in Taylor and Francis, IEEE, Elsevier, and EEMJ. Currently, she is a full-time professor at Universidad Autónoma de Baja California, at the Faculty of Engineering. She has been incorporated into CONACYT National Research System in 2015. She did receive the award of "Best session presentation" in WSECS2013 in San-Francisco, USA. She did receive as coauthor the award of "Outstanding Paper in the 2017 Emerald Literati Network Awards for Excellence". Her's interests include optoelectronics, robotics, artificial intelligence, measurement systems, and machine vision systems.

Jeffrey Yi-Lin Forrest is a professor of mathematics and the research coach for the School of Business at Slippery Rock University of Pennsylvania. His research interest covers a wide range of topics, including, but not limited to, economics, finance, mathematics, management, marketing and systems science. As of the end of 2020, he has published over 600 research works, 24 monographs and 27 special topic edited volumes.

Raksh Gangwar is working as Professor and Director in Women Institute of Technology, Dehradun. He is having more than 35 years of experience. He has guided many Ph.D and M.Tech scholars. He is also member of many committee of national/international repute. He has contributed many research papers. He has also contributed many patents under his name.

Ge Gao is a Professor at Zhuhai College of Science and Technology and Management School at Jilin University. Her research focuses on Blockchain application, Supply Chain Management, Big Data application, user interface management in mobile commerce, and Social electronic commerce.

Araceli Gárate-García is a full-time professor at the Universidad Politécnica de Baja California (UPBC) since 2017. She received her PhD in electronics and telecommunications in conjoint between the CICESE research center, Mexico and the IRCCyN research center of the ECN university, France in 2011, the M.Sc. degree in electronics and telecommunications from CICESE research center in 2006 and her bachelor degree in Electronic Engineering in 2003 from the ITM university. Her main research interests are the analysis and control of nonlinear systems with and without time delays and the symbolic computation.

María J. García G. is Bachelor in Chemistry and has a master in Operations Research (OR). Together others authors had increase their investigations, already two hundred and forty, mainly in the areas of Evaluation and Management of Projects, Knowledge Management, Managerial and Social Decision making and OR, especially in multi-criteria decision. They have been presented or published in different countries, having publications and offering their reports, chats or conferences in: Azerbaijan, Finland, Poland, Croatia, Switzerland, Greece, Germany, Italy, Czech Republic, Iceland, Lithuania, Spain, France, Portugal, United States, Panama, Uruguay, Brazil, Mexico, Argentina and Chile besides attending as guest speaker, in lectures to relevant events in Colombia, Peru, Spain and Venezuela. Among other works she is coauthor of: "Inventories control, the Inventory manager and Matrixes Of Weighing with multiplicative factors (MOWwMf)"; "A Methodology of the Decision Support Systems Applied to Other Projects of Investigation"; "Matrixes Of Weighing and catastrophes"; "Multiattribute Model with Multiplicative Factors and Matrixes Of Weighing and the Problem of the Potable Water"

Nuno Geada has a Master's degree in Systems Information Management by Polytechnic Institute of Setúbal - School of Business Sciences and Management -Setúbal, Degree in Industrial Management and Technology by Polytechnic Institute of Setúbal - School of Technology of Setubal. He has written chapters, and papers to journals about topics regarding information technology management and strategic change management. He is from the Editorial Board - Associate Editor from International Journal of Business Strategy and Automation (IJBSA). He is the Editor of the book Reviving Businesses with New Organizational Change Management Strategies. His main research interests in information systems management, strategy, knowledge management, change management, and information technology management adoption in business contexts throw models and frameworks. He works as a Professor and a Researcher.

Natheer K. Gharaibeh is currently Associate Professor at College of Computer Science & Engineering at Yanbu - Taibah University from June 2016. He has more than 17 years of experience: He worked as Assistant Professor at College of Computer Science & Engineering at Yanbu – Taibah University from September. 2013 till June 2016. Before that he worked as an Assistant Professor at Balqa Applied University. He also worked as part-time Lecturer at Jordan University of Science and Technology (JUST) and other Jordanian universities. He published many papers in International Journals and participated in several International Conferences. His current research interests are: Business Intelligence, NLP, IR, Software Engineering, and Knowledge Societies. He got a grant for a joint project from the DFG with Rostock Technical University - Germany. He is editorial board Member, reviewer, and Keynote speaker in many International Journals and Conferences, he also has membership in many International and Technical Societies.

Abichal Ghosh is a final year B.E. student pursuing his degree in Computer Science from BITS Pilani K.K. Birla Goa campus. His field of interest lies in the research areas of Artificial Intelligence, Machine Learning, Deep Learning, Image Processing, Computer Vision and their application in various fields such as Desalination by Membrane technology, Ozonation, and more. Recently, he has been working for the prediction of the optimal conditions of Thin Film Nanocomposite Membranes for efficient desalination. For the topics related to Computer Vision, he has previously worked in the topic of Segmentation and is also currently working on the topic of Learned Image Compression.

Christoph Glauser was born in Berne in 1964. After studying History, Political Science and Media Science in Berne and Law in Geneva, he obtained a doctorate at the University of Berne in 1994. Christoph Glauser then participated in the national research programme, NFP27 at the University of Geneva. As a lecturer in Journalism and Online Research, he worked at various universities. He lectured in the subject, „Organisational Learning" in Social Psychology at the University of Zurich and for six years, he was the leading researcher and lecturer at ETH Zurich. In 1997-1998 he was a Visiting Lecturer at the University of Washington in Seattle, for which he continued to lecture their graduate students in Rome until 2006. During that time, he was Visiting Lecturer for online research at various universities both in Switzerland and abroad. Since 1998, Christoph Glauser has developed a successful career as online expert, CEO and delegate of governing boards, in particular (delete 'of') MMS – Media Monitoring Switzerland AG - and in diverse IT companies. Since 1994, he has been running the Institute for Fundamental Studies in Computer-assisted Content Analyses IFAA in Berne. In 2001, Glauser founded the URL study factory for competition analyses, ArgYou (Arguments for You), in order to study content of websites on the internet and compare these via search engines with the searched-for content (online effect research). In 2006, this company evolved into ArgYou AG in Baar (Switzerland), where he has remained as Chair of the governing board up to the present. For some years, Glauser has been serving on several European committees as an expert in e-governance. Subsequently, in 2007, he was one of the sixteen members of the jury for the European Union e-Government award, which honours the best European e-government projects on behalf of the European Commission. Since 2014 he has been operating the IFAAR find-engine set up directly for purposes of digital evaluation.

Rajesh Godasu is pursuing a Ph.D. in information systems at Dakota State University, his research interest is Deep learning in medical images. He has worked with Dr. Zeng for the past three years on different Machine Learning, Data Science, and Predictive Analytics topics. Conducted research on the Topic "Transfer Learning in Medical Image Classification" and published two papers in Information systems conferences, MWAIS and AMCIS.

Jorge Gomes is a researcher at ADVANCE, ISEG, School of Economics & Management of the Universidade de Lisboa. He holds a PhD in Management from ISEG and a Masters in Management Sciences from ISCTE-IUL, He also have a post-graduation in Project Management from INDEG/ISCTE, and a degree in Geographic Engineering from the Faculty of Sciences of the Universidade de Lisboa. During the past 30 years, he has worked as an engineer, project manager, quality auditor and consultant. Teaches Management at ULHT, Lisboa. His research interests include Benefits Management, Project Management, Project Success, Maturity Models, IS/IT Investments, IS/IT in Healthcare, and IS/IT Management.

Hale Gonce Kocken is an Associate Professor in the Department of Mathematical Engineering at the Yildiz Technical University (YTU), Istanbul, Turkey. She has been a faculty member of YTU since 2004. She completed her Ph.D. entitled "Fuzzy approaches to network analysis" in Applied Mathematics (2011) from the same department. Her current area of research is mathematical programming, supply chain management, and some related Operational Research subjects in multi-criteria and fuzzy environments.

Rick Gorvett is Professor and Chair of the Mathematics Department at Bryant University. He is a Fellow of the Casualty Actuarial Society.

M. Govindarajan is currently an Associate Professor in the Department of Computer Science and Engineering, Annamalai University, Tamil Nadu, India. He received the B.E, M.E and Ph.D Degree in Computer Science and Engineering from Annamalai University, Tamil Nadu, India in 2001, 2005 and 2010 respectively. He did his post-doctoral research in the Department of Computing, Faculty of Engineering and Physical Sciences, University of Surrey, Guildford, Surrey, United Kingdom in 2011 and at CSIR Centre for Mathematical Modelling and Computer Simulation, Bangalore in 2013. He has visited countries like Czech Republic, Austria, Thailand, United Kingdom (twice), Malaysia, U.S.A (twice), and Singapore. He has presented and published more than 140 papers at Conferences and Journals and also received best paper awards. He has delivered invited talks at various national and international conferences. His current research interests include Data Mining and its applications, Web Mining, Text Mining, and Sentiment Mining. He has completed two major projects as principal investigator and has produced four Ph.Ds. He was the recipient of the Achievement Award for the field in the Conference in Bio-Engineering, Computer Science, Knowledge Mining (2006), Prague, Czech Republic. He received

Career Award for Young Teachers (2006), All India Council for Technical Education, New Delhi, India and Young Scientist International Travel Award (2012), Department of Science and Technology, Government of India, New Delhi. He is a Young Scientists awardee under Fast Track Scheme (2013), Department of Science and Technology, Government of India, New Delhi and also granted Young Scientist Fellowship (2013), Tamil Nadu State Council for Science and Technology, Government of Tamil Nadu, Chennai. He also received the Senior Scientist International Travel Award (2016), Department of Science and Technology, Government of India. He has published ten book chapters and also applied patent in the area of data mining. He is an active Member of various professional bodies and Editorial Board Member of various conferences and journals.

Ashwin Gupta has currently completed his BSc with Major in Computer Science from St. Xavier's College, Kolkata. His current research interest is Data Analytics and Machine Learning.

Neha Gupta is currently working as an Professor, Faculty of Computer Applications at Manav Rachna International Institute of Research and Studies, Faridabad campus. She has completed her PhD from Manav Rachna International University and has done R&D Project in CDAC-Noida. She has total of 12+ year of experience in teaching and research. She is a Life Member of ACM CSTA, Tech Republic and Professional Member of IEEE. She has authored and coauthored 30 research papers in SCI/ SCOPUS/Peer Reviewed Journals (Scopus indexed) and IEEE/IET Conference proceedings in areas of Web Content Mining, Mobile Computing, and Web Content Adaptation. She is a technical programme committee (TPC) member in various conferences across globe. She is an active reviewer for International Journal of Computer and Information Technology and in various IEEE Conferences around the world. She is one of the Editorial and review board members in International Journal of Research in Engineering and Technology.

Jafar Habibi is an associate professor at the Computer Engineering Department, Sharif University of Technology, Iran. He has been the head of the Computer Society of Iran and the Department of Computer Engineering. His main research interests are Internet of Things, Simulation, System Analysis and Design, and Social Network Analysis.

Christian Haertel studied business informatics at Otto von Guericke University Magdeburg. He joined the VLBA research team in 2021 and accompanies research projects with external partners (e.g., Google Cloud, Accenture Digital). The modelling and development of concepts in the areas of data science and cloud computing are his main areas of research.

J. Michael Hardin is the Provost and Vice President and Professor of Quantitative Analysis at Samford University. Dr. Hardin came to Samford University in July 2015 from the University of Alabama at Tuscaloosa, where he served as the Culverhouse College of Commerce and Business Administration dean. Dr. Hardin had previously served as Culverhouse's senior associate dean, associate dean for research, director of the University of Alabama's NIH Alabama EPSCoR Agency and director of Culverhouse's Institute of Business Intelligence. Dr. Hardin's service as a Culverhouse professor of quantitative analysis, business and statistics was widely credited for establishing the University of Alabama as an internationally-known resource in the field of data analytics. His Culverhouse career followed his numerous administrative and faculty appointments at the University of Alabama in Birmingham in biostatistics, biomathematics, health informatics and computer science. Dr. Hardin holds a Ph.D. in Applied Statistics from the University of Alabama, M.A. in Mathematics from the University of Alabama, M.S. in Research Design and Statistics from Florida State University's College of Education, B.A. in Mathematics from the University of West Florida, B.A. in Philosophy from the University of West Florida and M.Div. from New Orleans Baptist Theological Seminary. He is an ordained Southern Baptist minister. Dr. Hardin has authored or co-authored more than 150 papers in various journals, edited numerous professional journals, authored multiple book chapters, presented more than 250 abstracts at national meetings and given more than 150 invited lectures or talks. For 25 years he served as a National Institutes of Health (NIH) grant reviewer and participated as Investigator or co-Investigator on more than 100 U.S. Department of Health and Human Services/NIH-funded projects. He has served as a consultant for other national healthcare and financial organizations and was among the inventors receiving a U.S. patent licensed to MedMined, a Birmingham-based firm dedicated to controlling hospital infection rates and improving patient care.

Shanmugasundaram Hariharan received his B.E degree specialized in Computer Science and Engineering from Madurai Kammaraj University, Madurai, India in 2002, M.E degree specialized in the field of Computer Science and Engineering from Anna University, Chennai, India in 2004. He holds his Ph.D degree in the area of Information Retrieval from Anna University, Chennai, India. He is a member of IAENG, IACSIT, ISTE, CSTA and has 17 years of experience in teaching. Currently he is working as Professor in Department of Computer Science and Engineering, Vardhaman College of Engineering, India. His research interests include Information Retrieval, Data mining, Opinion Mining, Web mining. He has to his credit several papers in referred journals and conferences. He also serves as editorial board member and as program committee member for several international journals and conferences.

Budi Harsanto is a lecturer at Universitas Padjadjaran, Bandung, Indonesia. His research interests are in sustainability innovation, and operations and supply chain management.

Md Salleh Salleh Hassan, Prof., PhD, is a retired Professor at the Department of Communication, Faculty of Modern Languages and Communication, Universiti Putra Malaysia. He has graduated many PhD, master's and undergraduate students. He was once the Deputy Dean of the Faculty, and has published many research papers, attended many conferences both local and international.

Miralem Helmefalk, PhD, is an assistant senior lecturer at the Department of Marketing in School of Business and Economics at Linnaeus University in Sweden. Miralem's research interests lie in concepts within consumer psychology, digitalization, gamification as well as sensory marketing. He believes that machine learning represents the perfect storm for his research interests.

Gilberto J. Hernández is a Bachelor in Chemistry and have a master in Technology of foods. Together others authors had increase their investigations, mainly in the areas of Food technologies, Playful, in particular in the fantastic sports leagues, Knowledge Management, Managerial and Social Decision making, Logistics, Risk Management and Operations research, especially in multi-criteria decision and making decision under uncertainty and risk. They have been presented or published in different countries, having publications and offering their reports, chats or conferences in: Finland, Poland, Croatia, Switzerland, Greece, Czech Republic, Spain, Portugal and United States besides attending as guest speaker, in lectures to relevant events in Costa Rica and Venezuela. Among other works he is coauthor of: "Enterprise Logistics, Indicators and Physical Distribution Manager"; "Multiattribute Models with Multiplicative factors in the Fantasy Sports"; "The Industrial design manager of LoMoBaP and Knowledge Management"; "Dynamic knowledge: Diagnosis and Customer Service".

José Hernández Ramírez is a Chemical Engineer and have a master in Operations Research. Together others authors had increase their investigations, already above two hundred and forty, mainly in the areas of Knowledge Management, Managerial and Social Decision making, Logistics, Risk Management and Operations research, especially in multi-criteria decision. They have been presented or published in different countries, having publications and offering their reports, chats or conferences in: Azerbaijan, Finland, Croatia, Switzerland, Greece, Germany, Italy, Czech Republic, Iceland, Lithuania, Spain, France, Portugal, United States, Panama, Paraguay, Uruguay, Brazil, Cuba, Mexico, Argentina and Chile besides attending as guest speaker, in reiterated occasions, in lectures to relevant events in Colombia, Peru, Costa Rica, Brazil, Spain and Venezuela. Among other works he is coauthor of: "Teaching Enterprise Logistics through Indicators: Dispatch Manager"; "Enterprise diagnosis and the Environmental manager of LoMoBaP"; "Logistics, Marketing and Knowledge Management in the Community of Consumer".

Thanh Ho received M.S. degree in Computer Science from University of Information Technology, VNU-HCM, Vietnam in 2009 and PhD degree in Computer Science from University of Information Technology, VNU-HCM, Vietnam. He is currently lecturer in Faculty of Information Systems, University of Economics and Law, VNU-HCM, Vietnam in 2018. His research interests are Data mining, Data Analytics, Business Intelligence, Social Network Analysis, and Big Data.

Victoria Hodge is a Research Fellow and Software Developer in the Department of Computer Science at University of York. Her research interests include AI, outlier detection, and data mining. She is currently researching the safety assurance of machine learning for autonomous systems. A focus of this research is assuring robot navigation including localisation. She is on the editorial board of two journals and has authored over 60 refereed publications. She has worked in industry as a software architect for a medical diagnostics company; and as a software developer on condition monitoring in industrial environments, and deep learning for robot navigation.

Essam H. Houssein received his PhD degree in Computer Science in 2012. He is an associate professor at the Faculty of Computers and Information, Minia University, Egypt. He is the founder and chair of the Computing & Artificial Intelligence Research Group (CAIRG) in Egypt. He has more than 100 scientific research papers published in prestigious international journals in the topics for instance meta-heuristics optimization, artificial intelligence, image processing, IoT and its applications. Essam H. Houssein serves as a reviewer of more than 40 journals (Elsevier, Springer, IEEE, etc.). His research interests include WSNs, IoT, AI, Bioinformatics and Biomedical, Image processing, Data mining, and Meta-heuristics Optimization techniques.

Adamkolo Mohammed Ibrahim is a Lecturer at the Department of Mass Communication, University of Maiduguri, Nigeria and a PhD Research Scholar at Bayero University, Kano (BUK), Nigeria. He received his master's degree in Development Communication at Universiti Putra Malaysia (UPM) in 2017. In 2007, he had his first degree (BA Mass Communication) at the Department of Mass Communication, University of Maiduguri, Nigeria. Currently, he teaches mass communication at the University of Maiduguri. He conducts research and writes in ICT adoption for development, social media, cyberbullying, cyber terrorism/conflict, gender and ICT, gender and conflict and online shopping. He has published several journal articles, book chapters and a few books. His most recent work explores the impacts of fake news and hate speech in Nigerian democracy and proposes a theoretical model as a fact-checking tool. More details on his most recent works and all his other publications can be accessed on his website: https://unimaid.academia.edu/AdamkoloMohammedIbrahim. Malam Adamkolo is currently serving as an Editorial Board Member of Jurnal Komunikasi Ikatan Sarjana Komunikasi Indonesia (the Communication Journal of the Indonesian Association of Communication Scholars) and a co-researcher in a research project by The Kukah Centre, Abuja, Nigeria. The proposed title of the research is: "Engaging Local Communities for Peacebuilding, Social Cohesion, Preventing and Countering Violent Extremism in Nigeria's northeast". Adamkolo has received Publons Top Reviewer Award in 2018 (for being among the top 1% global peer reviewers in Psychiatry/Psychology). In 2017, Elsevier had awarded him a certificate of outstanding peer review with one of Elsevier's prestigious journals, Computers in Human Behaviour (CHB) which he reviews for; he also reviews for Emerald's Journal of Systems and Information Technology (JSIT) and several other journals. Much earlier, from 2000 to 2010, he worked as a broadcast journalist in Yobe Broadcasting Corporation (YBC) Damaturu, and from 2008 to 2010 was deployed to Sahel FM (formerly Pride FM, a subsidiary of YBC Damaturu as DJ-cum-producer/presenter/journalist). From 2008 to 2010, he worked as YBC's focal person on UNICEF and Partnership for the Revival of Routine Immunisation in Northern Nigeria-Maternal, newborn and Child Health (PRRINN-MNCH). From September to October 2018, he served as a consultant to ManienDanniels (West Africa Ltd.) and MNCH2 programme.

Funda Ipekten's research focused on a statistical analysis of high-throughput metabolomics data, multi-omics data integration, feature selection for multi-omics.

Adelina Ivanova is Assisted Professor Dr. in Department of Computer Systems and Informatics of University of Forestry, Sofia, Bulgaria. Her research interests are in the areas of ontology engineering, sustainable development, databases, and office information systems.

Sajan T. John is an Associate Professor of Industrial Engineering in the Department of Mechanical Engineering at Viswajyothi College of Engineering and Technology, Vazhakulam, Kerala. He received PhD from the National Institute of Technology Calicut in 2015. His research interests are in the areas of operations research, mathematical modelling, supply chain management and reverse logistics. He has published papers in international journals and proceedings of international and national conferences.

Rachid Kaleche is a PhD student of computer science since 2018. He is member of computer science laboratory (LIO) of Oran 1 university in Algeria. His current research interests deal with artificial intelligence, transportation system, logistic systems, machine learning, and bio-inspired approach. He is co-author of many publications and communications.

Reddi Kamesh received B.Tech in Chemical engineering from Acharya Nagarjuna University, Guntur, India, in 2011, and M.Tech and Ph.D. from Academy of and Innovative Research (AcSIR), CSIR-Indian Institute of Chemical Technology (IICT), Campus, Hyderabad, India, in 2014 and 2019 respectively. Dr. Kamesh has extensive experience in the field of Process Systems Engineering (PSE), Artificial Intelligence (AI) and Machine Learning methods, Integrated Multi-Scale Modelling methods, and Process Intensification. He is working as a scientist in CSIR-IICT since 2016. He has actively engaged in basic research as well as applied research. He has developed process model-based as well as AI-based methodologies to simulate, design, control, and optimize processes, for accelerated product and process design, and to achieve performance improvements to existing processes in terms of improving productivity and selectivity while maintaining their safety and environmental constraints. Dr. Kamesh was a recipient of the Ambuja Young Researchers Award in 2014 from Indian Institute of Chemical Engineers (IIChE).

Shri Kant has received his Ph. D. in applied mathematics from applied mathematics departments of institute of technology, Banaras Hindu University (BHU), Varanasi in 1981. He is working as a Professor and head of "Center of Cyber Security and cryptology", Department of Computer Science and Engineering of Sharda University, India and involved actively in teaching and research mainly in the area of cyber security and Machine learning. His areas of interest are Special Functions, Cryptology, Pattern Recognition, Cluster Analysis, Soft Computing Model, Machine Learning and Data Mining.

Nurdan Kara is an Assistant Prof. in the Department of Mathematics at National Defence University (MSU), Istanbul, Turkey. She has been a faculty member of Ankara University since 1998. She completed her Ph.D. entitled "Fuzzy approaches to multiobjective fractional transportation problem" in Applied Mathematics (2008) from Yildiz Technical University. Her current area of research is mathematical Programming, fractional programming, supply chain management and some related Operational Research subjects in multi criteria and fuzzy environments.

Prasanna Karhade is Associate Professor of IT Management, Shidler College Faculty Fellow and a Faculty Fellow at the Pacific Asian Center for Entrepreneurship [PACE] at the University of Hawai'i at Mānoa. His research interests include digital innovation and digital platforms in growing, rural, eastern, aspirational and transitional [GREAT] economies.

Bouamrane Karim received the PhD Degree in computer science from the Oran University in 2006. He is Professor of computer Science at Oran1 University. He is the head of "Decision and piloting system" team. His current research interests deal with decision support system and logistics in maritime transportation, urban transportation system, production system, health systems and application of bio-inspired based optimization metaheuristic. He participates in several scientific committees' international/national conferences in Algeria and others countries in the same domain and collaborated in Algerian-French scientific projects. He is co-author of more than 40 scientific publications.

Joseph Kasten is an Assistant Professor of Information Science and Technology at the Pennsylvania State University in York, PA. He earned a PhD in Information Science at Long Island University in Brookville, NY, an MBA at Dowling College in Oakdale, NY, and a BS in engineering at Florida Institute of Technology in Melbourne, FL. Before joining academia, Joe was a senior engineer with the Northrop-Grumman Corp. where he worked on various military and commercial projects such as the X-29 and the Boeing 777. His research interests center on the implementation of data analytics within the organization as well as the application of blockchain technology to emerging organizational requirements. Professor Kasten's recent research appears in the International Journal of Business Intelligence Research and International Journal of Healthcare Information Systems and Informatics.

Tolga Kaya is a full-time researcher and lecturer at the department of Management Engineering in Istanbul Technical University. His research areas are consumer modeling, statistical decision making, input-output modeling, multicriteria decision making, machine learning and fuzzy applications in business and management. He has published several papers and presented his research at a number of international conferences in these areas.

Wei Ke, Ph.D., is the Adjunct Associate Professor of Quantitative Revenue and Pricing Analytics at Columbia Business School. Previously, he was Managing Partner and the head of financial services practice in North America at Simon-Kucher & Partners. Wei received a Ph.D. in Decision, Risk, and Operations from Columbia Business School, and a BSc in Electrical Engineering & Applied Mathematics, summa cum laude, from Columbia University.

Vanessa Keppeler is a Senior Associate with PwC Germany's Financial Services Consulting practice. She specializes on the design and implementation of Data and AI Governance. Her research and studies focus on the practical enablement of Explainable AI in Financial Institutions. Vanessa holds a master's degree in Management (Finance).

Mehrnaz Khalaj Hedayati is an Assistant Professor of Management at Georgia College & State University, J. Whitney Bunting College of Business. Mehrnaz received her Ph.D. from the University of Rhode Island in 2020. Mehrnaz has published several academic journal articles. She is a Lean Six Sigma Certified from the URI College of Business. She has taught undergraduate and master's level courses in Business Quantitative Analysis, Business Statistics, and Operations Management. She has also served as ad-hoc reviewer for several academic journals.

Fahima Khanam is a Lecturer in the department of Aviation Operation Management at Bangabandhu Sheikh Mujibur Rahman Aviation and Aerospace University. Prior to joining the BSMRAAU, she served as Lecturer in the Department of Business Administration at Sheikh Burhanuddin Post Graduate College, European University, Victoria University and German University, Bangladesh where she taught Principles of Marketing, Marketing Management, Operations Management, International Business, and Business Communication. She also worked as a corporate professional in The Daily 'Prothom Alo', one of the top daily newspapers in Bangladesh. She holds an MBA in Marketing from University of Dhaka, Bangladesh. Her most recent publication appeared in the International Journal of Big Data and Analytics in Healthcare (IJBDAH). Her principal research interests include e-commerce, online shopping, social media marketing and branding strategy, marketing strategy and technology adoption.

Shardul Khandekar has his BE completed in E&TC and his research area includes machine learning and deep learning.

Mubina Khondkar serves as a Professor in the Department of Marketing at the University of Dhaka. She has interdisciplinary knowledge in the areas of marketing and development economics. She has both industry and research experiences with organizations including ANZ Grindlays Bank, Care Bangladesh, USAID, DFID, Concern, IFPRI, World Bank, SEDF, IFC, JICA, CIDA, UNICEF, BIDS, the University of Manchester, and the University of Cambridge. Her research interests include value chain analysis, marketing, poverty, microfinance, development economics, gender, and women's empowerment. Further details can be found here: https://www.researchgate.net/profile/Mubina-Khondkar.

Soumya Khurana has his BE completed in E&TC and his research area includes machine learning and deep learning.

Necla Koçhan is currently working as a postdoctoral researcher at Izmir Biomedicine and Genome Center, IBG. Her research interests are computational biology, statistical data analysis, fuzzy theory, classification, and biostatistics.

Koharudin is a master student in IPB University, Indonesia. In 2014 he joined the Bureau of Organization and Human Resource, Indonesian Institute of Sciences (LIPI), as IT Engineering. In 2020 He moved to Center for Scientific Data and Documentation, Indonesian Institute of Sciences (LIPI). His current roles include building and maintaining web applications, designing database architecture, integrating data and providing data through service point. He obtained his bachelor degree in Computer Science from the Sepuluh Nopember Institute of Technology in 2011. He has developed some applications such as Human Resources Information System, Mobile applications and API Gateway. His research interests include Bioinformatics, High Performance Computing and Machine Learning.

Tibor Koltay is Professor retired from the Institute of Learning Technologies at Eszterházy Károly Catholic University, in Hungary. He graduated from Eötvös Loránd University (Budapest, Hungary) in 1984 with an MA in Russian. He obtained there his PhD in 2002. In 1992 he was awarded the Certificate of Advanced Studies in Library and Information Science at Kent State University, Kent. OH.

Xiangfen Kong is an Associate Professor from the Civil Aviation University of China. Her research interests include smart airports, system reliability, operational research, and big data.

Elena Kornyshova is an Associate Professor at CNAM, Ph.D. in Economics and Management Sciences and Ph.D. in Computer Science. Her main research domains are method and process engineering, decision-making, enterprise architecture, and digitalization. She is/was involved in organization of multiple international conferences and workshops. She has significant experience in industry and consultancy sector mainly in the fields of IS engineering and enterprise architecture.

Maximiliano E. Korstanje is editor in chief of International Journal of Safety and Security in Tourism (UP Argentina) and Editor in Chief Emeritus of International Journal of Cyber Warfare and Terrorism (IGI-Global US). Korstanje is Senior Researchers in the Department of Economics at University of Palermo, Argentina. In 2015 he was awarded as Visiting Research Fellow at School of Sociology and Social Policy, University of Leeds, UK and the University of La Habana Cuba. In 2017 is elected as Foreign Faculty Member of AMIT, Mexican Academy in the study of Tourism, which is the most prominent institutions dedicated to tourism research in Mexico. He had a vast experience in editorial projects working as advisory member of Elsevier, Routledge, Springer, IGI global and Cambridge Scholar publishing. Korstanje had visited and given seminars in many important universities worldwide. He has also recently been selected to take part of the 2018 Albert Nelson Marquis Lifetime Achievement Award. a great distinction given by Marquis Who´s Who in the world.

Mika Kosonen is a graduate student in University of Lapland. He has bachelor's degree in social sciences and is currently finishing his master's degree. His bachelor's thesis was concerning artificial intelligence and ethics, and master's thesis contributes to morality in human-technology interaction, both with excellent grades. With strong interest in technology and human experience he is always wondering the world where technology mediates the reality, whether in suburbans or the wilderness found in northernmost parts of Europe.

Anjani Kumar is a Ph.D. student of computer science at the University of Nebraska at Omaha. He is working as a Data Scientist at Data Axle Inc. His primary research interests are in the fields of Big Data, Deep Learning, and Machine Learning.

Sameer Kumar is an Associate Professor at Universiti Malaya, Malaysia.

Madhusree Kundu is presently Professor, Department of Chemical Engineering, National Institute of Technology Rourkela, Orissa, India. Currently, HOD, Central Instrument Facility (CIF), NIT Rourkela. Experience: Worked as Process Engineer in Simon Carves India Limited (A Design Consultancy). First Academic Appointment: Assistant Professor, Birla Institute of Technology and Science (BITS) Pilani, Rajasthan, India. PhD: Indian Institute of Technology Kharagpur Research Interest: Fluid Phase equilibrium and its application, Modeling, & Simulation and Control, Chemommetrics/Machine Learning applications, Process Identification monitoring and Control, Biomimetic device development and Digitized Sustainable Agriculture.

Mascha Kurpicz-Briki obtained her PhD in the area of energy-efficient cloud computing at the University of Neuchâtel. After her PhD, she worked a few years in industry, in the area of open-source engineering, cloud computing and analytics. She is now professor for data engineering at the Bern University of Applied Sciences, investigating how to apply digital methods and in particular natural language processing to social and community challenges.

Kevin Kwak is an Information Systems and Accounting student at the University of Nebraska at Omaha. He received a Master's in Accounting and as of this writing is pursuing a Master's in Information Systems. His current interests of study are accounting, data security, and data mining. Currently, he has had five articles published in various journals.

Wikil Kwak is a Professor of Accounting at the University of Nebraska at Omaha. He received Ph.D. in Accounting from the University of Nebraska in Lincoln. Dr. Kwak's research interests include the areas of mathematical programming approaches in bankruptcy prediction, capital budgeting, transfer pricing, performance evaluation and Japanese capital market studies. He has published more than 57 articles in the Engineering Economist, Abacus, Contemporary Accounting Research, Review of Quantitative Finance and Accounting, Management Accountant, Journal of Petroleum Accounting and Financial Management, Business Intelligence and Data Mining, Review of Pacific Basin Financial Markets and Policies, and Multinational Business Review.

Georgios Lampropoulos received his BSc degree with the title of Information Technology Engineer specialized as a Software Engineer from the Department of Information Technology at Alexander

Technological Educational Institute of Thessaloniki (currently named International Hellenic University) in 2017 and he received his MSc in Web Intelligence from the same department in 2019. Currently, he is a PhD candidate and Visiting Lecturer in the Department of Information and Electronic Engineering at International Hellenic University and a MEd student in Education Sciences at Hellenic Open University. He has published his work in several peer reviewed journals and conferences, he has taken part in international research programs and he has also served as a reviewer and a member of the organizing and scientific committees of international conferences and international journals.

Torben Larsen is an MSc Econ from University of Aarhus and an international Degree in Strategic Management from University of Maryland-Tietgenskolen Dk. He has broad experience in regional planning of healthcare with Academic Awards from 1) Association of Hospital Managers in Norway, Lundbeck Fonden Dk and MIE96. He is a former Chief Research Consultant at University of Southern Denmark which included leadership of an EU-sponsored research project in Integrated Homecare. He has been involved with various courses and conferences and has written research papers in Health Economics, Neuroeconomics, Meditation and Biofeedback. 2017 he published "Homo Neuroeconomicus" (IJUDH(1)). 2020 he published "Neuroeconomic Pcyshology. 3 Modules for End-users . . . .", IJPCH Actually, he is giving guest lectures in cybernetic economics.

Matthias Lederer is Full Professor of Information Systems at the Technical University of Applied Sciences Amberg-Weiden. Prior to this, he was a professor at the ISM International School of Management Munich and at the same time Chief Process Officer at the IT Service Center of the Bavarian justice system. His previous positions include research assistant at the University of Erlangen-Nuremberg and strategy consultant at the German industrial company REHAU. His research and studies focus on business process management and IT management. Prof. Lederer holds a doctorate as well as a master's degree in international information systems and is the author of over 70 scientific publications in this field.

Eva Lee applies combinatorial optimization, math programming, game theory, and parallel computation to biological, medical, health systems, and logistics analyses. Her clinical decision-support systems (DSS) assist in disease diagnosis/prediction, treatment design, drug delivery, treatment and healthcare outcome analysis/prediction, and healthcare operations logistics. In logistics, she tackles operations planning and resource allocation, and her DSS addresses inventory control, vehicle dispatching, scheduling, transportation, telecom, portfolio investment, public health emergency treatment response, and facility location/planning. Dr. Lee is Director of the Center for Operations Research in Medicine and HealthCare, a center established through funds from the National Science Foundation and the Whitaker Foundation. The center focuses on biomedicine, public health and defense, translational medical research, medical delivery and preparedness, and the protection of critical infrastructures. She is a subject matter expert in medical systems and public health informatics, logistics and networks, and large-scale connected systems. She previously served as the Senior Health Systems Engineer and Professor for the U.S. Department of Veterans Affairs and was Co-Director for the Center for Health Organization Transformation. Dr. Lee has received numerous practice excellence awards, including the INFORMS Edelman Award on novel cancer therapeutics, the Wagner prize on vaccine immunity prediction, and the Pierskalla award on bioterrorism, emergency response, and mass casualty mitigation She is a fellow at INFORMS and AIMBE. Lee has served on NAE/NAS/IOM, NRC, NBSB, DTRA panel committees related to CBRN and WMD incidents, public health and medical preparedness, and healthcare systems innovation. She holds ten patents on medical systems and devices. Her work has been featured in the New York Times, London Times, disaster documentaries, and in other venues.

Jinha Lee is an Assistant Professor in the Department of Public and Allied Health at Bowling Green State University. His research interests include healthcare operations, data analytics, economic decision analysis, and system modeling in healthcare service. His work has examined practice variance and systems analysis for quality and process improvement and new clinical guidelines establishment. Also, his research has focused on economic analysis on industry networks, resource allocations, and the R&D process in healthcare services. His research primarily utilizes large datasets and clinical observations derived from various healthcare databases and field studies in clinical facilities. He has collaborated actively with hospitals, healthcare research institutes, and healthcare delivery organizations both in the U.S. and in foreign countries.

Ulli Leucht is a Manager in PwC Germany's Financial Services Technology Consulting team. He is an expert in AI and its use in Financial Institutions - which includes how AI use cases are identified, perceived, implemented, operated and surrounding governance, compliance, and legal requirements. Prior to joining PwC Germany, he worked with some of the most innovative FinTechs in the United Kingdom and the United States in the context of AI. Ulli's research and studies focus is the usage of AI in Financial Institutions. He holds a master's degree in Sensors and Cognitive Psychology.

Carson Leung is currently a Professor at the University of Manitoba, Canada. He has contributed more than 300 refereed publications on the topics of big data, computational intelligence, cognitive computing, data analytics, data mining, data science, fuzzy systems, machine learning, social network analysis, and visual analytics. These include eight chapters in IGI Global's books/encyclopedia (e.g., Encyclopedia of Organizational Knowledge, Administration, and Technology (2021)). He has also served on the Organizing Committee of the ACM CIKM, ACM SIGMOD, IEEE DSAA, IEEE ICDM, and other conferences.

Siyao Li is a student at the City University of Macau. She studies in the International Business program.

Gilson B. A. Lima is a Professor in the Industrial Engineering Department at Federal Fluminense University (UFF), Brazil. He received his PhD in the Rio de Janeiro Federal University, Brazil. His current research interests include industrial safety, risk management, industrial maintenance and industrial environmental management.

Yu-Wei Lin is an assistant professor in the Leavey School of Business, Santa Clara University. He received a Ph.D. in information systems at Gies College of Business, the University of Illinois at Urbana-Champaign. His research interests are in User-Generated Content, Healthcare Analytics, Online Review Analysis, Machine Learning, Decision Making, and Decision Support Systems.

Fangyao Liu is an assistant professor in the College of Electronic and Information at the Southwest Minzu University, China. He received Ph.D. in Information Technology from the University of Nebraska at Omaha, USA. Dr. Liu's research interests include the areas of data mining, artificial intelligence, and statistics. He has published more than 20 articles in the International journal of Computers Communications & Control, Journal of Urban Planning and Development, Journal of software, Journal of Asian Development, Journal of Contemporary Management, Procedia Computer Science, and several IEEE conferences.

Haoyu Liu is an assistant professor at the Faculty of Business, City University of Macau. He received an MPhil and a PhD in Operations Management from HKUST Business School in 2017 and 2020, respectively. He serves as a reviewer for Manufacturing & Service Operations Management (MSOM), Naval Research Logistics (NRL), International Journal of Applied Management Science (IJAMS), International Journal of Retail & Distribution Management (IJRDM), International Journal of E-Business Research (IJEBR), International Conference on Information Systems (ICIS), and INFORMS Conference on Service Science (ICSS). He has broad interests in issues related to healthcare, emerging technologies, charitable organizations, and marketing. In solving problems, he employs various techniques, ranging from game-theoretical and stochastic models to typical tools in empirical and experimental studies.

Ran Liu is an Assistant Professor in the Marketing department at Central Connecticut State University. His research focuses on online relationships, user-generated content (UGC), data modeling, and International businesses. He serves as Associate Editor (Asia) for Journal of Eastern European and Central Asian Research (JEECAR) and Faculty Advisor for American Marketing Association Collegiate Chapter.

Cèlia Llurba is currently a PhD student in Educational Technology in the Department of Pedagogy at the URV. Graduate in East Asian Studies from the UOC and a graduate in Mining Engineering from the UPC. She is currently a teacher of Technology in a high school in Cambrils (state employee) and also teaches in the subjects of Vocational Guidance and Citizenship, and Educational Processes and Contexts, within the Master's Degree in Teacher Training at the URV. Her main lines of research are: intellectual learning environments, data analytics and artificial intelligence in intellectual areas.

Manuel Lozano Rodriguez is American University of Sovereign Nations (AUSN) Visiting Prof. in his own discipline that takes bioethics off the medical hegemony to land it on social sciences, futurism, politics and pop culture through metaphysics of displacement. Born in Barcelona in 1978, Ph.D. in Bioethics, Sustainability and Global Public Health, AUSN; Master of Science in Sustainability, Peace and Development, AUSN; Graduate in Fundamentals of Sustainability Organizational, Harvard.

Lorenzo Magnani, philosopher, epistemologist, and cognitive scientist, is a professor of Philosophy of Science at the University of Pavia, Italy, and the director of its Computational Philosophy Laboratory. His previous positions have included: visiting researcher (Carnegie Mellon University, 1992; McGill University, 1992–93; University of Waterloo, 1993; and Georgia Institute of Technology, 1998–99) and visiting professor (visiting professor of Philosophy of Science and Theories of Ethics at Georgia Institute of Technology, 1999–2003; Weissman Distinguished Visiting Professor of Special Studies in Philosophy: Philosophy of Science at Baruch College, City University of New York, 2003). Visiting professor at the Sun Yat-sen University, Canton (Guangzhou), China from 2006 to 2012, in the event of the 50th anniversary of the re-building of the Philosophy Department of Sun Yat-sen University in 2010, an award was given to him to acknowledge his contributions to the areas of philosophy, philosophy of science, logic, and cognitive science. A Doctor Honoris Causa degree was awarded to Lorenzo Magnani by the Senate of the Ştefan cel Mare University, Suceava, Romania. In 2015 Lorenzo Magnani has been appointed member of the International Academy for the Philosophy of the Sciences (AIPS). He currently directs international research programs in the EU, USA, and China. His book Abduction, Reason, and Science (New York, 2001) has become a well-respected work in the field of human cognition. The book Morality in a Technological World (Cambridge, 2007) develops a philosophical and cognitive theory of the relationships between ethics and technology in a naturalistic perspective. The book Abductive Cognition. The Epistemological and Eco-Cognitive Dimensions of Hypothetical Reasoning and the last monograph Understanding Violence. The Intertwining of Morality, Religion, and Violence: A Philosophical Stance have been more recently published by Springer, in 2009 and 2011. A new monograph has been published by Springer in 2017, The Abductive Structure of Scientific Creativity. An Essay on the Ecology of Cognition, together with the Springer Handbook of Model-Based Science (edited with Tommaso Bertolotti). The last book Eco-Cognitive Computationalism. Cognitive Domestication of Ignorant Entities, published by Springer, offers an entirely new dynamic perspective on the nature of computation. He edited books in Chinese, 16 special issues of international academic journals, and 17 collective books, some of them deriving from international conferences. Since 1998, initially in collaboration with Nancy J. Nersessian and Paul Thagard, he created and promoted the MBR Conferences on Model-Based Reasoning. Since 2011 he is the editor of the Book Series Studies in Applied Philosophy, Epistemology and Rational Ethics (SAPERE), Springer, Heidelberg/Berlin.

Mazlina Abdul Majid is an Associate Professor in the Faculty of Computing at University Malaysia Pahang (UMP), Malaysia. She received her PHD in Computer Science from the University of Nottingham, UK. She held various managerial responsibilities as a Deputy Dean of Research and Graduate Studies and currently acts as the head of the Software Engineering Research Group in her Faculty. She also taught courses on the undergraduate and master's levels. She has published 130 research in local and international books, journals and conference proceedings. She is also a member of various committees of international conferences. Her research interests include simulation, software agent, software usability and testing.

Jasna D. Marković-Petrović received her B.Sc. (1992) and M.Sc. (2011) degrees in electrical engineering and her Ph.D. degree (2018) in technical sciences, all from the University of Belgrade, Serbia. She is with the Public Enterprise "Electric Power Industry of Serbia" for more than 25 years. Her activities involve implementation of the technical information system, participation in projects concerning upgrading the remote control system of the hydropower plant, and implementation of the SCADA security system. She is a member of the Serbian National CIGRÉ Study Committee D2. As author or coauthor, she published a number of book chapters, journal articles and conference papers in her field. Her main research interests involve smart grids, SCADA and industrial control systems security, and cyber risk management.

Roberto Marmo received the Laurea (cum laude) in Computer Science from Salerno University (Italy) and Ph.D. in Electronic and Computer Engineering obtained from the University of Pavia (Italy). He is presently contract teacher of computer science at Faculty of Engineering of Pavia University, Italy. His most recent work is concerned with mathematical models and software for social network analysis. He is author of "Social Media Mining", a textbook in Italian language on extraction of information from social media, website http://www.socialmediamining.it.

Nikolaos Matsatsinis is a full Professor of Information and Decision Support Systems in the School of Production Engineering and Management of the Technical University of Crete, Greece. He is President of the Hellenic Operational Research Society (HELORS). He is Director of DSS Lab and Postgraduate Programs. He has contributed as scientific or project coordinator on over of fifty national and international projects. He is chief editor of the Operational Research: An International Journal (Impact Factor 2020: 2.410) and International Journal of Decision Support Systems. He is the author or co-author/editor of 25 books and over of 120 articles in international scientific journals and books. He has organized and participated in the organization of over of ninety scientific conferences, including EURO 2021, and he has over of one hundred and ninety presentations in international and national scientific conferences. His research interests fall into the areas of Intelligent DSS, Multi-Agent Systems, Recommendation Systems, Multicriteria Decision Analysis, Group Decision Making, Operational Research, e-Marketing, Consumer Behaviour Analysis, Data Analysis, Business Intelligence & Business Analytics.

Hubert Maupas is graduated from Ecole Centrale de Lyon (France) and holds a PhD in Integrated Electronics, obtained with several patents and publications. He has spent most of his career in medical device industry and is currently working as COO of MUST, a all-in-one B2B Metaverse platform to manage DBE (Digital Business Ecosystem) embedding advanced matchmaking algorithms.

Iman Megahed is the AVP for Digital Transformation, Chief Strategy and Knowledge Officer at the American University in Cairo (AUC). She is currently responsible for all Information Technology, Information Security, Business Intelligence and institutional effectiveness functions. She co-founded the business intelligence and data governance functions to support informed based decision making. She also founded the office of Online Student Services which applied web services and portal technology to enhance student services. With a successful track record in technology and effectiveness administrative positions in Higher Education since 1992, Iman has accumulated extensive technical expertise, unique project management skills coupled with results-oriented leadership style and passion for informed based decision making. Iman earned her PhD in Organizational Behavior from Cairo University, MBA and BS in Computer Science from The American University in Cairo.

Natarajan Meghanathan is a tenured Full Professor of Computer Science at Jackson State University, Jackson, MS. He graduated with a Ph.D. in Computer Science from The University of Texas at Dallas in May 2005. Dr. Meghanathan has published more than 175 peer-reviewed articles (more than half of them being journal publications). He has also received federal education and research grants from the U. S. National Science Foundation, Army Research Lab and Air Force Research Lab. Dr. Meghanathan has been serving in the editorial board of several international journals and in the Technical Program Committees and Organization Committees of several international conferences. His research interests are Wireless Ad hoc Networks and Sensor Networks, Graph Theory and Network Science, Cyber Security, Machine Learning, Bioinformatics and Computational Biology. For more information, visit https:// www.jsums.edu/nmeghanathan.

Abelardo Mercado Herrera has a PhD from the National Institute of Astrophysics, Optics and Electronics (INAOE), specializing in Astrophysics, Postdoctorate in Astrophysics from the Institute of Astronomy from the National Autonomous University of Mexico (UNAM), Electronics Engineer from the Autonomous University of Baja California (UABC). He is a specialist in the mathematical-statistical description of stochastic processes and/or deterministic systems, nonlinear systems, complex systems, chaos theory, among others, as well as its application to physical phenomena such as astronomy, medicine, economics, finance, telecommunications, social sciences etc., in order to determine the dynamics underlying in such processes, and given the case, its connection with real physical variables and possible prediction. He has worked on the development of interfaces and programs to carry out electrical tests in industry, as well as in scientific instrumentation, applied to telemetry, infrared polarimetry, optics and spectroscopy. He has also specialized in image analysis, measurement techniques and noise reduction.

Shivlal Mewada is presently working as an Assistant Professor (contact) in the Dept. of CS, Govt. Holkar (Autonomous, Model) Science College, Indore, India. He shared the responsibility of research activities and coordinator of M.Phil.(CS) at Govt. Holkar Sci. Collage, Indore. He has also received JRF in 2010-11 for M.Phil. Programme under UGC Fellow scheme, New Delhi. He is a member of IEEE since 2013 and editorial member of the ISROSET since 2013. He is a technical committee and editorial member of various reputed journals including Taylor & Francis, Inderscience. He chaired 5 national and international conferences and seminars. He organized 2 special for international conferences. He also contributed to the organization of 2 national and 4 virtual international conferences. Mr. Mewada has published 3 book chapters and over 18 research articles in reputed journals like SCI, Scopus including IEEE conferences. His areas of interest include; cryptography, information security and computational intelligence.

Tanish Ambrishkumar Mishra is an undergraduate student at Sardar Patel College of Engineering, Mumbai, India. Currently pursuing his Bachelor of Technology (B.Tech) in Department of Mechanical Engineering. His research areas of interest are mobile robotics, biomimetic robot design, robotic prosthetic limb design, control systems and AI/ML.

Mayank Modashiya is a Data Scientist 1 at Kenco Group, Chattanooga, TN, USA. He earned is Bachelor's in Engineering in Mechanical Engineering, India. He earned his Masters in Industrial Engineering from the University of Texas at Arlington. Mayank has passion for applying machine learning (ML) and artificial Intelligence (AI) to solve complex supply chain problems. Mayank has more than 2 years' experience in developing and implementing AI/ML for problem solving. His research interest includes supply chain networks, logistics and manufacturing. He is member of INFORMS and IISE.

Jordi Mogas holds a PhD in Educational Technology and a Bachelor's in Information and Documentation with mention in information systems management. Currently, he is a postdoc researcher at GEPS research center (Globalisation, Education and Social Policies), at the Universitat Autònoma de Barcelona, and belongs to ARGET (Applied Research Group in Education and Technology). Dr. Mogas teaches at both the Department of Pedagogy at the Universitat Rovira i Virgili (professor associate) and at the Department of Education at the Universitat Oberta de Catalunya (professor collaborador). His main research lines are: Smart Learning Environments, Virtual Learning Environments and Self-Regulated Learning.

Siddhartha Moulik is working as a Scientist in CSIR-IICT. His field of specialization deals with wastewater treatment, cavitation based advanced oxidation processes, sonochemistry as well as in membrane separation technology along with experiences in practical field applications.

Adam Moyer is an Assistant Professor in the Department of Analytics and Information Systems at Ohio University's College of Business. Moyer received a BBA from Ohio University and has had experience managing information systems for non-profit organizations, has worked as a systems engineer, and has consulted for various companies. While earning an MS in Industrial & Systems Engineering at Ohio University, Adam developed and taught courses related to information systems, programming, system design and deployment, business intelligence, analytics, and cybersecurity at Ohio University. After gaining additional professional experience in the counterintelligence community, Moyer returned to Ohio University and earned a Ph.D. in Mechanical and Systems Engineering.

Anirban Mukherjee is faculty in marketing. He received a PhD in Marketing from The Samuel Curtis Johnson Graduate School of Management, Cornell University.

Anweshan Mukherjee has completed his BSc with Major in Computer Science from St. Xavier's College, Kolkata and is currently pursuing MSc in Computer Science from the same college. His current research interest is Data Analytics and Machine Learning.

Partha Mukherjee, assistant professor of data analytics, received his bachelor's degree in mechanical engineering in 1995 from Jadavpur University in India. He received his Master of Technology in Computer Science from Indian Statistical Institute in 2001. He earned his second graduate degree in computer Science from the University of Tulsa in 2008. He completed his Ph.D. from Penn State in information and technology with a minor in applied statistics in 2016.

Fabian N. Murrieta-Rico received B.Eng. and M.Eng. degrees from Instituto Tecnológico de Mexicali (ITM) in 2004 and 2013 respectively. In 2017, he received his PhD in Materials Physics at Centro de Investigación Científica y Educación Superior de Ensenada (CICESE). He has worked as an automation engineer, systems designer, as a university professor, and as postdoctoral researcher at Facultad de Ingeniería, Arquitectura y Diseño from Universidad Autónoma de Baja California (UABC) and at the Centro de Nanociencias y Nanotecnología from Universidad Nacional Autónoma de México (CNyN-UNAM), currently he works as professor at the Universidad Politécnica de Baja California. His research has been published in different journals and presented at international conferences since 2009. He has served as reviewer for different journals, some of them include IEEE Transactions on Industrial Electronics, IEEE Transactions on Instrumentation, Measurement and Sensor Review. His research interests are focused on the field of time and frequency metrology, the design of wireless sensor networks, automated systems, and highly sensitive chemical detectors.

Balsam A. J. Mustafa holds an MS.c in Information Systems from the UK and earned her Ph.D. in Computer Science (Software Engineering) from Malaysia. Her research interests are in the areas of empirical software engineering, intelligent health care systems, and data mining & analytics. Dr. Balsam has served on more than 25 international conference program committees and journal editorial boards, and has been a keynote and invited speaker at several international conferences. She is a member of IEEE and a professional member of the Association of Computing Machinery (ACM). Dr. Balsam has published 30 technical papers in various refereed journals and conference proceedings.

Ambika N. is an MCA, MPhil, Ph.D. in computer science. She completed her Ph.D. from Bharathiar university in the year 2015. She has 16 years of teaching experience and presently working for St.Francis College, Bangalore. She has guided BCA, MCA and M.Tech students in their projects. Her expertise includes wireless sensor network, Internet of things, cybersecurity. She gives guest lectures in her expertise. She is a reviewer of books, conferences (national/international), encyclopaedia and journals. She is advisory committee member of some conferences. She has many publications in National & international conferences, international books, national and international journals and encyclopaedias. She has some patent publications (National) in computer science division.

Jyotindra Narayan is a regular doctoral fellow at the Department of Mechanical Engineering, Indian Institute of Technology Guwahati, currently practicing and working on "Design, Development and Control Architecture of a Low-cost Lower-Limb Exoskeleton for Mobility Assistance and Gait Rehabilitation". Moreover, he employs the intelligent and soft computing algorithms in his research. He has a substantial experience in kinematics, dynamics and control of robotic devices for medical applications. He has published several journals, book chapters and conference papers on the broad topic of medical and rehabilitation devices.

Ghalia Nasserddine is a Ph.D in information technology and systems. She has been an assistant professor at Lebanese International University since 2010. In addition, she is active research in machine learning, belief function theory, renewable energy and High voltage transmission.

Son Nguyen earned his master's degree in applied mathematics and doctoral degree in mathematics, statistics emphasis, both at Ohio University. He is currently an assistant professor at the department of mathematics at Bryant University. His primary research interests lie in dimensionality reduction, imbalanced learning, and machine learning classification. In addition to the theoretical aspects, he is also interested in applying statistics to other areas such as finance and healthcare.

Van-Ho Nguyen received B.A. degree in Management Information System from Faculty of Information Systems, University of Economics and Law (VNU–HCM), Vietnam in 2015, and Master degree in MIS from School of Business Information Technology from University of Economics Ho Chi Minh City, Vietnam in 2020, respectively. His current research interests include Business Intelligence, Data Analytics, and Machine Learning.

Shivinder Nijjer, currently serving as Assistant Professor in Chitkara University, Punjab, has a doctorate in Business Analytics and Human Resource Management. She has authored books and book chapters in the field of Business Analytics, Information Systems and Strategy for eminent publication groups like Taylor and Francis, Emerald, Pearson and IGI Global. She is currently guiding two PhD candidates and is on reviewer panel of three Scopus indexed journals.

Roberto Nogueira is Grupo Globo Full Professor of Strategy at COPPEAD Graduate School of Business, The Federal University of Rio de Janeiro, where he is also executive director of the Strategy and Innovation Research Center. He joined COPPEAD in 1984 and since that teaches at the MSc, PhD and Executive Education courses. He was visiting professor at the University of San Diego (USA), San Jose State University (USA), Alma Business School (Italy), Audencia (France) and Stellenbosch (South

Africa). He is co-founder and board member of the Executive MBA Consortium for Global Business Innovation, encompassing Business Schools from five continents - Alma Business School (Italy), Cranfield (UK), Coppead (Brazil), ESAN (Peru), FIU (USA), Keio Business School (Japan), Kozminski (Poland), MIR (Russia), Munich Business School (Germany), San Jose State (Silicon Valley - USA) and Stellenbosch (South Africa) promoting the exchange of Executive MBA students. Nogueira wrote two books and has published dozens of scholarly articles on such topics as Corporate Strategy, Business Ecosystems, Innovation and Emerging Technologies and Business Reconfiguration, analyzing sectors such as Health, Energy, Education, Media and Entertainment and Space.

Cherie Noteboom is a Professor of Information Systems in the College of Business and Information Systems, Coordinator of the PhD in Information Systems and Co-Director of the Center of Excellence in Information Systems at Dakota State University. She holds a Ph.D. in Information Technology from the University of Nebraska-Omaha. In addition, she has earned an Education Doctorate in Adult & Higher Education & Administration & MBA from the University of South Dakota. She has a BS degree in computer science from South Dakota State University. She researches in the areas of Information Systems, Healthcare, and Project Management. Her industry experience runs the continuum from technical computer science endeavors to project management and formal management & leadership positions. She has significant experience working with Management Information Systems, Staff Development, Project Management, Application Development, Education, Healthcare, Mentoring, and Leadership.

Zinga Novais is a project manager. She holds a Master's in Project Management from ISEG, School of Economics & Management of the University of Lisbon. She also holds a post-graduation in Project Management and a postgraduation in Management & Business Consulting, both from ISEG - University of Lisbon; and a degree in Public Administration from ISCSP, School of Social and Political Sciences of the University of Lisbon.

Poonam Oberoi is an Associate Professor of Marketing at Excelia Business School. She joined Excelia Group in 2014 after successfully defending her thesis at Grenoble Ecole de Management the same year. On the research front, Dr. Oberoi's primary focus is in the area of innovation and technology management. Her work examines the technology and innovation sourcing decisions that firms make, and the consequences of these decisions. Since her appointment at Excelia Business School, she has published research papers on these topics in well-regarded, peer reviewed, international journals such as M@n@gement and Journal of Business Research. Furthermore, she has published many book chapters and case studies on related topics. For more information, please visit: https://www.excelia-group.com/faculty-research/faculty/oberoi.

Ibrahim Oguntola is a Research Assistant, Industrial Engineering, Dalhousie University, Canada.

Kamalendu Pal is with the Department of Computer Science, School of Science and Technology, City, University of London. Kamalendu received his BSc (Hons) degree in Physics from Calcutta University, India, Postgraduate Diploma in Computer Science from Pune, India, MSc degree in Software Systems Technology from the University of Sheffield, Postgraduate Diploma in Artificial Intelligence from the Kingston University, MPhil degree in Computer Science from the University College London, and MBA degree from the University of Hull, United Kingdom. He has published over seventy-five international research articles (including book chapters) widely in the scientific community with research papers in the ACM SIGMIS Database, Expert Systems with Applications, Decision Support Systems, and conferences. His research interests include knowledge-based systems, decision support systems, blockchain technology, software engineering, service-oriented computing, and ubiquitous computing. He is on the editorial board of an international computer science journal and is a member of the British Computer Society, the Institution of Engineering and Technology, and the IEEE Computer Society.

Ramon Palau is a researcher and lecturer in the Pedagogy Department of the Rovira and Virgili University. As a researcher he did internships in UNESCO París and Leipzig University. His current work as a researcher is in ARGET (Applied Research Group of Education Technology) focused in e-learning, digital technologies, digital competences and educational application of digital technologies. In this group he has participated in several research projects. Currently his research is centered in smart learning environments publishing the first fundings. He has worked as a content developer for several institutions as Universitat Oberta de Catalunya, Fundació URV, Fundació Paco Puerto, Editorial Barcanova and Universitat de Lleida. Previously of the works in academia, he has worked as a primary and secondary teacher as a civil servant. From 2003 until 2007 he had been a principal in a public school. Concerning teaching, in higher education level, he has taught in Master of Educational Technology in Universitat Rovira i Virgili and Universitat Oberta de Catalunya and the Master of Teaching in Secondary School where is the director of the program.

Adam Palmquist is an industrial PhDc at the department of Applied IT at Gothenburg University and works as Chief Scientific Officer (CSO) at the Swedish Gamification company Insert Coin. Palmquist has a background in learning and game design. He is the author of several books addressing the intersection of design, technology, and learning. Adam has worked as a gamification and learning advisor for several international companies in the technology and production industries. His PhD-project is a collaboration between Gothenburg University and Insert Coin concerning Gamified the World Engine (GWEN), a unique system-agnostic API constructed to make gamification designs scalable. The interdisciplinary project transpires at the intersection of Human-Computer Interaction, Design Science in Information Systems and Learning Analytics.

Chung-Yeung Pang received his Ph.D. from Cambridge University, England. He has over 30 years of software development experience in a variety of areas from device drivers, web, and mobile apps to large enterprise IT systems. He has experience in many programming languages, including low-level languages like Assembler and C, high-level languages like COBOL, Java and Ada, AI languages like LISP and Prolog, and mobile app languages like Javascript and Dart. For the past 20 years he has worked as a consultant in various corporate software projects. He worked in the fields of architecture design, development, coaching and management of IT projects. At one time he was a lead architect on a project with a budget of over $ 1 billion. In recent years, despite limited resources and high pressure in some projects, he has led many projects to complete on time and on budget.

Severin Pang completed a combined degree in mathematics, statistics, and economics at the University of Bern. He also received the Swiss federal state diploma for computer engineers. He has more than 10 years of experience in computing engineering in companies such as Swiss Re, Zurich Insurance and IBM. At IBM he implemented AI functionalities for a hovering robot to support ISS astronauts. Severin Pang is currently working as a data scientist at Cognitive Solutions & Innovation AG in Switzerland, where he formulates mathematical models for predictive maintenance of machines, develops an intelligent sensor to detect anomalies in the frequency spectrum, and verifies the effectiveness of fuel-saving measures for Airbus aircraft and optimizes the energy consumption of more than 6000 hotels around the world. He has contributed to a number of publications in the fields of data science, AI, and software engineering.

Renan Payer holds a PhD and a Master's degree in Production Engineering from Fluminense Federal University (Brazil). Graduated in Chemical Engineering (University of the State of Rio de Janeiro UERJ) in Industrial Chemistry (Fluminense Federal University - UFF). He has an MBA in Production and Quality Management. It carries out academic research in the area of sustainability, circular economy and digital transformation.

Jean-Eric Pelet holds a PhD in Marketing, an MBA in Information Systems and a BA (Hns) in Advertising. As an assistant professor in management, he works on problems concerning consumer behaviour when using a website or other information system (e-learning, knowledge management, e-commerce platforms), and how the interface can change that behavior. His main interest lies in the variables that enhance navigation in order to help people to be more efficient with these systems. He works as a visiting professor both in France and abroad (England, Switzerland) teaching e-marketing, ergonomics, usability, and consumer behaviour at Design Schools (Nantes), Business Schools (Paris, Reims), and Universities (Paris Dauphine – Nantes). Dr. Pelet has also actively participated in a number of European Community and National research projects. His current research interests focus on, social networks, interface design, and usability.

María A. Pérez received her M.S. and Ph.D. degrees in telecommunication engineering from the University of Valladolid, Spain, in 1996 and 1999, respectively. She is presently Associate Professor at University of Valladolid, and member of the Data Engineering Research Unit. Her research is focused on Big Data, Artificial Intelligence, Internet of Things, and the application of technology to the learning process. She has managed or participated in numerous international research projects. She is author or co-author of many publications in journals, books, and conferences. In addition, she has been involved as reviewer in several international research initiatives.

Vitalii Petranovskii received the Ph.D. degree in physical chemistry from the Moscow Institute of Crystallography in 1988. From 1993 to 1994, he worked as a Visiting Fellow at the National Institute of Materials Science and Chemical Research, Japan. Since 1995, he has been working with the Center for Nanotechnology and Nanotechnology, National University of Mexico, as the Head of the Department of Nanocatalysis, from 2006 to 2014. He is a member of the Mexican Academy of Sciences, the International Association of Zeolites, and the Russian Chemical Society. He has published over 160 articles in peer-reviewed journals and five invited book chapters. He is also a coauthor of the monograph Clusters and Matrix Isolated Clustered Superstructures (St. Petersburg, 1995). His research interests include the synthesis and properties of nanoparticles deposited on zeolite matrices, and the modification of the zeolite matrices themselves for their high-tech use.

Frederick E. Petry received BS and MS degrees in physics and a PhD in computer and information science from The Ohio State University. He is currently a computer scientist in the Naval Research Laboratory at the Stennis Space Center Mississippi. He has been on the faculty of the University of Alabama in Huntsville, the Ohio State University and Tulane University where he is an Emeritus Professor. His recent research interests include representation of imprecision via soft computing in databases, spatial and environmental and information systems and machine learning. Dr. Petry has over 350 scientific publications including 150 journal articles/book chapters and 9 books written or edited. For his research on the use of fuzzy sets for modeling imprecision in databases and information systems he was elected an IEEE Life Fellow, AAAS Fellow, IFSA Fellow and an ACM Distinguished Scientist. In 2016 he received the IEEE Computational Intelligence Society Pioneer Award.

Birgit Pilch studied Biology and then Technical Protection of Environment at Graz University and Graz University of Technology.

Matthias Pohl is a research associate in the Very Large Business Application Lab at the Otto von Guericke University Magdeburg since 2016. His main research and work interests are data science, statistical modeling and the efficient design of innovative IT solutions. Matthias Pohl studied Mathematics and Informatics and holds a Diplom degree in Mathematics from Otto von Guericke University Magdeburg.

Peter Poschmann, M.Sc., works as a research associate at the Chair of Logistics, Institute of Technology and Management, at the Technical University of Berlin. Within the scope of several research projects, he focuses on the technical application of Machine Learning to logistic problems, in particular the prediction of transport processes. Previously, he worked as a research associate at a Fraunhofer Institute with a focus on Data Science. He graduated in industrial engineering with a specialization in mechanical engineering at the Technical University of Darmstadt.

Brajkishore Prajapati is an associate Data Scientist at Azilen Technologies Pvt. Ltd. He is living in Gwalior, Madhya Pradesh. He is very passionate and loyal to his work and finishes his work on time. His dream is to become one of the great researchers in the field of Artificial Intelligence. He is a very big fan of cricket and reading.

Sabyasachi Pramanik is a Professional IEEE member. He obtained a PhD in Computer Science and Engineering from the Sri Satya Sai University of Technology and Medical Sciences, Bhopal, India. Presently, he is an Assistant Professor, Department of Computer Science and Engineering, Haldia Institute of Technology, India. He has many publications in various reputed international conferences, journals, and online book chapter contributions (Indexed by SCIE, Scopus, ESCI, etc.). He is doing research in the field of Artificial Intelligence, Data Privacy, Cybersecurity, Network Security, and Machine Learning. He is also serving as the editorial board member of many international journals. He is a reviewer of journal articles from IEEE, Springer, Elsevier, Inderscience, IET, and IGI Global. He has reviewed many conference papers, has been a keynote speaker, session chair and has been a technical program committee member in many international conferences. He has authored a book on Wireless Sensor Network. Currently, he is editing 6 books from IGI Global, CRC Press EAI/Springer and Scrivener-Wiley Publications.

Abdurrakhman Prasetyadi is a junior researcher at the Research Center for Data and Information Science, The Indonesia Institute of Sciences (LIPI), Indonesia since 2019. He was a researcher at the Center for Information Technology (UPT BIT LIPI) for 6 years. He obtained his bachelor's degree in

Library and Information Sciences from the University of Padjadjaran, Indonesia in 2008. He earned a Master's degree in Information Technology for Libraries from the IPB University in 2017. Abdurrakhman Prasetyadi's research interests include issues in the field of Library and Information Science, Social Informatics, and Informetrics.

Bitan Pratihar obtained his Bachelor of Technology degree in Chemical Engineering from National Institute of Technology Durgapur, India, in 2017. He completed his Master of Technology degree in Chemical Engineering department of National Institute of Technology Rourkela, India, in 2019. His research interests were the application of Fuzzy Logic in data mining, controller design, and soft sensor design for several chemical engineering applications and others. Currently, he is a doctoral student in Membrane Separation Laboratory of Chemical Engineering Department, Indian Institute of Technology Kharagpur, India.

Alessandro Puzzanghera is a PhD student at the University for foreigners "Dante Alighieri" in Reggio Calabria. He worked many years as legal assistant at the FIDLAW LLP a law firm in London. He successfully completed her studies in the Master of Studies (MSt) postgraduate level degree program of the European Law and Governance School at the European Public Law Organization in Athens. His fields of research include: Artificial Intelligence, Administrative law, Personal Data in particular about GDPR. He published papers for Hart publishing (Oxford), EPLO publication (Athens) and various italian scientific journals.

John Quinn is a Professor of Mathematics at Bryant University and has been teaching there since 1991. Prior to teaching, he was an engineer at the Naval Underwater Systems Center (now the Naval Undersea Warfare Center). He received his Sc.B. degree from Brown University in 1978, and his M.S. and Ph.D. degrees from Harvard University in 1987 and 1991, respectively. Professor Quinn has published in multiple areas. He has done previous research in mathematical programming methods and computable general equilibrium models. He currently does research in probability models and in data mining applications, including the prediction of rare events. He is also doing research in pension modeling, including the effects of health status on retirement payouts.

Parvathi R. is a Professor of School of Computing Science and Engineering at VIT University, Chennai since 2011. She received the Doctoral degree in the field of spatial data mining in the same year. Her teaching experience in the area of computer science includes more than two decades and her research interests include data mining, big data and computational biology.

Sreemathy R. is working as Associate Professor in Pune Institute of Computer Technology, Savitribai Phule Pune University, India. She has her Master's degree in Electronics Engineering from college of Engineering, Pune. Savitribai Phule Pune University and Doctoral degree in Electronics Engineering from Shivaji University, India. Her research areas include signal processing, image processing, Artificial Intelligence, Machine Learning and Deep Learning.

Kornelije Rabuzin is currently a Full Professor at the Faculty of organization and informatics, University of Zagreb, Croatia. He holds Bachelor, Master, and PhD degrees - all in Information Science. He performs research in the area of databases, particularly graph databases, as well as in the field of data warehousing and business intelligence. He has published four books and more than eighty scientific and professional papers.

Kaleche Rachid is a PhD student of computer science since 2018. He is member of computer science laboratory (LIO) of Oran1 university in Algeria. His current research interests deal with artificial intelligence, transportation system, logistic systems, machine learning, bio-inspired approach. He is co-author of many publications and communications.

Rulina Rachmawati earned a bachelor degree in Chemistry from the Sepuluh Nopember Institute of Technology, Indonesia, in 2009. She started her career as a technical librarian at the Library and Archive Agency of the Regional Government of Surabaya city, Indonesia. Her passion for librarianship brought her to pursue a Master of Information Management from RMIT University, Australia, in 2019. Presently, she is a librarian at the Center for Scientific Data and Documentation, the Indonesian Institute of Sciences. Her current roles include providing library services, providing content for the Indonesian Scientific Journal Database (ISJD), and researching data, documentation and information. Her research interests include bibliometrics, library services, information retrieval, and research data management.

Nayem Rahman is an Information Technology (IT) Professional. He has implemented several large projects using data warehousing and big data technologies. He holds a Ph.D. from the Department of Engineering and Technology Management at Portland State University, USA, an M.S. in Systems Science (Modeling & Simulation) from Portland State University, Oregon, USA, and an MBA in Management Information Systems (MIS), Project Management, and Marketing from Wright State University, Ohio, USA. He has authored 40 articles published in various conference proceedings and scholarly journals. He serves on the Editorial Review Board of the International Journal of End-User Computing and Development (IJEUCD). His principal research interests include Big Data Analytics, Big Data Technology Acceptance, Data Mining for Business Intelligence, and Simulation-based Decision Support System (DSS).

Vishnu Rajan is an Assistant Professor in the Production & Operations Management Division at XIME Kochi, Kerala, India. His current research interests include supply chain risk management, operations research, reliability engineering, manufacturing systems management, quantitative techniques and statistics. He has published research articles in reputed peer-reviewed international journals of Taylor & Francis, Emerald, Inderscience, Elsevier, IEEE and IIIE publications. He also has a scientific book chapter to his credit. Besides this, Vishnu serves as an editorial board member of the International Journal of Risk and Contingency Management (IJRCM) of IGI Global.

T. Rajeshwari is freelancer and Yagyopathy researcher. She usually writes up article in science forums related to Hindu Mythology and their scientific proofs. She belongs to Kolkata and travels across globe for social work and spreading the science of Hindu rituals.

P. N. Ram Kumar is Professor in the QM & OM area at the Indian Institute of Management Kozhikode. Prior to this appointment, he had worked as a Post-Doctoral Research Fellow in the School of Mechanical and Aerospace Engineering at the Nanyang Technological University, Singapore. He obtained his Bachelor in Mechanical Engineering from the JNTU Hyderabad in 2003, Master in Industrial Engineering from the PSG College of Technology, Coimbatore in 2005 and PhD from the IIT Madras in 2009.

His primary areas of research include, but not limited to, transportation network optimisation, military logistics, reliability engineering and supply chain management. He has authored several international journal papers and his work has been published in reputed journals such as Journal of the Operational Research Society, Defense and Security Analysis, Strategic Analysis, and Journal of Defense Modeling & Simulation, to name a few.

Perumal Ramasubramanian holds BE, ME from Computer Science and Engineering from Madurai Kamaraj University and PH.D Computer Science from Madurai Kamaraj University in the year 1989, 1996 and 2012. He has 31 years teaching experience in academia. He was published 55 papers in various international journal and conferences. He has authored 14 books and has 135 citations with h-index 5 and i10 index 4. He is also actively involved in various professional societies like Institution of Engineers(I), Computer Science Teachers Association, ISTE, ISRD, etc.

Célia M. Q. Ramos graduated in Computer Engineering from the University of Coimbra, obtained her Master in Electrical and Computers Engineering from the Higher Technical Institute, Lisbon University, and the PhD in Econometrics in the University of the Algarve (UALG), Faculty of Economics, Portugal. She is Associate Professor at School for Management, Hospitality and Tourism, also in the UALG, where she lectures computer science. Areas of research and special interest include the conception and development of business intelligence, information systems, tourism information systems, big data, tourism, machine learning, social media marketing, econometric modelling and panel-data models. Célia Ramos has published in the fields of information systems and tourism, namely, she has authored a book, several book chapters, conference papers and journal articles. At the level of applied research, she has participated in several funded projects.

Anshu Rani has more than 12 years of experience in teaching and learning at various reputed institutes. She is a researcher associated with the online consumer behaviour area.

Bindu Rani is a Ph.D. scholar from Department of Computer Science and Engineering, Sharda University, Greater Noida, India and works as assistant professor in Information Technology Department, Inderprastha Engineering College, Ghaziabad, Dr. A.P.J Abdul Kalam Technical University, India. She received Master in Computer Science and Application degree from Aligarh Muslim University (AMU), India. Her research interests are Data Mining, Big Data and Machine learning techniques.

N. Raghavendra Rao is an Advisor to FINAIT Consultancy Services India. He has a doctorate in the area of Finance. He has a rare distinction of having experience in the combined areas of Information Technology and Finance.

Zbigniew W. Ras is a Professor of Computer Science Department and the Director of the KDD Laboratory at the University of North Carolina, Charlotte. He also holds professorship position in the Institute of Computer Science at the Polish-Japanese Academy of Information Technology in Warsaw, Poland. His areas of specialization include knowledge discovery and data mining, recommender systems, health informatics, business analytics, flexible query answering, music information retrieval, and art.

Rohit Rastogi received his B.E. degree in Computer Science and Engineering from C.C.S.Univ. Meerut in 2003, the M.E. degree in Computer Science from NITTTR-Chandigarh (National Institute of Technical Teachers Training and Research-affiliated to MHRD, Govt. of India), Punjab Univ. Chandigarh in 2010. Currently he is pursuing his Ph.D. In computer science from Dayalbagh Educational Institute, Agra under renowned professor of Electrical Engineering Dr. D.K. Chaturvedi in area of spiritual consciousness. Dr. Santosh Satya of IIT-Delhi and dr. Navneet Arora of IIT-Roorkee have happily consented him to co supervise. He is also working presently with Dr. Piyush Trivedi of DSVV Hardwar, India in center of Scientific spirituality. He is a Associate Professor of CSE Dept. in ABES Engineering. College, Ghaziabad (U.P.-India), affiliated to Dr. A.P. J. Abdul Kalam Technical Univ. Lucknow (earlier Uttar Pradesh Tech. University). Also, he is preparing some interesting algorithms on Swarm Intelligence approaches like PSO, ACO and BCO etc.Rohit Rastogi is involved actively with Vichaar Krnati Abhiyaan and strongly believe that transformation starts within self.

Mark Rauch is a database administrator and a graduate student in the program for Database Management at the University of West Florida. Mark Rauch is actively working in the healthcare industry and has experience working with several Oracle database platforms as well as SQL Server. His experience extends across Oracle 11g, 12c, and 19c. He has also supported several aspects of Oracle Middleware including Oracle Data Integrator, Oracle Enterprise Manager, Web Logic, and Business Publisher.

Yuan Ren is an instructor in Shanghai Dianji University. He was born in 1984. He got his bachelor's degree in mathematics from Jilin University in 2007, and doctor's degree in computer software from Fudan University in 2013. His multidisciplinary research interests include image understanding, artificial intelligence, and data science.

M. Yudhi Rezaldi is a researcher at the Research Center for Informatics, National Research and Innovation Agency (BRIN). His academic qualifications were obtained from Pasundan Universiti Bandung for his bachelor degree, and Mater degree in Magister of Design from Institut Teknologi Bandung (ITB). He completed his PhD in 2020 at Computer Science from Universiti Kebangsaan Malaysia (UKM). And he is also an active member of Himpunan Peneliti Indonesia (Himpenindo). His research interests include visualization, modeling, computer graphics animation, multimedia design, Information Science, particularly disaster. He received an award The best researcher in the 2011 researcher and engineer incentive program in Indonesian Institute of Science (LIPI). and once received the Karya Satya award 10 years in 2018 from the Indonesian government for his services to the country.

Moisés Rivas López was born in June 1, 1960. He received the B.S. and M.S. degrees in Autonomous University of Baja California, México, in 1985, 1991, respectively. He received PhD degree in the same University, on specialty "Optical Scanning for Structural Health Monitoring", in 2010. He has written 5 book chapters and 148 Journal and Proceedings Conference papers. Since 1992 till the present time he has presented different works in several International Congresses of IEEE, ICROS, SICE, AMMAC in USA, England, Japan, turkey and Mexico. Dr. Rivas was Dean of Engineering Institute of Autonomous University Baja California, Since1997 to 2005; also was Rector of Polytechnic University of Baja California, Since2006 to 2010. Since 2012 to 208 was the head of physic engineering department, of Engineering Institute, Autonomous University of Baja California, Mexico. Since 2013 till the present time member of National Researcher System and now is Professor in the Polytechnic University of Baja California.

Julio C. Rodríguez-Quiñonez received the B.S. degree in CETYS, Mexico in 2007. He received the Ph.D. degree from Baja California Autonomous University, México, in 2013. He is currently Full Time Researcher-Professor in the Engineering Faculty of the Autonomous University of Baja California, and member of the National Research System Level 1. Since 2016 is Senior Member of IEEE. He is involved in the development of optical scanning prototype in the Applied Physics Department and research leader in the development of a new stereo vision system prototype. He has been thesis director of 3 Doctor's Degree students and 4 Master's degree students. He holds two patents referred to dynamic triangulation method, has been editor of 4 books, Guest Editor of Measurement, IEEE Sensors Journal, International Journal of Advanced Robotic Systems and Journal of Sensors, written over 70 papers, 8 book chapters and has been a reviewer for IEEE Sensors Journal, Optics and Lasers in Engineering, IEEE Transaction on Mechatronics and Neural Computing and Applications of Springer; he participated as a reviewer and Session Chair of IEEE ISIE conferences in 2014 (Turkey), 2015 (Brazil), 2016 (USA), 2017 (UK), 2019 (Canada), IECON 2018 (USA), IECON 2019 (Portugal), ISIE 2020 (Netherlands), ISIE 2021 (Japan). His current research interests include automated metrology, stereo vision systems, control systems, robot navigation and 3D laser scanners.

Mário José Batista Romão is an Associate Professor of Information Systems, with Aggregation, at ISEG – University of Lisbon. He is Director of the Masters program in Computer Science and Management. He holds a PhD in Management Sciences by ISCTE-IUL and by Computer Integrated Manufacturing at Cranfiel University (UK). He also holds a MsC in Telecommunications and Computer Science, at IST - Instituto Superior Técnico, University of Lisbon. He is Pos-Graduated in Project Management and holds the international certification Project Management Professional (PMP), by PMI – Project Management International. He has a degree in Electrotecnic Engineer by IST.

James Rotella did his BS in physics at Pennsylvania State University and MS in physics at the University of Pittsburgh. While at the University of Pittsburgh he focused on doing epigenetic research in the biophysics department. He went on to work for 4 years as a failure analysis engineer at a Dynamics Inc. working on improving their lines of flexible microelectronics. He focused on improving yield internally in the factory, and designing and carrying out accelerated life and field tests to improve field performance. After working at Dynamics, he moved on to begin work programming at K&L Gates where he maintains analytics pipelines, models, and databases. While at K&L Gates, he completed an Masters in Data Analytics at Pennsylvania State University.

Anirban Roy is the founder of Water-Energy Nexus Laboratory in BITS Pilani Goa Campus Founder and Promoter and CEO of Epione Swajal Solutions India LLP, focussing on Membrane Manufacturing. Experience in membrane synthesis, manufacturing, handling, devices, and prototypes.

Parimal Roy studied in Anthropology. Later he obtained papers on MBA, Project management, and Criminology (paper is better than a certificate) to enhance his knowledge. He is currently working in a state own institution in the field of Training & Development. Decolonizing, Marginal community, subaltern voice, Project management - all are interest arena in academic world. His written book is

Extra-marital love in folk songs. Co-author of Captive minded intellectual; Quantitative Ethnography in Indigenous Research Methodology; and so many book chapters and journals.

Saúl Rozada Raneros is a PhD candidate at University of Valladolid, who received his M.S. degrees in telecommunication engineering from the University of Valladolid, Spain. He is researcher of the Data Engineering Research Unit and his research is focused on Internet of Things, and Virtual Reality. Also, he is co-author of some publications in journals, dealing with topics related to his lines of his research.

Rauno Rusko is University lecturer at the University of Lapland. His research activities focus on cooperation, coopetition, strategic management, supply chain management and entrepreneurship mainly in the branches of information communication technology, forest industry and tourism. His articles appeared in the European Management Journal, Forest Policy and Economics, International Journal of Business Environment, Industrial Marketing Management, International Journal of Innovation in the Digital Economy and International Journal of Tourism Research among others.

Rashid bin Mohd Saad is an educationist and serving as an Assistant professor at the Department of Education at Universiti Malaya. At present, he is working in the Drug Discoveries of Indigenous communities in Bangladesh.

Sheelu Sagar is a research scholar pursuing her PhD in Management from Amity University (AUUP). She graduated with a Bachelor Degree of Science from Delhi University. She received her Post Graduate Degree in Master of Business Administration with distinction from Amity University Uttar Pradesh India in 2019. She is working at a post of Asst. Controller of Examinations, Amity University, Uttar Pradesh. She is associated with various NGOs - in India. She is an Active Member of Gayatri Teerth, ShantiKunj, Haridwar, Trustee - ChaturdhamVed Bhawan Nyas (having various centers all over India), Member Executive Body -Shree JeeGauSadan, Noida. She is a social worker and has been performing Yagya since last 35 years and working for revival of Indian Cultural Heritage through yagna (Hawan), meditation through Gayatri Mantra and pranayama. She is doing her research on Gayatri Mantra.

Rajarshi Saha has currently completed his BSc with Major in Computer Science from St. Xavier's College, Kolkata. His current research interest is Data Analytics and Machine Learning.

Sudipta Sahana is an Associate Professor at a renowned University in West Bengal. For more than 11 years he has worked in this region. He has passed his M.tech degree in Software Engineering and B.Tech Degree in Information Technology from West Bengal University of Technology with a great CGPA/DGPA in 2010 and 2012 respectively. He completed his Ph.D. from the University of Kalyani in 2020. He has published more than 60 papers in referred journals and conferences indexed by Scopus, DBLP, and Google Scholar and working as an editorial team member of many reputed journals. He is a life member of the Computer Society of India (CSI), Computer Science Teachers Association (CSTA), and also a member of the International Association of Computer Science and Information Technology (IACSIT).

Pavithra Salanke has more than a decade of experience in Teaching and she is an active member in the research area of HR using social media.

Hajara U. Sanda, PhD, is an Associate Professor at the Department of Mass Communication, Bayero University, Kano, Kano State, Nigeria. She is also a former Dean, Student Affairs of the university, and has published many research articles, presented many conference papers, and published a couple of books.

Enes Şanlıtürk holds B.S. in Industrial Engineering in Istanbul Technical University and M.S. in Management Engineering in Istanbul Technical University. Also, his Ph.D. education continues in Industrial Engineering in Istanbul Technical University. He has study in Machine Learning. His main contributions is enhancing defect prediction performance in machine learning on production systems. In addition, he works in private sector as an Analyst.

Loris Schmid was born in 1992 in Visp, Switzerland. Studying at the University of Berne he attained a Master of Science in Economics. During the UMUSE2 (User Monitoring of the US Election) project, Loris Schmid was employed by the University of Neuchâtel from August 2020 until February 2021 performing data analysis and processing. He works as an Analyst and Research Assistant at IFAAR since 2019.

Dara Schniederjans is an Associate Professor of Supply Chain Management at the University of Rhode Island, College of Business Administration. Dara received her Ph.D. from Texas Tech University in 2012. Dara has co-authored five books and published over thirty academic journal articles as well as numerous book chapters. Dara has served as a guest co-editor for a special issue on "Business ethics in Social Sciences" in the International Journal of Society Systems Science. She has also served as a website coordinator and new faculty development consortium co-coordinator for Decisions Sciences Institute.

Jaydip Sen obtained his Bachelor of Engineering (B.E) in Electrical Engineering with honors from Jadavpur University, Kolkata, India in 1988, and Master of Technology (M.Tech) in Computer Science with honors from Indian Statistical Institute, Kolkata in 2001. Currently, he is pursuing his PhD on "Security and Privacy in Internet of Things" in Jadavpur University, which is expected to be completed by December 2018. His research areas include security in wired and wireless networks, intrusion detection systems, secure routing protocols in wireless ad hoc and sensor networks, secure multicast and broadcast communication in next generation broadband wireless networks, trust and reputation based systems, sensor networks, and privacy issues in ubiquitous and pervasive communication. He has more than 100 publications in reputed international journals and referred conference proceedings (IEEE Xplore, ACM Digital Library, Springer LNCS etc.), and 6 book chapters in books published by internationally renowned publishing houses e.g. Springer, CRC press, IGI-Global etc. He is a Senior Member of ACM, USA a Member IEEE, USA.

Kishore Kumar Senapati's experiences at BIT, Mesra complement both teaching and research, which brought innovation culture at academia and Industry. He has significant Industry driven research and teaching experience in the leading organizations of the country working nearly two decades, including ≈ 16 years at current place as an Assistant Professor in the Department of Computer Science and Engineering at Birla Institute of Technology, MESRA, Ranchi, INDIA. He has obtained PhD in Engineering from Birla Institute of Technology, MESRA. He has Master of Technology in Computer Science from UTKAL University, ODISHA. He has more than 18 years of teaching and research experience. He has guided more than 41 students of ME & M. Tech and four PhD scholars are currently working under his supervision in Computer Science field. He has capabilities in the area of algorithm design, Image processing, Cyber Security and Machine learning. He has published more than 40 peer reviewed papers on various national and international journals of repute including conference presentations. He has delivered invited talks at various national and international seminars including conferences, symposium, and workshop. He is also professional member of national and international societies. He was also active members in various program committees of international conference and chaired the sessions. He serves as editor of International and National Journal of high repute. He has successfully conducted several workshops in his organization on various topics. He is an honorary computer science expert and serves the nation in multiple areas.

Oleg Yu. Sergiyenko was born in February, 9, 1969. He received the B.S., and M.S., degrees in Kharkiv National University of Automobiles and Highways, Kharkiv, Ukraine, in 1991, 1993, respectively. He received the Ph.D. degree in Kharkiv National Polytechnic University on specialty "Tools and methods of non-destructive control" in 1997. He received the DSc degree in Kharkiv National University of Radio electronics in 2018. He has been an editor of 7 books, written 24 book chapters, 160 papers indexed in Scopus and holds 2 patents of Ukraine and 1 in Mexico. Since 1994 till the present time he was represented by his research works in several International Congresses of IEEE, ICROS, SICE, IMEKO in USA, England, Japan, Canada, Italy, Brazil, Austria, Ukraine, and Mexico. Dr.Sergiyenko in December 2004 was invited by Engineering Institute of Baja California Autonomous University for researcher position. He is currently Head of Applied Physics Department of Engineering Institute of Baja California Autonomous University, Mexico, director of several Masters and Doctorate thesis. He was a member of Program Committees of various international and local conferences. He is member of Academy (Academician) of Applied Radio electronics of Bielorussia, Ukraine and Russia.

Martina Šestak received her Master's degree in Information and Software Engineering from the Faculty of Organization and Informatics, University of Zagreb in 2016. She is currently a Ph.D. student in Computer Science at Faculty of Electrical Engineering and Computer Science in Maribor. She is currently a Teaching Assistant and a member of Laboratory for Information Systems at the Faculty of Electrical Engineering and Computer Science, University of Maribor. Her main research interests include graph databases, data analytics and knowledge graphs.

Rohan Shah is a Director in the Financial Services practice at Simon-Kucher & Partners. Rohan holds a Master's degree in Operations Research, specializing in Financial and Managerial Applications from Columbia University in the City of New York.

Aakanksha Sharaff has completed her graduation in Computer Science and Engineering in 2010 from Government Engineering College, Bilaspur (C.G.). She has completed her post graduation Master of Technology in 2012 in Computer Science & Engineering (Specialization- Software Engineering) from National Institute of Technology, Rourkela and completed Ph.D. degree in Computer Science & Engineering in 2017 from National Institute of Technology Raipur, India. Her area of interest is Software Engineering, Data Mining, Text Mining, and Information Retrieval. She is currently working as an Assistant Professor at NIT Raipur India.

Michael J. Shaw joined the faculty of University of Illinois at Urbana-Champaign in 1984. He has been affiliated with the Gies College of Business, National Center for Supercomputing Applications, and the Information Trust Institute. His research interests include machine learning, digital transformation, and healthcare applications.

Yong Shi is a Professor of University of Nebraska at Omaha. He also serves as the Director, Chinese Academy of Sciences Research Center on Fictitious Economy & Data Science and the Director of the Key Lab of Big Data Mining and Knowledge Management, Chinese Academy of Sciences. He is the counselor of the State Council of PRC (2016), the elected member of the International Eurasian Academy of Science (2017), and elected fellow of the World Academy of Sciences for Advancement of Science in Developing Countries (2015). His research interests include business intelligence, data mining, and multiple criteria decision making. He has published more than 32 books, over 350 papers in various journals and numerous conferences/proceedings papers. He is the Editor-in-Chief of International Journal of Information Technology and Decision Making (SCI), Editor-in-Chief of Annals of Data Science (Springer) and a member of Editorial Board for several academic journals.

Dharmpal Singh received his Bachelor of Computer Science and Engineering and Master of Computer Science and Engineering from West Bengal University of Technology. He has about eight years of experience in teaching and research. At present, he is with JIS College of Engineering, Kalyani, and West Bengal, India as an Associate Professor. Currently, he had done his Ph. D from University of Kalyani. He has about 26 publications in national and international journals and conference proceedings. He is also the editorial board members of many reputed/ referred journal.

Aarushi Siri Agarwal is pursuing an undergraduate degree in Computer Science Engineering at Vellore Institute of Technology Chennai. Her interest is in using Machine Learning algorithms for data analysis, mainly in areas such as Cyber Security and Social Network Analysis.

R. Sridharan is a Professor of Industrial Engineering in the Department of Mechanical Engineering at National Institute of Technology Calicut, India. He received his PhD in 1995 from the Department of Mechanical Engineering at Indian Institute of Technology, Bombay, India. His research interests include modelling and analysis of decision problems in supply chain management, job shop production systems and flexible manufacturing systems. He has published papers in reputed journals such as IJPE, IJPR, JMTM, IJLM, IJAMT, etc. For the outstanding contribution to the field of industrial engineering and the institution, he has been conferred with the Fellowship award by the National Council of the Indian Institution of Industrial Engineering in 2017.

Karthik Srinivasan is an assistant professor of business analytics in the School of Business at University of Kansas (KU). He completed his PhD in Management Information Systems from University of Arizona and his master's in management from Indian Institute of Science. He has also worked as a software developer and a data scientist prior to joining academia. His research focuses on addressing novel and important analytics challenges using statistical machine learning, network science, and natural language processing. His research has been presented in top tier business and healthcare analytics conferences and journals. Karthik teaches database management, data warehousing, big data courses for undergraduates and masters students at KU.

Gautam Srivastava is working as an Assistant Professor with GL Bajaj Institute of Management and Research. He has 15+ years of academic experience. He has completed his Ph.D. from the University of Petroleum and Energy Studies, India. His area of specialization is Marketing. He has published and presented many research papers in national and international journals.

Daniel Staegemann studied computer science at Technical University Berlin (TUB). He received the master's degree in 2017. He is currently pursuing the Ph.D. degree with the Otto von Guericke University Magdeburg. Since 2018, he has been employed as a research associate with OVGU where he has authored numerous papers that have been published in prestigious journals and conferences, for which he is also an active reviewer. His research interest is primarily focused on big data, especially the testing.

Mirjana D. Stojanović received her B.Sc. (1985) and M.Sc. (1993) degrees in electrical engineering and her Ph.D. degree (2005) in technical sciences, all from the University of Belgrade, Serbia. She is currently full professor in Information and Communication Technologies at the Faculty of Transport and Traffic Engineering, University of Belgrade. Previously, she held research position at the Mihailo Pupin Institute, University of Belgrade, and was involved in developing telecommunication equipment and systems for regional power utilities and major Serbian corporate systems. Prof. Stojanović participated in a number of national and international R&D projects, including technical projects of the International Council on Large Electric Systems, CIGRÉ. As author or co-author she published more than 170 book chapters, journal articles, and conference papers in her field. She was lead editor of the book on ICS cyber security in the Future Internet environment. Mirjana Stojanović also published a monograph on teletraffic engineering and two university textbooks (in Serbian). Her research interests include communication protocols, cyber security, service and network management, and Future Internet technologies.

Frank Straube studied Industrial Engineering, received his doctorate in 1987 from the Department of Logistics at the Technical University of Berlin under Prof. Dr.-Ing. H. Baumgarten and subsequently worked in a scientifically oriented practice, including more than 10 years as head of a company with more than 100 employees planning logistics systems. After his habilitation (2004) at the University of St. Gallen, Prof. Straube followed the call to the TU Berlin and since then has been head of the logistics department at the Institute for Technology and Management. He is a member of the editorial boards of international logistics journals. Prof. Straube founded the "International Transfer Center for Logistics (ITCL)" in 2005 to realize innovative planning and training activities for companies. He is a member of different boards at companies and associations to bridge between science and practice.

Hamed Taherdoost is an award-winning leader and R&D professional. He is the founder of Hamta Group and sessional faculty member of University Canada West. He has over 20 years of experience in both industry and academia sectors. Dr. Hamed was lecturer at IAU and PNU universities, a scientific researcher and R&D and Academic Manager at IAU, Research Club, MDTH, NAAS, Pinmo, Tablokar, Requiti, and Hamta Academy. Hamed has authored over 120 scientific articles in peer-reviewed international journals and conference proceedings (h-index = 24; i10-index = 50; February 2021), as well as eight book chapters and seven books in the field of technology and research methodology. He is the author of the Research Skills book and his current papers have been published in Behaviour & Information Technology, Information and Computer Security, Electronics, Annual Data Science, Cogent Business & Management, Procedia Manufacturing, and International Journal of Intelligent Engineering Informatics. He is a Senior Member of the IEEE, IAEEEE, IASED & IEDRC, Working group member of IFIP TC and Member of CSIAC, ACT-IAC, and many other professional bodies. Currently, he is involved in several multidisciplinary research projects among which includes studying innovation in information technology & web development, people's behavior, and technology acceptance.

Toshifumi Takada, Professor of National Chung Cheng University, Taiwan, 2018 to present, and Professor Emeritus of Tohoku University Accounting School, served as a CPA examination commissioner from 2001 to 2003. He has held many important posts, including the special commissioner of the Business Accounting Council of the Financial Service Agency, councilor of the Japan Accounting Association, President of the Japan Audit Association, and Director of the Japan Internal Control Association. Professional Career: 1979-1997 Lecturer, Associate Professor, Professor of Fukushima University, Japan 1997-2018 Professor of Tohoku University, Japan 2018-present Professor of National Chung Cheng University, Taiwan.

Neeti Tandon is Yagypathy researcher, scholar of fundamental physics in Vikram University Ujjain. She is active Volunteer of Gayatri Parivaar and highly involved in philanthropic activities.

Ahmet Tezcan Tekin holds B.S. in Computer Science in Istanbul Technical University and Binghamton University, a M.S. and Ph.D. in Management Engineering in Istanbul Technical University. He has studies in Machine Learning, Fuzzy Clustering etc. He gives lectures on Database Management and Big Data Management in different programs. His main contributions in this research area is improving prediction performance in machine learning with the merging Ensemble Learning approach and fuzzy clustering approach.

Gizem Temelcan obtained her Ph.D. entitled "Optimization of the System Optimum Fuzzy Traffic Assignment Problem" in Mathematical Engineering from Yildiz Technical University in 2020. She is an Assistant Professor in the Department of Computer Engineering at Beykoz University, Istanbul, Turkey. Her research interests are operational research, optimization of linear and nonlinear programming problems in the fuzzy environment.

Ronak Tiwari is a graduate student of Industrial Engineering and Management in the Department of Mechanical Engineering at National Institute of Technology Calicut, India. He worked in the industry for two years after receiving his bachelor's degree. He received his bachelor's degree in Industrial Engineering, in 2018, from Pandit Deendayal Petroleum University, Gujarat, India. He also received a silver medal for his academic performance during his undergraduate studies. He received a Government of India Scholarship under INSPIRE scheme to pursue basic sciences. He is an active researcher, and his research interests are mainly in supply chain risk, supply chain resilience, location theory problems, and humanitarian logistics. He has also acted as a reviewer of some internationally reputed journals.

Carlos Torres is CEO of Power-MI, a cloud platform to manage Predictive Maintenance. Born in San Salvador, 1975. Mechanical Engineer, Universidad Centroamericana "José Simeon Cañas", El Salvador. Master in Science Mechatronics, Universität Siegen, Germany. INSEAD Certificate in Global Management, France. Harvard Business School graduated in Global Management Program, USA.

Cahyo Trianggoro is Junior Researcher at Research Center for Informatics, Indonesia Institute of Science (LIPI). Cahyo is completed study from University of Padjadjaran, where he received a Bachelor degree in Information and Library Science and currently pursue for master degree in graduate school University of Padjadjaran. Cahyo having research interest study in data governance, digital preservation, and social informatics.

B. K. Tripathy is now working as a Professor in SITE, school, VIT, Vellore, India. He has received research/academic fellowships from UGC, DST, SERC and DOE of Govt. of India. Dr. Tripathy has published more than 700 technical papers in international journals, proceedings of international conferences and edited research volumes. He has produced 30 PhDs, 13 MPhils and 5 M.S (By research) under his supervision. Dr. Tripathy has 10 edited volumes, published two text books on Soft Computing and Computer Graphics. He has served as the member of Advisory board or Technical Programme Committee member of more than 125 international conferences inside India and abroad. Also, he has edited 6 research volumes for different publications including IGI and CRC. He is a Fellow of IETE and life/senior member of IEEE, ACM, IRSS, CSI, ACEEE, OMS and IMS. Dr. Tripathy is an editorial board member/reviewer of more than 100 international journals of repute.

Gyananjaya Tripathy has completed his graduation in Information Technology in 2012 from Biju Patnaik University of Technology, Odisha. He has completed his post graduation Master of Technology in 2016 in Computer Science & Engineering (Specialization- Wireless Sensor Network) from Veer Surendra Sai University of Technology, Burla (Odisha) and pursuing his Ph.D. degree in Computer Science & Engineering from National Institute of Technology Raipur, India. His area of interest is Wireless Sensor Network and Sentiment Analysis.

Klaus Turowski (born 1966) studied Business and Engineering at the University of Karlsruhe, achieved his doctorate at the Institute for Business Informatics at the University of Münster and habilitated in Business Informatics at the Faculty of Computer Science at the Otto von Guericke University Magdeburg. In 2000, he deputized the Chair of Business Informatics at the University of the Federal Armed Forces München and, from 2001, he headed the Chair of Business Informatics and Systems Engineering at the University of Augsburg. Since 2011, he is heading the Chair of Business Informatics (AG WI) at the Otto von Guericke University Magdeburg, the Very Large Business Applications Lab (VLBA Lab) and the world's largest SAP University Competence Center (SAP UCC Magdeburg). Additionally, Klaus Turowski worked as a guest lecturer at several universities around the world and was a lecturer at the Universities of Darmstadt and Konstanz. He was a (co-) organizer of a multiplicity of national and international scientific congresses and workshops and acted as a member of several programme commitees, and expert Groups. In the context of his university activities as well as an independent consultant he gained practical experience in industry.

Mousami Turuk is working as Assistant Professor in Pune Institute of Computer Technology, Savitribai Phule Pune University, India. She has her Master's degree in Electronics Engineering from Walchand College of Engineering, Sangli, Shivaji University Kolhapur. She has Doctoral degree in Electronics Engineering from Sant Gadge Baba, Amaravati University India. Her research areas include computer vision, Machine Learning and Deep Learning.

M. Ali Ülkü, Ph.D., M.Sc., is a Full Professor and the Director of the Centre for Research in Sustainable Supply Chain Analytics (CRSSCA), in the Rowe School of Business at Dalhousie University, Canada. Dr. Ülkü's research is on sustainable and circular supply chain and logistics management, and analytical decision models.

Mahmud Ullah is an Associate Professor of Marketing at the Faculty of Business Studies, University of Dhaka, Bangladesh. He teaches Behavioral and Quantitative courses in Business, e.g., Psychology, Organizational Behavior, Consumer Behavior, Business Mathematics, Business Statistics, Quantitative Analyses in Business etc., in addition to the Basic and Specialized Marketing courses like Marketing Management, Non-Profit Marketing, E-Marketing etc. He also taught Basic & Advanced English, and IELTS in a couple of English language Schools in New Zealand during his stay over there between 2002 and 2006. He has conducted a number of research projects sponsored by different international and national organizations like the World Bank (RMB), UNICEF, UNFPA, USAID, JAICA, AUSAID, IPPF, PPD, Die Licht Brucke, Andheri Hilfe, BNSB, FPAB etc. He did most of his research in the field of Health, Education, and Environment. His research interests include ethical aspects of human behavior in all these relevant fields, specifically in the continuously evolving and changing field of Digital Business and Marketing.

Nivedita V. S. is an Assistant Professor in the Department of Computer Science and Technology at Bannari Amman Institute of Technology, India. She is pursuing her doctoral degree in Information and Communication Engineering at Anna University, India. She holds 6 years of professional experience in academic institutions affiliated under Anna University. Her research interests include information filtering and retrieval, explainable intelligence, big data, etc.

Satish Vadlamani is a Director of Data Science and BI at Kenco Group, Chattanooga, TN, USA. He earned B.Tech. in Electronics and Communications Engineering, India. A Masters and Ph.D. in Industrial and Systems Engineering from Mississippi State University, USA. Before joining Kenco, Dr. Vadlamani worked at other global supply chain companies like APLL and XPO. Dr. Vadlamani has passion for applying operations research, machine learning (ML) and artificial (AI) intelligence to solve complex supply chain problems. Dr. Vadlamani has seven years of experience applying ML and AI for problem solving. Dr. Vadlamani has published at multiple journals and conferences and teaches data science and analytics to people around the globe. His research interests include networks, wireless sensor networks, wireless ad-hoc networks, supply chain networks, network interdiction, location problems, transportation, and meta-heuristics. Dr. Vadlamani has been an invited speaker at various colleges, universities, and other professional organizations across the globe. He is a member of IEOM, INFORMS and IISE.

Phuong Vi was born in Thai Nguyen, Vietnam. She is a lecturer at the Faculty of Journalism - Communications, Thai Nguyen University of Science, Vietnam. Her current research focuses on the following: Media culture; Social Media; Journalism History; Online newspaper; Journalism and public opinion; Public Relations. Her research is articles about journalism - modern media; books and book chapters have been published in prestigious international journals. "I am a journalist, researcher, author, writer, and university lecturer that never tires of learning and learning and teaches others for posterity, and for social development."

Takis Vidalis completed his basic legal studies at the University of Athens. In 1995, he received his Ph.D. in law. In 2001 he was elected a senior researcher and legal advisor of the Hellenic National Bioethics Commission (now, Commission for Bioethics and Technoethics). He is the author (or co-author) of 7 books and more than 50 academic papers in topics related to ethics and law of advanced technologies, constitutional law, philosophy of law, and sociology of law. Currently, he teaches "Artificial Intelligence: Ethics and Law", at the Law School of the Univ. of Athens, and "Biolaw and Bioethics," at the International Hellenic University. He is the president of the Research Ethics Committee of the National Centre for Scientific Research "Democritos" (the largest multidisciplinary research centre of Greece), and a member of the European Group on Ethics in Science and New Technologies (European Commission).

Fabio Vitor is an Assistant Professor of operations research in the Department of Mathematical and Statistical Sciences at the University of Nebraska at Omaha. He received a Ph.D. in Industrial Engineering and M.S. in Operations Research from Kansas State University, and a B.S. in Industrial Engineering from Maua Institute of Technology, Brazil. Dr. Vitor has nearly 10 years of industry experience, working for companies such as Monsanto, Kalmar, and Volkswagen. Dr. Vitor's research includes both theoretical and applied topics in operations research. His theoretical research creates algorithms to more quickly solve continuous and discrete optimization problems while some of his applied research has involved the application of optimization models and other operations research tools to reduce inventory costs, improve delivery routings, optimize nursery planting allocation, improve airport operations, and create strategies to overcome human trafficking.

Rogan Vleming is the Head of Data Science & Engineering at Simon-Kucher & Partners. Rogan received an M.B.A. in Finance specializing in financial engineering from McMaster University's De-Groote School of Business, and a B.Sc. in Mechanical Engineering from McMaster University.

Haris Abd Wahab, PhD, is an Associate Professor in the Department of Social Administration and Justice, Faculty of Arts and Social Sciences, University of Malaya, Malaysia. He graduated in the field of human development and community development. He has conducted studies on community work, community development, volunteerism, and disability. He has extensive experience working as a medical social worker at the Ministry of Health, Malaysia.

Chaojie Wang works for The MITRE Corporation, an international thinktank and operator of Federally Funded Research and Development Centers (FFRDC). In his capacity as a principal systems engineer, Dr. Wang advises the federal government on IT Acquisition & Modernization, Data Analytics & Knowledge Management, Health IT and Informatics, and Emerging Technology Evaluation & Adoption. Dr. Wang currently serves as the Editor-in-Chief for the International Journal of Patient-Centered Healthcare (IJPCH) by IGI Global and is on the Editorial Review Board of the Issues in Information System (IIS) by the International Association for Computer Information Systems (IACIS). Dr. Wang teaches Data Science graduate courses at University of Maryland Baltimore County (UMBC) and Healthcare Informatics graduate courses at Harrisburg University of Science and Technology. Dr. Wang holds a Bachelor of Engineering in MIS from Tsinghua University, a Master of Art in Economics and a Master of Science in Statistics both from the University of Toledo, an MBA in Finance from Loyola University Maryland, and a Doctor of Science in Information Systems and Communications from Robert Morris University.

Di Wang received his B.S. and M.S. degree in electrical engineering from Fuzhou University, China and Tianjin University, China. He is currently pursuing his Ph.D. degree in the Industrial Engineering Department, University of Illinois at Chicago, USA. His current research interests include multi-agent systems, distributed control, and energy schedule in the smart city.

Yue Wang is a doctoral candidate at the Computer Network Information Center, Chinese Academy of Sciences. Her research interests cover data mining, machine learning, user behavior analysis, etc. She has been working at the intersection of machine learning and information management for several years. Recently, she is working on NEW ARP technical research. In this paper, she handles the research on the technologies of the NEW ARP.

Manuel Weinke works as a research associate at the Chair of Logistics, Institute of Technology and Management, at the Technical University of Berlin. Within the scope of several research projects, he focuses on the utilization of Machine Learning in logistics management. Previously, he worked as a senior consultant in a management consultancy. He graduated in industrial engineering with a major in logistics, project, and quality management at the Technical University of Berlin.

Thomas A. Woolman is a doctoral student at Indiana State University's Technology Management program, with a concentration in digital communication systems. Mr. Woolman also holds an MBA with a concentration in data analytics from Saint Joseph's University, a Master's degree in Data Analytics from Saint Joseph's University and a Master's degree in Physical Science from Emporia State University. He is the president of On Target Technologies, Inc., a data science and research analytics consulting firm based in Virginia, USA.

Brian G. Wu received his Bachelor of Arts in Mathematics & Piano Music from Albion College in 2014. He pursued his graduate education at Oakland University, where he received his MS in Applied Statistics in 2016 and his PhD in Applied Mathematical Sciences, Applied Statistics Specialization, in 2020. His PhD thesis addressed computational and modeling aspects of big time series data. He will continue his career as a Visiting Assistant Professor at Southwestern University in the 2021-22 academic year.

Tao Wu is an assistant professor of Computer Science at SUNY Oneonta. He has extensive research experience in the fields of data science, information science, wireless communications, wireless networks, and statistical signal processing. He is also an expert in computer hardware and programming.

Mengying Xia's research interests focus on molecular epidemiology and women's health. Her current research involves molecular predictors of ovarian cancer severity, recurrence, and prognosis.

Hang Xiao is a project manager in SSGM at State Street Corporation. He earned a M.S. in Information System from Northeastern University in 2012. His research interests include IoT, AI, Big Data, and Operational Research.

Khadidja Yachba (born in Oran, Algeria) is a Teacher (Assistant Professor) in Computer sciences department of University Centre Relizane and a research assistant at LIO Laboratory, Oran, Algeria. She received her Ph. D. in transport maritime and optimization at University of Oran 1, Ahmed Benbella in 2017. Her research interests are in Decision Support Systems (urban, road, maritime transportation, and health), Optimization, Simulation, Cooperative and Distributed System, Knowledge bases and Multi Criteria Decision Making. Khadidja Yachba has published in journals such as transport and telecommunication, International Journal of Decision Sciences, Risk and Management.

Ronald R. Yager has worked in the area of machine intelligence for over twenty-five years. He has published over 500 papers and more then thirty books in areas related to artificial intelligence, fuzzy sets, decision-making under uncertainty and the fusion of information. He is among the world's top 1% most highly cited researchers with over 85,000 citations. He was the recipient of the IEEE Computational Intelligence Society's highly prestigious Frank Rosenblatt Award in 2016. He was the recipient of the IEEE Systems, Man and Cybernetics Society 2018 Lotfi Zadeh Pioneer Award. He was also the recipient of the IEEE Computational Intelligence Society Pioneer award in Fuzzy Systems. He received honorary doctorates from the Azerbaijan Technical University, the State University of Information Technologies, Sofia Bulgaria and the Rostov on the Don University, Russia. Dr. Yager is a fellow of the IEEE and the Fuzzy Systems Association. He was given a lifetime achievement award by the Polish Academy of Sciences for his contributions. He served at the National Science Foundation as program director in the Information Sciences program. He was a NASA/Stanford visiting fellow and a research associate at the University of California, Berkeley. He has been a lecturer at NATO Advanced Study Institutes. He is a Distinguished Adjunct Professor at King Abdulaziz University, Jeddah, Saudi Arabia. He was a distinguished honorary professor at the Aalborg University Denmark. He was distinguished visiting scientist at King Saud University, Riyadh, Saudi Arabia. He received his undergraduate degree from the City College of New York and his Ph. D. from the Polytechnic University of New York. He was editor and chief of the International Journal of Intelligent Systems. He serves on the editorial board of numerous technology journals. Currently he is an Emeritus Professor at Iona College and is director of the Machine Intelligence.

Jing Yang is an associate professor of management information systems at the State University of New York at Oneonta. She has authored multiple research papers on consumer reviews that have been published in a variety of high-quality peer-reviewed journals, including Decision Support Systems, Nakai Business Review International, Wireless Personal Communications, and the International Journal of Operations Research and Information Systems.

Lanting Yang is a student at the City University of Macau. She studies in the International Business program.

Pi-Ying Yen is an assistant professor at the School of Business, Macau University of Science and Technology. She received her PhD in Industrial Engineering and Decision Analytics from HKUST in 2020. She serves as a reviewer for Manufacturing & Service Operations Management (MSOM) and Naval Research Logistics (NRL). Her research interests include socially responsible operations, supply chain management, and consumer behavior.

Iris Yeung received her B.Soc.Sc. Degree from the University of Hong Kong, M.Sc. degree from Imperial College, University of London, and a Ph.D. degree from University of Kent at Canterbury, UK. Her major research and teaching areas are time series analysis and multivariate data analysis. She has published articles in the Journal of Statistical Computation and Simulations, Statistica Sinica, Journal of Royal Statistical Society: Series C, Journal of Applied Statistical Science, Environmental Monitoring and Assessment, Environmental Science and Pollution Research, Waste Management, Marine Pollution Bulletin, Energy Policy, Applied Energy, Energy and Buildings, and Energy for Sustainable Development. She has participated in a number of consulting projects, including the British Council, Mass Transit Railway Corporation, Hong Kong Ferry (Holdings) Co. Ltd., Greenpeace East Asia, and Environmental Protection Department, The Government of the Hong Kong Special Administrative Region.

Selen Yılmaz Işıkhan carried out an integrated master and doctorate education in biostatistics department of Hacettepe University Faculty of Medicine. She has been working as a lecturer at the same university since 2010. Some examples of her research interests are machine learning, data mining, multivariate statistical analyses, regression analysis, meta analysis, and gut microbiota analysis.

Ambar Yoganingrum is a senior researcher at the Research Center for Informatics, National Research and Innovation Agency (BRIN), Indonesia, since 2019. She was a researcher in Center for Scientific Documentation and Information, Indonesian Institute of Sciences (PDII LIPI) for 18 years. She obtained her bachelor degree in Pharmaceutical Sciences from University of Padjadjaran, Indonesia in 1990. She earned a Master's degree in Health Informatics from the University of Indonesia in 2003 and a Doctorate in Information Systems from the same university in 2015. Ambar Yoganingrum's research interests include issues in the field of Library and Information Sciences, Information processing, Applied Informatics for Social Sciences purposes, and Multimedia.

M. Yossi is an Associate Professor and the Head of the Department of Industrial Engineering and Management at SCE – Shamoon College of Engineering. His areas of specialty are work-study, DEA, and ranking methods. He has published several papers and six books in these areas. He received his BSc, MSc, and Ph.D. (Summa Cum Laude) in Industrial Engineering from the Ben-Gurion University of the Negev, Israel.

William A. Young II is the Director of the Online Masters of Business Administration (OMBA) program, the Director of the Online Masters of Business Analytics (OMBAn), and a Charles G. O'Bleness Associate Professor of Business Analytics in the Department of Analytics and Information Systems. As an Associate Professor, Young received Ohio University's University Professor Award in 2020. Young earned his doctorate in Mechanical and Systems Engineering from Ohio University's Russ College of Engineering and Technology in 2010. William also received a bachelor's and master's degree in Electrical Engineering at Ohio University in 2002 and 2005, respectively. William has collaborated with multidisciplinary teams of faculty, students, and professionals on projects and programs that have been funded by General Electric Aviation, the National Science Foundation, Sogeti Netherlands, and Ohio's Department of Labor. Young's primary research and teaching interests relate to business analytics and operations management.

Jianjun Yu is currently the researcher, doctoral supervisor at the Computer Network Information Center, Chinese Academy of Sciences. His research interests cover big data analysis, collaborative filtering recommendations, and cloud computing. Recently, he is working on New ARP technical research.

Gokmen Zararsiz is a PhD researcher working in Dept. of Biostatistics, Faculty of Medicine, Erciyes University, Turkey.

Alex Zarifis is passionate about researching, teaching and practicing management in its many facets. He has taught in higher education for over ten years at universities including the University of Cambridge, University of Manchester and the University of Mannheim. His research is in the areas of information systems and management. Dr Alex first degree is a BSc in Management with Information Systems from the University of Leeds. His second an MSc in Business Information Technology and a PhD in Business Administration are both from the University of Manchester. The University of Manchester PhD in Business Administration is ranked 1st in the world according to the Financial Times.

David Zeng is a faculty member in College of Business and Information Systems at Dakota State University. David received his PhD at University of California, Irvine specializing in Information Systems. David's Teaching Interests include Predictive Analytics for Decision-making, Programming for Data Analytics (Python), Business Intelligence & Visualization, Deep Learning, AI Applications, Applied AI & applications, and Strategy & Application of AI in Organizations. David's research has been published at top-tier, peer-reviewed journals including MIS Quarterly, and has been funded by both internal and external grants. David received the Merrill D. Hunter Award of Excellence in Research in 2020. David is the Director of Center for Business Analytics Research (CBAR) at DSU.

Jin Zhang is a full professor at the School of Information Studies, University of Wisconsin-Milwaukee, U.S.A. He has published papers in journals such as Journal of the American Society for Information Science and Technology, Information Processing & Management, Journal of Documentation, Journal of Intelligent Information Systems, Online Information Review, etc. His book "Visualization for Information Retrieval" was published in the Information Retrieval Series by Springer in 2008. His research interests include visualization for information retrieval, information retrieval algorithm, metadata, search engine evaluation, consumer health informatics, social media, transaction log analysis, digital libraries, data mining, knowledge system evaluation, and human computer interface design.

Peng Zhao is a data science professional with experience in industry, teaching, and research. He has a broad range of practical data science experience in different industries, including finance, mobile device, consumer intelligence, big data technology, insurance, and biomedical industries. He is a leading machine learning expertise in a Big Data & AI company in New Jersey. He also manages a data scientist team providing a variety of data consulting services to individuals, businesses, and non-profit organizations.

Yuehua Zhao is a research assistant professor at the School of Information Management, Nanjing University, China. Her research interests include consumer health informatics, social network analysis, and social media research.

Index

D

F

G

H

I

N

O

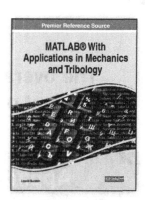

Ensure Quality Research is Introduced to the Academic Community

Become an Evaluator for IGI Global Authored Book Projects

Premier Reference Source

Stabilizing Currency and Preserving Economic Sovereignty Using the Grondona System

Patrick Collins

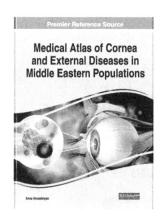

Premier Reference Source

Medical Atlas of Cornea and External Diseases in Middle Eastern Populations

Anna Hovakimyan

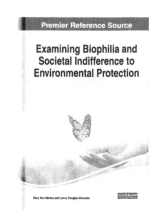

Premier Reference Source

Examining Biophilia and Societal Indifference to Environmental Protection

Mary Ann Markey and Lanny Douglas Meinecke

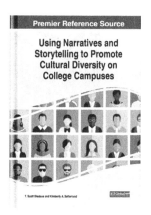

Premier Reference Source

Using Narratives and Storytelling to Promote Cultural Diversity on College Campuses

T. Scott Sledsoe and Kimberly A. Saffererund

The overall success of an authored book project is dependent on quality and timely manuscript evaluations.

Applications and Inquiries may be sent to:
development@igi-global.com

Applicants must have a doctorate (or equivalent degree) as well as publishing, research, and reviewing experience. Authored Book Evaluators are appointed for one-year terms and are expected to complete at least three evaluations per term. Upon successful completion of this term, evaluators can be considered for an additional term.

If you have a colleague that may be interested in this opportunity, we encourage you to share this information with them.

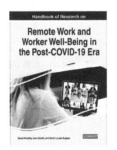

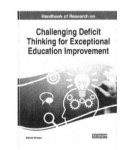

Printed in the United States
by Baker & Taylor Publisher Services